World Civilizations I

World Civilizations I

Boundless

World Civilizations I by Boundless *is licensed under a* Creative Commons Attribution-ShareAlike 4.0 International License, *except where otherwise noted.*

Cover Image: "World Map 1689." Located at: https://commons.wikimedia.org/wiki/File:World_Map_1689.JPG.

Published by SUNY OER Services
Milne Library
State University of New York at Geneseo
Geneseo, NY 14454

Distributed by State University of New York Press

Except where expressly noted otherwise, the contents of this course are based on materials originally published by Lumen Learning CC-BY-SA Creative Commons Attribution-ShareAlike License. The original version of the materials as published as World Civilizations may be access for free at https://courses.lumenlearning.com/suny-fmcc-boundless-worldhistory/.

ISBN: 978-1-64176-018-8

This book was produced using Pressbooks.com, and PDF rendering was done by PrinceXML.

Contents

About This Book   9

The Study of History and the Rise of Civilization

Precursors to Civilization   3
The Study of History   12

Ancient Mesopotamian Civilizations

The First Urban Civilizations   35
Akkadian Empire   43
Babylonia   55

Ancient Egypt

Introduction to Ancient Egypt   71
The Old Kingdom   75
The Middle Kingdom   84
The New Kingdom   93
Ancient Egyptian Society   110

Early Chinese Dynasties

The Mythical Period   139
The Shang Dynasty   147
The Zhou Dynasty   162
The Qin Dynasty   186
The Han Dynasty   190

Early Civilizations in the Indian Subcontinent

The Indus River Valley Civilizations   213
Indo-European Civilizations   233

Religion in the Indian Subcontinent	250

Ancient Greece and the Hellenistic World

Early Periods in Greek History	271
Sparta	281
The Persian Wars	290
Athens	298
Culture in Classical Greece	305
The Peloponnesian War	328
Macedonian Conquest	336

The Roman World

The Etruscans	357
Early Rome	368
The Roman Republic	379
The Roman Empire	407
The Flavian Dynasty	428
Christianity and the Late Roman Empire	448

The Byzantine Empire

Byzantium: The New Rome	473

The Rise and Spread of Islam

Pre-Islamic Arabia	491
Muhammad and the Rise of Islam	511
The Umayyad and Abbasid Empires	529

Crusades

The Crusades	555

The Development of Russia

The Princes of Rus	581
The Grand Duchy of Moscow	608

The Mongol Empire

The Mongol Empire	633
Genghis Khan	638

The Mongol Empire After Genghis Khan	651

Chinese Dynasties

The Tang Dynasty	667
The Song Dynasty	687

The Renaissance

The Renaissance	709
Italy During the Renaissance	714
Humanist Thought	727
Art in the Renaissance	739
Literature in the Renaissance	762
The Northern Renaissance	778

Civilizations in the Americas

The Inca	795
Early Civilizations of Mexico and Mesoamerica	816
The Maya	842
The Toltecs and the Aztecs	860

About This Book

Your World Civilizations I textbook is a compilation of articles written by instructors for universities around the country. The entire compilation is provided free of charge online through a Creative Commons license. You can access or even copy all the material here, for your own reference, even after the semester ends.

Different Versions

An electronic version is made available via your course at https://courses.lumenlearning.com/suny-fmcc-boundless-worldhistory/. You may also purchase a physical copy at the College Bookstore. The electronic version has access to multimedia content including video, slideshows, and interactive activities. The print version will have all the same reading material, but not include the multimedia content.

About the Author

There are many different authors; look to the "Licenses and Attributions" section at the end of each chapter to identify contributors. This compilation was edited by Anna Biel at Fulton-Montgomery Community College.

The Study of History and the Rise of Civilization

Precursors to Civilization

The Evolution of Humans

Human evolution is an ongoing and complex process that began seven million years ago.

Learning Objectives

To understand the process and timeline of human evolution

Key Takeaways

Key Points

- Humans began to evolve about seven million years ago, and progressed through four stages of evolution. Research shows that the first modern humans appeared 200,000 years ago.
- Neanderthals were a separate species from humans. Although they had larger brain capacity and interbred with humans, they eventually died out.
- A number of theories examine the relationship between environmental conditions and human evolution.
- The main human adaptations have included bipedalism, larger brain size, and reduced sexual dimorphism.

Key Terms

- **sexual dimorphism**: Differences in size or appearance between the sexes of an animal species.
- **encephalization**: An evolutionary increase in the complexity and/or size of the brain.

- **Red Queen hypothesis**: The theory that species must constantly evolve in order to compete with co-evolving animals around them.
- **turnover pulse hypothesis**: The theory that extinctions due to environmental conditions hurt specialist species more than generalist ones, leading to greater evolution among specialists.
- **savannah hypothesis**: The theory that hominins were forced out of the trees they lived in and onto the expanding savannah; as they did so, they began walking upright on two feet.
- **Toba catastrophe theory**: The theory that there was a near-extinction event for early humans about 70,000 years ago.
- **social brain hypothesis**: The theory that improving cognitive capabilities would allow hominins to influence local groups and control resources.
- **aridity hypothesis**: The theory that the savannah was expanding due to increasingly arid conditions, which then drove hominin adaptation.
- **hominids**: A primate of the family Hominidae that includes humans and their fossil ancestors.
- **bipedal**: Describing an animal that uses only two legs for walking.

Human evolution began with primates. Primate development diverged from other mammals about 85 million years ago. Various divergences among apes, gibbons, orangutans occurred during this period, with *Homini* (including early humans and chimpanzees) separating from *Gorillini* (gorillas) about 8 millions years ago. Humans and chimps then separated about 7.5 million years ago.

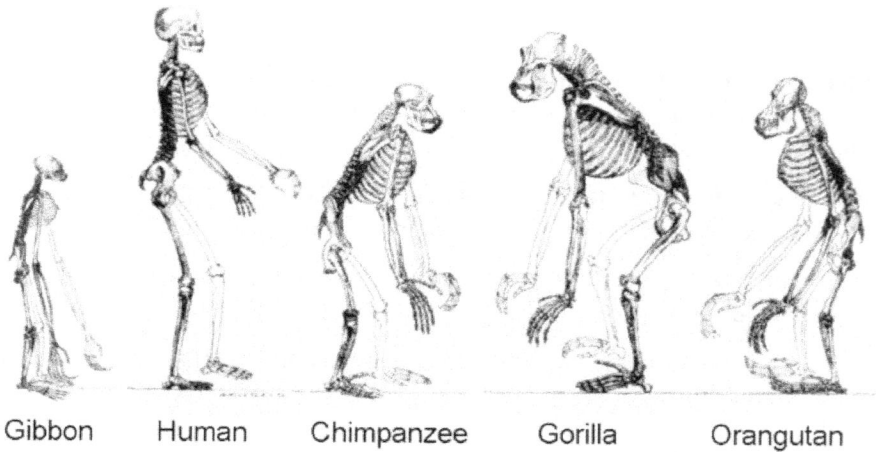

Skeletal structure of humans and other primates.: *A comparison of the skeletal structures of gibbons, humans, chimpanzees, gorillas and orangutans.*

Generally, it is believed that hominids first evolved in Africa and then migrated to other areas. There were four main stages of human evolution. The first, between four and seven million years ago, consisted of the proto hominins *Sahelanthropus*, *Orrorin* and *Ardipithecus*. These humans may have been bipedal, meaning they walked upright on two legs. The second stage, around four million years ago, was marked by the appearance of *Australopithecus*, and the third, around 2.7 million years ago, featured *Paranthropus*.

The fourth stage features the genus *Homo*, which existed between 1.8 and 2.5 million years ago. *Homo habilis*, which used stone tools and had a brain about the size of a chimpanzee, was an early hominin in this period. Coordinating fine hand movements needed for tool use may have led to increasing brain capacity. This was followed by *Homo erectus* and *Homo ergaster*, who had double the brain size and may have been the first to control fire and use more complex tools. *Homo heidelbergensis* appeared about 800,000 years ago, and modern humans, *Homo sapiens*, about 200,000 years ago. Humans acquired symbolic culture and language about 50,000 years ago.

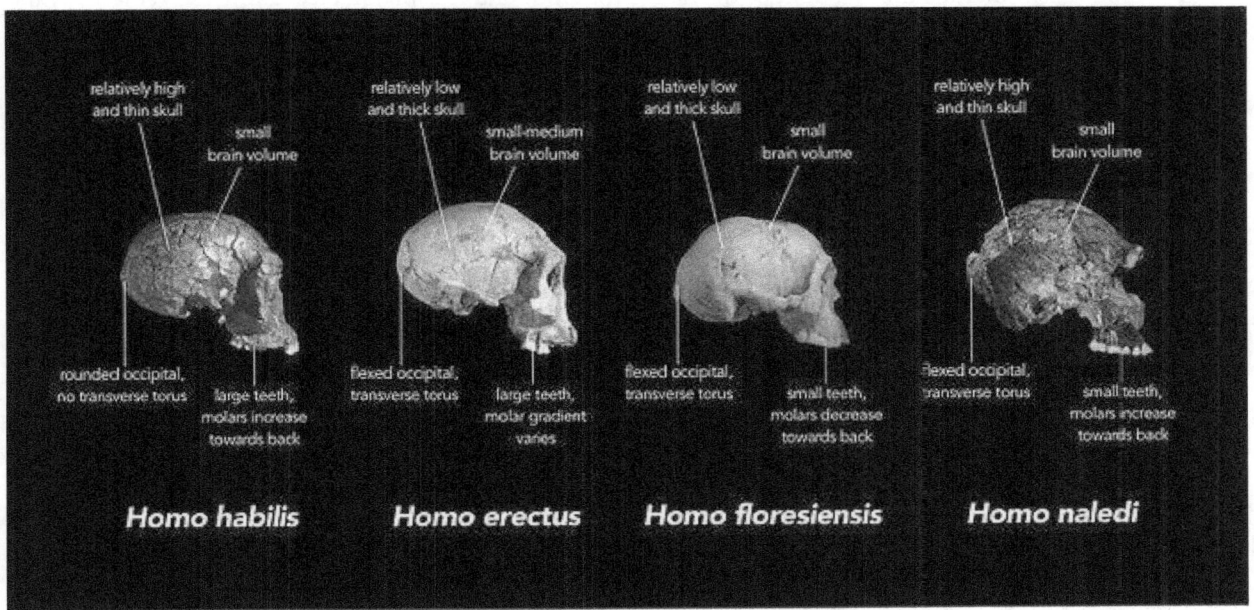

Comparison of skull features among early humans.: A comparison of Homo habilis, Homo erectus, Homo floresiensis and Homo naledi skull features.

Neanderthals

A separate species, *Homo neanderthalensis*, had a common ancestor with humans about 660,000 years ago, and engaged in interbreeding with *Homo sapiens* about 45,000 to 80,000 years ago. Although their brains were larger, Neanderthals had fewer social and technological innovations than humans, and they eventually died out.

Theories of Early Human Evolution

The savannah hypothesis states that hominins were forced out of the trees they lived in and onto the expanding savannah; as they did so, they began walking upright on two feet. This idea was expanded in the aridity hypothesis, which posited that the savannah was expanding due to increasingly arid conditions resulting in hominin adaptation. Thus, during periods of intense aridification, hominins also were pushed to evolve and adapt.

The turnover pulse hypothesis states that extinctions due to environmental conditions hurt specialist species more than generalist ones. While generalist species spread out when environmental conditions change, specialist species become more specialized and have a greater rate of evolution. The Red Queen hypothesis states that species must constantly evolve in order to compete with co-evolving animals around them. The social brain hypothesis states that improving cognitive capabilities would allow hominins to influence local groups and control resources. The Toba catastrophe theory states that there was a near-extinction event for early humans about 70,000 years ago.

Human Adaptations

Bipedalism, or walking upright, is one of the main human evolutionary adaptations. Advantages to be found in bipedalism include the freedom of the hands for labor and less physically taxing movement. Walking upright better allows for long distance travel and hunting, for a wider field of vision, a reduction of the amount of skin exposed to the sun, and overall thrives in a savannah environment. Bipedalism resulted in skeletal changes to the legs, knee and ankle joints, spinal vertebrae, toes, and arms. Most significantly, the pelvis became shorter and rounded, with a smaller birth canal, making birth more difficult for humans than other primates. In turn, this resulted in shorter gestation (as babies need to be born before their heads become too large), and more helpless infants who are not fully developed before birth.

Larger brain size, also called encephalization, began in early humans with *Homo habilis* and continued through the Neanderthal line (capacity of 1,200 – 1,900 cm3). The ability of the human brain to continue to grow after birth meant that social learning and language were possible. It is possible that a focus on eating meat, and cooking, allowed for brain growth. Modern humans have a brain volume of 1250 cm3.

Humans have reduced sexual dimorphism, or differences between males and females, and hidden estrus, which means the female is fertile year-round and shows no special sign of fertility. Human sexes still have some differences between them, with males being slightly larger and having more body hair and less body fat. These changes may be related to pair bonding for long-term raising of offspring.

Other adaptations include lessening of body hair, a chin, a descended larynx, and an emphasis on vision instead of smell.

The Neolithic Revolution

The Neolithic Revolution and invention of agriculture allowed humans to settle in groups, specialize, and develop civilizations.

Learning Objectives

Explain the significance of the Neolithic Revolution

Key Takeaways

Key Points

- During the Paleolithic Era, humans grouped together in small societies and subsisted by gathering plants, and fishing, hunting or scavenging wild animals.
- The Neolithic Revolution references a change from a largely nomadic hunter-gatherer way of life to a more settled, agrarian-based one, with the inception of the domestication of various plant and animal species—depending on species locally available and likely also influenced by local culture.
- There are several competing (but not mutually exclusive) theories as to the factors that drove populations to take up agriculture, including the Hilly Flanks hypothesis, the Feasting model, the Demographic theories, the evolutionary/intentionality theory, and the largely discredited Oasis Theory.
- The shift to agricultural food production supported a denser population, which in turn supported larger sedentary communities, the accumulation of goods and tools, and specialization in diverse forms of new labor.
- The nutritional standards of Neolithic populations were generally inferior to that of hunter-gatherers, and they worked longer hours and had shorter life expectancies.
- Life today, including our governments, specialized labor, and trade, is directly related to the advances made in the Neolithic Revolution.

Key Terms

- **Hilly Flanks hypothesis**: The theory that agriculture began in the hilly flanks of the Taurus and Zagros mountains, where the climate was not drier, and fertile land supported a variety of plants and animals amenable to domestication.
- **Evolutionary/Intentionality theory**: The theory that domestication was part of an evolutionary process between humans and plants.
- **Neolithic Revolution**: The world's first historically verifiable advancement in agriculture. It took place around 12,000 years ago.
- **Hunter-gatherer**: A nomadic lifestyle in which food is obtained from wild plants and animals; in contrast to an agricultural lifestyle, which relies mainly on domesticated species.
- **Paleolithic Era**: A period of history that spans from 2.5 million to 20,000 years ago, during which time humans evolved, used stone tools, and lived as hunter-gatherers.
- **Oasis Theory**: The theory that humans were forced into close association with animals due to changes in climate.
- **Feasting model**: The theory that displays of power through feasting drove agricultural technology.
- **specialization**: A process where laborers focused on one specialty area rather than creating all needed items.

> - **Demographic theories**: Theories about how sedentary populations may have driven agricultural changes.

Before the Rise of Civilization: The Paleolithic Era

The first humans evolved in Africa during the Paleolithic Era, or Stone Age, which spans the period of history from 2.5 million to about 10,000 BCE. During this time, humans lived in small groups as hunter-gatherers, with clear gender divisions for labor. The men hunted animals while the women gathered food, such as fruit, nuts and berries, from the local area. Simple tools made of stone, wood, and bone (such as hand axes, flints and spearheads) were used throughout the period. Fire was controlled, which created heat and light, and allowed for cooking.

Humankind gradually evolved from early members of the genus *Homo*—
such as *Homo habilis*,
who used simple stone tools— into fully behaviorally and anatomically modern humans (*Homo sapiens*) during the Paleolithic era. During the end of the Paleolithic, specifically the Middle and or Upper Paleolithic, humans began to produce the earliest works of art and engage in religious and spiritual behavior, such as burial and ritual. Paleolithic humans were nomads, who often moved their settlements as food became scarce. This eventually resulted in humans spreading out from Africa (beginning roughly 60,000 years ago) and into Eurasia, Southeast Asia, and Australia. By about 40,000 years ago, they had entered Europe, and by about 15,000 years ago, they had reached North America followed by South America.

Stone ball from a set of Paleolithic bolas:
Paleoliths (artifacts from the Paleolithic), such as this stone ball, demonstrate some of the stone technologies that the early humans used as tools and weapons.

During about 10,000 BCE, a major change occurred in the way humans lived; this would have a cascading effect on every part of human society and culture. That change was the Neolithic Revolution.

The Neolithic Revolution: From Hunter-Gatherer to Agriculturalist

The beginning of the Neolithic Revolution in different regions has been dated from perhaps 8,000 BCE in the Kuk Early Agricultural Site of Melanesia Kuk to 2,500 BCE in Subsaharan Africa, with some considering the developments of 9,000-7,000 BCE in the Fertile Crescent to be the most important. This transition everywhere is associated with the change from a largely nomadic hunter-gatherer way of life to a more settled, agrarian-based one, due to the inception of the domestication of various plant and animal species—depending on the species locally available, and probably also influenced by local culture.

It is not known why humans decided to begin cultivating plants and domesticating animals. While more labor-intensive, the people must have seen the relationship between cultivation of grains and an increase in population. The domestication of animals provided a new source of protein, through meat and milk, along with hides and wool, which allowed for the production of clothing and other objects.

There are several competing (but not mutually exclusive) theories about the factors that drove populations to take up agriculture. The most prominent of these are:

- The Oasis Theory, originally proposed by Raphael Pumpelly in 1908, and popularized by V. Gordon Childe in 1928, suggests as the climate got drier due to the Atlantic depressions shifting northward, communities contracted to oases where they were forced into close association with animals. These animals were then domesticated together with planting of seeds. However, this theory has little support amongst archaeologists today because subsequent climate data suggests that the region was getting wetter rather than drier.

- The Hilly Flanks hypothesis, proposed by Robert Braidwood in 1948, suggests that agriculture began in the hilly flanks of the Taurus and Zagros mountains, where the climate was not drier, as Childe had believed, and that fertile land supported a variety of plants and animals amenable to domestication.

- The Feasting model by Brian Hayden suggests that agriculture was driven by ostentatious displays of power, such as giving feasts, to exert dominance. This system required assembling large quantities of food, a demand which drove agricultural technology.

- The Demographic theories proposed by Carl Sauer and adapted by Lewis Binford and Kent Flannery posit that an increasingly sedentary population outgrew the resources in the local environment and required more food than could be gathered. Various social and economic factors helped drive the need for food.

- The Evolutionary/Intentionality theory, developed by David Rindos and others, views agriculture as an evolutionary adaptation of plants and humans. Starting with domestication by protection of wild plants, it led to specialization of location and then full-fledged domestication.

Effects of the Neolithic Revolution on Society

The traditional view is that the shift to agricultural food production supported a denser population, which in turn supported larger sedentary communities, the accumulation of goods and tools, and specialization in diverse forms of new labor. Overall a population could increase its size more rapidly when resources were more available. The resulting larger societies led to the development of different means of decision making and governmental organization. Food surpluses made possible the development of a social elite freed from labor, who dominated their communities and monopolized decision-making. There were deep social divisions and inequality between the sexes, with women's status declining as men took on greater roles as leaders and warriors. Social class was determined by occupation, with farmers and craftsmen at the lower end, and priests and warriors at the higher.

Effects of the Neolithic Revolution on Health

Neolithic populations generally had poorer nutrition, shorter life expectancies, and a more labor-intensive lifestyle than hunter-gatherers. Diseases jumped from animals to humans, and agriculturalists suffered from more anaemia, vitamin deficiencies, spinal deformations, and dental pathologies.

Overall Impact of the Neolithic Revolution on Modern Life

The way we live today is directly related to the advances made in the Neolithic Revolution. From the governments we live under, to the specialized work laborers do, to the trade of goods and food, humans were irrevocably changed by the switch to sedentary agriculture and domestication of animals. Human population swelled from five million to seven billion today.

Attributions

CC licensed content, Specific attribution

- Human Evolution. **Provided by**: Wikipedia. **Located at**: https://en.wikipedia.org/wiki/Human_evolution. **License**: *CC BY: Attribution*
- Evolution of Human Intelligence. **Provided by**: Wikipedia. **Located at**: https://en.wikipedia.org/wiki/Evolution_of_human_intelligence. **License**: *CC BY: Attribution*
- A synthesis of the theories and concepts of early human evolution. **Provided by**: The Royal Society Publishing. **Located at**: http://rstb.royalsocietypublishing.org/content/370/1663/20140064. **License**: *CC BY: Attribution*
- Ape_skeletons.png. **Provided by**: Wikipedia. **Located at**: https://www.google.com/url?sa=i&rct=j&q=&esrc=s&source=images&cd=&ved=0ahUKEwjS3MXKh8vNAhXCOiYKHVQwBREQjR-wIBw&url=%2Furl%3Fsa%3Di%26rct%3Dj%26q%3D%26esrc%3Ds%26source%3Dimages%26cd%3D%26ved%3D0ahUKEwjS3MXKh8vNAhXCOiYKHVQwBREQjR-wIBw%26url%3D%252Furl%253Fsa%253Di%2526rct%253Dj%2526q%253D%2526esrc%253Ds%2526source%253Dimages%2526cd%253D%2526ved%253D0ahUKEwjS3MXKh8vNAhXCOiYKHVQwBREQjR-wIBw%2526url%253D%25252Furl%25253Fsa%25253Di%252526rct%25253Dj%252526q%25253D%252526esrc%25253Ds%252526source%25253Dimages%252526cd%25253D%252526ved%25253D0ahUKEwjS3MXKh8vNAhXCOiYKHVQwBREQjR-wIBw%252526url%25253Dhttps%252525253A%2525252F%2525252Fen.wikipedia.org%2525252Fwiki%2525252FHuman_evolution%252526psig%25253DAFQjCNGE6UxF84hKzfCy6mE_EE6SHrjOPA%252526ust%25253D1467214896545125%2526psig%253DAFQjCNGE6UxF84hKzfCy6mE_EE6SHrjOPA%2526ust%253D1467214896545125%26psig%3DAFQjCNGE6UxF84hKzfCy6mE_EE6SHrjOPA%26ust%3D1467214896545125&psig=AFQjCNGE6UxF84hKzfCy6mE_EE6SHrjOPA&ust=1467214896545125. **License**: *CC BY: Attribution*
- Comparison_of_skull_features_of_Homo_naledi_and_other_early_human_species.jpg. **Provided by**: Wikipedia. **Located at**: https://en.wikipedia.org/wiki/Homo_naledi. **License**: *CC BY: Attribution*
- The Neolithic Revolution and Sumer. **Provided by**: Global Economics. **Located at**: http://globaleconomics.wikispaces.com/The+Neolithic+Revolution+and+Sumer. **License**: *CC BY: Attribution*
- Before the Rise of Civilization. **Provided by**: Wikibooks. **Located at**: http://en.wikibooks.org/wiki/World_History/Ancient_Civilizations%23Before_the_Rise_of_Civilization. **License**: *CC BY-SA: Attribution-ShareAlike*
- Civilization makes its du00e9but (8000 - 3000 BC). **Provided by**: Wikibooks. **Located at**: http://en.wikibooks.org/wiki/World_History/Ancient_Civilizations%23Civilization_makes_its_d.C3.A9but_.288000_-_3000_BC.29. **License**: *CC BY-SA: Attribution-ShareAlike*
- Paleolithic. **Provided by**: Wikipedia. **Located at**: http://en.wikipedia.org/wiki/Paleolithic. **License**: *CC BY-SA: Attribution-ShareAlike*
- Neolithic Revolution. **Provided by**: Wikipedia. **Located at**: http://en.wikipedia.org/wiki/Neolithic_Revolution. **License**: *CC BY-SA: Attribution-ShareAlike*
- Neolithic Revolution. **Provided by**: Wikipedia. **Located at**: http://en.wikipedia.org/wiki/Neolithic%20Revolution. **License**: *CC*

BY-SA: Attribution-ShareAlike

- **Boundless. Provided by**: Boundless Learning. **Located at**: http://www.boundless.com//sociology/definition/hunter-gatherer--2. **License**: *CC BY-SA: Attribution-ShareAlike*

- Ape_skeletons.png. **Provided by**: Wikipedia. **Located at**: https://www.google.com/url?sa=i&rct=j&q=&esrc=s&source=images&cd=&ved=0ahUKEwjS3MXKh8vNAhXCOiYKHVQwBREQjR-wIBw&url=%2Furl%3Fsa%3Di%26rct%3Dj%26q%3D%26esrc%3Ds%26source%3Dimages%26cd%3D%26ved%3D0ahUKEwjS3MXKh8vNAhXCOiYKHVQwBREQjR-wIBw%26url%3D%252Furl%253Fsa%253Di%2526rct%253Dj%2526q%253D%2526esrc%253Ds%2526source%253Dimages%2526cd%253D%2526ved%253D0ahUKEwjS3MXKh8vNAhXCOiYKHVQwBREQjR-wIBw%2526url%253D%25252Furl%25253Fsa%25253Di%252526rct%25253Dj%252526q%25253D%252526esrc%25253Ds%252526source%25253Dimages%252526cd%25253D%252526ved%25253D0ahUKEwjS3MXKh3vNAhXCOiYKHVQwBREQjR-wIBw%252526url%25253Dhttps%2525253A%2525252F%2525252Fen.wikipedia.org%2525252Fwiki%2525252FHuman_evolution%252526psig%25253DAFQjCNGE6UxF84hKzfCy6mE_EE6SHrjOPA%252526ust%25253D1467214896545125%2526psig%253DAFQjCNGE6UxF84hKzfCy6mE_EE6SHrjOPA%2526ust%253D1467214896545125%26psig%3DAFQjCNGE6UxF84hKzfCy6mE_EE6SHrjOPA%26ust%3D1467214896545125&psig=AFQjCNGE6UxF84hKzfCy6mE_EE6SHrjOPA&ust=1467214896545125. **License**: *CC BY: Attribution*

- Comparison_of_skull_features_of_Homo_naledi_and_other_early_human_species.jpg. **Provided by**: Wikipedia. **Located at**: https://en.wikipedia.org/wiki/Homo_naledi. **License**: *CC BY: Attribution*

- Paleolithic. **Provided by**: Wikipedia. **Located at**: http://en.wikipedia.org/wiki/Paleolithic_period. **License**: *CC BY-SA: Attribution-ShareAlike*

The Study of History

Splitting History

Periodization—the process of categorizing the past into discrete, quantified, named blocks of time in order to facilitate the study and analysis of history—is always arbitrary and rooted in particular regional perspectives, but serves to organize and systematize historical knowledge.

Learning Objectives

Analyze the complications inherent to splitting history for the purpose of academic study

Key Takeaways

Key Points

- The question of what kind of inquiries historians pose, what knowledge they seek, and how they interpret the evidence that they find remains controversial. Historians draw conclusions from the past approaches to history but in the end, they always write in the context of their own time, current dominant ideas of how to interpret the past, and even subjective viewpoints.
- All events that are remembered and preserved in some original form constitute the historical record. The task of historians is to identify the sources that can most usefully contribute to the production of accurate accounts of the past. These sources, known are primary sources or evidence, were produced at the time under study and constitute the foundation of historical inquiry.
- Periodization is the process of categorizing the past into discrete, quantified named blocks of time in order to facilitate the study and analysis of history. This results in descriptive abstractions that provide convenient terms for periods of time with relatively stable characteristics. All systems of periodization are arbitrary.

- The common general split between prehistory, ancient history, Middle Ages, modern history, and contemporary history is a Western division of the largest blocks of time agreed upon by Western historians. However, even within this largely accepted division the perspective of specific national developments and experiences often divides Western historians, as some periodizing labels will be applicable only to particular regions.
- The study of world history emerged as a distinct academic field in order to examine history from a global perspective rather than a solely national perspective of investigation. However, the field still struggles with an inherently Western periodization.
- World historians use a thematic approach to look for common patterns that emerge across all cultures. World history's periodization, as imperfect and biased as it is, serves as a way to organize and systematize knowledge.

Key Terms

- **periodization**: The process or study of categorizing the past into discrete, quantified named blocks of time in order to facilitate the study and analysis of history. This results in descriptive abstractions that provide convenient terms for periods of time with relatively stable characteristics. However, determining the precise beginning and ending to any period is usually arbitrary.
- **world history**: (Also global history or transnational history): emerged as a distinct academic field in the 1980s. It examines history from a global perspective. World history should not be confused with comparative history, which, like world history, deals with the history of multiple cultures and nations, but does not do so on a global scale. World history identifies common patterns that emerge across all cultures.
- **primary sources**: Original sources of information about a topic. In the study of history as an academic discipline, primary sources include artifact, document, diary, manuscript, autobiography, recording, or other source of information that was created at the time under study.

How Do We Write History?

The word *history* comes ultimately from Ancient Greek *historía*, meaning "inquiry," "knowledge from inquiry," or "judge." However, the question of what kind of inquiries historians pose, what knowledge they seek, and how they interpret the evidence that they find remains controversial.

Historians draw conclusions from past approaches to history, but in the end, they always write in the context of their own time, current dominant ideas of how to interpret the past, and even subjective viewpoints. Furthermore, current events and developments often trigger which past events, historical periods, or geographical regions are seen as critical and thus should be investigated. Finally, historical studies are designed to provide specific lessons for societies today. In the words of Benedetto Croce, Italian philosopher and historian, "All history is contemporary history."

All events that are remembered and preserved in some original form constitute the historical record. The task of historians is to identify the sources that can most usefully contribute to the production of accurate accounts of the past. These sources, known are primary sources or evidence, were produced at the time under study and constitute the foundation of historical inquiry. Ideally, a historian will use as many available primary sources as can be accessed, but in practice, sources may have been destroyed or may not be available for research. In some cases, the only eyewitness reports of an event may be memoirs, autobiographies, or oral interviews taken years later. Sometimes, the only evidence relating to an event or person in the distant past was written or copied decades or centuries later. Historians remain cautious when working with evidence recorded years, or even decades or centuries, after an event; this kind of evidence poses the question of to what extent witnesses remember events accurately. However, historians also point out that hardly any historical evidence can be seen as objective, as it is always a product of particular individuals, times, and dominant ideas. This is also why researchers try to find as many records of an event under investigation as possible, and it is not unusual that they find evidence that may present contradictory accounts of the same events. In general, the sources of historical knowledge can be separated into three categories: what is written, what is said, and what is physically preserved. Historians often consult all three.

Periodization

Periodization is the process of categorizing the past into discrete, quantified, named blocks of time in order to facilitate the study and analysis of history. This results in descriptive abstractions that provide convenient terms for periods of time with relatively stable characteristics.

To the extent that history is continuous and cannot be generalized, all systems of periodization are arbitrary. Moreover, determining the precise beginning and ending to any period is also a matter of arbitrary decisions. Eventually, periodizing labels are a reflection of very particular cultural and geographical perspectives, as well as specific subfields or themes of history (e.g., military history, social history, political history, intellectual history, cultural history, etc.). Consequently, not only do periodizing blocks inevitably overlap, but they also often seemingly conflict with or contradict one another. Some have a cultural usage (the Gilded Age), others refer to prominent historical events (the inter-war years: 1918–1939), yet others are defined by decimal numbering systems (the 1960s, the 17th century). Other periods are named after influential individuals whose impact may or may not have reached beyond certain geographic regions (the Victorian Era, the Edwardian Era, the Napoleonic Era).

Western Historical Periods

The common general split between prehistory (before written history), ancient history, Middle Ages, modern history, and contemporary history (history within the living memory) is a Western division of the largest blocks of time agreed upon by Western historians and representing the Western point of view. For example, the history of Asia or Africa cannot be neatly categorized following these periods.

However, even within this largely accepted division, the perspective of specific national developments and experiences often divides Western historians, as some periodizing labels will be applicable only to particular regions. This is especially true of labels derived from individuals or ruling dynasties, such as the Jacksonian Era in the United States, or the Merovingian Period in France. Cultural terms may also have a limited, even if larger, reach. For example, the concept of the Romantic period is largely meaningless outside of Europe and European-influenced cultures; even within those areas, different European regions may mark the beginning and the ending points of Romanticism differently. Likewise, the 1960s, although technically applicable to anywhere in the world according to Common Era numbering, has a certain set of specific cultural connotations in certain countries, including sexual revolution, counterculture, or youth rebellion. However, those never emerged in certain regions (e.g., in Spain under Francisco Franco's authoritarian regime). Some historians have also noted that the 1960s, as a descriptive historical period, actually began in the late 1950s and ended in the early 1970s, because the cultural and economic conditions that define the meaning of the period dominated longer than the actual decade of the 1960s.

Petrarch by Andrea del Castagno.

Petrarch, Italian poet and thinker, conceived of the idea of a European "Dark Age," which later evolved into the tripartite periodization of Western history into Ancient, Middle Ages and Modern.

While world history (also referred to as global history or transnational history) emerged as a distinct academic field of historical study in the 1980s in order to examine history from a global perspective rather than a solely national perspective of investigation, it still struggles with an inherently Western periodization. The common splits used when designing comprehensive college-level world history courses (and thus also used in history textbooks that are usually divided into volumes covering pre-modern and modern eras) are still a result of certain historical developments presented from the perspective of the Western world and particular national experiences. However, even the split between pre-modern and modern eras is problematic because it is complicated by the question of how history educators, textbook authors, and publishers decide to categorize what is known as the early modern era, which is traditionally a period between Renaissance and the end of the Age of Enlightenment. In the end, whether the early modern era is included in the first or the second part of a world history course frequently offered in U.S. colleges is a subjective decision of history educators. As a result, the same questions and choices apply to history textbooks written and published for the U.S. audience.

World historians use a thematic approach to identify common patterns that emerge across all cultures, with two major focal points: integration (how processes of world history have drawn people of the world together) and difference (how patterns of world history reveal the diversity of the human experiences). The periodization of world history, as imperfect and biased as it is, serves as a way to organize and systematize knowledge.
Without it, history would be nothing more than scattered events without a framework designed to help us understand the past.

Dates and Calendars

While various calendars were developed and used across millennia, cultures, and geographical regions, Western historical scholarship has unified the standards of determining dates based on the dominant Gregorian calendar.

Learning Objectives

Compare and contrast different calendars and how they affect our understanding of history

Key Takeaways

Key Points

- The first recorded calendars date to the Bronze

Age, including the Egyptian and Sumerian calendars. A larger number of calendar systems of the Ancient Near East became accessible in the Iron Age and were based on the Babylonian calendar. A great number of Hellenic calendars also developed in Classical Greece and influenced calendars outside of the immediate sphere of Greek influence, giving rise to the various Hindu calendars, as well as to the ancient Roman calendar.

- Despite various calendars used across millennia, cultures, and geographical regions, Western historical scholarship has unified the standards of determining dates based on the dominant Gregorian calendar.

- Julius Caesar effected drastic changes in the existing timekeeping system. The New Year in 709 AUC began on January first and ran over 365 days until December 31. Further adjustments were made under Augustus, who introduced the concept of the leap year in 737 AUC (4 CE). The resultant Julian calendar remained in almost universal use in Europe until 1582.

- The Gregorian calendar, also called the Western calendar and the Christian calendar, is internationally the most widely used civil calendar today. It is named after Pope Gregory XIII, who introduced it in October, 1582. The calendar was a refinement to the Julian calendar, amounting to a 0.002% correction in the length of the year.

- While the European Gregorian calendar eventually dominated the world and historiography, a number of other calendars have shaped
timekeeping systems that are still influential in some regions of the world. These include the Islamic calendar, various Hindu calendars, and the Mayan calendar.

- A calendar era that is often used as an alternative naming of the long-accepted *anno Domini* /before Christ system is Common Era or Current Era, abbreviated CE. While both systems are an accepted standard, the Common Era system is more neutral and inclusive of a non-Christian perspective.

Key Terms

- **Islamic calendar**: (Also Muslim calendar or Hijri calendar): A lunar calendar consisting of 12 months in a year of 354 or 355 days. It is used to date events in many Muslim countries (concurrently with the Gregorian calendar), and is used by Muslims everywhere to determine the proper days on which to observe the annual fasting, to attend Hajj, and to celebrate other Islamic holidays and festivals. The first year equals 622 CE, during which time the emigration of Muhammad from Mecca to Medina, known as the Hijra, occurred.

- **anno Domini**: The Medieval Latin term, which means in the year of the Lord but is often translated as in the year of our Lord. Dionysius Exiguus, of Scythia Minor, introduced the system based on this concept in 525, counting the years since the birth of Christ.

- **Mayan calendar**: A system of calendars used in pre-Columbian Mesoamerica, and in many modern communities in the Guatemalan highlands, Veracruz, Oaxaca and Chiapas, Mexico. The essentials of it are based upon a system that was in common use throughout the region, dating back to at least the fifth century BCE. It shares many aspects with calendars employed by other earlier Mesoamerican civilizations, such as the Zapotec and Olmec, and with contemporary or later calendars, such as the Mixtec and Aztec calen-

> dars.
>
> - **Julian calendar**: A calendar introduced by Julius Caesar in 46 BCE (708 AUC), which was a reform of the Roman calendar. It took effect in 45 BCE (AUC 709), shortly after the Roman conquest of Egypt. It was the predominant calendar in the Roman world, most of Europe, and in European settlements in the Americas and elsewhere, until it was refined and gradually replaced by the Gregorian calendar, promulgated in 1582 by Pope Gregory XIII.
> - **Gregorian calendar**: (Also the Western calendar and the Christian calendar): A calendar that is internationally the most widely used civil calendar today. It is named after Pope Gregory XIII, who introduced it in October 1582. The calendar was a refinement to the Julian calendar, amounting to a 0.002% correction in the length of the year.

Calendars and Writing History

Methods of timekeeping can be reconstructed for the prehistoric period from at least the Neolithic period. The natural units for timekeeping used by most historical societies are the day, the solar year, and the lunation. The first recorded calendars date to the Bronze Age, and include the Egyptian and Sumerian calendars. A larger number of calendar systems of the Ancient Near East became accessible in the Iron Age and were based on the Babylonian calendar. One of these was calendar of the Persian Empire, which in turn gave rise to the Zoroastrian calendar, as well as the Hebrew calendar.

A great number of Hellenic calendars were developed in Classical Greece and influenced calendars outside of the immediate sphere of Greek influence. These gave rise to the various Hindu calendars, as well as to the ancient Roman calendar, which contained very ancient remnants of a pre-Etruscan ten-month solar year. The Roman calendar was reformed by Julius Caesar in 45 BCE. The Julian calendar was no longer dependent on the observation of the new moon, but simply followed an algorithm of introducing a leap day every four years. This created a dissociation of the calendar month from the lunation. The Gregorian calendar was introduced as a refinement of the Julian calendar in 1582 and is today in worldwide use as the *de facto* calendar for secular purposes.

Despite various calendars used across millennia, cultures, and geographical regions, Western historical scholarship has unified the standards of determining dates based on the dominant Gregorian calendar. Regardless of what historical period or geographical areas Western historians investigate and write about, they adjust dates from the original timekeeping system to the Gregorian calendar. Occasionally, some historians decide to use both dates: the dates recorded under the original calendar used, and the date adjusted to the Gregorian calendar, easily recognizable to the Western student of history.

Julian Calendar

The old Roman year had 304 days divided into ten months, beginning with March. However, the ancient historian, Livy, gave credit to the second ancient Roman king, Numa Pompilious, for devising a calendar of twelve months. The extra months *Ianuarius* and *Februarius* had been invented, supposedly by Numa Pompilious, as stop-gaps. Julius Caesar realized that the system had become inoperable, so he effected drastic changes in the year of his third consulship. The New Year in 709 AUC (*ab urbe condita*— year from the founding of the City of Rome) began on January first and ran over 365 days until December 31.

Further adjustments were made under Augustus, who introduced the concept of the leap year in 737 AUC (4 CE). The resultant Julian calendar remained in almost universal use in Europe until 1582. Marcus Terentius Varro introduced the *Ab urbe condita* epoch, assuming a foundation of Rome in 753 BCE. The system remained in use during the early medieval period until the widespread adoption of the Dionysian era in the Carolingian period. The seven-day week has a tradition reaching back to the Ancient Near East, but the introduction of the planetary week, which remains in modern use, dates to the Roman Empire period.

Gregorian Calendar

The Gregorian calendar, also called the Western calendar and the Christian calendar, is internationally the most widely used civil calendar today. It is named after Pope Gregory XIII, who introduced it in October, 1582. The calendar was a refinement to the Julian calendar, amounting to a 0.002% correction in the length of the year. The motivation for the reform was to stop the drift of the calendar with respect to the equinoxes and solstices—particularly the vernal equinox, which set the date for Easter celebrations. Transition to the Gregorian calendar would restore the holiday to the time of the year in which it was celebrated when introduced by the early Church. The reform was adopted initially by the Catholic countries of Europe. Protestants and Eastern Orthodox countries continued to use the traditional Julian calendar, and eventually adopted the Gregorian reform for the sake of convenience in international trade. The last European country to adopt the reform was Greece in 1923.

The first page of the papal bull "Inter Gravissimas" by which Pope Gregory XIII introduced his calendar.

During the period between 1582, when the first countries adopted the Gregorian calendar, and 1923, when the last European country adopted it, it was often necessary to indicate the date of some event in both the Julian calendar and in the Gregorian calendar. Even before 1582, the year sometimes had to be double dated because of the different beginnings of the year in various countries.

Calendars Outside of Europe

While the European Gregorian calendar eventually dominated the world and historiography, a number of other calendars have shaped timekeeping systems that are still influential in some regions of the world. The Islamic calendar determines the first year in 622 CE, during which the emigration of Muhammad from Mecca to Medina, known as the Hijra, occurred. It is used to date events in many Muslim countries (concurrently with the Gregorian calendar), and is used by Muslims everywhere to determine the proper days on which to observe and celebrate Islamic religious practices (e.g., fasting), holidays, and festivals.

Various Hindu calendars developed in the medieval period with Gupta era astronomy as their common basis. Some of the more prominent regional Hindu calendars include the Nepali calendar, Assamese calendar, Bengali calendar, Malayalam calendar, Tamil calendar, the Vikrama Samvat (used in Northern India), and Shalivahana calendar. The common feature of all regional Hindu calendars is that the names of the twelve months are the same (because the names are based in Sanskrit) although the spelling and pronunciation have come to vary slightly from region to region over thousands of years. The month that starts the year also varies from region to region. The Buddhist calendar and the traditional lunisolar calendars of Cambodia, Laos, Myanmar, Sri Lanka, and Thailand are also based on an older version of the Hindu calendar.

Of all the ancient calendar systems, the Mayan and other Mesoamerican systems are the most complex. The Mayan calendar had two years, the 260-day Sacred Round, or *tzolkin*, and the 365-day Vague Year, or *haab*.

The essentials of the Mayan calendar are based upon a system that was in common use throughout the region, dating back to at least the fifth century BCE. It shares many aspects with calendars employed by other earlier Mesoamerican civilizations, such as the Zapotec and Olmec, and contemporary or later ones, such as the Mixtec and Aztec calendars. The Mayan calendar is still used in many modern communities in the Guatemalan highlands, Veracruz, Oaxaca and Chiapas, Mexico.

Islamic Calendar stamp issued at King Khaled airport (10 Rajab 1428 / 24 July 2007)

The first year was the Islamic year beginning in AD 622, during which the emigration of Muhammad from Mecca to Medina, known as the Hijra, occurred. Each numbered year is designated either "H" for *Hijra* or "AH" for the Latin *Anno Hegirae* ("in the year of the Hijra"). Hence, Muslims typically call their calendar the Hijri calendar.

Anno Domini v. Common Era

The terms *anno Domini* (AD) and before Christ (BC) are used to label or number years in the Julian and Gregorian calendars. The term *anno Domini* is Medieval Latin, which means *in the year of the Lord,* but is often translated as *in the year of our Lord*. It is occasionally set out more fully as *anno Domini nostri Iesu* (or *Jesu Christi* ("in the year of Our Lord Jesus Christ"). Dionysius Exiguus of Scythia Minor introduced the AD system in AD 525, counting the years since the birth of Christ. This calendar era is based on the traditionally recognized year of the conception or birth of Jesus of Nazareth, with AD counting years after the start of this epoch and BC denoting years before the start of the era. There is no year zero in this scheme, so the year AD 1 immediately follows the year 1 BC. This dating system was devised in 525, but was not widely used until after 800.

A calendar era that is often used as an alternative naming of the a*nno Domini* is Common Era or Current Era, abbreviated CE. The system uses BCE as an abbreviation for "before the Common (or Current) Era." The CE/BCE designation uses the same numeric values as the AD/BC system so the two notations (CE/BCE and AD/BC) are numerically equivalent. The expression "Common Era" can be found as early as 1708 in English and traced back to Latin usage among European Christians to 1615, as *vulgaris aerae,* and to 1635 in English as *Vulgar Era*.

Since the later 20th century, the use of CE and BCE have been popularized in academic and scientific publications, and more generally by authors and publishers wishing to emphasize secularism or sensitivity to non-Christians, because the system does not explicitly make use of religious titles for Jesus, such as "Christ" and *Dominus* ("Lord"), which are used in the BC/AD notation, nor does it give implicit expression to the Christian creed that Jesus is the Christ. While both systems are thus an accepted standard, the CE/BCE system is more neutral and inclusive of a non-Christian perspective.

The Imperfect Historical Record

While some primary sources are considered more reliable or trustworthy than others, hardly any historical evidence can be seen as fully objective since it is always a product of particular individuals, times, and dominant ideas.

Learning Objectives

Explain the consequences of the imperfect historical record

Key Takeaways

Key Points

- In the study of history as an academic discipline, a primary source is an artifact, document, diary, manuscript, autobiography, recording, or other source of information that was created at the time under study.
- History as an academic discipline is based on primary sources, as evaluated by the community of scholars for whom primary sources are absolutely fundamental to reconstructing the past. Ideally, a historian will use as many primary sources that were created during the time under study as can be accessed. In practice however, some sources have been destroyed, while others are not available for research.
- While some sources are considered more reliable or trustworthy than others, historians point out that hardly any historical evidence can be seen as fully objective since it is always a product of particular individuals, times, and dominant ideas.
- Historical method comprises the techniques and guidelines by which historians use primary sources and other evidence (including the evidence of archaeology) to research and write historical accounts of the past.
- Primary sources may remain in private hands or are located in archives, libraries, museums, historical societies, and special collections. Traditionally, historians attempt to answer historical questions through the study of written documents and oral accounts. They also use such sources as monuments, inscriptions, and pictures. In general, the sources of historical knowledge can be separated into three categories: what is written, what is said, and what is physically preserved. Historians often consult all three.
- Historians use various strategies to reconstruct the past when facing a lack of sources, including collaborating with experts from other academic disciplines, most notably archaeology.

Key Terms

- **secondary source**: A document or recording that relates or discusses information originally found in a primary source. It contrasts with a primary source, which is an original

> source of the information being discussed; a primary source can be a person with direct knowledge of a situation, or a document created by such a person. A secondary source involves generalization, analysis, synthesis, interpretation, or evaluation of the original information.
> - **primary source**: In the study of history as an academic discipline, an artifact, document, diary, manuscript, autobiography, recording, or other source of information that was created at the time under study. It serves as an original source of information about the topic.
> - **historical method**: A scholarly method that comprises the techniques and guidelines by which historians use primary sources and other evidence (including the evidence of archaeology) to research and write historical accounts of the past.

Primary Sources

In the study of history as an academic discipline, a primary source (also called original source or evidence) is an artifact, document, diary, manuscript, autobiography, recording, or other source of information that was created at the time under study. It serves as an original source of information about the topic. Primary sources are distinguished from secondary sources, which cite, comment on, or build upon primary sources. In some cases, a secondary source may also be a primary source, depending on how it is used. For example, a memoir would be considered a primary source in research concerning its author or about his or her friends characterized within it, but the same memoir would be a secondary source if it were used to examine the culture in which its author lived. "Primary" and "secondary" should be understood as relative terms, with sources categorized according to specific historical contexts and what is being studied.

Using Primary Sources: Historical Method

History as an academic discipline is based on primary sources, as evaluated by the community of scholars for whom primary sources are absolutely fundamental to reconstructing the past. Ideally, a historian will use as many primary sources that were created by the people involved at the time under study as can be accessed. In practice however, some sources have been destroyed, while others are not available for research. In some cases, the only eyewitness reports of an event may be memoirs, autobiographies, or oral interviews taken years later. Sometimes, the only evidence relating to an event or person in the distant past was written or copied decades or centuries later. Manuscripts that are sources for classical texts can be copies or fragments of documents. This is a common problem in classical studies, where sometimes only a summary of a book or letter, but not the actual book or letter, has survived. While some sources are considered more reliable or trustworthy than others (e.g., an original government document containing information about an event vs. a recording of a witness recalling the same event years later), historians point out that hardly any historical evidence can be seen as fully objective as it is always a product of particular individuals, times, and dominant ideas. This is also why researchers try to find as many records of an event under investigation as possible, and attempt to resolve evidence that may present contradictory accounts of the same events.

This wall painting (known as The portrait of Paquius Proculo and currently preserved at the Naples National Archaeological Museum) was found in the Roman city of Pompeii and serves as a complex example of a primary source.

The fresco would not tell much to historians without corresponding textual and archaeological evidence that helps to establish who the portrayed couple might have been. The man wears a toga, the mark of a Roman citizen, and holds a rotulus, suggesting he is involved in public and/or cultural affairs. The woman holds a stylus and wax tablet, emphasizing that she is educated and literate. It is suspected, based on the physical features of the couple, that they are Samnites, which may explain the desire to show off the status they have reached in Roman society.

Historical method comprises the techniques and guidelines by which historians use primary sources and other evidence (including the evidence of archaeology) to research and write historical accounts of the past. Historians continue to debate what aspects and practices of investigating primary sources should be considered, and what constitutes a primary source when developing the most effective historical method. The question of the nature, and even the possibility, of a sound historical method is so central that it has been continuously raised in the philosophy of history as a question of epistemology.

Finding Primary Sources

Primary sources may remain in private hands or are located in archives, libraries, museums, historical societies, and special collections. These can be public or private. Some are affiliated with universities and colleges, while others are government entities. Materials relating to one area might be spread over a large number of different institutions. These can be distant from the original source of the document. For example, the Huntington Library in California houses a large number of documents from the United Kingdom. While the development of technology has resulted in an increasing number of digitized sources, most primary source materials are not digitized and may only be represented online with a record or finding aid.

Traditionally, historians attempt to answer historical questions through the study of written documents and oral accounts. They also use such sources as monuments, inscriptions, and pictures. In general, the sources of historical knowledge can be separated into three categories: what is written, what is said, and what is physically preserved. Historians often consult all three. However, writing is the marker that separates history from what comes before

Archaeology is one discipline that is especially helpful to historians. By dealing with buried sites and objects, it contributes to the reconstruction of the past. However, archaeology is constituted by a range of methodologies and approaches that are independent from history. In other words, archaeology does not "fill the gaps" within textual sources but often contrasts its conclusions against those of contemporary textual sources.

Archaeology also provides an illustrative example of how historians can be helped when written records are missing. Unearthing artifacts and working with archaeologists to interpret them based on the expertise of a particular historical era and cultural or geographical area is one effective way to reconstruct the past. If written records are missing, historians often attempt to collect oral accounts of particular events, preferably by eyewitnesses, but sometimes, because of the passage of time, they are forced to work with the following generations. Thus, the question of the reliability of oral history has been widely debated.

When dealing with many government records, historians usually have to wait for a specific period of time before documents are declassified and available to researchers. For political reasons, many sensitive records may be destroyed, withdrawn from collections, or hidden, which may also encourage researchers to rely on oral histories. Missing records of events, or processes that historians believe took place based on very fragmentary evidence, forces historians to seek information in records that may not be a likely sources of information. As archival
research is always time-consuming and labor-intensive, this approach poses the risk of never producing desired results, despite the time and effort invested in finding informative and reliable resources. In some cases, historians are forced to speculate (this should be explicitly noted) or simply admit that we do not have sufficient information to reconstruct particular past events or processes.

Historical Bias

Biases have been part of historical investigation since the ancient beginnings of the discipline. While more recent scholarly practices attempt to remove earlier biases from history, no piece of historical scholarship can be fully free of biases.

Learning Objectives
Identify some examples of historical bias

Key Takeaways

Key Points

- Regardless of whether they are conscious or learned implicitly within cultural contexts, biases have been part of historical investigation since the ancient beginnings of the discipline. As such, history provides an excellent example of how biases change, evolve, and even disappear.
- Early attempts to make history an empirical, objective discipline (most notably by Voltaire) did not find many followers. Throughout the 18th and 19th centuries, European historians only strengthened their biases. As Europe gradually dominated the world through the self-imposed mission to colonize nearly all the other continents, Eurocentrism prevailed in history.
- Even within the Eurocentric perspective, not all Europeans were equal; Western historians largely ignored aspects of history, such as class, gender, or ethnicity. Until the rapid development of social history in the 1960s and 1970s, mainstream Western historical narratives focused on political and military history, while cultural or social history was written mostly from the perspective of the elites.
- The biased approach to history-writing transferred also to history-teaching. From the origins of national mass schooling systems in the 19th century, the teaching of history to promote national sentiment has been a high priority. History textbooks in most countries have been tools to foster nationalism and patriotism and to promote the most favorable version of national history.
- Germany attempts to be an example of how to remove nationalistic narratives from history education. The history curriculum in Germany is characterized by a transnational perspective that emphasizes the all-European heritage, minimizes the idea of national pride, and fosters the notion of civil society centered on democracy, human rights, and peace.
- Despite progress and increased focus on groups that have been traditionally excluded from mainstream historical narratives (people of color, women, the working class, the poor, the disabled, LGBTQI-identified people, etc.), bias remains a component of historical investigation.

Key Terms

- **Eurocentrism**: The practice of viewing the world from a European or generally Western perspective with an implied belief in the pre-eminence of Western culture. It may also be used to describe a view centered on the history or eminence of white people. The term was coined in the 1980s, referring to the notion of European exceptionalism and other Western equivalents, such as American exceptionalism.

Bias in Historical Writing

Bias is an inclination or outlook to present or hold a partial perspective, often accompanied by a refusal to consider the possible merits of alternative points of view. Regardless of whether conscious or learned implicitly within cultural contexts, biases have been part of historical investigation since the ancient beginnings of the discipline. As such, history provides an excellent example of how biases change, evolve, and even disappear.

History as a modern academic discipline based on empirical methods (in this case, studying primary sources in order to reconstruct the past based on available evidence), rose to prominence during the Age of Enlightenment. Voltaire, a French author and thinker, is credited to have developed a fresh outlook on history that broke from the tradition of narrating diplomatic and military events and emphasized customs, social history (the history of ordinary people) and achievements in the arts and sciences. His *Essay on Customs* traced the progress of world civilization in a universal context, thereby rejecting both nationalism and the traditional Christian frame of reference. Voltaire was also the first scholar to make a serious attempt to write the history of the world, eliminating theological frameworks and emphasizing economics, culture, and political history. He was the first to emphasize the debt of medieval culture to Middle Eastern civilization. Although he repeatedly warned against political bias on the part of the historian, he did not miss many opportunities to expose the intolerance and frauds of the Catholic Church over the ages— a topic that was Voltaire's life-long intellectual interest.

Voltaire's early attempts to make history an empirical, objective discipline did not find many followers. Throughout the 18th and 19th centuries, European historians only strengthened their biases. As Europe gradually benefited from the ongoing scientific progress and dominated the world in the self-imposed mission to colonize nearly all other continents, Eurocentrism prevailed in history. The practice of viewing and presenting the world from a European or generally Western perspective, with an implied belief in the pre-eminence of Western culture, dominated among European historians who contrasted the progressively mechanized character of European culture with traditional hunting, farming and herding societies in many of the areas of the world being newly conquered and colonized. These included the Americas, Asia, Africa and, later, the Pacific and Australasia. Many European writers of this time construed the history of Europe as paradigmatic for the rest of the world. Other cultures were identified as having reached a stage that Europe itself had already passed: primitive hunter-gatherer, farming, early civilization, feudalism and modern liberal-capitalism. Only Europe was considered to have achieved the last stage. With this assumption, Europeans were also presented as racially superior, and European history as a discipline became essentially the history of the dominance of white peoples.

However, even within the Eurocentric perspective, not all Europeans were equal; Western historians largely ignored aspects of history, such as class, gender, or ethnicity. Until relatively recently (particularly the rapid development of social history in the 1960s and 1970s), mainstream Western historical narratives focused on political and military history, while cultural or social history was written mostly from the perspective of the elites. Consequently, what was in fact an experience of a selected few (usually white males of upper classes, with some occasional mentions of their female counterparts), was typically presented as the illustrative experience of the entire society. In the United States, some of the first to break this approach were African American scholars who at the turn of the 20th century wrote histories of black Americans and called for their inclusion in the mainstream historical narrative.

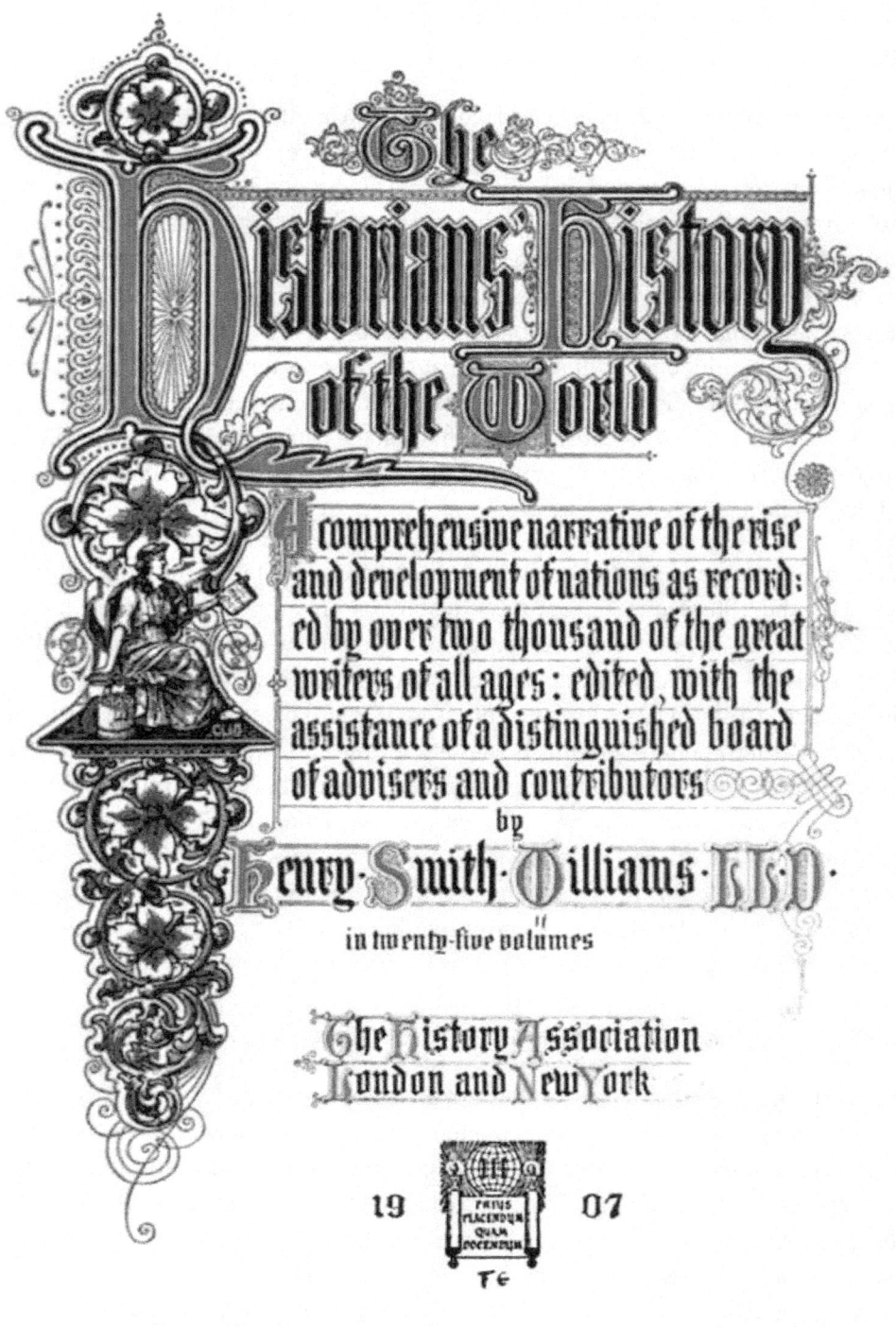

The title page to The Historians' History of the World: A Comprehensive Narrative of the Rise and Development of Nations as Recorded by over two thousand of the Great Writers of all Ages, 1907.

The Historians' History of the World is a 25-volume encyclopedia of world history originally published in English near the beginning of the 20th century. It is quite extensive but its perspective is entirely Western Eurocentric. For example, while four volumes focus on the history of England (with Scotland and Ireland included in one of them), "Poland, the Balkans, Turkey, minor Eastern states, China, Japan" are all described in one volume. It was compiled by Henry Smith Williams, a medical doctor and author, as well as other authorities on history, and published in New York in 1902 by Encyclopædia Britannica and the Outlook Company.

Bias in the Teaching of History

The biased approach to historical writing is present in the teaching of history as well. From the origins of national mass schooling systems in the 19th century, the teaching of history to promote national sentiment has been a high priority. Until today, in most countries history textbook are tools to foster nationalism and patriotism and promote the most favorable version of national history. In the United States, one of the most striking examples of this approach is the continuous narrative of the United States as a state established on the principles of personal liberty and democracy. Although aspects of U.S. history, such as slavery, genocide of American Indians, or disfranchisement of the large segments of the society for decades after the onset of the American statehood, are now taught in most (yet not all) American schools, they are presented as marginal in the larger narrative of liberty and democracy.

In many countries, history textbooks are sponsored by the national government and are written to put the national heritage in the most favorable light, although academic historians have often fought against the politicization of the textbooks, sometimes with success. Interestingly, the 21st-century Germany attempts to be an example of how to remove nationalistic narratives from history education. As the 20th-century history of Germany is filled with events and processes that are rarely a cause of national pride, the history curriculum in Germany (controlled by the 16 German states) is characterized by a transnational perspective that emphasizes the all-European heritage, minimizes the idea of national pride, and fosters the notion of civil society centered on democracy, human rights, and peace. Yet, even in the rather unusual German case, Eurocentrism continues to dominate.

The challenge to replace national, or even nationalist, perspectives with a more inclusive transnational or global view of human history is also still very present in college-level history curricula. In the United States after World War I, a strong movement emerged at the university level to teach courses in Western Civilization with the aim to give students a common heritage with Europe. After 1980, attention increasingly moved toward teaching world history or requiring students to take courses in non-western cultures. Yet, world history courses still struggle to move beyond the Eurocentric perspective, focusing heavily on the history of Europe and its links to the United States.

Despite all the progress and much more focus on the groups that have been traditionally excluded from mainstream historical narratives (people of color, women, the working class, the poor, the disabled, LGBTQI-identified people, etc.), bias remains a component of historical investigation, whether it is a product of nationalism, author's political views, or an agenda-driven interpretation of sources. It is only appropriate to state that the present world history book, while written in accordance with the most recent scholarly and educational practices, has been written and edited by authors trained in American universities and published in the United States. As such, it is also not free from both national (U.S.) and individual (authors') biases.

Attributions

CC licensed content, Specific attribution

- History. **Provided by**: Wikipedia. **Located at**: https://en.wikipedia.org/wiki/History. **License**: *CC BY-SA: Attribution-ShareAlike*

- Periodization. **Provided by**: Wikipedia. **Located at**: https://en.wikipedia.org/wiki/Periodization. **License**: *CC BY-SA: Attribution-ShareAlike*
- Historical method. **Provided by**: Wikipedia. **Located at**: https://en.wikipedia.org/wiki/Historical_method. **License**: *CC BY-SA: Attribution-ShareAlike*
- Early modern period. **Provided by**: Wikipedia. **Located at**: https://en.wikipedia.org/wiki/Early_modern_period. **License**: *CC BY-SA: Attribution-ShareAlike*
- World history. **Provided by**: Wikipedia. **Located at**: https://en.wikipedia.org/wiki/World_history. **License**: *CC BY-SA: Attribution-ShareAlike*
- Primary source. **Provided by**: Wikipedia. **Located at**: https://en.wikipedia.org/wiki/Primary_source. **License**: *CC BY-SA: Attribution-ShareAlike*
- Petrarch_by_Bargilla.jpg. **Provided by**: Wikipedia. **Located at**: https://en.wikipedia.org/wiki/Periodization#/media/File:Petrarch_by_Bargilla.jpg. **License**: *Public Domain: No Known Copyright*
- Common Era. **Provided by**: Wikipedia. **Located at**: https://en.wikipedia.org/wiki/Common_Era. **License**: *CC BY-SA: Attribution-ShareAlike*
- ab urbe condita. **Provided by**: Wikipedia. **Located at**: https://en.wikipedia.org/wiki/Ab_urbe_condita. **License**: *CC BY-SA: Attribution-ShareAlike*
- Julian calendar. **Provided by**: Wikipedia. **Located at**: https://en.wikipedia.org/wiki/Julian_calendar. **License**: *CC BY-SA: Attribution-ShareAlike*
- Gregorian calendar. **Provided by**: Wikipedia. **Located at**: https://en.wikipedia.org/wiki/Gregorian_calendar. **License**: *CC BY-SA: Attribution-ShareAlike*
- History of calendars. **Provided by**: Wikipedia. **Located at**: https://en.wikipedia.org/wiki/History_of_calendars. **License**: *CC BY-SA: Attribution-ShareAlike*
- Calendar. **Provided by**: Wikipedia. **Located at**: https://en.wikipedia.org/wiki/Calendar. **License**: *CC BY-SA: Attribution-ShareAlike*
- Maya calendar. **Provided by**: Wikipedia. **Located at**: https://en.wikipedia.org/wiki/Maya_calendar. **License**: *CC BY-SA: Attribution-ShareAlike*
- Anno Domini. **Provided by**: Wikipedia. **Located at**: https://en.wikipedia.org/wiki/Anno_Domini. **License**: *CC BY-SA: Attribution-ShareAlike*
- Islamic calendar. **Provided by**: Wikipedia. **Located at**: https://en.wikipedia.org/wiki/Islamic_calendar. **License**: *CC BY-SA: Attribution-ShareAlike*
- Petrarch_by_Bargilla.jpg. **Provided by**: Wikipedia. **Located at**: https://en.wikipedia.org/wiki/Periodization#/media/File:Petrarch_by_Bargilla.jpg. **License**: *Public Domain: No Known Copyright*
- Inter-grav.jpg. **Provided by**: Wikipedia. **Located at**: https://en.wikipedia.org/wiki/Gregorian_calendar#/media/File:Inter-grav.jpg. **License**: *Public Domain: No Known Copyright*
- King_Khaled_airport_exit_stamp.jpg. **Provided by**: Wikipedia. **Located at**: https://en.wikipedia.org/wiki/Islamic_calendar#/media/File:King_Khaled_airport_exit_stamp.jpg. **License**: *CC BY-SA: Attribution-ShareAlike*
- Historical method. **Provided by**: Wikipedia. **Located at**: https://en.wikipedia.org/wiki/Historical_method. **License**: *CC BY-SA: Attribution-ShareAlike*
- History. **Provided by**: Wikipedia. **Located at**: https://en.wikipedia.org/wiki/History. **License**: *CC BY-SA: Attribution-ShareAlike*
- Secondary source. **Provided by**: Wikipedia. **Located at**: https://en.wikipedia.org/wiki/Secondary_source. **License**: *CC BY-SA: Attribution-ShareAlike*
- Primary source. **Provided by**: Wikipedia. **Located at**: https://en.wikipedia.org/wiki/Primary_source. **License**: *CC BY-SA: Attribution-ShareAlike*
- Portrait of Paquius Proculo. **Provided by**: Wikipedia. **Located at**: https://en.wikipedia.org/wiki/Portrait_of_Paquius_Proculo. **License**: *CC BY-SA: Attribution-ShareAlike*
- Petrarch_by_Bargilla.jpg. **Provided by**: Wikipedia. **Located at**: https://en.wikipedia.org/wiki/Periodization#/media/File:Petrarch_by_Bargilla.jpg. **License**: *Public Domain: No Known Copyright*
- Inter-grav.jpg. **Provided by**: Wikipedia. **Located at**: https://en.wikipedia.org/wiki/Gregorian_calendar#/media/File:Inter-grav.jpg. **License**: *Public Domain: No Known Copyright*
- King_Khaled_airport_exit_stamp.jpg. **Provided by**: Wikipedia. **Located at**: https://en.wikipedia.org/wiki/Islamic_calendar#/media/File:King_Khaled_airport_exit_stamp.jpg. **License**: *CC BY-SA: Attribution-ShareAlike*
- Pompeii-couple.jpg. **Provided by**: Wikipedia. **Located at**: https://en.wikipedia.org/wiki/Primary_source#/media/File:Pompeii-cou-

- ple.jpg. **License:** *Public Domain: No Known Copyright*
- History. **Provided by:** Wikipedia. **Located at:** https://en.wikipedia.org/wiki/History. **License:** *CC BY-SA: Attribution-ShareAlike*
- The Historians' History of the World. **Provided by:** Wikipedia. **Located at:** https://en.wikipedia.org/wiki/The_Historians%27_History_of_the_World. **License:** *CC BY-SA: Attribution-ShareAlike*
- Social history. **Provided by:** Wikipedia. **Located at:** https://en.wikipedia.org/wiki/Social_history. **License:** *CC BY-SA: Attribution-ShareAlike*
- Voltaire. **Provided by:** Wikipedia. **Located at:** https://en.wikipedia.org/wiki/Voltaire#History. **License:** *CC BY-SA: Attribution-ShareAlike*
- Bias. **Provided by:** Wikipedia. **Located at:** https://en.wikipedia.org/wiki/Bias. **License:** *CC BY-SA: Attribution-ShareAlike*
- Eurocentrism. **Provided by:** Wikipedia. **Located at:** https://en.wikipedia.org/wiki/Eurocentrism. **License:** *CC BY-SA: Attribution-ShareAlike*
- Petrarch_by_Bargilla.jpg. **Provided by:** Wikipedia. **Located at:** https://en.wikipedia.org/wiki/Periodization#/media/File:Petrarch_by_Bargilla.jpg. **License:** *Public Domain: No Known Copyright*
- Inter-grav.jpg. **Provided by:** Wikipedia. **Located at:** https://en.wikipedia.org/wiki/Gregorian_calendar#/media/File:Inter-grav.jpg. **License:** *Public Domain: No Known Copyright*
- King_Khaled_airport_exit_stamp.jpg. **Provided by:** Wikipedia. **Located at:** https://en.wikipedia.org/wiki/Islamic_calendar#/media/File:King_Khaled_airport_exit_stamp.jpg. **License:** *CC BY-SA: Attribution-ShareAlike*
- Pompeii-couple.jpg. **Provided by:** Wikipedia. **Located at:** https://en.wikipedia.org/wiki/Primary_source#/media/File:Pompeii-couple.jpg. **License:** *Public Domain: No Known Copyright*
- 800px-The_Historians'_History_of_the_World_-_Title_Page.jpg. **Provided by:** Wikipedia. **Located at:** https://en.wikipedia.org/wiki/History#/media/File:The_Historians%27_History_of_the_World_-_Title_Page.jpg. **License:** *Public Domain: No Known Copyright*

Ancient Mesopotamian Civilizations

The First Urban Civilizations

The Sumerians

The Sumerian people lived in Mesopotamia from the 27th-20th century BCE. They were inventive and industrious, creating large city-states, trading goods, mass-producing pottery, and perfecting many forms of technology.

Learning Objectives

To understand the history and accomplishments of the Sumerian people

Key Takeaways

Key Points

- The Sumerians were a people living in Mesopotamia from the 27th-20th century BCE.
- The major periods in Sumerian history were the Ubaid period (6500-4100 BCE), the Uruk period (4100-2900 BCE), the Early Dynastic period (2900-2334 BCE), the Akkadian Empire period (2334 – 2218 BCE), the Gutian period (2218-2047 BCE), Sumerian Renaissance /Third Dynasty of Ur (2047-1940 BCE), and then decline.
- Many Sumerian clay tablets have been found with writing. Initially, pictograms were used, followed by cuneiform and then ideograms.
- Sumerians believed in anthropomorphic polytheism, or of many gods in human form that were specific to each city-state.
- Sumerians invented or perfected many forms of technology, including the wheel, mathematics, and cuneiform script.

> *Key Terms*
>
> - **Epic of Gilgamesh**: An epic poem from the Third Dynasty of Ur (circa 2100 BCE), which is seen as the earliest surviving great work of literature.
> - **pictograms**: A pictorial symbol for a word or phrase. They are the earliest known forms of writing.
> - **pantheon**: The collective gods of a people or religion.
> - **ideograms**: Written characters symbolizing an idea or entity without indicating the sounds used to say it.
> - **cuneiform script**: Wedge-shaped characters used in the ancient writing systems of Mesopotamia, surviving mainly on clay tablets.
> - **City-states**: A city that with its surrounding territory forms an independent state.
> - **anthropomorphic**: Having human characteristics.

"Sumerian" is the name given by the Semitic-speaking Akkadians to non-Semitic speaking people living in Mespotamia. City-states in the region, which were organized by canals and boundary stones and dedicated to a patron god or goddess, first rose to power during the prehistoric Ubaid and Uruk periods. Sumerian written history began in the 27th century BCE, but the first intelligible writing began in the 23rd century BCE. Classical Sumer ends with the rise of the Akkadian Empire in the 23rd century BCE, and only enjoys a brief renaissance in the 21st century BCE. The Sumerians were eventually absorbed into the Akkadian/Babylonian population.

Periods in Sumerian History

The Ubaid period (6500-4100 BCE) saw the first settlement in southern Mesopotamia by farmers who brought irrigation agriculture. Distinctive, finely painted pottery was evident during this time.

The Uruk period (4100-2900 BCE) saw several transitions. First, pottery began to be mass-produced. Second, trade goods began to flow down waterways in southern Mespotamia, and large, temple-centered cities (most likely theocratic and run by priests-kings) rose up to facilitate this trade. Slave labor was also utilized.

The Early Dynastic period (2900-2334 BCE) saw writing, in contrast to pictograms, become commonplace and decipherable. The Epic of Gilgamesh mentions several leaders, including Gilgamesh himself, who were likely historical kings. The first dynastic king was Etana, the 13th king of the first dynasty of Kish. War was on the increase, and cities erected walls for self-preservation. Sumerian culture began to spread from southern Mesopotamia into surrounding areas.

Sumerian Necklaces and Headgear: *Sumerian necklaces and headgear discovered in the royal (and individual) graves, showing the way they may have been worn.*

During the Akkadian Empire period (2334-2218 BCE), many in the region became bilingual in both Sumerian and Akkadian. Toward the end of the empire, though, Sumerian became increasingly a literary language.

The Gutian period (2218-2047 BCE) was marked by a period of chaos and decline, as Guti barbarians defeated the Akkadian military but were unable to support the civilizations in place.

The Sumerian Renaissance/Third Dynasty of Ur (2047-1940 BCE) saw the rulers Ur-Nammu and Shulgi, whose power extended into southern Assyria. However, the region was becoming more Semitic, and the Sumerian language became a religious language.

The Sumerian Renaissance ended with invasion by the Amorites, whose dynasty of Isin continued until 1700 BCE, at which point Mespotamia came under Babylonian rule.

Language and Writing

Many Sumerian clay tablets written in cuneiform script have been discovered. They are not the oldest example of writing, but nevertheless represent a great advance in the human ability to write down history and create literature. Initially, pictograms were used, followed by cuneiform, and then ideograms. Letters, receipts, hymns, prayers, and stories have all been found on clay tablets.

Bill of Sale on a Clay Tablet: *This clay tablet shows a bill of sale for a male slave and building, circa 2600 BCE.*

Religion

Sumerians believed in anthropomorphic polytheism, or of many gods in human form, which were specific to each city-state. The core pantheon consisted of An (heaven), Enki (a healer and friend to humans), Enlil (gave spells spirits must obey), Inanna (love and war), Utu (sun-god), and Sin (moon-god).

Technology

Sumerians invented or improved a wide range of technology, including the wheel, cuneiform script, arithmetic, geometry, irrigation, saws and other tools, sandals, chariots, harpoons, and beer.

The Assyrians

The Assyrians were a major Semitic empire of the Ancient Near East, who existed as an independent state for approximately nineteen centuries between c. 2500-605 BCE, enjoying widespread military success in its heyday.

Learning Objectives

Describe key characteristics and notable events of the Assyrian Empire

Key Takeaways

Key Points

- Centered on the Upper Tigris river in northern Mesopotamia, the Assyrians came to rule powerful empires at several times, the last of which grew to be the largest and most powerful empire the world had yet seen.
- At its peak, the Assyrian empire stretched from Cyprus in the Mediterranean Sea to Persia, and from the Caucasus Mountains (Armenia, Georgia, Azerbaijan) to the Arabian Peninsula and Egypt. It was at the height of technological, scientific, and cultural achievements for its time.
- In the Old Assyrian period, Assyria established colonies in Asia Minor and the Levant, and asserted itself over southern Mesopotamia under king Ilushuma.
- Assyria experienced fluctuating fortunes in the Middle Assyrian period, with some of its kings finding themselves under the influence of foreign rulers while others eclipsed neighboring empires.
- Assyria became a great military power during the Neo-Assyrian period, and saw the conquests of large empires, such as Egyptians, the Phoenicians, the Hittites, and the Persians, among others.
- After its fall in the late 600s BCE, Assyria remained a province and geo-political entity under various empires until the mid-7th century CE.

Key Terms

- **Aššur**: The original capital of the Assyrian Empire, which dates back to 2600 BCE.
- **Assyrian Empire**: A major Semitic kingdom of the Ancient Near East, which existed as an independent state for a period of approximately nineteen centuries from c. 2500-605 BCE.

The Assyrian Empire was a major Semitic kingdom, and often empire, of the Ancient Near East. It existed as an independent state for a period of approximately 19 centuries from c. 2500 BCE to 605 BCE, which spans the Early Bronze Age through to the late Iron Age. For a further 13 centuries, from the end of the 7th century BCE to the mid-7th century CE, it survived as a geo-political entity ruled, for the most part, by foreign powers (although a number of small Neo-Assyrian states arose at different times throughout this period).

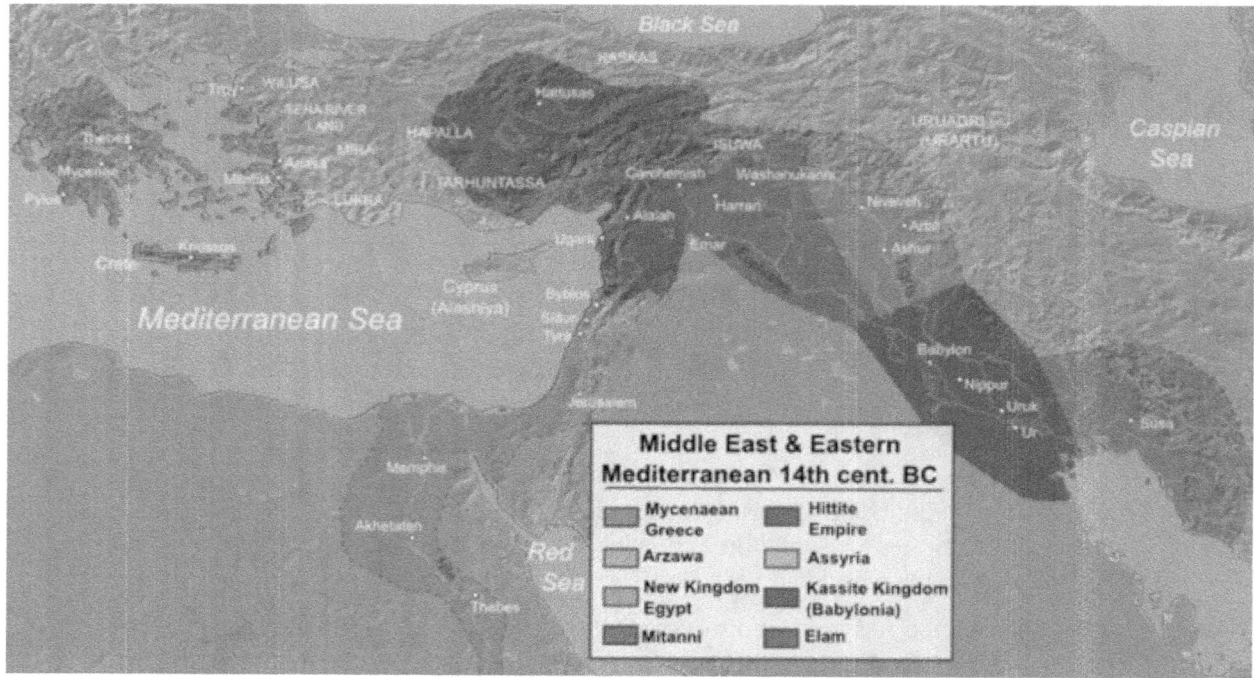

Map of the Ancient Near East during the 14th century BCE, showing the great powers of the day: This map shows the extent of the empires of Egypt (orange), Hatti (blue), the Kassite kingdom of Babylon (black), Assyria (yellow), and Mitanni (brown). The extent of the Achaean/Mycenaean civilization is shown in purple.

Centered on the Upper Tigris river, in northern Mesopotamia (northern Iraq, northeast Syria, and southeastern Turkey), the Assyrians came to rule powerful empires at several times, the last of which grew to be the largest and most powerful empire the world had yet seen.

As a substantial part of the greater Mesopotamian "Cradle of Civilization," Assyria was at the height of technological, scientific, and cultural achievements for its time. At its peak, the Assyrian empire stretched from Cyprus in the Mediterranean Sea to Persia (Iran), and from the Caucasus Mountains (Armenia, Georgia, Azerbaijan) to the Arabian Peninsula and Egypt. Assyria is named for its original capital, the ancient city of Ašur (a.k.a., Ashur) which dates to c. 2600 BCE and was located in what is now the Saladin Province of northern Iraq. Ashur was originally one of a number of Akkadian city states in Mesopotamia. In the late 24th century BCE, Assyrian kings were regional leaders under Sargon of Akkad, who united all the Akkadian Semites and Sumerian-speaking peoples of Mesopotamia under the Akkadian Empire (c. 2334 BC-2154 BCE). Following the fall of the Akkadian Empire, c. 2154 BCE, and the short-lived succeeding Sumerian Third Dynasty of Ur, which ruled southern Assyria, Assyria regained full independence.

The history of Assyria proper is roughly divided into three periods, known as Old Assyrian (late 21st-18th century BCE), Middle Assyrian (1365-1056 BCE), and Neo-Assyrian (911- 612BCE). These periods roughly correspond to the Middle Bronze Age, Late Bronze Age, and Early Iron Age, respectively. In the Old Assyrian period, Assyria established colonies in Asia Minor and the Levant. Under king Ilushuma, it asserted itself over southern Mesopotamia. From the late 19th century BCE, Assyria came into conflict with the newly created state of Babylonia, which eventually eclipsed the older Sumero-Akkadian states in the south, such as Ur, Isin, Larsa and Kish. Assyria experienced fluctuating fortunes in the Middle Assyrian period. Assyria had a period of empire under Shamshi-Adad I and Ishme-Dagan in the 19th and 18th centuries BCE. Following the reigns of these two kings, it found itself under Babylonian and Mitanni-Hurrian domination for short periods in the 18th and 15th centuries BCE, respectively.

However, a shift in the Assyrian's dominance occurred with the rise of the Middle Assyrian Empire (1365 BCE-1056 BCE). This period saw the reigns of great kings, such as Ashur-uballit I, Arik-den-ili, Tukulti-Ninurta I, and Tiglath-Pileser I. Additionally, during this period, Assyria overthrew Mitanni and eclipsed both the Hittite Empire and Egyptian Empire in the Near East. Long wars helped build Assyria into a warrior society, supported by landed nobility, which supplied horses to the military. All free male citizens were required to serve in the military, and women had very low status.

Beginning with the campaigns of Adad-nirari II from 911 BCE, Assyria again showed itself to be a great power over the next three centuries during the Neo-Assyrian period. It overthrew the Twenty-Fifth dynasty of Egypt, and conquered a number of other notable civilizations, including Babylonia, Elam, Media, Persia, Phoenicia/Canaan, Aramea (Syria), Arabia, Israel, and the Neo-Hittites. They drove the Ethiopians and Nubians from Egypt, defeated the Cimmerians and Scythians, and exacted tribute from Phrygia, Magan, and Punt, among others.

After its fall (between 612-605 BCE), Assyria remained a province and geo-political entity under the Babylonian, Median, Achaemenid, Seleucid, Parthian, Roman, and Sassanid Empires, until the Arab Islamic invasion and conquest of Mesopotamia in the mid-7th century CE when it was finally dissolved.

Assyria is mainly remembered for its military victories, technological advancements (such as using iron for weapons and building roads), use of torture to inspire fear, and a written history of conquests. Its military had not only general troops, but charioteers, cavalry, bowmen, and lancers.

Attributions

CC licensed content, Specific attribution

- The Epic of Gilgamesh. **Provided by**: Wikipedia. **Located at**: https://en.wikipedia.org/wiki/Epic_of_Gilgamesh. **License**: *CC BY-SA: Attribution-ShareAlike*
- Gutian Dynasty of Sumer. **Provided by**: Wikipedia. **Located at**: https://en.wikipedia.org/wiki/Gutian_dynasty_of_Sumer. **License**: *CC BY: Attribution*
- Cuneiform Script. **Provided by**: Wikipedia. **Located at**: https://en.wikipedia.org/wiki/Cuneiform_script. **License**: *CC BY: Attribution*
- Sumer. **Provided by**: Wikipedia. **Located at**: https://en.wikipedia.org/wiki/Sumer. **License**: *CC BY: Attribution*
- headdress.JPG. **Provided by**: Wikipedia. **Located at**: https://commons.wikimedia.org/wiki/File:Reconstructed_sumerian_headgear_necklaces_british_museum.JPG. **License**: *CC BY-SA: Attribution-ShareAlike*
- Bill_of_sale_Louvre_AO3765.jpg. **Provided by**: Wikipedia. **Located at**: https://www.google.com/url?sa=i&rct=j&q=&esrc=s&source=images&cd=&ved=0ahUKEwjakJWOwMvNAhUC7YMKHa03BbkQjR-wIBw&url=https%3A%2F%2Fen.wikipedia.org%2Fwiki%2FSumer&bvm=bv.125596728,d.eWE&psig=AFQjCNEusLcvhEBdzsQ5ZtrTTR7mnoIC3w&ust=1467227247872957. **License**: *CC BY: Attribution*
- History of the Assyrian People. **Provided by**: Wikipedia. **Located at**: https://en.wikipedia.org/wiki/History_of_the_Assyrian_people. **License**: *CC BY-SA: Attribution-ShareAlike*
- The Assyrian Empire. **Provided by**: CDA's World History Wiki. **Located at**: http://cdaworldhistory.wikidot.com/the-assyrian-empires. **License**: *CC BY: Attribution*
- Assyrians: Cavalry and Conquests. **Provided by**: Ancient Civilizations. **Located at**: http://www.ushistory.org/civ/4d.asp. **License**: *CC BY: Attribution*

- Assyria. **Provided by**: Wikipedia. **Located at**: http://en.wikipedia.org/wiki/Assyria. **License**: *CC BY-SA: Attribution-ShareAlike*
- headdress.JPG. **Provided by**: Wikipedia. **Located at**: https://commons.wikimedia.org/wiki/File:Reconstructed_sumerian_headgear_necklaces_british_museum.JPG. **License**: *CC BY-SA: Attribution-ShareAlike*
- Bill_of_sale_Louvre_AO3765.jpg. **Provided by**: Wikipedia. **Located at**: https://www.google.com/url?sa=i&rct=j&q=&esrc=s&source=images&cd=&ved=0ahUKEwjakJWOwMvNAhUC7YMKHa03BbkQjR-wIBw&url=https%3A%2F%2Fen.wikipedia.org%2Fwiki%2FSumer&bvm=bv.125596728,d.eWE&psig=AFQjCNEusLcvhEB-dzsQ5ZtrTTR7mnoIC3w&ust=1467227247872957. **License**: *CC BY: Attribution*
- Assyria. **Provided by**: Wikipedia. **Located at**: http://en.wikipedia.org/wiki/Assyria%23mediaviewer/File:14_century_BC_Eastern.png. **License**: *CC BY-SA: Attribution-ShareAlike*

Akkadian Empire

River Valley Civilizations

The first civilizations formed in river valleys, and were characterized by a caste system and a strong government that controlled water access and resources.

Learning Objectives

Explain why early civilizations arose on the banks of rivers

Key Takeaways

Key Points

- Rivers were attractive locations for the first civilizations because they provided a steady supply of drinking water and game, made the land fertile for growing crops, and allowed for easy transportation.
- Early river civilizations were all hydraulic empires that maintained power and control through exclusive control over access to water. This system of government arose through the need for flood control and irrigation, which requires central coordination and a specialized bureaucracy.
- Hydraulic hierarchies gave rise to the established permanent institution of impersonal government, since changes in ruling were usually in personnel, but not in the structure of government.

Key Terms

- **Water shortage**: Water is less available due to climate change, pollution, or overuse.
- **Water crisis**: There is not enough fresh, clean water to meet local demand.

- **caste**: A form of social stratification characterized by endogamy (hereditary transmission of a lifestyle). This lifestyle often includes an occupation, ritual status in a hierarchy, and customary social interaction and exclusion based on cultural notions of purity and pollution.
- **hydraulic empire**: A social or governmental structure that maintains power through exclusive control of water access.
- **Fertile Crescent**: A crescent-shaped region containing the comparatively moist and fertile land of otherwise arid and semi-arid Western Asia, and the Nile Valley and Nile Delta of northeast Africa. Often called the cradle of civilization.
- **Neolithic Revolution**: Also called the Agricultural Revolution, this was the wide-scale transition of human cultures from being hunter-gatherers to being settled agriculturalists.
- **Water stress**: Difficulty in finding fresh water, or the depletion of available water sources.

The First Civilizations

The first civilizations formed on the banks of rivers. The most notable examples are the Ancient Egyptians, who were based on the Nile, the Mesopotamians in the Fertile Crescent on the Tigris/Euphrates rivers, the Ancient Chinese on the Yellow River, and the Ancient India on the Indus. These early civilizations began to form around the time of the Neolithic Revolution (12000 BCE).

Rivers were attractive locations for the first civilizations because they provided a steady supply of drinking water and made the land fertile for growing crops. Moreover, goods and people could be transported easily, and the people in these civilizations could fish and hunt the animals that came to drink water. Additionally, those lost in the wilderness could return to civilization by traveling downstream, where the major centers of human population tend to concentrate.

The Nile River and Delta: *Most of the Ancient Egyptian settlements occurred along the northern part of the Nile, pictured in this satellite image taken from orbit by NASA.*

Hydraulic Empires

Though each civilization was uniquely different, we can see common patterns amongst these first civilizations since they were all based around rivers. Most notably, these early civilizations were all hydraulic empires. A hydraulic empire (also known as hydraulic despotism, or water monopoly empire) is a social or governmental structure which maintains power through exclusive control over water access. This system of government arises through the need for flood control and irrigation, which requires central coordination and a specialized bureaucracy. This political structure is commonly characterized by a system of hierarchy and control based around class or caste. Power, both over resources (food, water, energy) and a means of enforcement, such as the military, are vital for the maintenance of control. Most hydraulic empires exist in desert regions, but imperial China also had some such characteristics, due to the exacting needs of rice cultivation. The only hydraulic empire to exist in Africa was under the Ajuran State near the Jubba and Shebelle Rivers in the 15th century CE.

Karl August Wittfogel, the German scholar who first developed the notion of the hydraulic empire, argued in his book, *Oriental Despotism* (1957), that strong government control characterized these civilizations because a particular resource (in this case, river water) was both a central part of economic processes and environmentally limited. This fact made controlling supply and demand easier and allowed the establishment of a more complete monopoly, and also prevented the use of alternative resources to compensate.

However, it is also important to note that complex irrigation projects predated states in Madagascar, Mexico, China and Mesopotamia, and thus it cannot be said that a key, limited economic resource necessarily mandates a strong centralized bureaucracy.

According to Wittfogel, the typical hydraulic empire government has no trace of an independent aristocracy—
in contrast to the decentralized feudalism of medieval Europe. Though tribal societies had structures that were usually personal in nature, exercised by a patriarch over a tribal group related by various degrees of kinship, hydraulic hierarchies gave rise to the established permanent institution of impersonal government. Popular revolution in such a state was very difficult; a dynasty might die out or be overthrown by force, but the new regime would differ very little from the old one. Hydraulic empires were usually destroyed by foreign conquerors.

Water Scarcity Today

Access to water is still crucial to modern civilizations; water scarcity affects more than 2.8 billion people globally. Water stress is the term used to describe difficulty in finding fresh water or the depletion of available water sources. Water shortage is the term used when water is less available due to climate change, pollution, or overuse. Water crisis is the term used when there is not enough fresh, clean water to meet local demand. Water scarcity may be physical, meaning there are inadequate water resources available in a region, or economic, meaning governments are not managing available resources properly. The United Nations Development Programme has found that water scarcity generally results from the latter issue.

The Akkadian Empire

The Akkadian Empire flourished in the 24th and 22nd centuries BCE, ruled by Sargon and Naram-Sin. It eventually collapsed in 2154 BCE, due to the invasion of barbarian peoples and large-scale climatic changes.

Learning Objectives

Describe the key political characteristics of the Akkadian Empire

Key Takeaways

Key Points

- The Akkadian Empire was an ancient Semitic empire centered in the city of Akkad and its surrounding region in ancient Mesopotamia, which united all the indigenous Akkadian speaking Semites and the Sumerian speakers under one rule within a multilingual empire.

- King Sargon, the founder of the empire, conquered several regions in Mesopotamia and consolidated his power by instating Akaddian officials in new territories. He extended trade across Mesopotamia and strengthened the economy through rain-fed agriculture in northern Mesopotamia.
- The Akkadian Empire experienced a period of successful conquest under Naram-Sin due to benign climatic conditions, huge agricultural surpluses, and the confiscation of wealth.
- The empire collapsed after the invasion of the Gutians. Changing climatic conditions also contributed to internal rivalries and fragmentation, and the empire eventually split into the Assyrian Empire in the north and the Babylonian empire in the south.

Key Terms

- **Akkadian Empire**: An ancient Semitic empire centered in the city of Akkad and its surrounding region in ancient Mesopotamia.
- **Sargon**: The first king of the Akkadians. He conquered many of the surrounding regions to establish the massive multilingual empire.
- **Gutians**: A group of barbarians from the Zagros Mountains who invaded the Akkadian Empire and contributed to its collapse.
- **Cuneiform**: One of the earliest known systems of writing, distinguished by its wedge-shaped marks on clay tablets, and made by means of a blunt reed for a stylus.
- **Semites**: Today, the word "Semite" may be used to refer to any member of any of a number of peoples of ancient Southwest Asian descent, including the Akkadians, Phoenicians, Hebrews (Jews), Arabs, and their descendants.
- **Naram-Sin**: An Akkadian king who conquered Ebla, Armum, and Magan, and built a royal residence at Tell Brak.

The Akkadian Empire was an ancient Semitic empire centered in the city of Akkad, which united all the indigenous Akkadian speaking Semites and Sumerian speakers under one rule. The Empire controlled Mesopotamia, the Levant, and parts of Iran.

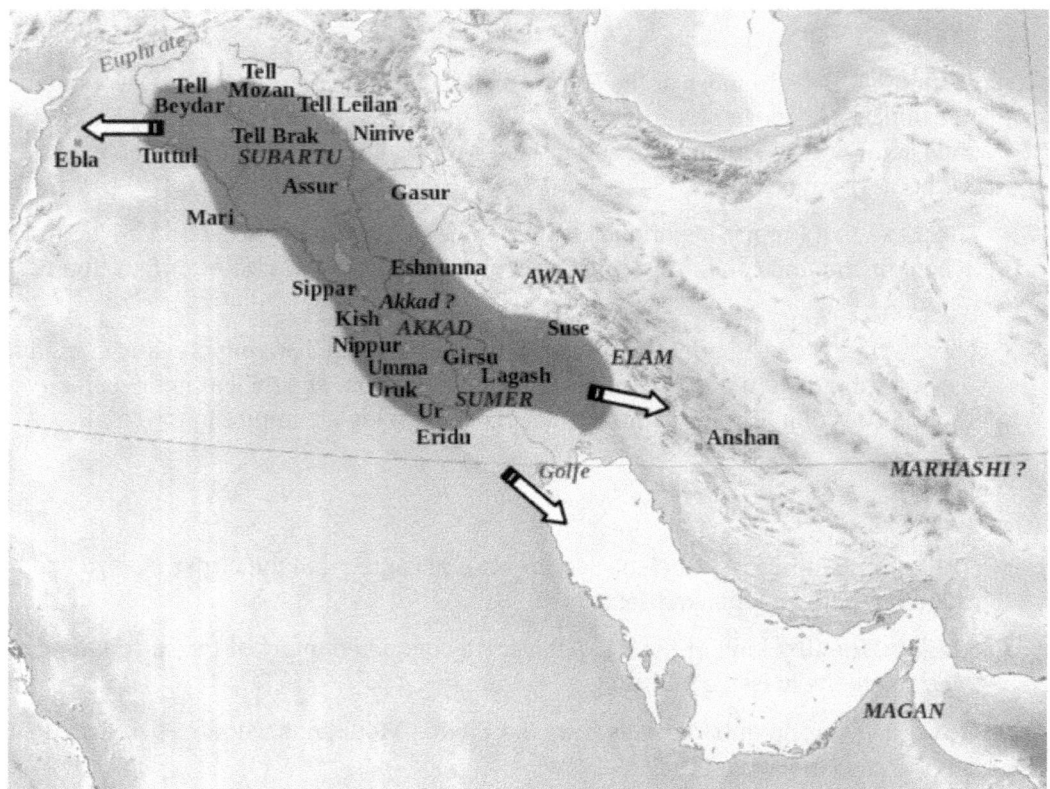

Map of the Akkadian Empire: *The Akkadian Empire is pictured in brown. The directions of the military campaigns are shown as yellow arrows.*

Its founder was Sargon of Akkad (2334–2279 BCE). Under Sargon and his successors, the Akkadian Empire reached its political peak between the 24th and 22nd centuries BCE. Akkad is sometimes regarded as the first empire in history.

Sargon and His Dynasty

Sargon claimed to be the son of La'ibum or Itti-Bel, a humble gardener, and possibly a *hierodule*, or priestess to Ishtar or Inanna. Some later claimed that his mother was an "entu" priestess (high priestess). Originally a cupbearer to king Ur-Zababa of Kish, Sargon became a gardener, which gave him access to a disciplined corps of workers who also may have served as his first soldiers. Displacing Ur-Zababa, Sargon was crowned king and began a career of foreign conquest. He invaded Syria and Canaan on four different campaigns, and spent three years subduing the countries of "the west" to unite them with Mesopotamia "into a single empire."

Sargon's empire reached westward as far as the Mediterranean Sea and perhaps Cyprus (Kaptara); northward as far as the mountains; eastward over Elam; and as far south as Magan (Oman)—a region over which he purportedly reigned for 56 years, though only four "year-names" survive. He replaced rulers with noble citizens of Akkad. Trade extended from the silver mines of Anatolia to the lapis lazuli mines in Afghanistan, and from the cedars of Lebanon to the copper of Magan. The empire's breadbasket was the rain-fed agricultural system of northern Mesopotamia (Assyria), and a chain of fortresses was built to control the imperial wheat production.

Sargon, throughout his long life, showed special deference to the Sumerian deities, particularly Inanna (Ishtar), his patroness, and Zababa, the warrior god of Kish. He called himself "the anointed priest of Anu" and "the great ensi of Enlil. "

Sargon managed to crush his opposition even in old age. Difficulties also broke out in the reign of his sons, Rimush (2278–2270 BCE), who was assassinated by his own courtiers, and Manishtushu (2269–2255 BCE), who reigned for 15 years. He, too, was likely assassinated in a palace conspiracy.

Bronze head of a king: *Bronze head of a king, most likely Sargon of Akkad but possibly Naram-Sin. Unearthed in Nineveh (now in Iraq).*

Naram-Sin

Manishtushu's son and successor, Naram-Sin (called, Beloved of Sin) (2254–2218 BCE), assumed the imperial title "King Naram-Sin, King of the Four Quarters." He was also, for the first time in Sumerian culture, addressed as "the god of Agade (Akkad)." This represents a marked shift away from the previous religious belief that kings were only representatives of the people toward the gods.

Naram-Sin conquered Ebla and Armum, and built a royal residence at Tell Brak, a crossroads at the heart of the Khabur River basin of the Jezirah. Naram-Sin also conquered Magan and created garrisons to protect the main roads. This productive period of Akkadian conquest may have been based upon benign climatic conditions, huge agricultural surpluses, and the confiscation of the wealth of other peoples.

Stele of Naram-Sin: This stele commemorates Naram-Sin's victory against the Lullubi from Zagros in 2260 BCE. Naram-Sin is depicted to be wearing a horned helmet, a symbol of divinity, and is also portrayed in a larger scale in comparison to others to emphasize his superiority.

Living in the Akkadian Empire

Future Mesopotamian states compared themselves to the Akkadian Empire, which they saw as a classical standard in governance. The economy was dependent on irrigated farmlands of southern Iraq, and rain-fed agriculture of Northern Iraq. There was often a surplus of agriculture but shortages of other goods, like metal ore, timber, and building stone. Art of the period often focused on kings, and depicted somber and grim conflict and subjugation to divinities. Sumerians and Akkadians were bilingual in each other's languages, but Akkadian gradually replaced Sumerian. The empire had a postal service, and a library featuring astronomical observations.

Collapse of the Akkadian Empire

The Empire of Akkad collapsed in 2154 BCE, within 180 years of its founding. The collapse ushered in a Dark Age period of regional decline that lasted until the rise of the Third Dynasty of Ur in 2112 BCE. By the end of the reign of Naram-Sin's son, Shar-kali-sharri (2217-2193 BCE), the empire had weakened significantly. There was a period of anarchy between 2192 BC and 2168 BCE. Some centralized authority may have been restored under Shu-Durul (2168-2154 BCE), but he was unable to prevent the empire collapsing outright from the invasion of barbarian peoples, known as the Gutians, from the Zagros Mountains.

Little is known about the Gutian period or for how long it lasted. Cuneiform sources suggest that the Gutians' administration showed little concern for maintaining agriculture, written records, or public safety; they reputedly released all farm animals to roam about Mesopotamia freely, and soon brought about famine and rocketing grain prices. The Sumerian king Ur-Nammu (2112-2095 BCE) later cleared the Gutians from Mesopotamia during his reign.

The collapse of rain-fed agriculture in the Upper Country due to drought meant the loss of the agrarian subsidies which had kept the Akkadian Empire solvent in southern Mesopotamia. Rivalries between pastoralists and farmers increased. Attempts to control access to water led to increased political instability; meanwhile, severe depopulation occurred.

After the fall of the Akkadian Empire, the Akkadian people coalesced into two major Akkadian speaking nations: Assyria in the north, and, a few centuries later, Babylonia in the south.

Ur

The city-state of Ur in Mesopotamia was important and wealthy, and featured highly centralized bureaucracy. It is famous for the Ziggurat of Ur, a temple whose ruins were discovered in modern day.

Learning Objectives

To understand the significance of the city-state of Ur

Key Takeaways

Key Points

- Ur was a major Sumerian city-state located in Mesopotamia, founded circa 3800 BCE.
- Cuneiform tablets show that Ur was a highly centralized, wealthy, bureaucratic state during the third millennium BCE.
- The Ziggurat of Ur was built in the 21st century BCE, during the reign of Ur-Nammu, and was reconstructed in the 6th century BCE by Nabonidus, the last king of Babylon.
- Control of Ur passed among various peoples until the Third Dynasty of Ur, which featured the strong kings Ur-Nammu and Shulgi.
- Ur was uninhabited by 500 BCE.

Key Terms

- **Sumerian**: A group of non-Semitic people living in ancient Mesopotamia.
- **Cuneiform**: Wedge-shaped characters imprinted onto clay tablets, used in ancient writing systems of Mesopotamia.
- **Sargon the Great**: A Semitic emperor of the Akkadian Empire, known for conquering Sumerian city-states in the 24th and 23rd centuries BCE.
- **Ziggurat**: A rectangular stepped tower, sometimes surmounted by a temple.

A Major Mesopotamian City

Ur was a major Sumerian city-state located in Mesopotamia, marked today by Tell el-Muqayyar in southern Iraq. It was founded circa 3800 BCE, and was recorded in written history from the 26th century BCE. Its patron god was Nanna, the moon god, and the city's name literally means "the abode of Nanna."

Cuneiform tablets show that Ur was, during the third millennium BCE, a highly centralized, wealthy, bureaucratic state. The discovery of the Royal Tombs, dating from about the 25th century BCE, showed that the area had luxury items made out of precious metals and semi-precious stones, which would have required importation. Some estimate that Ur was the largest city in the world from 2030-1980 BCE, with approximately 65,000 people.

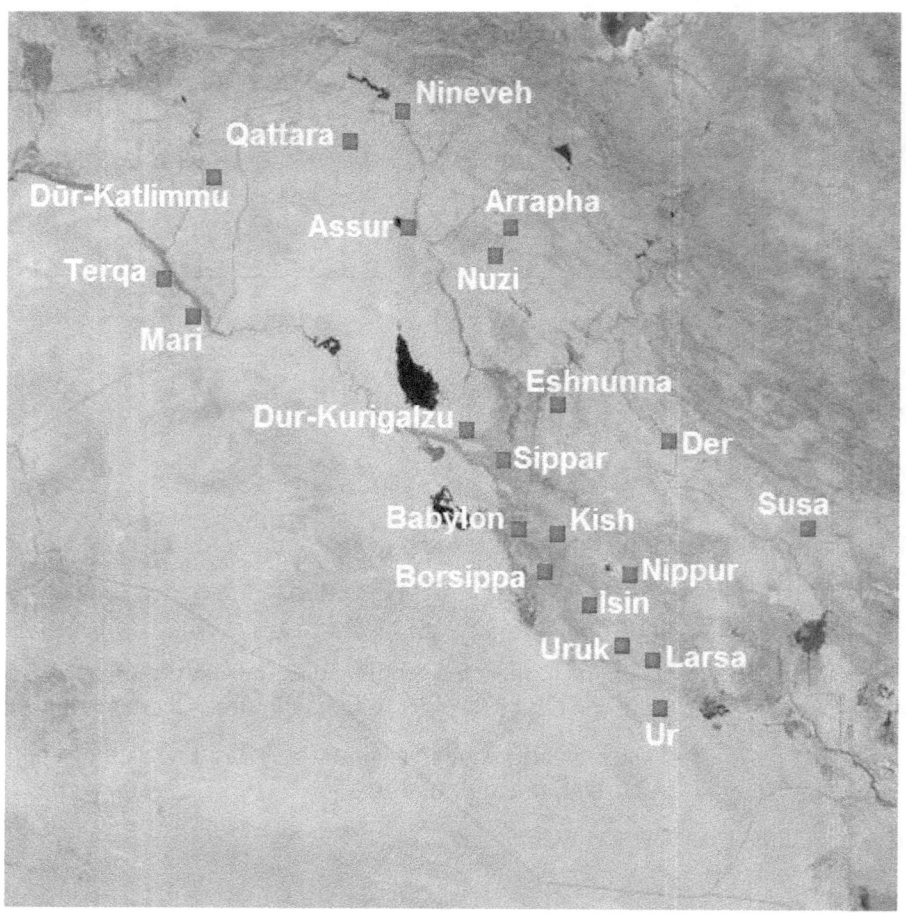

The City of Ur: *This map shows Mesopotamia in the third millennium BCE, with Ur in the south.*

The Ziggurat of Ur

The Ziggurat of Ur: *This is a reconstruction of Ur-Nammu's ziggurat.*

This temple was built in the 21st century BCE, during the reign of Ur-Nammu, and was reconstructed in the 6th century BCE by Nabonidus, the last king of Babylon. The ruins, which cover an area of 3,900 feet by 2,600 feet, were uncovered in the 1930s. It was part of a temple complex that served as an administrative center for the city of Ur, and was dedicated to Nanna, the moon god.

Control of Ur

Between the 24th and 22nd century BCE, Ur was controlled by Sargon the Great, of the Akkadian Empire. After the fall of this empire, Ur was ruled by the barbarian Gutians, until King Ur-Nammu came to power, circa 2047 – 2030 BCE (the Third Dynasty of Ur). Advances during this time included the building of temples, like the Ziggurat, better agricultural irrigation, and a code of laws, called the Code of Ur-Nammu, which preceded the Code of Hammurabi by 300 years.

Shulgi succeeded Ur-Nammu, and was able to increase Ur's power by creating a highly centralized bureaucratic state. Shulgi, who eventually declared himself a god, ruled from 2029-1982 BCE, and was well-known for at least two thousand years after.

Three more kings, Amar-Sin, Shu0Sin and Ibbi-Sin, ruled Ur before it fell to the Elamites in 1940 BCE. Although Ur lost its political power, it remained economically important. It was ruled by the first dynasty of Babylonia, then part of the Sealand Dynasty, then by the Kassites before falling to the Assyrian Empire from the 10th-7th century BE. After the 7th century BCE, it was ruled by the Chaldean Dynasty of Babylon. It began its final decline around 550 BCE, and was uninhabited by 500 BE. The final decline was likely due to drought, changing river patterns and the silting of the Persian Gulf.

Attributions

CC licensed content, Specific attribution

- Water Scarcity. **Provided by**: Wikipedia. **Located at**: https://en.wikipedia.org/wiki/Water_scarcity. **License**: *CC BY: Attribution*
- Hydraulic Empire. **Provided by**: Wikipedi. **Located at**: http://en.wikipedia.org/wiki/Hydraulic_empire. **License**: *CC BY-SA: Attribution-ShareAlike*
- River Civilization. **Provided by**: Wikipedia. **Located at**: http://en.wikipedia.org/wiki/River_civilization. **License**: *CC BY-SA: Attribution-ShareAlike*
- caste. **Provided by**: Wiktionary. **Located at**: http://en.wiktionary.org/wiki/caste. **License**: *CC BY-SA: Attribution-ShareAlike*
- Nile. **Provided by**: Wikipedia. **Located at**: http://en.wikipedia.org/wiki/File:Nile_River_and_delta_from_orbit.jpg. **License**: *Public Domain: No Known Copyright*
- Akkadian Empire. **Provided by**: Wikipedia. **Located at**: http://en.wikipedia.org/wiki/Akkadian_Empire. **License**: *CC BY-SA: Attribution-ShareAlike*
- Cuneiform. **Provided by**: Wikipedia. **Located at**: http://en.wikipedia.org/wiki/Cuneiform. **License**: *CC BY-SA: Attribution-ShareAlike*
- Nile. **Provided by**: Wikipedia. **Located at**: http://en.wikipedia.org/wiki/File:Nile_River_and_delta_from_orbit.jpg. **License**: *Public Domain: No Known Copyright*
- Sargon of Akkad. **Provided by**: Wikipedia. **Located at**: http://upload.wikimedia.org/wikipedia/commons/thumb/4/44/Sargon_of_Akkad.jpg/253px-Sargon_of_Akkad.jpg. **License**: *CC BY-SA: Attribution-ShareAlike*

- Akkadian Empire. **Provided by**: Wikipedia. **Located at**: http://en.wikipedia.org/wiki/Akkadian_Empire. **License**: *CC BY-SA: Attribution-ShareAlike*
- Akkadian Empire. **Provided by**: Wikipedia. **Located at**: http://en.wikipedia.org/wiki/Akkadian_Empire. **License**: *CC BY-SA: Attribution-ShareAlike*
- Ziggurat. **Provided by**: Wikipedia. **Located at**: https://en.wikipedia.org/wiki/Ziggurat. **License**: *CC BY-SA: Attribution-ShareAlike*
- Ur. **Provided by**: Wikipedia. **Located at**: https://en.wikipedia.org/wiki/Ur. **License**: *CC BY-SA: Attribution-ShareAlike*
- Ziggurat of Ur. **Provided by**: Wikipedia. **Located at**: https://en.wikipedia.org/wiki/Ziggurat_of_Ur. **License**: *CC BY-SA: Attribution-ShareAlike*
- Ur. **Provided by**: Wikipedia. **Located at**: https://en.wikipedia.org/wiki/Ur. **License**: *CC BY-SA: Attribution-ShareAlike*
- Shulgi. **Provided by**: Wikipedia. **Located at**: https://en.wikipedia.org/wiki/Shulgi. **License**: *CC BY-SA: Attribution-ShareAlike*
- Nile. **Provided by**: Wikipedia. **Located at**: http://en.wikipedia.org/wiki/File:Nile_River_and_delta_from_orbit.jpg. **License**: *Public Domain: No Known Copyright*
- Sargon of Akkad. **Provided by**: Wikipedia. **Located at**: http://upload.wikimedia.org/wikipedia/commons/thumb/4/44/Sargon_of_Akkad.jpg/253px-Sargon_of_Akkad.jpg. **License**: *CC BY-SA: Attribution-ShareAlike*
- Akkadian Empire. **Provided by**: Wikipedia. **Located at**: http://en.wikipedia.org/wiki/Akkadian_Empire. **License**: *CC BY-SA: Attribution-ShareAlike*
- Akkadian Empire. **Provided by**: Wikipedia. **Located at**: http://en.wikipedia.org/wiki/Akkadian_Empire. **License**: *CC BY-SA: Attribution-ShareAlike*
- Meso2mil-English.JPG. **Provided by**: Wikipedia. **Located at**: https://www.google.com/url?sa=i&rct=j&q=&esrc=s&source=images&cd=&ved=0ahUKEwicj9-Gh8zNAhUEKB4KHTeXABIQjR-wIBw&url=https%3A%2F%2Fen.wikipedia.org%2Fwiki%2FUr&bvm=bv.125801520,d.amc&psig=AFQjCNG86EuJUYhoThlxflV3vtV7rt6pkQ&ust=1467249119088837. **License**: *CC BY-SA: Attribution-ShareAlike*
- zigg.jpeg. **Provided by**: Wikipedia. **Located at**: https://www.google.com/url?sa=i&rct=j&q=&esrc=s&source=images&cd=&ved=0ahUKEwiZhY3Th8zNAhUKrB4KHQLqDowQjR-wIBw&url=https%3A%2F%2Fen.wikipedia.org%2Fwiki%2FZiggurat_of_Ur&bvm=bv.125801520,d.amc&psig=AFQjCNEgfbUndf-WZXxuRMW-7AUXHuHHGQ&ust=1467249270371533&cad=rja. **License**: *CC BY-SA: Attribution-ShareAlike*

Babylonia

Babylon

Following the collapse of the Akkadians, the Babylonian Empire flourished under Hammurabi, who conquered many surrounding peoples and empires, in addition to developing an extensive code of law and establishing Babylon as a "holy city" of southern Mesopotamia.

Learning Objectives

Describe key characteristics of the Babylonian Empire under Hammurabi

Key Takeaways

Key Points

- A series of conflicts between the Amorites and the Assyrians followed the collapse of the Akkadian Empire, out of which Babylon arose as a powerful city-state c. 1894 BCE.
- Babylon remained a minor territory for a century after it was founded, until the reign of its sixth Amorite ruler, Hammurabi (1792-1750 BCE), an extremely efficient ruler who established a bureaucracy with taxation and centralized government.
- Hammurabi also enjoyed various military successes over the whole of southern Mesopotamia, modern-day Iran and Syria, and the old Assyrian Empire in Asian Minor.
- After the death of Hammurabi, the First Babylonian Dynasty eventually fell due to attacks from outside its borders.

Key Terms

- **Marduk**: The south Mesopotamian god that rose to supremacy in the pantheon over the previous god, Enlil.

- **Hammurabi**: The sixth king of Babylon, who, under his rule, saw Babylonian advancements, both militarily and bureaucratically.
- **Code of Hammurabi**: A code of law that echoed and improved upon earlier written laws of Sumer, Akkad, and Assyria.
- **Amorites**: An ancient Semitic-speaking people from ancient Syria who also occupied large parts of Mesopotamia in the 21st Century BCE.

The Rise of the First Babylonian Dynasty

Following the disintegration of the Akkadian Empire, the Sumerians rose up with the Third Dynasty of Ur in the late 22nd century BCE, and ejected the barbarian Gutians from southern Mesopotamia. The Sumerian "Ur-III" dynasty eventually collapsed at the hands of the Elamites, another Semitic people, in 2002 BCE. Conflicts between the Amorites (Western Semitic nomads) and the Assyrians continued until Sargon I (1920-1881 BCE) succeeded as king in Assyria and withdrew Assyria from the region, leaving the Amorites in control (the Amorite period).

One of these Amorite dynasties founded the city-state of Babylon circa 1894 BCE, which would ultimately take over the others and form the short-lived first Babylonian empire, also called the Old Babylonian Period.

A chieftain named Sumuabum appropriated the then relatively small city of Babylon from the neighboring Mesopotamian city state of Kazallu, turning it into a state in its own right. Sumuabum appears never to have been given the title of King, however.

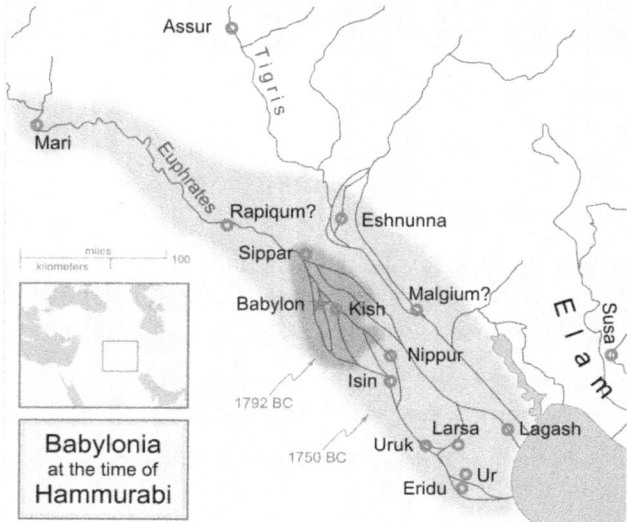

Babylonia under Hammurabi: *The extent of the Babylonian Empire at the start and end of Hammurabi's reign.*

The Babylonians Under Hammurabi

Babylon remained a minor territory for a century after it was founded, until the reign of its sixth Amorite ruler, Hammurabi (1792-1750 BCE). He was an efficient ruler, establishing a centralized bureaucracy with taxation. Hammurabi freed Babylon from Elamite dominance, and then conquered the whole of southern Mesopotamia, bringing stability and the name of Babylonia to the region.

The armies of Babylonia under Hammurabi were well-disciplined, and he was able to invade modern-day Iran to the east and conquer the pre-Iranic Elamites, Gutians and Kassites. To the west, Hammurabi enjoyed military success against the Semitic states of the Levant (modern Syria), including the powerful kingdom of Mari. Hammurabi also entered into a protracted war with the Old Assyrian Empire for control of Mesopotamia and the Near East. Assyria had extended control over parts of Asia Minor from the 21st century BCE, and from the latter part of the 19th century BCE had asserted itself over northeast Syria and central Mesopotamia as well. After a protracted, unresolved struggle over decades with the Assyrian king Ishme-Dagan, Hammurabi forced his successor, Mut-Ashkur, to pay tribute to Babylon c. 1751 BCE, thus giving Babylonia control over Assyria's centuries-old Hattian and Hurrian colonies in Asia Minor.

One of the most important works of this First Dynasty of Babylon was the compilation in about 1754 BCE of a code of laws, called the Code of Hammurabi, which echoed and improved upon the earlier written laws of Sumer, Akkad, and Assyria. It is one of the oldest deciphered writings of significant length in the world. The Code consists of 282 laws, with scaled punishments depending on social status, adjusting "an eye for an eye, a tooth for a tooth." Nearly one-half of the Code deals with matters of contract. A third of the code addresses issues concerning household and family relationships.

From before 3000 BC until the reign of Hammurabi, the major cultural and religious center of southern Mesopotamia had been the ancient city of Nippur, where the god Enlil reigned supreme. However, with the rise of Hammurabi, this honor was transferred to Babylon, and the god Marduk rose to supremacy (with the god Ashur remaining the dominant deity in Assyria). The city of Babylon became known as a "holy city," where any legitimate ruler of southern Mesopotamia had to be crowned. Hammurabi turned what had previously been a minor administrative town into a major city, increasing its size and population dramatically, and conducting a number of impressive architectural works.

The Decline of the First Babylonian Dynasty

Despite Hammurabi's various military successes, southern Mesopotamia had no natural, defensible boundaries, which made it vulnerable to attack. After the death of Hammurabi, his empire began to disintegrate rapidly. Under his successor Samsu-iluna (1749-1712 BCE), the far south of Mesopotamia was lost to a native Akkadian king, called Ilum-ma-ili, and became the Sealand Dynasty; it remained free of Babylon for the next 272 years.

Both the Babylonians and their Amorite rulers were driven from Assyria to the north by an Assyrian-Akkadian governor named Puzur-Sin, c. 1740 BCE. Amorite rule survived in a much-reduced Babylon, Samshu-iluna's successor, Abi-Eshuh, made a vain attempt to recapture the Sealand Dynasty for Babylon, but met defeat at the hands of king Damqi-ilishu II. By the end of his reign, Babylonia had shrunk to the small and relatively weak nation it had been upon its foundation.

Hammurabi's Code

The Code of Hammurabi was a collection of 282 laws, written in c. 1754 BCE in Babylon, which focused on contracts and family relationships, featuring a presumption of innocence and the presentation of evidence.

Learning Objectives
Describe the significance of Hammurabi's code

> ## Key Takeaways
>
> ### Key Points
>
> - The Code of Hammurabi is one of the oldest deciphered writings of length in the world (written c. 1754 BCE), and features a code of law from ancient Babylon in Mesopotamia.
> - The Code consisted of 282 laws, with punishments that varied based on social status (slaves, free men, and property owners).
> - Some have seen the Code as an early form of constitutional government, as an early form of the presumption of innocence, and as the ability to present evidence in one's case.
> - Major laws covered in the Code include slander, trade, slavery, the duties of workers, theft, liability, and divorce. Nearly half of the code focused on contracts, and a third on household relationships.
> - There were three social classes: the amelu (the elite), the mushkenu (free men) and ardu (slave).
> - Women had limited rights, and were mostly based around marriage contracts and divorce rights.
> - A stone stele featuring the Code was discovered in 1901, and is currently housed in the Louvre.
>
> ### Key Terms
>
> - **cuneiform**: Wedge-shaped characters used in the ancient writing systems of Mesopotamia, impressed on clay tablets.
> - **ardu**: In Babylon, a slave.
> - **mushkenu**: In Babylon, a free man who was probably landless.
> - **amelu**: In Babylon, an elite social class of people.
> - **stele**: A stone or wooden slab, generally taller than it is wide, erected as a monument.

The Code of Hammurabi is one of the oldest deciphered writings of length in the world, and features a code of law from ancient Babylon in Mesopotamia. Written in about 1754 BCE by the sixth king of Babylon, Hammurabi, the Code was written on stone stele and clay tablets. It consisted of 282 laws, with punishments that varied based on social status (slaves, free men, and property owners). It is most famous for the "an eye for an eye, a tooth for a tooth" (*lex talionis*) form of punishment. Other forms of codes of law had been in existence in the region around this time, including the Code of Ur-Nammu, king of Ur (c. 2050 BCE), the Laws of Eshnunna (c. 1930 BCE) and the codex of Lipit-Ishtar of Isin (c. 1870 BCE).

The laws were arranged in groups, so that citizens could easily read what was required of them. Some have seen the Code as an early form of constitutional government, and as an early form of the presumption of innocence, and the ability to present evidence in one's case. Intent was often recognized and affected punishment, with neglect severely punished. Some of the provisions may have been codification of Hammurabi's decisions, for the purpose of self-glorification. Nevertheless, the Code was studied, copied, and used as a model for legal reasoning for at least 1500 years after.

The prologue of the Code features Hammurabi stating that he wants "to make justice visible in the land, to destroy the wicked person and the evil-doer, that the strong might not injure the weak." Major laws covered in the Code include slander, trade, slavery, the duties of workers, theft, liability, and divorce. Nearly half of the code focused on contracts, such as wages to be paid, terms of transactions, and liability in case of property damage. A third of the code focused on household and family issues, including inheritance, divorce, paternity and sexual behavior. One section establishes that a judge who incorrectly decides an issue may be removed from his position permanently. A few sections address military service.

One of the most well-known sections of the Code was law #196: "If a man destroy the eye of another man, they shall destroy his eye. If one break a man's bone, they shall break his bone. If one destroy the eye of a freeman or break the bone of a freeman he shall pay one gold mina. If one destroy the eye of a man's slave or break a bone of a man's slave he shall pay one-half his price."

The Social Classes

Under Hammurabi's reign, there were three social classes. The *amelu* was originally an elite person with full civil rights, whose birth, marriage and death were recorded. Although he had certain privileges, he also was liable for harsher punishment and higher fines. The king and his court, high officials, professionals and craftsmen belonged to this group. The *mushkenu* was a free man who may have been landless. He was required to accept monetary compensation, paid smaller fines and lived in a separate section of the city. The *ardu* was a slave whose master paid for his upkeep, but also took his compensation. *Ardu* could own property and other slaves, and could purchase his own freedom.

Women's Rights

Women entered into marriage through a contract arranged by her family. She came with a dowry, and the gifts given by the groom to the bride also came with her. Divorce was up to the husband, but after divorce he then had to restore the dowry and provide her with an income, and any children came under the woman's custody. However, if the woman was considered a "bad wife" she might be sent away, or made a slave in the husband's house. If a wife brought action against her husband for cruelty and neglect, she could have a legal separation if the case was proved. Otherwise, she might be drowned as punishment. Adultery was punished with drowning of both parties, unless a husband was willing to pardon his wife.

Discovery of the Code

Archaeologists, including Egyptologist Gustave Jequier, discovered the code in 1901 at the ancient site of Susa in Khuzestan; a translation was published in 1902 by Jean-Vincent Scheil. A basalt stele containing the code in cuneiform script inscribed in the Akkadian language is currently on display in the Louvre, in Paris, France. Replicas are located at other museums throughout the world.

The Code of Hammurabi: *This basalt stele has the Code of Hammurabi inscribed in cuneiform script in the Akkadian language.*

Babylonian Culture

Hallmarks of Babylonian culture include mudbrick architecture, extensive astronomical records and logs, diagnostic medical handbooks, and translations of Sumerian literature.

Learning Objectives

Evaluate the extent and influence of Babylonian culture

Key Takeaways

Key Points

- Babylonian temples were massive structures of crude brick, supported by buttresses. Such uses of brick led to the early development of the pilaster and column, and of frescoes and enameled tiles.
- Certain pieces of Babylonian art featured crude three-dimensional statues, and gem-cutting was considered a high-perfection art.
- The Babylonians produced extensive compendiums of astronomical records containing catalogues of stars and constellations, as well as schemes for calculating various astro-

nomical coordinates and phenomena.
- Medicinally, the Babylonians introduced basic medical processes, such as diagnosis and prognosis, and also catalogued a variety of illnesses with their symptoms.
- Both Babylonian men and women learned to read and write, and much of Babylonian literature is translated from ancient Sumerian texts, such as the Epic of Gilgamesh.

Key Terms

- **mudbrick**: A brick mixture of loam, mud, sand, and water mixed with a binding material, such as rice husks or straw.
- **etiology**: Causation. In medicine, cause or origin of disease or condition.
- **pilaster**: An architectural element in classical architecture used to give the appearance of a supporting column and to articulate an extent of wall, with only an ornamental function.
- **Epic of Gilgamesh**: One of the most famous Babylonian works, a twelve-book saga translated from the original Sumerian.
- **Enūma Anu Enlil**: A series of cuneiform tablets containing centuries of Babylonian observations of celestial phenomena.
- **Diagnostic Handbook**: The most extensive Babylonian medical text, written by Esagil-kin-apli of Borsippa.

Art and Architecture

In Babylonia, an abundance of clay and lack of stone led to greater use of mudbrick. Babylonian temples were thus massive structures of crude brick, supported by buttresses. The use of brick led to the early development of the pilaster and column, and of frescoes and enameled tiles. The walls were brilliantly colored, and sometimes plated with zinc or gold, as well as with tiles. Painted terracotta cones for torches were also embedded in the plaster. In Babylonia, in place of the bas-relief, there was a preponderance of three-dimensional figures—the earliest examples being the Statues of Gudea—that were realistic, if also somewhat clumsy. The paucity of stone in Babylonia made every pebble a commodity and led to a high perfection in the art of gem-cutting.

Astronomy

During the 8th and 7th centuries BCE, Babylonian astronomers developed a new empirical approach to astronomy. They began studying philosophy dealing with the ideal nature of the universe and began employing an internal logic within their predictive planetary systems. This was an important contribution to astronomy and the philosophy of science, and some scholars have thus referred to this new approach as the first scientific revolution. Tablets dating back to the Old Babylonian period document the application of mathematics to variations in the length of daylight over a solar year. Centuries of Babylonian observations of celestial phenomena are recorded in a series of cuneiform tablets known as the " Enūma Anu Enlil." In fact, the oldest significant astronomical text known to mankind is Tablet 63 of the Enūma Anu Enlil, the Venus tablet of Ammi-saduqa, which lists the first and last visible risings of Venus over a period of about

21 years. This record is the earliest evidence that planets were recognized as periodic phenomena. The oldest rectangular astrolabe dates back to Babylonia c. 1100 BCE. The MUL.APIN contains catalogues of stars and constellations as well as schemes for predicting heliacal risings and the settings of the planets, as well as lengths of daylight measured by a water-clock, gnomon, shadows, and intercalations. The Babylonian GU text arranges stars in "strings" that lie along declination circles (thus measuring right-ascensions or time-intervals), and also employs the stars of the zenith, which are also separated by given right-ascensional differences.

Medicine

The oldest Babylonian texts on medicine date back to the First Babylonian Dynasty in the first half of the 2nd millennium BCE. The most extensive Babylonian medical text, however, is the Diagnostic Handbook written by the ummânū, or chief scholar, Esagil-kin-apli of Borsippa.

The Babylonians introduced the concepts of diagnosis, prognosis, physical examination, and prescriptions. The Diagnostic Handbook additionally introduced the methods of therapy and etiology outlining the use of empiricism, logic, and rationality in diagnosis, prognosis and treatment. For example, the text contains a list of medical symptoms and often detailed empirical observations along with logical rules used in combining observed symptoms on the body of a patient with its diagnosis and prognosis. In particular, Esagil-kin-apli discovered a variety of illnesses and diseases and described their symptoms in his Diagnostic Handbook, including those of many varieties of epilepsy and related ailments.

Literature

Libraries existed in most towns and temples. Women as well as men learned to read and write, and had knowledge of the extinct Sumerian language, along with a complicated and extensive syllabary.

A considerable amount of Babylonian literature was translated from Sumerian originals, and the language of religion and law long continued to be written in the old agglutinative language of Sumer. Vocabularies, grammars, and interlinear translations were compiled for the use of students, as well as commentaries on the older texts and explanations of obscure words and phrases. The characters of the syllabary were organized and named, and elaborate lists of them were drawn up.

There are many Babylonian literary works whose titles have come down to us. One of the most famous of these was the Epic of Gilgamesh, in twelve books, translated from the original Sumerian by a certain Sin-liqi-unninni, and arranged upon an astronomical principle. Each division contains the story of a single adventure in the career of King Gilgamesh. The whole story is a composite product, and it is probable that some of the stories are artificially attached to the central figure.

A Tablet from the Epic of Gilgamesh: The Deluge tablet of the Gilgamesh epic in Akkadian.

Philosophy

The origins of Babylonian philosophy can be traced back to early Mesopotamian wisdom literature, which embodied certain philosophies of life, particularly ethics, in the forms of dialectic, dialogs, epic poetry, folklore, hymns, lyrics, prose, and proverbs. Babylonian reasoning and rationality developed beyond empirical observation. It is possible that Babylonian philosophy had an influence on Greek philosophy, particularly Hellenistic philosophy. The Babylonian text Dialogue of Pessimism contains similarities to the agonistic thought of the sophists, the Heraclitean doctrine of contrasts, and the dialogs of Plato, as well as a precursor to the maieutic Socratic method of Socrates.

Neo-Babylonian Culture

The resurgence of Babylonian culture in the 7th and 6th century BCE resulted in a number of developments. In astronomy, a new approach was developed, based on the philosophy of the ideal nature of the early universe, and an internal logic within their predictive planetary systems. Some scholars have called this the first scientific revolution, and it was later adopted by Greek astronomers. The Babylonian astronomer Seleucus of Seleucia (b. 190 BCE) supported a heliocentric model of planetary motion. In mathematics, the Babylonians devised the base 60 numeral system, determined the square root of two correctly to seven places, and demonstrated knowledge of the Pythagorean theorem before Pythagoras.

Nebuchadnezzar and the Fall of Babylon

The Kassite Dynasty ruled Babylonia following the fall of Hammurabi and was succeeded by the Second Dynasty of Isin, during which time the Babylonians experienced military success and cultural upheavals under Nebuchadnezzar.

Learning Objectives

Describe the key characteristics of the Second Dynasty of Isin

Key Takeaways

Key Points

- Following the collapse of the First Babylonian Dynasty under Hammurabi, the Babylonian Empire entered a period of relatively weakened rule under the Kassites for 576 years. The Kassite Dynasty eventually fell itself due to the loss of territory and military weakness.
- The Kassites were succeeded by the Elamites, who themselves were conquered by Marduk-kabit-ahheshu, the founder of the Second Dynasty of Isin.
- Nebuchadnezzar I was the most famous ruler of the Second Dynasty of Isin. He enjoyed military successes for the first part of his career, then turned to peaceful building projects in his later years.
- The Babylonian Empire suffered major blows to its power when Nebuchadnezzar's sons lost a series of wars with Assyria, and their successors effectively became vassals of the Assyrian king. Babylonia descended into a period of chaos in 1026 BCE.

Key Terms

- **Elamites**: An ancient civilization centered in the far west and southwest of modern-day Iran.
- **Kassite Dynasty**: An ancient Near Eastern people who controlled Babylonia for nearly 600 years after the fall of the First Babylonian Dynasty.
- **Nebuchadnezzar I**: The most famous ruler of the Second Dynasty of Isin, who sacked the Elamite capital of Susa and devoted himself to peaceful building projects after securing Babylonia's borders.
- **Assyrian Empire**: A major Semitic empire of the Ancient Near East which existed as an

> independent state for a period of approximately nineteen centuries.
>
> - **Kudurru**: A type of stone document used as boundary stones and as records of land grants to vassals by the Kassites in ancient Babylonia.
> - **Marduk-kabit-ahheshu**: Overthrower of the Elamites and the founder of the Second Dynasty of Isin.

The Fall of the Kassite Dynasty and the Rise of the Second Dynasty of Isin

Following the collapse of the First Babylonian Dynasty under Hammurabi, the Babylonian Empire entered a period of relatively weakened rule under the Kassites for 576 years—
the longest dynasty in Babylonian history. The Kassite Dynasty eventually fell due to the loss of territory and military weakness, which resulted in the evident reduction in literacy and culture. In 1157 BCE, Babylon was conquered by Shutruk-Nahhunte of Elam.

The Elamites did not remain in control of Babylonia long, and Marduk-kabit-ahheshu (1155-1139 BCE) established the Second Dynasty of Isin. This dynasty was the very first native Akkadian-speaking south Mesopotamian dynasty to rule Babylon, and was to remain in power for some 125 years. The new king successfully drove out the Elamites and prevented any possible Kassite revival. Later in his reign, he went to war with Assyria and had some initial success before suffering defeat at the hands of the Assyrian king Ashur-Dan I. He was succeeded by his son Itti-Marduk-balatu in 1138 BCE, who was followed a year later by Ninurta-nadin-shumi in 1137 BCE.

The Reign of Nebuchadnezzar I and His Sons

Nebuchadnezzar I (1124-1103 BCE) was the most famous ruler of the Second Dynasty of Isin. He not only fought and defeated the Elamites and drove them from Babylonian territory but invaded Elam itself, sacked the Elamite capital Susa, and recovered the sacred statue of Marduk that had been carried off from Babylon. In the later years of his reign, he devoted himself to peaceful building projects and securing Babylonia's borders. His construction activities are memorialized in building inscriptions of the Ekituš-ḫegal-tila, the temple of Adad in Babylon, and on bricks from the temple of Enlil in Nippur. A late Babylonian inventory lists his donations of gold vessels in Ur. The earliest of three extant economic texts is dated to Nebuchadnezzar's eighth year; in addition to two kudurrus and a stone memorial tablet, they form the only existing commercial records. These artifacts evidence the dynasty's power as builders, craftsmen, and managers of the business of the empire.

The Kudurru of Nebuchadnezzar: *This detail depicts Nebuchadnezzar granting Marduk freedom from taxation.*

Nebuchadnezzar was succeeded by his two sons, firstly Enlil-nadin-apli (1103-1100 BCE), who lost territory to Assyria, and then Marduk-nadin-ahhe (1098-1081 BCE), who also went to war with Assyria. Some initial success in these conflicts gave way to catastrophic defeat at the hands of Tiglath-pileser I, who annexed huge swathes of Babylonian territory, thereby further expanding the Assyrian Empire. Following this military defeat, a terrible famine gripped Babylon, which invited attacks from Semitic Aramean tribes from the west.

In 1072 BCE, King Marduk-shapik-zeri signed a peace treaty with Ashur-bel-kala of Assyria. His successor, Kadašman-Buriaš, however, did not maintain his predecessor's peaceful intentions, and his actions prompted the Assyrian king to invade Babylonia and place his own man on the throne. Assyrian domination continued until c. 1050 BCE, with the two reigning Babylonian kings regarded as vassals of Assyria. Assyria descended into a period of civil war after 1050 BCE, which allowed Babylonia to once more largely free itself from the Assyrian yoke for a few decades.

However, Babylonia soon began to suffer repeated incursions from Semitic nomadic peoples migrating from the west, and large swathes of Babylonia were appropriated and occupied by these newly arrived Arameans, Chaldeans, and Suteans. Starting in 1026 and lasting till 911 BCE, Babylonia descended into a period of chaos.

Attributions

CC licensed content, Specific attribution

- Babylon. **Provided by**: Wikipedia. **Located at**: https://en.wikipedia.org/wiki/Babylon. **License**: *CC BY-SA: Attribution-ShareAlike*
- Mari, Syria. **Provided by**: Wikipedia. **Located at**: https://en.wikipedia.org/wiki/Mari,_Syria. **License**: *CC BY-SA: Attribution-ShareAlike*
- Code of Hammurabi. **Provided by**: Wikipedia. **Located at**: https://en.wikipedia.org/wiki/Code_of_Hammurabi. **License**: *CC BY-SA: Attribution-ShareAlike*
- Babylonia. **Provided by**: Wikipedia. **Located at**: http://en.wikipedia.org/wiki/Babylonia. **License**: *CC BY-SA: Attribution-ShareAlike*

- Babylonia. **Provided by**: Wikipedia. **Located at**: http://en.wikipedia.org/wiki/Babylonia. **License**: *CC BY-SA: Attribution-ShareAlike*
- Babylonian Law. **Provided by**: Wikipedia. **Located at**: https://en.wikipedia.org/wiki/Babylonian_law. **License**: *CC BY-SA: Attribution-ShareAlike*
- Hammurabi's Code: An Eye for an Eye. **Provided by**: Ancient Civilizations. **Located at**: http://www.ushistory.org/civ/4c.asp. **License**: *CC BY: Attribution*
- Code of Hammurabi. **Provided by**: Wikipedia. **Located at**: https://en.wikipedia.org/wiki/Code_of_Hammurabi. **License**: *CC BY-SA: Attribution-ShareAlike*
- Babylonia. **Provided by**: Wikipedia. **Located at**: http://en.wikipedia.org/wiki/Babylonia. **License**: *CC BY-SA: Attribution-ShareAlike*
- 220px-Code-de-Hammurabi-1.jpg. **Provided by**: Wikipedia. **Located at**: https://en.wikipedia.org/wiki/File:Code-de-Hammurabi-1.jpg. **License**: *CC BY: Attribution*
- Epic of Gilgamesh. **Provided by**: Wikipedia. **Located at**: http://en.wikipedia.org/wiki/Epic_of_gilgamesh. **License**: *CC BY-SA: Attribution-ShareAlike*
- Babylonia. **Provided by**: Wikipedia. **Located at**: http://en.wikipedia.org/wiki/Babylonia. **License**: *CC BY-SA: Attribution-ShareAlike*
- pilaster. **Provided by**: Wiktionary. **Located at**: http://en.wiktionary.org/wiki/pilaster. **License**: *CC BY-SA: Attribution-ShareAlike*
- etiology. **Provided by**: Wikipedia. **Located at**: http://en.wikipedia.org/wiki/etiology. **License**: *CC BY-SA: Attribution-ShareAlike*
- Babylonia. **Provided by**: Wikipedia. **Located at**: http://en.wikipedia.org/wiki/Babylonia. **License**: *CC BY-SA: Attribution-ShareAlike*
- 220px-Code-de-Hammurabi-1.jpg. **Provided by**: Wikipedia. **Located at**: https://en.wikipedia.org/wiki/File:Code-de-Hammurabi-1.jpg. **License**: *CC BY: Attribution*
- Epic of Gilgamesh. **Provided by**: Wikipedia. **Located at**: http://en.wikipedia.org/wiki/Epic_of_gilgamesh. **License**: *Public Domain: No Known Copyright*
- Babylonia. **Provided by**: Wikipedia. **Located at**: http://en.wikipedia.org/wiki/Babylonia. **License**: *CC BY-SA: Attribution-ShareAlike*
- Nebuchadnezzar I. **Provided by**: Wikipedia. **Located at**: http://en.wikipedia.org/wiki/Nebuchadnezzar_I. **License**: *CC BY-SA: Attribution-ShareAlike*
- Babylonia. **Provided by**: Wikipedia. **Located at**: http://en.wikipedia.org/wiki/Babylonia. **License**: *CC BY-SA: Attribution-ShareAlike*
- 220px-Code-de-Hammurabi-1.jpg. **Provided by**: Wikipedia. **Located at**: https://en.wikipedia.org/wiki/File:Code-de-Hammurabi-1.jpg. **License**: *CC BY: Attribution*
- Epic of Gilgamesh. **Provided by**: Wikipedia. **Located at**: http://en.wikipedia.org/wiki/Epic_of_gilgamesh. **License**: *Public Domain: No Known Copyright*
- Nebuchadnezzar I. **Provided by**: Wikipedia. **Located at**: http://en.wikipedia.org/wiki/Nebuchadnezzar_I. **License**: *Public Domain: No Known Copyright*

Ancient Egypt

Introduction to Ancient Egypt

The Rise of Egyptian Civilization

In prehistoric times (pre-3200 BCE), many different cultures lived in Egypt along the Nile River, and became progressively more sedentary and reliant on agriculture. By the time of the Early Dynastic Period, these cultures had solidified into a single state.

Learning Objectives

Describe the rise of civilization along the Nile River

Key Takeaways

Key Points

- The prehistory of Egypt spans from early human settlements to the beginning of the Early Dynastic Period of Egypt (c. 3100 BCE), and is equivalent to the Neolithic period.
- The Late Paleolithic in Egypt began around 30,000 BCE, and featured mobile buildings and tool-making industry.
- The Mesolithic saw the rise of various cultures, including Halfan, Qadan, Sebilian, and Harifian.
- The Neolithic saw the rise of cultures, including Merimde, El Omari, Maadi, Tasian, and Badarian.
- Three phases of Naqada culture included: the rise of new types of pottery (including blacktop-ware and white cross-line-ware), the use of mud-bricks, and increasingly sedentary lifestyles.
- During the Protodynastic period (3200-3000 BCE) powerful kings were in place, and unification of the state occurred, which led to the Early Dynastic Period.

> *Key Terms*
>
> - **nomadic pastoralism**: The herding of livestock to find fresh pasture to graze.
> - **Neolithic**: The later part of the Stone Age, during which ground or polished stone weapons and implements were used.
> - **Fertile Crescent**: Also known as the Cradle of Civilization, the Fertile Crescent is a crescent-shaped region containing the comparatively moist and fertile land of Western Asia, the Nile Valley, and the Nile Delta.
> - **serekhs**: An ornamental vignette combining a view of a palace facade and a top view of the royal courtyard. It was used as a royal crest.

The prehistory of Egypt spans from early human settlements to the beginning of the Early Dynastic Period of Egypt (c. 3100 BCE), which started with the first Pharoah Narmer (also known as Menes). It is equivalent to the Neolithic period, and is divided into cultural periods, named after locations where Egyptian settlements were found.

The Late Paleolithic

This period began around 30,000 BCE. Ancient, mobile buildings, capable of being disassembled and reassembled were found along the southern border near Wadi Halfa. Aterian tool-making industry reached Egypt around 40,000 BCE, and Khormusan industry began between 40,000 and 30,000 BCE.

The Mesolithic

Halfan culture arose along the Nile Valley of Egypt and in Nubia between 18,000 and 15,000 BCE. They appeared to be settled people, descended from the Khormusan people, and spawned the Ibero-Marusian industry. Material remains from these people include stone tools, flakes, and rock paintings.

The Qadan culture practiced wild-grain harvesting along the Nile, and developed sickles and grinding stones to collect and process these plants. These people were likely residents of Libya who were pushed into the Nile Valley due to desiccation in the Sahara. The Sebilian culture (also known as Esna) gathered wheat and barley.

The Harifian culture migrated out of the Fayyum and the Eastern deserts of Egypt to merge with the Pre-Pottery Neolithic B; this created the Circum-Arabian Nomadic Pastoral Complex, who invented nomadic pastoralism, and may have spread Proto-Semitic language throughout Mesopotamia.

The Neolithic

Expansion of the Sahara desert forced more people to settle around the Nile in a sedentary, agriculture-based lifestyle. Around 6000 BCE, Neolithic settlements began to appear in great number in this area, likely as migrants from the Fertile Crescent returned to the area. Weaving occurred for the first time in this period, and people buried their dead close to or within their settlements.

The Merimde culture (5000-4200 BCE) was located in Lower Egypt. People lived in small huts, created simple pottery, and had stone tools. They had cattle, sheep, goats, and pigs, and planted wheat, sorghum, and barley. The first Egyptian life-size clay head comes from this culture.

The El Omari culture (4000-3100 BCE) lived near modern-day Cairo. People lived in huts, and had undecorated pottery and stone tools. Metal was unknown.

The Maadi culture (also known as Buto Maadi) is the most important Lower Egyptian prehistoric culture. Copper was used, pottery was simple and undecorated, and people lived in huts. The dead were buried in cemeteries.

The Tasian culture (4500-3100 BCE) produced a kind of red, brown, and black pottery, called blacktop-ware. From this period on, Upper Egypt was strongly influenced by the culture of Lower Egypt.

The Badarian culture (4400-4000 BCE) was similar to the Tasian, except they improved blacktop-ware and used copper in addition to stone.

The Amratian culture (Naqada I) (4000-3500 BCE) continued making blacktop-ware, and added white cross-line-ware, which featured pottery with close, parallel, white, crossed lines. Mud-brick buildings were first seen in this period in small numbers.

Amratian (Naqada I) Terracotta Figure:
This terracotta female figure, c. 3500-3400 BCE, is housed at the Brooklyn Museum.

The Gerzean culture (Naqada II, 3500-3200 BCE) saw the laying of the foundation for Dynastic Egypt. It developed out of Amratian culture, moving south through Upper Egypt. Its pottery was painted dark red with pictures of animals, people and ships. Life was increasingly sedentary and focused on agriculture, as cities began to grow. Mud bricks were mass-produced, copper was used for tools and weapons, and silver, gold, lapis, and faience were used as decorations. The first Egyptian-style tombs were built.

Protodynastic Period (Naqada III) (3200 – 3000 BCE)

During this period, the process of state formation, begun in Naqada II, became clearer. Kings headed up powerful polities, but they were unrelated. Political unification was underway, which culminated in the formation of a single state in the Early Dynastic Period. Hieroglyphs may have first been used in this period, along with irrigation. Additionally, royal cemeteries and serekhs (royal crests) came into use.

Serekh of King Djet: *This serekh (royal crest) shows the Horus falcon.*

Attributions

CC licensed content, Specific attribution

- Serekh. **Provided by**: Wikipedia. **Located at**: https://en.wikipedia.org/wiki/Serekh. **License**: *CC BY: Attribution*
- Prehistoric Egypt. **Provided by**: Wikipedia. **Located at**: https://en.wikipedia.org/wiki/Prehistoric_Egypt. **License**: *CC BY: Attribution*
- Naqada III. **Provided by**: Wikipedia. **Located at**: https://en.wikipedia.org/wiki/Naqada_III. **License**: *CC BY: Attribution*
- Tasian Culture. **Provided by**: Wikipedia. **Located at**: https://en.wikipedia.org/wiki/Tasian_culture. **License**: *CC BY: Attribution*
- 291px-Egypte_louvre_290.jpg. **Provided by**: Wikipedia. **Located at**: https://en.wikipedia.org/wiki/Serekh#/media/File:Egypte_louvre_290.jpg. **License**: *CC BY: Attribution*
- 357px-Female_Figure_ca._3500-3400_B.C.E..jpg. **Provided by**: Wikipedia. **Located at**: https://en.wikipedia.org/wiki/Prehistoric_Egypt#/media/File:Female_Figure,_ca._3500-3400_B.C.E..jpg. **License**: *CC BY: Attribution*
- 360px-Egypte_louvre_317.jpg. **Provided by**: Wikipedia. **Located at**: https://en.wikipedia.org/wiki/Prehistoric_Egypt#/media/File:Egypte_louvre_317.jpg. **License**: *CC BY: Attribution*

The Old Kingdom

The Old Kingdom

The Old Kingdom, spanning the Third to Sixth Dynasties of Egypt (2686-2181 BCE), saw the prolific construction of pyramids, but declined due to civil instability, resource shortages, and a drop in precipitation.

Learning Objectives

Explain the reasons for the rise and fall of the Old Kingdom

Key Takeaways

Key Points

- The Old Kingdom is the name commonly given to the period when Egypt gained in complexity and achievement, spanning from the Third Dynasty through the Sixth Dynasty (2686-2181 BCE).
- The royal capital of Egypt during the Old Kingdom was located at Memphis, where the first notable king of the Old Kingdom, Djoser, established his court.
- In the Third Dynasty, formerly independent ancient Egyptian states became known as Nomes, which were ruled solely by the pharaoh. The former rulers of these states were subsequently forced to assume the role of governors, or otherwise work in tax collection.
- Egyptians during this Dynasty worshipped their pharaoh as a god, and believed that he ensured the stability of the cycles that were responsible for the annual flooding of the Nile. This flooding was necessary for their crops.
- The Fourth Dynasty saw multiple large-scale construction projects under pharaohs Sneferu, Khufu, and Khufu's sons Djedefra and Khafra, including the famous pyramid and Sphinx at Giza.
- The Fifth Dynasty saw changes in religious beliefs, including the rise of the cult of the

sun god Ra, and the deity Osiris.
- The Sixth Dynasty saw civil war and the loss of centralized power to nomarchs.

Key Terms

- **necropolis**: A cemetery, especially a large one belonging to an ancient city.
- **Osiris**: The Egyptian god of the underworld, and husband and brother of Isis.
- **Sneferu**: A king of the Fourth Dynasty, who used the greatest mass of stones in building pyramids.
- **Djoser**: An ancient Egyptian pharaoh of the Third Dynasty, and the founder of the Old Kingdom.
- **Old Kingdom**: Encompassing the Third to Eighth Dynasties, the name commonly given to the period in the 3rd millennium BCE, when Egypt attained its first continuous peak of complexity and achievement.
- **nomarchs**: Semi-feudal rulers of Ancient Egyptian provinces.
- **Nomes**: Subnational, administrative division of Ancient Egypt.
- **Ra**: The sun god, or the supreme Egyptian deity, worshipped as the creator of all life, and usually portrayed with a falcon's head bearing a solar disc.

The Old Kingdom is the name commonly given to the period from the Third Dynasty through the Sixth Dynasty (2686-2181 BCE), when Egypt gained in complexity and achievement. The Old Kingdom is the first of three so-called "Kingdom" periods that mark the high points of civilization in the Nile Valley. During this time, a new type of pyramid (the step) was created, as well as many other massive building projects, including the Sphinx. Additionally, trade became more widespread, new religious ideas were born, and the strong centralized government was subtly weakened and finally collapsed.

The king (not yet called Pharaoh) of Egypt during this period resided in the new royal capital, Memphis. He was considered a living god, and was believed to ensure the annual flooding of the Nile. This flooding was necessary for crop growth. The Old Kingdom is perhaps best known for a large number of pyramids, which were constructed as royal burial places. Thus, the period of the Old Kingdom is often called "The Age of the Pyramids."

Egypt's Old Kingdom was also a dynamic period in the development of Egyptian art. Sculptors created early portraits, the first life-size statues, and perfected the art of carving intricate relief decoration. These had two principal functions: to ensure an ordered existence, and to defeat death by preserving life in the next world.

The Beginning: Third Dynasty (c. 2650-2613 BCE)

The first notable king of the Old Kingdom was Djoser (reigned from 2691-2625 BCE) of the Third Dynasty, who ordered the construction of the step pyramid in Memphis' necropolis, Saqqara. It was in this era that formerly independent ancient Egyptian states became known as nomes, and were ruled solely by the king. The former rulers of these states were forced to assume the role of governors or tax collectors.

Golden Age: Fourth Dynasty (2613-2494 BCE)

The Old Kingdom and its royal power reached a zenith under the Fourth Dynasty, which began with Sneferu (2613-2589 BCE). Using a greater mass of stones than any other king, he built three pyramids: Meidum, the Bent Pyramid, and the Red Pyramid. He also sent his military into Sinai, Nubia and Libya, and began to trade with Lebanon for cedar.

Sneferu was succeeded by his (in)famous son, Khufu (2589-2566 BCE), who built the Great Pyramid of Giza. After Khufu's death, one of his sons built the second pyramid, and the Sphinx in Giza. Creating these massive projects required a centralized government with strong powers, sophistication and prosperity. Builders of the pyramids were not slaves but peasants, working in the farming off-season, along with specialists like stone cutters, mathematicians, and priests. Each household needed to provide a worker for these projects, although the wealthy could have a substitute.

The Pyramid of Khufu at Giza: *The Great Pyramid of Giza was built c. 2560 BCE, by Khufu during the Fourth Dynasty. It was built as a tomb for Khufu and constructed over a 20-year period. Modern estimates place construction efforts to require an average workforce of 14,567 people and a peak workforce of 40,000.*

Great Sphinx of Giza and the pyramid of Khafre: *The Sphinx is a limestone statue of a reclining mythical creature with a lion's body and a human head that stands on the Giza Plateau on the west bank of the Nile in Giza, Egypt. The face is generally believed to represent the face of King Khafra.*

The later kings of the Fourth Dynasty were king Menkaura (2532-2504 BCE), who built the smallest pyramid in Giza, Shepseskaf (2504-2498 BCE), and perhaps Djedefptah (2498-2496 BCE). During this period, there were military expeditions into Canaan and Nubia, spreading Egyptian influence along the Nile into modern-day Sudan.

Religious Changes: Fifth Dynasty (2494-2345 BCE)

The Fifth Dynasty began with Userkaf (2494-2487 BCE), and with several religious changes. The cult of the sun god Ra, and temples built for him, began to grow in importance during the Fifth Dynasty. This lessened efforts to build pyramids. Funerary prayers on royal tombs (called Pyramid Texts) appeared, and the cult of the deity Osiris ascended in importance.

Egyptians began to build ships to trade across maritime routes. Goods included ebony, incense, gold, and copper. They traded with Lebanon for cedar, and perhaps with modern-day Somalia for other goods. Ships were held together by tightly tied ropes.

Decline and Collapse: The Sixth Dynasty (2345-2181 BCE)

The power of the king and central government declined during this period, while that of nomarchs (regional governors) increased. These nomarchs were not part of the royal family. They passed down the title through their lineage, thus creating local dynasties that were not under the control of the king. Internal disorder resulted during and after the long reign of Pepi II (2278-2184 BCE), due to succession struggles, and eventually led to civil war. The final blow was a severe drought between 2200-2150 BCE, which prevented Nile flooding. Famine, conflict, and collapse beset the Old Kingdom for decades.

The First Intermediate Period

The First Intermediate Period, the Seventh to Eleventh dynasties, spanned approximately one hundred years (2181-2055 BCE), and was characterized by political instability and conflict between the Heracleopolitan and Theban Kings.

Learning Objectives

Describe the processes by which the First Intermediate Period occurred, and then transitioned into the Middle Kingdom

Key Takeaways

Key Points

- The First Intermediate Period was a dynamic time in history, when rule of Egypt was roughly divided between two competing power bases. One of those bases resided at Heracleopolis in Lower Egypt, a city just south of the Faiyum region. The other resided at Thebes in Upper Egypt.
- The Old Kingdom fell due to problems with succession from the Sixth Dynasty, the rising power of provincial monarchs, and a drier climate that resulted in widespread famine.
- Little is known about the Seventh and Eighth Dynasties due to a lack of evidence, but the Seventh Dynasty was most likely an oligarchy, while Eighth Dynasty rulers claimed to be the descendants of the Sixth Dynasty kings. Both ruled from Memphis.
- The Heracleopolitan Kings saw periods of both violence and peace under their rule, and eventually brought peace and order to the Nile Delta region.
- Siut princes to the south of the Heracleopolitan Kingdom became wealthy from a variety of agricultural and economic activities, and acted as a buffer during times of conflict between the northern and southern parts of Egypt.
- The Theban Kings enjoyed a string of military successes, the last of which was a victory against the Heracleopolitan Kings that unified Egypt under the Twelfth Dynasty.

> ### Key Terms
>
> - **Mentuhotep II**: A pharaoh of the Eleventh Dynasty, who defeated the Heracleopolitan Kings and unified Egypt. Often considered the first pharaoh of the Middle Kingdom.
> - **oligarchy**: A form of power structure in which power effectively rests with a small number of people who are distinguished by royalty, wealth, family ties, education, corporate, or military control.
> - **nomarchs**: Ancient Egyptian administration officials responsible for governing the provinces.
> - **First Intermediate Period**: A period of political conflict and instability lasting approximately 100 years and spanning the Seventh to Eleventh Dynasties.

The First Intermediate Period (c. 2181-2055 BCE), often described as a "dark period" in ancient Egyptian history after the end of the Old Kingdom, spanned approximately 100 years. It included the Seventh, Eighth, Ninth, Tenth, and part of the Eleventh dynasties.

The First Intermediate Period was a dynamic time in history when rule of Egypt was roughly divided between two competing power bases: Heracleopolis in Lower Egypt, and Thebes in Upper Egypt. It is believed that political chaos during this time resulted in temples being pillaged, artwork vandalized, and statues of kings destroyed. These two kingdoms eventually came into military conflict. The Theban kings conquered the north, which resulted in the reunification of Egypt under a single ruler during the second part of the Eleventh dynasty.

Events Leading to the First Intermediate Period

The Old Kingdom, which preceded this period, fell for numerous reasons. One was the extremely long reign of Pepi II (the last major king of the Sixth Dynasty), and the resulting succession issues. Another major problem was the rise in power of the provincial nomarchs. Toward the end of the Old Kingdom, the positions of the nomarchs had become hereditary, creating family legacies independent from the king. They erected tombs in their own domains and often raised armies, and engaged in local rivalries. A third reason for the dissolution of centralized kingship was the low level of the Nile inundation, which may have resulted in a drier climate, lower crop yields, and famine.

The Seventh and Eighth Dynasties at Memphis

The Seventh and Eighth dynasties are often overlooked because very little is known about the rulers of these two periods. The Seventh Dynasty was most likely an oligarchy based in Memphis that attempted to retain control of the country. The Eighth Dynasty rulers, claiming to be the descendants of the Sixth Dynasty kings, also ruled from Memphis.

The Heracleopolitan Kings

After the obscure reign of the Seventh and Eighth dynasty kings, a group of rulers rose out of Heracleopolis in Lower Egypt, and ruled for approximately 94 years. These kings comprise the Ninth and Tenth Dynasties, each with 19 rulers.

The founder of the Ninth Dynasty, Wahkare Khety I, is often described as an evil and violent ruler who caused much harm to the inhabitants of Egypt. He was seized with madness, and, as legend would have it, was eventually killed by a crocodile. Kheti I was succeeded by Kheti II, also known as Meryibre, whose reign was essentially peaceful but experienced problems in the Nile Delta. His successor, Kheti III, brought some degree of order to the Delta, although the power and influence of these Ninth Dynasty kings were still insignificant compared to that of the Old Kingdom kings.

A distinguished line of nomarchs rose out of Siut (or Asyut), which was a powerful and wealthy province in the south of the Heracleopolitan kingdom. These warrior princes maintained a close relationship with the kings of the Heracleopolitan royal household, as is evidenced by the inscriptions in their tombs. These inscriptions provide a glimpse at the political situation that was present during their reigns, and describe the Siut nomarchs digging canals, reducing taxation, reaping rich harvests, raising cattle herds, and maintaining an army and fleet. The Siut province acted as a buffer state between the northern and southern rulers and bore the brunt of the attacks from the Theban kings.

The Theban Kings

The Theban kings are believed to have been descendants of Intef or Inyotef, the nomarch of Thebes, often called the "Keeper of the Door of the South. " He is credited with organizing Upper Egypt into an independent ruling body in the south, although he himself did not appear to have tried to claim the title of king. Intef II began the Theban assault on northern Egypt, and his successor, Intef III, completed the attack and moved into Middle Egypt against the Heracleopolitan kings. The first three kings of the Eleventh Dynasty (all named Intef) were, therefore, also the last three kings of the First Intermediate Period. They were succeeded by a line of kings who were all called Mentuhotep. Mentuhotep II, also known as Nebhepetra, would eventually defeat the Heracleopolitan kings around 2033 BCE, and unify the country to continue the Eleventh Dynasty and bring Egypt into the Middle Kingdom.

Mentuhotep II: *Painted sandstone seated statue of Nebhepetre Mentuhotep II, Egyptian Museum, Cairo.*

Attributions

CC licensed content, Specific attribution

- Old Kingdom. **Provided by**: Ancient Egypt Wiki. **Located at**: http://ancientegypt.wikia.com/wiki/Old_Kingdom. **License**: *CC BY-SA: Attribution-ShareAlike*
- Fourth Dynasty of Egypt. **Provided by**: Wikipedia. **Located at**: https://en.wikipedia.org/wiki/Fourth_Dynasty_of_Egypt. **License**: *CC BY: Attribution*
- Third Dynasty of Egypt. **Provided by**: Wikipedia. **Located at**: https://en.wikipedia.org/wiki/Third_Dynasty_of_Egypt. **License**: *CC BY: Attribution*
- Fifth Dynasty of Egypt. **Provided by**: Wikipedia. **Located at**: https://en.wikipedia.org/wiki/Fifth_Dynasty_of_Egypt. **License**: *CC BY: Attribution*
- Old Kingdom of Egypt. **Provided by**: Wikipedia. **Located at**: http://en.wikipedia.org/wiki/Old_Kingdom_of_Egypt. **License**: *CC BY-SA: Attribution-ShareAlike*
- Great Pyramid of Giza. **Provided by**: Wikipedia. **Located at**: http://en.wikipedia.org/wiki/Pyramid_of_giza. **License**: *CC BY-SA: Attribution-ShareAlike*
- Great Sphinx of Giza. **Provided by**: Wikipedia. **Located at**: http://en.wikipedia.org/wiki/Great_Sphinx_of_Giza. **License**: *CC BY-SA: Attribution-ShareAlike*

- Egypt Giza Sphinx. **Provided by**: Wikipedia. **Located at**: http://upload.wikimedia.org/wikipedia/commons/thumb/6/6c/Egypt.Giza.Sphinx.02.jpg/640px-Egypt.Giza.Sphinx.02.jpg. **License**: *Public Domain: No Known Copyright*
- Great Pyramid of Giza. **Provided by**: Wikipedia. **Located at**: http://en.wikipedia.org/wiki/Pyramid_of_giza. **License**: *CC BY-SA: Attribution-ShareAlike*
- The First Intermediate Period. **Provided by**: Egyptology At Perk. **Located at**: https://egyptologyatperk.wikispaces.com/First+Intermediate+Period+(Dynasties+7+%E2%80%93+10). **License**: *CC BY: Attribution*
- First Intermediate Period. **Provided by**: Wikipedia. **Located at**: http://en.wikipedia.org/wiki/First_Intermediate_Period_of_Egypt. **License**: *CC BY-SA: Attribution-ShareAlike*
- First Intermediate Period. **Provided by**: Ancient Egypt Wiki. **Located at**: http://ancientegypt.wikia.com/wiki/First_Intermediate_Period. **License**: *CC BY-SA: Attribution-ShareAlike*
- oligarchy. **Provided by**: Wiktionary. **Located at**: http://en.wiktionary.org/wiki/oligarchy. **License**: *CC BY-SA: Attribution-ShareAlike*
- Egypt Giza Sphinx. **Provided by**: Wikipedia. **Located at**: http://upload.wikimedia.org/wikipedia/commons/thumb/6/6c/Egypt.Giza.Sphinx.02.jpg/640px-Egypt.Giza.Sphinx.02.jpg. **License**: *Public Domain: No Known Copyright*
- Great Pyramid of Giza. **Provided by**: Wikipedia. **Located at**: http://en.wikipedia.org/wiki/Pyramid_of_giza. **License**: *CC BY-SA: Attribution-ShareAlike*
- Mentuhotep II. **Provided by**: Wikipedia. **Located at**: http://en.wikipedia.org/wiki/Mentuhotep_II%23mediaviewer/File:Mentuhotep_Seated.jpg. **License**: *Public Domain: No Known Copyright*

The Middle Kingdom

The Middle Kingdom

The Middle Kingdom was a period of Egyptian history spanning the Eleventh through Twelfth Dynasty (2000-1700 BCE), when centralized power consolidated a unified Egypt.

Learning Objectives

Describe the various characteristics of Sensuret III's rule during the height of the Middle Kingdom

Key Takeaways

Key Points

- The Middle Kingdom had two phases: the end of the Eleventh Dynasty, which ruled from Thebes, and the Twelfth Dynasty onwards, which was centred around el-Lisht.
- During the First Intermediate Period, the governors of the nomes of Egypt— called nomarchs — gained considerable power. Amenemhet I also instituted a system of co-regency, which ensured a smooth transition from monarch to monarch and contributed to the stability of the Twelfth Dynasty.
- The height of the Middle Kingdom came under the rules of Sensuret III and Amenemhat III, the former of whom established clear boundaries for Egypt, and the latter of whom efficiently exploited Egyptian resources to bring about a period of economic prosperity.
- The Middle Kingdom declined into the Second Intermediate Period during the Thirteenth Dynasty, after a gradual loss of dynastic power and the disintegration of Egypt.

Key Terms

- **nomes**: Subnational administrative divisions within ancient Egypt.

> - **Amenemhat III**: Egyptian king who saw a great period of economic prosperity through efficient exploitation of natural resources.
> - **Middle Kingdom**: Period of unification in Ancient Egyptian history, stretching from the end of the Eleventh Dynasty to the Thirteenth Dynasty, roughly between 2030-1640 BCE.
> - **Senusret III**: Warrior-king during the Twelfth Dynasty, who centralized power within Egypt through various military successes.
> - **Sobekneferu,**: The first known female ruler of Egypt.
> - **genut**:
> - **waret**: Administrative divisions in Egypt.

The Middle Kingdom, also known as the Period of Reunification, is a period in the history of Ancient Egypt stretching from the end of the Eleventh Dynasty to the end of the Twelfth Dynasty, roughly between 2000-1700 BCE. There were two phases: the end of the Eleventh Dynasty, which ruled from Thebes, and the Twelfth Dynasty onwards, which was centred around el-Lisht.

The End of the Eleventh Dynasty and the Rise of the Twelfth Dynasty

Toward the end of the First Intermediate Period, Mentuhotep II and his successors unified Egypt under a single rule, and commanded such faraway locations as Nubia and the Sinai. He reigned for 51 years and restored the cult of the ruler, considering himself a god and wearing the headdresses of Amun and Min. His descendants ruled Egypt, until a vizier, Amenemhet I, came to power and initiated the Twelfth Dynasty.

From the Twelfth dynasty onward, pharaohs often kept well-trained standing armies, which formed the basis of larger forces raised for defense against invasion, or for expeditions up the Nile or across the Sinai. However, the Middle Kingdom remained defensive in its military strategy, with fortifications built at the First Cataract of the Nile, in the Delta and across the Sinai Isthmus.

Amenemhet I never held the absolute power commanded, in theory, by the Old Kingdom pharaohs. During the First Intermediate Period, the governors of the nomes of Egypt— nomarchs—gained considerable power. To strengthen his position, Amenemhet required registration of land, modified nome borders, and appointed nomarchs directly when offices became vacant. Generally, however, he acquiesced to the nomarch system, creating a strongly feudal organization.

In his 20th regnal year, Amenemhat established his son, Senusret I, as his co-regent. This instituted a practice that would be used throughout the Middle and New Kingdoms. The reign of Amenemhat II, successor to Senusret I, has been characterized as largely peaceful. It appears Amenemhet allowed nomarchs to become hereditary again. In his 33rd regnal year, he appointed his son, Senusret II, co-regent.

There is no evidence of military activity during the reign of Senusret II. Senusret instead appears to have focused on domestic issues, particularly the irrigation of the Faiyum. He reigned only fifteen years, and was succeeded by his son, Senusret III.

Height of the Middle Kingdom

Senusret III was a warrior-king, and launched a series of brutal campaigns in Nubia. After his victories, Senusret built a series of massive forts throughout the country as boundary markers; the locals were closely watched.

Statue head of Sensuret III: Statue head of Sensuret III, one of the kings in the Twelfth Dynasty.

Domestically, Senusret has been given credit for an administrative reform that put more power in the hands of appointees of the central government. Egypt was divided into three warets, or administrative divisions: North, South, and Head of the South (perhaps Lower Egypt, most of Upper Egypt, and the nomes of the original Theban kingdom during the war with Herakleopolis, respectively). The power of the nomarchs seems to drop off permanently during Sensuret's reign, which has been taken to indicate that the central government had finally suppressed them, though there is no record that Senusret took direct action against them.

The reign of Amenemhat III was the height of Middle Kingdom economic prosperity, and is remarkable for the degree to which Egypt exploited its resources. Mining camps in the Sinai, that had previously been used only by intermittent expeditions, were operated on a semi-permanent basis. After a reign of 45 years, Amenemhet III was succeeded by Amenemhet IV, under whom dynastic power began to weaken. Contemporary records of the Nile flood levels indicate that the end of the reign of Amenemhet III was dry, and crop failures may have helped to destabilize the dynasty. Furthermore, Amenemhet III had an inordinately long reign, which led to succession problems. Amenemhet IV was succeeded by Sobekneferu, the first historically attested female king of Egypt, who ruled for no more than four years. She apparently had no heirs, and when she died the Twelfth Dynasty came to a sudden end.

Decline into the Second Intermediate Period

After the death of Sobeknefru, Egypt was ruled by a series of ephemeral kings for about 10-15 years. Ancient Egyptian sources regard these as the first kings of the Thirteenth Dynasty.

After the initial dynastic chaos, a series of longer reigning, better attested kings ruled for about 50-80 years. The strongest king of this period, Neferhotep I, ruled for 11 years, maintained effective control of Upper Egypt, Nubia, and the Delta, and was even recognized as the suzerain of the ruler of Byblos. At some point during the Thirteenth Dynasty, the provinces of Xois and Avaris began governing themselves. Thus began the final portion of the Thirteenth Dynasty, when southern kings continued to reign over Upper Egypt; when the unity of Egypt fully disintegrated, however, the Middle Kingdom gave way to the Second Intermediate Period.

The Second Intermediate Period

The Second Intermediate Period (c. 1650-1550 BCE) spanned the Fourteenth to Seventeenth Dynasties, and was a period in which decentralized rule split Egypt between the Theban-based Seventeenth Dynasty in Upper Egypt and the Sixteenth Dynasty under the Hyksos in the north.

> **Learning Objectives**
>
> Explain the dynamics between the various groups of people vying for power during the Second Intermediate Period.

> ## Key Takeaways
>
> *Key Points*
>
> - The brilliant Twelfth Dynasty was succeeded by a weaker Thirteenth Dynasty, which experienced a splintering of power.
> - The Hyksos made their first appearance during the reign of Sobekhotep IV, and overran Egypt at the end of the Fourteenth Dynasty. They ruled through the Fifteenth and Sixteenth Dynasties.
> - The Abydos Dynasty was a short-lived Dynasty that ruled over part of Upper Egypt, and was contemporaneous with the Fifteenth and Sixteenth Dynasties.
> - The Seventeeth Dynasty established itself in Thebes around the time that the Hyksos took power in Egypt, and co-existed with the Hyksos through trade for a period of time. However, rulers from the Seventeenth Dynasty undertook several wars of liberation that eventually once again unified Egypt in the Eighteenth Dynasty.
>
> *Key Terms*
>
> - **Baal**: The native storm god of the Hyksos.
> - **Second Intermediate Period**: Spanning the Fourteenth to Seventeenth Dynasties, a period of Egyptian history where power was split between the Hyksos and a Theban-based dynasty in Upper Egypt.
> - **Hyksos**: An Asiatic people from West Asia who took over the eastern Nile Delta, ending the Thirteenth dynasty of Egypt and initiating the Second Intermediate Period.
> - **Abydos Dynasty**: A short-lived local dynasty ruling over parts of Upper Egypt during the Second Intermediate Period in Ancient Egypt.

The Second Intermediate Period (c. 1782-1550 BCE) marks a time when Ancient Egypt once again fell into disarray between the end of the Middle Kingdom, and the start of the New Kingdom. It is best known as the period when the Hyksos, who reigned during the Fifteenth and Sixteenth Dynasties, made their appearance in Egypt.

The Thirteenth Dynasty (1803 – 1649 BCE)

The brilliant Egyptian Twelfth Dynasty— and the Golden Age of the Middle Kingdom— came to an end around 1800 BCE with the death of Queen Sobekneferu (1806-1802 BCE), and was succeeded by the much weaker Thirteenth Dynasty (1803-1649 BCE). Pharoahs ruled from Memphis until the Hyksos conquered the capital in 1650 BCE.

The Fourteenth Dynasty (c. 1725-1650 BCE)

The Thirteenth Dynasty proved unable to hold onto the long land of Egypt, and the provincial ruling family in Xois, located in the marshes of the western Delta, broke away from the central authority to form the Fourteenth Dynasty. The capital of this dynasty was likely Avaris. It existed concurrently with the Thirteenth Dynasty, and its rulers seemed to be of Canaanite or West Semitic descent.

Fourteenth Dynasty Territory: *The area in orange is the territory possibly under control of the Fourteenth Dynasty.*

The Fifteenth Dynasty (c. 1650-1550 BCE)

The Hyksos made their first appearance in 1650 BCE and took control of the town of Avaris. They would also conquer the Sixteenth Dynasty in Thebes and a local dynasty in Abydos (see below). The Hyksos were of mixed Asiatic origin with mainly Semitic components, and their native storm god, Baal, became associated with the Egyptian storm god Seth. They brought technological innovation to Egypt, including bronze and pottery techniques, new breeds of animals and new crops, the horse and chariot, composite bow, battle-axes, and fortification techniques for warfare. These advances helped Egypt later rise to prominence.

Luxor Temple: *Thebes was the capital of many of the Sixteenth Dynasty pharaohs*

The Sixteenth Dynasty

This dynasty ruled the Theban region in Upper Egypt for 70 years, while the armies of the Fifteenth Dynasty advanced against southern enemies and encroached on Sixteenth territory. Famine was an issue during this period, most notably during the reign of Neferhotep III.

The Abydos Dynasty

The Abydos Dynasty was a short-lived local dynasty that ruled over part of Upper Egypt and was contemporaneous with the Fifteenth and Sixteenth Dynasties c. 1650-1600 BCE. The royal necropolis of the Abydos Dynasty was found in the southern part of Abydos, in an area called Anubis Mountain in ancient times, adjacent to the tombs of the Middle Kingdom rulers.

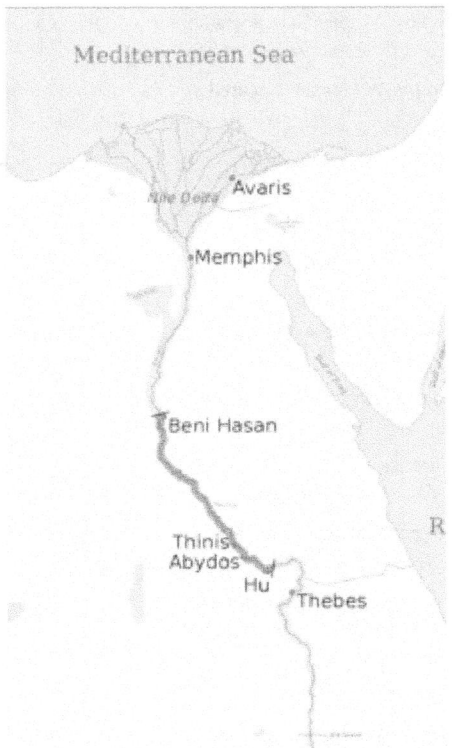

The Abydos Dynasty: *This map shows the possible extent of power of the Abydos Dynasty (in red).*

The Seventeenth Dynasty (c. 1580-1550 BCE)

Around the time Memphis and Itj-tawy fell to the Hyksos, the native Egyptian ruling house in Thebes declared its independence from Itj-tawy and became the Seventeenth Dynasty. This dynasty would eventually lead the war of liberation that drove the Hyksos back into Asia. The Theban-based Seventeenth Dynasty restored numerous temples throughout Upper Egypt while maintaining peaceful trading relations with the Hyksos kingdom in the north. Indeed, Senakhtenre Ahmose, the first king in the line of Ahmoside kings, even imported white limestone from the Hyksos-controlled region of Tura to make a granary door at the Temple of Karnak. However, his successors—the final two kings of this dynasty—,Seqenenre Tao and Kamose, defeated the Hyksos through several wars of liberation. With the creation of the Eighteenth Dynasty around 1550 BCE, the New Kingdom period of Egyptian history began with Ahmose I, its first pharaoh, who completed the expulsion of the Hyksos from Egypt and placed the country, once again, under centralized administrative control.

Attributions

CC licensed content, Specific attribution

- Middle Kingdom of Egypt. **Provided by**: Wikipedia. **Located at**: http://en.wikipedia.org/wiki/Middle_Kingdom_of_Egypt. **License**: *CC BY-SA: Attribution-ShareAlike*
- Middle Kingdom. **Provided by**: Wiktionary. **Located at**: http://en.wiktionary.org/wiki/Middle_Kingdom. **License**: *CC BY-SA: Attribution-ShareAlike*
- Middle Kingdom of Egypt. **Provided by**: Wikipedia. **Located at**: http://en.wikipedia.org/wiki/Middle_Kingdom_of_Egypt%23mediaviewer/File:GD-EG-Louxor-116.JPG. **License**: *CC BY-SA: Attribution-ShareAlike*

- Second Intermediate Period. **Provided by**: Wikipedia. **Located at**: http://en.wikipedia.org/wiki/Second_Intermediate_Period_of_Egypt. **License**: *CC BY-SA: Attribution-ShareAlike*
- Fifteenth Dynasty of Egypt. **Provided by**: Wikipedia. **Located at**: https://en.wikipedia.org/wiki/Fifteenth_Dynasty_of_Egypt. **License**: *CC BY: Attribution*
- Hyksos. **Provided by**: Wikipedia. **Located at**: https://en.wikipedia.org/wiki/Hyksos. **License**: *CC BY: Attribution*
- Thirteenth Dynasty of Egypt. **Provided by**: Wikipedia. **Located at**: https://en.wikipedia.org/wiki/Thirteenth_Dynasty_of_Egypt. **License**: *CC BY: Attribution*
- Abydos Dynasty. **Provided by**: Wikipedia. **Located at**: https://en.wikipedia.org/wiki/Abydos_Dynasty. **License**: *CC BY: Attribution*
- Seventeenth Dynasty. **Provided by**: Wikipedia. **Located at**: https://en.wikipedia.org/wiki/Seventeenth_Dynasty_of_Egypt. **License**: *CC BY: Attribution*
- Fourteenth Dynasty of Egypt. **Provided by**: Wikipedia. **Located at**: https://en.wikipedia.org/wiki/Fourteenth_Dynasty_of_Egypt. **License**: *CC BY: Attribution*
- The Second Intermediate Period (Dynasties 14-17). **Provided by**: Egyptology At Perk. **Located at**: https://egyptologyatperk.wikispaces.com/The+Second+Intermediate+Period+(Dynasties+14+%E2%80%93+17). **License**: *CC BY: Attribution*
- Middle Kingdom of Egypt. **Provided by**: Wikipedia. **Located at**: http://en.wikipedia.org/wiki/Middle_Kingdom_of_Egypt%23mediaviewer/File:GD-EG-Louxor-116.JPG. **License**: *CC BY-SA: Attribution-ShareAlike*
- 14th_dynasty_territory.png. **Provided by**: Wikipedia. **Located at**: https://en.wikipedia.org/wiki/File:14th_dynasty_territory.png. **License**: *CC BY: Attribution*
- Abydos_Dynasty.png. **Provided by**: Wikipedia. **Located at**: https://en.wikipedia.org/wiki/File:Abydos_Dynasty.png. **License**: *CC BY: Attribution*
- Second Intermediate Period. **Provided by**: Wikipedia. **Located at**: http://en.wikipedia.org/wiki/Second_Intermediate_Period_of_Egypt%23mediaviewer/File:Egypt.LuxorTemple.06.jpg. **License**: *Public Domain: No Known Copyright*

The New Kingdom

The New Kingdom

The New Kingdom of Egypt spanned the Eighteenth to Twentieth Dynasties (c. 1550-1077 BCE), and was Egypt's most prosperous time. It was ruled by pharaohs Hatshepsut, Thutmose III, Akhenaten, Tutankhamun and Ramesses II.

Learning Objectives

Explain the reasons for the collapse of the New Kingdom

Key Takeaways

Key Points

- The New Kingdom saw Egypt attempt to create a buffer against the Levant and by attaining its greatest territorial by extending into Nubia and the Near East. This was possibly a result of the foreign rule of the Hyksos during the Second Intermediate Period,
- The Eighteenth Dynasty contained some of Egypt's most famous pharaohs, including Hatshepsut, Akhenaten, Thutmose III, and Tutankhamun. Hatshepsut concentrated on expanding Egyptian trade, while Thutmose III consolidated power.
- Akhenaten's devotion to Aten defined his reign with religious fervor, while art flourished under his rule and attained an unprecedented level of realism.
- Due to Akenaten's lack of interest in international affairs, the Hittites gradually extended their influence into Phoenicia and Canaan.
- Ramesses II attempted war against the Hittites, but eventually agreed to a peace treaty after an indecisive result.
- The heavy cost of military efforts in addition to climatic changes resulted in a loss of centralized power at the end of the Twentieth Dynasty, leading to the Third Intermediate

> Period.
>
> *Key Terms*
>
> - **New Kingdom**: The period in ancient Egyptian history between the 16th century BCE and the 11th century BCE that covers the Eighteenth, Nineteenth, and Twentieth Dynasties of Egypt. Considered to be the peak of Egyptian power.
> - **Thutmose III**: The sixth pharaoh of the Eighteenth Dynasty, who greatly consolidated political power through a series of military conquests.
> - **Hatshepsut**: The fifth pharaoh of the Eighteenth Dynasty, who expanded Egyptian trade.
> - **Akhenaten**: Pharaoh of the Eighteenth Dynasty known for his religious fervor to the god Aten.
> - **Tutankhamun**: An Egyptian pharaoh of the 18th dynasty (ruled c. 1332 BC-1323 BC in the conventional chronology), during the period of Egyptian history known as the New Kingdom. He is popularly referred to as King Tut.
> - **Aten**: The disk of the sun in ancient Egyptian mythology, and originally an aspect of Ra.
> - **Ramesses II**: The third pharaoh of the Nineteenth Dynasty of Egypt, who made peace with the Hittites. Often regarded as the greatest, most celebrated, and most powerful pharaoh of the Egyptian Empire.

The New Kingdom of Egypt, also referred to as the Egyptian Empire, is the period in ancient Egyptian history between 1550-1070 BCE, covering the Eighteenth, Nineteenth, and Twentieth Dynasties of Egypt. The New Kingdom followed the Second Intermediate Period, and was succeeded by the Third Intermediate Period. It was Egypt's most prosperous time and marked the peak of its power.

The Nineteenth and Twentieth Dynasties (1292-1069 BCE) are also known as the Ramesside period, after the eleven pharaohs that took the name of Ramesses. The New Kingdom saw Egypt attempt to create a buffer against the Levant and attain its greatest territorial extent. This was possibly a result of the foreign rule of the Hyksos during the Second Intermediate Period

The Eighteenth Dynasty (c. 1543-1292 BCE)

The Eighteenth Dynasty, also known as the Thutmosid Dynasty, contained some of Egypt's most famous pharaohs, including Ahmose I, Hatshepsut, Thutmose III, Amenhotep III, Akhenaten (c. 1353-1336 BCE) and his queen Nefertiti, and Tutankhamun. Queen Hatshepsut (c. 1479 – 1458 BCE) concentrated on expanding Egypt's external trade by sending a commercial expedition to the land of Punt, and was the longest-reigning woman pharaoh of an indigenous dynasty. Thutmose III, who would become known as the greatest military pharoah, expanded Egypt's army and wielded it with great success to consolidate the empire created by his predecessors. These victories maximized Egyptian power and wealth during the reign of Amenhotep III. It was also during the reign of Thutmose III that the term "pharaoh," originally referring to the king's palace, became a form of address for the king.

One of the best-known Eighteenth Dynasty pharaohs is Amenhotep IV (c. 1353-1336 BCE), who changed his name to Akhenaten in honor of Aten and whose exclusive worship of the deity is often interpreted as the first instance of monotheism. Under his reign Egyptian art flourished and attained an unprecedented level of realism. Toward the end of this dynasty, the Hittites had expanded their influence into Phoenicia and Canaan, the outcome of which would be inherited by the rulers of the Nineteenth Dynasty.

Bust of Akhenaten: *Akhenaten, born Amenhotep IV, was the son of Queen Tiye. He rejected the old Egyptian religion and promoted the Aten as a supreme deity.*

The Nineteenth Dynasty (c. 1292-1187 BCE)

New Kingdom Egypt would reach the height of its power under Seti I and Ramesses II, who fought against the Libyans and Hittites. The city of Kadesh was a flashpoint, captured first by Seti I and then used as a peace bargain with the Hatti, and later attacked again by Ramesses II. Eventually, the Egyptians and Hittites signed a lasting peace treaty.

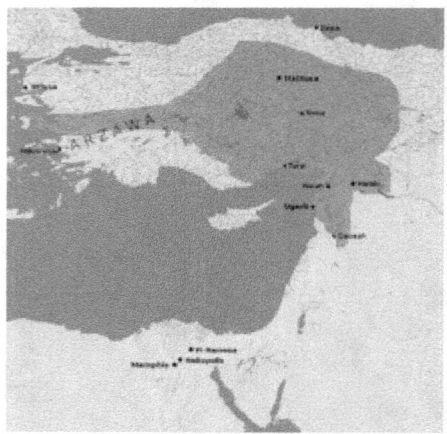

Egyptian and Hittite Empires: *This map shows the Egyptian (green) and Hittite (red) Empires around 1274 BCE.*

Ramesses II had a large number of children, and he built a massive funerary complex for his sons in the Valley of the Kings. The Nineteenth Dynasty ended in a revolt led by Setnakhte, the founder of the Twentieth Dynasty.

Temple of Ramesses II: *Detail of the Temple of Ramesses II.*

The Twentieth Dynasty (c. 1187-1064 BCE)

The last "great" pharaoh from the New Kingdom is widely regarded to be Ramesses III. In the eighth year of his reign, the Sea Peoples invaded Egypt by land and sea, but were defeated by Ramesses III.

The heavy cost of warfare slowly drained Egypt's treasury and contributed to the gradual decline of the Egyptian Empire in Asia. The severity of the difficulties is indicated by the fact that the first known labor strike in recorded history occurred during the 29th year of Ramesses III's reign, over food rations. Despite a palace conspiracy which may have killed Ramesses III, three of his sons ascended the throne successively as Ramesses IV, Ramesses VI and Ramesses VIII. Egypt was increasingly beset by droughts, below-normal flooding of the Nile, famine, civil unrest, and official corruption. The power of the last pharaoh of the dynasty, Ramesses XI, grew so weak that, in the south, the High Priests of Amun at Thebes became the de facto rulers of Upper Egypt. The Smendes controlled Lower Egypt even before Ramesses XI's death. Menes eventually founded the Twenty-first Dynasty at Tanis.

Hatshepsut

Hatshepsut ruled Egypt in the Eighteenth Dynasty (1478-1458 BCE), and brought wealth and a focus on large building projects. She was one of just a handful of female rulers.

Learning Objectives

Describe the achievements of Hatshepsut in Ancient Egypt.

Key Takeaways

Key Points

- Hatshepsut reigned Egypt from 1478-1458 BCE, during the Eighteenth Dynasty. She ruled longer than any other woman of an indigenous Egyptian dynasty.
- Hatshepsut established trade networks that helped build the wealth of the Eighteenth Dynasty.
- Hundreds of construction projects and statuary were commissioned by Hatshepsut, including obelisks and monuments at the Temple of Karnak.
- While not the first female ruler of Egypt, Hatshepsut's reign was longer and more prosperous; she oversaw a peaceful, wealthy era.
- The average woman in Egypt was quite liberated for the time, and had a variety of property and other rights.
- Hatshepsut died in 1458 BCE in middle age, possibly of diabetes and bone cancer. Her mummy was discovered in 1903 and identified in 2007.

> *Key Terms*
>
> - **kohl**: A black powder used as eye makeup.
> - **obelisks**: Stone pillars, typically having a square or rectangular cross section and a pyramidal tip, used as a monument.
> - **co-regent**: The situation wherein a monarchical position, normally held by one person, is held by two.

Hatshepsut reigned in Egypt from 1478-1458 BCE, during the Eighteenth Dynasty, longer than any other woman of an indigenous Egyptian dynasty. According to Egyptologist James Henry Breasted, she was "the first great woman in history of whom we are informed." She was the daughter of Thutmose I and his wife Ahmes. Hatshepsut's husband, Thutmose II, was also a child of Thutmose I, but was conceived with a different wife. Hatshepsut had a daughter named Neferure with her husband, Thutmose II. Thutmose II also fathered Thutmose III with Iset, a secondary wife. Hatshepsut ascended to the throne as co-regent with Thutmose III, who came to the throne as a two-year old child.

Statue of Hatshepsut: *This statue of Hatshepsut is housed at the Metropolitan Museum of Art in New York City.*

Trade Networks

Hatshepsut established trade networks that helped build the wealth of the Eighteenth Dynasty. This included a successful mission to the Land of Punt in the ninth year of her reign, which brought live myrrh trees and frankincense (which Hatshepsut used as kohl eyeliner) to Egypt. She also sent raiding expeditions to Byblos and Sinai, and may have led military campaigns against Nubia and Canaan.

Building Projects

Hatshepsut was a prolific builder, commissioning hundreds of construction projects and statuary. She had monuments constructed at the Temple of Karnak, and restored the original Precinct of Mut at Karnak, which had been ravaged during the Hyksos occupation of Egypt. She installed twin obelisks (the tallest in the world at that time) at the entrance to this temple, one of which still stands. Karnak's Red Chapel was intended as a shrine to her life, and may have stood with these obelisks.

The Temple of Pakhet was a monument to Bast and Sekhmet, lioness war goddesses. Later in the Nineteenth Dynasty, King Seti I attempted to take credit for this monument. However, Hatshepsut's masterpiece was a mortuary temple at Deir el-Bahri; the focal point was the Djeser-Djeseru ("the Sublime of Sublimes"), a colonnaded structure built 1,000 years before the Greek Parthenon. The Hatshepsut needle, a granite obelisk, is considered another great accomplishment.

Hatshepsut Temple: *The colonnaded design is evident in this temple.*

Female Rule

Hatshepsut was not the first female ruler of Egypt. She had been preceded by Merneith of the First Dynasty, Nimaathap of the Third Dynasty, Nitocris of the Sixth Dynasty, Sobekneferu of the Twelfth Dynasty,

Ahhotep I of the Seventeenth Dynasty, Ahmose-Nefertari, and others. However, Hatshepsut's reign was longer and more prosperous; she oversaw a peaceful, wealthy era. She was also proficient at self-promotion, which was enabled by her wealth.

Hieroglyphs of Thutmose III and Hatshepsut: *Hatshepsut, on the right, is shown having the trappings of a greater role.*

The word "king" was considered gender-neutral, and women could take the title. During her father's reign, she held the powerful office of God's Wife, and as wife to her husband, Thutmose II, she took an active role in administration of the kingdom. As pharaoh, she faced few challenges, even from her co-regent, who headed up the powerful Egyptian army and could have unseated her, had he chosen to do so.

Women's Status in Egypt

The average woman in Egypt was quite liberated for the time period. While her foremost role was as mother and wife, an average woman might have worked in weaving, perfume making, or entertainment. Women could own their own businesses, own and sell property, serve as witnesses in court cases, be in the company of men, divorce and remarry, and have access to one-third of their husband's property.

Hatshepsut's Death

Hatshepsut died in 1458 BCE in middle age; no cause of death is known, although she may have had diabetes and bone cancer, likely from a carcinogenic skin lotion. Her mummy was discovered in the Valley of the Kings by Howard Carer in 1903, although at the time, the mummy's identity was not known. In 2007, the mummy was found to be a match to a missing tooth known to have belonged to Hatshepsut.

Osirian Statues of Hatshepsut: *These statues of Hatshepsut at her tomb show her holding the crook and flail associated with Osiris.*

After her death, mostly during Thutmose III's reign, haphazard attempts were made to remove Hatshepsut from certain historical and pharaonic records. Amenhotep II, the son of Thutmose III, may have been responsible. The Tyldesley hypothesis states that Thutmose III may have decided to attempt to scale back Hatshepsut's role to that of regent rather than king.

The Third Intermediate Period

The Third Intermediate Period (c. 1069-664 BCE) spanned the Twenty-first to Twenty-sixth Dynasties, and was marked by internal divisions within Egypt, as well as conquest and rule by foreigners.

The New Kingdom

Learning Objectives

Describe the general landscape of the political chaos during Third Intermediate Period

Key Takeaways

Key Points

- The period of the Twenty-first Dynasty was characterized by the country's fracturing kingship, as power became split more and more between the pharaoh and the High Priests of Amun at Thebes.
- Egypt was temporarily reunified during the Twenty-second Dynasty, and experienced a period of stability, but shattered into two states after the reign of Osorkon II.
- Civil war raged in Thebes and was eventually quelled by Osorkon B, who founded the Upper Egyptian Libyan Dynasty. This dynasty collapsed, however, with the rise of local city-states.
- The Twenty-fourth Dynasty saw the conquest of the Nubians over native Egyptian rulers, and the Nubians ruled through the Twenty-Fifth Dynasty, when they expanded Egyptian power to the extent of the New Kingdom and restored many temples. Due to lacking military power, however, the Egyptians were conquered by the Assyrians toward the end of the Twenty-fifth Dynasty.
- The end of the Third Intermediate Period and the Twenty-sixth Dynasty saw Assyrian rule over Egypt. Although some measure of independence was regained, Egypt faced pressure and eventual defeat at the hands of the Persians.

Key Terms

- **Nubia**: A region along the Nile river, located in northern Sudan and southern Egypt.
- **Assyrians**: A major Mesopotamian East Semitic-speaking people.
- **High Priests of Amun**: The highest-ranking priest in the priesthood of the Ancient Egyptian god, Amun. Assumed significant power along with the pharaoh in the Twenty-First Dynasty.
- **Third Intermediate Period**: Spanning the Twenty-first to Twenty-sixth Dynasties. A period of Egyptian decline and political instability

The Third Intermediate Period of Ancient Egypt began with the death of the last pharaoh of the New Kingdom, Ramesses XI in 1070 BCE, and ended with the start of the Postdynastic Period. The Third Intermediate Period was one of decline and political instability. It was marked by a division of the state for much of the period, as well as conquest and rule by foreigners. However, many aspects of life for ordinary Egyptians changed relatively little.

The Twenty-First Dynasty (c. 1077-943 BCE)

The period of the Twenty-first Dynasty was characterized by the country's fracturing kingship. Even in Ramesses XI's day, the Twentieth Dynasty of Egypt was losing its grip on power in the city of Thebes, where priests were becoming increasingly powerful. The Amun priests of Thebes owned 2/3 of all the temple lands in Egypt, 90% of ships, and many other resources. Consequently, the Amun priests were as powerful as the Pharaoh, if not more so. After the death of Ramesses XI, his successor, Smendes I, ruled from the city of Tanis, but was mainly active only in Lower Egypt. Meanwhile, the High Priests of Amun at Thebes effectively ruled Middle and Upper Egypt in all but name. During this time, however, this division was relatively insignificant, due to the fact that both priests and pharaohs came from the same family.

The Twenty-Second (c. 943-716 BCE) and Twenty-Third (c. 880-720 BCE) Dynasties

The country was firmly reunited by the Twenty-second Dynasty, founded by Shoshenq I in approximately 943 BCE. Shoshenq I descended from Meshwesh immigrants originally from Ancient Libya. This unification brought stability to the country for well over a century, but after the reign of Osorkon II, the country had shattered in two states. Shoshenq III of the Twenty-Second Dynasty controlled Lower Egypt by 818 BCE, while Takelot II and his son Osorkon (the future Osorkon III) ruled Middle and Upper Egypt. In Thebes, a civil war engulfed the city between the forces of Pedubast I, a self-proclaimed pharaoh. Eventually Osorkon B defeated his enemies, and proceeded to found the Upper Egyptian Libyan Dynasty of Osorkon III, Takelot III, and Rudamun. This kingdom quickly fragmented after Rudamun's death with the rise of local city-states.

The Twenty-Fourth Dynasty (c. 732-720 BCE)

The Nubian kingdom to the south took full advantage of the division of the country. Nubia had already extended its influence into the Egyptian city of Thebes around 752 BCE, when the Nubian ruler Kashta coerced Shepenupet into adopting his own daughter Amenirdis as her successor. Twenty years later, around 732 BCE, these machinations bore fruit for Nubia when Kashta's successor Piye marched north in his Year 20 campaign into Egypt, and defeated the combined might of the native Egyptian rulers.

The Twenty-Fifth Dynasty (c. 760-656 BCE)

Following his military conquests, Piye established the Twenty-fifth Dynasty and appointed the defeated rulers as his provincial governors. Rulers under this dynasty originated in the Nubian Kingdom of Kush. Their reunification of Lower Egypt, Upper Egypt, and Kish created the largest Egyptian empire since the New Kingdom. They assimilated into Egyptian culture but also brought some aspects of Kushite culture. During this dynasty, the first widespread building of pyramids since the Middle Kingdom resumed. The Nubians were driven out of Egypt in 670 BCE by the Assyrians, who installed an initial puppet dynasty loyal to the Assyrians.

Nubian Pharaohs: *Statues of the Nubian Pharaohs of the Twenty-fifth Dynasty.*

End of the Third Intermediate Period

Upper Egypt remained under the rule of Tantamani for a time, while Lower Egypt was ruled by the Twenty-sixth Dynasty, starting in 664 BCE. Although originally established as clients of the Assyrians, the Twenty-sixth Dynasty managed to take advantage of the time of troubles facing the Assyrian empire to successfully bring about Egypt's political independence. In 656 BCE, Psamtik I (last of the Twenty-sixth Dynasty kings) occupied Thebes and became pharaoh, the King of Upper and Lower Egypt. He proceeded to reign over a united Egypt for 54 years from his capital at Sais. Four successive Saite kings continued guiding Egypt through a period of peace and prosperity from 610-525 BCE. Unfortunately for this dynasty, however, a new power was growing in the Near East: Persia. Pharaoh Psamtik III succeeded his father, Ahmose II, only six months before he had to face the Persian Empire at Pelusium. The new king was no match for the Persians, who had already taken Babylon. Psamtik III was defeated and briefly escaped to Memphis. He was ultimately imprisoned, and later executed at Susa, the capital of the Persian king Cambyses. With the Saite kings exterminated, Camybes assumed the formal title of Pharaoh.

The Decline of Ancient Egypt

Ancient Egypt went through a series of occupations and suffered a slow decline over a long period of time. First occupied by the Assyrians, then the Persians, and later the Macedonians and Romans, Egyptians would never again reach the glorious heights of self-rule they achieved during previous periods.

Learning Objectives

Explain why Ancient Egypt declined as an economic and political force

> ## Key Takeaways
>
> ### Key Points
>
> - After a renaissance in the 25th Dynasty, ancient Egypt was occupied by Assyrians, initiating the Late Period.
> - In 525 BCE, Egypt was conquered by Persia, and incorporated into the Achaemenid Persian Empire.
> - In 332 BCE, Egypt was given to Macedonia and Alexander the Great. During this period, the new capital of Alexandria flourished.
> - Egypt became a Roman province after the defeat of Marc Antony and Queen Cleopatra VII in 30 BCE. During this period, religious and other traditions slowly declined.
>
> ### Key Terms
>
> - **hieroglyphics**: A formal writing system used by ancient Egyptians, consisting of pictograms.
> - **pagan**: A person holding religious beliefs other than those of the main world religions, Christianity, Judaism, and Islam.
> - **Hellenistic**: Relating to Greek history, language, and culture, during the time between the death of Alexander the Great and the defeat of Mark Antony and Cleopatra in 31 BCE.

Ancient Egypt went through a series of occupations and suffered a slow decline over a long period of time. First occupied by the Assyrians, then the Persians, and later the Macedonians and Romans, Egyptians would never again reach the glorious heights of self-rule they achieved during previous periods.

Third Intermediate Period (1069-653 BCE)

After a renaissance in the Twenty-fifth dynasty, when religion, arts, and architecture (including pyramids) were restored, struggles against the Assyrians led to eventual conquest of Egypt by Esarhaddon in 671 BCE. Native Egyptian rulers were installed but could not retain control of the area, and former Pharaoh Taharqa seized control of southern Egypt for a time, until he was defeated again by the Assyrians. Taharqa's successor, Tanutamun, also made a failed attempt to regain Egypt, but was defeated.

Late Period (672-332 BCE)

Having been victorious in Egypt, the Assyrians installed a series of vassals known as the Saite kings of the Twenty-sixth Dynasty. In 653 BCE, one of these kings, Psamtik I, was able to achieve a peaceful separation from the Assyrians with the help of Lydian and Greek mercenaries. In 609 BCE, the Egyptians attempted to save the Assyrians, who were losing their war with the Babylonians, Chaldeans, Medians, and Scythians. However, they were unsuccessful.

In 525 BCE, the Persians, led by Cambyses II, invaded Egypt, capturing the Pharaoh Psamtik III. Egypt was joined with Cyprus and Phoenicia in the sixth satrapy of the Achaemenid Persian Empire, also called the Twenty-seventh Dynasty. This ended in 402 BCE, and the last native royal house of dynastic Egypt, known as the Thirtieth Dynasty, was ruled by Nectanebo II. Persian rule was restored briefly in 343 BCE, known as the Thirty-first Dynasty, but in 332 BCE, Egypt was handed over peacefully to the Macedonian ruler, Alexander the Great.

Macedonian and Ptolemaic Period (332-30 BCE)

Alexander the Great was welcomed into Egypt as a deliverer, and the new capital city of Alexandria was a showcase of Hellenistic rule, capped by the famous Library of Alexandria. Native Egyptian traditions were honored, but eventually local revolts, plus interest in Egyptian goods by the Romans, caused the Romans to wrest Egypt from the Macedonians.

Roman Period (30 BCE-641CE)

Egypt became a Roman province after the defeat of Marc Antony and Queen Cleopatra VII in 30 BCE. Some Egyptian traditions, including mummification and worship of local gods, continued, but local administration was handled exclusively by Romans. The spread of Christianity proved to be too powerful, and pagan rites were banned and temples closed. Egyptians continued to speak their language, but the ability to read hieroglyphics disappeared as temple priests diminished.

Attributions

CC licensed content, Specific attribution

- Nineteenth Dynasty of Egypt. **Provided by**: Wikipedia. **Located at**: https://en.wikipedia.org/wiki/Nineteenth_Dynasty_of_Egypt. **License**: *CC BY: Attribution*
- Twentieth Dynasty of Egypt. **Provided by**: Wikipedia. **Located at**: https://en.wikipedia.org/wiki/Twentieth_Dynasty_of_Egypt. **License**: *CC BY: Attribution*
- Eighteenth Dynasty of Egypt. **Provided by**: Wikipedia. **Located at**: https://en.wikipedia.org/wiki/Eighteenth_Dynasty_of_Egypt. **License**: *CC BY: Attribution*
- New Kingdom of Egypt. **Provided by**: Wikipedia. **Located at**: http://en.wikipedia.org/wiki/New_Kingdom_of_Egypt. **License**: *CC BY-SA: Attribution-ShareAlike*
- Hitt_Egypt_Perseus.png. **Provided by**: Wikipedia. **Located at**: https://en.wikipedia.org/wiki/File:Hitt_Egypt_Perseus.png. **License**: *CC BY: Attribution*
- New Kingdom of Egypt. **Provided by**: Wikipedia. **Located at**: http://en.wikipedia.org/wiki/New_Kingdom_of_Egypt%23mediaviewer/File:S_F-E-CAMERON_EGYPT_2006_FEB_00671.JPG. **License**: *CC BY-SA: Attribution-ShareAlike*
- New Kingdom of Egypt. **Provided by**: Wikipedia. **Located at**: http://en.wikipedia.org/wiki/New_Kingdom_of_Egypt%23mediaviewer/File:GD-EG-Caire-Mus%C3%A9e061.JPG. **License**: *CC BY-SA: Attribution-ShareAlike*
- Women of Ancient Egypt. **Provided by**: Ancient Civilizations. **Located at**: http://www.ushistory.org/civ/3f.asp. **License**: *CC BY-SA: Attribution-ShareAlike*
- Hatshepsut. **Provided by**: Wikipedia. **Located at**: https://en.wikipedia.org/wiki/Hatshepsut. **License**: *CC BY: Attribution*
- Hitt_Egypt_Perseus.png. **Provided by**: Wikipedia. **Located at**: https://en.wikipedia.org/wiki/File:Hitt_Egypt_Perseus.png. **License**: *CC BY: Attribution*
- New Kingdom of Egypt. **Provided by**: Wikipedia. **Located at**: http://en.wikipedia.org/wiki/New_Kingdom_of_Egypt%23mediaviewer/File:S_F-E-CAMERON_EGYPT_2006_FEB_00671.JPG. **License**: *CC BY-SA: Attribution-ShareAlike*
- New Kingdom of Egypt. **Provided by**: Wikipedia. **Located at**: http://en.wikipedia.org/wiki/New_Kingdom_of_Egypt%23mediaviewer/File:GD-EG-Caire-Mus%C3%A9e061.JPG. **License**: *CC BY-SA: Attribution-ShareAlike*
- Hatshepsut.jpg. **Provided by**: Wikipedia. **Located at**: https://en.wikipedia.org/wiki/Hatshepsut#/media/File:Hatshepsut.jpg. **License**: *CC BY: Attribution*

- 544px-Thutmose_III_and_Hatshepsut.jpg. **Provided by**: Wikipedia. **Located at**: https://en.wikipedia.org/wiki/Hatshepsut#/media/File:Thutmose_III_and_Hatshepsut.jpg. **License**: *CC BY: Attribution*
- 320px-S_F-E-CAMERON_2006-10-EGYPT-WESTBANK-0153.jpeg. **Provided by**: Wikipedia. **Located at**: https://en.wikipedia.org/wiki/Hatshepsut#/media/File:S_F-E-CAMERON_2006-10-EGYPT-WESTBANK-0153.JPG. **License**: *CC BY: Attribution*
- 640px-Il_tempio_di_Hatshepsut.jpeg. **Provided by**: Wikipedia. **Located at**: https://en.wikipedia.org/wiki/Hatshepsut#/media/File:Il_tempio_di_Hatshepsut.JPG. **License**: *CC BY: Attribution*
- Twenty-first Dynasty of Egypt. **Provided by**: Wikipedia. **Located at**: https://en.wikipedia.org/wiki/Twenty-first_Dynasty_of_Egypt. **License**: *CC BY: Attribution*
- Twenty-third Dynasty of Egypt. **Provided by**: Wikipedia. **Located at**: https://en.wikipedia.org/wiki/Twenty-third_Dynasty_of_Egypt. **License**: *CC BY: Attribution*
- Twenty-second Dynasty of Egypt. **Provided by**: Wikipedia. **Located at**: https://en.wikipedia.org/wiki/Twenty-second_Dynasty_of_Egypt. **License**: *CC BY: Attribution*
- Twenty-fifth Dynasty of Egypt. **Provided by**: Wikipedia. **Located at**: https://en.wikipedia.org/wiki/Twenty-fifth_Dynasty_of_Egypt. **License**: *CC BY: Attribution*
- Twenty-fourth Dynasty of Egypt. **Provided by**: Wikipedia. **Located at**: https://en.wikipedia.org/wiki/Twenty-fourth_Dynasty_of_Egypt. **License**: *CC BY: Attribution*
- Third Intermediate Period of Egypt. **Provided by**: Wikipedia. **Located at**: http://en.wikipedia.org/wiki/Third_Intermediate_Period_of_Egypt. **License**: *CC BY-SA: Attribution-ShareAlike*
- Amun. **Provided by**: Wikipedia. **Located at**: http://en.wikipedia.org/wiki/Amun. **License**: *CC BY-SA: Attribution-ShareAlike*
- Hitt_Egypt_Perseus.png. **Provided by**: Wikipedia. **Located at**: https://en.wikipedia.org/wiki/File:Hitt_Egypt_Perseus.png. **License**: *CC BY: Attribution*
- New Kingdom of Egypt. **Provided by**: Wikipedia. **Located at**: http://en.wikipedia.org/wiki/New_Kingdom_of_Egypt%23mediaviewer/File:S_F-E-CAMERON_EGYPT_2006_FEB_00671.JPG. **License**: *CC BY-SA: Attribution-ShareAlike*
- New Kingdom of Egypt. **Provided by**: Wikipedia. **Located at**: http://en.wikipedia.org/wiki/New_Kingdom_of_Egypt%23mediaviewer/File:GD-EG-Caire-Mus%C3%A9e061.JPG. **License**: *CC BY-SA: Attribution-ShareAlike*
- Hatshepsut.jpg. **Provided by**: Wikipedia. **Located at**: https://en.wikipedia.org/wiki/Hatshepsut#/media/File:Hatshepsut.jpg. **License**: *CC BY: Attribution*
- 544px-Thutmose_III_and_Hatshepsut.jpg. **Provided by**: Wikipedia. **Located at**: https://en.wikipedia.org/wiki/Hatshepsut#/media/File:Thutmose_III_and_Hatshepsut.jpg. **License**: *CC BY: Attribution*
- 320px-S_F-E-CAMERON_2006-10-EGYPT-WESTBANK-0153.jpeg. **Provided by**: Wikipedia. **Located at**: https://en.wikipedia.org/wiki/Hatshepsut#/media/File:S_F-E-CAMERON_2006-10-EGYPT-WESTBANK-0153.JPG. **License**: *CC BY: Attribution*
- 640px-Il_tempio_di_Hatshepsut.jpeg. **Provided by**: Wikipedia. **Located at**: https://en.wikipedia.org/wiki/Hatshepsut#/media/File:Il_tempio_di_Hatshepsut.JPG. **License**: *CC BY: Attribution*
- Third Intermediate Period of Egypt. **Provided by**: Wikipedia. **Located at**: http://en.wikipedia.org/wiki/Third_Intermediate_Period%23mediaviewer/File:NubianPharoahs.jpg. **License**: *Public Domain: No Known Copyright*
- History of Egypt. **Provided by**: Wikipedia. **Located at**: https://en.wikipedia.org/wiki/History_of_Egypt. **License**: *CC BY: Attribution*
- Ancient Egypt. **Provided by**: Wikipedia. **Located at**: https://en.wikipedia.org/wiki/Ancient_Egypt#Ptolemaic_Period. **License**: *CC BY: Attribution*
- Societal Collapse. **Provided by**: Wikipedia. **Located at**: https://en.wikipedia.org/wiki/Societal_collapse. **License**: *CC BY: Attribution*
- History of Ancient Egypt. **Provided by**: Wikipedia. **Located at**: https://en.wikipedia.org/wiki/History_of_ancient_Egypt. **License**: *CC BY: Attribution*
- Hitt_Egypt_Perseus.png. **Provided by**: Wikipedia. **Located at**: https://en.wikipedia.org/wiki/File:Hitt_Egypt_Perseus.png. **License**: *CC BY: Attribution*
- New Kingdom of Egypt. **Provided by**: Wikipedia. **Located at**: http://en.wikipedia.org/wiki/New_Kingdom_of_Egypt%23mediaviewer/File:S_F-E-CAMERON_EGYPT_2006_FEB_00671.JPG. **License**: *CC BY-SA: Attribution-ShareAlike*
- New Kingdom of Egypt. **Provided by**: Wikipedia. **Located at**: http://en.wikipedia.org/wiki/New_Kingdom_of_Egypt%23mediaviewer/File:GD-EG-Caire-Mus%C3%A9e061.JPG. **License**: *CC BY-SA: Attribution-ShareAlike*
- Hatshepsut.jpg. **Provided by**: Wikipedia. **Located at**: https://en.wikipedia.org/wiki/Hatshepsut#/media/File:Hatshepsut.jpg.

License: *CC BY: Attribution*

- 544px-Thutmose_III_and_Hatshepsut.jpg. **Provided by**: Wikipedia. **Located at**: https://en.wikipedia.org/wiki/Hatshepsut#/media/File:Thutmose_III_and_Hatshepsut.jpg. **License**: *CC BY: Attribution*

- 320px-S_F-E-CAMERON_2006-10-EGYPT-WESTBANK-0153.jpeg. **Provided by**: Wikipedia. **Located at**: https://en.wikipedia.org/wiki/Hatshepsut#/media/File:S_F-E-CAMERON_2006-10-EGYPT-WESTBANK-0153.JPG. **License**: *CC BY: Attribution*

- 640px-Il_tempio_di_Hatshepsut.jpeg. **Provided by**: Wikipedia. **Located at**: https://en.wikipedia.org/wiki/Hatshepsut#/media/File:Il_tempio_di_Hatshepsut.JPG. **License**: *CC BY: Attribution*

- Third Intermediate Period of Egypt. **Provided by**: Wikipedia. **Located at**: http://en.wikipedia.org/wiki/Third_Intermediate_Period%23mediaviewer/File:NubianPharoahs.jpg. **License**: *Public Domain: No Known Copyright*

Ancient Egyptian Society

Ancient Egyptian Religion

Ancient Egyptian religion lasted for more than 3,000 years, and consisted of a complex polytheism. The pharaoh's role was to sustain the gods in order to maintain order in the universe.

Learning Objectives

Describe the religious beliefs and practices of Ancient Egypt

---

Key Takeaways

Key Points

- The religion of Ancient Egypt lasted for more than 3,000 years, and was polytheistic, meaning there were a multitude of deities, who were believed to reside within and control the forces of nature.
- Formal religious practice centered on the pharaoh, or ruler, of Egypt, who was believed to be divine, and acted as intermediary between the people and the gods. His role was to sustain the gods so that they could maintain order in the universe.
- The Egyptian universe centered on Ma'at, which has several meanings in English, including truth, justice and order. It was fixed and eternal; without it the world would fall apart.
- The most important myth was of Osiris and Isis. The divine ruler Osiris was murdered by Set (god of chaos), then resurrected by his sister and wife Isis to conceive an heir, Horus. Osiris then became the ruler of the dead, while Horus eventually avenged his father and became king.
- Egyptians were very concerned about the fate of their souls after death. They believed ka (life-force) left the body upon death and needed to be fed. Ba, or personal spirituality,

remained in the body. The goal was to unite ka and ba to create akh.
- Artistic depictions of gods were not literal representations, as their true nature was considered mysterious. However, symbolic imagery was used to indicate this nature.
- Temples were the state's method of sustaining the gods, since their physical images were housed and cared for; temples were not a place for the average person to worship.
- Certain animals were worshipped and mummified as representatives of gods.
- Oracles were used by all classes.

Key Terms

- **polytheistic**: A religion with more than one worshipped god.
- **Duat**: The realm of the dead; residence of Osiris.
- **ka**: The spiritual part of an individual human being or god that survived after death.
- **pantheon**: The core actors of a religion.
- **heka**: The ability to use natural forces to create "magic."
- **Ma'at,**: The Egyptian universe.
- **ba**: The spiritual characteristics of an individual person that remained in the body after death. Ba could unite with the ka.
- **akh**: The combination of the ka and ba living in the afterlife.

The religion of Ancient Egypt lasted for more than 3,000 years, and was polytheistic, meaning there were a multitude of deities, who were believed to reside within and control the forces of nature. Religious practices were deeply embedded in the lives of Egyptians, as they attempted to provide for their gods and win their favor. The complexity of the religion was evident as some deities existed in different manifestations and had multiple mythological roles. The pantheon included gods with major roles in the universe, minor deities (or "demons"), foreign gods, and sometimes humans, including deceased Pharaohs.

Formal religious practice centered on the pharaoh, or ruler, of Egypt, who was believed to be divine, and acted as intermediary between the people and the gods. His role was to sustain the gods so that they could maintain order in the universe, and the state spent its resources generously to build temples and provide for rituals. The pharaoh was associated with Horus (and later Amun) and seen as the son of Ra. Upon death, the pharaoh was fully deified, directly identified with Ra and associated with Osiris, the god of death and rebirth. However, individuals could appeal directly to the gods for personal purposes through prayer or requests for magic; as the pharaoh's power declined, this personal form of practice became stronger. Popular religious practice also involved ceremonies around birth and naming. The people also invoked "magic" (called heka) to make things happen using natural forces.

Gods of the Pantheon: *This wall painting shows, from left to right, the gods Osiris, Anubis and Horus.*

Cosmology

The Egyptian universe centered on Ma'at, which has several meanings in English, including truth, justice and order. It was fixed and eternal (without it the world would fall apart), and there were constant threats of disorder requiring society to work to maintain it. Inhabitants of the cosmos included the gods, the spirits of deceased humans, and living humans, the most important of which was the pharaoh. Humans should cooperate to achieve this, and gods should function in balance. Ma'at was renewed by periodic events, such as the annual Nile flood, which echoed the original creation. Most important of these was the daily journey of the sun god Ra.

Egyptians saw the earth as flat land (the god Geb), over which arched the sky (goddess Nut); they were separated by Shu, the god of air. Underneath the earth was a parallel underworld and undersky, and beyond the skies lay Nu, the chaos before creation. Duat was a mysterious area associated with death and rebirth, and each day Ra passed through Duat after traveling over the earth during the day.

Egyptian Cosmology: *In this artwork, the air god Shu is assisted by other gods in holding up Nut, the sky, as Geb, the earth, lies beneath.*

Myths

Egyptian myths are mainly known from hymns, ritual and magical texts, funerary texts, and the writings of Greeks and Romans. The creation myth saw the world as emerging as a dry space in the primordial ocean of chaos, marked by the first rising of Ra. Other forms of the myth saw the primordial god Atum transforming into the elements of the world, and the creative speech of the intellectual god Ptah.

The most important myth was of Osiris and Isis. The divine ruler Osiris was murdered by Set (god of chaos), then resurrected by his sister and wife Isis to conceive an heir, Horus. Osiris then became the ruler of the dead, while Horus eventually avenged his father and became king. This myth set the Pharaohs, and their succession, as orderliness against chaos.

The Afterlife

Egyptians were very concerned about the fate of their souls after death, and built tombs, created grave goods and gave offerings to preserve the bodies and spirits of the dead. They believed humans possessed ka, or life-force, which left the body at death. To endure after death, the ka must continue to receive offerings of food; it could consume the spiritual essence of it. Humans also possessed a ba, a set of spiritual characteristics unique to each person, which remained in the body after death. Funeral rites were meant to release the ba so it could move, rejoin with the ka, and live on as an akh. However, the ba returned to the body at night, so the body must be preserved.

Mummification involved elaborate embalming practices, and wrapping in cloth, along with various rites, including the Opening of the Mouth ceremony. Tombs were originally mastabas (rectangular brick structures), and then pyramids.

However, this originally did not apply to the common person: they passed into a dark, bleak realm that was the opposite of life. Nobles did receive tombs and grave gifts from the pharaoh. Eventually, by about 2181 BCE, Egyptians began to believe every person had a ba and could access the afterlife. By the New Kingdom, the soul had to face dangers in the Duat before having a final judgment, called the Weighing of the Heart, where the gods compared the actions of the deceased while alive to Ma'at, to see if they were worthy. If so, the ka and ba were united into an akh, which then either traveled to the lush underworld, or traveled with Ra on his daily journey, or even returned to the world of the living to carry out magic.

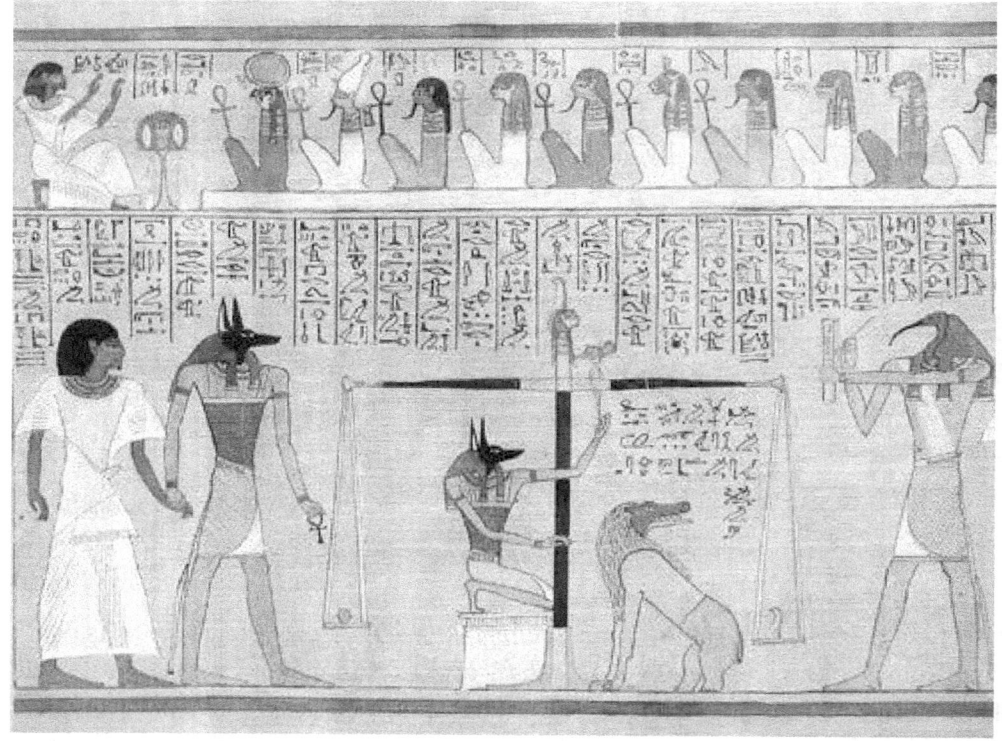

Funerary Text: In this section from the Book of the Dead for the scribe Hunefer, the Weighing of the Heart is shown.

Rise and Fall of Gods

Certain gods gained a primary status over time, and then fell as other gods overtook them. These included the sun god Ra, the creator god Amun, and the mother goddess Isis. There was even a period of time where Egypt was monotheistic, under Pharaoh Akhenaten, and his patron god Aten.

The Relationships of Deities

Just as the forces of nature had complex interrelationships, so did Egyptian deities. Minor deities might be linked, or deities might come together based on the meaning of numbers in Egyptian mythology (i.e., pairs represented duality). Deities might also be linked through syncretism, creating a composite deity.

Artistic Depictions of Gods

Artistic depictions of gods were not literal representations, since their true nature was considered mysterious. However, symbolic imagery was used to indicate this nature. An example was Anubis, a funerary god, who was shown as a jackal to counter its traditional meaning as a scavenger, and create protection for the mummy.

Temples

Temples were the state's method of sustaining the gods, as their physical images were housed and cared for; they were not a place for the average person to worship. They were both mortuary temples to serve deceased pharaohs and temples for patron gods. Starting as simple structures, they grew more elaborate, and were increasingly built from stone, with a common plan. Ritual duties were normally carried out by priests, or government officials serving in the role. In the New Kingdom, professional priesthood became common, and their wealth rivaled that of the pharaoh.

Rituals and Festivals

Aside from numerous temple rituals, including the morning offering ceremony and re-enactments of myths, there were coronation ceremonies and the sed festival, a renewal of the pharaoh's strength during his reign. The Opet Festival at Karnak involved a procession carrying the god's image to visit other significant sites.

Animal Worship

At many sites, Egyptians worshipped specific animals that they believed to be manifestations of deities. Examples include the Apis bull (of the god Ptah), and mummified cats and other animals.

Use of Oracles

Commoners and pharaohs asked questions of oracles, and answers could even be used during the New Kingdom to settle legal disputes. This might involve asking a question while a divine image was being carried, and interpreting movement, or drawing lots.

Ancient Egyptian Art

Ancient Egyptian art included painting, sculpture, pottery, glass work, and architecture. Many surviving art is related to tombs and monuments. Aside from the brief Amarna period, Egyptian art remained relatively unchanged for thousands of years.

Learning Objectives
Examine the development of Egyptian Art under the Old Kingdom.

Key Takeaways

Key Points

- Ancient Egyptian art includes painting, sculpture, architecture, and other forms of art, such as drawings on papyrus, created between 3000 BCE and 100 CE.

- Most of this art was highly stylized and symbolic. Much of the surviving forms come from tombs and monuments, and thus have a focus on life after death and preservation of knowledge.

- Symbolism meant order, shown through the pharaoh's regalia, or through the use of certain colors.

- In Egyptian art, the size of a figure indicates its relative importance.

- Paintings were often done on stone, and portrayed pleasant scenes of the afterlife in tombs.

- Ancient Egyptians created both monumental and smaller sculptures, using the technique of sunk relief.

- Ka statues, which were meant to provide a resting place for the ka part of the soul, were often made of wood and placed in tombs.

- Faience was sintered-quartz ceramic with surface vitrification, used to create relatively cheap small objects in many colors. Glass was originally a luxury item but became more common, and was used to make small jars, for perfume and other liquids, to be placed in tombs. Carvings of vases, amulets, and images of deities and animals were made of steatite. Pottery was sometimes covered with enamel, particularly in the color blue.

- Papyrus was used for writing and painting, and and was used to record every aspect of Egyptian life.

- Architects carefully planned buildings, aligning them with astronomically significant events, such as solstices and equinoxes. They used mainly sun-baked mud brick, limestone, sandstone, and granite.

- The Amarna period (1353-1336 BCE) represents an interruption in ancient Egyptian art style, subjects were represented more realistically, and scenes included portrayals of affection among the royal family.

Key Terms

- **papyrus**: A material prepared in ancient Egypt from the stem of a water plant, used in sheets for writing or painting on.
- **regalia**: The emblems or insignia of royalty.
- **sunk relief**: Sculptural technique in which the outlines of modeled forms are incised in a plane surface beyond which the forms do not project.
- **Ka**: The supposed spiritual part of an individual human being or god that survived after death, and could reside in a statue of the person.

> - **ushabti**: Ancient Egyptian funerary figure.
> - **Faience**: Glazed ceramic ware.
> - **scarabs**: Ancient Egyptian gem cut in the form of a scarab beetle

Ancient Egyptian art includes painting, sculpture, architecture, and other forms of art, such as drawings on papyrus, created between 3000 BCE and 100 AD. Most of this art was highly stylized and symbolic. Many of the surviving forms come from tombs and monuments, and thus have a focus on life after death and preservation of knowledge.

Symbolism

Symbolism in ancient Egyptian art conveyed a sense of order and the influence of natural elements. The regalia of the pharaoh symbolized his or her power to rule and maintain the order of the universe. Blue and gold indicated divinity because they were rare and were associated with precious materials, while black expressed the fertility of the Nile River.

Hierarchical Scale

In Egyptian art, the size of a figure indicates its relative importance. This meant gods or the pharaoh were usually bigger than other figures, followed by figures of high officials or the tomb owner; the smallest figures were servants, entertainers, animals, trees and architectural details.

Painting

Before painting a stone surface, it was whitewashed and sometimes covered with mud plaster. Pigments were made of mineral and able to stand up to strong sunlight with minimal fade. The binding medium is unknown; the paint was applied to dried plaster in the "fresco a secco" style. A varnish or resin was then applied as a protective coating, which, along with the dry climate of Egypt, protected the painting very well. The purpose of tomb paintings was to create a pleasant afterlife for the dead person, with themes such as journeying through the afterworld, or deities providing protection. The side view of the person or animal was generally shown, and paintings were often done in red, blue, green, gold, black and yellow.

Wall Painting of Nefertari: *In this wall painting of Nefertari, the side view is apparent.*

Sculpture

Ancient Egyptians created both monumental and smaller sculptures, using the technique of sunk relief. In this technique, the image is made by cutting the relief sculpture into a flat surface, set within a sunken area shaped around the image. In strong sunlight, this technique is very visible, emphasizing the outlines and forms by shadow. Figures are shown with the torso facing front, the head in side view, and the legs parted, with males sometimes darker than females. Large statues of deities (other than the pharaoh) were not common, although deities were often shown in paintings and reliefs.

Colossal sculpture on the scale of the Great Sphinx of Giza was not repeated, but smaller sphinxes and animals were found in temple complexes. The most sacred cult image of a temple's god was supposedly held in the naos in small boats, carved out of precious metal, but none have survived.

Ka statues, which were meant to provide a resting place for the ka part of the soul, were present in tombs as of Dynasty IV (2680-2565 BCE). These were often made of wood, and were called reserve heads, which were plain, hairless and naturalistic. Early tombs had small models of slaves, animals, buildings, and objects to provide life for the deceased in the afterworld. Later, ushabti figures were present as funerary figures to act as servants for the deceased, should he or she be called upon to do manual labor in the afterlife.

Ka Statue: *The ka statue was placed in the tomb to provide a physical place for the ka to manifest. This statue is found at the Egyptian Museum of Cairo.*

Many small carved objects have been discovered, from toys to utensils, and alabaster was used for the more expensive objects. In creating any statuary, strict conventions, accompanied by a rating system, were followed. This resulted in a rather timeless quality, as few changes were instituted over thousands of years.

Faience, Pottery, and Glass

Faience was sintered-quartz ceramic with surface vitrification used to create relatively cheap, small objects in many colors, but most commonly blue-green. It was often used for jewelry, scarabs, and figurines. Glass was originally a luxury item, but became more common, and was to used to make small jars, of perfume and other liquids, to be placed in tombs. Carvings of vases, amulets, and images of deities and animals were made of steatite. Pottery was sometimes covered with enamel, particularly in the color blue. In tombs, pottery was used to represent organs of the body removed during embalming, or to create cones, about ten inches tall, engraved with legends of the deceased.

Papyrus

Papyrus is very delicate and was used for writing and painting; it has only survived for long periods when buried in tombs. Every aspect of Egyptian life is found recorded on papyrus, from literary to administrative documents.

Architecture

Architects carefully planned buildings, aligning them with astronomically significant events, such as solstices and equinoxes, and used mainly sun-baked mud brick, limestone, sandstone, and granite. Stone was reserved for tombs and temples, while other buildings, such as palaces and fortresses, were made of bricks. Houses were made of mud from the Nile River that hardened in the sun. Many of these houses were destroyed in flooding or dismantled; examples of preserved structures include the village Deir al-Madinah and the fortress at Buhen.

The Giza Necropolis, built in the Fourth Dynasty, includes the Pyramid of Khufu (also known as the Great Pyramid or the Pyramid of Cheops), the Pyramid of Khafre, and the Pyramid of Menkaure, along with smaller "queen" pyramids and the Great Sphinx.

The Pyramids of Giza: *The Pyramid of Khufu (Great Pyramid) is the largest of the pyramids pictured here.*

The Temple of Karnak was first built in the 16th century BCE. About 30 pharaohs contributed to the buildings, creating an extremely large and diverse complex. It includes the Precincts of Amon-Re, Montu and Mut, and the Temple of Amehotep IV (dismantled).

The Temple of Karnak*: Shown here is the hypostyle hall of the Temple of Karnak.*

The Luxor Temple was constructed in the 14th century BCE by Amenhotep III in the ancient city of Thebes, now Luxor, with a major expansion by Ramesses II in the 13th century BCE. It includes the 79-foot high First Pylon, friezes, statues, and columns.

The Amarna Period (1353-1336 BCE)

During this period, which represents an interruption in ancient Egyptian art style, subjects were represented more realistically, and scenes included portrayals of affection among the royal family. There was a sense of movement in the images, with overlapping figures and large crowds. The style reflects Akhenaten's move to monotheism, but it disappeared after his death.

Ancient Egyptian Monuments

Ancient Egyptian monuments included pyramids, sphinxes, and temples. These buildings and statues required careful planning and resources, and showed the influence Egyptian religion had on the state and its people.

Learning Objectives

Describe the impressive attributes of the monuments erected by Egyptians in the Old Kingdom

Key Takeaways

Key Points

- Ancient Egyptian architects carefully planned buildings, aligning them with astronomically significant events, such as solstices and equinoxes, and used mainly sun-baked mud brick, limestone, sandstone, and granite.
- Egyptian pyramids were highly reflective, referenced the sun, and were usually placed on the West side of the Nile River.
- About 135 pyramids have been discovered in Egypt, with the largest (in Egypt and the world) being the Great Pyramid of Giza.
- The Great Sphinx of Giza is a reclining sphinx (a mythical creature with a lion's body and a human head); its face is meant to represent the Pharaoh Khafra. It is the world's oldest and largest monolith.
- Egyptian temples were used for official, formal worship of the gods by the state, and to commemorate pharaohs. The temple was the house of a particular god, and Egyptians would perform rituals, give offerings, re-enact myths, and keep order in the universe (ma'at).
- The Temple of Karnak was first built in the 16th century BCE. About 30 pharaohs contributed to the buildings, creating an extremely large and diverse complex.
- The Luxor Temple was constructed in the 14th century BCE by Amenhotep III in the ancient city of Thebes, now Luxor. It later received a major expansion by Ramesses II in the 13th century BCE.

Key Terms

- **solstices**: Either of the two times in the year (summer and winter) when the sun reaches its highest or lowest point in the sky at noon.
- **equinoxes**: Either of the two times in the year when the sun crosses the celestial equator, and day and night are of equal length.
- **Hypostyle halls**: In ancient Egypt, covered rooms with columns.
- **peristyle courts**: In ancient Egypt, courts that open to the sky.
- **pylon**: In ancient Egypt, two tapering towers with a less elevated section between them, forming a gateway.
- **friezes**: Broad, horizontal bands of sculpted or painted decoration.

- **monolith**: A large single upright block of stone, especially one shaped into, or serving as, a pillar or monument.
- **ma'at**: The ancient Egyptian concept of truth, balance, order, harmony, law, morality and justice.
- **obelisks**: Stone pillars, typically having a square or rectangular cross section and pyramidal top, used as monuments or landmarks.

Ancient Egyptian architects carefully planned buildings, aligning them with astronomically significant events, such as solstices and equinoxes. They used mainly sun-baked mud brick, limestone, sandstone, and granite. Stone was reserved for tombs and temples, while other buildings, such as palaces and fortresses, were made of bricks.

Pyramids

Egyptian pyramids referenced the rays of the sun, and appeared highly polished and reflective, with a capstone that was generally a hard stone like granite, sometimes plated with gold, silver or electrum. Most were placed west of the Nile, to allow the pharaoh's soul to join with the sun during its descent.

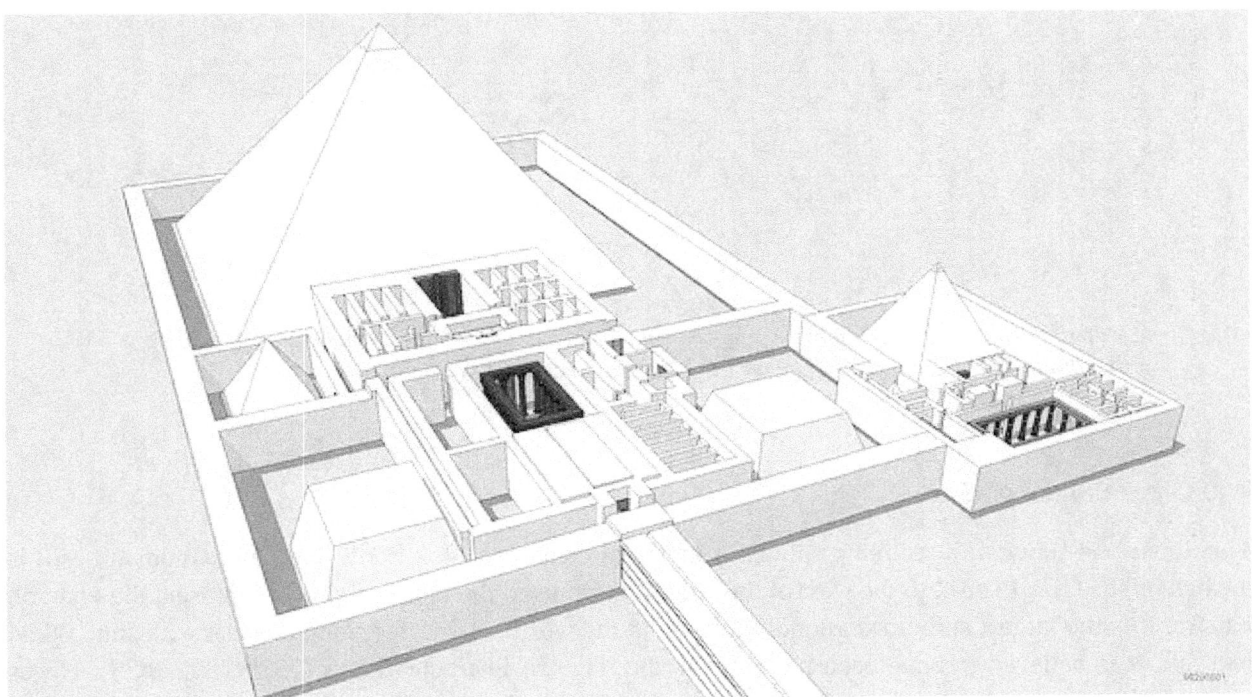

Old Kingdom Pyramid Temple Reconstruction: In this reconstruction, a causeway leads cut to the valley temple.

About 135 pyramids have been discovered in Egypt, with the largest (in Egypt and the world) being the Great Pyramid of Giza. Its base is over 566,000 square feet in area, and was one of the Seven Wonders of the Ancient World. The Giza Necropolis, built in the Fourth Dynasty, includes the Pyramid of Khufu (also known as the Great Pyramid or the Pyramid of Cheops), the Pyramid of Khafre and the Pyramid of Menkaure, along with smaller "queens" pyramids and the Great Sphinx.

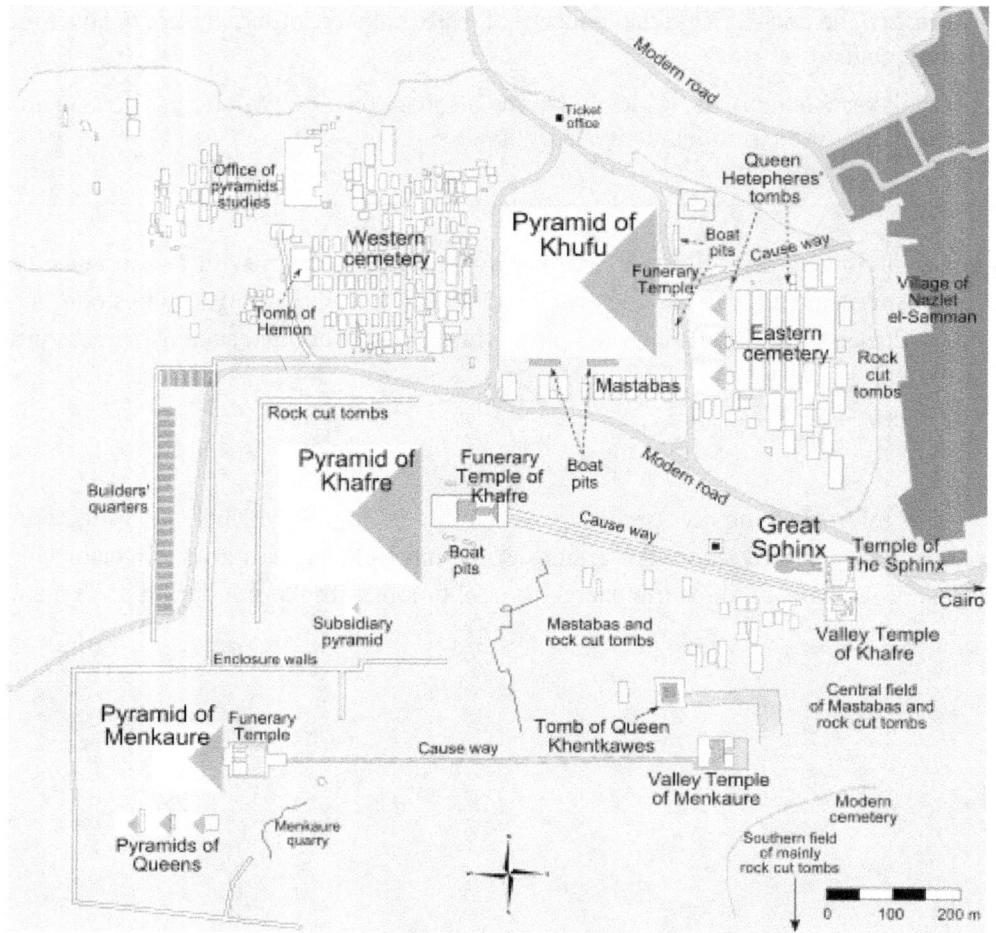

Map of Giza Pyramid Complex: *A map showing the layout of the Giza Pyramid area, including the Pyramids of Khufu, Khafre, Menkaure, and the Great Sphinx.*

The Great Sphinx of Giza

This limestone statue of a reclining sphinx (a mythical creature with a lion's body and a human head) is located on the Giza Plateau to the west of the Nile. It is believed the face is meant to represent the Pharaoh Khafra. It is the largest and oldest monolith statue in the world, at 241 feet long, 63 feet wide, and 66.34 feet tall. It is believed to have been built during the reign of Pharaoh Khafra (2558-2532 BCE). It was probably a focus of solar worship, as the lion is a symbol associated with the sun.

The Great Sphinx of Giza: *Here the Great Sphinx is shown against the Pyramid of Kahfre.*

Temples

Egyptian temples were used for official, formal worship of the gods by the state, and to commemorate pharaohs. The temple was the house dedicated to a particular god, and Egyptians would perform rituals there, give offerings, re-enact myths and keep order in the universe (ma'at). Pharaohs were in charge of caring for the gods, and they dedicated massive resources to this task. Priests assisted in this effort. The average citizen was not allowed into the inner sanctum of the temple, but might still go there to pray, give offerings, or ask questions of the gods.

The inner sanctuary had a cult image of the temple's god, as well as a series of surrounding rooms that became large and elaborate over time, evolving into massive stone edifices during the New Kingdom. Temples also often owned surrounding land and employed thousands of people to support its activities, creating a powerful institution. The designs emphasized order, symmetry and monumentality. Hypostyle halls (covered rooms filled with columns) led to peristyle courts (open courts), where the public could meet with priests. At the front of each court was a pylon (broad, flat towers) that held flagpoles. Outside the temple building was the temple enclosure, with a brick wall to symbolically protect from outside disorder; often a sacred lake would be found here. Decoration included reliefs (bas relief and sunken relief) of images and hieroglyphic text and sculpture, including obelisks, figures of gods (sometimes in sphinx form), and votive figures. Egyptian religions faced persecution by Christians, and the last temple was closed in 550 AD.

The Temple of Karnak was first built in the 16th century BCE. About 30 pharaohs contributed to the buildings, creating an extremely large and diverse complex. It includes the Precincts of Amon-Re, Montu and Mut, and the Temple of Amehotep IV (dismantled).

Temple of Karnak: *This view of the Temple of Karnak shows they hypostyle hall, with massive columns.*

The Luxor Temple was constructed in the 14th century BCE by Amenhotep III in the ancient city of Thebes, now Luxor, with a major expansion by Ramesses II in the 13th century BCE. It includes the 79-foot high First Pylon, friezes, statues, and columns.

Luxor Temple: *Shown here is the entrance pylon of Luxor Temple, one of the major New Kingdom temples.*

Ancient Egyptian Trade

Ancient Egyptians traded with their African and Mediterranean neighbors to obtain goods, such as cedar, lapis lazuli, gold, ivory, and more. They exported goods, such as papyrus, linen, and finished objects using a variety of land and maritime trading routes.

Learning Objectives
Describe the economic structure of ancient Egypt

Key Takeaways

Key Points

- Trade was occurring in the 5th century BCE onwards, especially with Canaan, Lebanon, Nubia and Punt.

- Just before the First Dynasty, Egypt had a colony in southern Canaan that produced Egyptian pottery for export to Egypt.
- In the Second Dynasty, Byblos provided quality timber that could not be found in Egypt.
- By the Fifth Dynasty, trade with Punt gave Egyptians gold, aromatic resins, ebony, ivory, and wild animals.
- A well-traveled land route from the Nile to the Red Sea crossed through the Wadi Hammamat. Another route, the Darb el-Arbain, was used from the time of the Old Kingdom of Egypt.
- Egyptians built ships as early as 3000 BCE by lashing planks of wood together and stuffing the gaps with reeds. They used them to import goods from Lebanon and Punt.

Key Terms

- **myrrh**: A fragrant gum resin obtained from certain trees, often used in perfumery, medicine and incense.
- **malachite**: A bright green mineral consisting of copper hydroxyl carbonate.
- **papyrus**: A material prepared in ancient Egypt from the stem of a water plant, used in sheets for writing, painting, or making rope, sandals, and boats.
- **obsidian**: A hard, dark, glasslike volcanic rock.
- **electrum**: A natural or artifical alloy of gold, with at least 20% silver, used for jewelry.

Early examples of ancient Egyptian trade included contact with Syria in the 5th century BCE, and importation of pottery and construction ideas from Canaan in the 4th century BCE. By this time, shipping was common, and the donkey, camel, and horse were domesticated and used for transportation. Lebanese cedar has been found in the tombs of Nekhen, dated to the Naqada I and II periods. Egyptians during this period also imported obsidian from Ethiopia, gold and incense from Nubia in the south, oil jugs from Palestine, and other goods from the oases of the western desert and the cultures of the eastern Mediterranean. Egyptian artifacts from this era have been found in Canaan and parts of the former Mesopotamia. In the latter half of the 4th century BCE, the gemstone lapis lazuli was being imported from Badakhshan (modern-day Afghanistan).

Just before the First Dynasty, Egypt had a colony in southern Canaan that produced Egyptian pottery for export to Egypt. In the Second Dynasty, Byblos provided quality timber that could not be found in Egypt. By the Fifth Dynasty, trade with Punt gave Egyptians gold, aromatic resins, ebony, ivory, and wild animals. Egypt also traded with Anatolia for tin and copper in order to make bronze. Mediterranean trading partners provided olive oil and other fine goods.

Egypt commonly exported grain, gold, linen, papyrus, and finished goods, such as glass and stone objects.

Depiction of Queen Hatshepsut's Expedition to Punt: *This painting shows Queen Hatshepsut's expedition to Punt.*

Land Trade Routes

A well-traveled land route from the Nile to the Red Sea crossed through the Wadi Hammamat, and was known from predynastic times. This route allowed travelers to move from Thebes to the Red Sea port of Elim, and led to the rise of ancient cities.

Another route, the Darb el-Arbain, was used from the time of the Old Kingdom of Egypt to trade gold, ivory, spices, wheat, animals, and plants. This route passed through Kharga in the south and Asyut in the north, and was a major route between Nubia and Egypt.

Maritime Trade Routes

Egyptians built ships as early as 3000 BCE by lashing planks of wood together and stuffing the gaps with reeds.

Egyptian Sailing Ship: This painting depicts an Egyptian ship from c. 1420 BCE.

Pharaoh Sahure, of the Fifth Dynasty, is known to have sent ships to Lebanon to import cedar, and to the Land of Punt for myrrh, malachite, and electrum. Queen Hatshepsut sent ships for myrrh in Punt, and extended Egyptian trade into modern-day Somalia and the Mediterranean.

Queen Hatshepsut: Queen Hatshepsut expanded trade into modern-day Somalia and the Mediterranean.

An ancient form of the Suez Canal is believed to have been started by Pharaoh Senusret II or III of the Twelfth Dynasty, in order to connect the Nile River with the Red Sea.

Ancient Egyptian Culture

The Middle Kingdom was a golden age for ancient Egypt, when arts, religion, and literature flourished. Two major innovations of the time were block statues and new forms of literature.

Learning Objectives

Examine the artistic and social developments of the Middle Kingdom

---

Key Takeaways

Key Points

- The Middle Kingdom (2134-1690 BCE) was a time of prosperity and stability, as well as a resurgence of art, literature, and architecture. Block statue was a new type of sculpture invented in the Middle Kingdom, and was often used as a funerary monument.
- Literature had new uses during the Middle Kingdom, and many classics were written during the period.

Key Terms

- **funerary monuments**: Sculpture meant to decorate a tomb within a pyramid.

The Middle Kingdom (2134-1690 BCE) was a time of prosperity and stability, as well as a resurgence of art, literature, and architecture. Two major innovations of the time were the block statue and new forms of literature.

The Block Statue

The block statue came into use during this period. This type of sculpture depicts a squatting man with knees drawn close to the chest and arms folded on top of the knees. The body may be adorned with a cloak, which makes the body appear to be a block shape. The feet may be covered by the cloak, or left uncovered. The head was often carved in great detail, and reflected Egyptian beauty ideals, including large ears and small breasts. The block statue became more popular over the years, with its high point in the Late Period, and was often used as funerary monuments of important, non-royal individuals. They may have been intended as guardians, and were often fully inscribed.

Example of Block Statue: *An example of a block statue from the Late Period, c. 650-633 BCE.*

Literature

In the Middle Kingdom period, due to growth of middle class and scribes, literature began to be written to entertain and provide intellectual stimulation. Previously, literature served the purposes of maintaining divine cults, preserving souls in the afterlife, and documenting practical activities. However, some Middle Kingdom literature may have been transcriptions of the oral literature and poetry of the Old Kingdom. Future generations of Egyptians often considered Middle Kingdom literature to be "classic," with the ultimate example being the Story of Sinuhe.

Attributions

CC licensed content, Specific attribution

- Ancient Egyptian Religion. **Provided by**: Wikipedia. **Located at**: https://en.wikipedia.org/wiki/Ancient_Egyptian_religion. **License**: *CC BY: Attribution*
- Egyptian Religion. **Provided by**: Archaeology of Ancient Egypt. **Located at**: http://anthropology.msu.edu/anp455-fs12/2012/10/11/egyptian-religion/. **License**: *CC BY: Attribution*
- Egyptian Social Structure. **Provided by**: Ancient Civilizations. **Located at**: http://www.ushistory.org/civ/3b.asp. **License**: *CC BY-SA: Attribution-ShareAlike*
- 347px-La_Tombe_de_Horemheb_cropped.jpg. **Provided by**: Wikipedia. **Located at**: https://en.wikipedia.org/wiki/Ancient_Egypt-

ian_religion#/media/File:La_Tombe_de_Horemheb_cropped.jpg. **License:** *CC BY: Attribution*

- 640px-Geb_Nut_Shu.jpg. **Provided by:** Wikipedia. **Located at:** https://en.wikipedia.org/wiki/Ancient_Egyptian_religion#/media/File:Geb,_Nut,_Shu.jpg. **License:** *CC BY: Attribution*
- BD_Hunefer_cropped_1.jpg. **Provided by:** Wikipedia. **Located at:** https://en.wikipedia.org/wiki/Ancient_Egyptian_religion#/media/File:BD_Hunefer_cropped_1.jpg. **License:** *CC BY: Attribution*
- Ushabti. **Provided by:** Wikipedia. **Located at:** https://en.wikipedia.org/wiki/Ushabti. **License:** *CC BY: Attribution*
- Egyptian Faience. **Provided by:** Wikipedia. **Located at:** https://en.wikipedia.org/wiki/Egyptian_faience. **License:** *CC BY: Attribution*
- Sunk Relief. **Provided by:** Wikipedia. **Located at:** https://en.wikipedia.org/wiki/Relief#Sunk_relief. **License:** *CC BY: Attribution*
- Amarna. **Provided by:** Wikipedia. **Located at:** https://en.wikipedia.org/wiki/Amarna. **License:** *CC BY: Attribution*
- Ancient Egyptian Architecture. **Provided by:** Wikipedia. **Located at:** https://en.wikipedia.org/wiki/Ancient_Egyptian_architecture. **License:** *CC BY: Attribution*
- Art of Ancient Egypt. **Provided by:** Wikipedia. **Located at:** https://en.wikipedia.org/wiki/Art_of_ancient_Egypt. **License:** *CC BY: Attribution*
- 347px-La_Tombe_de_Horemheb_cropped.jpg. **Provided by:** Wikipedia. **Located at:** https://en.wikipedia.org/wiki/Ancient_Egyptian_religion#/media/File:La_Tombe_de_Horemheb_cropped.jpg. **License:** *CC BY: Attribution*
- 640px-Geb_Nut_Shu.jpg. **Provided by:** Wikipedia. **Located at:** https://en.wikipedia.org/wiki/Ancient_Egyptian_religion#/media/File:Geb,_Nut,_Shu.jpg. **License:** *CC BY: Attribution*
- BD_Hunefer_cropped_1.jpg. **Provided by:** Wikipedia. **Located at:** https://en.wikipedia.org/wiki/Ancient_Egyptian_religion#/media/File:BD_Hunefer_cropped_1.jpg. **License:** *CC BY: Attribution*
- 326px-Maler_der_Grabkammer_der_Nefertari_004.jpg. **Provided by:** Wikipedia. **Located at:** https://en.wikipedia.org/wiki/Art_of_ancient_Egypt#/media/File:Maler_der_Grabkammer_der_Nefertari_004.jpg. **License:** *CC BY: Attribution*
- 640px-All_Gizah_Pyramids.jpg. **Provided by:** Wikipedia. **Located at:** https://en.wikipedia.org/wiki/Ancient_Egyptian_architecture#/media/File:All_Gizah_Pyramids.jpg. **License:** *CC BY: Attribution*
- 323px-Ka_Statue_of_horawibra.jpg. **Provided by:** Wikipedia. **Located at:** https://en.wikipedia.org/wiki/Art_of_ancient_Egypt#/media/File:Ka_Statue_of_horawibra.jpg. **License:** *CC BY: Attribution*
- 312px-Hypostyle_hall_Karnak_temple.jpg. **Provided by:** Wikipedia. **Located at:** https://en.wikipedia.org/wiki/Ancient_Egyptian_architecture#/media/File:Hypostyle_hall,_Karnak_temple.jpg. **License:** *CC BY: Attribution*
- Pyramid. **Provided by:** Wikipedia. **Located at:** https://en.wikipedia.org/wiki/Pyramid. **License:** *CC BY: Attribution*
- Great Sphinx of Giza. **Provided by:** Wikipedia. **Located at:** https://en.wikipedia.org/wiki/Great_Sphinx_of_Giza. **License:** *CC BY: Attribution*
- Egyptian Temple. **Provided by:** Wikipedia. **Located at:** https://en.wikipedia.org/wiki/Egyptian_temple. **License:** *CC BY: Attribution*
- Great Pyramid of Giza. **Provided by:** Wikipedia. **Located at:** https://en.wikipedia.org/wiki/Great_Pyramid_of_Giza. **License:** *CC BY: Attribution*
- 347px-La_Tombe_de_Horemheb_cropped.jpg. **Provided by:** Wikipedia. **Located at:** https://en.wikipedia.org/wiki/Ancient_Egyptian_religion#/media/File:La_Tombe_de_Horemheb_cropped.jpg. **License:** *CC BY: Attribution*
- 640px-Geb_Nut_Shu.jpg. **Provided by:** Wikipedia. **Located at:** https://en.wikipedia.org/wiki/Ancient_Egyptian_religion#/media/File:Geb,_Nut,_Shu.jpg. **License:** *CC BY: Attribution*
- BD_Hunefer_cropped_1.jpg. **Provided by:** Wikipedia. **Located at:** https://en.wikipedia.org/wiki/Ancient_Egyptian_religion#/media/File:BD_Hunefer_cropped_1.jpg. **License:** *CC BY: Attribution*
- 326px-Maler_der_Grabkammer_der_Nefertari_004.jpg. **Provided by:** Wikipedia. **Located at:** https://en.wikipedia.org/wiki/Art_of_ancient_Egypt#/media/File:Maler_der_Grabkammer_der_Nefertari_004.jpg. **License:** *CC BY: Attribution*
- 640px-All_Gizah_Pyramids.jpg. **Provided by:** Wikipedia. **Located at:** https://en.wikipedia.org/wiki/Ancient_Egyptian_architecture#/media/File:All_Gizah_Pyramids.jpg. **License:** *CC BY: Attribution*
- 323px-Ka_Statue_of_horawibra.jpg. **Provided by:** Wikipedia. **Located at:** https://en.wikipedia.org/wiki/Art_of_ancient_Egypt#/media/File:Ka_Statue_of_horawibra.jpg. **License:** *CC BY: Attribution*
- 312px-Hypostyle_hall_Karnak_temple.jpg. **Provided by:** Wikipedia. **Located at:** https://en.wikipedia.org/wiki/Ancient_Egyptian_architecture#/media/File:Hypostyle_hall,_Karnak_temple.jpg. **License:** *CC BY: Attribution*
- 491px-Giza_pyramid_complex_map.svg.png. **Provided by:** Wikipedia. **Located at:** https://en.wikipedia.org/wiki/Great_Pyramid_of_Giza#/media/File:Giza_pyramid_complex_(map).svg. **License:** *CC BY: Attribution*

- 640px-Karnak-Hypostyle3.jpg. **Provided by**: Wikipedia. **Located at**: https://en.wikipedia.org/wiki/Karnak#/media/File:Karnak-Hypostyle3.jpg. **License**: *CC BY: Attribution*
- 640px-Egypt.Giza.Sphinx.02.jpg. **Provided by**: Wikipedia. **Located at**: https://en.wikipedia.org/wiki/Great_Sphinx_of_Giza#/media/File:Egypt.Giza.Sphinx.02.jpg. **License**: *CC BY: Attribution*
- 640px-Pyramide_Djedkare_Isesi_3.jpg. **Provided by**: Wikipedia. **Located at**: https://en.wikipedia.org/wiki/Egyptian_temple#/media/File:Pyramide_Djedkare_Isesi_3.jpg. **License**: *CC BY: Attribution*
- 640px-Luxor07js.jpg. **Provided by**: Wikipedia. **Located at**: https://en.wikipedia.org/wiki/Egyptian_temple#/media/File:Luxor07(js).jpg. **License**: *CC BY: Attribution*
- Ancient Egyptian Trade. **Provided by**: Wikipedia. **Located at**: https://en.wikipedia.org/wiki/Ancient_Egyptian_trade. **License**: *CC BY: Attribution*
- Ancient Egypt. **Provided by**: Wikipedia. **Located at**: https://en.wikipedia.org/wiki/Ancient_Egypt. **License**: *CC BY: Attribution*
- History of Ancient Egypt. **Provided by**: Wikipedia. **Located at**: https://en.wikipedia.org/wiki/History_of_ancient_Egypt. **License**: *CC BY: Attribution*
- 347px-La_Tombe_de_Horemheb_cropped.jpg. **Provided by**: Wikipedia. **Located at**: https://en.wikipedia.org/wiki/Ancient_Egyptian_religion#/media/File:La_Tombe_de_Horemheb_cropped.jpg. **License**: *CC BY: Attribution*
- 640px-Geb_Nut_Shu.jpg. **Provided by**: Wikipedia. **Located at**: https://en.wikipedia.org/wiki/Ancient_Egyptian_religion#/media/File:Geb,_Nut,_Shu.jpg. **License**: *CC BY: Attribution*
- BD_Hunefer_cropped_1.jpg. **Provided by**: Wikipedia. **Located at**: https://en.wikipedia.org/wiki/Ancient_Egyptian_religion#/media/File:BD_Hunefer_cropped_1.jpg. **License**: *CC BY: Attribution*
- 326px-Maler_der_Grabkammer_der_Nefertari_004.jpg. **Provided by**: Wikipedia. **Located at**: https://en.wikipedia.org/wiki/Art_of_ancient_Egypt#/media/File:Maler_der_Grabkammer_der_Nefertari_004.jpg. **License**: *CC BY: Attribution*
- 640px-All_Gizah_Pyramids.jpg. **Provided by**: Wikipedia. **Located at**: https://en.wikipedia.org/wiki/Ancient_Egyptian_architecture#/media/File:All_Gizah_Pyramids.jpg. **License**: *CC BY: Attribution*
- 323px-Ka_Statue_of_horawibra.jpg. **Provided by**: Wikipedia. **Located at**: https://en.wikipedia.org/wiki/Art_of_ancient_Egypt#/media/File:Ka_Statue_of_horawibra.jpg. **License**: *CC BY: Attribution*
- 312px-Hypostyle_hall_Karnak_temple.jpg. **Provided by**: Wikipedia. **Located at**: https://en.wikipedia.org/wiki/Ancient_Egyptian_architecture#/media/File:Hypostyle_hall,_Karnak_temple.jpg. **License**: *CC BY: Attribution*
- 491px-Giza_pyramid_complex_map.svg.png. **Provided by**: Wikipedia. **Located at**: https://en.wikipedia.org/wiki/Great_Pyramid_of_Giza#/media/File:Giza_pyramid_complex_(map).svg. **License**: *CC BY: Attribution*
- 640px-Karnak-Hypostyle3.jpg. **Provided by**: Wikipedia. **Located at**: https://en.wikipedia.org/wiki/Karnak#/media/File:Karnak-Hypostyle3.jpg. **License**: *CC BY: Attribution*
- 640px-Egypt.Giza.Sphinx.02.jpg. **Provided by**: Wikipedia. **Located at**: https://en.wikipedia.org/wiki/Great_Sphinx_of_Giza#/media/File:Egypt.Giza.Sphinx.02.jpg. **License**: *CC BY: Attribution*
- 640px-Pyramide_Djedkare_Isesi_3.jpg. **Provided by**: Wikipedia. **Located at**: https://en.wikipedia.org/wiki/Egyptian_temple#/media/File:Pyramide_Djedkare_Isesi_3.jpg. **License**: *CC BY: Attribution*
- 640px-Luxor07js.jpg. **Provided by**: Wikipedia. **Located at**: https://en.wikipedia.org/wiki/Egyptian_temple#/media/File:Luxor07(js).jpg. **License**: *CC BY: Attribution*
- 640px-Relief_of_Hatshepsut's_expedition_to_the_Land_of_Punt_by_u03a3u03c4u03b1u03c5u0301u03c1u03bfu03c2.jpg. **Provided by**: Wikipedia. **Located at**: https://en.wikipedia.org/wiki/Land_of_Punt#/media/File:Relief_of_Hatshepsut%27s_expedition_to_the_Land_of_Punt_by_%CE%A3%CF%84%CE%B1%CF%8D%CF%81%CE%BF%CF%82.jpg. **License**: *CC BY: Attribution*
- 640px-Maler_der_Grabkammer_des_Menna_013.jpg. **Provided by**: Wikipedia. **Located at**: https://en.wikipedia.org/wiki/Ancient_maritime_history#/media/File:Maler_der_Grabkammer_des_Menna_013.jpg. **License**: *CC BY: Attribution*
- Hatshepsut.jpg. **Provided by**: Wikipedia. **Located at**: https://en.wikipedia.org/wiki/Hatshepsut#/media/File:Hatshepsut.jpg. **License**: *CC BY: Attribution*
- Block Statue. **Provided by**: Wikipedia. **Located at**: https://en.wikipedia.org/wiki/Block_statue. **License**: *CC BY: Attribution*
- Ancient Egypt. **Provided by**: Wikipedia. **Located at**: https://en.wikipedia.org/wiki/Ancient_Egypt#Middle_Kingdom_.282134.E2.80.931690_BC.29. **License**: *CC BY: Attribution*
- Middle Kingdom of Egypt. **Provided by**: Wikipedia. **Located at**: https://en.wikipedia.org/wiki/Middle_Kingdom_of_Egypt#Art. **License**: *CC BY: Attribution*
- 347px-La_Tombe_de_Horemheb_cropped.jpg. **Provided by**: Wikipedia. **Located at**: https://en.wikipedia.org/wiki/Ancient_Egyptian_religion#/media/File:La_Tombe_de_Horemheb_cropped.jpg. **License**: *CC BY: Attribution*

ANCIENT EGYPTIAN SOCIETY • 135

- 640px-Geb_Nut_Shu.jpg. **Provided by**: Wikipedia. **Located at**: https://en.wikipedia.org/wiki/Ancient_Egyptian_religion#/media/File:Geb,_Nut,_Shu.jpg. **License**: *CC BY: Attribution*
- BD_Hunefer_cropped_1.jpg. **Provided by**: Wikipedia. **Located at**: https://en.wikipedia.org/wiki/Ancient_Egyptian_religion#/media/File:BD_Hunefer_cropped_1.jpg. **License**: *CC BY: Attribution*
- 326px-Maler_der_Grabkammer_der_Nefertari_004.jpg. **Provided by**: Wikipedia. **Located at**: https://en.wikipedia.org/wiki/Art_of_ancient_Egypt#/media/File:Maler_der_Grabkammer_der_Nefertari_004.jpg. **License**: *CC BY: Attribution*
- 640px-All_Gizah_Pyramids.jpg. **Provided by**: Wikipedia. **Located at**: https://en.wikipedia.org/wiki/Ancient_Egyptian_architecture#/media/File:All_Gizah_Pyramids.jpg. **License**: *CC BY: Attribution*
- 323px-Ka_Statue_of_horawibra.jpg. **Provided by**: Wikipedia. **Located at**: https://en.wikipedia.org/wiki/Art_of_ancient_Egypt#/media/File:Ka_Statue_of_horawibra.jpg. **License**: *CC BY: Attribution*
- 312px-Hypostyle_hall_Karnak_temple.jpg. **Provided by**: Wikipedia. **Located at**: https://en.wikipedia.org/wiki/Ancient_Egyptian_architecture#/media/File:Hypostyle_hall,_Karnak_temple.jpg. **License**: *CC BY: Attribution*
- 491px-Giza_pyramid_complex_map.svg.png. **Provided by**: Wikipedia. **Located at**: https://en.wikipedia.org/wiki/Great_Pyramid_of_Giza#/media/File:Giza_pyramid_complex_(map).svg. **License**: *CC BY: Attribution*
- 640px-Karnak-Hypostyle3.jpg. **Provided by**: Wikipedia. **Located at**: https://en.wikipedia.org/wiki/Karnak#/media/File:Karnak-Hypostyle3.jpg. **License**: *CC BY: Attribution*
- 640px-Egypt.Giza.Sphinx.02.jpg. **Provided by**: Wikipedia. **Located at**: https://en.wikipedia.org/wiki/Great_Sphinx_of_Giza#/media/File:Egypt.Giza.Sphinx.02.jpg. **License**: *CC BY: Attribution*
- 640px-Pyramide_Djedkare_Isesi_3.jpg. **Provided by**: Wikipedia. **Located at**: https://en.wikipedia.org/wiki/Egyptian_temple#/media/File:Pyramide_Djedkare_Isesi_3.jpg. **License**: *CC BY: Attribution*
- 640px-Luxor07js.jpg. **Provided by**: Wikipedia. **Located at**: https://en.wikipedia.org/wiki/Egyptian_temple#/media/File:Luxor07(js).jpg. **License**: *CC BY: Attribution*
- 640px-Relief_of_Hatshepsut's_expedition_to_the_Land_of_Punt_by_u03a3u03c4u03b1u03c5u0301u03c1u03bfu03c2.jpg. **Provided by**: Wikipedia. **Located at**: https://en.wikipedia.org/wiki/Land_of_Punt#/media/File:Relief_of_Hatshepsut%27s_expedition_to_the_Land_of_Punt_by_%CE%A3%CF%84%CE%B1%CF%8D%CF%81%CE%BF%CF%82.jpg. **License**: *CC BY: Attribution*
- 640px-Maler_der_Grabkammer_des_Menna_013.jpg. **Provided by**: Wikipedia. **Located at**: https://en.wikipedia.org/wiki/Ancient_maritime_history#/media/File:Maler_der_Grabkammer_des_Menna_013.jpg. **License**: *CC BY: Attribution*
- Hatshepsut.jpg. **Provided by**: Wikipedia. **Located at**: https://en.wikipedia.org/wiki/Hatshepsut#/media/File:Hatshepsut.jpg. **License**: *CC BY: Attribution*
- 286px-Block_statue_Pa-Akh-Ra_CdM.jpg. **Provided by**: Wikipedia. **Located at**: https://en.wikipedia.org/wiki/Block_statue#/media/File:Block_statue_Pa-Akh-Ra_CdM.jpg. **License**: *CC BY: Attribution*

Early Chinese Dynasties

The Mythical Period

The Mythical Period

Early prehistoric China is called the "Mythical Period." It encompassed the legends of Pangu, and the rule of the Three Sovereigns, and the Five Emperors. The period ended when the last Emperor, Shun, left his throne to Yu the Great, and the Xia Dynasty began.

Learning Objectives

Recall what innovations emerged under the legendary rulers of China's Mythical Period

Key Takeaways

Key Points

- By 2000 BCE, cities developed in China, and the various cultures of the area began to merge into a larger, more unified Chinese culture.
- Most of what we know about the first part of prehistoric China is from Chinese mythology, which is why it's now known as the Mythical Period.
- The Mythical Period includes the rule of the Three Sovereigns and the Five Emperors.
- The last of the Five Emperors was Emperor Shun. He left his throne to Yu the Great, who founded the Xia dynasty and instituted the practice of passing rulership to a son.

Key Terms

- **Go**: An abstract strategy board game for two players, where the object is to surround more territory than the opponent.
- **millet**: Any of a group of various types of grass or its grains used as food, widely cultivated in the developing world.

- **urbanism**: The change in a country or region when its population migrates from rural to urban areas.
- **Pangu**: A mythical Chinese being who created the universe.
- **Yellow River**: Huang He in Chinese. A river of northern China which flows for 5,463 km (3,000 miles) to the Yellow Sea.
- **Yangtze**: The longest river in Asia, the Yangtze flows from the highlands of Tibet through central China, and empties into the Pacific Ocean at Shanghai.
- **Huai**: A major river in China located about midway between the Yellow and Yangtze Rivers.
- **Gilgamesh**: The hero of a Babylonian epic, and the legendary king of the Sumerian city state of Uruk.

History as Told by Archaeological Evidence

As in Mesopotamia, Egypt, and the Indus River valley, civilization in China developed around a great river. The Yellow River and the Huai and Yangtze Rivers, created fertile land, ripe for experimentation with agriculture. By around 4000 BCE, villages began to appear in these areas. The Neolithic Chinese cultivated a number of crops; the most important was a grain called millet. They also domesticated animals, such as pigs, dogs, and chickens. Silk production, through the domestication of silkworms, also likely began in this early period.

These villages influenced each other more and more over time, and by 2000 BCE a unified Chinese culture began to develop. There is also evidence of urbanism and the use of early writing d this time. These phenomena took place in China about 1000 years later than in Mesopotamia, Egypt, and the Indus River valley.

THE MYTHICAL PERIOD • 141

盤古氏

Pangu: Portrait of Pangu, the creator of the universe according to Chinese mythology. This portrait is from Sancai Tuhui, a Chinese encyclopedia published in 1609, during the Ming Dynasty.

History as Told by Chinese Legend

Chinese mythology tells a different story of the beginning of civilization. It holds that the universe was created by Pangu, the first living being. After his death, Pangu's left eye became the sun and his right eye became the moon. The Three Sovereigns and the Five Emperors, a series of legendary sage emperors and heroes, helped create man. These legendary rulers taught the ancient Chinese to speak, use fire, build houses, farm, and make clothing. Fuxi and his wife, Nüwa, were credited with introducing domesticated animals and creating the basic social structure of family life. Shennong was a divine farmer who gave the people knowledge of agriculture.

The existence of these emperors occurred before written Chinese history, and so the dates of reign are uncertain. The Five Emperors began with Huangdi, or the Yellow Emperor, whose reign is believed to be from 2698-2599 BCE. He was considered the founding ancestor of the Han Chinese ethnic group, and is credited with the invention of Chinese characters, silk, and traditional Chinese medicine.

The Yellow Emperor, or Huangdi.: *Portrait of the first of the Five Emperors, who was considered the original ancestor for Han Chinese.*

Next came Zhuanxu, who was credited with the invention of the Chinese calendar and the introduction of religion and astrology. Little is known about Emperor Ku's reign, believed to be from 2412-2343 BCE. Emperor Yao, whose reign was from 2317-2234 BCE, was credited with being a role model in dignity and diligence to future emperors, and was the inventor of the game "weiqi" (also known as "Go"). The last was Emperor Shun, whose reign was from 2233-2205 BCE, was known for his devotion. He left his throne to Yu the Great, who founded the Xia dynasty, and instituted the practice of passing rulership to a son. While these events are mythological, at their root there may be ancient memories of very early kings and rulers who emerged among the prehistoric Chinese, similar to the tales of Gilgamesh in Mesopotamia.

The Xia Dynasty

The final part of the Mythical Period was under the rule of the legendary Xia Dynasty, which may have been mythological. After the final ruler became corrupt, he was overthrown by Cheng Tang, who founded the Shang Dynasty.

Learning Objectives

- Recall characteristics of the Xia Dynasty

Key Takeaways

Key Points

- Sima Qian 's "Historical Records," the first comprehensive history of China, said that the last of the Five Emperors, Emperor Shun, left his throne to Yu the Great, who founded the Xia Dynasty.
- The Xia Dynasty was the first Chinese dynasty; it is still not known whether this dynasty existed or is only mythological.
- According to mythology, when the last Xia king became corrupt and cruel, Cheng Tang overthrew him in c. 1760 BCE and founded the Shang Dynasty.
- Many argue that the Zhou Dynasty, which ruled China much later, invented the idea of the Xia Dynasty to support their claim that China could only be, and had always been, ruled by one ruler.

Key Terms

- **Mandate of Heaven**: The Chinese philosophical concept of the circumstances under which a ruler is allowed to rule. Good rulers were allowed to rule under the Mandate of heaven, while despotic, unjust rulers had the Mandate revoked.
- **Sima Qian**: A renowned Chinese historiographer of the 2nd century BCE who wrote about the Xia Dynasty.
- **Shang Dynasty**: Also called the Yin Dynasty, succeeded the Xia Dynasty and followed the Zhou Dynasty. It existed in the second millennium BCE.

Sima Qian's Historical Records

The earliest comprehensive history of China is the Historical Records, written by Sima Qian, a renowned Chinese historiographer of the 2nd century BCE. This history begins around 3600 BCE, with an account of the Five Emperors. According to this history, the last of the great Five Emperors, Emperor Shun, left his throne to Yu the Great, who founded China's First Dynasty, the Xia Dynasty. Yu supposedly began the practice of inherited rule (passing power from father to son), a model that was perpetuated in the later Shang and Zhou dynasties.

Depiction of Yu the Great: *This hanging scroll shows Yu the Great, as imagined by Song Dynasty painter Ma Lin.*

According to mythology, Yu's descendants ruled China for nearly 500 years, until the last Xia king became corrupt and cruel. This led to his overthrow in c. 1760 BCE by Cheng Tang, who founded a new dynasty, the Shang Dynasty, in the Huang River Valley.

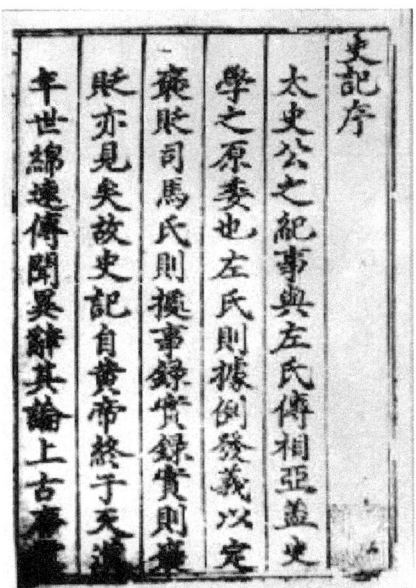

Sima Qian's Historical Records: *The first page of Sima Qian's Historical Records.*

Debate Over the Existence of the Xia Dynasty

There is much debate among scholars about how much of this mythology is true. Many argue that the Zhou Dynasty, which ruled China much later, invented the idea of the Xia Dynasty to support their claim that China could only be, and had always been, ruled by one ruler. The Zhou created the idea of the "Mandate of Heaven," which stated that there could be only one legitimate ruler of China at any given time. If he was a good ruler, he would have the support of heaven; if he was despotic, he would be overthrown. The various small states that had comprised Neolithic and Bronze Age China contradicted this version of history. Some people argue, therefore, that the Zhou may have created the idea of an ancient Xia Dynasty to support the idea that China always had one ruler.

Nonetheless, the Xia Dynasty may not be a complete fabrication; recent archaeological evidence may support its existence. (For a long time it was believed that the later Shang Dynasty may also have been purely mythological, until archaeology proved that it was real.) Archaeologists have discovered an advanced Bronze Age culture in China. Its capital, Erlitou, was a huge city around 2000 BCE. This may in fact be the people referred to in Chinese mythology as the Xia. It is believed that the Xia may have created a primitive writing system, though no evidence of this has been found. However, evidence does suggest that the Xia developed agricultural methods and experienced considerable prosperity. However, lack of irrigation and flood protection made the region prone to frequent floods and other natural disasters.

Attributions

CC licensed content, Specific attribution

- HIST101: Ancient Civilizations of the World. **Provided by**: Saylor. **Located at**: https://legacy.saylor.org/hist101/Intro/. **License**: *CC BY: Attribution*
- The First Chinese Dynasties. **Provided by**: Wikibooks. **Located at**: http://en.wikibooks.org/wiki/World_History/The_First_Chinese_Dynasties. **License**: *CC BY-SA: Attribution-ShareAlike*

- Ancient Chinese Civilization. **Provided by**: Wikibooks. **Located at**: http://en.wikibooks.org/wiki/World_History/Ancient_Civilizations%23Ancient_Chinese_Civilization. **License**: *CC BY-SA: Attribution-ShareAlike*
- Urbanization. **Provided by**: Wiktionary. **Located at**: http://en.wiktionary.org/wiki/urbanization. **License**: *CC BY-SA: Attribution-ShareAlike*
- Millet. **Provided by**: Wiktionary. **Located at**: http://en.wiktionary.org/wiki/millet. **License**: *CC BY-SA: Attribution-ShareAlike*
- Huang He. **Provided by**: Wiktionary. **Located at**: http://en.wiktionary.org/wiki/Huang_He%23English. **License**: *CC BY-SA: Attribution-ShareAlike*
- urbanism. **Provided by**: Wiktionary. **Located at**: http://en.wiktionary.org/wiki/urbanism. **License**: *CC BY-SA: Attribution-ShareAlike*
- Huai River. **Provided by**: Wikipedia. **Located at**: https://en.wikipedia.org/wiki/Huai_River. **License**: *CC BY: Attribution*
- Pangu. **Provided by**: Wikipedia. **Located at**: http://en.wikipedia.org/wiki/File:Pangu.jpg. **License**: *Public Domain: No Known Copyright*
- 362px-Huangti.jpg. **Provided by**: Wikipedia. **Located at**: https://en.wikipedia.org/wiki/Yellow_Emperor#/media/File:Huangti.jpg. **License**: *CC BY: Attribution*
- HIST101: Ancient Civilizations of the World. **Provided by:** Saylor. **Located at:** https://legacy.saylor.org/hist101/Intro/. **License**: *CC BY: Attribution*
- HIST101: Ancient Civilizations of the World. **Provided by:** Saylor. **Located at:** https://legacy.saylor.org/hist101/Intro/. **License**: *CC BY: Attribution*
- Mandate of Heaven. **Provided by:** Wiktionary. **Located at**: http://en.wiktionary.org/wiki/Mandate_of_Heaven. **License**: *CC BY-SA: Attribution-ShareAlike*
- The First Chinese Dynasties. **Provided by**: Wikibooks. **Located at**: http://en.wikibooks.org/wiki/World_History/The_First_Chinese_Dynasties. **License**: *CC BY-SA: Attribution-ShareAlike*
- Ancient Chinese Civilization. **Provided by**: Wikibooks. **Located at**: http://en.wikibooks.org/wiki/World_History/Ancient_Civilizations%23Ancient_Chinese_Civilization. **License**: *CC BY-SA: Attribution-ShareAlike*
- Pangu. **Provided by**: Wikipedia. **Located at**: http://en.wikipedia.org/wiki/File:Pangu.jpg. **License**: *Public Domain: No Known Copyright*
- 362px-Huangti.jpg. **Provided by**: Wikipedia. **Located at**: https://en.wikipedia.org/wiki/Yellow_Emperor#/media/File:Huangti.jpg. **License**: *CC BY: Attribution*
- 210px-King_Yu_of_Xia.jpg. **Provided by**: Wikipedia. **Located at**: https://en.wikipedia.org/wiki/Yu_the_Great#/media/File:King_Yu_of_Xia.jpg. **License**: *CC BY: Attribution*
- Shiji. **Provided by**: Wikipedia. **Located at**: http://en.wikipedia.org/wiki/File:Shiji.jpg. **License**: *Public Domain: No Known Copyright*

The Shang Dynasty

Introduction to the Shang Dynasty

The Shang Dynasty existed in the Yellow River Valley during the second millennium BCE. It built huge cities, monopolized bronze, and developed writing, until it was overthrown by the Zhou.

Learning Objectives

Compare the Shang Dynasty with the earlier Xia Dynasty

Key Takeaways

Key Points

- The Shang Dynasty (also called the Yin Dynasty) succeeded the Xia Dynasty, and was followed by the Zhou Dynasty. It was located in the Yellow River valley, during the second millennium BCE.
- The Shang Dynasty is the first period of prehistoric China that has been conclusively proven to have existed by archaeological evidence, such as excavated graves and oracle bones, the oldest substantial evidence of Chinese writing.
- Writing during the Shang Dynasty was already in an advanced form, suggesting that the written language had already existed for a long time.
- Under the Shang Dynasty, the Chinese built huge cities with strong social class divisions, expanded irrigation systems, and monopolized the use of bronze.
- The Shang Dynasty was overthrown in 1046 BCE by the Zhou, who established their own dynasty.

> Key Terms
>
> - **Oracle bones**: Inscriptions of divination records on the bones or shells of animals, dating to the Shang Dynasty of ancient China.
> - **Anyang**: A city from the Shang Dynasty, the excavation of which yielded large numbers of oracle bones. This helped prove the existence of the Shang Dynasty.
> - **Zhengzhou**: The modern-day area where the new capital of Shang was established during the Shang Dynasty.
> - **Xia Dynasty**: The first dynasty in traditional Chinese history.

The Shang Dynasty (also called the Yin Dynasty) succeeded the Xia Dynasty, and was followed by the Zhou Dynasty. It was located in the Yellow River valley during the second millennium BCE.

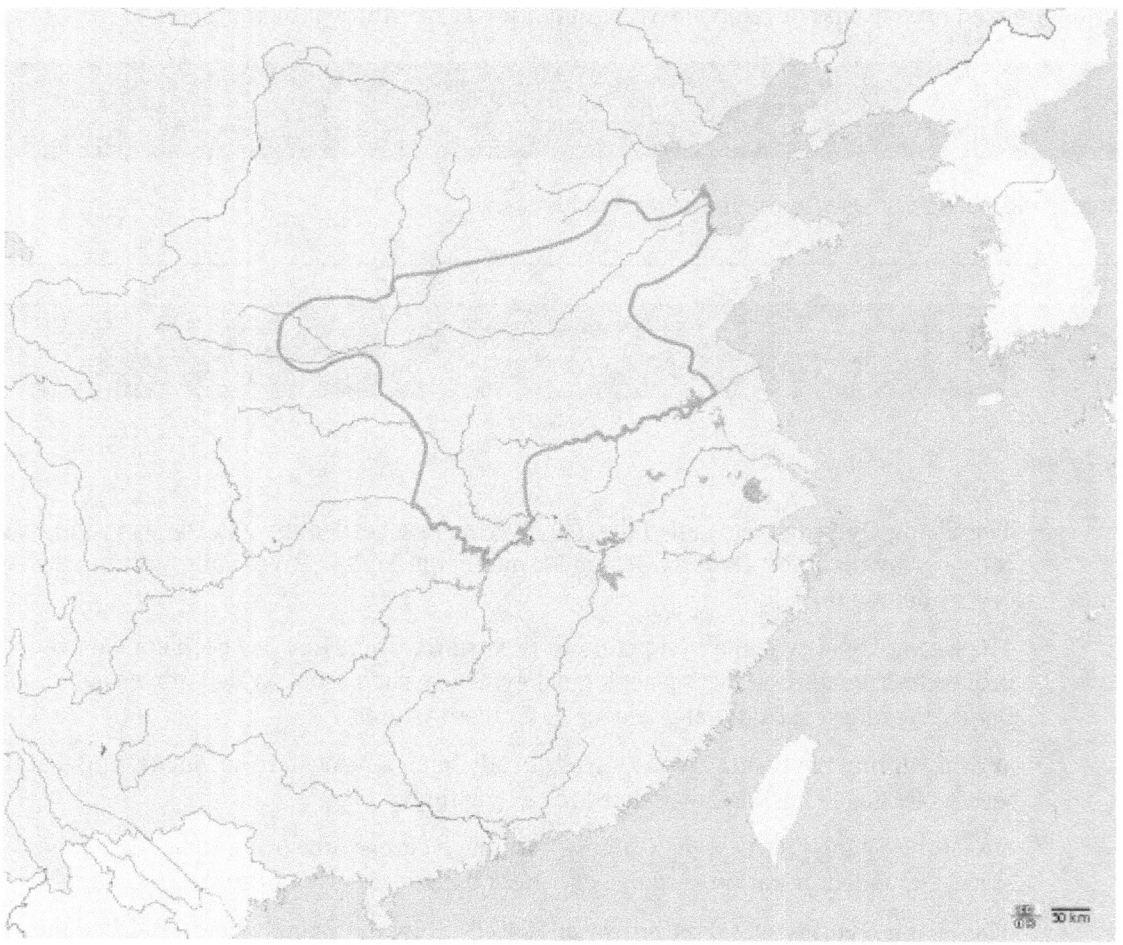

Map of Shang Dynasty: *This map shows the location of the Shang Dynasty in the Yellow River valley.*

Jie, the last king of the Xia Dynasty (the first Chinese dynasty), was overthrown c. 1760 BCE by Cheng Tang. It is estimated the Shang ruled from either 1766-1122 or 1556-1046 BCE.

While scholars still debate whether the Xia Dynasty actually existed, there is little doubt that the Shang Dynasty existed. The Shang Dynasty is, therefore, generally considered China's first historical dynasty.

Under the Shang Dynasty, a unified sense of Chinese culture emerged. This culture would continue to thrive and evolve, and many modern Chinese still see the Shang culture as China's dominant culture. Under the Shang Dynasty, the Chinese built huge cities with strong social class divisions, expanded irrigation systems, monopolized the use of bronze, and developed a system of writing. Shang kings were believed to fulfill sacred, not political, purposes. Instead, a council of chosen advisers administered various aspects of the government. The border territories of Shang rule were led by chieftains, who gained the right to govern through connections with royalty.

The Shang Dynasty was overthrown in 1046 BCE by the Zhou, a subject people living in the western part of the kingdom.

Archaeological Evidence

The Shang Dynasty is the oldest Chinese dynasty supported by archaeological finds. These have included 11 major Yin royal tombs and building sites of palaces and rituals, as well as weapons and remains of human and animal sacrifices, and artifacts, including bronze, jade, stone, bone, and ceramic.

The oldest surviving form of Chinese writing is inscriptions of divination records on the bones or shells of animals—so-called oracle bones. However, the writing on the oracle bones shows evidence of complex development, indicating that written language had existed for a long time. In fact, modern scholars are able to read it because the language was very similar to the modern Chinese writing system.

Archaeologists have also found ancient cities that correspond with the Shang Dynasty. When Cheng Tang overthrew the last king of the Xia Dynasty, he supposedly founded a new capital for his dynasty at a town called Shang, near modern-day Zhengzhou. Archaeological remains of this town may have been found—it seems to have functioned as a sacred capital, where the most sacred temples and religious objects were housed. This city also had palaces, workshops, and city walls.

Anyang, in modern-day Henan, is another important (but slightly later) Shang city that has been excavated. This site yielded large numbers of oracle bones that describe the travels of eleven named kings. The names and timeframes of these kings match traditional lists of Shang kings. Anyang was a huge city, with an extensive cemetery of thousands of graves and 11 large tombs—evidence of the city's labor force, which may have belonged to the 11 Shang kings.

Society Under the Shang Dynasty

The Shang Dynasty was located in the Yellow River valley in China during the second millennium BCE. It was a society that followed a class system of land-owners, soldiers, bronze workers, and peasants.

Learning Objectives
Summarize the social class system during the Shang Dynasty

> ## Key Takeaways
>
> ### Key Points
>
> - The Shang Dynasty (also called the Yin Dynasty) succeeded the Xia Dynasty, and was followed by the Zhou Dynasty. It was located in the Yellow River valley during the second millennium BCE. Citizens of the Shang Dynasty were classified into four social classes: the king and aristocracy, the military, artisans and craftsmen, and peasants.
> - Members of the aristocracy were the most respected social class, and were responsible for governing smaller areas of the dynasty.
> - Next in social status were the Shang military—both the infantry and the chariot warriors.
> - The Shang "middle class" were artisans and craftsmen, who mainly worked with bronze.
> - The poorest class in Shang society were the peasants, who were mostly farmers. Some scholars believe they functioned as slaves; others believe they were more like serfs.
>
> ### Key Terms
>
> - **aristocracy**: The nobility, or the hereditary ruling class.
> - **artisans**: Skilled manual workers, who use tools and machinery in a particular craft.
> - **peasants**: Members of the lowest social class, who toil on the land. This social class consisted of small farmers and tenants, sharecroppers, farmhands, and other laborers on the land, forming the main labor force in agriculture and horticulture.

The Shang Dynasty (also called the Yin Dynasty) succeeded the Xia Dynasty, and was followed by the Zhou Dynasty. It was located in the Yellow River valley during the second millennium BCE. It featured a stratified social system made up of aristocrats, soldiers, artisans and craftsmen, and peasants.

The Aristocracy and the Military

The aristocracy were centered around Anyang, the Shang capital, and conducted governmental affairs for the surrounding areas. Regional territories farther from the capital were also controlled by the wealthy.

The Shang military were next in social status, and who were respected and honored for their skill. There were two subdivisions of the military: the infantry (foot soldiers) and the chariot warriors. The latter were noted for their great skill in warfare and hunting. Archaeological evidence has supported the use of horses and other cavalry during the late Shang period, c. 1250 BCE.

Bronze battle-axe: *A bronze battle-axe dated to the Shang Dynasty.*

Artisans and Craftsmen

Artisans and craftsmen comprised the middle class of Shang society. Their largest contribution was their work with bronze, which the Chinese developed as early as 1500 BCE. Their work with bronze was a very important aspect of society. Bronze weapons and pottery were commonly made, but the most prominent creations included ritual vessels and treasures, many of which were discovered via archaeological findings in the 1920s and 1930s. Shang aristocrats and the royalty were likely buried with large numbers of bronze valuables, particularly wine vessels and other ornate structures.

152 • BOUNDLESS

Houmuwu Ding: *The "Houmuwu Ding" is the heaviest piece of bronze work found in China so far.*

Peasants

At the bottom of the social ladder were the peasants, the poorest of Chinese citizens. They comprised the majority of the population, and were limited to farming and selling crops for profit. Archaeological findings have shown that masses of peasants were buried with aristocrats, leading some scholars to believe that they were the equivalent of slaves. However, other scholars have countered that they may have been similar to serfs. Peasants were governed directly by local aristocrats.

Shang Religion

Shang religion was characterized by a combination of animism, shamanism, spiritual control of the world, divination, and respect and worship of dead ancestors, including through sacrifices.

Learning Objectives

Explain the religious foundation of Shang Dynasty culture

Key Points

- The Shang believed in spiritual control of the world by various gods. They also practiced ancestor worship. They appealed to the gods, including the supreme god Shangdi, and consulted their ancestors through oracle bones.
- The Shang established a lunar calendar using 29-day months, and 12-month years.
- There appears to have been a belief in the afterlife during the Shang Dynasty, evidenced by human and animal bodies and artifacts found in tombs.

Key Terms

- **animism**: The belief that spirits inhabit some or all classes of natural objects or phenomena, and that an immaterial force animates the universe.
- **shamanism**: A shaman is a person who is seen to have access to and influence in the world of spirits, and who typically enters a trance state during rituals, and practices divination and healing.
- **oracle bones**: Inscriptions of divination records on the bones or shells of animals, dating to the Shang Dynasty of ancient China.
- **divination**: The practice of seeking knowledge of the future or the unknown by supernatural means.

Shang Religion

Shang religion was characterized by a combination of animism, shamanism, spiritual control of the world, divination, and respect and worship of dead ancestors, including through sacrifice. Different gods represented natural and mythological symbols, such as the moon, sun, wind, rain, dragon, and phoenix. Peasants prayed to these gods for bountiful harvests. Festivals to celebrate gods were also common. In particular, the Shang kings, who considered themselves divine rulers, consulted the great god Shangdi (the "Supreme

Being" who ruled over humanity and nature) for advice and wisdom. The Shang believed that the ancestors could also confer good fortune, so they would also consult ancestors through oracle bones in order to seek approval for any major decision, and to learn about future success in harvesting, hunting, or battle.

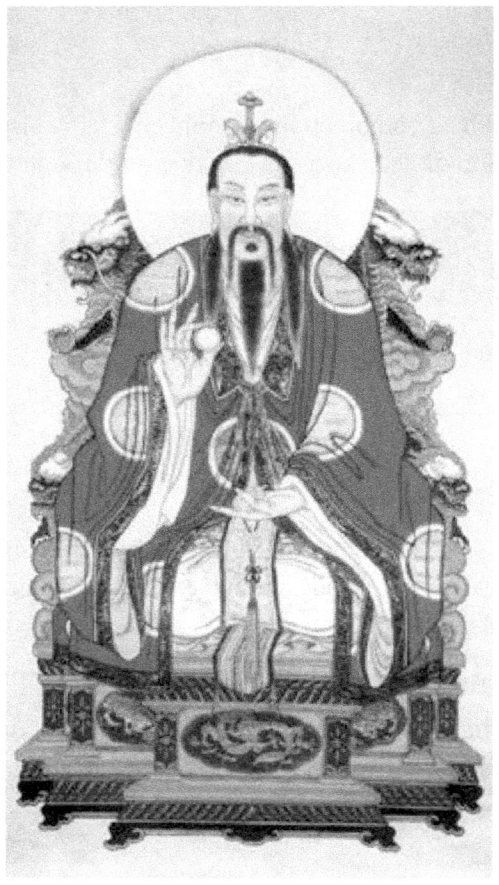

Shangdi: *One depiction of Shangdi, the Supreme Being who ruled over humanity and nature.*

Oracle Bones and Divination

The oldest surviving form of Chinese writing is inscriptions of divination records on the bones or shells of animals—so-called oracle bones. Oracle bones were pieces of bone or turtle shell used by the ancient Chinese, especially Chinese kings, in attempts to predict the future. The ancient kings would inscribe their name and the date on the bone along with a question. They would then heat the bone until it cracked, and then interpret the shape of the crack, which was believed to provide an answer to their question.

Questions were carved into oracle bones, such as, "Will we win the upcoming battle?", or "How many soldiers should we commit to the battle?" The bones reveal a great deal about what was important to Shang society. Many of the oracle bones ask questions about war, harvests, and childbirth.

Oracle Bone: *This oracle bone from the Shang Dynasty dates to the reign of King Wu Ding.*

The Afterlife

It appears that there was belief in the afterlife during the Shang Dynasty. Archaeologists have found Shang tombs surrounded by the skulls and bodies of human sacrifices. Some of these contain jade, which was seen to protect against decay and give immortality. Archaeologists believed that Shang tombs were very similar to those found in the Egyptian pyramids, in that they buried servants with them. Chinese archaeologists theorize that the Shang, like the ancient Egyptians, believed their servants would continue to serve them in the afterlife, so aristocrats' servants would be killed and buried with them when they died. Another interpretation is that these were enemy warriors captured in battle.

The Burial Pit at the Tomb of Lady Fu Hao: *This tomb is located in the ruins of the ancient Shang Dynasty capital, Yin.*

The Lunar Calendar

The Shang also established a lunar calendar that was used to predict and record events, such as harvests, births, and deaths (of rulers and peasants alike). The system assumed a 29-day month that began and ended with each new moon; twelve lunar months comprised one lunar year. Priests and astronomers were trained to recalculate the lunar year and add enough days so that each year lasted 365 days. Because the calendar was used to time both crop planting and the harvest, the king had to employ skilled astronomers to predict dates (and successes) of annual harvests; this would help him maintain support from the people.

Advancements Under the Shang

During the Shang Dynasty, bronze casting became more sophisticated. Military technology also advanced as horses were domesticated and chariots came into existence.

THE SHANG DYNASTY

Learning Objectives

Describe some of the technical advancements made under the Shang Dynasty

Key Takeaways

Key Points

- Bronze casting was perhaps the most important technology during the Shang Dynasty. The Shang made many objects out of bronze, including ceremonial tools, swords, and spearheads for the military.
- The Shang also domesticated horses and developed the chariot, which gave them a massive military advantage over their opponents.
- With these technologies, the Shang military expanded the kingdom's borders significantly.

Key Terms

- **chariot**: A two-wheeled, horse-drawn vehicle used in ancient warfare and racing.
- **Oracle bone**: Pieces of ox scapula or turtle plastron, used for divination in ancient China.

Shang Bronze Technology

The Shang ruled China during its Bronze Age; perhaps the most important technology at the time was bronze casting. The Shang cast bronze objects by
creating molds out of clay, carving a design into the clay, and then pouring molten bronze into the mold. They allowed the bronze to cool and then broke the clay off, revealing a completed bronze object.

Shang Dynasty Bronze: *This bronze ding vessel dates to the Shang Dynasty.*

The upper classes had the most access to bronze, and they used it for ceremonial objects, and to make offerings to ancestors. Bronze objects were also buried in the tombs of Shang elite. The Shang government used bronze for military weapons, such as swords and spearheads. These weapons gave them a distinct advantage over their enemies.

Shang Military Technology

The chariot was military technology that allowed the Shang to excel at war. Under the Shang, the Chinese domesticated the horse. Horses of that time were still too small to ride, but the Chinese gradually developed the chariot, which harnessed the horse's power. The chariot was a devastating weapon in battle, and it also allowed Shang soldiers to move vast distances at great speeds. A chariot burial site at Anyang (modern-day Henan) dates to the rule of King Wu Ding of the Shang Dynasty (c. 1200 BCE). Oracle bone inscriptions show that the Shang used chariots as mobile command vehicles and in royal hunts. Members of the royal household were often buried with a chariot, horses and a charioteer.

These military technologies were important, because the Shang were constantly at war. A significant number of Shang oracle bones were concerned
with battle. The Shang armies expanded the borders of the kingdom and captured precious resources and

prisoners of war, who could be enslaved or used as human sacrifice. The oracle bones also show deep concern over the "barbarians" living outside the empire, who were a constant threat to the safety and stability of the kingdom; the military had to be constantly ready to fight them.

Shang Dynasty Bronze Battle Axe: *This bronze axe is an example of Shang bronze work.*

Attributions

CC licensed content, Specific attribution

- The First Chinese Dynasties. **Provided by**: Wikibooks. **Located at**: http://en.wikibooks.org/wiki/World_History/The_First_Chinese_Dynasties. **License**: *CC BY-SA: Attribution-ShareAlike*
- HIST101: Ancient Civilizations of the World. **Provided by**: Saylor. **Located at**: https://legacy.saylor.org/hist101/Intro/ **License**: *CC BY: Attribution*
- HIST101: Ancient Civilizations of the World. **Provided by**: Saylor. **Located at**: https://legacy.saylor.org/hist101/Intro/ **License**: *CC BY: Attribution*
- HIST241: Pre-Modern Northeast Asia. **Provided by**: Saylor. **Located at**: https://legacy.saylor.org/hist241/Intro/. **License**: *CC BY: Attribution*
- Ancient Chinese Civilization. **Provided by**: Wikibooks. **Located at**: http://en.wikibooks.org/wiki/World_History/Ancient_Civilizations%23Ancient_Chinese_Civilization. **License**: *CC BY-SA: Attribution-ShareAlike*
- HIST101: Ancient Civilizations of the World. **Provided by**: Saylor. **Located at**: https://legacy.saylor.org/hist101/Intro/. **License**: *CC BY: Attribution*
- Oracle bones. **Provided by**: Wikipedia. **Located at**: http://en.wikipedia.org/wiki/Oracle%20bones. **License**: *CC BY-SA: Attribution-ShareAlike*

- Shang Dynasty. **Provided by**: Wikipedia. **Located at**: https://en.wikipedia.org/wiki/Shang_dynasty. **License**: *CC BY: Attribution*
- 557px-Shang_dynasty.svg.png. **Provided by**: Wikipedia. **Located at**: https://en.wikipedia.org/wiki/Shang_dynasty#/media/File:Shang_dynasty.svg. **License**: *CC BY: Attribution*
- Ancient Chinese Civilization. **Provided by**: Wikibooks. **Located at**: http://en.wikibooks.org/wiki/World_History/Ancient_Civilizations%23Ancient_Chinese_Civilization. **License**: *CC BY-SA: Attribution-ShareAlike*
- HIST101: Ancient Civilizations of the World. **Provided by**: Saylor. **Located at**: https://legacy.saylor.org/hist101/Intro/. **License**: *CC BY: Attribution*
- Aristocracy. **Provided by**: Wiktionary. **Located at**: http://en.wiktionary.org/wiki/aristocracy. **License**: *CC BY-SA: Attribution-ShareAlike*
- The First Chinese Dynasties. **Provided by**: Wikibooks. **Located at**: http://en.wikibooks.org/wiki/World_History/The_First_Chinese_Dynasties. **License**: *CC BY-SA: Attribution-ShareAlike*
- Artisan. **Provided by**: Wiktionary. **Located at**: http://en.wiktionary.org/wiki/artisan. **License**: *CC BY-SA: Attribution-ShareAlike*
- Peasant. **Provided by**: Wiktionary. **Located at**: http://en.wiktionary.org/wiki/peasant. **License**: *CC BY-SA: Attribution-ShareAlike*
- Shang Dynasty. **Provided by**: Wikipedia. **Located at**: https://en.wikipedia.org/wiki/Shang_dynasty. **License**: *CC BY: Attribution*
- 557px-Shang_dynasty.svg.png. **Provided by**: Wikipedia. **Located at**: https://en.wikipedia.org/wiki/Shang_dynasty#/media/File:Shang_dynasty.svg. **License**: *CC BY: Attribution*
- Hou Mu Wu Ding Full View. **Provided by**: Wikipedia. **Located at**: http://en.wikipedia.org/wiki/File:HouMuWuDingFullView.jpg. **License**: *CC BY-SA: Attribution-ShareAlike*
- Treasures of Ancient China exhibit - bronze battle axe. **Provided by**: Wikipedia. **Located at**: http://en.wikipedia.org/wiki/File:CMOC_Treasures_of_Ancient_China_exhibit_-_bronze_battle_axe.jpg. **License**: *CC BY-SA: Attribution-ShareAlike*
- The First Chinese Dynasties. **Provided by**: Wikibooks. **Located at**: http://en.wikibooks.org/wiki/World_History/The_First_Chinese_Dynasties. **License**: *CC BY-SA: Attribution-ShareAlike*
- HIST101: Ancient Civilizations of the World. **Provided by**: Saylor. **Located at**: https://legacy.saylor.org/hist101/Intro/. **License**: *CC BY: Attribution*
- HIST101: Ancient Civilizations of the World. **Provided by**: Saylor. **Located at**: https://legacy.saylor.org/hist101/Intro/. **License**: *CC BY: Attribution*
- Ancient Chinese Civilization. **Provided by**: Wikibooks. **Located at**: http://en.wikibooks.org/wiki/World_History/Ancient_Civilizations%23Ancient_Chinese_Civilization. **License**: *CC BY-SA: Attribution-ShareAlike*
- Animism. **Provided by**: Wiktionary. **Located at**: http://en.wiktionary.org/wiki/animism. **License**: *CC BY-SA: Attribution-ShareAlike*
- HIST241: Pre-Modern Northeast Asia. **Provided by**: Saylor. **Located at**: https://legacy.saylor.org/hist241/Intro/. **License**: *CC BY: Attribution*
- HIST101: Ancient Civilizations of the World. **Provided by**: Saylor. **Located at**: https://legacy.saylor.org/hist101/Intro/. **License**: *CC BY: Attribution*
- animism. **Provided by**: Wiktionary. **Located at**: http://en.wiktionary.org/wiki/animism. **License**: *CC BY-SA: Attribution-ShareAlike*
- Shang Dynasty. **Provided by**: Wikipedia. **Located at**: https://en.wikipedia.org/wiki/Shang_dynasty. **License**: *CC BY: Attribution*
- 557px-Shang_dynasty.svg.png. **Provided by**: Wikipedia. **Located at**: https://en.wikipedia.org/wiki/Shang_dynasty#/media/File:Shang_dynasty.svg. **License**: *CC BY: Attribution*
- Hou Mu Wu Ding Full View. **Provided by**: Wikipedia. **Located at**: http://en.wikipedia.org/wiki/File:HouMuWuDingFullView.jpg. **License**: *CC BY-SA: Attribution-ShareAlike*
- Treasures of Ancient China exhibit - bronze battle axe. **Provided by**: Wikipedia. **Located at**: http://en.wikipedia.org/wiki/File:CMOC_Treasures_of_Ancient_China_exhibit_-_bronze_battle_axe.jpg. **License**: *CC BY-SA: Attribution-ShareAlike*
- 312px-Shang_dynasty_inscribed_scapula.jpg. **Provided by**: Wikipedia. **Located at**: https://en.wikipedia.org/wiki/Oracle_bone#/media/File:Shang_dynasty_inscribed_scapula.jpg. **License**: *CC BY: Attribution*
- Tomb_Fu_Hao_YinXu.jpg. **Provided by**: Wikipedia. **Located at**: https://en.wikipedia.org/wiki/Tomb_of_Fu_Hao#/media/File:Tomb_Fu_Hao_YinXu.jpg. **License**: *CC BY: Attribution*
- Yuanshi Tianzun. **Provided by**: Wikipedia. **Located at**: http://en.wikipedia.org/wiki/File:YuanshiTianzun.jpg. **License**: *Public Domain: No Known Copyright*
- Shang Dynasty. **Provided by**: Wikipedia. **Located at**: https://en.wikipedia.org/wiki/Shang_dynasty. **License**: *CC BY: Attribution*
- Chariot. **Provided by**: Wikipedia. **Located at**: https://en.wikipedia.org/wiki/Chariot#China. **License**: *CC BY: Attribution*

- The First Chinese Dynasties. **Provided by**: Wikibooks. **Located at**: http://en.wikibooks.org/wiki/World_History/The_First_Chinese_Dynasties. **License**: *CC BY: Attribution*

- Shang Society and Shang Culture. **Provided by**: History 101. **Located at**: http://www.saylor.org/site/wp-content/uploads/2012/10/HIST101-3.2.1-ShangSociety-FINAL1.pdf. **License**: *CC BY: Attribution*

- 557px-Shang_dynasty.svg.png. **Provided by**: Wikipedia. **Located at**: https://en.wikipedia.org/wiki/Shang_dynasty#/media/File:Shang_dynasty.svg. **License**: *CC BY: Attribution*

- Hou Mu Wu Ding Full View. **Provided by**: Wikipedia. **Located at**: http://en.wikipedia.org/wiki/File:HouMuWuDingFullView.jpg. **License**: *CC BY-SA: Attribution-ShareAlike*

- Treasures of Ancient China exhibit - bronze battle axe. **Provided by**: Wikipedia. **Located at**: http://en.wikipedia.org/wiki/File:CMOC_Treasures_of_Ancient_China_exhibit_-_bronze_battle_axe.jpg. **License**: *CC BY-SA: Attribution-ShareAlike*

- 312px-Shang_dynasty_inscribed_scapula.jpg. **Provided by**: Wikipedia. **Located at**: https://en.wikipedia.org/wiki/Oracle_bone#/media/File:Shang_dynasty_inscribed_scapula.jpg. **License**: *CC BY: Attribution*

- Tomb_Fu_Hao_YinXu.jpg. **Provided by**: Wikipedia. **Located at**: https://en.wikipedia.org/wiki/Tomb_of_Fu_Hao#/media/File:Tomb_Fu_Hao_YinXu.jpg. **License**: *CC BY: Attribution*

- Yuanshi Tianzun. **Provided by**: Wikipedia. **Located at**: http://en.wikipedia.org/wiki/File:YuanshiTianzun.jpg. **License**: *Public Domain: No Known Copyright*

- 383px-Dinastia_shang_tipode_ding_biansato_xiii-xii_sec._ac.jpeg. **Provided by**: Wikipedia. **Located at**: https://en.wikipedia.org/wiki/Shang_dynasty#/media/File:Dinastia_shang,_tipode_ding_biansato,_xiii-xii_sec._ac.JPG. **License**: *CC BY: Attribution*

- 532px-CMOC_Treasures_of_Ancient_China_exhibit_-_bronze_battle_axe.jpg. **Provided by**: Wikipedia. **Located at**: https://en.wikipedia.org/wiki/Shang_dynasty#/media/File:CMOC_Treasures_of_Ancient_China_exhibit_-_bronze_battle_axe.jpg. **License**: *CC BY: Attribution*

The Zhou Dynasty

The Mandate of Heaven

The Zhou Dynasty overthrew the Shang Dynasty, and used the Mandate of Heaven as justification.

Learning Objectives

Describe the Zhou Dynasty's justification for overthrowing the Shang Dynasty

Key Takeaways

Key Points

- In 1046 BCE, the Shang Dynasty was overthrown at the Battle of Muye, and the Zhou Dynasty was established.
- The Zhou created the Mandate of Heaven: the idea that there could be only one legitimate ruler of China at a time, and that this ruler had the blessing of the gods. They used this Mandate to justify their overthrow of the Shang, and their subsequent rule.
- Some scholars think the earlier Xia Dynasty never existed—that it was invented by the Zhou to support their claim under the Mandate that there had always been only one ruler of China.

Key Terms

- **Battle of Muye**: The battle that resulted with the Zhou, a subject people living in the western part of the kingdom, overthrew the Shang Dynasty.
- **Mandate of Heaven**: The Chinese philosophical concept of the circumstances under which a ruler is allowed to rule. Good rulers were allowed to rule under the Mandate of Heaven, while despotic, unjust rulers had the Mandate revoked.

The Fall of the Shang

In 1046 BCE, the Zhou, a subject people living in the western part of the kingdom, overthrew the Shang Dynasty at the Battle of Muye. This was a battle between Shang and Zhou clans, over the Shang's expansion. They largely had the support of the Chinese people: Di Xin (the final king of the Shang Dynasty) had become cruel, spent state money on drinking and gambling, and ignored the state. The Zhou established authority by forging alliances with regional nobles, and founded their new dynasty with its capital at Fenghao (near present-day Xi'an, in western China).

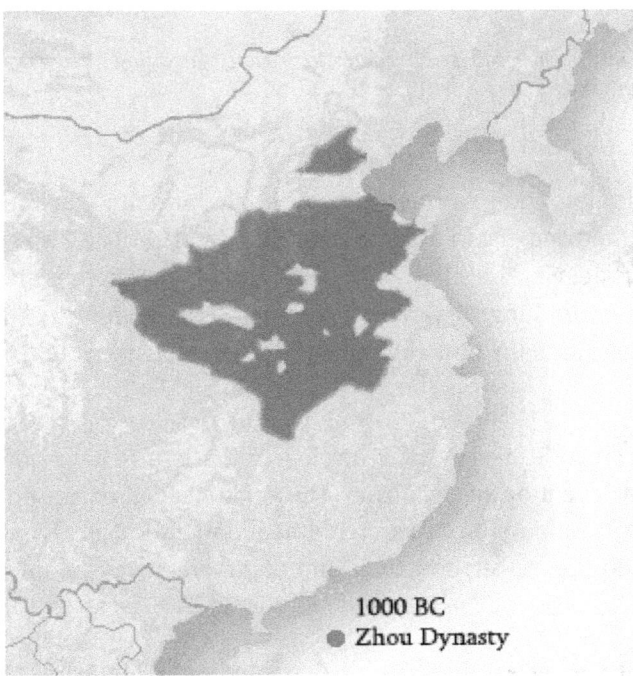

Map of Zhou Dynasty: This map shows the location of the ancient Zhou Dynasty.

The Mandate of Heaven

Under the Zhou Dynasty, China moved away from worship of Shangdi ("Celestial Lord") in favor of worship of Tian ("heaven"), and they created the Mandate of Heaven. According to this idea, there could be only one legitimate ruler of China at a time, and this ruler reigned as the "Son of Heaven" with the approval of the gods. If a king ruled unfairly he could lose this approval, which would result in his downfall. Overthrow, natural disasters, and famine were taken as a sign that the ruler had lost the Mandate of Heaven.

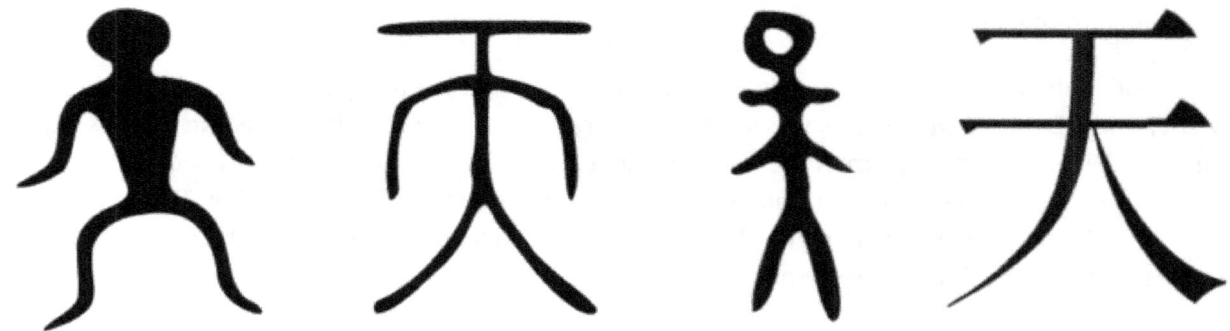

The Chinese Character for "Tian": *The Chinese character for "Tian," meaning "heaven," in (from left to right) Bronze script, Seal script, Oracle script, and modern simplified.*

The Mandate of Heaven did not require a ruler to be of noble birth, and had no time limitations. Instead, rulers were expected to be good and just in order to keep the Mandate. The Zhou claimed that their rule was justified by the Mandate of Heaven. In other words, the Zhou believed that the Shang kings had become immoral with their excessive drinking, luxuriant living, and cruelty, and so had lost their mandate. The gods' blessing was given instead to the new ruler under the Zhou Dynasty, which would rule China for the next 800 years.

The need for the Zhou to create a history of a unified China is also why some scholars think the Xia Dynasty may have been an invention of the Zhou. The Zhou needed to erase the various small states of prehistoric China from history, and replace them with the monocratic Xia Dynasty in order for their Mandate of Heaven to seem valid (i.e., to support the claim that there always would be, and always had been, only one ruler of China).

The Zhou ruled until 256 BCE, when the state of Qin captured Chengzhou. However, the Mandate of Heaven philosophy carried on throughout ancient China.

Society Under the Zhou Dynasty

Under the initial period of the Zhou Dynasty (called the Western Zhou period), a number of innovations were made, rulers were legitimized under the Mandate of Heaven, a feudal system developed, and new forms of irrigation allowed the population to expand.

> **Learning Objectives**
>
> Describe the main accomplishments of the Western Zhou period

> ## Key Takeaways
>
> ### Key Points
>
> - The first period of Zhou rule, during which the Zhou held undisputed power over China, is known as the Western Zhou period.
> - During the Western Zhou period, the focus of religion changed from the supreme god, Shangdi, to "Tian," or heaven; advances were made in farming technology; and the feudal system was established.
> - Under the feudal system, the monarchy would reward loyal nobles with large pieces of land.
> - Over time, the king grew weaker, and the lords of the feudal system grew stronger, until finally, in 711 BCE, one lord joined forces with an invading group of barbarians and killed the king.
>
> ### Key Terms
>
> - **Western Zhou period**: The first period of Zhou rule, during which the Zhou held undisputed power over China (1046-771 BCE).
> - **feudal system**: A social system based on personal ownership of resources and personal fealty between a suzerain (lord) and a vassal (subject). Defining characteristics include direct ownership of resources, personal loyalty, and a hierarchical social structure reinforced by religion.
> - **Duke of Zhou**: A regent to the king who established the feudal system, and held a lot of power during the Western Zhou period.

The first period of Zhou rule, during which the Zhou held undisputed power over China, is known as the Western Zhou period. This period ended when the capital was moved eastward. A number of important innovations took place during this period: the Zhou moved away from worship of Shangdi, the supreme god under the Shang, in favor of Tian ("heaven"); they legitimized rulers, through the Mandate of Heaven (divine right to rule); they moved to a feudal system; developed Chinese philosophy; and made new advances in irrigation that allowed more intensive farming and made it possible for the lands of China to sustain larger populations.

China created a substantial amount of literature during the Zhou Dynasty. These include The Book of History and The Book of Diviners, which was used by fortune tellers. Books dedicated to songs and ceremonial rites were also created. While many of these writings have been destroyed over time, their lasting impression on history is evidence of the strength of Zhou culture.

Like other river valley civilizations of the time, the people under the Zhou Dynasty followed patriarchal roles. Men chose which children would be educated and whom their daughters were married. The household usually consisted of the head male, his wife, his sons and unmarried daughters.

The feudal system in China was structurally similar to ones that followed, such as pre-imperial Macedon, Europe, and Japan. At the beginning of the Zhou Dynasty's rule, the Duke of Zhou, a regent to the king, held a lot of power, and the king rewarded the loyalty of nobles and generals with large pieces of land. Delegating regional control in this way allowed the Zhou to maintain control over a massive land area. Under this feudal (fengjian) system, land could be passed down within families, or broken up further and granted to more people.

Most importantly, the peasants who farmed the land were controlled by the feudal system. Slavery had been common during the Shang Dynasty, but this decreased and finally disappeared under the Zhou Dynasty, as social status became more fluid and transitory.

The Duke of Zhou: *Portrait of the Duke of Zhou in Sancai Tuhui, a Chinese encyclopedia published in 1609 during the Ming Dynasty.*

When the Duke of Zhou stepped down, China was united and at peace, leading to years of prosperity. But this only lasted for about seventy-five years. Over time, the central power of the Zhou Dynasty slowly weakened, and the lords of the fiefs originally bestowed by the Zhou came to equal the kings in wealth and influence. They began to actively compete with them for power, and the fiefs gained independence as individual states.

Finally, in 711 BCE, one rebellious noble, the Marquess of Shen, joined forces with invading barbarians, the Quanrong, to defeat the King You. No one came to the king's defense, and he was killed. The Zhou capital was sacked by the barbarians, and with this the Western Zhou period ended.

Art Under the Zhou Dynasty

Under the Zhou Dynasty, many art forms expanded and became more detailed, including bronze, bronze inscriptions, painting, and lacquerware.

Learning Objectives

Identify some of the art forms prevelant under the Zhou Dynasty

Key Takeaways

Key Points

- Work in bronze, including inscriptions, continued and expanded in the Zhou Dynasty.
- Few paintings have survived from this period, but we know that they were representations of the real world.
- The production of lacquerware expanded during this period.

Key Terms

- **lacquer**: A natural varnish, originating in China or Japan, and extracted from the sap of a sumac tree.

Bronze, Ceramics, and Jade

Chinese script cast onto bronzeware, such as bells and cauldrons, carried over from the Shang Dynasty into the Zhou; it showed continued changes in style over time, and by region. Under the Zhou, expansion of this form of writing continued, with the inclusion of patrons and ancestors.

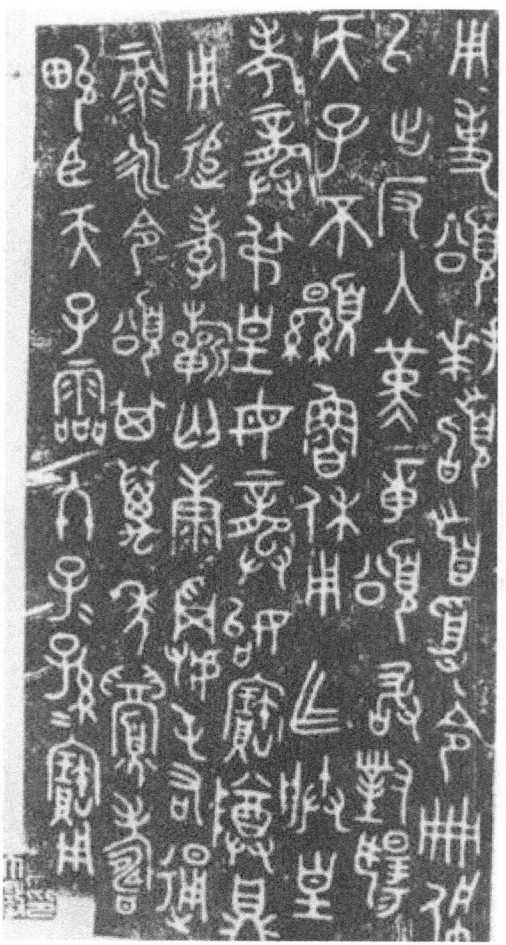

Example of Bronze Inscription: *This example of bronze inscription was cast on the Song ding, ca. 800 BCE. The text records the appointment of a man named Song (?) as supervisor of the storehouses in Chengzhou, and is repeated on at least 3 tripod pots (? dǐng), 5 tureens (? guǐ) and their lids, and 2 vases (? hú) and their lids.*

Other improvements to bronze objects under the Eastern Zhou included greater attention to detail and aesthetics. The casting process itself was improved by a new technique, called the lost wax method of production.

Example of Western Zhou Bronze: *A Chinese bronze "gui" ritual vessel on a pedestal, used as a container for grain. From the Western Zhou Dynasty, dated c. 1000 BC. The written inscription of 11 ancient Chinese characters on the bronze vessel states its use and ownership by Zhou royalty.*

Ceramic and Jade art continued from the Shang Dynasty, and was improved and refined, especially during the Warring States Period.

Paintings

Very few paintings from the Zhou have survived, however written descriptions of the works have remained. Representations of the real world, in the form of paintings of figures, portraits, and historical scenes, were common during the time. This was a new development. Painting was also done on pottery, tomb walls, and on silk.

Example of Silk Painting: *This example of silk painting shows a man riding a dragon, and has been dated to the 5th-3rd century BCE.*

Lacquerware

Lacquerware was a technique through which objects were decoratively covered by a wood finish and cured to a hard, durable finish. The lacquer itself might also be inlaid or carved. The Zhou continued and developed lacquer work done in the Shang Dynasty. During the Eastern Zhou period, a large quantity of lacquerware began to be produced.

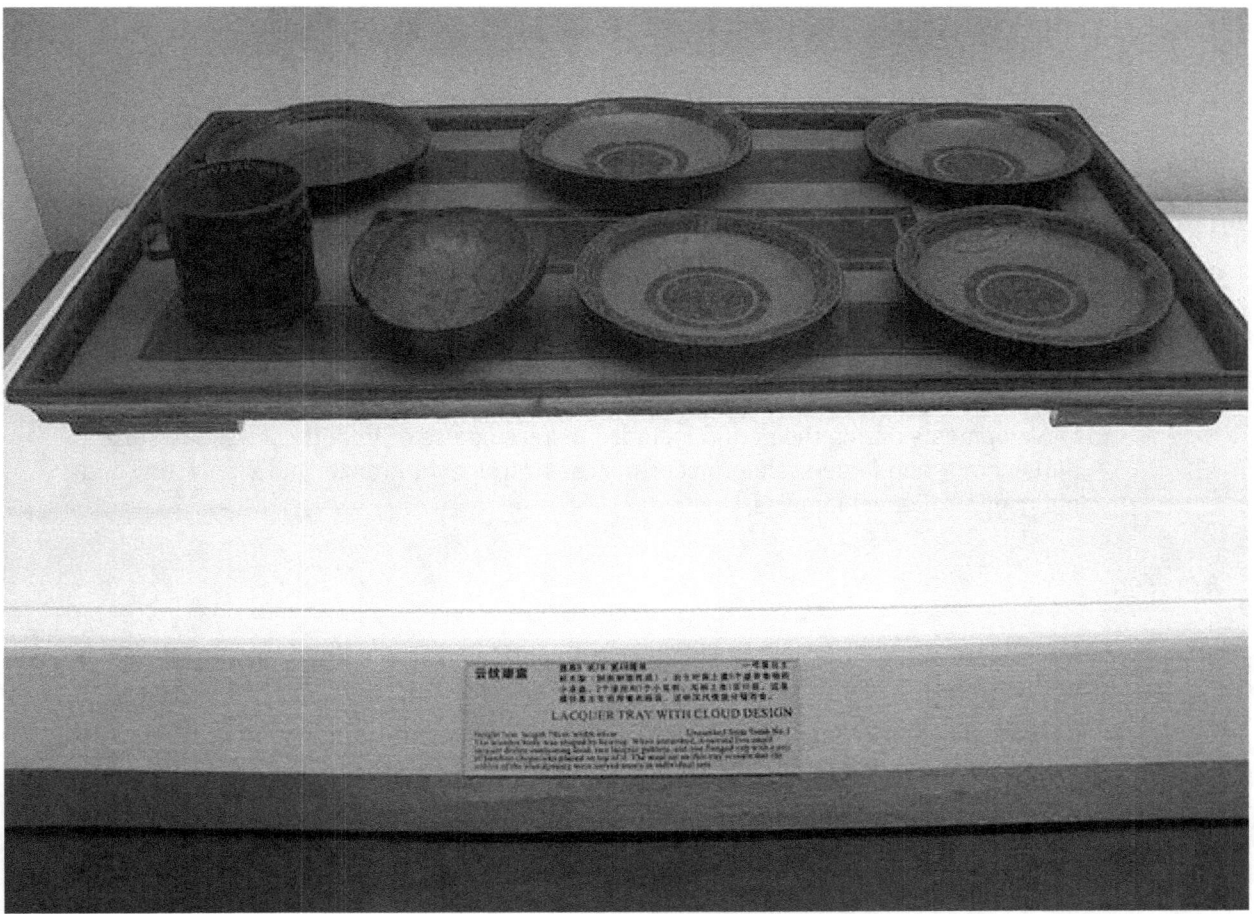

Example of Lacquerware: *These are Chinese Western Han (202 BC – 9 CE) era lacquerwares and lacquer tray unearthed from the 2nd-century-BCE Han Tomb No.1 at Mawangdui, Changsha, China in 1972.*

The Eastern Zhou Period

The Eastern Zhou period was divided into two halves. In the Spring and Autumn period, power became decentralized as nobles vied for power. In the Warring States period, strong states fought each other in large-scale war. During the period, there were substantial intellectual and military developments.

Learning Objectives

Explain the main political and military developments during the Eastern Zhou period

> ## Key Takeaways
>
> ### Key Points
>
> - During the first part of the Eastern Zhou period, called the Spring and Autumn period, the king became less powerful and the regional feudal became lords more so, until only seven consolidated powerful feudal states were left.
> - During the second part of the period, called the Warring States period, strong states vied for power until the Qin conquered them all and created a unified dynasty.
> - Developments during the period included increasing use of infantry, a trend toward bureaucracy and large-scale projects, the use of iron over bronze, and intellectual and philosophical developments.
>
> ### Key Terms
>
> - **feudalism**: A social system in which nobility hold lands from the King in exchange for military service, and peasants lived on the nobles' land and provided services.
> - **decentralized**: Moving away from a single point of administration to multiple locations, and usually giving them a degree of autonomy.
> - **infantry**: Soldiers marching or fighting on foot.
> - **Hegemony**: Domination, influence, or authority over another, especially by one political group over a society or by one nation over others.

The End of the Western Zhou Period

The first period of Zhou rule, which lasted from 1046-771 BCE and was referred to as the Western Zhou period, was characterized mostly by unified, peaceful rule. The lords under feudalism gained increasing power, and ultimately the Zhou King You was assassinated, and the capital, Haojing, was sacked in 770 BCE. The capital was quickly moved east to Chengzhou, near modern-day Luoyang, and the Zhou abandoned the western regions. Thus, the assassination marked the end of the Western Zhou period and the beginning of the Eastern Zhou period.

The Spring and Autumn Period of Eastern Zhou

The first part of the Eastern Zhou period is known as the Spring and Autumn period, named after the *Spring and Autumn Annals*, a text that narrated events on a year-by-year basis, and marked the beginning of China's deliberately recorded history. This period lasted from about 771-476 BCE. During this time, power became increasingly decentralized as regional feudal lords began to absorb smaller powers and vie for hegemony. The monarchy continued to lose power, and the people were nearly always at war.

The period from 685-591 BCE was called The Five Hegemons, and featured, in order, the Hegemony of Qi, Song, Jin, Qin, and Chu. By the end of 5th century BCE, the feudal system was consolidated into seven prominent and powerful states—Han, Wei, Zhao, Yue, Chu, Qi, and Qin—and China entered the Warring States period, when each state vied for complete control.

The Warring States Period

This period, in the second half of the Eastern Zhou, lasted from about 475-221 BCE, when China was united under the Qin Dynasty. The partition of the Jin state created seven major warring states. After a series of wars among these powerful states, King Zhao of Qin defeated King Nan of Zhou and conquered West Zhou in 256 BCE; his grandson, King Zhuangxiang of Qin, conquered East Zhou, bringing the Zhou Dynasty to an end.

A Map of the Warring States of China: *This map shows the Warring States late in the period. Qin has expanded southwest, Chu north and Zhao northwest.*

Developments During the Eastern Zhou

While the chariot remained in use, there was a shift during the period to infantry, possibly because of the invention of the crossbow. This meant that war became larger scale, as peasants were drafted to take the place of nobility as soldiers and needed complex logistical support. The aristocracy's importance dwindled as the king's became stronger, and strong central bureaucracies took hold. *The Art of War*, attributed to Sun Tzu, was written during this time; it remains a very influential book about strategy.

A sophisticated form of commercial arithmetic was in place during the period, as shown by a bundle of bamboo slips showing two digit decimal multiplication.

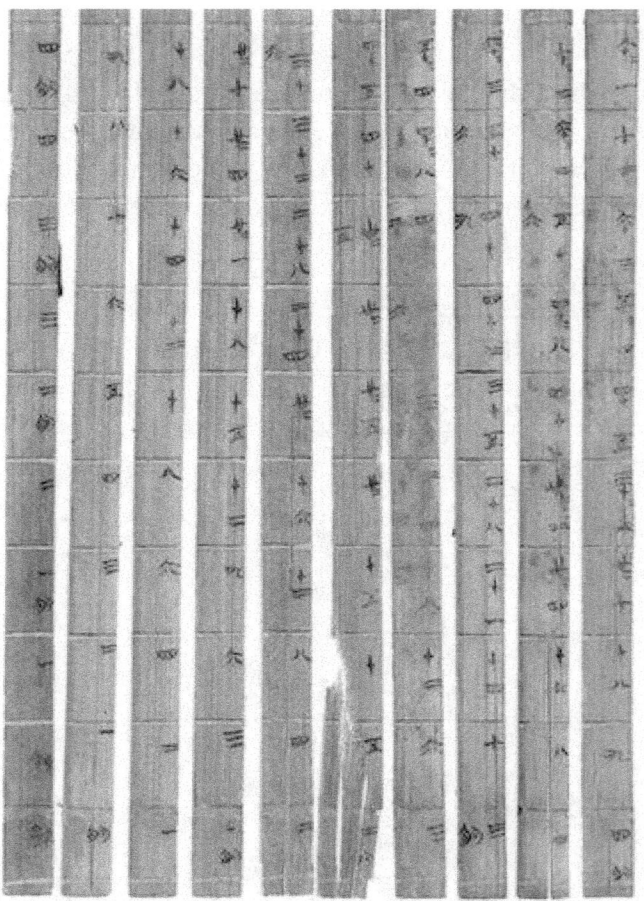

Bamboo Slips Showing Arithmetic: *These bamboo slips show a sophisticated two digit decimal multiplication table.*

A history of the Spring and Autumn Period, called the *Zuo Commentary on the Spring and Autumn Annals*, was published during this time.

Developments in iron work replaced bronze as the dominant metal used in warfare. Trade became increasingly important among states within China. Large-scale works, including the Dujiangyan Irrigation System and the Zhengguo Canal, were completed and increased agricultural production.

Iron Sword from the Warring States Period: *This iron sword is an example of the metal work done during this period.*

The Warring States Period

The Warring States period saw technological and philosophical development, and the emergence of the Qin Dynasty.

Learning Objectives
Demonstrate understanding of the main characteristics of the Warring States period

Key Takeaways

Key Points

- The second part of the Eastern Zhou period is known as the Warring States period. During this time, the seven states remaining from the Spring and Autumn period intensely and unrelentingly battled each other for total power.

- It was during this period that the Iron Age spread in China, leading to stronger tools and weapons made from iron instead of bronze.
- This period also saw the further development of Confucianism (by Mencius), Daoism, Legalism, and Mohism.
- By this time, two key Chinese social characteristics had solidified: l) the concept of the patrilineal family as the basic unit of society, and 2) the concept of natural social differentiation into classes.
- Iron replaced the use of bronze, sophisticated math came into use, and large-scale projects were undertaken.
- Ultimately, in 221 BCE, the Qin state emerged victorious and unified China once more under the Qin Dynasty.

Key Terms

- **crossbow**: A mechanised weapon, based on the bow and arrow, that fires bolts; it was invented during the Warring States period of the Zhou Dynasty, when its low cost and ease of use made it a preferable weapon to the chariot.

Over the course of the Spring and Autumn period, regional feudal lords consolidated and absorbed smaller powers; by 476 BCE, seven prominent states were left, all led by individual kings. The second part of the Eastern Zhou period is known as the Warring States period; during this time these few remaining states battled each other for total power.

Conflict Among the Seven States

The king by now was powerless, and the rulers of the seven independent states began to refer to themselves as kings as well. These major Chinese states were in constant competition. Since none of the states wanted any one rival to become too powerful, if one state became too strong, the others would join forces against it, so no state achieved dominance. This led to nearly 250 years of inconclusive warfare that became larger and larger in scale. It was also at this point that there first emerged the concept of a Chinese emperor who would rule over all the various kings, though the first Chinese emperors did not rule until China was unified under the later Qin Dynasty. The crossbow was invented, and its low cost and easy use (as compared to the expensive chariot) resulted in the increased conscription of peasants as expandable infantry.

Technological and Philosophical Development

The Iron Age had reached China by 600 CE, but it was during this period that the age spread and took root in China: by the time of the Warring States Period, China saw a widespread adoption of iron tools and weapons that were significantly stronger than their bronze counterparts.

This period also saw the further development of the philosophical movements that originated in the Hundred Schools of Thought of the Spring and Autumn period. Mencius further developed Confucian philosophy, expanding upon its doctrines and asserting the innate goodness of the individual and the importance of destiny. Daoism, Legalism, and Mohism became more developed. Archaic writing also gave way to a far more recognizable form of Chinese script.

Cultural, Economic, and Social Development

Two fundamental Chinese social characteristics had become apparent by this time: 1) the concept of the patrilineal family as the basic unit in society, with high importance placed on blood relations, and 2) the concept of natural social differentiation into classes, each regarded in terms of their contributions to society.

Large-scale projects, like the Dujiangyan Irrigation System and the Zhengguo Canal, were carried out. Sophisticated arithmetic was carried out, including two digit decimal multiplication.

The Zuo Commentary on the Spring and Autumn Annals was a literary achievement. In other literary works, sayings of philosophers of the period were recorded in the Analects and the Art of War.

The Rise of the Qin State and Resolution of the Warring States Period

Though the military rivalries and alliances in the Warring States period were complex and constantly in flux, over time the Qin state, under the leadership of King Zheng, emerged as the most powerful. The Qin were particularly strongly rooted in Legalist philosophy, which advocated the importance of the state at the expense of the individual. They were also known for being ruthless and ignoring etiquette and protocol of war in order to win at all costs. In particular, Shang Yang, adviser to Zheng, enacted laws to force subjects of the kingdom to act in ways that helped the state; he forced them to marry early, have many children, and produce certain quotas of food. Ultimately, in 221 BCE, the Qin state conquered the others and established the Qin Dynasty.

Chinese Philosophy

Confucianism, Daoism, Legalism, and Mohism all began during the Zhou Dynasty in the 6th century BCE, and had very strong influences on Chinese civilization.

Learning Objectives
Discuss Confucianism, Daoism, Legalism, and Mohism.

Key Takeaways
Key Points - Confucius stressed tradition and believed that an individual should strive to be virtuous

- and respectful, and to fit into his or her place in society.
- Confucianism remained prevalent in China from the Han Dynasty in 202 BCE to the end of dynastic rule in 1911.
- Lao-tzu was the legendary founder of Daoism, recorded in the form of the book the *Tao Te Ching*.
- Daoism advocated that the individual should follow a mysterious force, called The Way (dao), of the universe, and that all things were one.
- Legalism held that humans were inherently bad and needed to be kept in line by a strong state. According to Legalism, the state was far more important than the individual.
- Legalists could be divided into three types: those concerned with the position of ruler, those concerned with laws, and those concerned with tactics to keep the state safe.
- Mohism emerged under the philosopher Mozi, and its most well-known concept was "impartial care." Mohism also stated that all people should be equal in their material benefit, and in their protection from harm.

Key Terms

- **Five Classics**: The basis of civil examinations in imperial China and the Confucian canon. They consist of the Book of Odes, the Book of Documents, the Book of Changes, the Book of Rites, and the Spring and Autumn Annals.
- **Analects**: The document in which the students of Confucius recorded his teachings.
- **jen**: Human virtue, under Confucianism.
- **chi**: Life force or body energy, which supposedly circulates through the body along meridians.
- **Tao Te Ching**: The book which forms the basis of Daoist philosophy.

Confucianism

Confucius, who lived during the 6th century BCE, was one of the foremost Chinese philosophers. He looked back on the Western Zhou period, with its strong centralized state, as an ideal. He was pragmatic and sought to reform the existing government, encouraging a system of mutual duty between superiors and inferiors. Confucius stressed tradition and believed that an individual should strive to be virtuous and respectful, and to fit into his or her place in society. After his death in 479 BCE, his students wrote down his ethical and moral teachings in the *Lun-yü, or Analects* .

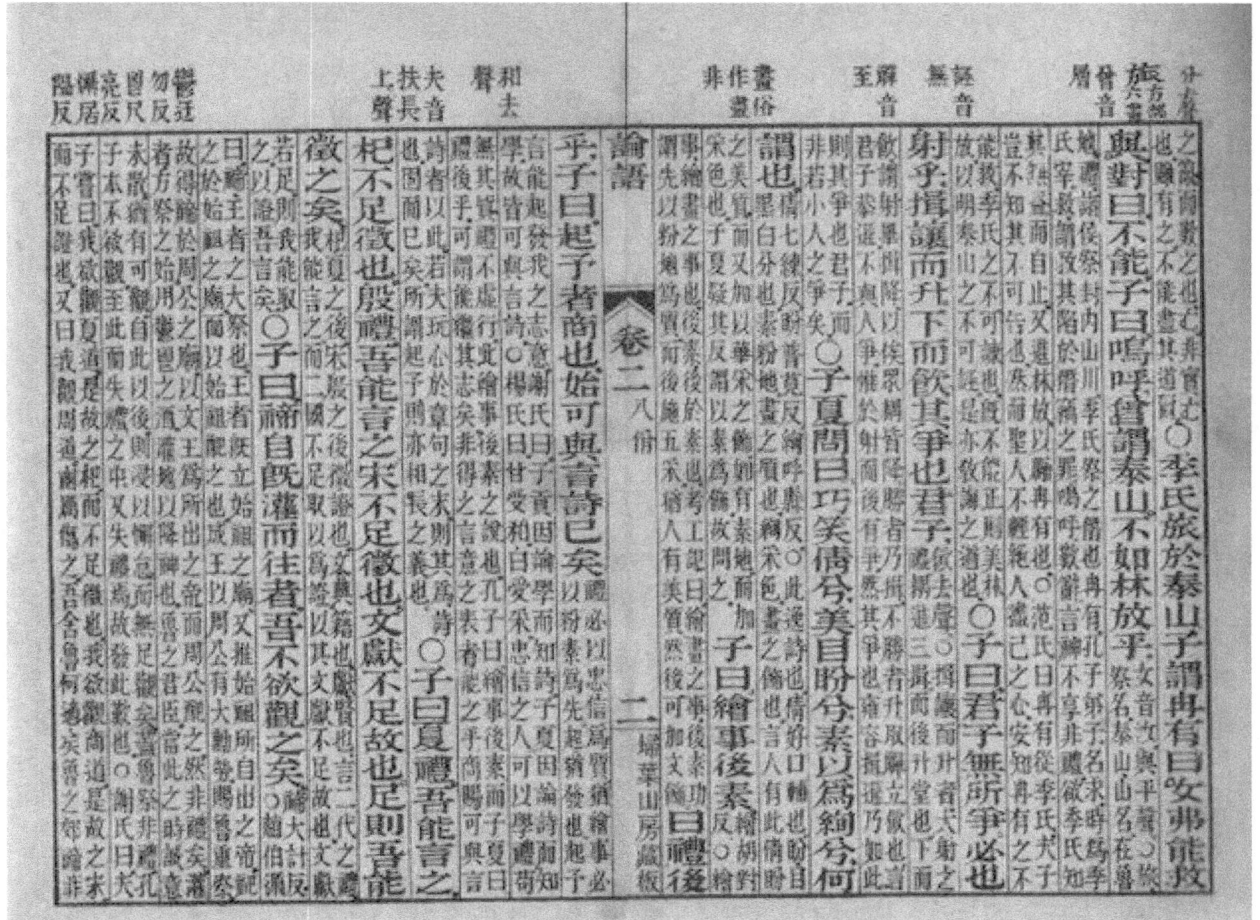

The Analects of Confucius: *The ethical and moral teachings of Confucius were written down by his students in this document.*

Being a good and virtuous human in every ordinary situation was the goal of Confucianism. This virtue was called "jen," and humans were seen as perfectible and basically good creatures. Ceremonies and rituals based on the Five Classics, especially the I Ching, were strongly instituted. Some ethical concepts included Yi (the moral disposition to do good), Lǐ (ritual norms for everyday life) and Zhì (the ability to see what is right in the behavior of others).

Confucianism remained prevalent in China from the Han Dynasty in 202 BCE to the end of dynastic rule in 1911. It was reformulated during the Tang Dynasty (618-907) as Neo-Confucianism, and became the basis of imperial exams.

Daoism

Another important philosopher in this period was Lao-tzu (also called Laozi), who founded Daoism (also called Taoism) during the same period as Confucianism. Lao-tzu is a legendary figure—it is uncertain if he actually existed. According to myth, Lao-tzu was born around 604 BCE as an old man. As he left his home to live a life of solitude, he was asked by the city gatekeeper to write down his thoughts. He did so in a book called *Tao Te Ching*, and was never seen again.

Lao-Tzu: *A depiction of Lao-Tzu, the founder of Daoism.*

Daoism advocated that the individual should follow a mysterious force, called The Way (dao), of the universe and act in accordance with nature. Daoism stressed the oneness of all things, and was strictly individualistic, as opposed to Confucianism, which advocated acting as society expected.

Daoism as a religion arose over time, and involved the worship of gods and ancestors, the cultivation of "chi" energy, a system of morals, and the use of alchemy to achieve immortality. It is still practice today.

Legalism

Although Confucianism and Daoism are the Chinese philosophies that have endured most to this day, even more important to this early period was a lesser-known philosophy called Legalism. This held that humans are inherently bad and need to be kept in line by a strong state. According to Legalism, the state was far more important than the individual. While Legalism held that laws should be clear and public and that everyone should be subject to them, it also contended that rulers had supreme power and must use stealth and secrecy to remain in power. Legalists also believed that society must strive to dominate other societies.

Legalists could be divided into three types. The first was concerned with *shi*, or the investment of the position of ruler with power (rather than the person) and the necessity of obtaining facts to rule well. The second was concerned with *fa*, or laws, regulations, and standards. This meant all were equal under the ruler, and the state was run by law, not a ruler. The third was the concept of *shu*, or tactics to keep the state safe. Legalism was generally in competition with Confucianism, which advocated a just and reciprocal relationship between the state and its subjects.

Depiction of Shang Yang: *Shang Yang was a Legalist reformer under the Qin.*

Mohism

Mohism emerged around the same time as the other philosophies discussed here, under the philosopher Mozi (c. 470-391 BCE). The most well-known concept under Mohism was "impartial care," also known as "universal love." This meant that people should care equally about other people, regardless of their true relationship to that person. This opposed the ideas of Confucianism, which said that love should be greater for close relationships. Mohism also stressed the ideas of self-restraint, reflection and authenticity.

Depiction of Mozi: *The Chinese philosopher who began Mohism is shown here.*

Mohism also stated that all people should be equal in their material benefit and in their protection from harm. Society could be improved by having it function like an organism, with a uniform moral compass. Those who were qualified should receive jobs, and thus the ruler would be surrounded by people of talent and skill. An unrighteous ruler would result in seven disasters for the state, including neglect of military defense, repression, illusions about strength, distrust, famine, and more.

Attributions

CC licensed content, Specific attribution

- The First Chinese Dynasties. **Provided by:** Wikibooks. **Located at:** http://en.wikibooks.org/wiki/World_History/The_First_Chinese_Dynasties. **License:** *CC BY-SA: Attribution-ShareAlike*
- HIST101: Ancient Civilizations of the World. **Provided by:** Saylor. **Located at:** https://legacy.saylor.org/hist101/Intro/. **License:** *CC BY: Attribution*
- Ancient Chinese Civilization. **Provided by:** Wikibooks. **Located at:** http://en.wikibooks.org/wiki/World_History/Ancient_Civilizations%23Ancient_Chinese_Civilization. **License:** *CC BY-SA: Attribution-ShareAlike*
- Mandate of Heaven. **Provided by:** Wiktionary. **Located at:** http://en.wiktionary.org/wiki/Mandate_of_Heaven. **License:** *CC BY-SA: Attribution-ShareAlike*
- Mandate of Heaven. **Provided by:** Wikipedia. **Located at:** https://en.wikipedia.org/wiki/Mandate_of_Heaven. **License:** *CC BY: Attribution*
- Tian. **Provided by:** Wikipedia. **Located at:** http://en.wikipedia.org/wiki/Tian. **License:** *Public Domain: No Known Copyright*
- Zhou_dynasty_1000_BC.png. **Provided by:** Wikipedia. **Located at:** https://en.wikipedia.org/wiki/Zhou_dynasty#/media/File:Zhou_dynasty_1000_BC.png. **License:** *CC BY: Attribution*

- The First Chinese Dynasties. **Provided by**: Wikibooks. **Located at**: http://en.wikibooks.org/wiki/World_History/The_First_Chinese_Dynasties. **License**: *CC BY-SA: Attribution-ShareAlike*
- Feudalism. **Provided by**: Wiktionary. **Located at**: http://en.wiktionary.org/wiki/feudalism. **License**: *CC BY-SA: Attribution-ShareAlike*
- HIST241: Pre-Modern Northeast Asia. **Provided by**: Saylor. **Located at**: https://legacy.saylor.org/hist241/Intro/. **License**: *CC BY: Attribution*
- HIST101: Ancient Civilizations of the World. **Provided by**: Saylor. **Located at**: https://legacy.saylor.org/hist101/Intro/. **License**: *CC BY: Attribution*
- HIST101: Ancient Civilizations of the World. **Provided by**: Saylor. **Located at**: https://legacy.saylor.org/hist101/Intro/. **License**: *CC BY: Attribution*
- Ancient Chinese Civilization. **Provided by**: Wikibooks. **Located at**: http://en.wikibooks.org/wiki/World_History/Ancient_Civilizations%23Ancient_Chinese_Civilization. **License**: *CC BY-SA: Attribution-ShareAlike*
- HIST101: Ancient Civilizations of the World. **Provided by**: Saylor. **Located at**: https://legacy.saylor.org/hist101/Intro/ **License**: *CC BY: Attribution*
- Zhou Dynasty. **Provided by**: Wikipedia. **Located at**: https://en.wikipedia.org/wiki/Zhou_dynasty. **License**: *CC BY: Attribution*
- Tian. **Provided by**: Wikipedia. **Located at**: http://en.wikipedia.org/wiki/Tian. **License**: *Public Domain: No Known Copyright*
- Zhou_dynasty_1000_BC.png. **Provided by**: Wikipedia. **Located at**: https://en.wikipedia.org/wiki/Zhou_dynasty#media/File:Zhou_dynasty_1000_BC.png. **License**: *CC BY: Attribution*
- Zhou Gong. **Provided by**: Wikipedia. **Located at**: http://en.wikipedia.org/wiki/File:Zhou_gong.jpg. **License**: *Public Domain: No Known Copyright*
- Zhou Dynasty. **Provided by**: Wikipedia. **Located at**: https://en.wikipedia.org/wiki/Zhou_dynasty. **License**: *CC BY: Attribution*
- Lacquerware. **Provided by**: Wikipedia. **Located at**: https://en.wikipedia.org/wiki/Lacquerware. **License**: *CC BY: Attribution*
- Chinese Ritual Bronze. **Provided by**: Wikipedia. **Located at**: https://en.wikipedia.org/wiki/Chinese_ritual_bronzes. **License**: *CC BY: Attribution*
- Chinese Bronze Inscriptions. **Provided by**: Wikipedia. **Located at**: https://en.wikipedia.org/wiki/Chinese_bronze_inscriptions#Zhou_dynasty_inscriptionsBron. **License**: *CC BY: Attribution*
- Tian. **Provided by**: Wikipedia. **Located at**: http://en.wikipedia.org/wiki/Tian. **License**: *Public Domain: No Known Copyright*
- Zhou_dynasty_1000_BC.png. **Provided by**: Wikipedia. **Located at**: https://en.wikipedia.org/wiki/Zhou_dynasty#media/File:Zhou_dynasty_1000_BC.png. **License**: *CC BY: Attribution*
- Zhou Gong. **Provided by**: Wikipedia. **Located at**: http://en.wikipedia.org/wiki/File:Zhou_gong.pg. **License**: *Public Domain: No Known Copyright*
- 247px-JinwenShisongding.jpg. **Provided by**: Wikimedia. **Located at**: https://commons.wikimedia.org/wiki/File:JinwenShisongding.jpg. **License**: *CC BY: Attribution*
- 472px-Western_Zhou_Gui_Vessel.jpg. **Provided by**: Wikimedia. **Located at**: https://commons.wikimedia.org/wiki/File:Western_Zhou_Gui_Vessel.jpg. **License**: *CC BY: Attribution*
- 640px-Mawangdui_lacquerwares_and_tray.jpg. **Provided by**: Wikimedia. **Located at**: https://commons.wikimedia.org/wiki/File:Mawangdui_lacquerwares_and_tray.jpg. **License**: *CC BY: Attribution*
- 349px-Changshadragon.jpg. **Provided by**: Wikimedia. **Located at**: https://commons.wikimedia.org/wiki/File:Changshadragon.jpg. **License**: *CC BY: Attribution*
- Ancient Chinese Civilization. **Provided by**: Wikibooks. **Located at**: http://en.wikibooks.org/wiki/World_History/Ancient_Civilizations%23Ancient_Chinese_Civilization. **License**: *CC BY-SA: Attribution-ShareAlike*
- Jack E. Maxfield, A Comprehensive Outline of World History (Organized by Region). November 23, 2009. **Provided by**: OpenStax CNX. **Located at**: http://cnx.org/contents/45ac7e52-e029-4436-895a-92b9e507b372@2.1. **License**: *CC BY: Attribution*
- HIST101: Ancient Civilizations of the World. **Provided by**: Saylor. **Located at**: https://legacy.saylor.org/hist101/Intro/. **License**: *CC BY: Attribution*
- HIST241: Pre-Modern Northeast Asia. **Provided by**: Saylor. **Located at**: https://legacy.saylor.org/hist241/Intro/. **License**: *CC BY: Attribution*
- The First Chinese Dynasties. **Provided by**: Wikibooks. **Located at**: http://en.wikibooks.org/wiki/World_History/The_First_Chinese_Dynasties. **License**: *CC BY-SA: Attribution-ShareAlike*
- Hegemony. **Provided by**: Wiktionary. **Located at**: http://en.wiktionary.org/wiki/hegemony. **License**: *CC BY-SA: Attribution-ShareAlike*

- Hegemony. **Provided by**: Wiktionary. **Located at**: http://en.wiktionary.org/wiki/Hegemony. **License**: *CC BY-SA: Attribution-ShareAlike*
- Warring States Period. **Provided by**: Wikipedia. **Located at**: https://en.wikipedia.org/wiki/Warring_States_period. **License**: *CC BY: Attribution*
- Western Zhou. **Provided by**: Wikipedia. **Located at**: https://en.wikipedia.org/wiki/Western_Zhou. **License**: *CC BY: Attribution*
- Spring and Autumn Period. **Provided by**: Wikipedia. **Located at**: https://en.wikipedia.org/wiki/Spring_and_Autumn_period. **License**: *CC BY: Attribution*
- Tian. **Provided by**: Wikipedia. **Located at**: http://en.wikipedia.org/wiki/Tian. **License**: *Public Domain: No Known Copyright*
- Zhou_dynasty_1000_BC.png. **Provided by**: Wikipedia. **Located at**: https://en.wikipedia.org/wiki/Zhou_dynasty#/media/File:Zhou_dynasty_1000_BC.png. **License**: *CC BY: Attribution*
- Zhou Gong. **Provided by**: Wikipedia. **Located at**: http://en.wikipedia.org/wiki/File:Zhou_gong.jpg. **License**: *Public Domain: No Known Copyright*
- 247px-JinwenShisongding.jpg. **Provided by**: Wikimedia. **Located at**: https://commons.wikimedia.org/wiki/File:Jinwen-Shisongding.jpg. **License**: *CC BY: Attribution*
- 472px-Western_Zhou_Gui_Vessel.jpg. **Provided by**: Wikimedia. **Located at**: https://commons.wikimedia.org/wiki/File:Western_Zhou_Gui_Vessel.jpg. **License**: *CC BY: Attribution*
- 640px-Mawangdui_lacquerwares_and_tray.jpg. **Provided by**: Wikimedia. **Located at**: https://commons.wikimedia.org/wiki/File:Mawangdui_lacquerwares_and_tray.jpg. **License**: *CC BY: Attribution*
- 349px-Changshadragon.jpg. **Provided by**: Wikimedia. **Located at**: https://commons.wikimedia.org/wiki/File:Changshadragon.jpg. **License**: *CC BY: Attribution*
- 522px-EN-WarringStatesAll260BCE.jpg. **Provided by**: Wikimedia. **Located at**: https://commons.wikimedia.org/wiki/File:EN-WarringStatesAll260BCE.jpg. **License**: *CC BY: Attribution*
- File:Qinghuajian, Suan Biao.jpg. **Provided by**: Wikimedia. **Located at**: https://commons.wikimedia.org/wiki/File:Qinghuajian,_Suan_Biao.jpg. **License**: *CC BY: Attribution*
- 640px-Warring_States_Iron_Sword.jpg. **Provided by**: Wikimedia. **Located at**: https://commons.wikimedia.org/wiki/File:Warring_States_Iron_Sword.jpg. **License**: *CC BY: Attribution*
- Warring States Period. **Provided by**: Wikipedia. **Located at**: https://en.wikipedia.org/wiki/Warring_States_period#Culture_and_society. **License**: *CC BY: Attribution*
- Ancient Chinese Civilization. **Provided by**: Wikibooks. **Located at**: http://en.wikibooks.org/wiki/World_History/Ancient_Civilizations%23Ancient_Chinese_Civilization. **License**: *CC BY-SA: Attribution-ShareAlike*
- The First Chinese Dynasties. **Provided by**: Wikibooks. **Located at**: http://en.wikibooks.org/wiki/World_History/The_First_Chinese_Dynasties. **License**: *CC BY-SA: Attribution-ShareAlike*
- Jack E. Maxfield, A Comprehensive Outline of World History (Organized by Region). November 23, 2009. **Provided by**: OpenStax CNX. **Located at**: http://cnx.org/contents/45ac7e52-e029-4436-895a-92b9e507b372@2.1. **License**: *CC BY: Attribution*
- HIST101: Ancient Civilizations of the World. **Provided by**: Saylor. **Located at**: https://legacy.saylor.org/hist101/Intro/. **License**: *CC BY: Attribution*
- HIST241: Pre-Modern Northeast Asia. **Provided by**: Saylor. **Located at**: https://legacy.saylor.org/hist241/Intro/. **License**: *CC BY: Attribution*
- Crossbow. **Provided by**: Wiktionary. **Located at**: http://en.wiktionary.org/wiki/crossbow. **License**: *CC BY-SA: Attribution-ShareAlike*
- Tian. **Provided by**: Wikipedia. **Located at**: http://en.wikipedia.org/wiki/Tian. **License**: *Public Domain: No Known Copyright*
- Zhou_dynasty_1000_BC.png. **Provided by**: Wikipedia. **Located at**: https://en.wikipedia.org/wiki/Zhou_dynasty#/media/File:Zhou_dynasty_1000_BC.png. **License**: *CC BY: Attribution*
- Zhou Gong. **Provided by**: Wikipedia. **Located at**: http://en.wikipedia.org/wiki/File:Zhou_gong.jpg. **License**: *Public Domain: No Known Copyright*
- 247px-JinwenShisongding.jpg. **Provided by**: Wikimedia. **Located at**: https://commons.wikimedia.org/wiki/File:Jinwen-Shisongding.jpg. **License**: *CC BY: Attribution*
- 472px-Western_Zhou_Gui_Vessel.jpg. **Provided by**: Wikimedia. **Located at**: https://commons.wikimedia.org/wiki/File:Western_Zhou_Gui_Vessel.jpg. **License**: *CC BY: Attribution*
- 640px-Mawangdui_lacquerwares_and_tray.jpg. **Provided by**: Wikimedia. **Located at**: https://commons.wikimedia.org/wiki/File:Mawangdui_lacquerwares_and_tray.jpg. **License**: *CC BY: Attribution*
- 349px-Changshadragon.jpg. **Provided by**: Wikimedia. **Located at**: https://commons.wikimedia.org/wiki/File:Changshadragon.jpg.

License: *CC BY: Attribution*

- **522px-EN-WarringStatesAll260BCE.jpg. Provided by**: Wikimedia. **Located at**: https://commons.wikimedia.org/wiki/File:EN-WarringStatesAll260BCE.jpg. **License**: *CC BY: Attribution*

- **File:Qinghuajian, Suan Biao.jpg. Provided by**: Wikimedia. **Located at**: https://commons.wikimedia.org/wiki/File:Qinghuajian,_Suan_Biao.jpg. **License**: *CC BY: Attribution*

- **640px-Warring_States_Iron_Sword.jpg. Provided by**: Wikimedia. **Located at**: https://commons.wikimedia.org/wiki/File:Warring_States_Iron_Sword.jpg. **License**: *CC BY: Attribution*

- **History of Taoism. Provided by**: Wikipedia. **Located at**: https://en.wikipedia.org/wiki/History_of_Taoism. **License**: *CC BY: Attribution*

- **Taoism and Confucianism - Ancient Philosophies. Provided by**: UShistory.org. **Located at**: http://www.ushistory.org/civ/9e.asp. **License**: *CC BY: Attribution*

- **Confucianism. Provided by**: Wikipedia. **Located at**: https://en.wikipedia.org/wiki/Confucianism. **License**: *CC BY: Attribution*

- **Mohism. Provided by**: Wikipedia. **Located at**: https://en.wikipedia.org/wiki/Mohism. **License**: *CC BY: Attribution*

- **Legalism (Chinese Philosophy). Provided by**: Wikipedia. **Located at**: https://en.wikipedia.org/wiki/Legalism_(Chinese_philosophy). **License**: *CC BY: Attribution*

- **Mozi. Provided by**: Wikipedia. **Located at**: https://en.wikipedia.org/wiki/Mozi. **License**: *CC BY: Attribution*

- **Tian. Provided by**: Wikipedia. **Located at**: http://en.wikipedia.org/wiki/Tian. **License**: *Public Domain: No Known Copyright*

- **Zhou_dynasty_1000_BC.png. Provided by**: Wikipedia. **Located at**: https://en.wikipedia.org/wiki/Zhou_dynasty#/media/File:Zhou_dynasty_1000_BC.png. **License**: *CC BY: Attribution*

- **Zhou Gong. Provided by**: Wikipedia. **Located at**: http://en.wikipedia.org/wiki/File:Zhou_gong.jpg. **License**: *Public Domain: No Known Copyright*

- **247px-JinwenShisongding.jpg. Provided by**: Wikimedia. **Located at**: https://commons.wikimedia.org/wiki/File:JinwenShisongding.jpg. **License**: *CC BY: Attribution*

- **472px-Western_Zhou_Gui_Vessel.jpg. Provided by**: Wikimedia. **Located at**: https://commons.wikimedia.org/wiki/File:Western_Zhou_Gui_Vessel.jpg. **License**: *CC BY: Attribution*

- **640px-Mawangdui_lacquerwares_and_tray.jpg. Provided by**: Wikimedia. **Located at**: https://commons.wikimedia.org/wiki/File:Mawangdui_lacquerwares_and_tray.jpg. **License**: *CC BY: Attribution*

- **349px-Changshadragon.jpg. Provided by**: Wikimedia. **Located at**: https://commons.wikimedia.org/wiki/File:Changshadragon.jpg. **License**: *CC BY: Attribution*

- **522px-EN-WarringStatesAll260BCE.jpg. Provided by**: Wikimedia. **Located at**: https://commons.wikimedia.org/wiki/File:EN-WarringStatesAll260BCE.jpg. **License**: *CC BY: Attribution*

- **File:Qinghuajian, Suan Biao.jpg. Provided by**: Wikimedia. **Located at**: https://commons.wikimedia.org/wiki/File:Qinghuajian,_Suan_Biao.jpg. **License**: *CC BY: Attribution*

- **640px-Warring_States_Iron_Sword.jpg. Provided by**: Wikimedia. **Located at**: https://commons.wikimedia.org/wiki/File:Warring_States_Iron_Sword.jpg. **License**: *CC BY: Attribution*

- **DaodeTianzun.jpg. Provided by**: Wikimedia. **Located at**: https://commons.wikimedia.org/wiki/File:DaodeTianzun.jpg. **License**: *CC BY: Attribution*

- **Mozi_drawing.jpg. Provided by**: Wikimedia. **Located at**: https://commons.wikimedia.org/wiki/File:Mozi_drawing.jpg. **License**: *CC BY: Attribution*

- **628px-Rongo_Analects_02.jpg. Provided by**: Wikimedia. **Located at**: https://commons.wikimedia.org/wiki/File:Rongo_Analects_02.jpg. **License**: *CC BY: Attribution*

- **323px-Shangyang.jpg. Provided by**: Wikimedia. **Located at**: https://commons.wikimedia.org/wiki/File:Shangyang.jpg. **License**: *CC BY: Attribution*

The Qin Dynasty

The Qin Dynasty

The Qin Dynasty saw rich cultural and technological innovation, but brutal rule, and gave way to the Han Dynasty after only 15 years.

Learning Objectives

Support the argument that the Qin Dynasty, though short-lived, was one of the most important periods of China's Classical Age

Key Takeaways

Key Points

- The leader of the victorious Qin state established the Qin Dynasty and recast himself as Shi Huangdi, the First Emperor of China.
- The Qin Dynasty was one of the shortest in all of Chinese history, lasting only about 15 years, but was also one of the most important. It was marked by a strong sense of unification and crucial technological and cultural innovation.
- Shi Huangdi standardized writing throughout the empire, built expansive infrastructure, such as highways and canals, standardized currency and measurement, conducted a census, and established a postal system.
- Legalism was the official philosophy, and other philosophies, such as Confucianism, were suppressed. Shi Huangdi also built the Great Wall of China, roughly 1,500 miles long and guarded by a massive army, to protect the nation against northern invaders.
- The Qin Dynasty collapsed after only 15 years. There was a brief period of chaos until the Han Dynasty was established.

> **Key Terms**
>
> - **Mandate of Heaven**: The belief, dating from ancient China, that heaven gives a ruler the right to rule fairly.
> - **Legalism**: A Chinese philosophy claiming that a strong state is necessary to curtail human self-interest.
> - **Great Wall of China**: An ancient Chinese fortification, almost 4,000 miles long, originally designed to protect China from the Mongols. Construction began during the Qin Dynasty, under Shi Huangdi.

When the Qin state emerged victorious from the Warring States period in 221 BCE, the state's leader, King Zheng, claimed the Mandate of Heaven and established the Qin Dynasty. He renamed himself Shi Huangdi (First Emperor), a far grander title than King, establishing the way in which China would be ruled for the next two millennia. Today he is known as Qin Shi Huang, meaning First Qin Emperor. He relied on brutal techniques and Legalist doctrine to consolidate and expand his power. The nobility were stripped of control and authority so that the independent and disloyal nobility that had plagued the Zhou would not pose a problem.

The Qin Dynasty was one of the shortest in all of Chinese history, lasting only about 15 years, but it was also one of the most important. With Qin Shi Huang's standardization of society and unification of the states, for the first time in centuries, into the first Chinese empire, he enabled the Chinese to think of themselves as members of a single kingdom. This laid the foundation for the consolidation of the Chinese territories that we know today, and resulted in a very bureaucratic state with a large economy, capable of supporting an expanded military.

Innovations of Emperor Shi Huangdi

The First Emperor divided China into provinces, with civil and military officials in a hierarchy of ranks. He built the Lingqu Canal, which joined the Yangtze River basin to the Canton area via the Li River. This canal helped send half a million Chinese troops to conquer the lands to the south.

Qin Shi Huang standardized writing, a crucial factor in the overcoming of cultural barriers between provinces, and unifying the empire. He also standardized systems of currency, weights, and measures, and conducted a census of his people. He established elaborate postal and irrigation systems, and built great highways.

In contrast, in line with his attempt to impose Legalism, Qin Shi Huang strongly discouraged philosophy (particularly Confucianism) and history—he buried 460 Confucian scholars alive and burned many of their philosophical texts, as well as many historical texts that were not about the Qin state. This burning of books and execution of philosophers marked the end of the Hundred Schools of Thought. The philosophy of Mohism in particular was completely wiped out.

Finally, Qin Shi Huang began the building of the Great Wall of China, one of the greatest construction feats of all time, to protect the nation against barbarians. Seven hundred thousand forced laborers were used in building the wall, and thousands of them were crushed beneath the massive gray rocks. The wall was roughly 1,500 miles long, and wide enough for six horses to gallop abreast along the top. The nation's first standing army, possibly consisting of millions, guarded the wall from northern invaders.

The Great Wall of China: *Sections of the Great Wall of China, from the part known as Jinshanling.*

The Terracotta Army: *A close-up of two soldiers in the terracotta army. Note how their faces differ from each other—each soldier was constructed to be unique.*

The Terracotta Army

Another of Qin Shi Huang's most impressive building projects was the preparation he made for his own death. He had a massive tomb created for him on Mount Li, near modern-day Xi'an, and was buried there when he died. The tomb was filled with thousands and thousands of life-sized (or larger) terracotta soldiers meant to guard the emperor in his afterlife. This terracotta army was rediscovered in the twentieth century. Each soldier was carved with a different face, and those that were armed had real weapons.

Collapse of the Qin Dynasty

Qin Shi Huang was paranoid about his death, and because of this he was able to survive numerous assassination attempts. He became increasingly obsessed with immortality and employed many alchemists and sorcerers. Ironically, he ultimately died by poisoning in 210 BCE, when he drank an "immortality potion."

The First Emperor's brutal techniques and tyranny produced resistance among the people, especially the conscripted peasants and farmers whose labors built the empire. Upon the First Emperor's death, China plunged into civil war, exacerbated by floods and droughts. In 207 BCE, Qin Shi Huang's son was killed, and the dynasty collapsed entirely. Chaos reigned until 202 BCE, when Gaozu, a petty official, became a general and reunited China under the Han Dynasty.

Attributions

CC licensed content, Specific attribution

- HIST101: Ancient Civilizations of the World. **Provided by**: Saylor. **Located at**: https://legacy.saylor.org/hist101/Intro/. **License**: *CC BY: Attribution*
- HIST241: Pre-Modern Northeast Asia. **Provided by**: Saylor. **Located at**: https://legacy.saylor.org/hist241/Intro/. **License**: *CC BY: Attribution*
- Jack E. Maxfield, A Comprehensive Outline of World History (Organized by Region). November 23, 2009. **Provided by**: OpenStax CNX. **Located at**: http://cnx.org/contents/45ac7e52-e029-4436-895a-92b9e507b372@2.1. **License**: *CC BY: Attribution*
- Great Wall of China. **Provided by**: Wiktionary. **Located at**: http://en.wiktionary.org/wiki/Great_Wall_of_China. **License**: *CC BY-SA: Attribution-ShareAlike*
- The Unification of China. **Provided by**: Wikibooks. **Located at**: http://en.wikibooks.org/wiki/World_History/The_Unification_of_China. **License**: *CC BY-SA: Attribution-ShareAlike*
- The Great Wall of China at Jinshanling. **Provided by**: Wikimedia. **Located at**: https://commons.wikimedia.org/wiki/File:The_Great_Wall_of_China_at_Jinshanling.jpg. **License**: *CC BY-SA: Attribution-ShareAlike*
- Terracotta PMorgan. **Provided by**: Wikimedia. **Located at**: https://commons.wikimedia.org/wiki/File:Terracotta_pmorgan.jpg. **License**: *CC BY: Attribution*

The Han Dynasty

The Rise of the Han Dynasty

The strong but benevolent Han Dynasty began a golden age of reform and expansion. The first period, called the Western Han, lasted until 9 CE.

Learning Objectives

Compare the Han Dynasty with the earlier Qin Dynasty, and explain the Western Han period

Key Takeaways

Key Points

- The Han Dynasty put an end to civil war and reunified China in 202 BCE, ushering in a golden age of peace and prosperity during which progress and cultural development took place.
- The Western Han period continued a lot of the Qin's policies, but modified them with Confucian ideals. Because of this, the Han lasted far longer than the harsher Qin Dynasty—
the Western Han period in particular lasted until 9 CE, when there was a brief rebellion.
- One of the most exalted Han emperors was Emperor Wu. He made Confucianism the official philosophy, encouraged reciprocity between the state and its people, reformed the economy and agriculture, made contact with India, defended China from the Huns, and doubled the size of the empire.
- Rebellions and external threats posed challenges to the Western Han, but it was able to survive.

Key Terms

- **four occupations**: A hierarchy in which aristocratic scholars had the highest social status, followed by farmers, then craftsmen and artisans, and finally merchants.
- **golden age**: A happy age of peace and prosperity; a time of great progress or achievement.
- **patrilineal**: Descent through the male line in a family.
- **xian**: Mythical afterlife paradise during the Han Dynasty.
- **socialism**: A political philosophy based on principles of community decision making, social equality, and the avoidance of economic and social exclusion, with preference to community goals over individual ones.
- **laissez-faire**: A policy of governmental non-interference in economic affairs.
- **Chu-Han Contention**: A four-year (206-202 BCE) civil war between the Chu and Han states.

Formation of the Han Dynasty

By the time the Qin Dynasty collapsed in 207 BCE, eighteen separate kingdoms had declared their independence. The Han and Chu states emerged as the most powerful, but the Han state was the victor of the Chu-Han Contention, a four-year civil war. Gaozu, who had been born a peasant, founded the Han Dynasty in 202 BCE, reunifying China.

Emperor Gaozu of the Han Dynasty: *Emperor Gaozu, formerly known as Liu Bang, founded the Han Dynasty.*

The Han Dynasty would become one of the most important and long-lasting dynasties in all of Chinese history. It would rule China for over four hundred years, from 206 BCE-220 CE, and ushered in a golden age of peace, prosperity, and development. Today, both the majority ethnic group in China and Chinese script are called Han.

Comparison of Han to Qin

In many ways, the Han carried on policies that began in the Qin. Provincial rule occurred in both, and the Han continued Legalist rule, although in much less stricter fashion. Confucianism was banned during the Qin, but resurrected during the Han. The Qin, with its focus on the power of the state, was not shaped by religion in the same way the Han was. The Han were considered with the afterlife, and worshipped their ancestors. Both had defined social classes, but in the Han, peasants were treated with greater respect and classes were based on occupations.

The Western Han Period and Political Reform

At first the Han Dynasty established its capital at Chang'an, in western China. This Western Han period would last from 206 BCE to 9 CE, when the dynasty's rule would be briefly interrupted by rebellion and the short-lived Xin Dynasty.

Throughout the Western Han period, the Han largely continued the governing policies of the Qin, continuing to expand the bureaucracy and encouraging a centralized state. There were, however, differences between the two dynasties, and it was perhaps these differences that allowed the Han to rule for so much longer than the Qin. The Han were more interested in the lives and well-being of their subjects, and they modified some of the harsher aspects of the earlier dynasty's rule with Confucian ideals of government. Freedom of speech and writing was restored, and the more laissez-faire style of governing allowed harmony, prosperity, and population growth.

This period also saw the further development of the four-class hierarchy, called the "four occupations," which gave aristocratic scholars the highest social status, followed by farmers, then craftsmen and artisans, and finally merchants.

The family during this time was patrilineal and featured a small number of nuclear family members. Arranged, monogamous marriages were the norm for most. Sons received equal shares of family property and were often sent away when married.

Ritual sacrifices of animals and food were made to deities, spirits, and ancestors at temples and shrines. Each person was seen as having a two-part soul. The spirit-soul, which went to the afterlife paradise of immortals, called xian, and the body-soul, which remained in its earthly tomb.

Other innovations included the first use of negative numbers in mathematics, the recording of stars and comets, the armillary sphere, which represented star movements in three dimensions, the waterwheel, and other engineering feats.

Emperor Wu

One of the most exalted Han emperors was Emperor Wu, who ruled from 141-87 BCE. He was responsible for a great number of innovations and political and military feats.

Emperor Wu of the Han Dynasty: *A portrait of Emperor Wu, one of the most influential rulers of the Han Dynasty.*

Emperor Wu experimented with socialism, and made Confucianism the single official philosophy. The Confucian classics were reassembled and transcribed. The Confucian ideal of each person accepting his social position helped legitimize the state and made people more willing to accept its power. At the same time, these ideals encouraged the state to act justly toward its people. There was reciprocity too in the fact that the state was funded partly by land taxes (a portion of the harvest); this meant that the prosperity of the agricultural estates determined the prosperity of the Han government.

Emperor Wu also founded great government industries and transportation and delivery services, developed governmental control of profit, and imposed a 5% income tax. He created civil-service examinations to test potential government officials on their knowledge of the Confucian classics, so that bureaucrats would be chosen for their intelligence instead of their social connections. Emperor Wu also reformed the Chinese economy and nationalized the salt and iron industries, and he initiated reforms that made farming more efficient.

Through Emperor Wu's southern and western conquests, the Han Dynasty made contact with the Indian cultural sphere. Emperor Wu repelled the invading barbarians (the Xiongnu, or Huns, a nomadic-pastoralist warrior people from the Eurasian steppe), and roughly doubled the size of the empire, claiming lands that included Korea, Manchuria, and even part of Turkistan. As China pushed its borders further, trade contacts were established with lands to the west, most notably via the Silk Road.

Challenges During the Western Han Period

Nonetheless, the Han faced many challenges. Emperor Gaozu rewarded his supporters with grants of land, which started again the same problems that had brought down the Zhou Dynasty. Several rebellions broke out, the most serious of which was the Rebellion of the Seven States. Nonetheless, the Han emperors stamped out the rebellions and gradually reduced the power of the small kingdoms (though never abolished them completely).

Another major danger to the Han was the external threat of the barbarians, the most dangerous of whom were the Huns. However, the Han Dynasty was able to face these internal and external threats and survive because of the strong centralized state they had established.

The Silk Road

The Silk Road was established by China's Han Dynasty, and led to cultural integration across a vast area of Asia. It persisted until the fall of the Mongolian Empire in 1360 CE.

Learning Objectives

Describe the importance of the Silk Road

Key Takeaways

Key Points

- The Silk Road was established by China's Han Dynasty (206 BCE-220 CE) through territorial expansion.
- The Silk Road was a series of trade and cultural transmission routes that were central to cultural interaction between the West and East.
- A great deal of protection and stability was provided on the Silk Road by the Han.
- A second *Pax Sinica* in 737 CE helped the Silk Road reach its golden age of cultural integration.
- The Mongol Empire, and *Pax Mongolica*, strengthened and re-established the Silk Road between 1207 and 1360 CE. However, as the Mongol Empire disintegrated, so did the Silk Road.

> *Key Terms*
>
> - **nomadic-pastoralist**: A lifestyle in which livestock are herded to find fresh grazing pastures in an irregular pattern of movement.
> - **Pax Sinica**: Latin term for "Chinese peace" maintained by Chinese hegemony.
> - **Tang Dynasty**: An imperial dynasty of China, from 618-907 CE.
> - **Pax Mongolica**: Latin term for "Mongolian peace" during their Empire.

Establishment of the Silk Road

Through southern and western conquests, the Han Dynasty of China (206 BCE-220 CE) made contact with the Indian cultural sphere.

Emperor Wu repelled the invading barbarians (the Xiongnu, or Huns, a nomadic-pastoralist warrior people from the Eurasian steppe) and roughly doubled the size of the empire, claiming lands that included Korea, Manchuria, and even part of Turkistan. As China pushed its borders further, trade contacts were established with lands to the west, most notably via the Silk Road.

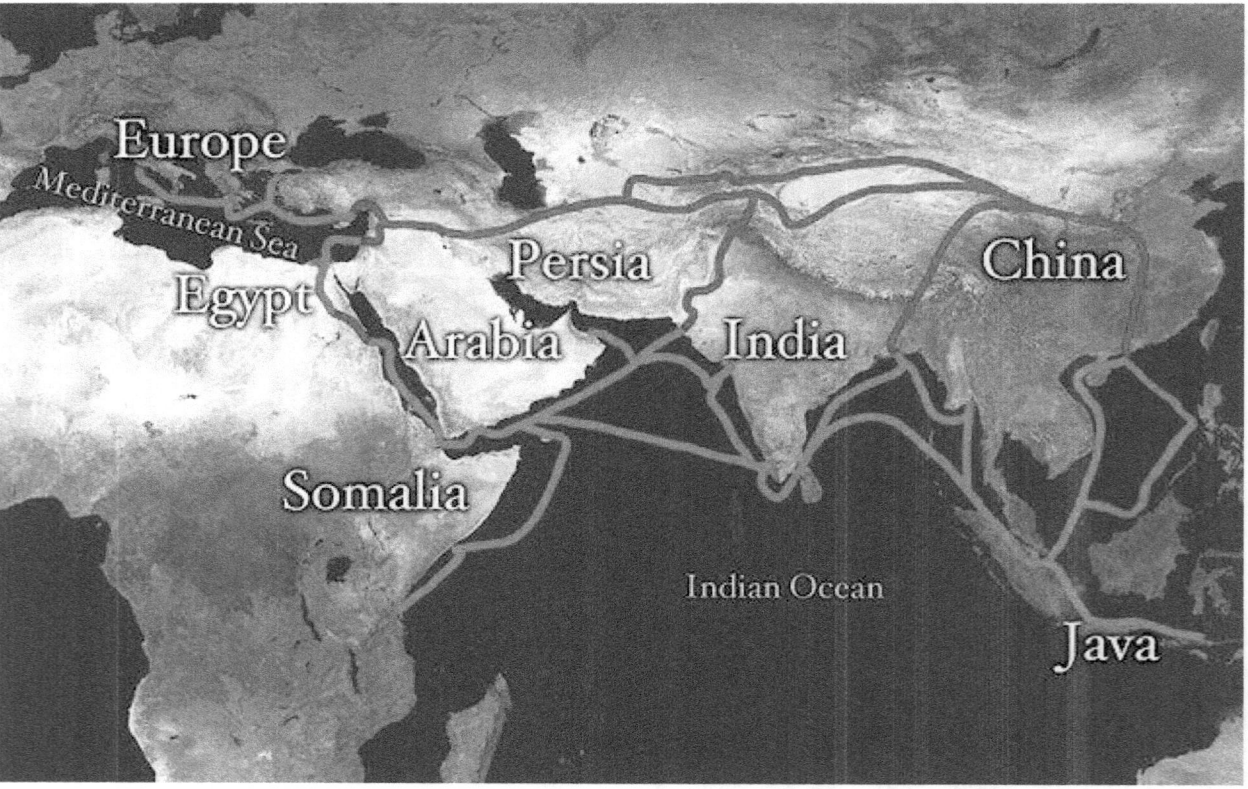

Map of Silk Road: *In this map of the Silk Road, red shows the land route and blue shows the maritime route.*

The Silk Road was a series of trade and cultural transmission routes that were central to cultural interaction between the West and East. Silk was certainly the major trade item from China, but many other goods were traded as well. These routes enabled strong trade relationships to develop with Persia, India, and the Roman Empire.

Example of Woven Silk Textile: *This woven silk textile from the Western Han era was found at Tomb No. 1 at Mawangdui, Changsha, Hunan Province.*

Chinese Control of the Silk Road

This expanded western territory became particularly important because of the silk routes. By this century, the Chinese had become very active in the silk trade, though until the Hans provided sufficient protection, the Silk Road had not functioned well because of nomad pirates. Expansion by the Han took place around 114 BCE, led mainly by imperial envoy Zhang Qian. The Great Wall of China was expanded to provide extra protection.

The Tang Dynasty reopened the route in 639 CE, but then lost it to the Tibetans in 678 CE. Control of the Silk Road would shuttle between China and Tibet until 737 CE. This second *Pax Sinica* helped the Silk Road reach its golden age. China was open to foreign cultures, and its urban areas could be quite cosmopolitan. The Silk Road helped to integrate cultures, but also exposed tribal and pastoral societies to new developments, sometimes causing them to become skilled warriors.

The Mongolian Empire and the Disintegration of the Silk Road

The Mongol Empire, and *Pax Mongolica*, strengthened and re-established the Silk Road between 1207 and 1360 CE. However, as the Mongol Empire disintegrated, so did the Silk Road. Gunpowder hastened the failing integration, and the Silk Road stopped being a shipping route for silk around 1453 CE. A lasting effect of this was to inspire Europeans to find alternate routes to Asia for trade, including Christopher Columbus ' famous overseas voyage in 1492.

The Eastern Han Period

The Eastern Han period was a time of reunification and prosperity that also saw the perfection of paper and porcelain.

Learning Objectives

Describe the Eastern Han period

Key Takeaways

Key Points

- The 400-year Han Dynasty was briefly interrupted by the rebellious Xin Dynasty. The first part of the Han Dynasty is known as the Western Han period; the Eastern Han period began when the Han overthrew the rebellion and reestablished the dynasty in 25 CE.
- Emperor Guangwu, the first emperor of the Eastern Han period, regained lost land and pacified the people.
- The Rule of Ming and Zhang was an era of prosperity; taxes were reduced, Confucian ideals were encouraged, the government was capable and strong, and the processes of creating paper and porcelain were perfected.
- A series of rebellions led to powerful generals who attempted to control the young emperor. Eventually, three states gained control and the Han Dynasty was ended.

Key Terms

- **Chimei**: A rebel army that ended the Xin dynasty after unrest.
- **regent**: A relative in a royal family who looks after the throne for an underaged king until he is mature enough to receive power.
- **porcelain**: A Chinese innovation perfected during the Eastern Han Period; durable, high-quality, and attractive ceramic ware.

Interruption by the Xin Dynasty

When the Western Han period ended in 9 CE, the regent to the prior emperor, Wang Mang, proclaimed his own new dynasty, the Xin Dynasty. He attempted a number of radical reforms, such as new forms of currency, a ban on slavery, and a return to old models of land distribution. A series of major floods on the Yellow River, however, displaced thousands of peasants, and caused massive unrest. A rebel army called the Chimei ("Red Eyebrows") developed out of the peasantry, and they defeated Wang Mang's armies and stormed the capital of Chang'an. They killed Wang Mang and put their own puppet ruler on the throne.

The Eastern Han Period

A new Han emperor, Emperor Guangwu, took control and ruled from Luoyang, in eastern China; thus began the Eastern Han period, which lasted from 25-220 CE. He defeated the Chimei rebels, as well as rival warlords, to reunify China again under the Han Dynasty.

Under Emperor Guangwu, the empire was strengthened considerably. Areas that had fallen away from Chinese control, such as Korea and Vietnam, were reconquered. The Hun Confederation, which had grown strong during China's period of instability, was pacified.

Emperor Guangwu: *Emperor Guangwu ruled during the Eastern Han Dynasty.*

Emperor Guangwu was succeeded by Emperor Ming, followed by Emperor Zhang. The Rule of Ming and Zhang, as it is called, is remembered for being an era of prosperity. Taxes were reduced, Confucian ideals were encouraged, and the emperors appointed able administrators. It was also in this period that paper, one of China's most important inventions, emerged. Though early forms of paper had existed for centuries, the process was now perfected. With paper, Chinese texts could circulate on a durable and relatively inexpensive medium, instead of on clay, silk, or bamboo. This allowed Chinese texts to become more readily available and encouraged learning. Another important innovation of this time was porcelain. Porcelain existed in previous forms for centuries, but was perfected in the Eastern Han period. The improvement of porcelain allowed for durable, high-quality, and attractive ceramic ware.

Ceramic Candle Holder from the Eastern Han Dynasty: *A ceramic candle holder from the Eastern Han Dynasty, with prancing animal figures.*

The Fall of the Eastern Han

A series of rebellions, including the Yellow Turban and Five Pecks of Rice, began in 184 CE. Military generals appointed during these crises kept their militia forces intact even after defeating the rebels. General-in-Chief He Jin plotted to overthrow palace eunuchs. He was discovered and killed, however, in the end 2,000 eunuchs were also killed. A series of generals attempted to control the young emperor, culminating in three spheres of influence. Cao Cao ruled the north, Sun Quan ruled the south, and Liu Bei controlled the west. After Cao Cao's death, his son Cao Pi forced Emperor Xian to give up his throne to him. This ended the Han Dynasty, and started a period of conflict between these three states, called Cao Wei, Eastern Wu and Shu Han.

Invention of Paper

Paper was invented by Cai Lun during the Han Dynasty of ancient China. It was used for a variety of purposes, including wrapping and writing, and eventually spread throughout the world.

Learning Objectives

Analyze the importance of paper and its invention

Key Takeaways

Key Points

- Cai Lun (202 BCE-220 CE), a Chinese official working in the Imperial court during the Han Dynasty, is attributed with the invention of paper.
- A basic process is still followed today that consists of creating felted sheets of fiber suspended in water, then draining the water and allowing the fibers to dry in a thin matted sheet.
- Early paper was used for wrapping and writing, as well as for toilet paper, tea bags, and napkins.
- After the Battle of Talas in 751 CE, during which the Chinese were defeated, two Chinese prisoners are believed to have leaked the secrets to making paper.

Key Terms

- **papyrus**: A material prepared in ancient Egypt from the pithy stem of a water plant, used in sheets throughout the ancient Mediterranean world as a surface for writing or painting.
- **bast fibers**: Fibrous material from the phloem of a plant, used as fiber in matting, cord, etc.

While the word "paper" is derived from papyrus, the early Egyptian thick writing sheets, it is made quite differently. While papyrus is made from the dried pith of the papyrus plant that has been woven, paper has been disintegrated and reformed.

During the Shang (1600-1050 BCE) and Zhou (1050-250 BCE) dynasties, bone, bamboo, and sometimes silk were used as writing tablets. Cai Lun (202 BCE-220 CE), a Chinese official working in the Imperial court during the Han Dynasty, is attributed with the invention of paper. However, earlier examples have been found, and he may have simply improved upon a known process. Legend states that he was inspired by the nests of paper wasps.

Portrait of Cai Lun: *This portrait of Cai Lun depicts the invention of paper.*

Cai Lun's paper was made using mulberry and other bast fibers along with fishnets, old rags, and hemp waste. The bark of the Paper Mulberry and Sandalwood were often used and highly valued during the period. His basic process of creating felted sheets of fiber suspended in water, then draining the water and allowing the fibers to dry in a thin matted sheet is still followed today.

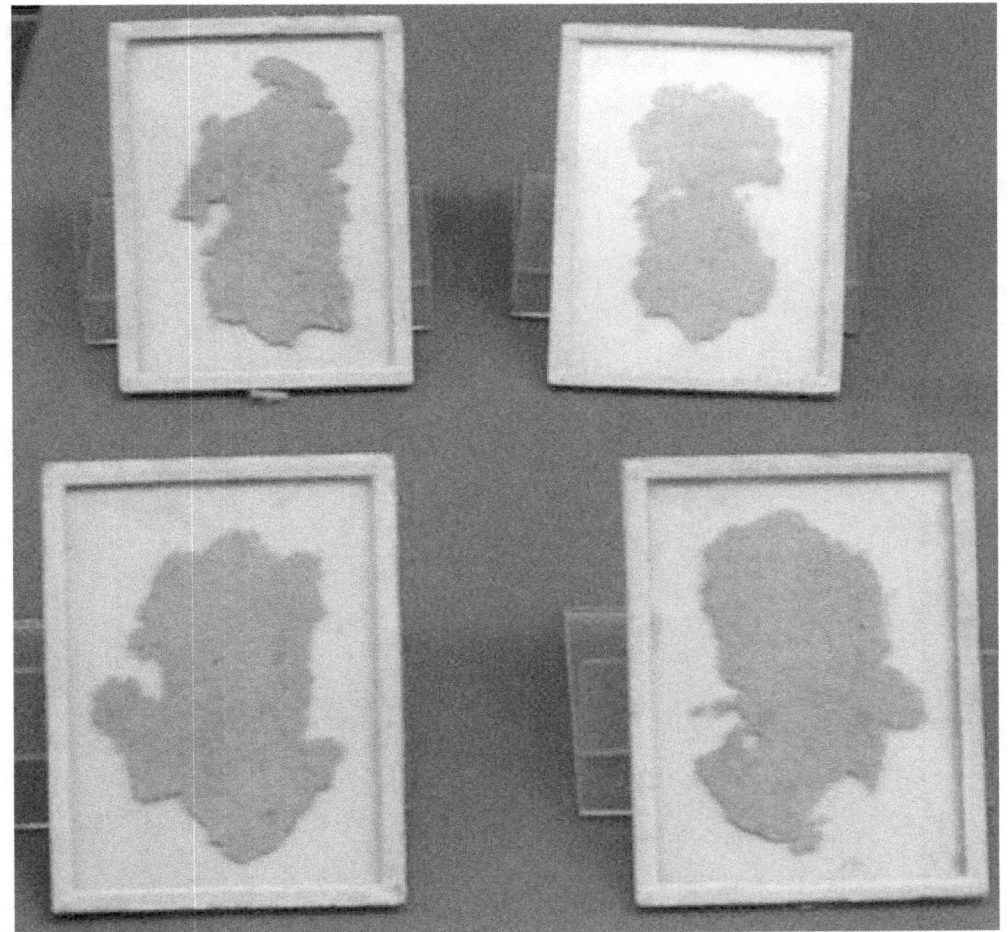

Chinese Hemp Wrapping Paper: *These examples of Chinese hemp wrapping paper date from 100 BCE.*

Uses of Paper

Paper was often used as a wrapping material. Paper used to wrap bronze mirrors has been dated to the reign of Emperor Wu in the 2nd century BCE. Paper was also used to wrap poisonous medicines. By the 3rd century CE, paper was commonly used for writing, and by 875 CE it was used as toilet paper. During the Tang dynasty (618-907 CE), paper was folded and sewn into tea bags, and used to make paper cups and napkins. During the Song dynasty (960-1279 CE), the world's first known paper money was produced, and often presented in special paper envelopes.

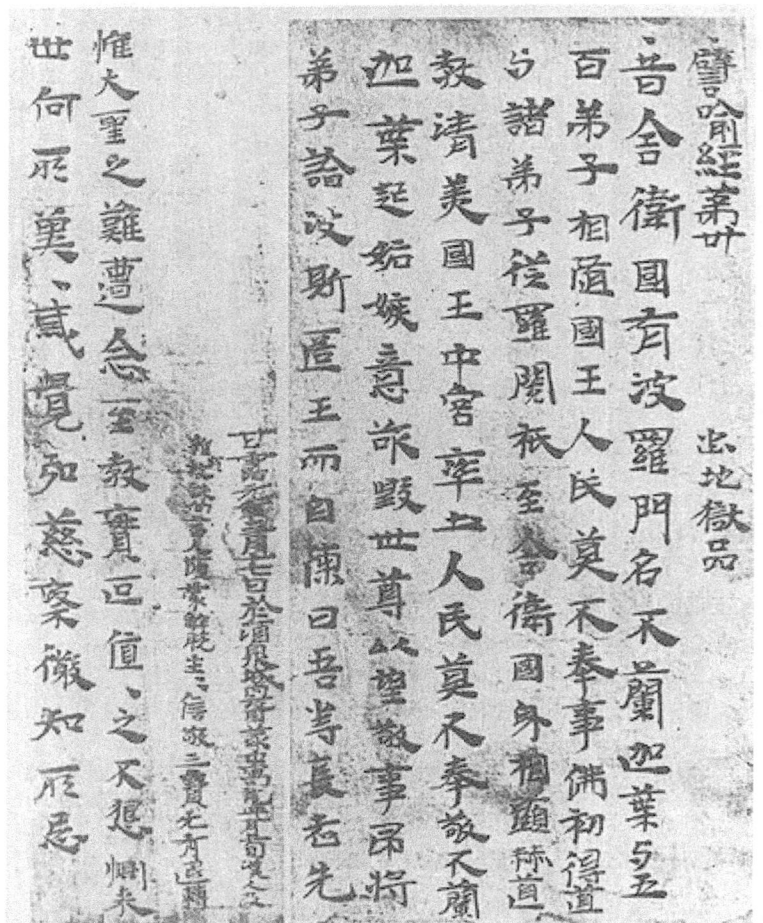

The Oldest Paper Book: This is the oldest paper book, dating to 256 CE.

Spread of Paper-making to the Islamic World

After the Battle of Talas in 751 CE, during which the Chinese were defeated, two Chinese prisoners are believed to have leaked the secrets to making paper. A paper mill was soon established, and many refinements were made to the process.

The Fall of the Han and the Three Kingdoms Period

As the Han Dynasty government weakened over time and ultimately collapsed, the empire fractured into the war-torn Three Kingdoms period.

Learning Objectives

Demonstrate the significance of the Battle of the Red Cliffs and the Three Kingdoms Period

> ## Key Takeaways
>
> ### Key Points
>
> - The Han government began to weaken and fracture by the end of the second century CE. General Dong Zhuo captured Emperor Shao and installed his own puppet ruler, Emperor Xian.
> - The warlord Cao Cao attempted to reunify China under the Han, but was defeated at the Battle of Red Cliffs.
> - The Han Dynasty ultimately collapsed in 220 CE, and China splintered into three warlord kingdoms in what is known as the Three Kingdoms period.
> - The Three Kingdoms period was war-torn, but also a time of great technological advancement.
>
> ### Key Terms
>
> - **hydraulic**: An engineering technique in which liquid is in motion and transmits energy.
> - **Battle of Red Cliffs**: A turning point in history that marked the last attempt to reunite the Han, and the beginning of a time of bloodshed for the Chinese.

After the death of Emperor Zhang (of the Eastern Han period's Rule of Ming and Zhang) in 88 CE, corrupt officials increasingly gained control of the state, while family feuds tore the dynasty apart. As the power of the emperor weakened, military commanders acted more independently and tried to secure power for themselves.

The Fall of the Han Dynasty

In 184 CE, two major Daoist rebellions—the Yellow Turban Rebellion and the Five Pecks of Rice Rebellion—broke out. In order to fight these rebellions Emperor Ling gave military commanders control over their own provinces, but this gave way to a long power struggle. In 189 CE, Emperor Ling died and was succeeded by his 13 year old son, Liu Bian, known as Emperor Shao. Empress Dowager He was regent, and her older brother, General-in-Chief He Jin, became the most powerful official in the court. He Jin wanted to exterminate the Ten Attendants, a group of influential eunuch officials. He summoned General Dong Zhuo to march on the city. The plot was discovered by the eunuchs, and He Jin was killed. In response the Emperor ordered indiscriminate killing of the eunuchs. The survivors kidnapped the Emperor and fled, only to later commit suicide upon General Dong Zhuo's arrival. The General would then replace Emperor Shao with the Prince of Cheniliu, known as Emperor Xian. Xian would be the last emperor of the Han Dynasty.

Portrait of Dong Zhuo: *This portrait of Dong Zhuo dates from a Qing Dynasty edition of the Romance of the Three Kingdoms.*

Dong Zhuo was eventually assassinated and was succeeded by another warlord, Cao Cao, who wanted to reunite the Han Empire by defeating the rebellious warlords. He nearly succeeded but was defeated in 208 CE at the Battle of Red Cliffs, a memorable turning point in history. With this defeat, most of the hope that the Han Empire would be reunited disappeared. When Cao Cao died in 220 CE, Emperor Xian abdicated the throne, claiming that he had failed to keep the Mandate of Heaven. China splintered into three kingdoms ruled by warlords; this marks the beginning of the Three Kingdoms period of Chinese history.

The Three Kingdoms Period

When the Han Dynasty collapsed in 220 CE, no one was powerful enough to reunify China under a single emperor. The result was the period of the Three Kingdoms, which lasted until 280 CE, when the Jin Dynasty took over. These three kingdoms, Wei, Shu, and Wu, battled for control in a long series of wars.

This was one of the bloodiest times in Chinese history—according to census data, the population decreased from 50 million to 16 million—but it also has long been romanticized in East Asian cultures and remembered as a time of chivalry and honor. It has been celebrated and popularized in operas, folk stories, and novels, and in more recent times, films, television, and video games.

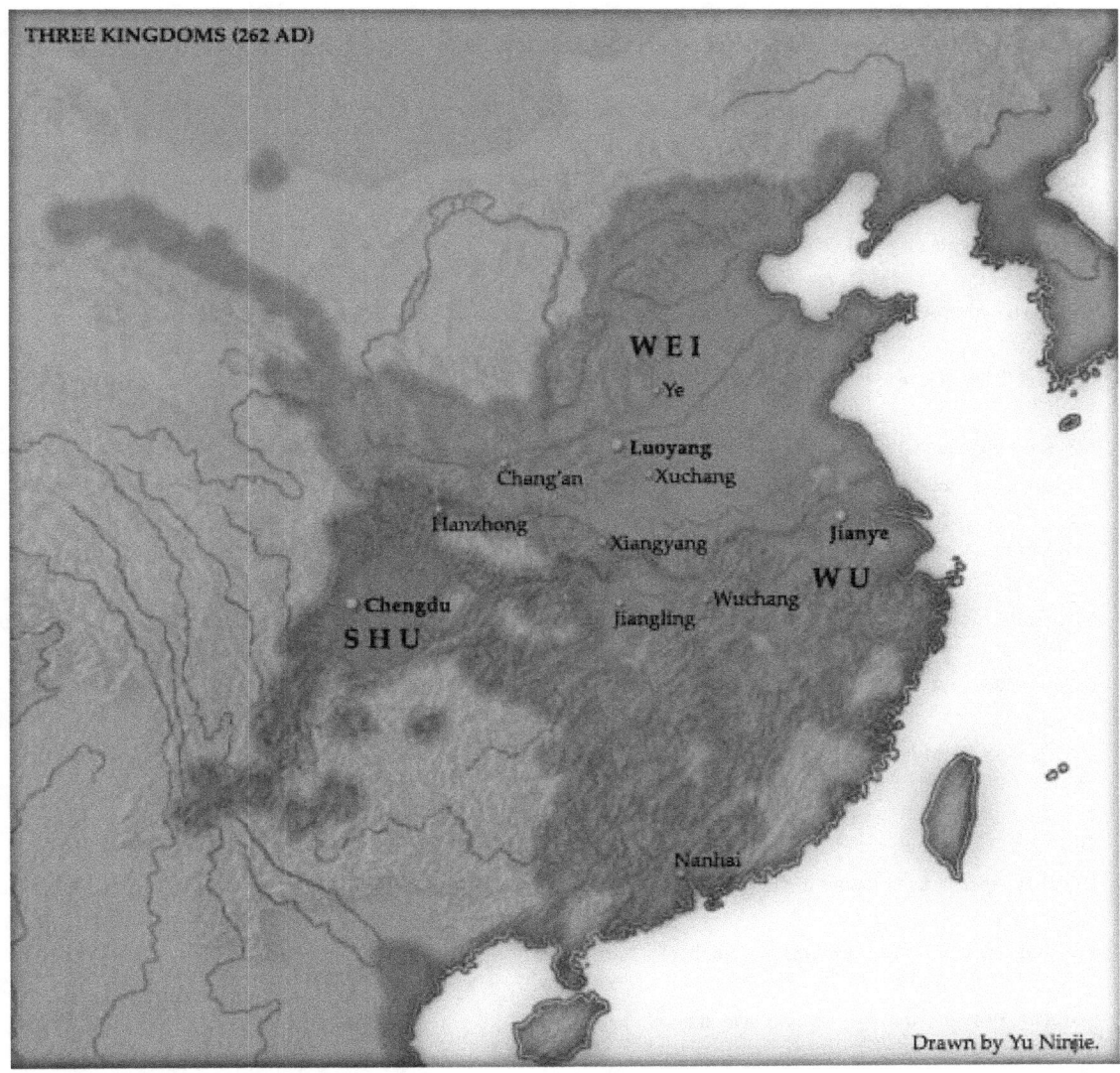

The Three Kingdoms: *The Three Kingdoms in 262 CE after the fall of the Han dynasty*

Technology advanced significantly during this period. Shu chancellor Zhuge Liang invented the wooden ox, suggested to be an early form of the wheelbarrow, and improved on the repeating crossbow. Wei mechanical engineer, Ma Jun, invented a hydraulic-powered, mechanical puppet theatre designed for his emperor. He also invented a new irrigation device, the south-pointing chariot, and a non-magnetic directional compass.

Attributions

CC licensed content, Specific attribution

- Han Dynasty. **Provided by**: Wikipedia. **Located at**: https://en.wikipedia.org/wiki/Han_dynasty. **License**: *CC BY: Attribution*
- HIST101: Ancient Civilizations of the World. **Provided by**: Saylor. **Located at**: https://legacy.saylor.org/hist101/Intro/. **License**: *CC BY: Attribution*

- Jack E. Maxfield, A Comprehensive Outline of World History (Organized by Region). November 23, 2009. **Provided by**: OpenStax CNX. **Located at**: http://cnx.org/contents/45ac7e52-e029-4436-895a-92b9e507b372@2.1. **License**: *CC BY: Attribution*
- Socialism. **Provided by**: Wiktionary. **Located at**: http://en.wiktionary.org/wiki/socialism. **License**: *CC BY-SA: Attribution-ShareAlike*
- Laissez-faire. **Provided by**: Wiktionary. **Located at**: http://en.wiktionary.org/wiki/laissez_faire%23English. **License**: *CC BY-SA: Attribution-ShareAlike*
- Golden age. **Provided by**: Wiktionary. **Located at**: http://en.wiktionary.org/wiki/golden_age. **License**: *CC BY-SA: Attribution-ShareAlike*
- The Unification of China. **Provided by**: Wikibooks. **Located at**: http://en.wikibooks.org/wiki/World_History/The_Unification_of_China. **License**: *CC BY-SA: Attribution-ShareAlike*
- laissez-faire. **Provided by**: Wikipedia. **Located at**: http://en.wikipedia.org/wiki/laissez-faire. **License**: *CC BY-SA: Attribution-ShareAlike*
- socialism. **Provided by**: Wiktionary. **Located at**: http://en.wiktionary.org/wiki/socialism. **License**: *CC BY-SA: Attribution-ShareAlike*
- Hangaozu.jpg. **Provided by**: Wikimedia. **Located at**: https://commons.wikimedia.org/wiki/File:Hangaozu.jpg. **License**: *CC BY: Attribution*
- 352px-u6f22u6b66u5e1d.jpg. **Provided by**: Wikimedia. **Located at**: https://commons.wikimedia.org/wiki/File:%E6%BC%A2%E6%AD%A6%E5%B8%9D.jpg. **License**: *CC BY: Attribution*
- Silk Road. **Provided by**: Wikipedia. **Located at**: https://en.wikipedia.org/wiki/Silk_Road. **License**: *CC BY: Attribution*
- Hangaozu.jpg. **Provided by**: Wikimedia. **Located at**: https://commons.wikimedia.org/wiki/File:Hangaozu.jpg. **License**: *CC BY: Attribution*
- 352px-u6f22u6b66u5e1d.jpg. **Provided by**: Wikimedia. **Located at**: https://commons.wikimedia.org/wiki/File:%E6%BC%A2%E6%AD%A6%E5%B8%9D.jpg. **License**: *CC BY: Attribution*
- 640px-Silk_route.jpg. **Provided by**: Wikimedia. **Located at**: https://commons.wikimedia.org/wiki/File:Silk_route.jpg. **License**: *CC BY: Attribution*
- 640px-Woven_silk_Western_Han_Dynasty.jpg. **Provided by**: Wikimedia. **Located at**: https://commons.wikimedia.org/wiki/File:Woven_silk,_Western_Han_Dynasty.jpg. **License**: *Public Domain: No Known Copyright*
- Han Dynasty. **Provided by**: Wikipedia. **Located at**: https://en.wikipedia.org/wiki/Han_dynasty#Eastern_Han. **License**: *CC BY: Attribution*
- Jack E. Maxfield, A Comprehensive Outline of World History (Organized by Region). November 23, 2009. **Provided by**: OpenStax CNX. **Located at**: http://cnx.org/contents/45ac7e52-e029-4436-895a-92b9e507b372@2.1. **License**: *CC BY: Attribution*
- HIST101: Ancient Civilizations of the World. **Provided by**: Saylor. **Located at**: https://legacy.saylor.org/hist101/Intro/. **License**: *CC BY: Attribution*
- The Unification of China. **Provided by**: Wikibooks. **Located at**: http://en.wikibooks.org/wiki/World_History/The_Unification_of_China. **License**: *CC BY-SA: Attribution-ShareAlike*
- porcelain. **Provided by**: Wiktionary. **Located at**: http://en.wiktionary.org/wiki/porcelain. **License**: *CC BY-SA: Attribution-ShareAlike*
- Hangaozu.jpg. **Provided by**: Wikimedia. **Located at**: https://commons.wikimedia.org/wiki/File:Hangaozu.jpg. **License**: *CC BY: Attribution*
- 352px-u6f22u6b66u5e1d.jpg. **Provided by**: Wikimedia. **Located at**: https://commons.wikimedia.org/wiki/File:%E6%BC%A2%E6%AD%A6%E5%B8%9D.jpg. **License**: *CC BY: Attribution*
- 640px-Silk_route.jpg. **Provided by**: Wikimedia. **Located at**: https://commons.wikimedia.org/wiki/File:Silk_route.jpg. **License**: *CC BY: Attribution*
- 640px-Woven_silk_Western_Han_Dynasty.jpg. **Provided by**: Wikimedia. **Located at**: https://commons.wikimedia.org/wiki/File:Woven_silk,_Western_Han_Dynasty.jpg. **License**: *Public Domain: No Known Copyright*
- 372px-Han_Guangwu_Di.jpg. **Provided by**: Wikimedia. **Located at**: https://commons.wikimedia.org/wiki/File:Han_Guangwu_Di.jpg. **License**: *Public Domain: No Known Copyright*
- Eastern Han pottery chandelier. **Provided by**: Wikimedia. **Located at**: https://commons.wikimedia.org/wiki/File:Eastern_Han_pottery_chandelier.JPG. **License**: *Public Domain: No Known Copyright*
- Cai Lun. **Provided by**: Wikipedia. **Located at**: https://en.wikipedia.org/wiki/Cai_Lun. **License**: *CC BY: Attribution*
- History of Paper. **Provided by**: Wikipedia. **Located at**: https://en.wikipedia.org/wiki/History_of_paper. **License**: *CC BY: Attribution*

THE HAN DYNASTY • 209

- Papermaking. **Provided by**: Wikipedia. **Located at**: https://en.wikipedia.org/wiki/Papermaking. **License**: *CC BY: Attribution*
- Hangaozu.jpg. **Provided by**: Wikimedia. **Located at**: https://commons.wikimedia.org/wiki/File:Hangaozu.jpg. **License**: *CC BY: Attribution*
- 352px-u6f22u6b66u5e1d.jpg. **Provided by**: Wikimedia. **Located at**: https://commons.wikimedia.org/wiki/File:%E6%BC%A2%E6%AD%A6%E5%B8%9D.jpg. **License**: *CC BY: Attribution*
- 640px-Silk_route.jpg. **Provided by**: Wikimedia. **Located at**: https://commons.wikimedia.org/wiki/File:Silk_route.jpg. **License**: *CC BY: Attribution*
- 640px-Woven_silk_Western_Han_Dynasty.jpg. **Provided by**: Wikimedia. **Located at**: https://commons.wikimedia.org/wiki/File:Woven_silk,_Western_Han_Dynasty.jpg. **License**: *Public Domain: No Known Copyright*
- 372px-Han_Guangwu_Di.jpg. **Provided by**: Wikimedia. **Located at**: https://commons.wikimedia.org/wiki/File:Han_Guangwu_Di.jpg. **License**: *Public Domain: No Known Copyright*
- Eastern Han pottery chandelier. **Provided by**: Wikimedia. **Located at**: https://commons.wikimedia.org/wiki/File:Eastern_Han_pottery_chandelier.JPG. **License**: *Public Domain: No Known Copyright*
- 494px-Chinese_hemp_paper_western_han.jpg. **Provided by**: Wikimedia. **Located at**: https://commons.wikimedia.org/wiki/File:Chinese_hemp_paper_western_han.jpg. **License**: *Public Domain: No Known Copyright*
- Cai-lun.jpg. **Provided by**: Wikimedia. **Located at**: https://commons.wikimedia.org/wiki/File:Cai-lun.jpg. **License**: *Public Domain: No Known Copyright*
- 374px-Paperbook256.jpg. **Provided by**: Wikimedia. **Located at**: https://commons.wikimedia.org/wiki/File:Paperbook%2B256.jpg. **License**: *Public Domain: No Known Copyright*
- End of the Han Dynasty. **Provided by**: Wikipedia. **Located at**: https://en.wikipedia.org/wiki/End_of_the_Han_dynasty. **License**: *CC BY: Attribution*
- Jack E. Maxfield, A Comprehensive Outline of World History (Organized by Region). November 23, 2009. **Provided by**: OpenStax CNX. **Located at**: http://cnx.org/contents/45ac7e52-e029-4436-895a-92b9e507b372@2.1. **License**: *CC BY: Attribution*
- The Unification of China. **Provided by**: Wikibooks. **Located at**: http://en.wikibooks.org/wiki/World_History/The_Unification_of_China. **License**: *CC BY-SA: Attribution-ShareAlike*
- HIST101: Ancient Civilizations of the World. **Provided by**: Saylor. **Located at**: https://legacy.saylor.org/hist101/Intro/. **License**: *CC BY: Attribution*
- HIST101: Ancient Civilizations of the World. **Provided by**: Saylor. **Located at**: https://legacy.saylor.org/hist101/Intro/. **License**: *CC BY: Attribution*
- Hydraulics. **Provided by**: Wiktionary. **Located at**: http://en.wiktionary.org/wiki/hydraulics. **License**: *CC BY-SA: Attribution-ShareAlike*
- hydraulic. **Provided by**: Wiktionary. **Located at**: http://en.wiktionary.org/wiki/hydraulic. **License**: *CC BY-SA: Attribution-ShareAlike*
- Hangaozu.jpg. **Provided by**: Wikimedia. **Located at**: https://commons.wikimedia.org/wiki/File:Hangaozu.jpg. **License**: *CC BY: Attribution*
- 352px-u6f22u6b66u5e1d.jpg. **Provided by**: Wikimedia. **Located at**: https://commons.wikimedia.org/wiki/File:%E6%BC%A2%E6%AD%A6%E5%B8%9D.jpg. **License**: *CC BY: Attribution*
- 640px-Silk_route.jpg. **Provided by**: Wikimedia. **Located at**: https://commons.wikimedia.org/wiki/File:Silk_route.jpg. **License**: *CC BY: Attribution*
- 640px-Woven_silk_Western_Han_Dynasty.jpg. **Provided by**: Wikimedia. **Located at**: https://commons.wikimedia.org/wiki/File:Woven_silk,_Western_Han_Dynasty.jpg. **License**: *Public Domain: No Known Copyright*
- 372px-Han_Guangwu_Di.jpg. **Provided by**: Wikimedia. **Located at**: https://commons.wikimedia.org/wiki/File:Han_Guangwu_Di.jpg. **License**: *Public Domain: No Known Copyright*
- Eastern Han pottery chandelier. **Provided by**: Wikimedia. **Located at**: https://commons.wikimedia.org/wiki/File:Eastern_Han_pottery_chandelier.JPG. **License**: *Public Domain: No Known Copyright*
- 494px-Chinese_hemp_paper_western_han.jpg. **Provided by**: Wikimedia. **Located at**: https://commons.wikimedia.org/wiki/File:Chinese_hemp_paper_western_han.jpg. **License**: *Public Domain: No Known Copyright*
- Cai-lun.jpg. **Provided by**: Wikimedia. **Located at**: https://commons.wikimedia.org/wiki/File:Cai-lun.jpg. **License**: *Public Domain: No Known Copyright*
- 374px-Paperbook256.jpg. **Provided by**: Wikimedia. **Located at**: https://commons.wikimedia.org/wiki/File:Paperbook%2B256.jpg. **License**: *Public Domain: No Known Copyright*
- Dong_Zhuo_Portrait.jpg. **Provided by**: Wikimedia. **Located at**: https://commons.wikimedia.org/wiki/File:Mohenjo-

daro_Sindh.jpeg. **License**: *CC BY-SA: Attribution-ShareAlike*

- China 5. **Provided by**: Wikimedia. **Located at**: https://en.wikipedia.org/wiki/File:China_5.jpg#/media/File:China_5.jpg. **License**: *Public Domain: No Known Copyright*

Early Civilizations in the Indian Subcontinent

The Indus River Valley Civilizations

The Indus River Valley Civilization

The Indus River Valley Civilization, located in modern Pakistan, was one of the world's three earliest widespread societies.

Learning Objectives

Identify the importance of the discovery of the Indus River Valley Civilization

---

Key Takeaways

Key Points

- The Indus Valley Civilization (also known as the Harappan Civilization) was a Bronze Age society extending from modern northeast Afghanistan to Pakistan and northwest India.
- The civilization developed in three phases: Early Harappan Phase (3300 BCE-2600 BCE), Mature Harappan Phase (2600 BCE-1900 BCE), and Late Harappan Phase (1900 BCE-1300 BCE).
- Inhabitants of the ancient Indus River valley developed new techniques in handicraft, including Carnelian products and seal carving, and metallurgy with copper, bronze, lead, and tin.
- Sir John Hubert Marshall led an excavation campaign in 1921-1922, during which he discovered the ruins of the city of Harappa. By 1931, the Mohenjo-daro site had been mostly excavated by Marshall and Sir Mortimer Wheeler. By 1999, over 1,056 cities and

> settlements of the Indus Civilization were located.
>
> *Key Terms*
>
> - **seal**: An emblem used as a means of authentication. Seal can refer to an impression in paper, wax, clay, or other medium. It can also refer to the device used.
> - **metallurgy**: The scientific and mechanical technique of working with bronze. copper, and tin.

The Indus Valley Civilization existed through its early years of 3300-1300 BCE, and its mature period of 2600-1900 BCE. The area of this civilization extended along the Indus River from what today is northeast Afghanistan, into Pakistan and northwest India. The Indus Civilization was the most widespread of the three early civilizations of the ancient world, along with Ancient Egypt and Mesopotamia. Harappa and Mohenjo-daro were thought to be the two great cities of the Indus Valley Civilization, emerging around 2600 BCE along the Indus River Valley in the Sindh and Punjab provinces of Pakistan. Their discovery and excavation in the 19th and 20th centuries provided important archaeological data about ancient cultures.

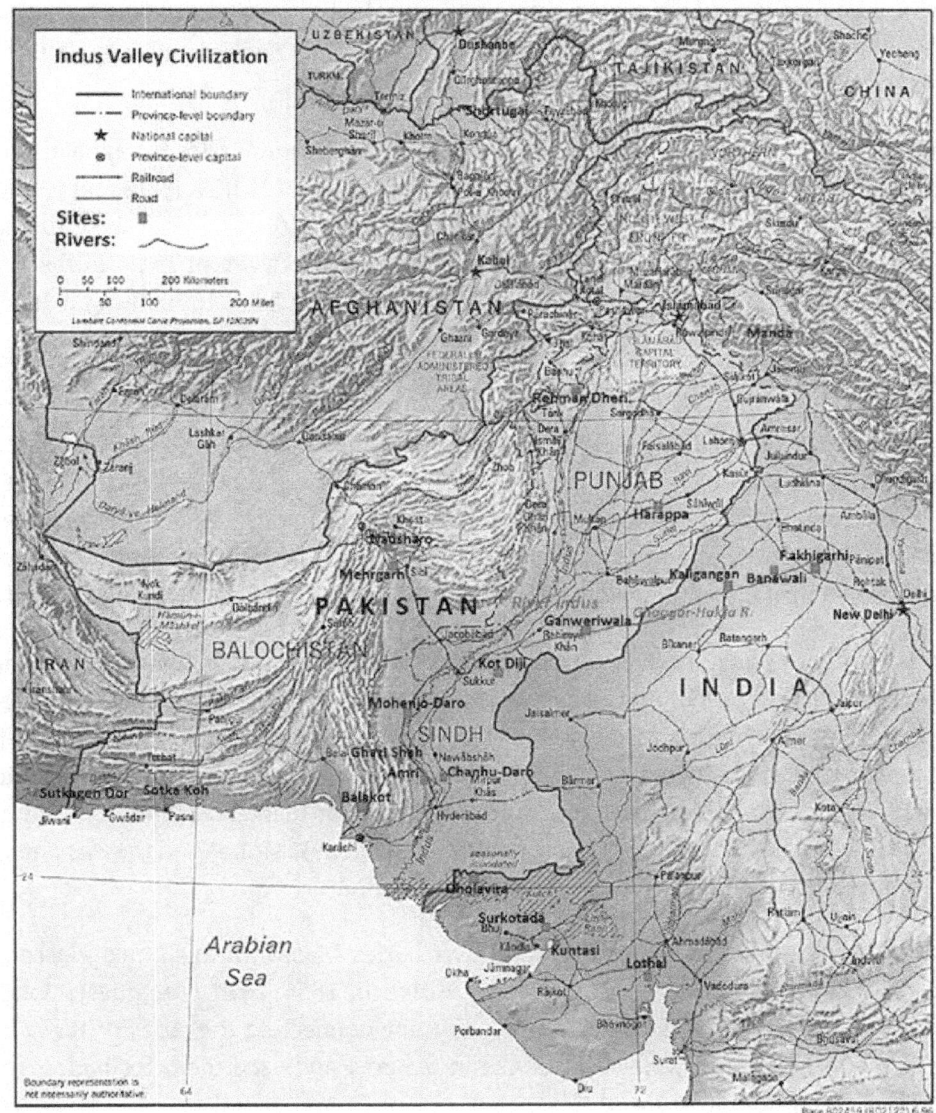

Map of the Indus Valley Civilization: *The major sites of the Indus Valley Civilization.*

Indus Valley Civilization

The Indus Valley Civilization was one of the three "Ancient East" societies that are considered to be the cradles of civilization of the old world of man, and are among the most widespread; the other two "Ancient East" societies are Mesopotamia and Pharonic Egypt. The lifespan of the Indus Valley Civilization is often separated into three phases: Early Harappan Phase (3300-2600 BCE), Mature Harappan Phase (2600-1900 BCE) and Late Harappan Phase (1900-1300 BCE).

At its peak, the Indus Valley Civilization may had a population of over five million people. It is considered a Bronze Age society, and inhabitants of the ancient Indus River Valley developed new techniques in metallurgy—the science of working with copper, bronze, lead, and tin. They also performed intricate handicraft, especially using products made of the semi-precious gemstone Carnelian, as well as seal carving—

the cutting
of patterns into the bottom face of a seal used for stamping. The Indus cities are noted for their urban planning, baked brick houses, elaborate drainage systems, water supply systems, and clusters of large, non-residential buildings.

The Indus Valley Civilization is also known as the Harappan Civilization, after Harappa, the first of its sites to be excavated in the 1920s, in what was then the Punjab province of British India and is now in Pakistan. The discoveries of Harappa, and the site of its fellow Indus city Mohenjo-daro, were the culmination of work beginning in 1861 with the founding of the Archaeological Survey of India in the British Raj, the common name for British imperial rule over the Indian subcontinent from 1858 through 1947.

Harappa and Mohenjo-daro

Harappa was a fortified city in modern-day Pakistan that is believed to have been home to as many as 23,500 residents living in sculpted houses with flat roofs made of red sand and clay. The city spread over 150 hectares (370 acres) and had fortified administrative and religious centers of the same type used in Mohenjo-daro. The modern village of Harappa, used as a railway station during the Raj, is six kilometers (3.7 miles) from the ancient city site, which suffered heavy damage during the British period of rule.

Mohenjo-daro is thought to have been built in the 26th century BCE and became not only the largest city of the Indus Valley Civilization but one of the world's earliest, major urban centers. Located west of the Indus River in the Larkana District, Mohenjo-daro was one of the most sophisticated cities of the period, with sophisticated engineering and urban planning. Cock-fighting was thought to have religious and ritual significance, with domesticated chickens bred for religion rather than food (although the city may have been a point of origin for the worldwide domestication of chickens). Mohenjo-daro was abandoned around 1900 BCE when the Indus Civilization went into sudden decline.

The ruins of Harappa were first described in 1842 by Charles Masson in his book, *Narrative of Various Journeys in Balochistan, Afghanistan, the Panjab, & Kalât*. In 1856, British engineers John and William Brunton were laying the East Indian Railway Company line connecting the cities of Karachi and Lahore, when their crew discovered hard, well-burnt bricks in the area and used them for ballast for the railroad track, unwittingly dismantling the ruins of the ancient city of Brahminabad.

Excavations

In 1912, John Faithfull Fleet, an English civil servant working with the Indian Civil Services, discovered several Harappan seals. This prompted an excavation campaign from 1921-1922 by Sir John Hubert Marshall, Director-General of the Archaeological Survey of India, which resulted in the discovery of Harappa. By 1931, much of
Mohenjo-Daro had been excavated, while the next director of the Archaeological Survey of India, Sir Mortimer Wheeler, led additional excavations.

Excavated Ruins of Mohenjo-daro: *The Great Bath at Mohenjo-daro, a city in the Indus River Valley Civilization.*

The Partition of India, in 1947, divided the country to create the new nation of Pakistan. The bulk of the archaeological finds that followed were inherited by Pakistan. By 1999, over 1,056 cities and settlements had been found, of which 96 have been excavated.

Cities of the Indus Valley Civilization

The Indus River Valley Civilization (IVC) contained urban centers with well-conceived and organized infrastructure, architecture, and systems of governance.

Learning Objectives

Explain the significance of the urban centers in the IVC

Key Takeaways

Key Points

- The Indus Valley Civilization contained more than 1,000 cities and settlements.
- These cities contained well-organized wastewater drainage systems, trash collection sys-

> tems, and possibly even public granaries and baths.
> - Although there were large walls and citadels, there is no evidence of monuments, palaces, or temples.
> - The uniformity of Harappan artifacts suggests some form of authority and governance to regulate seals, weights, and bricks.
>
> *Key Terms*
>
> - **granaries**: A storehouse or room in a barn for threshed grain or animal feed.
> - **citadels**: A central area in a city that is heavily fortified.
> - **Harappa and Mohenjo-daro**: Two of the major cities of the Indus Valley Civilization during the Bronze Age.
> - **urban planning**: A technical and political process concerned with the use of land and design of the urban environment that guides and ensures the orderly development of settlements and communities.

By 2600 BCE, the small Early Harappan communities had become large urban centers. These cities include Harappa, Ganeriwala, and Mohenjo-daro in modern-day Pakistan, and Dholavira, Kalibangan, Rakhigarhi, Rupar, and Lothal in modern-day India. In total, more than 1,052 cities and settlements have been found, mainly in the general region of the Indus River and its tributaries. The population of the Indus Valley Civilization may have once been as large as five million.

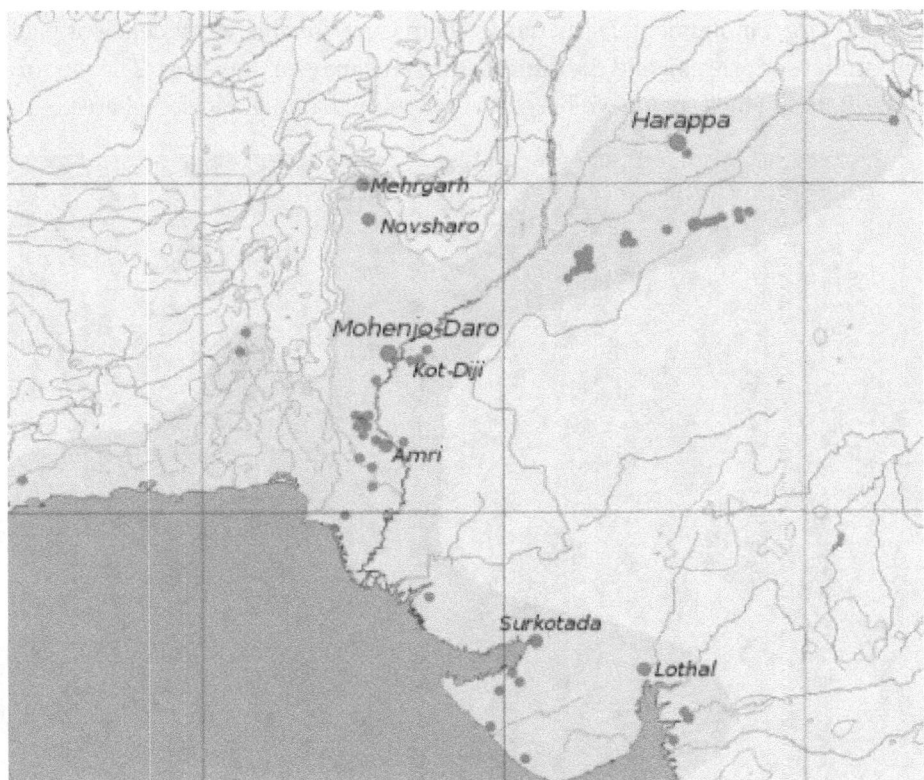

Indus Valley Civilization Sites: *This map shows a cluster of Indus Valley Civilization cities and excavation sites along the course of the Indus River in Pakistan.*

The remains of the Indus Valley Civilization cities indicate remarkable organization; there were well-ordered wastewater drainage and trash collection systems, and possibly even public granaries and baths. Most city-dwellers were artisans and merchants grouped together in distinct neighborhoods. The quality of urban planning suggests efficient municipal governments that placed a high priority on hygiene or religious ritual.

Infrastructure

Harappa, Mohenjo-daro, and the recently, partially-excavated Rakhigarhi demonstrate the world's first known urban sanitation systems. The ancient Indus systems of sewerage and drainage developed and used in cities throughout the Indus region were far more advanced than any found in contemporary urban sites in the Middle East, and even more efficient than those in many areas of Pakistan and India today. Individual homes drew water from wells, while waste water was directed to covered drains on the main streets. Houses opened only to inner courtyards and smaller lanes, and even the smallest homes on the city outskirts were believed to have been connected to the system, further supporting the conclusion that cleanliness was a matter of great importance.

Architecture

Harappans demonstrated advanced architecture with dockyards, granaries, warehouses, brick platforms, and protective walls. These massive walls likely protected the Harappans from floods and may have dissuaded military conflicts. Unlike Mesopotamia and Ancient Egypt, the inhabitants of the Indus Valley Civilization did not build large, monumental structures. There is no conclusive evidence of palaces or temples (or even of kings, armies, or priests), and the largest structures may be granaries. The city of Mohenjo-daro contains the "Great Bath," which may have been a large, public bathing and social area.

Sokhta Koh: *Sokhta Koh, a Harappan coastal settlement near Pasni, Pakistan, is depicted in a computer reconstruction. Sokhta Koh means "burnt hill," and corresponds to the browned-out earth due to extensive firing of pottery in open pit ovens.*

Authority and Governance

Archaeological records provide no immediate answers regarding a center of authority, or depictions of people in power in Harappan society. The extraordinary uniformity of Harappan artifacts is evident in pottery, seals, weights, and bricks with standardized sizes and weights, suggesting some form of authority and governance.

Over time, three major theories have developed concerning Harappan governance or system of rule. The first is that there was a single state encompassing all the communities of the civilization, given the similarity in artifacts, the evidence of planned settlements, the standardized ratio of brick size, and the apparent establishment of settlements near sources of raw material. The second theory posits that there was no single ruler, but a number of them representing each of the urban centers, including Mohenjo-daro, Harappa, and other communities. Finally, experts have theorized that the Indus Valley Civilization had no rulers as we understand them, with everyone enjoying equal status.

Harappan Culture

The Indus River Valley Civilization, also known as Harappan, included its own advanced technology, economy, and culture.

Learning Objectives

Identify how artifacts and ruins provided insight into the IRV's technology, economy, and culture

---

Key Takeaways

Key Points

- The Indus River Valley Civilization, also known as Harappan civilization, developed the first accurate system of standardized weights and measures, some as accurate as to 1.6 mm.
- Harappans created sculpture, seals, pottery, and jewelry from materials, such as terra-cotta, metal, and stone.
- Evidence shows Harappans participated in a vast maritime trade network extending from Central Asia to modern-day Iraq, Iran, Kuwait, and Syria.
- The Indus Script remains indecipherable without any comparable symbols, and is thought to have evolved independently of the writing in Mesopotamia and Ancient Egypt.

Key Terms

- **steatite**: Also known as Soapstone, steatite is a talc-schist, which is a type of metamorphic rock. It is very soft and has been a medium for carving for thousands of years.
- **Indus Script**: Symbols produced by the ancient Indus Valley Civilization.
- **chalcolithic period**: A period also known as the Copper Age, which lasted from 4300-3200 BCE.

The Indus Valley Civilization is the earliest known culture of the Indian subcontinent of the kind now called "urban" (or centered on large municipalities), and the largest of the four ancient civilizations, which also included Egypt, Mesopotamia, and China. The society of the Indus River Valley has been dated from the Bronze Age, the time period from approximately 3300-1300 BCE. It was located in modern-day India and Pakistan, and covered an area as large as Western Europe.

Harappa and Mohenjo-daro were the two great cities of the Indus Valley Civilization, emerging around 2600 BCE along the Indus River Valley in the Sindh and Punjab provinces of Pakistan. Their discovery and excavation in the 19th and 20th centuries provided important archaeological data regarding the civilization's technology, art, trade, transportation, writing, and religion.

Technology

The people of the Indus Valley, also known as Harappan (Harappa was the first city in the region found by archaeologists), achieved many notable advances in technology, including great accuracy in their systems and tools for measuring length and mass.

Harappans were among the first to develop a system of uniform weights and measures that conformed to a successive scale. The smallest division, approximately 1.6 mm, was marked on an ivory scale found in Lothal, a prominent Indus Valley city in the modern Indian state of Gujarat. It stands as the smallest division ever recorded on a Bronze Age scale. Another indication of an advanced measurement system is the fact that the bricks used to build Indus cities were uniform in size.

Harappans demonstrated advanced architecture with dockyards, granaries, warehouses, brick platforms, and protective walls. The ancient Indus systems of sewerage and drainage developed and used in cities throughout the region were far more advanced than any found in contemporary urban sites in the Middle East, and even more efficient than those in many areas of Pakistan and India today.

Harappans were thought to have been proficient in seal carving, the cutting of patterns into the bottom face of a seal, and used distinctive seals for the identification of property and to stamp clay on trade goods. Seals have been one of the most commonly discovered artifacts in Indus Valley cities, decorated with animal figures, such as elephants, tigers, and water buffalos.

Harappans also developed new techniques in metallurgy—the science of working with copper, bronze, lead, and tin—and performed intricate handicraft using products made of the semi-precious gemstone, Carnelian.

Art

Indus Valley excavation sites have revealed a number of distinct examples of the culture's art, including sculptures, seals, pottery, gold jewelry, and anatomically detailed figurines in terracotta, bronze, and steatite—more commonly known as Soapstone.

Among the various gold, terracotta, and stone figurines found, a figure of a "Priest-King" displayed a beard and patterned robe. Another figurine in bronze, known as the "Dancing Girl," is only 11 cm. high and shows a female figure in a pose that suggests the presence of some choreographed dance form enjoyed by members of the civilization. Terracotta works also included cows, bears, monkeys, and dogs. In addition to figurines, the Indus River Valley people are believed to have created necklaces, bangles, and other ornaments.

Miniature Votive Images or Toy Models from Harappa, c. 2500 BCE: *The Indus River Valley Civilization created figurines from terracotta, as well as bronze and steatite. It is still unknown whether these figurines have religious significance.*

Trade and Transportation

The civilization's economy appears to have depended significantly on trade, which was facilitated by major advances in transport technology. The Harappan Civilization may have been the first to use wheeled transport, in the form of bullock carts that are identical to those seen throughout South Asia today. It also appears they built boats and watercraft—a claim supported by archaeological discoveries of a massive, dredged canal, and what is regarded as a docking facility at the coastal city of Lothal.

The docks and canal in the ancient city of Lothal, located in modern India: *Archaeological evidence suggests that the Indus River Valley Civilization constructed boats and may have participated in an extensive maritime trade network.*

Trade focused on importing raw materials to be used in Harappan city workshops, including minerals from Iran and Afghanistan, lead and copper from other parts of India, jade from China, and cedar wood floated down rivers from the Himalayas and Kashmir. Other trade goods included terracotta pots, gold, silver, metals, beads, flints for making tools, seashells, pearls, and colored gem stones, such as lapis lazuli and turquoise.

There was an extensive maritime trade network operating between the Harappan and Mesopotamian civilizations. Harappan seals and jewelry have been found at archaeological sites in regions of Mesopotamia, which includes most of modern-day Iraq, Kuwait, and parts of Syria. Long-distance sea trade over bodies of water, such as the Arabian Sea, Red Sea and the Persian Gulf, may have become feasible with the development of plank watercraft that was equipped with a single central mast supporting a sail of woven rushes or cloth.

During 4300-3200 BCE of the Chalcolithic period, also known as the Copper Age, the Indus Valley Civilization area shows ceramic similarities with
southern Turkmenistan and northern Iran. During the Early Harappan period (about 3200-2600 BCE), cultural similarities in pottery, seals, figurines, and ornaments document caravan trade with Central Asia and the Iranian plateau.

Writing

Harappans are believed to have used Indus Script, a language consisting of symbols. A collection of written texts on clay and stone tablets unearthed at Harappa, which have been carbon dated 3300-3200 BCE, contain trident-shaped, plant-like markings. This Indus Script suggests that writing developed independently in the Indus River Valley Civilization from the script employed in Mesopotamia and Ancient Egypt.

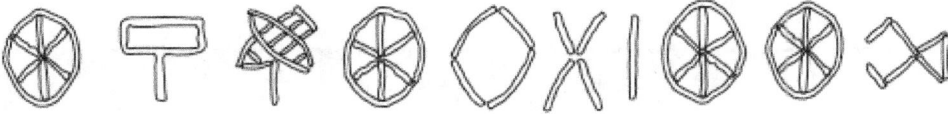

Indus Script: These ten Indus Script symbols were found on a "sign board" in the ancient city of Dholavira.

As many as 600 distinct Indus symbols have been found on seals, small tablets, ceramic pots, and more than a dozen other materials. Typical Indus inscriptions are no more than four or five characters in length, most of which are very small. The longest on a single surface, which is less than 1 inch (or 2.54 cm.) square, is 17 signs long. The characters are largely pictorial, but include many abstract signs that do not appear to have changed over time.

The inscriptions are thought to have been primarily written from right to left, but it is unclear whether this script constitutes a complete language. Without a "Rosetta Stone" to use as a comparison with other writing systems, the symbols have remained indecipherable to linguists and archaeologists.

A YouTube element has been excluded from this version of the text. You can view it online here: https://milnepublishing.geneseo.edu/suny-fmcc-boundless-worldhistory-print/?p=76

A Rosetta Stone for the Indus script, lecture by Rajesh Rao: Rajesh Rao is fascinated by "the mother of all crossword puzzles," how to decipher the 4,000-year-old Indus script. At TED 2011, he explained how he was enlisting modern computational techniques to read the Indus language. View full lesson: http://ed.ted.com/lessons/a-rosetta-stone-for-the-indus-script-rajesh-rao

Religion

The Harappan religion remains a topic of speculation. It has been widely suggested that the Harappans worshipped a mother goddess who symbolized fertility. In contrast to Egyptian and Mesopotamian civilizations, the Indus Valley Civilization seems to have lacked any temples or palaces that would give clear evidence of religious rites or specific deities. Some Indus Valley seals show a swastika symbol, which was included in later Indian religions including Hinduism, Buddhism, and Jainism.

Many Indus Valley seals also include the forms of animals, with some depicting them being carried in processions, while others showing chimeric creations, leading scholars to speculate about the role of animals in Indus Valley religions. One seal from Mohenjo-daro shows a half-human, half-buffalo monster attacking a tiger. This may be a reference to the Sumerian myth of a monster created by Aruru, the Sumerian earth and fertility goddess, to fight Gilgamesh, the hero of an ancient Mesopotamian epic poem. This is a further suggestion of international trade in Harappan culture.

The "Shiva Pashupati" seal: This seal was excavated in Mohenjo-daro and depicts a seated and possibly ithyphallic figure, surrounded by animals.

Disappearance of the Indus Valley Civilization

The Indus Valley Civilization declined around 1800 BCE due to climate change and migration.

Learning Objectives

Discuss the causes for the disappearance of the Indus Valley Civilization

Key Takeaways

Key Points

- One theory suggested that a nomadic, Indo-European tribe, called the Aryans, invaded and conquered the Indus Valley Civilization.
- Many scholars now believe the collapse of the Indus Valley Civilization was caused by climate change.
- The eastward shift of monsoons may have reduced the water supply, forcing the Harappans of the Indus River Valley to migrate and establish smaller villages and isolated farms.
- These small communities could not produce the agricultural surpluses needed to support cities, which where then abandoned.

Key Terms

- **Indo-Aryan Migration theory**: A theory suggesting the Harappan culture of the Indus River Valley was assimilated during a migration of the Aryan people into northwest India.
- **monsoon**: Seasonal changes in atmospheric circulation and precipitation; usually winds that bring heavy rain once a year.
- **Aryans**: A nomadic, Indo-European tribe called the Aryans suddenly overwhelmed and conquered the Indus Valley Civilization.

The great Indus Valley Civilization, located in modern-day India and Pakistan, began to decline around 1800 BCE. The civilization eventually disappeared along with its two great cities, Mohenjo-daro and Harappa. Harappa lends its name to the Indus Valley people because it was the civilization's first city to be discovered by modern archaeologists.

Archaeological evidence indicates that trade with Mesopotamia, located largely in modern Iraq, seemed to have ended. The advanced drainage system and baths of the great cities were built over or blocked. Writing began to disappear and the standardized weights and measures used for trade and taxation fell out of use.

Scholars have put forth differing theories to explain the disappearance of the Harappans, including an Aryan Invasion and climate change marked by overwhelming monsoons.

The Aryan Invasion Theory (c. 1800-1500 BC)

The Indus Valley Civilization may have met its demise due to invasion. According to one theory by British archaeologist Mortimer Wheeler, a nomadic, Indo-European tribe, called the Aryans, suddenly overwhelmed and conquered the Indus River Valley.

Wheeler, who was Director-General of the Archaeological Survey of India from 1944 to 1948, posited that many unburied corpses found in the top levels of the Mohenjo-daro archaeological site were victims of war. The theory suggested that by using horses and more advanced weapons against the peaceful Harappan people, the Aryans may have easily defeated them.

Yet shortly after Wheeler proposed his theory, other scholars dismissed it by explaining that the skeletons were not victims of invasion massacres, but rather the remains of hasty burials. Wheeler himself eventually admitted that the theory could not be proven and the skeletons indicated only a final phase of human occupation, with the decay of the city structures likely a result of it becoming uninhabited.

Later opponents of the invasion theory went so far as to state that adherents to the idea put forth in the 1940s were subtly justifying the British government's policy of intrusion into, and subsequent colonial rule over, India.

Various elements of the Indus Civilization are found in later cultures, suggesting the civilization did not disappear suddenly due to an invasion. Many scholars came to believe in an Indo-Aryan Migration theory stating that the Harappan culture was assimilated during a migration of the Aryan people into northwest India.

Aryans in India: *An early 20th-century depiction of Aryan people settling in agricultural villages in India.*

The Climate
Change Theory (c. 1800-1500 BC)

Other scholarship suggests the collapse of Harappan society resulted from climate change. Some experts believe the drying of the Saraswati River, which began around 1900 BCE, was the main cause for climate change, while others conclude that a great flood struck the area.

Any major environmental change, such as deforestation, flooding or droughts due to a river changing course, could have had disastrous effects on Harappan society, such as crop failures, starvation, and disease. Skeletal evidence suggests many people died from malaria, which is most often spread by mosquitoes. This also would have caused a breakdown in the economy and civic order within the urban areas.

Another disastrous change in the Harappan climate might have been eastward-moving monsoons, or winds that bring heavy rains. Monsoons can be both helpful and detrimental to a climate, depending on whether they support or destroy vegetation and agriculture. The monsoons that came to the Indus River Valley aided the growth of agricultural surpluses, which supported the development of cities, such as Harappa. The population came to rely on seasonal monsoons rather than irrigation, and as the monsoons shifted eastward, the water supply would have dried up.

Ruins of the city of Lothal: *Archaeological evidence shows that the site, which had been a major city before the downfall of the Indus Valley Civilization, continued to be inhabited by a much smaller population after the collapse. The few people who remained in Lothal did not repair the city, but lived in poorly-built houses and reed huts instead.*

By 1800 BCE, the Indus Valley climate grew cooler and drier, and a tectonic event may have diverted the Ghaggar Hakra river system toward the Ganges Plain. The Harappans may have migrated toward the Ganges basin in the east, where they established villages and isolated farms.

These small communities could not produce the same agricultural surpluses to support large cities. With the reduced production of goods, there was a decline in trade with Egypt and Mesopotamia. By around 1700 BCE, most of the Indus Valley Civilization cities had been abandoned.

Attributions

CC licensed content, Specific attribution

- Sir Mortimer Wheeler. **Provided by**: Wikipedia. **Located at**: https://en.wikipedia.org/wiki/Mortimer_Wheeler. **License**: *CC BY-SA: Attribution-ShareAlike*
- The Indus River Valley Civilizations (ca. 2800 - 1800 BC). **Provided by**: Wikibooks. **Located at**: http://en.wikibooks.org/wiki/World_History/Civilization_and_Empires_in_the_Indian_Subcontinent. **License**: *CC BY-SA: Attribution-ShareAlike*
- Harappa. **Provided by**: Wikipedia. **Located at**: https://en.wikipedia.org/wiki/Harappa. **License**: *CC BY-SA: Attribution-ShareAlike*
- Pakistan. **Provided by**: Wikipedia. **Located at**: https://en.wikipedia.org/wiki/Pakistan. **License**: *CC BY-SA: Attribution-ShareAlike*
- Metallurgy. **Provided by**: Wikipedia. **Located at**: https://en.wikipedia.org/wiki/Metallurgy. **License**: *CC BY-SA: Attribution-ShareAlike*
- Bronze Age. **Provided by**: Wikipedia. **Located at**: https://en.wikipedia.org/wiki/Bronze_Age. **License**: *CC BY-SA: Attribution-ShareAlike*
- Sir John Hubert Marshall. **Provided by**: Wikipedia. **Located at**: https://en.wikipedia.org/wiki/John_Marshall_(archaeologist). **License**: *CC BY-SA: Attribution-ShareAlike*

THE INDUS RIVER VALLEY CIVILIZATIONS • 231

- Mohenjo-dara. **Provided by**: Wikipedia. **Located at**: https://en.wikipedia.org/wiki/Mohenjo-daro. **License**: *CC BY-SA Attribution-ShareAlike*
- Indus Valley Civilization. **Provided by**: Wikipedia. **Located at**: https://en.wikipedia.org/wiki/Indus_Valley_Civilisation. **License**: *CC BY-SA: Attribution-ShareAlike*
- Indus Valley Civilization. **Provided by**: Wikimedia. **Located at**: https://commons.wikimedia.org/wiki/File:IVC-major-sites-2.jpg. **License**: *Public Domain: No Known Copyright*
- Mohenjodaro Sindh. **Provided by**: Wikimedia. **Located at**: https://commons.wikimedia.org/wiki/File:Mohenjodaro_Sindh.jpeg. **License**: *CC BY-SA: Attribution-ShareAlike*
- Indus River Valley Civilization. **Provided by**: Wikipedia. **Located at**: http://en.wikipedia.org/wiki/Indus_Valley_Civilization. **License**: *CC BY-SA: Attribution-ShareAlike*
- The Indus River Valley Civilizations. **Provided by**: Wikibooks. **Located at**: http://en.wikibooks.org/wiki/World_History/Civilization_and_Empires_in_the_Indian_Subcontinent. **License**: *CC BY-SA: Attribution-ShareAlike*
- Harappa. **Provided by**: Wikipedia. **Located at**: https://en.wikipedia.org/wiki/Harappa. **License**: *CC BY-SA: Attribution-ShareAlike*
- Mohenjo-daro. **Provided by**: Wikipedia. **Located at**: https://en.wikipedia.org/wiki/Mohenjo-daro. **License**: *CC BY-SA: Attribution-ShareAlike*
- Indus Valley Civilization. **Provided by**: Wikimedia. **Located at**: https://commons.wikimedia.org/wiki/File:IVC-major-sites-2.jpg. **License**: *Public Domain: No Known Copyright*
- Mohenjodaro Sindh. **Provided by**: Wikimedia. **Located at**: https://commons.wikimedia.org/wiki/File:Mohenjodaro_Sindh.jpeg. **License**: *CC BY-SA: Attribution-ShareAlike*
- IVC Map. **Provided by**: Wikimedia. **Located at**: https://commons.wikimedia.org/wiki/File:IVC_Map.png. **License**: *Public Domain: No Known Copyright*
- Sokhta Koh. **Provided by**: Wikipedia. **Located at**: http://en.wikipedia.org/wiki/File:Sokhta_Koh.jpg. **License**: *Public Domain: No Known Copyright*
- Indus Script. **Provided by**: Wikipedia. **Located at**: https://en.wikipedia.org/wiki/Indus_script. **License**: *CC BY-SA: Attribution-ShareAlike*
- Indus Valley Civilisation. **Provided by**: Wikipedia. **Located at**: https://en.wikipedia.org/wiki/Indus_Valley_Civilisation. **License**: *CC BY-SA: Attribution-ShareAlike*
- Harappa. **Provided by**: Wikipedia. **Located at**: https://en.wikipedia.org/wiki/Harappa. **License**: *CC BY-SA: Attribution-ShareAlike*
- Indus River Valley Civilization. **Provided by**: Wikibooks. **Located at**: http://en.wikibooks.org/wiki/World_History/Civilization_and_Empires_in_the_Indian_Subcontinent. **License**: *CC BY-SA: Attribution-ShareAlike*
- Rosetta Stone. **Provided by**: Wikipedia. **Located at**: https://en.wikipedia.org/wiki/Rosetta_Stone. **License**: *CC BY-SA: Attribution-ShareAlike*
- Indus Valley Civilization. **Provided by**: Wikimedia. **Located at**: https://commons.wikimedia.org/wiki/File:IVC-major-sites-2.jpg. **License**: *Public Domain: No Known Copyright*
- Mohenjodaro Sindh. **Provided by**: Wikimedia. **Located at**: https://commons.wikimedia.org/wiki/File:Mohenjodaro_Sindh.jpeg. **License**: *CC BY-SA: Attribution-ShareAlike*
- IVC Map. **Provided by**: Wikimedia. **Located at**: https://commons.wikimedia.org/wiki/File:IVC_Map.png. **License**: *Public Domain: No Known Copyright*
- Sokhta Koh. **Provided by**: Wikipedia. **Located at**: http://en.wikipedia.org/wiki/File:Sokhta_Koh.jpg. **License**: *Public Domain: No Known Copyright*
- A Rosetta Stone for the Indus script, lecture by Rajesh Rao. **Located at**: http://www.youtube.com/watch?v=a_-obTZO5pY. **License**: *Public Domain: No Known Copyright*. **License Terms**: Standard YouTube license
- Shiva Pashupati. **Provided by**: Wikimedia. **Located at**: https://commons.wikimedia.org/wiki/File:Shiva_Pashupati.jpg. **License**: *Public Domain: No Known Copyright*
- The 'Ten Indus Scripts' discovered near the northen gateway of the citadel Dholavira.svg. **Provided by**: Wikimedia. **Located at**: https://commons.wikimedia.org/wiki/File:The%27Ten_Indus_Scripts%27_discovered_near_the_northen_gateway_of_the_citadel_Dholavira.svg. **License**: *CC BY-SA: Attribution-ShareAlike*
- Harappan small figures. **Provided by**: Wikimedia. **Located at**: https://commons.wikimedia.org/wiki/File:Harappan_small_figures.jpg. **License**: *CC BY: Attribution*
- dock with canal in Lothal (India). **Provided by**: Wikimedia. **Located at**: https://commons.wikimedia.org/wiki/File:Lothal_dock.jpg. **License**: *Public Domain: No Known Copyright*
- Indo-Aryan Migration Theory. **Provided by**: Wikipedia. **Located at**: https://en.wikipedia.org/wiki/Indo-Aryan_migration_theory.

License: *CC BY-SA: Attribution-ShareAlike*

- Mortimer Wheeler. **Provided by**: Wikipedia. **Located at**: https://en.wikipedia.org/wiki/Mortimer_Wheeler. **License**: *CC BY-SA: Attribution-ShareAlike*
- Aryan Race. **Provided by**: Wikipedia. **Located at**: https://en.wikipedia.org/wiki/Aryan_race. **License**: *CC BY-SA: Attribution-ShareAlike*
- Monsoon. **Provided by**: Wikipedia. **Located at**: https://en.wikipedia.org/wiki/Monsoon. **License**: *CC BY-SA: Attribution-ShareAlike*
- Civilizations and Empires in the Indian Subcontinent. **Provided by**: Wikibooks. **Located at**: http://en.wikibooks.org/wiki/World_History/Civilization_and_Empires_in_the_Indian_Subcontinent. **License**: *CC BY-SA: Attribution-ShareAlike*
- Indus Valley Civilisation Collapse. **Provided by**: Wikipedia. **Located at**: https://en.wikipedia.org/wiki/Indus_Valley_Civilisation#Collapse_and_Late_Harappan. **License**: *CC BY-SA: Attribution-ShareAlike*
- Indus Valley Civilisation. **Provided by**: Wikipedia. **Located at**: https://en.wikipedia.org/wiki/Indus_Valley_Civilisation. **License**: *CC BY-SA: Attribution-ShareAlike*
- Indus Valley Civilization. **Provided by**: Wikimedia. **Located at**: https://commons.wikimedia.org/wiki/File:IVC-major-sites-2.jpg. **License**: *Public Domain: No Known Copyright*
- Mohenjodaro Sindh. **Provided by**: Wikimedia. **Located at**: https://commons.wikimedia.org/wiki/File:Mohenjodaro_Sindh.jpeg. **License**: *CC BY-SA: Attribution-ShareAlike*
- IVC Map. **Provided by**: Wikimedia. **Located at**: https://commons.wikimedia.org/wiki/File:IVC_Map.png. **License**: *Public Domain: No Known Copyright*
- Sokhta Koh. **Provided by**: Wikipedia. **Located at**: http://en.wikipedia.org/wiki/File:Sokhta_Koh.jpg. **License**: *Public Domain: No Known Copyright*
- A Rosetta Stone for the Indus script, lecture by Rajesh Rao. **Located at**: http://www.youtube.com/watch?v=a_-obTZO6pY. **License**: *Public Domain: No Known Copyright*. **License Terms**: Standard YouTube license
- Shiva Pashupati. **Provided by**: Wikimedia. **Located at**: https://commons.wikimedia.org/wiki/File:Shiva_Pashupati.jpg. **License**: *Public Domain: No Known Copyright*
- The'Ten Indus Scripts' discovered near the northen gateway of the citadel Dholavira.svg. **Provided by**: Wikimedia. **Located at**: https://commons.wikimedia.org/wiki/File:The%27Ten_Indus_Scripts%27_discovered_near_the_northen_gateway_of_the_citadel_Dholavira.svg. **License**: *CC BY-SA: Attribution-ShareAlike*
- Harappan small figures. **Provided by**: Wikimedia. **Located at**: https://commons.wikimedia.org/wiki/File:Harappan_small_figures.jpg. **License**: *CC BY: Attribution*
- dock with canal in Lothal (India). **Provided by**: Wikimedia. **Located at**: https://commons.wikimedia.org/wiki/File:Lothal_dock.jpg. **License**: *Public Domain: No Known Copyright*
- Aryans Settling in India. **Provided by**: Wikimedia. **Located at**: https://commons.wikimedia.org/wiki/File:Aryans_settling_in_India.jpg. **License**: *Public Domain: No Known Copyright*
- Lothal - bathroom structure. **Provided by**: Wikimedia. **Located at**: http://en.wikipedia.org/wiki/File:Lothal_-_bathroom_structure.jpg. **License**: *Public Domain: No Known Copyright*

Indo-European Civilizations

The Indo-Aryan Migration and the Vedic Period

Different theories explain the Vedic Period, c. 1200 BCE, when Indo-Aryan people on the Indian subcontinent migrated to the Ganges Plain.

Learning Objectives

Describe the defining characteristics of the Vedic Period and the cultural consequenes of the Indo-Aryan Migration

Key Takeaways

Key Points

- The Indo- Aryans were part of an expansion into the Indus Valley and Ganges Plain from 1800-1500 BCE. This is explained through Indo-Aryan Migration and Kurgan theories.
- The Indo-Aryans continued to settle the Ganges Plain, bringing their distinct religious beliefs and practices.
- The Vedic Period (c. 1750-500 BCE) is named for the Vedas, the oldest scriptures in Hinduism, which were composed during this period. The period can be divided into the Early Vedic (1750-1000 BCE) and Later Vedic (1000-500 BCE) periods.

Key Terms

- **Ganges Plain**: A large, fertile plain encompassing most of northern and eastern India, where the Indo-Aryans migrated.
- **Rig-Veda**: A sacred Indo-Aryan collection of Vedic Sanskrit hymns. It is counted among

> the four canonical sacred texts of Hinduism, known as the Vedas.
> - **the Vedas**: The oldest scriptures of Hinduism composed in Vedic Sanskrit, and originating in ancient India during the Vedic Period (c. 1750-500 BCE).

Scholars debate the origin of Indo-Aryan peoples in northern India. Many have rejected the claim of Indo-Aryan origin outside of India entirely, claiming the Indo-Aryan people and languages originated in India. Other origin hypotheses include an Indo-Aryan Migration in the period 1800-1500 BCE, and a fusion of the nomadic people known as Kurgans. Most history of this period is derived from the Vedas, the oldest scriptures in Hinduism, which help chart the timeline of an era from 1750-500 BCE, known as the Vedic Period.

The Indo-Aryan Migration (1800-1500 BCE)

Foreigners from the north are believed to have migrated to India and settled in the Indus Valley and Ganges Plain from 1800-1500 BCE. The most prominent of these groups spoke Indo-European languages and were called Aryans, or "noble people" in the Sanskrit language. These Indo-Aryans were a branch of the Indo-Iranians, who originated in present-day northern Afghanistan. By 1500 BCE, the Indo-Aryans had created small herding and agricultural communities across northern India.

These migrations took place over several centuries and likely did not involve an invasion, as hypothesized by British archaeologist Mortimer Wheeler in the mid-1940s. Wheeler, who was Director-General of the Archaeological Survey of India from 1944 to 1948, suggested that a nomadic, Indo-European tribe, called the Aryans, suddenly overwhelmed and conquered the Indus River Valley. He based his conclusions on the remains of unburied corpses found in the top levels of the archaeological site of Mohenjo-daro, one of the great cities of the Indus Valley Civilization, whom he said were victims of war. Yet shortly after Wheeler proposed his theory, other scholars dismissed it by explaining that the skeletons were not those of victims of invasion massacres, but rather the remains of hasty burials. Wheeler himself eventually admitted that the theory could not be proven.

The Kurgan Hypothesis

The Kurgan Hypothesis is the most widely accepted scenario of Indo-European origins. It postulates that people of a so-called Kurgan Culture, a grouping of the Yamna or Pit Grave culture and its predecessors, of the Pontic Steppe were the speakers of the Proto- Indo-European language. According to this theory, these nomadic pastoralists expanded throughout the Pontic-Caspian steppe and into Eastern Europe by early 3000 BCE. The Kurgan people may have been mobile because of their domestication of horses and later use of the chariot.

The Vedic Period (c. 1750-500 BCE)

The Vedic Period refers to the time in history from approximately 1750-500 BCE, during which Indo-Aryans settled into northern India, bringing with them specific religious traditions. Most history of this period is derived from the Vedas, the oldest scriptures in the Hindu religion, which were composed by the Aryans in Sanskrit.

Vedic Civilization is believed to have been centered in the northwestern parts of the Indian subcontinent and spread around 1200 to the Ganges Plain, a 255-million hectare area (630 million acres) of flat, fertile land named after the Ganges River and covering most of what is now northern and eastern India, eastern parts of Pakistan, and most of Bangladesh. Many scholars believe Vedic Civilization was a composite of the Indo-Aryan and Harappan, or Indus Valley, cultures.

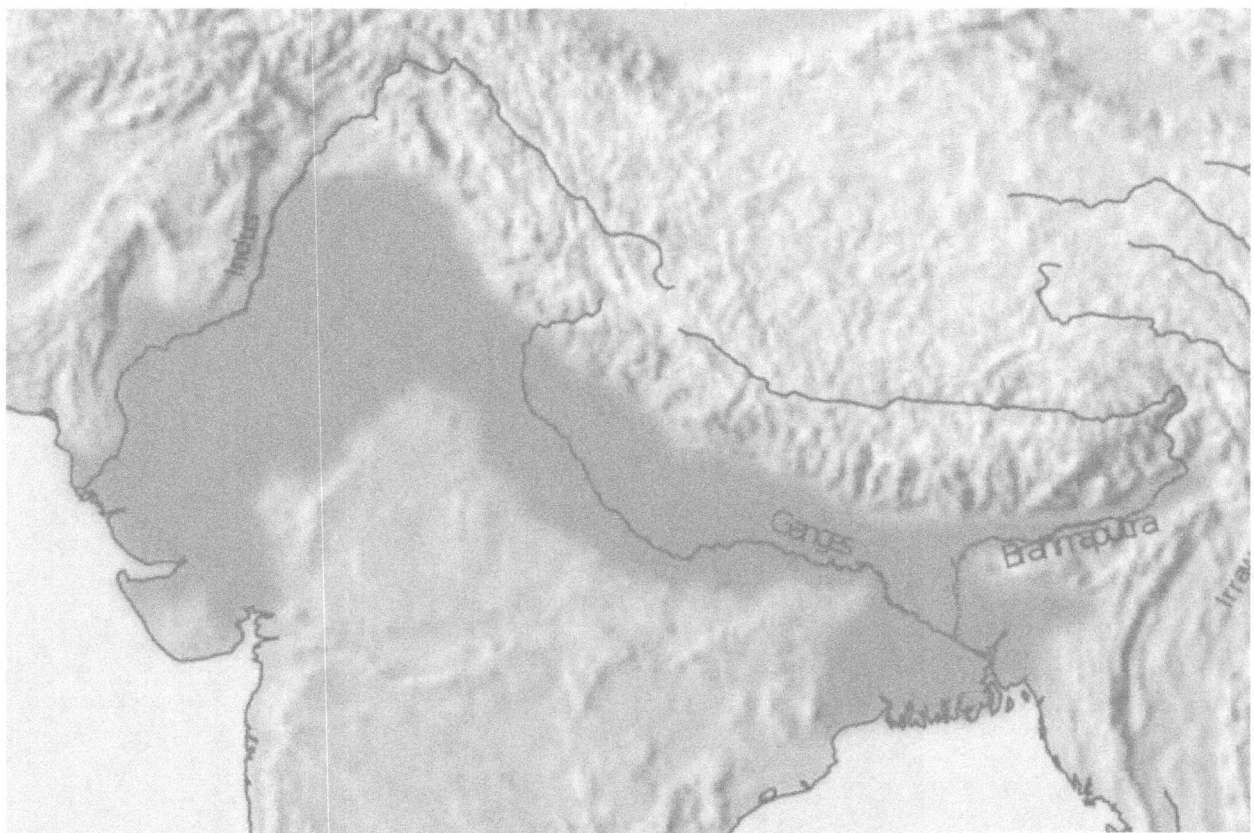

The Ganges Plain (Indo-Gangetic Plain): *The Ganges Plain is supported by the Indus and Ganges river systems. The Indo-Aryans settled various parts of the plain during their migration and the Vedic Period.*

Early Vedic Period (c. 1750-1000 BCE)

The Indo-Aryans in the Early Vedic Period, approximately 1750-1000 BCE, relied heavily on a pastoral, semi-nomadic economy with limited agriculture. They raised sheep, goats, and cattle, which became symbols of wealth.

The Indo-Aryans also preserved collections of religious and literary works by memorizing and reciting them, and handing them down from one generation to the next in their sacred language, Sanskrit. The *Rigveda*, which was likely composed during this time, contains several mythological and poetical accounts of the origins of the world, hymns praising the gods, and ancient prayers for life and prosperity.

Organized into tribes, the Vedic Aryans regularly clashed over land and resources. The Rigveda describes the most notable of these conflicts, the Battle of the Ten Kings, between the Bharatas tribe and a confederation of ten competing tribes on the banks of what is now the Ravi River in northwestern India and eastern Pakistan. Led by their king, Sudas, the Bharatas claimed victory and merged with the defeated Purus tribe to form the Kuru, a Vedic tribal union in northern India.

Later Vedic Period (c. 1000-500 BCE)

After the 12th century BCE, Vedic society transitioned from semi-nomadic to settled agriculture. From approximately 1000-500 BCE, the development of iron axes and ploughs enabled the Indo-Aryans to settle the thick forests on the western Ganges Plain.

This agricultural expansion led to an increase in trade and competition for resources, and many of the old tribes coalesced to form larger political units. The Indo-Aryans cultivated wheat, rice and barley and implemented new crafts, such as carpentry, leather work, tanning, pottery, jewelry crafting, textile dying, and wine making.

Ceramic goblet from Navdatoli, Malwa, c. 1300 BCE: As the Indo-Aryans developed an agricultural society during the Later Vedic Period (c. 1000-500), they further developed crafts, such as pottery.

Economic exchanges were conducted through gift giving, particularly between kings and priests, and barter using cattle as a unit of currency. While gold, silver, bronze, copper, tin, and lead are mentioned in some hymns as trade items, there is no indication of the use of coins.

The invasion of Darius I (a Persian ruler of the vast Achaemenid Empire that stretched into the Indus Valley) in the early 6th century BCE marked the beginning of outside influence in Vedic society. This continued into what became the Indo-Greek Kingdom, which covered various parts of South Asia and was centered mainly in modern Afghanistan and Pakistan.

The Caste System

A caste system developed among Indo-Aryans of the Vedic Period, splitting society into four major groups.

Learning Objectives

Explain the history of the caste system

Key Takeaways

Key Points

- The institution of the caste system, influenced by stories of the gods in the Rig-Veda epic, assumed and reinforced the idea that lifestyles, occupations, ritual statuses, and social statuses were inherited.
- Aryan society was patriarchal in the Vedic Period, with men in positions of authority and power handed down only through the male line.
- There were four classes in the caste system: Brahmins (priests and scholars), Kshatriyas (kings, governors, and warriors), Vaishyas (cattle herders, agriculturists, artisans, and merchants), and Shudras (laborers and service providers). A fifth group, Untouchables, was excluded from the caste system and historically performed the undesirable work.
- The caste system may have been more fluid in Aryan India than it is in modern-day India.

Key Terms

- **jatis**: The term used to denote the thousands of clans, tribes, religions, communities and sub-communities in India.
- **varnas**: The four broad ranks of the caste system in the Indo-Aryan culture, which included Brahmins (priests and scholars), Kshatriyas (kings, governors and warriors), Vaishyas (cattle herders, agriculturists, artisans, and merchants), and Shudras (laborers and service providers).

Caste systems through which social status was inherited developed independently in ancient societies all over the world, including the Middle East, Asia, and Africa. The caste system in ancient India was used to establish separate classes of inhabitants based upon their social positions and employment functions in the community. These roles and their importance, including the levels of power and significance based on patriarchy, were influenced by stories of the gods in the Rig-Veda epic.

Origins

The caste system in India may have several origins, possibly starting with the well-defined social orders of the Indo-Aryans in the Vedic Period, c. 1750-500 BCE. The Vedas were ancient scriptures, written in the Sanskrit language, which contained hymns, philosophies, and rituals handed down to the priests of the Vedic religion. One of these four sacred canonical texts, the Rig-Veda, described the origins of the world and points to the gods for the origin of the caste system.

The castes were a form of social stratification in Aryan India characterized by the hereditary transmission of lifestyle, occupation, ritual status, and social status. These social distinctions may have been more fluid in ancient Aryan civilizations than in modern India, where castes still exist but sociologists are observing inter-caste marriages and interactions becoming more fluid and less rigid.

The Rig-Veda: *A page of the Rig-Veda, one of the four sacred Veda texts, which described the origins of the world and the stories of the gods. The Rig-Veda influenced the development of the patriarchal society and the caste systems in Aryan India.*

Structure

The classes, known as varnas, enforced divisions in the populations that still affect this area of the world today. By around 1000 BCE, the Indo-Aryans developed four main caste distinctions: Brahamin, consisting of priests, scholars, and teachers; Kshatriyas, the kings, governors, and warriors; Vaishyas, comprising agriculturists, artisans, and merchants; and Sudras, the service providers and artisans who were originally non-Aryans but were admitted to Vedic society.

Each varna was divided into jatis, or sub-castes, which identified the individual's occupation and imposed marriage restrictions. Marriage was only possible between members of the same jati or two that were very close. Both varnas and jatis determined a person's purity level. Members of higher varnas or jatis had higher purity levels, and if contaminated by members of lower social groups, even by touch, they would have to undergo extensive cleansing rites.

Development of Patriarchy

Society during the Vedic Period (c.1750-500 BCE) was patriarchal and patrilineal, meaning to trace ancestral heritage through the male line. Marriage and childbearing were especially important to maintain male lineage. The institution of marriage was important, and different types of marriages—monogamy, polygyny and polyandry are mentioned in the Rig Veda. All priests, warriors, and tribal chiefs were men, and descent was always through the male line.

In other parts of society, women had no public authority; they only were able to influence affairs within their own homes. Women were to remain subject to the guidance of males in their lives, beginning with their father, then husband, and lastly their sons. Male gods were considered more important than female gods. These distinct gender roles may have contributed to the social stratification of the caste system.

Enduring Influence

The caste system that influenced the social structure of Aryan India has been maintained to some degree into modern-day India. The caste system survived for over two millennia, becoming one of the basic features of traditional Hindu society. Although the Constitution of India, the supreme law document of the Republic of India, formally abolished the caste system in 1950, some people maintain prejudices against members of lower social classes.

Gandhi at Madras, 1933: *Mahatma Gandhi visits Madras, now Chennai, during a tour of India in 1933. As leader of the Indian independence movement, Gandhi frequently spoke out against discrimination created by the caste system.*

Sanskrit

Vedic Sanskrit evolved to Classical Sanskrit, which has influenced modern Indian languages and is used in religious rites.

Learning Objectives
Explain the importance of Sanskrit

Key Takeaways

Key Points

- Sanskrit is originated as Vedic Sanskrit as early as 1700-1200 BCE, and was orally preserved as a part of the Vedic chanting tradition.
- The scholar Panini standardized Vedic Sanskrit into Classical Sanskrit when he defined the grammar, around 500 BCE.

- Vedic Sanskrit is the language of the Vedas, the oldest scriptures of Hinduism.
- Knowledge of Sanskrit became a marker of high social class during and after the Vedic Period.

Key Terms

- **Hinduism**: The dominant religion of the modern Indian subcontinent, which makes use of Sanskrit in its texts and practices.
- **Panini**: The scholar who standardized the grammar of Vedic Sanskrit to create Classical Sanskrit.

Sanskrit is the primary sacred language of Hinduism, and has been used as a philosophical language in the religions of Hinduism, Buddhism, and Jainism. Sanskrit is a standardized dialect of Old Indo-Aryan, originating as Vedic Sanskrit as early as 170001200 BCE.

One of the oldest Indo-European languages for which substantial documentation exists, Sanskrit is believed to have been the general language of the greater Indian Subcontinent in ancient times. It is still used today in Hindu religious rituals, Buddhist hymns and chants, and Jain texts.

Origins

Sanskrit traces its linguistic ancestry to Proto-Indo-Iranian and ultimately to Proto-Indo-European languages, meaning that it can be traced historically back to the people who spoke Indo-Iranian, also called the Aryan languages, as well as the Indo-European languages, a family of several hundred related languages and dialects. Today, an estimated 46% of humans speak some form of Indo-European language. The most widely-spoken Indo-European languages are English, Hindi, Bengali, Punjabi, Spanish, Portuguese, and Russian, each with over 100 million speakers.

Sanskrit manuscript on palm-leaf, in Bihar or Nepal, 11th century: *Sanskrit evolved from Proto-Indo-European languages and was used to write the Vedas, the Hindu religious texts compiled between 1500-500 BCE.*

Vedic Sanskrit is the language of the Vedas, the most ancient Hindu scripts, compiled c. 1500-500 BCE. The Vedas contain hymns, incantations called Samhitas, and theological and philosophical guidance for priests of the Vedic religion. Believed to be direct revelations to seers among the early Aryan people of India, the four chief collections are the Rig Veda, Sam Veda, Yajur Vedia, and Atharva Veda. (Depending on the source consulted, these are spelled, for example, either Rig Veda or Rigveda.)

Vedic Sanskrit was orally preserved as a part of the Vedic chanting tradition, predating alphabetic writing in India by several centuries. Modern linguists consider the metrical hymns of the Rigveda Samhita, the most ancient layer of text in the Vedas, to have been composed by many authors over several centuries of oral tradition.

Sanskrit Literature

Sanskrit Literature began with the spoken or sung literature of the Vedas from c. 1500 BCE, and continued with the oral tradition of the Sanskrit Epics of Iron Age India, the period after the Bronze Age began, around 1200 BCE. At approximately 1000 BCE, Vedic Sanskrit began the transition from a first language to a second language of religion and learning.

Around 500 BCE, the ancient scholar Panini standardized the grammar of Vedic Sanskrit, including 3,959 rules of syntax, semantics, and morphology (the study of words and how they are formed and relate to each other). Panini's *Astadhyayi* is the most important of the surviving texts of *Vyakarana*, the linguistic analysis of Sanskrit, consisting of eight chapters laying out his rules and their sources. Through this standardization, Panini helped create what is now known as Classical Sanskrit.

A 2004 Indian stamp honoring Panini, the great Sanskrit grammarian: The scholar Panini standardized the grammar of Vedic Sanskrit to create Classical Sanskrit. With this standardization, Sanskrit became a language of religion and learning.

The classical period of Sanskrit literature dates to the Gupta period and the successive pre-Islamic middle kingdoms of India, spanning approximately the 3rd to 8th centuries CE. Hindu Puranas, a genre of Indian literature that includes myths and legends, fall into the period of Classical Sanskrit.

Drama as a distinct genre of Sanskrit literature emerged in the final centuries BCE, influenced partly by Vedic mythology. Famous Sanskrit dramatists include Shudraka, Bhasa, Asvaghosa, and Kalidasa; their numerous plays are still available, although little is known about the authors themselves. Kalidasa's play, *Abhijnanasakuntalam*, is generally regarded as a masterpiece and was among the first Sanskrit works to be translated into English, as well as numerous other languages.

Works of Sanskrit literature, such as the Yoga-Sutras of Patanjali, which are still consulted by practitioners of yoga today, and the *Upanishads*, a series of sacred Hindu treatises, were translated into Arabic and Persian. Sanskrit fairy tales and fables were characterized by ethical reflections and proverbial philosophy, with a particular style making its way into Persian and Arabic literature and exerting influence over such famed tales as *One Thousand and One Nights*, better known in English as *Arabian Nights*.

Poetry was also a key feature of this period of the language. Kalidasa was the foremost Classical Sanskrit poet, with a simple but beautiful style, while later poetry shifted toward more intricate techniques including stanzas that read the same backwards and forwards, words that could be split to produce different meanings, and sophisticated metaphors.

Importance

Sanskrit is vital to Indian culture because of its extensive use in religious literature, primarily in Hinduism, and because most modern Indian languages have been directly derived from, or strongly influenced by, Sanskrit.

Knowledge of Sanskrit was a marker of social class and educational attainment in ancient India, and it was taught mainly to members of the higher castes (social groups based on birth and employment status). In the medieval era, Sanskrit continued to be spoken and written, particularly by Brahmins (the name for Hindu priests of the highest caste) for scholarly communication.

Today, Sanskrit is still used on the Indian Subcontinent. More than 3,000 Sanskrit works have been composed since India became independent in 1947, while more than 90 weekly, biweekly, and quarterly publications are published in Sanskrit. *Sudharma*, a daily newspaper written in Sanskrit, has been published in India since 1970. Sanskrit is used extensively in the Carnatic and Hindustani branches of classical music, and it continues to be used during worship in Hindu temples as well as in Buddhist and Jain religious practices.

Sanskrit is a major feature of the academic linguistic field of Indo-European studies, which focuses on both extinct and current Indo-European languages, and can be studied in major universities around the world.

The Vedas

The Vedas are the oldest texts of the Hindu religion and contain hymns, myths and rituals that still resonate in India today.

> ## Key Takeaways
>
> *Key Points*
>
> - The Vedas, meaning "knowledge," are the oldest texts of Hinduism.
> - They are derived from the ancient Indo- Aryan culture of the Indian Subcontinent and began as an oral tradition that was passed down through generations before finally being written in Vedic Sanskrit between 1500 and 500 BCE (Before Common Era).
> - The Vedas are structured in four different collections containing hymns, poems, prayers, and religious instruction.
> - The Indian caste system is based on a fable from the Vedas about the sacrifice of the deity Purusha.
>
> *Key Terms*
>
> - **Caste System**: An ancient social structure based upon one of the fables in the Vedas, castes persist in modern India.
> - **Rig Veda**: The oldest and most important of the four Vedas.
> - **Vedas**: The oldest scriptures of Hinduism, originally passed down orally but then written in Vedic Sanskrit between 1500 and 500 BCE.
> - **Hinduism**: A major world religion that began on the Indian Subcontinent.

The Indo-Aryan Vedas remain the oldest scriptures of Hinduism, which is considered one of the oldest religions in the world. Vedic ritualism, a composite of ancient Indo-Aryan and Harappan culture, contributed to the deities and traditions of Hinduism over time. The Vedas are split into four major texts and contain hymns, mythological accounts, poems, prayers, and formulas considered sacred to the Vedic religion.

Structure of the Vedas

Vedas, meaning "knowledge," were written in Vedic Sanskrit between 1500 and 500 BCE in the northwestern region the Indian Subcontinent. The Vedas were transmitted orally during the course of numerous subsequent generations before finally being archived in written form. Not much is known about the authors of the Vedas, as the focus is placed on the ideas found in Vedic tradition rather than those who originated the ideas. The oldest of the texts is the Rig Veda, and while it is not possible to establish precise dates for each of the ancient texts, it is believed the collection was completed by the end of the 2nd millennium BCE (Before Common Era).

There are four Indo-Aryan Vedas: the Rig Veda contains hymns about their mythology; the Sama Veda consists mainly of hymns about religious rituals; the Yajur Veda contains instructions for religious rituals; and the Atharva Veda consists of spells against enemies, sorcerers, and diseases. (Depending on the source consulted, these are spelled, for example, either Rig Veda or Rigveda.)

Rigveda Manuscript: *A manuscript copy of the Rigveda, the oldest and most important of the four Vedas of the Vedic religion, from the early 19th century.*

The Rig Veda is the largest and considered the most important of the collection, containing 1,028 hymns divided into 10 books called mandalas. The verses of the Sam Veda are taken almost completely from the Rig Veda, but arranged differently so they may be chanted. The Yajur Veda is divided into the White and Black halves and contains prose commentaries on how religious and sacrifices should be performed. The Atharva Veda includes charms and magic incantations written in the style of folklore.

Each Veda was further divided in two sections: the Brahmanas, instructions for religious rituals, and the Samhitas, mantras or hymns in praise of various deities. Modern linguists consider the metrical hymns of the Rigveda Samhita, the most ancient layer of text in the Vedas, to have been composed by many authors over several centuries of oral tradition.

Although the focus of the Vedas is on the message rather than the messengers, such as Buddha or Jesus Christ in their respective religions, the Vedic religion still held gods in high regard.

Vedic Religion

The Aryan pantheon of gods is described in great detail in the Rig Veda. However, the religious practices and deities are not uniformly consistent in these sacred texts, probably because the Aryans themselves were not a homogenous group. While spreading through the Indian Subcontinent, it is probable that their initial religious beliefs and practices were shaped by the absorption of local religious traditions.

According to the hymns of the Rig Veda, the most important deities were Agni, the god of Fire, intermediary between the gods and humans; Indra, the god of Heavens and War, protector of the Aryans against their enemies; Surya, the Sun god; Vayu, the god of Wind; and Prthivi, the goddess of Earth

Agni, God of Fire: *Agni, the Indian God of Fire from the ancient Vedic religion, shown riding a ram.*

Vedas and Castes

The Caste System, or groups based on birth or employment status, has been part of the social fabric of the Indian Subcontinent since ancient times. The castes are thought to have derived from a hymn found in the Vedas to the deity Purusha, who is believed to have been sacrificed by the other gods. Afterward Purusha's mind became the Moon, his eyes became the Sun, his head the Sky, and his feet the Earth.

The passage describing the classes of people derived from the sacrifice of Purusha is the first indication of a caste system. The Brahmins, or priests, came from Purusha's mouth; the Kshatriyas, or warrior rulers, came from Purusha's arms; the Vaishyas, or commoners such as landowners and merchants, came from Purusha's thighs; and the Shudras, or laborers and servants, came from Purusha's feet.

Today the castes still exist in the form of varna, or class system, based on the original four castes described in the Vedas. A fifth group known as Dalits, historically excluded from the varna system, are ostracized and called
untouchables. The caste system as it exists today is thought to be a product of developments following the collapse of British colonial rule in India. The system is frowned upon by many people in Indian society and was a focus of social justice campaigns during the 20th century by prominent progressive activists such as B. R. Ambedkar, an architect of the Indian Constitution, and Mahatma Gandhi, the revered leader of the nonviolent Indian independence movement.

Gandhi at Madras, 1933: Indian independence leader Mahatma Gandhi visits Madras, now Chennai, on a tour of India in 1933. During his appearances Gandhi frequently spoke out against the discrimination of the Indian caste system.

Attributions

CC licensed content, Specific attribution

- Indo-Gangetic Plain. **Provided by**: Wikipedia. **Located at**: https://en.wikipedia.org/wiki/Indo-Gangetic_Plain. **License**: *CC BY-SA: Attribution-ShareAlike*
- Aryan. **Provided by**: Wikipedia. **Located at**: http://en.wikipedia.org/wiki/Aryan. **License**: *CC BY-SA: Attribution-ShareAlike*
- Civilization and Empires in the Indian Subcontinent. **Provided by**: Wikibooks. **Located at**: http://en.wikibooks.org/wiki/World_History/Civilization_and_Empires_in_the_Indian_Subcontinent. **License**: *CC BY-SA: Attribution-ShareAlike*
- Vedic Period. **Provided by**: Wikipedia. **Located at**: https://en.wikipedia.org/wiki/Vedic_period. **License**: *CC BY-SA: Attribution-ShareAlike*

- Indo-Aryan Migration. **Provided by**: Wikipedia. **Located at**: http://en.wikipedia.org/wiki/Indo-Aryan_migration. **License**: *CC BY-SA: Attribution-ShareAlike*
- AP World History Wikispaces. **Provided by**: apworldhistorywiki Wikispace. **Located at**: http://apworldhistorywiki.wikispaces.com/South+Asia+87-99. **License**: *CC BY-SA: Attribution-ShareAlike*
- Kurgan Hypothesis. **Provided by**: Wikipedia. **Located at**: http://en.wikipedia.org/wiki/Kurgan_hypothesis. **License**: *CC BY-SA: Attribution-ShareAlike*
- Indo-Gangetic Plain. **Provided by**: Wikimedia. **Located at**: https://commons.wikimedia.org/wiki/File:Indo-Gangetic_Plain.png. **License**: *CC BY-SA: Attribution-ShareAlike*
- NavdatoliGoblet1300BCE. **Provided by**: Wikimedia. **Located at**: https://commons.wikimedia.org/wiki/File:NavdatoliGoblet1300BCE.jpg. **License**: *Public Domain: No Known Copyright*
- AP World History Wikispaces. **Provided by**: apworldhistorywiki Wikispace. **Located at**: http://apworldhistorywiki.wikispaces.com/South+Asia+87-99. **License**: *CC BY-SA: Attribution-ShareAlike*
- Vedic Age. **Provided by**: pgapworld Wikispace. **Located at**: https://pgapworld.wikispaces.com/Vedic+Age. **License**: *CC BY-SA: Attribution-ShareAlike*
- Vedic System. **Provided by**: Wikipedia. **Located at**: http://en.wikipedia.org/wiki/Vedic_period. **License**: *CC BY-SA: Attribution-ShareAlike*
- Mahatma Gandhi. **Provided by**: Wikipedia. **Located at**: https://en.wikipedia.org/wiki/Mahatma_Gandhi. **License**: *CC BY-SA: Attribution-ShareAlike*
- Varna. **Provided by**: Wikipedia. **Located at**: https://en.wikipedia.org/wiki/Varna_(Hinduism). **License**: *CC BY-SA: Attribution-ShareAlike*
- Vedas. **Provided by**: Wikipedia. **Located at**: https://en.wikipedia.org/wiki/Vedas. **License**: *CC BY-SA: Attribution-ShareAlike*
- Caste System in India. **Provided by**: Wikipedia. **Located at**: https://en.wikipedia.org/wiki/Caste_system_in_India. **License**: *CC BY-SA: Attribution-ShareAlike*
- Constitution of India. **Provided by**: Wikipedia. **Located at**: https://en.wikipedia.org/wiki/Constitution_of_India. **License**: *CC BY-SA: Attribution-ShareAlike*
- HIST101: Ancient Civilizations of the World. **Provided by**: Saylor. **Located at**: https://legacy.saylor.org/hist101/Intro/. **License**: *CC BY: Attribution*
- Indo-Gangetic Plain. **Provided by**: Wikimedia. **Located at**: https://commons.wikimedia.org/wiki/File:Indo-Gangetic_Plain.png. **License**: *CC BY-SA: Attribution-ShareAlike*
- NavdatoliGoblet1300BCE. **Provided by**: Wikimedia. **Located at**: https://commons.wikimedia.org/wiki/File:NavdatoliGoblet1300BCE.jpg. **License**: *Public Domain: No Known Copyright*
- Rigveda MS in Sanskrit on paper, India. **Provided by**: Wikimedia. **Located at**: https://commons.wikimedia.org/wiki/File:Rigveda_MS2097.jpg. **License**: *Public Domain: No Known Copyright*
- Gandhi at Madras, 1933. **Provided by**: Wikimedia. **Located at**: https://en.wikipedia.org/wiki/Caste_system_in_India#/media/File:Gandhi,_Harijan_Work_at_Madras.jpg. **License**: *Public Domain: No Known Copyright*
- Castes in India. **Provided by**: Wikimedia. **Located at**: https://commons.wikimedia.org/wiki/File:Seventy-two_Specimens_of_Castes_in_India_(18).jpg. **License**: *Public Domain: No Known Copyright*
- Panini. **Provided by**: Wikipedia. **Located at**: https://en.wikipedia.org/wiki/P%C4%81%E1%B9%87ini. **License**: *CC BY-SA: Attribution-ShareAlike*
- Kalidasa. **Provided by**: Wikipedia. **Located at**: https://en.wikipedia.org/wiki/K%C4%81lid%C4%81sa. **License**: *CC BY-SA: Attribution-ShareAlike*
- Indo-European Studies. **Provided by**: Wikipedia. **Located at**: https://en.wikipedia.org/wiki/Indo-European_studies. **License**: *CC BY-SA: Attribution-ShareAlike*
- Upanishads. **Provided by**: Wikipedia. **Located at**: https://en.wikipedia.org/wiki/Upanishads. **License**: *CC BY-SA: Attribution-ShareAlike*
- Vedic Sanskrit. **Provided by**: Wikipedia. **Located at**: https://en.wikipedia.org/wiki/Vedic_Sanskrit. **License**: *CC BY-SA: Attribution-ShareAlike*
- Indo-European Languages. **Provided by**: Wikipedia. **Located at**: https://en.wikipedia.org/wiki/Indo-European_languages. **License**: *CC BY-SA: Attribution-ShareAlike*
- Sanskrit Literature. **Provided by**: Wikipedia. **Located at**: https://en.wikipedia.org/wiki/Sanskrit_literature. **License**: *CC BY-SA: Attribution-ShareAlike*
- Sanskrit. **Provided by**: Wikipedia. **Located at**: http://en.wikipedia.org/wiki/Sanskrit. **License**: *CC BY-SA: Attribution-ShareAlike*

INDO-EUROPEAN CIVILIZATIONS • 249

- Indo-Gangetic Plain. **Provided by**: Wikimedia. **Located at**: https://commons.wikimedia.org/wiki/File:Indo-Gangetic_Plain.png. **License**: *CC BY-SA: Attribution-ShareAlike*

- NavdatoliGoblet1300BCE. **Provided by**: Wikimedia. **Located at**: https://commons.wikimedia.org/wiki/File:NavdatoliGoblet1300BCE.jpg. **License**: *Public Domain: No Known Copyright*

- Rigveda MS in Sanskrit on paper, India. **Provided by**: Wikimedia. **Located at**: https://commons.wikimedia.org/wiki/File:Rigveda_MS2097.jpg. **License**: *Public Domain: No Known Copyright*

- Gandhi at Madras, 1933. **Provided by**: Wikimedia. **Located at**: https://en.wikipedia.org/wiki/Caste_system_in_India#/media/File:Gandhi,_Harijan_Work_at_Madras.jpg. **License**: *Public Domain: No Known Copyright*

- Castes in India. **Provided by**: Wikimedia. **Located at**: https://commons.wikimedia.org/wiki/File:Seventy-two_Specimens_of_Castes_in_India_(18).jpg. **License**: *Public Domain: No Known Copyright*

- Devimahatmya Sanskrit MS Nepal 11c. **Provided by**: Wikimedia. **Located at**: http://en.wikipedia.org/wiki/File:Devimahatmya_Sanskrit_MS_Nepal_11c.jpg. **License**: *Public Domain: No Known Copyright*

- Panini, the great Sanskrit grammarian. **Provided by**: Wikimedia. **Located at**: http://en.wikipedia.org/wiki/File:Panini,_the_great_Sanskrit_grammarian..jpg. **License**: *Public Domain: No Known Copyright*

- Vedas. **Provided by**: Wikipedia. **Located at**: https://en.wikipedia.org/wiki/Vedas. **License**: *CC BY-SA: Attribution-ShareAlike*

- Rigveda. **Provided by**: Wikipedia. **Located at**: https://en.wikipedia.org/wiki/Rigveda. **License**: *CC BY-SA: Attribution-ShareAlike*

- Vedic Sanskrit. **Provided by**: Wikipedia. **Located at**: https://en.wikipedia.org/wiki/Vedic_Sanskrit. **License**: *CC BY-SA: Attribution-ShareAlike*

- Hinduism. **Provided by**: Wikipedia. **Located at**: https://en.wikipedia.org/wiki/Hinduism. **License**: *CC BY-SA: Attribution-ShareAlike*

- Caste System in India. **Provided by**: Wikipedia. **Located at**: https://en.wikipedia.org/wiki/Caste_system_in_India. **License**: *CC BY-SA: Attribution-ShareAlike*

- Indo-Gangetic Plain. **Provided by**: Wikimedia. **Located at**: https://commons.wikimedia.org/wiki/File:Indo-Gangetic_Plain.png. **License**: *CC BY-SA: Attribution-ShareAlike*

- NavdatoliGoblet1300BCE. **Provided by**: Wikimedia. **Located at**: https://commons.wikimedia.org/wiki/File:NavdatoliGoblet1300BCE.jpg. **License**: *Public Domain: No Known Copyright*

- Rigveda MS in Sanskrit on paper, India. **Provided by**: Wikimedia. **Located at**: https://commons.wikimedia.org/wiki/File:Rigveda_MS2097.jpg. **License**: *Public Domain: No Known Copyright*

- Gandhi at Madras, 1933. **Provided by**: Wikimedia. **Located at**: https://en.wikipedia.org/wiki/Caste_system_in_India#/media/File:Gandhi,_Harijan_Work_at_Madras.jpg. **License**: *Public Domain: No Known Copyright*

- Castes in India. **Provided by**: Wikimedia. **Located at**: https://commons.wikimedia.org/wiki/File:Seventy-two_Specimens_of_Castes_in_India_(18).jpg. **License**: *Public Domain: No Known Copyright*

- Devimahatmya Sanskrit MS Nepal 11c. **Provided by**: Wikimedia. **Located at**: http://en.wikipedia.org/wiki/File:Devimahatmya_Sanskrit_MS_Nepal_11c.jpg. **License**: *Public Domain: No Known Copyright*

- Panini, the great Sanskrit grammarian. **Provided by**: Wikimedia. **Located at**: http://en.wikipedia.org/wiki/File:Panini,_the_great_Sanskrit_grammarian..jpg. **License**: *Public Domain: No Known Copyright*

- Agni, God of Fire. **Provided by**: Wikipedia. **Located at**: https://commons.wikimedia.org/wiki/File:Agni_god_of_fire..pg. **License**: *Public Domain: No Known Copyright*

- Gandhi at Madras, 1933. **Provided by**: Wikipedia. **Located at**: https://en.wikipedia.org/wiki/Caste_system_in_India#/media/File:Gandhi,_Harijan_Work_at_Madras.jpg. **License**: *Public Domain: No Known Copyright*

- Rigveda Manuscript. **Provided by**: Wikipedia. **Located at**: https://en.wikipedia.org/wiki/Rigveda#/media/File:Rigveda_MS2097.jpg. **License**: *Public Domain: No Known Copyright*

Religion in the Indian Subcontinent

The Rise of Hinduism

Hinduism evolved as a synthesis of cultures and traditions, including the Indo-Aryan Vedic religion.

Learning Objectives

Explain the evolution of hinduism

Key Takeaways

Key Points

- The Vedic religion was influenced by local cultures and traditions adopted by Indo-Aryans as they spread throughout India. Vedic ritualism heavily influenced the rise of Hinduism, which rose to prominence after c. 400 BCE.
- The Vedas — the oldest texts of the Hindu religion—describe deities, mythology, and instructions for religious rituals.
- The Upanishads are a collection of Vedic texts particularly important to Hinduism that contain revealed truths concerning the nature of ultimate reality, and describing the character and form of human salvation.
- During the 14th and 15th centuries, the Hindu Vijayanagar Empire served as a barrier against Muslim invasion, fostering a reconstruction of Hindu life and administration. The Hindu Maratha Confederacy rose to power in the 18th century and eventually overthrew Muslim rule in India.

> *Key Terms*
>
> - **moksha**: The character and form of human salvation, as described in the Upanishads.
> - **Sramana**: Meaning "seeker," Sramana refers to several Indian religious movements that existed alongside the Vedic religion, the historical predecessor of modern Hinduism.
> - **brahman**: The nature of ultimate reality, as described in the Upanishads.
> - **Upanishads**: A collection of Vedic texts that contain the earliest emergence of some of the central religious concepts of Hinduism, Buddhism, and Jainism.

Hinduism is considered one of the oldest religions in the world. Western scholars regard Hinduism as a synthesis, or fusion, of various Indian cultures and traditions, with diverse roots and no stated founder. This synthesis is believed to have developed after Vedic times, between 500 BCE and 300 CE. However, Vedic ritualism, a composite of Indo-Aryan and Harappan culture, contributed to the deities and traditions of Hinduism. The Indo-Aryan Vedas remain the oldest scriptures of the Hindu religion, which has grown culturally and geographically through modern times to become one of the world's four major religions.

The Vedas

Vedas, meaning "knowledge," were written in Vedic Sanskrit between 1500 and 500 BCE in the northwestern region of the Indian Subcontinent. There are four Indo-Aryan Vedas: the Rig Veda contains hymns about mythology; the Sama Veda consists mainly of hymns about religious rituals; the Yajur Veda contains instructions for religious rituals; and the Atharva Veda consists of spells against enemies, sorcerers and diseases. (Depending on the source consulted, these are spelled, for example, either Sama Veda or Samaveda.) The Rig Veda is the largest and considered the most important of the collection, containing 1,028 hymns divided into ten books, called mandalas.

The Aryan pantheon of gods is described in great detail in the Rig Veda. However, the religious practices and deities are not uniformly consistent in these sacred texts, probably because the Aryans themselves were not a homogenous group. While spreading through the Indian subcontinent, it is probable their initial religious beliefs and practices were shaped by the absorption of local religious traditions.

According to the hymns of the Rig Veda, the most important deities were Agni, the god of Fire, and the intermediary between the gods and humans; Indra, the god of Heavens and War, protector of the Aryans against their enemies; Surya, the Sun god; Vayu, the god of Wind; and Prthivi, the goddess of Earth.

Modern Hindu representation of Agni, god of fire: *The Rig Veda describes the varied deities of Vedic religion. These gods persisted as Vedic religion was assimilated into Hinduism.*

The Upanishads

The Upanishads are a collection of Vedic texts that contain the earliest emergence of some of the central religious concepts of Hinduism, Buddhism, and Jainism. Also known as Vedanta, "the end of the Veda," the collection is one of the sacred texts of Hinduism thought to contain revealed truths concerning the nature of ultimate reality, or brahman, and describing the character and form of human salvation, called moksha. The Upanishads are found in the conclusion of the commentaries on the Vedas, and have been passed down by oral tradition.

Hindu Synthesis

Sramana, meaning "seeker," refers to several Indian religious movements, including Buddhism and Jainism, that existed alongside the Vedic religion—the historical predecessor of modern Hinduism. The Sramana traditions drove the so-called Hindu synthesis after the Vedic period that spread to southern Indian and parts of Southeast Asia. As it spread, this new Hinduism assimilated popular non-Vedic gods and other traditions from local cultures, and integrated societal divisions, called the caste system. It is also thought to have included both Buddhist and Sramana influences.

Splinter and Rise of Hinduism

During the reign of the Gupta Empire (between 320-550 CE), which included the period known as the Golden Age of India, the first known stone and cave temples dedicated to Hindu deities were built. After the Gupta period, central power disintegrated and religion became regionalized to an extent, with variants arising within Hinduism and competing with each other, as well as sects of Buddhism and Jainism. Over time, Buddhism declined but some of its practices were integrated into Hinduism, with large Hindu temples being built in South and Southeast Asia.

The Swaminarayan Akshardham Temple in Delhi, the world's largest Hindu temple: Hinduism evolved as a combination of various cultures and traditions, including Vedic religion and the Upanishads.

The Hindu religion maintained its presence and continued to grow despite a long period of Muslim rule in India, from 1200-1750 CE, during which Hindus endured violence as Islam grew to become what is now the second largest religion in India, behind Hinduism. Akbar I, emperor of the ruling Mughal Dynasty in India from 1556-1605 CE, ended official persecution of non-Muslims and recognized Hinduism, protected Hindu temples, and abolished discriminatory taxes against Hindus.

Hindu Prominence

During the 14th and 15th centuries, the Hindu Vijayanagar Empire had arisen and served as a barrier against invasion by Muslim rulers to the north, fostering a reconstruction of Hindu life and administration. Vidyaranya, a minister and mentor to three generations of kings in the Vijayanagar Empire beginning around 1336, helped spread the historical and cultural influence of Shankara—an Indian philosopher of the 8th century CE credited with unifying and establishing the main currents of thought in Hinduism.

The Hindu Maratha Confederacy rose to power in the 18th century and eventually overthrew Muslim rule in India. In the 19th century, the Indian subcontinent became a western colony during the period of the British Raj (the name of the British ruling government) beginning in 1858.

Through the period of the Raj, until its end in 1947, there was a Hindu resurgence, known as the Bengali Renaissance, in the Bengal region of India. It included a cultural, social, intellectual, and artistic movement. Indology, an academic study of Indian culture, was also established in the 19th century, and spread knowledge of Vedic philosophy and literature and promoted western interest in Hinduism.

In the 20th century, Hinduism gained prominence as a political force and source of national identity in India. According to the 2011 census, Hindus account for almost 80% of India's population of 1.21 billion people, with 960 million practitioners. Other nations with large Hindu populations include Nepal, with 23 million followers, and Bangladesh, with 15 million. Hinduism counts over 1 billion adherents across the globe, or approximately 15% of the world's population.

Singapore Diwali Decorations: *Diwali decorations in Little India are part of an annual Hindu celebration in Singapore, where there are over 260,000 Hindus.*

The Sramana Movement

Sramana broke with Vedic Hinduism over the authority of the Brahmins and the need to follow ascetic lives.

Learning Objectives

Understand the Sramana movement

Key Takeaways

Key Points

- Sramana was an ancient Indian religious movement with origins in the Vedic religion. However, it took a divergent path, rejecting Vedic Hindu ritualism and the authority of the Brahmins —the traditional priests of the Hindu religion.
- Sramanas were those who practiced an ascetic, or strict and self-denying, lifestyle in pursuit of spiritual liberation. They are commonly known as monks.
- The Sramana movement gave rise to Jainism and Buddhism.

Key Terms

- **Sramana**: An ancient Indian religious movement that began as an offshoot of the Vedic religion and focused on ascetic lifestyle and principles.
- **Vedic Religion**: The historical predecessor of modern Hinduism. The Vedas are the oldest scriptures in the Hindu religion.
- **Sramanas**: Sramana followers who renounced married and domestic life, and adopted an ascetic path. The Sramanas rejected the authority of the Brahmins.
- **Brahmin**: A member of a caste in Vedic Hinduism, consisting of priests and teachers who are held as intermediaries between deities and followers, and who are considered the protectors of the sacred learning found in the Vedas.
- **ascetic**: A person who practices severe self-discipline and abstention from worldly pleasures as a way of seeking spiritual enlightenment and freedom.

Sramana was an ancient Indian religious movement that began as an offshoot of the Vedic religion and gave rise to other similar but varying movements, including Buddhism and Jainism. Sramana, meaning "seeker," was a tradition that began around 800-600 BCE when new philosophical groups, who believed in a more austere path to spiritual freedom, rejected the authority of the Brahmins (the priests of Vedic Hinduism). Modern Hinduism can be regarded as a combination of Vedic and Sramana traditions; it is substantially influenced by both.

Vedic Roots

The Vedic Religion was the historical predecessor of modern Hinduism. The Vedic Period refers to the time period from approximately 1750-500 BCE, during which Indo- Aryans settled into northern India, bringing with them specific religious traditions. Most history of this period is derived from the Vedas, the oldest scriptures in the Hindu religion. Vedas, meaning "knowledge," were composed by the Aryans in Vedic Sanskrit between 1500 and 500 BCE, in the northwestern region the Indian subcontinent.

There are four Indo-Aryan Vedas: the Rig Veda contains hymns about their mythology; the Sama Veda consists mainly of hymns about religious rituals; the Yajur Veda contains instructions for religious rituals; and the Atharva Veda consists of spells against enemies, sorcerers, and diseases. (Depending on the source consulted, these are spelled, for example, either Rig Veda or Rigveda.)

Sramana Origins

Several Sramana movements are known to have existed in India before the 6th century BCE. Sramana existed in parallel to, but separate from, Vedic Hinduism. The dominant Vedic ritualism contrasted with the beliefs of the Sramanas followers who renounced married and domestic life and adopted an ascetic path, one of severe self-discipline and abstention from all indulgence, in order to achieve spiritual liberation. The Sramanas rejected the authority of the Brahmins, who were considered the protectors of the sacred learning found in the Vedas.

Brahmin is a caste, or social group, in Vedic Hinduism consisting of priests and teachers who are held as intermediaries between deities and followers. Brahmins are traditionally responsible for religious rituals in temples, and for reciting hymns and prayers during rite of passage rituals, such as weddings.

In India, Sramana originally referred to any ascetic, recluse, or religious practitioner who renounced secular life and society in order to focus solely on finding religious truth. Sramana evolved in India over two phases: the Paccekabuddha, the tradition of the individual ascetic, the "lone Buddha" who leaves the world behind; and the Savaka, the phase of disciples, or those who gather together as a community, such as a sect of monks.

Sramana Traditions

A "tradition" is a belief or behavior passed down within a group or society, with symbolic meaning or special significance. Sramana traditions drew upon established Brahmin concepts to formulate their own doctrines.

The Sramana traditions subscribe to diverse philosophies, and at times significantly disagree with each other, as well as with orthodox Hinduism and its six schools of Hindu philosophy. The differences range from a belief that every individual has a soul, to the assertion that there is no soul. In terms of lifestyle, Sramana traditions include a wide range of beliefs that can vary, from vegetarianism to meat eating, and from family life to extreme asceticism denying all worldly pleasures.

The varied Sramana movements arose in the same circles of ancient India that led to the development of Yogic practices, which include the Hindu philosophy of following a course of physical and mental discipline in order to attain liberation from the material world, and a union between the self and a supreme being or principle.

The Sramana traditions drove the so-called Hindu synthesis after the Vedic period, which spread to southern Indian and parts of Southeast Asia. As it spread, this new Hinduism assimilated popular non-Vedic gods and other traditions from local cultures, as well as the integrated societal divisions, called the caste system.

Sramaṇa traditions later gave rise to Yoga, Jainism, Buddhism, and some schools of Hinduism. They also led to popular concepts in all major Indian religions, such as saṃsāra, the cycle of birth and death, and *moksha*, liberation from that cycle.

Buddhism

After attaining Enlightenment, Siddhartha Gautama became known as the Buddha, and taught a Middle Way that became a major world religion, known as Buddhism.

Learning Objectives

Understand the development of Buddhism as a major world religion

Key Takeaways

Key Points

- Sramanas were those who practiced an ascetic, or strict and self-denying, lifestyle in pursuit of spiritual liberation. They are commonly known as monks.
- The Sramana movement gave rise to Buddhism, a non-theistic religion that encompasses a variety of traditions, beliefs, and practices, and arose when Siddhartha Gautama began following Sramana traditions in the 5th century BCE.
- Following his "Enlightenment," Siddhartha became known as Buddha, or "Awakened One." He began teaching a Middle Way to spiritual Nirvana, a release from all earthly burdens.
- Buddhism has spread to become one of the world's great religions, with an estimated 488 million followers.

Key Terms

- **Noble Eightfold Path**: The eight concepts taught by Buddha as the means to achieving Nirvana.
- **Nirvana**: A sublime state that marks the release from the cycle of rebirths, known in the Sramana tradition as samsara.
- **Sramana**: An offshoot of the Vedic religion that promoted an ascetic lifestyle; Sramana

> gave rise to Buddhism and other similar traditions.
> - **Siddhartha Gautama**: An aristocratic young man who gave up worldly comforts to follow Sramana, then attained Enlightenment and became known as the Buddha, teaching a Middle Way toward spiritual Nirvana.

Buddhism arose between 500-300 BCE, when Siddhartha Gautama, a young man from an aristocratic family, left behind his worldly comforts to seek spiritual enlightenment. He became a teacher commonly known as the Buddha, meaning "the awakened one," and Buddhism spread to become a non-theistic religion that encompasses a variety of traditions, beliefs, and practices largely based on his teachings.

Sramana Origins

Buddhism is based on an ancient Indian religious philosophy called Sramana, which began as an offshoot of the Vedic religion. Several Sramana movements are known to have existed in India before the 6th century BCE. Sramana existed in parallel to, but separate from, Vedic Hinduism, which followed the teachings and rituals found in the Vedas, the most ancient texts of the Vedic religion. Sramana, meaning "seeker," was a tradition that began when new philosophical groups who believed in a more austere path to spiritual freedom rejected the authority of the Vedas and the Brahmins, the priests of Vedic Hinduism, around 800-600 BCE.

Sramana promoted spiritual concepts that became popular in all major Indian religions, such as saṃsāra, the cycle of birth and death, and moksha , liberation from that cycle. The Sramanas renounced married and domestic life, and adopted an ascetic path— one of severe self-discipline and abstention from all indulgence—in order to achieve spiritual liberation. Sramaṇa traditions (or its religious and moral practices) later gave rise to varying schools of Hinduism, as well as Yoga, Jainism, and Buddhism.

Origins of Buddhism

Early texts suggest Siddhartha Gautama was born into the Shakya Clan, a community on the eastern edge of the Indian subcontinent in the 5th century BCE. His father was an elected chieftain, or oligarch, of the small republic. Gautama is thought to have been born in modern-day Nepal, and raised in the Shakya capital of Kapilvastu, which may have been in Nepal or India. Most scholars agree that he taught and founded a monastic order during the reign of the Magadha Empire. In addition to the Vedic Brahmins, the Buddha's lifetime coincided with the flourishing of influential Sramana schools of thought, including Jainism.

Buddhist teachings explain that Siddhartha was a young man from a respected family, who renounced his family and left his father's palace at age 29 in search of truth and enlightenment through Sramana. Siddhartha began this quest through a period of starvation and, according to legend, grew so thin he could feel his hands if he placed one on his back and the other on his stomach. This explains statues that depict Buddha as thin and withered, rather than the better known depiction of him seated with a large belly.

Emaciated Fasting Buddha: *This statue in Chiang Mai, Thailand, depicts the Buddha practicing severe asceticism before his Enlightenment.*

Buddha lived as a Sramana ascetic for approximately six years until he had an "awakening" in a place called Bodh Gaya, in the Gaya district of the modern Indian state of Bihar. Sitting under what became known as the Bodhi Tree, Siddhartha discovered what Buddhists call the Noble Eightfold Path, and attained Buddhatva, or Enlightenment, which is said to be a state of being completely free of lust (raga), hatred (dosa), and delusion (moha).

Siddhartha, thereafter known as Buddha, or "awakened one," was recognized by his followers, called Buddhists, as an enlightened teacher. He taught what he called the Middle Way or Middle Path, the character of the Noble Eightfold Path. This includes eight concepts to be sought after: right view, right resolve, right speech, right conduct, right livelihood, right effort, right mindfulness, and right samadhi (the state of intense concentration brought on through meditation).

His insights were intended to help sentient beings end their suffering through the elimination of ignorance and craving. This could be achieved through understanding the noble path, which is the way to achieve the sublime state of Nirvana. The literal meaning of Nirvana in the Sanskrit language is "blowing out" or "quenching," and is the ultimate spiritual goal of Buddhism. It marks the release from the cycle of rebirths, known in the Sramana tradition as samsara.

Another important Buddhist concept is Bodhisattva, a Sanskrit word for anyone who has been motivated by great compassion and a wish to attain buddhahood for the benefit of all sentient beings—those who have a conscious awareness of the self but are in contrast with buddhahood. Sentient beings are characteristically not yet enlightened and are thus confined to the death, rebirth and dukkha (suffering) found in the cycle of samsara. Bodhisattvas, therefore, are those who have set themselves on the path toward enlightenment and hope to benefit others through their journey. Depictions of the bodhisattva path are a popular subject in Buddhist art.

RELIGION IN THE INDIAN SUBCONTINENT • 261

Bodhisattva: *Clay sculpture of a bodhisattva, Afghanistan, 7th century.*

Rise of Buddhism

Buddha is thought to have died around 483 BCE, after 45 years of travel and teaching. Buddhists believe he passed into a state of Nirvana. Small communities of monks and nuns, known as bhikkus, sprung up along the routes Buddha traveled. Buddhism was overshadowed by the more dominant Hindu religion, but this began to change in the 3rd century BCE; this was when one of the Indian subcontinent's great rulers, Ashoka I of the Maurya Empire, renounced wars, despite having waged war to build his own kingdom. In a major break from others rulers of the time, he converted to Buddhism.

Ashoka promoted the religion's expansion by deploying monks to spread Buddha's teaching. This began a wave of conversion throughout India as well as in surrounding nations, such as Nepal, Tibet, and Burma, but also further afield in Asia, including in China and Japan. Over time Buddhism grew, as greater numbers of people became aware of its teachings, including those in western nations, eventually becoming one of the major religions practiced around the world.

Today, Buddhism is practiced by an estimated 488 million people. China is the nation with the largest number of Buddhists, approximately 244 million followers, or more than 18% of its total population. Other countries that have a large number of Buddhists among their populations include Myanmar with 48.4 million, Japan with 45.8 million, Sri Lanka with 14.2 million, Cambodia with 13.7 million, South Korea with 11 million, Thailand, Laos, Singapore, Taiwan, and Nepal. The United States is home to an estimated 1.2 million Buddhists, or 1.2% of the American population.

Jainism

Jainism is a pre-Buddhist religion with roots in the Sramana tradition. It focuses on karma.

Learning Objectives

- Understand the origins and principles of Jainism

Key Takeaways

Key Points

- Sramanas were those who practiced an ascetic, or strict and self-denying, lifestyle in pursuit of spiritual liberation. They are commonly known as monks.
- The Sramana movement gave rise to Jainism, which is considered an independent, pre-Buddhist religion with possible roots in the Indus Valley Civilization.
- The predominance of karma is one of the key features of Jainism. Karma is the sum of a person's actions in this and previous lives; it determines his or her fate in future existences.

Key Terms

- **karma**: The principle of causality in which intent and actions of an individual influence the future of that person; this is a key concept in Jainism, as well as in Hinduism and Buddhism.
- **ascetic**: A person who practices severe self-discipline and abstention from worldly pleasures in order to attain a higher level of spirituality.
- **Jainism**: An Indian religion that prescribes a path of non-violence toward all living beings, and emphasizes spiritual independence and equality between all forms of life.

> - **saṃsāra**: The repeating cycle of birth, life, and death (reincarnation) within Jainism, Hinduism, and Buddhism.

Jainism, one of the world's major religions, is believed to have roots in the Indus Valley Civilization, and follows aspects of the Sramana traditions of asceticism—self-denial and control in order to achieve a higher level of spirituality. Although Jainism is considered pre-Buddhist, the two religions have a link through a focus on karma—the concept that good deeds in one life will lead to a better existence in the next life. The ultimate aim of Jainism is to achieve liberation of the soul.

Sramana Origins

Jainism is based on an ancient Indian religious philosophy called Sramana, which began as an offshoot of the Vedic religion. Several Sramana movements are known to have existed in India before the 6th century BCE. Sramana existed in parallel to, but separate from, Vedic Hinduism, which followed the teachings and rituals found in the Vedas, the most ancient texts of the Vedic religion. Sramana, meaning "seeker," was a tradition that began around 800-600 BCE, when new philosophical groups, who believed in a more austere path to spiritual freedom, rejected the authority of the Vedas and the Brahmins (the priests of Vedic Hinduism).

Sramana promoted spiritual concepts that became popular in all major Indian religions, such as saṃsāra, the cycle of birth and death, and moksha, liberation from that cycle. The Sramanas renounced married and domestic life and adopted an ascetic path (one of severe self-discipline and abstention from all indulgence) in order to achieve spiritual liberation. Sramaṇa traditions (or religious and moral practices) later gave rise to varying schools of Hinduism, as well as Yoga, Buddhism, and Jainism.

Origins of Jainism

Jainism is considered an independent, pre-Buddhist religion that began c. 700 BCE, although its origins are disputed. Some scholars claim Jainism has its roots in the Indus Valley Civilization, reflecting native spirituality prior to the Indo-Aryan migration into India.

Various seals from Indus Valley Civilizations bear resemblance to Rishabha, the first Jain as the visual representation of Vishnu. Many relics depict Jain symbols, including standing nude male figures, images with serpent-heads, and the bull symbol of Vrshabadeva. However, other scholars believe the Sramana traditions were separate and contemporaneous with Indo-Aryan religious practices of the historical Vedic religion.

An Elaborate Mirpur Jain Temple Wall: *The Jain Temple in Mirpur, India, was built c. 800 CE.*

Jainism Beliefs

The distinguishing features of Jain philosophy are its belief in the independent existence of soul and matter; the denial of a creative and omnipotent God, combined with a belief in an eternal universe; and a strong emphasis on non-violence, morality, and ethics. The word Jain derives from the Sanskrit word jina, meaning conqueror, and the ultimate aim of Jain life is to achieve liberation of the soul.

The predominance of karma is one of the key features of Jainism. Karma is the sum of a person's actions in this and previous lives that determine his or her fate in future existences. A Sanskrit word, karma means action, word, or deed. Its focus is on the spiritual principle of cause and effect, with individual actions influencing individual effects. Good intent and good deeds contribute to good karma and future happiness, while bad intent and deeds produce bad karma and future suffering. Karma is a concept associated with rebirth, or the idea that death is the beginning of a new existence. This idea also appears in other Asian religions, including Buddhism.

The motto of Jainism is Parasparopagraho Jivanam, meaning "the function of souls is to help one another." This is associated with the idea of good deeds, and is incorporated into the main principles of Jainism: ahimsa, non-violence; anekantavada, non-absolutism; and aparigraha, non-possessiveness or non-attachment. Followers take five main vows that include ahimsa and aparigraha, as well as satya, not lying; asteya, not stealing; and brahmacharya, chastity. Jain monks and nuns adhere to these vows absolutely, placing Jainism squarely in the ascetic and self-discipline traditions of Sramana.

Jain Monk: *An image of a Jain monk meditating over religious texts.*

Jainism Followers

The majority of Jains live in India, which counts between 4 and 6 million followers. Some of the largest Jain communities outside India are in the United States, which has more than 79,000 followers; Kenya, which has nearly 69,000 adherents; the United Kingdom, which counts nearly 17,000 followers; and Canada, with approximately 12,000 followers. Other countries with notable Jain populations include Tanzania, Nepal, Uganda, Burma, Malaysia, South Africa, Fiji, Australia, and Japan.

Contemporary Jainism is divided into two major schools, or sects, called Digambara and Svetambara. The Svetambara, meaning "white clad," describes its ascetic adherents' practice of wearing white clothes, while the monks of the "sky clad" Digambara do not wear clothing at all, a practice upon which they disagree.

The most important religious festival of Jainism is Mahavir Jayanti, which celebrates the birth of Mahavira—the 24th and last Tirthankara, or teaching god. Other important festivals include Diwali, marking the Nirvana, or liberation, of Mahavira's soul; and the holy event of Paryushana, also known as Das Lakshana, which is a period of between eight and ten days in August or September of fasting, prayer, and meditation.

Paryushana Celebrations: *Followers of Jainism celebrate Paryushana at the Jain Center of America in New York City.*

Attributions

CC licensed content, Specific attribution

RELIGION IN THE INDIAN SUBCONTINENT • 267

- Adi Shankara. **Provided by**: Wikipedia. **Located at**: https://en.wikipedia.org/wiki/Adi_Shankara. **License**: *CC BY-SA: Attribution-ShareAlike*
- Sramana. **Provided by**: Wikipedia. **Located at**: https://en.wikipedia.org/wiki/%C5%9Arama%E1%B9%87a. **License**: *CC BY-SA: Attribution-ShareAlike*
- Hinduism by Country. **Provided by**: Wikipedia. **Located at**: https://en.wikipedia.org/wiki/Hinduism_by_country. **License**: *CC BY-SA: Attribution-ShareAlike*
- Akbar. **Provided by**: Wikipedia. **Located at**: https://en.wikipedia.org/wiki/Akbar. **License**: *CC BY-SA: Attribution-ShareAlike*
- Vidyaranya. **Provided by**: Wikipedia. **Located at**: https://en.wikipedia.org/wiki/Vidyaranya. **License**: *CC BY-SA: Attribution-ShareAlike*
- HIST101: Ancient Civilizations of the World. **Provided by**: Saylor. **Located at**: https://legacy.saylor.org/hist101/Intro/. **License**: *CC BY: Attribution*
- Hinduism. **Provided by**: Wikipedia. **Located at**: http://en.wikipedia.org/wiki/Hinduism. **License**: *CC BY-SA: Attribution-ShareAlike*
- Upanishads. **Provided by**: Wikipedia. **Located at**: http://en.wikipedia.org/wiki/Upanishads. **License**: *CC BY-SA: Attribution-ShareAlike*
- Singapore Diwali Decorations. **Provided by**: Wikimedia. **Located at**: https://commons.wikimedia.org/wiki/File:Singapore_Divali_Diwali_decorations_Little_India-_Serangoon_Road_2009.jpg. **License**: *CC BY: Attribution*
- Agni god of fire. **Provided by**: Wikimedia. **Located at**: https://commons.wikimedia.org/wiki/File:Agni_god_of_fire.jpg. **License**: *Public Domain: No Known Copyright*
- New Delhi Temple. **Provided by**: Wikimedia. **Located at**: http://en.wikipedia.org/wiki/File:New_Delhi_Temple.jpg. **License**: *CC BY-SA: Attribution-ShareAlike*
- Pratyekabuddha. **Provided by**: Wikipedia. **Located at**: https://en.wikipedia.org/wiki/Pratyekabuddha. **License**: *CC BY-SA: Attribution-ShareAlike*
- Asceticism. **Provided by**: Wikipedia. **Located at**: https://en.wikipedia.org/wiki/Asceticism. **License**: *CC BY-SA: Attribution-ShareAlike*
- Brahmin. **Provided by**: Wikipedia. **Located at**: https://en.wikipedia.org/wiki/Brahmin. **License**: *CC BY-SA: Attribution-ShareAlike*
- Hinduism. **Provided by**: Wikipedia. **Located at**: https://en.wikipedia.org/wiki/Hinduism. **License**: *CC BY-SA: Attribution-ShareAlike*
- Sravaka. **Provided by**: Wikipedia. **Located at**: https://en.wikipedia.org/wiki/%C5%9Ar%C4%81vaka. **License**: *CC BY-SA: Attribution-ShareAlike*
- Sramana. **Provided by**: Wikipedia. **Located at**: http://en.wikipedia.org/wiki/Sramana. **License**: *CC BY-SA: Attribution-ShareAlike*
- HIST101: Ancient Civilizations of the World. **Provided by**: Saylor. **Located at**: https://legacy.saylor.org/hist101/Intro/. **License**: *CC BY: Attribution*
- Singapore Diwali Decorations. **Provided by**: Wikimedia. **Located at**: https://commons.wikimedia.org/wiki/File:Singapore_Divali_Diwali_decorations_Little_India-_Serangoon_Road_2009.jpg. **License**: *CC BY: Attribution*
- Agni god of fire. **Provided by**: Wikimedia. **Located at**: https://commons.wikimedia.org/wiki/File:Agni_god_of_fire.jpg. **License**: *Public Domain: No Known Copyright*
- New Delhi Temple. **Provided by**: Wikimedia. **Located at**: http://en.wikipedia.org/wiki/File:New_Delhi_Temple.jpg. **License**: *CC BY-SA: Attribution-ShareAlike*
- Emaciated Fasting Buddha. **Provided by**: Wikimedia. **Located at**: https://commons.wikimedia.org/wiki/File:Emaciated_Siddhartha_Fasting_Gautama_Buddha.jpg. **License**: *CC BY: Attribution*
- Jain Monk. **Provided by**: Wikimedia. **Located at**: https://commons.wikimedia.org/wiki/File:Jain_Sthanakvasi_monk.jpg. **License**: *Public Domain: No Known Copyright*
- Buddhism By Country. **Provided by**: Wikipedia. **Located at**: https://en.wikipedia.org/wiki/Buddhism_by_country. **License**: *CC BY-SA: Attribution-ShareAlike*
- Gautama Buddha. **Provided by**: Wikipedia. **Located at**: https://en.wikipedia.org/wiki/Gautama_Buddha. **License**: *CC BY-SA: Attribution-ShareAlike*
- Middle Way. **Provided by**: Wikipedia. **Located at**: https://en.wikipedia.org/wiki/Middle_Way. **License**: *CC BY-SA: Attribution-ShareAlike*
- Sramana. **Provided by**: Wikipedia. **Located at**: https://en.wikipedia.org/wiki/%C5%9Arama%E1%B9%87a. **License**: *CC BY-SA: Attribution-ShareAlike*
- Asceticism. **Provided by**: Wikipedia. **Located at**: https://en.wikipedia.org/wiki/Asceticism. **License**: *CC BY-SA: Attribution-*

ShareAlike
- Bodhisattva. **Provided by**: Wikipedia. **Located at**: https://en.wikipedia.org/wiki/Bodhisattva. **License**: *CC BY-SA: Attribution-ShareAlike*
- Nirvana (Buddhism). **Provided by**: Wikipedia. **Located at**: https://en.wikipedia.org/wiki/Nirvana_(Buddhism). **License**: *CC BY-SA: Attribution-ShareAlike*
- Ashoka. **Provided by**: Wikipedia. **Located at**: https://en.wikipedia.org/wiki/Ashoka. **License**: *CC BY-SA: Attribution-ShareAlike*
- Singapore Diwali Decorations. **Provided by**: Wikimedia. **Located at**: https://commons.wikimedia.org/wiki/File:Singapore_Divali_Diwali_decorations_Little_India-_Serangoon_Road_2009.jpg. **License**: *CC BY: Attribution*
- Agni god of fire. **Provided by**: Wikimedia. **Located at**: https://commons.wikimedia.org/wiki/File:Agni_god_of_fire.jpg. **License**: *Public Domain: No Known Copyright*
- New Delhi Temple. **Provided by**: Wikimedia. **Located at**: http://en.wikipedia.org/wiki/File:New_Delhi_Temple.jpg. **License**: *CC BY-SA: Attribution-ShareAlike*
- Emaciated Fasting Buddha. **Provided by**: Wikimedia. **Located at**: https://commons.wikimedia.org/wiki/File:Emaciated_Siddhartha_Fasting_Gautama_Buddha.jpg. **License**: *CC BY: Attribution*
- Jain Monk. **Provided by**: Wikimedia. **Located at**: https://commons.wikimedia.org/wiki/File:Jain_Sthanakvasi_monk.jpg. **License**: *Public Domain: No Known Copyright*
- Bodhisattva. **Provided by**: Wikimedia. **Located at**: https://commons.wikimedia.org/wiki/File:Bodhisattva_Ghorband_Mus%C3%A9e_Guimet_2418.jpg. **License**: *Public Domain: No Known Copyright*
- Emaciated Fasting Buddha. **Provided by**: Wikimedia. **Located at**: https://commons.wikimedia.org/wiki/File:Emaciated_Siddhartha_Fasting_Gautama_Buddha.jpg. **License**: *CC BY: Attribution*
- Sramana. **Provided by**: Wikipedia. **Located at**: https://en.wikipedia.org/wiki/%C5%9Arama%E1%B9%87a. **License**: *CC BY-SA: Attribution-ShareAlike*
- Jainism. **Provided by**: Wikipedia. **Located at**: https://en.wikipedia.org/wiki/Jainism. **License**: *CC BY-SA: Attribution-ShareAlike*
- Svetambara. **Provided by**: Wikipedia. **Located at**: https://en.wikipedia.org/wiki/%C5%9Av%C4%93t%C4%81mbara. **License**: *CC BY-SA: Attribution-ShareAlike*
- Digambara. **Provided by**: Wikipedia. **Located at**: https://en.wikipedia.org/wiki/Digambara. **License**: *CC BY-SA: Attribution-ShareAlike*
- Karma. **Provided by**: Wikipedia. **Located at**: https://en.wikipedia.org/wiki/Karma. **License**: *CC BY-SA: Attribution-ShareAlike*
- Mahavir Jayanti. **Provided by**: Wikipedia. **Located at**: https://en.wikipedia.org/wiki/Mahavir_Jayanti. **License**: *CC BY-SA: Attribution-ShareAlike*
- Singapore Diwali Decorations. **Provided by**: Wikimedia. **Located at**: https://commons.wikimedia.org/wiki/File:Singapore_Divali_Diwali_decorations_Little_India-_Serangoon_Road_2009.jpg. **License**: *CC BY: Attribution*
- Agni god of fire. **Provided by**: Wikimedia. **Located at**: https://commons.wikimedia.org/wiki/File:Agni_god_of_fire.jpg. **License**: *Public Domain: No Known Copyright*
- New Delhi Temple. **Provided by**: Wikimedia. **Located at**: http://en.wikipedia.org/wiki/File:New_Delhi_Temple.jpg. **License**: *CC BY-SA: Attribution-ShareAlike*
- Emaciated Fasting Buddha. **Provided by**: Wikimedia. **Located at**: https://commons.wikimedia.org/wiki/File:Emaciated_Siddhartha_Fasting_Gautama_Buddha.jpg. **License**: *CC BY: Attribution*
- Jain Monk. **Provided by**: Wikimedia. **Located at**: https://commons.wikimedia.org/wiki/File:Jain_Sthanakvasi_monk.jpg. **License**: *Public Domain: No Known Copyright*
- Bodhisattva. **Provided by**: Wikimedia. **Located at**: https://commons.wikimedia.org/wiki/File:Bodhisattva_Ghorband_Mus%C3%A9e_Guimet_2418.jpg. **License**: *Public Domain: No Known Copyright*
- Emaciated Fasting Buddha. **Provided by**: Wikimedia. **Located at**: https://commons.wikimedia.org/wiki/File:Emaciated_Siddhartha_Fasting_Gautama_Buddha.jpg. **License**: *CC BY: Attribution*
- Paryushana Celebrations. **Provided by**: Wikimedia. **Located at**: https://commons.wikimedia.org/wiki/File:Das_Lakshana_(Paryusana)_celebrations,_New_York_City_Jain_temple.JPG. **License**: *CC BY-SA: Attribution-ShareAlike*
- Jain Monk. **Provided by**: Wikimedia. **Located at**: https://commons.wikimedia.org/wiki/File:Jain_Sthanakvasi_monk.jpg. **License**: *Public Domain: No Known Copyright*
- Mirpur Jain Temple Wall. **Provided by**: Wikimedia. **Located at**: https://commons.wikimedia.org/wiki/File:Mirpur_Jain_Temple_Elaborate_Wall.jpg. **License**: *CC BY-SA: Attribution-ShareAlike*

Ancient Greece and the Hellenistic World

Early Periods in Greek History

Greek Dark Ages

The Greek Dark Ages were ushered in by a period of violence, and characterized by the disruption of Greek cultural progress.

Learning Objectives

Understand the characteristics of the Greek Dark Ages

Key Takeaways

Key Points

- The Late Bronze Age collapse, also known as the Age of Calamities, was a transition in the Aegean Region, Eastern Mediterranean, and Southwestern Asia. It took place from the Late Bronze Age to the Early Iron Age. Historians believe this period was violent, sudden, and culturally disruptive.

- Many historians attribute the fall of the Mycenaeans, and overall Bronze Age collapse, to climatic or environmental catastrophe combined with an invasion by the Dorians (or Sea Peoples).

- During the Dark Ages, Greece was most likely divided into independent regions according to kinship groups, and the *oikoi*, or households.

- Toward the end of the Greek Dark Ages, communities began to develop that were governed by elite groups of aristocrats, as opposed to singular kings or chieftains of earlier periods. Additionally, trade with other communities in the Mediterranean and the Levant began to strengthen, based upon findings from archaeological sites.

> *Key Terms*
>
> - **oikoi**: The basic unit of society in most Greek city-states. In some usage, it refers to the line of descent from a father to a son throughout generations. Alternatively, it can refer to everybody living in a given house.
> - **Linear B**: Syllabic script that was used for writing Mycenaean Greek, the earliest documented form of the Greek language.
> - **palace economy**: A system of economic organization in which a substantial share of wealth flows into the control of a centralized administration (i.e., the palace), and then outward to the general population.

Age of Calamities

The Late Bronze Age collapse, or Age of Calamities, was a transition in the Aegean Region, Eastern Mediterranean, and Southwestern Asia that took place from the Late Bronze Age to the Early Iron Age. Historians believe this period was violent, sudden, and culturally disruptive. The palace economy of the Aegean Region that had characterized the Late Bronze Age, was replaced, after a hiatus, by the isolated village cultures of the Greek Dark Ages— a period that lasted for more than 400 years. Cities like Athens continued to be occupied, but with a more local sphere of influence, limited evidence of trade, and an impoverished culture, which took centuries to recover.

Fall of the Mycenaeans

Many historians attribute the fall of the Mycenaeans, and overall Bronze Age collapse, to climatic or environmental catastrophe, combined with an invasion by the Dorians or Sea Peoples—a group of people who possibly originated from different parts of the Mediterranean like the Black Sea, though their origins remain obscure. Historians also point to the widespread availability of edged iron weapons as an exasperating factor. Despite this, no single explanation fits all available archaeological evidence in explaining the fall of the Mycenaean culture.

Many large-scale revolts took place in several parts of the eastern Mediterranean during this time, and attempts to overthrow existing kingdoms were made as a result of economic and political instability by peoples already plagued with famine and hardship. Some regions in Greece, such as Attica, Euboea, and central Crete, recovered economically quicker from these events than other regions, but life for the poorest Greeks would have remained relatively unchanged. Farming, weaving, metalworking, and potting continued at lower levels of output and for local use. Some technical innovations were introduced around 1050 BCE with the start of the Proto-geometric style. However, the overall trend was toward simpler, less intricate pieces with fewer resources being devoted to the creation of art.

None of the Mycenaean palaces of the Late Bronze Age survived, with the possible exception of the Cyclopean fortifications on the Acropolis of Athens. The archaeological record shows that destruction was heaviest at palaces and fortified sites. Up to 90% of small sites in the Peloponnese were abandoned, suggesting major depopulation. The Linear B writing of the Greek language used by Mycenaean bureaucrats ceased, and decorations on Greek pottery after about 1100 BCE lacks the figurative decoration of the Mycenaeans, and was restricted to simpler geometric styles.

Society During the Greek Dark Ages

Greece was most likely divided into independent regions according to kinship groups and the *oikoi*, or households. Excavations of Dark Age communities, such as Nichoria in the Peloponnese, have shown how a Bronze Age town was abandoned in 1150 BCE, but then reemerged as a small village cluster by 1075 BCE. Archaeological evidence suggests that only 40 families lived in Nichoria and that there was abundant farming and grazing land. Some remains appear to have been the living quarters of a chieftain. High status individuals did exist during the Dark Ages; however, their standards of living were not significantly higher than others in their village.

By the mid- to late 8th century BCE, a new alphabet system was adopted by the Greek, and borrowed from the Phoenician writing system. This writing system introduced characters for vowel sounds, creating the first truly alphabetic (as opposed to abjad) writing system. The new system of writing spread throughout the Mediterranean, and was used not only to write in Greek, but also Phrygian and other languages.

It was previously believed that all contact had been lost between mainland Hellenes and foreign powers during this period; however, artifacts from excavations at Lefkandi in Euboea show that significant cultural and trade links with the east, especially the Levant coast, developed from approximately 900 BCE onward. Evidence has also emerged of a Hellenic presence in sub-Mycenaean Cyprus, and on the Syrian coast at Al Mina. The archaeological record of many sites demonstrates that the economic recovery of Greece was well advanced by the beginning of the 8th century BCE. Many burial sites contained offerings from the Near East, Egypt, and Italy. The decoration of pottery also became more elaborate, featuring figured scenes that parallel the stories of Homeric tradition. Iron tools and weapons also became better in quality, and communities began to develop that were governed by elite groups of aristocrats, as opposed to singular kings or chieftains of earlier periods.

Archaic Greece

The Archaic Period saw the increasing urbanization of Greek communities, and the development of the concept of the *polis*.

Learning Objectives

Understand the changes to Greek society during the Archaic Period

> ## Key Takeaways
>
> *Key Points*
>
> - The Archaic period saw significant urbanization, and the development of the concept of the *polis* , as it was used in classical Greece.
> - Archaic Greece, from the mid-seventh century onward, has been referred to as an "age of tyrants."
> - The Homeric Question concerns the doubts and consequent debate over the historicity of the *Iliad* and the *Odyssey,* as well as the identity of their author, Homer.
>
> *Key Terms*
>
> - **synoecism**: The amalgamation of several small settlements into a single urban center.
> - **polis**: The literal translation of this word from Greek is "city." It typically refers to the Greek city-states of the Archaic and Classical periods.

Archaic Greece

The Archaic period of Greek history lasted from the 8th century BCE to the second Persian invasion of Greece in 480 BCE. The period began with a massive increase in the Greek population and a structural revolution that established the Greek city-states, or *polis*. The Archaic period saw developments in Greek politics, economics, international relations, warfare, and culture. It also laid the groundwork for the classical period, both politically and culturally. During this time, the Greek alphabet developed, and the earliest surviving Greek literature was composed. Monumental sculpture and red-figure pottery also developed in Greece, and in Athens, the earliest institutions of democracy were implemented.

Some written accounts of life exist from this time period in the form of poetry, law codes, inscriptions on votive offerings, and epigrams inscribed on tombs. However, thorough written histories, such as those that exist from the Greek classical period, are lacking. Historians do have access to rich archaeological evidence from this period, however, that informs our understanding of Greek life during the Archaic period.

View from Philopappos, Acropolis Hill: The Acropolis of Athens, a noted polis of classical Greece.

Development of the Polis

The Archaic period saw significant urbanization and the development of the concept of the *polis* as it was used in classical Greece. However, the *polis* did not become the dominant form of sociopolitical organization throughout Greece during the Archaic period, and in the north and west of the country it did not become dominant until later in the classical period. The process of urbanization known as "synoecism" (or the amalgamation of several small settlements into a single urban center), took place in much of Greece during the 8th century. Both Athens and Argos, for example, coalesced into single settlements near the end of that century. In some settlements, physical unification was marked by the construction of defensive city walls. The increase in population, and evolution of the *polis* as a sociopolitical structure, necessitated a new form of political organization.

Age of Tyranny

Archaic Greece from the mid-7th century onward has been referred to as an "age of tyrants." Various explanations have been provided for the rise of tyranny in the 7th century. The most popular explanation dates back to Aristotle, who argued that tyrants were set up by the people in response to the nobility becoming less tolerable. Because there is no evidence from this time period demonstrating this to be the case, historians have looked for alternate explanations. Some argue that tyrannies were set up by individuals who controlled privates armies, and that early tyrants did not need the support of the people at all. Others suggest that tyrannies were established as a consequence of in-fighting between rival oligarchs, rather than as a result of fighting between oligarchs and the people.

Other historians question the existence of a 7th century "age of tyrants" altogether. In the Archaic period, the Greek word *tyrannos* did not have the negative connotations it had later in the classical period. Often the word could be used as synonymous with "king." As a result, many historians argue that Greek tyrants were not considered illegitimate rulers, and cannot be distinguished from any other rulers during the same period.

The Homeric Question

The Homeric Question concerns the doubts and consequent debate over the identity of Homer, the author of the *Iliad* and the *Odyssey*; it also questions the historicity of the two books. Many scholars agree that regardless of who authored Homer's works, it is highly likely that the poems attributed to him were part of a generations-old oral tradition, with many scholars believing the works to be transcribed some time in the 6th century BCE or earlier. Many estimates place the events of Homer's Trojan War as preceding the Greek Dark Ages, of approximately 1250 to 750 BCE. The *Iliad*, however, has been placed immediately following the Greek Dark Age period.

The Rise of Classical Greece

Classical Greece rose after the fall of the Athenian tyrants and the institution of Cleisthenes' democratic reforms, and lasted throughout the 5th and 4th centuries BCE.

Learning Objectives

Understand the significance of Cleisthenes' reforms to the rise of Classical Greece

Key Takeaways

Key Points

- The classical period followed the Archaic period, and was succeeded by the Hellenistic period.
- Much of modern Western politics, artistic and scientific thought, literature, and philosophy derives from this period of Greek history.
- Through Cleisthenes ' reforms, the people endowed their city with isonomic institutions, and established ostracism.
- A corpus of reforms made to Athenian political administration during this time led to the emergence of a wider democracy in the 460s and 450s BCE.

Key Terms

- **trittyes**: Population divisions in ancient Attica, established by the reforms of Cleisthenes

> in 508 BCE.
>
> - **ostracism**: A procedure under Athenian democracy by which any citizen could be expelled from the city-state of Athens for ten years.
> - **isonomic**: A word used by ancient Greek writers to refer to various kinds of popular government with the general goal of "equal rights."
> - **Cleisthenes**: A noble Athenian of the Alcmaeonid family, credited with reforming the constitution of ancient Athens, and setting it on a democratic footing in 508/7 BCE.
> - **Classical Greece**: A 200 year period in Greek culture, lasting from the 5th through 4th centuries BCE.

Classical Greece was a 200-year period in Greek culture lasting from the 5th to the 4th centuries BCE. This period saw the annexation of much of modern-day Greece by the Persian Empire, as well as its subsequent independence. Classical Greece also had a powerful influence on the Roman Empire, and greatly influenced the foundations of Western civilization. Much of modern Western politics, artistic and scientific thought, literature, and philosophy derives from this period of Greek history. The classical period was preceded by the Archaic period, and was succeeded by the Hellenistic period.

Rise of the City-States

The term " city-state," which is English in origin, does not fully translate the Greek term for these same entities, *polis*. *Poleis* were different from ancient city-states in that they were ruled by bodies of the citizens who lived there. Many were initially established, as in Sparta, via a network of villages, with a governance center being established in a central urban center. As notions of citizenship rose to prominence among landowners, *polis* came to embody an entire body of citizens and the term could be used to describe the populace of a place, rather than the physical location itself. Basic elements of a *polis* often included the following:

- Self-governance, autonomy, and independence
- A social hub and financial marketplace, called an *agora*
- Urban planning and architecture
- Temples, altars, and other sacred precincts, many of which would be dedicated to the patron deity of the city
- Public spaces, such as gymnasia and theaters
- Defensive walls to protect against invasion
- Coinage minted by the city

Polis were established and expanded by synoecism, or the absorption of nearby villages and tribes. Most cities were composed of several tribes that were in turn composed of groups sharing common ancestry, and their extended families. Territory was a less helpful means of thinking about the shape of a *polis* than regions of shared religious and political associations.

Dwellers of a *polis* were typically divided into four separate social classes, with an individual's status usually being determined at birth. Free adult men born of legitimate citizens were considered citizens with full legal and political rights, including the right to vote, be elected into office, and bear arms, with the obligation to serve in the army during wartime. The female relatives and underage children of full citizens were also considered citizens, but they had no formal political rights. They were typically represented within society by their adult male relatives. Citizens of other *poleis* who chose to reside in a different *polis* possessed full rights in their place of origin, but had no political rights in their new place of residence. Otherwise, such citizens had full personal and property rights subject to taxation. Finally, slaves were considered possessions of their owner and had no rights or privileges other than those granted by their owner.

Greco-Persian Wars

The Greco- Persian Wars, also referred to as the Persian Wars, were a series of conflicts that began in 499 BCE and lasted until 449 BCE, between the Achaemenid Empire of Persia (modern-day Iran) and Greek city-states. The conflict began when Cyrus the Great conquered the Greek-inhabited region of Ionia in 547 BCE. After struggling to control the cities of Ionia, the Persians appointed tyrants to rule each of them. When the tyrant of Miletus embarked on an unsuccessful expedition to conquer the island of Naxos with Persian support, however, a rebellion was incited throughout Hellenic Asia Minor against the Persians. This rebellion, known as the Ionian Revolt, lasted until 493 BCE, and drew increasingly more regions throughout Asia Minor into the conflict.

Eventually the Ionians suffered a decisive defeat and the rebellion collapsed. Subsequently, Darius the Great, the Persian ruler, sought to secure his empire from further revolts and interference from the mainland Greeks, and embarked upon a scheme to conquer all of Greece. The first Persian invasion of Greece began in 492 BCE, and was successful in conquering Macedon and re-subjugating Thrace. In 490 BCE, a second force was sent to Greece across the Aegean Sea, successfully subjugating the Cyclades. However, the Persians were defeated by the Athenians at the Battle of Marathon, putting a halt to Darius's plan until his death in 486 BCE.

In 480 BCE, Darius's son, Xerxes, personally led the second Persian invasion of Greece with one of the largest ancient armies ever assembled. His invasion was successful and Athens was burned. However, the following year, the Allied Greek states went on the offensive, defeating the Persian army at the Battle of Plataea and ending the invasion of Greece. The Greeks continued to expel Persian forces from Greece and surrounding areas, but the actions of Spartan General Pausanias at the siege of Byzantium alienated many of the Greek states from the Spartans, causing the anti-Persian alliance to be reconstituted around Athenian leadership in what became known as the Delian League. The Delian League continued the campaign against the Persians for the next three decades. Some historical sources suggest the end of hostilities between the Greeks and the Persians was marked by a peace treaty between Athens and Persia, called the Peace of Callias.

Athenian Democracy

Athenian democracy developed around the 5th century BCE, in the Greek city-state of Athens. It is the first known democracy in the world. Other Greek cities set up democracies, most following the Athenian model, but none are as well documented as Athens. Athenian democracy was a system of direct democracy, in which participating citizens voted directly on legislation and executive bills. Participation was open to adult, land-owning men, which historians estimate numbered between 30,000 and 50,000 individuals, out of a total population of approximately 250,000 to 300,000.

Before the first attempt at democratic government, Athens was ruled by a series of *archons*, or chief magistrates, and the Areopagus, which was made up of ex-*archons*. *Archons* were typically aristocrats who ruled to their own advantage. Additionally, a series of laws codified by Draco in 621 BCE reinforced the power of the aristocracy over all other citizens. A mediator called Solon reshaped the city-state by restructuring the way citizenship was defined in order to absorb the traditional aristocracy within it, and established the right of every Athenian to participate in meetings of governing assemblies. The Areopagus, however, retained ultimate lawmaking authorities.

Cleisthenes

In 510 BCE, Spartan troops helped the Athenians overthrow their king, the tyrant Hippias, son of Peisistratos. Cleomenes I, king of Sparta, put in place a pro-Spartan oligarchy headed by Isagoras. But his rival, Cleisthenes, with the support of the middle class and aided by democrats, managed to take over. Cleomenes intervened in 508 and 506 BCE, but could not stop Cleisthenes, who was then supported by the Athenians. Through his reforms, the people endowed their city with institutions furnished with equal rights (i.e., isonomic institutions), and established ostracism, a procedure by which any citizen could be expelled from the city-state of Athens for ten years.

Bust of Cleisthenes: Modern bust of Cleisthenes, known as "the father of Athenian democracy," on view at the Ohio Statehouse, Columbus, Ohio. Cleisthenes, the father of Greek democracy, reformed traditional Athenian government controlled by ruling tribes into the first government "of the people" (a demos, or democracy).

The isonomic and isegoric democracy was first organized into about 130 demes— political subdivisions created throughout Attica. Ten thousand citizens exercised their power via an assembly (the *ekklesia*, in

Greek), of which they all were a part, that was headed by a council of 500 citizens chosen at random. The city's administrative geography was reworked, the goal being to have mixed political groups—not federated by local interests linked to the sea, the city, or farming—whose decisions (declaration of war, etc.) would depend on their geographical situations. The territory of the city was subsequently divided into 30 trittyes. It was this corpus of reforms that would allow the emergence of a wider democracy in the 460s and 450s BCE.

Attributions

CC licensed content, Specific attribution

- Greek Dark Ages. **Provided by**: Wikipedia. **Located at**: https://en.wikipedia.org/wiki/Greek_Dark_Ages. **License**: *CC BY-SA: Attribution-ShareAlike*
- Palace economy. **Provided by**: Wikipedia. **Located at**: https://en.wikipedia.org/wiki/Palace_economy. **License**: *CC BY-SA: Attribution-ShareAlike*
- Late Bronze Age collapse. **Provided by**: Wikipedia. **Located at**: https://en.wikipedia.org/wiki/Late_Bronze_Age_collapse. **License**: *CC BY-SA: Attribution-ShareAlike*
- Archaic Greece. **Provided by**: Wikipedia. **Located at**: https://en.wikipedia.org/wiki/Archaic_Greece. **License**: *CC BY-SA: Attribution-ShareAlike*
- Polis. **Provided by**: Wikipedia. **Located at**: https://en.wikipedia.org/wiki/Polis. **License**: *CC BY-SA: Attribution-ShareAlike*
- Attica_06-13_Athens_50_View_from_Philopappos_-_Acropolis_Hill.jpg. **Provided by**: Wikipedia. **Located at**: https://en.wikipedia.org/wiki/File:Attica_06-13_Athens_50_View_from_Philopappos_-_Acropolis_Hill.jpg. **License**: *CC BY-SA: Attribution-ShareAlike*
- Isonomic. **Provided by**: Wikipedia. **Located at**: http://en.wikipedia.org/wiki/Isonomic. **License**: *CC BY-SA: Attribution-ShareAlike*
- The Delian League. **Provided by**: Wikipedia. **Located at**: http://en.wikipedia.org/wiki/Delian_League. **License**: *CC BY-SA: Attribution-ShareAlike*
- Ostracism. **Provided by**: Wikipedia. **Located at**: http://en.wikipedia.org/wiki/Ostracism. **License**: *CC BY-SA: Attribution-ShareAlike*
- Trittys. **Provided by**: Wikipedia. **Located at**: http://en.wikipedia.org/wiki/Trittys. **License**: *CC BY-SA: Attribution-ShareAlike*
- Polis. **Provided by**: Wikipedia. **Located at**: https://en.wikipedia.org/wiki/Polis. **License**: *CC BY-SA: Attribution-ShareAlike*
- Greco-Persian Wars. **Provided by**: Wikipedia. **Located at**: https://en.wikipedia.org/wiki/Greco-Persian_Wars. **License**: *CC BY-SA: Attribution-ShareAlike*
- Classical Greece. **Provided by**: Wikipedia. **Located at**: http://en.wikipedia.org/wiki/Classical_Greece. **License**: *CC BY-SA: Attribution-ShareAlike*
- Athenian democracy. **Provided by**: Wikipedia . **Located at**: https://en.wikipedia.org/wiki/Athenian_democracy. **License**: *CC BY-SA: Attribution-ShareAlike*
- Attica_06-13_Athens_50_View_from_Philopappos_-_Acropolis_Hill.jpg. **Provided by**: Wikipedia. **Located at**: https://en.wikipedia.org/wiki/File:Attica_06-13_Athens_50_View_from_Philopappos_-_Acropolis_Hill.jpg. **License**: *CC BY-SA: Attribution-ShareAlike*
- Cleisthenes. **Provided by**: Wikipedia. **Located at**: http://en.wikipedia.org/wiki/Cleisthenes%23mediaviewer/File:Cleisthenes.jpg. **License**: *Public Domain: No Known Copyright*

Sparta

Sparta

Sparta, known for its militaristic culture and unequaled women's rights, was a dominant military power in classical Greece.

Learning Objectives

Distinguish key differences between Athens and Sparta

Key Takeaways

Key Points

- Sparta was a prominent city-state in ancient Greece, situated on the banks of the Eurotas River in Laconia in southeastern Peloponnese.
- Given its military preeminence, Sparta was recognized as the overall leader of the combined Greek forces during the Greco-Persian Wars, and defeated Athens during the Peloponnesian War.
- Sparta's defeat by Thebes in the Battle of Leuctra in 371 BCE ended Sparta's prominent role in Greece, but it maintained its political independence until the Roman conquest of Greece in 146 BCE.
- Sparta functioned under an oligarchy of two hereditary kings.
- Unique in ancient Greece for its social system and constitution, Spartan society focused heavily on military training and excellence.
- Spartan women enjoyed status, power, and respect that was unequaled in the rest of the classical world.

> *Key Terms*
>
> - **Sparta**: A prominent city-state in ancient Greece situated on the banks of the Eurotas River in Laconia. The dominant military power in ancient Greece.
> - **agoge**: The rigorous education and training regimen mandated for all male Spartan citizens, except for the firstborn sons of the ruling houses Eurypontid and Agiad.

Sparta was a prominent city-state in ancient Greece situated on the banks of the Eurotas River in Laconia in southeastern Peloponnese. It emerged as a political entity around the 10th century BCE, when the invading Dorians subjugated the local, non-Dorian population. Around 650 BCE, it rose to become the dominant military power in ancient Greece. Given its military preeminence, Sparta was recognized as the overall leader of the combined Greek forces during the Greco-Persian Wars. Between 431 and 404 BCE, Sparta was the principal enemy of Athens during the Peloponnesian War, from which it emerged victorious, though at great cost. Sparta's defeat by Thebes in the Battle of Leuctra in 371 BCE ended Sparta's prominent role in Greece. However, it maintained its political independence until the Roman conquest of Greece in 146 BCE.

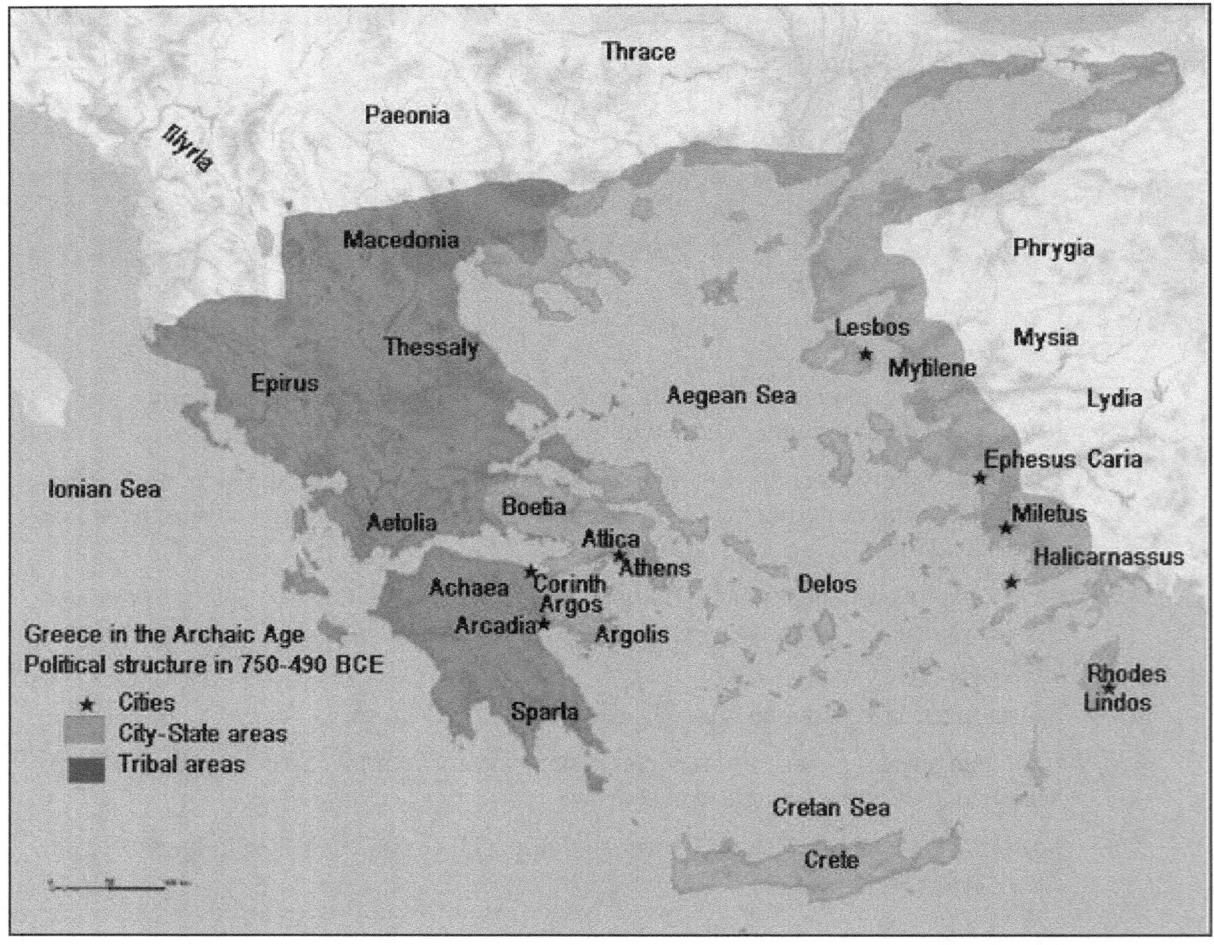

Political geography of ancient Greece: *The map shows the political structure of Greece in the Archaic Age.*

The Rise of Classical Sparta

The Spartans were already considered a land-fighting force to be reckoned with when, in 480 BCE, a small force of Spartans, Thespians, and Thebans made a legendary final stand at the Battle of Thermopylae against the massive Persian army during the Greco-Persian Wars. The Greek forces suffered very high casualties before finally being encircled and defeated. One year later, Sparta led a Greek alliance against the Persians at the Battle of Plataea where their superior weaponry, strategy, and bronze armor proved a huge asset in achieving a resounding victory. This decisive victory put an end to the Greco-Persian War, as well as Persian ambitions of spreading into Europe. Despite being fought as part of a alliance, the victory was credited to Sparta, which had been the de facto leader of the entire Greek expedition.

In the later classical period, Sparta fought amongst Athens, Thebes, and Persia for supremacy within the region. As a result of the Peloponnesian War, Sparta developed formidable naval power, enabling it to subdue many key Greek states and even overpower the elite Athenian navy. A period of Spartan Hegemony was inaugurated at the end of the 5th century BCE, when Sparta defeated the Athenian Empire and invaded Persian provinces in Anatolia.

Spartan Culture and Government

Sparta functioned under an oligarchy. The state was ruled by two hereditary kings of the Agiad and Eurypontid families, both supposedly descendants of Heracles, and equal in authority so that one could not act against the power and political enactments of his colleague. Unique in ancient Greece for its social system and constitution, Spartan society was completely focused on military training and excellence. Its inhabitants were classified as Spartiates (Spartan citizens who enjoyed full rights), Mothakes (non-Spartan, free men raised as Spartans), Perioikoi (freed men), and Helots (state-owned serfs, part of the enslaved, non-Spartan, local population).

Male Spartans began military training at age seven. The training was designed to encourage discipline and physical toughness, as well as emphasize the importance of the Spartan state. Boys lived in communal messes and, according to Xenophon, whose sons attended the *agoge*, the boys were fed "just the right amount for them never to become sluggish through being too full, while also giving them a taste of what it is not to have enough." Besides physical and weapons training, boys studied reading, writing, music, and dancing. Special punishments were imposed if boys failed to answer questions sufficiently laconically (i.e., briefly and wittily).

Spartan Hoplite: *Marble statue of a helmed hoplite (5th century BCE), Archaeological Museum of Sparta, Greece.*

At age 20, the Spartan citizen began his membership in one of the *syssitia* (dining messes or clubs), which were composed of about 15 members each, and were compulsory. Here each group learned how to bond and rely on one another. The Spartans were not eligible for election to public office until the age of 30. Only native Spartans were considered full citizens, and were obliged to undergo military training as prescribed by law, as well as participate in, and contribute financially to, one of the *syssitia*.

Spartan Women

Female Spartan citizens enjoyed status, power, and respect that was unequaled in the rest of the classical world. The higher status of females in Spartan society started at birth. Unlike in Athens, Spartan girls were fed the same food as their brothers. Nor were they confined to their father's house or prevented from exercising or getting fresh air. Spartan women even competed in sports. Most important, rather than being married at the age of 12 or 13, Spartan law forbade the marriage of a girl until she was in her late teens or early 20s. The reasons for delaying marriage were to ensure the birth of healthy children, but the effect was to spare Spartan women the hazards and lasting health damage associated with pregnancy among adolescents.

Spartan women, better fed from childhood and fit from exercise, stood a far better chance of reaching old age than their sisters in other Greek cities, where the median life expectancy was 34.6 years, or roughly ten years below that of men. Unlike Athenian women, who wore heavy, concealing clothes and were rarely seen outside the house, Spartan women wore dresses (*peplos*) slit up the side to allow freer movement, and moved freely about the city, either walking or driving chariots.

Culture in Classical Sparta

Although Spartan society was highly regimented, militarily and socially, enslaved classes and women were afforded greater privileges relative to the populations of other Greek city-states.

Learning Objectives

Understand the key characteristics of Sparta's society

Key Takeaways

Key Points

- Sparta was an oligarchic city-state, ruled by two hereditary kings equal in authority.
- Spartan society was largely structured around the military, and around military training.
- Inhabitants were classified as Spartiates (Spartan citizens, who enjoyed full rights), Mothakes (non-Spartan, free men raised as Spartans), Perioikoi (free, but non-citizen inhabitants), and Helots (state-owned serfs, part of the enslaved non-Spartan, local population).
- Spartiates began military training at the age of seven.
- At the age of 20, Spartiates were initiated into full citizenship and joined a *syssitia*.
- Helots were granted many privileges, in comparison to enslaved populations in other Greek city-states.
- The Helot population outnumbered the Spartiate population, and grew over time, causing societal tensions.
- Female Spartans enjoyed status, power, and respect that was unequaled in the rest of the classical world.

> *Key Terms*
>
> - **Delphi**: A famous ancient sanctuary that served as the seat of an oracle, who consulted on important decisions throughout the ancient classical world.
> - **ephors**: Ephors were ancient Spartan officials who shared power with the hereditary kings. Five individuals were elected annually to swear on behalf of the city, whereas kings served for a lifetime and swore only on their own behalf.
> - **gerousia**: The gerousia were a council of Spartan elders comprised of men over the age of 60, who were elected for life, and usually were members of one of the two kings' households.

The Spartan Political System

Sparta functioned under an oligarchy. The state was ruled by two hereditary kings of the Agiad and Eurypontid families, both supposedly descendants of Heracles, and equal in authority so that one could not act against the power and political enactments of his colleague. The duties of the kings were religious, judicial, and military in nature. They were the chief priests of the state, and maintained contact with Delphi, the sanctuary that exercised great authority in Spartan politics.

By 450 BCE, the kings' judicial authority was restricted to cases dealing with heiresses, adoptions, and public roads. Over time, royal prerogatives were curtailed further until, aside from their service as military generals, the kings became mere figureheads. For example, from the time of the Greco Persian Wars, the kings lost the right to declare war and were shadowed in the field by two officials, known as *ephors*. The *ephors* also supplanted the kings' leadership in the realm of foreign policy. Civil and criminal cases were also decided by *ephors*, as well as a council of 28 elders over the age of 60, called the *gerousia*. The *gerousia* were elected for life, and usually were members of one of the two kings' households. The *gerousia* discussed high state policy decisions, then proposed action alternatives to the *damos*—a collective body of Spartan citizenry, who would then select one of the options by voting.

Spartan Citizenship

Unique in ancient Greece for its social system, Spartan society was completely focused on military training and excellence. Its inhabitants were classified as Spartiates (Spartan citizens, who enjoyed full rights), Mothakes (non-Spartan, free men raised as Spartans), Perioikoi (free, but non-citizen inhabitants), and Helots (state-owned serfs, part of the enslaved, non-Spartan, local population).

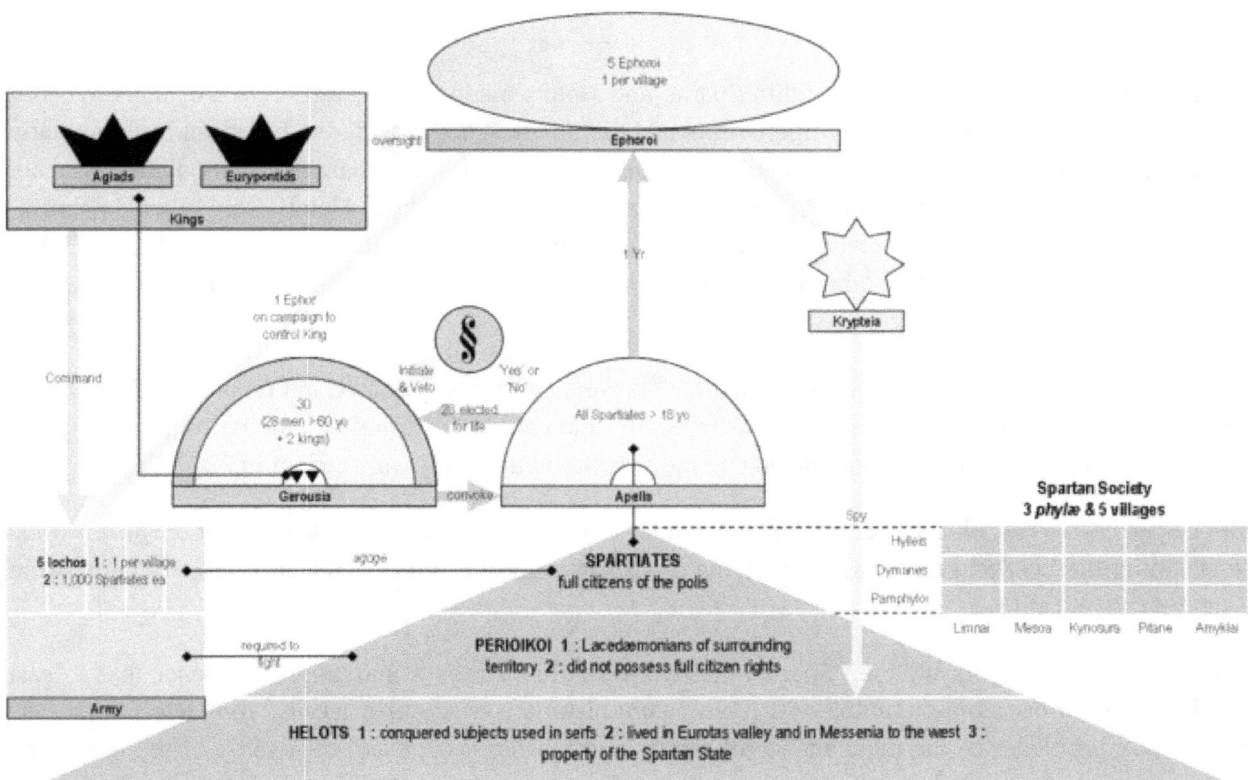

Structure of Spartan society: *Spartan society was highly regimented, with a clearly delineated class system.*

Male Spartans began military training at age seven. The training was designed to encourage discipline and physical toughness, as well as emphasize the importance of the Spartan state. Typically only men who were to become Spartiates underwent military training, although two exceptions existed to this rule. *Trophimoi*, or "foster sons," from other Greek city-states were allowed to attend training as foreign students. For example, the Athenian general Xenophon sent his two sons to Sparta as *trophimoi*. Additionally, sons of a Helot could enroll as a *syntrophos* if a Spartiate formally adopted him and paid his way. If a *syntrophos* did exceptionally well in training, he could be sponsored to become a Spartiate. Likewise, if a Spartan could not afford to pay the expenses associated with military training, they potentially could lose their right to citizenship.

Boys who underwent training lived in communal messes and, according to Xenophon, whose sons attended the *agoge*, the boys were fed "just the right amount for them never to become sluggish through being too full, while also giving them a taste of what it is not to have enough." Besides physical and weapons training, boys studied reading, writing, music, and dancing. Special punishments were imposed if boys failed to answer questions sufficiently laconically (i.e., briefly and wittily).

At age 20, the Spartan citizen began his membership in one of the *syssitia* (dining messes or clubs), which were composed of about 15 members each, and were compulsory. Here each group learned how to bond and rely on one another. The Spartans were not eligible for election to public office until the age of 30. Only native Spartans were considered full citizens, and were obliged to undergo military training as prescribed by law, as well as participate in, and contribute financially to, one of the *syssitia*.

Helots

Spartiates were actually a minority within Sparta, and Helots made up the largest class of inhabitants of the city-state. Helots were originally free Greeks that the Spartans had defeated in battle, and subsequently enslaved. In contrast to populations conquered by other Greek cities, the male Helot population was not exterminated, and women and children were not treated as chattel. Instead, Helots were given a subordinate position within Spartan society more comparable to the serfs of medieval Europe. Although Helots did not have voting rights, they otherwise enjoyed a relatively privileged position, in comparison to slave populations in other Greek city-states.

The Spartan poet, Tyrtaios, gives account that Helots were permitted to marry and retain half the fruits of their labor. They were also allowed religious freedoms and could own a limited amount of personal property. Up to 6,000 Helots even accumulated enough wealth to buy their own freedom in 227 BCE.

Since Spartiates were full-time soldiers, manual labor fell to the Helot population who worked as unskilled serfs, tilling the Spartan land or accompanying the Spartan army as non-combatants. Helot women were often used as wet nurses.

Relations between Helots and their Spartan masters were often strained, and there is evidence that at least one Helot revolt occurred circa 465-460 BCE. Many historians argue that because the Helots were permitted such privileges as the maintenance of family and kinship groups and ownership of property, they were better able to retain their identity as a conquered people and thus were more effective at organizing rebellions. Over time, the Spartiate population continued to decline and the Helot population grew, and the imbalance in power exasperated tensions that already existed.

Spartan Women

Female Spartans enjoyed status, power, and respect that was unequaled in the rest of the classical world. The higher status of females in Spartan society started at birth. Unlike in Athens, Spartan girls were fed the same food as their brothers. Nor were they confined to their father's house or prevented from exercising or getting fresh air. Spartan women even competed in sports. Most important, rather than being married at the age of 12 or 13, Spartan law forbade the marriage of a girl until she was in her late teens or early 20s. The reasons for delaying marriage were to ensure the birth of healthy children, but the effect was to spare Spartan women the hazards and lasting health damage associated with pregnancy among adolescents.

Spartan women, better fed from childhood and fit from exercise, stood a far better chance of reaching old age than their sisters in
other Greek cities where the median life expectancy was 34.6 years, or roughly ten years below that of men. Unlike Athenian women who wore heavy, concealing clothes and were rarely seen outside the house, Spartan women wore dresses (*peplos*) slit up the side to allow freer movement, and moved freely about the city, either walking or driving chariots.

Attributions

CC licensed content, Specific attribution

- Sparta. **Provided by**: Wikipedia. **Located at**: http://en.wikipedia.org/wiki/Sparta. **License**: *CC BY-SA: Attribution-ShareAlike*
- Sparta. **Provided by**: Wikipedia. **Located at**: http://en.wikipedia.org/wiki/Sparta%23mediaviewer/File:Helmed_Hoplite_Sparta.JPG. **License**: *CC BY-SA: Attribution-ShareAlike*
- Archaic Greece. **Provided by**: wikipedia. **Located at**: http://upload.wikimedia.org/wikipedia/commons/thumb/8/87/ArchaicGr.jpg/

603px-ArchaicGr.jpg. **License:** *Public Domain: No Known Copyright*
- Apella. **Provided by**: Wikipedia. **Located at**: https://en.wikipedia.org/wiki/Apella. **License**: *CC BY-SA: Attribution-ShareAlike*
- Spartan army. **Provided by**: Wikipedia. **Located at**: https://en.wikipedia.org/wiki/Spartan_army. **License**: *CC BY-SA: Attribution-ShareAlike*
- Sparta. **Provided by**: Wikipedia. **Located at**: https://en.wikipedia.org/wiki/Sparta. **License**: *CC BY-SA: Attribution-ShareAlike*
- Ephor. **Provided by**: Wikipedia. **Located at**: https://en.wikipedia.org/wiki/Ephor. **License**: *CC BY-SA: Attribution-ShareAlike*
- Delphi. **Provided by**: Wikipedia. **Located at**: https://en.wikipedia.org/wiki/Delphi. **License**: *CC BY-SA: Attribution-ShareAlike*
- Gerousia. **Provided by**: Wikipedia. **Located at**: https://en.wikipedia.org/wiki/Gerousia. **License**: *CC BY-SA: Attribution-ShareAlike*
- Sparta. **Provided by**: Wikipedia. **Located at**: http://en.wikipedia.org/wiki/Sparta%23mediaviewer/File:Helmed_Hoplite_Sparta.JPG. **License**: *CC BY-SA: Attribution-ShareAlike*
- Archaic Greece. **Provided by**: wikipedia. **Located at**: http://upload.wikimedia.org/wikipedia/commons/thumb/8/87/ArchaicGr.jpg/603px-ArchaicGr.jpg. **License**: *Public Domain: No Known Copyright*
- SpartaGreatRhetra.png. **Provided by**: Wikpedia. **Located at**: https://en.wikipedia.org/wiki/File:SpartaGreatRhetra.png. **License**: *CC BY-SA: Attribution-ShareAlike*

The Persian Wars

The Persian Wars

The Persian Wars led to the rise of Athens as the head of the Delian League.

Learning Objectives

Explain the consequences of the Persian Wars.

Key Takeaways

Key Points

- The Persian Wars began in 499 BCE, when Greeks in the Persian-controlled territory rose in the Ionian Revolt.
- Athens, and other Greek cities, sent aid, but were quickly forced to back down after defeat in 494 BCE.
- Subsequently, the Persians suffered many defeats at the hands of the Greeks, led by the Athenians.
- Silver mining contributed to the funding of a massive Greek army that was able to rebuke Persian assaults and eventually defeat the Persians entirely.
- The end of the Persian Wars led to the rise of Athens as the leader of the Delian League.

Key Terms

- **Persian Wars**: A series of conflicts, from 499-449 BCE, between the Achaemenid Empire of Persia and city-states of the Hellenic world.
- **hoplites**: A citizen-soldier of one of the ancient Greek city-states, armed primarily with

> spears and a shield.

The Persian Wars (499-449 BCE) were fought between the Achaemenid Empire and the Hellenic world during the Greek classical period. The conflict saw the rise of Athens, and led to its Golden Age.

Origins of the Conflict

Greeks of the classical period believed, and historians generally agree, that in the aftermath of the fall of Mycenaean civilization, many Greek tribes emigrated and settled in Asia Minor. These settlers were from three tribal groups: the Aeolians, Dorians, and Ionians. The Ionians settled along the coasts of Lydia and Caria, and founded 12 towns that remained politically separate from one another, although they did recognize a shared cultural heritage. This formed the basis for an exclusive Ionian "cultural league." The Lydians of western Asia Minor conquered the cities of Ionia, which put the region at conflict with the Median Empire, the precursor to the Achaemenid Empire of the Persian Wars, and a power that the Lydians opposed.

In 553 through 550 BCE, the Persian prince Cyrus led a successful revolt against the last Median king Astyages, and founded the Achaemenid Empire. Seeing an opportunity in the upheaval, the famous Lydian king Croesus asked the oracle at Delphi whether he should attack the Persians in order to extend his realm. According to Herodotus, he received the ambiguous answer that "if Croesus was to cross the Halys [River] he would destroy a great empire." Croesus chose to attack, and in the process he destroyed his own empire, with Lydia falling to Prince Cyrus. The Ionians sought to maintain autonomy under the Persians as they had under the Lydians, and resisted the Persians militarily for some time. However, due to their unwillingness to rise against the Lydians during previous conflicts, they were not granted special terms. Finding the Ionians difficult to rule, the Persians installed tyrants in every city, as a means of control.

Achaemenid Empire Map: *The Achaemenid Empire at its greatest extent.*

The Ionian Revolt

In 499 BCE, Greeks in the region rose up against Persian rule in the Ionian Revolt. At the heart of the rebellion lay a deep dissatisfaction with the tyrants who were appointed by the Persians to rule the local Greek communities. Specifically, the riot was incited by the Milesian tyrant Aristagoras, who in the wake of a failed expedition to conquer Naxos, utilized Greek unrest against Persian king Darius the Great to his own political purposes.

Athens and other Greek cities sent aid, but were quickly forced to back down after defeat in 494 BCE, at the Battle of Lade. As a result, Asia Minor returned to Persian control. Nonetheless, the Ionian Revolt remains significant as the first major conflict between Greece and the Persian Empire, as well as the first phase of the Persian Wars. Darius vowed to exact revenge against Athens, and developed a plan to conquer all Greeks in an attempt to secure the stability of his empire.

First Persian Invasion of Greece

In 492 BCE, the Persian general, Mardonius, led a campaign through Thrace and Macedonia. During this campaign, Mardonius re-subjugated Thrace and forced Macedonia to become a fully submissive client of the Persian Empire, whereas before they had maintained a broad degree of autonomy.
While victorious, he was wounded and forced to retreat back into Asia Minor. Additionally, he lost his 1200-ship naval fleet to a storm off the coast of Mount Athos. Darius sent ambassadors to all Greek cities to demand full submission in light of the recent Persian victory, and all cities submitted, with the exceptions of Athens and Sparta, both of which executed their respective ambassadors. These actions signaled Athens' continued defiance and brought Sparta into the conflict.

In 490 BCE, approximately 100,000 Persians landed in Attica intending to conquer Athens, but were defeated at the Battle of Marathon by a Greek army of 9,000 Athenian hoplites and 1,000 Plateans, led by the Athenian general, Miltiades. The Persian fleet continued to sail to Athens but, seeing it garrisoned, decided not to attempt an assault. The Battle of Marathon was a watershed moment in the Persian Wars, in that it demonstrated to the Greeks that the Persians could be defeated. It also demonstrated the superiority of the more heavily armed Greek hoplites.

Greek-Persian duel: Depiction of a Greek hoplite and a Persian warrior fighting each other on an ancient kylix.

Interbellum (490-480 BCE)

After the failure of the first Persian invasion, Darius raised a large army with the intent of invading Greece again. However, in 486 BCE, Darius's Egyptian subjects revolted, postponing any advancement against Greece. During preparations to march on Egypt, Darius died and his son, Xerxes I, inherited the throne. Xerxes quickly crushed the Egyptians and resumed preparations to invade Greece.

Second Invasion of Greece

In 480 BCE, Xerxes sent a much more powerful force of 300,000 soldiers by land, with 1,207 ships in support, across a double pontoon bridge over the Hellespont. This army took Thrace before descending on Thessaly and Boetia, whilst the Persian navy skirted the coast and resupplied the ground troops. The Greek fleet, meanwhile, dashed to block Cape Artemision. After being delayed by Leonidas I, the Spartan king of the Agiad Dynasty, at the Battle of Thermopylae (a battle made famous due to the sheer imbalance of forces, with 300 Spartans facing the entire Persian Army), Xerxes advanced into Attica, where he captured and burned Athens. But the Athenians had evacuated the city by sea, and under the command of Themistocles, defeated the Persian fleet at the Battle of Salamis.

In 483 BCE, during the period of peace between the two Persian invasions, a vein of silver ore had been discovered in the Laurion (a small mountain range near Athens), and the ore that was mined there paid for the construction of 200 warships to combat Aeginetan piracy. A year later, the Greeks, under the Spartan Pausanias, defeated the Persian army at Plataea. Meanwhile, the allied Greek navy won a decisive victory at the Battle of Mycale, destroying the Persian fleet, crippling Xerxe's sea power, and marking the ascendency of the Greek fleet. Following the Battle of Plataea and the Battle of Mycale, the Persians began withdrawing from Greece and never attempted an invasion again.

Greek Counterattack

The Battle of Mycale was in many ways a turning point, after which the Greeks went on the offensive against the Persian fleet. The Athenian fleet turned to chasing the Persians from the Aegean Sea, and in 478 BCE, the fleet then proceeded to capture Byzantium. In the course of doing so, Athens enrolled all the island states, and some mainland states, into an alliance called the Delian League— so named because its treasury was kept on the sacred island of Delos, whose purpose was to continue fighting the Persian Empire, prepare for future invasions, and organize a means of dividing the spoils of war. The Spartans, although they had taken part in the war, withdrew into isolation afterwards. The Spartans believed that the war's purpose had already been reached through the liberation of mainland Greece and the Greek cities of Asia Minor. Historians also speculate that Sparta was unconvinced of the ability of the Delian League to secure long-term security for Asian Greeks. The Spartan withdrawal from the League allowed Athens to establish unchallenged naval and commercial power within the Hellenic world.

Effects of the Persian Wars

Despite their victories in the Persian Wars, the Greek city-states emerged from the conflict more divided than united.

> **Learning Objectives**
>
> Understand the effect the Persian Wars had on the balance of power throughout the classical world

> ## Key Takeaways
>
> ### Key Points
>
> - After the second Persian invasion of Greece was halted, Sparta withdrew from the Delian League and reformed the Peloponnesian League with its original allies.
> - Many Greek city-states had been alienated from Sparta following the violent actions of Spartan leader Pausanias during the siege of Byzantium.
> - Following Sparta's departure from the Delian League, Athens was able to use the resources of the League to its own ends, which led it into conflict with less powerful members of the League.
> - The Persian Empire adopted a divide-and-rule strategy in relation to the Greek city-states in the wake of the Persian Wars, stoking already simmering conflicts, including the rivalry between Athens and Sparta, to protect the Persian Empire against further Greek attacks.
>
> ### Key Terms
>
> - **Peloponnesian League**: An alliance formed around Sparta in the Peloponnesus, from the 6th to 4th centuries BCE.
> - **Delian League**: An association of Greek city-states under the leadership of Athens, the purpose of which was to continue fighting the Persian Empire after the Greek victories at the end of the Second Persian invasion of Greece.
> - **hegemony**: The political, economic, or military predominance or control of one state over others.

Aftermath of the Persian Wars

As a result of the allied Greek success, a large contingent of the Persian fleet was destroyed and all Persian garrisons were expelled from Europe, marking an end of Persia's advance westward into the continent. The cities of Ionia were also liberated from Persian control. Despite their successes, however, the spoils of war caused greater inner conflict within the Hellenic world. The violent actions of Spartan leader Pausanias at the siege of Byzantium, for instance, alienated many of the Greek states from Sparta, and led to a shift in the military command of the Delian League from Sparta to Athens. This set the stage for Sparta's eventual withdrawal from the Delian League.

Two Leagues

Following the two Persian invasions of Greece, and during the Greek counterattacks that commenced after the Battles of Plataea and Mycale, Athens enrolled all island and some mainland city-states into an alliance, called the Delian League, the purpose of which was to pursue conflict with the Persian Empire, prepare for future invasions, and organize a means of dividing the spoils of war. The Spartans, although they had taken part in the war, withdrew from the Delian League early on, believing that the war's initial purpose had been met with the liberation of mainland Greece and the Greek cities of Asia Minor. Historians also

speculate that Sparta decided to leave the League for pragmatic reasons, remaining unconvinced that it was possible to secure long-term security for Greeks residing in Asia Minor, and as a result of their unease with Athenian efforts to increase their power. Once Sparta
withdrew from the Delian League after the Persian Wars, it reformed the Peloponnesian League, which had originally been formed in the 6th century and provided the blueprint for what was now the Delian League. The Spartan withdrawal from the League had the effect, however, of allowing Athens to establish unchallenged naval and commercial power, unrivaled throughout the Hellenic world. In fact, shortly after the League's inception, Athens began to use the League's navy for its own purposes, which frequently led it into conflict with other, less powerful League members.

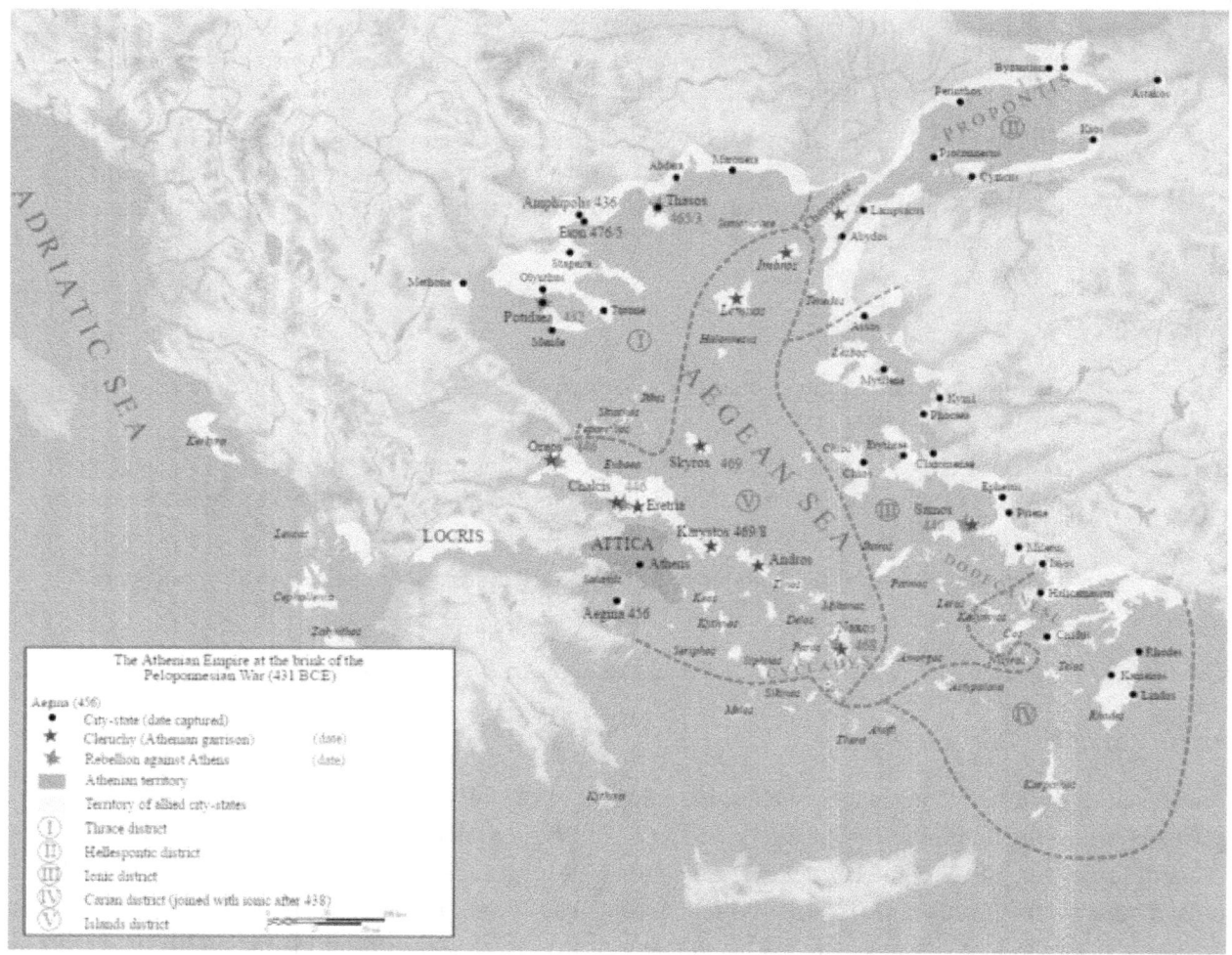

Map of the Athenian Empire c. 431 BCE: The Delian League was the basis for the Athenian Empire, shown here on the brink of the Peloponnesian War (c. 431 BCE).

Delian League Rebellions

A series of rebellions occurred between Athens and the smaller city-states that were members of the League. For example, Naxos was the first member of the League to attempt to secede, in approximately 471 BCE. It was later defeated and forced to tear down its defensive city walls, surrender its fleet, and lost voting privileges in the League. Thasos, another League member, also defected when, in 465 BCE, Athens founded the colony of Amphipolis on the Strymon River, which threatened Thasos' interests in the mines of Mt Pangaion. Thasos allied with Persia and petitioned Sparta for assistance, but Sparta was unable to help because it was facing the largest helot revolution in its history. Nonetheless, relations between Athens and Sparta were soured by the situation. After a three-year long siege, Thasos was recaptured and forced back into the Delian League, though it also lost its defensive walls and fleet, its mines were turned over to Athens, and the city-state was forced to pay yearly tribute and fines. According to Thucydides, the siege of Thasos marked the transformation of the League from an alliance into a hegemony.

Persia

Following their defeats at the hands of the Greeks, and plagued by internal rebellions that hindered their ability to fight foreign enemies, the Persians adopted a policy of divide-and-rule. Beginning in 449 BCE, the Persians attempted to aggravate the growing tensions between Athens and Sparta, and would even bribe politicians to achieve these aims. Their strategy was to keep the Greeks distracted with in-fighting, so as to stop the tide of counterattacks reaching the Persian Empire. Their strategy was largely successful, and there was no open conflict between the Greeks and Persia until 396 BCE, when the Spartan king Agesilaus briefly invaded Asia Minor.

Attributions

CC licensed content, Specific attribution

- Classical Greece. **Provided by**: Wikipedia. **Located at**: http://en.wikipedia.org/wiki/Classical_Greece%23The_Persian_Wars. **License**: *CC BY-SA: Attribution-ShareAlike*
- Achaemenid Empire. **Provided by**: WIkipedia. **Located at**: https://en.wikipedia.org/wiki/Achaemenid_Empire. **License**: *CC BY-SA: Attribution-ShareAlike*
- Greco-Persian Wars. **Provided by**: Wikipedia. **Located at**: http://en.wikipedia.org/wiki/Greco-Persian_Wars. **License**: *CC BY-SA: Attribution-ShareAlike*
- Hoplite. **Provided by**: Wikipedia. **Located at**: https://en.wikipedia.org/wiki/Hoplite. **License**: *CC BY-SA: Attribution-ShareAlike*
- Delian League. **Provided by**: Wikipedia. **Located at**: https://en.wikipedia.org/wiki/Delian_League. **License**: *CC BY-SA: Attribution-ShareAlike*
- Greek-Persian_duel.jpg. **Provided by**: Wikimedia. **Located at**: https://commons.wikimedia.org/wiki/File:Greek-Persian_duel.jpg. **License**: *Public Domain: No Known Copyright*
- AchaemenidMapBehistunInscription.png. **Provided by**: Wikipedia. **Located at**: https://en.wikipedia.org/wiki/File:AchaemenidMapBehistunInscription.png. **License**: *Public Domain: No Known Copyright*
- Delian League. **Provided by**: Wikipedia. **Located at**: https://en.wikipedia.org/wiki/Delian_League. **License**: *CC BY-SA: Attribution-ShareAlike*
- Hegemony. **Provided by**: Wikipedia. **Located at**: https://en.wikipedia.org/wiki/Hegemony. **License**: *CC BY-SA: Attribution-ShareAlike*
- Peloponnesian League. **Provided by**: Wikipedia. **Located at**: https://en.wikipedia.org/wiki/Peloponnesian_League. **License**: *CC BY-SA: Attribution-ShareAlike*
- Greco-Persian Wars. **Provided by**: Wikipedia. **Located at**: https://en.wikipedia.org/wiki/Greco-Persian_Wars. **License**: *CC BY-SA: Attribution-ShareAlike*
- Greek-Persian_duel.jpg. **Provided by**: Wikimedia. **Located at**: https://commons.wikimedia.org/wiki/File:Greek-Persian_duel.jpg. **License**: *Public Domain: No Known Copyright*
- AchaemenidMapBehistunInscription.png. **Provided by**: Wikipedia. **Located at**: https://en.wikipedia.org/wiki/File:AchaemenidMapBehistunInscription.png. **License**: *Public Domain: No Known Copyright*
- Map_athenian_empire_431_BC-en.svg. **Provided by**: Wikimedia. **Located at**: https://en.wikipedia.org/wiki/File:Map_athenian_empire_431_BC-en.svg. **License**: *CC BY-SA: Attribution-ShareAlike*

Athens

Athens

Athens attained its Golden Age under Pericles in the 5th century BCE, and flourished culturally as the hegemonic power of the Hellenic world.

Learning Objectives

Understand the factors contributing to the rise and fall of Athens

Key Takeaways

Key Points

- Cleisthenes overthrew the dictator Hippias in 511/510 BCE in order to establish democracy at Athen
- Athens entered its Golden Age in the 5th century BCE, when it abandoned the pretense of parity and relocated the treasury of the Delian League from Delos to Athens. This money funded the building of the Athenian Acropolis, put half the Athenian population on the public payroll, and allowed Athens to build and maintain the dominant naval power in the Greek world.
- With the empire's funds, military dominance, and its political fortunes as guided by statesman and orator Pericles, Athens produced some of the most influential and enduring cultural artifacts of the Western tradition.
- Tensions within the Delian League brought about the Peloponnesian War (431-404 BCE), during which Athens was defeated by its rival, Sparta. Athens lost further power when the armies of Philip II defeated an alliance of Greek city-states.

Key Terms

- **Pericles**: A prominent and influential Greek statesman, orator, and general of Athens during its Golden Age, in the time between the Persian and Peloponnesian wars.
- **Delian League**: Founded in 478 BCE, an association of Greek city-states under the leadership of Athens, whose purpose was to fight the Persian Empire during the Greco-Persian Wars.
- **Acropolis**: A settlement, especially a citadel, built upon an area of elevated ground, frequently a hill with precipitous sides, chosen for purposes of defense. Often the nuclei of large cities of classical antiquity.

The Rise of Athens (508-448 BCE)

In 514 BCE, the dictator Hippias established stability and prosperity with his rule of Athens, but remained very unpopular as a ruler. With the help of an army from Sparta in 511/510 BCE, he was overthrown by Cleisthenes, a radical politician of aristocratic background who established democracy in Athens.

Prior to the rise of Athens, Sparta, a city-state with a militaristic culture, considered itself the leader of the Greeks, and enforced an hegemony. In 499 BCE, Athens sent troops to aid the Ionian Greeks of Asia Minor, who were rebelling against the Persian Empire during the Ionian Revolt. This provoked two Persian invasions of Greece, both of which were repelled under the leadership of the soldier-statesmen Miltiades and Themistocles, during the Persian Wars. In the decades that followed, the Athenians, with the help of the Spartans and other allied Greek city-states, managed to rout the Persians. These victories enabled Athens to bring most of the Aegean, and many other parts of Greece, together in the Delian League, creating an Athenian-dominated alliance from which Sparta and its allies withdrew.

Greek-Persian Duel

Athenian Hegemony and the Age of Pericles

The 5th century BCE was a period of Athenian political hegemony, economic growth, and cultural flourishing that is sometimes referred to as the Golden Age of Athens. The latter part of this time period is often called The Age of Pericles. After peace was made with Persia in the 5th century BCE, what started as an alliance of independent city-states became an Athenian empire. Athens moved to abandon the pretense of parity among its allies, and relocated the Delian League treasury from Delos to Athens, where it funded the building of the Athenian Acropolis, put half its population on the public payroll, and maintained the dominant naval power in the Greek world. With the empire's funds, military dominance, and its political fortunes as guided by statesman and orator Pericles, Athens produced some of the most influential and enduring cultural artifacts of Western tradition, during what became known as the Golden Age of Athenian democracy, or the Age of Pericles. The playwrights Aeschylus, Sophocles, and Euripides all lived and worked in Athens during this time, as did historians Herodotus and Thucydides, the physician Hippocrates, and the philosopher Socrates.

Pericles was arguably the most prominent and influential Greek statesman, orator, and general of Athens during its Golden Age. One of his most popular reforms while in power was to allow *thetes* (Athenians without wealth) to occupy public office. Another success of his administration was the creation of the *misthophoria*, a special salary for the citizens that attended the courts as jurors. As Athens' ruler, he helped the city to prosper with a resplendent culture and democratic institutions.

5th century Athenian Political Institutions

The administration of the Athenian state was managed by a group of people referred to as magistrates, who were submitted to rigorous public control and chosen by lot. Only two magistrates were directly elected by the Popular Assembly: *strategos* (or generals), and magistrates of finance. All magistrates served for a year or less, with the exception of Pericles, who was elected year after year to public office. At the end of their service, magistrates were required to give an account of their administration and use of public finances.

The most elite posts in the Athenian political system belonged to archons. In ages past, they served as heads of the Athenian state, but in the Age of Pericles they lost much of their influence and power, though they still presided over tribunals. The Assembly of the People was the first organ of democracy in Athens. In theory, it was composed of all the citizens of Athens. However, it is estimated that the maximum number of participants it witnessed was 6,000. The Assembly met in front of the Acropolis and decided on laws and decrees. Once the Assembly gave its decision in a certain matter, the issue was raised to the Council, or *Boule*, to provide definitive approval.

The Council consisted of 500 members, 50 from each tribe, and functioned as an extension of the Assembly. Council members were chosen by lot in a similar manner to magistrates and supervised the work of the magistrates in addition to other legal projects and administrative details. They also oversaw the city-state's external affairs.

Athenian Defeat and Conquest By Macedon

Originally intended as an association of Greek city-states to continue the fight against the Persians, the Delian League soon turned into a vehicle for Athens's own imperial ambitions and empire-building. The resulting tensions brought about the Peloponnesian War (431-404 BCE), in which Athens was defeated by its rival, Sparta. By the mid-4th century BCE, the northern Greek kingdom of Macedon was becoming dominant in Athenian affairs. In 338 BCE, the armies of Philip II of Macedon defeated an alliance of some of the Greek city-states, including Athens and Thebes, at the Battle of Chaeronea, effectively ending Athenian independence.

Athenian Society

Classical Athenian society was structured as a democratic patriarchy that strived towards egalitarian ideals.

Learning Objectives

Understand the structures of Athenian society in the classical period

> ## Key Takeaways
>
> ### Key Points
>
> - The citizens of Athens decided matters of state in the Assembly of the People, the principle organ of Athen's democracy.
> - The Athenian democracy provided a number of governmental resources to its population in order to encourage participation in the democratic process.
> - Many governmental posts in classical Athens were chosen by lot, in an attempt to discourage corruption and patronage.
> - The Athenian elite lived relatively modestly, and wealth and land were not concentrated in the hands of the few, but rather distributed fairly evenly across the upper classes.
> - *Thetes* occupied the lowest rung of Athenian society, but were granted the right to hold public office during the reforms of Ephialtes and Pericles.
> - Athenian society was a patriarchy; men held all rights and advantages, such as access to education and power.
> - Athenian women were dedicated to the care and upkeep of the family home.
>
> ### Key Terms
>
> - **thetes**: The lowest social class of citizens in ancient Athens.
> - **Assembly of the People**: The democratic congregation of classical Athens, which, in theory, brought together all citizens to decide upon proposed laws and decrees.

Structure of the Athenian Government

In the Assembly of the People, Athenian citizens decided matters of state. In theory, it was composed of all the citizens of Athens; however, it is estimated that the maximum number of participants it included was 6,000. Since many citizens were incapable of exercising political rights, due to their poverty or ignorance, a number of governmental resources existed to encourage inclusivity. For example, the Athenian democracy provided the following to its population:

- Concession of salaries to public functionaries
- Help finding work for the poor
- Land grants for dispossessed villagers
- Public assistance for war widows, invalids, orphans, and indigents

In order to discourage corruption and patronage, most public offices that did not require specialized expertise were appointed by lot rather than by election. Offices were also rotated so that members could serve in all capacities in turn, in order to ensure that political functions were instituted as smoothly as possible regardless of each individual official's capacity.

When the Assembly of the People reached decisions on laws and decrees, the issue was raised to a body called the Council, or *Boule*, to provide definitive approval. The Council consisted of 500 members, 50 from each tribe, and functioned as an extension of the Assembly. Council members, who were chosen by lot, supervised the work of other government officials, legal projects, and other administrative details. They also oversaw the city-state's external affairs.

The Acropolis: *View of the Acropolis in Athens, Greece.*

Athenians in the Age of Pericles

The Athenian elite lived modestly and without great luxuries compared to the elites of other ancient societies. Wealth and land ownership was not typically concentrated in the hands of a few people. In fact, 71-73% of the citizen population owned 60-65% of the land. By contrast, *thetes* occupied the lowest social class of citizens in Athens. *Thetes* worked for wages or had less than 200 *medimnoi* as yearly income. Many held crucial roles in the Athenian navy as rowers, due to the preference of many ancient navies to rely on free men to row their galleys. During the reforms of Ephialtes and Pericles around 460-450 BCE, *thetes* were granted the right to hold public office.

Boys were educated at home until the age of seven, at which time they began formal schooling. Subjects included reading, writing, mathematics, and music, as well as physical education classes that were intended to prepare students for future military service. At the age of 18, service in the army was compulsory.

Athenian women were dedicated to the care and upkeep of the family home. Athenian society was a patriarchy; men held all rights and advantages, such as access to education and power. Nonetheless, some women, known as *hetaeras*, did receive an education with the specific purpose of entertaining men, similar to the Japanese geisha tradition. *Hetaeras* were considered higher in status than other women, but lower in status than men. One famous example of a *hetaera* is Pericles' mistress, Aspasia of Miletus, who is said to have debated with prominent writers and thinkers, including Socrates.

Attributions

CC licensed content, Specific attribution

- Caryatid. **Provided by**: Wikipedia. **Located at**: https://en.wikipedia.org/wiki/Caryatid. **License**: *CC BY-SA: Attribution-ShareAlike*
- Classical Athens. **Provided by**: Wikipedia. **Located at**: http://en.wikipedia.org/wiki/Classical_Athens. **License**: *CC BY-SA: Attribution-ShareAlike*
- Age of Pericles. **Provided by**: Wikipedia. **Located at**: http://en.wikipedia.org/wiki/Age_of_Pericles. **License**: *CC BY-SA: Attribution-ShareAlike*
- Delian League. **Provided by**: Wikipedia. **Located at**: http://en.wikipedia.org/wiki/Delian_League. **License**: *CC BY-SA: Attribution-ShareAlike*
- Acropolis. **Provided by**: Wikipedia. **Located at**: http://en.wikipedia.org/wiki/Acropolis. **License**: *CC BY-SA: Attribution-ShareAlike*
- Pericles. **Provided by**: Wiktionary. **Located at**: http://en.wiktionary.org/wiki/Pericles. **License**: *CC BY-SA: Attribution-ShareAlike*
- Fifth-century Athens. **Provided by**: Wikipedia. **Located at**: https://en.wikipedia.org/wiki/Fifth-century_Athens. **License**: *CC BY-SA: Attribution-ShareAlike*
- Athens. **Provided by**: Wikipedia. **Located at**: https://en.wikipedia.org/wiki/Athens. **License**: *CC BY-SA: Attribution-ShareAlike*
- Classical Athens. **Provided by**: Wikimedia. **Located at**: https://commons.wikimedia.org/wiki/File:Ath%C3%A8nes_Acropole_Caryatides.JPG. **License**: *Public Domain: No Known Copyright*
- Greek-Persian Duel. **Provided by**: Wikimedia. **Located at**: https://commons.wikimedia.org/wiki/File:Greek-Persian_duel.jpg. **License**: *Public Domain: No Known Copyright*
- Fifth-century Athens. **Provided by**: Wikipedia. **Located at**: https://en.wikipedia.org/wiki/Fifth-century_Athens. **License**: *CC BY-SA: Attribution-ShareAlike*
- Thetes. **Provided by**: Wikipedia. **Located at**: https://en.wikipedia.org/wiki/Thetes. **License**: *CC BY-SA: Attribution-ShareAlike*
- Classical Athens. **Provided by**: Wikimedia. **Located at**: https://commons.wikimedia.org/wiki/File:Ath%C3%A8nes_Acropole_Caryatides.JPG. **License**: *Public Domain: No Known Copyright*
- Greek-Persian Duel. **Provided by**: Wikimedia. **Located at**: https://commons.wikimedia.org/wiki/File:Greek-Persian_duel.jpg. **License**: *Public Domain: No Known Copyright*
- Lightmatter_acropolis.jpg. **Provided by**: Wikimedia. **Located at**: https://commons.wikimedia.org/wiki/File:Lightmatter_acropolis.jpg. **License**: *Public Domain: No Known Copyright*

Culture in Classical Greece

Classical Greek Philosophy

The three most famous Classical Greek philosophers are Socrates, Plato, and Aristotle.

Learning Objectives

Understand the main philosophical beliefs of Socrates, Plato, and Aristotle

Key Takeaways

Key Points

- Socrates is best known for having pursued a probing question-and-answer style of examination on a number of topics, usually attempting to arrive at a defensible and attractive definition of a virtue.
- In 399 BCE, Socrates was charged for his philosophical inquiries, convicted, and sentenced to death.
- Plato was a student of Socrates, and is the author of numerous dialogues and letters, as well as one of the primary sources available to modern scholars on Socrates' life.
- In his defining work, *The Republic,* Plato reaches the conclusion that a utopian city is likely impossible because philosophers would refuse to rule and the people would refuse to compel them to do so.
- Aristotle was a student of Plato, the tutor of Alexander the Great, and founder of the Lyceum and Peripatetic School of philosophy in Athens. He wrote on a number of subjects, including logic, physics, metaphysics, ethics, rhetoric, politics, and botany.

> *Key Terms*
>
> - **allegory of the cave**: A paradoxical analogy wherein Socrates argues that the invisible world is the most intelligible, and the visible world is the least knowable and obscure. Plato has Socrates describe a gathering of people who have lived chained to the wall of a cave all of their lives, facing a blank wall upon which shadows are projected. The shadows are as close as the prisoners get to viewing reality.
> - **aporia**: In philosophy, a paradox or state of puzzlement; in rhetoric, a useful expression of doubt.
> - **Socrates**: A classical Greek (Athenian) philosopher credited as one of the founders of Western philosophy. Known for a question-answer style of examination.
> - **Plato**: The student of Socrates and author of The Republic. A philosopher and mathematician in classical Greece.
> - **Aristotle**: The student of Plato, tutor to Alexander the Great, and founder of the Lyceum. A Greek philosopher who wrote on a number of topics, including logic, ethics, and metaphysics.

Classical Greece saw a flourishing of philosophers, especially in Athens during its Golden Age. Of these philosophers, the most famous are Socrates, Plato, and Aristotle.

Socrates

Socrates: *Bust of Socrates, currently in the Louvre.*

Socrates, born in Athens in the 5th century BCE, marks a watershed in ancient Greek philosophy. Athens was a center of learning, with sophists and philosophers traveling from across Greece to teach rhetoric, astronomy, cosmology, geometry, and the like. The great statesman Pericles was closely associated with these new teachings, however, and his political opponents struck at him by taking advantage of a conservative reaction against the philosophers. It became a crime to investigate issues above the heavens or below the earth because they were considered impious. While other philosophers, such as Anaxagoras, were forced to flee Athens, Socrates was the only documented individual charged under this law, convicted, and sentenced to death in 399 BCE. In the version of his defense speech presented by Plato, he claims that the envy others experience on account of his being a philosopher is what will lead to his conviction.

Many conversations involving Socrates (as recounted by Plato and Xenophon) end without having reached a firm conclusion, a style known as *aporia*. Socrates is said to have pursued this probing question-and-answer style of examination on a number of topics, usually attempting to arrive at a defensible and attractive definition of a virtue. While Socrates' recorded conversations rarely provide a definitive answer to the question under examination, several maxims or paradoxes for which he has become known recur. Socrates taught that no one desires what is bad, and so if anyone does something that truly is bad, it must be unwillingly or out of ignorance; consequently, all virtue is knowledge. He frequently remarks on his own ignorance (claiming that he does not know what courage is, for example). Plato presents Socrates as distinguishing himself from the common run of mankind by the fact that, while they know nothing noble and good, they do not know that they do not know, whereas Socrates knows and acknowledges that he knows nothing noble and good.

Socrates was morally, intellectually, and politically at odds with many of his fellow Athenians. When he was on trial, he used his method of *elenchos*, a dialectic method of inquiry that resembles the scientific method, to demonstrate to the jurors that their moral values are wrong-headed. He tells them they are concerned with their families, careers, and political responsibilities when they ought to be worried about the "welfare of their souls." Socrates' assertion that the gods had singled him out as a divine emissary seemed to provoke irritation, if not outright ridicule. Socrates also questioned the Sophistic doctrine that *arete* (virtue) can be taught. He liked to observe that successful fathers (such as the prominent military general Pericles) did not produce sons of their own quality. Socrates argued that moral excellence was more a matter of divine bequest than parental nurture.

Plato

Plato: *A copy of Plato's portrait bust by Silanion.*

Plato was an Athenian of the generation after Socrates. Ancient tradition ascribes 36 dialogues and 13 letters to him, although of these only 24 of the dialogues are now universally recognized as authentic. Most modern scholars believe that at least 28 dialogues, and two of the letters, were in fact written by Plato, although all of the 36 dialogues have some defenders. Plato's dialogues feature Socrates, although not always as the leader of the conversation. Along with Xenophon, Plato is the primary source of information about Socrates' life and beliefs, and it is not always easy to distinguish between the two.

Much of what is known about Plato's doctrines is derived from what Aristotle reports about them, and many of Plato's political doctrines are derived from Aristotle's works, *The Republic*, the *Laws*, and the *Statesman*. *The Republic* contains the suggestion that there will not be justice in cities unless they are ruled by philosopher kings; those responsible for enforcing the laws are compelled to hold their women, children, and property in common; and the individual is taught to pursue the common good through noble lies. *The Republic* determines that such a city is likely impossible, however, and generally assumes that philosophers would refuse to rule if the citizenry asked them to, and moreover, the citizenry would refuse to compel philosophers to rule in the first place.

"Platonism" is a term coined by scholars to refer to the intellectual consequences of denying, as Plato's Socrates often does, the reality of the material world. In several dialogues, most notably *The Republic*, Socrates inverts the common man's intuition about what is knowable and what is real. While most people take the objects of their senses to be real if anything is, Socrates is contemptuous of people who think that something has to be graspable in the hands to be real. Socrates's idea that reality is unavailable to those who use their senses is what puts him at odds with the common man and with common sense. Socrates says that he who sees with his eyes is blind, and this idea is most famously captured in his allegory of the cave, a paradoxical analogy wherein Socrates argues that the invisible world is the most intelligible and that the visible world is the least knowable and most obscure.

In the allegory, Socrates describes a gathering of people who have lived chained to the wall of a cave facing a blank wall. The people watch shadows projected on the wall from the fire burning behind them, and the people begin to name and describe the shadows, which are the closest images they have to reality. Socrates then explains that a philosopher is like a prisoner released from that cave who comes to understand the shadows on the wall are not reality.

Aristotle

Aristotle: *Roman copy in marble of a Greek bronze bust of Aristotle by Lysippus, c. 330 BCE. The alabaster mantle is modern.*

Aristotle moved to Athens from his native Stageira in 367 BCE, and began to study philosophy, and perhaps even rhetoric, under Isocrates. He eventually enrolled at Plato's Academy. He left Athens approximately twenty years later to study botany and zoology, became a tutor of Alexander the Great, and ultimately returned to Athens a decade later to establish his own school, the Lyceum. He is the founder of the Peripatetic School of philosophy, which aims to glean facts from experiences and explore the "why" in all things. In other words, he advocates learning by induction.

At least 29 of Aristotle's treatises have survived, known as the *corpus Aristotelicum*, and address a variety of subjects including logic, physics, optics, metaphysics, ethics, rhetoric, politics, poetry, botany, and zoology. Aristotle is often portrayed as disagreeing with his teacher, Plato. He criticizes the regimes described in Plato's *Republic* and *Laws*, and refers to the theory of forms as "empty words and poetic metaphors." He preferred utilizing empirical observation and practical concerns in his works. Aristotle did not consider virtue to be simple knowledge as Plato did, but founded in one's nature, habit, and reason. Virtue was gained by acting in accordance with nature and moderation.

Classical Greek Poetry and History

Homer, one of the greatest Greek poets, significantly influenced classical Greek historians as their field turned increasingly towards scientific evidence-gathering and analysis of cause and effect.

Learning Objectives

Explain how epic poetry influenced the development of classical Greek historical texts

Key Takeaways

Key Points

- The formative influence of the Homeric epics in shaping Greek culture was widely recognized, and Homer was described as the teacher of Greece.
- The *Iliad*, sometimes referred to as the *Song of Ilion* or *Song of Ilium*, is set during the Trojan War and recounts the battles and events surrounding a quarrel between King Agamemnon and the warrior Achilles.
- Herodotus is referred to as "The Father of History," and is the first historian known to have broken from Homeric tradition in order to treat historical subjects as a method of investigation arranged into a historiographic narrative.
- Thucydides, who had been trained in rhetoric, provided a model of historical prose-writing based more firmly in factual progression of a narrative, whereas Herodotus, due to frequent digressions and asides, appeared to minimize his authorial control.
- Thucydides is sometimes known as the father of "scientific history," or an early precursor to 20th century scientific positivism, because of his strict adherence to evidence-gathering and analysis of historical cause and effect without reference to divine intervention.
- Despite its heavy political slant, scholars cite strong literary and philosophical influences in Thucydides' work.

Key Terms

- **Homer**: A Greek poet of the 7th or 8th century BCE; author of the Iliad and the Odyssey.
- **dactylic hexameter**: A form of meter in poetry or a rhythmic scheme. Traditionally associated with the quantitative meter of classical epic poetry in both Greek and Latin, and consequently considered to be the grand style of classical poetry.

Homer

In the Western classical tradition, Homer is the author of the *Iliad* and the *Odyssey*, and is revered as the greatest of ancient Greek epic poets. These epics lie at the beginning of the Western canon of literature, and have had an enormous influence on the history of literature. Whether and when Homer lived is unknown. The ancient Greek author Herodotus estimates that Homer lived 400 years before his own time, which would place him at around 850 BCE, while other ancient sources claim that he lived much nearer to the supposed time of the Trojan War, in the early 12th century BCE. Most modern researchers place Homer in the 7th or 8th centuries BCE.

Homer: *Idealized portrayal of Homer dating to the Hellenistic period; located at the British Museum.*

The formative influence of the Homeric epics in shaping Greek culture was widely recognized, and Homer was described as the "Teacher of Greece." Homer's works, some 50% of which are speeches, provided models in persuasive speaking and writing that were emulated throughout the ancient and medieval Greek worlds. Fragments of Homer account for nearly half of all identifiable Greek literary papyrus finds.

The Iliad

The *Iliad* (sometimes referred to as the *Song of Ilion* or *Song of Ilium*) is an ancient Greek epic poem in dactylic hexameter. Set during the Trojan War (the ten-year siege of the city of Troy (Ilium) by a coalition of Greek states), it tells of the battles and events surrounding a quarrel between King Agamemnon and the warrior Achilles. Although the story covers only a few weeks in the final year of the war, the *Iliad* mentions or alludes to many of the Greek legends about the siege. The epic narrative describes events prophesied for the future, such as Achilles' looming death and the sack of Troy. The events are prefigured and alluded to more and more vividly, so that when the story reaches an end, the poem has told a more or less complete tale of the Trojan War.

Nineteenth century excavations at Hisarlik provided scholars with historical evidence for the events of the Trojan War, as told by Homer in the *Iliad*. Additionally, linguistic studies into oral epic traditions in nearby civilizations, and the deciphering of Linear B in the 1950s, provided further evidence that the Homeric poems could have been derived from oral transmissions of long-form tales about a war that actually took place. The likely historicity of the *Iliad* as a piece of literature, however, must be balanced against the creative license that would have been taken over years of transmission, as well as the alteration of historical fact to conform with tribal preferences and provide entertainment value to its intended audiences.

Herodotus

Herodotus was a Greek historian who was born in Halicarnassus (modern-day Bodrum, Turkey) and lived in the 5th century BCE. He was a contemporary of Socrates. He is referred to as "The Father of History" and is the first historian known to have broken from Homeric tradition in order to treat historical subjects as a method of investigation arranged into a historiographic narrative. His only known work is a history on the origins of the Greco-Persian Wars, entitled, *The Histories*. Herodotus states that he only reports that which was told to him, and some of his stories are fanciful and/or inaccurate; however, the majority of his information appears to be accurate.

Athenian tragic poets and storytellers appear to have provided heavy inspiration for Herodotus, as did Homer. Herodotus appears to have drawn on an Ionian tradition of storytelling, collecting and interpreting oral histories he happened upon during his travels in much the same way that oral poetry formed the basis for much of Homer's works. While these oral histories often contained folk-tale motifs and fed into a central moral, they also related verifiable facts relating to geography, anthropology, and history. For this reason, Herodotus drew criticism from his contemporaries, being touted as a mere storyteller and even a falsifier of information. In contrast to this type of approach, Thucydides, who had been trained in rhetoric, provided a model of historical prose-writing based more firmly in factual progression of a narrative, whereas Herodotus, due to frequent digressions and asides, appeared to minimize his authorial control.

Thucydides

Thucydides was an Athenian historian and general. His *History of the Peloponnesian War* recounts the 5th century BCE war between Athens and Sparta. Thucydides is sometimes known as the father of "scientific history," or an early precursor to 20th century scientific positivism, because of his strict adherence to evidence-gathering and analysis of historical cause and effect without reference to divine intervention. He is also considered the father of political realism, which is a school of thought within the realm of political science that views the political behavior of individuals and the relations between states to be governed by self-interest and fear. More generally, Thucydides' texts show concern with understanding why individuals react the way they do during such crises as plague, massacres, and civil war.

Unlike Herodotus, Thucydides did not view his historical accounts as a source of moral lessons, but rather as a factual reporting of contemporary political and military events. Thucydides viewed life in political terms rather than moral terms, and viewed history in political terms. Thucydides also tended to omit, or at least downplay, geographic and ethnographic aspects of events from his work, whereas Herodotus recorded all information as part of the narrative. Thucydides' accounts are generally held to be more unambiguous and reliable than those of Herodotus. However, unlike his predecessor, Thucydides does not reveal his sources. Curiously, although subsequent Greek historians, such as Plutarch, held up Thucydides' writings as a model for scholars of their field, many of them continued to view history as a source of moral lessons, as did Herodotus.

Despite its heavy political slant, scholars cite strong literary and philosophical influences in Thucydides' work. In particular, the *History of the Peloponnesian War* echoes the narrative tradition of Homer, and draws heavily from epic poetry and tragedy to construct what is essentially a positivistic account of world events. Additionally, it brings to the forefront themes of justice and suffering in a similar manner to the philosophical texts of Aristotle and Plato.

Classical Greek Theater

Classical Greek theater, whether tragic or comic, has had great influence on modern literature and drama.

Learning Objectives

Describe the common themes found in classical Greek plays

Key Takeaways

Key Points

- The city-state of Athens was the center of cultural power during this period, and held a drama festival in honor of the go Dionysus, called the Dionysia.
- Two dramatic genres to emerge from this era of Greek theater were tragedy and comedy, both of which rose to prominence around 500-490 BCE.
- Greek tragedy is an extension of the ancient rites carried out in honor of Dionysus; it heavily influenced the theater of ancient Rome and the Renaissance.
- Tragic plots were often based upon myths from the oral traditions of archaic epics, and took the form of narratives presented by actors.
- Aeschylus was the first tragedian to codify the basic rules of tragic drama, and is considered by many to be the "father of tragedy." Athenian comedy is divided into three periods: Old Comedy, Middle Comedy, and New Comedy.

Key Terms

- **chorus**: In the context of Greek theatre, a homogeneous, non-individualized group of performers who comment, with a collective voice, on dramatic action.
- **deus ex machina**: A plot device whereby a seemingly unsolvable problem is suddenly and abruptly resolved by the unexpected intervention of some new event, character, ability, or object.

> - **monody**: In the context of ancient Greek theater and literature, lyric poetry sung by a single performer rather than by a chorus.

The theatrical culture of ancient Greece flourished from approximately 700 BCE onward. The city-state of Athens was the center of cultural power during this period and held a drama festival in honor of the god Dionysus, called the Dionysia. This festival was exported to many of Athen's numerous colonies to promote a common cultural identity across the empire. Two dramatic genres to emerge from this era of Greek theater were tragedy and comedy, both of which rose to prominence around 500-490 BCE.

Greek Tragedy

Sometimes referred to as Attic tragedy, Greek tragedy is an extension of the ancient rites carried out in honor of Dionysus, and it heavily influenced the theater of ancient Rome and the Renaissance. Tragic plots were often based upon myths from the oral traditions of archaic epics, and took the form of narratives presented by actors. Tragedies typically began with a prologue, in which one or more characters introduce the plot and explain the background to the ensuing story. The prologue is then followed by *paraodos*, after which the story unfolds through three or more episodes. The episodes are interspersed by *stasima*, or choral interludes that explain or comment on the situation that is developing. The tragedy then ends with an *exodus*, which concludes the story.

Aeschylus and the Codification of Tragic Drama

Aeschylus was the first tragedian to codify the basic rules of tragic drama. He is often described as the father of tragedy. He is credited with inventing the trilogy, a series of three tragedies that tell one long story. Trilogies were often performed in sequence over the course of a day, from sunrise to sunset. At the end of the last play, a satyr play was staged to revive the spirits of the public after they had witnessed the heavy events of the tragedy that had preceded it.

Marble bust of Aeschylus

According to Aristotle, Aeschylus also expanded the number of actors in theater to allow for the dramatization of conflict on stage. Previously, it was standard for only one character to be present and interact with the homogeneous chorus, which commented in unison on the dramatic action unfolding on stage. Aeschylus's works show an evolution and enrichment in dialogue, contrasts, and theatrical effects over time, due to the rich competition that existed among playwrights of this era. Unfortunately, his plays, and those of Sophocles and Euripides, are the only works of classical Greek literature to have survived mostly intact, so there are not many rival texts to examine his works against.

The Reforms of Sophocles

Cast of Sophocles' bust in the Pushkin Museum

Sophocles was one such rival who triumphed against the famous and previously unchallenged Aeschylus. Sophocles introduced a third actor to staged tragedies, increased the chorus to 15 members, broke the cycle of trilogies (making possible the production of independent dramas), and introduced the concept of scenery to theater. Compared to the works of Aeschylus, choruses in Sophocles' plays did less explanatory work, shifting the focus to deeper character development and staged conflict. The events that took place were often left unexplained or unjustified, forcing the audience to reflect upon the human condition.

The Realism of Euripides

Euripides differs from Aeschylus and Sophocles in his search for technical experimentation and increased focus on feelings as a mechanism to elaborate the unfolding of tragic events. In Euripides' tragedies, there are three experimental aspects that reoccur. The first is the transition of the prologue to a monologue performed by an actor informing spectators of a story's background. The second is the introduction of *deus ex machina*, or a plot device whereby a seemingly unsolvable problem is suddenly and abruptly resolved by the unexpected intervention of some new event, character, ability, or object. Finally, the use of a chorus was minimized in favor of a monody sung by the characters.

Statue of Euripides

Another novelty introduced by Euripidean drama is the realism with which characters' psychological dynamics are portrayed. Unlike in Aeschylus or Sophocles' works, heroes in Euripides' plays were portrayed as insecure characters troubled by internal conflict rather than simply resolute. Female protagonists were also used to portray tormented sensitivity and irrational impulses that collided with the world of reason.

Greek Comedy

As Aristotle wrote in his *Poetics*, comedy is defined by the representation of laughable people, and involves some kind of blunder or ugliness that does not cause pain or disaster. Athenian comedy is divided into three periods: Old Comedy, Middle Comedy, and New Comedy. The Old Comedy period is largely represented by the 11 surviving plays of Aristophanes, whereas much of the work of the Middle Comedy period has been lost. New Comedy is known primarily by the substantial papyrus fragments of Menander. In general, the divisions between these periods is largely arbitrary, and ancient Greek comedy almost certainly developed constantly over the years.

Old Comedy and Aristophanes

Aristophanes, the most important Old Comic dramatist, wrote plays that abounded with political satire, as well as sexual and scatological innuendo. He lampooned the most important personalities and institutions of his day, including Socrates in *The Clouds*. His works are characterized as definitive to the genre of comedy even today.

Middle Comedy

Although the line between Old and Middle Comedy is not clearly marked chronologically, there are some important thematic differences between the two. For instance, the role of the chorus in Middle Comedy was largely diminished to the point where it had no influence on the plot. Additionally, public characters were no longer impersonated or personified onstage, and objects of ridicule tended to be more general rather than personal, and in many instances, literary rather than political. For some time, mythological burlesque was popular among Middle Comic poets. Stock characters also were employed during this period. In-depth assessment and critique of the styling of Middle Comedy is difficult, given the lack of complete bodies of work. However, given the revival of this style in Sicily and Magna Graecia, it appears that the works of this period did have considerable widespread literary and social impact.

New Comedy

The style of New Comedy is comparable to what is contemporarily referred to as situation comedy or comedy of manners. The playwrights of Greek New Comedy built upon the devices, characters, and situations their predecessors had developed. Prologues to shape the audience's understanding of events, messengers' speeches to announce offstage action, and *ex machina* endings were all well established tropes that were used in New Comedies. Satire and farce occupied less importance in the works of this time, and mythological themes and subjects were replaced by everyday concerns. Gods and goddesses were, at best, personified abstractions rather than actual characters, and no miracles or metamorphoses occurred. For the first time, love became a principal element in this type of theater.

Three playwrights are well known from this period: Menander, Philemon, and Diphilus. Menander was the most successful of the New Comedians. Menander's comedies focused on the fears and foibles of the ordinary man, as opposed to satirical accounts of political and public life, which perhaps lent to his comparative success within the genre. His comedies are the first to demonstrate the five-act structure later to become common in modern plays. Philemon's comedies dwell on philosophical issues, whereas Diphilus was noted for his use of farcical violence.

Classical Greek Architecture

Classical Greek architecture can be divided into three separate styles: the Doric Order, the Ionic Order, and the Corinthian Order.

Learning Objectives

Describe the distinguishing characteristics of Classical Greek Architecture

> ### Key Takeaways
>
> *Key Points*
>
> - Classical Greek architecture is best represented by substantially intact ruins of temples and open-air theaters.
> - The architectural style of classical Greece can be divided into three separate orders: the Doric Order, the Ionic Order, and the Corinthian Order. All three styles have had a profound impact on Western architecture of later periods.
> - While the three orders of Greek architecture are most easily recognizable by their capitals, the orders also governed the form, proportions, details, and relationships of the columns, entablature, pediment, and stylobate.
> - The Parthenon is considered the most important surviving building of classical Greece, and the zenith of Doric Order architecture.
>
> *Key Terms*
>
> - **stylobate**: In classical Greek architecture, a stylobate is the top step of a stepped platform upon which colonnades of temple columns are placed. In other words, the stylobate comprises the temple flooring.
> - **capitals**: In architecture, a capital forms the topmost member of a column.
> - **entablature**: An entablature is the superstructure of moldings and bands that lay horizontally above columns and rest on capitals.
> - **pediment**: A pediment is an element in classical, neoclassical, and baroque architecture that is placed above the horizontal structure of an entablature, and is typically supported by columns.

Classical Greek architecture is highly formalized in structure and decoration, and is best known for its temples, many of which are found throughout the region as substantially intact ruins. Each classical Greek temple appears to have been conceived as a sculptural entity within the landscape, and is usually raised on higher ground so that its proportions and the effects of light on its surface can be viewed from multiple angles. Open-air theaters are also an important type of building that survives throughout the Hellenic world, with the earliest dating from approximately 525-480 BCE.

Greek architectural style can be divided into three separate orders: the Doric Order, the Ionic Order, and the Corinthian Order. These styles have had a profound impact on Western architecture of later periods. In particular, the architecture of ancient Rome grew out of Greek architecture. Revivals of Classicism have also brought about renewed interest in the architectural styles of ancient Greece. While the three orders of Greek architecture are most easily recognizable by their capitals, the orders also governed the form, proportions, details, and relationships of the columns, entablature, pediment, and stylobate. Orders were applied to the whole range of buildings and monuments.

The Doric Order

The Doric Order developed on mainland Greece and spread to Italy. It is most easily recognized by its capital, which appears as a circular cushion placed on top of a column onto which a lintel rests. In early examples of the Doric Order, the cushion is splayed and flat, but over time, it became more refined, deeper, and with a greater curve.

Doric columns almost always feature fluting down the length of the column, numbering up to 20 flutes. The flutes meet at sharp edges, called arrises. Doric columns typically have no bases, with the exception of a few examples dating from the Hellenistic period. Columns of an early Doric temple, such as the Temple of Apollo at Syracuse, could have a column height to an entablature ratio of 2:1, and a column height to a base diameter ratio of only 4:1. Later, a column height to a diameter ratio of 6:1 became more usual, and there is a column height to an entablature ratio at the Parthenon oapproximately 3:1.

Doric entablatures consist of three parts: the architrave, the frieze, and the cornice. The architrave is composed of stone lintels that span the space between columns. On top of this rests the frieze, one of the major areas of sculptural decoration. The frieze is divided into triglyps and metopes. The triglyphs have three vertical grooves, similar to columnar fluting, and below them are guttae, small strips that appear to connect the triglyps to the architrave below. The triglyps are located above the center of each capital and the center of each lintel.

Pediments in the Doric style were decorated with figures in relief in early examples; however, by the time the sculptures on the Parthenon were created, many pediment decorations were freestanding.

The Parthenon

The Parthenon is considered the most important surviving building of classical Greece and the zenith of Doric Order architecture. It is a former temple on the Athenian Acropolis dedicated to the patron goddess of Athens, Athena. Construction began on the Parthenon in 447 BCE, when the Athenian Empire was at its peak. Construction was completed in 438 BCE, but decoration of the building continued until 432 BCE. Although most architectural elements of the Parthenon belong to the Doric Order, a continuous sculptured frieze in low relief that sits above the architrave belongs to the Ionic style.

The Parthenon: *The Parthenon under restoration in 2008.*

The Ionic Order

The Ionic Order coexisted with the Doric Order and was favored by Greek cities in Ionia, Asia Minor, and the Aegean Islands. It did not evolve into a clearly defined style until the mid-5th century BCE. Early Ionic temples in Asia Minor were particularly ambitious in scale.

The Ionic Order is most easily identified by its voluted capital. The cushion placed on top of the column is similarly shaped to that of the Doric Order, but is decorated with a stylized ornament and surmounted by a horizontal band that scrolls under to either side.

Ionic Order columns are fluted with narrow, shallow flutes that do not meet at a sharp edge, but have a flat band between them. The usual number of flutes is 24, but there can be as many as 44. The architrave is not always decorated, but more often it rises in three outwardly-stepped bands. The frieze runs in a continuous band and is separated from other members by rows of small projecting blocks.

The Ionic Order is lighter in appearance than the Doric Order, with columns that have a 9:1 ratio, and the diameter and the whole entablature appears much narrower and less heavy than those of the Doric. Decorations were distributed with some variation, and Ionic entablatures often featured formalized bands of motifs. The external frieze often contained a continuous band of figurative sculpture of ornament, though this was not always the case. Caryatids—draped female figures used as supporting members to the entablature—were also a feature of the Ionic Order.

The Erechteum on the Acropolis of Athens, Greece

Corner capital in the Ionic style with a diagonal volute, showing also details of the fluting separated by fillets.

The Corinthian Order

The Corinthian Order grew directly from the Ionic in the mid-5th century BCE, and was initially of a very similar style and proportion, with the only distinguishing factor being its more ornate capitals. The capitals of the Corinthian Order were much deeper than those of the Doric and Ionic Orders. They were shaped like a bell-shaped mixing bowl and ornamented with a double row of acanthus leaves above which rose splayed, voluted tendrils. The ratio of column height to diameter of the Corinthian Order is generally 10:1, with the capital taking up more than a tenth of the height. The ratio of capital height to diameter is generally about 1:16:1.

Initially the Corinthian Order was used internally in such sites as the Temple of Apollo Epicurius at Bassae. By the late 300s, features of the Corinthian Order began to be used externally at sites such as the Choragic Monument of Lysicrates and the Temple of Zeus Olympia, both in Athens. During the Hellenistic period, Corinthian columns were sometimes built without fluting. The Corinthian Order became popular among the Romans, who added a number of refinements and decorative details.

Scientific Advancements in the Classical Period

The Hellenistic Period witnessed significant scientific advancements, due to the mixing of Greek and Asian culture and royal patronage.

Learning Objectives

Describe the various scientific advancements made during the Hellenistic period

Key Takeaways

Key Points

- Great seats of learning rose during the Hellenistic Period, including those at Alexandria and Antioch.
- Scientific inquiries were often sponsored by royal patrons.
- The discoveries of several Greek mathematicians, including Pythagoras and Euclid, are still used in mathematical teaching today. Important developments include the basic rules of geometry, the idea of a formal mathematical proof, and discoveries in number theory, mathematical analysis, and applied mathematics.
- The Greeks also developed the field of astronomy, which they treated as a branch of mathematics to a highly sophisticated level.
- Hippocrates was a physician of the classical period, and is considered one of the most outstanding figures in the history of medicine. Most notably, he founded the Hippocratic school of medicine, which revolutionized medicine in ancient Greece by establishing it as a discipline distinct from other fields, and making medicine a profession.

Key Terms

- **Hellenistic period**: The period of ancient Greek and Mediterranean history between the death of Alexander the Great in 323 BCE and the emergence of the Roman Empire, as signified by the Battle of Actium in 31 BCE.
- **Alexandria**: An important seat of learning within the Hellenistic civilization and the capital of Hellenistic, Roman, and Byzantine Egypt for almost 1,000 years, until the Muslim conquest of Egypt in 641 CE.

Hellenistic Culture

Hellenistic culture produced seats of learning in Alexandria, Egypt and Antioch, Syria, along with Greek-speaking populations across several monarchies. Hellenistic science differed from Greek science in at least two ways. First, it benefited from the cross-fertilization of Greek ideas with those that had developed in the larger Hellenistic world. Secondly, to some extent, it was supported by royal patrons in the kingdoms founded by Alexander's successors.

Especially important to Hellenistic science was the city of Alexandria in Egypt, which became a major center of scientific research in the 3rd century BCE. Two institutions established there during the reigns of Ptolemy I Soter (reigned 323-283 BCE) and Ptolemy II Philadelphus (reigned 281-246 BCE) were the Library and the Museum. Unlike Plato 's Academy and Aristotle 's Lyceum, these institutions were officially supported by the Ptolemies, although the extent of patronage could be precarious, depending on the policies of the current ruler.

The Great Library of Alexandria: *The Great Library of Alexandria, O. Von Corven. 19th century.*

Mathematics and Astronomy

The discoveries of several Greek mathematicians, including Pythagoras and Euclid, are still used in mathematical teaching today. Important developments include the basic rules of geometry, the idea of a formal mathematical proof, and discoveries in number theory, mathematical analysis, and applied mathematics. Ancient Greek mathematicians also came close to establishing integral calculus.

The Greeks also developed the field of astronomy, which they treated as a branch of mathematics, to a highly sophisticated level. The first geometrical, three-dimensional models to explain the apparent motion of the planets was developed in the 4th century BCE, by Eudoxus of Cnidus and Callippus of Cyzicus.

Their younger contemporary, Heraclides Ponticus, proposed that the Earth rotates around its axis. In the 3rd century BCE, Aristarchus of Samos was the first to suggest a heliocentric system. In the 2nd century BCE, Hipparchus of Nicea made a number of contributions, including the first measurement of precession and the compilation of the first star catalog, in which he proposed the modern system of apparent magnitudes.

The Antikythera mechanism, a device for calculating the movements of the planets, was the first ancestor of the astronomical computer. It dates from about 80 BCE, and was discovered in an ancient shipwreck off the Greek island of Antikythera. The device became famous for its use of a differential gear, which was previously believed to have been invented in the 16th century, as well as the miniaturization and complexity of its parts, which has been compared to that of clocks produced in the 18th century.

The Medical Field

The ancient Greeks also made important discoveries in the medical field. Hippocrates was a physician of the classical period, and is considered one of the most outstanding figures in the history of medicine. He is sometimes even referred to as the "father of medicine." Most notably, he founded the Hippocratic school of medicine, whic revolutionized medicine in ancient Greece by establishing it as a discipline distinct from other fields, and making medicine a profession.

Other notable Hellenistic scientists and their achievements include:

- Herophilos (335-280 BCE), who was the first to base medical conclusions on dissection of the human body and to describe the nervous system
- Archimedes (c. 287-212 BCE), a geometer, physicist, and engineer who laid the foundations of hydrostatics and statics, and explained the principle of the lever
- Eratosthenes (c. 276 BCE-195/194 BCE), who measured the distance between the Sun and the Earth, as well as the size of the Earth

Attributions

CC licensed content, Specific attribution

- Socrates. **Provided by**: Wikipedia. **Located at**: http://en.wikipedia.org/wiki/Socrates. **License**: *CC BY-SA: Attribution-ShareAlike*
- Plato. **Provided by**: Wikipedia. **Located at**: http://en.wikipedia.org/wiki/Plato. **License**: *CC BY-SA: Attribution-ShareAlike*
- Ancient Greek Philosophy. **Provided by**: Wikipedia. **Located at**: http://en.wikipedia.org/wiki/Classical_Greek_philosophy%23Classical_Greek_philosophy. **License**: *CC BY-SA: Attribution-ShareAlike*
- Aporia. **Provided by**: Wikipedia. **Located at**: http://en.wikipedia.org/wiki/Aporia. **License**: *CC BY-SA: Attribution-ShareAlike*
- Aristotle. **Provided by**: Wiktionary. **Located at**: http://en.wiktionary.org/wiki/Aristotle. **License**: *CC BY-SA: Attribution-ShareAlike*
- Allegory of the Cave. **Provided by**: Wikipedia. **Located at**: http://en.wikipedia.org/wiki/Allegory_of_the_cave. **License**: *CC BY-SA: Attribution-ShareAlike*
- Peripatetic school. **Provided by**: Wikipedia. **Located at**: https://en.wikipedia.org/wiki/Peripatetic_school. **License**: *CC BY-SA: Attribution-ShareAlike*
- Socrates. **Provided by**: Wikipedia. **Located at**: http://en.wikipedia.org/wiki/Socrates%23mediaviewer/File:Socrates_Louvre.jpg. **License**: *CC BY-SA: Attribution-ShareAlike*
- Aristotle. **Provided by**: Wikipedia. **Located at**: http://en.wikipedia.org/wiki/Aristotle%23mediaviewer/File:Aristotle_Altemps_Inv8575.jpg. **License**: *Public Domain: No Known Copyright*
- Plato. **Provided by**: Wikipedia. **Located at**: http://en.wikipedia.org/wiki/Plato%23mediaviewer/File:Plato_Silanion_Musei_Capitolini_MC1377.jpg. **License**: *CC BY: Attribution*
- Iliad. **Provided by**: Wikipedia. **Located at**: http://en.wikipedia.org/wiki/Iliad. **License**: *CC BY-SA: Attribution-ShareAlike*

- Homer. **Provided by**: Wikipedia. **Located at**: http://en.wikipedia.org/wiki/Homer. **License**: *CC BY-SA: Attribution-ShareAlike*
- Dactylic Hexameter. **Provided by**: Wikipedia. **Located at**: http://en.wikipedia.org/wiki/Dactylic_hexameter. **License**: *CC BY-SA: Attribution-ShareAlike*
- Herodotus. **Provided by**: Wikipedia. **Located at**: https://en.wikipedia.org/wiki/Herodotus. **License**: *CC BY-SA: Attribution-ShareAlike*
- Thucydides. **Provided by**: Wikipedia. **Located at**: https://en.wikipedia.org/wiki/Thucydides. **License**: *CC BY-SA: Attribution-ShareAlike*
- Socrates. **Provided by**: Wikipedia. **Located at**: http://en.wikipedia.org/wiki/Socrates%23mediaviewer/File:Socrates_Louvre.jpg. **License**: *CC BY-SA: Attribution-ShareAlike*
- Aristotle. **Provided by**: Wikipedia. **Located at**: http://en.wikipedia.org/wiki/Aristotle%23mediaviewer/File:Aristotle_Altemps_Inv8575.jpg. **License**: *Public Domain: No Known Copyright*
- Plato. **Provided by**: Wikipedia. **Located at**: http://en.wikipedia.org/wiki/Plato%23mediaviewer/File:Plato_Silanion_Musei_Capitolini_MC1377.jpg. **License**: *CC BY: Attribution*
- Homer. **Provided by**: Wikipedia. **Located at**: http://upload.wikimedia.org/wikipedia/commons/1/1c/Homer_British_Museum.jpg. **License**: *CC BY-SA: Attribution-ShareAlike*
- Greek chorus. **Provided by**: Wikipedia. **Located at**: https://en.wikipedia.org/wiki/Greek_chorus. **License**: *CC BY-SA: Attribution-ShareAlike*
- Greek tragedy. **Provided by**: Wikipedia. **Located at**: https://en.wikipedia.org/wiki/Greek_tragedy. **License**: *CC BY-SA: Attribution-ShareAlike*
- Aeschylus. **Provided by**: Wikipedia. **Located at**: https://en.wikipedia.org/wiki/Aeschylus. **License**: *CC BY-SA: Attribution-ShareAlike*
- Monody. **Provided by**: Wikipedia. **Located at**: https://en.wikipedia.org/wiki/Monody. **License**: *CC BY-SA: Attribution-ShareAlike*
- Deus ex machina. **Provided by**: Wikipedia. **Located at**: https://en.wikipedia.org/wiki/Deus_ex_machina. **License**: *CC BY-SA: Attribution-ShareAlike*
- Ancient Greek comedy. **Provided by**: Wikipedia. **Located at**: https://en.wikipedia.org/wiki/Ancient_Greek_comedy. **License**: *CC BY-SA: Attribution-ShareAlike*
- Theatre of ancient Greece. **Provided by**: Wikipedia. **Located at**: https://en.wikipedia.org/wiki/Theatre_of_ancient_Greece. **License**: *CC BY-SA: Attribution-ShareAlike*
- Socrates. **Provided by**: Wikipedia. **Located at**: http://en.wikipedia.org/wiki/Socrates%23mediaviewer/File:Socrates_Louvre.jpg. **License**: *CC BY-SA: Attribution-ShareAlike*
- Aristotle. **Provided by**: Wikipedia. **Located at**: http://en.wikipedia.org/wiki/Aristotle%23mediaviewer/File:Aristotle_Altemps_Inv8575.jpg. **License**: *Public Domain: No Known Copyright*
- Plato. **Provided by**: Wikipedia. **Located at**: http://en.wikipedia.org/wiki/Plato%23mediaviewer/File:Plato_Silanion_Musei_Capitolini_MC1377.jpg. **License**: *CC BY: Attribution*
- Homer. **Provided by**: Wikipedia. **Located at**: http://upload.wikimedia.org/wikipedia/commons/1/1c/Homer_British_Museum.jpg. **License**: *CC BY-SA: Attribution-ShareAlike*
- Aischylos_BC3BCste.jpg. **Provided by**: Wikimedia. **Located at**: https://commons.wikimedia.org/wiki/File:Aischylos_B%C3%BCste.jpg. **License**: *Public Domain: No Known Copyright*
- Sophocles_pushkin.jpg. **Provided by**: Wikimedia. **Located at**: https://commons.wikimedia.org/wiki/File:Sophocles_pushkin.jpg. **License**: *CC BY-SA: Attribution-ShareAlike*
- Euripides_Statue.jpg. **Provided by**: Wikimedia. **Located at**: https://commons.wikimedia.org/wiki/File:Euripides_Statue.jpg. **License**: *Public Domain: No Known Copyright*
- Entablature. **Provided by**: Wikipedia. **Located at**: https://en.wikipedia.org/wiki/Entablature. **License**: *CC BY-SA: Attribution-ShareAlike*
- Pediment. **Provided by**: Wikipedia. **Located at**: https://en.wikipedia.org/wiki/Pediment. **License**: *CC BY-SA: Attribution-ShareAlike*
- Ancient Greek architecture. **Provided by**: Wikipedia. **Located at**: https://en.wikipedia.org/wiki/Ancient_Greek_architecture. **License**: *CC BY-SA: Attribution-ShareAlike*
- Capital (architecture). **Provided by**: Wikpedia. **Located at**: https://en.wikipedia.org/wiki/Capital_(architecture). **License**: *CC BY-SA: Attribution-ShareAlike*
- Stylobate. **Provided by**: Wikipedia. **Located at**: https://en.wikipedia.org/wiki/Stylobate. **License**: *CC BY-SA: Attribution-ShareAlike*

CULTURE IN CLASSICAL GREECE • 327

- Parthenon. **Provided by**: Wikipedia. **Located at**: https://en.wikipedia.org/wiki/Parthenon. **License**: *CC BY-SA: Attribution-ShareAlike*

- Socrates. **Provided by**: Wikipedia. **Located at**: http://en.wikipedia.org/wiki/Socrates%23mediaviewer/File:Socrates_Louvre.jpg. **License**: *CC BY-SA: Attribution-ShareAlike*

- Aristotle. **Provided by**: Wikipedia. **Located at**: http://en.wikipedia.org/wiki/Aristotle%23mediaviewer/File:Aristotle_Altemps_Inv8575.jpg. **License**: *Public Domain: No Known Copyright*

- Plato. **Provided by**: Wikipedia. **Located at**: http://en.wikipedia.org/wiki/Plato%23mediaviewer/File:Plato_Silanion_Musei_Capitolini_MC1377.jpg. **License**: *CC BY: Attribution*

- Homer. **Provided by**: Wikipedia. **Located at**: http://upload.wikimedia.org/wikipedia/commons/1/1c/Homer_British_Museum.jpg. **License**: *CC BY-SA: Attribution-ShareAlike*

- Aischylos_BC3BCste.jpg. **Provided by**: Wikimedia. **Located at**: https://commons.wikimedia.org/wiki/File:Aischylos_B%C3%BCste.jpg. **License**: *Public Domain: No Known Copyright*

- Sophocles_pushkin.jpg. **Provided by**: Wikimedia. **Located at**: https://commons.wikimedia.org/wiki/File:Sophocles_pushkin.jpg. **License**: *CC BY-SA: Attribution-ShareAlike*

- Euripides_Statue.jpg. **Provided by**: Wikimedia. **Located at**: https://commons.wikimedia.org/wiki/File:Euripides_Statue.jpg. **License**: *Public Domain: No Known Copyright*

- Parthenon-2008_entzerrt.jpg. **Provided by**: Wikipedia. **Located at**: https://en.wikipedia.org/wiki/File:Parthenon-2008_entzerrt.jpg. **License**: *CC BY-SA: Attribution-ShareAlike*

- Erechteion_-_chapiteau.jpg. **Provided by**: Wikipedia. **Located at**: https://en.wikipedia.org/wiki/File:Erechteion_-_chapiteau.jpg. **License**: *Public Domain: No Known Copyright*

- Eratosthenes. **Provided by**: Wikipedia. **Located at**: http://en.wikipedia.org/wiki/Eratosthenes. **License**: *CC BY-SA: Attribution-ShareAlike*

- Hellenistic Period. **Provided by**: Wikipedia. **Located at**: http://en.wikipedia.org/wiki/Hellenistic_period%23Culture. **License**: *CC BY-SA: Attribution-ShareAlike*

- Archimedes. **Provided by**: Wikipedia. **Located at**: http://en.wikipedia.org/wiki/Archimedes. **License**: *CC BY-SA: Attribution-ShareAlike*

- Hellenistic Period. **Provided by**: Wikipedia. **Located at**: http://en.wikipedia.org/wiki/Hellenistic_period%23Philosophy. **License**: *CC BY-SA: Attribution-ShareAlike*

- Ancient Greece. **Provided by**: Wikipedia. **Located at**: https://en.wikipedia.org/wiki/Ancient_Greece. **License**: *CC BY-SA: Attribution-ShareAlike*

- Socrates. **Provided by**: Wikipedia. **Located at**: http://en.wikipedia.org/wiki/Socrates%23mediaviewer/File:Socrates_Louvre.jpg. **License**: *CC BY-SA: Attribution-ShareAlike*

- Aristotle. **Provided by**: Wikipedia. **Located at**: http://en.wikipedia.org/wiki/Aristotle%23mediaviewer/File:Aristotle_Altemps_Inv8575.jpg. **License**: *Public Domain: No Known Copyright*

- Plato. **Provided by**: Wikipedia. **Located at**: http://en.wikipedia.org/wiki/Plato%23mediaviewer/File:Plato_Silanion_Musei_Capitolini_MC1377.jpg. **License**: *CC BY: Attribution*

- Homer. **Provided by**: Wikipedia. **Located at**: http://upload.wikimedia.org/wikipedia/commons/1/1c/Homer_British_Museum.jpg. **License**: *CC BY-SA: Attribution-ShareAlike*

- Aischylos_BC3BCste.jpg. **Provided by**: Wikimedia. **Located at**: https://commons.wikimedia.org/wiki/File:Aischylos_B%C3%BCste.jpg. **License**: *Public Domain: No Known Copyright*

- Sophocles_pushkin.jpg. **Provided by**: Wikimedia. **Located at**: https://commons.wikimedia.org/wiki/File:Sophocles_pushkin.jpg. **License**: *CC BY-SA: Attribution-ShareAlike*

- Euripides_Statue.jpg. **Provided by**: Wikimedia. **Located at**: https://commons.wikimedia.org/wiki/File:Euripides_Statue.jpg. **License**: *Public Domain: No Known Copyright*

- Parthenon-2008_entzerrt.jpg. **Provided by**: Wikipedia. **Located at**: https://en.wikipedia.org/wiki/File:Parthenon-2008_entzerrt.jpg. **License**: *CC BY-SA: Attribution-ShareAlike*

- Erechteion_-_chapiteau.jpg. **Provided by**: Wikipedia. **Located at**: https://en.wikipedia.org/wiki/File:Erechteion_-_chapiteau.jpg. **License**: *Public Domain: No Known Copyright*

- Library of Alexandria. **Provided by**: Wikimedia. **Located at**: https://commons.wikimedia.org/wiki/File:Ancientlibraryalex.jpg. **License**: *Public Domain: No Known Copyright*

The Peloponnesian War

Introduction to the Peloponnesian War

The Peloponnesian War provided a dramatic end to the 5th century BCE, shattering religious and cultural taboos, devastating vast swathes of countryside, and destroying whole cities.

Learning Objectives

Describe the events of the Peloponnesian War

Key Takeaways

Key Points

- The Peloponnesian War (431-404 BCE) was fought between Athens and its empire, known as the Delian League, and the Peloponnesian League, led by Sparta.
- During this conflict, Greek warfare evolved from an originally limited and formalized form of conflict, to all-out struggles between city-states, with large-scale atrocities.
- During the first phase, known as the Archidamian War, Sparta launched repeated invasions of Attica while Athens took advantage of its naval supremacy to raid the Peloponnese coast.
- Initially Athens' strategy, as guided by Pericles, was to avoid open battle with the more numerous and better trained Spartan hoplites, and to instead rely on Athens' superior naval fleet.
- In the aftermath of a devastating plague, Athenians turned against Pericles's defensive strategy in favor of a more aggressive one that would bring war directly to Sparta and its allies.
- The Peace of Nicias was signed in 421 BCE, and concluded the first phase of the war. The treaty was undermined, however, by continued fighting and calls for revolt through-

> out the Peloponnese.
> - The destruction of Athens' fleet at Aegospotami during the Decelean War effectively ended the Peloponnesian War. Athens surrendered a year later in 404 BCE.
>
> *Key Terms*
>
> - **helot**: Helots were a subjugated population group that formed the main population of Laconia and Messenia, the territories controlled by Sparta.
> - **hoplites**: Hoplites were citizen-soldiers of Ancient Greek city-states who were primarily armed with spears and shields.

The Peloponnesian War (431-404 BCE) was fought between Athens and its empire, known as the Delian League, and the Peloponnesian League, led by Sparta. During this conflict, Greek warfare evolved from an originally limited and formalized form of conflict, to all-out struggles between city-states, complete with large-scale atrocities. The Peloponnesian War provided a dramatic end to the 5th century BCE, shattering religious and cultural taboos, devastating vast swathes of countryside, and destroying whole cities. Historians have traditionally divided the war into several different phases.

The Archidamian War

During the first phase, known as the Archidamian War, Sparta launched repeated invasions of Attica while Athens took advantage of its naval supremacy to raid the Peloponnese coast. Sparta and its allies, with the exception of Corinth, were almost exclusively land-based powers, whereas the Athens empire, though based on a peninsula, had developed impressive naval power. As a result, the two powers were relatively unable to fight decisive battles. The Spartan strategy during the Archidamian War was to invade the land surrounding Athens, depriving Athenians of the productive land around their city. However, Athens maintained access to the sea and did not suffer much from this strategy, though many citizens of Attica abandoned their farms and moved inside the long walls connecting Athens to port Piraeus.

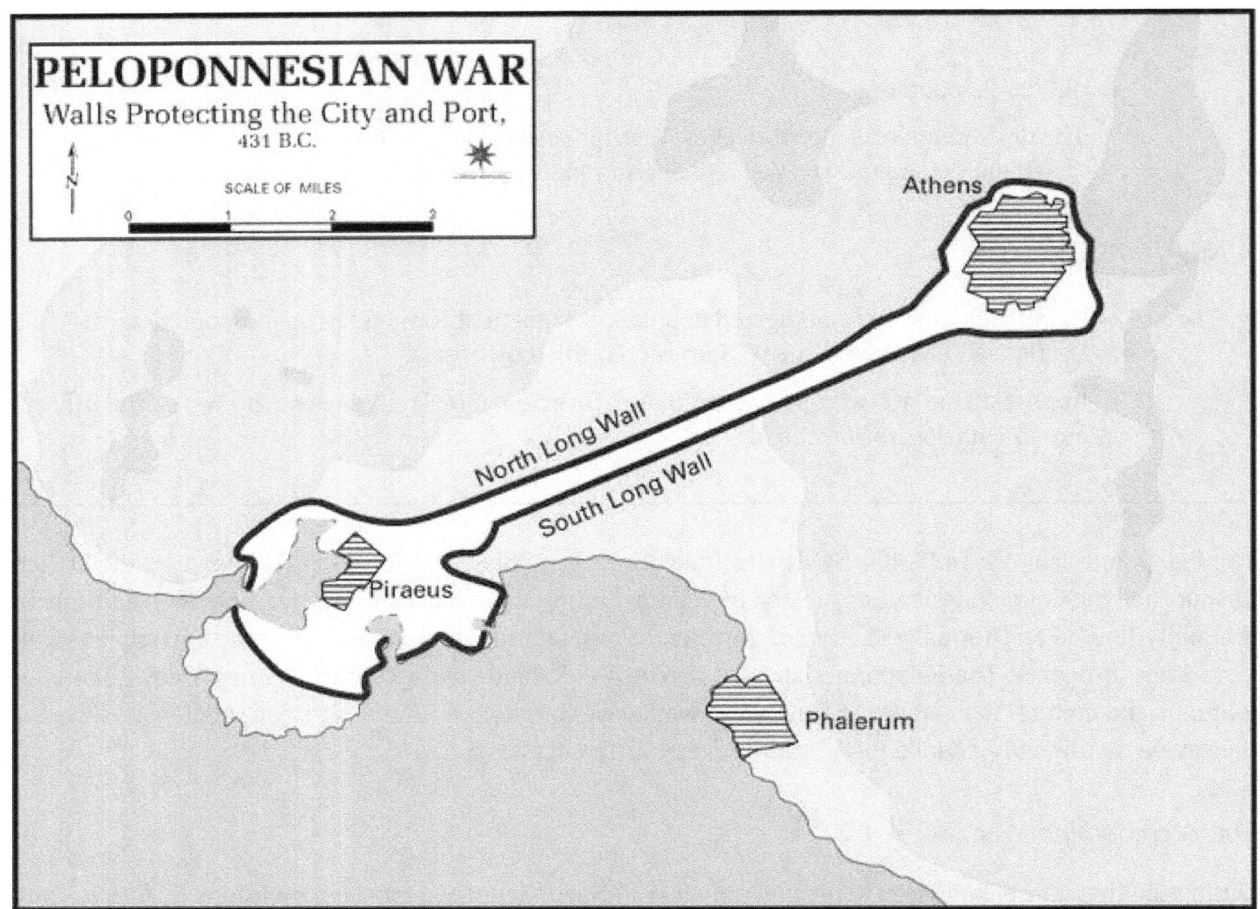

The Walls Protecting Athens: *The walls protecting Athens during the Peloponnesian War.*

Initially Athens' strategy, as guided by Pericles, was to avoid open battle with the more numerous, and better trained Spartan hoplites, and to instead rely on Athens' superior fleet. As a result, Athens' fleet went on the offensive, winning a victory at Naupactus. Their victory was short-lived, however, because in 430 BCE, an outbreak of plague hit Athens, ravaging the densely packed city and wiping out over 30,000 citizens, sailors, and soldiers, which amounted to roughly one-third to two-thirds of the Athenian population. As a result, Athenian manpower was drastically reduced, and due to widespread fears of plague, foreign mercenaries refused to hire themselves out to Athens. Sparta also abandoned its invasion of Attica during this time, unwilling to risk contact with their diseased enemy.

Pericles and his sons perished as a result of plague, and in the aftermath, Athenians turned against Pericles's defensive strategy in favor of a more aggressive one that would bring war directly to Sparta and its allies. Initially this strategy met with some success as Athens pursued naval raids throughout the Peloponnese. Their successes allowed them to fortify posts throughout the Peloponnese. One such post was near Pylos, on a tiny island called Sphacteria. It began attracting helot runaways from Sparta, which in turn raised Spartan fears that Athenian activities throughout the Peloponnese would incite a mass helot revolt. As a result, the Spartans were driven into action. During the ensuing conflicts, 300 to 400 Spartans were taken hostage, providing Athens with a bargaining chip.

In return, the Spartans raised an army of allies and helots and marched the length of Greece to the Athenian colony of Amphipolis, which controlled several nearby silver mines. These mines were particularly important because they provided much of the money that financed the Athenian war effort. The capture of this colony provided Sparta a bargaining chip as well, and the two rival city-states agreed to sign a truce, exchanging the Spartan hostages for Amphipolis and its silver mines.

Peace of Nicias

The Peace of Nicias was signed in 421 BCE, concluding the first phase of the war. Due to the loss of war hawks in both city-states during the previous conflict, the peace endured for approximately six years. The treaty was undermined, however, by continued fighting and calls for revolt throughout the Peloponnese. Although the Spartans refrained from such actions themselves, their allies remained vocal, particularly Argos. The Athenian supported the Argives and encouraged them to form a coalition of democratic states within the Peloponnese and separate from Sparta. Early Spartan attempts to thwart such a coalition ultimately failed, and the Argives, their allies, and a small Athenian force moved to seize the city of Tegea, near Sparta.

The Battle of Mantinea was the largest land battle fought within Greece during the Peloponnesian War. The Argive allied coalition initially utilized the sheer strength of their combined forces to score early successes, but failed to capitalize on them, providing the elite Spartan forces opportunities to defeat the coalition and save their city from a strategic defeat. The Argive democratic alliance was broken up, and most members were reincorporated into Sparta's Peloponnesian League, reestablishing Spartan hegemony throughout the region.

The Sicilian Expedition

During the 17th year of war, Athens received news that one of their distant allies in Sicily was under attack from Syracuse. The people of Syracuse were ethnically Dorian like the Spartans, and Sicily and their allies, the Athenians, were ethnically Ionian. In 415 BCE, Athens dispatched a massive expeditionary force to attack Syracuse in Sicily. The Athenian force consisted of more than 100 ships, approximately 5,000 infantry, and lightly armored troops. However, their cavalry was limited to about 30 horses, which proved to be no match for the large and highly trained Syracusan cavalry.

Meanwhile, the Syracusans petitioned Sparta for assistance in the matter, and Sparta sent their general, Gylippus, to Sicily with reinforcements. Subsequent Athenian attacks failed and Athens' entire force was destroyed by 413 BCE.

The Second War

This ushered in the final phase of the war, known as the Decelean War, or the Ionian War. By this time, Sparta was receiving support from Persia, and Sparta bolstered rebellions in Athens' Aegean Sea and Ionian subject states, in order to undermine Athens empire. This eventually led to the erosion of Athens' naval supremacy. The Lacedaemonians were no longer content with simply sending aid to Sicily as a means of supporting their ally. Instead, their focus shifted to an offensive strategy against Athens. As a result, Decelea, a town near Athens, was fortified in order to prevent the Athenians from making use of their land year-round, and to thwart overland shipments of supplies. Nearby silver mines were also disrupted, with Spartan hoplites freeing as many as 20,000 Athenian slaves in the vicinity. Due to this disruption in finance, Athens was forced to demand increased tribute from its subject allies, further increasing tension and the threat of rebellion throughout the Athenian empire.

Members of the Peloponnesian League continued to send reinforcements to Syracuse in hopes of driving off the Athenians, but instead, Athens sent another 100 ships and 5,000 troops to Sicily. Gylippus's forces, combined with those of the Syracusans, defeated the Athenians on land. The destruction of Athens' fleet at Aegospotami effectively ended the war, and Athens surrendered a year later in 404 BCE. Corinth and Thebes demanded that Athens be destroyed and all its citizens enslaved, but Sparta refused to destroy a city that had done good service at a time of great danger to Greece, and took Athens into their own alliance system.

Effects of the Peloponnesian War

Following the Peloponnesian War, Athens underwent a period of harsh oligarchic governance and Sparta enjoyed a brief hegemonic period.

Learning Objectives

Understand the effects of the Peloponnesian War on the Greek city-states

Key Takeaways

Key Points

- The Peloponnesian War ended in victory for Sparta and its allies, but signaled the demise of Athenian naval and political hegemony throughout the Mediterranean.
- Democracy in Athens was briefly overthrown in 411 BCE as a result of its poor handling of the Peloponnesian War. Lysander, the Spartan admiral who commanded the Spartan fleet at Aegospotami in 405 BCE, helped to organize the Thirty Tyrants as Athens' government for the 13 months they maintained power.
- Lysander established many pro-Spartan governments throughout the Aegean, where the ruling classes were more loyal to him than to Sparta as a whole. Eventually Spartan kings, Agis and Pausanias, abolished these Aegean decarchies, curbing Lysander's political influence.
- Agesilaus II was one of two Spartan kings during the period of Spartan hegemony, and is remembered for his multiple campaigns in the eastern Aegean and Persian territories.
- Agesilaus's loss at the Battle of Leuctra effectively ended Spartan hegemony throughout the region.

Key Terms

- **oligarchy**: A form of power structure in which a small group of people hold all power and influence in a state.
- **harmosts**: A Spartan term for a military governor.

> - **hegemony**: The political, economic, or military predominance or control of one state over others.

The Peloponnesian War ended in victory for Sparta and its allies, and led directly to the rising naval power of Sparta. However, it marked the demise of Athenian naval and political hegemony throughout the Mediterranean. The destruction from the Peloponnesian War weakened and divided the Greeks for years to come, eventually allowing the Macedonians an opportunity to conquer them in the mid-4th century BCE.

Athens

Democracy in Athens was briefly overthrown in 411 BCE as a result of its poor handling of the Peloponnesian War. Citizens reacted against Athens' defeat, blaming democratic politicians, such as Cleon and Cleophon. The Spartan army encouraged revolt, installing a pro-Spartan oligarchy within Athens, called the Thirty Tyrants, in 404 BCE. Lysander, the Spartan admiral who commanded the Spartan fleet at Aegospotami in 405 BCE, helped to organize the Thirty Tyrants as a government for the 13 months they maintained power.

During the Thirty Tyrants' rule, five percent of the Athenian population was killed, private property was confiscated, and democratic supporters were exiled. The Thirty appointed a council of 500 to serve the judicial functions that had formerly belonged to all citizens. Despite all this, not all Athenian men had their rights removed. In fact, 3,000 such men were chosen by the Thirty to share in the government of Athens. These men were permitted to carry weapons, entitled to jury trial, and allowed to reside with the city limits. This list of men was constantly being revised, and selection was most likely a reflection of loyalty to the regime, with the majority of Athenians not supporting the Thirty Tyrants' rule.

Nonetheless, the Thirty's regime was not met with much overt opposition for the majority of their rule, as a result of the harsh penalties placed on dissenters. Eventually, the level of violence and brutality carried out by the Thirty in Athens led to increased opposition, stemming primarily from a rebel group of exiles led by Thrasybulus, a former trierarch in the Athenian navy. The increased opposition culminated in a revolution that ultimately overthrew the Thirty's regime. In the aftermath, Athens gave amnesty to the 3,000 men who were given special treatment under the regime, with the exception of those who comprised the governing Thirty and their associated governmental officials. Athens struggled to recover from the upheaval caused by the Thirty Tyrants in the years that followed.

Sparta

As a result of the Peloponnesian War, Sparta, which had primarily been a continental culture, became a naval power. At its peak, Sparta overpowered many key Greek states, including the elite Athenian navy. By the end of the 5th century BCE, Sparta's successes against the Athenian Empire and ability to invade Persian provinces in Anatolia ushered in a period of Spartan hegemony. This hegemonic period was to be short-lived, however.

Lysander

After the end of the Peloponnesian War, Lysander established many pro-Spartan governments throughout the Aegean. Most of the ruling systems set up by Lysander were ten-man oligarchies, called decarchies, in which harmosts, Spartan military governors, were the heads of the government. Because Lysander appointed from within the ruling classes of these governments, the men were more loyal to Lysander than Sparta, making these Aegean outposts similar to a private empire.

Lysander and Spartan king Agis were in agreement with Corinth and Thebes that Athens should be totally destroyed in the aftermath of the Peloponnesian War, but they were opposed by a more moderate faction, headed by Pausanias. Eventually, Pausanias' moderate faction gained the upper hand and Athens was spared, though its defensive walls and port fortifications at Piraeus were demolished. Lysander also managed to require Athens to recall its exiles, causing political instability within the city-state, of which Lysander took advantage to establish the oligarchy that came to be known as the Thirty Tyrants. Because Lysander was also directly involved in the selection of the Thirty, these men were loyal to him over Sparta, causing King Agis and King Pausanias to agree to the abolishment of his Aegean decarchies, and eventually the restoration of democracy in Athens, which quickly curbed Lysander's political influence.

Lysander: *A 16th century engraving of Lysander*

Agesilaus and His Campaigns

Agesilaus II was one of two Spartan kings during the period of Spartan hegemony. Lysander was one of Agesilaus's biggest supporters, and was even a mentor. During his kingship, Agesilaus embarked on a number of military campaigns in the eastern Aegean and Persian territories. During these campaigns, the

Spartans under Agesilaus's command met with numerous rebelling Greek poleis, including the Thebans. The Thebans, Argives, Corinthians, and Athenians had rebelled during the Corinthian War from 395-386 BCE, and the Persians aided the Thebans, Corinthians, and Athenians against the Spartans.

During the winter of 379/378 BCE, a group of Theban exiles snuck into Thebes and succeeded in liberating it, despite resistance from a 1,500-strong Spartan garrison. This led to a number of Spartan expeditions against Thebes, known as The Boeotian War. The Greek city-states eventually attempted to broker peace, but Theban diplomat Epaminondas angered Agesilaus by arguing for the freedom of non-Spartan citizens within Laconia. As a result, Agesilaus excluded the Thebans from the treaty, and the Battle of Leuctra broke out in 371 BCE; the Spartans eventually lost. Sparta's international political influence precipitated quickly after their defeat.

Attributions

CC licensed content, Specific attribution

- Helots. **Provided by**: Wikipedia. **Located at**: https://en.wikipedia.org/wiki/Helots. **License**: *CC BY-SA: Attribution-ShareAlike*
- Hoplite. **Provided by**: Wikipedia. **Located at**: https://en.wikipedia.org/wiki/Hoplite. **License**: *CC BY-SA: Attribution-ShareAlike*
- Peloponnesian War. **Provided by**: Wikipedia. **Located at**: https://en.wikipedia.org/wiki/Peloponnesian_War. **License**: *CC BY-SA: Attribution-ShareAlike*
- Pelopennesian_War2C_Walls_Protecting_the_City2C_431_B.C..JPG. **Provided by**: Wikimedia. **Located at**: https://commons.wikimedia.org/wiki/File:Pelopennesian_War,_Walls_Protecting_the_City,_431_B.C..JPG. **License**: *Public Domain: No Known Copyright*
- Oligarchy. **Provided by**: Wikipedia. **Located at**: https://en.wikipedia.org/wiki/Oligarchy. **License**: *CC BY-SA: Attribution-ShareAlike*
- Sparta. **Provided by**: Wikipedia. **Located at**: https://en.wikipedia.org/wiki/Sparta. **License**: *CC BY-SA: Attribution-ShareAlike*
- Boeotian War. **Provided by**: Wikipedia. **Located at**: https://en.wikipedia.org/wiki/Boeotian_War. **License**: *CC BY-SA: Attribution-ShareAlike*
- Spartan hegemony. **Provided by**: Wikipedia. **Located at**: https://en.wikipedia.org/wiki/Spartan_hegemony. **License**: *CC BY-SA: Attribution-ShareAlike*
- Hegemony. **Provided by**: Wikipedia. **Located at**: https://en.wikipedia.org/wiki/Hegemony. **License**: *CC BY-SA: Attribution-ShareAlike*
- Peloponnesian War. **Provided by**: Wikipedia. **Located at**: https://en.wikipedia.org/wiki/Peloponnesian_War. **License**: *CC BY-SA: Attribution-ShareAlike*
- Harmost. **Provided by**: Wikipedia. **Located at**: https://en.wikipedia.org/wiki/Harmost. **License**: *CC BY-SA: Attribution-ShareAlike*
- History of Athens. **Provided by**: Wikipedia. **Located at**: https://en.wikipedia.org/wiki/History_of_Athens. **License**: *CC BY-SA: Attribution-ShareAlike*
- Lysander. **Provided by**: Wikipedia. **Located at**: https://en.wikipedia.org/wiki/Lysander. **License**: *CC BY-SA: Attribution-ShareAlike*
- Pelopennesian_War2C_Walls_Protecting_the_City2C_431_B.C..JPG. **Provided by**: Wikimedia. **Located at**: https://commons.wikimedia.org/wiki/File:Pelopennesian_War,_Walls_Protecting_the_City,_431_B.C..JPG. **License**: *Public Domain: No Known Copyright*
- Lysander-Sparta.jpg. **Provided by**: Wikimedia. **Located at**: https://commons.wikimedia.org/wiki/File:Lysander-Sparta.jpg. **License**: *Public Domain: No Known Copyright*

Macedonian Conquest

The Rise of the Macedon

Philip II's conquests during the Third Sacred War cemented his power, as well as the influence of Macedon, throughout the Hellenic world.

Learning Objectives

Describe Philip II's achievements and how he built up Macedon

Key Takeaways

Key Points

- The military skills Philip II learned while in Thebes, coupled with his expansionist vision of Macedonian greatness, brought him early successes when he ascended to the throne in 359 BCE.
- Philip earned immense prestige, and secured Macedon 's position in the Hellenic world during his involvement in the Third Sacred War, which began in Greece in 356 BCE.
- War with Athens would arise intermittently for the duration of Philip's campaigns, due to conflicts over land, and/or with allies.
- In 337 BCE, Philip created and led the League of Corinth, a federation of Greek states that aimed to invade the Persian Empire.
- In 336 BCE, Philip was assassinated during the earliest stages of the League of Corinth's Persian venture.
- Many Macedonian institutions and demonstrations of power mirrored established Achaemenid conventions.

> *Key Terms*
>
> - **sarissas**: A long spear or pike about 13-20 feet in length, used in ancient Greek and Hellenistic warfare, that was initially introduced by Philip II of Macedon.
>
> Macedon rose from a small kingdom on the periphery of classical Greek affairs, to a dominant player in the Hellenic world and beyond, within the span of 25 years between 359 and 336 BCE. Macedon's rise is largely attributable to the policies during Philip II's rule.

Background

In the aftermath of the Peloponnesian War, Sparta rose as a hegemonic power in classical Greece. Sparta's dominance was challenged by many Greek city-states who had traditionally been independent during the Corinthian War of 395-387 BCE. Sparta prevailed in the conflict, but only because Persia intervened on their behalf, demonstrating the fragility with which Sparta held its power over the other Greek city-states. In the next decade, the Thebans revolted against Sparta, successfully liberating their city-state, and later defeating the Spartans at the Battle of Leuctra (371 BCE). Theban general Epaminondas then led an invasion of the Peloponnesus in 370 BCE, invaded Messenia, and liberated the helots, permanently crippling Sparta.

These series of events allowed the Thebans to replace Spartan hegemonic power with their own. For the next nine years, Epaminondas and Theban general Pelopidas further extended Theban power and influence via a series of campaigns throughout Greece, bringing almost every city-state in Greece into the conflict. These years of war ultimately left Greece war-weary and depleted, and during Epaminondas's fourth invasion of the Peloponnesus in 362 BCE, Epaminondas was killed at the Battle of Mantinea. Although Thebes emerged victorious, their losses were heavy, and the Thebans returned to a defensive policy, allowing Athens to reclaim its position at the center of the Greek political system for the first time since the Peloponnesian War. The Athenians' second confederacy would be Macedon's main rivals for control of the lands of the north Aegean.

Philip II's Accession

Philip II of Macedon: *Bust of Philip II.*

While Philip was young, he was held hostage in Thebes, and received a military and diplomatic education from Epaminondas. By 364 BCE, Philip returned to Macedon, and the skills he learned while in Thebes, coupled with his expansionist vision of Macedonian greatness, brought him early successes when he ascended to the throne in 359 BCE. When he assumed the throne, the eastern regions of Macedonia had been sacked and invaded by the Paionians, and the Thracians and the Athenians had landed a contingent on the coast at Methoni. Philip pushed the Paionians and Thracians back, promising them tributes, and defeated the 3,000 Athenian hoplites at Methoni. In the interim between conflicts, Philip focused on strengthening his army and his overall position domestically, introducing the phalanx infantry corps and arming them with long spears, called sarissas.

A Macedonian Phalanx: Depiction of a Macedonian phalanx armed with sarissas.

In 358 BCE, Philip marched against the Illyrians, establishing his authority inland as far as Lake Ohrid. Subsequently, he agreed to lease the gold mines of Mount Pangaion to the Athenians in exchange for the return of the city of Pydna to Macedon. Ultimately, after conquering Amphipolis in 357 BCE, he reneged on his agreement, which led to war with Athens. During that conflict, Philip conquered Potidaea, but ceded it to the Chalkidian League of Olynthus, with which he was allied. A year later, he also conquered Crenides and changed its name to Philippi, using the gold from the mines there to finance subsequent campaigns.

Third Sacred War

Philip earned immense prestige and secured Macedon's position in the Hellenic world during his involvement in the Third Sacred War, which began in Greece in 356 BCE. Early in the war, Philip defeated the Thessalians at the Battle of Crocus Field, allowing him to acquire Pherae and Magnesia, which was the location of an important harbor, Pagasae. He did not attempt to advance further into central Greece, however, because the Athenians occupied Thermopylae. Although there were no open hostilities between the Athenians and Macedonians at the time, tensions had arisen as a result of Philip's recent land and resource acquisitions. Instead, Philip focused on subjugating the Balkan hill-country in the west and north, and attacking Greek coastal cities, many of which Philip maintained friendly relations with, until he had conquered their surrounding territories. Nonetheless, war with Athens would arise intermittently for the duration of Philip's campaigns, due to conflicts over land and/or with allies.

Persian Influences

For many Macedonian rulers, the Achaemenid Empire in Persia was a major sociopolitical influence, and Philip II was no exception. Many institutions and demonstrations of his power mirrored established Achaemenid conventions. For example, Philip established a Royal Secretary and Archive, as well as the institution of Royal Pages, which would mount the king on his horse in a manner very similar to the way in which Persian kings were mounted. He also aimed to make his power both political and religious in nature, utilizing a special throne stylized after those of the Achaemenid court, to demonstrate his elevated rank. Achaemenid administrative practices were also utilized in Macedonia rule of conquered lands, such as Thrace in 342-334 BCE.

In 337 BCE, Philip created and led the League of Corinth. Members of the league agreed not to engage in conflict with one another unless their aim was to suppress revolution. Another stated aim of the league was to invade the Persian Empire. Ironically, in 336 BCE, Philip was assassinated during the earliest stages of the Persian venture, during the marriage of his daughter Cleopatra to Alexander I of Epirus.

Alexander the Great

In a little over 30 years, Alexander the Great created one of the largest empires in the ancient world, using his military and tactical genius.

Learning Objectives

Examine Alexander the Great's successes and failures

Key Takeaways

Key Points

- Alexander the Great spent most of his ruling years on an unprecedented military campaign through Asia and northeast Africa. By the age of 30, he created an empire that stretched from Greece to Egypt, and into present-day Pakistan.
- Alexander inherited a strong kingdom and experienced army, both of which contributed to his successes.
- Alexander's legacy includes the cultural diffusion his engendered conquests, and the rise of Hellenistic culture as a result of his military campaigns.
- Alexander's impressive record was largely due to his smart use of terrain, phalanx and cavalry tactics, bold and adaptive strategy, and the fierce loyalty of his troops.

Key Terms

- **phalanx**: A rectangular mass military formation, usually composed entirely of heavy infantry armed with spears, pikes, sarissas, or similar weapons.
- **Alexander the Great**: Formally Alexander III of Macedon, a Macedonian king who was undefeated in battle and is considered one of history's most successful commanders.
- **Philip II**: A king of the Greek kingdom of Macedon from 359 BCE until his assassination in 336 BCE. He was the father of Alexander the Great.

Following the decline of the Greek city-states, the Greek kingdom of Macedon rose to power under Philip II. Alexander III, commonly known as Alexander the Great, was born to Philip II in Pella in 356 BCE, and succeeded his father to the throne at the age of 20. He spent most of his ruling years on an unprecedented military campaign through Asia and northeast Africa, and by the age of 30, had created one of the largest empires of the ancient world, which stretched from Greece to Egypt and into present-day Pakistan. He was undefeated in battle and is considered one of history's most successful commanders.

Alexander the Great: *Bust of a young Alexander the Great from the Hellenistic era, now at the British Museum.*

During his youth, Alexander was tutored by the philosopher Aristotle, until the age of 16. When he succeeded his father to the throne in 336 BCE, after Philip was assassinated, Alexander inherited a strong kingdom and an experienced army. He had been awarded the generalship of Greece, and used this authority to launch his father's military expansion plans. In 334 BCE, he invaded the Achaemenid Empire, ruled Asia Minor, and began a series of campaigns that lasted ten years. Alexander broke the power of Persia in a series of decisive battles, most notably the battles of Issus and Gaugamela. He overthrew the Persian King Darius III, and conquered the entirety of the Persian Empire. At that point, his empire stretched from the Adriatic Sea to the Indus River.

Seeking to reach the "ends of the world and the Great Outer Sea," he invaded India in 326 BCE, but was eventually forced to turn back at the demand of his troops. Alexander died in Babylon in 323 BCE, the city he planned to establish as his capital, without executing a series of planned campaigns that would have begun with an invasion of Arabia. In the years following his death, a series of civil wars tore his empire apart, resulting in several states ruled by the Diadochi, Alexander's surviving generals and heirs. Alexander's legacy includes the cultural diffusion his engendered conquests. He founded some 20 cities that bore his name, the most notable being Alexandria in Egypt. Alexander's settlement of Greek colonists, and the spread of Greek culture in the east, resulted in a new Hellenistic civilization, aspects of which were still evident in the traditions of the Byzantine Empire in the mid-15th century. Alexander became legendary as a classical hero in the mold of Achilles, and he features prominently in the history and myth of Greek and non-Greek cultures. He became the measure against which military leaders compared themselves, and military academies throughout the world still teach his tactics.

Military Generalship

Alexander earned the honorific epithet "the Great" due to his unparalleled success as a military commander. He never lost a battle, despite typically being outnumbered. His impressive record was largely due to his smart use of terrain, phalanx and cavalry tactics, bold strategy, and the fierce loyalty of his troops. The Macedonian phalanx, armed with the *sarissa*, a spear up to 20 feet long, had been developed and perfected by Alexander's father, Philip II. Alexander used its speed and maneuverability to great effect against larger, but more disparate, Persian forces. Alexander also recognized the potential for disunity among his diverse army, due to the various languages, cultures, and preferred weapons individual soldiers wielded. He overcame the possibility of unrest among his troops by being personally involved in battles, as was common among Macedonian kings.

In his first battle in Asia, at Granicus, Alexander used only a small part of his forces— perhaps 13,000 infantry, with 5,000 cavalry—against a much larger Persian force of 40,000. Alexander placed the phalanx at the center, and cavalry and archers on the wings, so that his line matched the length of the Persian cavalry line. By contrast, the Persian infantry was stationed behind its cavalry. Alexander's military positioning ensured that his troops would not be outflanked; further, his phalanx, armed with long pikes, had a considerable advantage over the Persians' scimitars and javelins. Macedonian losses were negligible compared to those of the Persians.

At Issus in 333 BCE, his first confrontation with Darius, he used the same deployment, and again the central phalanx pushed through. Alexander personally led the charge in the center and routed the opposing army. At the decisive encounter with Alexander at Gaugamela, Darius equipped his chariots with scythes on the wheels to break up the phalanx and equipped his cavalry with pikes. Alexander in turn arranged a double phalanx, with the center advancing at an angle, which parted when the chariots bore down and reformed once they had passed. The advance proved successful and broke Darius's center, and Darius was forced to retreat once again.

When faced with opponents who used unfamiliar fighting techniques, such as in Central Asia and India, Alexander adapted his forces to his opponents' style. For example, in Bactria and Sogdiana, Alexander successfully used his javelin throwers and archers to prevent outflanking movements, while massing his cavalry at the center. In India, confronted by Porus's elephant corps, the Macedonians opened their ranks to envelop the elephants, and used their sarissas to strike upwards and dislodge the elephants' handlers.

Alexander's Empire

Alexander the Great's legacy was the dissemination of Greek culture throughout Asia.

Learning Objectives

Describe the legacy Alexander left within his conquered territories

Key Takeaways

Key Points

- Alexander's campaigns greatly increased contacts and trade between the East and West, and vast areas to the east were significantly exposed to Greek civilization and influence. Successor states remained dominant for the next 300 years during the Hellenistic period.
- Over the course of his conquests, Alexander founded some 20 cities that bore his name, and these cities became centers of culture and diversity. The most famous of these cities is Egypt's Mediterranean port of Alexandria.
- Hellenization refers to the spread of Greek language, culture, and population into the former Persian empire after Alexander's conquest.
- Alexander's death was sudden and his empire disintegrated into a 40-year period of war and chaos in 321 BCE. The Hellenistic world eventually settled into four stable power blocks: the Ptolemaic Kingdom of Egypt, the Seleucid Empire in the east, the Kingdom of Pergamon in Asia Minor, and Macedon.

Key Terms

- **Hellenization**: The spread of Greek language, culture, and population into the former Persian empire after Alexander's conquests.

Alexander's legacy extended beyond his military conquests. His campaigns greatly increased contacts and trade between the East and West, and vast areas to the east were exposed to Greek civilization and influence. Some of the cities he founded became major cultural centers, and many survived into the 21st century. His chroniclers recorded valuable information about the areas through which he marched, while the Greeks themselves attained a sense of belonging to a world beyond the Mediterranean.

Hellenistic Kingdoms

Alexander's most immediate legacy was the introduction of Macedonian rule to huge swathes of Asia. Many of the areas he conquered remained in Macedonian hands or under Greek influence for the next 200 to 300 years. The successor states that emerged were, at least initially, dominant forces, and this 300 year period is often referred to as the Hellenistic period.

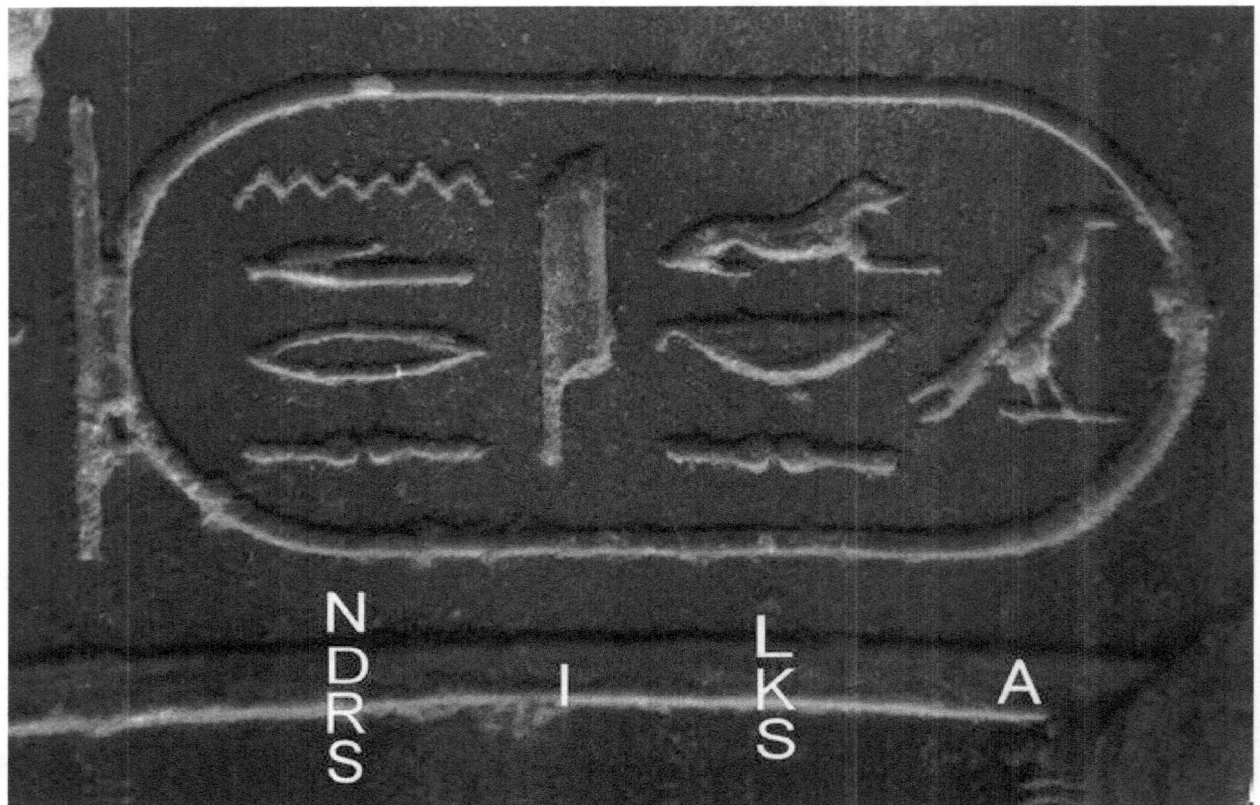

Alexander's name in hieroglyphics: *Name of Alexander the Great in Egyptian hieroglyphs (written from right to left), c. 330 BCE, Egypt; Louvre Museum.*

The eastern borders of Alexander's empire began to collapse during his lifetime. However, the power vacuum he left in the northwest of the Indian subcontinent directly gave rise to one of the most powerful Indian dynasties in history. Taking advantage of this, Chandragupta Maurya (referred to in Greek sources as *Sandrokottos*), of relatively humble origin, took control of the Punjab, and with that power base proceeded to conquer the Nanda Empire.

Hellenization

The term "Hellenization" was coined to denote the spread of Greek language, culture, and population into the former Persian empire after Alexander's conquest. Alexander deliberately pursued Hellenization policies in the communities he conquered. While his intentions may have simply been to disseminate Greek culture, it is more likely that his policies were pragmatic in nature and intended to aid in the rule of his enormous empire via cultural homogenization. Alexander's Hellenization policies can also be viewed as a result of his probable megalomania. Later his successors explicitly rejected these policies. Nevertheless, Hellenization occurred throughout the region, accompanied by a distinct and opposite "Orientalization" of the successor states.

The core of Hellenistic culture was essentially Athenian. The close association of men from across Greece in Alexander's army directly led to the emergence of the largely Attic-based *koine* (or "common") Greek dialect. *Koine* spread throughout the Hellenistic world, becoming the *lingua franca* of Hellenistic lands, and eventually the ancestor of modern Greek. Furthermore, town planning, education, local government, and art during the Hellenistic periods were all based on classical Greek ideals, evolving into distinct new forms commonly grouped as Hellenistic.

The Founding of Cities

Over the course of his conquests, Alexander founded some 20 cities that bore his name, most of them east of the Tigris River. The first, and greatest, was Alexandria in Egypt, which would become one of the leading Mediterranean cities. The cities' locations reflected trade routes, as well as defensive positions. At first, the cities must have been inhospitable, and little more than defensive garrisons. Following Alexander's death, many Greeks who had settled there tried to return to Greece. However, a century or so after Alexander's death, many of these cities were thriving with elaborate public buildings and substantial populations that included both Greek and local peoples.

Alexander's cities were most likely intended to be administrative headquarters for his empire, primarily settled by Greeks, many of whom would have served in Alexander's military campaigns. The purpose of these administrative centers was to control the newly conquered subject populations. Alexander attempted to create a unified ruling class in conquered territories like Persia, often using marriage ties to intermingle the conquered with conquerors. He also adopted elements of the Persian court culture, adopting his own version of their royal robes, and imitating some court ceremonies. Many Macedonians resented these policies, believing hybridization of Greek and foreign cultures to be irreverent.

Alexander's attempts at unification also extended to his army. He placed Persian soldiers, some of who had been trained in the Macedonian style, within Macedonian ranks, solving chronic manpower problems.

Division of the Empire

Alexander's death was so sudden that when reports of his death reached Greece, they were not immediately believed. Alexander had no obvious or legitimate heir because his son, Alexander IV, was born after Alexander's death. According to Diodorus, an ancient Greek historian, Alexander's companions asked him on his deathbed to whom he bequeathed his kingdom. His laconic reply was, *tôi kratistôi* ("to the strongest"). Another, more plausible, story claims that Alexander passed his signet ring to Perdiccas, a bodyguard and leader of the companion cavalry, thereby nominating him as his official successor.

Perdiccas initially did not claim power, instead suggesting that Alexander's unborn baby would be king, if male. He also offered himself, Craterus, Leonnatus, and Antipater, as guardians of Alexander's unborn child. However, the infantry rejected this arrangement since they had been excluded from the discussion. Instead, they supported Alexander's half-brother, Philip Arrhidaeus, as Alexander's successor. Eventually the two sides reconciled, and after the birth of Alexander IV, Perdiccas and Philip III were appointed joint kings, albeit in name only.

Dissension and rivalry soon afflicted the Macedonians. After the assassination of Perdiccas in 321 BCE, Macedonian unity collapsed, and 40 years of war between "The Successors" (*Diadochi*) ensued, before the Hellenistic world settled into four stable power blocks: the Ptolemaic Kingdom of Egypt, the Seleucid Empire in the east, the Kingdom of Pergamon in Asia Minor, and Macedon. In the process, both Alexander IV and Philip III were murdered.

The Legacy of Alexander the Great

Four stable power blocks emerged following the death of Alexander the Great: the Ptolemaic Kingdom of Egypt, the Seleucid Empire, the Attalid Dynasty of the Kingdom of Pergamon, and Macedon.

Learning Objectives

Evaluate Alexander the Great's legacy as carried out by his successors

Key Takeaways

Key Points

- After the assassination of Perdiccas in 321 BCE, Macedonian unity collapsed, and 40 years of war between "The Successors" (Diadochi) ensued before the Hellenistic world settled into four stable power blocks: the Ptolemaic Kingdom of Egypt, the Seleucid Empire, the Kingdom of Pergamon in Asia Minor, and Macedon.
- The Ptolemaic Kingdom was ruled by the Ptolemaic dynasty, starting with Ptolemy I Soter's accession to the throne following the death of Alexander the Great. The dynasty survived until the death of Cleopatra VII in 30 BCE, at which point Egypt was conquered by the Romans.
- Although the Ptolemaic Kingdom observed the Egyptian religion and customs, Greek inhabitants were treated as a privileged minority.
- The Seleucid Empire was a major center of Hellenistic culture where Greek customs prevailed and the Greek political elite dominated, though mostly in urban areas.
- The Attalid kingdom of Pergamon began as a rump state, but was expanded by subsequent rulers.
- The Attalids were some of the most loyal supporters of Rome in the Hellenistic world and were known for their generous and intelligent rule.
- The Macedonian regime is the only successor state to Alexander the Great's empire that maintained archaic perceptions of kingship, and elided the adoption of Hellenistic monarchical customs.

Key Terms

- **proskynesis**: A traditional Persian act of bowing or prostrating oneself before a person of higher social rank.
- **satrap**: A governor of a province in the Hellenistic empire. The word is also used metaphorically to refer to leaders who are heavily influenced by larger superpowers or hegemonies, and regionally act as a surrogate for those larger players.

Background

Alexander's death was so sudden that when reports of his death reached Greece, they were not immediately believed. Alexander had no obvious or legitimate heir because his son, Alexander IV, was born after Alexander's death. According to Diodorus, an ancient Greek historian, Alexander's companions asked him on his deathbed to whom he bequeathed his kingdom. His laconic reply was tôi kratistôi ("to the strongest"). Another, more plausible, story claims that Alexander passed his signet ring to Perdiccas, a bodyguard and leader of the companion cavalry, thereby nominating him as his official successor.

Perdiccas initially did not claim power, instead suggesting that Alexander's unborn baby would be king, if male. He also offered himself, Craterus, Leonnatus, and Antipater, as guardians of Alexander's unborn child. However, the infantry rejected this arrangement since they had been excluded from the discussion. Instead, they supported Alexander's half-brother, Philip Arrhidaeus, as Alexander's successor. Eventually the two sides reconciled, and after the birth of Alexander IV, Perdiccas and Philip III were appointed joint kings, albeit in name only.

Dissension and rivalry soon afflicted the Macedonians. After the assassination of Perdiccas in 321 BCE, Macedonian unity collapsed, and 40 years of war between "The Successors" (Diadochi) ensued before the Hellenistic world settled into four stable power blocks: the Ptolemaic Kingdom of Egypt, the Seleucid Empire in the east, the Kingdom of Pergamon in Asia Minor, and Macedon. In the process, both Alexander IV and Philip III were murdered.

The Ptolemaic Kingdom of Egypt

The Ptolemaic Kingdom was a Hellenistic kingdom based in Egypt, and ruled by the Ptolemaic dynasty, starting with Ptolemy I Soter's accession to the throne following the death of Alexander the Great. The Ptolemaic dynasty survived until the death of Cleopatra VII in 30 BCE, at which point Egypt was conquered by the Romans. Ptolemy was appointed as satrap of Egypt in 323 BCE, by Perdiccas during the succession crisis that erupted following Alexander the Great. From that time, Ptolemy ruled Egypt nominally in the name of joint kings Philip III and Alexander IV. As Alexander the Great's empire disintegrated, however, Ptolemy established himself as a ruler in his own right. In 321 BCE, Ptolemy defended Egypt against an invasion by Perdiccas. During the Wars of the Diadochi (322-301 BCE), Ptolemy further consolidated his position within Egypt and the region by taking the title of King.

Ptolemy I Soter: *Bust of Ptolemy I Soter, king of Egypt (305-282 BCE) and founder of the Ptolemaic dynasty. The identification is based upon coin effigies.*

Early in the Ptolemaic dyansty, Egyptian religion and customs were observed, and magnificent new temples were built in the style of the old pharaohs. During the reign of Ptolemies II and III, thousands of Macedonian veterans were rewarded with farm land grants, and settled in colonies and garrisons throughout the country. Within a century, Greek influence had spread throughout the country and intermarriage produced a large Greco-Egyptian educated class. Despite this, the Greeks remained a privileged minority in Ptolemaic Egypt. Greek individuals lived under Greek law, received a Greek education, were tried in Greek courts, and were citizens of Greek cities, rather than Egyptian cities.

The Seleucid Empire

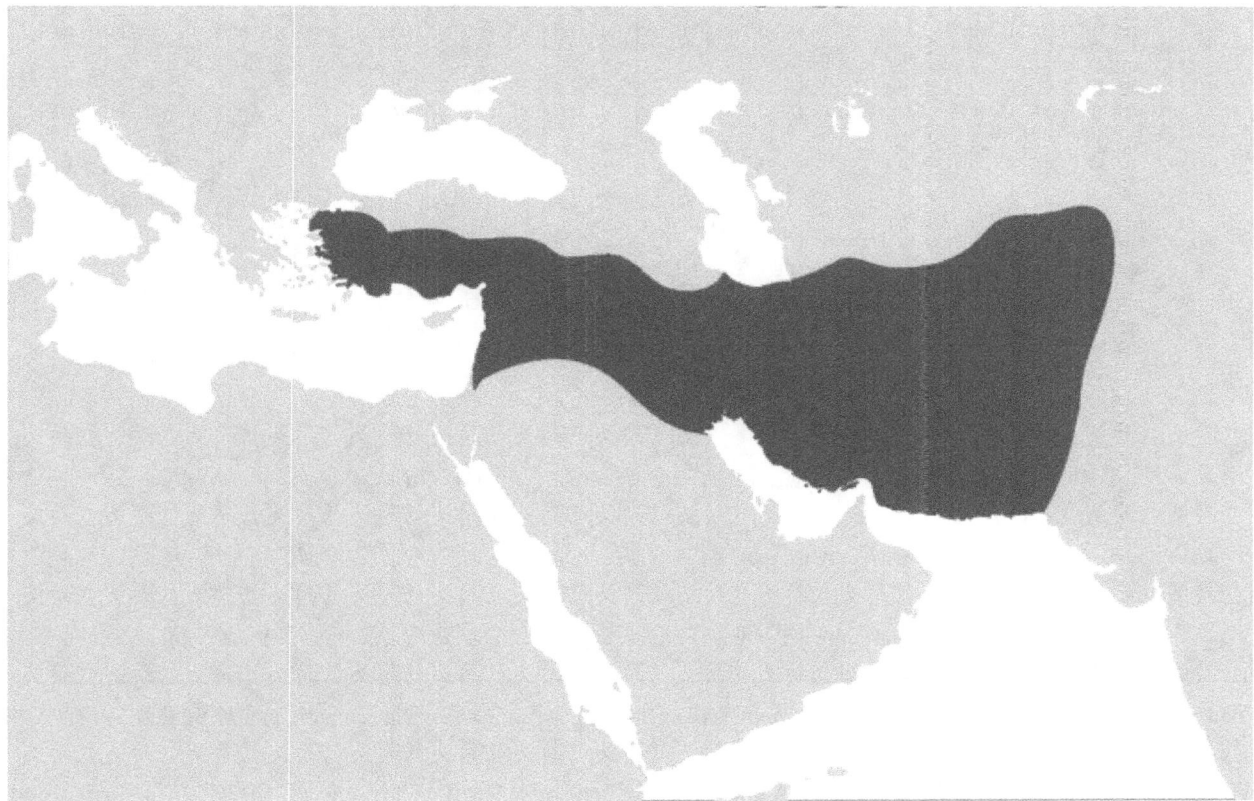

Seleucid Empire: *Seleucid Empire at its greatest extent, 281 BCE.*

The Seleucid Empire was a Hellenistic state ruled by the Seleucid Dynasty, which existed from 312 BCE-63 BCE. It was founded by Seleucus I Nicator following the dissolution of Alexander the Great's empire. Following Ptolemy's successes in the Wars of the Diadochi, Seleucus, then a senior officer in the Macedonian Royal Army, received Babylonia. From there, he expanded his dominion to include much of Alexander's near eastern territories. At the height of its power, the Seleucid Empire encompassed central Anatolia, Persia, the Levant, Mesopotamia, and what is now Kuwait, Afghanistan, and parts of Pakistan and Turkmenistan. Seleucus himself traveled as far as India in his campaigns. Seleucid expansion into Anatolia and Greece was halted, however, after decisive defeats at the hands of the Roman army.

The Seleucid Empire was a major center of Hellenistic culture, where Greek customs prevailed and the Greek political elite dominated, though mostly in urban areas. Existing Greek populations within the empire were supplemented with Greek immigrants.

The Kingdom of Pergamon

Asia Minor, 188 BCE: *The Kingdom of Pergamon (colored olive), shown at its greatest extent in 188 BCE.*

The ancient Greek city of Pergamon was taken by Lysimachus, King of Thrace, in 301 BCE, a short-lived possession that ended when the kingdom of Thrace collapsed. It became the capital of a new kingdom of Pergamon, which Philetaerus founded in 281 BCE, thus beginning the rule of the Attalid Dynasty. The Attalid kingdom began as a rump state, but was expanded by subsequent rulers. The Attalids themselves were some of the most loyal supporters of Rome in the Hellenistic world. Under Attalus I (r. 241-197 BCE), the Attalids allied with Rome against Philip V of Macedon, during the first and second Macedonian Wars. They allied with Rome again under Eumenes II (r. 197-158 BCE) against Perseus of Macedon, during the Third Macedonian War. Additionally, in exchange for their support against the Seleucids, the Attalids were given all former Seleucid domains in Asia Minor.

The Attalids were known for their intelligent and generous rule. Many historical documents from the era demonstrate that the Attalids supported the growth of towns by sending in skilled artisans and remitting taxes. They also allowed Greek cities to maintain nominal independence and sent gifts to Greek cultural sites, such as Delphi, Delos, and Athens, and even remodeled the Acropolis of Pergamon after the Acropolis in Athens. When Attalus III (r. 138-133 BCE) died without an heir, he bequeathed his entire kingdom to Rome to prevent civil war.

Macedon

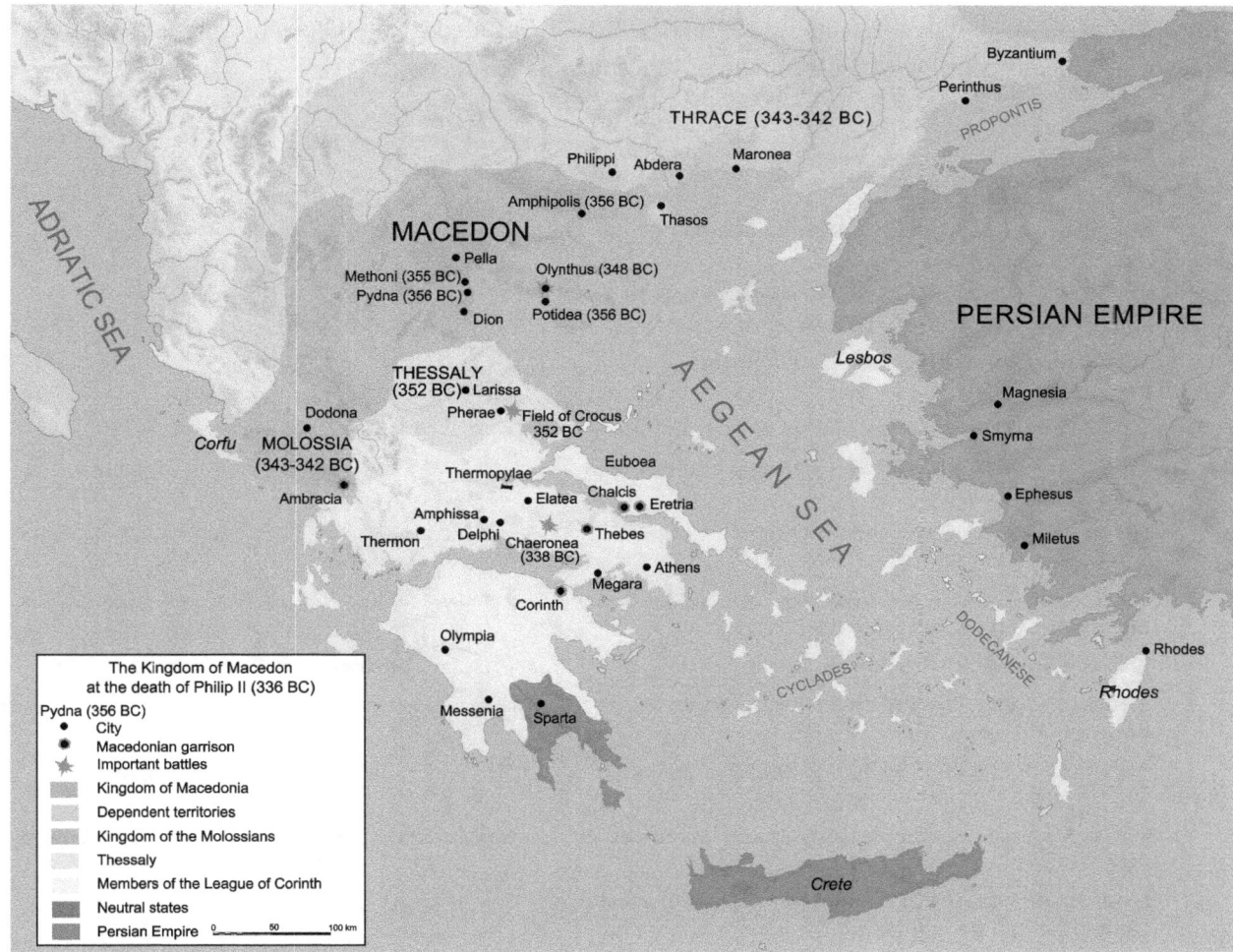

The Kingdom of Macedon at the death of Philip II (336 BCE)

Macedon, or Macedonia, was the dominant state of Hellenistic Greece. In the partition of Alexander's empire among the Diadochi, Macedon fell to the Antipatrid Dynasty, which was headed by Antipater and his son, Cassander. Following Cassander's death in 297 BCE, Macedon slid into a long period of civil strife. Antigonus II (r. 277-239 BCE) successfully restored order and prosperity in the region, and established a stable monarchy under the Antigonid Dynasty, though he lost control of many Greek city-states in the process.

Notably, the Macedonian regime is the only successor state to Alexander the Great's empire that maintained archaic perceptions of kingship, and elided the adoption of Hellenistic monarchical customs. The Macedonian king was never deified in the same way that kings of the Ptolemaic and Seleucic Dynasties had been. Additionally, the custom of proskynesis, a traditional Persian act of bowing or prostrating oneself before a person of higher social rank, was never adopted. Instead, Macedonian subjects addressed their kings in a far more casual manner, and kings still consulted with their aristocracy in the process of making decisions.

During the reigns of Philip V (r. 221-179 BCE) and his son Perseus (r. 179-168 BCE), Macedon clashed with the rising Roman republic. During the 2nd and 1st centuries BCE, Macedon fought a series of wars against Rome. Two decisive defeats in 197 and 168 BCE resulted in the deposition of the Antigonid Dynasty, and the dismantling of the kingdom of Macedon.

Attributions

CC licensed content, Specific attribution

- Rise of Macedon. **Provided by**: Wikipedia. **Located at**: https://en.wikipedia.org/wiki/Rise_of_Macedon. **License**: *CC BY-SA: Attribution-ShareAlike*
- Classical Greece: Rise of Macedon. **Provided by**: Wikipedia. **Located at**: https://en.wikipedia.org/wiki/Classical_Greece#Rise_of_Macedon. **License**: *CC BY-SA: Attribution-ShareAlike*
- Epaminondas. **Provided by**: Wikipedia. **Located at**: https://en.wikipedia.org/wiki/Epaminondas. **License**: *CC BY-SA: Attribution-ShareAlike*
- Sarissa. **Provided by**: Wikipedia. **Located at**: https://en.wikipedia.org/wiki/Sarissa. **License**: *CC BY-SA: Attribution-ShareAlike*
- Philip II of Macedon. **Provided by**: Wikipedia. **Located at**: https://en.wikipedia.org/wiki/Philip_II_of_Macedon. **License**: *CC BY-SA: Attribution-ShareAlike*
- Filip_II_Macedonia.jpg. **Provided by**: Wikipedia. **Located at**: https://en.wikipedia.org/wiki/File:Filip_II_Macedonia.jpg. **License**: *Public Domain: No Known Copyright*
- Makedonische_phalanx.png. **Provided by**: Wikipedia. **Located at**: https://en.wikipedia.org/wiki/File:Makedonische_phalanx.png. **License**: *Public Domain: No Known Copyright*
- Phalanx. **Provided by**: Wikipedia. **Located at**: http://en.wikipedia.org/wiki/Phalanx. **License**: *CC BY-SA: Attribution-ShareAlike*
- Alexander the Great. **Provided by**: Wikipedia. **Located at**: http://en.wikipedia.org/wiki/Alexander_the_great%23Character. **License**: *CC BY-SA: Attribution-ShareAlike*
- Alexander the Great. **Provided by**: Wiktionary. **Located at**: http://en.wiktionary.org/wiki/Alexander_the_Great. **License**: *CC BY-SA: Attribution-ShareAlike*
- Filip_II_Macedonia.jpg. **Provided by**: Wikipedia. **Located at**: https://en.wikipedia.org/wiki/File:Filip_II_Macedonia.jpg. **License**: *Public Domain: No Known Copyright*
- Makedonische_phalanx.png. **Provided by**: Wikipedia. **Located at**: https://en.wikipedia.org/wiki/File:Makedonische_phalanx.png. **License**: *Public Domain: No Known Copyright*
- Alexander the Great. **Provided by**: Wikipedia. **Located at**: http://en.wikipedia.org/wiki/Alexander_the_great%23mediaviewer/File:AlexanderTheGreat_Bust.jpg. **License**: *CC BY-SA: Attribution-ShareAlike*
- Alexander the Great. **Provided by**: Wikipedia. **Located at**: http://en.wikipedia.org/wiki/Alexander_the_Great. **License**: *CC BY-SA: Attribution-ShareAlike*
- Filip_II_Macedonia.jpg. **Provided by**: Wikipedia. **Located at**: https://en.wikipedia.org/wiki/File:Filip_II_Macedonia.jpg. **License**: *Public Domain: No Known Copyright*
- Makedonische_phalanx.png. **Provided by**: Wikipedia. **Located at**: https://en.wikipedia.org/wiki/File:Makedonische_phalanx.png. **License**: *Public Domain: No Known Copyright*
- Alexander the Great. **Provided by**: Wikipedia. **Located at**: http://en.wikipedia.org/wiki/Alexander_the_great%23mediaviewer/File:AlexanderTheGreat_Bust.jpg. **License**: *CC BY-SA: Attribution-ShareAlike*
- Alexander the Great. **Provided by**: Wikipedia. **Located at**: http://en.wikipedia.org/wiki/Alexander_the_Great%23mediaviewer/File:Name_of_Alexander_the_Great_in_Hieroglyphs_circa_330_BCE.jpg. **License**: *CC BY-SA: Attribution-ShareAlike*
- Seleucid Empire. **Provided by**: Wikipedia. **Located at**: https://en.wikipedia.org/wiki/Seleucid_Empire. **License**: *CC BY-SA: Attribution-ShareAlike*
- Proskynesis. **Provided by**: Wikipedia. **Located at**: https://en.wikipedia.org/wiki/Proskynesis. **License**: *CC BY-SA: Attribution-ShareAlike*
- Pergamon. **Provided by**: Wikipedia. **Located at**: https://en.wikipedia.org/wiki/Pergamon. **License**: *CC BY-SA: Attribution-ShareAlike*
- Attalid dynasty. **Provided by**: Wikipedia. **Located at**: https://en.wikipedia.org/wiki/Attalid_dynasty. **License**: *CC BY-SA: Attribution-ShareAlike*
- Macedonia (ancient kingdom). **Provided by**: Wikipedia. **Located at**: https://en.wikipedia.org/wiki/Macedonia_(ancient_kingdom). **License**: *CC BY-SA: Attribution-ShareAlike*

- Ptolemaic Kingdom. **Provided by**: Wikipedia. **Located at**: https://en.wikipedia.org/wiki/Ptolemaic_Kingdom. **License**: *CC BY-SA: Attribution-ShareAlike*
- Satrap. **Provided by**: Wikipedia. **Located at**: https://en.wikipedia.org/wiki/Satrap. **License**: *CC BY-SA: Attribution-ShareAlike*
- Filip_II_Macedonia.jpg. **Provided by**: Wikipedia. **Located at**: https://en.wikipedia.org/wiki/File:Filip_II_Macedonia.jpg. **License**: *Public Domain: No Known Copyright*
- Makedonische_phalanx.png. **Provided by**: Wikipedia. **Located at**: https://en.wikipedia.org/wiki/File:Makedonische_phalanx.png. **License**: *Public Domain: No Known Copyright*
- Alexander the Great. **Provided by**: Wikipedia. **Located at**: http://en.wikipedia.org/wiki/Alexander_the_great%23mediaviewer/File:AlexanderTheGreat_Bust.jpg. **License**: *CC BY-SA: Attribution-ShareAlike*
- Alexander the Great. **Provided by**: Wikipedia. **Located at**: http://en.wikipedia.org/wiki/Alexander_the_Great%23mediaviewer/File:Name_of_Alexander_the_Great_in_Hieroglyphs_circa_330_BCE.jpg. **License**: *CC BY-SA: Attribution-ShareAlike*
- Map_Macedonia_336_BC-en.svg. **Provided by**: Wikimedia. **Located at**: https://commons.wikimedia.org/wiki/File:Map_Macedonia_336_BC-en.svg. **License**: *CC BY-SA: Attribution-ShareAlike*
- Seleucid_Empire_28flat_map29.svg. **Provided by**: Wikimedia. **Located at**: https://commons.wikimedia.org/wiki/File:Seleucid_Empire_(flat_map).svg. **License**: *CC BY-SA: Attribution-ShareAlike*
- Ptolemy_I_Soter_Louvre_Ma849.jpg. **Provided by**: Wikimedia. **Located at**: https://commons.wikimedia.org/wiki/File:Ptolemy_I_Soter_Louvre_Ma849.jpg. **License**: *Public Domain: No Known Copyright*
- Asia_Minor_188_BCE.jpg. **Provided by**: Wikimedia. **Located at**: https://commons.wikimedia.org/wiki/File:Asia_Minor_188_BCE.jpg. **License**: *Public Domain: No Known Copyright*

The Roman World

The Etruscans

The Origins of Etruria

The Etruscans were a Mediterranean civilization during the 6th to 3rd century BCE, from whom the Romans derived a great deal of cultural influence.

Learning Objectives

Explain the relationship between the Etruscan and Roman civilizations

Key Takeaways

Key Points

- The prevailing view is that Rome was founded by Italics who later merged with Etruscans. Rome was likely a small settlement until the arrival of the Etruscans, who then established Rome's urban infrastructure.
- The Etruscans were indigenous to the Mediterranean area, probably stemming from the Villanovan culture.
- The mining and commerce of metal, especially copper and iron, led to an enrichment of the Etruscans, and to the expansion of their influence in the Italian Peninsula and the western Mediterranean Sea. Conflicts with the Greeks led the Etruscans to ally themselves with the Carthaginians.
- The Etruscans governed within a state system, with only remnants of the chiefdom or tribal forms. The Etruscan state government was essentially a theocracy.
- Aristocratic families were important within Etruscan society, and women enjoyed, comparatively, many freedoms within society.
- The Etruscan system of belief was an immanent polytheism that incorporated indigenous, Indo-European, and Greek influences.

- It is believed that the Etruscans spoke a non-Indo-European language, probably related to what is called the Tyrsenian language family, which is itself an isolate family, or in other words, unrelated directly to other known language groups.

Key Terms

- **theocracy**: A form of government in which a deity is officially recognized as the civil ruler, and official policy is governed by officials regarded as divinely guided, or is pursuant to the doctrine of a particular religion or religious group.
- **Etruscan**: The modern name given to a civilization of ancient Italy in the area corresponding roughly to Tuscany, western Umbria, and northern Latium.
- **oligarchic**: A form of power structure in which power effectively rests with a small number of people. These people could be distinguished by royalty, wealth, family ties, education, corporate, or military control. Such states are often controlled by a few prominent families who typically pass their influence from one generation to the next; however, inheritance is not a necessary condition for the application of this term.

Those who subscribe to an Italic (a diverse group of people who inhabited pre-Roman Italy) foundation of Rome, followed by an Etruscan invasion, typically speak of an Etruscan "influence" on Roman culture; that is, cultural objects that were adopted by Rome from neighboring Etruria. The prevailing view is that Rome was founded by Italics who later merged with Etruscans. In that case, Etruscan cultural objects are not a heritage but are, instead, influences. Rome was likely a small settlement until the arrival of the Etruscans, who then established its initial urban infrastructure.

Origins

The origins of the Etruscans are mostly lost in prehistory. Historians have no literature, and no original texts of religion or philosophy. Therefore, much of what is known about this civilization is derived from grave goods and tomb findings. The main hypotheses state that the Etruscans were indigenous to the region, probably stemming from the Villanovan culture or from the Near East. Etruscan expansion was focused both to the north, beyond the Apennines, and into Campania. The mining and commerce of metal, especially copper and iron, led to an enrichment of the Etruscans, and to the expansion of their influence in the Italian Peninsula and the western Mediterranean Sea. Here, their interests collided with those of the Greeks, especially in the 6th century BCE, when Phoceans of Italy founded colonies along the coast of Sardinia, Spain, and Corsica. This led the Etruscans to ally themselves with the Carthaginians, whose interests also collided with the Greeks.

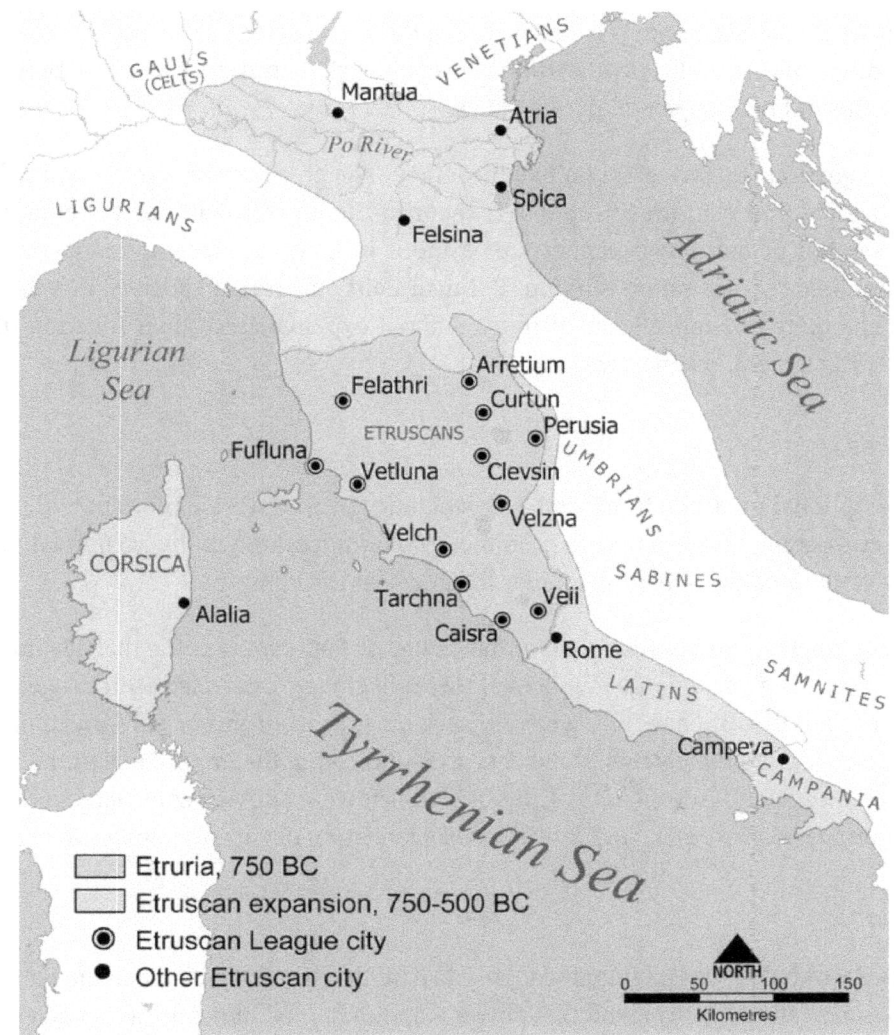

Map of the Etruscan Civilization: *Extent of Etruscan civilization and the 12 Etruscan League cities.*

Around 540 BCE, the Battle of Alalia led to a new distribution of power in the western Mediterranean Sea. Though the battle had no clear winner, Carthage managed to expand its sphere of influence at the expense of the Greeks, and Etruria saw itself relegated to the northern Tyrrhenian Sea with full ownership of Corsica. From the first half of the 5th century BCE, the new international political situation signaled the beginning of Etruscan decline after they had lost their southern provinces. In 480 BCE, Etruria's ally, Carthage, was defeated by a coalition of Magna Graecia cities led by Syracuse. A few years later, in 474 BCE, Syracuse's tyrant, Hiero, defeated the Etruscans at the Battle of Cumae. Etruria's influence over the cities of Latium and Campania weakened, and it was taken over by the Romans and Samnites. In the 4th century, Etruria saw a Gallic invasion end its influence over the Po valley and the Adriatic coast. Meanwhile, Rome had started annexing Etruscan cities. These events led to the loss of the Northern Etruscan provinces. Etruria was conquered by Rome in the 3rd century BCE.

Etruscan Government

The Etruscans governed using a state system of society, with only remnants of the chiefdom and tribal forms. In this way, they were different from the surrounding Italics. Rome was, in a sense, the first Italic state, but it began as an Etruscan one. It is believed that the Etruscan government style changed from total monarchy to an oligarchic republic (as the Roman Republic did) in the 6th century BCE, although it is important to note this did not happen to all city-states.

The Etruscan state government was essentially a theocracy. The government was viewed as being a central authority over all tribal and clan organizations. It retained the power of life and death; in fact, the gorgon, an ancient symbol of that power, appears as a motif in Etruscan decoration. The adherents to this state power were united by a common religion. Political unity in Etruscan society was the city-state, and Etruscan texts name quite a number of magistrates without explanation of their function (the camthi, the parnich, the purth, the tamera, the macstrev, etc.).

Etruscan Families

According to inscriptional evidence from tombs, aristocratic families were important within Etruscan society. Most likely, aristocratic families rose to prominence over time through the accumulation of wealth via trade, with many of the wealthiest Etruscan cities located near the coast.

The Etruscan name for family was *lautn*, and at the center of the *lautn* was the married couple. Etruscans were monogamous, and the lids of large numbers of sarcophagi were decorated with images of smiling couples in the prime of their life, often reclining next to each other or in an embrace. Many tombs also included funerary inscriptions naming the parents of the deceased, indicating the importance of the mother's side of the family in Etruscan society. Additionally, Etruscan women were allowed considerable freedoms in comparison to Greek and Roman women, and mixed-sex socialization outside the domestic realm occurred.

Etruscan Religion

The Etruscan system of belief was an immanent polytheism; that is, all visible phenomena were considered to be a manifestation of divine power, and that power was subdivided into deities that acted continually on the world of man and could be dissuaded or persuaded in favor of human affairs. Three layers of deities are evident in the extensive Etruscan art motifs. One appears to be divinities of an indigenous nature: Catha and Usil, the sun; Tivr, the moon; Selvans, a civil god; Turan, the goddess of love; Laran, the god of war; Leinth, the goddess of death; Maris; Thalna; Turms; and the ever-popular Fufluns, whose name is related in an unknown way to the city of Populonia and the *populus Romanus*, the Roman people.

Ruling over this pantheon of lesser deities were higher ones that seem to reflect the Indo-European system: Tin or Tinia, the sky; Uni, his wife (Juno); and Cel, the earth goddess. In addition the Greek gods were taken into the Etruscan system: Aritimi (Artemis), Menrva (Minerva), and Pacha (Bacchus). The Greek heroes taken from Homer also appear extensively in art motifs.

The Greek polytheistic approach was similar to the Etruscan religious and cultural base. As the Romans emerged from the legacy created by both of these groups, it shared in a belief system of many gods and deities.

Etruscan Language and Etymology

Knowledge of the Etruscan language is still far from complete. It is believed that the Etruscans spoke a non-Indo-European language, probably related to what is called the Tyrsenian language family, which is itself an isolate family, or in other words, unrelated directly to other known language groups. No etymology exists for *Rasna*, the Etruscans' name for themselves, though Italian historic linguist, Massimo Pittau, has proposed that it meant "shaved" or "beardless." The hypothesized etymology for *Tusci*, a root for "Tuscan" or "Etruscan," suggests a connection to the Latin and Greek words for "tower," illustrating the *Tusci* people as those who built towers. This was possibly based upon the Etruscan preference for building hill towns on high precipices that were enhanced by walls. The word may also be related to the city of Troy, which was also a city of towers, suggesting large numbers of migrants from that region into Etruria.

Etruscan Artifacts

Historians have no literature, or original Etruscan religious or philosophical texts, on which to base knowledge of their civilization. So much of what is known is derived from grave goods and tomb findings.

Learning Objectives

Explain the importance of Etruscan artifacts to our understanding of their history

Key Takeaways

Key Points

- Princely tombs did not house individuals, but families who were interred over long periods.
- Although many Etruscan cities were later assimilated by Italic, Celtlic, or Roman ethnic groups, the Etruscan names and inscriptions that survive within the ruins provide historic evidence as to the range of settlements that the Etruscans constructed.
- It is unclear whether Etruscan cultural objects are influences upon Roman culture or part of native Roman heritage. The criterion for deciding whether or not an object originated in Rome or descended to the Romans from the Etruscans is the date of the object and the opinion of ancient sources regarding the provenance of the object's style.
- Although Diodorus of Sicily wrote, in the 1st century, of the great achievements of the Etruscans, little survives or is known of it.

Key Terms

- **sarcophagi**: A box-like funeral receptacle for a corpse, most commonly carved in stone and displayed above ground.
- **oligarchic**: A form of power structure in which power effectively rests with a small number of people. These people could be distinguished by royalty, wealth, family ties, education, corporate, or military control. Such states are often controlled by a few prominent families who typically pass their influence from one generation to the next, but inheritance is not a necessary condition for the application of this term.

Historians have no literature or original Etruscan religious or philosophical texts on which to base knowledge of their civilization, so much of what is known is derived from grave goods and tomb findings. Princely tombs did not house individuals, but families who were interred over long periods. The decorations and objects included at these sites paint a picture of Etruscan social and political life. For instance, wealth from trade seems to have supported the rise of aristocratic families who, in turn, were likely foundational to the Etruscan oligarchic system of governance. Indeed, at some Etruscan tombs, physical evidence of trade has been found in the form of grave goods, including fine faience ware cups, which was likely the result of trade with Egypt. Additionally, the depiction of married couples on many sarcophagi provide insight into the respect and freedoms granted to women within Etruscan society, as well as the emphasis placed on romantic love as a basis for marriage pairings.

Sarcophagus of the Spouses: *Sarcophagus of an Etruscan couple in the Louvre, Room 18.*

Although many Etruscan cities were later assimilated by Italic, Celtic, or Roman ethnic groups, the Etruscan names and inscriptions that survive within the ruins provide historic evidence of the range of settlements constructed by the Etruscans. Etruscan cities flourished over most of Italy during the Roman Iron Age. According to ancient sources, some cities were founded by the Etruscans in prehistoric times, and bore entirely Etruscan names. Others were later colonized by the Etruscans from Italic groups.

Nonetheless, relatively little is known about the architecture of the ancient Etruscans. What is known is that they adapted the native Italic styles with influence from the external appearance of Greek architecture. Etruscan architecture is not generally considered part of the body of Greco-Roman classical architecture.

Though the houses of the wealthy were evidently very large and comfortable, the burial chambers of tombs, and the grave-goods that filled them, survived in greater numbers. In the southern Etruscan area, tombs contain large, rock-cut chambers under a tumulus in large necropoli.

There is some debate among historians as to whether Rome was founded by Italic cultures and then invaded by the Etruscans, or whether Etruscan cultural objects were adopted subsequently by Roman peoples. In other words, it is unclear whether Etruscan cultural objects are influences upon Roman culture, or part of native Roman heritage. Among archaeologists, the main criteria for deciding whether or not an object originated in Rome, or descended to the Romans from the Etruscans, is the date of the object, which is often determined by process of carbon dating. After this process, the opinion of ancient sources is consulted.

Although Diodorus of Sicily wrote in the 1st century of the great achievements of the Etruscans, little survives or is known of it. Most Etruscan script that does survive are fragments of religious and funeral texts. However, it is evident, from Etruscan visual art, that Greek myths were well known.

Etruscan Religion

The Etruscan belief system was heavily influenced by other religions in the region, and placed heavy emphasis on the divination of the gods' wills to guide human affairs.

Learning Objectives

Describe some of the key characteristics of the Etruscan belief system

Key Takeaways

Key Points

- The Etruscan system of belief was an immanent polytheism, meaning all visible phenomena were considered to be a manifestation of divine power, and that power was subdivided into deities that acted continually on the world of man.
- The Etruscan scriptures were a corpus of texts termed the *Etrusca Disciplina*, a set of rules for the conduct of all divination.
- Three layers of deities are evident in the extensive Etruscan art motifs: indigenous, Indo-European, and Greek.
- Etruscan beliefs concerning the afterlife were influenced by a number of sources, particularly those of the early Mediterranean region.

Key Terms

- **Etrusca Disciplina**: A corpus of texts that comprised the Etruscan scriptures, which

> essentially provided a systematic guide to divination.
>
> - **polytheism**: The worship of, or belief in, multiple deities, usually assembled into a pantheon of gods and goddesses, each with their own specific religions and rituals.

The Etruscan system of belief was an immanent polytheism; that is, all visible phenomena were considered to be a manifestation of divine power and that power was subdivided into deities that acted continually on the world of man, and could be dissuaded or persuaded in favor of human affairs. The Greek polytheistic approach was similar to the Etruscan religious and cultural base. As the Romans emerged from the legacy created by both of these groups, it shared in a belief system of many gods and deities.

Etrusca Disciplina

The Etruscan scriptures were a corpus of texts, termed the *Etrusca Disciplina*. These texts were not scriptures in the typical sense, and foretold no prophecies. The Etruscans did not appear to have a systematic rubric for ethics or morals. Instead, they concerned themselves with the problem of understanding the will of the gods, which the Etruscans considered inscrutable. The Etruscans did not attempt to rationalize or explain divine actions or intentions, but to simply divine what the gods' wills were through an elaborate system of divination. Therefore, the *Etrusca Disciplina* is mainly a set of rules for the conduct of all sorts of divination. It does not dictate what laws shall be made or how humans are to behave, but instead elaborates rules for how to ask the gods these questions and receive their answers.

Divinations were conducted by priests, who the Romans called *haruspices* or *sacerdotes*. A special magistrate was designated to look after sacred items, but every man had religious responsibilities. In this way, the Etruscans placed special emphasis upon intimate contact with divinity, consulting with the gods and seeking signs from them before embarking upon a task.

Spirits and Deities

Three layers of deities are evident in the extensive Etruscan art motifs. One appears to be divinities of an indigenous nature: Catha and Usil, the sun; Tivr, the moon; Selvans, a civil god; Turan, the goddess of love; Laran, the god of war; Leinth, the goddess of death; Maris; Thalna; Turms; and the ever-popular Fufluns, whose name is related in some unknown way to the city of Populonia and the *populus Romanus* (the Roman people). Ruling over this pantheon of lesser deities were higher ones that seem to reflect the Indo European system: Tin or Tinia, the sky; Uni, his wife (Juno); and Cel, the earth goddess. In addition, the Greek gods were taken into the Etruscan system: Aritimi (Artemis), Menrva (Minerva), and Pacha (Bacchus). The Greek heroes taken from Homer also appear extensively in art motifs.

Mars of Todi: *The Mars of Todi, a life-sized Etruscan bronze sculpture of a soldier making a votive offering, most likely to Laran, the Etruscan god of war; late 5th to early 4th century BCE.*

The Afterlife

Etruscan beliefs concerning the afterlife seem to be influenced by a number of sources. The Etruscans shared in general early Mediterranean beliefs. For instance, much like the Egyptians, the Etruscans believed that survival and prosperity in the afterlife depended on the treatment of the deceased's remains. Souls of ancestors are found depicted around Etruscan tombs, and after the 5th century BCE, the deceased are depicted in iconography as traveling to the underworld. In several instances, spirits of the dead are referred to as *hinthial*, or one who is underneath. The transmigrational world beyond the grave was patterned after the Greek Hades and ruled by Aita. The deceased were guided there by Charun, the equivalent of Death, who was blue and wielded a hammer. The Etruscan version of Hades was populated by Greek mythological figures, some of which were of composite appearance to those in Greek mythology.

Etruscan tombs imitated domestic structures, contained wall paintings and even furniture, and were spacious. The deceased was depicted in the tomb at the prime of their life, and often with a spouse. Not everyone had a sarcophagus, however. Some deceased individuals were laid out on stone benches, and depending on the proportion of inhumation, versus cremation, rites followed, cremated ashes and bones might be put into an urn in the shape of a house, or in a representation of the deceased.

Reconstruction of an Etruscan Temple: *19th century reconstruction of an Etruscan temple, in the courtyard of the Villa Giulia Museum in Rome, Italy.*

Attributions

CC licensed content, Specific attribution

- Etruscan society. **Provided by**: Wikipedia. **Located at**: https://en.wikipedia.org/wiki/Etruscan_society. **License**: *CC BY-SA: Attribution-ShareAlike*
- Theocracy. **Provided by**: Wikipedia. **Located at**: http://en.wikipedia.org/wiki/Theocracy. **License**: *CC BY-SA: Attribution-ShareAlike*
- Etruscan Civilization. **Provided by**: Wikipedia. **Located at**: http://en.wikipedia.org/wiki/Etruscan_civilization. **License**: *CC BY-SA: Attribution-ShareAlike*
- theocracy. **Provided by**: Wiktionary. **Located at**: http://en.wiktionary.org/wiki/theocracy. **License**: *CC BY-SA: Attribution-ShareAlike*
- Oligarchy. **Provided by**: Wikipedia. **Located at**: http://en.wikipedia.org/wiki/Oligarchy. **License**: *CC BY-SA: Attribution-ShareAlike*
- Etruscan Civliization Map. **Provided by**: Wikimedia. **Located at**: https://commons.wikimedia.org/wiki/File:Etruscan_civilization_map.png. **License**: *Public Domain: No Known Copyright*
- Etruscan civilization. **Provided by**: Wikipedia. **Located at**: https://en.wikipedia.org/wiki/Etruscan_civilization. **License**: *CC BY-SA: Attribution-ShareAlike*
- Etruria. **Provided by**: Wikipedia. **Located at**: https://en.wikipedia.org/wiki/Etruria. **License**: *CC BY-SA: Attribution-ShareAlike*
- Sarcophagus. **Provided by**: Wikipedia. **Located at**: https://en.wikipedia.org/wiki/Sarcophagus. **License**: *CC BY-SA: Attribution-ShareAlike*
- Etruscan Civliization Map. **Provided by**: Wikimedia. **Located at**: https://commons.wikimedia.org/wiki/File:Etruscan_civilization_map.png. **License**: *Public Domain: No Known Copyright*
- Paris_-_Louvre_-_Sarcophage.jpg. **Provided by**: Wikipedia. **Located at**: https://en.wikipedia.org/wiki/File:Paris_-_Louvre_-_Sarcophage.jpg. **License**: *Public Domain: No Known Copyright*
- Etruscan mythology. **Provided by**: Wikipedia. **Located at**: https://en.wikipedia.org/wiki/Etruscan_mythology. **License**: *CC BY-SA: Attribution-ShareAlike*
- Polytheism. **Provided by**: Wikipedia. **Located at**: https://en.wikipedia.org/wiki/Polytheism. **License**: *CC BY-SA: Attribution-ShareAlike*
- Etruscan Civliization Map. **Provided by**: Wikimedia. **Located at**: https://commons.wikimedia.org/wiki/File:Etruscan_civilization_map.png. **License**: *Public Domain: No Known Copyright*
- Paris_-_Louvre_-_Sarcophage.jpg. **Provided by**: Wikipedia. **Located at**: https://en.wikipedia.org/wiki/File:Paris_-_Louvre_-_Sarcophage.jpg. **License**: *Public Domain: No Known Copyright*
- Villa_Giulia_ricostruzione_del_tempio_etrusco_03.JPG. **Provided by**: Wikipedia. **Located at**: https://en.wikipedia.org/wiki/File:Villa_Giulia_ricostruzione_del_tempio_etrusco_03.JPG. **License**: *Public Domain: No Known Copyright*
- 0_Mars_de_Todi_-_Museo_Gregoriano_Etruscano_28129.JPG. **Provided by**: Wikipedia. **Located at**: https://en.wikipedia.org/wiki/File:0_Mars_de_Todi_-_Museo_Gregoriano_Etruscano_(1).JPG. **License**: *CC BY-SA: Attribution-ShareAlike*

Early Rome

The Founding of Rome

Myths surrounding the founding of Rome describe the city's origins through the lens of later figures and events.

Learning Objectives

Explain how the founding of Rome is rooted in mythology

Key Takeaways

Key Points

- The national epic poem of mythical Rome, the *Aeneid* by Virgil, tells the story of how the Trojan prince, Aeneas, came to Italy. The *Aeneid* was written under the emperor Augustus, who, through Julius Caesar, claimed ancestry from Aeneas.
- The Alba Longan line, begun by Iulus, Aeneas's son, extends to King Procas, who fathered two sons, Numitor and Amulius. According to the myth of Romulus and Remus,
  Amulius captured Numitor, sent him to prison, and forced the daughter of Numitor, Rhea Silvia, to become a virgin priestess among the Vestals.
- Despite Amulius' best efforts, Rhea Silvia had twin boys, Romulus and Remus, by Mars. Romulus and Remus eventually overthrew Amulius, and restored Numitor.
- In the course of a dispute during the founding of the city of Rome, Romulus killed Remus. Thus Rome began with a fratricide, a story that was later taken to represent the city's history of internecine political strife and bloodshed.
- According to the archaeological record of the region, the development of Rome itself is presumed to have coalesced around the migrations of various Italic tribes, who originally

inhabited the Alban Hills as they moved into the agriculturally-superior valley near the Tiber River.
- The discovery of a series of fortification walls on the north slope of Palatine Hill, most likely dating to the middle of the 8th century BCE, provide the strongest evidence of the original site and date of the founding of the city of Rome.

Key Terms

- **Romulus**: The founder of Rome, and one of two twin sons of Rhea Silvia and Mars.
- **Aeneas**: A Trojan survivor of the Trojan War who, according to legend, journeyed to Italy and founded the bloodline that would eventually lead to the Julio-Claudian emperors.
- **Rome**: An Italic civilization that began on the Italian Peninsula as early as the 8th century BCE. Located along the Mediterranean Sea, and centered on one city, it expanded to become one of the largest empires in the ancient world.

The founding of Rome can be investigated through archaeology, but traditional stories, handed down by the ancient Romans themselves, explain the earliest history of their city in terms of legend and myth. The most familiar of these myths, and perhaps the most famous of all Roman myths, is the story of Romulus and Remus, the twins who were suckled by a she-wolf. This story had to be reconciled with a dual tradition, set earlier in time.

Romulus and the Founding of Rome

The Capitoline Wolf: *The iconic sculpture of Romulus and Remus being suckled by the she-wolf who raised them. Traditional scholarship says the wolf-figure is Etruscan, 5th century BCE, with figures of Romulus and Remus added in the 15th century CE by Antonio Pollaiuolo. Recent studies suggest that the wolf may be a medieval sculpture dating from the 13th century CE.*

Romulus and Remus were purported to be sons of Rhea Silvia and Mars, the god of war. Because of a prophecy that they would overthrow their great-uncle Amulius, who had overthrown Silvia's father, Numitor, they were, in the manner of many mythological heroes, abandoned at birth. Both sons were left to die on the Tiber River, but were saved by a number of miraculous interventions. After being carried to safety by the river itself, the twins were nurtured by a she-wolf and fed by a woodpecker, until a shepherd, named Faustulus, found them and took them as his sons.

When Remus and Romulus became adults and learned the truth about their birth and upbringing, they killed Amulius and restored Numitor to the throne. Rather than wait to inherit Alba Longa, the city of their birth, the twins decided to establish their own city. They quarreled, however, over where to locate the new city, and in the process of their dispute, Romulus killed his brother. Thus Rome began with a fratricide, a story that was later taken to represent the city's history of internecine political strife and bloodshed.

Aeneas and the Aeneid

The national epic of mythical Rome, the *Aeneid* by Virgil, tells the story of how the Trojan prince, Aeneas, came to Italy. Although the Aeneid was written under the emperor Augustus between 29 and 19 BCE, it tells the story of the founding of Rome centuries before Augustus's time. The hero, Aeneas, was already well known within Greco-Roman legend and myth, having been a character in the *Iliad*. But Virgil took the disconnected tales of Aeneas's wanderings, and his vague association with the foundation of Rome, and fashioned it into a compelling foundation myth or national epic. The story tied Rome to the legends of Troy, explained the Punic Wars, glorified traditional Roman virtues, and legitimized the Julio-Claudian dynasty as descendants of the founders, heroes, and gods of Rome and Troy.

Virgil makes use of symbolism to draw comparisons between the emperor Augustus and Aeneas, painting them both as founders of Rome. The Aeneid also contains prophecies about Rome's future, the deeds of Augustus, his ancestors, and other famous Romans. The shield of Aeneas even depicts Augustus's victory at Actium in 31 BCE. Virgil wrote the Aeneid during a time of major political and social change in Rome, with the fall of the republic and the Final War of the Roman Republic tearing through society and causing many to question Rome's inherent greatness. In this context, Augustus instituted a new era of prosperity and peace through the reintroduction of traditional Roman moral values. The Aeneid was seen as reflecting this aim by depicting Aeneas as a man devoted and loyal to his country and its greatness, rather than being concerned with his own personal gains. The *Aeneid* also gives mythic legitimization to the rule of Julius Caesar, and by extension, to his adopted son, Augustus, by immortalizing the tradition that renamed Aeneas's son Iulus, making him an ancestor to the family of Julius Caesar.

According to the *Aeneid*, the survivors from the fallen city of Troy banded together under Aeneas, underwent a series of adventures around the Mediterranean Sea, including a stop at newly founded Carthage under the rule of Queen Dido, and eventually reached the Italian coast. The Trojans were thought to have landed in an area between modern Anzio and Fiumicino, southwest of Rome, probably at Laurentum, or in other versions, at Lavinium, a place named for Lavinia, the daughter of King Latinus, who Aeneas married. Aeneas' arrival started a series of armed conflicts with Turnus over the marriage of Lavinia. Before the arrival of Aeneas, Turnus was engaged to Lavinia, who then married Aeneas, which began the conflict. Aeneas eventually won the war and killed Turnus, which granted the Trojans the right to stay and to assimilate with the local peoples. The young son of Aeneas, Ascanius, also known as Iulus, went on to found Alba Longa and the line of Alban kings who filled the chronological gap between the Trojan saga and the traditional founding of Rome in the 8th century BCE.

Toward the end of this line, King Procas appears as the father of Numitor and Amulius. At Procas' death, Numitor became king of Alba Longa, but Amulius captured him and sent him to prison. He also forced the daughter of Numitor, Rhea Silvia, to become a virgin priestess among the Vestals. For many years, Amulius was the king. The tortuous nature of the chronology is indicated by Rhea Silvia's ordination among the Vestals, whose order was traditionally said to have been founded by the successor of Romulus, Numa Pompilius.

The Archaeological Record

According to the archaeological record of the region, the Italic tribes who originally inhabited the Alban Hills moved down into the valleys, which provided better land for agriculture. The area around the Tiber River was particularly advantageous and offered many strategic resources. For instance, the river itself provided a natural border on one side of the settlement, and the hills on the other side provided another defensive position for the townspeople. A settlement in this area would have also allowed for control of the river, including commercial and military traffic, as well as a natural observation point at Isola Tiberina. This was especially important, since Rome was at the intersection of the principal roads to the sea from Sabinum and Etruria, and traffic from those roads could not be as easily controlled.

The development of Rome itself is presumed to have coalesced around the migrations of these various tribes into the valley, as evidenced by differences in pottery and burial techniques. The discovery of a series of fortification walls on the north slope of Palatine Hill, most likely dating to the middle of the 8th century BCE, provide the strongest evidence for the original site and date of the founding of the city of Rome.

The Seven Kings

For its first 200 years, Rome was ruled by seven kings, each of whom is credited either with establishing a key Roman tradition or constructing an important building.

Learning Objectives

Explain the significance of the Seven Kings of Rome to Roman culture

Key Takeaways

Key Points

- Romulus was Rome's first king and the city's founder. He is best known for the Rape of the Sabine Women and the establishment of the Senate, as well as various voting practices.
- Numa Pompilius was a just, pious king who established the cult of the Vestal Virgins at Rome, and the position of Pontifex Maximus. His reign was characterized by peace.

- Tullus Hostilius had little regard for the Roman gods, and focused entirely on military expansion. He constructed the home of the Roman Senate, the *Curia Hostilia*.
- Ancus Marcius ruled peacefully and only fought wars when Roman territories needed defending.
- Lucius Tarquinius Priscus increased the size of the Senate and began major construction works, including the Temple to Jupiter Optimus Maximus, and the Circus Maximus.
- Servius Tullius built the first *pomerium*—walls that fully encircled the Seven Hills of Rome. He also made organizational changes to the Roman army, and implemented a new constitution for the Romans, further developing the citizen classes.
- Lucius Tarquinius Superbus's reign is remembered for his use of violence and intimidation, as well as his disrespect of Roman custom and the Roman Senate. He was eventually overthrown, thus leading to the establishment of the Roman Republic.

Key Terms

- **absolute monarchy**: A monarchical form of government in which the monarch has absolute power among his or her people. This amounts to unrestricted political power over a sovereign state and its people.
- **patrician**: A group of elite families in ancient Rome.

The first 200 years of Roman history occurred under a monarchy. Rome was ruled by seven kings over this period of time, and each of their reigns were characterized by the personality of the ruler in question. Each of these kings is credited either with establishing a key Roman tradition, or constructing an important building. None of the seven kings were known to be dynasts, and no reference is made to the hereditary nature of kingdom until after the fifth king, Tarquinius Priscus.

The king of Rome possessed absolute power over the people, and the Senate provided only a weak, oligarchic counterbalance to his power, primarily exercising only minor administrative powers. For these reasons, the kingdom of Rome is considered an absolute monarchy. Despite this, Roman kings, with the exception of Romulus, were elected by citizens of Rome who occupied the Curiate Assembly. There, members would vote on candidates that had been nominated by a chosen member of the Senate, called an interrex. Candidates could be chosen from any source.

Romulus

Romulus was Rome's legendary first king and the city's founder. In 753 BCE, Romulus began building the city upon the Palatine Hill. After founding and naming Rome, as the story goes, he permitted men of all classes to come to Rome as citizens, including slaves and freemen, without distinction. To provide his citizens with wives, Romulus invited the neighboring tribes to a festival in Rome where he abducted the young women amongst them (this is known as The Rape of the Sabine Women). After the ensuing war with the Sabines, Romulus shared the kingship with the Sabine king, Titus Tatius. Romulus selected 100 of the most noble men to form the Roman Senate as an advisory council to the king. These men were called *patres* (from *pater:* father, head), and their descendants became the patricians. He also established voting, and class structures that would define sociopolitical proceedings throughout the Roman Republic and Empire.

Numa Pompilius

After the death of Romulus, there was an *interregnum* for one year, during which ten men chosen from the senate governed Rome as successive *interreges*. Numa Pompilius, a Sabine, was eventually chosen by the senate to succeed Romulus because of his reputation for justice and piety. Numa's reign was marked by peace and religious reform. Numa constructed a new temple to Janus and, after establishing peace with Rome's neighbors, shut the doors of the temple to indicate a state of peace. The doors of the temple remained closed for the balance of his reign. He established the cult of the Vestal Virgins at Rome, as well as the "leaping priests," known as the Salii, and three flamines, or priests, assigned to Jupiter, Mars, and Quirinus. He also established the office and duties of Pontifex Maximus, the head priest of the Roman state religion.

Tullus Hostilius

Tullus Hostilius was much like Romulus in his warlike behavior, and completely unlike Numa in his lack of respect for the gods. Tullus waged war against Alba Longa, Fidenae and Veii, and the Sabines. It was during Tullus' reign that the city of Alba Longa was completely destroyed, after which Tullus integrated its population into Rome. According to the Roman historian Livy, Tullus neglected the worship of the gods until, towards the end of his reign, he fell ill and became superstitious. However, when Tullus called upon Jupiter and begged assistance, Jupiter responded with a bolt of lightning that burned the king and his house to ashes. Tullus is attributed with constructing a new home for the Senate, the *Curia Hostilia,* which survived for 562 years after his death.

Ancus Marcius

Following the death of Tullus, the Romans elected a peaceful and religious king in his place—Numa's grandson, Ancus Marcius. Much like his grandfather, Ancus did little to expand the borders of Rome, and only fought war when his territories needed defending.

Lucius Tarquinius Priscus

Lucius Tarquinius Priscus was the fifth king of Rome and the first of Etruscan birth. After immigrating to Rome, he gained favor with Ancus, who later adopted him as his son. Upon ascending the throne, he waged wars against the Sabines and Etruscans, doubling the size of Rome and bringing great treasures to the city. One of his first reforms was to add 100 new members to the Senate from the conquered Etruscan tribes, bringing the total number of senators to 200. He used the treasures Rome had acquired from conquests to build great monuments for Rome, including the Roman Forum, the temple to Jupiter on the Capitoline Hill, and the Circus Maximus. His reign is best remembered for the introduction of Etruscan symbols of military distinction and civilian authority into the Roman tradition, including the scepter of the king, the rings worn by senators, and the use of the tuba for military purposes.

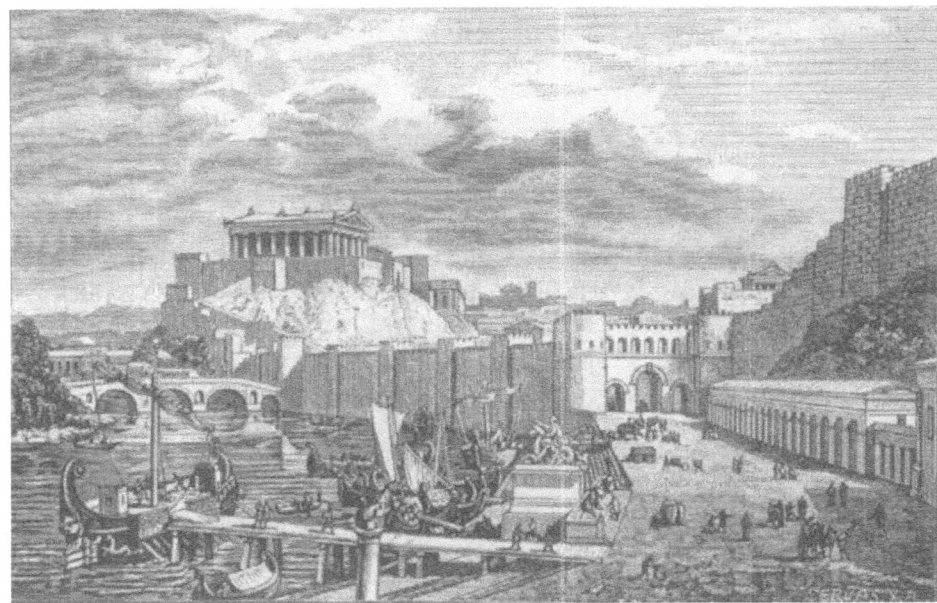

The Temple of Jupiter Optimus Maximus: *19th century illustration depicting the Temple of Jupiter Optimus Maximus above the Tiber River during the Roman Republic.*

Servius Tullus

Following Priscus's death, his son-in-law, Servius Tullius, succeeded him to the throne. Like his father-in-law before him, Servius fought successful wars against the Etruscans. He used the treasure from his campaigns to build the first *pomerium*—walls that fully encircled the Seven Hills of Rome. He also made organizational changes to the Roman army, and was renowned for implementing a new constitution for the Romans and further developing the citizen classes. Servius's reforms brought about a major change in Roman life—voting rights were now based on socioeconomic status, transferring much of the power into the hands of the Roman elite. The 44-year reign of Servius came to an abrupt end when he was assassinated in a conspiracy led by his own daughter, Tullia, and her husband, Lucius Tarquinius Superbus.

Lucius Tarquinius Superbus

While in power, Tarquinius conducted a number of wars against Rome's neighbors, including the Volsci, Gabii, and the Rutuli. Tarquinius also engaged in a series of public works, notably the completion of the Temple of Jupiter Optimus Maximus on the Capitoline Hill. Tarquin's reign, however, is best remembered for his use of violence and intimidation in his attempts to maintain control over Rome, as well as his disrespect of Roman custom and the Roman Senate. Tensions came to a head when the king's son, Sextus Tarquinius, raped Lucretia, wife and daughter to powerful Roman nobles. Lucretia then told her relatives about the attack and subsequently committed suicide to avoid the dishonor of the episode. Four men, led by Lucius Junius Brutus, incited a revolution, and as a result, Tarquinius and his family were deposed and expelled from Rome in 509 BCE. Because of his actions and the way they were viewed by the people, the word for King, *rex*, held a negative connotation in Roman culture until the fall of the Roman Empire. Brutus and Collatinus became Rome's first consuls, marking the beginning of the Roman Republic. This new government would survive for the next 500 years, until the rise of Julius Caesar and Caesar Augustus, and cover a period in which Rome's authority and area of control extended to cover great areas of Europe, North Africa, and the Middle East.

Early Roman Society

Multiple, overlapping hierarchies characterized Roman society, which was also highly patriarchal.

Learning Objectives

Describe what Roman society was like in its early years

Key Takeaways

Key Points

- Roman society was extremely patriarchal and hierarchical. The adult male head of a household had special legal powers and privileges that gave him jurisdiction over all the members of his family.
- The status of freeborn Romans was established by their ancestry, census ranking, and citizenship.
- The most important division within Roman society was between patricians, a small elite who monopolized political power, and plebeians, who comprised the majority of Roman society.
- The Roman census divided citizens into six complex classes based on property holdings.
- Most adult, free-born men within the city limits of Rome held Roman citizenship. Classes of non-citizens existed and held different legal rights.

Key Terms

- **plebeians**: A general body of free Roman citizens who were part of the lower strata of society.
- **patricians**: A group of ruling class families in ancient Rome.
- **tax farming**: A technique of financial management in which future, uncertain revenue streams are fixed into periodic rents via assignment by legal contract to a third party.

Roman society was extremely patriarchal and hierarchical. The adult male head of a household had special legal powers and privileges that gave him jurisdiction over all the members of his family, including his wife, adult sons, adult married daughters, and slaves, but there were multiple, overlapping hierarchies at play within society at large. An individual's relative position in one hierarchy might have been higher or lower than it was in another. The status of freeborn Romans was established by the following:

- Their ancestry
- Their census rank, which in turn was determined by the individual's wealth and political privi-

lege
- Citizenship, of which there were grades with varying rights and privileges

Ancestry

The most important division within Roman society was between patricians, a small elite who monopolized political power, and plebeians, who comprised the majority of Roman society. These designations were established at birth, with patricians tracing their ancestry back to the first Senate established under Romulus. Adult, male non-citizens fell outside the realms of these divisions, but women and children, who were also not considered formal citizens, took the social status of their father or husband. Originally, all public offices were only open to patricians and the classes could not intermarry, but, over time, the differentiation between patrician and plebeian statuses became less pronounced, particularly after the establishment of the Roman republic.

Census Rankings

The Roman census divided citizens into six complex classes based on property holdings. The richest class was called the senatorial class, with wealth based on ownership of large agricultural estates, since members of the highest social classes did not traditionally engage in commercial activity. Below the senatorial class was the equestrian order, comprised of members who held the same volume of wealth as the senatorial classes, but who engaged in commerce, making them an influential early business class. Certain political and quasi-political positions were filled by members of the equestrian order, including tax farming and leadership of the Praetorian Guard. Three additional property-owning classes occupied the rungs beneath the equestrian order. Finally, the *proletarii* occupied the bottom rung with the lowest property values in the kingdom.

Citizenship

Citizenship in ancient Rome afforded political and legal privileges to free individuals with respect to laws, property, and governance. Most adult, free-born men within the city limits of Rome held Roman citizenship. Men who lived in towns outside of Rome might also hold citizenship, but some lacked the right to vote. Free-born, foreign subjects during this period were known as *peregrini*, and special laws existed to govern their conduct and disputes, though they were not considered Roman citizens during the Roman kingdom period. Free-born women in ancient Rome were considered citizens, but they could not vote or hold political office. The status of woman's citizenship affected the citizenship of her offspring. For example, in a type of Roman marriage called *conubium*, both spouses must be citizens in order to marry. Additionally, the phrase *ex duobus civibus Romanis natos*, translated to mean "children born of two Roman citizens," reinforces the importance of both parents' legal status in determining that of their offspring.

Roman citizenship: *The toga, shown here on a statue restored with the head of Nerva, was the distinctive garb of Roman citizens*

Classes of non-citizens existed and held different legal rights. Under Roman law, slaves were considered property and held no rights. However, certain laws did regulate the institution of slavery, and extended protections to slaves that were not granted to other forms of property. Slaves who had been manumitted became freedmen and enjoyed largely the same rights and protections as free-born citizens. Many slaves descended from debtors or prisoners of war, especially women and children who were captured during foreign military campaigns and sieges.

Ironically, many slaves originated from Rome's conquest of Greece, and yet Greek culture was considered, in some respects by the Romans, to be superior to their own. In this way, it seems Romans regarded slavery as a circumstance of birth, misfortune, or war, rather than being limited to, or defined by, ethnicity or race. Because it was defined mainly in terms of a lack of legal rights and status, it was also not considered a permanent or inescapable position. Some who had received educations or learned skills that allowed them to earn their own living were manumitted upon the death of their
owner, or allowed to earn money to buy their freedom during their owner's lifetime. Some slave owners also freed slaves who they believed to be their natural children. Nonetheless, many worked under harsh conditions, and/or suffered inhumanely under their owners during their enslavement.

Most freed slaves joined the lower plebeian classes, and worked as farmers or tradesmen, though as time progressed and their numbers increased, many were also accepted into the equestrian class. Some went on to populate the civil service, whereas others engaged in commerce, amassing vast fortunes that were rivaled only by those in the wealthiest classes.

Attributions

CC licensed content, Specific attribution

- Aeneid. **Provided by**: Wikipedia. **Located at**: https://en.wikipedia.org/wiki/Aeneid. **License**: *CC BY-SA: Attribution-ShareAlike*
- Romulus and Remus. **Provided by**: Wikipedia. **Located at**: https://en.wikipedia.org/wiki/Romulus_and_Remus. **License**: *CC BY-SA: Attribution-ShareAlike*
- The Founding of Rome. **Provided by**: Wikipedia. **Located at**: http://en.wikipedia.org/wiki/Founding_of_Rome%23Aeneas. **License**: *CC BY-SA: Attribution-ShareAlike*
- Rome. **Provided by**: Wiktionary. **Located at**: http://en.wiktionary.org/wiki/Rome. **License**: *CC BY-SA: Attribution-ShareAlike*
- Lupa Capitolina. **Provided by**: Wikipedia. **Located at**: http://en.wikipedia.org/wiki/Romulus_and_Remus%23mediaviewer/File:0_Lupa_Capitolina_(2).JPG. **License**: *CC BY-SA: Attribution-ShareAlike*
- King of Rome. **Provided by**: Wikipedia. **Located at**: https://en.wikipedia.org/wiki/King_of_Rome. **License**: *CC BY-SA: Attribution-ShareAlike*
- Absolute monarchy. **Provided by**: Wikipedia. **Located at**: https://en.wikipedia.org/wiki/Absolute_monarchy. **License**: *CC BY-SA: Attribution-ShareAlike*
- Seven Kings of Rome. **Provided by**: Wikipedia. **Located at**: http://en.wikipedia.org/wiki/Seven_Kings_of_Rome. **License**: *CC BY-SA: Attribution-ShareAlike*
- Patrician (ancient Rome). **Provided by**: Wikpedia. **Located at**: http://en.wikipedia.org/wiki/Patrician_(ancient_Rome). **License**: *CC BY-SA: Attribution-ShareAlike*
- patrician. **Provided by**: Wiktionary. **Located at**: http://en.wiktionary.org/wiki/patrician. **License**: *CC BY-SA: Attribution-ShareAlike*
- Lupa Capitolina. **Provided by**: Wikipedia. **Located at**: http://en.wikipedia.org/wiki/Romulus_and_Remus%23mediaviewer/File:0_Lupa_Capitolina_(2).JPG. **License**: *CC BY-SA: Attribution-ShareAlike*
- City of Rome during time of republic. **Provided by**: Wikimedia. **Located at**: https://commons.wikimedia.org/wiki/File:City_of_Rome_during_time_of_republic.jpg. **License**: *Public Domain: No Known Copyright*
- Roman citizenship. **Provided by**: Wikipedia. **Located at**: https://en.wikipedia.org/wiki/Roman_citizenship. **License**: *CC BY-SA: Attribution-ShareAlike*
- Social class in ancient Rome. **Provided by**: Wikipedia. **Located at**: https://en.wikipedia.org/wiki/Social_class_in_ancient_Rome. **License**: *CC BY-SA: Attribution-ShareAlike*
- Plebs. **Provided by**: Wikipedia. **Located at**: https://en.wikipedia.org/wiki/Plebs. **License**: *CC BY-SA: Attribution-ShareAlike*
- Farm (revenue leasing). **Provided by**: Wikipedia. **Located at**: https://en.wikipedia.org/wiki/Farm_(revenue_leasing). **License**: *CC BY-SA: Attribution-ShareAlike*
- Patrician (ancient Rome). **Provided by**: Wikipedia. **Located at**: https://en.wikipedia.org/wiki/Patrician_(ancient_Rome). **License**: *CC BY-SA: Attribution-ShareAlike*
- Lupa Capitolina. **Provided by**: Wikipedia. **Located at**: http://en.wikipedia.org/wiki/Romulus_and_Remus%23mediaviewer/File:0_Lupa_Capitolina_(2).JPG. **License**: *CC BY-SA: Attribution-ShareAlike*
- City of Rome during time of republic. **Provided by**: Wikimedia. **Located at**: https://commons.wikimedia.org/wiki/File:City_of_Rome_during_time_of_republic.jpg. **License**: *Public Domain: No Known Copyright*
- 220px-Togato,_I_sec_dc._con_testa_di_restauro_da_un_ritratto_di_nerva,_inv._2286.JPG. **Provided by**: Wikimedia. **Located at**: https://commons.wikimedia.org/wiki/File:Togato,_I_sec_dc._con_testa_di_restauro_da_un_ritratto_di_nerva,_inv._2286.JPG. **License**: *Public Domain: No Known Copyright*

The Roman Republic

The Establishment of the Roman Republic

After the publicoutcry that arose as a result of the rape of Lucretia, Romans overthrew the unpopular king, Lucius Tarquinius Superbus, and established a republican form of government.

Learning Objectives

Explain why and how Rome transitioned from a monarchy to a republic

Key Takeaways

Key Points

- The Roman monarchy was overthrown around 509 BCE, during a political revolution that resulted in the expulsion of Lucius Tarquinius Superbus, the last king of Rome.
- Despite waging a number of successful campaigns against Rome's neighbors, securing Rome's position as head of the Latin cities, and engaging in a series of public works, Tarquinius was a very unpopular king, due to his violence and abuses of power.
- When word spread that Tarquinius's son raped Lucretia, the wife of the governor of Collatia, an uprising occurred in which a number of prominent patricians argued for a change in government.
- A general election was held during a legal assembly, and participants voted in favor of the establishment of a Roman republic.
- Subsequently, all Tarquins were exiled from Rome and an interrex and two consuls were established to lead the new republic.

> *Key Terms*
>
> - **patricians**: A group of ruling class families in ancient Rome.
> - **plebeians**: A general body of free Roman citizens who were part of the lower strata of society.
> - **interrex**: Literally, this translates to mean a ruler that presides over the period between the rule of two separate kings; or, in other words, a short-term regent.

The Roman monarchy was overthrown around 509 BCE, during a political revolution that resulted in the expulsion of Lucius Tarquinius Superbus, the last king of Rome. Subsequently, the Roman Republic was established.

Background

Tarquinius was the son of Lucius Tarquinius Priscus, the fifth king of Rome's Seven Kings period. Tarquinius was married to Tullia Minor, the daughter of Servius Tullius, the sixth king of Rome's Seven Kings period. Around 535 BCE, Tarquinius and his wife, Tullia Minor, arranged for the murder of his father-in-law. Tarquinius became king following Servius Tullius's death.

Tarquinius waged a number of successful campaigns against Rome's neighbors, including the Volsci, Gabii, and the Rutuli. He also secured Rome's position as head of the Latin cities, and in a series of public works, such as the completion of the Temple of Jupiter Optimus Maximus. However, Tarquinius remained an unpopular king for a number of reasons. He refused to bury his predecessor and executed a number of leading senators whom he suspected remained loyal to Servius. Following these actions, he refused to replace the senators he executed and refused to consult the Senate in matters of government going forward, thus diminishing the size and influence of the Senate greatly. He also went on to judge capital criminal cases without the advice of his counselors, stoking fear among his political opponents that they would be unfairly targeted.

The Rape of Lucretia and An Uprising

Titian's Tarquin and Lucretia (1571).

Tarquin and Lucretia

During Tarquinius's war with the Rutuli, his son, Sextus Tarquinius, was sent on a military errand to Collatia, where he was received with great hospitality at the governor's mansion. The governor's wife, Lucretia, hosted Sextus while the governor was away at war. During the night, Sextus entered her bedroom and raped her. The next day, Lucretia traveled to her father, Spurius Lucretius, a distinguished prefect in Rome, and, before witnesses, informed him of what had happened. Because her father was a chief magistrate of Rome, her pleas for justice and vengeance could not be ignored. At the end of her pleas, she stabbed herself in the heart with a dagger, ultimately dying in her own father's arms. The scene struck those who had witnessed it with such horror that they collectively vowed to publicly defend their liberty against the outrages of such tyrants.

Lucius Junius Brutus, a leading citizen and the grandson of Rome's fifth king, Tarquinius Priscus, publicly opened a debate on the form of government that Rome should have in place of the existing monarchy. A number of patricians attended the debate, in which Brutus
proposed the banishment of the Tarquins from all territories of Rome, and the appointment of an interrex to nominate new magistrates and to oversee an election of ratification. It was decided that a republican form of government should temporarily replace the monarchy, with two consuls replacing the king and executing the will of a patrician senate. Spurius Lucretius was elected interrex, and he proposed Brutus, and Lucius Tarquinius Collatinus, a leading citizen who was also related to Tarquinius Priscus, as the first two consuls. His choice was ratified by the *comitia curiata*, an organization of patrician families who primarily ratified decrees of the king.

In order to rally the plebeians to their cause, all were summoned to a legal assembly in the forum, and Lucretia's body was paraded through the streets. Brutus gave a speech and a general election was held. The results were in favor of a republic. Brutus left Lucretius in command of the city as interrex, and pursued the king in Ardea where he had been positioned with his army on campaign. Tarquinius, however, who had heard of developments in Rome, fled the camp before Brutus arrived, and the army received Brutus favorably, expelling the king's sons from their encampment. Tarquinius was subsequently refused entry into Rome and lived as an exile with his family.

The Establishment of the Republic

Brutus and Lucretia: *The statue shows Brutus holding the knife and swearing the oath, with Lucretia.*

Although there is no scholarly agreement as to whether or not it actually took place, Plutarch and Appian both claim that Brutus's first act as consul was to initiate an oath for the people, swearing never again to allow a king to rule Rome. What is known for certain is that he replenished the Senate to its original number of 300 senators, recruiting men from among the equestrian class. The new consuls also created a separate office, called the rex sacrorum, to carry out and oversee religious duties, a task that had previously fallen to the king.

The two consuls continued to be elected annually by Roman citizens and advised by the senate. Both consuls were elected for one-year terms and could veto each other's actions. Initially, they were endowed with all the powers of kings past, though over time these were broken down further by the addition of magistrates to the governmental system. The first magistrate added was the praetor, an office that assumed judicial authority from the consuls. After the praetor, the censor was established, who assumed the power to conduct the Roman census.

Structure of the Republic

The Roman Republic was composed of the Senate, a number of legislative assemblies, and elected magistrates.

Learning Objectives

Describe the political structure of the Roman Republic

Key Takeaways

Key Points

- The Constitution of the Roman Republic was a set of guidelines and principles passed down, mainly through precedent. The constitution was largely unwritten and uncodified, and evolved over time.
- Roman citizenship was a vital prerequisite to possessing many important legal rights. The Senate passed decrees that were called *senatus consulta*, ostensibly "advice" from the senate to a magistrate. The focus of the Roman Senate was usually foreign policy.
- There were two types of legislative assemblies. The first was the *comitia* ("committees"), which were assemblies of all Roman citizens. The second was the *concilia* ("councils"), which were assemblies of specific groups of citizens.
- The *comitia centuriata* was the assembly of the centuries (soldiers), and they elected magistrates who had imperium powers (consuls and praetors). The *comitia tributa*, or assembly of the tribes (the citizens of Rome), was presided over by a consul and composed of 35 tribes. They elected quaestors, curule aediles, and military tribunes.
- Dictators were sometimes elected during times of military emergency, during which the constitutional government would be disbanded.

Key Terms

- **patricians**: A group of ruling class families in ancient Rome.
- **plebeian**: A general body of free Roman citizens who were part of the lower strata of society.
- **Roman Senate**: A political institution in the ancient Roman Republic. It was not an elected body, but one whose members were appointed by the consuls, and later by the censors.

The Constitution of the Roman Republic was a set of guidelines and principles passed down, mainly through precedent. The constitution was largely unwritten and uncodified, and evolved over time. Rather than creating a government that was primarily a democracy (as was ancient Athens), an aristocracy (as was ancient Sparta), or a monarchy (as was Rome before, and in many respects after, the Republic), the Roman constitution mixed these three elements of governance into their overall political system. The democratic element took the form of legislative assemblies; the aristocratic element took the form of the Senate; and the monarchical element took the form of the many term-limited consuls.

The Roman SPQR Banner: "SPQR" (senatus populusque romanus) was the Roman motto, which stood for "the Senate and people of Rome".

The Roman Senate

The Senate's ultimate authority derived from the esteem and prestige of the senators, and was based on both precedent and custom. The Senate passed decrees, which were called *senatus consulta*, ostensibly "advice" handed down from the senate to a magistrate. In practice, the magistrates usually followed the *senatus consulta*. The focus of the Roman Senate was usually foreign policy. However, the power of the Senate expanded over time as the power of the legislative assemblies declined, and eventually the Senate took a greater role in civil law-making. Senators were usually appointed by Roman censors, but during times of military emergency, such as the civil wars of the 1st century BCE, this practice became less prevalent, and the Roman dictator, triumvir, or the Senate itself would select its members.

Curia Iulia – The Roman Senate House: *The Curia Julia in the Roman Forum, the seat of the imperial Senate.*

Legislative Assemblies

Roman citizenship was a vital prerequisite to possessing many important legal rights, such as the rights to trial and appeal, marriage, suffrage, to hold office, to enter binding contracts, and to enjoy special tax exemptions. An adult male citizen with full legal and political rights was called *optimo jure*. The *optimo jure* elected assemblies, and the assemblies elected magistrates, enacted legislation, presided over trials in capital cases, declared war and peace, and forged or dissolved treaties. There were two types of legislative assemblies. The first was the *comitia* ("committees"), which were assemblies of all *optimo jure*. The second was the *concilia* ("councils"), which were assemblies of specific groups of *optimo jure*.

Citizens on these assemblies were organized further on the basis of curiae (familial groupings), centuries (for military purposes), and tribes (for civil purposes), and each would each gather into their own assemblies. The Curiate Assembly served only a symbolic purpose in the late Republic, though the assembly was used to ratify the powers of newly elected magistrates by passing laws known as *leges curiatae*. The *comitia centuriata* was the assembly of the centuries (soldiers). The president of the *comi-*

tia centuriata was usually a consul, and the *comitia centuriata* would elect magistrates who had imperium powers (consuls and praetors). It also elected censors. Only the *comitia centuriata* could declare war and ratify the results of a census. It also served as the highest court of appeal in certain judicial cases.

The assembly of the tribes, the *comitia tributa*, was presided over by a consul, and was composed of 35 tribes. The tribes were not ethnic or kinship groups, but rather geographical subdivisions. While it did not pass many laws, the *comitia tributa* did elect quaestors, curule aediles, and military tribunes. The Plebeian Council was identical to the assembly of the tribes, but excluded the patricians. They elected their own officers, plebeian tribunes, and plebeian aediles. Usually a plebeian tribune would preside over the assembly. This assembly passed most laws, and could also act as a court of appeal.

Since the tribunes were considered to be the embodiment of the plebeians, they were sacrosanct. Their sacrosanctness was enforced by a pledge, taken by the plebeians, to kill any person who harmed or interfered with a tribune during his term of office. As such, it was considered a capital offense to harm a tribune, to disregard his veto, or to interfere with his actions. In times of military emergency, a dictator would be appointed for a term of six months. The constitutional government would be dissolved, and the dictator would be the absolute master of the state. When the dictator's term ended, constitutional government would be restored.

Executive Magistrates

Magistrates were the elected officials of the Roman republic. Each magistrate was vested with a degree of power, and the dictator, when there was one, had the highest level of power. Below the dictator was the censor (when they existed), and the consuls, the highest ranking ordinary magistrates. Two were elected every year and wielded supreme power in both civil and military powers. The ranking among both consuls flipped every month, with one outranking the other.

Below the consuls were the praetors, who administered civil law, presided over the courts, and commanded provincial armies. Censors conducted the Roman census, during which time they could appoint people to the Senate. Curule aediles were officers elected to conduct domestic affairs in Rome, who were vested with powers over the markets, public games, and shows. Finally, at the bottom of magistrate rankings were the quaestors, who usually assisted the consuls in Rome and the governors in the provinces with financial tasks. Plebeian tribunes and plebeian aediles were considered representatives of the people, and acted as a popular check over the Senate through use of their veto powers, thus safeguarding the civil liberties of all Roman citizens.

Each magistrate could only veto an action that was taken by an equal or lower ranked magistrate. The most significant constitutional power a magistrate could hold was that of imperium or command, which was held only by consuls and praetors. This gave the magistrate in question the constitutional authority to issue commands, military or otherwise.

Election to a magisterial office resulted in automatic membership in the Senate for life, unless impeached. Once a magistrate's annual term in office expired, he had to wait at least ten years before serving in that office again. Occasionally, however, a magistrate would have his command powers extended through prorogation, which effectively allowed him to retain the powers of his office as a promagistrate.

Roman Society Under the Republic

The bulk of Roman politics prior to the 1st century BCE focused on inequalities among the orders.

Learning Objectives

Describe the relationship between the government and the people in the time of the Roman Republic

Key Takeaways

Key Points

- A number of developments affected the relationship between Rome's republican government and
society, particularly in regard to how that relationship differed among patricians and plebeians.
- In 494 BCE, plebeian soldiers refused to march against a wartime enemy, in order to demand the right to elect their own officials.
- The passage of Lex Trebonia forbade the co-opting of colleagues to fill vacant positions on tribunes in order to sway voting in favor of patrician blocs over plebeians.
- Throughout the 4th century BCE, a series of reforms were passed that required all laws passed by the plebeian council to have the full force of law over the entire population. This gave the plebeian tribunes a positive political impact over the entire population for the first time in Roman history.
- In 445 BCE, the plebeians demanded the right to stand for election as consul. Ultimately, a compromise was reached in which consular command authority was granted to a select number of military tribunes.
- The Licinio-Sextian law was passed in 367 BCE; it addressed the economic plight of the plebeians and prevented the election of further patrician magistrates.
- In the decades following the passage of the Licinio-Sextian law, further legislation was enacted that granted political equality to the plebeians. Nonetheless, it remained difficult for a plebeian from an unknown family to enter the Senate, due to the rise of a new patricio-plebeian aristocracy that was less interested in the plight of the average plebeian.

Key Terms

- **patricians**: A group of ruling class families in ancient Rome.
- **plebeian**: A general body of free Roman citizens who were part of the lower strata of society.

In the first few centuries of the Roman Republic, a number of developments affected the relationship between the government and the Roman people, particularly in regard to how that relationship differed across the separate strata of society.

The Patrician Era (509-367 BCE)

The last king of Rome, Lucius Tarquinius Superbus, was overthrown in 509 BCE. One of the biggest changes that occurred as a result was the establishment of two chief magistrates, called consuls, who were elected by the citizens of Rome for an annual term. This stood in stark contrast to the previous system, in which a king was elected by senators, for life. Built in to the consul system were checks on authority, since each consul could provide balance to the decisions made by his colleague. Their limited terms of office also opened them up to the possibility of prosecution in the event of abuses of power. However, when consuls exercised their political powers in tandem, the magnitude and influence they wielded was hardly different from that of the old kings.

In 494 BCE, Rome was at war with two neighboring tribes, and plebeian soldiers refused to march against the enemy, instead seceding to the Aventine Hill. There, the plebeian soldiers took advantage of the situation to demand the right to elect their own officials. The patricians assented to their demands, and the plebeian soldiers returned to battle. The new offices that were created as a result came to be known as "plebeian tribunes," and they were to be assisted by "plebeian aediles."

In the early years of the republic, plebeians were not permitted to hold magisterial office. Tribunes and aediles were technically not magistrates, since they were only elected by fellow plebeians, as opposed to the unified population of plebeians and patricians. Although plebeian tribunes regularly attempted to block legislation they considered unfavorable, patricians could still override their veto with the support of one or more other tribunes. Tension over this imbalance of power led to the passage of Lex Trebonia, which forbade the co-opting of colleagues to fill vacant positions on tribunes in order to sway voting in favor of one or another bloc. Throughout the 4th century BCE, a series of reforms were passed that required all laws passed by the plebeian council to have equal force over the entire population, regardless of status as patrician or plebeian. This gave the plebeian tribunes a positive political impact over the entire population for the first time in Roman history.

Gaius Gracchus: *This 18th century drawing shows Gaius Gracchus, tribune of the people, presiding over the plebeian council.*

In 445 BCE, the plebeians demanded the right to stand for election as consul. The Roman Senate initially refused them this right, but ultimately a compromise was reached in which consular command authority was granted to a select number of military tribunes, who, in turn, were elected by the centuriate assembly with veto power being retained by the senate.

Around 400 BCE, during a series of wars that were fought against neighboring tribes, the plebeians demanded concessions for the disenfranchisement they experienced as foot soldiers fighting for spoils of war that they were never to see. As a result, the Licinio-Sextian law was eventually passed in 367 BCE, which addressed the economic plight of the plebeians and prevented the election of further patrician magistrates.

The Conflict of the Orders Ends (367-287 BCE)

In the decades following the passage of the Licinio-Sextian law, further legislation was enacted that granted political equality to the plebeians. Nonetheless, it remained difficult for a plebeian from an unknown family to enter the Senate. In fact, the very presence of a long-standing nobility, and the Roman population's deep respect for it, made it very difficult for individuals from unknown families to be elected to high office. Additionally, elections could be expensive, neither senators nor magistrates were paid for their services, and the Senate usually did not reimburse magistrates for expenses incurred during their official duties, providing many barriers to the entry of high political office by the non-affluent.

Ultimately, a new patricio-plebeian aristocracy emerged and replaced the old patrician nobility. Whereas the old patrician nobility existed simply on the basis of being able to run for office, the new aristocracy existed on the basis of affluence. Although a small number of plebeians had achieved the same standing as the patrician families of the past, new plebeian aristocrats were less interested in the plight of the average plebeian than were the old patrician aristocrats. For a time, the plebeian plight was mitigated, due higher employment, income, and patriotism that was wrought by a series of wars in which Rome was engaged; these things eliminated the threat of plebeian unrest. But by 287 BCE, the economic conditions of the plebeians deteriorated as a result of widespread indebtedness, and the plebeians sought relief. Roman senators, most of whom were also creditors, refused to give in to the plebeians' demands, resulting in the first plebeian secession to Janiculum Hill.

In order to end the plebeian secession, a dictator, Quintus Hortensius, was appointed. Hortensius, who was himself a plebeian, passed a law known as the "Hortensian Law." This law ended the requirement that an *auctoritas patrum* be passed before a bill could be considered by either the plebeian council or the tribal assembly, thus removing the final patrician senatorial check on the plebeian council. The requirement was not changed, however, in the centuriate assembly. This provided a loophole through which the patrician senate could still deter plebeian legislative influence.

Art and Literature in the Roman Republic

Culture flourished during the Roman Republic with the emergence of great authors, such as Cicero and Lucretius, and with the development of Roman relief and portraiture sculpture.

Learning Objectives

Recognize the wide extent of art and literature created during the Roman Republic

Key Takeaways

Key Points

- Roman literature was, from its very inception, influenced heavily by Greek authors. Some of the earliest works we possess are of historical epics that tell the early military history of Rome. However, authors diversified their genres as the Republic expanded.
- Cicero is one of the most famous Republican authors, and his letters provide detailed information about an important period in Roman history.
- Romans typically produced historical sculptures in relief, as opposed to Greek freestanding sculpture. Small sculptures were considered luxury items, while moulded relief decoration in pottery vessels and small figurines were produced in great quantities for a wider section of the population.
- The most well-known surviving examples of Roman painting consist of the wall paintings from Pompeii and Herculaneum that were preserved in the aftermath of the fatal eruption of Mount Vesuvius in 79 CE.
- Veristic portraiture is a hallmark of Roman art during the Republic, though its use began to diminish during the 1st century BCE as civil wars threatened the empire and individ-

ual strong men began amassing more power.

Key Terms

- **Cicero**: A Roman philosopher, politician, lawyer, orator, political theorist, consul, and constitutionalist.
- **veristic portraiture**: A hyper-realistic portrayal of the subject's facial characteristics; a common style of portraiture in the early to mid-Republic.

Literature

Roman literature was, from its very inception, heavily influenced by Greek authors. Some of the earliest works we possess are historical epics telling the early military history of Rome, similar to the Greek epic narratives of Homer, Herodotus, and Thucydides. Virgil, though generally considered to be an Augustan poet, represents the pinnacle of Roman epic poetry. His *Aeneid* tells the story of the flight of Aeneas from Troy, and his settlement of the city that would become Rome. As the Republic expanded, authors began to produce poetry, comedy, history, and tragedy. Lucretius, in his *De rerum natura (On the Nature of Things)*, attempted to explicate science in an epic poem. The genre of satire was also common in Rome, and satires were written by, among others, Juvenal and Persius.

The Age of Cicero

Bust of Cicero: A mid-first century CE bust of Cicero, in the Capitoline Museums, Rome.

Cicero has traditionally been considered the master of Latin prose. The writing he produced from approximately 80 BCE until his death in 43 BCE, exceeds that of any Latin author whose work survives, in terms of quantity and variety of genre and subject matter. It also possesses unsurpassed stylistic excellence. Cicero's many works can be divided into four groups: letters, rhetorical treatises, philosophical works, and orations. His letters provide detailed information about an important period in Roman history, and offers a vivid picture of public and private life among the Roman governing class. Cicero's works on oratory are our most valuable Latin sources for ancient theories on education and rhetoric. His philosophical works were the basis of moral philosophy during the Middle Ages, and his speeches inspired many European political leaders, as well as the founders of the United States.

Art

Early Roman art was greatly influenced by the art of Greece and the neighboring Etruscans, who were also greatly influenced by Greek art via trade. As the Roman Republic conquered Greek territory, expanding its imperial domain throughout the Hellenistic world, official and patrician sculpture grew out of the Hellenistic style that many Romans encountered during their campaigns, making it difficult to distinguish truly Roman elements from elements of Greek style. This was especially true since much of what survives of Greek sculpture are actually copies made of Greek originals by Romans. By the 2nd century BCE, most sculptors working within Rome were Greek, many of whom were enslaved following military conquests, and whose names were rarely recorded with the work they created. Vast numbers of Greek statues were also imported to Rome as a result of conquest as well as trade.

Rather than create free-standing works depicting heroic exploits from history or mythology, as the Greeks had, the Romans produced historical works in relief. Small sculptures were considered luxury items and were frequently the object of client-patron relationships. The silver Warren Cup and glass Lycurgus cup are examples of the high quality works that were produced during this period. For a wider section of the population, moulded relief decoration in pottery vessels and small figurines were produced in great quantities, and were often of great quality.

In the 3rd century BCE, Greek art taken during wars became popular, and many Roman homes were decorated with landscapes by Greek artists.

Of the vast body of Roman painting that once existed, only a few examples survive to the modern-age. The most well-known surviving examples of Roman painting are the wall paintings from Pompeii and Herculaneum, that were preserved in the aftermath of the fatal eruption of Mount Vesuvius in 79 CE. A large number of paintings also survived in the catacombs of Rome, dating from the 3rd century CE to 400, prior to the Christian age, demonstrating a continuation of the domestic decorative tradition for use in humble burial chambers. Wall painting was not considered high art in either Greece or Rome. Sculpture and panel painting, usually consisting of tempera or encaustic painting on wooden panels, were considered more prestigious art forms.

A large number of Fayum mummy portraits, bust portraits on wood added to the outside of mummies by the Romanized middle class, exist in Roman Egypt. Although these are in some ways distinctively local, they are also broadly representative of the Roman style of painted portraits.

Roman portraiture during the Republic is identified by its considerable realism, known as veristic portraiture. Verism refers to a hyper-realistic portrayal of the subject's facial characteristics. The style originated from Hellenistic Greece; however, its use in Republican Rome and survival throughout much of the Republic is due to Roman values, customs, and political life. As with other forms of Roman art, Roman portraiture borrowed certain details from Greek art, but adapted these to their own needs. Veristic images often show their male subject with receding hairlines, deep winkles, and even with warts. While the face of the portrait was often shown with incredible detail and likeness, the body of the subject would be idealized, and did not seem to correspond to the age shown in the face.

Bust of an Old Man: *Veristic portraiture of an Old Man. Verism refers to a hyper-realistic portrayal of the subject's facial characteristics.*

Portrait sculpture during the period utilized youthful and classical proportions, evolving later into a mixture of realism and idealism. Advancements were also made in relief sculptures, often depicting Roman victories. The Romans, however, completely lacked a tradition of figurative vase-painting comparable to that of the ancient Greeks, which the Etruscans had also emulated.

The Late Republic

The use of veristic portraiture began to diminish during the Late Republic in the 1st century BCE. During this time, civil wars threatened the empire and individual men began to gain more power. The portraits of Pompey the Great and Julius Caesar, two political rivals who were also the most powerful generals in the Republic, began to change the style of portraits and their use. The portraits of Pompey the Great were neither fully idealized, nor were they created in the same veristic style of Republican senators. Pompey borrowed a specific parting and curl of his hair from Alexander the Great, linking Pompey visually to Alexander's likeness, and triggering his audience to associate him with Alexander's characteristics and qualities.

Bust of Pompey the Great: *The portraits of Pompey the Great were neither fully idealized, nor were they created in the same veristic style of Republican senators. This bust clearly shows the specific parting and curl of his hair that would have likened him to Alexander the Great.*

Republican Wars and Conquest

By the end of the mid-Republic, Rome had achieved military dominance on both the Italian peninsula and within the Mediterranean.

Learning Objectives

Describe the key results and effects of major Republican wars

Key Takeaways

Key Points

- Early Roman Republican wars were wars of both expansion and defense, aimed at protecting Rome from neighboring cities and nations, and establishing its territory within the region.
- The Samnite Wars were fought against the Etruscans and effectively finished off all vestiges of Etruscan power by 282 BCE.

- By the middle of the 3rd century and the end of the Pyrrhic War, Rome had effectively dominated the Italian peninsula and won an international military reputation.
- Over the course of the three Punic Wars, Rome completely defeated Hannibal and razed Carthage to the ground, thereby acquiring all of Carthage's North African and Spanish territories.
- After four Macedonian Wars, Rome had established its first permanent foothold in the Greek world, and divided the Macedonian Kingdom into four client republics.

Key Terms

- **Punic Wars**: A series of three wars fought between Rome and Carthage, from 264 BCE to 146 BCE, that resulted in the complete destruction of Carthage.
- **Pyrrhus**: Greek general and statesman of the Hellenistic era. Later he became king of Epirus (r. 306-302, 297-272 BCE) and Macedon (r. 288-284, 273-272 BCE). He was one of the strongest opponents of early Rome. Some of his battles, though successful, cost him heavy losses, from which the term "Pyrrhic victory" was coined.

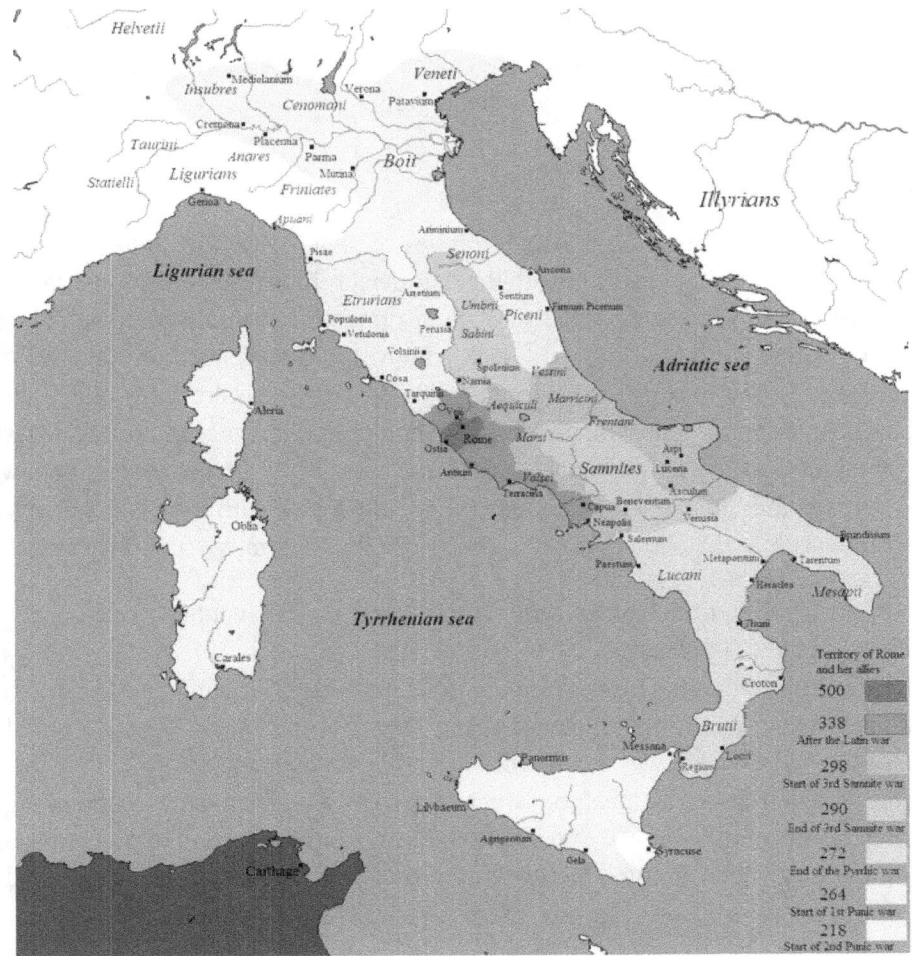

Roman Conquest of the Italian Peninsula: *This map shows the expansion of Roman territory through the various wars fought during the Republican period.*

Early Republic

Early Campaigns (458-396 BCE)

The first Roman Republican wars were wars of both expansion and defense, aimed at protecting Rome from neighboring cities and nations, as well as establishing its territory in the region. Initially, Rome's immediate neighbors were either Latin towns and villages or tribal Sabines from the Apennine hills beyond. One by one, Rome defeated both the persistent Sabines and the nearby Etruscan and Latin cities. By the end of this period, Rome had effectively secured its position against all immediate threats.

Expansion into Italy and the Samnite Wars (343-282 BCE)

The First Samnite War, of 343 BCE-341 BCE, was a relatively short affair. The Romans beat the Samnites in two battles, but were forced to withdraw from the war before they could pursue the conflict further, due to the revolt of several of their Latin allies in the Latin War. The Second Samnite War, from 327 BCE-304 BCE, was much longer and more serious for both the Romans and Samnites, but by 304 BCE the Romans had effectively annexed the greater part of the Samnite territory and founded several colonies therein. Seven years after their defeat, with Roman dominance of the area seemingly assured, the Samnites rose again and defeated a Roman army in 298 BCE, to open the Third Samnite War. With this success in hand, they managed to bring together a coalition of several of Rome's enemies, but by 282 BCE, Rome finished off the last vestiges of Etruscan power in the region.

Pyrrhic War (280-275 BCE)

By the beginning of the 3rd century BCE, Rome had established itself as a major power on the Italian Peninsula, but had not yet come into conflict with the dominant military powers in the Mediterranean Basin at the time: the Carthage and Greek kingdoms. When a diplomatic dispute between Rome and a Greek colony erupted into a naval confrontation, the Greek colony appealed for military aid to Pyrrhus, ruler of the northwestern Greek kingdom of Epirus. Motivated by a personal desire for military accomplishment, Pyrrhus landed a Greek army of approximately 25,000 men on Italian soil in 280 BCE. Despite early victories, Pyrrhus found his position in Italy untenable. Rome steadfastly refused to negotiate with Pyrrhus as long as his army remained in Italy. Facing unacceptably heavy losses with each encounter with the Roman army, Pyrrhus withdrew from the peninsula (thus giving rise to the term "pyrrhic victory").

In 275 BCE, Pyrrhus again met the Roman army at the Battle of Beneventum. While Beneventum's outcome was indecisive, it led to Pyrrhus's
complete withdrawal from Italy, due to the decimation of his army following years of foreign campaigns, and the diminishing likelihood of further material gains. These conflicts with Pyrrhus would have a positive effect on Rome. Rome had shown it was capable of pitting its armies successfully against the dominant military powers of the Mediterranean, and that the Greek kingdoms were incapable of defending their colonies in Italy and abroad. Rome quickly moved into southern Italia, subjugating and dividing the Greek colonies. By the middle of the 3rd century, Rome effectively dominated the Italian peninsula, and had won an international military reputation.

Mid-Republic

Punic Wars

The First Punic War began in 264 BCE, when Rome and Carthage became interested in using settlements within Sicily to solve their own internal conflicts. The war saw land battles in Sicily early on, but focus soon shifted to naval battles around Sicily and Africa. Before the First Punic War, there was essentially no Roman navy. The new war in Sicily against Carthage, a great naval power, forced Rome to quickly build a fleet and train sailors. Though the first few naval battles of the First Punic War were catastrophic disasters for Rome, Rome was eventually able to beat the Carthaginians and leave them without a fleet or sufficient funds to raise another. For a maritime power, the loss of Carthage's access to the Mediterranean stung financially and psychologically, leading the Carthaginians to sue for peace.

Continuing distrust led to the renewal of hostilities in the Second Punic War, when, in 218 BCE, Carthaginian commander Hannibal attacked a Spanish town with diplomatic ties to Rome. Hannibal then crossed the Italian Alps to invade Italy. Hannibal's successes in Italy began immediately, but his brother, Hasdrubal, was defeated after he crossed the Alps on the Metaurus River. Unable to defeat Hannibal on Italian soil, the Romans boldly sent an army to Africa under Scipio Africanus, with the intention of threatening the Carthaginian capital. As a result, Hannibal was recalled to Africa, and defeated at the Battle of Zama.

Carthage never managed to recover after the Second Punic War, and the Third Punic War that followed was, in reality, a simple punitive mission to raze the city of Carthage to the ground. Carthage was almost defenseless, and when besieged offered immediate surrender, conceding to a string of outrageous Roman demands. The Romans refused the surrender and the city was stormed and completely destroyed after a short siege. Ultimately, all of Carthage's North African and Spanish territories were acquired by Rome.

Hannibal's Famous Crossing of the Alps: *Depiction of Hannibal and his army crossing the Alps during the Second Punic War.*

Macedon and Greece

Rome's preoccupation with its war in Carthage provided an opportunity for Philip V of the kingdom of Macedonia, located in the northern part of the Greek peninsula, to attempt to extend his power westward. Over the next several decades, Rome clashed with Macedon to protect their Greek allies throughout the First, Second, and Third Macedonian Wars. By 168 BCE, the Macedonians had been thoroughly defeated, and Rome divided the Macedonian Kingdom into four client republics. After a Fourth Macedonian War, and nearly a century of constant crisis management in Greece (which almost always was a result of internal instability when Rome pulled out), Rome decided to divide Macedonia into two new Roman provinces, Achaea and Epirus.

Crises of the Republic

The 1st century BCE saw tensions between patricians and plebeians erupt into violence, as the Republic became increasingly more divided and unstable.

Learning Objectives

Explain how crises in the 1st century BCE further destabilized the Roman Republic

Key Takeaways

Key Points

- Though the causes and attributes of individual crises varied throughout the decades, an underlying theme of conflict between the aristocracy and ordinary citizens drove the majority of actions.
- The Gracchi brothers, Tiberius and Gaius, introduced a number of populist agrarian and land reforms in the 130s and 120s BCE that were heavily opposed by the patrician Senate. Both brothers were murdered by mob violence after political stalemates.
- Political instability continued, as populist Marius and optimate Sulla engaged in a series of conflicts that culminated in Sulla seizing power and marching to Asia Minor against the decrees of the Senate, and Marius seizing power in a coup back at Rome.
- The Catilinarian Conspiracy discredited the populist party, in turn repairing the image of the Senate, which had come to be seen as weak and not worthy of such violent attack.
- Under the terms of the First Triumvirate, Pompey's arrangements would be ratified and Caesar would be elected consul in 59 BCE; he subsequently served as governor of Gaul for five years. Crassus was promised the consulship later.
- The triumvirate crumbled in the wake of growing political violence and Crassus and Caesar's daughter's death.
- A resolution was passed by the Senate that declared that if Caesar did not lay down his arms by July 49 BCE, he would be considered an enemy of the Republic. Meanwhile, Pompey was granted dictatorial powers over the Republic.
- On January 10, 49 BCE, Caesar crossed the Rubicon and marched towards Rome. Pompey, the consuls, and the Senate all abandoned Rome for Greece, and Caesar entered the city unopposed.

Key Terms

- **Gracchi Brothers**: Brothers Tiberius and Gaius, Roman plebeian nobiles who both served as tribunes in the late 2nd century BCE. They attempted to pass land reform legislation that would redistribute the major patrician landholdings among the plebeians.

- **plebeian**: A general body of free Roman citizens who were part of the lower strata of society.
- **patrician**: A group of ruling class families in ancient Rome.

The Crises of the Roman Republic refers to an extended period of political instability and social unrest that culminated in the demise of the Roman Republic, and the advent of the Roman Empire from about 134 BCE-44 BCE. The exact dates of this period of crisis are unclear or are in dispute from scholar to scholar. Though the causes and attributes of individual crises varied throughout the decades, an underlying theme of conflict between the aristocracy and ordinary citizens drove the majority of actions.

Optimates were a traditionalist majority of the late Roman Republic. They wished to limit the power of the popular assemblies and the Tribune of the Plebeians, and to extend the power of the Senate, which was viewed as more dedicated to the interests of the aristocrats. In particular, they were concerned with the rise of individual generals, who, backed by the tribunate, the assemblies, and their own soldiers, could shift power from the Senate and aristocracy. Many members of this faction were so-classified because they used the backing of the aristocracy and the Senate to achieve personal
goals, not necessarily because they favored the aristocracy over the lower classes. Similarly, the populists did not necessarily champion the lower classes, but often used their support to achieve personal goals.

Following a period of great military successes and economic failures of the early Republican period, many plebeian calls for reform among the classes had been quieted. However, many new slaves were being imported from abroad, causing an unemployment crisis among the lower classes. A flood of unemployed citizens entered Rome, giving rise to populist ideas throughout the city.

The Gracchi Brothers

Tiberius Gracchus took office as a tribune of the plebeians in late 134 BCE. At the time, Roman society was a highly stratified class system with tensions bubbling below the surface. This system consisted of noble families of the senatorial rank (patricians), the knight or equestrian class, citizens (grouped into two or three classes of self-governing allies of Rome: landowners; and plebs, or tenant freemen, depending on the time period), non-citizens who lived outside of southwestern Italy, and at the bottom, slaves. The government owned large tracts of farm land that it had gained through invasion or escheat. This land was rented out to either large landowners whose slaves tilled the land, or small tenant farmers who occupied the property on the basis of a sub-lease. Beginning in 133 BCE, Tiberius tried to redress the grievances of displaced small tenant farmers. He bypassed the Roman Senate, and passed a law limiting the amount of land belonging to the state that any individual could farm, which resulted in the dissolution of large plantations maintained by rich landowners on public land.

A political back-and-forth ensued in the Senate as the other tribune, Octavius, blocked Tiberius's initiatives, and the Senate denied funds needed for land reform. When Tiberius sought re-election to his one-year term (an unprecedented action), the oligarchic nobles responded by murdering Tiberius, and mass riots broke out in the city in reaction to the assassination. About nine years later, Tiberius Gracchus's younger brother, Gaius, passed more radical reforms in favor of the poorer plebeians. Once again, the situation ended in violence and murder as Gaius fled Rome and was either murdered by oligarchs or committed suicide. The deaths of the Gracchi brothers marked the beginning of a late Republic trend in which tensions and conflicts erupted in violence.

Gaius Gracchus Addressing the People: *Silvestre David Mirys' rendition of the the tribune, Gaius Gracchus, addressing the people of Rome.*

Marius and Sulla

The next major reformer of the time was Gaius Marius, who like the Gracchi, was a populist who championed the lower classes. He was a general who abolished the property requirement for becoming a soldier, which allowed the poor to enlist in large numbers. Lucius Cornelius Sulla was appointed as Marius's quaestor (supervisor of the financial affairs of the state) in 107 BCE, and later competed with Marius for supreme power. Over the next few decades, he and Marius engaged in a series of conflicts that culminated in Sulla seizing power and marching to Asia Minor against the decrees of the Senate. Marius launched a coup in Sulla's absence, putting to death some of his enemies and instituting a populist regime, but died soon after.

Bust of Sulla: *The bust of Lucius Cornelius Sulla, an optimate who marched against Rome and installed himself as dictator in 82-81 BCE.*

Pompey, Crassus, and the Catilinarian Conspiracy

In 77 BCE, two of Sulla's former lieutenants, Gnaeus Pompeius Magnus ("Pompey the Great") and Marcus Licinius Crassus, had left Rome to put down uprisings and found the populist party, attacking Sulla's constitution upon their return. In an attempt to forge an agreement with the populist party, both lieutenants promised to dismantle components of Sulla's constitution that the populists found disagreeable, in return for being elected consul. The two were elected in 70 BCE and held true to their word. Four years later, in 66 BCE, a movement to use peaceful means to address the plights of the various classes arose; however, after several failures in achieving their goals, the movement, headed by Lucius Sergius Catilina and based in Faesulae, a hotbed of agrarian agitation, decided to march to Rome and instigate an uprising. Marcus Tullius Cicero, the consul at the time, intercepted messages regarding recruitment and plans, leading the Senate to authorize the assassination of many Catilinarian conspirators in Rome, an action that was seen as stemming from dubious authority. This effectively disrupted the conspiracy and discredited the populist party, in turn repairing the image of the Senate, which had come to be seen as weak and not worthy of such violent attack.

First Triumvirate

In 62 BCE, Pompey returned from campaigning in Asia to find that the Senate, elated by its successes against the Catiline conspirators, was unwilling to ratify any of Pompey's arrangements, leaving Pompey powerless. Julius Caesar returned from his governorship in Spain a year later and, along with Crassus, established a private agreement with Pompey known as the First Triumvirate. Under the terms of this agreement, Pompey's arrangements would be ratified and Caesar would be elected consul in 59 BCE, subsequently serving as governor of Gaul for five years. Crassus was promised the consulship later.

When Caesar became consul, he saw the passage of Pompey's arrangements through the Senate, at times using violent means to ensure their passage. Caesar also facilitated the election of patrician Publius Clodius Pulcher to the tribunate in 58 BCE, and Clodius sidelined Caesar's senatorial opponents, Cato and Cicero. Clodius eventually formed armed gangs that terrorized Rome and began to attack Pompey's followers, who formed counter-gangs in response, marking the end of the political alliance between Pompey and Caeser. Though the triumvirate was briefly renewed in the face of political opposition for the consulship from Domitius Ahenobarbus, Crassus's death during an expedition against the Kingdom of Parthia, and the death of Pompey's wife, Julia, who was also Caesar's daughter, severed any remaining bonds between Pompey and Caesar.

Beginning in the summer of 54 BCE, a wave of political corruption and violence swept Rome, reaching a climax in January 52 BCE, when Clodius was murdered in a gang war. Caesar presented an ultimatum to the Senate on January 1, 49 BCE, which was ultimately rejected. Subsequently, a resolution was passed that declared that if Caesar did not lay down his arms by July, he would be considered an enemy of the Republic. The senators adopted Pompey as their champion, and on January 7, Pompey was granted dictatorial powers over the Republic by the Senate. Pompey's army, however, was composed mainly of untested conscripts, and on January 10, Caesar crossed the Rubicon with his more experienced forces in defiance of Roman laws, and marched towards Rome. Pompey, the consuls, and the Senate all abandoned Rome for Greece, in the face of Caeser's rapidly advancing forces, and Caesar entered the city unopposed.

Attributions

CC licensed content, Specific attribution

- Roman Republic. **Provided by**: Wikipedia. **Located at**: https://en.wikipedia.org/wiki/Roman_Republic. **License**: *CC BY-SA: Attribution-ShareAlike*
- Interrex. **Provided by**: Wikipedia. **Located at**: https://en.wikipedia.org/wiki/Interrex. **License**: *CC BY-SA: Attribution-ShareAlike*
- Overthrow of the Roman monarchy. **Provided by**: Wikipedia. **Located at**: https://en.wikipedia.org/wiki/Overthrow_of_the_Roman_monarchy. **License**: *CC BY-SA: Attribution-ShareAlike*
- Roman Kingdom. **Provided by**: Wikipedia. **Located at**: https://en.wikipedia.org/wiki/Roman_Kingdom. **License**: *CC BY-SA: Attribution-ShareAlike*
- N03Brutus-u-Lucretia.jpg. **Provided by**: Wikipedia. **Located at**: https://en.wikipedia.org/wiki/File:N03Brutus-u-Lucretia.jpg. **License**: *Public Domain: No Known Copyright*
- Tizian_094.jpg. **Provided by**: Wikimedia. **Located at**: https://commons.wikimedia.org/wiki/File:Tizian_094.jpg. **License**: *Public Domain: No Known Copyright*
- Senate of the Roman Republic. **Provided by**: Wikipedia. **Located at**: http://en.wikipedia.org/wiki/Senate_of_the_Roman_Republic. **License**: *CC BY-SA: Attribution-ShareAlike*
- Constitution of the Roman Republic. **Provided by**: Wikipedia. **Located at**: http://en.wikipedia.org/wiki/Constitution_of_the_Roman_Republic. **License**: *CC BY-SA: Attribution-ShareAlike*
- N03Brutus-u-Lucretia.jpg. **Provided by**: Wikipedia. **Located at**: https://en.wikipedia.org/wiki/File:N03Brutus-u-Lucretia.jpg. **License**: *Public Domain: No Known Copyright*
- Tizian_094.jpg. **Provided by**: Wikimedia. **Located at**: https://commons.wikimedia.org/wiki/File:Tizian_094.jpg. **License**: *Public*

Domain: No Known Copyright

- Curia Iulia - The Roman Senate House. **Provided by**: Wikipedia. **Located at**: http://en.wikipedia.org/wiki/Roman_Senate%23mediaviewer/File:Curia_Iulia.JPG. **License**: *CC BY-SA: Attribution-ShareAlike*
- Roman SPQR Banner. **Provided by**: Wikipedia. **Located at**: http://en.wikipedia.org/wiki/Spqr%23mediaviewer/File:Roman_SPQR_banner.svg. **License**: *CC BY: Attribution*
- Roman Republic. **Provided by**: Wikipedia. **Located at**: https://en.wikipedia.org/wiki/Roman_Republic. **License**: *CC BY-SA: Attribution-ShareAlike*
- Social class in ancient Rome. **Provided by**: Wikipedia. **Located at**: https://en.wikipedia.org/wiki/Social_class_in_ancient_Rome. **License**: *CC BY-SA: Attribution-ShareAlike*
- Conflict of the Orders. **Provided by**: Wikipedia. **Located at**: https://en.wikipedia.org/wiki/Conflict_of_the_Orders **License**: *CC BY-SA: Attribution-ShareAlike*
- Lex Licinia Sextia. **Provided by**: Wikipedia. **Located at**: https://en.wikipedia.org/wiki/Lex_Licinia_Sextia. **License**: *CC BY-SA: Attribution-ShareAlike*
- Lex Trebonia (448 BC). **Provided by**: Wikipedia. **Located at**: https://en.wikipedia.org/wiki/Lex_Trebonia_(448_BC). **License**: *CC BY-SA: Attribution-ShareAlike*
- N03Brutus-u-Lucretia.jpg. **Provided by**: Wikipedia. **Located at**: https://en.wikipedia.org/wiki/File:N03Brutus-u-Lucretia.jpg. **License**: *Public Domain: No Known Copyright*
- Tizian_094.jpg. **Provided by**: Wikimedia. **Located at**: https://commons.wikimedia.org/wiki/File:Tizian_094.jpg. **License**: *Public Domain: No Known Copyright*
- Curia Iulia - The Roman Senate House. **Provided by**: Wikipedia. **Located at**: http://en.wikipedia.org/wiki/Roman_Senate%23mediaviewer/File:Curia_Iulia.JPG. **License**: *CC BY-SA: Attribution-ShareAlike*
- Roman SPQR Banner. **Provided by**: Wikipedia. **Located at**: http://en.wikipedia.org/wiki/Spqr%23mediaviewer/File:Roman_SPQR_banner.svg. **License**: *CC BY: Attribution*
- Gaius_Gracchus_Tribune_of_the_People.jpg. **Provided by**: Wikimedia. **Located at**: https://commons.wikimedia.org/wiki/File:Gaius_Gracchus_Tribune_of_the_People.jpg. **License**: *Public Domain: No Known Copyright*
- Roman art. **Provided by**: Wikipedia. **Located at**: https://en.wikipedia.org/wiki/Roman_art. **License**: *CC BY-SA: Attribution-ShareAlike*
- Roman Republic: The arts. **Provided by**: Wikipedia. **Located at**: https://en.wikipedia.org/wiki/Roman_Republic#The_arts. **License**: *CC BY-SA: Attribution-ShareAlike*
- N03Brutus-u-Lucretia.jpg. **Provided by**: Wikipedia. **Located at**: https://en.wikipedia.org/wiki/File:N03Brutus-u-Lucretia.jpg. **License**: *Public Domain: No Known Copyright*
- Tizian_094.jpg. **Provided by**: Wikimedia. **Located at**: https://commons.wikimedia.org/wiki/File:Tizian_094.jpg. **License**: *Public Domain: No Known Copyright*
- Curia Iulia - The Roman Senate House. **Provided by**: Wikipedia. **Located at**: http://en.wikipedia.org/wiki/Roman_Senate%23mediaviewer/File:Curia_Iulia.JPG. **License**: *CC BY-SA: Attribution-ShareAlike*
- Roman SPQR Banner. **Provided by**: Wikipedia. **Located at**: http://en.wikipedia.org/wiki/Spqr%23mediaviewer/File:Roman_SPQR_banner.svg. **License**: *CC BY: Attribution*
- Gaius_Gracchus_Tribune_of_the_People.jpg. **Provided by**: Wikimedia. **Located at**: https://commons.wikimedia.org/wiki/File:Gaius_Gracchus_Tribune_of_the_People.jpg. **License**: *Public Domain: No Known Copyright*
- Pompeius. **Provided by**: Wikimedia Commons. **Located at**: http://commons.wikimedia.org/wiki/File:Pompejus.JPG. **License**: *Public Domain: No Known Copyright*
- Cicero - Musei Capitolini. **Provided by**: Wikipedia. **Located at**: http://en.wikipedia.org/wiki/Cicero%23mediaviewer/File:Cicero_-_Musei_Capitolini.JPG. **License**: *CC BY-SA: Attribution-ShareAlike*
- Old man Vatican. **Provided by**: Wikimedia Commons. **Located at**: http://commons.wikimedia.org/wiki/File:Old_man_vatican_pushkin01.jpg. **License**: *CC BY-SA: Attribution-ShareAlike*
- Punic Wars. **Provided by**: Wikipedia. **Located at**: http://en.wikipedia.org/wiki/Punic_Wars. **License**: *CC BY-SA: Attribution-ShareAlike*
- Roman Republic. **Provided by**: Wikipedia. **Located at**: http://en.wikipedia.org/wiki/Roman_Republic. **License**: *CC BY-SA: Attribution-ShareAlike*
- N03Brutus-u-Lucretia.jpg. **Provided by**: Wikipedia. **Located at**: https://en.wikipedia.org/wiki/File:N03Brutus-u-Lucretia.jpg. **License**: *Public Domain: No Known Copyright*
- Tizian_094.jpg. **Provided by**: Wikimedia. **Located at**: https://commons.wikimedia.org/wiki/File:Tizian_094.jpg. **License**: *Public*

Domain: No Known Copyright

- Curia Iulia - The Roman Senate House. **Provided by**: Wikipedia. **Located at**: http://en.wikipedia.org/wiki/Roman_Senate%23mediaviewer/File:Curia_Iulia.JPG. **License**: *CC BY-SA: Attribution-ShareAlike*
- Roman SPQR Banner. **Provided by**: Wikipedia. **Located at**: http://en.wikipedia.org/wiki/Spqr%23mediaviewer/File:Roman_SPQR_banner.svg. **License**: *CC BY: Attribution*
- Gaius_Gracchus_Tribune_of_the_People.jpg. **Provided by**: Wikimedia. **Located at**: https://commons.wikimedia.org/wiki/File:Gaius_Gracchus_Tribune_of_the_People.jpg. **License**: *Public Domain: No Known Copyright*
- Pompeius. **Provided by**: Wikimedia Commons. **Located at**: http://commons.wikimedia.org/wiki/File:Pompejus.JPG. **License**: *Public Domain: No Known Copyright*
- Cicero - Musei Capitolini. **Provided by**: Wikipedia. **Located at**: http://en.wikipedia.org/wiki/Cicero%23mediaviewer/File:Cicero_-_Musei_Capitolini.JPG. **License**: *CC BY-SA: Attribution-ShareAlike*
- Old man Vatican. **Provided by**: Wikimedia Commons. **Located at**: http://commons.wikimedia.org/wiki/File:Old_man_vatican_pushkin01.jpg. **License**: *CC BY-SA: Attribution-ShareAlike*
- Depiction of Hannibal. **Provided by**: Wikipedia. **Located at**: http://en.wikipedia.org/wiki/Punic_Wars%23mediaviewer/File:Hannibal3.jpg. **License**: *Public Domain: No Known Copyright*
- Roman Conquest of Italy. **Provided by**: Wikimedia. **Located at**: https://commons.wikimedia.org/wiki/File:Roman_conquest_of_Italy.PNG. **License**: *Public Domain: No Known Copyright*
- Roman Republic. **Provided by**: Wikipedia. **Located at**: https://en.wikipedia.org/wiki/Roman_Republic. **License**: *CC BY-SA: Attribution-ShareAlike*
- Plebs. **Provided by**: Wikipedia. **Located at**: http://en.wikipedia.org/wiki/Plebs. **License**: *CC BY-SA: Attribution-ShareAlike*
- Sulla. **Provided by**: Wikipedia. **Located at**: http://en.wikipedia.org/wiki/Sulla. **License**: *CC BY-SA: Attribution-ShareAlike*
- Crisis of the Roman Republic. **Provided by**: Wikipedia. **Located at**: http://en.wikipedia.org/wiki/Crisis_of_the_Roman_Republic. **License**: *CC BY-SA: Attribution-ShareAlike*
- Gracchi. **Provided by**: Wikipedia. **Located at**: http://en.wikipedia.org/wiki/Gracchi. **License**: *CC BY-SA: Attribution-ShareAlike*
- plebeian. **Provided by**: Wiktionary. **Located at**: http://en.wiktionary.org/wiki/plebeian. **License**: *CC BY-SA: Attribution-ShareAlike*
- patrician. **Provided by**: Wiktionary. **Located at**: http://en.wiktionary.org/wiki/patrician. **License**: *CC BY-SA: Attribution-ShareAlike*
- N03Brutus-u-Lucretia.jpg. **Provided by**: Wikipedia. **Located at**: https://en.wikipedia.org/wiki/File:N03Brutus-u-Lucretia.jpg. **License**: *Public Domain: No Known Copyright*
- Tizian_094.jpg. **Provided by**: Wikimedia. **Located at**: https://commons.wikimedia.org/wiki/File:Tizian_094.jpg. **License**: *Public Domain: No Known Copyright*
- Curia Iulia - The Roman Senate House. **Provided by**: Wikipedia. **Located at**: http://en.wikipedia.org/wiki/Roman_Senate%23mediaviewer/File:Curia_Iulia.JPG. **License**: *CC BY-SA: Attribution-ShareAlike*
- Roman SPQR Banner. **Provided by**: Wikipedia. **Located at**: http://en.wikipedia.org/wiki/Spqr%23mediaviewer/File:Roman_SPQR_banner.svg. **License**: *CC BY: Attribution*
- Gaius_Gracchus_Tribune_of_the_People.jpg. **Provided by**: Wikimedia. **Located at**: https://commons.wikimedia.org/wiki/File:Gaius_Gracchus_Tribune_of_the_People.jpg. **License**: *Public Domain: No Known Copyright*
- Pompeius. **Provided by**: Wikimedia Commons. **Located at**: http://commons.wikimedia.org/wiki/File:Pompejus.JPG. **License**: *Public Domain: No Known Copyright*
- Cicero - Musei Capitolini. **Provided by**: Wikipedia. **Located at**: http://en.wikipedia.org/wiki/Cicero%23mediaviewer/File:Cicero_-_Musei_Capitolini.JPG. **License**: *CC BY-SA: Attribution-ShareAlike*
- Old man Vatican. **Provided by**: Wikimedia Commons. **Located at**: http://commons.wikimedia.org/wiki/File:Old_man_vatican_pushkin01.jpg. **License**: *CC BY-SA: Attribution-ShareAlike*
- Depiction of Hannibal. **Provided by**: Wikipedia. **Located at**: http://en.wikipedia.org/wiki/Punic_Wars%23mediaviewer/File:Hannibal3.jpg. **License**: *Public Domain: No Known Copyright*
- Roman Conquest of Italy. **Provided by**: Wikimedia. **Located at**: https://commons.wikimedia.org/wiki/File:Roman_conquest_of_Italy.PNG. **License**: *Public Domain: No Known Copyright*
- Sulla Glyptothek Munich. **Provided by**: Wikipedia. **Located at**: http://en.wikipedia.org/wiki/Sulla%23mediaviewer/File:Sulla_Glyptothek_Munich_309.jpg. **License**: *Public Domain: No Known Copyright*
- Gaius Gracchus Tribune of the People. **Provided by**: Wikipedia. **Located at**: http://en.wikipedia.org/wiki/Gracchi%23mediaviewer/File:Gaius_Gracchus_Tribune_of_the_People.jpg. **License**: *Public Domain: No Known Copyright*

The Roman Empire

Julius Caesar

Julius Caesar was a late Republic statesman and general who waged civil war against the Roman Senate, defeating many patrician conservatives before he declared himself dictator.

Learning Objectives
Explain the rise of Julius Caesar and his various successes

Key Takeaways

Key Points

- In 60 BCE, Julius Caesar, Marcus Licinius Crassus, and Gnaeus Pompeius Magnus (Pompey the Great) formed a political alliance, known as the First Triumvirate, that was to dominate Roman politics for several years, though their populist tactics were opposed by the conservative Senate.

- Caesar enjoyed great success as commander in the Gallic Wars. Upon conclusion of the wars, he refused to return to Rome as ordered by the Senate, and instead, crossed the Rubicon in 49 BCE with a legion, entering Roman territory under arms.

- Caesar fought in a civil war against his old colleague, Pompey, who had aligned himself with conservative interests in the Senate. Caesar quickly defeated his rival and many other Senate conservatives who had previously opposed him.

- With most of his enemies gone, Caesar installed himself as dictator in perpetuity. As dictator, he instituted a series of reforms and, most notably, created the Julian calendar.

- Caesar was assassinated in 44 BCE by his remaining enemies in the Senate, throwing Rome into another period of chaos and civil war.

> ### Key Terms
>
> - **dictator**: During Caesar's time, in the late Roman Republic, ruler for life. In the early Republic, by contrast, a dictator was a general appointed by the Senate, who served temporarily during a national emergency.
> - **Julius Caesar**: A Roman general, statesman, consul, and author, who played a critical role in the events that led to the demise of the Roman Republic and the rise of the Roman Empire.
> - **Pompey**: A military and political leader of the late Roman Republic, who represented the Roman Senate in a civil war against Julius Caesar.

Gaius Julius Caesar was a Roman general, statesman, consul, and notable author of Latin prose. He played a critical role in the events that led to the demise of the Roman Republic and the rise of the Roman Empire. In 60 BCE, Caesar, Marcus Licinius Crassus, and Gnaeus Pompeius Magnus (Pompey the Great) formed a political alliance, known as the First Triumvirate, that was to dominate Roman politics for several years. Caesar made the initial overtures that led to the informal alliance. An acclaimed military commander who had also served in a variety of political offices, Caesar sought election as consul in 59 BCE, along with two other candidates. The election was particularly contentious, with corruption occurring on all sides. Caesar won, as well as conservative Marcus Bibulus, but saw that he could further his political influence with Crassus and Pompey. Their attempts to amass power through populist tactics were opposed by the conservative ruling class within the Roman Senate, among them Cato the Younger and Cicero. Meanwhile, Caesar's victories in the Gallic Wars, completed by 51 BCE, extended Rome's territory to the English Channel and the Rhine River. Caesar became the first Roman general to cross both when he built a bridge across the Rhine and conducted the first invasion of Britain.

These achievements granted Caesar unmatched military power and threatened to eclipse the standing of his colleague, Pompey, who had realigned himself with the Senate after the death of Crassus in 53 BCE. With the Gallic Wars concluded, the Senate ordered Caesar to step down from his military command and return to Rome. Caesar refused and marked his defiance in 49 BCE by crossing the Rubicon (shallow river in northern Italy) with a legion. In doing so, he deliberately broke the law on imperium and engaged in an open act of insurrection and treason. Civil War ensued, with Pompey representing the Roman Senate forces against Caesar, but Caesar quickly defeated Pompey in 48 BCE, and dispatched Pompey's supporters in the following year. During this time, many staunch Senate conservatives, such as Cato the Younger, were either killed or committed suicide, thereby greatly decreasing the number of optimates in Rome.

Caesar as Dictator

Bust of Julius Caesar: *Gaius Julius Caesar was a Roman general, statesman, consul, and notable author of Latin prose.*

After assuming control of the government upon the defeat of his enemies in 45 BCE, Caesar began a program of social and governmental reforms that included the creation of the Julian calendar. He centralized the bureaucracy of the Republic and eventually proclaimed himself "dictator in perpetuity." It is important to note that Caesar did not declare himself *rex* (king), but instead, claimed the title of dictator. Contrary to the negative connotations that the modern use of the word evokes, the Roman dictator was appointed by the Senate during times of emergency as a unilateral decision-maker who could act more quickly than the usual bureaucratic processes that the Republican government would allow. Upon bringing the Roman state out of trouble, the dictator would then resign and restore power back to the Senate. Thus, Caesar's declaration ostensibly remained within the Republican framework of power, though the huge amounts of power he had gathered for himself in practice set him up similar to a monarch.

Caesar used his powers to fill the Senate with his own partisans. He also increased the number of magistrates who were elected each year, which created a large pool of experienced magistrates and allowed Caesar to reward his supporters. He used his powers to appoint many new senators, which eventually raised the Senate's membership to 900. All the appointments were of his own partisans, which robbed the senatorial aristocracy of its prestige and made the Senate increasingly subservient to him. To minimize the risk that another general might attempt to challenge him, Caesar passed a law that subjected governors to term limits. All of these changes watered down the power of the Senate, which infuriated those used to aristocratic privilege. Such anger proved to be fuel for Caesar's eventual assassination.

Despite the defeat of most of his conservative enemies, however, underlying political conflicts had not been resolved. On the Ides of March (March 15) 44 BCE, Caesar was scheduled to appear at a session of the Senate, and a group of senators led by Marcus Junius Brutus and Gaius Cassius Longinus conspired to assassinate him. Though some of his assassins may have had ulterior personal vendettas against Caesar, Brutus is said to have acted out of concern for the Republic in the face of what he considered to be a monarchical tyrant. Mark Antony, one of Caesar's generals and administrator of Italy during Caesar's campaigns abroad, learned such a plan existed the night before, and attempted to intercept Caesar, but the plotters anticipated this and arranged to meet him outside the site of the session and detain him him there. Caesar was stabbed 23 times and lay dead on the ground for some time before officials removed his body.

A new series of civil wars broke out following Caesar's assassination, and the constitutional government of the Republic was never restored. Caesar's adopted heir, Octavian, later known as Augustus, rose to sole power, and the era of the Roman Empire began.

Founding of the Roman Empire

Augustus rose to power after Julius Caesar's assassination, through a series of political and military maneuvers, eventually establishing himself as the first emperor of Rome.

Learning Objectives

Explain the key features of Augustus's reign and the reasons for its successes

Key Takeaways

Key Points

- Following the assassination of his maternal great-uncle Julius Caesar in 44 BCE, Caesar's will named Octavian as his adopted son and heir when Octavian was only 19 years old.
- By ingratiating himself with his father's legions, Octavian was able to fulfill the military demands of the Roman Senate. He quickly gained both power and prestige and formed the Second Triumvirate with Antony and Lepidus in 43 BCE.
- By 31 BCE, Octavian had emerged as the sole ruler of Rome, upon the political and military defeat of the two other triumvirs.

> *Key Terms*
>
> - **Mark Antony**: Julius Caesar's right hand man, and a member of the Second Triumvirate. He was eventually defeated by Octavian at the Battle of Actium in 31 BCE
> - **Augustus**: The founder of the Roman Empire, known as Octavian during his early years and during his rise to power.

Augustus is regarded by many scholars as the founder and first emperor of the Roman Empire. He ruled from 27 BCE until his death in 14 CE.

Rise to Power

Augustus was born Gaius Octavius, and in his early years was known as Octavian. He was from an old and wealthy equestrian branch of the plebeian Octavii family. Following the assassination of his maternal great-uncle, Julius Caesar, in 44 BCE, Caesar's will named Octavian as his adopted son and heir when Octavian was only 19 years old. The young Octavian quickly took advantage of the situation and ingratiated himself with both the Roman people and his adoptive father's legions, thereby elevating his status and importance within Rome. Octavian found Mark Antony, Julius Caesar's former colleague and the current consul of Rome, in an uneasy truce with Caesar's assassins, who had been granted general amnesty for their part in the plot. Nonetheless, Antony eventually succeeded in driving most of them out of Rome, using Caesar's eulogy as an opportunity to mount public opinion against the assassins.

Mark Antony began amassing political support, and Octavian set about rivaling it. Eventually, many Caesarian sympathizers began to view Octavian as the lesser evil of the two. Octavian allied himself with optimate factions, despite their opposition to Caesar when he was alive. The optimate orator, Marcus Tullius Cicero, began attacking Antony in a series of speeches, portraying him as a threat to the republican order of Rome. As public opinion against him mounted, Antony fled to Cisalpine Gaul at the end of his consular year.

Octavian further established himself both politically and militarily in the following months. He was declared a senator and granted the power of military command, *imperium*, in 43 BCE, and was further able to leverage his successes to obtain the vacant consulships left by the two defeated consuls of that year.

Octavian eventually reached an uneasy truce with Mark Antony and Marcus Lepidus in October 43 BCE, and together, the three formed the Second Triumvirate to defeat the assassins of Caesar. Following their victory against Brutus at Phillipi, the Triumvirate divided the Roman Republic among themselves and ruled as military dictators. Relations within the Triumvirate were strained as the various members sought greater political power. Civil war between Antony and Octavian was averted in 40 BCE, when Antony married Octavian's sister, Octavia Minor. Despite his marriage, Antony continued a love affair with Cleopatra, the former lover of Caesar and queen of Egypt, further straining political ties to Rome. Octavian used Antony's relationship with Cleopatra to his own advantage, portraying Antony as less committed to Rome. With Lepidus expelled in 36 BCE, the Triumvirate finally disintegrated in the year 33. Finally, disagreements between Octavian and Antony erupted into civil war in the year 31 BCE.

The Roman Senate, at Octavian's direction, declared war on Cleopatra's regime in Egypt and proclaimed Antony a traitor. Antony was defeated by Octavian at the naval Battle of Actium the same year. Defeated, Antony fled with Cleopatra to Alexandria where they both committed suicide. With Antony dead, Octavian was left as the undisputed master of the Roman world. Octavian would assume the title Augustus, and reign as the first Roman Emperor.

Augustus of Prima Porta: *The statue of Augustus of Prima Porta is perhaps one of the best known images of the Emperor Augustus. It portrays the emperor as perpetually youthful, and depicts many of the key propaganda messages that Augustus put forth during his time as emperor.*

The Pax Romana

The Pax Romana, which began under Augustus, was a 200-year period of peace in which Rome experienced minimal expansion by military forces.

Learning Objectives

Describe the key reasons for and characteristics of the Pax Romana

Key Takeaways

Key Points

- The Pax Romana was established under Augustus, and for that reason it is sometimes referred to as the Pax Augusta.
- Augustus closed the Gates of Janus three times to signify the onset of peace: in 29 BCE, 25 BCE, and 13 BCE, likely in conjunction with the Ara Pacis ceremony.
- The Romans regarded peace not as an absence of war, but as the rare situation that existed when all opponents had been beaten down and lost the ability to resist. Thus, Augustus had to persuade Romans that the prosperity they could achieve in the absence of warfare was better for the Empire than the potential wealth and honor acquired when fighting a risky war.
- The Ara Pacis is a prime example of the propaganda Augustus employed to promote the Pax Romana, and depicts images of Roman gods and the city of Rome personified amidst wealth and prosperity.

Key Terms

- **Ara Pacis Augustae**: The Altar of Augustan Peace, a sacrificial altar that displays imagery of the peace and prosperity Augustus achieved during the Pax Romana.
- **Pax Romana**: The long period of relative peace and minimal expansion by military force experienced by the Roman Empire in the 1st and 2nd centuries CE. Also sometimes known as the Pax Augusta.

Augustus's Constitutional Reforms

After the demise of the Second Triumvirate, Augustus restored the outward facade of the free Republic with governmental power vested in the Roman
Senate, the executive magistrates, and the legislative assemblies. In reality, however, he retained his autocratic power over the Republic as a military dictator. By law, Augustus held powers granted to him for life

by the Senate, including supreme military command and those of tribune and censor. It took several years for Augustus to develop the framework within which a formally republican state could be led under his sole rule.

Augustus passed a series of laws between the years 30 and 2 BCE that transformed the constitution of the Roman Republic into the constitution of the Roman Empire. During this time, Augustus reformed the Roman system of taxation, developed networks of roads with an official courier system, established a standing army, established the Praetorian Guard, created official police and fire-fighting services for Rome, and rebuilt much of the city during his reign.

First Settlement

During the First Settlement, Augustus modified the Roman political system to make it more palatable to the senatorial classes, eschewing the open authoritarianism exhibited by Julius Caesar and Mark Anthony. In 28 BCE, in a calculated move, Augustus eradicated the emergency powers he held as dictator and returned all powers and provinces to the Senate and the Roman people. Members of the Senate were unhappy with this prospect, and in order to appease them, Augustus agreed to a ten-year extension of responsibilities over disorderly provinces. As a result of this, Augustus retained *imperium* over the provinces where the majority of Rome's soldiers were stationed. Augustus also rejected monarchical titles, instead calling himself *princeps civitatis* ("First Citizen"). The resulting constitutional framework became known as the Principate, the first phase of the Roman Empire.

At this time, Augustus was given honorifics that made his full name *Imperator Caesar divi filius Augustus*. *Imperator* stressed military power and victory and emphasized his role as commander-in-chief. *Divi filius* roughly translates to "son of the divine," enhancing his legitimacy as ruler without deifying him completely. The use of Caesar provided a link between himself and Julius Caesar, who was still very popular among lower classes. Finally, the name Augustus raised associations to Rome's illustrious and majestic traditions, without creating heavy authoritarian overtones.

By the end of the first settlement, Augustus was in an ideal political position. Although he no longer held dictatorial powers, he had created an identity of such influence that authority followed naturally.

Second Settlement

In the wake of Augustus's poor health, a second settlement was announced in 23 BCE. During this time, Augustus outwardly appeared to rein
in his constitutional powers, but really continued to extend his dominion throughout the Empire. Augustus renounced his ten-year consulship, but in return, secured the following concessions for himself.

- A seat on the consuls's platform at the front of the Curia
- The right to speak first in a Senate meeting, or *ius primae relationis*
- The right to summon a meeting of the Senate, which was a useful tool for policy making
- Care of Rome's grain supply, or *cura annonae*, which gave him sweeping patronage powers over the plebs

Augustus was also granted the role of *tribunicia potestas*, which enabled him to act as the guardian of the citizens of Rome. This position came with a number of benefits, including the right to propose laws to the Senate whenever he wanted, veto power of laws, and the ability to grant amnesty to any citizen accused of a crime. Though the role of *tribunicia potestas* effectively gave Augustus legislative supremacy, it also had many positive connotations hearkening back to the Republic, making Augustus's position less offensive to the aristocracy. Beyond Rome, Augustus was granted *maius imperium*, meaning greater (proconsular) power. This position enabled him to effectively override the orders of any other provincial governor in the Roman Empire, in addition to governing his own provinces and armies.

Augustus and the Pax Romana

The *Pax Romana* (Latin for "Roman peace") was a long period of relative peace and minimal expansion by military forces experienced by the Roman Empire in the 1st and 2nd centuries CE. Since this period was initiated during
Augustus's reign, it is sometimes called Pax Augusta. Its span was approximately 206 years (27 BCE to 180 CE).

The Pax Romana started after Augustus, then Octavian, met and defeated Mark Antony in the Battle of Actium in 31 BCE. Augustus created a junta of the greatest military magnates and gave himself the titular honor. By binding together these leading magnates into a single title, he eliminated the prospect of civil war. The Pax Romana was not immediate, despite the end of the civil war, because fighting continued in Hispania and in the Alps.

Despite continuous wars of imperial expansion on the Empire's frontiers and one year-long civil war over the imperial succession, the Roman world was largely free from large-scale conflict for more than two centuries. Augustus dramatically enlarged the Empire, annexing Egypt, Dalmatia, Pannonia, Noricum, and Raetia, expanded possessions in Africa as well as into Germania, and completed the conquest of Hispania. Beyond Rome's frontiers, he secured the Empire with a buffer region of client states, and made peace with the troublesome Parthian Empire through diplomacy.

Augustus closed the Gates of Janus (the set of gates to the Temple of Janus, which was closed in times of peace and opened in times of war) three times. The first time was in 29 BCE and the second in 25 BCE. The third closure is undocumented, but scholars have persuasively dated the event to 13 BCE during the Ara Pacis ceremony, which was held after Augustus and Agrippa jointly returned from pacifying the provinces.

Augustus faced some trouble making peace an acceptable mode of life for the Romans, who had been at war with one power or another continuously for 200 years prior to this period. The Romans regarded peace not as an absence of war, but the rare situation that existed when all opponents had been beaten down and lost the ability to resist. Augustus's challenge was to persuade Romans that the prosperity they could achieve in the absence of war was better for the Empire than the potential wealth and honor acquired from fighting. Augustus succeeded by means of skillful propaganda. Subsequent emperors followed his lead, sometimes producing lavish ceremonies to close the Gates of Janus, issuing coins with Pax on the reverse, and patronizing literature extolling the benefits of the Pax Romana.

The Ara Pacis Augustae

The Ara Pacis Augustae, or Altar of Augustan Peace, is one of the best examples of Augustan artistic propaganda and the prime symbol of the new Pax Romana. It was commissioned by the Senate in 13 BCE to honor the peace and bounty established by Augustus following his return from Spain and Gaul. The theme of peace is seen most notably in the east and west walls of the Ara Pacis, each of which had two panels, although only small fragments remain for one panel on each side. On the east side sits an unidentified goddess presumed by scholars to be Tellus, Venus, or Peace within an allegorical scene of prosperity and fertility. Twins sit on her lap along with a cornucopia of fruits. Personifications of the wind and sea surround her, each riding on a bird or a sea monster. Beneath the women rests a bull and lamb, both sacrificial animals, and flowering plants fill the empty space. The nearly incomplete second eastern panel appears to depict a female warrior, possibly Roma, amid the spoils of conquest.

The Tellus Mater Panel of the Ara Pacis: *The eastern wall of the Ara Pacis, which depicts the Tellus Mater surrounded by symbols of fertility and prosperity.*

Augustus died in 14 CE at the age of 75. He may have died from natural causes, although unconfirmed rumors swirled that his wife Livia poisoned him. His adopted son (also stepson and former son-in-law), Tiberius, succeeded him to the throne.

The Julio-Claudian Emperors

The Julio-Claudian emperors expanded the boundaries of the Roman Empire and engaged in ambitious construction projects. However, they were met with mixed public reception due to their unique ruling methods.

Learning Objectives

Describe the reigns of the emperors who followed Augustus

Key Takeaways

Key Points

- Tiberius was the second emperor of the Roman Empire, and was considered one of Rome's greatest generals.
- Tiberius conquered Pannonia, Dalmatia, Raetia, and temporarily, parts of Germania. His conquests laid the foundations for the northern frontier.
- When Tiberius died on March 16, 37 CE, his estate and titles were left to Caligula and Tiberius's grandson, Gemellus. However, Caligula's first act as Princeps was to to void Tiberius's will and have Gemellus executed.
- Although Caligula is described as a noble and moderate ruler during the first six months of his reign, sources portray him as a cruel and sadistic tyrant, immediately thereafter.
- In 38 CE, Caligula focused his attention on political and public reform; however, by 39 CE, a financial crisis had emerged as a result of Caligula's use of political payments, which had overextended the state's treasury. Despite financial difficulties, Caligula began a number of construction projects during this time.
- In 41 CE, Caligula was assassinated as part of a conspiracy by officers of the Praetorian Guard, senators, and courtiers.
- Claudius, the fourth emperor of the Roman Empire, was the first Roman Emperor to be born outside of Italy.
- Despite his lack of experience, Claudius was an able and efficient administrator, as well as an ambitious builder. He constructed many roads, aqueducts, and canals across the Empire.
- Claudius's appointment as emperor by the Praetorian Guard damaged his reputation. This was amplified when Claudius became the first emperor to resort to bribery as a means to secure army loyalty. Claudius also rewarded the Praetorian Guard that had named him emperor with 15,000 sesterces.

Key Terms

- **Praetorian Guard**: A force of bodyguards used by the Roman emperors. They also served as secret police, and participated in wars.
- **Julio-Claudian dynasty**: The first five Roman emperors who ruled the Roman Empire, including Augustus, Tiberius, Caligula, Claudius, and Nero.

Tiberius

Tiberius was the second emperor of the Roman Empire and reigned from 14 to 37 CE. The previous emperor, Augustus, was his stepfather; this officially made him a Julian. However, his biological father was Tiberius Claudius Nero, making him a Claudian by birth. Subsequent emperors would continue the blended dynasty of both families for the next 30 years, leading historians to name it the Julio-Claudian Dynasty. Tiberius is also the grand-uncle of Caligula, his successor, the paternal uncle of Claudius, and the great-grand uncle of Nero.

Tiberius is considered one of Rome's greatest generals. During his reign, he conquered Pannonia, Dalmatia, Raetia, and temporarily, parts of Germania. His conquests laid the foundations for the northern frontier. However, he was known by contemporaries to be dark, reclusive, and somber—a ruler who never really wanted to be emperor. The tone was set early in his reign when the Senate convened to validate his position as Princeps. During the proceedings, Tiberius attempted to play the part of the reluctant public servant, but came across as derisive and obstructive. His direct orders appeared vague, inspiring more debate than action and leaving the Senate to act on its own. After the death of Tiberius's son in 23 CE, the emperor became even more reclusive, leaving the administration largely in the hands of his unscrupulous Praetorian Prefects.

Tiberius: *Tiberius, Romisch-Germanisches Museum, Cologne*

Caligula

When Tiberius died on March 16, 37 CE, his estate and titles were left to Caligula and Tiberius's grandson, Gemellus, with the intention that they would rule as joint heirs. However, Caligula's first act as Princeps was to to void Tiberius's will and have Gemellus executed. When Tiberius died, he had not been well liked. Caligula, on the other hand, was almost universally heralded upon his assumption of the throne. There are few surviving sources on Caligula's reign. Caligula's first acts as emperor were generous in spirit, but political in nature. He granted bonuses to the military, including the Praetorian Guard, city troops, and the army outside of Italy. He destroyed Tiberius's treason papers and declared that treason trials would no longer continue as a practice, even going so far as to recall those who had already been sent into exile for treason. He also helped those who had been adversely affected by the imperial tax system, banished certain sexual deviants, and put on large public spectacles, such as gladiatorial games, for the common people.

Although he is described as a noble and moderate ruler during the first six months of his reign, sources portray him as a cruel and sadistic tyrant immediately thereafter. The transitional point seems to center around an illness Caligula experienced in October of 37 CE. It is unclear whether the incident was merely an illness, or if Caligula had been poisoned. Either way, following the incident, the young emperor began dealing with what he considered to be serious threats, by killing or exiling those who were close to him. During the remainder of his reign, he worked to increase the personal power of the emperor during his short reign, and devoted much of his attention to ambitious construction projects and luxurious dwellings for himself.

In 38 CE, Caligula focused his attention on political and public reform. He published the accounts of public funds, which had not been done under Tiberius's reign, provided aid to those who lost property in fires, and abolished certain taxes. He also allowed new members into the equestrian and senatorial orders. Perhaps most significantly, he restored the practice of democratic elections, which delighted much of the public but was a cause for concern among the aristocracy.

By 39 CE, a financial crisis had emerged as a result of Caligula's use of political payments, which had overextended the state's treasury. In order to to restock the treasury, Caligula began falsely accusing, fining, and even killing individuals in order to seize their estates. He also asked the public to lend the state money, and raised taxes on lawsuits, weddings, and prostitution, as well as auctioning the lives of gladiators at shows. Wills that left items to Tiberius were also reinterpreted as having left said items to Caligula. Centurions who had acquired property by plunder were also forced to turn over their spoils to the state, and highway commissioners were accused of incompetence and embezzlement and forced to repay money that they might not have taken in the first place. Around the same time, a brief famine occurred, possibly as a result of the financial crisis, though its causes remain unclear.

Despite financial difficulties, Caligula began a number of construction projects during this time. He initiated the construction of two aqueducts in Rome, Awua Claudia and Anio Novus, which were considered contemporary engineering marvels. In 39 CE, he ordered the construction of a temporary floating bridge between the resort of Baiae and the port of Puteoli, which rivaled the bridge Persian king Xerxes had constructed across the Hellespont. Caligula had two large ships constructed for himself that were among the largest constructed in the ancient world. The larger of the two was essentially an elaborate floating palace with marble floors and plumbing. He also improved the harbors at Rhegium and Sicily, which allowed for increased grain imports from Egypt, possibly in response to the famine Rome experienced.

During his reign, the Empire annexed the Kingdom of Mauretania as a province. Mauretania had previously been a client kingdom ruled by Ptolemy of Mauretania. Details on how and why Mauretania was ultimately annexed remain unclear. Ptolemy was had been invited to Rome by Caligula and suddenly executed in what was seemingly a personal political move, rather than a calculated response to military of economic needs. However, Roman possession of Mauretania ultimately proved to be a boon to the territory, as the subsequent rebellion of Tacfarinas demonstrated how exposed the African Proconsularis was on its western borders. There also was a northern campaign to Britannia that was aborted during Caligula's reign, though there is not a cohesive narrative of the event.

In 39 CE, relations between Caligula and the Senate deteriorated. Caligula ordered a new set of treason investigations and trials, replacing the consul and putting a number of senators to death. Many other senators were reportedly treated in a degrading fashion and humiliated by Caligula. In 41 CE, Caligula was assassinated as part of a conspiracy by officers of the Praetorian Guard, senators, and courtiers. The conspirators used the assassination as an opportunity to re-institute the Republic, but were ultimately unsuccessful.

Caligula: *Emperor Caligula, Ny Carlsberg Glyptotek.*

Claudius

Claudius, the fourth emperor of the Roman Empire, was the first Roman Emperor to be born outside of Italy. He was afflicted with a limp and slight deafness, which caused his family to ostracize him and exclude him from public office until he shared the consulship with his nephew, Caligula, in 37 CE. Due to Claudius's afflictions, it is likely he was spared from the many purges of Tiberius and Caligula's reigns. As a result, Claudius was declared Emperor by the Praetorian Guard after Caligula's assassination, due to his position as the last man in the Julio-Claudian line.

Despite his lack of experience, Claudius was an able and efficient administrator, as well as an ambitious builder; he constructed many roads, aqueducts, and canals across the Empire. His reign also saw the beginning of the conquest of Britain. Additionally, Claudius presided over many public trials, and issued up to 20 edicts a day. However, in spite of his capable rule, Claudius continued to be viewed as vulnerable by the Roman nobility throughout his reign, forcing Claudius to constantly defend his position. He did so by emphasizing his place within the Julio-Claudian family, dropping the cognomen, Nero, from his name, and replacing it with Caesar.

Nonetheless, his appointment as emperor by the Praetorian Guard caused damage to his reputation, and this was amplified when Claudius became the first emperor to resort to bribery as a means to secure army loyalty. Claudius also rewarded the Praetorian Guard that had named him emperor with 15,000 sesterces.

Claudius: Bust of Emperor Claudius.

The Last Julio-Claudian Emperors

Nero's consolidation of personal power led to rebellion, civil war, and a year-long period of upheaval, during which four separate emperors ruled Rome.

Learning Objectives

Explain how Nero and other factors contributed to the fall of the Julio-Claudian Dynasty

Key Takeaways

Key Points

- Nero reigned as Roman Emperor from 54 to 68 CE, and was the last emperor in the Julio-Claudian Dynasty.
- Very early in Nero's rule, problems arose, due to his mother, Agrippina the Younger's competition for influence with Nero's two main advisers, Seneca and Burrus.
- Nero minimized the influence of all of his advisers and effectively eliminating all rivals to his throne. He also slowly removed power from the Senate, despite having promised to grant them with powers equivalent to those they had under republican rule.
- In March 68, Gaius Gulius Vindex, the governor of Gallia Lugdunensis, rebelled against Nero's tax policies and called upon the support of Servius Sulpicius Galba, the governor of Hispania Tarraconensis, who not only joined the rebellion, but also declared himself emperor in opposition to Nero. Galba would become the first emperor in what was known as the Year of the Four Emperors.
- Vespasian was the fourth and final emperor to rule in the year 69 CE, and established the stable Flavian Dynasty, that was to succeed the Julio-Claudians.

Key Terms

- **Flavian dynasty**: A Roman imperial dynasty that ruled the Roman Empire from 69 to 96 CE, encompassing the reigns of Vespasian and his two sons, Titus and Domitian.
- **Julio-Claudian dynasty**: The first five Roman emperors who ruled the Roman Empire, including Augustus, Tiberius, Caligula, Claudius, and Nero.
- **Praetorian Guard**: A force of bodyguards used by the Roman emperors. They also served as secret police and participated in wars.

Nero

Nero reigned as Roman Emperor from 54 to 68 CE, and was the last emperor in the Julio-Claudian Dynasty. Nero focused on diplomacy, trade, and enhancing the cultural life of the Empire during his rule. He ordered theaters to be built and promoted athletic games. However, according to Tacitus, a historian writing one generation after Nero's rule, Nero was viewed by many Romans as compulsive and corrupt. Suetonius, another historian writing a generation after Nero's rule, claims that Nero began the Great Fire of Rome in 64 CE, in order to clear land for a palatial complex he was planning.

Nero: *A marble bust of Nero, at the Antiquarium of the Palatine.*

Early Rule

When Claudius died in 54, Nero was established as the new emperor. According to some ancient historians, Agrippina the Younger, Nero's mother, poisoned Claudius in order to make Nero the youngest Roman emperor (at the age of 17). Very early in Nero's rule, problems arose due to Agrippina's competition for influence with Nero's two main advisers, Seneca and Burrus. For example, in the year 54, Agrippina caused a scandal by attempting to sit with Nero while he met with the Armenian envoy, an unheard of act, since women were not permitted to be in the same room as men while official business was being conducted. The next year, Agrippina attempted to intervene on behalf of Nero's wife, Octavia, with whom Nero was dissatisfied and cheating on with a former slave. With the help of his adviser, Seneca, Nero managed to resist his mother's interference yet again.

Sensing his resistance to her influence, Agrippina began pushing for Britannicus, Nero's stepbrother, to become emperor. Britannicus was still shy of 14 years old, and legally still a minor, but because he was the son of the previous emperor, Claudius, by blood, Agrippina held hope that he would be accepted as the true heir to the throne. Her efforts were thwarted, however, when Britannicus mysteriously died one day short of becoming a legal adult. Many ancient historians claim that Britannicus was poisoned by his stepbrother, Nero. Shortly thereafter, Agrippina was ordered out of the imperial residence.

Consolidation of Power

Over time, Nero began minimizing the influence of all advisers and effectively eliminating all rivals to his throne. Even Seneca and Burrus were accused of conspiring against, and embezzling from the emperor; they were eventually acquitted, reducing their roles from careful management of the government to mere moderation of Nero's actions on the throne. In 58 CE, Nero became romantically involved with Poppaea Sabina, the wife of his friend and future emperor, Otho. Because divorcing his current wife and marrying Poppaea did not seem politically feasible with his mother still alive, Nero ordered Agrippina's murder the following year.

Nero's consolidation of power included a slow usurpation of authority from the Senate. Although he had promised the Senate powers equivalent to those it had under republican rule, over the course of the first decade of Nero's rule, the Senate was divested of all its authority, which led directly to the Pisonian Conspiracy of 65. Gaius Calpurnius Piso, a Roman statesman, organized the conspiracy against Nero with the help of Subrius Flavus, a tribune, and Sulpicius Asper, a centurion of the Praetorian Guard, in order to restore the Republic and wrest power from the emperor. However, the conspiracy failed when it was discovered by a freedman, who reported the details to Nero's secretary. This led to the execution of all conspirators. Seneca was also ordered to commit suicide after he admitted to having prior knowledge of the plot.

Vindex and Galba's Revolt

In March 68, Gaius Gulius Vindex, the governor of Gallia Lugdunensis, rebelled against Nero's tax policies and called upon the support of Servius Sulpicius Galba, the governor of Hispania Tarraconensis, who not only joined the rebellion, but also declared himself emperor in opposition to Nero. Two months later, Vindex's forces were defeated at the Battle of Vesontio, and Vindex committed suicide. The legions that defeated Vindex then attempted to proclaim their own commander, Verginius, as emperor, but Verginius refused to act against Nero. Meanwhile, public support for Galba grew despite his being officially declared a public enemy. In response, Nero began to flee Rome only to turn back when the army officers that were with him refused to obey his commands. When Nero returned, he received word that the Senate had declared him a public enemy and intended to beat him to death—although in actuality, the Senate remained open to mediating an end to the conflict, and many senators felt a sense of loyalty to Nero, even if only on account of him being the last of the Julio-Claudian line. However, Nero was unaware of this and convinced his private secretary to help him take his own life.

Year of the Four Emperors

The suicide of Emperor Nero was followed by a brief period of civil war. Then, between June 68 and December 69, four emperors ruled in succession: Galba, Otho, Vitellius, and Vespasian.

Galba was recognized as emperor following Nero's suicide, but he did not remain popular for long. On his march to Rome, he either destroyed or took enormous fines from towns that did not accept him immediately. Once in Rome, Galba made many of Nero's reforms redundant, including ones that benefited important people within Roman society. Galba executed many senators and equites without trial, in a paranoid attempt to consolidate his power, which unsettled many, including the Praetorian Guard. Finally, the legions of Germania Inferior refused to swear allegiance and obedience to Galba, instead proclaiming the governor Vitellius as emperor.

This caused Galba to panic and name Lucius Calpurnius Piso Licinianus, a young senator, as his successor. This upset many people, but especially Marcus Salvius Otho, who had coveted after the title for himself. Otho bribed the Praetorian Guard to support him and embarked upon a coup d'etat, during which Galba was killed by the Praetorians. Otho was recognized as emperor by the Senate the same day and was expected by many to be a fair ruler. Unfortunately, soon thereafter, Vitellius declared himself Imperator in Germania, and dispatched half his army to march on Italy.

Otho attempted to broker a peace, but Vitellius was uninterested, especially because his legions were some of the finest in the empire, which gave him a great advantage over Otho. Indeed, Otho was eventually defeated at the Battle of Bedriacum, and rather than flee and attempt a counterattack, Otho committed suicide. He had been emperor for little more than three months. Vitellius was recognized as emperor by the Senate. Very quickly thereafter, he proceeded to bankrupt the imperial treasury by throwing a series of feasts, banquets, and triumphal parades. He tortured and executed money lenders who demanded payment and killed any citizens who named him as their heir. He also lured many political rivals to his palace in order to assassinate them.

Meanwhile, many of the legions in the African province of Egypt, and the Middle East provinces of Iudaea and Syria, including the governor of Syria, acclaimed Vespasian as their emperor. A force marched from the Middle East to Rome, and Vespasian traveled to Alexandria, where he was officially named Emperor. From there, Vespasian invaded Italy and won a crushing victory over Vitellius's army at the Second Battle of Bedriacum. Vitellius was found by Vespasian's men at the imperial palace and put to death. The Senate acknowledged Vespasian as emperor the next day, marking the beginning of the Flavian Dynasty, which was to succeed the Julio-Claudian line. Vespasian remained emperor for the rest of his natural life.

Vespasian: *A plaster cast of Vespasian in the Pushkin Museum, after an original held in the Louvre.*

Attributions

CC licensed content, Specific attribution

- Pompey. **Provided by**: Wikipedia. **Located at**: http://en.wikipedia.org/wiki/Pompey. **License**: *CC BY-SA: Attribution-ShareAlike*
- Julius Caesar. **Provided by**: Wikipedia. **Located at**: http://en.wikipedia.org/wiki/Julius_Caesar. **License**: *CC BY-SA: Attribution-ShareAlike*
- Gaius Julius Caesar (100-44 BC). **Provided by**: Wikipedia. **Located at**: http://en.wikipedia.org/wiki/Julius_Caesar%23mediaviewer/File:Gaius_Julius_Caesar_(100-44_BC).JPG. **License**: *Public Domain: No Known Copyright*
- Mark Antony. **Provided by**: Wikipedia. **Located at**: http://en.wikipedia.org/wiki/Mark_Antony. **License**: *CC BY-SA: Attribution-ShareAlike*
- Augustus. **Provided by**: Wikipedia. **Located at**: http://en.wikipedia.org/wiki/Augustus. **License**: *CC BY-SA: Attribution-ShareAlike*
- Gaius Julius Caesar (100-44 BC). **Provided by**: Wikipedia. **Located at**: http://en.wikipedia.org/wiki/Julius_Caesar%23mediaviewer/File:Gaius_Julius_Caesar_(100-44_BC).JPG. **License**: *Public Domain: No Known Copyright*
- Statue-Augustus. **Provided by**: Wikipedia. **Located at**: http://en.wikipedia.org/wiki/Augustus%23mediaviewer/File:Statue-Augustus.jpg. **License**: *CC BY-SA: Attribution-ShareAlike*
- Pax Romana. **Provided by**: Wiktionary. **Located at**: http://en.wiktionary.org/wiki/Pax_Romana. **License**: *CC BY-SA: Attribution-ShareAlike*
- Constitutional reforms of Augustus. **Provided by**: Wikipedia. **Located at**: https://en.wikipedia.org/wiki/Constitutional_reforms_of_Augustus. **License**: *CC BY-SA: Attribution-ShareAlike*
- Ara Pacis. **Provided by**: Wikipedia. **Located at**: http://en.wikipedia.org/wiki/Ara_Pacis. **License**: *CC BY-SA: Attribution-ShareAlike*
- Gaius Julius Caesar (100-44 BC). **Provided by**: Wikipedia. **Located at**: http://en.wikipedia.org/wiki/Julius_Caesar%23mediaviewer/File:Gaius_Julius_Caesar_(100-44_BC).JPG. **License**: *Public Domain: No Known Copyright*
- Statue-Augustus. **Provided by**: Wikipedia. **Located at**: http://en.wikipedia.org/wiki/Augustus%23mediaviewer/File:Statue-Augustus.jpg. **License**: *CC BY-SA: Attribution-ShareAlike*
- Ara Pacis Panel Tellus Mater. **Provided by**: Wikimedia Commons. **Located at**: http://commons.wikimedia.org/wiki/File:AraPacisReliefTellusMater.JPG. **License**: *Public Domain: No Known Copyright*
- Tiberius. **Provided by**: Wikipedia. **Located at**: https://en.wikipedia.org/wiki/Tiberius. **License**: *CC BY-SA: Attribution-ShareAlike*
- Julio-Claudian Dynasty. **Provided by**: Wikipedia. **Located at**: https://en.wikipedia.org/wiki/Julio-Claudian_dynasty. **License**: *CC BY-SA: Attribution-ShareAlike*
- Praetorian Guard. **Provided by**: Wikipedia. **Located at**: https://en.wikipedia.org/wiki/Praetorian_Guard. **License**: *CC BY-SA: Attribution-ShareAlike*
- Claudius. **Provided by**: Wikipedia. **Located at**: https://en.wikipedia.org/wiki/Claudius. **License**: *CC BY-SA: Attribution-ShareAlike*
- Caligula. **Provided by**: Wikipedia. **Located at**: https://en.wikipedia.org/wiki/Caligula. **License**: *CC BY-SA: Attribution-ShareAlike*
- Gaius Julius Caesar (100-44 BC). **Provided by**: Wikipedia. **Located at**: http://en.wikipedia.org/wiki/Julius_Caesar%23mediaviewer/File:Gaius_Julius_Caesar_(100-44_BC).JPG. **License**: *Public Domain: No Known Copyright*
- Statue-Augustus. **Provided by**: Wikipedia. **Located at**: http://en.wikipedia.org/wiki/Augustus%23mediaviewer/File:Statue-Augustus.jpg. **License**: *CC BY-SA: Attribution-ShareAlike*
- Ara Pacis Panel Tellus Mater. **Provided by**: Wikimedia Commons. **Located at**: http://commons.wikimedia.org/wiki/File:AraPacisReliefTellusMater.JPG. **License**: *Public Domain: No Known Copyright*
- 438px-Gaius_Caesar_Caligula.jpg. **Provided by**: Wikimedia. **Located at**: https://commons.wikimedia.org/wiki/File:Gaius_Caesar_Caligula.jpg. **License**: *CC BY-SA: Attribution-ShareAlike*
- 454px-Claudius_crop.jpg. **Provided by**: Wikimedia. **Located at**: https://commons.wikimedia.org/wiki/File:Claudius_crop.jpg. **License**: *CC BY-SA: Attribution-ShareAlike*
- Tiberius,_Romisch-Germanisches_Museum,_Cologne_(8115606671).jpg. **Provided by**: Wikimedia. **Located at**: https://commons.wikimedia.org/wiki/File:Tiberius,_Romisch-Germanisches_Museum,_Cologne_(8115606671).jpg. **License**: *CC BY-SA: Attribution-ShareAlike*
- Nero. **Provided by**: Wikipedia. **Located at**: https://en.wikipedia.org/wiki/Nero. **License**: *CC BY-SA: Attribution-ShareAlike*
- Year of the Four Emperors. **Provided by**: Wikipedia. **Located at**: https://en.wikipedia.org/wiki/Year_of_the_Four_Emperors. **License**: *CC BY-SA: Attribution-ShareAlike*
- Flavian dynasty. **Provided by**: Wikipedia. **Located at**: https://en.wikipedia.org/wiki/Flavian_dynasty. **License**: *CC BY-SA: Attribu-*

tion-ShareAlike

- Gaius Julius Caesar (100-44 BC). **Provided by**: Wikipedia. **Located at**: http://en.wikipedia.org/wiki/Julius_Caesar%23mediaviewer/File:Gaius_Julius_Caesar_(100-44_BC).JPG. **License**: *Public Domain: No Known Copyright*
- Statue-Augustus. **Provided by**: Wikipedia. **Located at**: http://en.wikipedia.org/wiki/Augustus%23mediaviewer/File:Statue-Augustus.jpg. **License**: *CC BY-SA: Attribution-ShareAlike*
- Ara Pacis Panel Tellus Mater. **Provided by**: Wikimedia Commons. **Located at**: http://commons.wikimedia.org/wiki/File:AraPacis-ReliefTellusMater.JPG. **License**: *Public Domain: No Known Copyright*
- 438px-Gaius_Caesar_Caligula.jpg. **Provided by**: Wikimedia. **Located at**: https://commons.wikimedia.org/wiki/File:Gaius_Caesar_Caligula.jpg. **License**: *CC BY-SA: Attribution-ShareAlike*
- 454px-Claudius_crop.jpg. **Provided by**: Wikimedia. **Located at**: https://commons.wikimedia.org/wiki/File:Claudius_crop.jpg. **License**: *CC BY-SA: Attribution-ShareAlike*
- Tiberius,_Romisch-Germanisches_Museum,_Cologne_(8115606671).jpg. **Provided by**: Wikimedia. **Located at**: https://commons.wikimedia.org/wiki/File:Tiberius,_Romisch-Germanisches_Museum,_Cologne_(8115606671).jpg. **License**: *CC BY-SA: Attribution-ShareAlike*
- Vespasianus02_pushkin.jpg. **Provided by**: Wikimedia. **Located at**: https://commons.wikimedia.org/wiki/File:Vespasianus02_pushkin.jpg. **License**: *CC BY-SA: Attribution-ShareAlike*
- Nero_Palatino_Inv618.jpg. **Provided by**: Wikimedia. **Located at**: https://commons.wikimedia.org/wiki/File:Nero_Palatino_Inv618.jpg. **License**: *Public Domain: No Known Copyright*

The Flavian Dynasty

The Flavian Dynasty

The Flavian Dynasty, which began under the rule of Vespasian during the Year of the Four Emperors, is known for several significant historic, economic, and military events.

Learning Objectives

Analyze how Vespasian consolidated control over the empire

Key Takeaways

Key Points

- Vespasian, a general for the Roman army, founded the Flavian Dynasty, which ruled the Empire for 27 years.
- While Vespasian besieged Jerusalem during the Jewish rebellion, emperor Nero committed suicide and plunged Rome into a year of civil war, known as the Year of the Four Emperors.
- After Galba and Otho perished in quick succession, Vitellius became the third emperor in April 69 CE.
- The Roman legions of Roman Egypt and Judaea reacted by declaring Vespasian, their commander, emperor on July 1, 69 CE.
- In his bid for imperial power, Vespasian joined forces with Mucianus, the governor of Syria, and Primus, a general in Pannonia, leaving his son, Titus, to command the besieging forces at Jerusalem; Primus and Mucianus led the Flavian forces against Vitellius, while Vespasian took control of Egypt.
- On December 20, 69, Vitellius was defeated, and the following day, Vespasian was declared Emperor by the Senate.

- Little information survives about the government during Vespasian's ten-year rule; he reformed the financial system at Rome after the campaign against Judaea ended successfully, and initiated several ambitious construction projects.

Key Terms

- **Praetorian Guard**: A force of bodyguards used by Roman Emperors, who also served as secret police and participated in wars.
- **Year of the Four Emperors**: A year in the history of the Roman Empire, 69 CE, in which four emperors ruled in succession: Galba, Otho, Vitellius, and Vespasian.
- **Colosseum**: Also known as the Flavian Amphitheater, an oval amphitheater in the center of the city of Rome, Italy, built of concrete and sand. The largest amphitheater ever built, used for gladiatorial contests and public spectacles, such as mock sea battles, animal hunts, executions, re-enactments of famous battles, and dramas based on Classical mythology.

Overview

The Flavian Dynasty was a Roman imperial dynasty that ruled the Roman Empire between 69 CE and 96 CE, encompassing the reigns of Vespasian (69-79 CE), and his two sons Titus (79-81 CE) and Domitian (81-96 CE). The Flavians rose to power during the civil war of 69, known as the Year of the Four Emperors. After Galba and Otho died in quick succession, Vitellius became emperor in mid 69 CE. His claim to the throne was quickly challenged by legions stationed in the Eastern provinces, who declared their commander, Vespasian, emperor in his place. The Second Battle of Bedriacum tilted the balance decisively in favor of the Flavian forces, who entered Rome on December 20. The following day, the Roman Senate officially declared Vespasian emperor of the Roman Empire, thus commencing the Flavian Dynasty. Although the dynasty proved to be short-lived, several significant historic, economic, and military events took place during their reign.

The Flavians initiated economic and cultural reforms. Under Vespasian, new taxes were devised to restore the Empire's finances, while Domitian revalued the Roman coinage by increasing its silver content. A massive building program was enacted to celebrate the ascent of the Flavian Dynasty, leaving multiple enduring landmarks in the city of Rome, the most spectacular of which was the Flavian Amphitheater, better known as the Colosseum.

Rise to Power

On June 9, 68 CE, amidst growing opposition of the Senate and the army, Nero committed suicide, and with him the Julio-Claudian Dynasty came to an end. Chaos ensued, leading to a year of brutal civil war, known as the Year of the Four Emperors, during which the four most influential generals in the Roman Empire—Galba, Otho, Vitellius and Vespasian—successively vied for imperial power. News of Nero's death reached Vespasian as he was preparing to besiege the city of Jerusalem. Almost simultaneously the Senate had declared Galba, then governor of Hispania Tarraconensis (modern Spain), as Emperor of Rome. Rather than continue his campaign, Vespasian decided to await further orders and send Titus to greet the new Emperor. Before reaching Italy however, Titus learned that Galba had been murdered and replaced by

Otho, the governor of Lusitania (modern Portugal). At the same time, Vitellius and his armies in Germania had risen in revolt, and prepared to march on Rome, intent on overthrowing Otho. Not wanting to risk being taken hostage by one side or the other, Titus abandoned the journey to Rome and rejoined his father in Judaea.

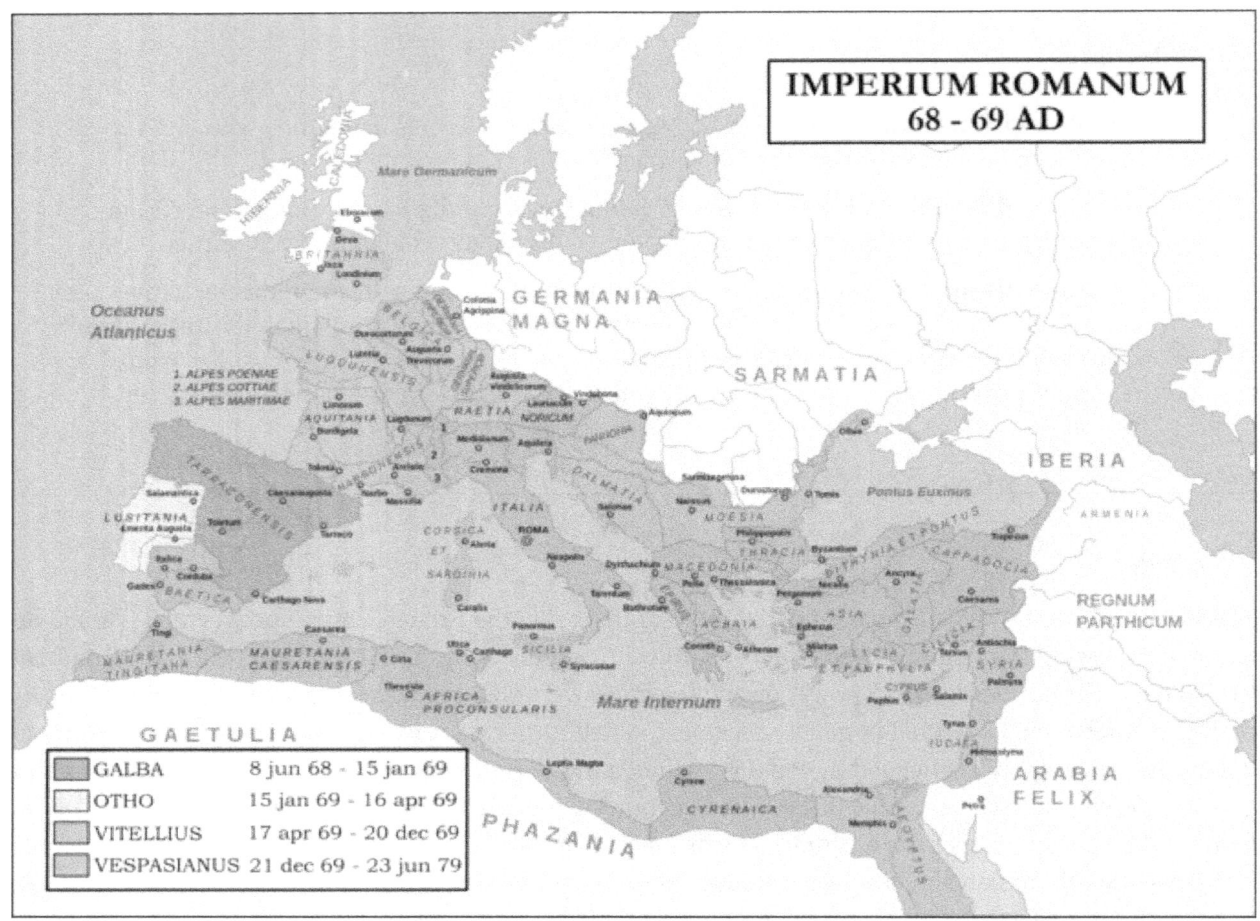

Roman Empire in 69 CE: *The Roman Empire during the Year of the Four Emperors (69 CE). Purple areas indicate provinces loyal to Vespasian and Gaius Licinius Mucianus. Green areas indicate provinces loyal to Vitellius.*

Otho and Vitellius realized the potential threat posed by the Flavian faction. With four legions at his disposal, Vespasian commanded a strength of nearly 80,000 soldiers. His position in Judaea further granted him the advantage of being nearest to the vital province of Egypt, which controlled the grain supply to Rome. His brother, Titus Flavius Sabinus II, as city prefect, commanded the entire city garrison of Rome. Tensions among the Flavian troops ran high, but as long as Galba and Otho remained in power, Vespasian refused to take action. When Otho was defeated by Vitellius at the First Battle of Bedriacum however, the armies in Judaea and Egypt took matters into their own hands, and declared Vespasian emperor on July 1, 69. Vespasian accepted, and entered an alliance with Gaius Licinius Mucianus, the governor of Syria, against Vitellius. A strong force drawn from the Judaean and Syrian legions marched on Rome under the command of Mucianus, while Vespasian himself travelled to Alexandria, leaving Titus in charge of ending the Jewish rebellion.

Meanwhile in Rome, Domitian was placed under house arrest by Vitellius, as a safeguard against future Flavian aggression. Support for the old emperor was waning however, as more legions throughout the empire pledged their allegiance to Vespasian. On October 24, 69, the forces of Vitellius and Vespasian clashed at the Second Battle of Bedriacum, which ended in a crushing defeat for the armies of Vitellius. In despair, he attempted to negotiate a surrender. Terms of peace, including a voluntary abdication, were agreed upon with Titus Flavius Sabinus II, but the soldiers of the Praetorian Guard—the imperial bodyguard—considered such a resignation disgraceful, and prevented Vitellius from carrying out the treaty. After several skirmishes between the factions, eventually Vitellius was killed and on December 21, the Senate proclaimed Vespasian emperor of the Roman Empire.

Although the war had officially ended, a state of anarchy and lawlessness pervaded in the first days following the demise of Vitellius. In early 70 AD, order was properly restored by Mucianus, who headed an interim government with Domitian as the representative of the Flavian family in the Senate. Upon receiving the tidings of his rival's defeat and death at Alexandria, the new Emperor at once forwarded supplies of urgently needed grain to Rome, along with an edict or a declaration of policy, in which he gave assurance of an entire reversal of the laws of Nero, especially those relating to treason. However, in early 70, Vespasian was still in Egypt, continuing to consolidate support from the Egyptians before departing. By the end of the year, he finally returned to Rome, and was properly installed as Emperor.

Vespasian's Rule

Little factual information survives about Vespasian's government during the ten years he was Emperor. Vespasian spent his first year as a ruler in Egypt, during which the administration of the empire was given to Mucianus, aided by Vespasian's son, Domitian. Modern historians believe that Vespasian remained there, in order to consolidate support from the Egyptians. In mid-70, Vespasian first came to Rome and immediately embarked on a widespread propaganda campaign to consolidate his power and promote the new dynasty. His reign is best known for financial reforms following the demise of the Julio-Claudian Dynasty, such as the institution of the tax on urinals, and the numerous military campaigns fought during the 70s. The most significant of these was the First Jewish-Roman War, which ended in the destruction of the city of Jerusalem by Titus. In addition, Vespasian faced several uprisings in Egypt, Gaul, and Germania, and reportedly survived several conspiracies against him. Vespasian helped rebuild Rome after the civil war, adding a temple of peace, and beginning construction of the Flavian Amphitheater, better known as the Colosseum.

Many modern historians note the increased amount of propaganda that appeared during Vespasian's reign. Stories of a supernatural emperor, who was destined to rule, circulated in the empire. Nearly one-third of all coins minted in Rome under Vespasian celebrated military victory or peace. The word *vindex* was removed from coins so as not to remind the public of rebellious Vindex. Construction projects bore inscriptions praising Vespasian and condemning previous emperors. A temple of peace was constructed in the forum as well. Vespasian approved histories written under his reign, ensuring biases against him were removed.

Vespasian also gave financial rewards to writers. The ancient historians who lived through the period, such as Tacitus, Suetonius, Josephus, and Pliny the Elder, speak suspiciously well of Vespasian, while condemning the emperors who came before him. Tacitus admits that his status was elevated by Vespasian, Josephus identifies Vespasian as a patron and savior, and Pliny dedicated his Natural Histories to Vespasian's son, Titus.

Those who spoke against Vespasian were punished. A number of stoic philosophers were accused of corrupting students with inappropriate teachings and were expelled from Rome. Helvidius Priscus, a pro-republic philosopher, was executed for his teachings.

Vespasian died of natural causes on June 23, 79, and was immediately succeeded by his eldest son, Titus.

Bust of Vespasian: *Vespasian founded the Flavian Dynasty, which ruled the Empire for twenty-seven years.*

Military Achievements of the Flavians

The Flavian Dynasty's military witnessed the siege and destruction of Jerusalem by Titus in 70 CE, and substantial conquests in Great Britain under command of Gnaeus Julius Agricola between 77 and 83 CE.

THE FLAVIAN DYNASTY

Learning Objectives

Describe some of the military achievements and challenges of the Flavian emperors

Key Takeaways

Key Points

- The most significant military campaign undertaken during the Flavian period was the siege and destruction of Jerusalem in 70 CE by Titus; it was a response to a failed Jewish rebellion in 66.
- Contemporary estimates claimed that 1,100,000 people were killed during the siege, of which a majority were Jewish.
- Substantial conquests were made in Great Britain under command of Gnaeus Julius Agricola, between 77 and 83.
- The military campaigns undertaken during Domitian's reign were usually defensive in nature, as the Emperor rejected the idea of expansionist warfare, and the few battles were mainly fought with Germanic tribes, especially the Dacians.

Key Terms

- **the Forum**: A a rectangular forum (plaza) surrounded by the ruins of several important ancient government buildings at the center of the city of Rome, originally a large marketplace.
- **Torah**: The central text of the religious Judaic tradition, often referring specifically to the first five books of the twenty-four books of the Tanakh.
- **Limes Germanicus**: A line of frontier fortifications that bounded the ancient Roman provinces of Germania Inferior, Germania Superior and Raetia, dividing the Roman Empire and the unsubdued Germanic tribes, from the years 83 to about 260 CE.

Overview

The Flavian Dynasty's military witnessed the siege and destruction of Jerusalem by Titus in 70 CE, following the failed Jewish rebellion of 66. Substantial conquests were made in Great Britain under command of Gnaeus Julius Agricola between 77 and 83, while Domitian was unable to procure a decisive victory against King Decebalus in the war against the Dacians. In addition, the Empire strengthened its border defenses by expanding the fortifications along the Limes Germanicus.

Siege of Jerusalem

The most significant military campaign undertaken during the Flavian period was the siege and destruction of Jerusalem in 70 by Titus. The destruction of the city was the culmination of the Roman campaign in Judaea following the Jewish uprising of 66. The Second Temple was completely demolished, after which Titus's soldiers proclaimed him *imperator,* an honorific meaning "commander," in honor of the victory. Jerusalem was sacked and much of the population killed or dispersed. Josephus claims that 1,100,000 people were killed during the siege, of which a majority were Jewish. 97,000 were captured and enslaved, including Simon Bar Giora and John of Gischala. Many fled to areas around the Mediterranean.

Titus reportedly refused to accept a wreath of victory, as there is "no merit in vanquishing people forsaken by their own God." Upon his return to Rome in 71, Titus was awarded a triumph. Accompanied by Vespasian and Domitian, he rode into the city, enthusiastically saluted by the Roman populace, and preceded by a lavish parade containing treasures and captives from the war. Josephus describes a procession with large amounts of gold and silver carried along the route, followed by elaborate re-enactments of the war, Jewish prisoners, and finally the treasures taken from the Temple of Jerusalem, including the Menorah and the Torah. Leaders of the resistance were executed in the Forum, after which the procession closed with religious sacrifices at the Temple of Jupiter. The triumphal Arch of Titus, which stands at one entrance to the Forum, memorializes the victory of Titus.

Siege of Jerusalem: *This relief from the Arch of Titus depicts Roman soldiers carrying treasures from the Temple of Jerusalem, including the Menorah. The city was besieged and destroyed by Titus in 70 CE.*

Conquest of Britain

The conquest of Britain continued under command of Gnaeus Julius Agricola, who expanded the Roman Empire as far as Caledonia, or modern day Scotland, between 77 and 84 AD. In 82, Agricola crossed an unidentified body of water and defeated peoples unknown to the Romans until then. He fortified the coast facing Ireland, and Tacitus recalled that his father-in-law often claimed the island could be conquered with a single legion and a few auxiliaries. He had given refuge to an exiled Irish king whom he hoped he might use as the excuse for conquest. This conquest never happened, but some historians believe that the crossing referred to was in fact a small-scale exploratory or punitive expedition to Ireland. The following year, Agricola raised a fleet and pushed beyond the Forth into Caledonia. To aid the advance, an expansive legionary fortress was constructed at Inchtuthil. In the summer of 84, Agricola faced the armies of the Caledonians, led by Calgacus, at the Battle of Mons Graupius. Although the Romans inflicted heavy losses on the Calidonians, two-thirds of their army managed to escape and hide in the Scottish marshes and Highlands, ultimately preventing Agricola from bringing the entire British island under his control.

Other Military Activity

The military campaigns undertaken during Domitian's reign were usually defensive in nature, as the Emperor rejected the idea of expansionist warfare. His most significant military contribution was the development of the Limes Germanicus, which encompassed a vast network of roads, forts, and watchtowers constructed along the Rhine river to defend the Empire from the unsubdued Germanic tribes. Nevertheless, several important wars were fought in Gaul, against the Chatti, and across the Danube frontier against the Suebi, the Sarmatians, and the Dacians. Led by King Decebalus, the Dacians invaded the province of Moesia around 84 or 85, wreaking considerable havoc and killing the Moesian governor Oppius Sabinus. Domitian immediately launched a counteroffensive, which resulted in the destruction of a legion during an ill-fated expedition into Dacia. Their commander, Cornelius Fuscus, was killed, and the battle standard of the Praetorian Guard lost.

In 87, the Romans invaded Dacia once more, this time under command of Tettius Julianus, and finally managed to defeat Decebalus late in 88, at the same site where Fuscus had previously been killed. An attack on Dacia's capital was cancelled, however, when a crisis arose on the German frontier. This forced Domitian to sign a peace treaty with Decebalus that was severely criticized by contemporary authors. For the remainder of Domitian's reign, Dacia remained a relatively peaceful client kingdom, but Decebalus used the Roman money to fortify his defenses, and continued to defy Rome. It was not until the reign of Trajan, in 106, that a decisive victory against Decebalus was procured. Again, the Roman army sustained heavy losses, but Trajan succeeded in capturing Sarmizegetusa and, importantly, annexed the gold and silver mines of Dacia.

Eruptions of Vesuvius and Pompeii

The eruption of Mount Vesuvius in 79 CE was one of the most catastrophic volcanic eruptions in European history, with several Roman settlements obliterated and buried, and thereby preserved, under ash.

Learning Objectives

Describe the events surrounding the Eruption of Mount Vesuvius

Key Takeaways

Key Points

- The eruption of Mount Vesuvius in 79 CE, during the reign of Emperor Titus, was one of the most catastrophic volcanic eruptions in European history.
- Historians have learned about the eruption from the eyewitness account of Pliny the Younger, a Roman administrator and poet.
- Mount Vesuvius spewed a deadly cloud of volcanic gas, stones, and ash to a height of 21 miles, ejecting molten rock and pulverized pumice at the rate of 1.5 million tons per second, ultimately releasing a hundred thousand times the thermal energy of the Hiroshima bombing.
- Several Roman settlements were obliterated and buried underneath massive pyroclastic surges and ashfall deposits, the most well known of which are Pompeii and Herculaneum.
- The preserved remains of about 1,500 people have been found at Pompeii and Herculaneum, but the overall death toll is still unknown.

Key Terms

- **Pompeii**: An ancient Roman town-city near modern Naples, in the Campania region of Italy, destroyed during the eruption of Mount Vesuvius.
- **pyroclastic surge**: A fluidized mass of turbulent gas and rock fragments, ejected during some volcanic eruptions.
- **Pliny the Younger**: A lawyer, author, and magistrate of Ancient Rome who witnessed the eruption of Mount Vesuvius.

Overview

Although his administration was marked by a relative absence of major military or political conflicts, Titus faced a number of major disasters during his brief reign. On August 24, 79 CE, barely two months after his accession, Mount Vesuvius erupted, resulting in the almost complete destruction of life and property in the cities and resort communities around the Bay of Naples. The cities of Pompeii and Herculaneum were buried under meters of stone and lava, killing thousands of citizens. Titus appointed two ex-consuls to organize and coordinate the relief effort, while personally donating large amounts of money from the imperial treasury to aid the victims of the volcano. Additionally, he visited Pompeii once after the eruption and again the following year.

The city was lost for nearly 1,700 years before its accidental rediscovery in 1748. Since then, its excavation has provided an extraordinarily detailed insight into the life of a city at the height of the Roman Empire, frozen at the moment it was buried on August 24, 79. The Forum, the baths, many houses, and some out-of-town villas, like the Villa of the Mysteries, remain surprisingly well preserved. Today, it is one of the most popular tourist attractions of Italy and a UNESCO World Heritage Site. On-going excavations reveal new insights into the Roman history and culture.

The Eruption

Reconstructions of the eruption and its effects vary considerably in the details but have the same overall features. The eruption lasted for two days. The morning of the first day, August 24, was perceived as normal by the only eyewitness to leave a surviving document, Pliny the Younger, who at that point was staying at Misenum, on the other side of the Bay of Naples, about 19 miles from the volcano, which may have prevented him from noticing the early signs of the eruption. He was not to have any opportunity, during the next two days, to talk to people who had witnessed the eruption from Pompeii or Herculaneum (indeed he never mentions Pompeii in his letter), so he would not have noticed early, smaller fissures and releases of ash and smoke on the mountain, if such had occurred earlier in the morning.

Around 1:00 p.m., Mount Vesuvius violently exploded, throwing up a high-altitude column from which ash began to fall, blanketing the area. Rescues and escapes occurred during this time. At some time in the night or early the next day, August 25, pyroclastic flows in the close vicinity of the volcano began. Lights seen on the mountain were interpreted as fires. People as far away as Misenum fled for their lives. The flows were rapid-moving, dense, and very hot, knocking down wholly or partly all structures in their path, incinerating or suffocating all population remaining there and altering the landscape, including the coastline. These were accompanied by additional light tremors and a mild tsunami in the Bay of Naples. By evening of the second day the eruption was over, leaving only haze in the atmosphere, through which the sun shone weakly.

Pliny the Younger wrote an account of the eruption:

> Broad sheets of flame were lighting up many parts of Vesuvius; their light and brightness were the more vivid for the darkness of the night… it was daylight now elsewhere in the world, but there the darkness was darker and thicker than any night.

Casualties

In Pompeii, the eruption destroyed the city, killing its inhabitants and burying it under tons of ash. Evidence for the destruction originally came from a surviving letter by Pliny the Younger, who saw the eruption from a distance and described the death of his uncle, Pliny the Elder, an admiral of the Roman fleet, who tried to rescue citizens. The site was lost for about 1,500 years until its initial rediscovery in 1599, and broader rediscovery almost 150 years later by Spanish engineer Rocque Joaquin de Alcubierre in 1748. The objects that lay beneath the city have been preserved for centuries because of the lack of air and moisture. These artifacts provide an extraordinarily detailed insight into the life of a city during the Pax Romana. During the excavation, plaster was used to fill in the voids in the ash layers that once held human bodies. This allowed archaeologists to see the exact position the person was in when he or she died.

Pompeii's "Garden of the Fugitives": *Plaster casts of victims still in situ; many casts are in the Archaeological Museum of Naples.*

By 2003, around 1,044 casts made from impressions of bodies in the ash deposits had been recovered in and around Pompeii, with the scattered bones of another 100. The remains of about 332 bodies have been found at Herculaneum (300 in arched vaults discovered in 1980). The percentage these numbers represent of the total dead, or the percentage of the dead to the total number at risk, remain completely unknown.

Thirty-eight percent of the 1,044 were found in the ash fall deposits, the majority inside buildings. These are thought to have been killed mainly by roof collapses, with the smaller number of victims found outside buildings probably killed by falling roof slates, or by larger rocks thrown out by the volcano. This differs from modern experience, since over the last four hundred years only around 4% of victims have been killed by ash falls during explosive eruptions. The remaining 62% of remains found at Pompeii were in the pyroclastic surge deposits, and thus were probably killed by them. It was initially believed that due to the state of the bodies found at Pompeii, and the outline of clothes on the bodies, it was unlikely that high temperatures were a significant cause. But in 2010, studies indicated that during the fourth pyroclastic surge–the first surge to reach Pompeii–temperatures reached 572 °F. Volcanologist Giuseppe Mastrolorenzo, who led the study, noted that "[The temperature was] enough to kill hundreds of people in a fraction of a second." In reference as to why the bodies were frozen in suspended action, he said, "The contorted postures are not the effects of a long agony, but of the cadaveric spasm, a consequence of heat shock on corpses."

Ring Lady: *The skeletal remains of a young woman killed by the eruption of Mount Vesuvius in 79 CE. The skeleton, unearthed from the ruins of Herculaneum in 1982, was named the "Ring Lady" because of the emerald and ruby rings found on the woman's left hand. Two gold bracelets and gold earrings were also found by the woman's side.*

Flavian Architecture

Under the Flavian Dynasty, a massive building program was undertaken, leaving multiple enduring landmarks in the city of Rome, the most spectacular of which was the Flavian Amphitheater, better known as the Colosseum.

> ### Learning Objectives
>
> Identify some of the key structures erected by the Flavian emperors

> ### Key Takeaways
>
> *Key Points*
>
> - Perhaps the most enduring legacy of the Flavian Dynasty was their massive building program, which not only erected new buildings to celebrate their successes, but also renovated buildings, statues, and monuments throughout Rome.
> - The most spectacular of these buildings was the Flavian Amphitheater, better known as the Colosseum, built from the spoils of the Siege of Jerusalem.
> - The Colosseum was used for gladiatorial contests and public spectacles, such as mock sea battles, animal hunts, executions, re-enactments of famous battles, and dramas based on Classical mythology.
> - The bulk of the Flavian construction projects was carried out during the reign of Domitian, who spent lavishly to restore and embellish the city of Rome.
>
> *Key Terms*
>
> - **Flavian Amphitheatre**: Better known as the Colosseum, an oval amphitheater in the center of the city of Rome, Italy; used for gladiatorial games, among other activities.
> - **Apollo**: One of the most important and complex of the Olympian deities, variously recognized as a god of music, truth and prophecy, healing, the sun and light, plague, poetry, and more.

Overview

The Flavian Dynasty is perhaps best known for its vast construction program on the city of Rome, intended to restore the capital from the damage it had suffered during the Great Fire of 64, and the civil war of 69. Vespasian added the temple of Peace and the temple to the deified Claudius. In 75, a colossal statue of Apollo, begun under Nero as a statue of himself, was finished on Vespasian's orders, and he also dedicated a stage of the theater of Marcellus. Construction of the Flavian Amphitheater, presently better known as the Colosseum (probably after the nearby statue), was begun in 70 CE under Vespasian, and finally completed in 80 under Titus. In addition to providing spectacular entertainments to the Roman populace, the building was also conceived as a gigantic triumphal monument to commemorate the military achievements of the Flavians during the Jewish wars. Adjacent to the amphitheater, within the precinct of Nero's Golden House, Titus also ordered the construction of a new public bath-house, which was to bear his name. Construction of this building was hastily finished to coincide with the completion of the Flavian Amphitheater.

The bulk of the Flavian construction projects was carried out during the reign of Domitian, who spent lavishly to restore and embellish the city of Rome. Much more than a renovation project however, Domitian's building program was intended to be the crowning achievement of an Empire-wide cultural renaissance. Around 50 structures were erected, restored, or completed, a number second only to the amount erected under Augustus. Among the most important new structures were an odeum, a stadium, and an expansive palace on the Palatine Hill, known as the Flavian Palace, which was designed by Domitian's master architect, Rabirius. The most important building Domitian restored was the Temple of Jupiter on the Capitoline Hill, which was said to have been covered with a gilded roof. Among those he completed were the Temple of Vespasian and Titus, the Arch of Titus, and the Colosseum, to which he added a fourth level and finished the interior seating area.

The Colosseum

The Colosseum is an oval amphitheater in the center of the city of Rome, Italy. Built of concrete and sand, it is the largest amphitheater ever built. The Colosseum is situated just east of the Roman Forum. Construction began under the emperor Vespasian in 72 CE, and was completed in 80 CE under his successor and heir, Titus. Further modifications were made during the reign of Domitian (81-96).

The Colosseum could hold, it is estimated, between 50,000 and 80,000 spectators, with an average audience of some 65,000; it was used for gladiatorial contests and public spectacles, such as mock sea battles (for only a short time, as the hypogeum was soon filled in with mechanisms to support the other activities), animal hunts, executions, re-enactments of famous battles, and dramas based on Classical mythology.

Construction was funded by the opulent spoils taken from the Jewish Temple after the Great Jewish Revolt in 70 CE led to the Siege of Jerusalem. According to a reconstructed inscription found on the site, "the emperor Vespasian ordered this new amphitheater to be erected from his general's share of the booty." Along with the spoils, estimated 100,000 Jewish prisoners were brought back to Rome after the war, and many contributed to the massive workforce needed for construction. The slaves undertook manual labor, such as working in the quarries at Tivoli where the travertine was quarried, along with lifting and transporting the quarried stones 20 miles from Tivoli to Rome. Along with this free source of unskilled labor, teams of professional Roman builders, engineers, artists, painters and decorators undertook the more specialized tasks necessary for building the Colosseum.

The Flavian Amphitheater: *The most enduring landmark of the Flavian Dynasty was the Flavian Amphitheater, better known as the Colosseum. Its construction was begun by Vespasian, and ultimately finished by Titus and Domitian, financed from the spoils of the destruction of the Second Jerusalem Temple.*

Fall of the Flavian Emperors

Domitian, the last of the Flavian emperors, was a ruthless autocrat who had many enemies, some of whom eventually assassinated him, giving rise to the long-lived Nerva-Antonine Dynasty.

Learning Objectives

Analyze the factors that led to the fall of the Flavian Dynasty

Key Takeaways

Key Points

- Flavian rule came to an end on September 18, 96, when Domitian was assassinated and was succeeded by the longtime Flavian supporter and advisor Marcus Cocceius Nerva, who founded the long-lived Nerva-Antonine Dynasty.
- Domitian's government exhibited totalitarian characteristics, which caused disapproval of the Roman Senate, among others.
- He dealt with several revolts during his rule, the last one being a successful assassination.

- The Senate rejoiced at the death of Domitian, and immediately following Nerva's accession as Emperor, passed *damnatio memoriae* on his memory: his coins and statues were melted, his arches were torn down, and his name was erased from all public records.

Key Terms

- **damnatio memoriae**: Latin for "condemnation of memory," a form of dishonor that could be passed by the Roman Senate on traitors or others who brought discredit to the Roman State; the intent was to erase the malefactor from history, a task somewhat easier in ancient times, when documentation was limited.
- **Marcus Cocceius Nerva**: Succeeded Domitian as emperor the same day as his assassination. Founded the Nerva-Antonine Dynasty.
- **Roman Senate**: A political institution in ancient Rome, and one of the most enduring institutions in Roman history, established in the first days of the city. By the time of the Roman Empire, it had lost much of its political power as well as its prestige.

Flavian rule came to an end on September 18, 96, when Domitian was assassinated. He was succeeded by the longtime Flavian supporter and advisor, Marcus Cocceius Nerva, who founded the long-lived Nerva-Antonine Dynasty.

Opposition to Domitian

Domitian's government exhibited totalitarian characteristics; he saw himself as the new Augustus, an enlightened despot destined to guide the Roman Empire into a new era of brilliance. Religious, military, and cultural propaganda fostered a cult of personality, and by nominating himself perpetual censor, he sought to control public and private morals. As a consequence, Domitian was popular with the people and army, but considered a tyrant by members of the Roman Senate.

Since the fall of the Republic, the authority of the Roman Senate had largely eroded under the quasi-monarchical system of government established by Augustus, known as the Principate. The Principate allowed the existence of a de facto dictatorial regime, while maintaining the formal framework of the Roman Republic. Most Emperors upheld the public facade of democracy, and in return the Senate implicitly acknowledged the Emperor's status as a de facto monarch.

Some rulers handled this arrangement with less subtlety than others. Domitian was not so subtle. From the outset of his reign, he stressed the reality of his autocracy. He disliked aristocrats and had no fear of showing it, withdrawing every decision-making power from the Senate, and instead relying on a small set of friends and equestrians to control the important offices of state.

The dislike was mutual. After Domitian's assassination, the senators of Rome rushed to the Senate house, where they immediately passed a motion condemning his memory to oblivion. Under the rulers of the Nervan-Antonian Dynasty, senatorial authors published histories that elaborated on the view of Domitian as a tyrant. Modern revisionists have instead characterized Domitian as a ruthless but efficient autocrat, whose cultural, economic, and political program provided the foundation of the peaceful 2nd century.

Assassination

Domitian dealt with several revolts during his rule, the last of which was a successful plot to assassinate him. Domitian was assassinated on September 18, 96, in a palace conspiracy organized by court officials. A highly detailed account of the plot and the assassination is provided by Suetonius, who alleges that Domitian's chamberlain, Parthenius, was the chief instigator behind the conspiracy, citing the recent execution of Domitian's secretary, Epaphroditus, as the primary motive. The murder itself was carried out by a freedman of Parthenius, named Maximus, and a steward of Domitian's niece Flavia Domitilla, named Stephanus.

The precise involvement of the Praetorian Guard is less clear. At the time, the Guard was commanded by Titus Flavius Norbanus and Titus Petronius Secundus, and the latter was almost certainly aware of the plot. Cassius Dio, writing nearly a hundred years after the assassination, includes Domitia Longina among the conspirators, but in light of her attested devotion to Domitian—even years after her husband had died—her involvement in the plot seems highly unlikely.

Dio further suggests that the assassination was improvised, while Suetonius implies a well-organized conspiracy. For some days before the attack took place, Stephanus feigned an injury so as to be able to conceal a dagger beneath his bandages. On the day of the assassination, the doors to the servants' quarters were locked while Domitian's personal weapon of last resort, a sword he concealed beneath his pillow, had been removed in advance.

Domitian and Stephanus wrestled on the ground for some time, until the Emperor was finally overpowered and fatally stabbed by the conspirators; Stephanus was stabbed by Domitian during the struggle and died shortly afterward. Around noon, Domitian, just one month short of his 45th birthday, was dead. His body was carried away on a common bier, and unceremoniously cremated by his nurse Phyllis, who later mingled the ashes with those of his niece Julia, at the Flavian temple.

The End of the Flavian Dynasty

The same day as Domitian's death, the Senate proclaimed Marcus Cocceius Nerva to be emperor. Despite his political experience, this was a remarkable choice. Nerva was old and childless, and had spent much of his career out of the public light, prompting both ancient and modern authors to speculate on his involvement in Domitian's assassination.

According to Cassius Dio, the conspirators approached Nerva as a potential successor prior to the assassination, suggesting that he was at least aware of the plot. He does not appear in Suetonius' version of the events, but this may be understandable, since his works were published under Nerva's direct descendants, Trajan and Hadrian. To suggest the dynasty owed its accession to murder would have been less than sensitive.

On the other hand, Nerva lacked widespread support in the Empire, and as a known Flavian loyalist, his track record would not have recommended him to the conspirators. The precise facts have been obscured by history, but modern historians believe Nerva was proclaimed emperor solely on the initiative of the Senate, within hours after the news of the assassination broke. The decision may have been hasty so as to avoid civil war, but neither appears to have been involved in the conspiracy.

The Senate nonetheless rejoiced at the death of Domitian, and immediately following Nerva's accession as Emperor, passed *damnatio memoriae* on his memory: his coins and statues were melted, his arches were torn down, and his name was erased from all public records. Domitian and, over a century later, Publius Septimius Geta, were the only emperors known to have officially received a *damnatio memoriae*, though others may have received de facto ones. In many instances, existing portraits of Domitian, such as those found on the Cancelleria Reliefs, were simply recarved to fit the likeness of Nerva, which allowed quick production of new images and recycling of previous material. Yet the order of the Senate was only partially executed in Rome, and wholly disregarded in most of the provinces outside Italy.

Although Nerva's brief reign was marred by financial difficulties and his inability to assert his authority over the Roman army (who were still loyal to Domitian), his greatest success was his ability to ensure a peaceful transition of power after his death, thus founding the Nerva-Antonine Dynasty.

Domitian: Domitian as Emperor (Vatican Museums), possibly recut from a statue of Nero.

Attributions

CC licensed content, Specific attribution

- Flavian dynasty. **Provided by**: Wikipedia. **Located at**: https://en.wikipedia.org/wiki/Flavian_dynasty. **License**: *CC BY-SA: Attribution-ShareAlike*
- Vespasian. **Provided by**: Wikipedia. **Located at**: https://en.wikipedia.org/wiki/Vespasian. **License**: *CC BY-SA: Attribution-ShareAlike*
- Moesia. **Provided by**: Wikipedia. **Located at**: https://en.wikipedia.org/wiki/Moesia. **License**: *CC BY-SA: Attribution-ShareAlike*
- Dalmatia. **Provided by**: Wikipedia. **Located at**: https://en.wikipedia.org/wiki/Dalmatia. **License**: *CC BY-SA: Attribution-ShareAlike*
- Egypt (Roman province). **Provided by**: Wikipedia. **Located at**: https://en.wikipedia.org/wiki/Egypt_(Roman_province). **License**: *CC BY-SA: Attribution-ShareAlike*
- Judea (Roman province). **Provided by**: Wikipedia. **Located at**: https://en.wikipedia.org/wiki/Judea_(Roman_province). **License**:

CC BY-SA: Attribution-ShareAlike

- Pannonia. **Provided by**: Wikipedia. **Located at**: https://en.wikipedia.org/wiki/Pannonia. **License**: *CC BY-SA: Attribution-ShareAlike*
- Roman_Empire_69.svg.png. **Provided by**: Wikimedia. **Located at**: https://commons.wikimedia.org/wiki/File:Roman_Empire_69.svg. **License**: *CC BY-SA: Attribution-ShareAlike*
- 440px-Vespasianus01_pushkin_edit.png. **Provided by**: Wikimedia. **Located at**: https://commons.wikimedia.org/wiki/File:Vespasianus01_pushkin_edit.png. **License**: *CC BY-SA: Attribution-ShareAlike*
- Siege of Jerusalem. **Provided by**: Wikipedia. **Located at**: https://en.wikipedia.org/wiki/Siege_of_Jerusalem_(AD_70). **License**: *CC BY-SA: Attribution-ShareAlike*
- Flavian dynasty. **Provided by**: Wikipedia. **Located at**: https://en.wikipedia.org/wiki/Flavian_dynasty. **License**: *CC BY-SA: Attribution-ShareAlike*
- Roman_Empire_69.svg.png. **Provided by**: Wikimedia. **Located at**: https://commons.wikimedia.org/wiki/File:Roman_Empire_69.svg. **License**: *CC BY-SA: Attribution-ShareAlike*
- 440px-Vespasianus01_pushkin_edit.png. **Provided by**: Wikimedia. **Located at**: https://commons.wikimedia.org/wiki/File:Vespasianus01_pushkin_edit.png. **License**: *CC BY-SA: Attribution-ShareAlike*
- 660px-Arch_of_Titus_Menorah.png. **Provided by**: Wikimedia. **Located at**: https://commons.wikimedia.org/wiki/File:Arch_of_Titus_Menorah.png. **License**: *CC BY-SA: Attribution-ShareAlike*
- Pompeii. **Provided by**: Wikipedia. **Located at**: https://en.wikipedia.org/wiki/Pompeii. **License**: *CC BY-SA: Attribution-ShareAlike*
- Flavian dynasty. **Provided by**: Wikipedia. **Located at**: https://en.wikipedia.org/wiki/Flavian_dynasty. **License**: *CC BY-SA: Attribution-ShareAlike*
- Eruption of Mount Vesuvius. **Provided by**: Wikipedia. **Located at**: https://en.wikipedia.org/wiki/Eruption_of_Mount_Vesuvius_in_79. **License**: *CC BY-SA: Attribution-ShareAlike*
- Roman_Empire_69.svg.png. **Provided by**: Wikimedia. **Located at**: https://commons.wikimedia.org/wiki/File:Roman_Empire_69.svg. **License**: *CC BY-SA: Attribution-ShareAlike*
- 440px-Vespasianus01_pushkin_edit.png. **Provided by**: Wikimedia. **Located at**: https://commons.wikimedia.org/wiki/File:Vespasianus01_pushkin_edit.png. **License**: *CC BY-SA: Attribution-ShareAlike*
- 660px-Arch_of_Titus_Menorah.png. **Provided by**: Wikimedia. **Located at**: https://commons.wikimedia.org/wiki/File:Arch_of_Titus_Menorah.png. **License**: *CC BY-SA: Attribution-ShareAlike*
- Ring_Lady.JPG. **Provided by**: Wikipedia. **Located at**: https://en.wikipedia.org/wiki/File:Ring_Lady.JPG. **License**: *CC BY-SA: Attribution-ShareAlike*
- Pompeii_Garden_of_the_Fugitives_02.jpg. **Provided by**: Wikimedia. **Located at**: https://commons.wikimedia.org/wiki/File:Pompeii_Garden_of_the_Fugitives_02.jpg. **License**: *Public Domain: No Known Copyright*
- Flavian dynasty. **Provided by**: Wikipedia. **Located at**: https://en.wikipedia.org/wiki/Flavian_dynasty#Construction. **License**: *CC BY-SA: Attribution-ShareAlike*
- Colosseum. **Provided by**: Wikipedia. **Located at**: https://en.wikipedia.org/wiki/Colosseum. **License**: *CC BY-SA: Attribution-ShareAlike*
- Roman_Empire_69.svg.png. **Provided by**: Wikimedia. **Located at**: https://commons.wikimedia.org/wiki/File:Roman_Empire_69.svg. **License**: *CC BY-SA: Attribution-ShareAlike*
- 440px-Vespasianus01_pushkin_edit.png. **Provided by**: Wikimedia. **Located at**: https://commons.wikimedia.org/wiki/File:Vespasianus01_pushkin_edit.png. **License**: *CC BY-SA: Attribution-ShareAlike*
- 660px-Arch_of_Titus_Menorah.png. **Provided by**: Wikimedia. **Located at**: https://commons.wikimedia.org/wiki/File:Arch_of_Titus_Menorah.png. **License**: *CC BY-SA: Attribution-ShareAlike*
- Ring_Lady.JPG. **Provided by**: Wikipedia. **Located at**: https://en.wikipedia.org/wiki/File:Ring_Lady.JPG. **License**: *CC BY-SA: Attribution-ShareAlike*
- Pompeii_Garden_of_the_Fugitives_02.jpg. **Provided by**: Wikimedia. **Located at**: https://commons.wikimedia.org/wiki/File:Pompeii_Garden_of_the_Fugitives_02.jpg. **License**: *Public Domain: No Known Copyright*
- Colosseum_in_Rome,_Italy_-_April_2007.jpg. **Provided by**: Wikimedia. **Located at**: https://commons.wikimedia.org/wiki/File:Colosseum_in_Rome,_Italy_-_April_2007.jpg. **License**: *CC BY-SA: Attribution-ShareAlike*
- Domitian. **Provided by**: Wikipedia. **Located at**: https://en.wikipedia.org/wiki/Domitian. **License**: *CC BY-SA: Attribution-ShareAlike*
- Flavian dynasty. **Provided by**: Wikipedia. **Located at**: https://en.wikipedia.org/wiki/Flavian_dynasty. **License**: *CC BY-SA: Attribution-ShareAlike*

- Roman_Empire_69.svg.png. **Provided by**: Wikimedia. **Located at**: https://commons.wikimedia.org/wiki/File:Roman_Empire_69.svg. **License**: *CC BY-SA: Attribution-ShareAlike*

- 440px-Vespasianus01_pushkin_edit.png. **Provided by**: Wikimedia. **Located at**: https://commons.wikimedia.org/wiki/File:Vespasianus01_pushkin_edit.png. **License**: *CC BY-SA: Attribution-ShareAlike*

- 660px-Arch_of_Titus_Menorah.png. **Provided by**: Wikimedia. **Located at**: https://commons.wikimedia.org/wiki/File:Arch_of_Titus_Menorah.png. **License**: *CC BY-SA: Attribution-ShareAlike*

- Ring_Lady.JPG. **Provided by**: Wikipedia. **Located at**: https://en.wikipedia.org/wiki/File:Ring_Lady.JPG. **License**: *CC BY-SA: Attribution-ShareAlike*

- Pompeii_Garden_of_the_Fugitives_02.jpg. **Provided by**: Wikimedia. **Located at**: https://commons.wikimedia.org/wiki/File:Pompeii_Garden_of_the_Fugitives_02.jpg. **License**: *Public Domain: No Known Copyright*

- Colosseum_in_Rome,_Italy_-_April_2007.jpg. **Provided by**: Wikimedia. **Located at**: https://commons.wikimedia.org/wiki/File:Colosseum_in_Rome,_Italy_-_April_2007.jpg. **License**: *CC BY-SA: Attribution-ShareAlike*

- Domitian_statue_Vatican.png. **Provided by**: Wikimedia. **Located at**: https://commons.wikimedia.org/wiki/File:Domitian_statue_Vatican.png. **License**: *CC BY-SA: Attribution-ShareAlike*

Christianity and the Late Roman Empire

Crises of the Roman Empire

The Crisis of the Third Century was a period in which the Roman Empire nearly collapsed under the combined pressures of invasion, civil war, plague, and economic depression.

Learning Objectives

Describe the problems afflicting the Roman Empire during the third century

Key Takeaways

Key Points

- The situation of the Roman Empire became dire in 235 CE, when emperor Alexander Severus was murdered by his own troops after defeat by Germanic tribes.
- In the years following the emperor's death, generals of the Roman army fought each other for control of the Empire, and neglected their duties of defending the empire from invasion. As a result, various provinces became victims of frequent raids.
- By 268, the Empire had split into three competing states: the Gallic Empire, including the Roman provinces of Gaul, Britannia, and Hispania; the Palmyrene Empire, including the eastern provinces of Syria Palaestina and Aegyptus; and the Italian-centered and independent Roman Empire proper.
- One of the most profound and lasting effects of the Crisis of the Third Century was the disruption of Rome 's extensive internal trade network under the Pax Romana.

- The continuing problems of the Empire would be radically addressed by Diocletian, allowing the Empire to continue to survive in the West for over a century, and in the East for over a millennium.

Key Terms

- **Crisis of the Third Century**: A period in which the Roman Empire nearly collapsed under the combined pressures of invasion, civil war, plague, and economic depression.
- **coloni**: A tenant farmer from the late Roman Empire and Early Middle Ages; sharecroppers.
- **Pax Romana**: The long period of relative peacefulness and minimal expansion by the Roman military force that was experienced by the Roman Empire after the end of the Final War of the Roman Republic, and before the beginning of the Crisis of the Third Century.

Overview

The Crisis of the Third Century, also known as Military Anarchy or the Imperial Crisis, (235-284 CE) was a period in which the Roman Empire nearly collapsed under the combined pressures of invasion, civil war, plague, and economic depression. The Crisis began with the assassination of Emperor Severus Alexander by his own troops in 235, initiating a 50-year period in which there were at least 26 claimants to the title of Emperor, mostly prominent Roman army generals, who assumed imperial power over all or part of the Empire. Twenty-six men were officially accepted by the Roman Senate as emperor during this period, and thus became legitimate emperors.

By 268, the Empire had split into three competing states: the Gallic Empire, including the Roman provinces of Gaul, Britannia, and (briefly) Hispania; the Palmyrene Empire, including the eastern provinces of Syria Palaestina and Aegyptus; and the Italian-centered and independent Roman Empire proper, between them. Later, Aurelian (270-275) reunited the empire; the Crisis ended with the ascension and reforms of Diocletian in 284.

The Crisis resulted in such profound changes in the Empire's institutions, society, economic life, and, eventually, religion, that it is increasingly seen by most historians as defining the transition between the historical periods of classical antiquity and late antiquity.

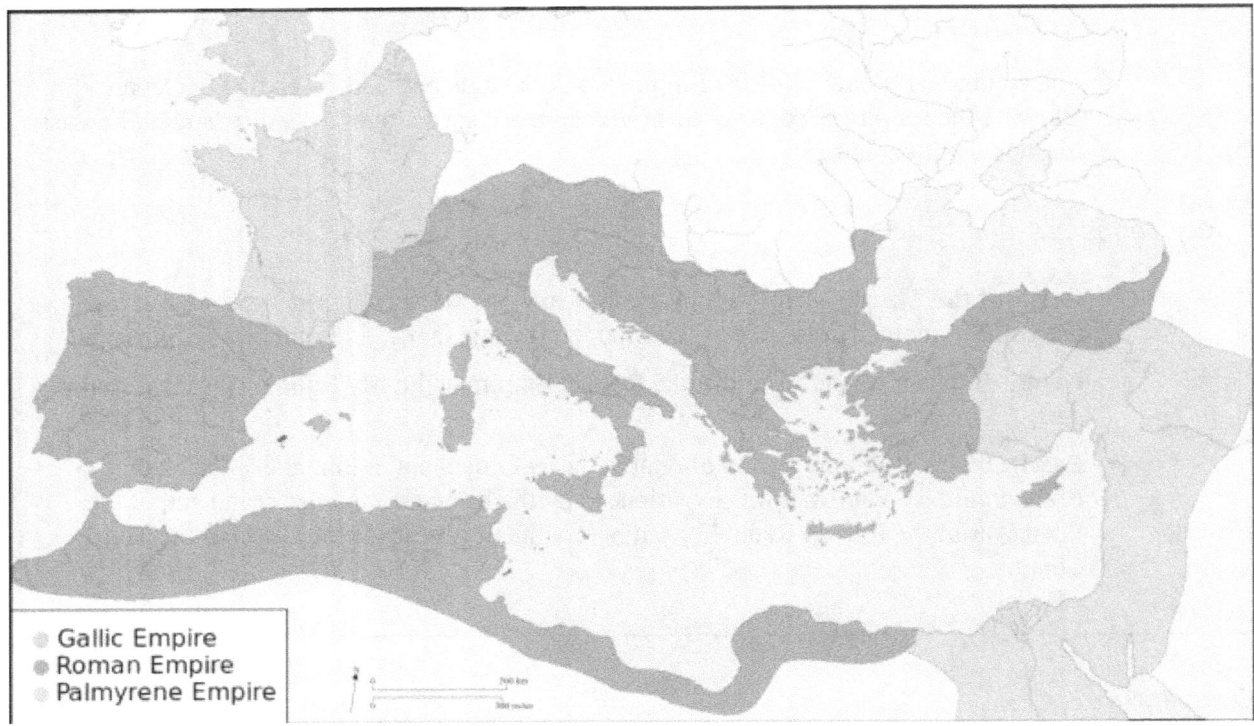

The Roman Empire in 271 CE: *The divided Empire during the Crisis of the Third Century.*

History of the Crisis

The situation of the Roman Empire became dire in 235 CE, when Emperor Alexander Severus was murdered by his own troops. Many Roman legions had been defeated during a campaign against Germanic peoples raiding across the borders, while the emperor was focused primarily on the dangers from the Sassanid Persian Empire. Leading his troops personally, Alexander Severus resorted to diplomacy and paying tribute, in an attempt to pacify the Germanic chieftains quickly. According to Herodian, this cost him the respect of his troops, who may have felt they should be punishing the tribes who were intruding on Rome's territory.

In the years following the emperor's death, generals of the Roman army fought each other for control of the Empire and neglected their duties of defending the empire from invasion. Provincials became victims of frequent raids along the length of the Rhine and Danube rivers, by such foreign tribes as the Carpians, Goths, Vandals, and Alamanni, and attacks from Sassanids in the east. Climate changes and a rise in sea levels ruined the agriculture of what is now the Low Countries, forcing tribes to migrate. Additionally, in 251, the Plague of Cyprian (possibly smallpox) broke out, causing large-scale death, and possibly weakened the ability of the Empire to defend itself.

After the loss of Valerian in 260, the Roman Empire was beset by usurpers, who broke it up into three competing states. The Roman provinces of Gaul, Britain, and Hispania broke off to form the Gallic Empire. After the death of Odaenathus in 267, the eastern provinces of Syria, Palestine, and Aegyptus became independent as the Palmyrene Empire, leaving the remaining Italian-centered Roman Empire proper in the middle.

An invasion by a vast host of Goths was defeated at the Battle of Naissus in 268 or 269. This victory was significant as the turning point of the crisis, when a series of tough, energetic soldier-emperors took power.

Victories by Emperor Claudius II Gothicus over the next two years drove back the Alamanni and recovered Hispania from the Gallic Empire. When Claudius died in 270 of the plague, Aurelian, who had commanded the cavalry at Naissus, succeeded him as the emperor and continued the restoration of the Empire.

Aurelian reigned (270-275) through the worst of the crisis, defeating the Vandals, the Visigoths, the Palmyrenes, the Persians, and then the remainder of the Gallic Empire. By late 274, the Roman Empire was reunited into a single entity, and the frontier troops were back in place. More than a century would pass before Rome again lost military ascendancy over its external enemies. However, dozens of formerly thriving cities, especially in the Western Empire, had been ruined, their populations dispersed and, with the breakdown of the economic system, could not be rebuilt. Major cities and towns, even Rome itself, had not needed fortifications for many centuries; many then surrounded themselves with thick walls.

Finally, although Aurelian had played a significant role in restoring the Empire's borders from external threat, more fundamental problems remained. In particular, the right of succession had never been clearly defined in the Roman Empire, leading to continuous civil wars as competing factions in the military, Senate, and other parties put forward their favored candidate for emperor. Another issue was the sheer size of the Empire, which made it difficult for a single autocratic ruler to effectively manage multiple threats at the same time. These continuing problems would be radically addressed by Diocletian, allowing the Empire to continue to survive in the West for over a century, and in the East for over a millennium.

Impact

One of the most profound and lasting effects of the Crisis of the Third Century was the disruption of Rome's extensive internal trade network. Ever since the Pax Romana, starting with Augustus, the Empire's economy had depended in large part on trade between Mediterranean ports and across the extensive road systems to the Empire's interior. Merchants could travel from one end of the Empire to the other in relative safety within a few weeks, moving agricultural goods produced in the provinces to the cities, and manufactured goods produced by the great cities of the East to the more rural provinces.

With the onset of the Crisis of the Third Century, however, this vast internal trade network broke down. The widespread civil unrest made it no longer safe for merchants to travel as they once had, and the financial crisis that struck made exchange very difficult with the debased currency. This produced profound changes that, in many ways, foreshadowed the very decentralized economic character of the coming Middle Ages.

Large landowners, no longer able to successfully export their crops over long distances, began producing food for subsistence and local barter. Rather than import manufactured goods from the Empire's great urban areas, they began to manufacture many goods locally, often on their own estates, thus beginning the self-sufficient "house economy" that would become commonplace in later centuries, reaching its final form in the Middle Ages' manorialism. The common free people of the Roman cities, meanwhile, began to move out into the countryside in search of food and better protection.

Made desperate by economic necessity, many of these former city dwellers, as well as many small farmers, were forced to give up hard-earned, basic civil rights in order to receive protection from large land-holders. In doing so, they became a half-free class of Roman citizen known as *coloni*. They were tied to the land, and in later Imperial law their status was made hereditary. This provided an early model for serfdom, the origins of medieval feudal society and of the medieval peasantry.

Diocletian and the Tetrarchy

Facing the pressures of civil war, plague, invasion, and economic depression, Diocletian was able to stabilize the Roman Empire for another hundred years through economic reform and the establishment of the Tetrarchy.

Learning Objectives

Describe the change in attitudes towards Christians and their statuses within the Roman Empire

Key Takeaways

Key Points

- Diocletian secured the empire's borders and purged it of all threats to his power. He separated and enlarged the empire's civil and military services, and reorganized the empire's provincial divisions, establishing the largest and most bureaucratic government in the history of the empire.
- Diocletian also restructured the Roman government by establishing the Tetrarchy, a system of rule in which four men shared rule over the massive Roman Empire. The empire was effectively divided in two, with an Augustus and a subordinate Caesar in each half.
- Diocletian established administrative capitals for each of the Tetrarchs, which were located closer to the empire's borders. Though Rome retained its unique Prefect of the City, it was no longer the administrative capital.
- By 313, therefore, there remained only two emperors: Constantine in the west and Licinius in the east. The tetrarchic system was at an end, although it took until 324 for Constantine to finally defeat Licinius, reunite the two halves of the Roman Empire, and declare himself sole Augustus.

Key Terms

- **Diocletian**: Roman emperor from 284 to 305 CE. Established the tetrarchy and instituted economic and tax reforms to stabilize the Roman Empire.
- **tetrarchy**: A form of government in which power is divided between four individuals. In ancient Rome, a system of government instituted by Diocletian that split power between two rulers in the east, and two rulers in the west.

Diocletian and the Stabilization of the Roman Empire

Diocletian was Roman emperor from 284 to 305 CE. Born to a family of low status in the Roman province of Dalmatia, Diocletian rose through the ranks of the military to become cavalry commander to the Emperor Carus. After the deaths of Carus and his son Numerian on campaign in Persia, Diocletian was proclaimed emperor. Diocletian's reign stabilized the empire, and marked the end of the Crisis of the Third Century. He appointed fellow officer, Maximian, as Augustus, co-emperor, in 286. Diocletian delegated further in 293, appointing Galerius and Constantius as caesars, junior co-emperors. Under this "tetrarchy," or "rule of four," each emperor would rule over a quarter-division of the empire. Diocletian further secured the empire's borders and purged it of all threats to his power.

He separated and enlarged the empire's civil and military services and reorganized the empire's provincial divisions, establishing the largest and most bureaucratic government in the history of the empire. He established new administrative centers in Nicomedia, Mediolanum, Antioch, and Trier, closer to the empire's frontiers than the traditional capital at Rome had been. Building on third-century trends towards absolutism, he styled himself an autocrat, elevating himself above the empire's masses with imposing forms of court ceremonies and architecture. Bureaucratic and military growth, constant campaigning, and construction projects increased the state's expenditures and necessitated a comprehensive tax reform. From at least 297 on, imperial taxation was standardized, made more equitable, and levied at generally higher rates.

While it is referred to as a "palace" because of its intended use as the retirement residence of Diocletian, the term can be misleading as the structure is massive and more resembles a large fortress: about half of it was for Diocletian's personal use, and the rest housed the military garrison.

The Tetrarchy

The first phase of Diocletian's government restructuring, sometimes referred to as the diarchy ("rule of two"), involved the designation of the general Maximian as co-emperor—first as Caesar (junior emperor) in 285, then Augustus in 286. This reorganization allowed Diocletian to take care of matters in the eastern regions of the empire, while Maximian similarly took charge of the western regions, thereby halving the administrative work required to oversee an empire as large as Rome's. In 293, feeling more focus was needed on both civic and military problems, Diocletian, with Maximian's consent, expanded the imperial college by appointing two Caesars (one responsible to each Augustus)—Galerius and Constantius Chlorus.

In 305, the senior emperors jointly abdicated and retired, allowing Constantius and Galerius to be elevated in rank to Augusti. They in turn appointed two new Caesars—Severus II in the west under Constantius, and Maximinus in the east under Galerius—thereby creating the second tetrarchy.

The four tetrarchs based themselves not at Rome but in other cities closer to the frontiers, mainly intended as headquarters for the defense of the empire against bordering rivals. Although Rome ceased to be an operational capital, it continued to be the nominal capital of the entire Roman Empire, not reduced to the status of a province, but under its own, unique Prefect of the City (*praefectus urbis*).

Zones of Influence in the Roman Tetrarchy: *This map shows the four zones of influence under Diocletian's tetrarchy.*

In terms of regional jurisdiction, there was no precise division between the four tetrarchs, and this period did not see the Roman state actually split up into four distinct sub-empires. Each emperor had his zone of influence within the Roman Empire, but this influence mainly applied to the theater of war. The tetrarch was himself often in the field, while delegating most of the administration to the hierarchic bureaucracy headed by his respective Praetorian Prefect. The Praetorian Prefect was the title of a high office in the Roman Empire, originating as the commander of the Praetorian Guard, the office gradually acquired extensive legal and administrative functions, with its holders becoming the emperor's chief aides.

Demise of the Tetrarchy

When, in 305, the 20-year term of Diocletian and Maximian ended, both abdicated. Their Caesares, Galerius and Constantius Chlorus, were both raised to the rank of Augustus, and two new Caesares were appointed: Maximinus (Caesar to Galerius) and Flavius Valerius Severus (Caesar to Constantius). These four formed the second tetrarchy.

However, the system broke down very quickly thereafter. When Constantius died in 306, Galerius promoted Severus to Augustus while Constantine, Constantius' son, was proclaimed Augustus by his father's troops. At the same time, Maxentius, the son of Maximian, who also resented being left out of the new arrangements, defeated Severus before forcing him to abdicate and then arranging his murder in 307. Maxentius and Maximian both then declared themselves Augusti. By 308, there were therefore no fewer than four claimants to the rank of Augustus (Galerius, Constantine, Maximian and Maxentius), and only one to that of Caesar (Maximinus).

In 308, Galerius, together with the retired emperor Diocletian and the supposedly retired Maximian, called an imperial "conference" at Carnuntum on the River Danube. The council agreed that Licinius would become Augustus in the West, with Constantine as his Caesar. In the East, Galerius remained Augustus, and Maximinus remained his Caesar. Maximian was to retire, and Maxentius was declared an usurper. This agreement proved disastrous: by 308 Maxentius had become de facto ruler of Italy and Africa even without any imperial rank, and neither Constantine nor Maximinus—who had both been Caesares since 306 and 305, respectively—were prepared to tolerate the promotion of the Augustus Licinius as their superior.

After an abortive attempt to placate both Constantine and Maximinus with the meaningless title *filius Augusti* ("son of the Augustus," essentially an alternative title for Caesar), they both had to be recognized as Augusti in 309. However, four full Augusti all at odds with each other did not bode well for the tetrarchic system.

Between 309 and 313, most of the claimants to the imperial office died or were killed in various civil wars. Constantine forced Maximian's suicide in 310. Galerius died naturally in 311. Maxentius was defeated by Constantine at the Battle of the Milvian Bridge in 312, and subsequently killed. Maximinus committed suicide at Tarsus in 313, after being defeated in battle by Licinius.

By 313, therefore, there remained only two emperors: Constantine in the west and Licinius in the east. The tetrarchic system was at an end, although it took until 324 for Constantine to finally defeat Licinius, reunite the two halves of the Roman Empire, and declare himself sole Augustus.

The Rise of Christianity

Though the early Christians were persecuted under some emperors, such as Nero and Diocletian, the religion continued to thrive and grow, eventually becoming the official religion of the Roman Empire under Constantine.

Learning Objectives

Describe the challenges Christians faced in the Roman Empire

Key Takeaways

Key Points

- Christians suffered from sporadic and localized persecutions over a period of two and a half centuries, as their refusal to participate in Imperial Cult of Rome was considered an

> act of treason, and was thus punishable by execution.
>
> - The Diocletianic, or Great Persecution, was the last and most severe persecution of Christians in the Roman Empire, which lasted from 302-311 CE. Galerius issued an edict of toleration in 311, which granted Christians the right to practice their religion, but did not restore any taken property back to them.
> - The Edict of Milan in 313 made the empire officially neutral with regard to religious worship; it neither made the traditional religions illegal nor made Christianity the state religion.
>
> Key Terms
>
> - **the Great Persecution**: The last and most severe persecution of Christians in the Roman Empire.
> - **Edict of Milan**: An agreement in 313 CE by Constantine and Licinius to treat Christians benevolently within the Roman Empire.

Persecution of Early Christians

Christianity posed a serious threat to the traditional Romans. The idea of monotheism was considered offensive against the polytheistic Roman pantheon, and came into further conflict with the Imperial Cult, in which emperors and some members of their families were worshipped as divine. As such, Christianity was considered criminal and was punished harshly.

The first recorded official persecution of Christians on behalf of the Roman Empire was in 64 CE, when, as reported by the Roman historian Tacitus, Emperor Nero blamed Christians for the Great Fire of Rome. According to Church tradition, it was during the reign of Nero that Peter and Paul were martyred in Rome. However, modern historians debate whether the Roman government distinguished between Christians and Jews prior to Nerva's modification of the Fiscus Judaicus in 96, from which point practicing Jews paid the tax and Christians did not.

The Diocletianic or Great Persecution was the last and most severe persecution of Christians in the Roman Empire, which lasted from 302-311 CE. In 303, the emperors Diocletian, Maximian, Galerius, and Constantius issued a series of edicts rescinding the legal rights of Christians and demanding that they comply with traditional Roman religious practices. Later edicts targeted the clergy and ordered all inhabitants to sacrifice to the Roman gods (a policy known as universal sacrifice). The persecution varied in intensity across the empire—it was weakest in Gaul and Britain, where only the first edict was applied, and strongest in the Eastern provinces. Persecutory laws were nullified by different emperors at different times, but Constantine and Licinius's Edict of Milan (313) has traditionally marked the end of the persecution.

During the Great Persecution, Diocletian ordered Christian buildings and the homes of Christians torn down, and their sacred books collected and burned during the Great Persecution. Christians were arrested, tortured, mutilated, burned, starved, and condemned to gladiatorial contests to amuse spectators. The Great Persecution officially ended in April of 311, when Galerius, senior emperor of the Tetrarchy, issued an edict of toleration which granted Christians the right to practice their religion, though it did not restore any property to them. Constantine, Caesar in the western empire, and Licinius, Caesar in the east, also were signatories to the edict of toleration. It has been speculated that Galerius' reversal of his long-standing policy of Christian persecution has been attributable to one or both of these co-Caesars.

The Rise of Christianity

The Diocletianic persecution was ultimately unsuccessful. As one modern historian has put it, it was simply "too little and too late." Christians were never purged systematically in any part of the empire, and Christian evasion continually undermined the edicts' enforcement. Although the persecution resulted in death, torture, imprisonment, or dislocation for many Christians, the majority of the empire's Christians avoided punishment. Some bribed their way to freedom or fled. In the end, the persecution failed to check the rise of the church. By 324, Constantine was sole ruler of the empire, and Christianity had become his favored religion.

By 324, Constantine, the Christian convert, ruled the entire empire alone. Christianity became the greatest beneficiary of imperial largesse. The persecutors had been routed. As the historian J. Liebeschuetz has written: "The final result of the Great Persecution provided a testimonial to the truth of Christianity, which it could have won in no other way." After Constantine, the Christianization of the Roman empire would continue apace. Under Theodosius I (r. 378-395), Christianity became the state religion. By the 5th century, Christianity was the empire's predominant faith, and filled the same role paganism had at the end of the 3rd century. Because of the persecution, however, a number of Christian communities were riven between those who had complied with imperial authorities (*traditores*) and those who had refused. In Africa, the Donatists, who protested the election of the alleged traditor, Caecilian, to the bishopric of Carthage, continued to resist the authority of the central church until after 411. The Melitians in Egypt left the Egyptian Church similarly divided.

The Edict of Milan

In 313, Constantine and Licinius announced in the Edict of Milan "that it was proper that the Christians and all others should have liberty to follow that mode of religion which to each of them appeared best," thereby granting tolerance to all religions, including Christianity. The Edict of Milan went a step further than the earlier Edict of Toleration by Galerius in 311, and returned confiscated Church property. This edict made the empire officially neutral with regard to religious worship; it neither made the traditional religions illegal, nor made Christianity the state religion (as did the later Edict of Thessalonica in 380 CE). The Edict of Milan did, however, raise the stock of Christianity within the empire, and it reaffirmed the importance of religious worship to the welfare of the state.

Constantine

Constantine the Great was a Roman Emperor from 306 to 337 CE; he adopted Christianity and declared it the religion of the Roman Empire.

> **Learning Objectives**
>
> Type your learning objectives here.
>
> - First
> - Second

> **Key Takeaways**
>
> *Key Points*
>
> - The age of Constantine marked a distinct epoch in the history of the Roman Empire, both for founding Byzantium in the east, as well as his adoption of Christianity as a state religion.
> - As emperor, Constantine enacted many administrative, financial, social, and military reforms to strengthen the empire.
> - Constantine experienced a dramatic event in 312 at the Battle of the Milvian Bridge, after which Constantine claimed the emperorship in the west and converted to Christianity.
> - According to some sources, on the evening of October 27, with the armies preparing for battle, Constantine had a vision of a cross, which led him to fight under the protection of the Christian god.
> - The accession of Constantine was a turning point for early Christianity; after his victory, Constantine took over the role of patron of the Christian faith.
>
> *Key Terms*
>
> - **Edict of Milan**: The February 313 CE agreement to treat Christians benevolently within the Roman Empire, thereby ending years of persecution.
> - **Chi-Rho**: One of the earliest forms of christogram, which is used by some Christians, and was used by the Roman emperor, Constantine I (r. 306-337), as part of a military standard.
> - **Battle of the Milvian Bridge**: A battle that took place between the Roman Emperors, Constantine I and Maxentius, on October 28, 312, and is often seen as the beginning of Constantine's conversion to Christianity.

Constantine the Great was a Roman Emperor from 306-337 CE. Constantine was the son of Flavius Valerius Constantius, a Roman army officer, and his consort, Helena. His father became Caesar, the deputy emperor in the west, in 293 CE. Constantine was sent east, where he rose through the ranks to become a military tribune under the emperors Diocletian and Galerius. In 305, Constantius was raised to the rank of Augustus, senior western emperor, and Constantine was recalled west to campaign under his father in Britannia (modern Great Britain). Acclaimed as emperor by the army at Eboracum (modern-day York) after his father's death in 306 CE, Constantine emerged victorious in a series of civil wars against the emperors Maxentius and Licinius, to become sole ruler of both west and east by 324 CE.

As emperor, Constantine enacted many administrative, financial, social, and military reforms to strengthen the empire. The government was restructured and civil and military authority separated. A new gold coin, the solidus, was introduced to combat inflation. It would become the standard for Byzantine and European currencies for more than a thousand years. As the first Roman emperor to claim conversion to Christianity, Constantine played an influential role in the proclamation of the Edict of Milan in 313, which decreed tolerance for Christianity in the empire. He called the First Council of Nicaea in 325, at which the Nicene Creed was professed by Christians. In military matters, the Roman army was reorganized to consist of mobile field units and garrison soldiers capable of countering internal threats and barbarian invasions. Constantine pursued successful campaigns against the tribes on the Roman frontiers—the Franks, the Alamanni, the Goths, and the Sarmatians—even resettling territories abandoned by his predecessors during the Crisis of the Third Century.

Constantine's reputation flourished during the lifetime of his children and for centuries after his reign. The medieval church upheld him as a paragon of virtue, while secular rulers invoked him as a prototype, a point of reference, and the symbol of imperial legitimacy and identity. One of his major political legacies, aside from moving the capital of the empire to Constantinople, was that, in leaving the empire to his sons, he replaced Diocletian's tetrarchy with the principle of dynastic succession.

The Battle of the Milvian Bridge

Eusebius of Caesarea, and other Christian sources, record that Constantine experienced a dramatic event in 312 at the Battle of the Milvian Bridge, after which Constantine claimed the emperorship in the west, and converted to Christianity. The Battle of the Milvian Bridge took place between the Roman Emperors, Constantine I and Maxentius, on October 28, 312. It takes its name from the Milvian Bridge, an important route over the Tiber. Constantine won the battle and started on the path that led him to end the tetrarchy and become the sole ruler of the Roman Empire. Maxentius drowned in the Tiber during the battle, and his body was later taken from the river and decapitated.

According to chroniclers, such as Eusebius of Caesarea and Lactantius, the battle marked the beginning of Constantine's conversion to Christianity. Eusebius of Caesarea recounts that Constantine looked up to the sun before the battle and saw a cross of light above it, and with it the Greek words Ἐν Τούτῳ Νίκα ("in this sign, conquer!"), often rendered in a Latin version, "*in hoc signo vinces.*" Constantine commanded his troops to adorn their shields with a Christian symbol (the Chi-Rho), and thereafter they were victorious. The Arch of Constantine, erected in celebration of the victory, certainly attributes Constantine's success to divine intervention; however, the monument does not display any overtly Christian symbolism, so there is no scholarly consensus on the events' relation to Constantine's conversion to Christianity.

Constantine: *Missorium depicting Constantine's son Constantius II, accompanied by a guardsman with the Chi Rho monogram depicted on his shield.*

Following the battle, Constantine ignored the altars to the gods prepared on the Capitoline, and did not carry out the customary sacrifices to celebrate a general's victorious entry into Rome, instead heading directly to the imperial palace. Most influential people in the empire, however, especially high military officials, had not been converted to Christianity, and still participated in the traditional religions of Rome; Constantine's rule exhibited at least a willingness to appease these factions. The Roman coins minted up to eight years after the battle still bore the images of Roman gods. The monuments he first commissioned, such as the Arch of Constantine, contained no reference to Christianity.

Constantine and Christianity

While the Roman Emperor Constantine the Great reigned (306-337 CE), Christianity began to transition to the dominant religion of the Roman Empire. Historians remain uncertain about Constantine's reasons for favoring Christianity, and theologians and historians have argued about which form of Early Christianity he subscribed to. There is no consensus among scholars as to whether he adopted his mother Helena's Christianity in his youth, or (as claimed by Eusebius of Caesarea) encouraged her to convert to the faith himself. Some scholars question the extent to which he should be considered a Christian emperor: "Constantine saw himself as an 'emperor of the Christian people.' If this made him a Christian is the subject of debate," although he allegedly received a baptism shortly before his death.

Constantine's decision to cease the persecution of Christians in the Roman Empire was a turning point for early Christianity, sometimes referred to as the Triumph of the Church, the Peace of the Church, or the Constantinian Shift. In 313, Constantine and Licinius issued the Edict of Milan, decriminalizing Christian worship. The emperor became a great patron of the Church and set a precedent for the position of the Christian emperor within the Church, and the notion of orthodoxy, Christendom, ecumenical councils, and the state church of the Roman Empire, declared by edict in 380. He is revered as a saint and isapostolos in the Eastern Orthodox Church and Oriental Orthodox Church for his example as a "Christian monarch."

The Shift East

Constantine built a new imperial residence in Byzantium and renamed the city Constantinople after himself; the city eventually became the capital of the empire for over one thousand years.

Learning Objectives

Explain why Constantine moved the capital of the empire to Constantinople, and the consequences that had for the empire as a whole

Key Takeaways

Key Points

- After defeating Maxentius and his rebellion, Constantine gradually consolidated his military superiority over his rivals in the crumbling Tetrarchy, in particular Licinius.
- Eventually, Constantine defeated Licinius, making him the sole emperor of the empire, thereby ending the tetrarchy.
- Licinius' defeat came to represent the defeat of a rival center of Pagan and Greek-speaking political activity in the east, and it was proposed that a new eastern capital should represent the integration of the east into the Roman Empire as a whole; Constantine chose Byzantium.
- The city was thus founded in 324, dedicated on May 11, 330, and renamed Constantinople.
- The Byzantine Empire considered Constantine its founder, and the Holy Roman Empire reckoned him among the venerable figures of its tradition.

> **Key Terms**
>
> - **Byzantium**: An ancient Greek colony on the site that later became Constantinople, and eventually Istanbul.
> - **Byzantine Empire**: Also referred to as the Eastern Roman Empire, was the continuation of the Roman Empire in the east during Late Antiquity and the Middle Ages, when the empire's capital city was Constantinople.

The age of Constantine marked a distinct epoch in the history of the Roman Empire. He built a new imperial residence at Byzantium, and renamed the city Constantinople after himself (the laudatory epithet of "New Rome " came later, and was never an official title). It would later become the capital of the empire for over one thousand years; for this reason the later Eastern Empire would come to be known as the Byzantine Empire.

Background: War With Licinius

After defeating Maxentius, Constantine gradually consolidated his military superiority over his rivals in the crumbling tetrarchy. In 313, he met Licinius in Milan to secure their alliance by the marriage of Licinius and Constantine's half-sister, Constantia. During this meeting, the emperors agreed on the so-called Edict of Milan, officially granting full tolerance to Christianity and all religions in the Empire. In the year 320, Licinius allegedly reneged on the religious freedom promised by the Edict of Milan in 313, and began to oppress Christians anew, generally without bloodshed, but resorting to confiscations and sacking of Christian office-holders.

This dubious arrangement eventually became a challenge to Constantine in the west, climaxing in the great civil war of 324. Licinius, aided by Goth mercenaries, represented the past and the ancient Pagan faiths. Constantine and his Franks marched under the standard of the *labarum* Chi-Rho, and both sides saw the battle in religious terms. Outnumbered, but fired by their zeal, Constantine's army emerged victorious in the Battle of Adrianople. Licinius fled across the Bosphorus and appointed Martius Martinianus, the commander of his bodyguard, as Caesar, but Constantine next won the Battle of the Hellespont, and finally the Battle of Chrysopolis on September 18, 324. Licinius and Martinianus surrendered to Constantine at Nicomedia on the promise their lives would be spared: they were sent to live as private citizens in Thessalonica and Cappadocia, respectively, but in 325, Constantine accused Licinius of plotting against him and had them both arrested and hanged. Licinius's son (the son of Constantine's half-sister) was also killed. Thus, Constantine became the sole emperor of the Roman Empire.

Foundation of Constantinople

Licinius' defeat came to represent the defeat of a rival center of Pagan and Greek-speaking political activity in the east, as opposed to the Christian and Latin-speaking Rome, and it was proposed that a new eastern capital should represent the integration of the east into the Roman Empire as a whole, as a center of learning, prosperity, and cultural preservation for the whole of the eastern Roman Empire. Among the various locations proposed for this alternative capital, Constantine appears to have toyed earlier with Serdica (present-day Sofia), as he was reported saying that "Serdica is my Rome." Sirmium and Thessalonica were also considered. Eventually, however, Constantine decided to work on the Greek city of Byzantium, which offered the advantage of having already been extensively rebuilt on Roman patterns of urbanism, during the preceding century, by Septimius Severus and Caracalla, who had already acknowledged its strategic importance.

The city was thus founded in 324, dedicated on May 11, 330, and renamed *Constantinopolis* ("Constantine's City" or Constantinople in English). Special commemorative coins were issued in 330 to honor the event. The new city was protected by the relics of the True Cross, the Rod of Moses, and other holy relics, though a cameo now at the Hermitage Museum also represented Constantine crowned by the tyche of the new city. The figures of old gods were either replaced or assimilated into a framework of Christian symbolism. Constantine built the new Church of the Holy Apostles on the site of a temple to Aphrodite. Generations later there was the story that a divine vision led Constantine to this spot, and an angel no one else could see led him on a circuit of the new walls. The capital would often be compared to the 'old' Rome as *Nova Roma Constantinopolitana*, the "New Rome of Constantinople." Constantinople was a superb base from which to guard the Danube River, and it was reasonably close to the eastern frontiers. Constantine also began the building of the great fortified walls, which were expanded and rebuilt in subsequent ages.

Constantinopolis Coin: *Coin struck by Constantine I to commemorate the founding of Constantinople.*

Legacy

Historian J.B. Bury asserts that "the foundation of Constantinople [...] inaugurated a permanent division between the Eastern and Western, the Greek and the Latin, halves of the empire—a division to which events had already pointed—and affected decisively the whole subsequent history of Europe."

The Byzantine Empire considered Constantine its founder, and the Holy Roman Empire reckoned him among the venerable figures of its tradition. In the later Byzantine state, it had become a great honor for an emperor to be hailed as a "new Constantine." Ten emperors, including the last emperor of the Eastern Roman Empire, carried the name. Monumental Constantinian forms were used at the court of Charlemagne to suggest that he was Constantine's successor and equal. Constantine acquired a mythic role as a warrior against "heathens."

The Decline and Fall of the Roman Empire

The Fall of the Western Roman Empire was the period of decline during which the empire disintegrated and split into numerous successor states.

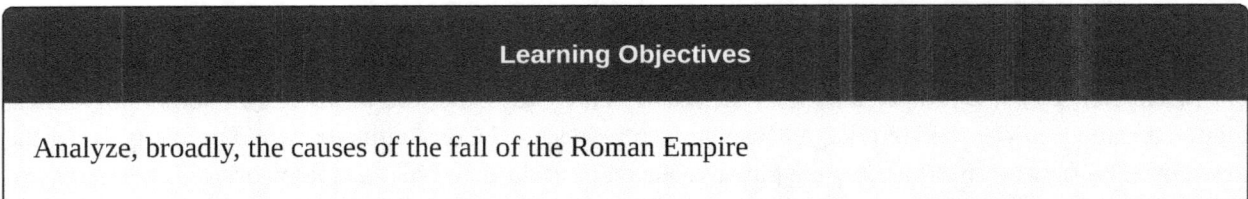

Key Points

- Throughout the 5th century, the empire's territories in western Europe and northwestern Africa, including Italy, fell to various invading or indigenous peoples, in what is sometimes called the Migration Period.
- By the late 3rd century, the city of Rome no longer served as an effective capital for the emperor, and various cities were used as new administrative capitals. Successive emperors, starting with Constantine, privileged the eastern city of Byzantium, which he had entirely rebuilt after a siege.
- In 476, after being refused lands in Italy, Odacer and his Germanic mercenaries took Ravenna, the Western Roman capital at the time, and deposed Western Emperor Romulus Augustus. The whole of Italy was quickly conquered, and Odoacer's rule became recognized in the Eastern Empire.
- Four broad schools of thought exist on the decline and fall of the Roman Empire: decay owing to general malaise, monocausal decay, catastrophic collapse, and transformation.

Key Terms

- **Odoacer**: A soldier, who came to power in the Western Roman Empire in 476 CE. His reign is commonly seen as marking the end of the Western Roman Empire.
- **Migration Period**: Also known as the period of the Barbarian Invasions, it was a period of intensified human migration in Europe from about 400 to 800 CE, during the transition from Late Antiquity to the Early Middle Ages.

The Fall of the Western Roman Empire was the process of decline during which the empire failed to enforce its rule, and its vast territory was divided into several successor polities. The Roman Empire lost the strengths that had allowed it to exercise effective control; modern historians mention factors including the effectiveness and numbers of the army, the health and numbers of the Roman population, the strength of the economy, the competence of the emperor, the religious changes of the period, and the efficiency of the civil administration. Increasing pressure from barbarians outside Roman culture also contributed greatly to the collapse. The reasons for the collapse are major subjects of the historiography of the ancient world, and they inform much modern discourse on state failure.

By 476 CE, when Odoacer deposed Emperor Romulus, the Western Roman Empire wielded negligible military, political, or financial power and had no effective control over the scattered western domains that could still be described as Roman. Invading "barbarians" had established their own polities on most of the area of the Western Empire. While its legitimacy lasted for centuries longer and its cultural influence remains today, the Western Empire never had the strength to rise again.

It is important to note, however, that the so-called fall of the Roman Empire specifically refers to the fall of the *Western* Roman Empire, since the Eastern Roman Empire, or what became known as the Byzantine Empire, whose capital was founded by Constantine, remained for another 1,000 years. Theodosius was the last emperor who ruled over the whole empire. After his death in 395, he gave the two halves of the empire to his two sons, Arcadius and Honorius; Arcadius became ruler in the east, with his capital in Constantinople, and Honorius became ruler in the west, with his capital in Milan, and later Ravenna.

Rome in the 5th Century CE

Throughout the 5th century, the empire's territories in western Europe and northwestern Africa, including Italy, fell to various invading or indigenous peoples in what is sometimes called the Migration Period, also known as the Barbarian Invasions, from the Roman and South European perspective. The first migrations of peoples were made by Germanic tribes, such as the Goths, Vandals, Angles, Saxons, Lombards, Suebi, Frisii, Jutes and Franks; they were later pushed westwards by the Huns, Avars, Slavs, and Bulgars.

Although the eastern half still survived with borders essentially intact for several centuries (until the Muslim conquests), the Empire as a whole had initiated major cultural and political transformations since the Crisis of the Third Century, with the shift towards a more openly autocratic and ritualized form of government, the adoption of Christianity as the state religion, and a general rejection of the traditions and values of Classical Antiquity.

The reasons for the decline of the Empire are still debated today, and are likely multiple. Historians infer that the population appears to have diminished in many provinces (especially western Europe), judging from the diminishing size of fortifications built to protect the cities from barbarian incursions from the 3rd century on. Some historians even have suggested that parts of the periphery were no longer inhabited, because these fortifications were restricted to the center of the city only. By the late 3rd century, the city of Rome no longer served as an effective capital for the emperor, and various cities were used as new administrative capitals. Successive emperors, starting with Constantine, privileged the eastern city of Byzantium, which he had entirely rebuilt after a siege. Later renamed Constantinople, and protected by formidable walls in the late 4th and early 5th centuries, it was to become the largest and most powerful city of Christian Europe in the Early Middle Ages. Since the Crisis of the Third Century, the empire was intermittently ruled by more than one emperor at once (usually two), presiding over different regions.

The Latin-speaking west, under dreadful demographic crisis, and the wealthier Greek-speaking east, also began to diverge politically and culturally. Although this was a gradual process, still incomplete when Italy came under the rule of barbarian chieftains in the last quarter of the 5th century, it deepened further afterward, and had lasting consequences for the medieval history of Europe.

In 476, after being refused lands in Italy, Orestes' Germanic mercenaries, under the leadership of the chieftain Odoacer, captured and executed Orestes and took Ravenna, the Western Roman capital at the time, deposing Western Emperor Romulus Augustus. The whole of Italy was quickly conquered, and Odoacer's rule became recognized in the Eastern Empire. Meanwhile, much of the rest of the Western provinces were conquered by waves of Germanic invasions, most of them being disconnected politically from the east altogether, and continuing a slow decline. Although Roman political authority in the west was lost, Roman culture would last in most parts of the former western provinces into the 6th century and beyond.

Romulus Augustus Resigns the Crown: *Charlotte Mary Yonge's 1880 artist rendition of Romulus Augustus resigning the crown to Odoacer.*

Theories on the Decline and Fall

The various theories and explanations for the fall of the Roman Empire in the west may be very broadly classified into four schools of thought (although the classification is not without overlap):

- Decay owing to general malaise
- Monocausal decay
- Catastrophic collapse
- Transformation

The tradition positing general malaise goes back to the historian, Edward Gibbon, who argued that the edifice of the Roman Empire had been built on unsound foundations from the beginning. According to Gibbon, the fall was—in the final analysis—inevitable. On the other hand, Gibbon had assigned a major portion of the responsibility for the decay to the influence of Christianity, and is often, though perhaps unjustly, seen as the founding father of the school of monocausal explanation. On the other hand, the school of catastrophic collapse holds that the fall of the empire had not been a pre-determined event and need not be taken for granted. Rather, it was due to the combined effect of a number of adverse processes, many of them set in motion by the Migration Period, that together applied too much stress to the empire's basically sound structure. Finally, the transformation school challenges the whole notion of the 'fall' of the empire, asking instead to distinguish between the fall into disuse of a particular political dispensation, anyway unworkable towards its end; and the fate of the Roman civilization that under-girded the empire. According to this school, drawing its basic premise from the Pirenne thesis, the Roman world underwent a gradual (though often violent) series of transformations, morphing into the medieval world. The historians belonging to this school often prefer to speak of Late Antiquity, instead of the Fall of the Roman Empire.

Ostrogothic Kingdom: *The Ostrogothic Kingdom, which rose from the ruins of the Western Roman Empire.*

Attributions

CC licensed content, Specific attribution

- Crisis of the Third Century. **Provided by**: Wikipedia. **Located at**: https://en.wikipedia.org/wiki/Crisis_of_the_Third_Century. **License**: *CC BY-SA: Attribution-ShareAlike*
- History of the Roman Empire. **Provided by**: Wikipedia. **Located at**: https://en.wikipedia.org/wiki/History_of_the_Roman_Empire. **License**: *CC BY-SA: Attribution-ShareAlike*
- 800px-Map_of_Ancient_Rome_271_AD.svg.png. **Provided by**: Wikimedia. **Located at**: https://commons.wikimedia.org/wiki/File:Map_of_Ancient_Rome_271_AD.svg. **License**: *Public Domain: No Known Copyright*
- Diocletian's Palace. **Provided by**: Wikipedia. **Located at**: https://en.wikipedia.org/wiki/Diocletian%27s_Palace. **License**: *CC BY-SA: Attribution-ShareAlike*
- Diocletian. **Provided by**: Wikipedia. **Located at**: http://en.wikipedia.org/wiki/Diocletian%23Tetrarchy. **License**: *CC BY-SA: Attribution-ShareAlike*
- Tetrarchy. **Provided by**: Wikipedia. **Located at**: http://en.wikipedia.org/wiki/Tetrarchy%23mediaviewer/File:Tetrarchy_map3.jpg. **License**: *CC BY-SA: Attribution-ShareAlike*
- Crisis of the Third Century. **Provided by**: Wikipedia. **Located at**: http://en.wikipedia.org/wiki/Crisis_of_the_Third_Century. **License**: *CC BY-SA: Attribution-ShareAlike*
- tetrarchy. **Provided by**: Wiktionary. **Located at**: http://en.wiktionary.org/wiki/tetrarchy. **License**: *CC BY-SA: Attribution-ShareAlike*
- Praetorian Prefect. **Provided by**: Wikipedia. **Located at**: http://en.wikipedia.org/wiki/Praetorian_prefect. **License**: *CC BY-SA:*

Attribution-ShareAlike

- 800px-Map_of_Ancient_Rome_271_AD.svg.png. **Provided by**: Wikimedia. **Located at**: https://commons.wikimedia.org/wiki/File:Map_of_Ancient_Rome_271_AD.svg. **License**: *Public Domain: No Known Copyright*
- Tetrarchy Map. **Provided by**: Wikimedia. **Located at**: https://commons.wikimedia.org/wiki/File:Tetrarchy_map3.jpg. **License**: *Public Domain: No Known Copyright*
- Diocletianic Persecution. **Provided by**: Wikipedia. **Located at**: https://en.wikipedia.org/wiki/Diocletianic_Persecution. **License**: *CC BY-SA: Attribution-ShareAlike*
- Constantine the Great and Christanity. **Provided by**: Wikipedia. **Located at**: http://en.wikipedia.org/wiki/Constantine_the_Great_and_Christianity. **License**: *CC BY-SA: Attribution-ShareAlike*
- Edict of Milan. **Provided by**: Wikipedia. **Located at**: http://en.wikipedia.org/wiki/Edict_of_milan. **License**: *CC BY-SA: Attribution-ShareAlike*
- 800px-Map_of_Ancient_Rome_271_AD.svg.png. **Provided by**: Wikimedia. **Located at**: https://commons.wikimedia.org/wiki/File:Map_of_Ancient_Rome_271_AD.svg. **License**: *Public Domain: No Known Copyright*
- Tetrarchy Map. **Provided by**: Wikimedia. **Located at**: https://commons.wikimedia.org/wiki/File:Tetrarchy_map3.jpg. **License**: *Public Domain: No Known Copyright*
- Battle of the Milvian Bridge. **Provided by**: Wikipedia. **Located at**: https://en.wikipedia.org/wiki/Battle_of_the_Milvian_Bridge. **License**: *CC BY-SA: Attribution-ShareAlike*
- Constantine the Great and Christianity. **Provided by**: Wikipedia. **Located at**: https://en.wikipedia.org/wiki/Constantine_the_Great_and_Christianity. **License**: *CC BY-SA: Attribution-ShareAlike*
- Constantine the Great. **Provided by**: Wikipedia. **Located at**: https://en.wikipedia.org/wiki/Constantine_the_Great. **License**: *CC BY-SA: Attribution-ShareAlike*
- 800px-Map_of_Ancient_Rome_271_AD.svg.png. **Provided by**: Wikimedia. **Located at**: https://commons.wikimedia.org/wiki/File:Map_of_Ancient_Rome_271_AD.svg. **License**: *Public Domain: No Known Copyright*
- Tetrarchy Map. **Provided by**: Wikimedia. **Located at**: https://commons.wikimedia.org/wiki/File:Tetrarchy_map3.jpg. **License**: *Public Domain: No Known Copyright*
- 1280px-Missorium_Kerch.jpg. **Provided by**: Wikipedia. **Located at**: https://en.wikipedia.org/wiki/Battle_of_the_Milvian_Bridge#/media/File:Missorium_Kerch.jpg. **License**: *CC BY-SA: Attribution-ShareAlike*
- Constantine the Great. **Provided by**: Wikipedia. **Located at**: https://en.wikipedia.org/wiki/Constantine_the_Great. **License**: *CC BY-SA: Attribution-ShareAlike*
- Byzantine Empire. **Provided by**: Wikipedia. **Located at**: https://en.wikipedia.org/wiki/Byzantine_Empire#History. **License**: *CC BY-SA: Attribution-ShareAlike*
- 800px-Map_of_Ancient_Rome_271_AD.svg.png. **Provided by**: Wikimedia. **Located at**: https://commons.wikimedia.org/wiki/File:Map_of_Ancient_Rome_271_AD.svg. **License**: *Public Domain: No Known Copyright*
- Tetrarchy Map. **Provided by**: Wikimedia. **Located at**: https://commons.wikimedia.org/wiki/File:Tetrarchy_map3.jpg. **License**: *Public Domain: No Known Copyright*
- 1280px-Missorium_Kerch.jpg. **Provided by**: Wikipedia. **Located at**: https://en.wikipedia.org/wiki/Battle_of_the_Milvian_Bridge#/media/File:Missorium_Kerch.jpg. **License**: *CC BY-SA: Attribution-ShareAlike*
- Constantinopolis_coin.jpg. **Provided by**: Wikipedia. **Located at**: https://en.wikipedia.org/wiki/Constantine_the_Great#/media/File:Constantinopolis_coin.jpg. **License**: *CC BY-SA: Attribution-ShareAlike*
- Ostrogothic Kingdom. **Provided by**: Wikipedia. **Located at**: https://en.wikipedia.org/wiki/Ostrogothic_Kingdom. **License**: *CC BY-SA: Attribution-ShareAlike*
- Fall of the Western Roman Emi. **Provided by**: Wikipedia. **Located at**: http://en.wikipedia.org/wiki/Fall_of_the_Western_Roman_Empire. **License**: *CC BY-SA: Attribution-ShareAlike*
- Migration Period. **Provided by**: Wikipedia. **Located at**: http://en.wikipedia.org/wiki/Migration_period. **License**: *CC BY-SA: Attribution-ShareAlike*
- Odoacer. **Provided by**: Wikipedia. **Located at**: http://en.wikipedia.org/wiki/Odoacer. **License**: *CC BY-SA: Attribution-ShareAlike*
- Decline of the Roman Empire. **Provided by**: Wikipedia. **Located at**: http://en.wikipedia.org/wiki/Decline_of_the_Roman_Empire%23Theories_of_a_fall.2C_decline.2C_transition_and_continuity. **License**: *CC BY-SA: Attribution-ShareAlike*
- 800px-Map_of_Ancient_Rome_271_AD.svg.png. **Provided by**: Wikimedia. **Located at**: https://commons.wikimedia.org/wiki/File:Map_of_Ancient_Rome_271_AD.svg. **License**: *Public Domain: No Known Copyright*
- Tetrarchy Map. **Provided by**: Wikimedia. **Located at**: https://commons.wikimedia.org/wiki/File:Tetrarchy_map3.jpg. **License**:

Public Domain: No Known Copyright

- 1280px-Missorium_Kerch.jpg. **Provided by**: Wikipedia. **Located at**: https://en.wikipedia.org/wiki/Battle_of_the_Milvian_Bridge#/media/File:Missorium_Kerch.jpg. **License**: *CC BY-SA: Attribution-ShareAlike*
- Constantinopolis_coin.jpg. **Provided by**: Wikipedia. **Located at**: https://en.wikipedia.org/wiki/Constantine_the_Great#/media/File:Constantinopolis_coin.jpg. **License**: *CC BY-SA: Attribution-ShareAlike*
- Young Folks' History of Rome. **Provided by**: Wikimedia. **Located at**: https://commons.wikimedia.org/wiki/File:Young_Folks%27_History_of_Rome_illus420.png. **License**: *Public Domain: No Known Copyright*
- Ostrogothic Kingdom. **Provided by**: Wikimedia. **Located at**: https://commons.wikimedia.org/wiki/File:Ostrogothic_Kingdom.png. **License**: *Public Domain: No Known Copyright*

The Byzantine Empire

Byzantium: The New Rome

Naming of the Byzantine Empire

While the Western Roman Empire fell, the Eastern Roman Empire, now known as the Byzantine Empire, thrived.

Learning Objectives

Describe identifying characteristics of the Byzantine Empire

Key Takeaways

Key Points

- While the Western Roman Empire fell in 476 CE, the Eastern Roman Empire, centered on the city of Constantinople, survived and thrived.
- After the Eastern Roman Empire's much later fall in 1453 CE, western scholars began calling it the " Byzantine Empire " to emphasize its distinction from the earlier, Latin-speaking Roman Empire centered on Rome.
- The "Byzantine Empire" is now the standard term used among historians to refer to the Eastern Roman Empire.
- Although the Byzantine Empire had a multi-ethnic character during most of its history and preserved Romano-Hellenistic traditions, it became identified with its increasingly predominant Greek element and its own unique cultural developments.

Key Terms

- **Constantinople**: Formerly Byzantium, the capital of the Byzantine Empire as established by its first emperor, Constantine the Great. (Today the city is known as Istanbul.)

The Byzantine Empire, sometimes referred to as the Eastern Roman Empire, was the continuation of the Roman Empire in the east during Late Antiquity and the Middle Ages, when its capital city was Constantinople (modern-day Istanbul, originally founded as Byzantium). It survived the fragmentation and fall of the Western Roman Empire in the 5th century CE, and continued to exist for an additional thousand years until it fell to the Ottoman Turks in 1453. During most of its existence, the empire was the most powerful economic, cultural, and military force in Europe. Both "Byzantine Empire" and "Eastern Roman Empire" are historiographical terms created after the end of the realm; its citizens continued to refer to their empire as the Roman Empire, and thought of themselves as Romans. Although the people living in the Eastern Roman Empire referred to themselves as Romans, they were distinguished by their Greek heritage, Orthodox Christianity, and their regional connections. Over time, the culture of the Eastern Roman Empire transformed. Greek replaced Latin as the language of the empire. Christianity became more important in daily life, although the culture's pagan Roman past still exerted an influence.

Several signal events from the 4th to 6th centuries mark the period of transition during which the Roman Empire's Greek east and Latin west divided. Constantine I (r. 324-337) reorganized the empire, made Constantinople the new capital, and legalized Christianity. Under Theodosius I (r. 379-395), Christianity became the empire's official state religion, and other religious practices were proscribed. Finally, under the reign of Heraclius (r. 610-641), the empire's military and administration were restructured and adopted Greek for official use instead of Latin. Thus, although the Roman state continued and Roman state traditions were maintained, modern historians distinguish Byzantium from ancient Rome insofar as it was centered on Constantinople, oriented towards Greek rather than Latin culture, and characterized by Orthodox Christianity.

Just as the Byzantine Empire represented the political continuation of the Roman Empire, Byzantine art and culture developed directly out of the art of the Roman Empire, which was itself profoundly influenced by ancient Greek art. Byzantine art never lost sight of this classical heritage. For example, the Byzantine capital, Constantinople, was adorned with a large number of classical sculptures, although they eventually became an object of some puzzlement for its inhabitants. And indeed, the art produced during the Byzantine Empire, although marked by periodic revivals of a classical aesthetic, was above all marked by the development of a new aesthetic. Thus, although the Byzantine Empire had a multi-ethnic character during most of its history, and preserved Romano-Hellenistic traditions, it became identified by its western and northern contemporaries with its increasingly predominant Greek element and its own unique cultural developments.

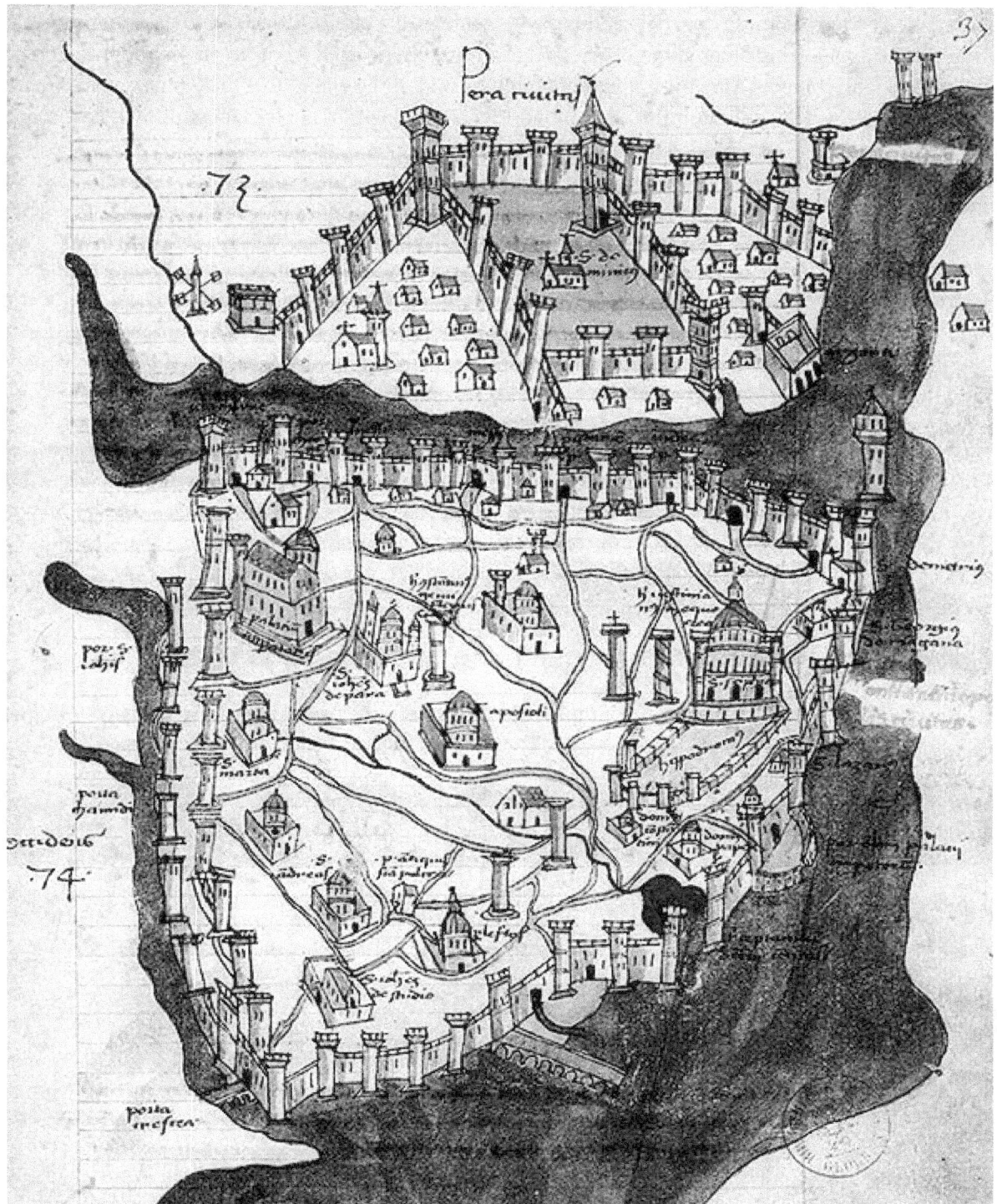

Map of Constantinople: *A map of Constantinople, the capital and founding city of the Byzantine Empire, drawn in 1422 CE by Florentine cartographer Cristoforo Buondelmonti. This is the oldest surviving map of the city and the only one that predates the Turkish conquest of the city in 1453 CE.*

Nomenclature

The first use of the term "Byzantine" to label the later years of the Roman Empire was in 1557, when the German historian Hieronymus Wolf published his work, *Corpus Historiæ Byzantinæ*, a collection of historical sources. The term comes from "Byzantium," the name of the city of Constantinople before it became Constantine's capital. This older name of the city would rarely be used from this point onward except in historical or poetic contexts. However, it was not until the mid-19th century that the term came into general use in the western world; calling it the "Byzantine Empire" helped to emphasize its differences from the earlier Latin-speaking Roman Empire, centered on Rome.

The term "Byzantine" was also useful to the many western European states that also claimed to be the true successors of the Roman Empire, as it was used to delegitimize the claims of the Byzantines as true Romans. In modern times, the term "Byzantine" has also come to have a pejorative sense, used to describe things that are overly complex or arcane. "Byzantine diplomacy" has come to mean excess use of trickery and behind-the-scenes manipulation. These are all based on medieval stereotypes about the Byzantine Empire that developed as western Europeans came into contact with the Byzantines, and were perplexed by their more structured government.

No such distinction existed in the Islamic and Slavic worlds, where the empire was more straightforwardly seen as the continuation of the Roman Empire. In the Islamic world, the Roman Empire was known primarily as Rûm. The name millet-i Rûm, or "Roman nation," was used by the Ottomans through the 20th century to refer to the former subjects of the Byzantine Empire, that is, the Orthodox Christian community within Ottoman realms.

The Eastern Roman Empire, Constantine the Great, and Byzantium

The Christian, Greek-speaking Byzantine Empire had its capital at Constantinople, established by Emperor Constantine the Great.

Learning Objectives

Explain the role of Constantine in Byzantine Empire history

Key Takeaways

Key Points

- The Byzantine Empire (the Eastern Roman Empire) was distinct from the Western Roman Empire in several ways; most importantly, the Byzantines were Christians and spoke Greek instead of Latin.
- The founder of the Byzantine Empire and its first emperor, Constantine the Great, moved the capital of the Roman Empire to the city of Byzantium in 330 CE, and renamed it Constantinople.
- Constantine the Great also legalized Christianity, which had previously been persecuted in the Roman Empire. Christianity would become a major element of Byzantine culture.

- Constantinople became the largest city in the empire and a major commercial center, while the Western Roman Empire fell in 476 CE.

Key Terms

- **Germanic barbarians**: An uncivilized or uncultured person, originally compared to the hellenistic Greco-Roman civilization; often associated with fighting or other such shows of strength.
- **Christianity**: An Abrahamic religion based on the teachings of Jesus Christ and various scholars who wrote the Christian Bible. It was legalized in the Byzantine Empire by Constantine the Great, and the religion became a major element of Byzantine culture.

Constantine the Great and the Beginning of Byzantium

It is a matter of debate when the Roman Empire officially ended and transformed into the Byzantine Empire. Most scholars accept that it did not happen at one time, but that it was a slow process; thus, late Roman history overlaps with early Byzantine history. Constantine I ("the Great") is usually held to be the founder of the Byzantine Empire. He was responsible for several major changes that would help create a Byzantine culture distinct from the Roman past.

As emperor, Constantine enacted many administrative, financial, social, and military reforms to strengthen the empire. The government was restructured and civil and military authority separated. A new gold coin, the *solidus*, was introduced to combat inflation. It would become the standard for Byzantine and European currencies for more than a thousand years. As the first Roman emperor to claim conversion to Christianity, Constantine played an influential role in the development of Christianity as the religion of the empire. In military matters, the Roman army was reorganized to consist of mobile field units and garrison soldiers capable of countering internal threats and barbarian invasions. Constantine pursued successful campaigns against the tribes on the Roman frontiers—the Franks, the Alamanni, the Goths, and the Sarmatians—, and even resettled territories abandoned by his predecessors during the turmoil of the previous century.

The age of Constantine marked a distinct epoch in the history of the Roman Empire. He built a new imperial residence at Byzantium and renamed the city Constantinople after himself (the laudatory epithet of "New Rome " came later, and was never an official title). It would later become the capital of the empire for over one thousand years; for this reason the later Eastern Empire would come to be known as the Byzantine Empire. His more immediate political legacy was that, in leaving the empire to his sons, he replaced Diocletian 's tetrarchy (government where power is divided among four individuals) with the principle of dynastic succession. His reputation flourished during the lifetime of his children, and for centuries after his reign. The medieval church upheld him as a paragon of virtue, while secular rulers invoked him as a prototype, a point of reference, and the symbol of imperial legitimacy and identity.

Constantine the Great: *Byzantine Emperor Constantine the Great presents a representation of the city of Constantinople as tribute to an enthroned Mary and Christ Child in this church mosaic. St Sophia, c. 1000 CE.*

Constantinople and Civil Reform

Constantine moved the seat of the empire, and introduced important changes into its civil and religious constitution. In 330, he founded Constantinople as a second Rome on the site of Byzantium, which was well-positioned astride the trade routes between east and west; it was a superb base from which to guard the Danube river, and was reasonably close to the eastern frontiers. Constantine also began the building of the great fortified walls, which were expanded and rebuilt in subsequent ages. J. B. Bury asserts that "the foundation of Constantinople [...] inaugurated a permanent division between the Eastern and Western, the Greek and the Latin, halves of the empire—a division to which events had already pointed—and affected decisively the whole subsequent history of Europe."

Constantine built upon the administrative reforms introduced by Diocletian. He stabilized the coinage (the gold *solidus* that he introduced became a highly prized and stable currency), and made changes to the structure of the army. Under Constantine, the empire had recovered much of its military strength and enjoyed a period of stability and prosperity. He also reconquered southern parts of Dacia, after defeating the Visigoths in 332, and he was planning a campaign against Sassanid Persia as well. To divide administrative responsibilities, Constantine replaced the single praetorian prefect, who had traditionally exercised both military and civil functions, with regional prefects enjoying civil authority alone. In the course of the 4th century, four great sections emerged from these Constantinian beginnings, and the practice of separating civil from military authority persisted until the 7th century.

Constantine and Christianity

Constantine was the first emperor to stop Christian persecutions and to legalize Christianity, as well as all other religions and cults in the Roman Empire.

In February 313, Constantine met with Licinius in Milan, where they developed the Edict of Milan. The edict stated that Christians should be allowed to follow the faith without oppression. This removed penalties for professing Christianity, under which many had been martyred previously, and returned confiscated Church property. The edict protected from religious persecution not only Christians but all religions, allowing anyone to worship whichever deity they chose.

Scholars debate whether Constantine adopted Christianity in his youth from his mother, St. Helena,, or whether he adopted it gradually over the course of his life. According to Christian writers, Constantine was over 40 when he finally declared himself a Christian, writing to Christians to make clear that he believed he owed his successes to the protection of the Christian High God alone. Throughout his rule, Constantine supported the Church financially, built basilicas, granted privileges to clergy (e.g. exemption from certain taxes), promoted Christians to high office, and returned property confiscated during the Diocletianic persecution. His most famous building projects include the Church of the Holy Sepulchre, and Old Saint Peter's Basilica.

The reign of Constantine established a precedent for the position of the emperor as having great influence and ultimate regulatory authority within the religious discussions involving the early Christian councils of that time (most notably, the dispute over Arianism, and the nature of God). Constantine himself disliked the risks to societal stability that religious disputes and controversies brought with them, preferring where possible to establish an orthodoxy. One way in which Constantine used his influence over the early Church councils was to seek to establish a consensus over the oft debated and argued issue over the nature of God. In 325, he summoned the Council of Nicaea, effectively the first Ecumenical Council. The Council of Nicaea is most known for its dealing with Arianism and for instituting the Nicene Creed, which is still used today by Christians.

The Fall of the Western Roman Empire

After Constantine, few emperors ruled the entire Roman Empire. It was too big and was under attack from too many directions. Usually, there was an emperor of the Western Roman Empire ruling from Italy or Gaul, and an emperor of the Eastern Roman Empire ruling from Constantinople. While the Western Empire was overrun by Germanic barbarians (its lands in Italy were conquered by the Ostrogoths, Spain was conquered by the Visigoths, North Africa was conquered by the Vandals, and Gaul was conquered by the Franks), the Eastern Empire thrived. Constantinople became the largest city in the empire and a major commercial center. In 476 CE, the last Western Roman Emperor was deposed and the Western Roman Empire was no more. Thus the Eastern Roman Empire was the only Roman Empire left standing.

Justinian and Theodora

Emperor Justinian was responsible for substantial expansion, a legal code, and the Hagia Sophia, but suffered defeats against the Persians.

Learning Objectives

Discuss the accomplishments and failures of Emperor Justinian the Great

Key Takeaways

Key Points

- Emperor Justinian the Great was responsible for substantial expansion of the Byzantine Empire, and for conquering Africa, Spain, Rome, and most of Italy.
- Justinian was responsible for the construction of the Hagia Sophia, the center of Christianity in Constantinople. Even today, the Hagia Sophia is recognized as one of the greatest buildings in the world.
- Justinian also systematized the Roman legal code that served as the basis for law in the Byzantine Empire.
- After a plague reduced the Byzantine population, they lost Rome and Italy to the Ostrogoths, and several important cities to the Persians.

Key Terms

- **Hagia Sophia**: A church built by Byzantine Emperor Justinian; the center of Christianity in Constantinople and one of the greatest buildings in the world to this day. It is now a mosque in the Muslim Istanbul.
- **Nika riots**: When angry racing fans, already angry over rising taxes, became enraged at Emperor Justinian for arresting two popular charioteers, and tried to depose him in 532 CE.

Byzantine Empire from Constantine to Justinian

One of Constantine's successors, Theodosius I (379-395), was the last emperor to rule both the Eastern and Western halves of the empire. In 391 and 392, he issued a series of edicts essentially banning pagan religion. Pagan festivals and sacrifices were banned, as was access to all pagan temples and places of worship. The state of the empire in 395 may be described in terms of the outcome of Constantine's work. The dynastic principle was established so firmly that the emperor who died in that year, Theodosius I, could bequeath the imperial office jointly to his sons, Arcadius in the East and Honorius in the West.

The Eastern Empire was largely spared the difficulties faced by the west in the third and fourth centuries, due in part to a more firmly established urban culture and greater financial resources, which allowed it to placate invaders with tribute and pay foreign mercenaries. Throughout the fifth century, various invading armies overran the Western Empire but spared the east. Theodosius II further fortified the walls of Constantinople, leaving the city impervious to most attacks; the walls were not breached until 1204.

To fend off the Huns, Theodosius had to pay an enormous annual tribute to Attila. His successor, Marcian, refused to continue to pay the tribute, but Attila had already diverted his attention to the west. After his death in 453, the Hunnic Empire collapsed, and many of the remaining Huns were often hired as mercenaries by Constantinople.

Leo I succeeded Marcian as emperor, and after the fall of Attila, the true chief in Constantinople was the Alan general, Aspar. Leo I managed to free himself from the influence of the non-Orthodox chief by supporting the rise of the Isaurians, a semi-barbarian tribe living in southern Anatolia. Aspar and his son, Ardabur, were murdered in a riot in 471, and henceforth, Constantinople restored Orthodox leadership for centuries.

When Leo died in 474, Zeno and Ariadne's younger son succeeded to the throne as Leo II, with Zeno as regent. When Leo II died later that year, Zeno became emperor. The end of the Western Empire is sometimes dated to 476, early in Zeno's reign, when the Germanic Roman general, Odoacer, deposed the titular Western Emperor Romulus Augustulus, but declined to replace him with another puppet.

Emperor Justinian I

In 527 CE, Justinian I came to the throne in Constantinople. He dreamed of reconquering the lands of the Western Roman Empire and ruling a single, united Roman Empire from his seat in Constantinople.

Emperor Justinian: Byzantine Emperor Justinian I depicted on one of the famous mosaics of the Basilica of San Vitale, Ravenna.

The western conquests began in 533, as Justinian sent his general, Belisarius, to reclaim the former province of Africa from the Vandals, who had been in control since 429 with their capital at Carthage. Belisarius successfully defeated the Vandals and claimed Africa for Constantinople. Next, Justinian sent him to take Italy from the Ostrogoths in 535 CE. Belisarius defeated the Ostrogoths in a series of battles and reclaimed Rome. By 540 CE, most of Italy was in Justinian's hands. He sent another army to conquer Spain.

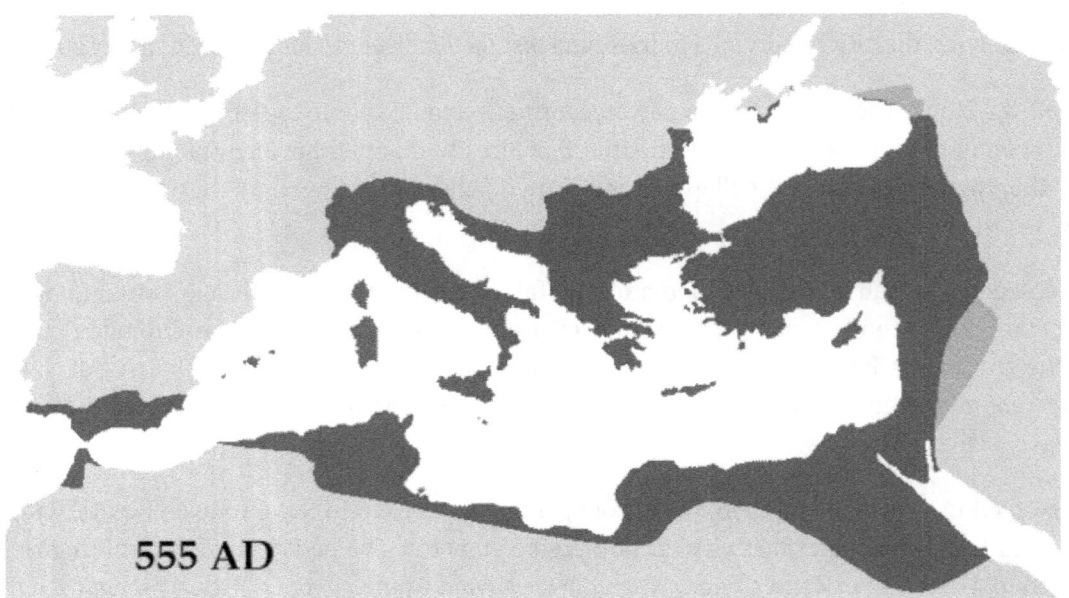

The Byzantine Empire under Justinian: *The Byzantine Empire at its greatest extent, in 555 CE under Justinian the Great.*

Accomplishments in Byzantium

Justinian also undertook many important projects at home. Much of Constantinople was burned down early in Justinian's reign after a series of riots called the Nika riots, in 532 CE, when angry racing fans became enraged at Justinian for arresting two popular charioteers (though this was really just the last straw for a populace increasingly angry over rising taxes) and tried to depose him. The riots were put down, and Justinian set about rebuilding the city on a grander scale. His greatest accomplishment was the Hagia Sophia, the most important church of the city. The Hagia Sophia was a staggering work of Byzantine architecture, intended to awe all who set foot in the church. It was the largest church in the world for nearly a thousand years, and for the rest of Byzantine history it was the center of Christian worship in Constantinople.

The Hagia Sophia: *Byzantine Emperor Justinian built the Greek Orthodox Church of the Holy Wisdom of God, the Hagia Sophia, which was completed in only four and a half years (532 CE-537 CE). Even now, it is universally acknowledged as one of the greatest buildings in the world.*

Emperor Justinian's most important contribution, perhaps, was a unified Roman legal code. Prior to his reign, Roman laws had differed from region to region, and many contradicted one another. The Romans had attempted to systematize the legal code in the fifth century but had not completed the effort. Justinian set up a commission of lawyers to put together a single code, listing each law by subject so that it could be easily referenced. This not only served as the basis for law in the Byzantine Empire, but it was the main influence on the Catholic Church's development of canon law, and went on to become the basis of law in many European countries. Justinian's law code continues to have a major influence on public international law to this day.

The impact of a more unified legal code and military conflicts was the increased ability for the Byzantine Empire to establish trade and improve their economic standing. Byzantine merchants traded not only all over the Mediterranean region, but also throughout regions to the east. These included areas around the Black Sea, the Red Sea, and the Indian Ocean.

Theodora

Theodora was empress of the Byzantine Empire and the wife of Emperor Justinian I. She was one of the most influential and powerful of the Byzantine empresses. Some sources mention her as empress regnant, with Justinian I as her co-regent. Along with her husband, she is a saint in the Eastern Orthodox Church, commemorated on November 14.

Theodora participated in Justinian's legal and spiritual reforms, and her involvement in the increase of the rights of women was substantial. She had laws passed that prohibited forced prostitution and closed brothels. She created a convent on the Asian side of the Dardanelles called the Metanoia (Repentance), where the ex-prostitutes could support themselves. She also expanded the rights of women in divorce and property ownership, instituted the death penalty for rape, forbade exposure of unwanted infants, gave mothers some guardianship rights over their children, and forbade the killing of a wife who committed adultery.

Justinian's Difficulties

A terrible plague swept through the empire, killing Theodora and almost killing him. The plague wiped out huge numbers of the empire's population, leaving villages empty and crops unharvested. The army was also afflicted, and the Ostrogoths were able to effectively regain Italy in 546 CE, through guerrilla warfare against the Byzantine occupiers.

With Justinian's army bogged down fighting in Italy, the empire's defenses against the Persians on its eastern frontiers were weakened. In the Roman-Persian Wars, the Persians invaded and destroyed a number of important cities. Justinian was forced to establish a humiliating 50-year peace treaty with them in 561 CE.

Still, Justinian kept the empire from collapse. He sent a new general, Narses, to Italy with a small force. Narses finally defeated the Ostrogoths and drove them back out of Italy. By the time the war was over, Italy, once one of the most prosperous lands in the ancient world, was wrecked. The city of Rome changed hands multiple times, and most of the cities of Italy were abandoned or fell into a long period of decline. The impoverishment of Italy and the weakened Byzantine military made it impossible for the empire to hold the peninsula. Soon a new Germanic tribe, the Lombards, came in and conquered most of Italy, though Rome, Naples, and Ravenna remained isolated pockets of Byzantine control. At the same time, another new barbarian enemy, the Slavs, appeared from north of the Danube. They devastated Greece and the Balkans, and in the absence of strong Byzantine military might, they settled in small communities in these lands.

The Justinian Code

Justinian I achieved lasting fame through his judicial reforms, particularly through the complete revision of all Roman law that was compiled in what is known today as the *Corpus juris civilis*.

Learning Objectives

Explain the historical significance of Justinian's legal reforms

Key Takeaways

Key Points

- Shortly after Justinian became emperor in 527, he decided the empire's legal system

> needed repair.
> - Early in his reign, Justinian appointed an official, Tribonian, to oversee this task.
> - The project as a whole became known as *Corpus juris civilis*, or the Justinian Code.
> - It consists of the *Codex Iustinianus*, the *Digesta*, the *Institutiones*, and the *Novellae*.
> - Many of the laws contained in the Codex were aimed at regulating religious practice.
> - The *Corpus* formed the basis not only of Roman jurisprudence (including ecclesiastical Canon Law), but also influenced civil law throughout the Middle Ages and into modern nation states.
>
> *Key Terms*
>
> - **Corpus juris civilis**: The modern name for a collection of fundamental works in jurisprudence, issued from 529 to 534 by order of Justinian I, Eastern Roman Emperor.
> - **Justinian I**: A Byzantine emperor from 527 to 565. During his reign, he sought to revive the empire's greatness and reconquer the lost western half of the historical Roman Empire; he also enacted important legal codes.

Byzantine Emperor Justinian I achieved lasting fame through his judicial reforms, particularly through the complete revision of all Roman law, something that had not previously been attempted. There existed three codices of imperial laws and other individual laws, many of which conflicted or were out of date. The total of Justinian's legislature is known today as the *Corpus juris civilis*.

The work as planned had three parts:

1. *Codex:* a compilation, by selection and extraction, of imperial enactments to date, going back to Hadrian in the 2nd century CE.
2. *Digesta:* an encyclopedia composed of mostly brief extracts from the writings of Roman jurists. Fragments were taken out of various legal treatises and opinions and inserted in the *Digesta*.
3. *Institutiones:* a student textbook, mainly introducing the *Codex*, although it has important conceptual elements that are less developed in the *Codex* or the *Digesta*.

All three parts, even the textbook, were given force of law. They were intended to be, together, the sole source of law; reference to any other source, including the original texts from which the *Codex* and the *Digesta* had been taken, was forbidden. Nonetheless, Justinian found himself having to enact further laws, and today these are counted as a fourth part of the *Corpus*, the *Novellae Constitutiones*. As opposed to the rest of the *Corpus*, the *Novellae* appeared in Greek, the common language of the Eastern Empire.

The work was directed by Tribonian, an official in Justinian's court. His team was authorized to edit what they included. How far they made amendments is not recorded and, in the main, cannot be known because most of the originals have not survived. The text was composed and distributed almost entirely in Latin, which was still the official language of the government of the Byzantine Empire in 529-534, whereas the prevalent language of merchants, farmers, seamen, and other citizens was Greek.

Many of the laws contained in the *Codex* were aimed at regulating religious practice, included numerous provisions served to secure the status of Christianity as the state religion of the empire, uniting church and state, and making anyone who was not connected to the Christian church a non-citizen. It also contained laws forbidding particular pagan practices; for example, all persons present at a pagan sacrifice may be indicted as if for murder. Other laws, some influenced by his wife, Theodora, include those to protect prostitutes from exploitation, and women from being forced into prostitution. Rapists were treated severely. Further, by his policies, women charged with major crimes should be guarded by other women to prevent sexual abuse; if a woman was widowed, her dowry should be returned; and a husband could not take on a major debt without his wife giving her consent twice.

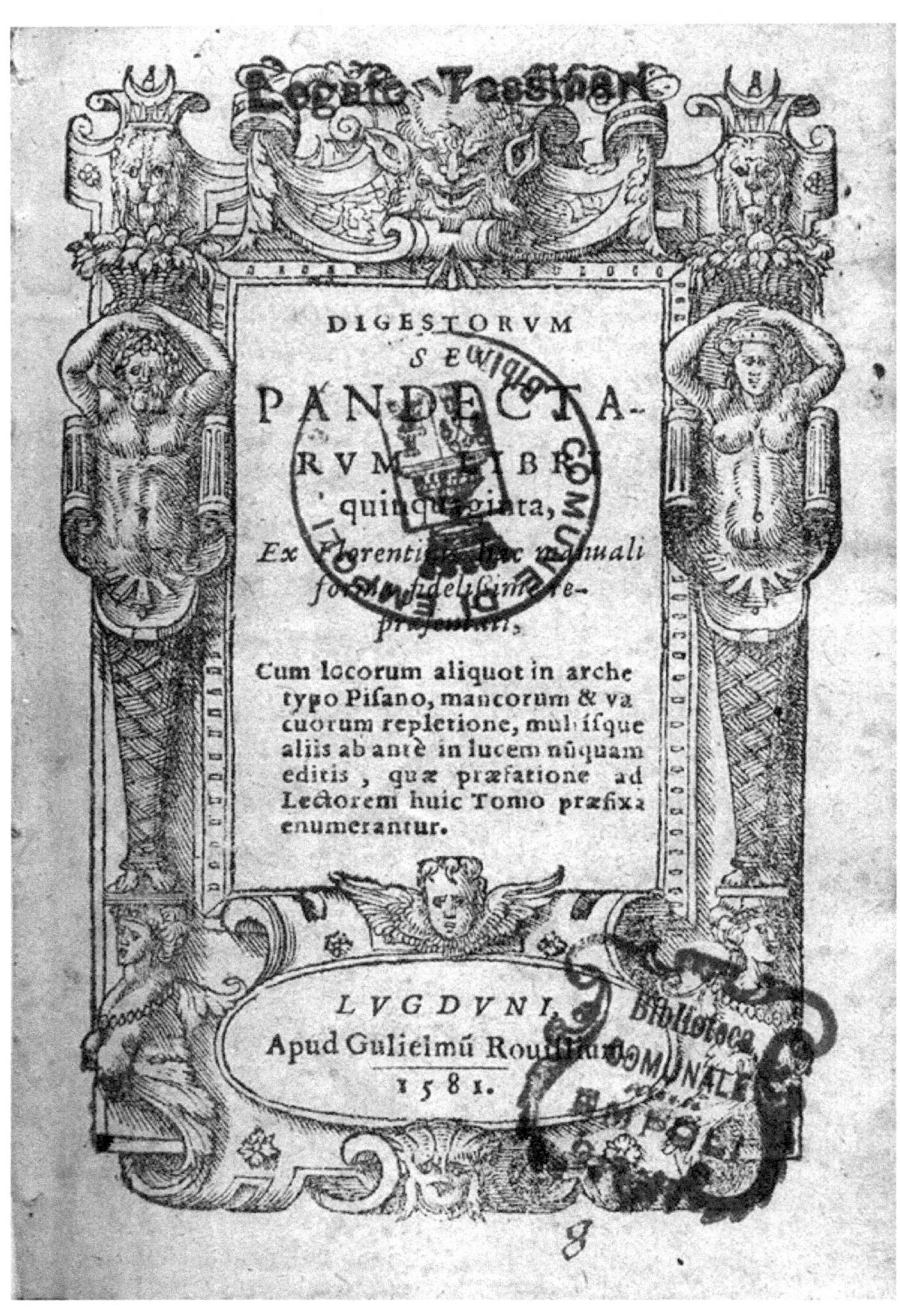

Justinian Digesta: *A later copy of Justinian's Digesta: Digestorum, seu Pandectarum libri quinquaginta. Lugduni apud Gulielmum Rouillium, 1581. From Biblioteca Comunale "Renato Fucini" di Empoli.*

Legacy

The *Corpus* forms the basis of Latin jurisprudence (including ecclesiastical Canon Law) and, for historians, provides a valuable insight into the concerns and activities of the later Roman Empire. As a collection, it gathers together the many sources in which the laws and the other rules were expressed or published (proper laws, senatorial consults, imperial decrees, case law, and jurists' opinions and interpretations). It formed the basis of later Byzantine law, as expressed in the *Basilika* of Basil I and Leo VI the Wise. The only western province where the Justinian Code was introduced was Italy, from where it was to pass to western Europe in the 12th century, and become the basis of much European law code. It eventually passed to eastern Europe, where it appeared in Slavic editions, and it also passed on to Russia.

It was not in general use during the Early Middle Ages. After the Early Middle Ages, interest in it revived. It was "received" or imitated as private law, and its public law content was quarried for arguments by both secular and ecclesiastical authorities. The revived Roman law, in turn, became the foundation of law in all civil law jurisdictions. The provisions of the *Corpus Juris Civilis* also influenced the canon law of the Roman Catholic Church; it was said that *ecclesia vivit lege romana*—the church lives by Roman law. Its influence on common law legal systems has been much smaller, although some basic concepts from the *Corpus* have survived through Norman law—such as the contrast, especially in the Institutes, between "law" (statute) and custom. The *Corpus* continues to have a major influence on public international law. Its four parts thus constitute the foundation documents of the western legal tradition.

Attributions

CC licensed content, Specific attribution

- HIST101: Ancient Civilizations of the World. **Provided by**: Saylor. **Located at**: https://legacy.saylor.org/hist101/Intro/. **License**: *CC BY: Attribution*
- HIST101: Ancient Civilizations of the World. **Provided by**: Saylor. **Located at**: https://legacy.saylor.org/hist101/Intro/. **License**: *CC BY: Attribution*
- Map of Constantinople (1422) by Florentine cartographer Cristoforo Buondelmonte. **Provided by**: Wikimedia. **Located at**: https://commons.wikimedia.org/wiki/File:Map_of_Constantinople_(1422)_by_Florentine_cartographer_Cristoforo_Buondelmonte.jpg. **License**: *Public Domain: No Known Copyright*
- HIST101: Ancient Civilizations of the World. **Provided by**: Saylor. **Located at**: https://legacy.saylor.org/hist101/Intro/. **License**: *CC BY: Attribution*
- HIST101: Ancient Civilizations of the World. **Provided by**: Saylor. **Located at**: https://legacy.saylor.org/hist101/Intro/. **License**: *CC BY: Attribution*
- Byzantine Empire. **Provided by**: Wikipedia. **Located at**: http://en.wikipedia.org/wiki/Byzantine_Empire. **License**: *CC BY-SA: Attribution-ShareAlike*
- Christianity. **Provided by**: Wiktionary. **Located at**: http://en.wiktionary.org/wiki/Christianity. **License**: *CC BY-SA: Attribution-ShareAlike*
- barbarian definition. **Provided by**: Wiktionary.org. **Located at**: http://en.wiktionary.org/wiki/barbarian. **License**: *CC BY-SA: Attribution-ShareAlike*
- Christianity. **Provided by**: Wiktionary. **Located at**: http://en.wiktionary.org/wiki/Christianity. **License**: *CC BY-SA: Attribution-ShareAlike*
- Map of Constantinople (1422) by Florentine cartographer Cristoforo Buondelmonte. **Provided by**: Wikimedia. **Located at**: https://commons.wikimedia.org/wiki/File:Map_of_Constantinople_(1422)_by_Florentine_cartographer_Cristoforo_Buondelmonte.jpg. **License**: *Public Domain: No Known Copyright*
- Constantine I Hagia Sophia. **Provided by**: Wikimedia. **Located at**: https://commons.wikimedia.org/wiki/File:Constantine_I_Hagia_Sophia.jpg. **License**: *Public Domain: No Known Copyright*
- HIST101: Ancient Civilizations of the World. **Provided by**: Saylor. **Located at**: https://legacy.saylor.org/hist101/Intro/. **License**: *CC BY: Attribution*
- Byzantine Empire. **Provided by**: Wikipedia. **Located at**: http://en.wikipedia.org/wiki/Byzantine_Empire. **License**: *CC BY-SA:*

Attribution-ShareAlike

- Hagia Sophia. **Provided by**: Wiktionary. **Located at**: http://en.wiktionary.org/wiki/Hagia_Sophia. **License**: *CC BY-SA: Attribution-ShareAlike*
- Map of Constantinople (1422) by Florentine cartographer Cristoforo Buondelmonte. **Provided by**: Wikimedia. **Located at**: https://commons.wikimedia.org/wiki/File:Map_of_Constantinople_(1422)_by_Florentine_cartographer_Cristoforo_Buondelmonte.jpg. **License**: *Public Domain: No Known Copyright*
- Constantine I Hagia Sophia. **Provided by**: Wikimedia. **Located at**: https://commons.wikimedia.org/wiki/File:Constantine_I_Hagia_Sophia.jpg. **License**: *Public Domain: No Known Copyright*
- Justinian 555 AD. **Provided by**: Wikimedia. **Located at**: https://commons.wikimedia.org/wiki/File:Justinian555AD.png. **License**: *CC BY-SA: Attribution-ShareAlike*
- Aya Sofya. **Provided by**: Wikimedia. **Located at**: https://commons.wikimedia.org/wiki/File:Aya_sofya.jpg. **License**: *Public Domain: No Known Copyright*
- Justinian. **Provided by**: Wikimedia. **Located at**: https://commons.wikimedia.org/wiki/File:Justinian.jpg. **License**: *CC BY-SA: Attribution-ShareAlike*
- Codex Justinianus. **Provided by**: Wikipedia. **Located at**: https://en.wikipedia.org/wiki/Codex_Justinianus. **License**: *CC BY-SA: Attribution-ShareAlike*
- Byzantine Empire under the Justinian dynasty. **Provided by**: Wikipedia. **Located at**: https://en.wikipedia.org/wiki/Byzantine_Empire_under_the_Justinian_dynasty. **License**: *CC BY-SA: Attribution-ShareAlike*
- Corpus Juris Civilis. **Provided by**: Wikipedia. **Located at**: https://en.wikipedia.org/wiki/Corpus_Juris_Civilis. **License**: *CC BY-SA: Attribution-ShareAlike*
- Byzantine Empire. **Provided by**: Wikipedia. **Located at**: https://en.wikipedia.org/wiki/Byzantine_Empire. **License**: *CC BY-SA: Attribution-ShareAlike*
- Justinian I. **Provided by**: Wikipedia. **Located at**: https://en.wikipedia.org/wiki/Justinian_I#Legislative_activities. **License**: *CC BY-SA: Attribution-ShareAlike*
- Map of Constantinople (1422) by Florentine cartographer Cristoforo Buondelmonte. **Provided by**: Wikimedia. **Located at**: https://commons.wikimedia.org/wiki/File:Map_of_Constantinople_(1422)_by_Florentine_cartographer_Cristoforo_Buondelmonte.jpg. **License**: *Public Domain: No Known Copyright*
- Constantine I Hagia Sophia. **Provided by**: Wikimedia. **Located at**: https://commons.wikimedia.org/wiki/File:Constantine_I_Hagia_Sophia.jpg. **License**: *Public Domain: No Known Copyright*
- Justinian 555 AD. **Provided by**: Wikimedia. **Located at**: https://commons.wikimedia.org/wiki/File:Justinian555AD.png. **License**: *CC BY-SA: Attribution-ShareAlike*
- Aya Sofya. **Provided by**: Wikimedia. **Located at**: https://commons.wikimedia.org/wiki/File:Aya_sofya.jpg. **License**: *Public Domain: No Known Copyright*
- Justinian. **Provided by**: Wikimedia. **Located at**: https://commons.wikimedia.org/wiki/File:Justinian.jpg. **License**: *CC BY-SA: Attribution-ShareAlike*
- Digesto_02.jpg. **Provided by**: Wikimedia. **Located at**: https://commons.wikimedia.org/wiki/File:Digesto_02.jpg. **License**: *Public Domain: No Known Copyright*

The Rise and Spread of Islam

Pre-Islamic Arabia

The Nomadic Tribes of Arabia

The nomadic pastoralist Bedouin tribes inhabited the Arabian Peninsula before the rise of Islam around 700 CE.

Learning Objectives

Describe the societal structure of tribes in Arabia

Key Takeaways

Key Points

- Nomadic Bedouin tribes dominated the Arabian Peninsula before the rise of Islam.
- Family groups called clans formed larger tribal units, which reinforced family cooperation in the difficult living conditions on the Arabian peninsula and protected its members against other tribes.
- The Bedouin tribes were nomadic pastoralists who relied on their herds of goats, sheep, and camels for meat, milk, cheese, blood, fur/wool, and other sustenance.
- The pre-Islamic Bedouins also hunted, served as bodyguards, escorted caravans, worked as mercenaries, and traded or raided to gain animals, women, gold, fabric, and other luxury items.
- Arab tribes begin to appear in the south Syrian deserts and southern Jordan around 200 CE, but spread from the central Arabian Peninsula after the rise of Islam in the 630s CE.

Key Terms

- **Nabatean**: an ancient Semitic people who inhabited northern Arabia and Southern Lev-

> ant, ca. 37–100 CE.
> - **Bedouin**: a predominantly desert-dwelling Arabian ethnic group traditionally divided into tribes or clans.

Pre-Islamic Arabia

Pre-Islamic Arabia refers to the Arabian Peninsula prior to the rise of Islam in the 630s.

Some of the settled communities in the Arabian Peninsula developed into distinctive civilizations. Sources for these civilizations are not extensive, and are limited to archaeological evidence, accounts written outside of Arabia, and Arab oral traditions later recorded by Islamic scholars. Among the most prominent civilizations were Thamud, which arose around 3000 BCE and lasted to about 300 CE, and Dilmun, which arose around the end of the fourth millennium and lasted to about 600 CE. Additionally, from the beginning of the first millennium BCE, Southern Arabia was the home to a number of kingdoms, such as the Sabaean kingdom, and the coastal areas of Eastern Arabia were controlled by the Iranian Parthians and Sassanians from 300 BCE.

Pre-Islamic religion in Arabia consisted of indigenous polytheistic beliefs, Ancient Arabian Christianity, Nestorian Christianity, Judaism, and Zoroastrianism. Christianity existed in the Arabian Peninsula, and was established first by the early Arab traders who heard the gospel from Peter the apostle at Jerusalem (Acts 2:11), as well as those evangelized by Paul's ministry in Arabia (Galatians 1:17) and by St Thomas. While ancient Arabian Christianity was strong in areas of Southern Arabia, especially with Najran being an important center of Christianity, Nestorian Christianity was the dominant religion in Eastern Arabia prior to the advent of Islam.

Tribes in the Arabian Peninsula c. 600 CE: *Approximate locations of some of the important tribes and Empire of the Arabian Peninsula before the dawn of Islam. Family groups called clans formed larger tribal units, which reinforced family cooperation in the difficulty living conditions on the Arabian peninsula and protected its members against other tribes.*

Nomadic Tribes in Pre-Islamic Arabia

One of the major cultures that dominated the Arabian Peninsula just before the rise of Islam was that of the nomadic Bedouin people. The polytheistic Bedouin clans placed heavy emphasis on kin-related groups, with each clan clustered under tribes. The immediate family shared one tent and can also be called a clan. Many of these tents and their associated familial relations comprised a tribe. Although clans were made up of family members, a tribe might take in a non-related member and give them familial status. Society was patriarchal, with inheritance through the male lines. Tribes provided a means of protection for its members; death to one clan member meant brutal retaliation.

Non-members of the tribe were viewed as outsiders or enemies. Tribes shared common ethical understandings and provided an individual with an identity. Warfare between tribes was common among the Bedouin, and warfare was given a high honor. The difficult living conditions in the Arabian Peninsula created a heavy emphasis on family cooperation, further strengthening the clan system.

Bedouin shepherd in the Syrian desert: *While most modern Bedouins have abandoned their nomadic and tribal traditions for modern urban lifestyles, they retain traditional Bedouin culture with traditional music, poetry, dances, and other cultural practices.*

The Bedouin tribes in pre-Islamic Arabia were nomadic-pastoralists. Pastoralists depend on their small herds of goats, sheep, camels, horses, or other animals for meat, milk, cheese, blood, fur/wool, and other sustenance. Because of the harsh climate and the seasonal migrations required to obtain resources, the Bedouin nomadic tribes generally raised sheep, goats, and camels. Each member of the family had a specific role in taking care of the animals, from guarding the herd to making cheese from milk. The nomads also hunted, served as bodyguards, escorted caravans, and worked as mercenaries. Some tribes traded with towns in order to gain goods, while others raided other tribes for animals, women, gold, fabric, and other luxury items.

Bedouin tribes raised camels as part of their nomadic-pastoralist lifestyle: *Tribes migrated seasonally to reach resources for their herds of sheep, goats, and camels. Each member of the family had a specific role in taking care of the animals, from guarding the herd to making cheese from milk.*

Origin of Jewish and Other Tribes

The first mention of Jews in the areas of modern-day Saudi Arabia dates back, by some accounts, to the time of the First Temple. Immigration to the Arabian Peninsula began in earnest in the 2nd century CE, and by the 6th and 7th centuries there was a considerable Jewish population in Hejaz, mostly in and around Medina. This was partly because of the embrace of Judaism by leaders such as Abu Karib Asad and Dhu Nuwas, who was very aggressive about converting his subjects to Judaism, and who persecuted Christians in his kingdom as a reaction to Christian persecution of Jews there by the local Christians. Before the rise of Islam, there were three main Jewish tribes in the city of Medina: the Banu Nadir, the Banu Qainuqa, and the Banu Qurayza. Arab tribes, most notably the Ghassanids and Lakhmids, began to appear in the south Syrian deserts and southern Jordan from the mid 3rd century CE, during the mid to later stages of the Roman Empire and Sassanid Empire. The Nabatean civilization in Jordan was an Aramaic-speaking ethnic mix of Canaanites, Arameans, and Arabs. According to tradition, the Saudi Bedouin are descendants of two groups. One group, the Yemenis, settled in southwestern Arabia, in the mountains of Yemen, and claimed they descended from a semi-legendary ancestral figure, Qahtan (or Joktan). The second group, the Qaysis, settled in north-central Arabia and claimed they were descendants of the Biblical Ishmael.

Arabian Cities

Cities like Mecca and Medina acted as important centers of trade and religion in pre-Islamic Arabia.

Learning Objectives

Examine the historical significance of Mecca and Medina

Key Takeaways

Key Points

- As sea trade routes became more dangerous, several tribes built the Arabian city of Mecca into a center of trade to direct more secure overland caravan routes.
- Once a year, the nomadic tribes would declare a truce and converge upon Mecca in a pilgrimage to pay homage to their idols at the Kaaba and drink from the Zamzam Well.
- The oasis city of Yathrib, also known as Medina, was ruled by several Jewish tribes until Arab tribes gained political power around 400 CE.

Key Terms

- **Ishmael**: A figure in the Hebrew Bible and the Qur'an, and Abraham's first son according to Jews, Christians, and Muslims. He was born of Abraham's marriage to Sarah's handmaiden Hagar.
- **Zamzam Well**: A well located in the city of Mecca that, according to Islamic belief, is a miraculously generated source of water from God.
- **Kaaba**: A sacred building in the city of Mecca that housed the tribal idols until the rise of Islam in 7th century, when it became the center of Islam's most sacred mosque.

Although the majority of pre-Islamic Arabia was nomadic, there were several important cities that came into being as centers of trade and religion, such as Mecca, Medina (Yathrib), Karbala, and Damascus. The most important of these cities was Mecca, which was an important center of trade in the area, as well as the location of the Kaaba (or Ka'ba), one of the most revered shrines in polytheistic Arabia. After the rise of Islam, the Kaaba became the most sacred place in Islam.

Islamic tradition attributes the beginning of Mecca to Ishmael 's descendants. Many Muslims point to the Old Testament chapter Psalm 84:3–6 and a mention of a pilgrimage at the Valley of Baca, which is interpreted as a reference to Mecca as Bakkah in Qur'an Surah 3:96. The Greek historian Diodorus Siculus, who lived between 60 BCE and 30 BCE, wrote about the isolated region of Arabia in his work *Bibliotheca historica*, describing a holy shrine that Muslims see as Kaaba at Mecca: "And a temple has been set up there, which is very holy and exceedingly revered by all Arabians." Some time in the 5th century, the Kaaba was a place to worship the deities of Arabia's pagan tribes. Mecca's most important pagan deity was Hubal, whose idol had been placed there by the ruling Quraysh tribe and remained until the 7th century.

The City of Mecca

In the 5th century, the Quraysh tribes took control of Mecca and became skilled merchants and traders. In the 6th century, they joined the lucrative spice trade, since battles in other parts of the world were causing traders to divert from the dangerous sea routes to the more secure overland routes. The Byzantine Empire had previously controlled the Red Sea, but piracy had been increasing. Another previous route, which ran through the Persian Gulf via the Tigris and Euphrates rivers, was also threatened by exploitations from the Sassanid Empire, and disrupted by the Lakhmids, the Ghassanids, and the Roman–Persian Wars.

Mecca's prominence as a trading center eventually surpassed the cities of Petra and Palmyra. Historical accounts also provide some indication that goods from other continents may also have flowed through Mecca. Camel caravans, said to have first been used by Muhammad's great-grandfather, were a major part of Mecca's bustling economy. Alliances were struck between the merchants in Mecca and the local nomadic tribes, who would bring goods—leather, livestock, and metals mined in the local mountains—to Mecca to be loaded on the caravans and carried to cities in Syria and Iraq. Historical accounts provide some indication that goods from other continents may also have flowed through Mecca. Goods from Africa and the Far East passed through en route to Syria. The Meccans signed treaties with both the Byzantines and the Bedouins to negotiate safe passages for caravans and give them water and pasture rights. Mecca became the center of a loose confederation of client tribes, which included those of the Banu Tamim. Other regional powers such as the Abyssinian, Ghassan, and Lakhm were in decline, leaving Meccan trade to be the primary binding force in Arabia in the late 6th century.

The harsh conditions and terrain of the Arabian peninsula meant a near-constant state of conflict between the local tribes, but once a year they would declare a truce and converge upon Mecca in a pilgrimage. Up to the 7th century, this journey was undertaken by the pagan Arabs to pay homage to their shrine and drink from the Zamzam Well. However, it was also the time each year when disputes would be arbitrated, debts would be resolved, and trading would occur at Meccan fairs. These annual events gave the tribes a sense of common identity and made Mecca an important focus for the peninsula.

A modern-day caravan crossing the Arabian Peninsula: As sea trade routes became more dangerous, several tribes built the Arabian city of Mecca into a center of trade to direct more secure overland caravan routes.

The City of Medina (Yathrib)

Although the city of Medina did not have any great distinction until the introduction of Islam, it has always held an important place in trade and agriculture because of its location in a fertile region of the Hejaz. The city was able to maintain decent amounts of food and water, and therefore was an important pit stop for trade caravans traveling along the Red Sea. This was especially important given the merchant culture of Arabia. Along with the port of Jidda, Medina and Mecca thrived through years of pilgrimage.

During the pre-Islamic period up until 622 CE, Medina was known as Yathrib, an oasis city. Yathrib was dominated by Jewish tribes until around 400 CE, when several Arab tribes gained political power. Medina is celebrated for containing the mosque of Muhammad. Medina is 210 miles (340 km) north of Mecca and about 120 miles (190 km) from the Red Sea coast. It is situated in the most fertile part of the Hejaz territory, where the streams of the vicinity converge. An immense plain extends to the south; in every direction the view is bounded by hills and mountains.

In 622 CE, Muhammad and around 70 Meccan Muhajirun believers left Mecca for sanctuary in Yathrib, an event that transformed the religious and political landscape of the city completely. The longstanding enmity between the Aus and Khazraj tribes was dampened as many tribe members, and some local Jews, embraced Islam. Muhammad, linked to the Khazraj through his great-grandmother, was agreed on as civic leader.

The Muslim converts native to Yathrib—whether pagan Arab or Jewish—were called Ansar ("the Patrons" or "the Helpers"). According to Ibn Ishaq, the local pagan Arab tribes, the Muslim Muhajirun from Mecca, the local Muslims (Ansar), and the Jews of the area signed an agreement, the Constitution of Medina, which committed all parties to mutual cooperation under the leadership of Muhammad. The nature of this document as recorded by Ibn Ishaq and transmitted by Ibn Hisham is the subject of dispute among modern Western historians. Many maintain that this "treaty" is possibly a collage of different agreements, oral rather than written, of different dates, and that it is not clear when they were made. Other scholars, however, both Western and Muslim, argue that the text of the agreement—whether it was originally a single document or several—is possibly one of the oldest Islamic texts we possess.

Medina: Old depiction of Medina during Ottoman times.

Culture and Religion in Pre-Islamic Arabia

The nomadic tribes of pre-Islamic Arabia primarily practiced polytheism, although some tribes converted to Judaism and Christianity.

Learning Objectives

Explain the significance of polytheism and monotheism in pre-Islamic Arabia

Key Takeaways

Key Points

- Before the rise of the monotheistic religions of Judaism, Christianity, and Islam, most Bedouin tribes practiced polytheism in the form of animism and idolatry.
- Three of the ruling tribes of Yathrib (Medina) were Jewish, one of the oldest monotheistic religions.
- Christianity spread to Arabia after Constantinople conquered Byzantium in 324 CE, and it was adopted by several Bedouin tribes.
- Poetry was a large part of tribal culture and communication, and it was often used as propaganda against other tribes.

Key Terms

- **polytheism**: The worship of or belief in multiple deities usually assembled into a pantheon of gods and goddesses, along with their own religions and rituals.
- **Ka'aba**: A building at the center of Islam's most sacred mosque, Al-Masjid al-Haram, in Mecca, al-Hejaz, Saudi Arabia. It is the most sacred Muslim site in the world.
- **monotheism**: The belief in the existence of a single god.
- **idolatry**: The worship of an idol or a physical object, such as a cult image, as a god.
- **animism**: The worldview that non-human entities (animals, plants, and inanimate objects or phenomena) possess a spiritual essence; often practiced by tribal groups before organized religion.

Overview

Religion in pre-Islamic Arabia was a mix of polytheism, Christianity, Judaism, and Iranian religions. Arab polytheism, the dominant belief system, was based on the belief in deities and other supernatural beings such as djinn. Gods and goddesses were worshipped at local shrines, such as the Kaaba in Mecca. Some scholars postulate that Allah may have been one of the gods of the Meccan religion to whom the shrine was dedicated, although it seems he had little relevance in the religion. Many of the physical descriptions of the pre-Islamic gods are traced to idols, especially near the Kaaba, which is believed to have contained up to 360 of them.

The Kaaba: *The Kaaba is a cube-shaped building in Mecca held to be sacred both by Muslims and pre-Islamic polytheistic tribes.*

Other religions were represented to varying, lesser degrees. The influence of the adjacent Roman, Axumite, and Sasanian empires resulted in Christian communities in the northwest, northeast, and south of Arabia. Christianity made a lesser impact, but secured some conversions in the remainder of the peninsula. With the exception of Nestorianism in the northeast and the Persian Gulf, the dominant form of Christianity was Monophysitism. The Arabian peninsula had been subject to Jewish migration since Roman times, which had resulted in a diaspora community supplemented by local converts. Additionally, the influence of the Sasanian Empire resulted in the presence Iranian religions. Zoroastrianism existed in the east and south, and there is evidence of Manichaeism or possibly Mazdakism being practiced in Mecca.

Polytheism in Pre-Islamic Arabia

Before the rise of Islam, most Bedouin tribes practiced polytheism, most often in the form of animism. Animists believe that non-human entities (animals, plants, and inanimate objects or phenomena) possess a spiritual essence. Totemism and idolatry, or worship of totems or idols representing natural phenomena, were also common religious practices in the pre-Islamic world. Idols were housed in the Kaaba, an ancient sanctuary in the city of Mecca. The site housed about 360 idols and attracted worshippers from all over Arabia. According to the holy Muslim text the Quran, Ibrahim, together with his son Ishmael, raised the foundations of a house and began work on the Kaaba around 2130 BCE.

The chief god in pre-Islamic Arabia was Hubal, the Syrian god of the moon. The three daughters of Hubal were the chief goddesses of Meccan Arabian mythology: Allāt, Al-'Uzzá, and Manāt. Allāt was the goddess associated with the underworld. Al-'Uzzá, "The Mightiest One" or "The Strong," was a fertility goddess, and she was called upon for protection and victory before war. Manāt was the goddess of fate; the Book of Idols describes her as the most ancient of all these idols. The Book of Idols describes gods and rites of Arabian religion, but criticizes the idolatry of pre-Islamic religion.

Relief of the goddess Allāt, one of the three patron gods of the city of Mecca: Before the rise of the monotheistic religions of Judaism, Christianity, and Islam, most Bedouin tribes practiced polytheism in the form of animism and idolatry.

Monotheism in Pre-Islamic Arabia

Judaism

The most well-known monotheists were the Hebrews, although the Persians and the Medes had also developed monotheism. Judaism is one of the oldest monotheistic religions.

A thriving community of Jewish tribes existed in pre-Islamic Arabia and included both sedentary and nomadic communities. Jews migrated into Arabia starting Roman times. Arabian Jews spoke Arabic as well as Hebrew and Aramaic and had contact with Jewish religious centers in Babylonia and Palestine.

The Yemeni Himyarites converted to Judaism in the 4th century, and some of the Kindah, a tribe in central Arabia who were the Himyarites' vassals, were also converted in the 4th/5th century. There is evidence that Jewish converts in the Hejaz were regarded as Jews by other Jews and non-Jews alike, and sought advice from Babylonian rabbis on matters of attire and kosher food. In at least one case, it is known that an Arab tribe agreed to adopt Judaism as a condition for settling in a town dominated by Jewish inhabitants. Some Arab women in Yathrib/Medina are said to have vowed to make their child a Jew if the child survived, since they considered the Jews to be people "of knowledge and the book." Historian Philip Hitti infers from proper names and agricultural vocabulary that the Jewish tribes of Yathrib consisted mostly of Judaized clans of Arabian and Aramaean origin.

Christianity

After Constantine conquered Byzantium in 324 CE, Christianity spread to Arabia. The principal tribes that embraced Christianity were the Himyar, Ghassan, Rabi'a, Tagh'ab, Bahra, and Tunukh, parts of the Tay and Khud'a, the inhabitants of Najran, and the Arabs of Hira. Traditionally, both Jews and Christians believe in the God of Abraham, Isaac and Jacob, for Jews the God of the Tanakh, for Christians the God of the Old Testament, the creator of the universe. Both religions reject the view that God is entirely transcendent, and thus separate from the world, as the pre-Christian Greek Unknown God. Both religions also reject atheism on one hand and polytheism on the other.

The main areas of Christian influence in Arabia were on the northeastern and northwestern borders and in what was to become Yemen in the south. The northwest was under the influence of Christian missionary activity from the Roman Empire, where the Ghassanids, residents of a client kingdom of the Romans, were converted to Christianity. In the south, particularly at Najran, a center of Christianity developed as a result of the influence of the Christian kingdom of Axum based on the other side of the Red Sea in Ethiopia. Both the Ghassanids and the Christians in the south adopted Monophysitism. The spread of Christianity was halted in 622 CE by the rise of Islam, though the city of Mecca provided a central location for an intermingling of the two cultures. For example, in addition to the animistic idols, the pre-Islamic Kaaba housed statues of Jesus and his holy mother, Mary.

Nomadic Culture and Poetry

Like later cultures in the region, the Bedouin tribes placed heavy importance on poetry and oral tradition as a means of communication. Poetry was used to communicate within the community and sometimes promoted tribal propaganda. Tribes constructed verses against their enemies, often discrediting their people or fighting abilities. Poets maintained sacred places in their tribes and communities because they were thought to be divinely inspired. Poets often wrote in classical Arabic, which differed from the common tribal dialect. Poetry was also a form of entertainment, as many poets constructed prose about the nature and beauty surrounding their nomadic lives.

Music

Arabian music extended from the Islamic peoples in Arabia to North Africa, Persia, and Syria. Although the major writings on Arabian music appeared after the dawn of Islam (622 CE), music had already been cultivated for thousands of years. Pre-Islamic Arabian music was primarily vocal, and it may have developed from simple caravan songs (huda) to a more sophisticated secular song (nasb). Instruments were generally used alone and served only to accompany the singer. The short lute ('ud), long lute (tunbur), flute (qussaba), tambourine (duff), and drum (tabl) were the most popular instruments.

Women in Pre-Islamic Arabia

Women had almost no legal status under tribal law in pre-Islamic Arabia.

Learning Objectives

Assess the role and rights of women in Islamic and pre-Islamic Arabia

Key Takeaways

Key Points

- In the nomadic Bedouin tribes, tribal law determined women's rights, while in the Christian and Jewish southern Arabian Peninsula, Christian and Hebrew edicts determined women's rights.
- Under the customary tribal law existing in Arabia before the rise of Islam, women, as a general rule, had virtually no legal status; fathers sold their daughters into marriage for a price, the husband could terminate the union at will, and women had little or no property or succession rights.
- One of the most important roles for women was to produce children, especially male offspring; women also cooked meals, milked animals, washed clothes, prepared butter and cheese, spun wool, and wove fabric for tents.
- Upper-class women usually had more rights than tribal women and might own property or even inherit from relatives.
- In many modern-day Islamic countries, politics and religion are linked by Sharia law, including the mandatory wearing of the hijab in countries like Saudi Arabia.

Key Terms

- **Sharia**: (Islamic law) deals with many topics addressed by secular law, including crime, politics, and economics, as well as personal matters such as sexual intercourse, hygiene, diet, prayer, everyday etiquette and fasting. Historically, adherence to Islamic law has served as one of the distinguishing characteristics of the Muslim faith.
- **Jahiliyyah**: The period of ignorance before the rise of Islam.
- **hijab**: A veil that covers the head and chest, which is particularly worn by some Muslim women in the presence of adult males outside of their immediate family.

In pre-Islamic Arabia, women's status varied widely according to the laws and cultural norms of the tribes in which they lived. In the prosperous southern region of the Arabian Peninsula, for example, the religious edicts of Christianity and Judaism held sway among the Sabians and Himyarites. In other places, such as the city of Mecca, and in the nomadic Bedouin tribes, tribal law determined women's rights. Therefore, there was no single definition of the roles played and rights held by women prior to the advent of Islam.

Depiction of the costumes of women in the 4th-6th centuries: *Under the customary tribal law existing in Arabia before the rise of Islam, as a general rule women had virtually no legal status; fathers sold their daughters into marriage for a price, the husband could terminate the union at will, and women had little or no property or succession rights.*

Tribal Law

Under the customary tribal law existing in Arabia at the advent of Islam, as a general rule women had virtually no legal status. The tribe acted as the main functional unit of Arabian society and was composed of people with connections to a common relative. These tribes were patriarchal and inheritance was passed through the male lines; women could not inherit property. The tribal leader enforced the tribe's spoken rules, which generally limited the rights of the women. Women were often considered property to be inherited or seized in a tribal conflict.

There were also patterns of homicidal abuse of women and girls, including instances of killing female infants if they were considered a liability. The Quran mentions that the Arabs in Jahiliyyah (the period of ignorance or pre-Islamic period) used to bury their daughters alive. The motives were twofold: the fear that an increase in female offspring would result in economic burden, and the fear of the humiliation frequently caused when girls were captured by a hostile tribe and subsequently preferring their captors to their parents and brothers.

Women in Islam and the Hijab

After the rise of Islam, the Quran (the word of God) and the Hadith (the traditions of the prophet Muhammad) developed into Sharia, or Islamic religious law. Sharia dictates that women should cover themselves with a veil. Women who follow these traditions feel it wearing the hijab is their claim to respectability and piety. One of the relevant passages from the Quran translates as "O Prophet! Tell thy wives and daughters, and the believing women, that they should cast their outer garments over their persons, that are most convenient, that they should be known and not molested. And Allah is Oft-Forgiving, Most Merciful" (Quran Surat Al-Ahzab 33:59). These areas of the body are known as "awrah" (parts of the body that should be covered) and are referred to in both the Quran and the Hadith. "Hijab" can also be used to refer to the seclusion of women from men in the public sphere.

Modern-day female art students in Afghanistan: *In many modern Islamic countries, Sharia combines politics and religion. For example, in Saudi Arabia it is mandatory for women to wear the hijab, while in Afghanistan it is very common but not legally required by the state.*

The practice of women covering themselves with veils was also known during pre-Islamic times. In the Byzantine Empire and pre-Islamic Persia, a veil was a symbol of respect worn by the elite and upper-class women.

Standing woman holding her veil. Terracotta figurine, c. 400–375 BC: Veils were present in the Byzantine Empire and pre-Islamic Persia, and veil wearing is now a basic principle of the Islamic faith.

Marriage

In pre-Islamic Arabian culture, women had little control over their marriages and were rarely allowed to divorce their husbands. Marriages usually consisted of an agreement between a man and his future wife's family, and occurred either within the tribe or between two families of different tribes. As part of the agreement, the man's family might offer property such as camels or horses in exchange for the woman. Upon marriage, the woman would leave her family and reside permanently in the tribe of her husband. Marriage by capture, or "Ba'al," was also a common pre-Islamic practice.

Under Islam, polygyny (the marriage of multiple women to one man) is allowed, but not widespread. In some Islamic countries, such as Iran, a woman's husband may enter into temporary marriages in addition to permanent marriage. Islam forbids Muslim women from marrying non-Muslims.

Family Structure

One of the most important roles for women in pre-Islamic tribes was to produce children, especially male offspring. A woman's male children could inherit property and increased the wealth of the tribe. While men often tended the herds of livestock and guarded the tribe, women played integral roles within tribal society. Women cooked meals, milked animals, washed clothes, prepared butter and cheese, spun wool, and wove fabric for tents.

Upper-Class Women

While the general population of women in pre-Islamic Arabia did not enjoy the luxury of many rights, many women of upper-class status did. They married into comfortable homes and were sometimes able to own property or even inherit from relatives.

Attributions

CC licensed content, Specific attribution

- Pre-Islamic Arabia. **Provided by**: Wikipedia. **Located at**: http://en.wikipedia.org/wiki/Pre-Islamic_Arabia. **License**: *CC BY-SA: Attribution-ShareAlike*
- Bedouin. **Provided by**: Wikipedia. **Located at**: http://en.wikipedia.org/wiki/Bedouin. **License**: *CC BY-SA: Attribution-ShareAlike*
- Arabians. **Provided by**: Wikipedia. **Located at**: http://en.wikipedia.org/wiki/Arabians. **License**: *CC BY-SA: Attribution-ShareAlike*
- Middle Eastern Empires. **Provided by**: Wikibooks. **Located at**: http://en.wikibooks.org/wiki/World_History/Middle_Eastern_Empires. **License**: *CC BY-SA: Attribution-ShareAlike*
- Culture Pre-Islamic Arabia. **Provided by**: iah211dspring2010 Wikispace. **Located at**: http://iah211dspring2010.wikispaces.com/Group+2-1+Pre-Islamic+Arabia. **License**: *CC BY-SA: Attribution-ShareAlike*
- Muhammad. **Provided by**: Wikipedia. **Located at**: http://en.wikipedia.org/wiki/Muhammad. **License**: *CC BY-SA: Attribution-ShareAlike*
- Kaaba. **Provided by**: Wikipedia. **Located at**: http://en.wikipedia.org/wiki/Kaaba. **License**: *CC BY-SA: Attribution-ShareAlike*
- History of Jews in the Arabian Peninsula. **Provided by**: wikipedia. **Located at**: http://en.wikipedia.org/wiki/History_of_the_Jews_in_the_Arabian_Peninsula. **License**: *CC BY-SA: Attribution-ShareAlike*
- Map of Arabia 600 AD. **Provided by**: Wikimedia. **Located at**: http://en.wikipedia.org/wiki/File:Map_of_Arabia_600_AD.svg. **License**: *Public Domain: No Known Copyright*
- Syrian Bedouin Shepherd. **Provided by**: Wikimedia. **Located at**: http://en.wikipedia.org/wiki/File:Syrian_Bedouin_Shepherd.jpg. **License**: *CC BY-SA: Attribution-ShareAlike*
- Camels in Dubai 2. **Provided by**: Wikimedia. **Located at**: http://en.wikipedia.org/wiki/File:Camels_in_Dubai_2.jpg. **License**: *CC BY-SA: Attribution-ShareAlike*
- Pre-Islamic Arabia Culture. **Provided by**: iah211dspring2010 Wikispace. **Located at**: http://iah211dspring2010.wikispaces.com/Group+2-1+Pre-Islamic+Arabia. **License**: *CC BY-SA: Attribution-ShareAlike*
- Mecca. **Provided by**: Wikipedia. **Located at**: http://en.wikipedia.org/wiki/Mecca. **License**: *CC BY-SA: Attribution-ShareAlike*
- Medina. **Provided by**: Wikipedia. **Located at**: http://en.wikipedia.org/wiki/Medina. **License**: *CC BY-SA: Attribution-ShareAlike*
- Kaaba. **Provided by**: Wikipedia. **Located at**: http://en.wikipedia.org/wiki/Kaaba. **License**: *CC BY-SA: Attribution-ShareAlike*
- Zamzam Well. **Provided by**: Wikipedia. **Located at**: http://en.wikipedia.org/wiki/Zamzam_Well. **License**: *CC BY-SA: Attribution-ShareAlike*
- Ishmael. **Provided by**: Wikipedia. **Located at**: http://en.wikipedia.org/wiki/Ishmael. **License**: *CC BY-SA: Attribution-ShareAlike*
- Map of Arabia 600 AD. **Provided by**: Wikimedia. **Located at**: http://en.wikipedia.org/wiki/File:Map_of_Arabia_600_AD.svg. **License**: *Public Domain: No Known Copyright*
- Syrian Bedouin Shepherd. **Provided by**: Wikimedia. **Located at**: http://en.wikipedia.org/wiki/File:Syrian_Bedouin_Shepherd.jpg. **License**: *CC BY-SA: Attribution-ShareAlike*
- Camels in Dubai 2. **Provided by**: Wikimedia. **Located at**: http://en.wikipedia.org/wiki/File:Camels_in_Dubai_2.jpg. **License**: *CC BY-SA: Attribution-ShareAlike*
- Madina_Munavara.JPG. **Provided by**: Wikipedia. **Located at**: https://en.wikipedia.org/wiki/Medina#/media/File:Madina_Munavara.JPG. **License**: *CC BY-SA: Attribution-ShareAlike*
- A Journey. **Provided by**: Wikimedia. **Located at**: http://commons.wikimedia.org/wiki/File:A_journey.jpg. **License**: *Public Domain: No Known Copyright*
- Arabians. **Provided by**: Wikipedia. **Located at**: http://en.wikipedia.org/wiki/Arabians. **License**: *CC BY-SA: Attribution-ShareAlike*
- Pre-Islamic Culture. **Provided by**: iah211dspring2010 Wikispace. **Located at**: http://iah211dspring2010.wikispaces.com/Group+2-1+Pre-Islamic+Arabia. **License**: *CC BY-SA: Attribution-ShareAlike*
- Middle Eastern Empires. **Provided by**: Wikibooks. **Located at**: http://en.wikibooks.org/wiki/World_History/Middle_Eastern_Empires. **License**: *CC BY-SA: Attribution-ShareAlike*

PRE-ISLAMIC ARABIA • 509

- Book of Idols. **Provided by**: Wikipedia. **Located at**: http://en.wikipedia.org/wiki/Book_of_Idols. **License**: *CC BY-SA: Attribution-ShareAlike*
- Animism. **Provided by**: Wikipedia. **Located at**: http://en.wikipedia.org/wiki/Animism. **License**: *CC BY-SA: Attribution-ShareAlike*
- Arabian Polytheism. **Provided by**: Wikipedia. **Located at**: http://en.wikipedia.org/wiki/Arabian_polytheism. **License**: *CC BY-SA: Attribution-ShareAlike*
- Pre-Islamic Arabia. **Provided by**: Wikipedia. **Located at**: http://en.wikipedia.org/wiki/Pre-Islamic_Arabia. **License**: *CC BY-SA: Attribution-ShareAlike*
- Polytheism. **Provided by**: Wikipedia. **Located at**: http://en.wikipedia.org/wiki/Polytheism. **License**: *CC BY-SA: Attribution-ShareAlike*
- monotheism. **Provided by**: Wiktionary. **Located at**: http://en.wiktionary.org/wiki/monotheism. **License**: *CC BY-SA: Attribution-ShareAlike*
- polytheism. **Provided by**: Wiktionary. **Located at**: http://en.wiktionary.org/wiki/polytheism. **License**: *CC BY-SA: Attribution-ShareAlike*
- idolatry. **Provided by**: Wiktionary. **Located at**: http://en.wiktionary.org/wiki/idolatry. **License**: *CC BY-SA: Attribution-ShareAlike*
- animism. **Provided by**: Wiktionary. **Located at**: http://en.wiktionary.org/wiki/animism. **License**: *CC BY-SA: Attribution-ShareAlike*
- Christianity and Judaism. **Provided by**: Wikipedia. **Located at**: http://en.wikipedia.org/wiki/Christianity_and_Judaism. **License**: *CC BY-SA: Attribution-ShareAlike*
- Map of Arabia 600 AD. **Provided by**: Wikimedia. **Located at**: http://en.wikipedia.org/wiki/File:Map_of_Arabia_600_AD.svg. **License**: *Public Domain: No Known Copyright*
- Syrian Bedouin Shepherd. **Provided by**: Wikimedia. **Located at**: http://en.wikipedia.org/wiki/File:Syrian_Bedouin_Shepherd.jpg. **License**: *CC BY-SA: Attribution-ShareAlike*
- Camels in Dubai 2. **Provided by**: Wikimedia. **Located at**: http://en.wikipedia.org/wiki/File:Camels_in_Dubai_2.jpg. **License**: *CC BY-SA: Attribution-ShareAlike*
- Madina_Munavara.JPG. **Provided by**: Wikipedia. **Located at**: https://en.wikipedia.org/wiki/Medina#/media/File:Madina_Munavara.JPG. **License**: *CC BY-SA: Attribution-ShareAlike*
- A Journey. **Provided by**: Wikimedia. **Located at**: http://commons.wikimedia.org/wiki/File:A_journey.jpg. **License**: *Public Domain: No Known Copyright*
- Allat Palmyra RGZM 3369. **Provided by**: Wikimedia. **Located at**: http://commons.wikimedia.org/wiki/Category:Allat%23mediaviewer/File:Allat_Palmyra_RGZM_3369.jpg. **License**: *CC BY-SA: Attribution-ShareAlike*
- Mosquu00e9e_Masjid_el_Haram_u00e0_la_Mecque.jpg. **Provided by**: Wikipedia. **Located at**: https://en.wikipedia.org/wiki/Kaaba. **License**: *CC BY-SA: Attribution-ShareAlike*
- Pre-Islamic Arabia Culture. **Provided by**: iah211dspring2010 Wikispace. **Located at**: http://iah211dspring2010.wikispaces.com/Group+2-1+Pre-Islamic+Arabia. **License**: *CC BY-SA: Attribution-ShareAlike*
- Women in Early Islam. **Provided by**: iah211dspring2010 Wikispace. **Located at**: http://iah211dspring2010.wikispaces.com/Group+4-1+Women+in+Early+Islam. **License**: *CC BY-SA: Attribution-ShareAlike*
- Women in Arab Societies. **Provided by**: Wikipedia. **Located at**: http://en.wikipedia.org/wiki/Women_in_Arab_societies. **License**: *CC BY-SA: Attribution-ShareAlike*
- Pre-Islamic Arabia. **Provided by**: Wikipedia. **Located at**: http://en.wikipedia.org/wiki/Pre-Islamic_Arabia. **License**: *CC BY-SA: Attribution-ShareAlike*
- Women in Islam. **Provided by**: Wikipedia. **Located at**: http://en.wikipedia.org/wiki/Women_in_islam. **License**: *CC BY-SA: Attribution-ShareAlike*
- Hijab. **Provided by**: Wikipedia. **Located at**: http://en.wikipedia.org/wiki/Hijab. **License**: *CC BY-SA: Attribution-ShareAlike*
- Map of Arabia 600 AD. **Provided by**: Wikimedia. **Located at**: http://en.wikipedia.org/wiki/File:Map_of_Arabia_600_AD.svg. **License**: *Public Domain: No Known Copyright*
- Syrian Bedouin Shepherd. **Provided by**: Wikimedia. **Located at**: http://en.wikipedia.org/wiki/File:Syrian_Bedouin_Shepherd.jpg. **License**: *CC BY-SA: Attribution-ShareAlike*
- Camels in Dubai 2. **Provided by**: Wikimedia. **Located at**: http://en.wikipedia.org/wiki/File:Camels_in_Dubai_2.jpg. **License**: *CC BY-SA: Attribution-ShareAlike*
- Madina_Munavara.JPG. **Provided by**: Wikipedia. **Located at**: https://en.wikipedia.org/wiki/Medina#/media/File:Madina_Munavara.JPG. **License**: *CC BY-SA: Attribution-ShareAlike*

- A Journey. **Provided by**: Wikimedia. **Located at**: http://commons.wikimedia.org/wiki/File:A_journey.jpg. **License**: *Public Domain: No Known Copyright*
- Allat Palmyra RGZM 3369. **Provided by**: Wikimedia. **Located at**: http://commons.wikimedia.org/wiki/Category:Allat%23mediaviewer/File:Allat_Palmyra_RGZM_3369.jpg. **License**: *CC BY-SA: Attribution-ShareAlike*
- Mosquu00e9e_Masjid_el_Haram_u00e0_la_Mecque.jpg. **Provided by**: Wikipedia. **Located at**: https://en.wikipedia.org/wiki/Kaaba. **License**: *CC BY-SA: Attribution-ShareAlike*
- Veil. **Provided by**: Wikipedia. **Located at**: http://en.wikipedia.org/wiki/Veil. **License**: *CC BY-SA: Attribution-ShareAlike*
- Center for Contemporary Arts Afghanistan in 2010. **Provided by**: Wikimedia Commons. **Located at**: http://en.wikipedia.org/wiki/Hijab%23mediaviewer/File:Center_for_Contemporary_Arts_Afghanistan_in_2010.jpg. **License**: *Public Domain: No Known Copyright*
- PLATE8CX. **Provided by**: Wikimedia. **Located at**: http://en.wikipedia.org/wiki/Women_in_Arab_societies%23mediaviewer/File:PLATE8CX.jpg. **License**: *Public Domain: No Known Copyright*

Muhammad and the Rise of Islam

Early Life of Muhammad

Born c. 570 CE in Mecca, Muhammad was raised by his uncle Abu Talib and later worked as a merchant.

Learning Objectives
Describe Muhammad's life before 622 CE

Key Takeaways

Key Points

- Muhammad was born in or around the year 570 CE to the Banu Hashim clan of the Quraysh tribe, one of Mecca's prominent families.
- Muhammad was orphaned at an early age and brought up under the care of his paternal uncle Abu Talib.
- Muhammad worked mostly as a merchant, as well as a shepherd, and married Khadijah, a 40-year-old widow, in 595 CE when he was twenty-five.
- In 605 CE, Muhammad honored all the Meccan clan leaders and set the Black Stone back into the correct spot in the Ka'aba.

Key Terms

- **the Black Stone**: The eastern cornerstone of the Kaaba, the ancient stone building located in the center of the Grand Mosque in Mecca, Saudi Arabia. It is revered by Mus-

> lims as an Islamic relic that, according to Muslim tradition, dates back to the time of Adam and Eve.
> - **Quraysh tribe**: A powerful merchant group that controlled Mecca and the Kaaba.

Overview

Muhammad unified Arabia into a single religious polity under Islam. Muslims and Bahá'ís believe he is a messenger and prophet of God. The Quran, the central religious text in Islam, alludes to Muhammad's life. Muhammad's life is traditionally defined into two periods: pre-hijra (emigration) in Mecca (from 570 to 622 CE) and post-hijra in Medina (from 622 until 632 CE). There are also traditional Muslim biographies of Muhammad (the sira literature), which provide additional information about Muhammad's life. Muhammad is almost universally considered by Muslims as the last prophet sent by God to mankind. While non-Muslims regard Muhammad as the founder of Islam, Muslims consider him to have restored the unaltered original monotheistic faith of Adam, Noah, Abraham, Moses, Jesus, and other prophets.

Childhood

Muhammad was born around the year 570 CE to the Banu Hashim clan of the Quraysh tribe, one of Mecca's prominent families. His father, Abdullah, died almost six months before Muhammad was born. According to Islamic tradition, Muhammad was sent to live with a Bedouin family in the desert, as desert life was considered healthier for infants. Muhammad stayed with his foster mother, Halimah bint Abi Dhuayb, and her husband until he was two years old. At the age of six, Muhammad lost his biological mother, Amina, to illness and was raised by his paternal grandfather, Abd al-Muttalib, until he died when Muhammad was eight. He then came under the care of his uncle Abu Talib, the new leader of Banu Hashim.

Adolescence and Early Adulthood

While still in his teens, Muhammad accompanied his uncle on trading journeys to Syria, gaining experience in commercial trade, which was the only career open to him as an orphan. Islamic tradition states that when Muhammad was either nine or twelve, while accompanying a caravan to Syria he met a Christian monk or hermit named Bahira, who is said to have foreseen Muhammed's career as a prophet of God. Little is known of Muhammad during his later youth; available information is fragmented, and it is difficult to separate history from legend. It is known that he became a merchant and "was involved in trade between the Indian ocean and the Mediterranean Sea." Due to his upright character during this time, he acquired the nickname "al-Amin," meaning "faithful, trustworthy," and "al-Sadiq," meaning "truthful."

Muhammad worked as a trader for Khadija, a widow, until he married her in 595 CE at the age of 25. The marriage lasted for 25 years and was reported to be a happy one. Muhammad relied upon Khadija and did not enter into a marriage with another woman during his first marriage. After Khadija's death, Khawla bint Hakim suggested that Muhammad that should marry Sawda bint Zama, a Muslim widow, or Aisha, daughter of Um Ruman and Abu Bakr of Mecca. Muhammad is said to have asked for arrangements to marry both.

According to a text collected by historian Ibn Ishaq, Muhammad was involved with a well-known story about setting the Black Stone in place in the wall of the Kaaba in 605 CE. The Black Stone, a sacred object, had been removed to facilitate renovations to the Kaaba. The leaders of Mecca could not agree on which clan should have the honor of setting the Black Stone back in its place. They agreed to wait for the next man to come through the gate and ask him to choose. That man was the 35-year-old Muhammad, five years before his first revelation. He asked for a cloth and put the Black Stone in its center. The clan leaders held the corners of the cloth and together carried the Black Stone to the right spot; then Muhammad set the stone in place, satisfying all who were present.

Muhammad and the Black Stone: *An illustration from c. 1315 depicting Muhammad's role in re-setting the Black Stone in 605 CE.*

Occasionally he would retreat to a cave in the mountains for several nights of seclusion and prayer; it is reported that it was at this spot that he was visited by Gabriel and received his first revelation from God.

The Quran

Muhammad received revelations from 609-632 CE, and they became the basis for the Quran, the central religious text of Islam.

Learning Objectives

Discuss the origins of the first Muslim converts

Key Takeaways

Key Points

- Muhammad first received revelations in 609 CE in a cave on Mount Hira, near Mecca.
- Muslims regard the Quran as the most important miracle of Muhammad, the proof of his prophethood, and the culmination of a series of divine messages revealed by the angel Gabriel from 609–632 CE.
- The key themes of the early Quranic verses included the responsibility of man towards his creator; the resurrection of the dead, God's final judgment followed by vivid descriptions of the tortures in Hell and pleasures in Paradise; and the signs of God in all aspects of life. Religious duties included belief in God, asking for forgiveness of sins, offering frequent prayers, assisting others particularly those in need, rejecting cheating and the love of wealth, being chaste, and not killing newborn girls.
- Muhammad's immediate family were the first to believe he was a prophet, followed by three main groups of early converts to Islam: younger brothers and sons of great merchants, people who had fallen out of the first rank in their tribe or failed to attain it, and unprotected foreigners.
- Muslims believe the Quran to be both the unaltered and the final revelation of God. Religious concepts and practices include the five pillars of Islam, which are obligatory acts of worship, and following Islamic law, which touches on virtually every aspect of life and society, from banking and welfare to the status of women and the environment.

Key Terms

- **Quran**: Literally meaning "the recitation," it is the central religious text of Islam, which Muslims believe to be a revelation from God.
- **Khadijah**: The first wife of Muhammad.
- **Five Pillars of Islam**: Five basic acts in Islam, considered mandatory by believers and are the foundation of Muslim life.

Muhammad's First Revelations

When he was nearly 40, Muhammad began spending many hours alone in prayer and speculating over the aspects of creation. He was concerned with the "ignorance of divine guidance" (*Jahiliyyah*), social unrest, injustice, widespread discrimination (particularly against women), fighting among tribes, and abuse of tribal authorities prevalent in pre-Islamic Arabia. The moral degeneration of his fellow people, and his own quest for a true religion, further lent fuel to this, with the result that he began to withdraw periodically to a cave called Mount Hira, three miles north of Mecca, for contemplation and reflection. During this period Muhammad began to have dreams replete with spiritual significance that were fulfilled according to their true import; this was the commencement of his divine revelation. Islamic tradition holds that during one of his visits to Mount Hira in the year 609 CE, the angel Gabriel appeared to him and commanded Muhammad to recite verses that would later be included in the Quran. Upon receiving his first revelations, Muhammad was deeply distressed. When he returned home, he was consoled and reassured by Khadijah and her Christian cousin. Muhammad feared that others would dismiss his claims as evidence of him being possessed. On the other hand, Shi'a tradition maintains that Muhammad was neither surprised nor frightened at the appearance of Gabriel, but rather welcomed him as if he was expected.

The cave Hira: *The cave Hira in the mountain Jabal al-Nour where, according to Muslim belief, Muhammad received his first revelation from the angel Gabriel.*

The initial revelation was followed by a pause of three years (a period known as *fatra*) during which Muhammad felt depressed and further gave himself to prayers and spiritual practices. When the revelations resumed, he was reassured and began preaching.

The Quran

Quran Al-Qur'n ?: Arabic calligraphy for "Quran"

Muslims believe that the Quran was verbally revealed from God to Muhammad through the angel Gabriel gradually over a period of approximately 23 years, beginning on 22 December 609 CE, when Muhammad was 40, and concluding in 632 CE, the year of his death. At the beginning of these revelations, Muhammad was confident that he could distinguish his own thoughts from the messages. Sahih al-Bukhari narrates Muhammad describing the revelations as, "Sometimes it is (revealed) like the ringing of a bell," and Aisha reported, "I saw the Prophet being inspired Divinely on a very cold day and noticed the sweat dropping from his forehead (as the Inspiration was over)."

Muhammad's first revelation, according to the Quran, was accompanied by a vision. The agent of revelation is mentioned as the "one mighty in power," the one who "grew clear to view when he was on the uppermost horizon. Then he drew nigh and came down till he was (distant) two bows' length or even nearer." The Islamic studies scholar Welch states in the *Encyclopaedia of Islam* that he believes the graphic descriptions of Muhammad's condition at these moments may be regarded as genuine, because he was severely disturbed after these revelations. According to Welch, these seizures would have been seen by those around him as evidence for the superhuman origin of Muhammad's inspirations. However, Muhammad's critics accused him of being a possessed man, a soothsayer or a magician, since his experiences were similar to those claimed by such figures well known in ancient Arabia. Welch additionally states that it remains uncertain whether these experiences occurred before or after Muhammad's initial claim of prophethood.

The Quran describes Muhammad as "ummi," which is traditionally interpreted as "illiterate," but the meaning is more complex. Medieval commentators such as Al-Tabari maintained that the term induced two meanings: firstly, the inability to read or write in general, and secondly, the inexperience or ignorance of books or scriptures. However, priority was given to the first meaning. Muhammad's illiteracy was taken as a sign of the genuineness of his prophethood. For example, according to Fakhr al-Din al-Razi, if Muhammad had mastered writing and reading he possibly would have been suspected of having studied the books of the ancestors. Some scholars such as Watt prefer the second meaning.

According to the Quran, one of the main roles of Muhammad is to warn the unbelievers of their punishment at the end of the world. The Quran does not explicitly refer to Judgment Day, but provided examples from the history of extinct communities and warns Muhammad's contemporaries of similar calamities. Muhammad did not only warn those who rejected God's revelation, but also dispensed good news for those who abandoned evil, listening to the divine words and serving God. Muhammad's mission also involves preaching monotheism; the Quran commands Muhammad to proclaim and praise the name of his Lord and instructs him not to worship idols or associate other deities with God.

A depiction of Muhammad receiving his first revelation from the angel Gabriel: Muslims regard the Quran as the most important miracle of Muhammad, the proof of his prophethood, and the culmination of a series of divine messages revealed by the angel Gabriel from 609–632 CE. (From the manuscript Jami' al-tawarikh by Rashid-al-Din Hamadani, 1307, Ilkhanate period)

The key themes of the early Quranic verses included the responsibility of man towards his creator; the resurrection of the dead, God's final judgment followed by vivid descriptions of the tortures in Hell and pleasures in Paradise; and the signs of God in all aspects of life. Religious duties required of the believers at this time were few: belief in God, asking for forgiveness of sins, offering frequent prayers, assisting others, particularly those in need, rejecting cheating and the love of wealth (considered to be significant in the commercial life of Mecca), being chaste, and not killing newborn girls.

Rise of Islam in Mecca

According to Muslim tradition, Muhammad's wife Khadija was the first to believe he was a prophet. She was followed by Muhammad's ten-year-old cousin Ali ibn Abi Talib, close friend Abu Bakr, and adopted son Zaid. Around 613, Muhammad began to preach to the public. Most Meccans ignored and mocked him, but he did begin to gain followers. There were three main groups of early converts to Islam: younger brothers and sons of great merchants; people who had fallen out of the first rank in their tribe or failed to attain it; and the weak, mostly unprotected foreigners.

Basic Tenets and Practices of Islam

Islam is a monotheistic and Abrahamic religion articulated by the Quran, which is considered by its adherents to be the verbatim word of God (Allah), and, for the vast majority of adherents, by the teachings and normative example (called the *sunnah*, composed of accounts called *hadith*) of Muhammad. An adherent of Islam is called a Muslim. Muslims believe that God is one and incomparable and that the purpose of existence is to worship God. Nearly all Muslims consider Muhammad to be the last prophet of God.

Muslims also believe that Islam is the complete and universal version of a primordial faith that was revealed many times before through prophets including Adam, Noah, Abraham, Moses, and Jesus. Muslims believe the Quran to be both the unaltered and the final revelation of God. Religious concepts and practices include the Five Pillars of Islam and following Islamic law, which touches on virtually every aspect of life and society, from banking and welfare to the status of women and the environment.

The Five Pillars of Islam are five basic acts in Islam; they are considered mandatory by believers and are the foundation of Muslim life. They are summarized in the famous *hadith* of Gabriel. The Five Pillars are:

1. *Shahada* (faith): there is only one God (Allah), and Muhammad is God's messenger. It is a set statement normally recited in Arabic: lā ʾilāha ʾillā-llāhu muḥammadun rasūlu-llāh (لَا إِلٰهَ إِلَّا اللّٰه مُحَمَّدٌ رَسُولُ اللّٰه) "There is no god but God (and) Muhammad is the messenger of God."

2. *Salat* (prayer): consists of five daily prayers, the names referring to the prayer times: *Fajr* (dawn), *Dhuhr* (noon), *ʿAṣr* (afternoon), *Maghrib* (evening), and *ʿIshāʾ* (night). All of these prayers are recited while facing in the direction of the Kaaba in Mecca, and are accompanied by a series of set positions including bowing with hands on knees, standing, prostrating, and sitting in a special position.

3. *Zakāt* (charity): the practice of charitable giving based on accumulated wealth. It is the personal responsibility of each Muslim to ease the economic hardship of others and to strive towards eliminating inequality. *Zakāt* consists of spending a portion of one's wealth for the benefit of the poor or needy, like debtors or travelers.

4. *Sawm* (fasting): three types of fasting are recognized by the Quran: ritual fasting, fasting as compensation for repentance, and ascetic fasting. Ritual fasting is an obligatory act during the month of Ramadan. The fast is meant to allow Muslims to seek nearness to and look for forgiveness from God, to express their gratitude to and dependence on him, to atone for their past sins, and to remind them of the needy.

5. *Hajj* (pilgrimage to Mecca): every able-bodied Muslim is obliged to make the pilgrimage to Mecca at least once in his or her life. The main rituals of the *Hajj* include walking seven times around the Kaaba, termed *Tawaf*; touching the Black Stone, termed *Istilam*; traveling seven times between Mount Safa and Mount Marwah, termed *Saʾyee*; and symbolically stoning the Devil in Mina, termed *Ramee*.

Flight from Mecca to Medina

As Islam faced more political and religious opposition in Mecca, Muhammad and his followers migrated to Medina in 622 CE.

Learning Objectives

Explain the basis for opposition to Muhammad

Key Takeaways

Key Points

- As Islam spread in Mecca, the ruling tribes began to oppose Muhammad 's preaching and his condemnation of idolatry.
- The Quraysh tribe controlled the Kaaba and drew their religious and political power from its polytheistic shrines, so they began to persecute the Muslims and many of Muhammad's followers became martyrs.
- When Muhammad's wife Khadijah and uncle Abu Talib both died in 619 CE, Abu Lahab assumed leadership of the Banu Hashim clan and withdrew the clan's protection from Muhammad.
- In 622 CE, Muhammad and his followers migrated to Yathrib in the Hijra to escape persecution, renaming the city Medina in honor of the prophet.
- Among the first things Muhammad did to ease the longstanding grievances among the tribes of Medina was draft a document known as the Constitution of Medina.

Key Terms

- **Mecca**: The birthplace of Muhammad and the site of Muhammad's first revelation of the Quran, this city is regarded as the holiest city in the religion of Islam.
- **Banu Hashim clan**: One of Mecca's prominent families and part of the Quraysh tribe.
- **Medina**: Muhammad's destination during the Hijra, which became the power base of Islam in its first century (renamed from Yathrib).
- **Hijra**: The migration or journey of the Islamic prophet Muhammad and his followers from Mecca to Medina in June 622 CE.

Muhammad Starts Preaching

During the first three years of his ministry, Muhammad preached Islam privately, mainly among his near relatives and close acquaintances. According to Muslim tradition, Muhammad's wife Khadija was the first to believe he was a prophet. She was followed by Muhammad's ten-year-old cousin Ali ibn Abi Talib, close friend Abu Bakr, and adopted son Zaid. According to Islamic belief, in the fourth year of Muhammad's prophethood, around 613, he was ordered by God to make his propagation of this monotheistic faith public. Muhammad's earliest teachings were marked by his insistence on the oneness of God, the denunciation of polytheism, belief in the last judgment and its recompense, and social and economic justice.

Most Meccans ignored and mocked him, though a few became his followers. There were three main groups of early converts to Islam: younger brothers and sons of great merchants; people who had fallen out of the first rank in their tribe or failed to attain it; and the weak, mostly unprotected foreigners.

Opposition in Mecca

According to Ibn Sad, one of Muhammad's companions, the opposition in Mecca started when Muhammad delivered verses that condemned idol worship and polytheism. However, the Quran maintains that it began when Muhammad started public preaching. As Islam spread, Muhammad threatened the local tribes and Meccan rulers because their wealth depended on the Kaaba. Muhammad's preaching was particularly offensive to his own Quraysh tribe because they guarded the Kaaba and drew their political and religious power from its polytheistic shrines.

The ruling tribes of Mecca perceived Muhammad as a danger that might cause tensions similar to the rivalry of Judaism and Bedouin Polytheism in Yathrib. The powerful merchants in Mecca attempted to convince Muhammad to abandon his preaching by offering him admission into the inner circle of merchants and an advantageous marriage. However, Muhammad turned down both offers.

The last ayah from the sura An-Najm in the Quran: *Muhammad's message of monotheism challenged the traditional social order in Mecca. The Quraysh tribe controlled the Kaaba and drew their religious and political power from its polytheistic shrines, so they began to persecute the Muslims and many of Muhammad's followers became martyrs.*

At first, the opposition was confined to ridicule and sarcasm, but later morphed into active persecution that forced a section of new converts to migrate to neighboring Abyssinia (present day Ethiopia). Upset by the rate at which Muhammad was gaining new followers, the Quraysh proposed adopting a common form of worship, which was denounced by the Quran.

Muhammad himself was protected from physical harm as long as he belonged to the Banu Hashim clan, but his followers were not so lucky. Sumayyah bint Khabbab, a slave of the prominent Meccan leader Abu Jahl, is famous as the first martyr of Islam; her master killed her with a spear when she refused to give up her faith. Bilal, another Muslim slave, was tortured by Umayyah ibn Khalaf, who placed more and more rocks on his chest to force his conversion, until he died.

Death of Khadijah and Abu Talib in 619 CE

Muhammad's wife Khadijah and uncle Abu Talib both died in 619 CE, the year that became known as the "year of sorrow." With the death of Abu Talib, Abu Lahab assumed leadership of the Banu Hashim clan. Soon after, Abu Lahab withdrew the clan's protection from Muhammad, endangering him and his followers. Muhammad took this opportunity to look for a new home for himself and his followers. After several unsuccessful negotiations, he found hope with some men from Yathrib (later called Medina). The Arab population of Yathrib were familiar with monotheism and were prepared for the appearance of a prophet because a Jewish community existed there as well. They also hoped, by the means of Muhammad and the new faith, to gain supremacy over Mecca; the Yathrib were jealous of its importance as the place of pilgrimage. Converts to Islam came from nearly all Arab tribes in Medina; by June of the subsequent year, seventy-five Muslims came to Mecca for pilgrimage and to meet Muhammad.

The Delegation from Medina

A delegation from Medina, consisting of the representatives of the twelve important clans of Medina, invited Muhammad as a neutral outsider to serve as the chief arbitrator for the entire community. There was fighting in Yathrib (Medina) mainly involving its Arab and Jewish inhabitants for around a hundred years before 620. The recurring slaughters and disagreements over the resulting claims, especially after the battle of Bu'ath, in which all the clans were involved, made it obvious that the tribal conceptions of blood feud and an eye for an eye were no longer workable unless there was one man with authority to adjudicate in disputed cases. The delegation from Medina pledged themselves and their fellow citizens to accept Muhammad into their community and physically protect him as one of their own.

The Hijra in 622 CE

The Hijra is the migration of Muhammad and his followers from Mecca to Medina, 320 kilometers (200 miles) north, in 622 CE. Muhammad instructed his followers to emigrate to Medina until nearly all of them left Mecca. According to tradition, the Meccans, alarmed at the departure, plotted to assassinate Muhammad. In June 622, when he was warned of the plot, Muhammad slipped out of Mecca with his companion, Abu Bakr.

On the night of his departure, Muhammad's house was besieged by the appointed men of Quraysh. It is said that when Muhammad emerged from his house, he recited the a verse from the Quran and threw a handful of dust in the direction of the besiegers, which prevented them seeing him. When the Quraysh learned of Muhammad's escape, they announced a large reward for bringing him back to them, alive or dead, and pursuers scattered in all directions. After eight days' journey, Muhammad entered the outskirts of Medina, but did not enter the city directly. He stopped at a place called Quba, some miles from the main city, and established a mosque there. After a fourteen-days stay at Quba, Muhammad started for Medina, participating in his first Friday prayer on the way, and upon reaching the city was greeted cordially by its people.

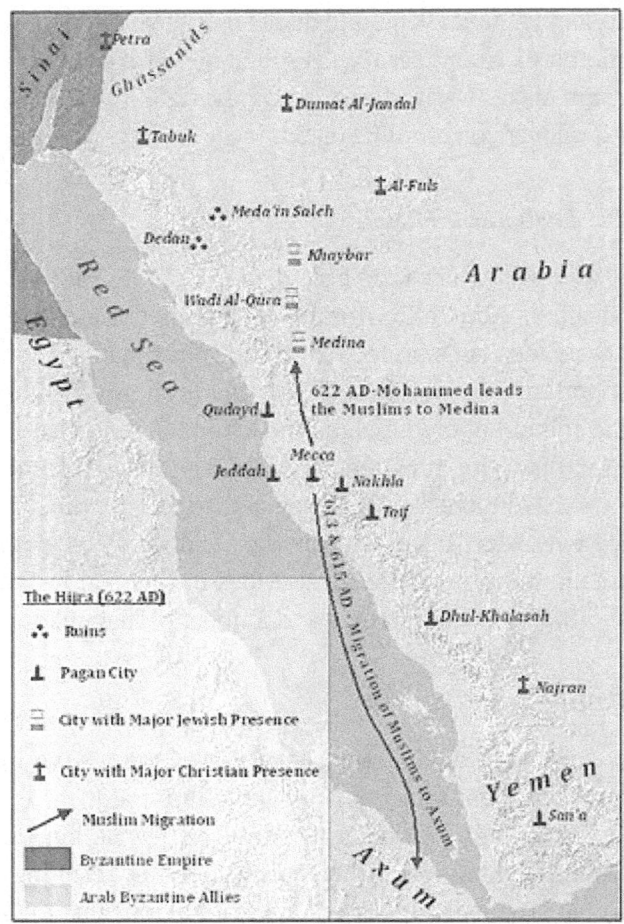

The Hijra and other early Muslim migrations: *The Hijra is the migration or journey of the Islamic prophet Muhammad and his followers from Mecca to Yathrib, which he later renamed Medina, in 622 CE.*

Muhammad in Medina

Among the first things Muhammad did to ease the longstanding grievances among the tribes of Medina was draft a document known as the Constitution of Medina, "establishing a kind of alliance or federation" among the eight Medinan tribes and Muslim emigrants from Mecca. The document specified rights and duties of all citizens and the relationship of the different communities in Medina (including between the Muslim community and other communities, specifically the Jews and other "Peoples of the Book"). The community defined in the Constitution of Medina, *Ummah,* had a religious outlook, also shaped by practical considerations, and substantially preserved the legal forms of the old Arab tribes.

The first group of pagan converts to Islam in Medina were the clans who had not produced great leaders for themselves but had suffered from warlike leaders from other clans. This was followed by the general acceptance of Islam by the pagan population of Medina, with some exceptions.

Reconciliation and Consolidation of the Islamic State

Around 628 CE, the nascent Islamic state was somewhat consolidated when Muhammad left Medina to perform pilgrimage at Mecca. The Quraysh intercepted him en route and made a treaty with the Muslims. Though the terms of the Hudaybiyyah treaty may have been unfavorable to the Muslims of Medina, the Quran declared it a clear victory. Muslim historians suggest that the treaty mobilized the contact between the Meccan pagans and the Muslims of Medina. The treaty demonstrated that the Quraysh recognized Muhammad as their equal and Islam as a rising power.

Islam Ascendant

After eight years of warring with Mecca and finally conquering the city in 630 CE, Muhammad united Arabia into a single Islamic state.

Learning Objectives

Discuss the rise of Islam under Muhammad

Key Takeaways

Key Points

- Muhammad created the first Islamic state when he wrote the Constitution of Medina, a formal agreement between Muhammad and all of the significant tribes and families of Medina, including Muslims, Jews, Christians, and pagans.
- The Battle of Badr was a key battle in the early days of Islam and a turning point in Muhammad's struggle with his opponents among the Quraysh in Mecca.
- The Battle of Uḥud in 625 CE was the second military encounter between the Meccans and the Muslims, but the Muslims suffered defeat and withdrew.
- After eight years of fighting with the Meccan tribes, Muhammad gathered an army of 10,000 followers and conquered the city of Mecca, destroying the pagan idols in the Kaaba.
- By the time of Muhammad's unexpected death in 632 CE, he had united Arabia into a single Muslim religious polity.

> *Key Terms*
>
> - **Constitution of Medina**: A formal agreement between Muhammad and all of the significant tribes and families of Medina, including Muslims, Jews, Christians, and pagans, that formed the basis of the first Islamic state.
> - **Ummah**: The collective community of Islamic peoples.
> - **Farewell Pilgrimage**: The only Hajj pilgrimage to Mecca by the Islamic prophet Muhammad, in 632 CE.

The Constitution of Medina

Upon his arrival in Medina, Muhammad unified the tribes by drafting the Constitution of Medina, which was a formal agreement between Muhammad and all of the significant tribes and families of Medina, including Muslims, Jews, Christians, and pagans. This constitution instituted rights and responsibilities and united the different Medina communities into the first Islamic state, the Ummah.

An important feature of the Constitution of Medina is the redefinition of ties between Muslims. It set faith relationships above blood ties and emphasized individual responsibility. Tribal identities were still important, and were used to refer to different groups, but the constitution declared that the "main binding tie" for the newly created Ummah was religion. This contrasts with the norms of pre-Islamic Arabia, which was a thoroughly tribal society. This was an important event in the development of the small group of Muslims in Medina to the larger Muslim community and empire. While praying in the Masjid al-Qiblatain in Medina in 624 CE, Muhammad received revelations that he should be facing Mecca rather than Jerusalem during prayer. Muhammad adjusted to the new direction, and his companions praying with him followed his lead, beginning the tradition of facing Mecca during prayer.

The Masjid al-Qiblatain, where Muhammad established the new Qibla, or direction of prayer: Muhammad received revelations that he should face Mecca, rather than Jerusalem, in 624 CE.

Beginning of Armed Conflict

Economically uprooted by their Meccan persecutors and with no available profession, the Muslim migrants turned to raiding Meccan caravans. This response to persecution and effort to provide sustenance for Muslim families initiated armed conflict between the Muslims and the pagan Quraysh of Mecca. Muhammad delivered Quranic verses permitting the Muslims, "those who have been expelled from their homes," to fight the Meccans in opposition to persecution. The caravan attacks provoked and pressured Mecca by interfering with trade, and allowed the Muslims to acquire wealth, power, and prestige while working toward their ultimate goal of inducing Mecca's submission to the new faith.

Battle of Badr

In March 624, Muhammad led three hundred warriors in a raid on a Meccan merchant caravan. The Muslims set an ambush for the caravan at Badr, but a Meccan force intervened and the Battle of Badr commenced. Although outnumbered more than three to one, the Muslims won the battle, killing at least forty-five Meccans. Muhammad and his followers saw the victory as confirmation of their faith, and Muhammad said the victory was assisted by an invisible host of angels. The victory strengthened Muhammad's position in Medina and dispelled earlier doubts among his followers.

Battle of Uhud

To maintain economic prosperity, the Meccans needed to restore their prestige after their defeat at Badr. Abu Sufyan, the leader of the ruling Quraysh tribe, gathered an army of 3,000 men and set out for an attack on Medina. Muhammad led his Muslim force to the Meccans to fight the Battle of Uhud on March 23, 625 CE. When the battle seemed close to a decisive Muslim victory, the Muslim archers left their assigned posts to raid the Meccan camp. Meccan war veteran Khalid ibn al-Walid led a surprise attack, which killed many Muslims and injured Muhammad. The Muslims withdrew up the slopes of Uḥud. The Meccans did not pursue the Muslims further, but marched back to Mecca declaring victory.

For the Muslims, the battle was a significant setback. According to the Quran, the loss at Uhud was partly a punishment and partly a test for steadfastness.

Conquest of Mecca and Arabia

After eight years of fighting with the Meccan tribes, Muhammad gathered an army of 10,000 Muslim converts and marched on the city of Mecca. The attack went largely uncontested and Muhammad took over the city with little bloodshed. Most Meccans converted to Islam. Muhammad declared an amnesty for past offenses, except for ten men and women who had mocked and made fun of him in songs and verses. Some of these people were later pardoned. Muhammad destroyed the pagan idols in the Kaaba and then sent his followers out to destroy all of the remaining pagan temples in Eastern Arabia.

Following the conquest of Mecca, Muhammad was alarmed by a military threat from the confederate tribes of Hawazin, who were raising an army twice the size of Muhammad's. The Banu Hawazin were old enemies of the Meccans. They were joined by the Banu Thaqif, who adopted an anti-Meccan policy due to the decline of the prestige of Meccans. Muhammad defeated the Hawazin and Thaqif tribes in the Battle of Hunayn.

At the end of the 10th year after the migration to Medina, Muhammad performed his first truly Islamic pilgrimage, thereby teaching his followers the rules governing the various ceremonies of the annual Great Pilgrimage. In 632, a few months after returning to Medina from the Farewell Pilgrimage, Muhammad fell ill and died. By the time Muhammad died, most of the Arabian Peninsula had converted to Islam, and he had united Arabia into a single Muslim religious polity.

Attributions

CC licensed content, Specific attribution

- Middle Eastern Empires. **Provided by**: Wikibooks. **Located at**: http://en.wikibooks.org/wiki/World_History/Middle_Eastern_Empires. **License**: *CC BY-SA: Attribution-ShareAlike*
- Muhammad. **Provided by**: Wikipedia. **Located at**: http://en.wikipedia.org/wiki/Muhammad. **License**: *CC BY-SA: Attribution-ShareAlike*
- Quraysh tribe. **Provided by**: Wikipedia. **Located at**: http://en.wikipedia.org/wiki/Quraysh_tribe. **License**: *CC BY-SA: Attribution-ShareAlike*
- Mohammed kaaba 1315. **Provided by**: Wikimedia. **Located at**: http://en.wikipedia.org/wiki/File:Mohammed_kaaba_1315.jpg. **License**: *Public Domain: No Known Copyright*
- Middle Eastern Empires. **Provided by**: Wikibooks. **Located at**: http://en.wikibooks.org/wiki/World_History/Middle_Eastern_Empires. **License**: *CC BY-SA: Attribution-ShareAlike*
- Quran. **Provided by**: Wikipedia. **Located at**: http://en.wikipedia.org/wiki/Quran. **License**: *CC BY-SA: Attribution-ShareAlike*
- Muhammad. **Provided by**: Wikipedia. **Located at**: http://en.wikipedia.org/wiki/Muhammad. **License**: *CC BY-SA: Attribution-ShareAlike*
- Abu Bakr. **Provided by**: Wikipedia. **Located at**: http://en.wikipedia.org/wiki/Abu_Bakr. **License**: *CC BY-SA: Attribution-ShareAlike*
- Mohammed kaaba 1315. **Provided by**: Wikimedia. **Located at**: http://en.wikipedia.org/wiki/File:Mohammed_kaaba_1315.jpg. **License**: *Public Domain: No Known Copyright*

- Cave Hira. **Provided by**: Wikimedia. **Located at**: http://en.wikipedia.org/wiki/File:Cave_Hira.jpg. **License**: *Public Domain: No Known Copyright*
- Qu'ran. **Provided by**: Wikipedia. **Located at**: http://en.wikipedia.org/wiki/Quran%23mediaviewer/File:Quran2.png. **License**: *CC BY-SA: Attribution-ShareAlike*
- Mohammed receiving revelation from the angel Gabriel. **Provided by**: Wikimedia. **Located at**: http://en.wikipedia.org/wiki/File:Mohammed_receiving_revelation_from_the_angel_Gabriel.jpg. **License**: *Public Domain: No Known Copyright*
- Middle Eastern Empires. **Provided by**: Wikibooks. **Located at**: http://en.wikibooks.org/wiki/World_History/Middle_Eastern_Empires. **License**: *CC BY-SA: Attribution-ShareAlike*
- Medina. **Provided by**: Wikipedia. **Located at**: http://en.wikipedia.org/wiki/Medina. **License**: *CC BY-SA: Attribution-ShareAlike*
- Mecca. **Provided by**: Wikipedia. **Located at**: http://en.wikipedia.org/wiki/Mecca. **License**: *CC BY-SA: Attribution-ShareAlike*
- Hijra (islam). **Provided by**: Wikipedia. **Located at**: http://en.wikipedia.org/wiki/Hijra_(Islam). **License**: *CC BY-SA: Attribution-ShareAlike*
- Muhammad. **Provided by**: Wikipedia. **Located at**: http://en.wikipedia.org/wiki/Muhammad. **License**: *CC BY-SA: Attribution-ShareAlike*
- Mohammed kaaba 1315. **Provided by**: Wikimedia. **Located at**: http://en.wikipedia.org/wiki/File:Mohammed_kaaba_1315.jpg. **License**: *Public Domain: No Known Copyright*
- Cave Hira. **Provided by**: Wikimedia. **Located at**: http://en.wikipedia.org/wiki/File:Cave_Hira.jpg. **License**: *Public Domain: No Known Copyright*
- Qu'ran. **Provided by**: Wikipedia. **Located at**: http://en.wikipedia.org/wiki/Quran%23mediaviewer/File:Quran2.png. **License**: *CC BY-SA: Attribution-ShareAlike*
- Mohammed receiving revelation from the angel Gabriel. **Provided by**: Wikimedia. **Located at**: http://en.wikipedia.org/wiki/File:Mohammed_receiving_revelation_from_the_angel_Gabriel.jpg. **License**: *Public Domain: No Known Copyright*
- Surat An-Najm. **Provided by**: Wikipedia. **Located at**: http://en.wikipedia.org/wiki/File:Surat_An-Najm.jpg. **License**: *CC BY-SA: Attribution-ShareAlike*
- Hejira. **Provided by**: wikipedia. **Located at**: http://upload.wikimedia.org/wikipedia/commons/thumb/6/64/Hejaz622.jpg/316px-Hejaz622.jpg. **License**: *CC BY-SA: Attribution-ShareAlike*
- Masjid al-Qiblatayn. **Provided by**: Wikipedia. **Located at**: https://en.wikipedia.org/wiki/Masjid_al-Qiblatayn. **License**: *CC BY-SA: Attribution-ShareAlike*
- Constitution of Medina. **Provided by**: Wikipedia. **Located at**: http://en.wikipedia.org/wiki/Constitution_of_medina. **License**: *CC BY-SA: Attribution-ShareAlike*
- Ummah. **Provided by**: Wikipedia. **Located at**: http://en.wikipedia.org/wiki/Ummah. **License**: *CC BY-SA: Attribution-ShareAlike*
- Battle of Uhud. **Provided by**: Wikipedia. **Located at**: http://en.wikipedia.org/wiki/Battle_of_Uhud. **License**: *CC BY-SA: Attribution-ShareAlike*
- Battle of Badr. **Provided by**: Wikipedia. **Located at**: http://en.wikipedia.org/wiki/Battle_of_badr. **License**: *CC BY-SA: Attribution-ShareAlike*
- Conquest of Mecca. **Provided by**: Wikipedia. **Located at**: http://en.wikipedia.org/wiki/Conquest_of_Mecca. **License**: *CC BY-SA: Attribution-ShareAlike*
- Farewell Pilgrimage. **Provided by**: Wikipedia. **Located at**: http://en.wikipedia.org/wiki/Farewell_Pilgrimage. **License**: *CC BY-SA: Attribution-ShareAlike*
- Middle Eastern Empires. **Provided by**: Wikibooks. **Located at**: http://en.wikibooks.org/wiki/World_History/Middle_Eastern_Empires. **License**: *CC BY-SA: Attribution-ShareAlike*
- Muhammad. **Provided by**: Wikipedia. **Located at**: http://en.wikipedia.org/wiki/Muhammad. **License**: *CC BY-SA: Attribution-ShareAlike*
- Hadith. **Provided by**: Wikipedia. **Located at**: http://en.wikipedia.org/wiki/Hadith. **License**: *CC BY-SA: Attribution-ShareAlike*
- Sharia. **Provided by**: Wikipedia. **Located at**: http://en.wikipedia.org/wiki/Sharia. **License**: *CC BY-SA: Attribution-ShareAlike*
- Sunnah. **Provided by**: Wikipedia. **Located at**: http://en.wikipedia.org/wiki/Sunnah. **License**: *CC BY-SA: Attribution-ShareAlike*
- Hijab. **Provided by**: Wikipedia. **Located at**: http://en.wikipedia.org/wiki/Hijab. **License**: *CC BY-SA: Attribution-ShareAlike*
- Mohammed kaaba 1315. **Provided by**: Wikimedia. **Located at**: http://en.wikipedia.org/wiki/File:Mohammed_kaaba_1315.jpg. **License**: *Public Domain: No Known Copyright*
- Cave Hira. **Provided by**: Wikimedia. **Located at**: http://en.wikipedia.org/wiki/File:Cave_Hira.jpg. **License**: *Public Domain: No Known Copyright*

- Qu'ran. **Provided by**: Wikipedia. **Located at**: http://en.wikipedia.org/wiki/Quran%23mediaviewer/File:Quran2.png. **License**: *CC BY-SA: Attribution-ShareAlike*
- Mohammed receiving revelation from the angel Gabriel. **Provided by**: Wikimedia. **Located at**: http://en.wikipedia.org/wiki/File:Mohammed_receiving_revelation_from_the_angel_Gabriel.jpg. **License**: *Public Domain: No Known Copyright*
- Surat An-Najm. **Provided by**: Wikipedia. **Located at**: http://en.wikipedia.org/wiki/File:Surat_An-Najm.jpg. **License**: *CC BY-SA: Attribution-ShareAlike*
- Hejira. **Provided by**: wikipedia. **Located at**: http://upload.wikimedia.org/wikipedia/commons/thumb/6/64/Hejaz622.jpg/316px-Hejaz622.jpg. **License**: *CC BY-SA: Attribution-ShareAlike*
- Masjid al-Qiblatain. **Provided by**: Wikimedia. **Located at**: http://en.wikipedia.org/wiki/File:Masjid_al-Qiblatain.jpg. **License**: *CC BY-SA: Attribution-ShareAlike*

The Umayyad and Abbasid Empires

Muhammad's Successors

After Muhammad's death in 632 CE, there were conflicts among his followers as to who would become his successor, which created a split in Islam between the Sunni and Shi'a sects.

Learning Objectives

Assess the Caliphates' rise to power

Key Takeaways

Key Points

- After Muhammad 's death in 632 CE, his friend Abu Bakr was named caliph and ruler of the Islamic community, or Ummah.
- Sunni Muslims believe that Abu Bakr was the proper successor, while Shi'a Muslims believe that Ali should have succeed Muhammad as caliph.
- After Muhammad's death and the rebellion of several tribes, Abu Bakr initiated several military campaigns to bring Arabia under Islam and into the caliphate.
- The Rashidun Caliphate (632–661) was led by Abu Bakr, then by Umar ibn Khattab as the second caliph, Uthman Ibn Affan as the third caliph, and Ali as the fourth caliph.
- Muslim armies conquered most of Arabia by 633, followed by north Africa, Mesopotamia, and Persia, significantly shaping the history of the world through the spread of Islam.

> *Key Terms*
>
> - **Sunni**: The branch of Islam that believes that a caliph should be elected by Muslims or their representatives and that Abu Bakr was the first caliph.
> - **Ummah**: An Arabic word meaning "nation" or "community;" usually refers to the collective community of Islamic peoples.
> - **Shi'a**: The minority Islamic branch that believes Muhammad appointed his cousin Ali as his successor and that the caliph should be decided based on this family lineage.
> - **caliph**: The head of state in a caliphate, and the title for the ruler of the Islamic Ummah; a successor of Muhammad.

Succession after Muhammad's Death

Muhammad united the tribes of Arabia into a single Arab Muslim religious polity in the last years of his life. He established a new unified Arabian Peninsula, which led to the Rashidun and Umayyad Caliphates and the rapid expansion of Muslim power over the next century.

With Muhammad's death in 632 CE, disagreement broke out among his followers over deciding his successor. Muhammad's prominent companion Umar ibn al-Khattab nominated Abu Bakr, Muhammad's friend and collaborator. With additional support, Abu Bakr was confirmed as the first caliph (religious successor to Muhammad) that same year. This choice was disputed by some of Muhammad's companions, who held that Ali ibn Abi Talib, his cousin and son-in-law, had been designated the successor by Muhammad at Ghadir Khumm. Ali was Muhammad's first cousin and closest living male relative, as well as his son-in-law, having married Muhammad's daughter Fatimah. Ali would eventually become the fourth Sunni caliph. These disagreements over Muhammad's true successor led to a major split in Islam between what became the Sunni and Shi'a denominations, a division that still holds to this day.

Sunni Muslims believe and confirm that Abu Bakr was chosen by the community and that this was the proper procedure. Sunnis further argue that a caliph should ideally be chosen by election or community consensus. Shi'a Muslims believe that just as God alone appoints a prophet, only God has the prerogative to appoint the successor to his prophet. They believe God chose Ali to be Muhammad's successor and the first caliph of Islam.

Rise of the Caliphates

After Muhammad's death, many Arabian tribes rejected Islam or withheld the alms tax established by Muhammad. Many tribes claimed that they had submitted to Muhammad and that with Muhammad's death, their allegiance had ended. Caliph Abu Bakr insisted that they had not just submitted to a leader, but joined the Islamic community of Ummah.

To retain the cohesion of the Islamic state, Abu Bakr divided his Muslim army to force the Arabian tribes into submission. After a series of successful campaigns, Abu Bakr's general Khalid ibn Walid defeated a competing prophet and the Arabian peninsula was united under the caliphate in Medina. Once the rebellions had been quelled, Abu Bakr began a war of conquest. In just a few short decades, his campaigns led to one of the largest empires in history. Muslim armies conquered most of Arabia by 633, followed by north Africa, Mesopotamia, and Persia, significantly shaping the history of the world through the spread of Islam.

Rashidun Caliphate (632–661)

Abu Bakr nominated Umar as his successor on his deathbed. Umar ibn Khattab, the second caliph, was killed by a Persian named Piruz Nahavandi. Umar's successor, Uthman Ibn Affan, was elected by a council of electors (Majlis). Uthman was killed by members of a disaffected group. Ali then took control, but was not universally accepted as caliph by the governors of Egypt, and later by some of his own guard. He faced two major rebellions and was assassinated by Abdl-alRahman, a Kharijite. Ali's tumultuous rule lasted only five years. This period is known as the Fitna, or the first Islamic civil war.

The followers of Ali later became the Shi'a minority sect of Islam, which rejects the legitimacy of the first three caliphs. The followers of all four Rashidun caliphs (Abu Bakr, Umar, Uthman, and Ali) became the majority Sunni sect. Under the Rashidun, each region (Sultanate) of the caliphate had its own governor (Sultan). Muawiyah, a relative of Uthman and governor (Wali) of Syria, became one of Ali's challengers, and after Ali's assassination managed to overcome the other claimants to the caliphate. Muawiyah transformed the caliphate into a hereditary office, thus founding the Umayyad dynasty. In areas that were previously under Sassanid Persian or Byzantine rule, the caliphs lowered taxes, provided greater local autonomy (to their delegated governors), granted greater religious freedom for Jews and some indigenous Christians, and brought peace to peoples demoralized and disaffected by the casualties and heavy taxation that resulted from the decades of Byzantine-Persian warfare.

Expansion Under the Umayyad Caliphates

The Umayyad Caliphate, the second of the four major Arab caliphates established after the death of Muhammad, expanded the territory of the Islamic state to one of the largest empires in history.

Learning Objectives

Describe the advancements made under the Umayyad Caliphate

Key Takeaways

Key Points

- The Umayyad Caliphate, which emerged after the Rashidun Caliphate collapsed, was characterized by hereditary elections and territory expansion.
- The Umayyad Caliphate became one of the largest unitary states in history and one of the few states to ever extend direct rule over three continents.

- When the Abbasid dynasty revolted against the Umayyads and killed many of their ruling family members, a few Umayyads escaped to the Iberian peninsula and founded the Cordoba Caliphate, characterized by peaceful diplomacy, religious tolerance, and cultural flourishing.

Key Terms

- **Al-Andalus**: Also known as Muslim Spain or Islamic Iberia, a medieval Muslim territory and cultural domain occupying at its peak most of modern-day Spain and Portugal.
- **Dome of the Rock**: A shrine located on the Temple Mount in the Old City of Jerusalem.
- **Umayyad Caliphate**: The second of the four major Arab caliphates established after the death of Muhammad.

Umayyad Caliphate (661–750)

The Umayyad Caliphate was the second of the four major Arab caliphates established after the death of Muhammad. This caliphate was centered on the Umayyad dynasty, hailing from Mecca. The Umayyad family had first come to power under the third caliph, Uthman ibn Affan (r. 644–656), but the Umayyad regime was founded by Muawiya ibn Abi Sufyan, long-time governor of Syria, after the end of the First Muslim Civil War in 661 CE. Syria remained the Umayyads' main power base thereafter, and Damascus was their capital.

Under the Umayyads, the caliphate territory grew rapidly. The Islamic Caliphate became one of the largest unitary states in history, and one of the few states to ever extend direct rule over three continents (Africa, Europe, and Asia). The Umayyads incorporated the Caucasus, Transoxiana, Sindh, the Maghreb, and the Iberian Peninsula (Al-Andalus) into the Muslim world. At its greatest extent, the Umayyad Caliphate covered 5.79 million square miles and included 62 million people (29% of the world's population), making it the fifth largest empire in history in both area and proportion of the world's population. Although the Umayyad Caliphate did not rule all of the Sahara, nomadic Berber tribes paid homage to the caliph. However, although these vast areas may have recognized the supremacy of the caliph, de facto power was in the hands of local sultans and emirs.

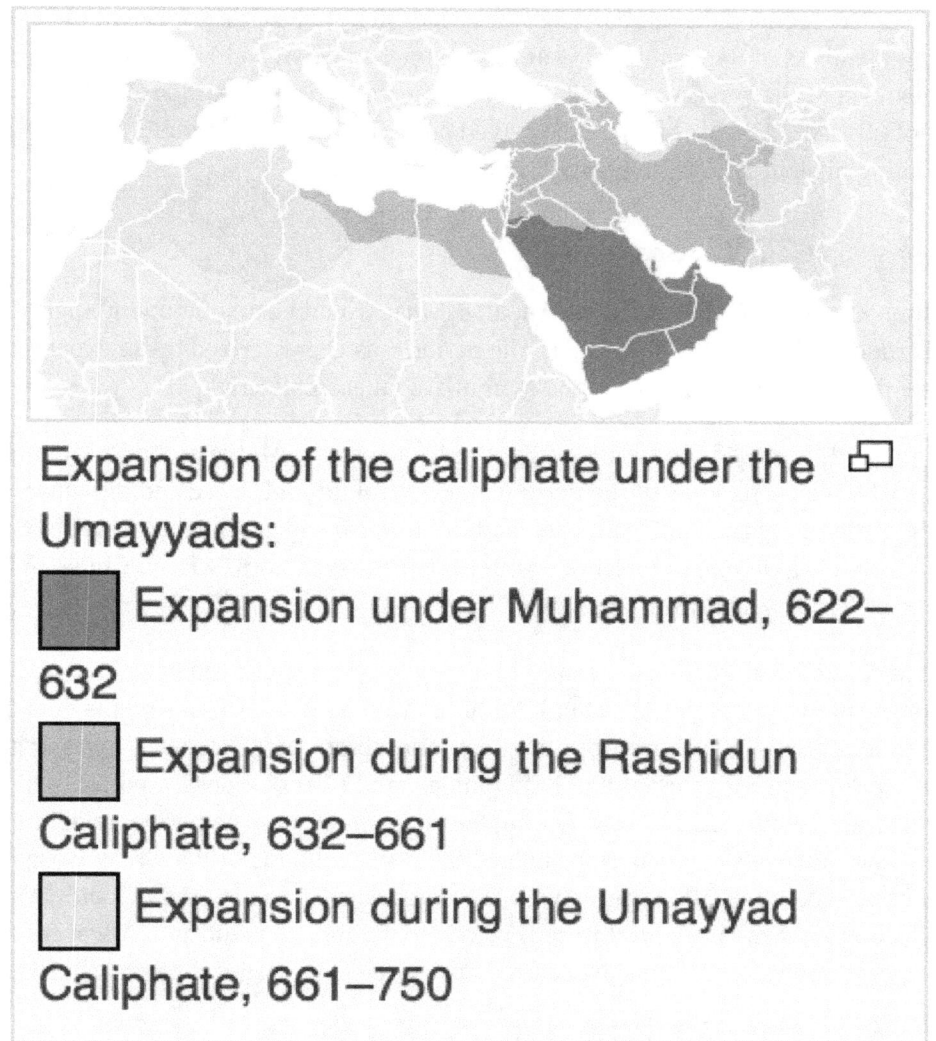

Expansion of the caliphate: *This map shows the extension of Islamic rule under Muhammad, the Rashidun Caliphate, and the Umayyad Caliphate*

The Umayyad dynasty was not universally supported within the Muslim community for a variety of reasons, including their hereditary election and suggestions of impious behavior. Some Muslims felt that only members of Muhammad's Banu Hashim clan or those of his own lineage, such as the descendants of Ali, should rule. Some Muslims thought that Umayyad taxation and administrative practices were unjust. While the non-Muslim population had autonomy, their judicial matters were dealt with in accordance with their own laws and by their own religious heads or their appointees. Non-Muslims paid a poll tax for policing to the central state. Muhammad had stated explicitly during his lifetime that each religious minority should be allowed to practice its own religion and govern itself, and the policy had on the whole continued.

There were numerous rebellions against the Umayyads, as well as splits within the Umayyad ranks, which notably included the rivalry between Yaman and Qays. Allegedly, The Sunnis killed Ali's son Hussein and his family at the Battle of Karbala in 680, solidifying the Shi'a-Sunni split. Eventually, supporters of the Banu Hashim and the supporters of the lineage of Ali united to bring down the Umayyads in 750. However, the Shi'at 'Alī, "the Party of Ali," were again disappointed when the Abbasid dynasty took power, as the Abbasids were descended from Muhammad's uncle `Abbas ibn `Abd al-Muttalib, and not from Ali.

The Abbasid victors desecrated the tombs of the Umayyads in Syria, sparing only that of Umar II, and most of the remaining members of the Umayyad family were tracked down and killed. When Abbasids declared amnesty for members of the Umayyad family, eighty gathered to receive pardons, and all were massacred. One grandson of Hisham, Abd al-Rahman I, survived and established a kingdom in Al-Andalus (Moorish Iberia), proclaiming his family to be the Umayyad Caliphate revived.

Umayyad Dynasty in Cordoba, Spain

The revival of the Umayyad Caliphate in Al-Andalus (what would become modern Spain) was called the Caliphate of Córdoba, which lasted until 1031. The period was characterized by an expansion of trade and culture, and saw the construction of masterpieces of al-Andalus architecture.

The caliphate enjoyed increased prosperity during the 10th century. Abd-ar-Rahman III united al-Andalus and brought the Christian kingdoms of the north under control through force and diplomacy. Abd-ar-Rahman stopped the Fatimid advance into caliphate land in Morocco and al-Andalus. This period of prosperity was marked by increasing diplomatic relations with Berber tribes in north Africa, Christian kings from the north, and France, Germany, and Constantinople.

Córdoba was the cultural and intellectual center of al-Andalus. Mosques, such as the Great Mosque, were the focus of many caliphs' attention. The caliph's palace, Medina Azahara, was on the outskirts of the city, and had many rooms filled with riches from the East. The library of Al-Ḥakam II was one of the largest libraries in the world, housing at least 400,000 volumes, and Córdoba possessed translations of ancient Greek texts into Arabic, Latin and Hebrew. During the Umayyad Caliphate period, relations between Jews and Arabs were cordial; Jewish stonemasons helped build the columns of the Great Mosque. Al-Andalus was subject to eastern cultural influences as well. The musician Ziryab is credited with bringing hair and clothing styles, toothpaste, and deodorant from Baghdad to the Iberian peninsula. Advances in science, history, geography, philosophy, and language occurred during the Umayyad Caliphate as well.

Mosque: Interior of the Mezquita (Mosque), one of the finest examples of Umayyad architecture in Spain.

Legacy of the Umayyad Caliphate

The Umayyad caliphate was marked both by territorial expansion and by the administrative and cultural problems that such expansion created. Despite some notable exceptions, the Umayyads tended to favor the rights of the old Arab families, and in particular their own, over those of newly converted Muslims (mawali). Therefore, they held to a less universalist conception of Islam than did many of their rivals.

During the period of the Umayyads, Arabic became the administrative language, in which state documents and currency were issued. Mass conversions brought a large influx of Muslims to the caliphate. The Umayyads also constructed famous buildings such as the Dome of the Rock at Jerusalem and the Umayyad Mosque at Damascus.

According to one common view, the Umayyads transformed the caliphate from a religious institution (during the Rashidun) to a dynastic one. However, the Umayyad caliphs do seem to have understood themselves as the representatives of God on Earth.

The Umayyads have met with a largely negative reception from later Islamic historians, who have accused them of promoting a kingship (*mulk*, a term with connotations of tyranny) instead of a true caliphate (*khilafa*). In this respect it is notable that the Umayyad caliphs referred to themselves not as *khalifat rasul Allah* ("successor of the messenger of God," the title preferred by the tradition), but rather as *khalifat Allah* ("deputy of God").

Many Muslims criticized the Umayyads for having too many non-Muslim, former Roman administrators in their government. St. John of Damascus was also a high administrator in the Umayyad administration. As the Muslims took over cities, they left the people's political representatives and the Roman tax collectors and administrators. The people's political representatives calculated and negotiated taxes. The central government and the local governments got paid respectively for the services they provided. Many Christian cities used some of the taxes to maintain their churches and run their own organizations. Later, the Umayyads were criticized by some Muslims for not reducing the taxes of the people who converted to Islam.

Spread of Islam

In the years following the Prophet Muhammad's death, the expansion of Islam was carried out by his successor caliphates, who increased the territory of the Islamic state and sought converts from both polytheistic and monotheistic religions.

Learning Objectives

Discuss the spread of Islam and identify how the caliphs maintained authority over conquered territories.

Key Takeaways

Key Points

- The expansion of the Arab Empire in the years following the Prophet Muhammad 's death led to the creation of caliphates, who occupied a vast geographical area and sought converts to Islamic faith.
- The people of the Islamic world created numerous sophisticated centers of culture and science with far-reaching mercantile networks, travelers, scientists, hunters, mathematicians, doctors, and philosophers.
- Historians distinguish between two separate strands of converts of the time. One is animists and polytheists of tribal societies of the Arabian Peninsula and the Fertile crescent; the other is the monotheistic populations of the Middle Eastern agrarian and urbanized societies.
- The Arab conquerors generally respected the traditional middle-Eastern pattern of religious pluralism with regard to the conquered populations, respecting the practice of other faiths in Arab territory, although widespread conversions to Islam came about as a result of the breakdown of historically religiously organized societies.

Key Terms

- **Zoroastrianism**: an ancient Iranian religion and religious philosophy that arose in the eastern ancient Persian Empire, when the religious philosopher Zoroaster simplified the pantheon of early Iranian gods into two opposing forces.
- **Imam**: An Islamic leadership position, most commonly in the context of a worship leader of a mosque and Sunni Muslim community.

Overview

The expansion of the Arab Empire in the years following the Prophet Muhammad's death led to the creation of caliphates occupying a vast geographical area. Conversion to Islam was boosted by missionary activities, particularly those of Imams, who easily intermingled with local populace to propagate religious teachings. These early caliphates, coupled with Muslim economics and trading and the later expansion of the Ottoman Empire, resulted in Islam's spread outwards from Mecca towards both the Atlantic and Pacific oceans and the creation of the Muslim world. Trading played an important role in the spread of Islam in several parts of the world, notably southeast Asia.

Muslim dynasties were soon established and subsequent empires such as those of the Abbasids, Fatimids, Almoravids, Seljukids, and Ajurans, Adal and Warsangali in Somalia, Mughals in India, Safavids in Persia, and Ottomans in Anatolia were among the largest and most powerful in the world. The people of the Islamic world created numerous sophisticated centers of culture and science with far-reaching mercantile networks, travelers, scientists, hunters, mathematicians, doctors, and philosophers, all contributing to the Golden Age of Islam. Islamic expansion in South and East Asia fostered cosmopolitan and eclectic Muslim cultures in the Indian subcontinent, Malaysia, Indonesia, and China.

Within the first century of the establishment of Islam upon the Arabian Peninsula and the subsequent rapid expansion of the Arab Empire during the Muslim conquests, one of the most significant empires in world history was formed. For the subjects of this new empire, formerly subjects of the greatly reduced Byzantine and obliterated Sassanid empires, not much changed in practice. The objective of the conquests was of a practical nature more than anything else, as fertile land and water were scarce in the Arabian Peninsula. A real Islamization therefore only came about in the subsequent centuries.

Conversions to Islam

Historians distinguish between two separate strands of converts of the time. One is animists and polytheists of tribal societies of the Arabian Peninsula and the Fertile crescent; the other is the monotheistic populations of the Middle Eastern agrarian and urbanized societies.

For the polytheistic and pagan societies, apart from the religious and spiritual reasons each individual may have had, conversion to Islam "represented the response of a tribal, pastoral population to the need for a larger framework for political and economic integration, a more stable state, and a more imaginative and encompassing moral vision to cope with the problems of a tumultuous society." In contrast, for sedentary and often already monotheistic societies, "Islam was substituted for a Byzantine or Sassanian political identity and for a Christian, Jewish or Zoroastrian religious affiliation." Initially, conversion was neither required nor necessarily wished for: "[The Arab conquerors] did not require the conversion as much as the subordination of non-Muslim peoples. At the outset, they were hostile to conversions because new Muslims diluted the economic and status advantages of the Arabs."

Only in subsequent centuries, with the development of the religious doctrine of Islam and with that the understanding of the Muslim Ummah, did mass conversion take place. The new understanding by the religious and political leadership led in many cases to a weakening or breakdown of the social and religious structures of parallel religious communities such as Christians and Jews. With the weakening of many churches, for example, and with the favoring of Islam and the migration of substantial Muslim Turkish populations into the areas of Anatolia and the Balkans, the "social and cultural relevance of Islam" were enhanced and a large number of peoples were converted.

During the Abbasid Caliphate, expansion ceased and the central disciplines of Islamic philosophy, theology, law, and mysticism became more widespread, and the gradual conversions of the populations within the empire occurred. Significant conversions also occurred beyond the extents of the empire, such as that of the Turkic tribes in Central Asia and peoples living in regions south of the Sahara in Africa through contact with Muslim traders active in the area and Sufi orders. In Africa it spread along three routes—across the Sahara via trading towns such as Timbuktu, up the Nile Valley through the Sudan up to Uganda, and across the Red Sea and down East Africa through settlements such as Mombasa and Zanzibar. These initial conversions were of a flexible nature.

The Arab-Muslim conquests followed a general pattern of nomadic conquests of settled regions, whereby conquering peoples became the new military elite and reached a compromise with the old elites by allowing them to retain local political, religious, and financial authority. Peasants, workers, and merchants paid taxes, while members of the old and new elites collected them.

The Great Mosque of Kairouan: *The Great Mosque of Kairouan, founded in 670 CE by the Arab general and conqueror Uqba Ibn Nafi, is the oldest mosque in western Islamic lands and represents an architectural symbol of the spread of Islam in North Africa, situated in Kairouan, Tunisia.*

Policy Toward Non-Muslims

The Arab conquerors did not repeat the mistake made by the Byzantine and Sasanian empires, who had tried and failed to impose an official religion on subject populations, which had caused resentments that made the Muslim conquests more acceptable to them. Instead, the rulers of the new empire generally respected the traditional middle-Eastern pattern of religious pluralism, which was not one of equality but rather of dominance by one group over the others. After the end of military operations, which involved the sacking of some monasteries and confiscation of Zoroastrian fire temples in Syria and Iraq, the early caliphate was characterized by religious tolerance, and people of all ethnicities and religions blended in public life. Before Muslims were ready to build mosques in Syria, they accepted Christian churches as holy places and shared them with local Christians. In Iraq and Egypt, Muslim authorities cooperated with Christian religious leaders. Numerous churches were repaired and new ones built during the Umayyad era.

Some non-Muslim populations did experience persecution, however. After the Muslim conquest of Persia, Zoroastrians were given dhimmi (non-Muslim) status and subjected to persecutions; discrimination and harassment began in the form of sparse violence. Zoroastrians were made to pay an extra tax called Jizya; if they failed, they were killed, enslaved, or imprisoned. Those paying Jizya were subjected to insults and humiliation by the tax collectors. Zoroastrians who were captured as slaves in wars were given their freedom if they converted to Islam.

The Islamic Golden Age

Abbasid leadership cultivated intellectual, cultural, and scientific developments in the Islamic Golden Age.

Learning Objectives

Identify the causes of, and developments during, the Islamic Golden Age

Key Takeaways

Key Points

- The Islamic Golden Age started with the rise of Islam and establishment of the first Islamic state in 622.
- The introduction of paper in the 10th century enabled Islamic scholars to easily write manuscripts; Arab scholars also saved classic works of antiquity by translating them into various languages.
- The Arabs assimilated the scientific knowledge of the civilizations they had overrun, including the ancient Greek, Roman, Persian, Chinese, Indian, Egyptian, and Phoenician civilizations.
- Scientists advanced the fields of algebra, calculus, geometry, chemistry, biology, medicine, and astronomy.
- Many forms of art flourished during the Islamic Golden Age, including ceramics, metalwork, textiles, illuminated manuscripts, woodwork, and calligraphy.

Key Terms

- **calligraphy**: A visual art related to writing—the design and execution of lettering with a broad tip instrument or brush in one stroke.
- **arabesque**: A form of artistic decoration consisting of surface decorations based on rhythmic linear patterns of scrolling and interlacing foliage, tendrils, and other elements.
- **Averroës**: A medieval Andalusian polymath famous for his translations and commentaries of Aristotle.

Overview

The Islamic Golden Age refers to a period in the history of Islam, traditionally dated from the 8th century to the 13th century, during which much of the historically Islamic world was ruled by various caliphates and science, economic development, and cultural works flourished. This period is traditionally understood to have begun during the reign of the Abbasid caliph Harun al-Rashid (786–809) with the inauguration of the House of Wisdom in Baghdad, where scholars from various parts of the world with different cultural backgrounds were mandated to gather and translate all of the world's classical knowledge into the Arabic language.

The end of the age is variously given as 1258 with the Mongolian Sack of Baghdad, or 1492 with the completion of the Christian Reconquista of the Emirate of Granada in Al-Andalus, Iberian Peninsula. During the Golden Age, the major Islamic capital cities of Baghdad, Cairo, and Córdoba became the main intellectual centers for science, philosophy, medicine, and education. The government heavily patronized scholars, and the best scholars and notable translators, such as Hunayn ibn Ishaq, had salaries estimated to be the equivalent of those of professional athletes today.

The School of Nisibis and later the School of Edessa became centers of learning and transmission of classical wisdom. The House of Wisdom was a library, translation institute, and academy, and the Library of Alexandria and the Imperial Library of Constantinople housed new works of literature. Nestorian Christians played an important role in the formation of Arab culture, with the Jundishapur hospital and medical academy prominent in the late Sassanid, Umayyad, and early Abbasid periods. Notably, eight generations of the Nestorian Bukhtishu family served as private doctors to caliphs and sultans between the 8th and 11th centuries.

Literature and Philosophy

With the introduction of paper, information was democratized and it became possible to make a living from simply writing and selling books. The use of paper spread from China into Muslim regions in the 8th century, and then to Spain (and then the rest of Europe) in the 10th century. Paper was easier to manufacture than parchment and less likely to crack than papyrus, and could absorb ink, making it difficult to erase and ideal for keeping records. Islamic paper makers devised assembly-line methods of hand-copying manuscripts to turn out editions far larger than any available in Europe for centuries. The best known fiction from the Islamic world is *The Book of One Thousand and One Nights*, which took form in the 10th century and reached its final form by the 14th century, although the number and type of tales vary.

Painting of the Ali Baba story in The Book of One Thousand and One Nights by Maxfield Parrish: *The introduction of paper in the 10th century enabled Islamic scholars to easily write manuscripts, including The Book of One Thousand and One Nights. Arab scholars also saved classic works of antiquity by translating them into various languages.*

Christians (particularly Nestorian Christians) contributed to the Arab Islamic civilization during the Ummayad and the Abbasid periods by translating works of Greek philosophers to Syriac and then to Arabic. During the 4th through the 7th centuries, scholarly work in the Syriac and Greek languages was either newly initiated or carried on from the Hellenistic period. Many classic works of antiquity might have been lost if Arab scholars had not translated them into Arabic and Persian and later into Turkish, Hebrew, and Latin. Islamic scholars also absorbed ideas from China and India, and in turn Arabic philosophic literature contributed to the development of modern European philosophy.

Ibn Rushd

Ibn Rushd, also known by his Latinized name Averroës (April 14, 1126–December 10, 1198), was an Al-Andalus Muslim polymath, a master of Aristotelian philosophy, Islamic philosophy, Islamic theology, Maliki law and jurisprudence, logic, psychology, politics, Andalusian classical music theory, medicine, astronomy, geography, mathematics, physics, and celestial mechanics. Averroes was born in Córdoba, Al-Andalus, present-day Spain, and died in Marrakesh, present-day Morocco.

The 13th-century philosophical movement based on Averroes' work is called Averroism. Both Ibn Rushd and the scholar Ibn Sina played a major role in saving the works of Aristotle, whose ideas came to dominate the non-religious thought of the Christian and Muslim worlds. Ibn Rushd has been described as the "founding father of secular thought in Western Europe." He tried to reconcile Aristotle's system of thought with Islam. According to him, there is no conflict between religion and philosophy; rather they are different ways of reaching the same truth. He believed in the eternity of the universe. Ibn Ruhd also held that the soul is divided into two parts, one individual and one divine; while the individual soul is not eternal, all humans at the basic level share one and the same divine soul.

Science and Mathematics

The Arabs assimilated the scientific knowledge of the civilizations they had conquered, including the ancient Greek, Roman, Persian, Chinese, Indian, Egyptian, and Phoenician civilizations. Scientists recovered the Alexandrian mathematical, geometric, and astronomical knowledge, such as that of Euclid and Claudius Ptolemy.

Persian scientist Muhammad ibn Mūsā al-Khwārizmī significantly developed algebra in in his landmark text, *Kitab al-Jabr wa-l-Muqabala*, from which the term "algebra" is derived. The term "algorithm" is derived from the name of the scholar al-Khwarizmi, who was also responsible for introducing the Arabic numerals and Hindu-Arabic numeral system beyond the Indian subcontinent. In calculus, the scholar Alhazen discovered the sum formula for the fourth power, using a method readily generalizable to determine the sum for any integral power. He used this to find the volume of a paraboloid.

Medicine

Medicine was a central part of medieval Islamic culture. Responding to circumstances of time and place, Islamic physicians and scholars developed a large and complex medical literature exploring and synthesizing the theory and practice of medicine. Islamic medicine was built on tradition, chiefly the theoretical and practical knowledge developed in India, Greece, Persia, and Rome. Islamic scholars translated their writings from Syriac, Greek, and Sanskrit into Arabic and then produced new medical knowledge based on those texts. In order to make the Greek tradition more accessible, understandable, and teachable, Islamic scholars organized the Greco-Roman medical knowledge into encyclopedias.

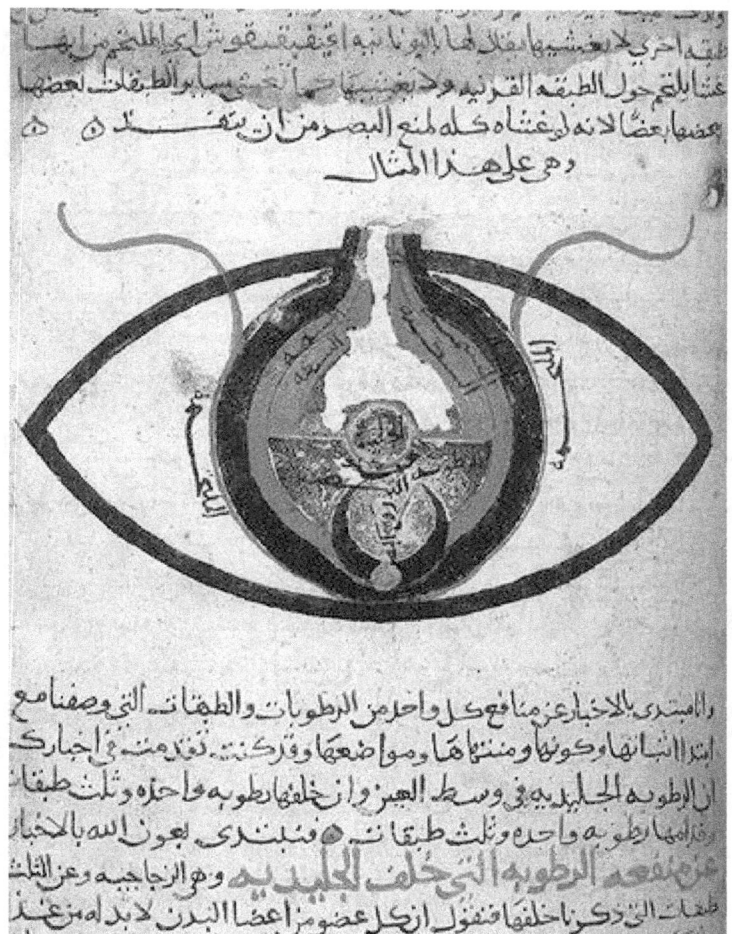

The eye, according to Hunain ibn Ishaq: *Scholars developed large encyclopedias of medical knowledge during the Islamic Golden Age, such as this one from a manuscript dated circa 1200.*

Art

Ceramics, glass, metalwork, textiles, illuminated manuscripts, and woodwork flourished during the Islamic Golden Age. Manuscript illumination became an important and greatly respected art, and portrait miniature painting flourished in Persia. Calligraphy, an essential aspect of written Arabic, developed in manuscripts and architectural decoration.

Arabesque

Typically, though not entirely, Islamic art depicts nature patterns and Arabic calligraphy, rather than figures, because many Muslims feared that the depiction of the human form is idolatry and thereby a sin against God, forbidden in the Quran. There are repeating elements in Islamic art, such as the use of geometrical floral or vegetal designs in a repetition known as the arabesque. The arabesque in Islamic art is often used to symbolize the transcendent, indivisible, and infinite nature of God. Mistakes in repetitions may be intentionally introduced as a show of humility by artists who believe only God can produce perfection, although this theory is disputed.

Detail of arabesque decoration at the Alhambra in Spain: Arabesque in Islamic art is often used to symbolize the transcendent, indivisible, and infinite nature of God.

Calligraphy

The traditional instrument of the Arabic calligrapher is the qalam, a pen made of dried reed or bamboo. Qalam ink is often in color, and chosen such that its intensity can vary greatly, so that the greater strokes of the compositions can be very dynamic in their effect. Islamic calligraphy is applied on a wide range of decorative mediums other than paper, such as tiles, vessels, carpets, and inscriptions. Before the advent of paper, papyrus and parchment were used for writing.

Coins were another support for calligraphy. Beginning in 692, the Islamic caliphate reformed the coinage of the Near East by replacing visual depiction with words. This was especially true for dinars, or gold coins of high value, which were inscribed with quotes from the Quran.

By the 10th century, the Persians, who had converted to Islam, began weaving inscriptions on elaborately patterned silks. These calligraphic-inscribed textiles were so precious that Crusaders brought them to Europe as prized possessions. A notable example is the Suaire de Saint-Josse, used to wrap the bones of St. Josse in the abbey of St. Josse-sur-Mer near Caen in northwestern France.

Architecture and Tilework

There were many advances in architectural construction, and mosques, tombs, palaces, and forts were inspired by Persian and Byzantine architecture. Islamic mosaic art anticipated principles of quasicrystalline geometry, which would not be discovered for 500 more years. This art used symmetric polygonal shapes to create patterns that can continue indefinitely without repeating. These patterns have even helped modern scientists understand quasicrystals at the atomic levels.

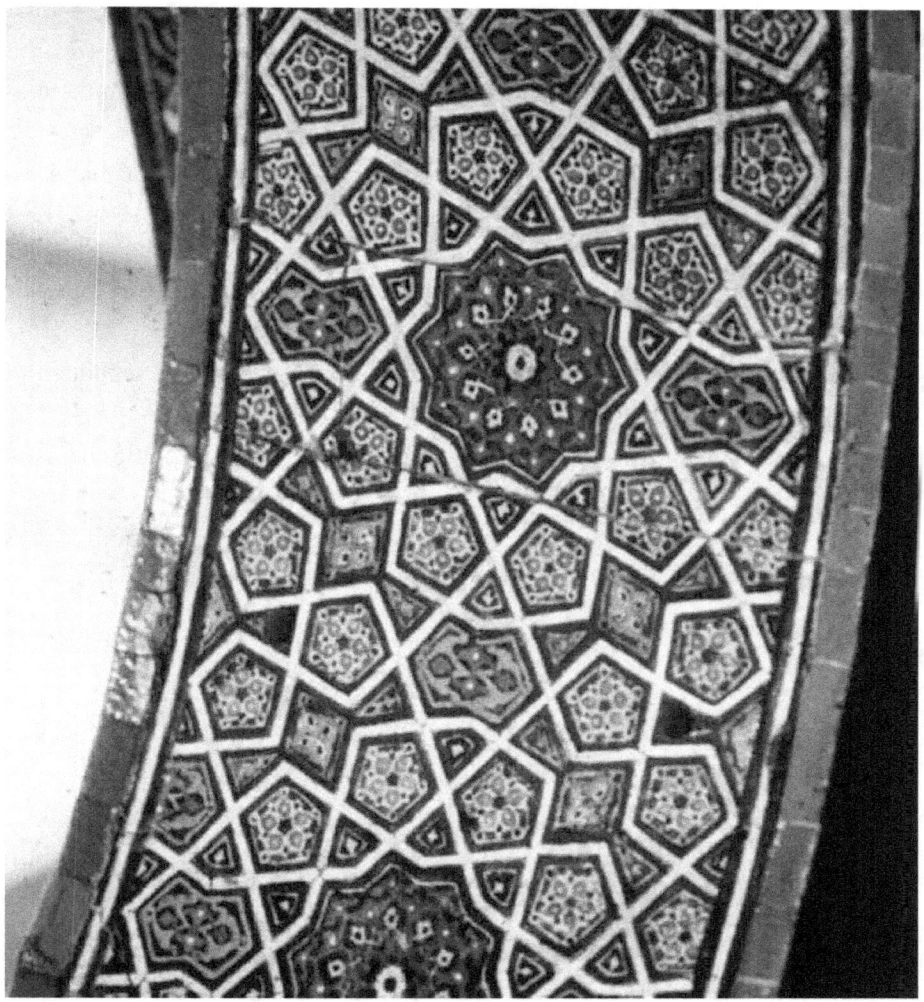

Mosque Archway: Geometric patterns: an archway in the Sultan's lodge in the Ottoman Green Mosque in Bursa, Turkey (1424), its girih strapwork forming 10-point stars and pentagons.

The Abbasid Empire

The Abbasid Caliphate was the third of the Islamic caliphates to succeed the Islamic prophet Muhammad in 750 CE, and ruled over a large, flourishing empire for three centuries.

Learning Objectives

Discuss the political stability during the Abbasid Era and the Abbasids' rise to power

Key Takeaways

Key Points

- The Abbasids overthrew the Umayyad dynasty in 750 CE, supporting the mawali, or non-Arab Muslims, by moving the capital to Baghdad in 762 CE.
- The Persian bureaucracy slowly replaced the old Arab aristocracy as the Abbasids established the new positions of vizier and emir to delegate their central authority.
- The Abbasids maintained an unbroken line of caliphs for over three centuries, consolidating Islamic rule and cultivating great intellectual and cultural developments in the Middle East in the Golden Age of Islam.
- The Fatimid dynasty broke from the Abbasids in 909 and created separate line of caliphs in Morocco, Algeria, Tunisia, Libya, Egypt, and Palestine until 1171 CE.
- Abbasid control eventually disintegrated, and the edges of the empire declared local autonomy.
- Though lacking in political power, the dynasty continued to claim authority in religious matters until after the Ottoman conquest of Egypt in 1517.

Key Terms

- **mawali**: Non-Arab Muslims.
- **vizier**: A high-ranking political advisor or minister in the Muslim world.
- **emir**: A title of high office used in a variety of places in the Muslim world.
- **Fatimid dynasty**: A Shi'a Islamic caliphate that spanned a large area of North Africa, from the Red Sea in the east to the Atlantic Ocean in the west; they claimed lineage from Muhammad's daughter.

Rise of the Abbasid Empire (c. 750 CE)

The Umayyad dynasty was overthrown by another family of Meccan origin, the Abbasids, in 750 CE. The Abbasids distinguished themselves from the Umayyads by attacking their moral character and administration. In particular, they appealed to non-Arab Muslims, known as mawali, who remained outside the kinship-based society of the Arabs and were perceived as a lower class within the Umayyad empire. The Abbasid dynasty descended from Muhammad 's youngest uncle, Abbas ibn Abd al-Muttalib (566–653 CE), from whom the dynasty takes its name. Muhammad ibn 'Ali, a great-grandson of Abbas, began to campaign for the return of power to the family of Muhammad, the Hashimites, in Persia during the reign of Umar II, an Umayyad caliph who ruled from 717–720 CE.

Coin of the Abbasids, Baghdad, Iraq, 765 CE

Power in Baghdad

The Abbasids moved the empire's capital from Damascus, in modern-day Syria, to Baghdad, in modern-day Iraq, in 762 CE. The Abbasids had depended heavily on the support of Persians in their overthrow of the Umayyads, and the geographic power shift appeased the Persian mawali support base. Abu al-'Abbas's successor, Al-Mansur, welcomed non-Arab Muslims to his court. While this helped integrate Arab and Persian cultures, it alienated the Arabs who had supported the Abbasids in their battles against the Umayyads. The Abbasids established the new position of vizier to delegate central authority, and delegated even greater authority to local emirs. As the viziers exerted greater influence, many Abbasid caliphs were relegated to a more ceremonial role as Persian bureaucracy slowly replaced the old Arab aristocracy.

The Abbasids, who ruled from Baghdad, had an unbroken line of caliphs for over three centuries, consolidating Islamic rule and cultivating great intellectual and cultural developments in the Middle East in the Golden Age of Islam. By 940 CE, however, the power of the caliphate under the Abbasids began waning as non-Arabs gained influence and the various subordinate sultans and emirs became increasingly independent.

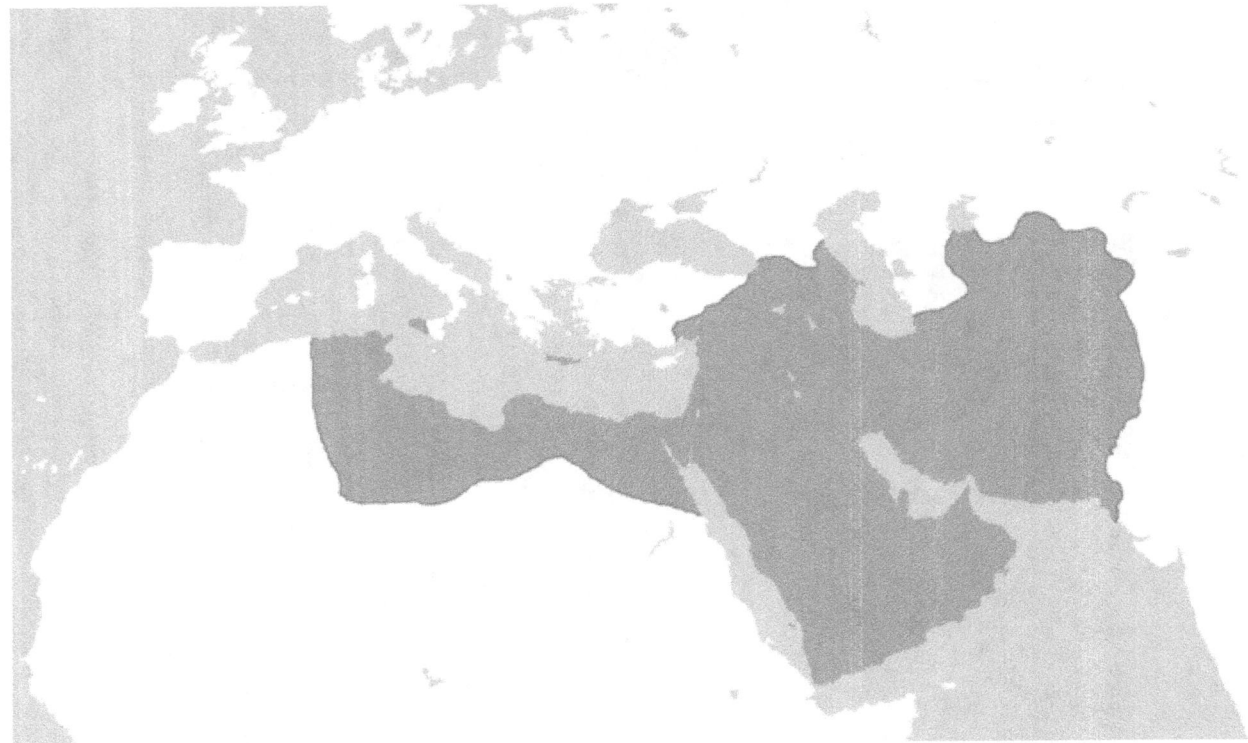

Map of the Abbasid Caliphate at its greatest extent, c. 850 CE: The Abbasid dynasty ruled as caliphs from their capital in Baghdad, in modern Iraq, after taking over authority of the Muslim empire from the Umayyads in 750 CE.

Decline of the Abbasid Empire

The Abbasid leadership worked to overcome the political challenges of a large empire with limited communication in the last half of the 8th century (750–800 CE). While the Byzantine Empire was fighting Abbasid rule in Syria and Anatolia, the caliphate's military operations were focused on internal unrest. Local governors had begun to exert greater autonomy, using their increasing power to make their positions hereditary. Simultaneously, former supporters of the Abbasids had broken away to create a separate kingdom around Khorosan in northern Persia.

Several factions left the empire to exercise independent authority. In 793 CE, the Shi'a (also called Shi'ite) dynasty of Idrisids gained authored over Fez in Morocco. The Berber Kharijites set up an independent state in North Africa in 801 CE. A family of governors under the Abbasids became increasingly independent until they founded the Aghlabid Emirate in the 830s. Within 50 years, the Idrisids in the Maghreb, the Aghlabids of Ifriqiya, and the Tulunids and Ikshidids of Misr became independent in Africa.

By the 860s governors in Egypt set up their own Tulunid Emirate, so named for its founder Ahmad ibn Tulun, starting a dynastic rule separate from the caliph. In the eastern territories, local governors decreased their ties to the central Abbasid rule. The Saffarids of Herat and the Samanids of Bukhara seceded in the 870s to cultivate a more Persian culture and rule. The Tulinid dynasty managed Palestine, the Hijaz, and parts of Egypt. By 900 CE, the Abbasids controlled only central Mesopotamia, and the Byzantine Empire began to reconquer western Anatolia.

The Fatimid Caliphate (909–1171 CE)

Several factions challenged the Abbasids' claims to the caliphate. Most Shi'a Muslims had supported the Abbasid war against the Umayyads because the Abbasids claimed legitimacy with their familial connection to Muhammad, an important issue for Shi'a. However, once in power, the Abbasids embraced Sunni Islam and disavowed any support for Shi'a beliefs.

The Shi'a Ubayd Allah al-Mahdi Billah of the Fatimid dynasty, who claimed descent from Muhammad's daughter, declared himself Caliph in 909 CE and created a separate line of caliphs in North Africa. The Fatimid caliphs initially controlled Morocco, Algeria, Tunisia, and Libya, and they expanded for the next 150 years, taking Egypt and Palestine. The Abbasid dynasty finally challenged Fatimid rule, limiting them to Egypt. By the 920s, a Shi'a sect that only recognized the first five Imams and could trace its roots to Muhammad's daughter Fatima, took control of Idrisi and then Aghlabid domains. This group advanced to Egypt in 969 CE, establishing their capital near Fustat in Cairo, which they built as a bastion of Shi'a learning and politics. By 1000 CE, they had become the chief political and ideological challenge to Abbasid Sunni Islam. At this point, the Abbasid dynasty had fragmented into several governorships that were mostly autonomous, although they official recognized caliphal authority from Baghdad. The caliph himself was under "protection" of the Buyid Emirs, who possessed all of Iraq and western Iran, and were quietly Shi'a in their sympathies.

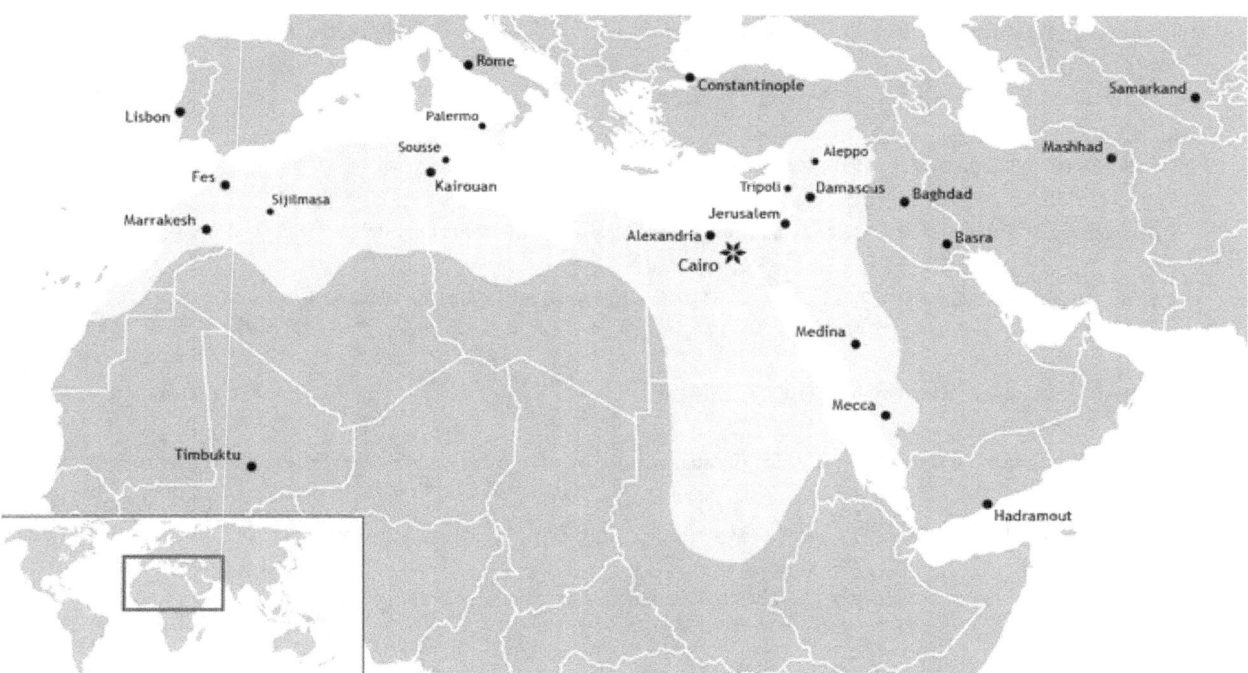

The Fatimid Caliphate at its height, c. 969 CE: *The Fatimid dynasty broke from the Abbasids in 909 CE and created separate lines of caliphs in Morocco, Algeria, Tunisia, Libya, Egypt, and Palestine until 1171 CE.*

Outside Iraq, all the autonomous provinces slowly became states with hereditary rulers, armies, and revenues. They operated under only nominal caliph authority, with emirs ruling their own provinces from their own capitals. Mahmud of Ghazni took the title of "sultan," instead of "emir," signifying the Ghaznavid Empire's independence from caliphal authority, despite Mahmud's ostentatious displays of Sunni orthodoxy and ritual submission to the caliph. In the 11th century, the loss of respect for the caliphs continued, as some Islamic rulers no longer mentioned the caliph's name in the Friday khutba, or struck it off their coinage. The political power of the Abbasids largely ended with the rise of the Buyids and the Seljuq Turks in 1258 CE. Though lacking in political power, the dynasty continued to claim authority in religious matters until after the Ottoman conquest of Egypt in 1517.

Attributions

CC licensed content, Specific attribution

- Middle Eastern Empires. **Provided by**: Wikibooks. **Located at**: http://en.wikibooks.org/wiki/World_History/Middle_Eastern_Empires. **License**: *CC BY-SA: Attribution-ShareAlike*
- Muhammad. **Provided by**: Wikipedia. **Located at**: http://en.wikipedia.org/wiki/Muhammad. **License**: *CC BY-SA: Attribution-ShareAlike*
- Muslim Conquests. **Provided by**: Wikipedia. **Located at**: http://en.wikipedia.org/wiki/Muslim_conquests. **License**: *CC BY-SA: Attribution-ShareAlike*
- Succession to Muhammad. **Provided by**: Wikipedia. **Located at**: http://en.wikipedia.org/wiki/Succession_to_Muhammad. **License**: *CC BY-SA: Attribution-ShareAlike*
- Rashidun Caliphate. **Provided by**: Wikipedia. **Located at**: http://en.wikipedia.org/wiki/Rashidun_Caliphate. **License**: *CC BY-SA: Attribution-ShareAlike*
- Caliph. **Provided by**: Wikipedia. **Located at**: http://en.wikipedia.org/wiki/Caliph. **License**: *CC BY-SA: Attribution-ShareAlike*
- Caliphate. **Provided by**: Wikipedia. **Located at**: http://en.wikipedia.org/wiki/Caliphate. **License**: *CC BY-SA: Attribution-ShareAlike*
- Sunni. **Provided by**: Wiktionary. **Located at**: http://en.wiktionary.org/wiki/Sunni. **License**: *CC BY-SA: Attribution-ShareAlike*
- Shia Islam. **Provided by**: Wikipedia. **Located at**: http://en.wikipedia.org/wiki/Shia_Islam. **License**: *CC BY-SA: Attribution-ShareAlike*
- Umayyad Caliphate. **Provided by**: Wikipedia. **Located at**: https://en.wikipedia.org/wiki/Umayyad_Caliphate. **License**: *CC BY-SA: Attribution-ShareAlike*
- Caliphate of Cu00f3rdoba. **Provided by**: Wikipedia. **Located at**: https://en.wikipedia.org/wiki/Caliphate_of_Cordoba. **License**: *CC BY-SA: Attribution-ShareAlike*
- Screen Shot 2016-08-12 at 12.52.52 PM.png. **Provided by**: Wikipedia. **Located at**: https://en.wikipedia.org/wiki/Umayyad_Caliphate. **License**: *CC BY-SA: Attribution-ShareAlike*
- Spain_Andalusia_Cordoba_BW_2015-10-27_13-54-14.jpg. **Provided by**: Wikipedia. **Located at**: https://en.wikipedia.org/wiki/Caliphate_of_Cordoba#/media/File:Spain_Andalusia_Cordoba_BW_2015-10-27_13-54-14.jpg. **License**: *CC BY-SA: Attribution-ShareAlike*
- Muslim Conquests. **Provided by**: Wikipedia. **Located at**: http://en.wikipedia.org/wiki/Muslim_conquests. **License**: *CC BY-SA: Attribution-ShareAlike*
- Rashidun Caliphate. **Provided by**: Wikipedia. **Located at**: http://en.wikipedia.org/wiki/Rashidun_Caliphate. **License**: *CC BY-SA: Attribution-ShareAlike*
- Caliphates. **Provided by**: Wikipedia. **Located at**: http://en.wikipedia.org/wiki/Caliphates. **License**: *CC BY-SA: Attribution-ShareAlike*
- Middle Eastern Empires. **Provided by**: Wikibooks. **Located at**: http://en.wikibooks.org/wiki/World_History/Middle_Eastern_Empires. **License**: *CC BY-SA: Attribution-ShareAlike*
- Zoroastrianism. **Provided by**: Wikipedia. **Located at**: http://en.wikipedia.org/wiki/Zoroastrianism. **License**: *CC BY-SA: Attribution-ShareAlike*
- Muslim Conquest of Persia. **Provided by**: Wikipedia. **Located at**: http://en.wikipedia.org/wiki/Rashidun_conquest_of_the_Sassanian_Empire. **License**: *CC BY-SA: Attribution-ShareAlike*
- Screen Shot 2016-08-12 at 12.52.52 PM.png. **Provided by**: Wikipedia. **Located at**: https://en.wikipedia.org/wiki/Umayyad_Caliphate. **License**: *CC BY-SA: Attribution-ShareAlike*
- Spain_Andalusia_Cordoba_BW_2015-10-27_13-54-14.jpg. **Provided by**: Wikipedia. **Located at**: https://en.wikipedia.org/wiki/Caliphate_of_Cordoba#/media/File:Spain_Andalusia_Cordoba_BW_2015-10-27_13-54-14.jpg. **License**: *CC BY-SA: Attribution-ShareAlike*
- Kairouan_Mosque_Courtyard.jpg. **Provided by**: Wikipedia. **Located at**: https://en.wikipedia.org/wiki/Spread_of_Islam. **License**: *CC BY-SA: Attribution-ShareAlike*
- Islamic Golden Age. **Provided by**: Wikipedia. **Located at**: http://en.wikipedia.org/wiki/Islamic_Golden_Age. **License**: *CC BY-SA:*

- Islamic Architecture. **Provided by**: Wikipedia. **Located at**: http://en.wikipedia.org/wiki/Islamic_architecture. **License**: *CC BY-SA: Attribution-ShareAlike*
- Abbasid Caliphate. **Provided by**: Wikipedia. **Located at**: http://en.wikipedia.org/wiki/Abbasid_Caliphate. **License** *CC BY-SA: Attribution-ShareAlike*
- calligraphy. **Provided by**: Wiktionary. **Located at**: http://en.wiktionary.org/wiki/calligraphy. **License**: *CC BY-SA: Attribution-ShareAlike*
- Averroes. **Provided by**: Wikipedia. **Located at**: http://en.wikipedia.org/wiki/Ibn_Rushd. **License**: *CC BY-SA: Attribution-ShareAlike*
- Islamic Calligraphy. **Provided by**: Wikipedia. **Located at**: http://en.wikipedia.org/wiki/Islamic_calligraphy. **License**: *CC BY-SA: Attribution-ShareAlike*
- Islamic Art. **Provided by**: Wikipedia. **Located at**: http://en.wikipedia.org/wiki/Islamic_art. **License**: *CC BY-SA: Attribution-ShareAlike*
- Arabesque (Islamic Art). **Provided by**: Wikipedia. **Located at**: http://en.wikipedia.org/wiki/Arabesque_(Islamic_art). **License**: *CC BY-SA: Attribution-ShareAlike*
- Screen Shot 2016-08-12 at 12.52.52 PM.png. **Provided by**: Wikipedia. **Located at**: https://en.wikipedia.org/wiki/Umayyad_Caliphate. **License**: *CC BY-SA: Attribution-ShareAlike*
- Spain_Andalusia_Cordoba_BW_2015-10-27_13-54-14.jpg. **Provided by**: Wikipedia. **Located at**: https://en.wikipedia.org/wiki/Caliphate_of_Cordoba#/media/File:Spain_Andalusia_Cordoba_BW_2015-10-27_13-54-14.jpg. **License**: *CC BY-SA: Attribution-ShareAlike*
- Kairouan_Mosque_Courtyard.jpg. **Provided by**: Wikipedia. **Located at**: https://en.wikipedia.org/wiki/Spread_of_Islam. **License**: *CC BY-SA: Attribution-ShareAlike*
- Cheshm Manuscript. **Provided by**: Wikipedia. **Located at**: http://upload.wikimedia.org/wikipedia/commons/thumb/a/a6/Cheshm_manuscript.jpg/360px-Cheshm_manuscript.jpg. **License**: *CC BY-SA: Attribution-ShareAlike*
- Ali Bab. **Provided by**: Wikimedia. **Located at**: http://en.wikipedia.org/wiki/File:Ali-Baba.jpg. **License**: *Public Domain: No Known Copyright*
- Arabesque. **Provided by**: Wikipedia. **Located at**: http://upload.wikimedia.org/wikipedia/commons/thumb/2/2f/Atauriques.jpg/640px-Atauriques.jpg. **License**: *CC BY-SA: Attribution-ShareAlike*
- Green_mosque_archway.JPG. **Provided by**: Wikipedia. **Located at**: https://en.wikipedia.org/wiki/Islamic_Golden_Age#/media/File:Green_mosque_archway.JPG. **License**: *CC BY-SA: Attribution-ShareAlike*
- Caliphates. **Provided by**: Wikipedia. **Located at**: http://en.wikipedia.org/wiki/Caliphates. **License**: *CC BY-SA: Attribution-ShareAlike*
- Emir. **Provided by**: Wikipedia. **Located at**: http://en.wikipedia.org/wiki/Emir. **License**: *CC BY-SA: Attribution-ShareAlike*
- Middle Eastern Empires. **Provided by**: Wikibooks. **Located at**: http://en.wikibooks.org/wiki/World_History/Middle_Eastern_Empires. **License**: *CC BY-SA: Attribution-ShareAlike*
- Abbasid Caliphate. **Provided by**: Wikipedia. **Located at**: http://en.wikipedia.org/wiki/Abbasid_Caliphate. **License**: *CC BY-SA: Attribution-ShareAlike*
- Anatolia. **Provided by**: Wikipedia. **Located at**: http://en.wikipedia.org/wiki/Anatolia. **License**: *CC BY-SA: Attribution-ShareAlike*
- Fatimid Caliphate. **Provided by**: Wikipedia. **Located at**: http://en.wikipedia.org/wiki/Fatimid_Caliphate. **License**: *CC BY-SA: Attribution-ShareAlike*
- Screen Shot 2016-08-12 at 12.52.52 PM.png. **Provided by**: Wikipedia. **Located at**: https://en.wikipedia.org/wiki/Umayyad_Caliphate. **License**: *CC BY-SA: Attribution-ShareAlike*
- Spain_Andalusia_Cordoba_BW_2015-10-27_13-54-14.jpg. **Provided by**: Wikipedia. **Located at**: https://en.wikipedia.org/wiki/Caliphate_of_Cordoba#/media/File:Spain_Andalusia_Cordoba_BW_2015-10-27_13-54-14.jpg. **License**: *CC BY-SA: Attribution-ShareAlike*
- Kairouan_Mosque_Courtyard.jpg. **Provided by**: Wikipedia. **Located at**: https://en.wikipedia.org/wiki/Spread_of_Islam. **License**: *CC BY-SA: Attribution-ShareAlike*
- Cheshm Manuscript. **Provided by**: Wikipedia. **Located at**: http://upload.wikimedia.org/wikipedia/commons/thumb/a/a6/Cheshm_manuscript.jpg/360px-Cheshm_manuscript.jpg. **License**: *CC BY-SA: Attribution-ShareAlike*
- Ali Bab. **Provided by**: Wikimedia. **Located at**: http://en.wikipedia.org/wiki/File:Ali-Baba.jpg. **License**: *Public Domain: No Known Copyright*
- Arabesque. **Provided by**: Wikipedia. **Located at**: http://upload.wikimedia.org/wikipedia/commons/thumb/2/2f/Atauriques.jpg/

640px-Atauriques.jpg. **License**: *CC BY-SA: Attribution-ShareAlike*

- Green_mosque_archway.JPG. **Provided by**: Wikipedia. **Located at**: https://en.wikipedia.org/wiki/Islamic_Golden_Age#/media/File:Green_mosque_archway.JPG. **License**: *CC BY-SA: Attribution-ShareAlike*
- Abbasids850. **Provided by**: Wikimedia. **Located at**: http://commons.wikimedia.org/wiki/File:Abbasids850.png. **License**: *CC BY-SA: Attribution-ShareAlike*
- Fatimid Islamic Caliphate. **Provided by**: Wikimedia Commons. **Located at**: http://en.wikipedia.org/wiki/Fatimid_Caliphate%23mediaviewer/File:Fatimid_Islamic_Caliphate.png. **License**: *Public Domain: No Known Copyright*
- Abbasids_Baghdad_Iraq_765.jpg. **Provided by**: Wikipedia. **Located at**: https://en.wikipedia.org/wiki/Abbasid_Caliphate#/media/File:Abbasids_Baghdad_Iraq_765.jpg. **License**: *CC BY-SA: Attribution-ShareAlike*

Crusades

The Crusades

The Crusades

The Crusades were military campaigns sanctioned by the Roman Catholic Church during the High and Late Middle Ages.

Learning Objectives

Describe the origins of the Crusades

Key Takeaways

Key Points

- The Crusades were a series of military conflicts conducted by Christian knights to defend Christians and the Christian empire against Muslim forces.
- The Holy Land was part of the Roman Empire until the Islamic conquests of the 7th and 8th centuries. Thereafter, Christians were permitted to visit parts of the Holy Land until 1071, when Christian pilgrimages were stopped by the Seljuq Turks.
- The Seljuq Turks had taken over much of Byzantium after the Byzantine defeat at the Battle of Manzikert in 1071.
- In 1095 at the Council of Piacenza, Byzantine Emperor Alexios I Komnenos requested military aid from Urban II to fight the Turks.
- In July 1095, Urban turned to his homeland of France to recruit men for the expedition. His travels there culminated in the Council of Clermont in November, where he gave speeches combining the idea of pilgrimage to the Holy Land with that of waging a holy war against infidels, which received an enthusiastic response.

> *Key Terms*
>
> - **Seljuq Empire**: A medieval Turko-Persian Sunni Muslim empire that controlled a vast area stretching from the Hindu Kush to eastern Anatolia and from Central Asia to the Persian Gulf. The Seljuq Turk attack on Byzantium helped spur the crusades.
> - **heretical**: Relating to departure from established beliefs or customs.
> - **Byzantine Empire**: The predominantly Greek-speaking continuation of the eastern half of the Roman Empire during Late Antiquity and the Middle Ages.
> - **schism**: A division or a split, usually between groups belonging to a religious denomination.

The Crusades were a series of military conflicts conducted by Christian knights for the defense of Christians and for the expansion of Christian domains between the 11th and 15th centuries. Generally, the Crusades refer to the campaigns in the Holy Land sponsored by the papacy against Muslim forces. There were other crusades against Islamic forces in southern Spain, southern Italy, and Sicily, as well as campaigns of Teutonic knights against pagan strongholds in Eastern Europe. A few crusades, such as the Fourth Crusade, were waged within Christendom against groups that were considered heretical and schismatic. Crusades were fought for many reasons—to capture Jerusalem, recapture Christian territory, or defend Christians in non-Christian lands; as a means of conflict resolution among Roman Catholics; for political or territorial advantage; and to combat paganism and heresy.

Origin of the Crusades

The origin of the Crusades in general, and particularly of the First Crusade, is widely debated among historians. The confusion is partially due to the numerous armies in the First Crusade, and their lack of direct unity. The similar ideologies held the armies to similar goals, but the connections were rarely strong, and unity broke down often. The Crusades are most commonly linked to the political and social situation in 11th-century Europe, the rise of a reform movement within the papacy, and the political and religious confrontation of Christianity and Islam in Europe and the Middle East. Christianity had spread throughout Europe, Africa, and the Middle East in Late Antiquity, but by the early 8th century Christian rule had become limited to Europe and Anatolia after the Muslim conquests.

Background in Europe

The Holy Land had been part of the Roman Empire, and thus the Byzantine Empire, until the Islamic conquests. In the 7th and 8th centuries, Islam was introduced in the Arabian Peninsula by the Islamic prophet Muhammad and his followers. This formed a unified Muslim polity, which led to a rapid expansion of Arab power, the influence of which stretched from the northwest Indian subcontinent, across Central Asia, the Middle East, North Africa, southern Italy, and the Iberian Peninsula, to the Pyrenees. Tolerance, trade, and political relationships between the Arabs and the Christian states of Europe waxed and waned. For example, the Fatimid caliph al-Hakim bi-Amr Allah destroyed the Church of the Holy Sepulchre, but his successor allowed the Byzantine Empire to rebuild it. Pilgrimages by Catholics to sacred sites were permitted, resident Christians were given certain legal rights and protections under Dhimmi status, and interfaith marriages were not uncommon. Cultures and creeds coexisted and competed, but the frontier conditions became increasingly inhospitable to Catholic pilgrims and merchants.

At the western edge of Europe and of Islamic expansion, the Reconquista (recapture of the Iberian Peninsula from the Muslims) was well underway by the 11th century, reaching its turning point in 1085 when Alfonso VI of León and Castile retook Toledo from Muslim rule. Increasingly in the 11th century, foreign knights, mostly from France, visited Iberia to assist the Christians in their efforts.

The heart of Western Europe had been stabilized after the Christianization of the Saxon, Viking, and Hungarian peoples by the end of the 10th century. However, the breakdown of the Carolingian Empire gave rise to an entire class of warriors who now had little to do but fight among themselves. The random violence of the knightly class was regularly condemned by the church, and so it established the Peace and Truce of God to prohibit fighting on certain days of the year.

At the same time, the reform-minded papacy came into conflict with the Holy Roman Emperors, resulting in the Investiture Controversy. The papacy began to assert its independence from secular rulers, marshaling arguments for the proper use of armed force by Catholics. Popes such as Gregory VII justified the subsequent warfare against the emperor's partisans in theological terms. It became acceptable for the pope to utilize knights in the name of Christendom, not only against political enemies of the papacy, but also against Al-Andalus, or, theoretically, against the Seljuq dynasty in the east. The result was intense piety, an interest in religious affairs, and religious propaganda advocating a just war to reclaim Palestine from the Muslims. Participation in such a war was seen as a form of penance that could counterbalance sin.

Aid to Byzantium

To the east of Europe lay the Byzantine Empire, composed of Christians who had long followed a separate Orthodox rite; the Eastern Orthodox and Roman Catholic churches had been in schism since 1054. Historians have argued that the desire to impose Roman church authority in the east may have been one of the goals of the Crusades, although Urban II, who launched the First Crusade, never refers to such a goal in his letters on crusading. The Seljuq Empire had taken over almost all of Anatolia after the Byzantine defeat at the Battle of Manzikert in 1071; however, their conquests were piecemeal and led by semi-independent warlords, rather than by the sultan. A dramatic collapse of the empire's position on the eve of the Council of Clermont brought Byzantium to the brink of disaster. By the mid-1090s, the Byzantine Empire was largely confined to Balkan Europe and the northwestern fringe of Anatolia, and faced Norman enemies in the west as well as Turks in the east. In response to the defeat at Manzikert and subsequent Byzantine losses in Anatolia in 1074, Pope Gregory VII had called for the *milites Christi* ("soldiers of Christ") to go to Byzantium's aid.

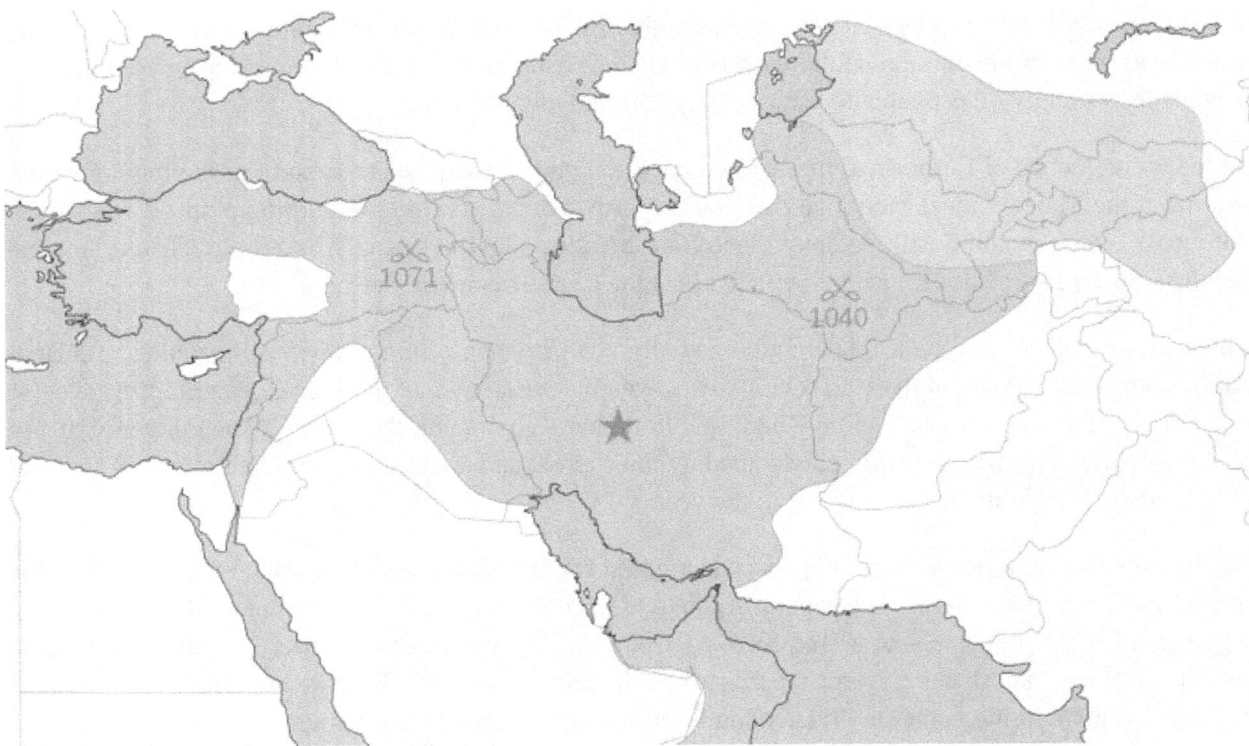

Seljuq Empire: *The Great Seljuq Empire at its greatest extent (1092).*

While the Crusades had causes deeply rooted in the social and political situations of 11th-century Europe, the event actually triggering the First Crusade was a request for assistance from Byzantine emperor Alexios I Komnenos. Alexios was worried about the advances of the Seljuqs, who had reached as far west as Nicaea, not far from Constantinople. In March 1095, Alexios sent envoys to the Council of Piacenza to ask Pope Urban II for aid against the Turks.

Urban responded favorably, perhaps hoping to heal the Great Schism of forty years earlier, and to reunite the Church under papal primacy by helping the eastern churches in their time of need. Alexios and Urban had previously been in close contact in 1089 and later, and had openly discussed the prospect of the (re)union of the Christian church. There were signs of considerable co-operation between Rome and Constantinople in the years immediately before the Crusade.

In July 1095, Urban turned to his homeland of France to recruit men for the expedition. His travels there culminated in the Council of Clermont in November, where, according to the various speeches attributed to him, he gave an impassioned sermon to a large audience of French nobles and clergy, graphically detailing the fantastical atrocities being committed against pilgrims and eastern Christians. Urban talked about the violence of European society and the necessity of maintaining the Peace of God; about helping the Greeks, who had asked for assistance; about the crimes being committed against Christians in the east; and about a new kind of war, an armed pilgrimage, and of rewards in heaven, where remission of sins was offered to any who might die in the undertaking. Combining the idea of pilgrimage to the Holy Land with that of waging a holy war against infidels, Urban received an enthusiastic response to his speeches and soon after began collecting military forces to begin the First Crusade.

Council of Clermont: *Pope Urban II at the Council of Clermont, where he gave speeches in favor of a Crusade.*

The First Crusade

The First Crusade (1095–1099) was a military expedition by Roman Catholic Europe to regain the Holy Lands taken in Muslim conquests, ultimately resulting in the recapture of Jerusalem.

Learning Objectives

Evaluate the events of the First Crusade

Key Takeaways

Key Points

- The First Crusade (1095–1099), called for by Pope Urban II, was the first of a number of crusades that attempted to recapture the Holy Lands.
- It was launched on November 27, 1095, by Pope Urban II with the primary goal of responding to an appeal from Byzantine Emperor Alexios I Komnenos, who had been

- defeated by Turkish forces.
- An additional goal soon became the principal objective—the Christian reconquest of the sacred city of Jerusalem and the Holy Land and the freeing of the Eastern Christians from Muslim rule.
- The first object of the campaign was Nicaea, previously a city under Byzantine rule, which the Crusaders captured on June 18, 1097, by defeating the troops of Kilij Arslan.
- After marching through the Mediterranean region, the Crusaders arrived at Jerusalem, launched an assault on the city, and captured it in July 1099, massacring many of the city's Muslim and Jewish inhabitants.
- In the end, they established the crusader states of the Kingdom of Jerusalem, the County of Tripoli, the Principality of Antioch, and the County of Edessa.

Key Terms

- **Church of the Holy Sepulchre**: A church within the Christian Quarter of the Old City of Jerusalem that contains, according to traditions dating back to at least the 4th century, the two holiest sites in Christendom—the site where Jesus of Nazareth was crucified and Jesus's empty tomb, where he is said to have been buried and resurrected.
- **Pope Urban II**: Pope from March 12, 1088, to his death in 1099, he is best known for initiating the First Crusade.
- **People's Crusade**: An expedition seen as the prelude to the First Crusade that lasted roughly six months, from April to October 1096, and was led mostly by peasants.
- **Alexios I Komnenos**: Byzantine emperor from 1081 to 1118, whose appeals to Western Europe for help against the Turks were also the catalyst that likely contributed to the convoking of the Crusades.

Overview

The First Crusade (1095–1099), called for by Pope Urban II, was the first of a number of crusades intended to recapture the Holy Lands. It started as a widespread pilgrimage in western Christendom and ended as a military expedition by Roman Catholic Europe to regain the Holy Lands taken in the Muslim conquests of the Mediterranean (632–661), ultimately resulting in the recapture of Jerusalem in 1099.

It was launched on November 27, 1095, by Pope Urban II with the primary goal of responding to an appeal from Byzantine Emperor Alexios I Komnenos, who requested that western volunteers come to his aid and help to repel the invading Seljuq Turks from Anatolia (modern-day Turkey). An additional goal soon became the principal objective—the Christian reconquest of the sacred city of Jerusalem and the Holy Land and the freeing of the Eastern Christians from Muslim rule.

During the crusade, knights, peasants, and serfs from many regions of Western Europe travelled over land and by sea, first to Constantinople and then on toward Jerusalem. The Crusaders arrived at Jerusalem, launched an assault on the city, and captured it in July 1099, massacring many of the city's Muslim and Jewish inhabitants. They also established the crusader states of the Kingdom of Jerusalem, the County of Tripoli, the Principality of Antioch, and the County of Edessa.

People's Crusade

Pope Urban II planned the departure of the crusade for August 15, 1096; before this, a number of unexpected bands of peasants and low-ranking knights organized and set off for Jerusalem on their own, on an expedition known as the People's Crusade, led by a monk named Peter the Hermit. The peasant population had been afflicted by drought, famine, and disease for many years before 1096, and some of them seem to have envisioned the crusade as an escape from these hardships. Spurring them on had been a number of meteorological occurrences beginning in 1095 that seemed to be a divine blessing for the movement—a meteor shower, an aurorae, a lunar eclipse, and a comet, among other events. An outbreak of ergotism had also occurred just before the Council of Clermont. Millenarianism, the belief that the end of the world was imminent, widespread in the early 11th century, experienced a resurgence in popularity. The response was beyond expectations; while Urban might have expected a few thousand knights, he ended up with a migration numbering up to 40,000 Crusaders of mostly unskilled fighters, including women and children.

Lacking military discipline in what likely seemed a strange land (Eastern Europe), Peter's fledgling army quickly found itself in trouble despite the fact that they were still in Christian territory. This unruly mob began to attack and pillage outside Constantinople in search of supplies and food, prompting Alexios to hurriedly ferry the gathering across the Bosporus one week later. After crossing into Asia Minor, the crusaders split up and began to plunder the countryside, wandering into Seljuq territory around Nicaea, where they were massacred by an overwhelming group of Turks.

People's Crusade massacre: *An illustration showing the defeat of the People's Crusade by the Turks.*

The First Crusade

The four main Crusader armies left Europe around the appointed time in August 1096. They took different paths to Constantinople and gathered outside the city walls between November 1096 and April 1097; Hugh of Vermandois arrived first, followed by Godfrey, Raymond, and Bohemond. This time, Emperor Alexios was more prepared for the Crusaders; there were fewer incidents of violence along the way.

The Crusaders may have expected Alexios to become their leader, but he had no interest in joining them, and was mainly concerned with transporting them into Asia Minor as quickly as possible. In return for food and supplies, Alexios requested that the leaders to swear fealty to him and promise to return to the Byzantine Empire any land recovered from the Turks. Before ensuring that the various armies were shuttled across the Bosporus, Alexios advised the leaders on how best to deal with the Seljuq armies they would soon encounter.

Siege of Nicaea and March to Jerusalem

The Crusader armies crossed over into Asia Minor during the first half of 1097, where they were joined by Peter the Hermit and the remainder of his little army. Alexios also sent two of his own generals, Manuel Boutoumites and Tatikios, to assist the Crusaders. The first object of their campaign was Nicaea, previously a city under Byzantine rule, but which had become the capital of the Seljuq Sultanate of Rum under Kilij Arslan I. Arslan was away campaigning against the Danishmends in central Anatolia at the time, and had left behind his treasury and his family, underestimating the strength of these new Crusaders.

Subsequently, upon the Crusaders' arrival, the city was subjected to a lengthy siege, and when Arslan had word of it he rushed back to Nicaea and attacked the Crusader army on May 16. He was driven back by the unexpectedly large Crusader force, with heavy losses suffered on both sides in the ensuing battle. The siege continued, but the Crusaders had little success as they found they could not blockade Lake Iznik, which the city was situated on, and from which it could be provisioned. To break the city, Alexios had the Crusaders' ships rolled over land on logs, and at the sight of them the Turkish garrison finally surrendered, 18 June 18. The city was handed over to the Byzantine troops.

At the end of June, the Crusaders marched on through Anatolia. They were accompanied by some Byzantine troops under Tatikios, and still harbored the hope that Alexios would send a full Byzantine army after them. After a battle with Kilij Arslan, the Crusaders marched through Anatolia unopposed, but the journey was unpleasant, as Arslan had burned and destroyed everything he left behind in his army's flight. It was the middle of summer, and the Crusaders had very little food and water; many men and horses died. Fellow Christians sometimes gave them gifts of food and money, but more often than not the Crusaders simply looted and pillaged whenever the opportunity presented itself.

Proceeding down the Mediterranean coast, the crusaders encountered little resistance, as local rulers preferred to make peace with them and furnish them with supplies rather than fight.

Capture of Jerusalem

On June 7, the Crusaders reached Jerusalem, which had been recaptured from the Seljuqs by the Fatimids only the year before. Many Crusaders wept upon seeing the city they had journeyed so long to reach. The arrival at Jerusalem revealed an arid countryside, lacking in water or food supplies. Here there was no prospect of relief, even as they feared an imminent attack by the local Fatimid rulers. The Crusaders resolved to take the city by assault. They might have been left with little choice, as it has been estimated that only about 12,000 men, including 1,500 cavalry, remained by the time the army reached Jerusalem.

After the failure of the initial assault, a meeting between the various leaders was organized in which it was agreed upon that a more concerted attack would be required in the future. On June 17, a party of Genoese mariners under Guglielmo Embriaco arrived at Jaffa and provided the Crusaders with skilled engineers, and perhaps more critically, supplies of timber (cannibalized from the ships) with which to build siege engines. The Crusaders' morale was raised when a priest, Peter Desiderius, claimed to have had a divine vision of Bishop Adhemar instructing them to fast and then march in a barefoot procession around the city walls, after which the city would fall, following the Biblical story of Joshua at the siege of Jericho.

The final assault on Jerusalem began on July 13; Raymond's troops attacked the south gate while the other contingents attacked the northern wall. Initially the Provençals at the southern gate made little headway, but the contingents at the northern wall fared better, with a slow but steady attrition of the defense. On July 15, a final push was launched at both ends of the city, and eventually the inner rampart of the northern wall was captured. In the ensuing panic, the defenders abandoned the walls of the city at both ends, allowing the Crusaders to finally enter.

Capture of Jerusalem: *A depiction of the capture of Jerusalem in 1099 from a medieval manuscript. The burning buildings of Jerusalem are centered in the image. The various Crusaders are surrounding and besieging the village armed for an attack.*

The massacre that followed the capture of Jerusalem has attained particular notoriety, as a "juxtaposition of extreme violence and anguished faith." The eyewitness accounts from the Crusaders themselves leave little doubt that there was a great slaughter in the aftermath of the siege. Nevertheless, some historians propose that the scale of the massacre was exaggerated in later medieval sources. The slaughter lasted a day;

Muslims were indiscriminately killed, and Jews who had taken refuge in their synagogue died when it was burnt down by the Crusaders. The following day, Tancred's prisoners in the mosque were slaughtered. Still, it is clear that some Muslims and Jews of the city survived the massacre, either escaping or being taken prisoner to be ransomed. The Eastern Christian population of the city had been expelled before the siege by the governor, and thus escaped the massacre.

On July 22, a council was held in the Church of the Holy Sepulchre to establish a king for the newly created Kingdom of Jerusalem. Raymond IV of Toulouse and Godfrey of Bouillon were recognized as the leaders of the crusade and the siege of Jerusalem. Raymond was the wealthier and more powerful of the two, but at first he refused to become king, perhaps attempting to show his piety and probably hoping that the other nobles would insist upon his election anyway. The more popular Godfrey did not hesitate like Raymond, and accepted a position as secular leader.

Having captured Jerusalem and the Church of the Holy Sepulchre, the Crusaders had fulfilled their vow.

The Second Crusade

The Second Crusade (1147–1149) was the second major crusade launched against Islam by Catholic Europe, started in response to the fall of the County of Edessa founded in the First Crusade; it was largely a failure for the Europeans.

Learning Objectives

Explain the successes and failures of the Second Crusade

Key Takeaways

Key Points

- The Second Crusade was started in 1147 in response to the fall of the County of Edessa the previous year to the forces of Zengi; Edessa was founded during the First Crusade.
- The Second Crusade was led by two European kings— Louis VII of France and Conrad III of Germany.
- The German and French armies took separate routes to Anatolia, fighting skirmishes along the way, and both were defeated separately by the Seljuq Turks.
- Louis and Conrad and the remnants of their armies eventually reached Jerusalem and participated in an ill-advised attack on Damascus in 1148.
- The Second Crusade was a failure for the Crusaders and a great victory for the Muslims.

> *Key Terms*
>
> - **Moors**: The Muslim inhabitants of the Maghreb, North Africa and the Iberian Peninsula, Sicily, and Malta during the Middle Ages, who initially were Berber and Arab peoples of North African descent.
> - **Conrad III**: First German king of the Hohenstaufen dynasty, who led troops in the Second Crusade.
> - **Manuel I Komneno**: A Byzantine Emperor of the 12th century who reigned over a crucial turning point in the history of Byzantium and the Mediterranean, including the Second Crusade.
> - **Louis VII**: A Capetian king of the Franks from 1137 until his death who led troops in the Second Crusade.

The Second Crusade

The Second Crusade (1147–1149) was the second major crusade launched from Europe as a Catholic holy war against Islam. The Second Crusade was started in 1147 in response to the fall of the County of Edessa the previous year to the forces of Zengi. The county had been founded during the First Crusade by King Baldwin of Boulogne in 1098. While it was the first Crusader state to be founded, it was also the first to fall.

The Second Crusade was announced by Pope Eugene III, and was the first of the crusades to be led by European kings, namely Louis VII of France and Conrad III of Germany, who had help from a number of other European nobles. The armies of the two kings marched separately across Europe. After crossing Byzantine territory into Anatolia, both armies were separately defeated by the Seljuq Turks. The main Western Christian source, Odo of Deuil, and Syriac Christian sources claim that the Byzantine Emperor Manuel I Komnenos secretly hindered the Crusaders' progress, particularly in Anatolia, where he is alleged to have deliberately ordered Turks to attack them. Louis and Conrad and the remnants of their armies reached Jerusalem and participated in an ill-advised attack on Damascus in 1148. The Crusade in the east was a failure for the Crusaders and a great victory for the Muslims. It would ultimately have a key influence on the fall of Jerusalem and give rise to the Third Crusade at the end of the 12th century.

The only Christian success of the Second Crusade came to a combined force of 13,000 Flemish, Frisian, Norman, English, Scottish, and German Crusaders in 1147. Traveling by ship from England to the Holy Land, the army stopped and helped the smaller (7,000) Portuguese army capture Lisbon, expelling its Moorish occupants.

Crusade in the East

Joscelin II had tried to take back Edessa, but Nur ad-Din defeated him in November 1146. On February 16, 1147, the French Crusaders met to discuss their route. The Germans had already decided to travel overland through Hungary, as the sea route was politically impractical because Roger II, king of Sicily, was an enemy of Conrad. Many of the French nobles distrusted the land route, which would take them through the Byzantine Empire, the reputation of which still suffered from the accounts of the First Crusaders. Nevertheless, it was decided to follow Conrad, and to set out on June 15.

German Route

The German crusaders, accompanied by the papal legate and Cardinal Theodwin, intended to meet the French in Constantinople. Ottokar III of Styria joined Conrad at Vienna, and Conrad's enemy Géza II of Hungary allowed them to pass through unharmed. When the German army of 20,000 men arrived in Byzantine territory, Emperor Manuel I Komnenos feared they were going to attack him, and Byzantine troops were posted to ensure that there was no trouble. On September 10, the Germans arrived at Constantinople, where relations with Manuel were poor. There was a battle, after which the Germans were convinced that they should cross into Asia Minor as quickly as possible.

In Asia Minor, Conrad decided not to wait for the French, and marched towards Iconium, capital of the Seljuq Sultanate of Rûm. Conrad split his army into two divisions. The authority of the Byzantine Empire in the western provinces of Asia Minor was more nominal than real, with much of the provinces being a no-man's land controlled by Turkish nomads. Conrad underestimated the length of the march against Anatolia, and anyhow assumed that the authority of Emperor Manuel was greater in Anatolia than was in fact the case. Conrad took the knights and the best troops with him to march overland and sent the camp followers with Otto of Freising to follow the coastal road. The king's contingent was almost totally destroyed by the Seljuqs on October 25, 1147, at the second Battle of Dorylaeum.

French Route

The French crusaders departed from Metz in June 1147, led by Louis, Thierry of Alsace, Renaut I of Bar, Amadeus III, Count of Savoy and his half-brother William V of Montferrat, William VII of Auvergne, and others, along with armies from Lorraine, Brittany, Burgundy, and Aquitaine. A force from Provence, led by Alphonse of Toulouse, chose to wait until August and cross by sea. At Worms, Louis joined with crusaders from Normandy and England.

They followed Conrad's route fairly peacefully, although Louis came into conflict with King Geza of Hungary when Geza discovered Louis had allowed an attempted Hungarian usurper to join his army. Relations within Byzantine territory were grim, and the Lorrainers, who had marched ahead of the rest of the French, also came into conflict with the slower Germans whom they met on the way.

The French met the remnants of Conrad's army at Lopadion, and Conrad joined Louis's force. They followed Otto of Freising's route, moving closer to the Mediterranean coast, and they arrived at Ephesus in December, where they learned that the Turks were preparing to attack them. Manuel had sent ambassadors complaining about the pillaging and plundering that Louis had done along the way, and there was no guarantee that the Byzantines would assist them against the Turks. Meanwhile, Conrad fell sick and returned to Constantinople, where Manuel attended to him personally, and Louis, paying no attention to the warnings of a Turkish attack, marched out from Ephesus with the French and German survivors. The Turks were indeed waiting to attack, but in a small battle outside Ephesus, the French and Germans were victorious.

They reached Laodicea on the Lycus early in January 1148, around the same time Otto of Freising's army had been destroyed in the same area. After resuming the march, the vanguard under Amadeus of Savoy was separated from the rest of the army at Mount Cadmus, and Louis's troops suffered heavy losses from the Turks. After being delayed for a month by storms, most of the promised ships from Provence did not arrive at all. Louis and his associates claimed the ships that did make it for themselves, while the rest of the army had to resume the long march to Antioch. The army was almost entirely destroyed, either by the Turks or by sickness.

Siege of Damascus

The remains of the German and French armies eventually continued on to Jerusalem, where they planned an attack on the Muslim forces in Damascus. The Crusaders decided to attack Damascus from the west, where orchards would provide them with a constant food supply. They arrived at Daraiya on July 23. The following day, the well-prepared Muslims constantly attacked the army advancing through the orchards outside Damascus. The defenders had sought help from Saif ad-Din Ghazi I of Mosul and Nur ad-Din of Aleppo, who personally led an attack on the Crusader camp. The Crusaders were pushed back from the walls into the orchards, where they were prone to ambushes and guerrilla attacks.

According to William of Tyre, on July 27 the Crusaders decided to move to the plain on the eastern side of the city, which was less heavily fortified, but also had much less food and water. Some records indicate that Unur had bribed the leaders to move to a less defensible position, and that Unur had promised to break off his alliance with Nur ad-Din if the Crusaders went home. Meanwhile, Nur ad-Din and Saif ad-Din had by now arrived. With Nur ad-Din in the field it was impossible for the Crusaders to return to their better position. The local Crusader lords refused to carry on with the siege, and the three kings had no choice but to abandon the city. First Conrad, then the rest of the army, decided to retreat to Jerusalem on July 28, and they were followed the whole way by Turkish archers, who constantly harassed them.

Siege of Damascus: *A print of the Siege of Damascus.*

Aftermath

Each of the Christian forces felt betrayed by the other. In Germany, the Crusade was seen as a huge debacle, with many monks writing that it could only have been the work of the Devil. Despite the distaste for the memory of the Second Crusade, the experience had notable impact on German literature, with many epic poems of the late 12th century featuring battle scenes clearly inspired by the fighting in the crusade. The cultural impact of the Second Crusade was even greater in France. Unlike Conrad, the Louis's image was improved by the crusade, with many of the French seeing him as a suffering pilgrim king who quietly bore God's punishments.

Relations between the Eastern Roman Empire and the French were badly damaged by the Second Crusade. Louis and other French leaders openly accused Emperor Manuel I of colluding with Turkish attackers during the march across Asia Minor. The memory of the Second Crusade was to color French views of the Byzantines for the rest of the 12th and 13th centuries.

The Third Crusade

The Third Crusade (1189–1192) was an attempt by European leaders to reconquer the Holy Land from the Muslim sultan Saladin; it resulted in the capture of the important cities Acre and Jaffa, but failed to capture Jerusalem, the main motivation of the crusade.

Learning Objectives

Compare and contrast the Third Crusade with the first two

Key Takeaways

Key Points

- After the failure of the Second Crusade, the Zengid dynasty controlled a unified Syria and engaged in a successful conflict with the Fatimid rulers of Egypt; the Egyptian and Syrian forces were ultimately unified under Saladin, who employed them to reduce the Christian states and recapture Jerusalem in 1187.
- The Crusaders, mainly under the leadership of King Richard of England, captured Acre and Jaffa on their way to Jerusalem.
- Because of conflict with King Richard and to settle succession disputes, the German and French armies left the crusade early, weakening the Christian forces.
- After trying to overtake Jerusalem and having Jaffa change hands several times, Richard and Saladin finalized a treaty granting Muslim control over Jerusalem but allowing unarmed Christian pilgrims and merchants to visit the city.
- The Third Crusade differed from the First Crusade in several ways: kings led the armies into battle, it was in response to European losses, and it resulted in a treaty.

> *Key Terms*
>
> - **Richard the Lionheart**: King of England from July 6, 1189, until his death; famous for his reputation as a great military leader and warrior.
> - **Saladin**: The first sultan of Egypt and Syria and the founder of the Ayyubid dynasty; he led the Muslim military campaign against the Crusader states in the Levant.

Overview

The Third Crusade (1189–1192), also known as The Kings' Crusade, was an attempt by European leaders to reconquer the Holy Land from Saladin. The campaign was largely successful, capturing the important cities of Acre and Jaffa, and reversing most of Saladin's conquests, but it failed to capture Jerusalem, the emotional and spiritual motivation of the crusade.

After the failure of the Second Crusade, the Zengid dynasty controlled a unified Syria and engaged in a conflict with the Fatimid rulers of Egypt. The Egyptian and Syrian forces were ultimately unified under Saladin, who employed them to reduce the Christian states and recapture Jerusalem in 1187. Spurred by religious zeal, King Henry II of England and King Philip II of France (known as Philip Augustus) ended their conflict with each other to lead a new crusade. The death of Henry in 1189, however, meant the English contingent came under the command of his successor, King Richard I of England (known as Richard the Lionheart). The elderly Holy Roman Emperor Frederick Barbarossa also responded to the call to arms, leading a massive army across Anatolia, but he drowned in a river in Asia Minor on June 10, 1190, before reaching the Holy Land. His death caused tremendous grief among the German Crusaders, and most of his troops returned home.

After the Crusaders had driven the Muslims from Acre, Philip and Frederick's successor, Leopold V, Duke of Austria (known as Leopold the Virtuous), left the Holy Land in August 1191. On September 2, 1192, Richard and Saladin finalized a treaty granting Muslim control over Jerusalem but allowing unarmed Christian pilgrims and merchants to visit the city. Richard departed the Holy Land on October 2. The successes of the Third Crusade allowed the Crusaders to maintain considerable states in Cyprus and on the Syrian coast. However, the failure to recapture Jerusalem would lead to the Fourth Crusade.

Background

One of the major differences between the First and Third Crusades is that by the time of the Third Crusade, and to a certain degree during the Second, the Muslim opponents had unified under a single powerful leader. At the time of the First Crusade, the Middle East was severely divided by warring rulers. Without a unified front opposing them, the Christian troops were able to conquer Jerusalem, as well as the other Crusader states. But under the powerful force of the Seljuq Turks during the Second Crusade and the even more unified power of Saladin during the Third, the Europeans were unable to achieve their ultimate aim of holding Jerusalem.

After the failure of the Second Crusade, Nur ad-Din Zangi had control of Damascus and a unified Syria. Nur ad-Din also took over Egypt through an alliance, and appointed Saladin the sultan of these territories.

After Nur ad-Din's death, Saladin also took over Acre and Jerusalem, thereby wresting control of Palestine from the Crusaders, who had conquered the area 88 years earlier. Pope Urban III is said to have collapsed and died upon hearing this news, but it is not actually feasible that tidings of the fall of Jerusalem could have reached him by the time he died, although he did know of the battle of Hattin and the fall of Acre.

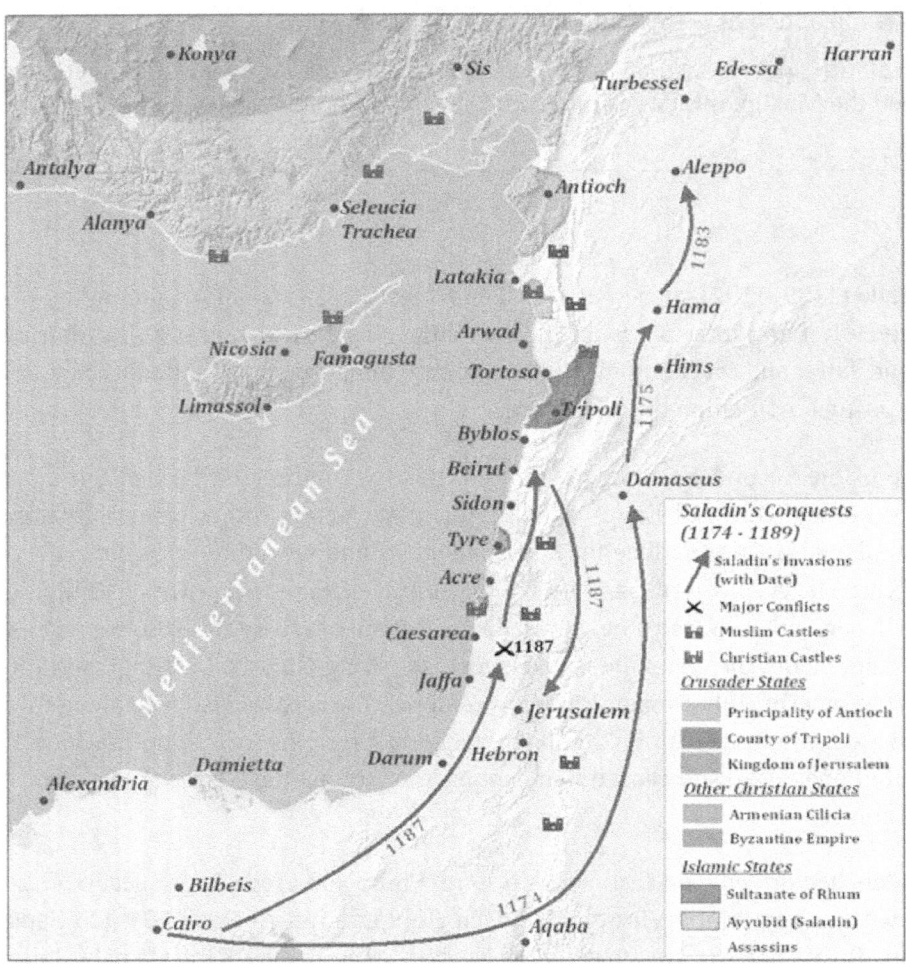

Saladin's Conquest (1174-1189): *Map of Saladin's Conquest into the Levant, including invasions routes, major conflicts, strongholds, and occupations.*

Siege of Acre

The Siege of Acre was one of the first confrontations of the Third Crusade, and a key victory for the Crusaders but a serious defeat for Saladin, who had hoped to destroy the whole of the Crusader kingdom.

Richard arrived at Acre on June 8, 1191, and immediately began supervising the construction of siege weapons to assault the city, which was captured on July 12. Richard, Philip, and Leopold quarreled over the spoils of the victory. Richard cast down the German flag from the city, slighting Leopold. The rest of the German army returned home.

On July 31, Philip also returned home, to settle the succession in Vermandois and Flanders, and Richard was left in sole charge of the Christian expeditionary forces. As in the Second Crusade, these disagreements and divisions within the European armies led to a weakening of the Christian forces.

Siege of Acre: *The Siege of Acre was the first major confrontation of the Third Crusade.*

Battle of Arsuf

After the capture of Acre, Richard decided to march to the city of Jaffa. Control of Jaffa was necessary before an attack on Jerusalem could be attempted. On September 7, 1191, however, Saladin attacked Richard's army at Arsuf, thirty miles north of Jaffa. Richard then ordered a general counterattack, which won the battle. Arsuf was an important victory. The Muslim army was not destroyed, despite the considerable casualties it suffered, but it was scattered; this was considered shameful by the Muslims and boosted the morale of the Crusaders. Richard was able to take, defend, and hold Jaffa, a strategically crucial move toward securing Jerusalem. By depriving Saladin of the coast, Richard seriously threatened his hold on Jerusalem.

Advances on Jerusalem and Negotiations

Following his victory at Arsuf, Richard took Jaffa and established his new headquarters there. In November 1191 the Crusader army advanced inland toward Jerusalem. On December 12 Saladin was forced by pressure from his emirs to disband the greater part of his army. Learning this, Richard pushed his army forward, spending Christmas at Latrun. The army then marched to Beit Nuba, only twelve miles from Jerusalem. Muslim morale in Jerusalem was so low that the arrival of the Crusaders would probably have caused the city to fall quickly. Appallingly bad weather—cold with heavy rain and hailstorms—combined with fear that if the Crusader army besieged Jerusalem it might be trapped by a relieving force, led to the decision to retreat back to the coast. In July 1192, Saladin's army suddenly attacked and captured Jaffa with thousands of men.

Richard was intending to return to England when he heard the news that Saladin and his army had captured Jaffa. Richard and a small force of little more than 2,000 men went to Jaffa by sea in a surprise attack. They stormed Jaffa from their ships and the Ayyubids, who had been unprepared for a naval attack, were driven from the city.

On September 2, 1192, following his defeat at Jaffa, Saladin was forced to finalize a treaty with Richard providing that Jerusalem would remain under Muslim control, but allowing unarmed Christian pilgrims and traders to visit the city. The city of Ascalon was a contentious issue, as it threatened communication between Saladin's dominions in Egypt and Syria; it was eventually agreed that Ascalon, with its defenses demolished, be returned to Saladin's control. Richard departed the Holy Land on October 9, 1192.

Aftermath and Comparisons

Neither side was entirely satisfied with the results of the war. Though Richard's victories had deprived the Muslims of important coastal territories and re-established a viable Frankish state in Palestine, many Christians in the Latin West felt disappointed that Richard had elected not to pursue the recapture of Jerusalem. Likewise, many in the Islamic world felt disturbed that Saladin had failed to drive the Christians out of Syria and Palestine. However, trade flourished throughout the Middle East and in port cities along the Mediterranean coastline.

The motivations and results of the Third Crusade differed from those of the First in several ways. Many historians contend that the motivations for the Third Crusade were more political than religious, thereby giving rise to the disagreements between the German, French, and English armies throughout the crusade. By the end, only Richard of England was left, and his small force was unable to finally overtake Saladin, despite successes at Acre and Jaffa. This infighting severely weakened the power of the European forces.

In addition, unlike the First Crusade, in the Second and Third Crusades kings led Crusaders into battle. The presence of European kings in battle set the armies up for instability, for the monarchs had to ensure their own territories were not threatened during their absence. During the Third Crusade, both the German and French armies were forced to return home to settle succession disputes and stabilize their kingdoms.

Furthermore, both the Second and Third Crusades were in response to European losses, first the fall of the Kingdom of Edessa and then the fall of Jerusalem to Saladin. These defensive expeditions could be seen as lacking the religious fervor and initiative of the First Crusade, which was entirely on the terms of the Christian armies.

Finally, the Third Crusade resulted in a treaty that left Jerusalem under Muslim dominion but allowed Christians access for trading and pilgrimage. In the past two crusades, the result had been to conquer and massacre or retreat, with no compromise or middle ground achieved. Despite the agreement in the Third Crusade, the failure to overtake Jerusalem led to still another crusade soon after.

The Fourth Crusade

Crusading became increasingly widespread in terms of geography and objectives during the 13th century and beyond, and crusades were aimed more at maintaining political and religious control over Europe than reclaiming the Holy Land.

Learning Objectives

Describe the failures of the Fourth Crusade

Key Takeaways

Key Terms

- **Crusader states**: A number of mostly 12th- and 13th-century feudal states created by Western European crusaders in Asia Minor, Greece, and the Holy Land, and in the eastern Baltic area during the Northern Crusades.
- **Great Schism**: The break of communion between what are now the Eastern Orthodox and Catholic churches, which has lasted since the 11th century.
- **Knights Templar**: Among the wealthiest and most powerful of the Western Christian military orders; prominent actors in the Crusades.
- **heretics**: People who holds beliefs or theories that are strongly at variance with established beliefs or customs, especially those held by the Roman Catholic Church.

Evolution of the Crusades

The Crusades were a series of religious wars undertaken by the Latin church between the 11th and 15th centuries. Crusades were fought for many reasons: to capture Jerusalem, recapture Christian territory, or defend Christians in non-Christian lands; as a means of conflict resolution among Roman Catholics; for political or territorial advantage; and to combat paganism and heresy.

The First Crusade arose after a call to arms in 1095 sermons by Pope Urban II. Urban urged military support for the Byzantine Empire and its Emperor, Alexios I, who needed reinforcements for his conflict with westward-migrating Turks in Anatolia. One of Urban's main aims was to guarantee pilgrims access to the holy sites in the Holy Land that were under Muslim control. Urban's wider strategy may have been to unite the eastern and western branches of Christendom, which had been divided since their split in 1054, and establish himself as head of the unified church. Regardless of the motivation, the response to Urban's preaching by people of many different classes across Western Europe established the precedent for later crusades.

As a result of the First Crusade, four primary Crusader states were created: the Kingdom of Jerusalem, the County of Edessa, the Principality of Antioch, and the County of Tripoli. On a popular level, the First Crusade unleashed a wave of impassioned, pious Catholic fury, which was expressed in the massacres of Jews that accompanied the Crusades and the violent treatment of the "schismatic" Orthodox Christians of the east.

Under the papacies of Calixtus II, Honorius II, Eugenius III, and Innocent II, smaller-scale crusading continued around the Crusader states in the early 12th century. The Knights Templar were recognized, and grants of crusading indulgences to those who opposed papal enemies are seen by some historians as the beginning of politically motivated crusades. The loss of Edessa in 1144 to Imad ad-Din Zengi led to preaching for what subsequently became known as the Second Crusade. King Louis VII and Conrad III led armies from France and Germany to Jerusalem and Damascus without winning any major victories. Bernard of Clairvaux, who had encouraged the Second Crusade in his preachings, was upset with the violence and slaughter directed toward the Jewish population of the Rhineland.

In 1187 Saladin united the enemies of the Crusader states, was victorious at the Battle of Hattin, and retook Jerusalem. According to Benedict of Peterborough, Pope Urban III died of deep sadness on October 19, 1187, upon hearing news of the defeat. His successor, Pope Gregory VIII, issued a papal bull that proposed a third crusade to recapture Jerusalem. This crusade failed to win control of Jerusalem from the Muslims, but did result in a treaty that allowed trading and pilgrimage there for Europeans.

Crusading became increasingly widespread in terms of geography and objectives during the 13th century; crusades were aimed at maintaining political and religious control over Europe and beyond and were not exclusively focused on the Holy Land. In Northern Europe the Catholic church continued to battle peoples whom they considered pagans; Popes such as Celestine III, Innocent III, Honorius III, and Gregory IX preached crusade against the Livonians, Prussians, and Russians. In the early 13th century, Albert of Riga established Riga as the seat of the Bishopric of Riga and formed the Livonian Brothers of the Sword to convert the pagans to Catholicism and protect German commerce.

Fourth Crusade

Innocent III began preaching what became the Fourth Crusade in 1200 in France, England, and Germany, but primarily in France. The Fourth Crusade (1202–1204) was a Western European armed expedition originally intended to conquer Muslim-controlled Jerusalem by means of an invasion through Egypt. Instead, a sequence of events culminated in the Crusaders sacking the city of Constantinople, the capital of the Christian-controlled Byzantine Empire. The Fourth Crusade never came to within 1,000 miles of its objective of Jerusalem, instead conquering Byzantium twice before being routed by the Bulgars at Adrianople.

In January 1203, en route to Jerusalem, the majority of the Crusader leadership entered into an agreement with the Byzantine prince Alexios Angelos to divert to Constantinople and restore his deposed father as emperor. The intention of the Crusaders was then to continue to the Holy Land with promised Byzantine financial and military assistance. On June 23, 1203, the main Crusader fleet reached Constantinople. Smaller contingents continued to Acre.

In August 1203, following clashes outside Constantinople, Alexios Angelos was crowned co-emperor (as Alexios IV Angelos) with Crusader support. However, in January 1204, he was deposed by a popular uprising in Constantinople. The Western Crusaders were no longer able to receive their promised payments, and when Alexios was murdered on February 8, 1204, the Crusaders and Venetians decided on the outright conquest of Constantinople. In April 1204, they captured and brutally sacked the city and set up a new Latin Empire, as well as partitioned other Byzantine territories among themselves.

Byzantine resistance based in unconquered sections of the empire such as Nicaea, Trebizond, and Epirus ultimately recovered Constantinople in 1261.

The Fourth Crusade is considered to be one of the final acts in the Great Schism between the Eastern Orthodox Church and Roman Catholic Church, and a key turning point in the decline of the Byzantine Empire and Christianity in the Near East.

Conquest of Constantinople: *A Medieval painting of the Conquest of Constantinople by the Crusaders in 1204.*

Later Crusades

After the failure of the Fourth Crusade to hold Constantinople or reach Jerusalem, Innocent III launched the first crusade against heretics, the Albigensian Crusade, against the Cathars in France and the County of Toulouse. Over the early decades of the century the Cathars were driven underground while the French monarchy asserted control over the region. Andrew II of Hungary waged the Bosnian Crusade against the Bosnian church, which was theologically Catholic but in long-term schism with the Roman Catholic Church. The conflict only ended with the Mongol invasion of Hungary in 1241. In the Iberian peninsula, Crusader privileges were given to those aiding the Templars, the Hospitallers, and the Iberian orders that merged with the Order of Calatrava and the Order of Santiago. The papacy declared frequent Iberian crusades, and from 1212 to 1265 the Christian kingdoms drove the Muslims back to the Emirate of Granada, which held out until 1492, when the Muslims and Jews were expelled from the peninsula.

Around this time, popularity and energy for the Crusades declined. One factor in the decline was the disunity and conflict among Latin Christian interests in the eastern Mediterranean. Pope Martin IV compromised the papacy by supporting Charles of Anjou, and tarnished its spiritual luster with botched secular "crusades" against Sicily and Aragon. The collapse of the papacy's moral authority and the rise of nationalism rang the death knell for crusading, ultimately leading to the Avignon Papacy and the Western Schism. The mainland Crusader states were extinguished with the fall of Tripoli in 1289 and the fall of Acre in 1291.

Centuries later, during the middle of the 15th century, the Latin church tried to organize a new crusade aimed at restoring the Eastern Roman or Byzantine Empire, which was gradually being torn down by the advancing Ottoman Turks. The attempt failed, however, as the vast majority of Greek civilians and a growing part of their clergy refused to recognize and accept the short-lived near-union of the churches of East and West signed at the Council of Florence and Ferrara by the Ecumenical patriarch Joseph II of Constantinople. The Greek population, reacting to the Latin conquest, believed that the Byzantine civilization that revolved around the Orthodox faith would be more secure under Ottoman Islamic rule. Overall, religious-observant Greeks preferred to sacrifice their political freedom and political independence in order to preserve their faith's traditions and rituals in separation from the Roman See.

In the late-14th and early-15th centuries, "crusades" on a limited scale were organized by the kingdoms of Hungary, Poland, Wallachia, and Serbia. These were not the traditional expeditions aimed at the recovery of Jerusalem but rather defensive campaigns intended to prevent further expansion to the west by the Ottoman Empire.

Attributions

CC licensed content, Specific attribution

- History of Christianity of the Middle Ages. **Provided by**: Wikipedia. **Located at**: http://en.wikipedia.org/wiki/History_of_Christianity_of_the_Middle_Ages%23Crusades. **License**: *CC BY-SA: Attribution-ShareAlike*
- Crusades. **Provided by**: Wikipedia. **Located at**: http://en.wikipedia.org/wiki/Crusades. **License**: *CC BY-SA: Attribution-ShareAlike*
- Schism. **Provided by**: Wikipedia. **Located at**: http://en.wikipedia.org/wiki/Schism. **License**: *CC BY-SA: Attribution-ShareAlike*
- Apotheosis. **Provided by**: Wikipedia. **Located at**: http://en.wikipedia.org/wiki/Apotheosis. **License**: *CC BY-SA: Attribution-ShareAlike*
- Zionism. **Provided by**: Wikipedia. **Located at**: http://en.wikipedia.org/wiki/Zionism. **License**: *CC BY-SA: Attribution-ShareAlike*
- Byzantine Empire. **Provided by**: Wikipedia. **Located at**: http://en.wikipedia.org/wiki/Byzantine_Empire. **License**: *CC BY-SA: Attribution-ShareAlike*
- Germanic peoples. **Provided by**: Wikipedia. **Located at**: http://en.wikipedia.org/wiki/Germanic_peoples. **License**: *CC BY-SA: Attribution-ShareAlike*
- Heresy. **Provided by**: Wikipedia. **Located at**: http://en.wikipedia.org/wiki/Heresy. **License**: *CC BY-SA: Attribution-ShareAlike*
- CouncilofClermont.jpg. **Provided by**: Wikipedia. **Located at**: https://en.wikipedia.org/wiki/First_Crusade. **License**: *CC BY-SA: Attribution-ShareAlike*
- Seljuk_Empire_locator_map.svg.png. **Provided by**: Wikipedia. **Located at**: https://en.wikipedia.org/wiki/Crusades. **License**: *CC BY-SA: Attribution-ShareAlike*
- Kingdom of Jerusalem. **Provided by**: Wikipedia. **Located at**: https://en.wikipedia.org/wiki/Kingdom_of_Jerusalem. **License**: *CC BY-SA: Attribution-ShareAlike*
- People's Crusade. **Provided by**: Wikipedia. **Located at**: https://en.wikipedia.org/wiki/People%27s_Crusade. **License**: *CC BY-SA: Attribution-ShareAlike*
- First Crusade. **Provided by**: Wikipedia. **Located at**: https://en.wikipedia.org/wiki/First_Crusade#Princes.27_Crusade. **License**: *CC BY-SA: Attribution-ShareAlike*
- CouncilofClermont.jpg. **Provided by**: Wikipedia. **Located at**: https://en.wikipedia.org/wiki/First_Crusade. **License**: *CC BY-SA: Attribution-ShareAlike*
- Seljuk_Empire_locator_map.svg.png. **Provided by**: Wikipedia. **Located at**: https://en.wikipedia.org/wiki/Crusades. **License**: *CC BY-SA: Attribution-ShareAlike*
- PeoplesCrusadeMassacre.jpg. **Provided by**: Wikipedia. **Located at**: https://en.wikipedia.org/wiki/First_Crusade#/media/File:PeoplesCrusadeMassacre.jpg. **License**: *CC BY-SA: Attribution-ShareAlike*
- 1099jerusalem.jpg. **Provided by**: Wikipedia. **Located at**: https://en.wikipedia.org/wiki/First_Crusade#/media/File:1099jerusalem.jpg. **License**: *CC BY-SA: Attribution-ShareAlike*
- Second Crusade. **Provided by**: Wikipedia. **Located at**: https://en.wikipedia.org/wiki/Second_Crusade. **License**: *CC BY-SA: Attribution-ShareAlike*

THE CRUSADES • 577

- CouncilofClermont.jpg. **Provided by**: Wikipedia. **Located at**: https://en.wikipedia.org/wiki/First_Crusade. **License**: *CC BY-SA: Attribution-ShareAlike*
- Seljuk_Empire_locator_map.svg.png. **Provided by**: Wikipedia. **Located at**: https://en.wikipedia.org/wiki/Crusades. **License**: *CC BY-SA: Attribution-ShareAlike*
- PeoplesCrusadeMassacre.jpg. **Provided by**: Wikipedia. **Located at**: https://en.wikipedia.org/wiki/First_Crusade#/media/File:PeoplesCrusadeMassacre.jpg. **License**: *CC BY-SA: Attribution-ShareAlike*
- 1099jerusalem.jpg. **Provided by**: Wikipedia. **Located at**: https://en.wikipedia.org/wiki/First_Crusade#/media/File:1099jerusalem.jpg. **License**: *CC BY-SA: Attribution-ShareAlike*
- Siege_of_Damascus.jpg. **Provided by**: Wikipedia. **Located at**: https://en.wikipedia.org/wiki/Second_Crusade#/media/File:Siege_of_Damascus.jpg. **License**: *CC BY-SA: Attribution-ShareAlike*
- Third Crusade. **Provided by**: Wikipedia. **Located at**: https://en.wikipedia.org/wiki/Third_Crusade. **License**: *CC BY-SA: Attribution-ShareAlike*
- Saladin. **Provided by**: Wikipedi. **Located at**: https://en.wikipedia.org/wiki/Saladin. **License**: *CC BY-SA: Attribution-ShareAlike*
- Siege of Acre. **Provided by**: Wikipedia. **Located at**: https://www.wikipedia.org/wiki/Siege_of_Acre. **License**: *CC BY-SA: Attribution-ShareAlike*
- CouncilofClermont.jpg. **Provided by**: Wikipedia. **Located at**: https://en.wikipedia.org/wiki/First_Crusade. **License**: *CC BY-SA: Attribution-ShareAlike*
- Seljuk_Empire_locator_map.svg.png. **Provided by**: Wikipedia. **Located at**: https://en.wikipedia.org/wiki/Crusades. **License**: *CC BY-SA: Attribution-ShareAlike*
- PeoplesCrusadeMassacre.jpg. **Provided by**: Wikipedia. **Located at**: https://en.wikipedia.org/wiki/First_Crusade#/media/File:PeoplesCrusadeMassacre.jpg. **License**: *CC BY-SA: Attribution-ShareAlike*
- 1099jerusalem.jpg. **Provided by**: Wikipedia. **Located at**: https://en.wikipedia.org/wiki/First_Crusade#/media/File:1099jerusalem.jpg. **License**: *CC BY-SA: Attribution-ShareAlike*
- Siege_of_Damascus.jpg. **Provided by**: Wikipedia. **Located at**: https://en.wikipedia.org/wiki/Second_Crusade#/media/File:Siege_of_Damascus.jpg. **License**: *CC BY-SA: Attribution-ShareAlike*
- Saladin's_Conquest_(1174-1189).jpg. **Provided by**: Wikipedia. **Located at**: https://en.wikipedia.org/wiki/Second_Crusade#/media/File:Saladin%27s_Conquest_(1174-1189).jpg. **License**: *CC BY-SA: Attribution-ShareAlike*
- 400px-Siege_of_Acre.jpg. **Provided by**: Wikipedia. **Located at**: https://en.wikipedia.org/wiki/Third_Crusade#/media/File:Siege_of_Acre.jpg. **License**: *CC BY-SA: Attribution-ShareAlike*
- Fourth Crusade. **Provided by**: Wikipedia. **Located at**: https://en.wikipedia.org/wiki/Fourth_Crusade. **License**: *CC BY-SA: Attribution-ShareAlike*
- Crusades. **Provided by**: Wikipedia. **Located at**: https://en.wikipedia.org/wiki/Crusades. **License**: *CC BY-SA: Attribution-ShareAlike*
- CouncilofClermont.jpg. **Provided by**: Wikipedia. **Located at**: https://en.wikipedia.org/wiki/First_Crusade. **License**: *CC BY-SA: Attribution-ShareAlike*
- Seljuk_Empire_locator_map.svg.png. **Provided by**: Wikipedia. **Located at**: https://en.wikipedia.org/wiki/Crusades. **License**: *CC BY-SA: Attribution-ShareAlike*
- PeoplesCrusadeMassacre.jpg. **Provided by**: Wikipedia. **Located at**: https://en.wikipedia.org/wiki/First_Crusade#/media/File:PeoplesCrusadeMassacre.jpg. **License**: *CC BY-SA: Attribution-ShareAlike*
- 1099jerusalem.jpg. **Provided by**: Wikipedia. **Located at**: https://en.wikipedia.org/wiki/First_Crusade#/media/File:1099jerusalem.jpg. **License**: *CC BY-SA: Attribution-ShareAlike*
- Siege_of_Damascus.jpg. **Provided by**: Wikipedia. **Located at**: https://en.wikipedia.org/wiki/Second_Crusade#/media/File:Siege_of_Damascus.jpg. **License**: *CC BY-SA: Attribution-ShareAlike*
- Saladin's_Conquest_(1174-1189).jpg. **Provided by**: Wikipedia. **Located at**: https://en.wikipedia.org/wiki/Second_Crusade#/media/File:Saladin%27s_Conquest_(1174-1189).jpg. **License**: *CC BY-SA: Attribution-ShareAlike*
- 400px-Siege_of_Acre.jpg. **Provided by**: Wikipedia. **Located at**: https://en.wikipedia.org/wiki/Third_Crusade#/media/File:Siege_of_Acre.jpg. **License**: *CC BY-SA: Attribution-ShareAlike*
- ConquestOfConstantinopleByTheCrusadersIn1204.jpg. **Provided by**: Wikipedia. **Located at**: https://en.wikipedia.org/wiki/Fourth_Crusade#/media/File:ConquestOfConstantinopleByTheCrusadersIn1204.jpg. **License**: *CC BY-SA: Attribution-ShareAlike*

The Development of Russia

The Princes of Rus

Rurik and the Foundation of Rus'

Rurik was a Varangian chieftain who established the first ruling dynasty in Russian history called the Rurik Dynasty in 862 near Novgorod. This dynasty went on to to establish Kievan Rus'.

Learning Objectives

Understand the key aspects of Rurik's rise to power and the establishment of Kievan Rus'

Key Takeaways

Key Points

- Rurik and his followers likely originated in Scandinavia and were related to Norse Vikings.
- The Primary Chronicle is one of the few written documents available that tells us how Rurik came to power.
- Local leaders most likely invited Rurik to establish order in the Ladoga region around 862, beginning a powerful legacy of Varangian leaders.
- The capital of Kievan Rus' moved from Novgorod to Kiev after Rurik's successor, Oleg, captured this southern city.

Key Terms

- **Primary Chronicle**: A text written in the 12th century that relates a detailed history of Rurik's rise to power.
- **Varangians**: Norse Vikings who established trade routes throughout Eurasia and eventually established a powerful dynasty in Russia.

> - **Rurik Dynasty**: The founders of Kievan Rus' who stayed in power until 1598 and established the first incarnation of a unified Russia.

Rurik

Rurik (also spelled Riurik) was a Varangian chieftain who arrived in the Ladoga region in modern-day Russia in 862. He built the Holmgard settlement = near Novgorod in the 860s and founded the first significant dynasty in Russian history called the Rurik Dynasty. Rurik and his heirs also established a significant geographical and political formation known as Kievan Rus', the first incarnation of modern Russia. The Rurik rulers continued to rule Russia into the 16th century and the mythology surrounding the man Rurik is often referred to as the official beginning of Russian history.

Primary Chronicle

The identity of the mythic leader Rurik remains obscure and unknown. His original birthplace, family history, and titles are shrouded in mystery with very few historical clues. Some 19th-century scholars attempted to identify him as Rorik of Dorestad (a Viking-Age trading outpost situated in the northern part of modern-day Germany). However, no concrete evidence exists to confirm this particular origin story.

A page from the Primary Chronicle or The Tale of Bygone Years: This rare written document was created in the 12th century and provides the most promising clues as to the arrival of Rurik in Ladoga.

The debate also continues as to how Rurik came to control the Novgorod region. However, some clues are available from the *Primary Chronicle*. This document is also known as *The Tale of Bygone Years* and was compiled in Kiev around 1113 by the monk Nestor. It relates the history of Kievan Rus' from 850 to 1110 with various updates and edits made throughout the 12th century by scholarly monks. It is difficult to untangle legend from fact, but this document provides the most promising clues regarding Rurik. *The Primary Chronicle* contends the Varangians were a Viking group, most likely from Sweden or northern Germany, who controlled trade routes across northern Russia and tied together various cultures across Eurasia.

A monument celebrating the millennial anniversary of the arrival of Rurik in Russia: *This modern interpretation of Rurik illustrates his powerful place in Russian history and lore.*

The various tribal groups, including Chuds, Eastern Slavs, Merias, Veses, and Krivichs, along the northern trade routes near Novgorod often cooperated with the Varangian Rus' leaders. But in the late 850s they rose up in rebellion, according to the P*rimary Chronicle*. However, soon after this rebellion, the local tribes near the Novgorod region began to experience internal disorder and conflict. These events prompted local tribal leaders to invite Rurik and his Varangian leaders back to the region in 862 to reinstate peace and order. This moment in history is known as the *Invitation of the Varangians* and is commonly regarded as the starting point of official Russian history.

Development of Kievan Rus'

According to legend, at the call of the local tribal leaders Rurik, along with his brothers Truvor and Sineus, founded the Holmgard settlement in Ladoga. This settlement is supposed to be at the site of modern-day Novgorod. However, newer archeological evidence suggests that Novgorod was not regularly settled until the 10th century, leading some to speculate that Holmgard refers to a smaller settlement just southeast of the city. The founding of Holmgard signaled a new era in Russian history and the three brothers became the famous founders of the first Rus' ruling dynasty.

Kievan Rus' in 1015: *The expansion and shifting borders of Kievan Rus' become apparent when looking at this map, which includes the two centers of power in Novgorod and Kiev.*

Rurik died in 879 and his successor, Oleg, continued the Varangian Rus' expansion in 882 by taking the southern city of Kiev from the Khasars and establishing the medieval state of Kievan Rus'. The capital officially moved to Kiev at this point. With this shift in power, there were two distinct capitals in Kievan Rus', the northern seat of Novgorod and the southern center in Kiev. In Kievan Rus' tradition, the heir apparent would oversee the northern site of Novgorod while the ruling Rus' king stayed in Kiev. Over the next 100 years local tribes consolidated and unified under the Rurik Dynasty, although local fractures and cultural differences continued to play a significant role in the attempt to maintain order under Varangian rule.

Vladimir I and Christianization

Vladimir I ruled from 980 to 1015 and was the first Kievan Rus' ruler to officially establish Orthodox Christianity as the new religion of the region.

> **Learning Objectives**
>
> Outline the shift from pagan culture to Orthodox Christianity under the rule of Vladimir I

> **Key Takeaways**
>
> *Key Points*
>
> - Vladimir I became the ruler of Kievan Rus' after overthrowing his brother Yaropolk in 978.
> - Vladimir I formed an alliance with Basil II of the Byzantine Empire and married his sister Anna in 988.
> - After his marriage Vladimir I officially changed the state religion to Orthodox Christianity and destroyed pagan temples and icons.
> - He built the first stone church in Kiev in 989, called the Church of the Tithes.
>
> *Key Terms*
>
> - **Constantinople**: The capital of the Byzantine Empire.
> - **Perun**: The pagan thunder god that many locals, and possibly Vladimir I, worshipped before Christianization.
> - **Basil II**: The Byzantine emperor who encouraged Vladimir to convert to Christianity and offered a political marriage alliance with his sister, Anna.

Vladimir I

Vladimir I, also known as Vladimir the Great or Vladimir Sviatoslavich the Great, ruled Kievan Rus' from 980 to 1015 and is famous for Christianizing this territory during his reign. Before he gained the throne in 980, he had been the Prince of Novgorod while his father, Sviatoslav of the Rurik Dynasty, ruled over Kiev. During his rule as the Prince of Novgorod in the 970s, and by the time Vladimir claimed power after his father's death, he had consolidated power between modern-day Ukraine and the Baltic Sea. He also successfully bolstered his frontiers against incursions from Bulgarian, Baltic, and Eastern nomads during his reign.

Early Myths of Christianization

The original Rus' territory was comprised of hundreds of small towns and regions, each with its own beliefs and religious practices. Many of these practices were based on pagan and localized traditions. The first mention of any attempts to bring Christianity to Rus' appears around 860. The Byzantine Patriarch Photius penned a letter in the year 867 that described the Rus' region right after the Rus'-Byzantine War of 860. According to Photius, the people of the region appeared enthusiastic about the new religion and he claims to have sent a bishop to convert the population. However, this low-ranking official did not successfully convert the population of Rus' and it would take another twenty years before a significant change in religious practices would come about.

The stories regarding these first Byzantine missions to Rus' during the 860s vary greatly and there is no official record to substantiate the claims of the Byzantine patriarchs. Any local people in small villages who embraced Christian practices would have had to contend with fears of change from their neighbors.

Vladimir I and His Rise to Power

The major player in the Christianization of the Rus' world is traditionally considered Vladimir I. He was born in 958, the youngest of three sons, to the Rus' king Sviatoslav. He ascended to the position of Prince of Novgorod around 969 while his oldest brother, Yaropolk, became the designated heir to the throne in Kiev. Sviatoslav died in 972, leaving behind a fragile political scene among his three sons. Vladimir was forced to flee to Scandinavia in 976 after Yaropolk murdered their brother Oleg and violently took control of Rus'.

Vladimir I: *A Christian representation of Vladimir I, who was the first Rus' leader to officially bring Christianity to the region.*

Vladimir fled to his kinsman Haakon Sigurdsson, who ruled Norway at the time. Together they gathered an army with the intent to regain control of
Rus' and establish Vladimir as the ruler. In 978, Vladimir returned to Kievan Rus' and successfully recaptured the territory. He also slew his brother Yaropolk in Kiev in the name of treason and, in turn, became the ruler of all of Kievan Rus'.

Constantinople and Conversion

Vladimir spent the next decade expanding his holdings, bolstering his military might, and establishing stronger borders against outside invasions.

He also remained a practicing pagan during these first years of his rule. He continued to build shrines to pagan gods, traveled with multiple wives and concubines, and most likely continued to promote the worship of the thunder god Perun. However, the *Primary Chronicle* (one of the few written documents about this time) states that in 987 Vladimir decided to send envoys to investigate the various religions neighboring Kievan Rus'.

According to the limited documentation from the time, the envoys that came back from Constantinople reported that the festivities and the presence of
God in the Christian Orthodox faith were more beautiful than anything they had ever seen, convincing Vladimir of his future religion.

Another version of events claims that Basil II of Byzantine needed a military and political ally in the face of a local uprising near Constantinople. In this version of the story, Vladimir demanded a royal marriage in return for his military help. He also announced he would Christianize Kievan Rus' if he was offered a desirable marriage tie. In either version of events, Vladimir vied for the hand of Anna, the sister of the ruling Byzantine emperor, Basil II. In order to marry her he was baptized in the Orthodox faith with the name Basil, a nod to his future brother-in-law.

17th-century Church of the Tithes: *The original stone Church of the Tithes collapsed from fire and sacking in the 12th century. However, two later versions were erected and destroyed in the 17th and 19th centuries.*

He returned to Kiev with his bride in 988 and proceeded to destroy all pagan temples and monuments. He also built the first stone church in Kiev named the Church of the Tithes starting in 989. These moves confirmed a deep political alliance between the Byzantine Empire and Rus' for years to come.

Baptism of Kiev

On his return in 988, Vladimir baptized his twelve sons and many boyars in official recognition of the new faith. He also sent out a message to all residents of Kiev, both rich and poor, to appear at the Dnieper River the following day. The next day the residents of Kiev who appeared were baptized in the river while Orthodox priests prayed. This event became known as the Baptism of Kiev.

Monument of Saint Vladimir in Kiev: *This statue sits close to the site of the original Baptism of Kiev.*

Pagan uprisings continued throughout Kievan Rus' for at least another century. Many local populations violently rejected the new religion and a particularly brutal uprising occurred in Novgorod in 1071. However, Vladimir became a symbol of the Russian Orthodox religion, and when he died in 1015 his body parts were distributed throughout the country to serve as holy relics.

Yaroslav the Wise

Yaroslav I, also known as Yaroslav the Wise, developed the first legal codes, beautified Kievan Rus', and formed major political alliances with the West during his nearly 40-year reign.

Learning Objectives

Outline the key elements of Yaroslav the Wise's reign and cultural influence

Key Takeaways

Key Points

- Yaroslav I came to power after a bloody civil war between brothers.
- He captured the Kievan throne because of the devotion of the Novgorodian and Varangian troops to his cause.
- Grand Prince Yaroslav was the first Kievan ruler to codify legal customs into the Pravda Yaroslava.
- He bolstered borders and encouraged political alliances with other major European powers during his reign.

Key Terms

- **primogeniture**: A policy that designates the oldest son as the heir to the throne upon the death of the father.
- **Novgorod Republic**: The northern stronghold of Kievan Rus' where Yaroslav gained early support for his cause.

Yaroslav the Wise

Yaroslav the Wise was the Grand Prince of Kiev from 1016 until his death in 1954. He was also vice-regent of Novgorod from 1010 to 1015 before his father, Vladimir the Great, died. During his reign he was known for spreading Christianity to the people of Rus', founding the first monasteries in the country, encouraging foreign alliances, and translating Greek texts in Church Slavonic. He also created some of the first legal codes in Kievan Rus'. These accomplishments during his lengthy rule granted him the title of Yaroslav the Wise in early chronicles of his life, and his legacy endures in both political and religious Russian history.

Youth and Rise to Power

Yaroslav was the son of the Varangian Grand Prince Vladimir the Great and most likely his second son with Rogneda of Polotsk. His youth remains
shrouded in mystery. Evidence from the *Primary Chronicle* and examination of his skeleton suggests he is one of the youngest sons of Vladimir, and possibly a son from a different mother. He was most likely born around the year 978.

Facial reconstruction of Yaroslav I by Mikhail Gerasimov

He was set as vice-regent of Novgorod in 1010, as befitted a senior heir to the throne. In this same time period Vladimir the Great granted the Kievan throne to his younger son, Boris. Relations were strained in this family. Yaroslav refused to pay Novgorodian tribute to Kiev in 1014, and only Vladimir's death in 1015 prevented a severe war between these two regions. However, the next few years were spent in a bitter civil war between the brothers. Yarsolav was vying for the seat in Kiev against his brother Sviatopolk I, who was supported by Duke Boleslaw I of Chrobry. In the ensuing years of carnage, three of his brothers were murdered (Boris, Gleb, and Svyatoslav). Yaroslav won the first battle at Kiev against Sviatopolk in 1016 and Sviatopolk was forced to flee to Poland.

After this significant triumph Yaroslav's ascent to greatness began, and he granted freedoms and privileges to the Novgorod Republic, who had
helped him gain the Kievan throne. These first steps also most likely led to the first legal code in Kievan Rus' under Yaroslav. He was chronicled as Yaroslav the Wise in retellings of these events because of his even-handed dealing with the wars, but it is highly possible he was involved in the murder of his brothers and other gruesome acts of war.

Wise Reign

The civil war did not completely end in 1016. Sviatopolk returned in 1018 and retook Kiev. However, Varangian and Novgorodian troops recaptured the capital and Sviatopolk fled to the West never to return. Another fraternal conflict arose in 1024 when another brother of Yaroslav's, Mstislav of Chernigov, attempted to capture Kiev. After this conflict, the brothers split the Kievan Rus' holdings, with Mstislav ruling over the region left of the Dnieper River.

Yaroslav the Wise was instrumental in defending borders and expanding the holdings of Kievan Rus'. He protected the southern borders from nomadic tribes, such as the Pechenegs, by constructing a line of military forts. He also successfully laid claim to Chersonesus in the Crimea and came to a peaceful agreement with the Byzantine Empire after many years of conflict and disagreements over land holdings.

Saint Sophia Cathedral in Kiev: *This iconic cathedral fell into disrepair and was almost destroyed during the Soviet era, but it was saved and restored to its former glory.*

Yaroslav the Wise garnered his thoughtful reputation due to his prolific years in power. He was a ruler that loved literature, religion, and the written language. His many accomplishments included:

- Building the Saint Sophia Cathedral and the first monasteries in Russia, named Saint George and Saint Irene.
- Founding a library and a school at the Saint Sophia Cathedral and encouraging the translation of Greek texts into Church Slavonic.
- Developing a more established hierarchy within the Russian Orthodox Church, including a statute outlining the rights of the clergy and establishing the sobor of bishops.
- Beautifying Kiev with elements of design taken from the Byzantine Empire, including the Golden Gate of Kiev.
- Compiling the first book of laws in Kievan Rus', called the Pravda Yaroslava. This first compi-

lation set down clear laws that reflected the feudal landscape of the 11th century. This initial legal code would live on and be refined into the Russkaya Pravda in the 12th century.

- Establishing primogeniture, which meant that his eldest son would succeed him as Grand Prince over Novgorod and Kiev, hoping that future conflict between his children would be avoided.

Golden Gate of Kiev in 2016: *This important monument was one of the great architectural accomplishments created under Yaroslav the Wise, and now features a monument to the ruler, seen in the foreground.*

Family and Death

Yaroslav married Ingegerd Olofsdotter, the daughter of the king of Sweden, in 1019. He had many sons and encouraged them to remain on good terms,
after all the years of warfare and bloodshed with his own brothers. He also married three of his daughters to European royalty. Elizabeth, Anna, and Anastasia married Harald III of Norway, Henry I of France, and Andrew I of Hungary respectively. These marriages forged powerful alliances with European states.

Daughters of Yaroslav the Wise: *This 11th-century fresco in Saint Sophia's Cathedral shows four of Yaroslav's daughter, probably Anne, Anastasia, Elizabeth, and Agatha.*

The Grand Prince Yaroslav I died in 1054 and was buried in Saint Sophia's Cathedral. His expansion of culture and military might, along with his unification of Kievan Rus', left a powerful impression on Russian history. Many towns and monuments remain dedicated to this leader.

The Mongol Threat

The Mongol Empire expanded its holdings in the 13th century and established its rule over most of the major Kievan Rus' principalities after brutal military invasions over the course of many years.

Learning Objectives

Describe the attacks by th Mongols on the Russian principality

> ## Key Takeaways
>
> ### Key Points
>
> - The major principalities of Kievan Rus' became increasingly fractured and independent after the death of Yaroslav the Wise in 1054.
> - The first Mongol attempt to capture Kievan territories occurred in 1223 at the Battle of the Kalka River.
> - The Mongol forces began a heavy military campaign on Kievan Rus' in 1237 under the rule of Batu Khan.
> - Kiev was sacked and taken in 1240, starting a long era of Mongol rule in the region.
>
> ### Key Terms
>
> - **Tatar yoke**: The name given to the years of Mongol rule in Kievan Rus', which meant heavy taxation and the possibility of local invasions at any time.
> - **Golden Horde**: The western section of the Mongol Empire that included Kievan Rus' and parts of Eastern Europe.
> - **Sarai**: The new capital of the Mongol Empire in the southern part of Kievan Rus'.

Mongol Invasion

The Mongol invasion of the Kievan Rus' principalities began in 1223 at the Battle of the Kalka River. However, the Mongol armies ended up focusing their military might on other regions after this bloody meeting, only to return in 1237. For the next three years the Mongol forces took over the major princely cities of Kievan Rus' and finally forced most principalities to submit to foreign rule and taxation. Rus' became part of what is known as the Golden Horde, the western extension of the Mongol Empire located in the eastern Slavic region. Some of the new taxes and rules of law lasted until 1480 and had a lasting impact on the shape and character of modern Russia.

Fragmented Kievan Rus'

After the end of the unifying reign of Yaroslav the Wise, Kievan Rus' became fragmented and power was focused on smaller polities. The great ruler's death in 1054 brought about major power struggles between his sons and princes in outlying provinces. By the 12th century, after years of fighting amongst the princes, power was centered around smaller principalities. This unsettled trend left Kievan Rus' much more fragmented. Power was passed down to the eldest in the local ruling dynasty and cities were responsible for their own defenses. The Byzantine Empire was also facing major upheaval, which meant a central Russian ally and trading partner was weakened, which, in turn, weakened the strength and wealth of Kievan Rus'.

The principalities of Kievan Rus' at its height, 1054-1132: *The princely regions were relatively unified into the 12th century but slowly separated and became more localized as fights over regions and power among the nobility continued.*

Mongol Invasion

The already fragile alliances between the smaller Rus' principalities faced further tension when the nomadic invaders, the Mongols, arrived on the scene during this fractured era. These invaders originated on the steppes of central Asia and were unified under the infamous warrior and leader Genghis Khan. The Mongols began to expand their power across the continent. The Battle of the Kalka River in 1223 initiated the first attempt of the Mongol forces to capture Kievan Rus'. It was a bloody battle that ended with the execution of Mstislav of Kiev executed the Kievan forces greatly weakened. The Mongols were superior in their military tactics and stretched the Rus' forces considerably, however after executing the Kievan prince, the forces went back to Asia to rejoin Genghis Khan. However, the Mongol threat was far from over, and they returned in 1237.

The Sacking of Suzdal in 1238 by Batu Khan: *This 16th-century depiction of the Mongol invasion highlights the bloodshed and military might of the invaders.*

Over the course of the years 1237 and 1238, the Mongol leader, Batu Khan, led his 35,000 mounted archers to burn down Moscow and Kolomna. Then he split his army into smaller units that tackled the princely polities one at a time. Only Novgorod and Pskov were spared major destruction during this time. Refugees from the southern principalities, where destruction was widespread and devastating, were forced to flee to the harsh northern forests, where good soil and resources were scarce. The final victory for Batu Khan came in December 1240 when he stormed the great capital of Kiev and prevailed.

Tatar Rule and the Golden Horde

The Mongols, also known as the Tatars, built their new capital, Sarai, in the south along the Volga River. All the major principalities, such as Novgorod, Smolensk, and Pskov, submitted to Mongol rule. The age of this economic and cultural rule is often called the Tatar yoke, but over the course of 200 years, it was a relatively peaceful rule. The Tatars followed in the footsteps of Genghis Khan and refrained from settling the entire region or forcing local populations to adopt specific religious or cultural traditions. However, Rus' principalities paid tribute and taxes to the Mongol rulers regularly, under the umbrella of the Golden Horde (the western portion of the Mongol Empire). Around 1259 this tribute was organized into a census that was enforced by the locals Rus' princes on a regular schedule, collected, and taken to the capital of Sarai for the Mongol leaders.

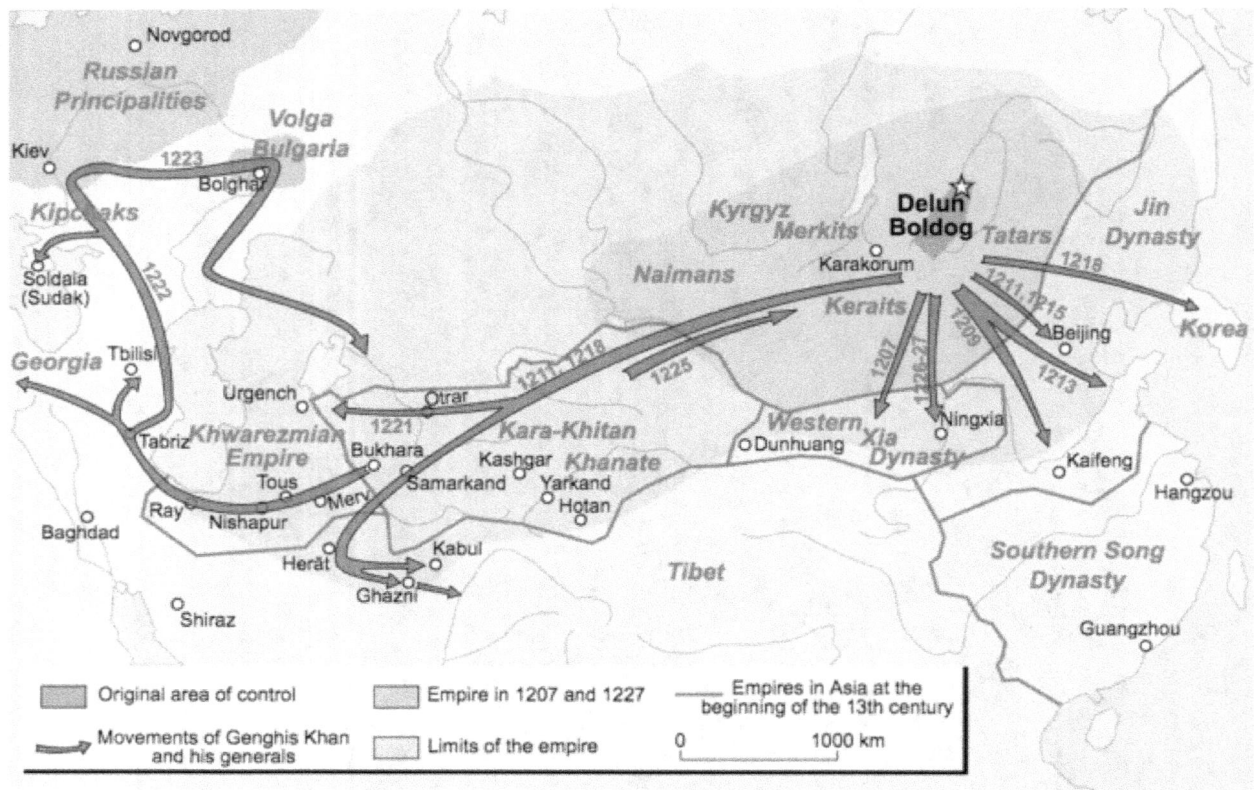

A map of the Mongol Empire as it expanded: This illustration shows the rapid expansion of the Mongol Empire as it traveled west into what became known as the Golden Horde.

Effects of Mongol Rule

Despite the fact that the established Tatar rule was relatively peaceful, demanding taxation and the devastation from years of invasion left many major cities in disrepair for decades. It took years to rebuild Kiev and Pskov. However, Novgorod continued to flourish and the relatively new city centers of the Moscow and Tver began to prosper. Another downside to the Tatar presence was the continued threat of invasion and destruction, which happened sporadically during their presence. Each new military invasion meant heavy tolls on the local population and years of reconstruction.

Culturally, the Mongol rule brought about major shifts during the first century of their presence. Extensive postal road systems, military organization, and powerful dynasties were established by Tatar alliances.

Capital punishment and torture also became more widespread during the years of Tatar rule. Some noblemen also changed their names and adopted the Tatar language, bringing about a shift in the aesthetic, linguistic, and cultural ties of Russia life. Many scholars also note that the Mongol rule was a major cause of the division of East Slavic people in Rus' into three distinctive modern-day nations, Russia, Ukraine, and Belarus.

Ivan I and the Rise of Moscow

The small trading outpost of Moscow in the north of Rus' transformed into a wealthy cultural center in the 14th century under the leadership of Ivan I.

Learning Objectives

Outline the key points that helped Moscow become so powerful and how Ivan I accomplished these major victories

Key Takeaways

Key Points

- Moscow was considered a small trading outpost under the principality of Vladimir-Suzdal into the 13th century.
- Power struggles and constant raids under the Mongol Empire's Golden Horde caused once powerful cities, such as Kiev, to struggle financially and culturally.
- Ivan I utilized the relative calm and safety of the northern city of Moscow to entice a larger population and wealth to move there.
- Alliances between Golden Horde leaders and Ivan I saved Moscow from many of the raids and destruction of other centers, like Tver.

Key Terms

- **Tver**: A rival city to Moscow that eventually lost favor under the Golden Horde.
- **Grand Prince of Vladimir**: The title given to the ruler of this northern province, where Moscow was situated.

The Rise of Moscow

Moscow was only a small trading outpost in the principality of Vladimir-Suzdal in Kievan Rus' before the invasion of Mongol forces during the 13th century. However, due to the unstable environment of the

Golden Horde, and the deft leadership of Ivan I at a critical time during the 13th century, Moscow became a safe haven of prosperity during his reign. It also became the new seat of power of the Russian Orthodox Church.

Ivan I

Ivan I (also known as Ivan Kalita) was born around 1288 to the Prince of Moscow, Daniil Aleksandrovich. He was born during a time of devastation and upheaval in Rus'. Kiev had been overtaken by the invading Mongol forces in 1240, and most of the Rus' principalities had been absorbed into the Golden Horde of the Mongol Empire by the time Ivan was born. He ascended to the seat of Prince of Moscow after the death of his father, and then the death of his older brother Yury.

Ivan I: *He was born around 1288 and died in either 1340 or 1341, still holding the title of Grand Prince of Vladimir.*

Ivan I stepped into a role that had already been expanded by his predecessors. Both his older brother and his father had captured nearby lands, including Kolomna and Mozhaisk. Yury had also made a successful alliance with the Mongol leader Uzbeg Khan and married his sister, securing more power and advantages within the hierarchy of the Golden Horde.

Ivan I continued the family tradition and petitioned the leaders of the Golden Horde to gain the seat of Grand Prince of Vladimir. His other three rivals, all princes of Tver, had previously been granted the title in prior years. However they were all subsequently deprived of the title and all three aspiring princes also eventually ended up murdered. Ivan I, on the other hand, garnered the title from Khan Muhammad Ozbeg in 1328. This new title, which he kept until his death around 1340, meant he could collect taxes from the Russian lands as a ruling prince and position his tiny city as a major player in the Vladimir region.

Moscow's Rise

During this time of upheaval, the tiny outpost of Moscow had multiple advantages that repositioned this town and set it up for future prosperity under Ivan I. Three major contributing factors helped Ivan I relocate power to this area:

- It was situated in between other major principalities on the east and west so it was often protected from the more devastating invasions.
- This relative safety, compared to Tver and Ryazan, for example, started to bring in tax-paying citizens who wanted a safe place to build a home and earn a livelihood.
- Finally, Moscow was set up perfectly along the trade route from Novgorod to the Volga River, giving it an economic advantage from the start.

Ivan I also spurred on the growth of Moscow by actively recruiting people to move to the region. Inaddition, he bought the freedom of people who had been captured by the extensive Mongol raids. These recruits further bolstered the population of Moscow. Finally, he focused his attention on establishing peace and routing out thieves and raiding parties in the region, making for a safe and calm metaphorical island in a storm of unsettled political and military upsets.

Kievan Rus' 1220-1240: *This map illustrates the power dynamics at play during the 13th century shortly before Ivan I was born. Sarai, the capital of the Golden Horde, sat to the southeast, while Moscow (not visible on this map) was tucked up in the northern forests of Vladimir-Suzdal.*

Ivan I knew that the peace of his region depended upon keeping up an alliance with the Golden Horde, which he did faithfully. Moscow's increased wealth during this era also allowed him to loan money to neighboring principalities. These regions then became indebted to Moscow, bolstering its political and financial position.

In addition, a few neighboring cities and villages were subsumed into Moscow during the 1320s and 1330s, including Uglich, Belozero, and Galich. These shifts slowly transformed the tiny trading outpost into a bustling city center in the northern forests of what was once Kievan Rus'.

Russian Orthodox Church and The Center of Moscow

Ivan I committed some of Moscow's new wealth to building a splendid city center and creating an iconic religious setting. He built stone churches in the center of Moscow with his newly gained wealth. Ivan I also tempted one of the most important religious leaders in Rus', the Orthodox Metropolitan Peter, to the city of Moscow. Before the rule of the Golden Horde the original Russian Orthodox Church was based in Kiev. After years of devastation, Metropolitan Peter transferred the seat of power to Moscow where a new Renaissance of culture was blossoming. This perfectly timed transformation of Moscow coincided with the decades of devastation in Kiev, effectively transferring power to the north once again.

Peter of Moscow and scenes from his life as depicted in a 15th-century icon: This religious leader helped bring cultural power to Moscow by moving the seat of the Russian Orthodox Church there during Ivan I's reign.

One of the most lasting accomplishments of Ivan I was to petition the Khan based in Sarai to designate his son, who would become Simeon the Proud, as the heir to the title of Grand Prince of Vladimir. This agreement a line of succession that meant the ruling head of Moscow would almost always hold power over the principality of Vladimir, ensuring Moscow held a powerful position for decades to come.

Attributions

CC licensed content, Specific attribution

- Rurik. **Provided by**: Wikipedia. **Located at**: https://en.wikipedia.org/wiki/Rurik. **License**: *CC BY-SA: Attribution-ShareAlike*
- Varangians. **Provided by**: Wikipedia. **Located at**: https://en.wikipedia.org/wiki/Varangians. **License**: *CC BY-SA: Attribution-ShareAlike*
- Primary Chronicle. **Provided by**: Wikipedia. **Located at**: https://en.wikipedia.org/wiki/Primary_Chronicle. **License**: *CC BY-SA: Attribution-ShareAlike*
- Kievan Rus. **Provided by**: Wikipedia. **Located at**: https://en.wikipedia.org/wiki/Kievan_Rus. **License**: *CC BY-SA: Attribution-ShareAlike*
- Veliky Novgorod. **Provided by**: Wikipedia. **Located at**: https://en.wikipedia.org/wiki/Veliky_Novgorod. **License**: *CC BY-SA: Attribution-ShareAlike*
- Rurik Dynasty. **Provided by**: Wikipedia. **Located at**: https://en.wikipedia.org/wiki/Rurik_dynasty. **License**: *CC BY-SA: Attribution-ShareAlike*
- Tale of Bygone Years. **Provided by**: Wikipedia. **Located at**: https://en.wikipedia.org/wiki/Primary_Chronicle#/media/File:14_2_List_of_Radzivill_Chron.jpg. **License**: *Public Domain: No Known Copyright*
- Rurik. **Provided by**: Wikipedia. **Located at**: https://en.wikipedia.org/wiki/Rurik#/media/File:1000_Rurik.JPG. **License**: *CC BY-SA: Attribution-ShareAlike*
- Location of Rus'. **Provided by**: Wikipedia. **Located at**: https://en.wikipedia.org/wiki/Kievan_Rus%27#/media/File:Kievan-rus-1015-1113-(en).png. **License**: *CC BY-SA: Attribution-ShareAlike*
- Christianization of Kievan Rus. **Provided by**: Wikipedia. **Located at**: https://en.wikipedia.org/wiki/Christianization_of_Kievan_Rus%27. **License**: *CC BY-SA: Attribution-ShareAlike*
- Church of the Tithes. **Provided by**: Wikipedia. **Located at**: https://en.wikipedia.org/wiki/Church_of_the_Tithes. **License**: *CC BY-SA: Attribution-ShareAlike*
- Vladimir the Great. **Provided by**: Wikipedia. **Located at**: https://en.wikipedia.org/wiki/Vladimir_the_Great. **License**: *CC BY-SA: Attribution-ShareAlike*
- Constantinople. **Provided by**: Wikipedia. **Located at**: https://en.wikipedia.org/wiki/Constantinople. **License**: *CC BY-SA: Attribution-ShareAlike*
- Christianization of the Rus' Khaganate. **Provided by**: Wikipedia. **Located at**: https://en.wikipedia.org/wiki/Christianization_of_the_Rus%27_Khaganate. **License**: *CC BY-SA: Attribution-ShareAlike*
- Tale of Bygone Years. **Provided by**: Wikipedia. **Located at**: https://en.wikipedia.org/wiki/Primary_Chronicle#/media/File:14_2_List_of_Radzivill_Chron.jpg. **License**: *Public Domain: No Known Copyright*
- Rurik. **Provided by**: Wikipedia. **Located at**: https://en.wikipedia.org/wiki/Rurik#/media/File:1000_Rurik.JPG. **License**: *CC BY-SA: Attribution-ShareAlike*
- Location of Rus'. **Provided by**: Wikipedia. **Located at**: https://en.wikipedia.org/wiki/Kievan_Rus%27#/media/File:Kievan-rus-1015-1113-(en).png. **License**: *CC BY-SA: Attribution-ShareAlike*
- Vladimir I Sviatoslavich. **Provided by**: Wikipedia. **Located at**: https://en.wikipedia.org/wiki/Vladimir_the_Great#/media/File:Vladimir-I-Sviatoslavich.jpg. **License**: *Public Domain: No Known Copyright*
- Saint Vladimir Monument. **Provided by**: Wikipedia. **Located at**: https://en.wikipedia.org/wiki/Christianization_of_Kievan_Rus%27#/media/File:%D0%92%D0%BE%D0%BB%D0%BE%D0%B4%D0%B8%D0%BC%D0%B8%D1%80_%D0%92%D0%B5%D0%BB%D0%B8%D0%BA%D0%B8%D0%B9.JPG. **License**: *CC BY-SA: Attribution-ShareAlike*
- The 17th-century Church of the Tithes. **Provided by**: Wikipedia. **Located at**: https://en.wikipedia.org/wiki/Church_of_the_Tithes#/media/File:De%C5%9Batynna_cerkva.png. **License**: *Public Domain: No Known Copyright*
- Saint Sophia's Cathedral. **Provided by**: Wikipedia. **Located at**: https://en.wikipedia.org/wiki/Saint_Sophia%27s_Cathedral,_Kiev. **License**: *CC BY-SA: Attribution-ShareAlike*
- Golden Gate of Kiev. **Provided by**: Wikipedia. **Located at**: https://en.wikipedia.org/wiki/Golden_Gate,_Kiev. **License**: *CC BY-SA: Attribution-ShareAlike*
- Yaroslav the Wise. **Provided by**: Wikipedia. **Located at**: https://en.wikipedia.org/wiki/Yaroslav_the_Wise. **License**: *CC BY-SA: Attribution-ShareAlike*
- Russkaya Pravda. **Provided by**: Wikipedia. **Located at**: https://en.wikipedia.org/wiki/Russkaya_Pravda. **License**: *CC BY-SA: Attribution-ShareAlike*
- Tale of Bygone Years. **Provided by**: Wikipedia. **Located at**: https://en.wikipedia.org/wiki/Primary_Chronicle#/media/File:14_2_List_of_Radzivill_Chron.jpg. **License**: *Public Domain: No Known Copyright*
- Rurik. **Provided by**: Wikipedia. **Located at**: https://en.wikipedia.org/wiki/Rurik#/media/File:1000_Rurik.JPG. **License**: *CC BY-*

- Location of Rus'. **Provided by**: Wikipedia. **Located at**: https://en.wikipedia.org/wiki/Kievan_Rus%27#/media/File:Kievan-rus-1015-1113-(en).png. **License**: *CC BY-SA: Attribution-ShareAlike*
- Vladimir I Sviatoslavich. **Provided by**: Wikipedia. **Located at**: https://en.wikipedia.org/wiki/Vladimir_the_Great#/media/File:Vladimir-I-Sviatoslavich.jpg. **License**: *Public Domain: No Known Copyright*
- Saint Vladimir Monument. **Provided by**: Wikipedia. **Located at**: https://en.wikipedia.org/wiki/Christianization_of_Kievan_Rus%27#/media/File:%D0%92%D0%BE%D0%BB%D0%BE%D0%B4%D0%B8%D0%BC%D0%B8%D1%80_%D0%92%D0%B5%D0%BB%D0%B8%D0%BA%D0%B8%D0%B9.JPG. **License**: *CC BY-SA: Attribution-ShareAlike*
- The 17th-century Church of the Tithes. **Provided by**: Wikipedia. **Located at**: https://en.wikipedia.org/wiki/Church_of_the_Tithes#/media/File:De%C5%9Batynna_cerkva.png. **License**: *Public Domain: No Known Copyright*
- Daughters of Yaroslav the Wise. **Provided by**: Wikipedia. **Located at**: https://en.wikipedia.org/wiki/Yaroslav_the_Wise#/media/File:Daughters_of_Yaroslav_the_Wise.jpg. **License**: *Public Domain: No Known Copyright*
- Facial Reconstruction of Yaroslav. **Provided by**: Wikipedia. **Located at**: https://en.wikipedia.org/wiki/Yaroslav_the_Wise#/media/File:Yaroslav_recontruccion.png. **License**: *CC BY-SA: Attribution-ShareAlike*
- Saint Sophia Cathedral in Kiev. **Provided by**: Wikipedia. **Located at**: https://en.wikipedia.org/wiki/Saint_Sophia%27s_Cathedral,_Kiev#/media/File:Kij%C3%B3w_-_Sob%C3%B3r_M%C4%85dro%C5%9Bci_Bo%C5%BCej_02.jpg. **License**: *CC BY-SA: Attribution-ShareAlike*
- Golden Gate of Kiev in 2016. **Provided by**: Wikipedia. **Located at**: https://en.wikipedia.org/wiki/Golden_Gate,_Kiev#/media/File:GoldenGate2016.jpg. **License**: *CC BY-SA: Attribution-ShareAlike*
- Sarai (city). **Provided by**: Wikipedia. **Located at**: https://en.wikipedia.org/wiki/Sarai_%28city%29. **License**: *CC BY-SA: Attribution-ShareAlike*
- Mongol Invasion of Rus'. **Provided by**: Wikipedia. **Located at**: https://en.wikipedia.org/wiki/Mongol_invasion_of_Rus%27. **License**: *CC BY-SA: Attribution-ShareAlike*
- Kievan Rus'. **Provided by**: Wikipedia. **Located at**: https://en.wikipedia.org/wiki/Kievan_Rus%27. **License**: *CC BY-SA: Attribution-ShareAlike*
- Mongol Empire. **Provided by**: Wikipedia. **Located at**: https://en.wikipedia.org/wiki/Mongol_Empire. **License**: *CC BY-SA: Attribution-ShareAlike*
- Yuri II of Vladimir. **Provided by**: Wikipedia. **Located at**: https://en.wikipedia.org/wiki/Yuri_II_of_Vladimir. **License**: *CC BY-SA: Attribution-ShareAlike*
- Battle of the Kalka River. **Provided by**: Wikipedia. **Located at**: https://en.wikipedia.org/wiki/Battle_of_the_Kalka_River. **License**: *CC BY-SA: Attribution-ShareAlike*
- Batu Khan. **Provided by**: Wikipedia. **Located at**: https://en.wikipedia.org/wiki/Batu_Khan. **License**: *CC BY-SA: Attribution-ShareAlike*
- Tale of Bygone Years. **Provided by**: Wikipedia. **Located at**: https://en.wikipedia.org/wiki/Primary_Chronicle#/media/File:14_2_List_of_Radzivill_Chron.jpg. **License**: *Public Domain: No Known Copyright*
- Rurik. **Provided by**: Wikipedia. **Located at**: https://en.wikipedia.org/wiki/Rurik#/media/File:1000_Rurik.JPG. **License**: *CC BY-SA: Attribution-ShareAlike*
- Location of Rus'. **Provided by**: Wikipedia. **Located at**: https://en.wikipedia.org/wiki/Kievan_Rus%27#/media/File:Kievan-rus-1015-1113-(en).png. **License**: *CC BY-SA: Attribution-ShareAlike*
- Vladimir I Sviatoslavich. **Provided by**: Wikipedia. **Located at**: https://en.wikipedia.org/wiki/Vladimir_the_Great#/media/File:Vladimir-I-Sviatoslavich.jpg. **License**: *Public Domain: No Known Copyright*
- Saint Vladimir Monument. **Provided by**: Wikipedia. **Located at**: https://en.wikipedia.org/wiki/Christianization_of_Kievan_Rus%27#/media/File:%D0%92%D0%BE%D0%BB%D0%BE%D0%B4%D0%B8%D0%BC%D0%B8%D1%80_%D0%92%D0%B5%D0%BB%D0%B8%D0%BA%D0%B8%D0%B9.JPG. **License**: *CC BY-SA: Attribution-ShareAlike*
- The 17th-century Church of the Tithes. **Provided by**: Wikipedia. **Located at**: https://en.wikipedia.org/wiki/Church_of_the_Tithes#/media/File:De%C5%9Batynna_cerkva.png. **License**: *Public Domain: No Known Copyright*
- Daughters of Yaroslav the Wise. **Provided by**: Wikipedia. **Located at**: https://en.wikipedia.org/wiki/Yaroslav_the_Wise#/media/File:Daughters_of_Yaroslav_the_Wise.jpg. **License**: *Public Domain: No Known Copyright*
- Facial Reconstruction of Yaroslav. **Provided by**: Wikipedia. **Located at**: https://en.wikipedia.org/wiki/Yaroslav_the_Wise#/media/File:Yaroslav_recontruccion.png. **License**: *CC BY-SA: Attribution-ShareAlike*
- Saint Sophia Cathedral in Kiev. **Provided by**: Wikipedia. **Located at**: https://en.wikipedia.org/wiki/Saint_Sophia%27s_Cathe-

- dral,_Kiev#/media/File:Kij%C3%B3w_-_Sob%C3%B3r_M%C4%85dro%C5%9Bci_Bo%C5%BCej_02.jpg. **License**: *CC BY-SA: Attribution-ShareAlike*
- Golden Gate of Kiev in 2016. **Provided by**: Wikipedia. **Located at**: https://en.wikipedia.org/wiki/Golden_Gate,_Kiev#/media/File:GoldenGate2016.jpg. **License**: *CC BY-SA: Attribution-ShareAlike*
- Sacking_of_Suzdal_by_Batu_Khan.jpg. **Provided by**: Wikipedia. **Located at**: https://en.wikipedia.org/wiki/Mongol_invasion_of_Rus%27#/media/File:Sacking_of_Suzdal_by_Batu_Khan.jpg. **License**: *Public Domain: No Known Copyright*
- Genghis Khan Mongol Empire. **Provided by**: Wikipedia. **Located at**: https://en.wikipedia.org/wiki/Mongol_invasion_of_Rus%27#/media/File:Genghis_Khan_empire-en.svg. **License**: *CC BY-SA: Attribution-ShareAlike*
- Principalities of Kievan Rus'. **Provided by**: Wikipedia. **Located at**: https://en.wikipedia.org/wiki/Kievan_Rus%27#/media/File:Principalities_of_Kievan_Rus%27_(1054-1132).jpg. **License**: *CC BY-SA: Attribution-ShareAlike*
- Moscow. **Provided by**: Wikipedia. **Located at**: https://en.wikipedia.org/wiki/Moscow. **License**: *CC BY-SA: Attribution-ShareAlike*
- Daniel of Moscow. **Provided by**: Wikipedia. **Located at**: https://en.wikipedia.org/wiki/Daniel_of_Moscow. **License**: *CC BY-SA: Attribution-ShareAlike*
- Peter of Moscow. **Provided by**: Wikipedia. **Located at**: https://en.wikipedia.org/wiki/Peter_of_Moscow. **License**: *CC BY-SA: Attribution-ShareAlike*
- Yury of Moscow. **Provided by**: Wikipedia. **Located at**: https://en.wikipedia.org/wiki/Yury_of_Moscow. **License**: *CC BY-SA: Attribution-ShareAlike*
- Grand Duchy of Moscow. **Provided by**: Wikipedia. **Located at**: https://en.wikipedia.org/wiki/Grand_Duchy_of_Moscow. **License**: *CC BY-SA: Attribution-ShareAlike*
- Vladimir-Suzdal. **Provided by**: Wikipedia. **Located at**: https://en.wikipedia.org/wiki/Vladimir-Suzdal. **License**: *CC BY-SA: Attribution-ShareAlike*
- Ivan I of Moscow. **Provided by**: Wikipedia. **Located at**: https://en.wikipedia.org/wiki/Ivan_I_of_Moscow. **License**: *CC BY-SA: Attribution-ShareAlike*
- Tale of Bygone Years. **Provided by**: Wikipedia. **Located at**: https://en.wikipedia.org/wiki/Primary_Chronicle#/media/File:14_2_List_of_Radzivill_Chron.jpg. **License**: *Public Domain: No Known Copyright*
- Rurik. **Provided by**: Wikipedia. **Located at**: https://en.wikipedia.org/wiki/Rurik#/media/File:1000_Rurik.JPG. **License**: *CC BY-SA: Attribution-ShareAlike*
- Location of Rus'. **Provided by**: Wikipedia. **Located at**: https://en.wikipedia.org/wiki/Kievan_Rus%27#/media/File:Kievan-rus-1015-1113-(en).png. **License**: *CC BY-SA: Attribution-ShareAlike*
- Vladimir I Sviatoslavich. **Provided by**: Wikipedia. **Located at**: https://en.wikipedia.org/wiki/Vladimir_the_Great#/media/File:Vladimir-I-Sviatoslavich.jpg. **License**: *Public Domain: No Known Copyright*
- Saint Vladimir Monument. **Provided by**: Wikipedia. **Located at**: https://en.wikipedia.org/wiki/Christianization_of_Kievan_Rus%27#/media/File:%D0%92%D0%BE%D0%BB%D0%BE%D0%B4%D0%B8%D0%BC%D0%B8%D1%80_%D0%92%D0%B5%D0%BB%D0%B8%D0%BA%D0%B8%D0%B9.JPG. **License**: *CC BY-SA: Attribution-ShareAlike*
- The 17th-century Church of the Tithes. **Provided by**: Wikipedia. **Located at**: https://en.wikipedia.org/wiki/Church_of_the_Tithes#/media/File:De%C5%9Batynna_cerkva.png. **License**: *Public Domain: No Known Copyright*
- Daughters of Yaroslav the Wise. **Provided by**: Wikipedia. **Located at**: https://en.wikipedia.org/wiki/Yaroslav_the_Wise#/media/File:Daughters_of_Yaroslav_the_Wise.jpg. **License**: *Public Domain: No Known Copyright*
- Facial Reconstruction of Yaroslav. **Provided by**: Wikipedia. **Located at**: https://en.wikipedia.org/wiki/Yaroslav_the_Wise#/media/File:Yaroslav_recontruccion.png. **License**: *CC BY-SA: Attribution-ShareAlike*
- Saint Sophia Cathedral in Kiev. **Provided by**: Wikipedia. **Located at**: https://en.wikipedia.org/wiki/Saint_Sophia%27s_Cathedral,_Kiev#/media/File:Kij%C3%B3w_-_Sob%C3%B3r_M%C4%85dro%C5%9Bci_Bo%C5%BCej_02.jpg. **License**: *CC BY-SA: Attribution-ShareAlike*
- Golden Gate of Kiev in 2016. **Provided by**: Wikipedia. **Located at**: https://en.wikipedia.org/wiki/Golden_Gate,_Kiev#/media/File:GoldenGate2016.jpg. **License**: *CC BY-SA: Attribution-ShareAlike*
- Sacking_of_Suzdal_by_Batu_Khan.jpg. **Provided by**: Wikipedia. **Located at**: https://en.wikipedia.org/wiki/Mongol_invasion_of_Rus%27#/media/File:Sacking_of_Suzdal_by_Batu_Khan.jpg. **License**: *Public Domain: No Known Copyright*
- Genghis Khan Mongol Empire. **Provided by**: Wikipedia. **Located at**: https://en.wikipedia.org/wiki/Mongol_invasion_of_Rus%27#/media/File:Genghis_Khan_empire-en.svg. **License**: *CC BY-SA: Attribution-ShareAlike*
- Principalities of Kievan Rus'. **Provided by**: Wikipedia. **Located at**: https://en.wikipedia.org/wiki/Kievan_Rus%27#/media/File:Principalities_of_Kievan_Rus%27_(1054-1132).jpg. **License**: *CC BY-SA: Attribution-ShareAlike*

- Ivan I. **Provided by**: Wikipedia. **Located at**: https://en.wikipedia.org/wiki/Ivan_I_of_Moscow#/media/File:Ivan_Kalita.jpg. **License**: *Public Domain: No Known Copyright*
- Kievan Rus' 1220-1240. **Provided by**: Wikipedia. **Located at**: https://en.wikipedia.org/wiki/Moscow#/media/File:Kyivan_Rus%27_1220-1240.png. **License**: *CC BY-SA: Attribution-ShareAlike*
- Peter of Moscow. **Provided by**: Wikipedia. **Located at**: https://en.wikipedia.org/wiki/Peter_cf_Moscow#/media/File:PietrodiMosca.jpg. **License**: *CC BY-SA: Attribution-ShareAlike*

The Grand Duchy of Moscow

The Formation of Russia

Ivan III became Grand Prince of Moscow in 1462 and proceeded to refuse the Tatar yoke, collect surrounding lands, and consolidate political power around Moscow. His son, Vasili III, continued in his footsteps marking an era known as the "Gathering of the Russian Lands."

Learning Objectives

Outline the key points that led to a consolidated northern region under Ivan III and Vasili III in Moscow

Key Takeaways

Key Points

- Moscow had risen to a powerful position in the north due to its location and relative wealth and stability during the height of the Golden Horde.
- Ivan III overtook Novgorod, along with his four brothers' landholdings, which began a process consolidating power under the Grand Prince of Moscow.
- Ivan III was the first prince of Rus' to style himself as the Tsar in the grand tradition of the Orthodox Byzantine Empire.
- Vasili III followed in his father's footsteps and continued a regime of consolidating land and practicing domestic intolerance that suppressed any attempts to disobey the seat of Moscow.

Key Terms

- **Muscovite Sudebnik**: The legal code crafted by Ivan III that further consolidated his

> power and outlined harsh punishments for disobedience.
> - **Novgorod**: Moscow's most prominent rival in the northern region.
> - **boyars**: Members of the highest ruling class in feudal Rus', second only to the princes.

Gathering of the Russian Lands

Ivan III was the first Muscovite prince to consolidate Moscow's position of power and successfully incorporate the rival cities of Tver and Novgorod under the umbrella of Moscow's rule. These shifts in power in the Northern provinces created the first semblance of a "Russian" state (though that name would not be utilized for another century). Ivan the Great was also the first Rus' prince to style himself a Tsar, thereby setting up a strong start for his successor son, Vasili III. Between the two leaders, what would become known as the "Gathering of the Russian Lands" would occur and begin a new era of Russian history after the Mongol Empire's Golden Horde.

Ivan III and the End of the Golden Horde

Ivan III Vasilyevich, also known as Ivan the Great, was born in Moscow in 1440 and became Grand Prince of Moscow in 1462. He ruled from this seat of power until his death in 1505. He came into power when Moscow had many economic and cultural advantages in the norther provinces. His predecessors had expanded Moscow's holdings from a mere 600 miles to 15,000. The seat of the Russian Orthodox Church was also centered in Moscow starting in the 14th century. In addition, Moscow had long been a loyal ally to the ruling Mongol Empire and had an optimal position along major trade routes between Novgorod and the Volga River.

Ivan III: *He held the title of Grand Prince of Moscow between 1462 and 1505.*

However, one of Ivan the Great's most substantial accomplishments was refusing the Tatar yoke (as the Mongol Empire's stranglehold on Rus' lands has been called) in 1476. Moscow refused to pay its normal Golden Horde taxes starting in that year, which spurred Khan Ahmed to wage war against the city in 1480. It took a number of months before the Khan retreated back to the steppe. During the following year, internal fractures within the Mongol Empire greatly weakened the hold of Mongol rulers on the northeastern Rus' lands, which effectively freed Moscow from its old duties.

Moscow's Land Grab

The other major political change that Ivan III instigated was a major consolidation of power in the northern principalities, often called the "Gathering of the Russian Lands." Moscow's primary rival, Novgorod, became Ivan the Great's first order of business. The two grand cities had been locked in dispute for over a century, but Ivan III waged a harsh war that forced Novgorod to cede its land to Moscow after many uprisings and attempted alliances between Novgorod and Lithuania. The official state document accepting Moscow's rule was signed by Archbishop Feofil of Novgorod in 1478. Any revolts that arose out of Novgorod over the next decade were swiftly put down and any disobedient Novgorodian royal family members were removed to Moscow or other outposts to discourage further outbursts.

In addition to capturing his greatest rival city, Ivan III also collected his four brothers' local lands over the course of his rule, further expanding and consolidating the land under the power of the Grand Prince of Moscow. Ivan III also levied his political, economic, and military might over the course of his reign to gain control of Yaroslavl, Rostov, Tver, and Vyatka, forming one of the most unified political formations in the region since Vladimir the Great. This new political formation was in contrast to centuries of local princes ruling over their regions relatively autonomously.

Palace of Facets pillar: *This decadent pillar resides in the Palace of Facets built by Italian architects in stone in the mostly wooden Moscow Kremlin. This banquet hall was only one of many major architectural feats Ivan III built during his reign in Moscow.*

Ivan the Great also greatly shaped the future of the Rus' lands. These major shifts included:

- Styling himself the "Tsar and Autocrat" in Byzantine style, essentially stepping into the new leadership position in Orthodoxy after the fall of the Byzantine Empire. These changes also occurred after he married Sophia Paleologue of Constantinople, who had brought court and religious rituals from the Byzantine Empire.

- He stripped the boyars of theirlocalized and state power and essentially created a sovereign state that paid homage to Moscow.

- He oversaw the creation of a new legal code, called Muscovite Sudebnik in 1497, which further consolidated his place as the highest ruler of the northern Rus' lands and instated harsh penalties for disobedience, sacrilege, or attempts to undermine the crown.

- The princes of formerly powerful principalities now under Moscow's rule were placed in the role of service nobility, rather than sovereign rulers as they once were.

- Ivan III's power was partly due to his alliance with Russian Orthodoxy, which created an atmos-

Vasili III

Vasili III was the son of Sophia Paleologue and Ivan the Great and the Grand Prince of Moscow from 1505 to 1533. He followed in his father's footsteps and continued to expand Moscow's landholdings and political clout. He annexed, Pskov, Volokolamsk, Ryazan, and Novgorod-Seversky during his reign. His most spectacular grab for power was his capture of Smolensk, the great stronghold of Lithuania. He utilized a rebellious ally in the form of the Lithuanian prince Mikhail Glinski to gain this major victory.

Vasili III: *This piece was created by a contemporary artist and depicts Vasili III as a scholar and leader.*

Vasili III also followed in his father's oppressive footsteps. He utilized alliances with the Orthodox Church to put down any rebellions or feudal disputes. He limited the power of the boyars and the once-powerful Rurikid dynasties in newly conquered provinces. He also increased the gentry's landholdings, once more consolidating power around Moscow. In general, Vasili III's reign was marked by an oppressive atmosphere; he carried out harsh penalties for speaking out against the power structure or showing the slightest disobedience to the crown.

Ivan the Terrible

Ivan IV, or Ivan the Terrible, reigned from 1547 to 1584 and became the first tsar of Russia. His reign was punctuated with severe oppression and cultural and political expansion, leaving behind a complex legacy.

Learning Objectives

Outline the key points of Ivan IV's policies and examine the positive and negative aspects of his rule

Key Takeaways

Key Points

- Ivan IV is often known as Ivan the Terrible, even though the more correct translation is akin to Ivan the Fearsome or Ivan the Awesome.
- Ivan IV was the first Rus' prince to title himself "Tsar of All the Russias" beginning the long tradition of rule under the tsars.
- Lands in the Crimea, Siberia, and modern-day Tatarstan were all subsumed into Russian lands under Ivan IV.
- The persecution of the boyars during Ivan IV's reign began under the harsh regulations of the oprichnina.

Key Terms

- **Moscow Print Yard**: The first publishing house in Russia, which was opened in 1553.
- **boyar**: A member of the feudal ruling elite who was second only to the princes in Russian territories.
- **oprichnina**: A state policy enacted by Ivan IV that made him absolute monarch of much of the north and hailed in an era of boyar persecution. Ivan IV successfully grabbed large chunks of land from the nobility and created his own personal guard, the oprichniki, during this era.

Ivan IV

Ivan IV Vasileyevich is widely known as Ivan the Terrible or Ivan the Fearsome. He was the Grand Prince of Moscow from 1533 to 1547 and reigned as the "Tsar of all the Russias" from 1547 until he died in 1584. His complex years in power precipitated military conquests, including Kazan and Astrakhan, that changed the shape and demographic character of Russia forever. He also reshaped the political formation of the Russian state, oversaw a cultural Renaissance in Russia, and shifted power to the head of state, the tsar, a title that had never before been given to a prince in the Rus' lands.

Rise to Power

Ivan IV was born in 1530 to Vasili III and Elena Glinskaya. He was three when he was named the Grand Prince of Moscow after his father's death. Some say his years as the child vice-regent of Moscow under manipulative boyar powers shaped his views for life. In 1547, at the age of sixteen, he was crowned "Tsar of All the Russias" and was the first person to be coronated with that title. This title claimed the heritage of Kievan Rus' while firmly establishing a new unified Russian state. He also married Anastasia Romanovna, which tied him to the powerful Romanov family.

18th-century portrait of Ivan IV: *Images of Ivan IV often display a prominent brow and a frowning mouth.*

Domestic Innovations and Changes

Despite Ivan IV's reputation as a paranoid and moody ruler, he also contributed to the cultural and political shifts that would shape Russia for centuries. Among these initial changes in relatively peaceful times he:

- Revised the law code, the Sudebnik of 1550, which initiated a standing army, known as the streltsy. This army would help him in future military conquests.

- Developed the Zemsky Sobor, a Russian parliament, along with the council of the nobles, known as the Chosen Council.

- Regulated the Church more effectively with the Council of the Hundred Chapters, which regulated Church traditions and the hierarchy.

- Established the Moscow Print Yard in 1553 and brought the first printing press to Russia.
- Oversaw the construction of St. Basil's Cathedral in Moscow.

St. Basil's Cathedral: *This iconic structure was one cultural accomplishment created under Ivan IV's rule.*

Oprichnina and Absolute Monarchy

The 1560s were difficult with Russia facing drought and famine, along with a number of Tatar invasions, and a sea-trading blockade from the Swedes and Poles. Ivan IV's wife, Anastasia, was also likely poisoned and died in 1560, leaving Ivan shaken and, some sources say, mentally unstable. Ivan IV threatened to abdicate and fled from Moscow in 1564. However, a group of boyars went to beg Ivan to return in order to keep the peace. Ivan agreed to return with the understanding he would be granted absolute power and then instituted what is known as the oprichnina.

1911 painting by Apollinary Vasnetsov: *This painting represents people fleeing from the Oprichniki, the secret service and military oppressors of Ivan IV's reign.*

This agreement changed the way the Russian state worked and began an era of oppression, executions, and state surveillance. It split the Russian lands into two distinct spheres, with the northern region around the former Novgorod Republic placed under the absolute power of Ivan IV. The boyar council oversaw the rest of the Russian lands. This new proclamation also started a wave of persecution and against the boyars. Ivan IV executed, exiled, or forcibly removed hundreds of boyars from power, solidifying his legacy as a paranoid and unstable ruler.

Military
Conquests and Foreign Relations

Ivan IV established a powerful trade agreement with England and even asked for asylum, should he need it in his fights with the boyars, from Elizabeth I. However, Ivan IV's greatest legacy remains his conquests, which reshaped Russia and pushed back Tatar powers who had been dominating and invading the region for centuries.

His first conquest was the Kazan Khanate, which had been raiding the northeast region of Russia for decades. This territory sits in modern-day Tatarstan. A faction of Russian supporters were already rising up in the region but Ivan IV led his army of 150,000 to battle in June of 1552. After months of siege and blocking Kazan's water supply, the city fell in October. The conquest of the entire Kazan Khanate reshaped relations between the nomadic people and the Russian state. It also created a more diverse population under the fold of the Russian state and the Church.

Ivan IV also embarked on the Livonian War, which lasted 24 years. The war pitted Russia against the Swedish Empire, the Polish-Lithuanian Commonwealth, and Poland. The Polish leader, Stefan Batory, was an ally of the Ottoman Empire in the south, which was also in a tug-of-war with Russia over territory. These two powerful entities on each edge of Russian lands, and the prolonged wars, left the economy in Moscow strained and Russian resources scarce in the 1570s.

Ivan IV also oversaw two decisive territorial victories during his reign. The first was the defeat of the Crimean horde, which meant the southern lands were once again under Russian leadership. The second expansion of Russian territory was headed by Cossack leader Yermak Timofeyevich. He led expeditions into Siberian territories that had never been under Russian rule. Between 1577 and 1580 many new Siberian regions had reached agreements with Russian leaders, allowing Ivan IV to style himself "Tsar of Siberia" in his last years.

Ivan IV's throne: *This decadent throne mirrors Ivan the Terrible's love of power and opulence.*

Madness and Legacy

Ivan IV left behind a compelling and contradictory legacy. Even his nickname "terrible" is a source for confusion. In Russian the word *grozny* means "awesome," "powerful" or "thundering," rather than "terrible" or "mad." However, Ivan IV often behaved in ruthless and paranoid ways that favors the less flattering interpretation. He persecuted the long-ruling boyars and often accused people of attempting to murder him (which makes some sense when you look at his family's history). His often reckless foreign policies, such as the drawn out Livonian War, left the economy unstable and fertile lands a wreck. Legend also suggests he murdered his son Ivan Ivanovich, whom he had groomed for the throne, in 1581, leaving the throne to his childless son Feodor Ivanovich. However, his dedication to culture and innovation reshaped Russia and solidified its place in the East.

The Time of Troubles

The Time of Troubles occurred between 1598 and 1613 and was caused by severe famine, prolonged dynastic disputes, and outside invasions from Poland and Sweden. The worst of it ended with the coronation of Michael I in 1613.

Learning Objectives

Outline the distinctive features of the Time of Troubles and how they eventually ended

Key Takeaways

Key Points

- The Time of Troubles started with the death of the childless Tsar Feodor Ivanovich, which spurred an ongoing dynastic dispute.
- Famine between 1601 and 1603 caused massive starvation and further strained Russia.
- Two false heirs to the throne, known as False Dmitris, were backed by the Polish-Lithuanian Commonwealth that wanted to grab power in Moscow.
- Rurikid Prince Dmitry Pozharsky and Novgorod merchant Kuzma Minin led the final resistance against Polish invasion that ended the dynastic dispute and reclaimed Moscow in 1613.

Key Terms

- **Feodor Ivanovich**: The last tsar of the Rurik Dynasty, whose death spurred on a major dynastic dispute.
- **Dmitry Pozharsky**: The Rurikid prince that successfully ousted Polish forces from Moscow.
- **Zemsky Sobor**: A form of Russian parliament that met to vote on major state decisions, and was comprised of nobility, Orthodox clergy, and merchant representatives.

The Time of Troubles was an era of Russian history dominated by a dynastic crisis and exacerbated by ongoing wars with Poland and Sweden, as well as a devastating famine. It began with the death of the childless last Russian Tsar of the Rurik Dynasty, Feodor Ivanovich, in 1598 and continued until the establishment of the Romanov Dynasty in 1613. It took another six years to end two of the wars that had started during the Time of Troubles, including the Dymitriads against the Polish-Lithuanian Commonwealth.

Famine and Unrest

At the death of Feodor Ivanovich, the last Rurikid Tsar, in 1598, his brother-in-law and trusted advisor, Boris Godunov, was elected his successor by the Zemsky Sobor (Great National Assembly). Godunov was a leading boyar and had accomplished a great deal under the reign of the mentally-challenged and childless Feodor. However, his position as a boyar caused unrest among the Romanov clan who saw it as an affront to follow a lowly boyar. Due to the political unrest, strained resources, and factions against his rule, he was not able to accomplish much during his short reign, which only lasted until 1605.

Tsar Boris Godunov: *His short-lived reign was beset by famine and resistance from the boyars.*

While Godunov was attempting to keep the country stitched together, a devastating famine swept across Russian from 1601 to 1603. Most likely caused by a volcanic eruption in Peru in 1600, the temperatures stayed well below normal during the summer months and often went below freezing at night. Crops failed and about two million Russians, a third of the population, perished during this famine. This famine also caused people to flock to Moscow for food supplies, straining the capital both socially and financially.

Dynastic Uncertainty and False Dmitris

The troubles did not cease after the famine subsided. In fact, 1603 brought about new political and dynastic struggles. Feodor Ivanovich's younger brother was reportedly stabbed to death before the Tsar's death, but somepeople still believed he had fled and was alive. The first of the nicknamed False Dmitris appeared in the Polish-Lithuanian Commonwealth in 1603 claiming he was the lost young brother of Ivan the Terrible. Polish forces saw this pretender's appearance as an opportunity to regain land and influence in Russia and the some 4,000 troops comprised of Russian exiles, Lithuanians, and Cossacks crossed the border and began what is known as the Dymitriad wars.

Vasili IV of Russia: *He was the last member of the Rurikid Dynasty to rule in Moscow between 1606 and 1610.*

False Dmitri was supported by enough Polish and Russian rebels hoping for a rich reward that he was married to Marina Mniszech and ascended to the throne in Moscow at Boris Godunov's death in 1605. Within a year Vasily Shuisky (a Rurikid prince) staged an uprising against False Dmitri, murdered him, and seized control of power in Moscow for himself. He ruled between 1606 and 1610 and was known as Vasili IV. However, the boyars and mercenaries were still displeased with this new ruler. At the same time as Shuisky's ascent, a new False Dmitri appeared on the scene with the backing of the Polish-Lithuanian magnates.

An Empty Throne and Wars

Shuisky retained power long enough to make a treaty with Sweden, which spurred a worried Poland into officially beginning the Polish-Muscovite War that lasted from 1605 to 1618. The struggle over who would gain control of Moscow became entangled and complex once Poland became an acting participant. Shuisky was still on the throne, both the second False Dmitri and the son of the Polish king, Władysław, were attempting to take control.

None of the three pretenders succeeded, however, when the Polish king himself, Sigismund III, decided he would take the seat in Moscow.

Russia was stretched to its limit by 1611. Within the five years after Boris Godunov's death powers had shifted considerably:

- The boyars quarreled amongst themselves over who should rule Moscow while the throne remained empty.
- Russian Orthodoxy was imperiled and many Orthodox religious leaders were imprisoned.
- Catholic Polish forces occupied the Kremlin in Moscow and Smolensk.
- Swedish forces had taken over Novgorod in retaliation to Polish forces attempting to ally with Russia.
- Tatar raids continued in the south leaving many people dead and stretched for resources.

The End of Troubles

Two strong leaders arose out of the chaos of the first decade of the 17th century to combat the Polish invasion and settle the dynastic dispute. The powerful Novgordian merchant Kuzma Minin along with the Rurikid Prince Dmitry Pozharsky rallied enough forces to push back the Polish forces in Russia. The new Russian rebellion first pushed Polish forces back to the Kremlin, and between November 3rd and 6th (New Style) Prince Pozharsky had forced the garrison to surrender in Moscow. November 4 is known as National Unity Day, however it fell out of favor during Communism, only to be reinstated in 2005.

The dynastic wars finally came to an end when the Grand National Assembly elected Michael Romanov, the son of the metropolitan Philaret, to the throne in 1613. The new Romanov Tsar, Michael I, quickly had the second False Dmitri's son and wife killed, to stifle further uprisings.

Michael I: *The first Romanov Tsar to be crowned in 1613.*

Despite the end to internal unrest, the wars with Sweden and Poland would last until 1618 and 1619 respectively, when peace treaties were finally enacted. These treaties forced Russia to cede some lands, but the dynastic resolution and the ousting of foreign powers unified most people in Russia behind the new Romanov Tsar and started a new era.

The Romanovs

The Romanov Dynasty was officially founded at the coronation of Michael I in 1613. It was the second royal dynasty in Russia after the Rurikid princes of the Middle Ages. The Romanov name stayed in power until the abdication of Tsar Nicholas II in 1917.

> ## Learning Objectives
>
> Explain the rise of power of the House of Romanov and the first major Russian Tsars of this dynasty

> ## Key Takeaways
>
> ### Key Points
>
> - The Romanovs were exiled during the Time of Troubles but brought back when Romanovs Patriarch Philaret and his son Michael were politically advantageous.
> - Michael I was the first Romanov Tsar and began a long line of powerful rulers.
> - Alexis I successfully navigated Russia through multiple uprisings and wars and created long-lasting political bureaus.
> - After a long dynastic dispute, Peter the Great rose to power and changed Russia with the new capital of St. Petersburg and western influences.
>
> ### Key Terms
>
> - **Old Believers**: Followers of the Orthodox faith the way it was practiced before Alexis I convened the Great Moscow Synod and changed the traditions.
> - **Duma chancellory**: The first provincial administrative bureau created under Alexis I. In Russian it is called Razryadny Prikaz.
> - **Rurikid**: A descendent of the Rurik Dynasty, which dominated seats of power throughout Russian lands for over six centuries before the Romanov Dynasty began.

The House of Romanov

The House of Romanov was the second major royal dynasty in Russia, and arose after the Rurikid Dynasty. It was founded in 1613 with the coronation of Michael I and ended in 1917 with the abdication of Tsar Nicholas II. However, the direct male blood line of the Romanov Dynasty ended when Elizabeth of Russia died in 1762, and Peter III, followed by Catherine the Great, were placed in power, both German-born royalty.

Roots of the Romanovs

The earliest common ancestor for the Romanov clan goes back to Andrei Kobyla. Sources say he was a boyar under the leadership of the Rurikid prince Semyon I of Moscow in 1347. This figure remains somewhat mysterious with some sources claiming he was the high-born son of a Rus' prince. Others point to the name Kobyla, which means horse, suggesting he was descended from the Master of Horse in the royal household.

Whatever the real origins of this patriarch-like figure, his descendants split into about a dozen different branches over the next couple of centuries. One such descendent, Roman Yurievich Zakharyin-Yuriev, gave the Romanov Dynasty its name. Grandchildren of this patriarch changed their name to Romanov and it remained there until they rose to power.

Michael I

The Romanov Dynasty proper was founded after the Time of Troubles, an era between 1598 and 1613, which included a dynastic struggle, wars with Sweden and Poland, and severe famine. Tsar Boris Godunov's rule, which lasted until 1605, saw the Romanov families exiled to the Urals and other remote areas. Michael I's father was forced to take monastic vows and adopt the name Philaret. Two impostors attempting to gain the throne in Moscow attempted to leverage Romanov power after Godunov died in 1605. And by 1613, the Romanov family had again become a popular name in the running for power.

Patriarch Philaret's son, Michael I, was voted into power by the zemsky sober in July 1613, ending a long dynastic dispute. He unified the boyars and satisfied the Moscow royalty as the son of Feodor Nikitich Romanov (now Patriarch Philaret) and the nephew of the Rurikid Tsar Feodor I. He was only sixteen at his coronation, and both he and his mother were afraid of his future in such a difficult political position.

Representation of a young Michael I: *He rose to power in Moscow when he was just sixteen and went on to become an influential leader in Russian history.*

Michael I reinstated order in Moscow over his first years in power and also developed two major government offices, the Posolsky Prikaz (Foreign Office) and the Razryadny Prikaz (Duma chancellory, or provincial administration office). These two offices remained essential to Russian order for a many decades.

Alexis I

Michael I ruled until his death in 1645 and his son, Alexis, took over the throne at the age of sixteen, just like his father. His reign would last over 30 years and ended at his death in 1676. His reign was marked by riots in cities such Pskov and Novgorod, as well as continued wars with Sweden and Poland.

Alexis I of Russian in the 1670s: *His policies toward the Church and peasant uprisings created new legal codes and traditions that lasted well into the 19th century.*

However, Alexis I established a new legal code called Subornoye Ulozheniye, which created a serf class, made hereditary class unchangeable, and required official state documentation to travel between towns. These codes stayed in effect well into the 19th century. Under Alexis I's rule, the Orthodox Church also convened the Great Moscow Synod, which created new customs and traditions. This historic moment created a schism between what are termed Old Believers (those attached to the previous hierarchy and traditions of the Church) and the new Church traditions. Alexis I's legacy paints him as a peaceful and reflective ruler, with a propensity for progressive ideas.

Dynastic Dispute and Peter the Great

At the death of Alexis I in 1676, a dynastic dispute erupted between the children of his first wife, namely Fyodor III, Sofia Alexeyevna, Ivan V, and the son of his second wife, Peter Alexeyevich (later Peter the Great). The crown was quickly passed down through the children of his first wife. Fyodor III died from illness after ruling for only six years. Between 1682 and 1689 power was contested between Sofia Alexeyevna, Ivan V, and Peter. Sofia served as regent from 1682 to 1689. She actively opposed Peter's claim to the throne in favor of her own brother, Ivan. However, Ivan V and Peter shared the throne until Ivan's death in 1696.

This portrait was a gift to the King of England and displays a western style that was rarely scene in royal portraits before this time. He is not wearing a beard or the traditional caps and robes that marked Russian nobility before his rule.

Peter went on to rule over Russia, and even style himself Emperor of all Russia in 1721, and ruled until his death in 1725. He built a new capital in St. Petersburg, where he built a navy and attempted to wrest control of the Baltic Sea. He is also remembered for bringing western culture and Enlightenment ideas to Russia, as well as limiting the control of the Church.

Attributions

CC licensed content, Specific attribution

- Boyar. **Provided by**: Wikipedia. **Located at**: https://en.wikipedia.org/wiki/Boyar. **License**: *CC BY-SA: Attribution-ShareAlike*
- Palace of Facets. **Provided by**: Wikipedia. **Located at**: https://en.wikipedia.org/wiki/Palace_of_Facets. **License**: *CC BY-SA: Attribution-ShareAlike*
- Sudebnik. **Provided by**: Wikipedia. **Located at**: https://en.wikipedia.org/wiki/Sudebnik. **License**: *CC BY-SA: Attribution-ShareAlike*
- Ivan III of Russia. **Provided by**: Wikipedia. **Located at**: https://en.wikipedia.org/wiki/Ivan_III_of_Russia. **License**: *CC BY-SA: Attribution-ShareAlike*
- Vasili III of Russia. **Provided by**: Wikipedia. **Located at**: https://en.wikipedia.org/wiki/Vasili_III_of_Russia. **License**: *CC BY-SA: Attribution-ShareAlike*
- Ivan III of Russia. **Provided by**: Wikipedia. **Located at**: https://en.wikipedia.org/wiki/Ivan_III_of_Russia#/media/File:Ivan_III_of_Russia_3.jpg. **License**: *Public Domain: No Known Copyright*
- Palace of facets pillars. **Provided by**: Wikipedia. **Located at**: https://en.wikipedia.org/wiki/Palace_of_Facets#/media/File:Palace_of_facets_pillar.jpg. **License**: *CC BY-SA: Attribution-ShareAlike*
- Vasili III of Russia. **Provided by**: Wikipedia. **Located at**: https://en.wikipedia.org/wiki/Vasili_III_of_Russia#/media/File:Vasili_III_of_Russia.jpg. **License**: *Public Domain: No Known Copyright*
- Boyar. **Provided by**: Wikipedia. **Located at**: https://en.wikipedia.org/wiki/Boyar. **License**: *CC BY-SA: Attribution-ShareAlike*
- Yermak Timofeyevich. **Provided by**: Wikipedia. **Located at**: https://en.wikipedia.org/wiki/Yermak_Timofeyevich. **License**: *CC BY-SA: Attribution-ShareAlike*
- Oprichnina. **Provided by**: Wikipedia. **Located at**: https://en.wikipedia.org/wiki/Oprichnina. **License**: *CC BY-SA: Attribution-ShareAlike*
- Sudebnik of 1550. **Provided by**: Wikipedia. **Located at**: https://en.wikipedia.org/wiki/Sudebnik_of_1550. **License**: *CC BY-SA: Attribution-ShareAlike*
- Moscow Print Yard. **Provided by**: Wikipedia. **Located at**: https://en.wikipedia.org/wiki/Moscow_Print_Yard. **License**: *CC BY-SA: Attribution-ShareAlike*
- Saint Basil's Cathedral. **Provided by**: Wikipedia. **Located at**: https://en.wikipedia.org/wiki/Saint_Basil%27s_Cathedral. **License**: *CC BY-SA: Attribution-ShareAlike*
- Khanate of Kazan. **Provided by**: Wikipedia. **Located at**: https://en.wikipedia.org/wiki/Khanate_of_Kazan. **License**: *CC BY-SA: Attribution-ShareAlike*
- Ivan the Terrible. **Provided by**: Wikipedia. **Located at**: https://en.wikipedia.org/wiki/Ivan_the_Terrible. **License**: *CC BY-SA: Attribution-ShareAlike*
- Ivan III of Russia. **Provided by**: Wikipedia. **Located at**: https://en.wikipedia.org/wiki/Ivan_III_of_Russia#/media/File:Ivan_III_of_Russia_3.jpg. **License**: *Public Domain: No Known Copyright*
- Palace of facets pillars. **Provided by**: Wikipedia. **Located at**: https://en.wikipedia.org/wiki/Palace_of_Facets#/media/File:Palace_of_facets_pillar.jpg. **License**: *CC BY-SA: Attribution-ShareAlike*
- Vasili III of Russia. **Provided by**: Wikipedia. **Located at**: https://en.wikipedia.org/wiki/Vasili_III_of_Russia#/media/File:Vasili_III_of_Russia.jpg. **License**: *Public Domain: No Known Copyright*
- Ivan_IV_by_anonim_18th_c._GIM.jpg. **Provided by**: Wikipedia. **Located at**: https://en.wikipedia.org/wiki/Ivan_the_Terrible#/media/File:Ivan_IV_by_anonim_(18th_c.,_GIM).jpg. **License**: *Public Domain: No Known Copyright*
- Moscow St. Basil's Cathedral. **Provided by**: Wikipedia. **Located at**: https://en.wikipedia.org/wiki/Saint_Basil%27s_Cathedral#/media/File:Moscow_StBasilCathedral_d18.jpg. **License**: *CC BY-SA: Attribution-ShareAlike*
- Oprichnik by Vasnetsov. **Provided by**: Wikipedia. **Located at**: https://en.wikipedia.org/wiki/Oprichnina#/media/File:Oprichnik_by_Vasnetsov.jpg. **License**: *Public Domain: No Known Copyright*
- Ivan's Ivory Throne. **Provided by**: Wikipedia. **Located at**: https://en.wikipedia.org/wiki/Ivan_the_Terrible#/media/File:Ivans_ivory_throne.jpg. **License**: *CC BY-SA: Attribution-ShareAlike*

- Polish-Lithuanian Commonwealth. **Provided by**: Wikipedia. **Located at**: https://en.wikipedia.org/wiki/Polish%E2%80%93Lithuanian_Commonwealth. **License**: *CC BY-SA: Attribution-ShareAlike*
- Michael I of Russia. **Provided by**: Wikipedia. **Located at**: https://en.wikipedia.org/wiki/Michael_I_of_Russia. **License**: *CC BY-SA: Attribution-ShareAlike*
- Kuzma Minin. **Provided by**: Wikipedia. **Located at**: https://en.wikipedia.org/wiki/Kuzma_Minin. **License**: *CC BY-SA: Attribution-ShareAlike*
- Dmitry Pozharsky. **Provided by**: Wikipedia. **Located at**: https://en.wikipedia.org/wiki/Dmitry_Pozharsky. **License**: *CC BY-SA: Attribution-ShareAlike*
- Wu0142adysu0142aw IV Vasa. **Provided by**: Wikipedia. **Located at**: https://en.wikipedia.org/wiki/W%C5%82adys%C5%82aw_IV_Vasa. **License**: *CC BY-SA: Attribution-ShareAlike*
- Polish-Muscovite War. **Provided by**: Wikipedia. **Located at**: https://en.wikipedia.org/wiki/Polish%E2%80%93Muscovite_War_%281605%E2%80%9318%29. **License**: *CC BY-SA: Attribution-ShareAlike*
- Time of Troubles. **Provided by**: Wikipedia. **Located at**: https://en.wikipedia.org/wiki/Time_of_Troubles. **License**: *CC BY-SA: Attribution-ShareAlike*
- Vasili IV of Russia. **Provided by**: Wikipedia. **Located at**: https://en.wikipedia.org/wiki/Vasili_IV_of_Russia. **License**: *CC BY-SA: Attribution-ShareAlike*
- Ivan III of Russia. **Provided by**: Wikipedia. **Located at**: https://en.wikipedia.org/wiki/Ivan_III_of_Russia#/media/File:Ivan_III_of_Russia_3.jpg. **License**: *Public Domain: No Known Copyright*
- Palace of facets pillars. **Provided by**: Wikipedia. **Located at**: https://en.wikipedia.org/wiki/Palace_of_Facets#/media/File:Palace_of_facets_pillar.jpg. **License**: *CC BY-SA: Attribution-ShareAlike*
- Vasili III of Russia. **Provided by**: Wikipedia. **Located at**: https://en.wikipedia.org/wiki/Vasili_III_of_Russia#/media/File:Vasili_III_of_Russia.jpg. **License**: *Public Domain: No Known Copyright*
- Ivan_IV_by_anonim_18th_c._GIM.jpg. **Provided by**: Wikipedia. **Located at**: https://en.wikipedia.org/wiki/Ivan_the_Terrible#/media/File:Ivan_IV_by_anonim_(18th_c._GIM).jpg. **License**: *Public Domain: No Known Copyright*
- Moscow St. Basil's Cathedral. **Provided by**: Wikipedia. **Located at**: https://en.wikipedia.org/wiki/Saint_Basil%27s_Cathedral#/media/File:Moscow_StBasilCathedral_d18.jpg. **License**: *CC BY-SA: Attribution-ShareAlike*
- Oprichnik by Vasnetsov. **Provided by**: Wikipedia. **Located at**: https://en.wikipedia.org/wiki/Oprichnina#/media/File:Oprichnik_by_Vasnetsov.jpg. **License**: *Public Domain: No Known Copyright*
- Ivan's Ivory Throne. **Provided by**: Wikipedia. **Located at**: https://en.wikipedia.org/wiki/Ivan_the_Terrible#/media/File:Ivans_ivory_throne.jpg. **License**: *CC BY-SA: Attribution-ShareAlike*
- Vasili IV of Russia. **Provided by**: Wikipedia. **Located at**: https://en.wikipedia.org/wiki/Vasili_IV_of_Russia#/media/File:Vasili_IV_of_Russia.PNG. **License**: *Public Domain: No Known Copyright*
- Boris Godunov by anon 17th Century. **Provided by**: Wikipedia. **Located at**: https://en.wikipedia.org/wiki/Boris_Godunov#/media/File:Boris_Godunov_by_anonim_(17th_c._GIM).jpg. **License**: *Public Domain: No Known Copyright*
- Michail I Romanov. **Provided by**: Wikipedia. **Located at**: https://en.wikipedia.org/wiki/Michael_I_of_Russia#/media/File:Michail_I._Romanov.jpg. **License**: *CC BY-SA: Attribution-ShareAlike*
- Alexis of Russia. **Provided by**: Wikipedia. **Located at**: https://en.wikipedia.org/wiki/Alexis_of_Russia. **License**: *CC BY-SA: Attribution-ShareAlike*
- Sofia Alekseyevna of Russia. **Provided by**: Wikipedia. **Located at**: https://en.wikipedia.org/wiki/Sofia_Alekseyevna_of_Russia. **License**: *CC BY-SA: Attribution-ShareAlike*
- Sobornoye Ulozheniye. **Provided by**: Wikipedia. **Located at**: https://en.wikipedia.org/wiki/Sobornoye_Ulozheniye. **License**: *CC BY-SA: Attribution-ShareAlike*
- Feodor III of Russia. **Provided by**: Wikipedia. **Located at**: https://en.wikipedia.org/wiki/Feodor_III_of_Russia. **License**: *CC BY-SA: Attribution-ShareAlike*
- Peter the Great. **Provided by**: Wikipedia. **Located at**: https://en.wikipedia.org/wiki/Peter_the_Great. **License**: *CC BY-SA: Attribution-ShareAlike*
- Anastasia Romanovna. **Provided by**: Wikipedia. **Located at**: https://en.wikipedia.org/wiki/Anastasia_Romanovna. **License**: *CC BY-SA: Attribution-ShareAlike*
- Patriarch Philaret of Moscow. **Provided by**: Wikipedia. **Located at**: https://en.wikipedia.org/wiki/Patriarch_Philaret_of_Moscow. **License**: *CC BY-SA: Attribution-ShareAlike*
- Ivan V of Russia. **Provided by**: Wikipedia. **Located at**: https://en.wikipedia.org/wiki/Ivan_V_of_Russia. **License**: *CC BY-SA: Attribution-ShareAlike*

- Michael I of Russia. **Provided by**: Wikipedia. **Located at**: https://en.wikipedia.org/wiki/Michael_I_of_Russia. **License**: *CC BY-SA: Attribution-ShareAlike*
- House of Romanov. **Provided by**: Wikipedia. **Located at**: https://en.wikipedia.org/wiki/House_of_Romanov. **License**: *CC BY-SA: Attribution-ShareAlike*
- Ivan III of Russia. **Provided by**: Wikipedia. **Located at**: https://en.wikipedia.org/wiki/Ivan_III_of_Russia#/media/File:Ivan_III_of_Russia_3.jpg. **License**: *Public Domain: No Known Copyright*
- Palace of facets pillars. **Provided by**: Wikipedia. **Located at**: https://en.wikipedia.org/wiki/Palace_of_Facets#/media/File:Palace_of_facets_pillar.jpg. **License**: *CC BY-SA: Attribution-ShareAlike*
- Vasili III of Russia. **Provided by**: Wikipedia. **Located at**: https://en.wikipedia.org/wiki/Vasili_III_of_Russia#/media/File:Vasili_III_of_Russia.jpg. **License**: *Public Domain: No Known Copyright*
- Ivan_IV_by_anonim_18th_c._GIM.jpg. **Provided by**: Wikipedia. **Located at**: https://en.wikipedia.org/wiki/Ivan_the_Terrible#/media/File:Ivan_IV_by_anonim_(18th_c.,_GIM).jpg. **License**: *Public Domain: No Known Copyright*
- Moscow St. Basil's Cathedral. **Provided by**: Wikipedia. **Located at**: https://en.wikipedia.org/wiki/Saint_Basil%27s_Cathedral#/media/File:Moscow_StBasilCathedral_d18.jpg. **License**: *CC BY-SA: Attribution-ShareAlike*
- Oprichnik by Vasnetsov. **Provided by**: Wikipedia. **Located at**: https://en.wikipedia.org/wiki/Oprichnina#/media/File:Oprichnik_by_Vasnetsov.jpg. **License**: *Public Domain: No Known Copyright*
- Ivan's Ivory Throne. **Provided by**: Wikipedia. **Located at**: https://en.wikipedia.org/wiki/Ivan_the_Terrible#/media/File:Ivans_ivory_throne.jpg. **License**: *CC BY-SA: Attribution-ShareAlike*
- Vasili IV of Russia. **Provided by**: Wikipedia. **Located at**: https://en.wikipedia.org/wiki/Vasili_IV_of_Russia#/media/File:Vasili_IV_of_Russia.PNG. **License**: *Public Domain: No Known Copyright*
- Boris Godunov by anon 17th Century. **Provided by**: Wikipedia. **Located at**: https://en.wikipedia.org/wiki/Boris_Godunov#/media/File:Boris_Godunov_by_anonim_(17th_c.,_GIM).jpg. **License**: *Public Domain: No Known Copyright*
- Michail I Romanov. **Provided by**: Wikipedia. **Located at**: https://en.wikipedia.org/wiki/Michael_I_of_Russia#/media/File:Michail_I._Romanov.jpg. **License**: *CC BY-SA: Attribution-ShareAlike*
- Alexis I of Russia 1670s Ptuj Ormozu030c Regional Museum. **Provided by**: Wikipedia. **Located at**: https://en.wikipedia.org/wiki/Alexis_of_Russia#/media/File:Alexis_I_of_Russia_(1670s,_Ptuj_Ormo%C5%BE_Regional_Museum).jpg. **License**: *Public Domain: No Known Copyright*
- Tsar Mikhail I cropped. **Provided by**: Wikipedia. **Located at**: https://en.wikipedia.org/wiki/Michael_I_of_Russia#/media/File:Tsar_Mikhail_I_-cropped.JPG. **License**: *Public Domain: No Known Copyright*
- Peter I by Kneller. **Provided by**: Wikipedia. **Located at**: https://en.wikipedia.org/wiki/Peter_the_Great#/media/File:Peter_I_by_Kneller.jpg. **License**: *Public Domain: No Known Copyright*

The Mongol Empire

The Mongol Empire

Overview of the Mongol Empire

The Mongol Empire expanded through brutal raids and invasions, but also established routes of trade and technology between East and West.

Learning Objectives

Define the significance of the Pax Mongolica

Key Takeaways

Key Points

- The Mongol Empire existed during the 13th and 14th centuries and was the largest land empire in history.
- The empire unified the nomadic Mongol and Turkic tribes of historical Mongolia.
- The empire sent invasions in every direction, ultimately connecting the East with the West with the *Pax Mongolica*, or Mongol Peace, which allowed trade, technologies, commodities, and ideologies to be disseminated and exchanged across Eurasia.
- The Mongol raids and invasions were some of the deadliest and most terrifying conflicts in human history.
- Ultimately, the empire started to fragment; it dissolved in 1368, at which point the Han Chinese Ming Dynasty took control.

Key Terms

- **tributary states**: Pre-modern states subordinate to a more powerful state.

- **Pax Mongolica**: Also known as the Mongol Peace, this agreement allowed trade, technologies, commodities, and ideologies to be disseminated and exchanged across Eurasia.
- **High Middle Ages**: A time between the 10th and 12th centuries when the core cultural and social characteristics of the Middle Ages were firmly set.

Rise of the Mongol Empire

During Europe's High Middle Ages the Mongol Empire, the largest contiguous land empire in history, began to emerge. The Mongol Empire began in the Central Asian steppes and lasted throughout the 13th and 14th centuries. At its greatest extent it included all of modern-day Mongolia, China, parts of Burma, Romania, Pakistan, Siberia, Ukraine, Belarus, Cilicia, Anatolia, Georgia, Armenia, Persia, Iraq, Central Asia, and much or all of Russia. Many additional countries became tributary states of the Mongol Empire.

The empire unified the nomadic Mongol and Turkic tribes of historical Mongolia under the leadership of Genghis Khan, who was proclaimed ruler of all Mongols in 1206. The empire grew rapidly under his rule and then under his descendants, who sent invasions in every direction. The vast transcontinental empire connected the east with the west with an enforced *Pax Mongolica*, or Mongol Peace, allowing trade, technologies, commodities, and ideologies to be disseminated and exchanged across Eurasia.

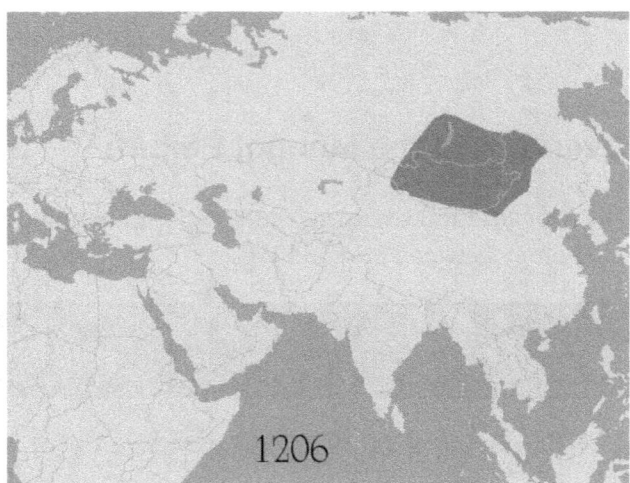

The Mongol Empire: Expansion of the Mongol empire from 1206 CE-1294 CE.

Mongol invasions and conquests progressed over the next century, until 1300, by which time the vast empire covered much of Asia and Eastern Europe. Historians regard the Mongol raids and invasions as some of the deadliest and most terrifying conflicts in human history. The Mongols spread panic ahead of them and induced population displacement on an unprecedented scale.

Impact of the Pax Mongolica

The Pax Mongolica refers to the relative stabilization of the regions under Mongol control during the height of the empire in the 13th and 14th centuries. The Mongol rulers maintained peace and relative stability in such varied regions because they did not force subjects to adopt religious or cultural traditions. However, they still enforced a legal code known as the Yassa (Great Law), which stopped feudal disagreements at local levels and made outright disobedience a dubious prospect. It also ensured that it was easy to create an army in short time and gave the khans access to the daughters of local leaders.

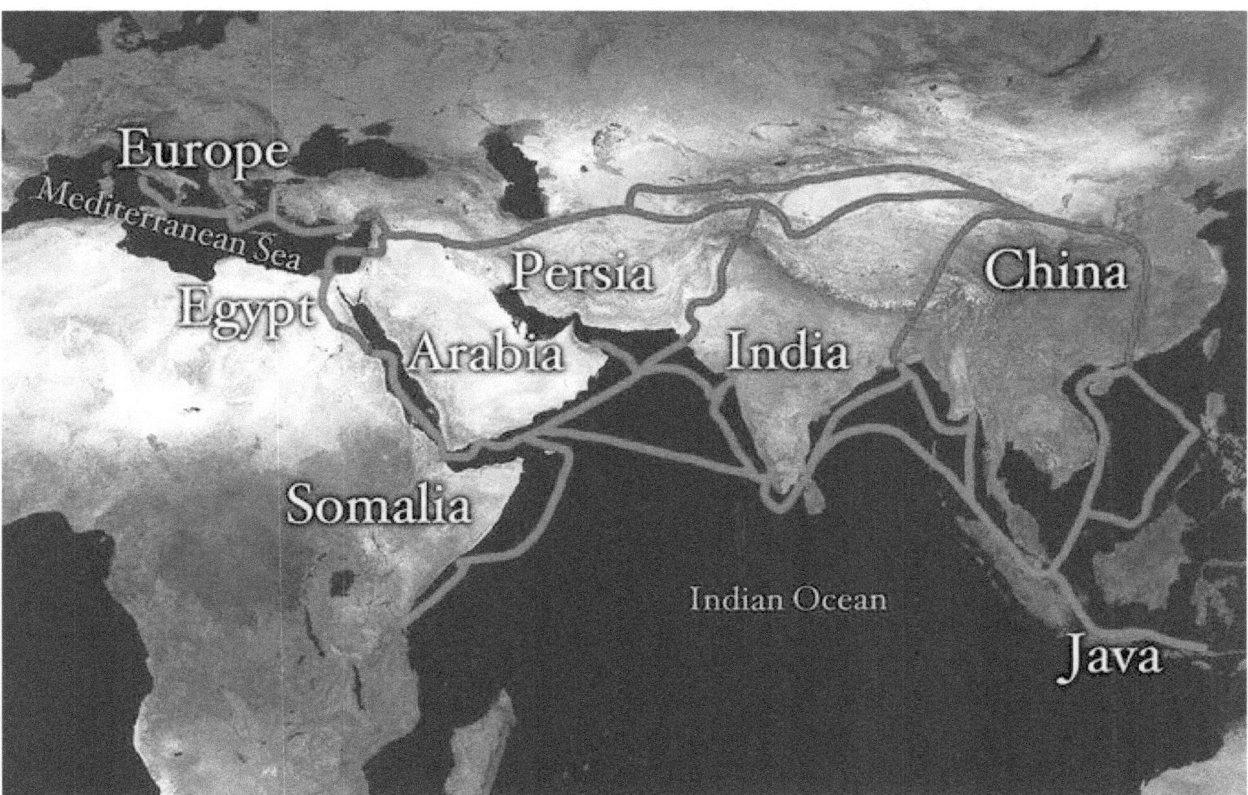

The Silk Road: *At its height these trade routes stretched between Europe, Persia, and China. They connected ideas, materials, and people in new and exciting ways that allowed for innovations.*

The constant presence of troops across the empire also ensured that people followed Yassa edicts and maintained enough stability for goods and for people to travel long distances along these routes. In this environment the largest empire to ever exist helped one of the most influential trade routes in the world, known as the Silk Road, to flourish. This route allowed commodities such as silk, pepper, cinnamon, precious stones, linen, and leather goods to travel between Europe, the Steppe, India, and China.

Marco Polo in a Tatar costume: *This style of dress, with the fur hat, long coat, and saber, would have been popular in regions in and around Russian, Eurasia, and Turkey.*

Ideas also traveled along the trade route, including major discoveries and innovations in mathematics, astronomy, paper-making, and banking systems from various parts of the world. Famous explorers, such as Marco Polo, also enjoyed the freedom and stability the Pax Mongolica provided, and were able to bring back valuable information about the East and the Mongol Empire to Europe.

The Empire Starts to Fragment

Tatar and Mongol raids against Russian states continued well into the later 1200's. Elsewhere, the Mongols' territorial gains in China persisted into the 14th century under the Yuan Dynasty, while those in Persia persisted into the 15th century under the Timurid Dynasty. In India, the Mongols' gains survived into the 19th century as the Mughal Empire.

However, the Battle of Ain Jalut in 1260 was a turning point. It was the first time a Mongol advance had ever been beaten back in direct combat on the battlefield, and it marked the beginning of the fragmentation of the empire due to wars over succession. The grandchildren of Genghis Khan disputed whether the royal line should follow from his son and initial heir Ögedei or one of his other sons. After long rivalries and civil war, Kublai Khan took power in 1271 when he established the Yuan Dynasty, but civil war ensued again as he sought unsuccessfully to regain control of the followers of Genghis Khan's other descendants.

By the time of Kublai's death in 1294, the Mongol Empire had fractured into four separate empires, or khanates. This weakness allowed the Han Chinese Ming Dynasty to take control in 1368, while Russian princes also slowly developed independence over the 14th and 15th centuries, and the Mongol Empire finally dissolved.

Attributions

CC licensed content, Specific attribution

- Yassa. **Provided by**: Wikipedia. **Located at**: https://en.wikipedia.org/wiki/Yassa. **License**: *CC BY-SA: Attribution-ShareAlike*
- Silk Road. **Provided by**: Wikipedia. **Located at**: https://en.wikipedia.org/wiki/Silk_Road. **License**: *CC BY-SA: Attribution-ShareAlike*
- Mongol invasions and conquests. **Provided by**: Wikipedia. **Located at**: http://en.wikipedia.org/wiki/Mongol_conquest. **License**: *CC BY-SA: Attribution-ShareAlike*
- HIST302: Medieval Europe. **Provided by**: Saylor. **Located at**: https://legacy.saylor.org/hist302/Intro/. **License**: *CC BY: Attribution*
- Tributary state. **Provided by**: Wikipedia. **Located at**: http://en.wikipedia.org/wiki/Tributary_state. **License**: *CC BY-SA: Attribution-ShareAlike*
- Changes in Eurasia - Mongol Conquest and Aftermath. **Provided by**: Wikibooks. **Located at**: http://en.wikibooks.org/wiki/World_History/Changes_in_Eurasia_-_Mongol_Conquest_and_Aftermath. **License**: *CC BY-SA: Attribution-ShareAlike*
- Mongol Empire. **Provided by**: Wikipedia. **Located at**: http://en.wikipedia.org/wiki/Mongol_Empire. **License**: *CC BY-SA: Attribution-ShareAlike*
- Pax Mongolica. **Provided by**: Wikipedia. **Located at**: http://en.wikipedia.org/wiki/Pax%20Mongolica. **License**: *CC BY-SA: Attribution-ShareAlike*
- Mongol Empire map. **Provided by**: Wikipedia. **Located at**: http://en.wikipedia.org/wiki/File:Mongol_Empire_map.gif. **License**: *Public Domain: No Known Copyright*
- Extent of the Silk Road. **Provided by**: Wikipedia. **Located at**: https://en.wikipedia.org/wiki/Silk_Road#/media/File:Silk_route.jpg. **License**: *Public Domain: No Known Copyright*
- Marco Polo costume tartare. **Provided by**: Wikipedia. **Located at**: https://en.wikipedia.org/wiki/Marco_Polo#/media/File:Marco_Polo_-_costume_tartare.jpg. **License**: *Public Domain: No Known Copyright*

Genghis Khan

Genghis Khan

Genghis Khan ruled between 1206 and 1227, expanding trade across Asia and into eastern Europe, enacting relatively tolerant social and religious laws, and leading devastating military campaigns that left local populations depleted and fearful of the brutal Mongol forces.

Learning Objectives

Outline the major cultural contributions and complex role played by Genghis Khan in the development of the Mongol Empire

Key Takeaways

Key Points

- Genghis Khan was the first leader, or Khan, of the Mongol Empire, from 1206 CE–1227 CE.
- Genghis Khan generally advocated literacy, religious freedom, and trade, although many local customs were frowned upon or discarded once Mongol rule was implemented.
- In terms of social policy, he forbade selling of women, theft of property, and fighting.
- This ruler used groundbreaking siege warfare and spy techniques to understand his enemies and more successfully conquer and subsume them under his rule.
- Genghis Khan led merciless conquests of the Western Xia Dynasty, the Jin Dynasty in 1234, the Kara-Khitan Khanate, and the Khwarazmian Empire. Many local people across Asia considered Genghis Khan a dark historical figure.

> *Key Terms*
>
> - **Khan**: The universal leader of the Mongol tribes.
> - **Temujin**: Ghengis Khan's birth name.
> - **Uyghur-Mongolian script**: The first writing system created specifically for the Mongolian language and the most successful until the introduction of Cyrillic in 1946. This is a true alphabet with separate letters for consonants and vowels, alphabets based on this script are used in Inner Mongolia and other parts of China to this day.

The First Khan and the Mongol Empire

Before Genghis Khan became the leader of Mongolia, he was known as Temujin. He was born around 1162 in modern-day northern Mongolia into a nomadic tribe with noble ties and powerful alliances. These fortunate circumstances helped him unite dozens of tribes in his adulthood via alliances. In his early 20s he married his young wife Börte, a bride from another powerful tribe. Soon, bubbling tensions erupted and she was kidnapped by a rival tribe. During this era, and possibly spurred by the capture of his wife, Temujin united the nomadic, previously ever-rivaling Mongol tribes under his rule through political manipulation and military might, and also reclaimed his bride from the rebellious tribe.

As Temujin gained power, he forbade looting of his enemies without permission, and he implemented a policy of sharing spoils with his warriors and their families instead of giving it all to the aristocrats. His meritocratic policies tended to gain a broader range of followers, compared to his rival brother, Jamukha, who also hoped to rule over greater swaths of Mongolian territory. This split in policies created conflict with his uncles and brothers, who were also legitimate heirs to Mongol succession, as well as his generals.

War ensued, and Temujin prevailed, destroying all the remaining rival tribes from 1203–1205 and bringing them under his sway. In 1206, Temujin was crowned as the leader of the Great Mongol Nation. It was then that he assumed the title of Genghis Khan, meaning universal leader, marking the start of the Mongol Empire. The first great khan was able to grasp power over such varied populations through bloody siege warfare and elaborate spy systems, which allowed him to better understand his enemy. He also utilized a lenient policy toward religious and local traditions, which convinced many people to follow his lead with promises of amnesty and neutrality.

Genghis Khan: *Genghis Khan as portrayed in a 14th-century Yuan-era album. He was the first leader of the unified Mongols and first emperor under the Mongolian Empire.*

Innovations Under Genghis Khan

As a ruler over a vast network of tribal groups, Genghis Khan innovated the way he ruled and garnered power as he expanded his holdings. These unprecedented innovations encouraged a relatively peaceful reign and helped to develop stabler trading routes and alliances, marking his rule as one of the most successful political entities of the era. He also successfully brought technology, language, and goods farther west. Some of his major accomplishments include:

- Organizing his army by dividing it into decimal subsections of 10, 100, 1,000, and 10,000, and discarded the lineage-based, tribal bands that once dominated warfare.

- Founding the Imperial Guard and rewarding loyalty with high positions as heads of army units and households no matter the class of the individual.

- Proclaiming a new law of the empire, called the Yassa, which outlawed the theft of property, fighting amongst the population, and hunting animals during the breeding season, among many other things.

- Forbidding the selling of women. He also encouraged women to discuss major, public decisions. Unlike other leaders in the region, Ghengis allowed his wives to sit at the table with him and encouraged them to voice their opinions.

- Appointing his adopted brother as supreme judge, ordering him to keep detailed records of the empire.

- Decreeing religious freedom and exempting the poor and the clergy from taxation. Because of this, Muslims, Buddhists, and Christians from Manchuria, North China, India, and Persia were more likely to acquiesce to Mongol intrusions and takeovers.
- Encouraging literacy and adopting the Uyghur script, which would form the Empire's Uyghur-Mongolian script.

Destruction and Expansion Under Genghis Khan

Despite his many successful political and social changes, Genghis was also a destructive and intimidating leader. He initially forged the Mongol Empire in Central Asia with the unification of the Mongol and Turkic confederations on the Mongolian plateau in 1206. Then Mongol forces invaded westward into Central Asia including:

- Western Xia Dynasty in 1209
- Kara-Khitan Khanate in 1218
- Khwarazmian Empire in 1221

These conquests seriously depopulated large areas of central Asia and northeastern Iran, complicating the image of Genghis Khan as a peaceful ruler practicing religious tolerance. Any city or town that resisted the Mongols was subject to destruction. Each soldier was required to execute a certain number of persons in cities that did not cooperate. For example, after the conquest of the city of Urgench, each Mongol warrior, in an army that might have consisted of 20,000 soldiers, was required to execute 24 people.

Sack of Baghdad: *Illustrations of Mongol advances show the deeply militaristic reality of this empire's success, and the darker side of Genghis Khan's rule.*

By 1260, the armies of the Mongol Empire had swept across and outward from the Asian steppes. The dark side of Genghis Khan's rule can be seen in the destruction of ancient and powerful kingdoms in the Middle East, Egypt, and Poland. During the same period, Mongol assaults on China replaced the Sung Dynasty with the Yuan Dynasty. Many local populations in what is now India, Pakistan, and Iran considered the great khan to be a blood-thirsty warlord set on destruction.

The Mongols' military tactics, based on the swift and ferocious use of mounted cavalry, cannons, and siege warfare crushed even the strongest European and Islamic forces and left a trail of devastation behind. Even populations that appreciated the new legal code and relative religious tolerance did not have much free will when it came to Mongol advances. Many times Jewish kosher traditions and Muslim halal traditions were also cast aside in favor of Mongol dining and social customs.

Genghis Khan died in 1227 under mysterious circumstances in possession of one of the largest empires in history. He left these vast holdings in the hands of his sons and heirs, Ögedei and Jochi, who continued to expand outward with attacks and political alliances in every direction.

Expansion Throughout Eastern Asia

Under Genghis Khan and his son Ögedei, the Mongol Empire conquered both the Western Xia Dynasty and the Jin Dynasty to the west.

Learning Objectives

Recall the significance and consequences of the Mongol Empire's battles with the Western Xia and Jin Dynasties.

Key Takeaways

Key Points

- Under Genghis Khan, the Mongol Empire conquered the Tanguts' Western Xia Dynasty in 1209.
- Afterward, Genghis Khan began the conquest of the neighboring Jin Dynasty in 1211.
- The Jin Dynasty would finally be successfully conquered by Genghis' son, Ögedei Khan, in 1234.

Key Terms

- **ethnocide**: The destruction of a national or localized culture in the wake of a population's destruction.
- **Zhongdu**: The capital of the Jin Dynasty before the Mongol attacks, situated where

modern-day Beijing sits.

- **Badger Pass**: The location of the battle between Genghis Khan's Mongol Empire and the Jin Dynasty, where the Mongols massacred thousands of Jin troops.

At the time of the political rise of Genghis Khan in 1206 CE, the Mongol Empire shared its western borders with the Western Xia Dynasty of the Tanguts. To the east and south was the Jin Dynasty of northern China. These two regions offered valuable resources and would serve as vassal-states over time as Genghis gained power over these two large territories. His relentless battle tactics also revealed his ruthless viewpoints when it came to disobedient enemy forces and gaining complete control of a region.

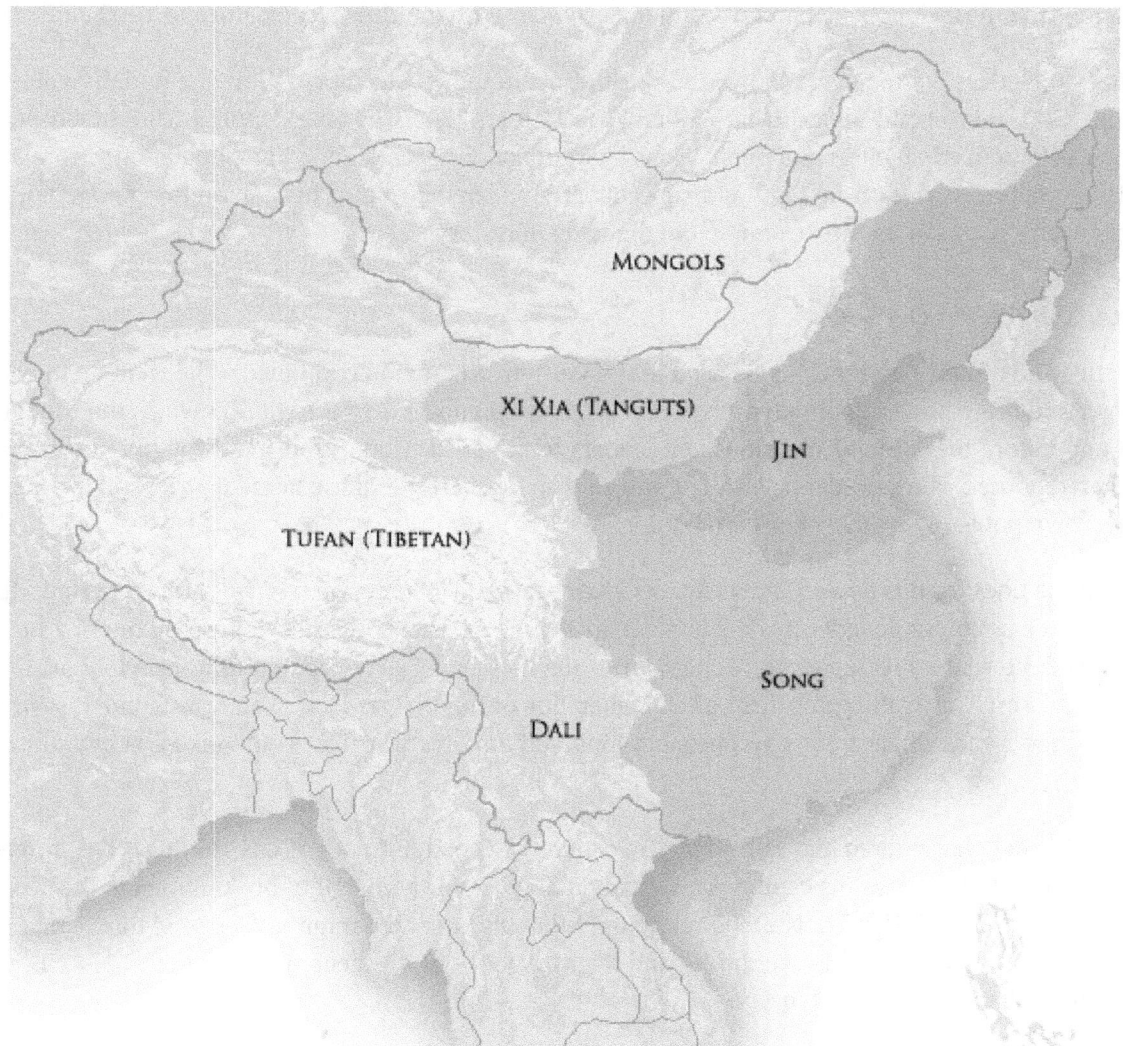

Map illustrating the neighboring Xia and Jin regions: *These two regions were directly adjacent to Genghis Khan's newly unified Mongol territories in the late 12th and early 13th centuries.*

Conquest of the Western Xia Dynasty

The Western Xia Dynasty (also known as the Xi-Xia Dynasty) was located in what is modern-day northern China and sat along the southern border of the Mongol territories. It emerged in 1038 but often struggled to retain independent status from neighboring dynasties. The Xia Dynasty also shared a complex history with the neighboring Jin Dynasty, even serving as a vassal state to the Jin for a period before the arrival of Mongol forces.

Genghis Khan first planned for war with the Western Xia, correctly believing that the young, more powerful ruler of the Jin Dynasty would not come to the Western Xia Dynasty's aid. His very first attempt to gain power started in 1205, the year before he was named supreme ruler on Mongol lands, and his initial attacks were based on a flimsy political pretext. However, he realized that this region would be an ideal gateway to conquering the Jin Dynasty to the south and east. Despite initial difficulties in capturing the Western Xia's well-defended cities, Genghis Khan forced their surrender with multiple siege battles in 1209 and 1210.

Genghis's relentless battle tactics showed to great effect in the Xia territory. While he initially gained territory in 1209, the second invasion in Western Xia in the 1220s was an example of the bloodshed and slaughter he practiced on cities and populations that did not obey his orders. The population was relatively demolished before his death in 1227 and subsequently under the rule of his son and heir, Ögedei. Some scholars even say this is the first example of ethnocide in history.

Conquest of the Jin Dynasty

The tactics and military might Genghis used in the Western Xia region continued as he went on to conquer the larger and more powerful Jin Dynasty in 1211 CE, beginning a 23-year war known as the Mongol-Jin War. Long before the Mongol invasions, Jin leaders took vassal tribute from the Mongolian tribes along their shared border. These leaders even encouraged disputes between these nomadic tribes in order to bolster their own power along their northern border.

However, the tides for this powerful dynasty decidedly shifted when the war started during the first Mongol invasion. Jin's army commander made a tactical mistake in not attacking the Mongols at the first opportunity. Instead, he sent a messenger to Mongols. But the messenger defected and told the Mongols that the Jin Dynasty army was waiting for them on the other side of the Badger Pass. This was where the Mongols massacred thousands of Jin troops and began a long and arduous war that would take a heavy toll on the region.

In 1215 CE Genghis captured and sacked the Jin capital of Zhongdu (modern-day Beijing). This forced the Emperor Xuanzong to move his capital south, abandoning the northern half of his kingdom to the Mongols. Between 1232 CE and 1233 CE, Kaifeng fell to the Mongols under the reign of Genghis' third son, Ögedei Khan. The last major battle between the Jin and the Mongols was the siege of Caizhou in 1234 CE, which marked the collapse of the Jin Dynasty.

The years of war took a heavy toll on the population of the Jin Dynasty, as it had in the Western Xia. Mongol warriors were reported to take the livestock from the small towns and villages along their path and kill the owners.

Despite the hardship of war and the siege and heavy cavalry tactics utilized by Mongol forces, the unifying and centralizing effects of the Mongol Empire created an expansive trade route and opened up these far eastern regions to western influence and goods. More stability along the trade route known as the Silk Road allowed goods and ideas to travel long distances and established a connection between eastern European principalities like the Russian territories.

Jar from the Jin Dynasty: *Hunping jar of the Jin Dynasty, with Buddhist figures.*

Expansion Throughout Central and Western Asia

Under Genghis Khan, the Mongols, who began using catapults and gunpowder in their invasions, conquered the Kara-Khitan Khanate and the Khwarazmian Empire.

Learning Objectives

Assess the factors in Genghis Khan's successful conquest of the Khwarazmian Empire and the Kara-Khitan

> ## Key Takeaways
>
> ### Key Points
>
> - Under Genghis Khan, the Mongol Empire conquered the Kara-Khitan Khanate in Central Asia in 1218 CE. This was a relatively easy conquest because the prince of Kara-Khitan, Küchlüg, had become unpopular with his people due to his persecution of Islam.
> - The empire now had a border with the Khwarazmian Empire, which they proceeded to conquer as well in 1221 CE.
> - The Mongol Empire's conquest of the Khwarazmian Empire saw huge numbers of civilians massacred and enslaved.
> - During this time, the empire used catapults to hurl gunpowder bombs. The Mongol Empire is often given credit for introducing gunpowder to Europe.
> - By the time of Genghis Khan's death in 1227 CE, the Mongol Empire was twice the size of the Roman Empire and the Muslim Caliphate.
>
> ### Key Terms
>
> - **catapult**: A device or weapon for throwing or launching large objects. Used by Genghis Khan during the Mongol invasion of the Khwarazmian Empire.
> - **Samarkand**: The capital of the Khwarazm region, which was captured by Mongol forces around 1221.
> - **gunpowder**: An explosive substance; can be used to form bombs. Was introduced to Europe by the Mongols.
> - **huochong**: A Chinese mortar used in the Central Asia campaign

Genghis Khan created an efficient military regime after his unifying rise to power in the nomadic Mongol territories of northeastern Asia in 1206 CE. These forces were no longer grouped by tribe or familial affiliation, but rather were organized into armies of multiples of ten soldiers that could be sent where needed in the name of Mongol expansion. Genghis Khan sent forces in every direction, including westward into central Asia. While he was fighting the Western Xia and Jin Dynasties in the east, he was also attempting to gain more land to the west in the Kara-Khitan Khanate and the Khwarazmian Empire, regions that comprise modern-day Iran, Iraq, and Uzbekistan.

Conquest of the Kara-Khitan Khanate

The Mongol Empire conquered the Kara-Khitan Khanate, an empire comprised of former nomads in Central Asia, in the years 1216-1218 CE. The khanate was under the rule of Prince Küchlüg, who had converted to Buddhism and had been persecuting the Muslim majority among the Khitan. This alienated him from most of his people, creating ideal circumstances for a takeover by Genghis Khan.

The Kara-Khitai attracted Genghis Khan's attention when they besieged Almaliq, a city belonging to vassals of the Mongol Empire. Genghis Khan dispatched an army, who, under the command of General Jebe, defeated the Kara-Khitai at their capital, Balasagun, and Küchlüg fled. Jebe gained support from the Kara-Khitan populace by announcing that Küchlüg's oppressive policy of religious persecution had ended. When his army followed Küchlüg to Kashgar in 1217, the populace revolted and turned on Küchlüg, forcing him to flee again for his life. Jebe pursued Küchlüg into modern Afghanistan. According to Persian historian Ata-Malik Juvayni, a group of hunters caught Küchlüg in 1218 and handed him over to the Mongols, who promptly beheaded him.

With Küchlüg's death, the Mongol Empire secured control over the Kara-Khitai and surrounding areas. The Mongols now had a firm outpost in Central Asia directly bordering the Khwarazmian Empire, in Greater Iran. Relations with the Khwarazms would quickly break down, leading to the Mongol invasion of that territory in 1219.

Kara-Khitans Hunting: *Kara-Khitans using eagles to hunt, painted during the Chinese Song Dynasty.*

Conquest of the Khwarazmian Empire

In the early 13th century, the Khwarazmian Empire was governed by Shah Ala ad-Din Muhammad. Genghis Khan saw the potential advantage in Khwarazmia as a commercial trading partner using the Silk Road, and he sent a caravan to establish official trade ties with the empire. However, a Khwarazmian governor attacked the caravan, claiming that it contained spies. Genghis Khan sent a second group of ambassadors to meet the Shah himself instead of the governor. The Shah had all the men shaved and the Muslim ambassador beheaded and sent his head back with the two remaining ambassadors.

Outraged, Genghis Khan organized one of his largest and most brutal invasion campaigns, fought by 200,000 soldiers in three divisions. He left a commander and troops in China, designated his successors to be his family members, and set out for Khwarazmia. Before he left, he divided his empire among his sons and immediate family and declared that his heir should be his charismatic third son, Ögedei. His invasion of Khwarazmia would last from 1219-1221 CE. His son Jochi led the first division into the northeast, and the second division under Jebe marched secretly to the southeast to form, with the first division, a pincer attack on Samarkand. The third division under Genghis Khan and Tolui moved in from the northwest. The Shah's army, in contrast, was fragmented, a decisive factor in their defeat—the Mongols were not facing a unified defense.

The Mongol tactics were precise and often brutally efficient, including heavy cavalry, siege tactics, and even gunpowder weapons. The attack on the Khwarazm capital, Samarkand, was decisive and left the local population depleted and in tatters. Generally speaking, Mongol forces would enslave or massacre populations after a victorious capture of a city or region, establishing a new rule of law and highlighting Mongol dominance. Legend tells that the often flamboyant Genghis Khan executed the Khwarazm governor by pouring molten silver into his ears and eyes. Eventually the Shah fled rather than surrender, and he died shortly after, possibly killed by the Mongols. After their victory, Genghis Khan ordered two of his generals and their forces to completely destroy the remnants of the empire, including not only royal buildings but entire towns, populations, and even vast swaths of farmland.

The assault on the wealthy trading city of Urgench proved to be the most difficult battle of the Mongol invasion. Mongolian casualties were higher than normal because most battles they fought were in less densely packed urban settings. However, they were successful, and after an extensive invasion such as this one, young women and children were often given to the Mongol soldiers as slaves. Persian scholar Juvayni states that 50,000 Mongol soldiers were given the task of executing 24 Urgench citizens each. If Juvanyi's estimation is true, 1.2 million people were killed, making it one of the bloodiest invasions in history.

During the invasion of Transoxania in 1219, along with the main Mongol force, Genghis Khan used a Chinese specialist catapult unit in battle, adding to the powerful tactics already in use by Mongol forces. They were used again in 1220 in Transoxania. The Chinese may have used these same catapults to hurl gunpowder bombs. In fact, historians have suggested that the Mongol invasion brought Chinese gunpowder weapons to Central Asia. One of these was the huochong, a Chinese mortar.

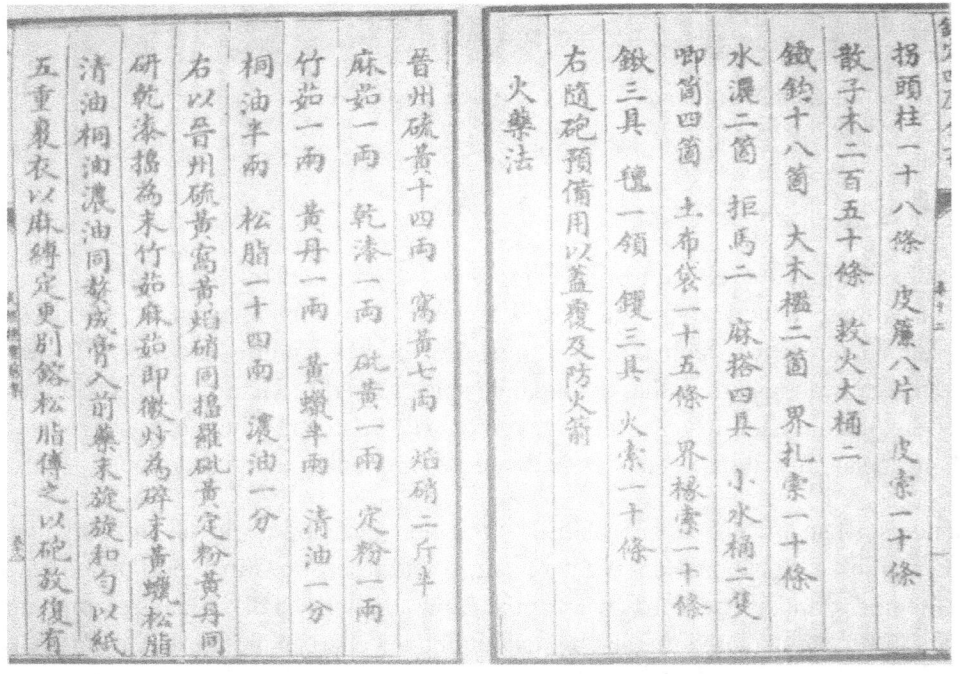

Chinese Formula for Gunpowder: *The earliest known written formula for gunpowder, from the Chinese Wujing Zongyao, a military compendium, of 1044 CE.*

By the time of Genghis Khan's death in 1227, the Mongol Empire ruled from the Pacific Ocean to the Caspian Sea, an empire twice the size of the Roman Empire and Muslim Caliphate.

Pushing Farther West

The Mongols conquered the areas today known as Iran, Iraq, Syria, Caucasus and parts of Turkey. Further Mongol raids reached southwards as far as Gaza into the Palestine region in 1260 and 1300. The major battles were the Siege of Baghdad in 1258, when the Mongols sacked the city that for 500 years had been the center of Islamic power, and the Battle of Ain Jalut in 1260, when the Muslim Egyptians were for the first time able to stop the Mongol advance.

The Mongols were never able to expand farther west than the Middle East due to a combination of political and environmental factors, such as lack of sufficient grazing room for their horses.

Attributions

CC licensed content, Specific attribution

- Mongol invasions and conquests. **Provided by**: Wikipedia. **Located at**: http://en.wikipedia.org/wiki/Mongol_conquest. **License**: *CC BY-SA: Attribution-ShareAlike*
- Mongol invasion of Central Asia. **Provided by**: Wikipedia. **Located at**: http://en.wikipedia.org/wiki/Mongol_invasion_of_Central_Asia. **License**: *CC BY-SA: Attribution-ShareAlike*
- Mongol conquest of the Kara-Khitai. **Provided by**: Wikipedia. **Located at**: http://en.wikipedia.org/wiki/Mongol_conquest_of_the_Kara-Khitai. **License**: *CC BY-SA: Attribution-ShareAlike*
- Changes in Eurasia - Mongol Conquest and Aftermath. **Provided by**: Wikibooks. **Located at**: http://en.wikibooks.org/wiki/World_History/Changes_in_Eurasia_-_Mongol_Conquest_and_Aftermath. **License**: *CC BY-SA: Attribution-ShareAlike*
- Mongolian script. **Provided by**: Wikipedia. **Located at**: http://en.wikipedia.org/wiki/Mongolian_script. **License**: *CC BY-SA: Attribution-ShareAlike*
- HIST302: Medieval Europe. **Provided by**: Saylor. **Located at**: https://legacy.saylor.org/hist302/Intro/. **License**: *CC BY: Attribution*
- Mongol Empire. **Provided by**: Wikipedia. **Located at**: http://en.wikipedia.org/wiki/Mongol_Empire. **License**: *CC BY-SA: Attribution-ShareAlike*
- Mongol Empire. **Provided by**: Wikipedia. **Located at**: https://en.wikipedia.org/wiki/Mongol_Empire#/media/File:DiezAlbumsFallOfBaghdad.jpg. **License**: *Public Domain: No Known Copyright*
- Yuan Emperor Album Genghis Portrait. **Provided by**: Wikipedia. **Located at**: http://en.wikipedia.org/wiki/File:YuanEmperorAlbumGenghisPortrait.jpg. **License**: *Public Domain: No Known Copyright*
- Changes in Eurasia - Mongol Conquest and Aftermath. **Provided by**: Wikibooks. **Located at**: http://en.wikibooks.org/wiki/World_History/Changes_in_Eurasia_-_Mongol_Conquest_and_Aftermath. **License**: *CC BY-SA: Attribution-ShareAlike*
- HIST302: Medieval Europe. **Provided by**: Saylor. **Located at**: https://legacy.saylor.org/hist302/Intro/. **License**: *CC BY: Attribution*
- Mongol invasions and conquests. **Provided by**: Wikipedia. **Located at**: http://en.wikipedia.org/wiki/Mongol_conquest. **License**: *CC BY-SA: Attribution-ShareAlike*
- Jin Jar. **Provided by**: Wikipedia. **Located at**: http://en.wikipedia.org/wiki/File:JinJar.JPG. **License**: *Public Domain: No Known Copyright*
- Mongol Empire. **Provided by**: WIkipedia. **Located at**: http://en.wikipedia.org/wiki/Mongol_Empire. **License**: *CC BY-SA: Attribution-ShareAlike*
- Mongol invasion of Central Asia. **Provided by**: Wikipedia. **Located at**: http://en.wikipedia.org/wiki/Mongol_invasion_of_Central_Asia. **License**: *CC BY-SA: Attribution-ShareAlike*
- Mongol Empire. **Provided by**: Wikipedia. **Located at**: https://en.wikipedia.org/wiki/Mongol_Empire#/media/File:DiezAlbumsFallOfBaghdad.jpg. **License**: *Public Domain: No Known Copyright*
- Yuan Emperor Album Genghis Portrait. **Provided by**: Wikipedia. **Located at**: http://en.wikipedia.org/wiki/File:YuanEmperorAlbumGenghisPortrait.jpg. **License**: *Public Domain: No Known Copyright*
- Sung Dynasty 1141. **Provided by**: Wikipedia. **Located at**: https://en.wikipedia.org/wiki/File:Sung_Dynasty_1141.png. **License**: *CC BY-SA: Attribution-ShareAlike*

- Jin Jar. **Provided by**: Wikipedia. **Located at**: http://en.wikipedia.org/wiki/File:JinJar.JPG. **License**: *Public Domain: No Known Copyright*
- Mongol conquest of the Kara-Khitai. **Provided by**: Wikipedia. **Located at**: http://en.wikipedia.org/wiki/Mongol_conquest_of_the_Kara-Khitai. **License**: *CC BY-SA: Attribution-ShareAlike*
- Mongol invasions and conquests. **Provided by**: Wikipedia. **Located at**: http://en.wikipedia.org/wiki/Mongol_conquest. **License**: *CC BY-SA: Attribution-ShareAlike*
- HIST302: Medieval Europe. **Provided by**: Saylor. **Located at**: https://legacy.saylor.org/hist302/Intro/. **License**: *CC BY: Attribution*
- Mongol Empire. **Provided by**: Wikipedia. **Located at**: http://en.wikipedia.org/wiki/Mongol_Empire. **License**: *CC BY-SA: Attribution-ShareAlike*
- Mongol invasion of Central Asia. **Provided by**: Wikipedia. **Located at**: http://en.wikipedia.org/wiki/Mongol_invasion_of_Central_Asia. **License**: *CC BY-SA: Attribution-ShareAlike*
- Changes in Eurasia - Mongol Conquest and Aftermath. **Provided by**: Wikibooks. **Located at**: http://en.wikibooks.org/wiki/World_History/Changes_in_Eurasia_-_Mongol_Conquest_and_Aftermath. **License**: *CC BY-SA: Attribution-ShareAlike*
- Mongol Empire. **Provided by**: Wikipedia. **Located at**: https://en.wikipedia.org/wiki/Mongol_Empire#/media/File:DiezAlbumsFallOfBaghdad.jpg. **License**: *Public Domain: No Known Copyright*
- Yuan Emperor Album Genghis Portrait. **Provided by**: Wikipedia. **Located at**: http://en.wikipedia.org/wiki/File:YuanEmperorAlbumGenghisPortrait.jpg. **License**: *Public Domain: No Known Copyright*
- Sung Dynasty 1141. **Provided by**: Wikipedia. **Located at**: https://en.wikipedia.org/wiki/File:Sung_Dynasty_1141.png. **License**: *CC BY-SA: Attribution-ShareAlike*
- Jin Jar. **Provided by**: Wikipedia. **Located at**: http://en.wikipedia.org/wiki/File:JinJar.JPG. **License**: *Public Domain: No Known Copyright*
- Chinese Gunpowder Formula. **Provided by**: Wikipedia. **Located at**: http://en.wikipedia.org/wiki/File:Chinese_Gunpowder_Formula.JPG. **License**: *Public Domain: No Known Copyright*
- Mongol Hunters Song. **Provided by**: Wikipedia. **Located at**: http://en.wikipedia.org/wiki/File:MongolHuntersSong.jpg. **License**: *Public Domain: No Known Copyright*

The Mongol Empire After Genghis Khan

The Mongols in Eastern Europe

Under Ögedei, the Mongol Empire conquered Eastern Europe. Various tactical errors and unexpected cultural and environmental factors stopped the Mongol forces from moving into Western Europe in 1241.

Learning Objectives
Recognize the European territories conquered by Ögedei and why the Mongols halted their expansion into Western Europe

Key Takeaways

Key Points

- Ögedei Khan, Genghis Khan's third son, ruled the Mongol Empire from 1227 CE-1241 CE.
- Under Ögedei, the Mongol Empire conquered Eastern Europe by invading Russia and Bulgaria; Poland, at the Battle of Legnica; and Hungary, at the Battle of Mohi.
- Changes in the terrain and resources, which limited their cavalry abilities, along with the death of a charismatic leader Ögedei in 1241, brought these forces to a halt before they reached Western Europe.

Key Terms

- **Rus'**: Early Russia; encompassed modern-day Russia, Ukraine, Poland, Belarus, and the

Baltic states.

- **steppe**: The grasslands of Eastern Europe and Asia. Similar to the North American prairie and the African savannah.

Expansion of the Mongol Empire Under Ögedei

Ögedei, Genghis Khan's third son, took over from his father and ruled the Mongol Empire from 1227 CE-1241 CE. One of his most important contributions to the empire was his conquest of Eastern Europe. These conquests involved invasions of Russia, Hungary, Volga Bulgaria, Poland, Dalmatia, and Wallachia. Over the course of four years (1237–1241), the Mongols quickly overtook most of the major eastern European cities, only sparing Novgorod and Pskov. As a result of the successful invasions, many of the conquered territories would become part of the Mongol Empire. This conquered region is sometimes referred to as the Golden Horde.

The operations were masterminded by General Subutai and commanded by Batu Khan and Kadan, both grandsons of Genghis Khan. The Mongols had acquired Chinese gunpowder, which they deployed in battle during the invasion of Europe to great success, in the form of bombs hurled via catapults. The Mongols have been credited for introducing gunpowder and associated weapons into Europe. They were also masters at cavalry invasions and siege warfare, which threatened many of the principalities the Mongols hoped to capture.

"Coronation of Ögedei": *"Coronation Of Ögedei,"* 1229, by Rashid al-Din.

Invasion and Conquest of Russian Lands

Ögedei Khan ordered his nephew (and grandson of Genghis Khan) Batu Khan to conquer Russia in 1235. (The territory was then called Rus' and encompassed modern-day Russia, Ukraine, Poland, Belarus, and the Baltic states. Territories and cities were ruled over by princely dynasties, which often meant these regions were fragmented politically.) The main force arrived at Ryazan in December 1237. Ryazan refused to surrender, and the Mongols sacked it and then stormed through other Russian cities, including Vladimir Suzdal in the north, and Pereyaslav and Chernihiv in the south. Other major Russian cities—such as Torzhok, and Kozelsk—were captured between 1238 and 1240. Some cities, such as Novgorod in the north, were not attacked due to the dense march and forest land surrounding it. However, the princes ruling Novgorod acted as tax collectors for the Mongol Empire in the coming decades.

Afterward, the Mongols turned their attention to the steppe, crushing various tribes and sacking Crimea to the west. They returned to Russia in 1239 and sacked several more cities and finally took the southern Rus' capital of Kiev, leaving behind their trademark destruction of both the population and city structures. This final attack sealed the Rus' principalities' fate, forcing princes to flee their regions or capitulate to Mongol taxation and rule.

Invasion into Central Europe

The Mongols continued to invade Central Europe with three armies. One army defeated the fragmented Poland at the Battle of Legnica in 1241. Two days later the armies regrouped and crushed the Hungarian army at the Battle of Mohi, killing up to a quarter of the population and destroying as much as half of the habitable dwellings. This decisive victory was partially due to the fact that Hungary was unprepared for an invasion and did not having a standing army ready to fight. It took a number of months for the Mongol army to subdue various power centers in Hungary. A major battle called the Mongol's Siege of Esztergom in the capital of Hungary forced people to flee and a new capital was moved to Budapest. However, the Mongols had a difficult time capturing fortified cities throughout Hungarian territories, which kept

The Battle of Legnica: *A depiction of the Battle of Legnica by Matthäus Merian the Elder, painted 1630.*

a total takeover from occurring. The Hungarian king Bela IV fled to Croatia during the initial attacks on his cities, and fortified structures throughout this territory helped keep the king and the local populations safe. However, Zagreb was sacked and destroyed in pursuit of the fugitive king and further territorial gains.

While the Mongol armies were fighting in Hungary and Croatia, they also pushed their forces into Austria, Dalmatia, and Moravia. Where they found local resistance, they ruthlessly killed the population. Where the locale offered no resistance, they forced the men into servitude in the Mongol army. They also ransacked Moldavia and Wallachia, plundering food stores and leaving the population in a precarious state.

End of the Mongol Advance

Although the Mongol forces were well-versed in cavalry and siege attacks, these two strategies also served as their weak points as they went farther westward. Many people in Hungary, Croatia, and Dalmatia had food stores at the ready for the long siege battles of the Mongol armies. Fortified cities and boggy or mountainous terrain also slowed down the light cavalry of the Mongol forces and gave European cities an advantage. Although politically fractured, European powers were uniting; even Hungarians who had survived the initial attack, or never engaged in battle, had begun a guerilla attack lead by survivors of the Hungarian royal family.

The Klis Fortress in Croatia: *This type of rocky, fortified city posed a serious challenge to Mongol forces who were often mounted on horses. This particular city defeated the Mongol army in 1242.*

Along with all of these tactical challenges the charismatic Mongol leader, Ögedei, died in December 1241. His death forced the Mongol armies to halt their westward expansion, especially in the face of mounting difficulties, and hasten back the thousands of miles to Karakorum, their capital in Mongolia, to elect his successor. Although the expansion did not extend into Western Europe, the Mongol forces retained power over many major Eastern European cities for many decades. However, after Ögedei's death, power disputes plagued the Mongol Empire and eventually weakened their extensive hold on such vast territories.

The Mongol Empire after Genghis Khan • 655

Administrative Reform in the Mongol Empire

Möngke was generally a popular ruler of the Mongol Empire; he met debts, controlled spending, conducted a census, and protected civilians.

Learning Objectives

Choose the best summary of Möngke's achievements

Key Takeaways

Key Points

- After Ögedei's death, Genghis Khan 's descendants Güyük and Batu Khan fought about who would rule until Batu Khan's death, at which point Genghis' grandson Möngke took control.
- Möngke was generally a popular ruler. He generously met all Güyük's outstanding debts, an unprecedented move.
- Möngke also forbade extravagant spending, imposed taxes (which incited some rebellions), and punished the unauthorized plundering of civilians. He established the Department of Monetary Affairs and standardized a system of measurement.
- Möngke conducted a census of the Mongol Empire and its land.

Key Terms

- **ingot**: A block of steel, gold, or other metal oblong in shape and used for currency.
- **Department of Monetary Affairs**: Möngke established this body to control the issuance of paper money in order to eliminate the overissue of currency that had been a problem since Ögedei's reign.

From Ögedei's death in 1241 CE until 1246 CE the Mongol Empire was ruled under the regency of Ögedei's widow, Töregene Khatun. She set the stage for the ascension of her son, Güyük, as Great Khan, and he would take control in 1246. He and Ögedei's nephew Batu Khan (both grandsons of Genghis Khan) fought bitterly for power; Güyük died in 1248 on the way to confront Batu.

Another nephew of Ögedei's (and so a third grandson of Genghis Khan's), Möngke, then took the throne in 1251 with Batu's approval. In 1255, well into Möngke's reign, Batu had repaired his relationship with the Great Khan and so finally felt secure enough to prepare invasions westward into Europe. Fortunately for the Europeans, however, he died before his plans could be implemented.

The Mongol Empire Under Möngke

Möngke's rule established some of the most consistent monetary and administrative policies since Genghis Khan. In the mercantile department he:

- Forbade extravagant spending and limited gifts to the princes.
- Made merchants subject to taxes.
- Prohibited the demanding of goods and services from civilian populations by merchants.
- Punished the unauthorized plundering of civilians by generals and princes (including his own son).

In 1253, Möngke established the Department of Monetary Affairs to control the issuance of paper money. This new department contributed to better econimic stability including:

- Limiting the overissue of currency, which had been a problem since Ögedei's reign.
- Standardizing a system of measurement based on the silver ingot.
- Paying out all debts drawn by high-rank Mongol elites to important foreign and local merchants.

Möngke recognized that if he did not meet his predecessor's, Güyük's, financial obligations, it would make merchants reluctant to continue business with the Mongols. Like many other rules around the world at this time, his hope was to take advantage of the budding commercial revolution in Europe and the Middle East. Ata-Malik Juvaini, a 13th-century Persian historian, commented on the virtue of this move, saying, "And from what book of history has it been read or heard…that a king paid the debt of another king? "

The Mongol Empire's administration followed a trend that was occurring in the Western Europe, in which kings and emperors were finding efficient ways to manage their administrative and legals systems and fund crusades, conquests, and wars. From 1252–1259, Möngke conducted a census of the Mongol Empire including Iran, Afghanistan, Georgia, Armenia, Russia, Central Asia and North China. The new census counted not only households but also the number of men aged 15–60 and the number of fields, livestock, vineyards, and orchards.

Möngke also tried to create a fixed poll tax collected by imperial agents, which could be forwarded to the needy units. He taxed the wealthiest people most severely. But the census and taxation sparked popular riots and resistance in the western districts and in the more independent regions under the Mongol umbrella. These rebellions were ultimately put down, and Möngke would continue to rule.

Expansion and Khanates

At the death of Genghis Khan in 1226, the empire was already large enough that one ruler could not oversee the administrative aspects of each region. Genghis realized this and created appanages, or khanates, for his sons, daughters, and grandsons to rule over in order to keep a consistent rule of law. Möngke's administrative policies extended to these regions during his reign, often causing local unrest due to Mongol occupation and taxation. Some khanates were more closely linked to centralized Mongol policies than others, depending on their location, who oversaw them, and the amount of resistance in each region.

Painting of the Battle of Mohi in 1241: *Möngke might have been present at this battle, which took place in the kingdom of Hungary, during one of the many Mongol invasions and attacks that expanded the Mongol Empire.*

It should also be noted that the vast religious and cultural traditions of these khanates, including Islam, Judaism, Taoism, Orthodoxy, and Buddhism, were often at odds with the khanate rulers and their demands. Some of the most essential khanates to exist under Möngke's administrative years included:

- The Golden Horde, which contained the Rus' principalities and large chunks of modern-day Eastern Europe, including Ukraine, Belarus, and Romania. Many Russian princes capitulated with Mongol rule and a relatively stable alliance existed in the 1250s in some principalities.
- Chagatai Khanate was a Turkic region which was ruled over by Chagatai, Odegei's second son, until 1242 at his death. This region was clearly Islamic and functioned as an outlying region of the central Mongol government until 1259, when Möngke died.
- Ilkhanate was the major southwestern khanate of the Mongol Empire and encompassed parts of modern-day Iran, Azerbaijan, Armenia, and Turkey and the heartland of Persian culture. Möngke's brother, Hulagu, ruled over this region and his descendants continued to oversee this khanate into the 14th century.

Möngke's Death

Möngke died while conducting war in China on August 11, 1259. He was possibly a victim of cholera or dysentery, however there is no confirmed record of the cause of his death. His son Asutai conducted him back to Mongolia to be buried. The ruler's death sparked the four-year Toluid Civil War between his two younger brothers, Kublai and Ariq Böke, and also spurred on the division of the Mongol Empire.

Kublai Khan

Kublai Khan came to power in 1260. By 1271 he had renamed the Empire the Yuan Dynasty and conquered the Song dynasty and with it, all of China. However, Chinese forces ultimately overthrew the Mongols to form the Ming Dynasty.

Learning Objectives

Identify Kublai Khan's most significant achievements

Key Takeaways

Key Points

- Möngke's death led to civil war (or Toluid Civil War) between his two younger brothers; ultimately, Kublai Khan emerged victorious and renamed the empire as the Yuan Dynasty in 1271.
- Kublai also renamed himself Emperor of China in order to win over millions of Chinese subjects.
- Ultimately, under Kublai Khan, the Mongols were the first non-Chinese people to conquer all of China. However, their conquests of Japan and Java failed.
- At the time of Kublai's death, the Mongol Empire fractured into four separate empires; this made it easy for the Han Chinese to overthrow them in 1368 and establish the Ming Dynasty.

Möngke's death in 1259 led to civil war (often referred to as the Toluid Civil War) between his two younger brothers, Kublai Khan and Ariq Böke. Kublai Khan emerged victorious and established the Yuan Dynasty in China in 1271, perhaps the Mongols' greatest triumph, though it would eventually be overthrown in 1368 by the native Han Chinese, who would launch their own Ming Dynasty.

Establishment of the Yuan Dynasty

After Kublai took over control of the Chinese territories with the blessings of Möngke Khan around 1251, he sought to establish a firmer hold on these vast regions. Rivaling dynasties loomed throughout the Chinese territories making for a contentious political background to Kublai's rule. His greatest obstacle was the powerful Song dynasty in the south. He stabilized the northern regions by placing a hostage puppet leader in Korea named Wonjong in 1259. After the death of Möngke in that same year, and the following civil war, Kublai was named the Great Khan and successor of Möngke. This new powerful position allowed Kublai to oversee uprisings and wars between the western khanates and assist rulers (often family members) to oversee these regions. However, his tenuous hold in the east occupied most of his resources.

Kublai Khan: *A portrait of a young Kublai Khan by Anige, a Nepali artist in Kublai's court.*

In 1271, as he continued to consolidate his power over the vast and varying Chinese subjects and outlying regions, Kublai Khan renamed his khanate the Yuan Dynasty. His newly named dynasty appeared to be successful after the fall of the major southern center Xiangyang in 1273 to Mongol forces after five years of struggle. The final piece of the puzzle for Kublai was the conquest of the Song Dynasty in southern China. He finally garnered this sought-after southern region in 1276 and the last Song emperor died in 1279 after years of costly battles. With this success, the Mongols became the first non-Chinese people to conquer all of the Chinese territories. Kublai moved his headquarters to Dadu, what later became the modern city of Beijing. His establishment of a capital there was a controversial move to many Mongols who accused him of being too closely tied to Chinese culture. However, the Yuan Dynasty often functioned as an independent khanate from the rest of the western Mongol-dominated regions.

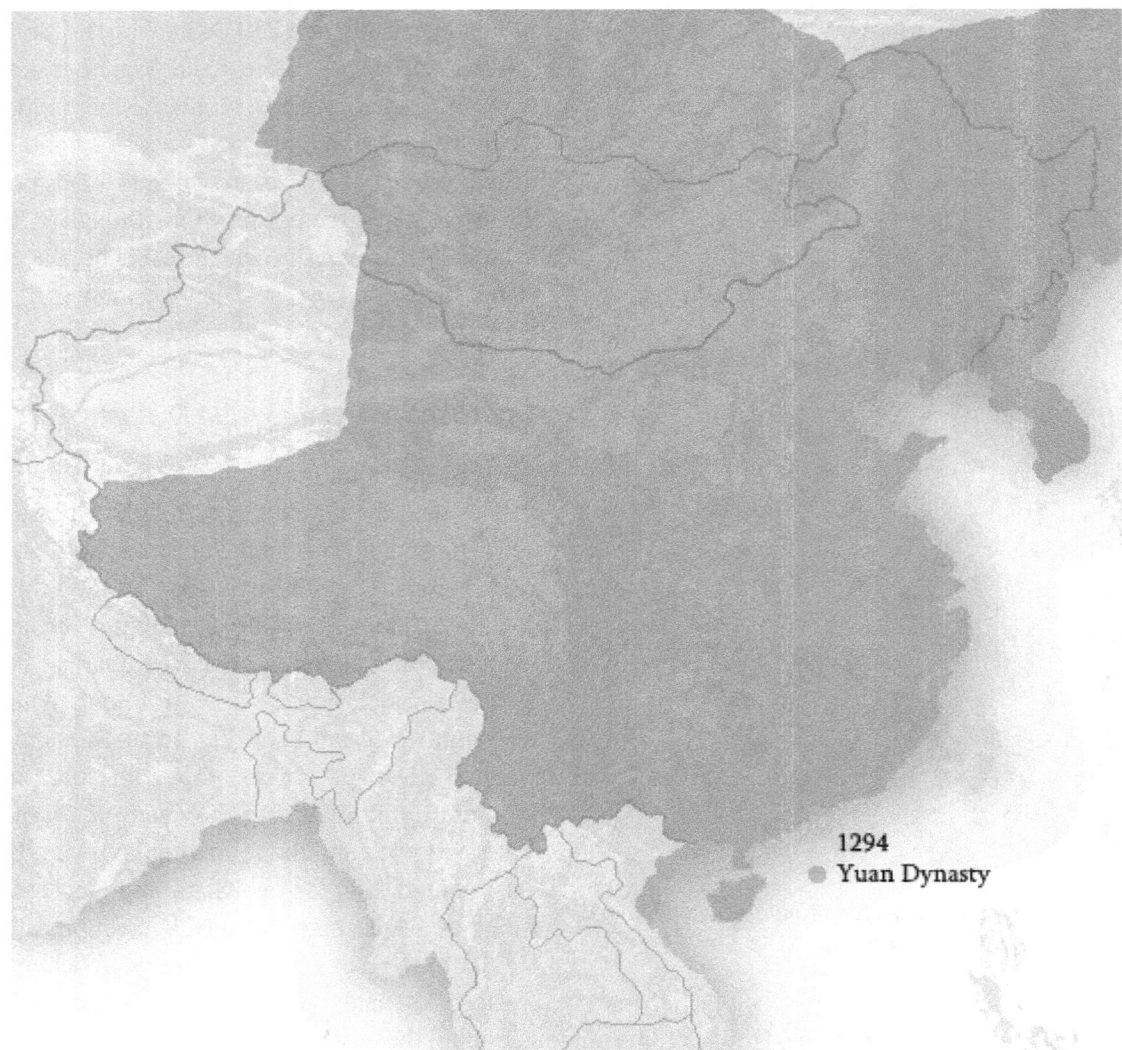

Yuan Dynasty circa 1292: *The sheer scale of this khanate required extensive military support and often strained the Mongol treasury in order to keep populations under its influence.*

Extended Invasions

Kublai Khan's costly invasions of many territories in the east did not go smoothly and some went on for many years, draining the Mongol treasury and utilizing precious resources. Although the invasions of Burma in 1277, 1283, and 1287 forced the population to eventually capitulate, they were never more than a vassal state. Similarly, the Yuan forces invaded Sakhalin Island off the coast of modern-day Russia multiple times between 1264 and 1308, and the various tribal groups also eventually became a vassals after long years of turmoil. Southern Asian regions often agreed to Yuan rule and taxation only in the face of more bloodshed and terror. Conversely, Mongol invasions of Japan (1274 and 1280) and Java (1293) under Kublai Khan ultimately failed and illustrated the costly effects of constant invasive military tactics.

Yuan Dynasty Administration

Kublai Khan made significant reforms to existing institutions under the Yuan Dynasty. He divided the Dynasty's territory into a central region and peripheral regions that were under the control of various officials. He created an academy, offices, trade ports and canals, and sponsored arts and science. Mongol records also list 20,166 public schools created during his reign. He also, along with engineers, invented the Muslim trebuchet (hui-hui pao), a counterweight-based weapon that was highly successful in battle.

He also continued to welcome trade and travel throughout his empire. Marco Polo, Marco Polo's father (an Italian merchant), and his father's trade partner traveled to China during this time. They met Kublai Khan and lived amongst his court to establish trade relations. Polo generally praised the wealth and extravagance of Khan and the Mongol Empire. Some historians also speculate that trade was so accessible between the empire and Europe, that it may have contributed to the flow of disease, especially the black plague in the mid-1300s.

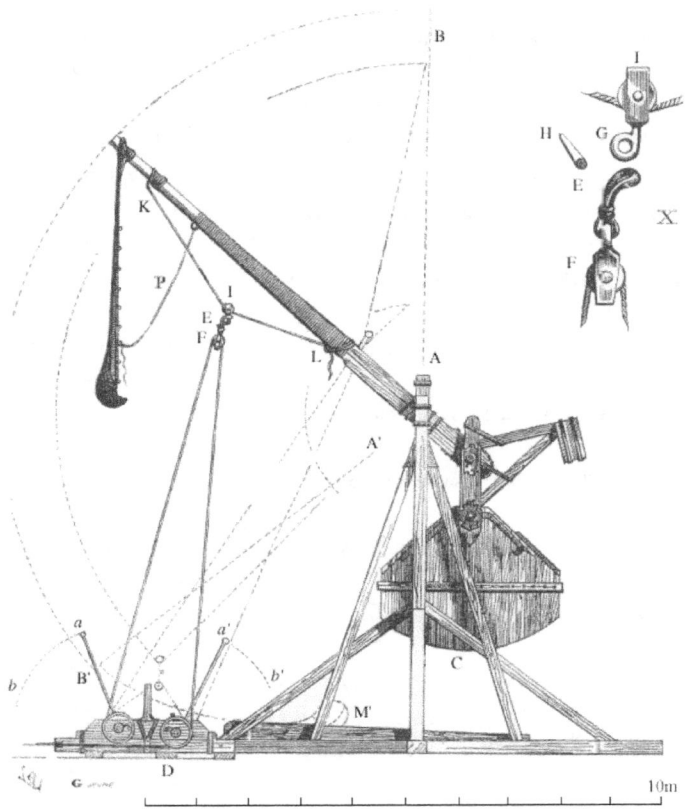

Trebuchet: *The scheme of the "Muslim trebuchet" (hui-hui pao), invented during Kublai Khan's rule.*

By the time of Kublai's death in 1294, the Mongol Empire had fractured into four separate empires, which were based on administrative zones Genghis had created. The four empires were known as khanates, each pursuing its own separate interests and objectives: the Golden Horde Khanate in the northwest, the Chagatai Khanate in the west, the Ilkhanate in the southwest, and the Yuan Dynasty, based in modern-day Beijing. In 1304, the three western khanates briefly accepted the rule of the Yuan Dynasty in name, but when the Dynasty was overthrown by the Han Chinese Ming Dynasty in 1368, and with increasing local unrest in the Golden Horde, the Mongol Empire finally dissolved.

Attributions

CC licensed content, Specific attribution

- Battle of Mohi. **Provided by**: Wikipedia. **Located at**: https://en.wikipedia.org/wiki/Battle_of_Mohi. **License**: *CC BY-SA: Attribution-ShareAlike*
- u00d6gedei Khan. **Provided by**: Wikipedia. **Located at**: https://en.wikipedia.org/wiki/%C3%96gedei_Khan. **License**: *CC BY-SA: Attribution-ShareAlike*
- HIST201: History of Europe, 1000 to 1800. **Provided by**: Saylor. **Located at**: https://legacy.saylor.org/hist201/Intro/. **License**: *CC BY: Attribution*
- Steppe. **Provided by**: Wiktionary. **Located at**: http://en.wiktionary.org/wiki/steppe. **License**: *CC BY-SA: Attribution-ShareAlike*
- Mongol Empire. **Provided by**: Wikipedia. **Located at**: http://en.wikipedia.org/wiki/Mongol_Empire. **License**: *CC BY-SA: Attribution-ShareAlike*
- Mongol invasion of Europe. **Provided by**: Wikipedia. **Located at**: http://en.wikipedia.org/wiki/Mongol_invasion_of_Europe. **License**: *CC BY-SA: Attribution-ShareAlike*
- Muscovy. **Provided by**: Saylor. **Located at**: http://www.saylor.org/site/wp-content/uploads/2011/01/Muscovy.pdf. **License**: *CC BY: Attribution*
- Mongol invasions and conquests. **Provided by**: Wikipedia. **Located at**: http://en.wikipedia.org/wiki/Mongol_conquest. **License**: *CC BY-SA: Attribution-ShareAlike*
- Changes in Eurasia - Mongol Conquest and Aftermath. **Provided by**: Wikibooks. **Located at**: http://en.wikibooks.org/wiki/World_History/Changes_in_Eurasia_-_Mongol_Conquest_and_Aftermath. **License**: *CC BY-SA: Attribution-ShareAlike*
- steppe. **Provided by**: Wiktionary. **Located at**: http://en.wiktionary.org/wiki/steppe. **License**: *CC BY-SA: Attribution-ShareAlike*
- Mongol Invasion of Europe. **Provided by**: Wikipedia. **Located at**: https://en.wikipedia.org/wiki/Mongol_invasion_of_Europe#/media/File:Klis_0807_3.jpg. **License**: *CC BY-SA: Attribution-ShareAlike*
- Coronation Of Ogodei 1229. **Provided by**: Wikipedia. **Located at**: http://en.wikipedia.org/wiki/File:CoronationOfOgodei1229.jpg. **License**: *Public Domain: No Known Copyright*
- Bitwa pod Legnicu0105. **Provided by**: Wikipedia. **Located at**: http://en.wikipedia.org/wiki/File:Bitwa_pod_Legnic%C4%85.jpg. **License**: *Public Domain: No Known Copyright*
- Division of the Mongol Empire. **Provided by**: Wikipedia. **Located at**: https://en.wikipedia.org/wiki/Division_of_the_Mongol_Empire. **License**: *CC BY-SA: Attribution-ShareAlike*
- HIST201: History of Europe, 1000 to 1800. **Provided by**: Saylor. **Located at**: https://legacy.saylor.org/hist201/Intro/. **License**: *CC BY: Attribution*
- Changes in Eurasia - Mongol Conquest and Aftermath. **Provided by**: Wikibooks. **Located at**: http://en.wikibooks.org/wiki/World_History/Changes_in_Eurasia_-_Mongol_Conquest_and_Aftermath. **License**: *CC BY-SA: Attribution-ShareAlike*
- Muscovy. **Provided by**: Saylor. **Located at**: http://www.saylor.org/site/wp-content/uploads/2011/01/Muscovy.pdf. **License**: *CC BY: Attribution*
- Mongol invasions and conquests. **Provided by**: Wikipedia. **Located at**: http://en.wikipedia.org/wiki/Mongol_conquest. **License**: *CC BY-SA: Attribution-ShareAlike*
- Mongol invasion of Europe. **Provided by**: Wikipedia. **Located at**: http://en.wikipedia.org/wiki/Mongol_invasion_of_Europe. **License**: *CC BY-SA: Attribution-ShareAlike*
- Mongol Empire. **Provided by**: Wikipedia. **Located at**: http://en.wikipedia.org/wiki/Mongol_Empire. **License**: *CC BY-SA: Attribution-ShareAlike*
- Mongol Invasion of Europe. **Provided by**: Wikipedia. **Located at**: https://en.wikipedia.org/wiki/Mongol_invasion_of_Europe#/media/File:Klis_0807_3.jpg. **License**: *CC BY-SA: Attribution-ShareAlike*
- Coronation Of Ogodei 1229. **Provided by**: Wikipedia. **Located at**: http://en.wikipedia.org/wiki/File:CoronationOfOgodei1229.jpg. **License**: *Public Domain: No Known Copyright*
- Bitwa pod Legnicu0105. **Provided by**: Wikipedia. **Located at**: http://en.wikipedia.org/wiki/File:Bitwa_pod_Legnic%C4%85.jpg. **License**: *Public Domain: No Known Copyright*
- Battle of Mohi 1241. **Provided by**: Wikipedia. **Located at**: https://en.wikipedia.org/wiki/M%C3%B6ngke_Khan#/media/File:Battle_of_Mohi_1241.PNG. **License**: *Public Domain: No Known Copyright*
- Kublai Khan. **Provided by**: Wikipedia. **Located at**: https://en.wikipedia.org/wiki/Kublai_Khan. **License**: *CC BY-SA: Attribution-ShareAlike*
- Song dynasty. **Provided by**: Wikipedia. **Located at**: https://en.wikipedia.org/wiki/Song_dynasty. **License**: *CC BY-SA: Attribution-ShareAlike*
- HIST302: Medieval Europe. **Provided by**: Saylor. **Located at**: https://legacy.saylor.org/hist302/Intro/. **License**: *CC BY: Attribution*
- Yuan dynasty. **Provided by**: Wikipedia. **Located at**: http://en.wikipedia.org/wiki/Yuan_Dynasty. **License**: *CC BY-SA: Attribution-*

ShareAlike

- Changes in Eurasia - Mongol Conquest and Aftermath. **Provided by**: Wikibooks. **Located at**: http://en.wikibooks.org/wiki/World_History/Changes_in_Eurasia_-_Mongol_Conquest_and_Aftermath. **License**: *CC BY-SA: Attribution-ShareAlike*
- Mongol invasions and conquests. **Provided by**: Wikipedia. **Located at**: http://en.wikipedia.org/wiki/Mongol_conquest. **License**: *CC BY-SA: Attribution-ShareAlike*
- Mongol Empire. **Provided by**: Wikipedia. **Located at**: http://en.wikipedia.org/wiki/Mongol_Empire. **License**: *CC BY-SA: Attribution-ShareAlike*
- Mongol Invasion of Europe. **Provided by**: Wikipedia. **Located at**: https://en.wikipedia.org/wiki/Mongol_invasion_of_Europe#/media/File:Klis_0807_3.jpg. **License**: *CC BY-SA: Attribution-ShareAlike*
- Coronation Of Ogodei 1229. **Provided by**: Wikipedia. **Located at**: http://en.wikipedia.org/wiki/File:CoronationOfOgodei1229.jpg. **License**: *Public Domain: No Known Copyright*
- Bitwa pod Legnicu0105. **Provided by**: Wikipedia. **Located at**: http://en.wikipedia.org/wiki/File:Bitwa_pod_Legric%C4%85.jpg. **License**: *Public Domain: No Known Copyright*
- Battle of Mohi 1241. **Provided by**: Wikipedia. **Located at**: https://en.wikipedia.org/wiki/M%C3%B6ngke_Khan#/media/File:Battle_of_Mohi_1241.PNG. **License**: *Public Domain: No Known Copyright*
- Yuan Dynasty 1294. **Provided by**: Wikipedia. **Located at**: https://en.wikipedia.org/wiki/Yuan_dynasty#/media/File:Yuan_Dynasty_1294.png. **License**: *CC BY-SA: Attribution-ShareAlike*
- Trebuchet 2. **Provided by**: Wikipedia. **Located at**: http://en.wikipedia.org/wiki/File:Trebuchet2.png. **License**: *Public Domain: No Known Copyright*
- Qubilai Setsen Khaan. **Provided by**: Wikipedia. **Located at**: http://en.wikipedia.org/wiki/File:Qubilai_Setsen_Khaan.JPG. **License**: *Public Domain: No Known Copyright*

Chinese Dynasties

The Tang Dynasty

Rise of the Tang Dynasty

The Tang dynasty, generally regarded as a golden age of Chinese culture, was founded by the Lǐ family, who seized power during the decline and collapse of the Sui dynasty.

Learning Objectives

Explain the events that led to the Tang dynasty coming to power

Key Takeaways

Key Points

- The short-lived Sui dynasty had profound effects on the development of China as an imperial power, consolidating the ethnic and cultural character of the people and uniting the Northern and Southern dynasties.
- After a series of costly and disastrous military campaigns against one of the Three Kingdoms of Korea, the Sui dynasty disintegrated under a sequence of popular revolts culminating in the assassination of Emperor Yang by his ministers in 618.
- The Tang dynasty was founded by the Li Yuan, a duke who seized power during the decline and collapse of the Sui dynasty.
- For the next hundred years, several Tang leaders ruled, including a woman, Empress Wu, whose rise to power was achieved through cruel and calculating tactics but made room for the prominent role of women in the imperial court.
- During the forty-four-year reign of Emperor Xuanzong, who came to power in 712, the Tang dynasty reached its height, a golden age with low economic inflation and a toned down lifestyle for the imperial court.

> ### Key Terms
>
> - **sinicization**: A process whereby non-Han Chinese societies come under the influence of Han Chinese state and society.
> - **Han Chinese**: An ethnic group native to East Asia; the Chinese peoples especially as distinguished from non-Chinese (such as Mongolian) people in the population.
> - **Confucianism**: A tradition, philosophy, religion, humanistic, or rationalistic religion, a way of governing, and a way of life based on the teachings of Confucius.

Overview of the Tang Dynasty

The Tang dynasty (Chinese: ??) was an imperial dynasty of China preceded by the Sui dynasty and followed by the Five Dynasties and Ten Kingdoms period. It is generally regarded as a high point in Chinese civilization and a golden age of cosmopolitan culture. Its territory, acquired through the military campaigns of its early rulers, rivaled that of the Han dynasty, and the Tang capital at Chang'an (present-day Xi'an) was the most populous city in the world.

With its large population base, the dynasty was able to raise professional and conscripted armies of hundreds of thousands of troops to contend with nomadic powers in dominating Inner Asia and the lucrative trade routes along the Silk Road. Various kingdoms and states paid tribute to the Tang court, and the Tang also conquered or subdued several regions that it indirectly controlled through a protectorate system. Besides political hegemony, the Tang also exerted a powerful cultural influence over neighboring states such as those in Korea, Japan, and Vietnam.

The Tang dynasty was largely a period of progress and stability in the first half of its rule, followed by the An Lushan Rebellion and the decline of central authority in the later half of the dynasty. Like the previous Sui dynasty, the Tang dynasty maintained a civil service system by recruiting scholar-officials through standardized examinations and recommendations to office. Chinese culture flourished and further matured during the Tang era; it is considered the greatest age for Chinese poetry. Two of China's most famous poets, Li Bai and Du Fu, belonged to this age, as did many famous painters such as Han Gan, Zhang Xuan, and Zhou Fang. There were many notable innovations during the Tang, including the development of woodblock printing.

Decline of the Sui Dynasty and the Founding of the Tang

The Sui dynasty was a short-lived imperial dynasty of pivotal significance. The Sui unified the Northern and Southern dynasties and reinstalled the rule of ethnic Han Chinese in the entirety of China proper, as well as sinicized former nomadic ethnic minorities within its territory. By the middle of the Sui dynasty, the newly unified empire entered an age of prosperity with vast agricultural surplus that supported acute population growth. Wide-ranging reforms and construction projects were undertaken to consolidate the newly unified state, with long-lasting influences beyond the short dynastic reign. The Sui dynasty was succeeded by the Tang dynasty, which largely inherited its foundation.

After a series of costly and disastrous military campaigns against Goguryeo, one of the Three Kingdoms of Korea, ended in defeat by 614, the Sui dynasty disintegrated under a sequence of popular revolts culminating in the assassination of Emperor Yang by his ministers in 618. The dynasty, which lasted only thirty-seven years, was undermined by ambitious wars and construction projects, which overstretched its resources. Particularly under Emperor Yang, heavy taxation and compulsory labor duties eventually induced widespread revolts and a brief civil war following the fall of the dynasty.

Emperor Yang of Sui: *Portrait painting of Emperor Yang of Sui, the last emperor of the Sui dynasty, commissioned in 643 by Taizong, painted by Yan Liben (600–673).*

After Yang's death, the Sui dynasty's territories were carved into a handful of short-lived states by its officials, generals, and agrarian rebel leaders, and the process of elimination and annexation that followed ultimately culminated in the consolidation of the Tang dynasty by the former Sui general Li Yuan.

Li Yuan was duke of Tang and governor of Taiyuan during the Sui dynasty's collapse. He had prestige and military experience, and was a first cousin of Emperor Yang of Sui. Li Yuan rose in rebellion in 617, along with his son and his equally militant daughter Princess Pingyang, who raised and commanded her own troops. In the winter of 617, Li Yuan occupied Chang'an, relegated Emperor Yang to the position of Taishang Huang or retired emperor, and acted as regent to the puppet child-emperor, Emperor Gong of Sui. On the news of Emperor Yang's murder by General Yuwen Huaji on June 18, 618, Li Yuan declared himself the emperor of a new dynasty, the Tang.

Early Tang Dynasty and the Rise to Prosperity

Li Yuan, known as Emperor Gaozu of Tang, ruled until 626, when he was forcefully deposed by his son Li Shimin, the Prince of Qin, conventionally known by his temple name Taizong. Although killing two brothers and deposing his father contradicted the Confucian value of filial piety, Taizong showed himself to be a capable leader who listened to the advice of the wisest members of his council.

Emperor Taizong: *Emperor Taizong (r. 626–649) receives Gar Tongtsen Yülsung, ambassador of Tibet, at his court; painted in 641 by Yan Liben (600–673)*

For the next hundred years, several Tang leaders ruled, including a woman, Empress Wu, whose rise to power was achieved through cruel and calculating tactics but made room for the prominent role of women in the imperial court. Wu's rule was actually a short break in the Tang dynasty, as she established the short-lived Zhou dynasty; the Tang dynasty was restored after her rule. In 706 the wife of Emperor Zhongzong of Tang, Empress Wei, persuaded her husband to staff government offices with his sister and her daughters, and in 709 requested that he grant women the right to bequeath hereditary privileges to their sons (which before was a male right only). Just as Emperor Zhongzong was dominated by Empress Wei, so too was Ruizong dominated by Princess Taiping. This was finally ended when Princess Taiping's coup failed in 712 (she later hanged herself in 713) and Emperor Ruizong abdicated to Emperor Xuanzong.

During the forty-four-year reign of Emperor Xuanzong, the Tang dynasty reached its height, a golden age with low economic inflation and a toned down lifestyle for the imperial court. Seen as a progressive and benevolent ruler, Xuanzong even abolished the death penalty in the year 747; all executions had to be approved beforehand by the emperor himself. Xuanzong bowed to the consensus of his ministers on policy decisions and made efforts to staff government ministries fairly with different political factions. His staunch Confucian chancellor Zhang Jiuling (673–740) worked to reduce deflation and increase the money supply by upholding the use of private coinage, while his aristocratic and technocratic successor, Li Linfu

(d. 753) favored government monopoly over the issuance of coinage. After 737 most of Xuanzong's confidence rested in his long-standing chancellor Li Linfu, who championed a more aggressive foreign policy employing non-Chinese generals. This policy ultimately created the conditions for a massive rebellion against Xuanzong.

Trade Under the Tang Dynasty

By reopening the Silk Road and increasing maritime trade by sail at sea, the Tang were able to gain many new technologies, cultural practices, rare luxuries, and foreign items.

Learning Objectives

Describe how the Tang dynasty prospered from trade

Key Takeaways

Key Points

- Although the Silk Road from China to the West was initially formulated during the reign of Emperor Wu of Han (141–87 BCE), it was reopened by the Tang Empire in 639 CE when Hou Junji conquered the West, and remained open for almost four decades.
- The Silk Road was the most important pre-modern Eurasian trade route, opening long-distance political and economic relations between the civilizations.
- Though silk was certainly the major trade item exported from China, many other goods were traded, and religions, syncretic philosophies, and various technologies, as well as diseases, also spread along the Silk Road.
- In addition to economic trade, the Silk Road served as a means of carrying out cultural trade among the civilizations along its network.
- Chinese maritime presence increased dramatically during the Tang period, giving rise to large seaports and trade relations with Africa, India, and beyond.

Key Terms

- **Pax Sinica**: A period of peace in East Asia, maintained by Chinese hegemony, during which long-distance trade flourished, cities ballooned, standards of living rose, and the population surged.
- **Silk Road**: An ancient network of trade routes that for centuries were central to cultural interaction through regions of the Asian continent connecting the West and East from China to the Mediterranean Sea.

Overview

Through use of land trade along the Silk Road and maritime trade by sail at sea, the Tang were able to gain many new technologies, cultural practices, rare luxuries, and contemporary items. From the Middle East, India, Persia, and Central Asia the Tang were able to acquire new ideas in fashion, new types of ceramics, and improved silver-smithing. The Chinese also gradually adopted the foreign concept of stools and chairs as seating, whereas before they had always sat on mats placed on the floor. In the Middle East, the Islamic world coveted and purchased in bulk Chinese goods such as silks, lacquerwares, and porcelain wares. Songs, dances, and musical instruments from foreign regions became popular in China during the Tang dynasty. These musical instruments included oboes, flutes, and small lacquered drums from Kucha in the Tarim Basin, and percussion instruments from India such as cymbals. At the court there were nine musical ensembles (expanded from seven in the Sui dynasty) representing music from throughout Asia.

There was great contact with and interest in India as a hub for Buddhist knowledge, with famous travelers such as Xuanzang (d. 664) visiting the South Asian subcontinent. After a seventeen-year-long trip, Xuanzang managed to bring back valuable Sanskrit texts to be translated into Chinese. There was also a Turkic–Chinese dictionary available for serious scholars and students, and Turkic folksongs gave inspiration to some Chinese poetry. In the interior of China, trade was facilitated by the Grand Canal and the Tang government's rationalization of the greater canal system that reduced costs of transporting grain and other commodities. The state also managed roughly 32,100 km (19,900 mi) of postal service routes by horse and boat.

The Silk Road

Although the Silk Road from China to the West was initially formulated during the reign of Emperor Wu (141–87 BCE) during the Han dynasty, it was reopened by the Tang in 639 CE when Hou Junji (d. 643) conquered the West, and remained open for almost four decades. It was closed after the Tibetans captured it in 678, but in 699, during Empress Wu's period, it reopened when the Tang reconquered the Four Garrisons of Anxi originally installed in 640, once again connecting China directly to the West for land-based trade.

The Silk Road was the most important pre-modern Eurasian trade route. The Tang dynasty established a second Pax Sinica and the Silk Road reached its golden age, whereby Persian and Sogdian merchants benefited from the commerce between East and West. At the same time, the Chinese empire welcomed foreign cultures, making it very cosmopolitan in its urban centers.

The Tang captured the vital route through the Gilgit Valley from Tibet in 722, lost it to the Tibetans in 737, and regained it under the command of the Goguryeo-Korean General Gao Xianzhi. When the An Lushan Rebellion ended in 763, the Tang Empire had once again lost control over its western lands, as the Tibetan Empire largely cut off China's direct access to the Silk Road. An internal rebellion in 848 ousted the Tibetan rulers, and Tang China regained its northwestern prefectures from Tibet in 851. These lands contained crucial grazing areas and pastures for raising horses that the Tang dynasty desperately needed.

Despite the many western travelers coming into China to live and trade, many travelers, mainly religious monks, recorded the strict border laws that the Chinese enforced. As the monk Xuanzang and many other monk travelers attested to, there were many Chinese government checkpoints along the Silk Road where travel permits into the Tang Empire were examined. Furthermore, banditry was a problem along the checkpoints and oasis towns, as Xuanzang also recorded that his group of travelers was assaulted by bandits on multiple occasions.

The Silk Road also affected Tang dynasty art. Horses became a significant symbol of prosperity and power as well as an instrument of military and diplomatic policy. Horses were also revered as a relative of the dragon.

Tang period jar: *A Tang period gilt-silver jar, shaped in the style of northern nomad's leather bag, decorated with a horse dancing with a cup of wine in its mouth, as the horses of Emperor Xuanzong were trained to do.*

Seaports and Maritime Trade

Chinese envoys had been sailing through the Indian Ocean to India since perhaps the 2nd century BC, but it was during the Tang dynasty that a strong Chinese maritime presence was found in the Persian Gulf and Red Sea, into Persia, Mesopotamia, Arabia, Egypt, Aksum (Ethiopia), and Somalia in the Horn of Africa.

During the Tang dynasty, thousands of foreigners came and lived in numerous Chinese cities for trade and commercial ties with China, including Persians, Arabs, Hindu Indians, Malays, Bengalis, Sinhalese, Khmers, Chams, Jews and Nestorian Christians of the Near East, and many others. In 748, the Buddhist monk Jian Zhen described Guangzhou as a bustling mercantile center where many large and impressive foreign ships came to dock.

During the An Lushan Rebellion Arab and Persian pirates burned and looted Guangzhou in 758, and foreigners were massacred at Yangzhou in 760. The Tang government reacted by shutting the port of Canton down for roughly five decades, and foreign vessels docked at Hanoi instead. However, when the port reopened it thrived. In 851 the Arab merchant Sulaiman al-Tajir observed the manufacturing of Chinese porcelain in Guangzhou and admired its transparent quality. He also provided a description of Guangzhou's mosque, its granaries, its local government administration, some of its written records, and the treatment of travelers, along with the use of ceramics, rice-wine, and tea. However, in another bloody episode at Guangzhou in 879, the Chinese rebel Huang Chao sacked the city and purportedly slaughtered thousands of native Chinese, along with foreign Jews, Christians, Zoroastrians, and Muslims in the process. Huang's rebellion was eventually suppressed in 884.

The Chinese engaged in large-scale production for overseas export by at least the time of the Tang. This was proven by the discovery of the Belitung shipwreck, a silt-preserved shipwrecked Arabian dhow in the Gaspar Strait near Belitung, which contained 63,000 pieces of Tang ceramics, silver, and gold. Beginning in 785, the Chinese began to call regularly at Sufala on the East African coast in order to cut out Arab middlemen, with various contemporary Chinese sources giving detailed descriptions of trade in Africa. In 863 the Chinese author Duan Chengshi (d. 863) provided a detailed description of the slave trade, ivory trade, and ambergris trade in a country called Bobali, which historians suggest was Berbera in Somalia. In Fustat (old Cairo), Egypt, the fame of Chinese ceramics there led to an enormous demand for Chinese goods; hence Chinese often traveled there. During this time period, the Arab merchant Shulama wrote of his admiration for Chinese seafaring junks, but noted that their draft was too deep for them to enter the Euphrates River, which forced them to ferry passengers and cargo in small boats. Shulama also noted that Chinese ships were often very large, with capacities of up to 600–700 passengers.

Foreign merchant: *Figurine of a Sogdian merchant of the Tang dynasty, 7th-century.*

Religion Under the Tang Dynasty

Religion in the Tang dynasty was diverse, and emperors sought support and legitimation from some local religious leaders, but persecuted others.

Learning Objectives

Analyze why the emperors of the Tang dynasty were interested in the promotion of certain religions

Key Takeaways

Key Points

- Taoism was the official religion of the Tang; it is a native Chinese religious and philosophical tradition, based on the writings of Laozi.
- Taoism was combined with ancient Chinese folk religions, medical practices, Buddhism, and martial arts to create a complex and syncretic spirituality.
- Li Yuan, the founder of the Tang dynasty, had attracted a following by claiming descent from the Taoist sage Laozi.
- Buddhism, originating in India around the time of Confucius, continued its influence during the Tang period and was accepted by some members of the imperial family, becoming thoroughly sinicized and a permanent part of Chinese traditional culture.
- The prominent status of Buddhism in Chinese culture began to decline as the dynasty and central government declined during the late-8th century and 9th century, and many Buddhists experienced persecution.
- The Tang dynasty also officially recognized various foreign religions, such as the Nestorian Christian Church.

Key Terms

- **Taoism**: A religious or philosophical tradition of Chinese origin with an emphasis on living in harmony and accordance with the natural flow or cosmic structural order of the universe.
- **Confucianism**: A Chinese humanistic religion that teaches that human beings are fundamentally good, and teachable, improvable, and perfectible through personal and communal endeavors, especially self-cultivation and self-creation; focuses on the cultivation of virtue, maintenance of ethics, and familial and social harmony.
- **Chan Buddhism**: A school of Mahayana Buddhism that originated in China during the Tang dynasty, was strongly influenced by Taoism, and later became Zen when it travelled to Japan.

Taoism

Taoism was the official religion of the Tang. It is a native Chinese religious and philosophical tradition with an emphasis on living in harmony and accordance with the natural flow or cosmic structural order of the universe commonly referred to as the *Tao*. It has its roots in the book of the *Tao Te Ching* (attributed to Laozi in the 6th century BCE) and the *Zhuangzi*. The ruling Li family of the Tang dynasty actually claimed descent from the ancient Laozi.

Taoism has had a profound influence on Chinese culture, and clerics of institutionalized Taoism usually take care to note distinctions between their ritual tradition and the customs and practices found in Chinese folk religion, as these distinctions sometimes appear blurred. Chinese alchemy, Chinese astrology, Chan Buddhism, several martial arts, traditional Chinese medicine, feng shui, and many styles of qigong have been intertwined with Taoism throughout history.

During the Tang dynasty, the Chinese continued to combine their ancient folk religion with Taoism and incorporated many deities into religious practice. The Chinese believed the Tao and the afterlife were a reality parallel to the living world, complete with a bureaucracy and an afterlife currency needed by dead ancestors. Funerary practices included providing the deceased with everything they might need in the afterlife, including animals, servants, entertainers, hunters, homes, and officials. This is reflected in Tang dynasty art and in many short stories written in the Tang about people accidentally winding up in the realm of the dead, only to come back and report their experiences.

Buddhism

Buddhism, originating in India around the time of Confucius, continued its influence during the Tang period and was accepted by some members of the imperial family, becoming thoroughly sinicized and a permanent part of Chinese traditional culture. In an age before Neo- Confucianism and figures such as Zhu Xi (1130–1200), Buddhism began to flourish in China during the Northern and Southern dynasties, and became the dominant ideology during the prosperous Tang. Buddhist monasteries played an integral role in Chinese society, offering lodging for travelers in remote areas, schools for children throughout the country, and a place for urban literati to stage social events and gatherings such as going-away parties. Buddhist monasteries were also engaged in the economy, since their land and serfs gave them enough revenue to set up mills, oil presses, and other enterprises. Although the monasteries retained "serfs," these monastery dependents could actually own property and employ others to help them in their work, and could even own slaves.

Tang period Bodhisattva: *A Tang dynasty sculpture of a Bodhisattva, a being who, motivated by great compassion, has generated bodhicitta, a spontaneous wish to attain buddhahood for the benefit of all sentient beings.*

The prominent status of Buddhism in Chinese culture began to decline as the dynasty and central government declined during the late 8th century and 9th century. Buddhist convents and temples that had been exempt from state taxes were targeted for taxation. In 845 Emperor Wuzong of Tang finally shut down 4,600 Buddhist monasteries and 40,000 temples and shrines, forcing 260,000 Buddhist monks and nuns to return to secular life. This episode would later be dubbed one of the Four Buddhist Persecutions in China. Although the ban would be lifted just a few years later, Buddhism never regained its once dominant status in Chinese culture.

This situation also came about through a revival of interest in native Chinese philosophies, such as Confucianism and Taoism. Han Yu (786–824)—who Arthur F. Wright stated was a "brilliant polemicist and ardent xenophobe"—was one of the first men of the Tang to denounce Buddhism. Although his contemporaries found him crude and obnoxious, he foreshadowed the later persecution of Buddhism in the Tang, as well as the revival of Confucian theory with the rise of Neo-Confucianism of the Song dynasty. Nonetheless, Chan Buddhism gained popularity amongst the educated elite. There were also many famous Chan monks from the Tang era, such as Mazu Daoyi, Baizhang, and Huangbo Xiyun. The sect of Pure Land Buddhism initiated by the Chinese monk Huiyuan (334–416) was also just as popular as Chan Buddhism during the Tang.

Christianity

The Tang dynasty also officially recognized various foreign religions. The Assyrian Church of the East, otherwise known as the Nestorian Christian Church, was given recognition by the Tang court. In 781, the Nestorian Stele was created in order to honor the achievements of their community in China. The stele contains a long inscription in Chinese with Syriac glosses, composed by the cleric Adam, probably the metropolitan of Beth Sinaye. The inscription describes the eventful progress of the Nestorian mission in China since Alopen's arrival. A Christian monastery was established in Shaanxi province where the Daqin Pagoda still stands, and inside the pagoda there is Christian-themed artwork. Although the religion largely died out after the Tang, it was revived in China following the Mongol invasions of the 13th century.

Nestorian Stele: *The Nestorian Stele, erected in Chang'an 781.*

Religion and Politics

From the outset, religion played a role in Tang politics. In his bid for power, Li Yuan had attracted a following by claiming descent from the Taoist sage Laozi (6th century BCE). People bidding for office would have monks from Buddhist temples pray for them in public in return for cash donations or gifts if the person was selected. Before the persecution of Buddhism in the 9th century, Buddhism and Taoism were accepted side by side, and Emperor Xuanzong (r. 712–56) invited monks and clerics of both religions to his court. At the same time Xuanzong exalted the ancient Laozi by granting him grand titles and writing commentary on him, set up a school to prepare candidates for examinations on Taoist scriptures, and called upon the Indian monk Vajrabodhi (671–741) to perform Tantric rites to avert a drought in the year 726. In 742 Emperor Xuanzong personally held the incense burner during a ceremony led by Amoghavajra (705–74, patriarch of the Shingon school) reciting "mystical incantations to secure the victory of Tang forces."

While religion played a role in politics, politics also played a role in religion. In the year 714, Emperor Xuanzong forbade shops and vendors in the city of Chang'an to sell copied Buddhist sutras, instead giving the Buddhist clergy of the monasteries the sole right to distribute sutras to the laity. In the previous year of 713, Emperor Xuanzong had liquidated the highly lucrative Inexhaustible Treasury, which was run by a prominent Buddhist monastery in Chang'an. This monastery collected vast amounts of money, silk, and treasures through multitudes of anonymous people's repentances, leaving the donations on the monastery's premise. Although the monastery was generous in donations, Emperor Xuanzong issued a decree abolishing their treasury on grounds that their banking practices were fraudulent. He collected their riches and distributed the wealth to various other Buddhist monasteries and Taoist abbeys, and used it to repair statues, halls, and bridges in the city.

The Literati

Scholar-officials, also known as the Chinese *literati*, were civil servants appointed by the emperor of China to perform day-to-day governance, and came into special prominence during the Tang dynasty.

Learning Objectives

Describe the role of the literati in the Tang dynasty's administration

Key Takeaways

Key Points

- The Tang dynasty was largely a period of progress and stability in the first half of the dynasty's rule, which was established as a civil service system by recruiting scholar-officials through standardized examinations and recommendations to office.
- These scholar-officials, also known as the literati, performed the day-to-day governance of the state from the Han dynasty to the end of the Qing dynasty, China's last imperial dynasty, in 1912, but came to special prominence during the Tang period.
- Since only a limited number could become court or local officials, the majority of scholar-officials stayed in villages or cities as social leaders and teachers.
- The imperial examinations were a civil service examination system to select scholar-officials in imperial China.
- Wu Zetian, later Empress Wu, reformed the imperial examinations to include a new class of elite bureaucrats derived from humbler origins.

Key Terms

- **literati**: Also known as scholar-officials, they were civil servants appointed by the emperor of China to perform day-to-day governance.
- **Wu Zetian**: A Chinese sovereign who ruled unofficially as empress consort and empress dowager, and then officially as empress regnan during the brief Zhou dynasty, which interrupted the Tang dynasty.

Scholar-Officials

The first half of the Tang dynasty was largely a period of progress and stability. Like the previous Sui dynasty, the Tang dynasty maintained a civil service system by recruiting scholar-officials through standardized examinations and recommendations to office. These scholar-officials, also known as the literati, performed the day-to-day governance of the state from the Han dynasty to the end of the Qing dynasty, China's last imperial dynasty, in 1912, but came to special prominence during the Tang period. The scholar-officials were schooled in calligraphy and Confucian texts.

Since only a limited number could become court or local officials, the majority of scholar-officials stayed in villages or cities as social leaders. The scholar-officials carried out social welfare measures, taught in private schools, helped negotiate minor legal disputes, supervised community projects, maintained local law and order, conducted Confucian ceremonies, assisted in the government's collection of taxes, and preached Confucian moral teachings. As a class, these scholars claimed to represent morality and virtue. The district magistrate, who by regulation was not allowed to serve in his home district, depended on local scholars for advice and for carrying out projects, giving them power to benefit themselves and their clients.

Imperial Examinations

The imperial examinations were a civil service examination system to select scholar-officials for the state bureaucracy in imperial China. Although there were imperial exams as early as the Han dynasty, the system became the major path to office only in the mid-Tang dynasty, and remained so until its abolition in 1905. Since the exams were based on knowledge of the classics and literary style, not technical expertise, successful candidates, and even those who failed, were generalists who shared a common language and culture. This common culture helped to unify the empire and the ideal of achievement by merit gave legitimacy to imperial rule.

Imperial exam results: Candidates gathering around the wall where the results are posted. This announcement was known as "releasing the roll."

The examination system helped to shape China's intellectual, cultural, and political life. The increased reliance on the exam system was in part responsible for the Tang dynasty shifting from a military aristocracy to a gentry class of scholar-bureaucrats.

The entire premise of the scholarly meritocracy was based on mastery of the Confucian classics. This had important effects on Chinese society. Theoretically, this system would result in a highly meritocratic ruling class, with the best students running the country. The examinations gave many people the opportunity to pursue political power and honor, and thus encouraged serious pursuit of formal education. Since the system did not formally discriminate based on social status, it provided an avenue for upward social mobility regardless of age or social class.

However, even though the examination-based bureaucracy's heavy emphasis on Confucian literature ensured that the most eloquent writers and erudite scholars achieved high positions, the system lacked formal safeguards against political corruption, besides the Confucian moral teachings tested by the examinations. Once their political futures were secured by success in the examinations, high-ranking officials were often tempted to corruption and abuse of power. Moreover, the relatively low status of military professionals in Confucian society discouraged similar efficiency and meritocracy within the military.

Examination cells: *Chinese examination cells at the South River School (Nanjiangxue) Nanjing (China). Shown without curtains or other furnishings.*

Wu Zetian's Reforms

A pivotal point in the development of imperial examinations emerged with the rise of Wu Zetian, later Empress Wu. Up until that point, the rulers of the Tang dynasty were all male members of the Li family. Wu Zetian was exceptional; a woman not of the Li family, she came to occupy the seat of the emperor in an official manner in 690, and even before that she had begun to stretch her power within the imperial courts behind the scenes. Reform of the imperial examinations to include a new class of elite bureaucrats derived from humbler origins became a keystone of Wu's gamble to retain power.

In 655, Wu Zetian graduated forty-four candidates with the *jinshi* degree, and during one seven-year period the annual average of exam takers graduated with a *jinshi* degree was greater than fifty-eight persons per year. Wu lavished favors on the newly graduated *jinshi* degree-holders, increasing the prestige associated with this path of attaining a government career. This clearly began a process of opening up opportunities to success for a wider population pool, including inhabitants of China's less prestigious southeast area. Most of the Li family's supporters were located to the northwest, particularly around the capital city of Chang'an. Wu's progressive accumulation of political power through enhancement of the examination system involved attaining the allegiance of previously under-represented regions, alleviating frustrations of the literati, and encouraging education in various locales so even people in the remote corners of the empire would work on their studies in order to pass the imperial exams. Wu thus developed a nucleus of elite bureaucrats useful from the perspective of control by the central government.

Decline of the Tang Dynasty

After the difficult suppression of the An Lushan Rebellion, the *jiedushi* increased their powers and accelerated the disintegration of the Tang dynasty.

Learning Objectives

Describe the reasons for the eventual fall of the Tang dynasty

Key Takeaways

Key Points

- The An Lushan Rebellion was a devastating rebellion against the Tang dynasty of China; it significantly weakened the dynasty.
- The power of the *jiedushi*, or provincial military governors, increased greatly after imperial troops crushed the rebels, taking administrative power away from the scholar-officials.
- In addition to natural calamities and *jiedushi* amassing autonomous control, the Huang Chao Rebellion resulted in the sacking of both Chang'an and Luoyang, and took an

> entire decade to suppress; although the rebellion was defeated by the Tang, the dynasty never recovered from that crucial blow, weakening it for future military powers to take over.
> - Eventually the *jiedushi* ushered in the political division of the Five Dynasties and Ten Kingdoms period, a period marked by continuous infighting among the rival kingdoms, dynasties, and regional regimes established by rival *jiedushi*.
>
> Key Terms
>
> - **jiedushi**: Regional military governors in China during the Tang dynasty and the Five Dynasties and Ten Kingdoms period.
> - **An Lushan Rebellion**: A devastating rebellion against the Tang dynasty of China that began on December 16, 755, when general An Lushan declared himself emperor in Northern China, thus establishing a rival Yan dynasty, and ended when the Yan fell on February 17, 763.

An Lushan Rebellion

The Tang dynasty, established in 618 CE, after experiencing its golden age entered its long decline, beginning with the An Lushan Rebellion by Sogdian general An Lushan. The rebellion spanned the reigns of three Tang emperors before it was finally quashed, and involved a wide range of regional powers; besides the Tang dynasty loyalists, others involved were anti-Tang families, especially in An Lushan's base area in Hebei, and Arab, Uyghur, and Sogdian forces or influences, among others. The rebellion and subsequent disorder resulted in a huge loss of life and large-scale destruction. It significantly weakened the Tang dynasty and led to the loss of the Western Regions.

The power of the *jiedushi*, or provincial military governors, increased greatly after imperial troops crushed the rebels, taking administrative power away from the scholar-officials. The discipline of these generals also decayed as their power increased and the resentment of common people against the incapacity of the government grew, and their grievances exploded into several rebellions during the mid-9th century. Eventually the *jiedushi* ushered in the political division of the Five Dynasties and Ten Kingdoms period, a period marked by continuous infighting among the rival kingdoms, dynasties, and regional regimes established by rival *jiedushi*. Many impoverished farmers, tax-burdened landowners, and merchants, as well as many large salt smuggling operations, formed the base of the anti-government rebellions of this period.

Tang warrior: *A Tang pottery warrior from Duan's Tomb, Shaanxi.*

The An Lushan Rebellion and its aftermath greatly weakened the centralized bureaucracy of the Tang dynasty, especially in regards to its perimeters. Virtually autonomous provinces and ad hoc financial organizations arose, reducing the influence of the regular bureaucracy in Chang'an. The Tang dynasty's desire for political stability in this turbulent period also resulted in the pardoning of many rebels. Indeed, some were even given their own garrisons to command. Political and economic control of the northeast region became intermittent or was lost, and the emperor became a sort of puppet, set to do the bidding of the strongest garrison. Furthermore, the Tang government also lost most of its control over the Western Regions due to troop withdrawal to central China to attempt to crush the rebellion and deal with subsequent disturbances. Continued military and economic weakness resulted in further erosions of Tang territorial control during the ensuing years, particularly in regard to the Uighur and Tibetan empires. By 790 Chinese control over the Tarim Basin area was completely lost.

The political decline was paralleled by economic decline, including large Tang governmental debt to Uighur money lenders. In addition to being politically and economically detrimental to the empire, the An Lushan Rebellion also affected the intellectual culture of the Tang dynasty. Many intellectuals had their careers interrupted, giving them time to ponder the causes of the unrest. Some lost faith in themselves, concluding that a lack of moral seriousness in intellectual culture had been the cause of the rebellion.

Collapse of the Tang Dynasty

In addition to natural calamities and *jiedushi* amassing autonomous control, the Huang Chao Rebellion (874–884) resulted in the sacking of both Chang'an and Luoyang, and took an entire decade to suppress. Although the rebellion was defeated by the Tang, the dynasty never recovered from that crucial blow, weakening it for future military powers to take over. There were also groups of bandits, the size of small armies, that ravaged the countryside in the last years of the Tang. These bandits smuggled illicit salt, ambushed merchants and convoys, and even besieged several walled cities.

Zhu Wen, originally a salt smuggler who had served under the rebel Huang, surrendered to Tang forces. For helping to defeat Huang, he was granted a series of rapid military promotions. In 907 the Tang dynasty was ended when Zhu Wen, now a military governor, deposed the last emperor of Tang, Emperor Ai of Tang, and took the throne for himself. A year later the deposed Emperor Ai was poisoned by Zhu Wen, and died. Zhu Wen was known posthumously as Emperor Taizu of Later Liang. He established the Later Liang, which inaugurated the Five Dynasties and Ten Kingdoms period.

Attributions

CC licensed content, Specific attribution

- Tang dynasty. **Provided by**: Wikipedia. **Located at**: https://en.wikipedia.org/wiki/Tang_dynasty. **License**: *CC BY-SA: Attribution-ShareAlike*
- Sui dynasty. **Provided by**: Wikipedia. **Located at**: https://en.wikipedia.org/wiki/Sui_dynasty. **License**: *CC BY-SA: Attribution-ShareAlike*
- Transition from Sui to Tang. **Provided by**: Wikipedia. **Located at**: https://en.wikipedia.org/wiki/Transition_from_Sui_to_Tang. **License**: *CC BY-SA: Attribution-ShareAlike*
- 440px-Sui_Yangdi_Tang.jpg. **Provided by**: Wikimedia. **Located at**: https://commons.wikimedia.org/wiki/File:Sui_Yangdi_Tang.jpg. **License**: *CC BY-SA: Attribution-ShareAlike*
- Emperor_Taizong_gives_an_audience_to_the_ambassador_of_Tibet.jpg. **Provided by**: Wikimedia. **Located at**: https://commons.wikimedia.org/wiki/File:Emperor_Taizong_gives_an_audience_to_the_ambassador_of_Tibet.jpg. **License** *CC BY-SA: Attribution-ShareAlike*
- Tang dynasty. **Provided by**: Wikipedia. **Located at**: https://en.wikipedia.org/wiki/Tang_dynasty. **License**: *CC BY-SA: Attribution-ShareAlike*
- Silk Road. **Provided by**: Wikipedia. **Located at**: https://en.wikipedia.org/wiki/Silk_Road. **License**: *CC BY-SA: Attribution-ShareAlike*
- 440px-Sui_Yangdi_Tang.jpg. **Provided by**: Wikimedia. **Located at**: https://commons.wikimedia.org/wiki/File:Sui_Yangdi_Tang.jpg. **License**: *CC BY-SA: Attribution-ShareAlike*
- Emperor_Taizong_gives_an_audience_to_the_ambassador_of_Tibet.jpg. **Provided by**: Wikimedia. **Located at**: https://commons.wikimedia.org/wiki/File:Emperor_Taizong_gives_an_audience_to_the_ambassador_of_Tibet.jpg. **License**: *CC BY-SA: Attribution-ShareAlike*
- Gilt_silver_jar_with_pattern_of_dancing_horses.jpg. **Provided by**: Wikimedia. **Located at**: https://commons.wikimedia.org/wiki/File:Gilt_silver_jar_with_pattern_of_dancing_horses.jpg. **License**: *CC BY-SA: Attribution-ShareAlike*
- ForeignMerchant.jpg. **Provided by**: Wikimedia. **Located at**: https://commons.wikimedia.org/wiki/File:ForeignMerchant.jpg. **License**: *CC BY-SA: Attribution-ShareAlike*
- Taoism. **Provided by**: Wikipedia. **Located at**: https://en.wikipedia.org/wiki/Taoism. **License**: *CC BY-SA: Attribution-ShareAlike*
- Tang dynasty. **Provided by**: Wikipedia. **Located at**: https://en.wikipedia.org/wiki/Tang_dynasty. **License**: *CC BY-SA: Attribution-ShareAlike*
- Church of the East in Chine. **Provided by**: Wikipedia. **Located at**: https://en.wikipedia.org/wiki/Church_of_the_East_in_China. **License**: *CC BY-SA: Attribution-ShareAlike*
- 440px-Sui_Yangdi_Tang.jpg. **Provided by**: Wikimedia. **Located at**: https://commons.wikimedia.org/wiki/File:Sui_Yangdi_Tang.jpg. **License**: *CC BY-SA: Attribution-ShareAlike*
- Emperor_Taizong_gives_an_audience_to_the_ambassador_of_Tibet.jpg. **Provided by**: Wikimedia. **Located at**: https://commons.wikimedia.org/wiki/File:Emperor_Taizong_gives_an_audience_to_the_ambassador_of_Tibet.jpg. **License**: *CC BY-SA: Attribution-ShareAlike*
- Gilt_silver_jar_with_pattern_of_dancing_horses.jpg. **Provided by**: Wikimedia. **Located at**: https://commons.wikimedia.org/wiki/File:Gilt_silver_jar_with_pattern_of_dancing_horses.jpg. **License**: *CC BY-SA: Attribution-ShareAlike*
- ForeignMerchant.jpg. **Provided by**: Wikimedia. **Located at**: https://commons.wikimedia.org/wiki/File:ForeignMerchant.jpg. **License**: *CC BY-SA: Attribution-ShareAlike*

- TangBodhisattva.JPG. **Provided by**: Wikimedia. **Located at**: https://commons.wikimedia.org/wiki/File:TangBodhisattva.JPG. **License**: *CC BY-SA: Attribution-ShareAlike*
- Nestorian-Stele-Budge-plate-X.jpg. **Provided by**: Wikimedia. **Located at**: https://commons.wikimedia.org/wiki/File:Nestorian-Stele-Budge-plate-X.jpg. **License**: *CC BY-SA: Attribution-ShareAlike*
- Scholar-official. **Provided by**: Wikipedia. **Located at**: https://en.wikipedia.org/wiki/Scholar-official. **License**: *CC BY-SA: Attribution-ShareAlike*
- Imperial Examination. **Provided by**: Wikipedia. **Located at**: https://en.wikipedia.org/wiki/Imperial_examination. **License**: *CC BY-SA: Attribution-ShareAlike*
- 440px-Sui_Yangdi_Tang.jpg. **Provided by**: Wikimedia. **Located at**: https://commons.wikimedia.org/wiki/File:Sui_Yangdi_Tang.jpg. **License**: *CC BY-SA: Attribution-ShareAlike*
- Emperor_Taizong_gives_an_audience_to_the_ambassador_of_Tibet.jpg. **Provided by**: Wikimedia. **Located at**: https://commons.wikimedia.org/wiki/File:Emperor_Taizong_gives_an_audience_to_the_ambassador_of_Tibet.jpg. **License**: *CC BY-SA: Attribution-ShareAlike*
- Gilt_silver_jar_with_pattern_of_dancing_horses.jpg. **Provided by**: Wikimedia. **Located at**: https://commons.wikimedia.org/wiki/File:Gilt_silver_jar_with_pattern_of_dancing_horses.jpg. **License**: *CC BY-SA: Attribution-ShareAlike*
- ForeignMerchant.jpg. **Provided by**: Wikimedia. **Located at**: https://commons.wikimedia.org/wiki/File:ForeignMerchant.jpg. **License**: *CC BY-SA: Attribution-ShareAlike*
- TangBodhisattva.JPG. **Provided by**: Wikimedia. **Located at**: https://commons.wikimedia.org/wiki/File:TangBodhisattva.JPG. **License**: *CC BY-SA: Attribution-ShareAlike*
- Nestorian-Stele-Budge-plate-X.jpg. **Provided by**: Wikimedia. **Located at**: https://commons.wikimedia.org/wiki/File:Nestorian-Stele-Budge-plate-X.jpg. **License**: *CC BY-SA: Attribution-ShareAlike*
- Civilserviceexam1.jpg. **Provided by**: Wikimedia. **Located at**: https://commons.wikimedia.org/wiki/File:Civilserviceexam1.jpg. **License**: *Public Domain: No Known Copyright*
- 1024px-Pru00fcfungszellen-Nanking.jpg. **Provided by**: Wikipedia. **Located at**: https://en.wikipedia.org/wiki/Imperial_examination#/media/File:Pr%C3%BCfungszellen-Nanking.jpg. **License**: *CC BY-SA: Attribution-ShareAlike*
- Tang Dynasty. **Provided by**: Wikipedia. **Located at**: https://en.wikipedia.org/wiki/Tang_dynasty#End_of_the_dynasty. **License**: *CC BY-SA: Attribution-ShareAlike*
- An Lushan Rebellion. **Provided by**: Wikipedia. **Located at**: https://en.wikipedia.org/wiki/An_Lushan_Rebellion. **License**: *CC BY-SA: Attribution-ShareAlike*
- Jiedushi. **Provided by**: Wikipedia. **Located at**: https://en.wikipedia.org/wiki/Jiedushi. **License**: *CC BY-SA: Attribution-ShareAlike*
- Huang Chao. **Provided by**: Wikipedia. **Located at**: https://en.wikipedia.org/wiki/Huang_Chao. **License**: *CC BY-SA: Attribution-ShareAlike*
- 440px-Sui_Yangdi_Tang.jpg. **Provided by**: Wikimedia. **Located at**: https://commons.wikimedia.org/wiki/File:Sui_Yangdi_Tang.jpg. **License**: *CC BY-SA: Attribution-ShareAlike*
- Emperor_Taizong_gives_an_audience_to_the_ambassador_of_Tibet.jpg. **Provided by**: Wikimedia. **Located at**: https://commons.wikimedia.org/wiki/File:Emperor_Taizong_gives_an_audience_to_the_ambassador_of_Tibet.jpg. **License**: *CC BY-SA: Attribution-ShareAlike*
- Gilt_silver_jar_with_pattern_of_dancing_horses.jpg. **Provided by**: Wikimedia. **Located at**: https://commons.wikimedia.org/wiki/File:Gilt_silver_jar_with_pattern_of_dancing_horses.jpg. **License**: *CC BY-SA: Attribution-ShareAlike*
- ForeignMerchant.jpg. **Provided by**: Wikimedia. **Located at**: https://commons.wikimedia.org/wiki/File:ForeignMerchant.jpg. **License**: *CC BY-SA: Attribution-ShareAlike*
- TangBodhisattva.JPG. **Provided by**: Wikimedia. **Located at**: https://commons.wikimedia.org/wiki/File:TangBodhisattva.JPG. **License**: *CC BY-SA: Attribution-ShareAlike*
- Nestorian-Stele-Budge-plate-X.jpg. **Provided by**: Wikimedia. **Located at**: https://commons.wikimedia.org/wiki/File:Nestorian-Stele-Budge-plate-X.jpg. **License**: *CC BY-SA: Attribution-ShareAlike*
- Civilserviceexam1.jpg. **Provided by**: Wikimedia. **Located at**: https://commons.wikimedia.org/wiki/File:Civilserviceexam1.jpg. **License**: *Public Domain: No Known Copyright*
- 1024px-Pru00fcfungszellen-Nanking.jpg. **Provided by**: Wikipedia. **Located at**: https://en.wikipedia.org/wiki/Imperial_examination#/media/File:Pr%C3%BCfungszellen-Nanking.jpg. **License**: *CC BY-SA: Attribution-ShareAlike*
- Tang_Pottery_Warrior.jpg. **Provided by**: Wikipedia. **Located at**: https://en.wikipedia.org/wiki/Tang_dynasty#/media/File:Tang_Pottery_Warrior.jpg. **License**: *CC BY-SA: Attribution-ShareAlike*

The Song Dynasty

Origins of the Song Dynasty

The Song dynasty was an era of Chinese history that began in 960 and continued until 1279; it succeeded the tumultuous Five Dynasties and Ten Kingdoms period and saw many technological and cultural innovations.

Learning Objectives

Describe who the Song were and how they rose to power

Key Takeaways

Key Points

- The Song dynasty was an era of Chinese history that began in 960, directly after the chaotic Five Dynasties and Ten Kingdoms period.
- It was the first government in world history to issue banknotes and the first Chinese government to establish a permanent standing navy; it saw the first known use of gunpowder and the first recognition of true north using a compass.
- The Song dynasty was divided into two distinct periods, Northern (960–1127) and Southern (1127–1279).
- Social life during the Song was vibrant, and included public artworks, the spread of literature, and the growth of philosophy.
- Zhao Kuangyin, later known as Emperor Taizu (r. 960–976), usurped the throne from the Zhou dynasty with the support of military commanders in 960, initiating the Song dynasty and ending the Five Dynasties period.
- Upon taking the throne, his first goal was the reunification of China after half a century of political division.

> *Key Terms*
>
> - **Emperor Taizu**: Personal name Zhao Kuangyin; he was the founder and first emperor of the Song dynasty in China.
> - **Five Dynasties and Ten Kingdoms**: An era of political upheaval in 10th-century imperial China; during this period, five states quickly succeeded one another in the Chinese Central Plain, while more than a dozen concurrent states were established elsewhere, mainly in south China.

Overview

The Song dynasty was an era of Chinese history that began in 960 and continued until 1279. It succeeded the Five Dynasties and Ten Kingdoms period, and was followed by the Yuan dynasty. It was the first government in world history to issue banknotes or true paper money nationally and the first Chinese government to establish a permanent standing navy. This dynasty also saw the first known use of gunpowder as well as the first discernment of true north using a compass.

The Song dynasty was divided into two distinct periods, Northern and Southern. During the Northern Song (960–1127), the Song capital was in the northern city of Bianjing (now Kaifeng), and the dynasty controlled most of what is now Eastern China. The Southern Song (1127–1279) refers to the period after the Song lost control of its northern half to the Jurchen Jin dynasty in the Jin-Song Wars. During this time, the Song court retreated south of the Yangtze and established its capital at Lin'an (now Hangzhou). Although the Song dynasty had lost control of the traditional "birthplace of Chinese civilization" along the Yellow River, the Song economy was still strong, as the Southern Song empire contained a large population and productive agricultural land. The Southern Song dynasty considerably bolstered its naval strength to defend its waters and land borders and to conduct maritime missions abroad.

Social life during the Song was vibrant. Citizens gathered to view and trade precious artworks, the populace intermingled at public festivals and private clubs, and cities had lively entertainment quarters. The spread of literature and knowledge was enhanced by the rapid expansion of woodblock printing and the 11th-century invention of movable-type printing. Technology, science, philosophy, mathematics, and engineering flourished over the course of the Song. Philosophers such as Cheng Yi and Zhu Xi reinvigorated Confucianism with new commentary infused with Buddhist ideals, and emphasized a new organization of classic texts that brought out the core doctrine of Neo-Confucianism. Although the institution of the civil service examinations had existed since the Sui dynasty, it became much more prominent in the Song period. The officials who gained power by succeeding in the exams became a leading factor in the shift from a military-aristocratic elite to a bureaucratic elite.

Founding of the Song Dynasty

The Later Zhou was the last of the Five Dynasties that had controlled northern China after the fall of the Tang dynasty in 907. Zhao Kuangyin, later known as Emperor Taizu (r. 960–976), usurped the throne from the Zhou with the support of military commanders in 960, initiating the Song dynasty. Upon taking the throne, his first goal was the reunification of China after half a century of political division. This included the conquests of Nanping, Wu-Yue, Southern Han, Later Shu, and Southern Tang in the south as well as the Northern Han and the Sixteen Prefectures in the north. With capable military officers such as Yang Ye (d. 986), Liu Tingrang (929–987), Cao Bin (931–999) and Huyan Zan (d. 1000), the early Song military became the dominant force in China. Innovative military tactics, such as defending supply lines across floating pontoon bridges, led to success in battle. One such success was the Song assault against the Southern Tang state while crossing the Yangtze River in 974. Using a mass of arrow fire from crossbowmen, Song forces were able to defeat the renowned war elephant corps of the Southern Han on January 23, 971, thus forcing the submission of Southern Han and terminating the first and last elephant corps to make up a regular division within a Chinese army.

Consolidation in the south was completed in 978, with the conquest of Wu-Yue. Song military forces then turned north against the Northern Han, which fell to Song forces in 979. However, efforts to take the Sixteen Prefectures were unsuccessful, and they were incorporated into the Liao state based in Manchuria to the immediate north instead. To the far northwest, the Tanguts had been in power over northern Shaanxi since 881, after the earlier Tang court appointed a Tangut chief as a military governor (*jiedushi*) over the region, a seat that became hereditary (forming the Xi-Xia dynasty). Although the Song state was evenly matched against the Liao dynasty, the Song gained significant military victories against the Western Xia (who would eventually fall to the Mongol conquest of Genghis Khan in 1227).

Emperor Taizu: *A court painting of Emperor Taizu of Song (r. 960–976), who founded the Song dynasty and unified China.*

The Northern Song Era

During the Northern Song (960-1127), the Song capital was in the northern city of Kaifeng, and the dynasty controlled most of what is now Eastern China.

> **Learning Objectives**
>
> Describe the successes and setbacks of the Northern Song Dynasty

> **Key Takeaways**
>
> *Key Points*
>
> - Emperor Taizu of Song unified the empire by conquering other lands during his reign, ending the upheaval of the Five Dynasties and Ten Kingdoms period and beginning the Song dynasty.
> - The Song court maintained diplomatic relations with Chola India, the Fatimid Caliphate, Srivijaya, the Kara-Khanid Khanate of Central Asia, and other countries that were also trade partners with Japan.
> - From its inception under Taizu, the Song dynasty alternated between warfare and diplomacy with the ethnic Khitans of the Liao dynasty in the northeast and with the Tanguts of the Western Xia in the northwest.
> - During the 11th century, political rivalries divided members of the court due to the ministers' differing approaches, opinions, and policies regarding the handling of the Song's complex society and thriving economy.
> - After the Jurchen conquest of North China and a shift of capitals from Kaifeng to Lin'an, the Northern Song transitioned into the Southern Song dynasty.
>
> *Key Terms*
>
> - **New Policies**: A series of reforms initiated by the Northern Song dynasty reformer Wang Anshi when he served as minister under Emperor Shenzong from 1069–1076.
> - **Jin dynasty**: This dynasty lasted from 1115–1234 as one of the last dynasties in Chinese history to predate the Mongol invasion of China; they warred with the Song dynasty.

Beginning of the Song Dynasty

Emperor Taizu of Song (r. 960–976) had unified the empire by conquering other lands during his reign, ending the upheaval of the Five Dynasties and Ten Kingdoms period. In Kaifeng he established a strong central government over the empire. He ensured administrative stability by promoting the civil service examination system of drafting state bureaucrats by skill and merit (instead of aristocratic or military position) and promoted projects that ensured efficiency in communication throughout the empire. In one such project, cartographers created detailed maps of each province and city that were then collected in a large atlas. Emperor Taizu also promoted groundbreaking scientific and technological innovations by supporting such works as the astronomical clock tower designed and built by the engineer Zhang Sixun.

Diplomacy and War

The Song court maintained diplomatic relations with Chola India, the Fatimid Caliphate, Srivijaya, the Kara-Khanid Khanate of Central Asia, and other countries that were also trade partners with Japan. However, China's closest neighboring states affected its domestic and foreign policy the most. From its inception under Taizu, the Song dynasty alternated between warfare and diplomacy with the ethnic Khitans of the Liao dynasty in the northeast and with the Tanguts of the Western Xia in the northwest. The Song dynasty used military force in an attempt to quell the Liao dynasty and recapture the

Sixteen Prefectures, a territory under Khitan control that was traditionally considered part of China proper. Song forces were repulsed by the Liao forces, who engaged in aggressive yearly campaigns into Northern Song territory until 1005, when the signing of the Shanyuan Treaty ended these northern border clashes. The Song were forced to provide tribute to the Khitans, although this did little damage to the Song economy since the Khitans were economically dependent upon importing massive amounts of goods from the Song. More significantly, the Song state recognized the Liao state as its diplomatic equal.

The Song dynasty managed to win several military victories over the Tanguts in the early 11th century, culminating in a campaign led by the polymath scientist, general, and statesman Shen Kuo (1031–1095). However, this campaign was ultimately a failure due to a rival military officer of Shen disobeying direct orders, and the territory gained from the Western Xia was eventually lost. There

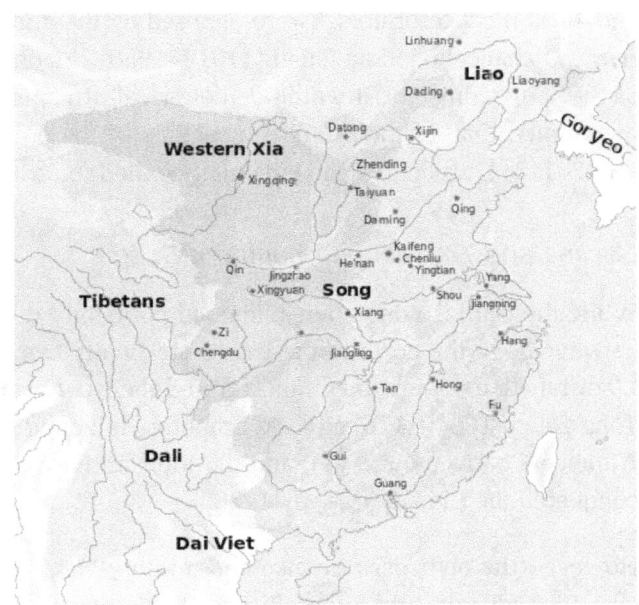

Northern Song dynasty: *The extent of the land holdings of the Northern Song dynasty in 1111.*

was also a significant war fought against the Lý dynasty of Vietnam from 1075 to 1077 over a border dispute and the Song's severing of commercial relations with the Đại Việt kingdom. After Lý forces inflicted heavy damages in a raid on Guangxi, the Song commander Guo Kui (1022–1088) penetrated as far as Thăng Long (modern Hanoi). Heavy losses on both sides prompted the Lý commander Thường Kiệt (1019–1105) to make peace overtures, allowing both sides to withdraw from the war effort; captured territories held by both Song and Lý were mutually exchanged in 1082, along with prisoners of war.

Political Rivalries

During the 11th century, political rivalries divided members of the court due to the ministers' differing approaches, opinions, and policies regarding the handling of the Song's complex society and thriving economy. The idealist Chancellor Fan Zhongyan (989–1052) was the first to experience a heated political backlash when he attempted to institute the Qingli Reforms, which included measures such as improving the recruitment system of officials, increasing the salaries for minor officials, and establishing sponsorship programs to allow a wider range of people to be well educated and eligible for state service.

After Fan was forced to step down from his office, Wang Anshi (1021–1086) became chancellor of the imperial court. With the backing of Emperor Shenzong (1067–1085), Wang Anshi severely criticized the educational system and state bureaucracy. Seeking to resolve what he saw as state corruption and negligence, Wang implemented a series of reforms called the New Policies. These involved land value tax reform, the establishment of several government monopolies, the support of local militias, and the creation of higher standards for the Imperial examination to make it more practical for men skilled in statecraft to pass.

The reforms created political factions in the court. Wang Anshi's "New Policies Group" (Xin Fa), also known as the "Reformers," were opposed by the ministers in the "Conservative" faction led by the historian and chancellor Sima Guang (1019–1086). As one faction supplanted another in the majority position of the court ministers, it would demote rival officials and exile them to govern remote frontier regions of the empire. One of the prominent victims of the political rivalry, the famous poet and statesman Su Shi (1037–1101), was jailed and eventually exiled for criticizing Wang's reforms.

Decline and Transition to Southern Song

While the central Song court remained politically divided and focused upon its internal affairs, alarming new events to the north in the Liao state finally came to its attention. The Jurchen, a subject tribe of the Liao, rebelled against them and formed their own state, the Jin dynasty (1115–1234). The Song official Tong Guan (1054–1126) advised Emperor Huizong (1100–1125) to form an alliance with the Jurchens (the Alliance Conducted at Sea), and the joint military campaign under this alliance toppled and completely conquered the Liao dynasty by 1125.

However, the poor performance and military weakness of the Song army was observed by the Jurchens, who immediately broke the alliance, beginning the Jin–Song Wars of 1125 and 1127; during the latter invasion, the Jurchens captured not only the capital, but also the retired Emperor Huizong, his successor Emperor Qinzong, and most of the imperial court. This took place in the year of Jingkang and it is known as the Jingkang Incident.

The remaining Song forces regrouped under the self-proclaimed Emperor Gaozong of Song (1127–1162) and withdrew south of the Yangtze to establish a new capital at Lin'an (modern Hangzhou). The Jurchen conquest of northern China and the shift of capitals from Kaifeng to Lin'an was the dividing line between the Northern and Southern Song dynasties.

The Southern Song Era

The Southern Song (1127–1279) was the period after the Song lost control of its northern half to the Jurchen Jin dynasty in the Jin–Song Wars and retreated south of the Yangtze, establishing a capital at Lin'an.

Learning Objectives

Compare and contrast the Southern Song era with the Northern Song era

Key Takeaways

Key Points

- After the Jins captured the Northern Song capital of Kaifeng, they went on to conquer the rest of northern China, while the Song Chinese court fled south and founded the Southern Song dynasty.
- Although weakened and pushed south beyond the Huai River, the Southern Song found new ways to bolster its strong economy and defend itself against the Jin dynasty, especially through the creation of the first standing navy of China.
- The Jin-Song Wars engendered an era of technological, cultural, and demographic changes in China, including the introduction of gunpowder into weaponry.
- Though the Song dynasty was able to hold back the Jin from their southern territory, a new foe came to power over the steppe, deserts, and plains north of the Jin dynasty—the Mongols led by Genghis Khan.
- The Mongols were at one time allied with the Song, but this alliance was broken when the Song recaptured the former imperial capitals of Kaifeng, Luoyang, and Chang'an at the collapse of the Jin dynasty.
- The Mongols continued to war with the Song, eventually founding the Yuan dynasty under Kublai Khan, thus ending the Song dynasty.

Key Terms

- **Kublai Khan**: The fifth Great Khan of the Mongol Empire and founder of the Yuan dynasty in China as a conquest dynasty in 1271; he ruled as the first Yuan emperor until his death in 1294.
- **Mongols**: An East-Central Asian ethnic group native to Mongolia.
- **Genghis Khan**: The founder and Great Khan (emperor) of the Mongol Empire, which became the largest contiguous empire in history after his death.

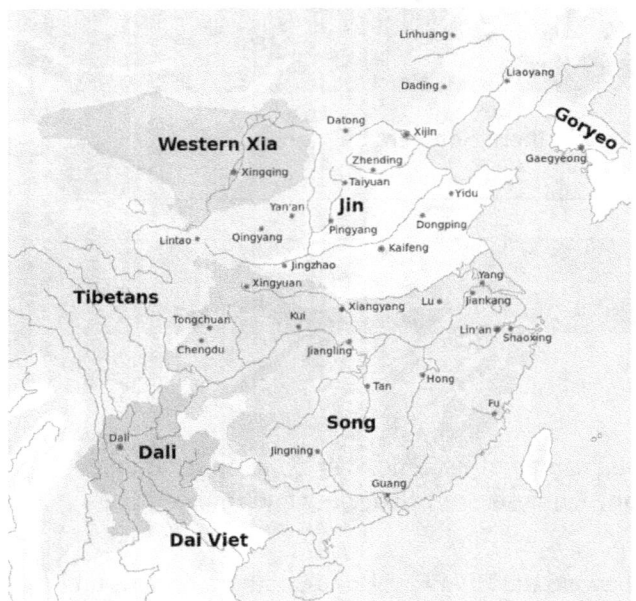

Southern Song in 1142: *The extent of the land holdings of the Southern Song dynasty, significantly reduced from Northern Song's holdings by the Jin dynasty.*

Founding of the Southern Song

After capturing Kaifeng, the Jurchens went on to conquer the rest of northern China, while the Song Chinese court fled south. They took up temporary residence at Nanjing, where a surviving prince was named Emperor Gaozong of Song in 1127. Jin forces halted at the Yangtze River, but staged continual raids south of the river until a later boundary was fixed at the Huai River further north. With the border fixed at the Huai, the Song government promoted an immigration policy of repopulating and resettling territories north of the Yangtze River, since vast tracts of vacant land between the Yangtze and the Huai were open for landless peasants found in the Jiangsu, Zhejiang, Jiangxi, and Fujian provinces of the south.

Continued War with the Jin

Though weakened and pushed south beyond the Huai River, the Southern Song found new ways to bolster its strong economy and defend itself against the Jin dynasty. It had able military officers such as Yue Fei and Han Shizhong. The government sponsored massive shipbuilding, harbor-improvement projects, and the construction of beacons and seaport warehouses to support maritime trade abroad, including at the major international seaports, such as Quanzhou, Guangzhou, and Xiamen, that were sustaining China's commerce. To protect and support the multitude of ships sailing for maritime interests into the waters of the East China Sea and Yellow Sea (to Korea and Japan), Southeast Asia, the Indian Ocean, and the Red Sea, it was necessary to establish an official standing navy. The Song dynasty therefore established China's first permanent navy in 1132, with a headquarters at Dinghai.

With a permanent navy, the Song were prepared to face the naval forces of the Jin on the Yangtze River in 1161, in the Battle of Tangdao and the Battle of Caishi. During these battles the Song navy employed swift paddle-wheel driven naval vessels armed with trebuchet catapults aboard the decks that launched gunpowder bombs. Although the Jin forces commanded by Wanyan Liang (the Prince of Hailing) boasted 70,000 men on 600 warships, and the Song forces only 3,000 men on 120 warships, the Song forces were victorious in both battles due to the destructive power of the bombs and the rapid assaults by paddle-wheel ships. The strength of the navy was heavily emphasized after that. A century after the navy was founded it had grown in size to 52,000 fighting marines.

Southern Song era ship: *A Song era junk ship, 13th century; Chinese ships of the Song period featured hulls with watertight compartments.*

The Jin-Song Wars engendered an era of technological, cultural, and demographic changes in China. Battles between the Song and Jin brought about the introduction of various gunpowder weapons. The siege of De'an in 1132 was the first recorded appearance of the fire lance, an early ancestor of firearms. There were also reports of battles fought with primitive gunpowder bombs like the incendiary *huopao* or the exploding *tiehuopao*, flammable arrows, and other related weapons.

The Song government confiscated portions of land owned by the gentry in order to raise revenue for military and naval projects, an act which caused dissension and loss of loyalty amongst leading members of Song society, but did not stop the Song's defensive preparations. Financial matters were made worse by the fact that many wealthy, land-owning families—some of which had members working as officials for the government—used their social connections with those in office to obtain tax-exempt status.

The Mongols

Although the Song dynasty was able to hold back the Jin, a new foe came to power over the steppe, deserts, and plains north of the Jin dynasty. The Mongols, led by Genghis Khan (r. 1206–1227), initially invaded the Jin dynasty in 1205 and 1209, engaging in large raids across its borders, and in 1211 an enormous Mongol army was assembled to invade the Jin. The Jin dynasty was forced to submit and pay tribute to the Mongols as vassals; when the Jin suddenly moved their capital city from Beijing to Kaifeng, the Mongols saw this as a revolt. Under the leadership of Ögedei Khan (r.1229–1241), Mongol forces conquered both the Jin dynasty and Western Xia dynasty. The Mongols also invaded Korea, the Abbasid Caliphate of the Middle East, and Kievan Rus'.

The Mongols were at one time allied with the Song, but this alliance was broken when the Song recaptured the former imperial capitals of Kaifeng, Luoyang, and Chang'an at the collapse of the Jin dynasty. The Mongol leader Möngke Khan led a campaign against the Song in 1259, but died on August 11 during the Battle of Diaoyu Fortress in Chongqing. Möngke's death and the ensuing succession crisis prompted Hulagu Khan to pull the bulk of the Mongol forces out of the Middle East, where they were poised to fight the Egyptian Mamluks (who defeated the remaining Mongols at Ain Jalut). Although Hulagu was allied with Kublai Khan, his forces were unable to help in the assault against the Song due to Hulagu's war with the Golden Horde.

Kublai continued the assault against the Song, gaining a temporary foothold on the southern banks of the Yangtze. Kublai made preparations to take Ezhou, but a pending civil war with his brother Ariq Böke—a rival claimant to the Mongol Khaganate—forced Kublai to move back north with the bulk of his forces. In Kublai's absence, the Song forces were ordered by Chancellor Jia Sidao to make an opportune assault, and succeeded in pushing the Mongol forces back to the northern banks of the Yangtze. There were minor border skirmishes until 1265, when Kublai won a significant battle in Sichuan. From 1268 to 1273, Kublai blockaded the Yangtze River with his navy and besieged Xiangyang, the last obstacle in his way to invading the rich Yangtze River basin.

The End of the Southern Song

Kublai Khan officially declared the creation of the Yuan dynasty in 1271. In 1275, a Song force of 130,000 troops under Chancellor Jia Sidao was defeated by Kublai's newly appointed commander-in-chief, General Bayan. By 1276, most of the Song territory had been captured by Yuan forces. In the Battle of Yamen on the Pearl River Delta in 1279, the Yuan army, led by General Zhang Hongfan, finally crushed the Song resistance. The last remaining ruler, the 8-year-old emperor Emperor Huaizong of Song, committed suicide, as did Prime Minister Lu Xiufu and 800 members of the royal clan. On Kublai's orders carried out by his commander Bayan, the rest of the former imperial family of Song were unharmed; the deposed Emperor Gong was demoted, given the title "Duke of Ying," but was eventually exiled to Tibet, where he took up a monastic life. The former emperor would eventually be forced to commit suicide under the orders of Kublai's great-great grandson Gegeen Khan, who feared that Emperor Gong would stage a coup to restore his reign. Other members of the Song imperial family continued to live in the Yuan dynasty, including Zhao Mengfu and Zhao Yong.

Culture Under the Song Dynasty

Social life and culture during the Song was vibrant and diverse, with important achievements in the arts and lively popular entertainment.

Learning Objectives

Explain cultural aspects of the Song dynasty

Key Takeaways

Key Points

- The Song dynasty was an era of administrative sophistication and complex social organization that brought rise to a rich and diverse social life and culture.
- Citizens gathered to view and trade precious artworks, the populace intermingled at public festivals and private clubs, and cities had lively entertainment quarters.
- Although women were on a lower social tier than men, they enjoyed many social and legal privileges and wielded considerable power at home and in their own small businesses, and some women became famous artists and writers.
- Ancient Chinese Taoism, ancestor worship, and foreign-originated Buddhism were the most prominent religious practices in the Song period.
- Chinese literature during the Song period contained a range of different genres and was enriched by the social complexity of the period.
- The visual arts during the Song dynasty were heightened by new developments in areas such as landscape and portrait painting.

Key Terms

- **antiquarian**: An aficionado or student of antiquities or things of the past; or relating to such interests.

> - **Pear Garden**: The first known royal acting and musical academy in China, founded during the Tang dynasty by Emperor Xuanzong.
> - **Manichaean**: Of or relating to a major religion founded in Iran that taught an elaborate dualistic cosmology describing the struggle between a good, spiritual world of light, and an evil, material world of darkness.

Society during the Song Dynasty

The Song dynasty was an era of administrative sophistication and complex social organization. Some of the largest cities in the world were found in China during this period (Kaifeng and Hangzhou had populations of over a million). People enjoyed various social clubs and entertainment in the cities, and there were many schools and temples to provide the people with education and religious services. The Song government supported social welfare programs, including the establishment of retirement homes, public clinics, and paupers' graveyards. The Song dynasty supported a widespread postal service, modeled on the earlier Han dynasty (202 BCE–CE 220) postal system, to provide swift communication throughout the empire. The central government employed thousands of postal workers of various ranks to provide service for post offices and larger postal stations. In rural areas, farming peasants either owned their own plots of land, paid rents as tenant farmers, or were serfs on large estates.

Women in the Song Dynasty

Although women were on a lower social tier than men (according to Confucian ethics), they enjoyed many social and legal privileges and wielded considerable power at home and in their own small businesses. As Song society became more and more prosperous and parents on the bride's side of the family provided larger dowries for her marriage, women naturally gained many new legal rights in the ownership of property. Under certain circumstances, an unmarried daughter without brothers, or a surviving mother without sons, could inherit one-half of her father's share of undivided family property. There were many notable and well-educated women, and it was a common practice for women to educate their sons during their earliest youth. The mother of the scientist, general, diplomat, and statesman Shen Kuo taught him essentials of military strategy. There were also exceptional women writers and poets such as Li Qingzhao (1084–1151), who became famous even in her lifetime.

Empress of Zhenzong of Song: *Official court portrait painting of the empress and wife of Zhenzong. Notice the heavy ceremonial facial painting and elaborate clothing, typical of royal women.*

Men dominated the public sphere, while affluent wives spent most of their time indoors enjoying leisure activities and managing the household. However, women of the lower and middle classes were not solely bound to the domestic sphere. It was common for women to manage town inns and restaurants, farmers' daughters to weave mats and sell them on their own behalf, midwives to deliver babies, Buddhist nuns to study religious texts and sutras, and female nurses to assist physicians. Many women kept a close eye on their own financial matters; there are legal case documents that describe childless widows who accused their nephews of stealing their property.

Social Life in the Song

The populace engaged in a vibrant social and domestic life, enjoying such public festivals as the Lantern Festival and the Qingming Festival. There were entertainment quarters in the cities providing a constant array of amusements. There were puppeteers, acrobats, theatre actors, sword swallowers, snake charmers, storytellers, singers and musicians, and prostitutes, and places to relax, including tea houses, restaurants, and organized banquets. People attended social clubs in large numbers; there were tea clubs, exotic food clubs, antiquarian and art collectors' clubs, horse-loving clubs, poetry clubs, and music clubs. There were regional styles of cooking and cuisine, as well as of performing arts. Theatrical drama was very popular amongst the elite and general populace, although Classical Chinese—not the vernacular language—was spoken by actors on stage. The four largest drama theaters in Kaifeng could hold audiences of several thousand each. There were also notable domestic pastimes, as people at home enjoyed activities such as the go and xiangqi board games.

Religion and Philosophy

Religion in China during this period had a great effect on people's lives, beliefs, and daily activities, and Chinese literature on spirituality was popular. The major deities of Taoism and Buddhism, ancestral spirits, and the many deities of Chinese folk religion were worshipped with sacrificial offerings. Tansen Sen asserts that more Buddhist monks from India travelled to China during the Song than in the previous Tang dynasty (618–907). With many ethnic foreigners traveling to China to conduct trade or live permanently, there came many foreign religions; religious minorities in China included Middle Eastern Muslims, Kaifeng Jews, and Persian Manichaeans.

Song intellectuals sought answers to all philosophical and political questions in the Confucian Classics. This renewed interest in the Confucian ideals and society of ancient times coincided with the decline of Buddhism, which was then largely regarded as foreign and as offering few solutions for practical problems. However, Buddhism in this period continued as a cultural underlay to the more-accepted Confucianism and even Taoism, both seen as native and pure by conservative Neo-Confucians. The continuing popularity of Buddhism is evidenced by achievements in the arts, such as the one-hundred painting set of the Five Hundred Luohan, completed by Lin Tinggui and Zhou Jichang in 1178.

A Luohan painting: *One of the Five Hundred Luohan, painted in 1207 by Liu Songnian, Southern Song period.*

Chinese folk religion continued as a tradition in China, drawing upon aspects of both ancient Chinese mythology and ancestor worship. Many people believed that spirits and deities of the spirit realm regularly interacted with the realm of the living. This subject was popular in Song literature. People in Song China believed that many of their daily misfortunes and blessings were caused by an array of different deities and spirits who interfered with their daily lives. These deities included the nationally accepted deities of Buddhism and Taoism, as well as the local deities and demons from specific geographic locations. If one displeased a long-dead relative, the dissatisfied ancestor would allegedly inflict natural ailments and illnesses. People also believed in mischievous demons and malevolent spirits who had the capability to extort sacrificial offerings meant for ancestors—in essence these were bullies of the spiritual realm.

Arts and Literature

Chinese painting during the Song dynasty reached a new level of sophistication with further development of landscape painting. The shan shui style painting—"shan" meaning mountain, and "shui" meaning river—became prominent features in Chinese landscape art. The emphasis laid upon landscape painting in the Song period was grounded in Chinese philosophy; Taoism stressed that humans were but tiny specks among vast and greater cosmos, while Neo-Confucianist writers often pursued the discovery of patterns and principles that they believed caused all social and natural phenomena. The making of glazed and translucent porcelain and celadon wares with complex use of enamels was also developed further during the Song period. Longquan celadon wares were particularly popular in the Song period. Black and red lacquerwares of the Song period featured beautifully carved artwork of miniature nature scenes, landscapes, or simple decorative motifs.

Song-era painting: *A Song-era painting that exemplifies new styles of landscape paintings, depicting humans as small aspects of grand landscapes.*

The gentry elite engaged in the arts as accepted pastimes of the cultured scholar-official; these pastimes included painting, composing poetry, and writing calligraphy. Poetry and literature profited from the rising popularity and development of the ci poetry form. Enormous encyclopedic volumes were compiled, such as works of historiography and dozens of treatises on technical subjects. This included the universal history text of the Zizhi Tongjian, compiled into 1000 volumes of 9.4-million written Chinese characters. The genre of Chinese travel literature also became popular with the writings of the geographers Fan Chengda (1126–1193) and Su Shi, the latter of whom wrote the "daytrip essay" known as Record of Stone Bell Mountain, which used persuasive writing to argue for a philosophical point. Although an early form of the local geographic gazetteer had existed in China since the 1st century, the matured form known as "treatise on a place," or fangzhi, replaced the old "map guide," or tujing, during the Song dynasty.

Theater and drama in China trace their roots back to the academy of music known as the Pear Garden, founded in the early 8th century during the Tang dynasty. However, historian Stephen H. West asserts that the Northern Song era capital Kaifeng was the first real center where the performing arts became "an industry, a conglomerate involving theatre, gambling, prostitution, and food." The rise in consumption by merchants and scholar-officials, he states, "accelerated the growth of both the performance and the food industries," asserting a direct link between the two due to their close proximity within the cities. Of the fifty-some theaters located in the "pleasure districts" of Kaifeng, four were large enough to entertain audiences of several thousand each, drawing huge crowds that nearby businesses thrived upon. The chief crowd that gathered was composed of those from the merchant class, while government officials only went to restaurants and attended theater performances during holidays.

Technological Advancements under the Song

The Song dynasty provided some of the most significant technological advances in Chinese history.

Learning Objectives

Identify some of the technological advancements made under the Song

Key Takeaways

Key Points

- Notable advances in civil engineering, nautics, and metallurgy were made in Song China.
- Advances in moveable type made the printing of texts easier and faster, thereby making the dissemination of ideas and learning more widespread.
- The application of new weapons using gunpowder enabled the Song to ward off its militant enemies.
- In Song China, topographical elevation, a formal rectangular grid system, and use of a

standard graduated scale of distances were applied to terrain maps.

Key Terms

- **metallurgy**: The branch of science and technology concerned with the properties of metals and their production and purification.
- **Cartography**: The study and practice of making maps.

Overview

The Song dynasty provided some of the most significant technological advances in Chinese history, many of which came from talented statesmen drafted by the government through imperial examinations.

The ingenuity of advanced mechanical engineering has a long tradition in China. The Song engineer Su Song admitted that he and his contemporaries were building upon the achievements of the ancients such as Zhang Heng (78–139), an astronomer, inventor, and early master of mechanical gears. The application of movable type printing advanced the already widespread use of woodblock printing to educate and amuse Confucian students and the masses. The application of new weapons using gunpowder enabled the Song to ward off its militant enemies—the Liao, Western Xia, and Jin—with weapons such as cannons until its collapse to the Mongol forces of Kublai Khan in the late 13th century.

Notable advances in civil engineering, nautics, and metallurgy were made in Song China, and the windmill was introduced in China during the 13th century. These advances, along with the introduction of paper-printed money, helped revolutionize and sustain the economy of the Song dynasty.

Gunpowder and New Weaponry

Advancements in weapons technology enhanced by gunpowder, including the evolution of the early flamethrower, explosive grenade, firearm, cannon, and land mine, enabled the Song Chinese to ward off their militant enemies until the Song's ultimate collapse in the late 13th century. The *Wujing Zongyao* manuscript of 1044 was the first book in history to provide formulas for gunpowder and their specified use in different types of bombs. While engaged in a war with the Mongols, in 1259 the official Li Zengbo wrote in his *Kezhai Zagao, Xugaohou* that the city of Qingzhou was manufacturing one- to two-thousand strong iron-cased bomb shells a month, dispatching to Xiangyang and Yingzhou about ten- to twenty-thousand such bombs at a time. In turn, the invading Mongols employed northern Chinese soldiers and used this same type of gunpowder weapons against the Song. By the 14th century the firearm and cannon could also be found in Europe, India, and the Islamic Middle East, during the early age of gunpowder warfare.

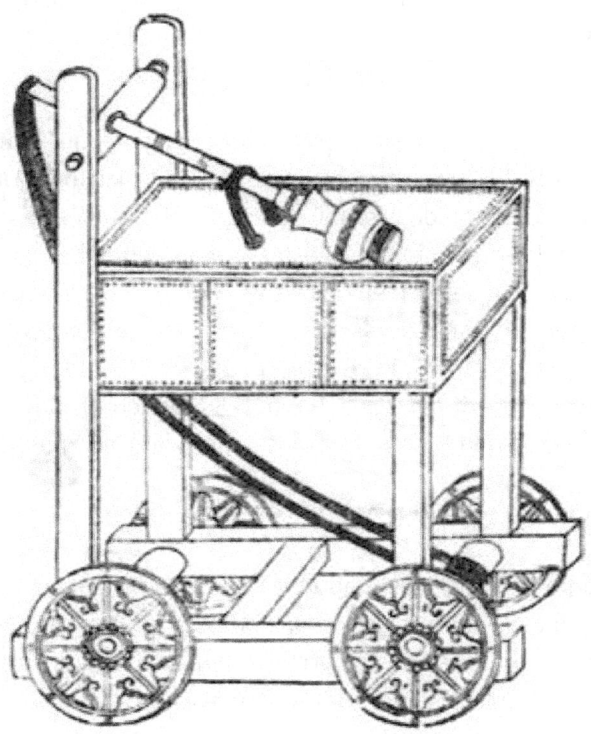

Trebuchet: *An illustration of a trebuchet catapult from the Wujing Zongyao manuscript of 1044. Trebuchets like this were used to launch the earliest type of explosive bombs.*

Advances in Navigation

As early as the Han dynasty, when the state needed to effectively measure distances traveled throughout the empire, the Chinese relied on the mechanical odometer device. The Chinese odometer came in the form of a wheeled-carriage, its inner gears functioning off the rotated motion of the wheels, and specific units of distance—the Chinese li—marked by the mechanical striking of a drum or bell for auditory alarm. The specifications for the 11th century odometer were written by Chief Chamberlain Lu Daolong, who is quoted extensively in the historical text of the Song Shi (compiled by 1345). In the Song period, the odometer vehicle was also combined with another old complex mechanical device known as the south-pointing chariot. This device, originally crafted by Ma Jun in the 3rd century, incorporated a differential gear that allowed a figure mounted on the vehicle to always point south, no matter how the vehicle's wheels turned about. The device concept of the differential gear for this navigational vehicle is now found in modern automobiles in order to apply the equal amount of torque to wheels rotating at different speeds.

Mathematics and Cartography

There were many notable improvements to Chinese mathematics during the Song era. Mathematician Yang Hui's 1261 book provided the earliest Chinese illustration of Pascal's triangle, although it had earlier been described by Jia Xian in around 1100. Yang Hui also provided rules for constructing combinatorial arrangements in magic squares, provided theoretical proof for Euclid 's forty-third proposition about parallelograms, and was the first to use negative coefficients of "x" in quadratic equations. Yang's contemporary Qin Jiushao (c. 1202–1261) was the first to introduce the zero symbol into Chinese mathematics; before this blank spaces were used instead of zeroes in the system of counting rods.

Geometry was essential to surveying and cartography. The earliest extant Chinese maps date to the 4th century BCE, yet it was not until the time of Pei Xiu (224–271) that topographical elevation, a formal rectangular grid system, and use of a standard graduated scale of distances were applied to terrain maps. Following a long tradition, Shen Kuo created a raised-relief map, while his other maps featured a uniform graduated scale of 1:900,000. A 3-ft squared map of 1137—carved into a stone block—followed a uniform grid scale of 100 li for each gridded square, and accurately mapped the outline of the coasts and river systems of China, extending all the way to India. Furthermore, the world's oldest known terrain map in printed form comes from the edited encyclopedia of Yang Jia in 1155, which displays western China without the formal grid system that was characteristic of more professionally made Chinese maps.

Moveable Type Printing

The innovation of movable type printing was made by the artisan Bi Sheng (990–1051), first described by the scientist and statesman Shen Kuo in his *Dream Pool Essays* of 1088. Movable type enhanced the already widespread use of woodblock methods of printing thousands of documents and volumes of written literature, which were then consumed eagerly by an increasingly literate public. The advancement of printing deeply affected education and the scholar-official class; since more books could be made faster, printed books were cheaper than laboriously handwritten copies. The enhancement of widespread printing and print culture in the Song period was thus a direct catalyst in the rise of social mobility and expansion of the educated class of scholar elites, the latter of which expanded dramatically in size from the 11th to 13th centuries.

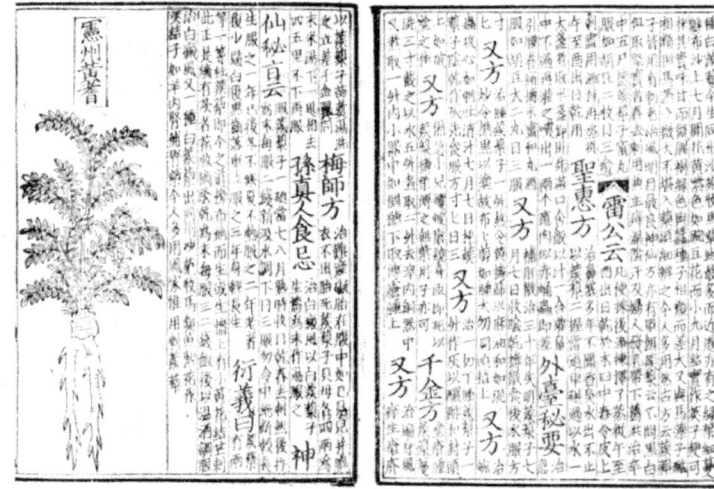

Woodblock printing: *The Bencao on traditional Chinese medicine; printed with woodblock in 1249, Song dynasty.*

Attributions

CC licensed content, Specific attribution

- Song dynasty. **Provided by**: Wikipedia. **Located at**: https://en.wikipedia.org/wiki/Song_dynasty. **License**: *CC BY-SA: Attribution-*

- ShareAlike
- History of the Song dynasty. **Provided by**: Wikipedia. **Located at**: https://en.wikipedia.org/wiki/History_of_the_Song_dynasty. **License**: *CC BY-SA: Attribution-ShareAlike*
- 340px-Song_Taizu.jpg. **Provided by**: Wikipedia. **Located at**: https://en.wikipedia.org/wiki/Song_dynasty#/media/File:Song_Taizu.jpg. **License**: *CC BY-SA: Attribution-ShareAlike*
- History of the Song dynasty. **Provided by**: Wikipedia. **Located at**: https://en.wikipedia.org/wiki/History_of_the_Song_dynasty. **License**: *CC BY-SA: Attribution-ShareAlike*
- Song dynasty. **Provided by**: Wikipedia. **Located at**: https://en.wikipedia.org/wiki/Song_dynasty. **License**: *CC BY-SA: Attribution-ShareAlike*
- 340px-Song_Taizu.jpg. **Provided by**: Wikipedia. **Located at**: https://en.wikipedia.org/wiki/Song_dynasty#/media/File:Song_Taizu.jpg. **License**: *CC BY-SA: Attribution-ShareAlike*
- China_-_Song_Dynasty-en.svg.png. **Provided by**: Wikimedia. **Located at**: https://commons.wikimedia.org/wiki/File:China_-_Song_Dynasty-en.svg. **License**: *CC BY-SA: Attribution-ShareAlike*
- History of the Song dynasty. **Provided by**: Wikipedia. **Located at**: https://en.wikipedia.org/wiki/History_of_the_Song_dynasty. **License**: *CC BY-SA: Attribution-ShareAlike*
- Jin-Song Wars. **Provided by**: Wikipedia. **Located at**: https://en.wikipedia.org/wiki/Jin_Song_Wars. **License**: *CC BY-SA: Attribution-ShareAlike*
- Song dynasty. **Provided by**: Wikipedia. **Located at**: https://en.wikipedia.org/wiki/Song_dynasty. **License**: *CC BY-SA: Attribution-ShareAlike*
- 340px-Song_Taizu.jpg. **Provided by**: Wikipedia. **Located at**: https://en.wikipedia.org/wiki/Song_dynasty#/media/File:Song_Taizu.jpg. **License**: *CC BY-SA: Attribution-ShareAlike*
- China_-_Song_Dynasty-en.svg.png. **Provided by**: Wikimedia. **Located at**: https://commons.wikimedia.org/wiki/File:China_-_Song_Dynasty-en.svg. **License**: *CC BY-SA: Attribution-ShareAlike*
- SongJunk.jpg. **Provided by**: Wikimedia. **Located at**: https://commons.wikimedia.org/wiki/File:SongJunk.jpg. **License**: *Public Domain: No Known Copyright*
- https://commons.wikimedia.org/wiki/File:China_-_Southern_Song_Dynasty-en.svg. **Provided by**: Wikimedia. **Located at**: https://en.wikipedia.org/wiki/Song_dynasty#/media/File:China_-_Southern_Song_Dynasty-en.svg. **License**: *CC BY-SA: Attribution-ShareAlike*
- Society of the Song dynasty. **Provided by**: Wikipedia. **Located at**: https://en.wikipedia.org/wiki/Society_of_the_Song_dynasty. **License**: *CC BY-SA: Attribution-ShareAlike*
- Song dynasty. **Provided by**: Wikipedia. **Located at**: https://en.wikipedia.org/wiki/Song_dynasty. **License**: *CC BY-SA: Attribution-ShareAlike*
- Culture of the Song dynasty. **Provided by**: Wikipedia. **Located at**: https://en.wikipedia.org/wiki/Culture_of_the_Song_dynasty. **License**: *CC BY-SA: Attribution-ShareAlike*
- 340px-Song_Taizu.jpg. **Provided by**: Wikipedia. **Located at**: https://en.wikipedia.org/wiki/Song_dynasty#/media/File:Song_Taizu.jpg. **License**: *CC BY-SA: Attribution-ShareAlike*
- China_-_Song_Dynasty-en.svg.png. **Provided by**: Wikimedia. **Located at**: https://commons.wikimedia.org/wiki/File:China_-_Song_Dynasty-en.svg. **License**: *CC BY-SA: Attribution-ShareAlike*
- SongJunk.jpg. **Provided by**: Wikimedia. **Located at**: https://commons.wikimedia.org/wiki/File:SongJunk.jpg. **License**: *Public Domain: No Known Copyright*
- https://commons.wikimedia.org/wiki/File:China_-_Southern_Song_Dynasty-en.svg. **Provided by**: Wikimedia. **Located at**: https://en.wikipedia.org/wiki/Song_dynasty#/media/File:China_-_Southern_Song_Dynasty-en.svg. **License**: *CC BY-SA: Attribution-ShareAlike*
- 1024px-Empress_of_Zhenzong_of_Song.jpg. **Provided by**: Wikimedia. **Located at**: https://commons.wikimedia.org/wiki/File:Empress_of_Zhenzong_of_Song.jpg. **License**: *Public Domain: No Known Copyright*
- Li_Zhao_Dao_Tang_Ming_Huang_to_Shu.jpg. **Provided by**: Wikimedia. **Located at**: https://commons.wikimedia.org/wiki/File:Li_Zhao_Dao_Tang_Ming_Huang_to_Shu.jpg. **License**: *Public Domain: No Known Copyright*
- 800px-Liu_Songnian-Luohan.jpg. **Provided by**: Wikimedia. **Located at**: https://commons.wikimedia.org/wiki/File:Empress_of_Zhenzong_of_Song.jpg. **License**: *Public Domain: No Known Copyright*
- Song dynasty. **Provided by**: Wikipedia. **Located at**: https://en.wikipedia.org/wiki/Song_dynasty. **License**: *CC BY-SA: Attribution-ShareAlike*
- Science and technology of the Song dynasty. **Provided by**: Wikipedia. **Located at**: https://en.wikipedia.org/wiki/Sci-

- ence_and_technology_of_the_Song_dynasty. **License**: *CC BY-SA: Attribution-ShareAlike*
- 340px-Song_Taizu.jpg. **Provided by**: Wikipedia. **Located at**: https://en.wikipedia.org/wiki/Song_dynasty#/media/File:Song_Taizu.jpg. **License**: *CC BY-SA: Attribution-ShareAlike*
- China_-_Song_Dynasty-en.svg.png. **Provided by**: Wikimedia. **Located at**: https://commons.wikimedia.org/wiki/File:China_-_Song_Dynasty-en.svg. **License**: *CC BY-SA: Attribution-ShareAlike*
- SongJunk.jpg. **Provided by**: Wikimedia. **Located at**: https://commons.wikimedia.org/wiki/File:SongJunk.jpg. **License**: *Public Domain: No Known Copyright*
- https://commons.wikimedia.org/wiki/File:China_-_Southern_Song_Dynasty-en.svg. **Provided by**: Wikimedia. **Located at**: https://en.wikipedia.org/wiki/Song_dynasty#/media/File:China_-_Southern_Song_Dynasty-en.svg. **License**: *CC BY-SA: Attribution-ShareAlike*
- 1024px-Empress_of_Zhenzong_of_Song.jpg. **Provided by**: Wikimedia. **Located at**: https://commons.wikimedia.org/wiki/File:Empress_of_Zhenzong_of_Song.jpg. **License**: *Public Domain: No Known Copyright*
- Li_Zhao_Dao_Tang_Ming_Huang_to_Shu.jpg. **Provided by**: Wikimedia. **Located at**: https://commons.wikimedia.org/wiki/File:Li_Zhao_Dao_Tang_Ming_Huang_to_Shu.jpg. **License**: *Public Domain: No Known Copyright*
- 800px-Liu_Songnian-Luohan.jpg. **Provided by**: Wikimedia. **Located at**: https://commons.wikimedia.org/wiki/File:Empress_of_Zhenzong_of_Song.jpg. **License**: *Public Domain: No Known Copyright*
- Trebuchet1-intransit.jpg. **Provided by**: Wikimedia. **Located at**: https://commons.wikimedia.org/wiki/File:Trebuchet1-intransit.jpg. **License**: *CC BY-SA: Attribution-ShareAlike*
- Pen_ts'ao,_woodblock_book_1249-ce.png. **Provided by**: Wikimedia. **Located at**: https://commons.wikimedia.org/wiki/File:Pen_ts%27ao,_woodblock_book_1249-ce.png. **License**: *Public Domain: No Known Copyright*

The Renaissance

The Renaissance

Introduction to the Renaissance

The Renaissance was a cultural movement that began in Italy in the 14th century, and spread to the rest of Europe during the 15th and 16th centuries.

Learning Objectives

Describe the influences of the Renaissance and historical perspectives by modern-day writers

Key Takeaways

Key Points

- There is a consensus that the Renaissance began in Florence, Italy, in the 14th century, most likely due to the political structure and the civil and social nature of the city. The Renaissance encompassed the flowering of Latin languages, a change in artistic style, and gradual, widespread educational reform.
- The development of conventions of diplomacy and an increased reliance on observation in science were also markers of the Renaissance.
- The Renaissance is probably best known for its artistic developments and for the development of " Humanism," a movement that emphasized the importance of creating citizens who were able to engage in the civil life of their community.
- Some historians debate the 19th-century glorification of the Renaissance and individual culture heroes as "Renaissance men."
- Some have called into question whether the Renaissance was a cultural "advance" from the Middle Ages, instead seeing it as a period of pessimism and nostalgia for classical antiquity.

> *Key Terms*
>
> - **Medici**: The last name of a powerful and influential aristocratic Florentine family from the 13th to the 17th century.
> - **studia humanitatis**: Specifically, a cultural and intellectual movement in 14th–16th century Europe characterized by attention to classical culture and a promotion of vernacular texts, notably during the Renaissance.
> - **Renaissance**: A cultural movement from the 14th to the 17th century, beginning in Italy and later spreading to the rest of Europe.
> - **Petrarch**: An Italian scholar and poet in Renaissance Italy, and one of the earliest humanists.

Overview

The Renaissance was a period in Europe, from the 14th to the 17th century, regarded as the cultural bridge between the Middle Ages and modern history. It started as a cultural movement in Italy, specifically in Florence, in the late medieval period and later spread to the rest of Europe, marking the beginning of the early modern age.

The intellectual basis of the Renaissance was its own invented version of humanism, derived from the rediscovery of classical Greek philosophy, such as that of Protagoras, who said that "Man is the measure of all things." This new thinking became manifest in art, architecture, politics, science, and literature. Early examples were the development of perspective in oil painting and the recycled knowledge of how to make concrete. Though availability of paper and the invention of metal movable type sped the dissemination of ideas from the later 15th century, the changes of the Renaissance were not uniformly experienced across Europe.

Cultural, Political, and Intellectual Influences

As a cultural movement, the Renaissance encompassed the innovative flowering of Latin and vernacular literatures, beginning with the 14th-century resurgence of learning based on classical sources, which contemporaries credited to Petrarch; the development of linear perspective and other techniques of rendering a more natural reality in painting; and gradual but widespread educational reform.

In politics, the Renaissance contributed the development of the conventions of diplomacy, and in science an increased reliance on observation. Although the Renaissance saw revolutions in many intellectual pursuits, as well as social and political upheaval, it is perhaps best known for its artistic developments and the contributions of such polymaths as Leonardo da Vinci and Michelangelo, who inspired the term "Renaissance man."

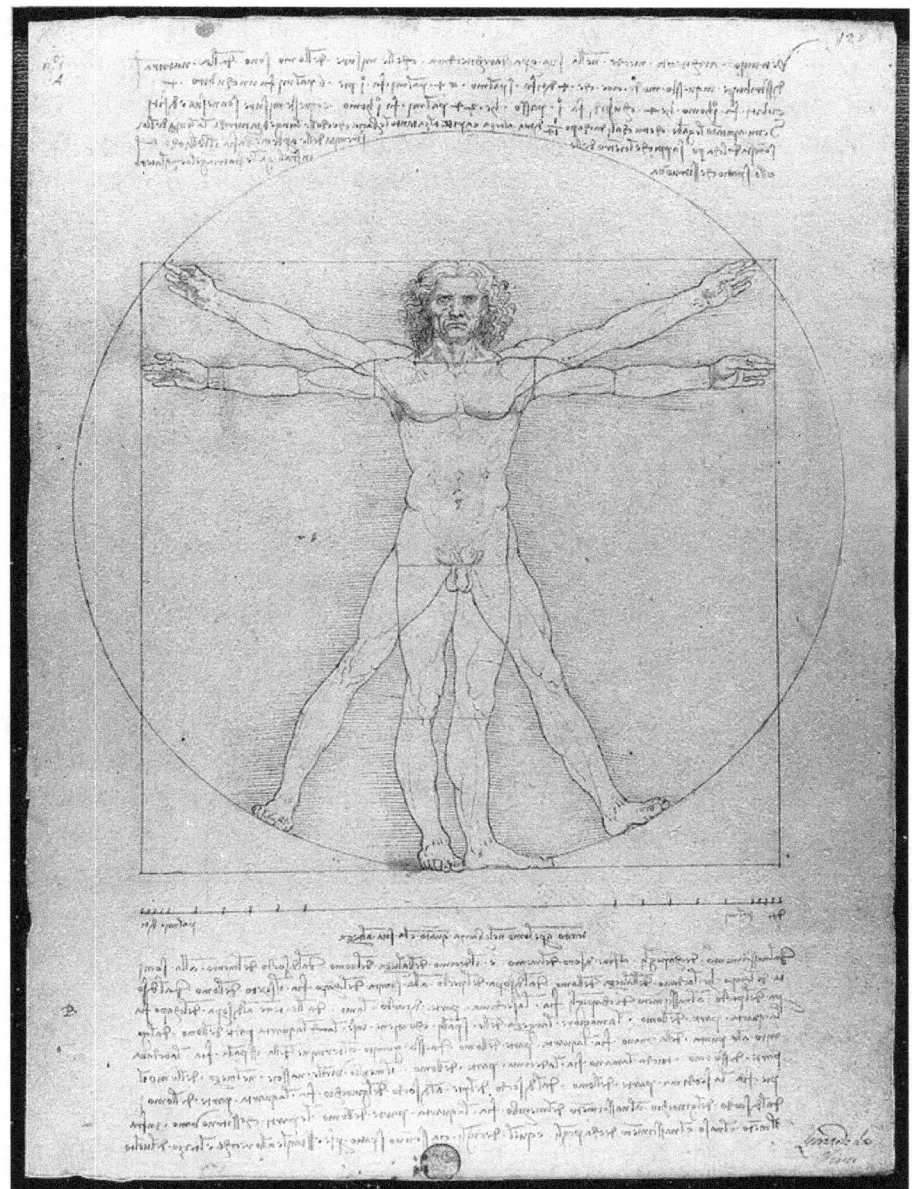

Leonardo da Vinci's Vitruvian Man: *Leonardo da Vinci's Vitruvian Man shows clearly the effect writers of Antiquity had on Renaissance thinkers. Based on the specifications in Vitruvius' De architectura (1st century BCE), Leonardo tried to draw the perfectly proportioned man.*

Beginnings

Various theories have been proposed to account for the origins and characteristics of the Renaissance, focusing on a variety of factors, including the social and civic peculiarities of Florence at the time; its political structure; the patronage of its dominant family, the Medici; and the migration of Greek scholars and texts to Italy following the Fall of Constantinople at the hands of the Ottoman Turks.

Many argue that the ideas characterizing the Renaissance had their origin in late 13th-century Florence, in particular in the writings of Dante Alighieri (1265–1321) and Petrarch (1304–1374), as well as the paintings of Giotto di Bondone (1267–1337). Some writers date the Renaissance quite precisely; one proposed starting point is 1401, when the rival geniuses Lorenzo Ghiberti and Filippo Brunelleschi competed for the contract to build the bronze doors for the Baptistery of the Florence Cathedral (Ghiberti won). Others see more general competition between artists and polymaths such as Brunelleschi, Ghiberti, Donatello, and Masaccio for artistic commissions as sparking the creativity of the Renaissance. Yet it remains much debated why the Renaissance began in Italy, and why it began when it did. Accordingly, several theories have been put forward to explain its origins.

Historical Perspectives on the Renaissance

The Renaissance has a long and complex historiography, and in line with general skepticism of discrete periodizations there has been much debate among historians reacting to the 19th-century glorification of the Renaissance and individual culture heroes as "Renaissance men," questioning the usefulness of "Renaissance" as a term and as a historical delineation.

Some observers have called into question whether the Renaissance was a cultural advance from the Middle Ages, seeing it instead as a period of pessimism and nostalgia for classical antiquity, while social and economic historians, especially of the longue durée (long-term) have focused on the continuity between the two eras, which are linked, as Panofsky observed, "by a thousand ties."

The word "Renaissance," whose literal translation from French into English is "Rebirth," appears in English writing from the 1830s. The word occurs in Jules Michelet's 1855 work, *Histoire de France*. The word "Renaissance" has also been extended to other historical and cultural movements, such as the Carolingian Renaissance and the Renaissance of the 12th century.

A YouTube element has been excluded from this version of the text. You can view it online here: https://milnepublishing.geneseo.edu/suny-fmcc-boundless-worldhistory-print/?p=256

The Renaissance: Was it a Thing? – Crash Course World History #22: European learning changed the world in the 15th and 16th centuries, but was it a cultural revolution, or an evolution? We'd argue that any cultural shift that occurs over a couple of hundred years isn't too overwhelming to the people who live through it. In retrospect though, the cultural bloom in Europe during this time was pretty impressive.

Attributions

CC licensed content, Specific attribution

- Vitruvian Man. **Provided by**: Wikipedia. **Located at**: https://en.wikipedia.org/wiki/Vitruvian_Man. **License**: *CC BY-SA: Attribution-ShareAlike*
- Petrarch. **Provided by**: Wikipedia. **Located at**: http://en.wikipedia.org/wiki/Petrarch. **License**: *CC BY-SA: Attribution-ShareAlike*
- Humanism. **Provided by**: Wiktionary. **Located at**: http://en.wiktionary.org/wiki/humanism. **License**: *CC BY-SA: Attribution-ShareAlike*
- Renaissance. **Provided by**: Wikipedia. **Located at**: http://en.wikipedia.org/wiki/Renaissance. **License**: *CC BY-SA: Attribution-*

ShareAlike
- Medici. **Provided by**: Wiktionary. **Located at**: http://en.wiktionary.org/wiki/Medici. **License**: *CC BY-SA: Attribution-ShareAlike*
- Renaissance. **Provided by**: Wiktionary. **Located at**: http://en.wiktionary.org/wiki/Renaissance. **License**: *CC BY-SA: Attribution-ShareAlike*
- Da Vinci Vitruve Luc Viatour. **Provided by**: Wikimedia. **Located at**: https://commons.wikimedia.org/wiki/File:Da_Vinci_Vitruve_Luc_Viatour.jpg. **License**: *Public Domain: No Known Copyright*
- The Renaissance: Was it a Thing? - Crash Course World History #22. **Located at**: http://www.youtube.com/watch?v=Vufba_ZcoR0. **License**: *Public Domain: No Known Copyright*. **License Terms**: Standard YouTube license

Italy During the Renaissance

Italian Trade Cities

Italian city-states trading during the late Middle Ages set the stage for the Renaissance by moving resources, culture, and knowledge from the East.

Learning Objectives

Show how Northern Italy and the wealthy city-states within it became such huge European powers

---

Key Takeaways

Key Points

- While Northern Italy was not richer in resources than many other parts of Europe, the level of development, stimulated by trade, allowed it to prosper. In particular, Florence became one of the wealthiest cities in Northern Italy.
- Florence became the center of this financial industry, and the gold florin became the main currency of international trade.
- Luxury goods bought in the Levant, such as spices, dyes, and silks, were imported to Italy and then resold throughout Europe.
- The Italian trade routes that covered the Mediterranean and beyond were also major conduits of culture and knowledge.

Key Terms

- **Vitruvius**: A Roman author, architect, and civil engineer (born c. 80–70 BC, died after c. 15 BCE), perhaps best known for his multi-volume work entitled De Architectura.
- **Hanseatic League**: A commercial and defensive confederation of merchant guilds and

> their market towns that dominated trade along the coast of Northern Europe.
> - **Tacitus**: A senator and a historian of the Roman Empire (c. 56–after 117 CE).
> - **Levant**: The countries bordering the eastern Mediterranean Sea.
> - **city-state**: A political phenomenon of small independent states mostly in the central and northern Italian peninsula between the 9th and 15th centuries.

Prosperous City-States

During the late Middle Ages, Northern and Central Italy became far more prosperous than the south of Italy, with the city-states, such as Venice and Genoa, among the wealthiest in Europe. The Crusades had built lasting trade links to the Levant, and the Fourth Crusade had done much to destroy the Byzantine Roman Empire as a commercial rival to the Venetians and Genoese.

The main trade routes from the east passed through the Byzantine Empire or the Arab lands and onwards to the ports of Genoa, Pisa, and Venice. Luxury goods bought in the Levant, such as spices, dyes, and silks, were imported to Italy and then resold throughout Europe. Moreover, the inland city-states profited from the rich agricultural land of the Po valley.

From France, Germany, and the Low Countries, through the medium of the Champagne fairs, land and river trade routes brought goods such as wool, wheat, and precious metals into the region. The extensive trade that stretched from Egypt to the Baltic generated substantial surpluses that allowed significant investment in mining and agriculture.

Thus, while Northern Italy was not richer in resources than many other parts of Europe, the level of development, stimulated by trade, allowed it to prosper. In particular, Florence became one of the wealthiest cities in Northern Italy, due mainly to its woolen textile production, developed under the supervision of its dominant trade guild, the *Arte della Lana*. Wool was imported from Northern Europe (and in the 16th century from Spain), and together with dyes from the east was used to make high quality textiles.

Revitalizing Trade Routes

In the 13th century, much of Europe experienced strong economic growth. The trade routes of the Italian states linked with those of established Mediterranean ports, and eventually the Hanseatic League of the Baltic and northern regions of Europe, to create a network economy in Europe for the first time since the 4th century. The city-states of Italy expanded greatly during this period, and grew in power to become de facto fully independent of the Holy Roman Empire; apart from the Kingdom of Naples, outside powers kept their armies out of Italy. During this period, the modern commercial infrastructure developed, with double-entry bookkeeping, joint stock companies, an international banking system, a systematized foreign exchange market, insurance, and government debt. Florence became the center of this financial industry, and the gold florin became the main currency of international trade.

While Roman urban republican sensibilities persisted, there were many movements and changes afoot. Italy first felt the changes in Europe from the 11th to the 13th centuries. Typically there was:

- A rise in population—the population doubled in this period (the demographic explosion)
- An emergence of huge cities (Venice, Florence, and Milan had over 100,000 inhabitants by the 13th century, and many others, such as Genoa, Bologna, and Verona, had over 50,000)
- Rebuilding of the great cathedrals
- Substantial migration from country to city (in Italy the rate of urbanization reached 20%, making it the most urbanized society in the world at that time)
- An agrarian revolution
- Development of commerce

The decline of feudalism and the rise of cities influenced each other; for example, the demand for luxury goods led to an increase in trade, which led to greater numbers of tradesmen becoming wealthy, who, in turn, demanded more luxury goods.

Palazzo della Signoria e Uffizzi, Florence: *Florence was one of the most important city-states in Italy.*

The Transfer of Culture and Knowledge

The Italian trade routes that covered the Mediterranean and beyond were also major conduits of culture and knowledge. The recovery of lost Greek texts, which had been preserved by Arab scholars, following the Crusader conquest of the Byzantine heartlands revitalized medieval philosophy in the Renaissance of the 12th century. Additionally, Byzantine scholars migrated to Italy during and following the Ottoman conquest of the Byzantines between the 12th and 15th centuries, and were important in sparking the new linguistic studies of the Renaissance, in newly created academies in Florence and Venice. Humanist scholars searched monastic libraries for ancient manuscripts and recovered Tacitus and other Latin authors. The rediscovery of Vitruvius meant that the architectural principles of Antiquity could be observed once more, and Renaissance artists were encouraged, in the atmosphere of humanist optimism, to excel the achievements of the Ancients, like Apelles, of whom they read.

A YouTube element has been excluded from this version of the text. You can view it online here: https://milnepublishing.geneseo.edu/suny-fmcc-boundless-worldhistory-print/?p=257

Venice and the Ottoman Empire: Crash Course World History #19: John Green discusses the strange and mutually beneficial relationship between a republic, the city-state of Venice, and an Empire, the Ottomans—and how studying history can help you to be a better boyfriend and/or girlfriend. Together, the Ottoman Empire and Venice grew wealthy by facilitating trade: The Venetians had ships and nautical expertise; the Ottomans had access to many of the most valuable goods in the world, especially pepper and grain. Working together across cultural and religious divides, they both become very rich, and the Ottomans became one of the most powerful political entities in the world.

Italian Politics

Italian politics during the time of the Renaissance was dominated by the rising merchant class, especially one family, the House of Medici, whose power in Florence was nearly absolute.

Learning Objectives
Describe the intricacies of Italian politics during this time

Key Takeaways
Key Points • Northern and Central Italy became prosperous in the late Middle Ages through the

> growth of international trade and the rise of the merchant class, who eventually gained almost complete control of the governments of the Italian city-states.
>
> - A popular explanation for the Italian Renaissance is the thesis that the primary impetus of the early Renaissance was the long-running series of wars between Florence and Milan, whereby the leading figures of Florence rallied the people by presenting the war as one between the free republic and a despotic monarchy.
> - The House of Medici was an Italian banking family, political dynasty, and later royal house in Florence who were the major sponsors of art and architecture in the early and High Renaissance.
>
> Key Terms
>
> - **House of Medici**: An Italian banking family, political dynasty, and later royal house in the Republic of Florence during the first half of the 15th century that had a major impact on the rise of the Italian Renaissance.
> - **Hundred Years' War**: A series of conflicts waged from 1337 to 1453 by the House of Plantagenet, rulers of the Kingdom of England, against the House of Valois, rulers of the Kingdom of France, for control of the Kingdom of France.

Italy in the Late Middle Ages

By the Late Middle Ages (circa 1300 onward), Latium, the former heartland of the Roman Empire, and southern Italy were generally poorer than the north. Rome was a city of ancient ruins, and the Papal States were loosely administered and vulnerable to external interference such as that of France, and later Spain. The papacy was affronted when the Avignon Papacy was created in southern France as a consequence of pressure from King Philip the Fair of France. In the south, Sicily had for some time been under foreign domination, by the Arabs and then the Normans. Sicily had prospered for 150 years during the Emirate of Sicily, and later for two centuries during the Norman Kingdom and the Hohenstaufen Kingdom, but had declined by the late Middle Ages.

The Rise of the Merchant Class

In contrast, Northern and Central Italy had become far more prosperous, and it has been calculated that the region was among the richest in Europe. The new mercantile governing class, who gained their position through financial skill, adapted to their purposes the feudal aristocratic model that had dominated Europe in the Middle Ages. A feature of the High Middle Ages in Northern Italy was the rise of the urban communes, which had broken from the control of bishops and local counts. In much of the region, the landed nobility was poorer than the urban patriarchs in the high medieval money economy, whose inflationary rise left land-holding aristocrats impoverished. The increase in trade during the early Renaissance enhanced these characteristics.

This change also gave the merchants almost complete control of the governments of the Italian city-states, again enhancing trade. One of the most important effects of this political control was security. Those that grew extremely wealthy in a feudal state ran constant risk of running afoul of the monarchy and having their lands confiscated, as famously occurred to Jacques Coeur in France. The northern states also kept many medieval laws that severely hampered commerce, such as those against usury and prohibitions on trading with non-Christians. In the city-states of Italy, these laws were repealed or rewritten.

The 14th century saw a series of catastrophes that caused the European economy to go into recession, including the Hundred Years' War, the Black Death, and numerous famines. It was during this period of instability that the Renaissance authors such as Dante and Petrarch lived, and the first stirrings of Renaissance art were to be seen, notably in the realism of Giotto. Paradoxically, some of these disasters would help establish the Renaissance. The Black Death wiped out a third of Europe's population. The resulting labor shortage increased wages, and the reduced population was therefore much wealthier and better fed, and, significantly, had more surplus money to spend on luxury goods. As incidences of the plague began to decline in the early 15th century, Europe's devastated population once again began to grow. The new demand for products and services also helped create a growing class of bankers, merchants, and skilled artisans.

Warring Italians

Northern Italy and upper Central Italy were divided into a number of warring city-states, the most powerful being Milan, Florence, Pisa, Siena, Genoa, Ferrara, Mantua, Verona, and Venice. High medieval Northern Italy was further divided by the long-running battle for supremacy between the forces of the papacy and of the Holy Roman Empire; each city aligned itself with one faction or the other, yet was divided internally between the two warring parties, Guelfs and Ghibellines. Warfare between the states was common, but invasion from outside Italy was confined to intermittent sorties of Holy Roman emperors. Renaissance politics developed from this background. Since the 13th century, as armies became primarily composed of mercenaries, prosperous city-states could field considerable forces, despite their low populations. In the course of the 15th century, the most powerful city-states annexed their smaller neighbors. Florence took Pisa in 1406, Venice captured Padua and Verona, and the Duchy of Milan annexed a number of nearby areas, including Pavia and Parma.

A popular explanation for the Italian Renaissance is the thesis, first advanced by historian Hans Baron, that the primary impetus of the early Renaissance was the long-running series of wars between Florence and Milan. By the late 14th century, Milan had become a centralized monarchy under the control of the Visconti family. Giangaleazzo Visconti, who ruled the city from 1378 to 1402, was renowned both for his cruelty and for his abilities, and set about building an empire in Northern Italy. He launched a long series of wars, with Milan steadily conquering neighboring states and defeating the various coalitions led by Florence that sought in vain to halt the advance. This culminated in the 1402 siege of Florence, when it looked as though the city was doomed to fall, before Giangaleazzo suddenly died and his empire collapsed.

Baron's thesis suggests that during these long wars, the leading figures of Florence rallied the people by presenting the war as one between the free republic and a despotic monarchy, between the ideals of the Greek and Roman Republics and those of the Roman Empire and medieval kingdoms. For Baron, the most important figure in crafting this ideology was Leonardo Bruni. This time of crisis in Florence was the period when the most influential figures of the early Renaissance were coming of age, such as Ghiberti, Donatello, Masolino, and Brunelleschi. Inculcated with this republican ideology, they later went on to advocate republican ideas that were to have an enormous impact on the Renaissance.

The Medici Family

The House of Medici was an Italian banking family, political dynasty, and later royal house that first began to gather prominence under Cosimo de' Medici in the Republic of Florence during the first half of the 15th century. The family originated in the Mugello region of the Tuscan countryside, gradually rising until they were able to fund the Medici Bank. The bank was the largest in Europe during the 15th century, which helped the Medici gain political power in Florence—though officially they remained citizens rather than monarchs. The biggest accomplishments of the Medici were in the sponsorship of art and architecture, mainly early and High Renaissance art and architecture. The Medici were responsible for the majority of Florentine art during their reign.

Their wealth and influence initially derived from the textile trade guided by the guild of the *Arte della Lana*. Like other signore families, they dominated their city's government, they were able to bring Florence under their family's power, and they created an environment where art and Humanism could flourish. They, along with other families of Italy, such as the Visconti and Sforza of Milan, the Este of Ferrara, and the Gonzaga of Mantua, fostered and inspired the birth of the Italian Renaissance. The Medici family was connected to most other elite families of the time through marriages of convenience, partnerships, or employment, so the family had a central position in the social network. Several families had systematic access to the rest of the elite families only through the Medici, perhaps similar to banking relationships.

The Medici Bank was one of the most prosperous and most respected institutions in Europe. There are some estimates that the Medici family were the wealthiest family in Europe for a time. From this base, they acquired political power initially in Florence and later in wider Italy and Europe. A notable contribution to the profession of accounting was the improvement of the general ledger system through the development of the double-entry bookkeeping system for tracking credits and debits. The Medici family were among the earliest businesses to use the system.

Cosimo di Giovanni de' Medici was the first of the Medici political dynasty, and had tremendous political power in Florence. Despite his influence, his power was not absolute; Florence's legislative councils at times resisted his proposals, something that would not have been tolerated by the Visconti of Milan, for instance. Throughout his life he was always *primus inter pares*, or first among equals. His power over Florence stemmed from his wealth, which he used to control votes. As Florence was proud of its "democracy," Medici pretended to have little political ambition, and did not often hold public office. Aeneas Sylvius, Bishop of Siena and later Pope Pius II, said of him, "Political questions are settled in [Cosimo's] house. The man he chooses holds office… He it is who decides peace and war… He is king in all but name."

Cosimo di Giovanni de' Medici: *Portrait of Cosimo de' Medici, the found of the House of Medici, by Jacopo Pontormo; the laurel branch (il Broncone) was a symbol used also by his heirs.*

The Church During the Italian Renaissance

The new Humanist ideals of the Renaissance, although more secular in many aspects, developed against a Christian backdrop, and the church patronized many works of Renaissance art.

Learning Objectives
Analyze the church's role in Italy at the time of the Renaissance

> ## Key Takeaways
>
> *Key Points*
>
> - The Renaissance began in times of religious turmoil, especially surrounding the papacy, which culminated in the Western Schism, in which three men simultaneously claimed to be the true pope.
> - The new engagement with Greek Christian works during the Renaissance, and particularly the return to the original Greek of the New Testament promoted by Humanists Lorenzo Valla and Erasmus, helped pave the way for the Protestant Reformation.
> - In addition to being the head of the church, the pope became one of Italy's most important secular rulers, and pontiffs such as Julius II often waged campaigns to protect and expand their temporal domains.
> - The Counter-Reformation was a period of Catholic resurgence initiated in response to the Protestant Reformation.
>
> *Key Terms*
>
> - **neo-Platonism**: A tradition of philosophy that arose in the 3rd century CE, based on the philosophy of Plato, which involved describing the derivation of the whole of reality from a single principle, "the One." Plotinus is traditionally identified as the founder of this school.
> - **Western Schism**: A split within the Roman Catholic Church that lasted from 1378 to 1417, when three men simultaneously claimed to be the true pope.
> - **Counter-Reformation**: A period of Catholic resurgence initiated in response to the Protestant Reformation.

The Church in the Late Middle Ages

The Renaissance began in times of religious turmoil. The late Middle Ages was a period of political intrigue surrounding the papacy, culminating in the Western Schism, in which three men simultaneously claimed to be the true pope. While the schism was resolved by the Council of Constance (1414), a resulting reform movement known as Conciliarism sought to limit the power of the pope. Although the papacy eventually emerged supreme in ecclesiastical matters by the Fifth Council of the Lateran (1511), it was dogged by continued accusations of corruption, most famously in the person of Pope Alexander VI, who was accused variously of simony, nepotism, and fathering four children.

Pope Alexander VI: Alexander VI, a Borgia pope infamous for his corruption.

Churchmen such as Erasmus and Luther proposed reform to the church, often based on Humanist textual criticism of the New Testament. In October 1517 Luther published the *Ninety-five Theses*, challenging papal authority and criticizing its perceived corruption, particularly with regard to instances of sold indulgences. The *Ninety-five Theses* led to the Reformation, a break with the Roman Catholic Church that previously claimed hegemony in Western Europe. Humanism and the Renaissance therefore played a direct role in sparking the Reformation, as well as in many other contemporaneous religious debates and conflicts.

Pope Paul III came to the papal throne (1534–1549) after the sack of Rome in 1527, with uncertainties prevalent in the Catholic Church following the Protestant Reformation. Nicolaus Copernicus dedicated *De revolutionibus orbium coelestium* (On the Revolutions of the Celestial Spheres) to Paul III, who became the grandfather of Alessandro Farnese (cardinal), who had paintings by Titian, Michelangelo, and Raphael, as well as an important collection of drawings, and who commissioned the masterpiece of Giulio Clovio, arguably the last major illuminated manuscript, the Farnese Hours.

The Church and the Renaissance

The city of Rome, the papacy, and the Papal States were all affected by the Renaissance. On the one hand, it was a time of great artistic patronage and architectural magnificence, when the church pardoned and even sponsored such artists as Michelangelo, Brunelleschi, Bramante, Raphael, Fra Angelico, Donatello, and da Vinci. On the other hand, wealthy Italian families often secured episcopal offices, including the papacy, for their own members, some of whom were known for immorality.

In the revival of neo-Platonism and other ancient philosophies, Renaissance Humanists did not reject Christianity; quite to the contrary, many of the Renaissance's greatest works were devoted to it, and the church patronized many works of Renaissance art. The new ideals of Humanism, although more secular in some aspects, developed against a Christian backdrop, especially in the Northern Renaissance. In turn, the Renaissance had a profound effect on contemporary theology, particularly in the way people perceived the relationship between man and God.

Michelangelo's Pietà in St. Peter's Basilica, Vatican City: Michelangelo's Pietà exemplifies the character of Renaissance art, combining the classical aesthetic of Greek art with religious imagery, in this case Mother Mary holding the body of Jesus after the crucifixion.

In addition to being the head of the church, the pope became one of Italy's most important secular rulers, and pontiffs such as Julius II often waged campaigns to protect and expand their temporal domains. Furthermore, the popes, in a spirit of refined competition with other Italian lords, spent lavishly both on private luxuries and public works, repairing or building churches, bridges, and a magnificent system of aqueducts in Rome that still function today.

From 1505 to 1626, St. Peter's Basilica, perhaps the most recognized Christian church, was built on the site of the old Constantinian basilica in Rome. This was a time of increased contact with Greek culture, opening up new avenues of learning, especially in the fields of philosophy, poetry, classics, rhetoric, and political science, fostering a spirit of Humanism—all of which would influence the church.

Counter-Reformation

The Counter-Reformation, also called the Catholic Reformation or the Catholic Revival, was the period of Catholic resurgence initiated in response to the Protestant Reformation, beginning with the Council of Trent (1545–1563) and ending at the close of the Thirty Years' War (1648). The Counter-Reformation was a comprehensive effort composed of four major elements—ecclesiastical or structural reconfigurations, new religious orders (such as the Jesuits), spiritual movements, and political reform.

Such reforms included the foundation of seminaries for the proper training of priests in the spiritual life and the theological traditions of the church, the reform of religious life by returning orders to their spiritual foundations, and new spiritual movements focusing on the devotional life and a personal relationship with Christ, including the Spanish mystics and the French school of spirituality. It also involved political activities that included the Roman Inquisition. One primary emphasis of the Counter-Reformation was a mission to reach parts of the world that had been colonized as predominantly Catholic, and also try to reconvert areas, such as Sweden and England, that were at one time Catholic but had been Protestantized during the Reformation.

Attributions

CC licensed content, Specific attribution

- Piazza della Signoria. **Provided by**: Wikimedia. **Located at**: https://en.wikipedia.org/wiki/Piazza_della_Signoria. **License**: *CC BY-SA: Attribution-ShareAlike*
- Hanseatic League. **Provided by**: Wikipedia. **Located at**: http://en.wikipedia.org/wiki/Hanseatic_League. **License**: *CC BY-SA: Attribution-ShareAlike*
- Vitruvius. **Provided by**: Wikipedia. **Located at**: http://en.wikipedia.org/wiki/Vitruvius. **License**: *CC BY-SA: Attribution-ShareAlike*
- Tacitus. **Provided by**: Wikipedia. **Located at**: http://en.wikipedia.org/wiki/Tacitus. **License**: *CC BY-SA: Attribution-ShareAlike*
- Italian Renaissance. **Provided by**: Wikipedia. **Located at**: http://en.wikipedia.org/wiki/Italian_Renaissance. **License**: *CC BY-SA: Attribution-ShareAlike*
- Levant. **Provided by**: Wiktionary. **Located at**: http://en.wiktionary.org/wiki/Levant. **License**: *CC BY-SA: Attribution-ShareAlike*
- Italian city-states. **Provided by**: Wikipedia. **Located at**: http://en.wikipedia.org/wiki/Italian_city-states. **License**: *CC BY-SA: Attribution-ShareAlike*
- Humanist. **Provided by**: Wiktionary. **Located at**: http://en.wiktionary.org/wiki/humanism. **License**: *CC BY-SA: Attribution-ShareAlike*
- Venice and the Ottoman Empire: Crash Course World History #19. **Located at**: http://www.youtube.com/watch?v=UN-II_jBzzo. **License**: *Public Domain: No Known Copyright*. **License Terms**: Standard YouTube license
- FirenzeIMG0281 bordercropped. **Provided by**: Wikimedia. **Located at**: https://commons.wikimedia.org/wiki/File:FirenzeIMG0281_bordercropped.jpg. **License**: *CC BY-SA: Attribution-ShareAlike*
- Italian Renaissance. **Provided by**: Wikipedia. **Located at**: https://en.wikipedia.org/wiki/Italian_Renaissance. **License**: *CC BY-SA: Attribution-ShareAlike*
- Cosimo de' Medici. **Provided by**: Wikipedia. **Located at**: https://en.wikipedia.org/wiki/Cosimo_de%27_Medici. **License**: *CC BY-SA: Attribution-ShareAlike*
- House of Medici. **Provided by**: Wikipedia. **Located at**: https://en.wikipedia.org/wiki/House_of_Medici. **License**: *CC BY-SA: Attribution-ShareAlike*
- Italy in the Middle Ages. **Provided by**: Wikipedia. **Located at**: https://en.wikipedia.org/wiki/Italy_in_the_Middle_Ages. **License**: *CC BY-SA: Attribution-ShareAlike*
- Venice and the Ottoman Empire: Crash Course World History #19. **Located at**: http://www.youtube.com/watch?v=UN-II_jBzzo. **License**: *Public Domain: No Known Copyright*. **License Terms**: Standard YouTube license
- FirenzeIMG0281 bordercropped. **Provided by**: Wikimedia. **Located at**: https://commons.wikimedia.org/wiki/File:FirenzeIMG0281_bordercropped.jpg. **License**: *CC BY-SA: Attribution-ShareAlike*
- 1024px-Pontormo_-_Ritratto_di_Cosimo_il_Vecchio_-_Google_Art_Project.jpg. **Provided by**: Wikipedia. **Located at**:

https://en.wikipedia.org/wiki/Cosimo_de%27_Medici#/media/File:Pontormo_-_Ritratto_di_Cosimo_il_Vecchio_-_Google_Art_Project.jpg. **License:** *CC BY-SA: Attribution-ShareAlike*

- History of the Catholic Church. **Provided by**: Wikipedia. **Located at**: https://en.wikipedia.org/wiki/History_of_the_Catholic_Church#Renaissance_and_reforms. **License:** *CC BY-SA: Attribution-ShareAlike*
- Renaissance. **Provided by**: Wikipedia. **Located at**: https://en.wikipedia.org/wiki/Renaissance. **License:** *CC BY-SA: Attribution-ShareAlike*
- Counter-Reformation. **Provided by**: Wikipedia. **Located at**: https://en.wikipedia.org/wiki/Counter-Reformation. **License:** *CC BY-SA: Attribution-ShareAlike*
- Venice and the Ottoman Empire: Crash Course World History #19. **Located at**: http://www.youtube.com/watch?v=UN-II_jBzzo. **License:** *Public Domain: No Known Copyright*. **License Terms**: Standard YouTube license
- FirenzeIMG0281 bordercropped. **Provided by**: Wikimedia. **Located at**: https://commons.wikimedia.org/wiki/File:FirenzeIMG0281_bordercropped.jpg. **License:** *CC BY-SA: Attribution-ShareAlike*
- 1024px-Pontormo_-_Ritratto_di_Cosimo_il_Vecchio_-_Google_Art_Project.jpg. **Provided by**: Wikipedia. **Located at**: https://en.wikipedia.org/wiki/Cosimo_de%27_Medici#/media/File:Pontormo_-_Ritratto_di_Cosimo_il_Vecchio_-_Google_Art_Project.jpg. **License:** *CC BY-SA: Attribution-ShareAlike*
- 440px-Alexander_VI_-_Pinturicchio_detail.jpg. **Provided by**: Wikipedia. **Located at**: https://en.wikipedia.org/wiki/Renaissance#/media/File:Alexander_VI_-_Pinturicchio_detail.jpg. **License:** *CC BY-SA: Attribution-ShareAlike*
- 400px-Michelangelo's_Pieta_5450_cut_out_black.jpg. **Provided by**: Wikipedia. **Located at**: https://en.wikipedia.org/wiki/History_of_Christianity#/media/File:Michelangelo%27s_Pieta_5450_cut_out_black.jpg. **License:** *CC BY-SA: Attribution-ShareAlike*

Humanist Thought

Petrarch

Petrarch is often called the "Father of Humanism," both for his discovery of important classical texts and his personal commitment to the way of life found in ancient literature and philosophy.

Learning Objectives

Explain Petrarch's contributions to the Renaissance

Key Takeaways

Key Points

- Petrarch is traditionally called the "Father of Humanism," both for his influential philosophical attitudes, found in his numerous personal letters, and his discovery and compilation of classical texts.
- Petrarch was born in the Tuscan city of Arezzo in 1304, and spent his early childhood near Florence, but his family moved to Avignon to follow Pope Clement V, who moved there in 1309 to begin the Avignon Papacy.
- He traveled widely in Europe and, during his travels, collected crumbling Latin manuscripts, whose discovery, especially Cicero 's letters, helped spark the Renaissance.
- A highly introspective man, he shaped the nascent Humanist movement a great deal because many of the internal conflicts and musings expressed in his writings were seized upon by Renaissance Humanist philosophers and argued continually for the next 200 years.

> *Key Terms*
>
> - **Dark Ages**: An imprecise term of historical periodization that was once used to refer to the Middle Ages but is latterly most commonly used in relation to the early medieval period, i.e., the centuries following the collapse of the Western Roman Empire; the term was coined by Petrarch.
> - **Humanism**: The study of classical antiquity, at first in Italy and then spreading across Western Europe in the 14th, 15th, and 16th centuries.
> - **Avignon Papacy**: The period from 1309 to 1377, during which seven successive popes resided in Avignon, France.

Overview

Francesco Petrarca (July 20, 1304–July 19, 1374), commonly anglicized as Petrarch, was an Italian scholar and poet in Renaissance Italy, and one of the earliest Humanists. Petrarch's rediscovery of Cicero's letters is often credited for initiating the 14th-century Renaissance. Petrarch is often considered the founder of Humanism. Petrarch's sonnets were admired and imitated throughout Europe during the Renaissance and became a model for lyrical poetry. In the 16th century, Pietro Bembo created the model for the modern Italian language based on Petrarch's works.

Petrarch was born in the Tuscan city of Arezzo in 1304. Petrarch spent his early childhood in the village of Incisa, near Florence. He spent much of his early life at Avignon and nearby Carpentras, where his family moved to follow Pope Clement V, who moved there in 1309 to begin the Avignon Papacy. Petrarch studied law at the University of Montpellier (1316–1320) and the University of Bologna (1320–23); because his father was in the profession of law he insisted that Petrarch and his brother study law also. Petrarch, however, was primarily interested in writing and Latin literature, and considered these seven years wasted.

He traveled widely in Europe, served as an ambassador, and has been called "the first tourist" because he traveled just for pleasure. During his travels, he collected crumbling Latin manuscripts and was a prime mover in the recovery of knowledge from writers of Rome and Greece. He encouraged and advised Leontius Pilatus's translation of Homer from a manuscript purchased by Boccaccio, although he was severely critical of the result. In 1345 he personally discovered a collection of Cicero's letters not previously known to have existed, the collection *ad Atticum*.

Disdaining what he believed to be the ignorance of the centuries preceding the era in which he lived, Petrarch is credited or charged with creating the concept of a historical "Dark Ages."

Francesco Petrarca: *Statue of Petrarch on the Uffizi Palace, in Florence.*

Father of Humanism

Petrarch is traditionally called the "Father of Humanism," and considered by many to more generally be the "Father of the Renaissance." This honorific is so given both for his influential philosophical attitudes, found in his numerous personal letters, and his discovery and compilation of classical texts.

In his work *Secretum meum* he points out that secular achievements did not necessarily preclude an authentic relationship with God. Petrarch argued instead that God had given humans their vast intellectual and creative potential to be used to their fullest. He inspired Humanist philosophy, which led to the intellectual flowering of the Renaissance. He believed in the immense moral and practical value of the study of ancient history and literature—that is, the study of human thought and action. Petrarch was a devout Catholic and did not see a conflict between realizing humanity's potential and having religious faith.

A highly introspective man, he shaped the nascent Humanist movement a great deal, because many of the internal conflicts and musings expressed in his writings were seized upon by Renaissance Humanist philosophers and argued continually for the next 200 years. For example, Petrarch struggled with the proper relation between the active and contemplative life, and tended to emphasize the importance of solitude and study. In a clear disagreement with Dante, in 1346 Petrarch argued in his *De vita solitaria* that Pope Celestine V's refusal of the papacy in 1294 was a virtuous example of solitary life. Later, the politician and thinker Leonardo Bruni argued for the active life, or "civic humanism." As a result, a number of political, military, and religious leaders during the Renaissance were inculcated with the notion that their pursuit of personal fulfillment should be grounded in classical example and philosophical contemplation.

Humanism

Humanism was an intellectual movement embraced by scholars, writers, and civic leaders in 14th century Italy.

Learning Objectives

Assess how Humanism gave rise to the art of the Renaissance

Key Takeaways

Key Points

- Humanists reacted against the utilitarian approach to education, seeking to create a citizenry who were able to speak and write with eloquence and thus able to engage the civic life of their communities.
- The movement was largely founded on the ideals of Italian scholar and poet Francesco Petrarca, which were often centered around humanity's potential for achievement.
- While Humanism initially began as a predominantly literary movement, its influence quickly pervaded the general culture of the time, reintroducing classical Greek and Roman art forms and leading to the Renaissance.
- Donatello became renowned as the greatest sculptor of the Early Renaissance, known especially for his Humanist, and unusually erotic, statue of David.
- While medieval society viewed artists as servants and craftspeople, Renaissance artists were trained intellectuals, and their art reflected this newfound point of view.
- In humanist painting, the treatment of the elements of perspective and depiction of light became of particular concern.

> *Key Terms*
>
> - **High Renaissance**: The period in art history denoting the apogee of the visual arts in the Italian Renaissance. The High Renaissance period is traditionally thought to have begun in the 1490s—with Leonardo's fresco of The Last Supper in Milan and the death of Lorenzo de' Medici in Florence—and to have ended in 1527, with the Sack of Rome by the troops of Charles V.

Overview

Humanism, also known as Renaissance Humanism, was an intellectual movement embraced by scholars, writers, and civic leaders in 14th- and early-15th-century Italy. The movement developed in response to the medieval scholastic conventions in education at the time, which emphasized practical, pre-professional, and scientific studies engaged in solely for job preparation, and typically by men alone. Humanists reacted against this utilitarian approach, seeking to create a citizenry who were able to speak and write with eloquence and thus able to engage the civic life of their communities. This was to be accomplished through the study of the *"studia humanitatis,"* known today as the humanities: grammar, rhetoric, history, poetry, and moral philosophy. Humanism introduced a program to revive the cultural—and particularly the literary—legacy and moral philosophy of classical antiquity. The movement was largely founded on the ideals of Italian scholar and poet Francesco Petrarca, which were often centered around humanity's potential for achievement.

While Humanism initially began as a predominantly literary movement, its influence quickly pervaded the general culture of the time, re-introducing classical Greek and Roman art forms and contributing to the development of the Renaissance. Humanists considered the ancient world to be the pinnacle of human achievement, and thought its accomplishments should serve as the model for contemporary Europe. There were important centers of Humanism in Florence, Naples, Rome, Venice, Genoa, Mantua, Ferrara, and Urbino.

Humanism was an optimistic philosophy that saw man as a rational and sentient being, with the ability to decide and think for himself. It saw man as inherently good by nature, which was in tension with the Christian view of man as the original sinner needing redemption. It provoked fresh insight into the nature of reality, questioning beyond God and spirituality, and provided knowledge about history beyond Christian history.

Humanist Art

Renaissance Humanists saw no conflict between their study of the Ancients and Christianity. The lack of perceived conflict allowed Early Renaissance artists to combine classical forms, classical themes, and Christian theology freely. Early Renaissance sculpture is a great vehicle to explore the emerging Renaissance style. The leading artists of this medium were Donatello, Filippo Brunelleschi, and Lorenzo Ghiberti. Donatello became renowned as the greatest sculptor of the Early Renaissance, known especially for his classical, and unusually erotic, statue of David, which became one of the icons of the Florentine republic.

Donatello's David: *Donatello's David is regarded as an iconic Humanist work of art.*

Humanism affected the artistic community and how artists were perceived. While medieval society viewed artists as servants and craftspeople, Renaissance artists were trained intellectuals, and their art reflected this newfound point of view. Patronage of the arts became an important activity, and commissions included secular subject matter as well as religious. Important patrons, such as Cosimo de' Medici, emerged and contributed largely to the expanding artistic production of the time.

In painting, the treatment of the elements of perspective and light became of particular concern. Paolo Uccello, for example, who is best known for "The Battle of San Romano," was obsessed by his interest in perspective, and would stay up all night in his study trying to grasp the exact vanishing point. He used perspective in order to create a feeling of depth in his paintings. In addition, the use of oil paint had its beginnings in the early part of the 16th century, and its use continued to be explored extensively throughout the High Renaissance.

"The Battle of San Romano" by Paolo Uccello: *Italian Humanist paintings were largely concerned with the depiction of perspective and light.*

Origins

Some of the first Humanists were great collectors of antique manuscripts, including Petrarch, Giovanni Boccaccio, Coluccio Salutati, and Poggio Bracciolini. Of the three, Petrarch was dubbed the "Father of Humanism" because of his devotion to Greek and Roman scrolls. Many worked for the organized church and were in holy orders (like Petrarch), while others were lawyers and chancellors of Italian cities (such as Petrarch's disciple Salutati, the Chancellor of Florence) and thus had access to book-copying workshops.

In Italy, the Humanist educational program won rapid acceptance and, by the mid-15th century, many of the upper classes had received Humanist educations, possibly in addition to traditional scholastic ones. Some of the highest officials of the church were Humanists with the resources to amass important libraries. Such was Cardinal Basilios Bessarion, a convert to the Latin church from Greek Orthodoxy, who was considered for the papacy and was one of the most learned scholars of his time.

Following the Crusader sacking of Constantinople and the end of the Byzantine Empire in 1453, the migration of Byzantine Greek scholars and émigrés, who had greater familiarity with ancient languages and works, furthered the revival of Greek and Roman literature and science.

Education and Humanism

Humanism played a major role in education during the Renaissance, with the goal of cultivating the moral and intellectual character of citizens.

Learning Objectives

Define Humanism and its goals as a movement in education

Key Takeaways

Key Points

- The Humanists of the Renaissance created schools to teach their ideas and wrote books all about education.
- One of the most profound and important schools was established and created by Vittorino da Feltre in 1423 in Mantua to provide the children of the ruler of Mantua with a Humanist education.
- Humanists sought to create a citizenry able to speak and write with eloquence and clarity, thus capable of engaging in the civic life of their communities and persuading others to virtuous and prudent actions.
- Humanist schools combined Christianity and classical texts to produce a model of education for all of Europe.

Key Terms

- **Humanism**: A cultural and intellectual movement in 14th–16th century Europe characterized by attention to Classical culture and a promotion of vernacular texts, notably during the Renaissance.
- **Vittorino da Feltre**: An Italian humanist and teacher who started an important humanist school in Mantua.
- **Liberal arts**: Those areas of learning that require and cultivate general intellectual ability rather than technical skills; the humanities.
- **Cicero**: A Roman philosopher, politician, lawyer, orator, political theorist, consul, and constitutionalist who lived from 106–43 BCE.

Overview

During the Renaissance, Humanism played a major role in education. Humanists —proponents or practitioners of Humanism during the Renaissance—believed that human beings could be dramatically changed by education. The Humanists of the Renaissance created schools to teach their ideas and wrote books all about education. Humanists sought to create a citizenry able to speak and write with eloquence and clarity, thus capable of engaging in the civic life of their communities and persuading others to virtuous and prudent actions. This was to be accomplished through the study of the humanities: grammar, rhetoric, history, poetry, and moral philosophy.

The Humanists believed that it was important to transcend to the afterlife with a perfect mind and body, which could be attained with education. The purpose of Humanism was to create a universal man whose person combined intellectual and physical excellence and who was capable of functioning honorably in virtually any situation. This ideology was referred to as the *uomo universale*, an ancient Greco-Roman ideal. Education during the Renaissance was mainly composed of ancient literature and history, as it was thought that the classics provided moral instruction and an intensive understanding of human behavior.

The educational curriculum of Humanism spread throughout Europe during the 16th century and became the educational foundation for the schooling of European elites, the functionaries of political administration, the clergy of the various legally recognized churches, and the learned professionals of law and medicine.

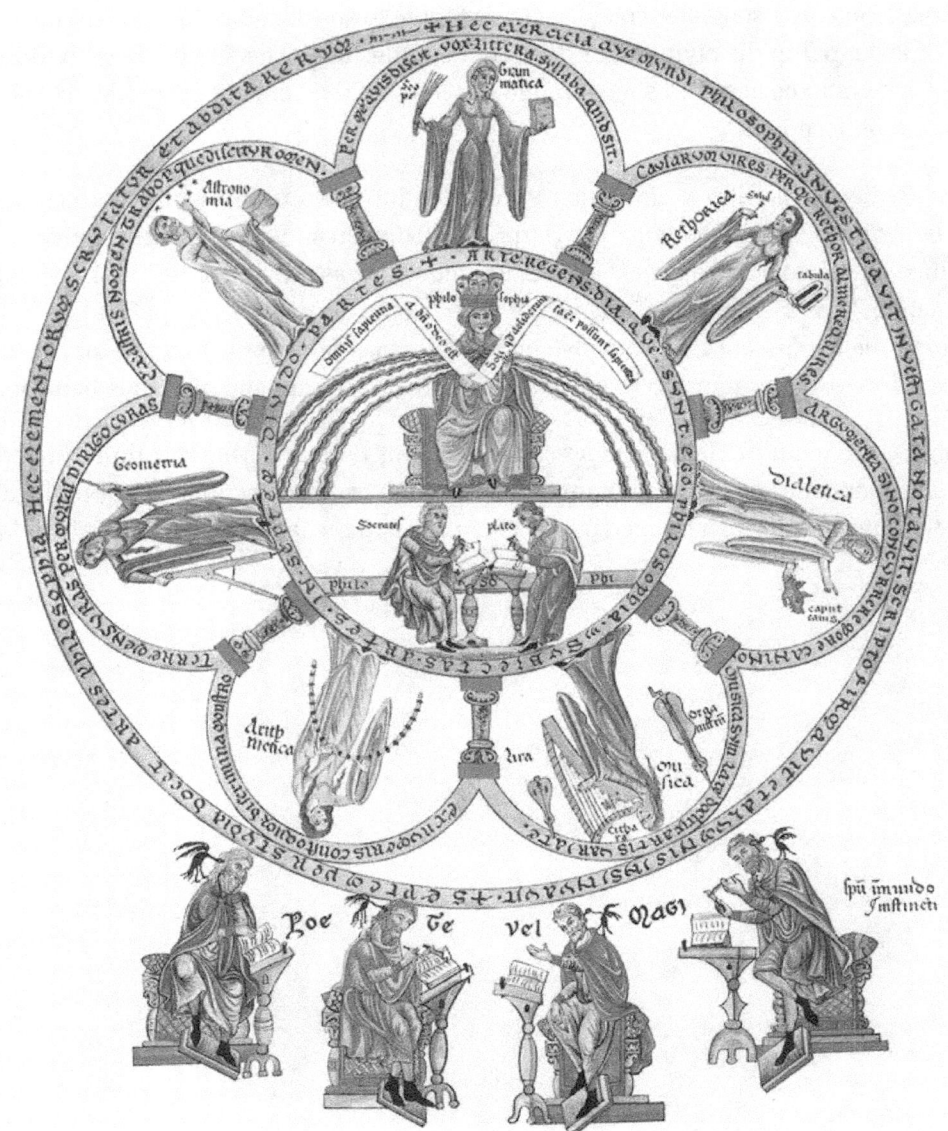

Philosophia et septem artes liberales

A painting symbolizing the liberal arts, depicting individuals representing the seven areas of liberal arts study, all circling around Plato and Socrates.

Humanist Schools

One of the most important Humanist schools was established by Vittorino da Feltre in 1423. The school was in Mantua, which is a small Italian state. The ruler of Mantua had always wanted to provide a Humanist education for his children, and the school was a way to help him.

Most of Feltre's ideas were based on those of previous classical authors, such as Cicero and Quintilian. The main foundation of the school was liberal studies. Liberal arts were viewed as the key to freedom, which allowed humans to achieve their goals and reach their full potential. Liberal studies included philosophy, history, rhetoric, letters, mathematics, poetry, music, and astronomy. Based on the Greek idea of a "sound mind," the school in Mantua offered physical education as well. This included archery, dance, hunting, and swimming.

The children that attended the schools were generally from upper-class families, though some seats were reserved for poor but talented students. Females were not usually allowed to attend, but were encouraged to know history, learn dance, and appreciate poetry. Some important females that were educated during the Renaissance were Isotta Nogarola, Cassandra Fedele of Venice, and Laura Cereta.

Overall, Humanist education was thought at the time to be an important factor in the preparation of life. Its main goal was to improve the lives of citizens and help their communities. Humanist schools combined Christianity and the classics to produce a model of education for all of Europe.

Laura Cereta: *Laura Cereta (1469–1499) was a Renaissance Humanist and feminist. Most of her writing was in the form of letters to other intellectuals.*

Attributions

CC licensed content, Specific attribution

- Petrarch. **Provided by**: Wikipedia. **Located at**: https://en.wikipedia.org/wiki/Petrarch. **License**: *CC BY-SA: Attribution-ShareAlike*
- Renaissance. **Provided by**: Wikipedia. **Located at**: https://en.wikipedia.org/wiki/Renaissance#Humanism. **License**: *CC BY-SA: Attribution-ShareAlike*
- 340px-Francesco_Petrarca2.jpg. **Provided by**: Wikipedia. **Located at**: https://en.wikipedia.org/wiki/Petrarch#/media/File:Francesco_Petrarca2.jpg. **License**: *CC BY-SA: Attribution-ShareAlike*
- Paolo Uccello. **Provided by**: Wikipedia. **Located at**: https://en.wikipedia.org/wiki/Paolo_Uccello. **License**: *CC BY-SA: Attribution-ShareAlike*
- David (Donatello). **Provided by**: Wikipedia. **Located at**: https://en.wikipedia.org/wiki/David_(Donatello). **License**: *CC BY-SA: Attribution-ShareAlike*
- The Battle of San Romano. **Provided by**: Wikipedia. **Located at**: https://en.wikipedia.org/wiki/The_Battle_of_San_Romano. **License**: *CC BY-SA: Attribution-ShareAlike*
- Humanism. **Provided by**: Wikipedia. **Located at**: http://en.wikipedia.org/wiki/Humanism. **License**: *CC BY-SA: Attribution-ShareAlike*
- High Renaissance. **Provided by**: Wikipedia. **Located at**: http://en.wikipedia.org/wiki/High%20Renaissance. **License**: *CC BY-SA: Attribution-ShareAlike*
- 340px-Francesco_Petrarca2.jpg. **Provided by**: Wikipedia. **Located at**: https://en.wikipedia.org/wiki/Petrarch#/media/File:Francesco_Petrarca2.jpg. **License**: *CC BY-SA: Attribution-ShareAlike*
- Uccello Battle of San Romano Uffizi. **Provided by**: Wikipedia. **Located at**: http://en.wikipedia.org/wiki/File:Uccello_Battle_of_San_Romano_Uffizi.jpg. **License**: *CC BY-SA: Attribution-ShareAlike*
- Donatello - David - Florenu00e7a. **Provided by**: Wikimedia. **Located at**: https://commons.wikimedia.org/wiki/File:Donatello_-_David_-_Floren%C3%A7a.jpg. **License**: *CC BY-SA: Attribution-ShareAlike*
- Humanism. **Provided by**: Wikipedia. **Located at**: http://en.wikipedia.org/wiki/Humanism. **License**: *CC BY-SA: Attribution-ShareAlike*
- Vittorino da Feltre. **Provided by**: Wikipedia. **Located at**: http://en.wikipedia.org/wiki/Vittorino_da_Feltre. **License**: *CC BY-SA: Attribution-ShareAlike*
- Education and humanism. **Provided by**: Wikipedia. **Located at**: http://en.wikipedia.org/wiki/Education_and_Humanism. **License**: *CC BY-SA: Attribution-ShareAlike*
- Cicero. **Provided by**: Wikipedia. **Located at**: http://en.wikipedia.org/wiki/Cicero. **License**: *CC BY-SA: Attribution-ShareAlike*
- liberal arts. **Provided by**: Wiktionary. **Located at**: http://en.wiktionary.org/wiki/liberal_arts. **License**: *CC BY-SA: Attribution-ShareAlike*
- 340px-Francesco_Petrarca2.jpg. **Provided by**: Wikipedia. **Located at**: https://en.wikipedia.org/wiki/Petrarch#/media/File:Francesco_Petrarca2.jpg. **License**: *CC BY-SA: Attribution-ShareAlike*
- Uccello Battle of San Romano Uffizi. **Provided by**: Wikipedia. **Located at**: http://en.wikipedia.org/wiki/File:Uccello_Battle_of_San_Romano_Uffizi.jpg. **License**: *CC BY-SA: Attribution-ShareAlike*
- Donatello - David - Florenu00e7a. **Provided by**: Wikimedia. **Located at**: https://commons.wikimedia.org/wiki/File:Donatello_-_David_-_Floren%C3%A7a.jpg. **License**: *CC BY-SA: Attribution-ShareAlike*
- Hortus_Deliciarum,_Die_Philosophie_mit_den_sieben_freien_Ku00fcnsten.JPG. **Provided by**: Wikipedia. **Located at**: https://en.wikipedia.org/wiki/Liberal_arts_education#/media/File:Hortus_Deliciarum,_Die_Philosophie_mit_den_sieben_freien_Kunsten.JPG. **License**: *CC BY-SA: Attribution-ShareAlike*
- Laura Cereta. **Provided by**: Wikipedia. **Located at**: http://en.wikipedia.org/wiki/Laura_Cereta%23mediaviewer/File:LauraCereta.jpg. **License**: *Public Domain: No Known Copyright*

Art in the Renaissance

The Italian Renaissance

Learning Objectives

The art of the Italian Renaissance was influential throughout Europe for centuries.

Key Takeaways

Key Points

- The Florence school of painting became the dominant style during the Renaissance. Renaissance artworks depicted more secular subject matter than previous artistic movements.
- Michelangelo, da Vinci, and Rafael are among the best known painters of the High Renaissance.
- The High Renaissance was followed by the Mannerist movement, known for elongated figures.

Key Terms

- **fresco**: A type of wall painting in which color pigments are mixed with water and applied to wet plaster. As the plaster and pigments dry, they fuse together and the painting becomes a part of the wall itself.
- **Mannerism**: A style of art developed at the end of the High Renaissance, characterized by the deliberate distortion and exaggeration of perspective, especially the elongation of figures.

The Renaissance began during the 14th century and remained the dominate style in Italy, and in much of Europe, until the 16th century. The term "renaissance" was developed during the 19th century in order to describe this period of time and its accompanying artistic style. However, people who were living during the Renaissance did see themselves as different from their Medieval predecessors. Through a variety of texts that survive, we know that people living during the Renaissance saw themselves as different largely because they were deliberately trying to imitate the Ancients in art and architecture.

Florence and the Renaissance

When you hear the term "Renaissance" and picture a style of art, you are probably picturing the Renaissance style that was developed in Florence, which became the dominate style of art during the Renaissance. During the Middle Ages and the Renaissance, Italy was divided into a number of different city states. Each city state had its own government, culture, economy, and artistic style. There were many different styles of art and architecture that were developed in Italy during the Renaissance. Siena, which was a political ally of France, for example, retained a Gothic element to its art for much of the Renaissance.

Certain conditions aided the development of the Renaissance style in Florence during this time period. In the 15th century, Florence became a major mercantile center. The production of cloth drove their economy and a merchant class emerged. Humanism, which had developed during the 14th century, remained an important intellectual movement that impacted art production as well.

Early Renaissance

During the Early Renaissance, artists began to reject the Byzantine style of religious painting and strove to create realism in their depiction of the human form and space. This aim toward realism began with Cimabue and Giotto, and reached its peak in the art of the "Perfect" artists, such as Andrea Mantegna and Paolo Uccello, who created works that employed one point perspective and played with perspective for their educated, art knowledgeable viewer.

During the Early Renaissance we also see important developments in subject matter, in addition to style. While religion was an important element in the daily life of people living during the Renaissance, and remained a driving factor behind artistic production, we also see a new avenue open to panting—mythological subject matter. Many scholars point to Botticelli's *Birth of Venus* as the very first panel painting of a mythological scene. While the tradition itself likely arose from cassone painting, which typically featured scenes from mythology and romantic texts, the development of mythological panel painting would open a world for artistic patronage, production, and themes.

Birth of Venus: *Botticelli's Birth of Venus was among the most important works of the early Renaissance.*

High Renaissance

The period known as the High Renaissance represents the culmination of the goals of the Early Renaissance, namely the realistic representation of figures in space rendered with credible motion and in an appropriately decorous style. The most well known artists from this phase are Leonardo da Vinci, Raphael, Titian, and Michelangelo. Their paintings and frescoes are among the most widely known works of art in the world. Da Vinci's *Last Supper*, Raphael's *The School of Athens* and Michelangelo's Sistine Chapel Ceiling paintings are the masterpieces of this period and embody the elements of the High Renaissance.

Marriage of the Virgin, by Raphael: *The painting depicts a marriage ceremony between Mary and Joseph.*

Mannerism

High Renaissance painting evolved into Mannerism in Florence. Mannerist artists, who consciously rebelled against the principles of High Renaissance, tended to represent elongated figures in illogical spaces. Modern scholarship has recognized the capacity of Mannerist art to convey strong, often religious, emotion where the High Renaissance failed to do so. Some of the main artists of this period are Pontormo, Bronzino, Rosso Fiorentino, Parmigianino and Raphael's pupil, Giulio Romano.

Art and Patronage

The Medici family used their vast fortune to control the Florentine political system and sponsor a series of artistic accomplishments.

Learning Objectives

Discuss the relationship between art, patronage, and politics during the Renaissance

Key Takeaways

Key Points

- Although the Renaissance was underway before the Medici family came to power in Florence, their patronage and political support of the arts helped catalyze the Renaissance into a fully fledged cultural movement.
- The Medici wealth and influence initially derived from the textile trade guided by the guild of the Arte della Lana; through financial superiority, the Medici dominated their city's government.
- Medici patronage was responsible for the majority of Florentine art during their reign, as artists generally only made their works when they received commissions in advance.
- Although none of the Medici themselves were scientists, the family is well known to have been the patrons of the famous Galileo Galilei, who tutored multiple generations of Medici children.

Key Terms

- **Lorenzo de' Medici**: An Italian statesman and de facto ruler of the Florentine Republic, who was one of the most powerful and enthusiastic patrons of the Renaissance.
- **patronage**: The support, encouragement, privilege, or financial aid that an organization or individual bestows on another, especially in the arts.

Overview

It has long been a matter of debate why the Renaissance began in Florence, and not elsewhere in Italy. Scholars have noted several features unique to Florentine cultural life that may have caused such a cultural movement. Many have emphasized the role played by the Medici, a banking family and later ducal ruling house, in patronizing and stimulating the arts. Lorenzo de' Medici (1449–1492) was the catalyst for an enormous amount of arts patronage, encouraging his countrymen to commission works from the leading artists of Florence, including Leonardo da Vinci, Sandro Botticelli, and Michelangelo Buonarroti. Works by Neri di Bicci, Botticelli, da Vinci, and Filippino Lippi had been commissioned additionally by the convent di San Donato agli Scopeti of the Augustinians order in Florence.

The Medici House Patronage

The House of Medici was an Italian banking family, political dynasty, and later royal house that first began to gather prominence under Cosimo de' Medici in the Republic of Florence during the first half of the 15th century. Their wealth and influence initially derived from the textile trade guided by the guild of the Arte della Lana. Like other signore families, they dominated their city's government, they were able to bring Florence under their family's power, and they created an environment where art and Humanism could flourish. They, along with other families of Italy, such as the Visconti and Sforza of Milan, the Este of Ferrara, and the Gonzaga of Mantua, fostered and inspired the birth of the Italian Renaissance.

The biggest accomplishments of the Medici were in the sponsorship of art and architecture, mainly early and High Renaissance art and architecture. The Medici were responsible for the majority of Florentine art during their reign. Their money was significant because during this period, artists generally only made their works when they received commissions in advance. Giovanni di Bicci de' Medici, the first patron of the arts in the family, aided Masaccio and commissioned Brunelleschi for the reconstruction of the Basilica of San Lorenzo, Florence, in 1419. Cosimo the Elder's notable artistic associates were Donatello and Fra Angelico. The most significant addition to the list over the years was Michelangelo Buonarroti (1475–1564), who produced work for a number of Medici, beginning with Lorenzo the Magnificent, who was said to be extremely fond of the young Michelangelo, inviting him to study the family collection of antique sculpture. Lorenzo also served as patron of Leonardo da Vinci (1452–1519) for seven years. Indeed, Lorenzo was an artist in his own right, and an author of poetry and song; his support of the arts and letters is seen as a high point in Medici patronage.

The Medici House: *Medici family members placed allegorically in the entourage of a king from the Three Wise Men in the Tuscan countryside in a Benozzo Gozzoli fresco, c. 1459.*

In architecture, the Medici are responsible for some notable features of Florence, including the Uffizi Gallery, the Boboli Gardens, the Belvedere, the Medici Chapel, and the Palazzo Medici. Later, in Rome, the Medici Popes continued in the family tradition by patronizing artists in Rome. Pope Leo X would chiefly commission works from Raphael. Pope Clement VII commissioned Michelangelo to paint the altar wall of the Sistine Chapel just before the pontiff's death in 1534. Eleanor of Toledo, princess of Spain and wife of Cosimo I the Great, purchased the Pitti Palace from Buonaccorso Pitti in 1550. Cosimo in turn patronized Vasari, who erected the Uffizi Gallery in 1560 and founded the Accademia delle Arti del Disegno ("Academy of the Arts of Drawing") in 1563. Marie de' Medici, widow of Henry IV of France and mother of Louis XIII, is the subject of a commissioned cycle of paintings known as the Marie de' Medici cycle, painted for the Luxembourg Palace by court painter Peter Paul Rubens in 1622–1623.

Although none of the Medici themselves were scientists, the family is well known to have been the patrons of the famous Galileo Galilei, who tutored multiple generations of Medici children and was an important figurehead for his patron's quest for power. Galileo's patronage was eventually abandoned by Ferdinando II when the Inquisition accused Galileo of heresy. However, the Medici family did afford the scientist a safe haven for many years. Galileo named the four largest moons of Jupiter after four Medici children he tutored, although the names Galileo used are not the names currently used.

Leonardo da Vinci

While Leonardo da Vinci is admired as a scientist, an academic, and an inventor, he is most famous for his achievements as the painter of several Renaissance masterpieces.

Learning Objectives

Describe the works of Leonardo da Vinci that demonstrate his most innovative techniques as an artist

---

Key Takeaways

Key Points

- Among the qualities that make da Vinci's work unique are the innovative techniques that he used in laying on the paint, his detailed knowledge of anatomy, his innovative use of the human form in figurative composition, and his use of sfumato.
- Among the most famous works created by da Vinci is the small portrait titled the *Mona Lisa*, known for the elusive smile on the woman's face, brought about by the fact that da Vinci subtly shadowed the corners of the mouth and eyes so that the exact nature of the smile cannot be determined.
- Despite his famous paintings, da Vinci was not a prolific painter; he was a prolific draftsman, keeping journals full of small sketches and detailed drawings recording all manner of things that interested him.

Key Terms

- **sfumato**: In painting, the application of subtle layers of translucent paint so that there is no visible transition between colors, tones, and often objects.

While Leonardo da Vinci is greatly admired as a scientist, an academic, and an inventor, he is most famous for his achievements as the painter of several Renaissance masterpieces. His paintings were groundbreaking for a variety of reasons and his works have been imitated by students and discussed at great length by connoisseurs and critics.

Among the qualities that make da Vinci's work unique are the innovative techniques that he used in laying on the paint, his detailed knowledge of anatomy, his use of the human form in figurative composition, and his use of sfumato. All of these qualities are present in his most celebrated works, the *Mona Lisa*, *The Last Supper*, and the *Virgin of the Rocks*.

***The Virgin of the Rocks*, Leonardo da Vinci, 1483–1486:** *This painting shows the Madonna and Child Jesus with the infant John the Baptist and an angel, in a rocky setting.*

The Last Supper

Da Vinci's most celebrated painting of the 1490s is *The Last Supper*, which was painted for the refectory of the Convent of Santa Maria della Grazie in Milan. The painting depicts the last meal shared by Jesus and the 12 Apostles where he announces that one of the them will betray him. When finished, the painting was acclaimed as a masterpiece of design. This work demonstrates something that da Vinci did very well: taking a very traditional subject matter, such as the Last Supper, and completely re-inventing it.

Prior to this moment in art history, every representation of the Last Supper followed the same visual tradition: Jesus and the Apostles seated at a table. Judas is placed on the opposite side of the table of everyone else and is effortlessly identified by the viewer. When da Vinci painted The Last Supper he placed Judas on the same side of the table as Christ and the Apostles, who are shown reacting to Jesus as he announces that one of them will betray him. They are depicted as alarmed, upset, and trying to determine who will commit the act. The viewer also has to determine which figure is Judas, who will betray Christ. By depicting the scene in this manner, da Vinci has infused psychology into the work.

Unfortunately, this masterpiece of the Renaissance began to deteriorate immediately after da Vinci finished painting, due largely to the painting technique that he had chosen. Instead of using the technique of fresco, da Vinci had used tempera over a ground that was mainly gesso in an attempt to bring the subtle effects of oil paint to fresco. His new technique was not successful, and resulted in a surface that was subject to mold and flaking.

The Last Supper: *Leonardo da Vinci's Last Supper, although much deteriorated, demonstrates the painter's mastery of the human form in figurative composition.*

Mona Lisa

Among the works created by da Vinci in the 16th century is the small portrait known as the *Mona Lisa,* or *La Gioconda,* "the laughing one." In the present era it is arguably the most famous painting in the world. Its fame rests, in particular, on the elusive smile on the woman's face—its mysterious quality brought about perhaps by the fact that the artist has subtly shadowed the corners of the mouth and eyes so that the exact nature of the smile cannot be determined.

The shadowy quality for which the work is renowned came to be called sfumato, the application of subtle layers of translucent paint so that there is no visible transition between colors, tones, and often objects. Other characteristics found in this work are the unadorned dress, in which the eyes and hands have no competition from other details; the dramatic landscape background, in which the world seems to be in a state of flux; the subdued coloring; and the extremely smooth nature of the painterly technique, employing oils, but applied much like tempera and blended on the surface so that the brushstrokes are indistinguishable. And again, da Vinci is innovating upon a type of painting here. Portraits were very common in the Renaissance. However, portraits of women were always in profile, which was seen as proper and modest. Here, da Vinci present a portrait of a woman who not only faces the viewer but follows them with her eyes.

Mona Lisa: *In the Mona Lisa, da Vinci incorporates his sfumato technique to create a shadowy quality.*

Virgin and Child with St. Anne

In the painting *Virgin and Child with St. Anne*, da Vinci's composition again picks up the theme of figures in a landscape. What makes this painting unusual is that there are two obliquely set figures superimposed. Mary is seated on the knee of her mother, St. Anne. She leans forward to restrain the Christ Child as he plays roughly with a lamb, the sign of his own impending sacrifice. This painting influenced many contemporaries, including Michelangelo, Raphael, and Andrea del Sarto. The trends in its composition were adopted in particular by the Venetian painters Tintoretto and Veronese.

Virgin and Child with Saint Anne: *Virgin and Child with St. Anne (c. 1510) by Leonardo da Vinci, Louvre Museum.*

Michelangelo

Michelangelo was a 16th century Florentine artist renowned for his masterpieces in sculpture, painting, and architectural design.

Learning Objectives

Discuss Michelangelo's achievements in sculpture, painting, and architecture

Key Takeaways

Key Points

- Michelangelo created his colossal marble statue, the David, out of a single block of marble, which established his prominence as a sculptor of extraordinary technical skill and strength of symbolic imagination.
- In painting, Michelangelo is renowned for the ceiling and *The Last Judgement* of the Sistine Chapel, where he depicted a complex scheme representing Creation, the Downfall of Man, the Salvation of Man, and the Genealogy of Christ.
- Michelangelo's chief contribution to Saint Peter's Basilica was the use of a Greek Cross form and an external masonry of massive proportions, with every corner filled in by a stairwell or small vestry. The effect is a continuous wall-surface that appears fractured or folded at different angles.

Key Terms

- **contrapposto**: The standing position of a human figure where most of the weight is placed on one foot, and the other leg is relaxed. The effect of contrapposto in art makes figures look very naturalistic.
- **Sistine Chapel**: The best-known chapel in the Apostolic Palace.

Michelangelo was a 16th century Florentine artist renowned for his masterpieces in sculpture, painting, and architectural design. His most well known works are the *David*, the *Last Judgment*, and the *Basilica of Saint Peter's* in the Vatican.

Sculpture: David

In 1504, Michelangelo was commissioned to create a colossal marble statue portraying David as a symbol of Florentine freedom. The subsequent masterpiece, *David*, established the artist's prominence as a sculptor of extraordinary technical skill and strength of symbolic imagination. *David* was created out of a single marble block, and stands larger than life, as it was originally intended to adorn the Florence Cathedral. The work differs from previous representations in that the Biblical hero is not depicted with the head of the slain Goliath, as he is in Donatello's and Verrocchio's statues; both had represented the hero standing victorious over the head of Goliath. No earlier Florentine artist had omitted the giant altogether. Instead of appearing victorious over a foe, David's face looks tense and ready for combat. The tendons in his neck stand out tautly, his brow is furrowed, and his eyes seem to focus intently on something in the distance.

Veins bulge out of his lowered right hand, but his body is in a relaxed *contrapposto* pose, and he carries his sling casually thrown over his left shoulder. In the Renaissance, *contrapposto* poses were thought of as a distinctive feature of antique sculpture.

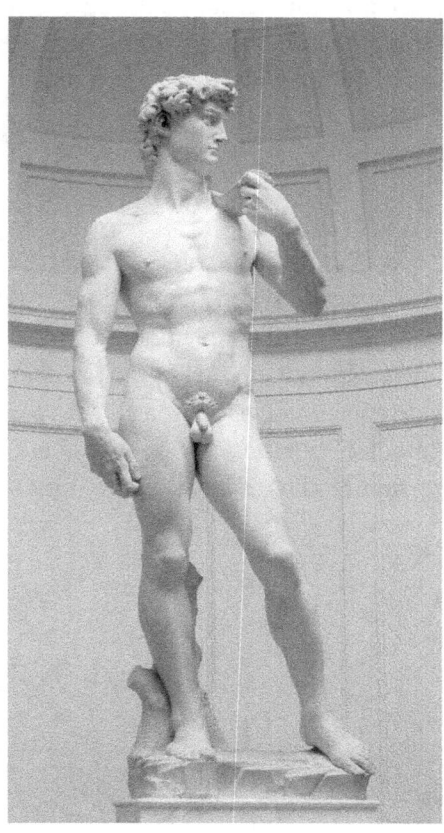

The David by Michelangelo, 1504: *Michelangelo's David stands in contrapposto pose.*

The sculpture was intended to be placed on the exterior of the Duomo, and has become one of the most recognized works of Renaissance sculpture.

Painting: The Last Judgement

In painting, Michelangelo is renowned for his work in the Sistine Chapel. He was originally commissioned to paint tromp-l'oeil coffers after the original ceiling developed a crack. Michelangelo lobbied for a different and more complex scheme, representing Creation, the Downfall of Man, the Promise of Salvation through the prophets, and the Genealogy of Christ. The work is part of a larger scheme of decoration within the chapel that represents much of the doctrine of the Catholic Church.

The composition eventually contained over 300 figures, and had at its center nine episodes from the Book of Genesis, divided into three groups: God's Creation of the Earth, God's Creation of Humankind, and their fall from God's grace, and lastly, the state of Humanity as represented by Noah and his family. Twelve men and women who prophesied the coming of the Jesus are painted on the pendentives supporting the ceiling. Among the most famous paintings on the ceiling are The Creation of Adam, Adam and Eve in the Garden of Eden, the Great Flood, the Prophet Isaiah and the Cumaean Sibyl. The ancestors of Christ are painted around the windows.

The fresco of *The Last Judgment* on the altar wall of the Sistine Chapel was commissioned by Pope Clement VII, and Michelangelo labored on the project from 1536–1541. The work is located on the altar wall of the Sistine Chapel, which is not a traditional placement for the subject. Typically, last judgement scenes were placed on the exit wall of churches as a way to remind the viewer of eternal punishments as they left worship. *The Last Judgment* is a depiction of the second coming of Christ and the apocalypse; where the souls of humanity rise and are assigned to their various fates, as judged by Christ, surrounded by the Saints. In contrast to the earlier figures Michelangelo painted on the ceiling, the figures in *The Last Judgement* are heavily muscled and are in much more artificial poses, demonstrating how this work is in the Mannerist style.

In this work Michelangelo has rejected the orderly depiction of the last judgement as established by Medieval tradition in favor of a swirling scene of chaos as each soul is judged. When the painting was revealed it was heavily criticized for its inclusion of classical imagery as well as for the amount of nude figures in somewhat suggestive poses. The ill reception that the work received may be tied to the Counter Reformation and the Council of Trent, which lead to a preference for more conservative religious art devoid of classical references. Although a number of figures were made more modest with the addition of drapery, the changes were not made until after the death of Michelangelo, demonstrating the respect and admiration that was afforded to him during his lifetime.

The Last Judgement: *The fresco of The Last Judgment on the altar wall of the Sistine Chapel was commissioned by Pope Clement VII. Michelangelo worked on the project from 1534–1541.*

Architecture: St. Peter's Basilica

Finally, although other architects were involved, Michelangelo is given credit for designing St. Peter's Basilica. Michelangelo's chief contribution was the use of a symmetrical plan of a Greek Cross form and an external masonry of massive proportions, with every corner filled in by a stairwell or small vestry. The effect is of a continuous wall surface that is folded or fractured at different angles, lacking the right angles that usually define change of direction at the corners of a building. This exterior is surrounded by a giant order of Corinthian pilasters all set at slightly different angles to each other, in keeping with the ever-changing angles of the wall's surface. Above them the huge cornice ripples in a continuous band, giving the appearance of keeping the whole building in a state of compression.

St. Peter's Basillica: *Michelangelo designed the dome of St. Peter's Basilica on or before 1564, although it was unfinished when he died.*

Mannerism

Mannerist artists began to reject the harmony and ideal proportions of the Renaissance in favor of irrational settings, artificial colors, unclear subject matters, and elongated forms.

Learning Objectives

Describe the Mannerist style, how it differs from the Renaissance, and reasons why it emerged.

> **Key Takeaways**
>
> *Key Points*
>
> - Mannerism came after the High Renaissance and before the Baroque.
> - The artists who came a generation after Raphael and Michelangelo had a dilemma. They could not surpass the great works that had already been created by Leonardo da Vinci, Raphael, and Michelangelo. This is when we start to see Mannerism emerge.
> - Jacopo da Pontormo (1494–1557) represents the shift from the Renaissance to the Mannerist style.
>
> *Key Terms*
>
> - **Mannerism**: Style of art in Europe from c. 1520–1600. Mannerism came after the High Renaissance and before the Baroque. Not every artist painting during this period is considered a Mannerist artist.

Mannerism is the name given to a style of art in Europe from c. 1520–1600. Mannerism came after the High Renaissance and before the Baroque. Not every artist painting during this period is considered a Mannerist artist, however, and there is much debate among scholars over whether Mannerism should be considered a separate movement from the High Renaissance, or a stylistic phase of the High Renaissance. Mannerism will be treated as a separate art movement here as there are many differences between the High Renaissance and the Mannerist styles.

Style

What makes a work of art Mannerist? First we must understand the ideals and goals of the Renaissance. During the Renaissance artists were engaging with classical antiquity in a new way. In addition, they developed theories on perspective, and in all ways strived to create works of art that were perfect, harmonious, and showed ideal depictions of the natural world. Leonardo da Vinci, Raphael, and Michelangelo are considered the artists who reached the greatest achievements in art during the Renaissance.

The Renaissance stressed harmony and beauty and no one could create more beautiful works than the great three artists listed above. The artists who came a generation after had a dilemma; they could not surpass the great works that had already been created by da Vinci, Raphael, and Michelangelo. This is when we start to see Mannerism emerge. Younger artists trying to do something new and different began to reject harmony and ideal proportions in favor of irrational settings, artificial colors, unclear subject matters, and elongated forms.

Jacopo da Pontormo

Jacopo da Pontormo (1494–1557) represents the shift from the Renaissance to the Mannerist style. Take for example his *Deposition from the Cross*, an altarpiece that was painted for a chapel in the Church of Santa Felicita, Florence. The figures of Mary and Jesus appear to be a direct reference to Michelangelo's

Pieta. Although the work is called a *"Deposition,"* there is no cross. Scholars also refer to this work as the "Entombment" but there is no tomb. This lack of clarity on subject matter is a hallmark of Mannerist painting. In addition, the setting is irrational, almost as if it is not in this world, and the colors are far from naturalistic. This work could not have been produced by a Renaissance artist. The Mannerist movement stresses different goals and this work of art by Pontormo demonstrates this new, and different style.

Pontormo, Deposition from the Cross, 1525-1528, Church of Santa Felicita, Florence: *This work of art by Pontormo demonstrates the hallmarks of the Mannerist style: unclear subject matter, irrational setting, and artificial colors.*

Attributions

CC licensed content, Specific attribution

- The Marriage of the Virgin (Raphael). **Provided by**: Wikipedia. **Located at**: https://en.wikipedia.org/wiki/The_Marriage_of_the_Virgin_(Raphael). **License**: *CC BY-SA: Attribution-ShareAlike*
- Mannerism. **Provided by**: Wiktionary. **Located at**: http://en.wiktionary.org/wiki/Mannerism. **License**: *CC BY-SA: Attribution-ShareAlike*
- Italian Renaissance. **Provided by**: Wikipedia. **Located at**: http://en.wikipedia.org/wiki/Italian_Renaissance. **License**: *CC BY-SA: Attribution-ShareAlike*
- The Birth of Venus (Botticelli). **Provided by**: Wikipedia. **Located at**: http://en.wikipedia.org/wiki/The_Birth_of_Venus_(Botticelli). **License**: *CC BY-SA: Attribution-ShareAlike*
- fresco. **Provided by**: Wiktionary. **Located at**: http://en.wiktionary.org/wiki/fresco. **License**: *CC BY-SA: Attribution-ShareAlike*
- sfumato. **Provided by**: Wiktionary. **Located at**: http://en.wiktionary.org/wiki/sfumato. **License**: *CC BY-SA: Attribution-ShareAlike*
- Italian Renaissance painting. **Provided by**: Wikipedia. **Located at**: http://en.wikipedia.org/wiki/Italian_Renaissance_painting. **License**: *Public Domain: No Known Copyright*
- Sandro Botticelli - La nascita di Venere - Google Art Project - edited. **Provided by**: Wikipedia. **Located at**: http://en.wikipedia.org/wiki/File:Sandro_Botticelli_-_La_nascita_di_Venere_-_Google_Art_Project_-_edited.jpg. **License**: *Public Domain: No Known Copyright*
- House of Medici. **Provided by**: Wikipedia. **Located at**: https://en.wikipedia.org/wiki/House_of_Medici. **License**: *CC BY-SA: Attribution-ShareAlike*
- Renaissance. **Provided by**: Wikipedia. **Located at**: https://en.wikipedia.org/wiki/Renaissance#Cultural_conditions_in_Florence. **License**: *CC BY-SA: Attribution-ShareAlike*
- Italian Renaissance painting. **Provided by**: Wikipedia. **Located at**: http://en.wikipedia.org/wiki/Italian_Renaissance_painting. **License**: *Public Domain: No Known Copyright*
- Sandro Botticelli - La nascita di Venere - Google Art Project - edited. **Provided by**: Wikipedia. **Located at**: http://en.wikipedia.org/wiki/File:Sandro_Botticelli_-_La_nascita_di_Venere_-_Google_Art_Project_-_edited.jpg. **License**: *Public Domain: No Known Copyright*
- Gozzoli_magi.jpg. **Provided by**: Wikipedia. **Located at**: https://en.wikipedia.org/wiki/House_of_Medici#/media/File:Gozzoli_magi.jpg. **License**: *CC BY-SA: Attribution-ShareAlike*
- Leonardo da Vinci. **Provided by**: Wikipedia. **Located at**: http://en.wikipedia.org/wiki/Leonardo_da_Vinci%23Painting. **License**: *CC BY-SA: Attribution-ShareAlike*
- sfumato. **Provided by**: Wiktionary. **Located at**: http://en.wiktionary.org/wiki/sfumato. **License**: *CC BY-SA: Attribution-ShareAlike*
- Leonardo Da Vinci. **Provided by**: Wikipedia. **Located at**: http://en.wikipedia.org/wiki/Leonardo%20Da%20Vinci. **License**: *CC BY-SA: Attribution-ShareAlike*
- Italian Renaissance painting. **Provided by**: Wikipedia. **Located at**: http://en.wikipedia.org/wiki/Italian_Renaissance_painting. **License**: *Public Domain: No Known Copyright*
- Sandro Botticelli - La nascita di Venere - Google Art Project - edited. **Provided by**: Wikipedia. **Located at**: http://en.wikipedia.org/wiki/File:Sandro_Botticelli_-_La_nascita_di_Venere_-_Google_Art_Project_-_edited.jpg. **License**: *Public Domain: No Known Copyright*
- Gozzoli_magi.jpg. **Provided by**: Wikipedia. **Located at**: https://en.wikipedia.org/wiki/House_of_Medici#/media/File:Gozzoli_magi.jpg. **License**: *CC BY-SA: Attribution-ShareAlike*
- Leonardo_Da_Vinci_-_Vergine_delle_Rocce_28Louvre29.jpg. **Provided by**: Wikipedia. **Located at**: https://en.wikipedia.org/wiki/Virgin_of_the_Rocks. **License**: *Public Domain: No Known Copyright*
- u00daltima Cena - Da Vinci 5. **Provided by**: Wikipedia. **Located at**: http://en.wikipedia.org/wiki/File:%C3%9Altima_Cena_-_Da_Vinci_5.jpg. **License**: *Public Domain: No Known Copyright*
- Mona Lisa, by Leonardo da Vinci, from C2RMF retouched. **Provided by**: Wikipedia. **Located at**: http://en.wikipedia.org/wiki/File:Mona_Lisa,_by_Leonardo_da_Vinci,_from_C2RMF_retouched.jpg. **License**: *Public Domain: No Known Copyright*
- Leonardo da vinci, The Virgin and Child with Saint Anne 01. **Provided by**: Wikipedia. **Located at**: http://en.wikipedia.org/wiki/File:Leonardo_da_vinci,_The_Virgin_and_Child_with_Saint_Anne_01.jpg. **License**: *Public Domain: No Known Copyright*
- David (Michelangelo). **Provided by**: Wikipedia. **Located at**: http://en.wikipedia.org/wiki/David_(Michelangelo)%23Interpretation. **License**: *CC BY-SA: Attribution-ShareAlike*
- St Peter's Basilica. **Provided by**: Wikipedia. **Located at**: http://en.wikipedia.org/wiki/St_Peter's_Basilica%23Michelangelo.27s_contribution. **License**: *CC BY-SA: Attribution-ShareAlike*
- Michelangelo. **Provided by**: Wikipedia. **Located at**: http://en.wikipedia.org/wiki/Michelangelo%23Life_and_works. **License**: *CC*

BY-SA: Attribution-ShareAlike

- contrapposto. **Provided by**: Wiktionary. **Located at**: http://en.wiktionary.org/wiki/contrapposto. **License**: *CC BY-SA: Attribution-ShareAlike*
- Sistine Chapel. **Provided by**: Wikipedia. **Located at**: http://en.wikipedia.org/wiki/Sistine%20Chapel. **License**: *CC BY-SA: Attribution-ShareAlike*
- Italian Renaissance painting. **Provided by**: Wikipedia. **Located at**: http://en.wikipedia.org/wiki/Italian_Renaissance_painting. **License**: *Public Domain: No Known Copyright*
- Sandro Botticelli - La nascita di Venere - Google Art Project - edited. **Provided by**: Wikipedia. **Located at**: http://en.wikipedia.org/wiki/File:Sandro_Botticelli_-_La_nascita_di_Venere_-_Google_Art_Project_-_edited.jpg. **License**: *Public Domain: No Known Copyright*
- Gozzoli_magi.jpg. **Provided by**: Wikipedia. **Located at**: https://en.wikipedia.org/wiki/House_of_Medici#/media/File:Gozzoli_magi.jpg. **License**: *CC BY-SA: Attribution-ShareAlike*
- Leonardo_Da_Vinci_-_Vergine_delle_Rocce_28Louvre29.jpg. **Provided by**: Wikipedia. **Located at**: https://en.wikipedia.org/wiki/Virgin_of_the_Rocks. **License**: *Public Domain: No Known Copyright*
- u00daltima Cena - Da Vinci 5. **Provided by**: Wikipedia. **Located at**: http://en.wikipedia.org/wiki/File:%C3%9Altima_Cena_-_Da_Vinci_5.jpg. **License**: *Public Domain: No Known Copyright*
- Mona Lisa, by Leonardo da Vinci, from C2RMF retouched. **Provided by**: Wikipedia. **Located at**: http://en.wikipedia.org/wiki/File:Mona_Lisa,_by_Leonardo_da_Vinci,_from_C2RMF_retouched.jpg. **License**: *Public Domain: No Known Copyright*
- Leonardo da vinci, The Virgin and Child with Saint Anne 01. **Provided by**: Wikipedia. **Located at**: http://en.wikipedia.org/wiki/File:Leonardo_da_vinci,_The_Virgin_and_Child_with_Saint_Anne_01.jpg. **License**: *Public Domain: No Known Copyright*
- David von Michelangelo. **Provided by**: Wikipedia. **Located at**: http://en.wikipedia.org/wiki/File:David_von_Michelangelo.jpg. **License**: *CC BY-SA: Attribution-ShareAlike*
- Petersdom von Engelsburg gesehen. **Provided by**: Wikipedia. **Located at**: http://en.wikipedia.org/wiki/File:Petersdom_von_Engelsburg_gesehen.jpg. **License**: *Public Domain: No Known Copyright*
- Michelangelo, Giudizio Universale 02. **Provided by**: Wikipedia. **Located at**: http://en.wikipedia.org/wiki/File:Michelangelo,_Giudizio_Universale_02.jpg. **License**: *Public Domain: No Known Copyright*
- Pontormo. **Provided by**: Wikipedia. **Located at**: https://en.wikipedia.org/wiki/Pontormo. **License**: *CC BY-SA: Attribution-ShareAlike*
- The Deposition from the Cross (Pontormo). **Provided by**: Wikipedia. **Located at**: https://en.wikipedia.org/wiki/The_Deposition_from_the_Cross_(Pontormo). **License**: *CC BY-SA: Attribution-ShareAlike*
- Mannerism. **Provided by**: wikipedia. **Located at**: https://en.wikipedia.org/wiki/Mannerism. **License**: *CC BY-SA: Attribution-ShareAlike*
- Pontormo. **Provided by**: Wikipedia. **Located at**: https://en.wikipedia.org/wiki/Pontormo. **License**: *CC BY-SA: Attribution-ShareAlike*
- Mannerism. **Provided by**: Wikipedia. **Located at**: https://en.wikipedia.org/wiki/Mannerism. **License**: *CC BY-SA: Attribution-ShareAlike*
- Italian Renaissance painting. **Provided by**: Wikipedia. **Located at**: http://en.wikipedia.org/wiki/Italian_Renaissance_painting. **License**: *Public Domain: No Known Copyright*
- Sandro Botticelli - La nascita di Venere - Google Art Project - edited. **Provided by**: Wikipedia. **Located at**: http://en.wikipedia.org/wiki/File:Sandro_Botticelli_-_La_nascita_di_Venere_-_Google_Art_Project_-_edited.jpg. **License**: *Public Domain: No Known Copyright*
- Gozzoli_magi.jpg. **Provided by**: Wikipedia. **Located at**: https://en.wikipedia.org/wiki/House_of_Medici#/media/File:Gozzoli_magi.jpg. **License**: *CC BY-SA: Attribution-ShareAlike*
- Leonardo_Da_Vinci_-_Vergine_delle_Rocce_28Louvre29.jpg. **Provided by**: Wikipedia. **Located at**: https://en.wikipedia.org/wiki/Virgin_of_the_Rocks. **License**: *Public Domain: No Known Copyright*
- u00daltima Cena - Da Vinci 5. **Provided by**: Wikipedia. **Located at**: http://en.wikipedia.org/wiki/File:%C3%9Altima_Cena_-_Da_Vinci_5.jpg. **License**: *Public Domain: No Known Copyright*
- Mona Lisa, by Leonardo da Vinci, from C2RMF retouched. **Provided by**: Wikipedia. **Located at**: http://en.wikipedia.org/wiki/File:Mona_Lisa,_by_Leonardo_da_Vinci,_from_C2RMF_retouched.jpg. **License**: *Public Domain: No Known Copyright*
- Leonardo da vinci, The Virgin and Child with Saint Anne 01. **Provided by**: Wikipedia. **Located at**: http://en.wikipedia.org/wiki/File:Leonardo_da_vinci,_The_Virgin_and_Child_with_Saint_Anne_01.jpg. **License**: *Public Domain: No Known Copyright*
- David von Michelangelo. **Provided by**: Wikipedia. **Located at**: http://en.wikipedia.org/wiki/File:David_von_Michelangelo.jpg.

License: *CC BY-SA: Attribution-ShareAlike*
- Petersdom von Engelsburg gesehen. **Provided by**: Wikipedia. **Located at**: http://en.wikipedia.org/wiki/File:Petersdom_von_Engelsburg_gesehen.jpg. **License**: *Public Domain: No Known Copyright*
- Michelangelo, Giudizio Universale 02. **Provided by**: Wikipedia. **Located at**: http://en.wikipedia.org/wiki/File:M_chelangelo,_Giudizio_Universale_02.jpg. **License**: *Public Domain: No Known Copyright*
- Deposition_from_the_Cross__artble.com. **Provided by**: artble. **Located at**: http://www.artble.com/artists/rosso_fiorentino/paintings/deposition_from_the_cross. **License**: *Public Domain: No Known Copyright*

Literature in the Renaissance

The Rise of the Vernacular

Renaissance literature refers to European literature that was influenced by the intellectual and cultural tendencies of the Renaissance.

Learning Objectives

Evaluate the influence of the different people, styles, and ideas that influenced Renaissance literature

Key Takeaways

Key Points

- In the 13th century, Italian authors began writing in their native vernacular language rather than in Latin, French, or Provençal. The earliest Renaissance literature appeared in 14th century Italy; Dante, Petrarch, and Machiavelli are notable examples of Italian Renaissance writers.
- From Italy the influence of the Renaissance spread across Europe; the scholarly writings of Erasmus and the plays of Shakespeare can be considered Renaissance in character.
- Renaissance literature is characterized by the adoption of a Humanist philosophy and the recovery of the classical literature of Antiquity, and benefited from the spread of printing in the latter part of the 15th century.

Key Terms

- **Spenserian stanza**: Fixed verse form invented by Edmund Spenser for his epic poem "The Faerie Queene." Each stanza contains nine lines in total; the rhyme scheme of these lines is "ababbcbcc."

- **vernacular**: The native language or native dialect of a specific population, especially as distinguished from a literary, national, or standard variety of the language.
- **anthropocentric**: Believing human beings to be the central or most significant species on the planet, or the assessing reality through an exclusively human perspective.

Overview

The 13th century Italian literary revolution helped set the stage for the Renaissance. Prior to the Renaissance, the Italian language was not the literary language in Italy. It was only in the 13th century that Italian authors began writing in their native vernacular language rather than in Latin, French, or Provençal. The 1250s saw a major change in Italian poetry as the Dolce Stil Novo (Sweet New Style, which emphasized Platonic rather than courtly love) came into its own, pioneered by poets like Guittone d'Arezzo and Guido Guinizelli. Especially in poetry, major changes in Italian literature had been taking place decades before the Renaissance truly began.

With the printing of books initiated in Venice by Aldus Manutius, an increasing number of works began to be published in the Italian language, in addition to the flood of Latin and Greek texts that constituted the mainstream of the Italian Renaissance. The source for these works expanded beyond works of theology and towards the pre-Christian eras of Imperial Rome and Ancient Greece. This is not to say that no religious works were published in this period; Dante Alighieri's *The Divine Comedy* reflects a distinctly medieval world view. Christianity remained a major influence for artists and authors, with the classics coming into their own as a second primary influence.

At Florence the most celebrated Humanists wrote also in the vulgar tongue, and commented on Dante and Petrarch and defended them from their enemies. Leone Battista Alberti, the learned Greek and Latin scholar, wrote in the vernacular, and Vespasiano da Bisticci, while he was constantly absorbed in Greek and Latin manuscripts, wrote the Vite di uomini illustri, valuable for their historical contents and rivaling the best works of the 14th century in their candor and simplicity.

Renaissance Literature

The earliest Renaissance literature appeared in 14th century Italy; Dante, Petrarch, and Machiavelli are notable examples of Italian Renaissance writers. From Italy the influence of the Renaissance spread at different rates to other countries, and continued to spread throughout Europe through the 17th century. The English Renaissance and the Renaissance in Scotland date from the late 15th century to the early 17th century. In northern Europe the scholarly writings of Erasmus, the plays of Shakespeare, the poems of Edmund Spenser, and the writings of Sir Philip Sidney may be considered Renaissance in character.

The literature of the Renaissance was written within the general movement of the Renaissance that arose in 13th century Italy and continued until the 16th century while being diffused into the western world. It is characterized by the adoption of a Humanist philosophy and the recovery of the classical literature of Antiquity and benefited from the spread of printing in the latter part of the 15th century. For the writers of the Renaissance, Greco-Roman inspiration was shown both in the themes of their writing and in the literary forms they used. The world was considered from an anthropocentric perspective. Platonic ideas were revived and put to the service of Christianity. The search for pleasures of the senses and a critical and rational spirit completed the ideological panorama of the period. New literary genres such as the essay and new metrical forms such as the sonnet and Spenserian stanza made their appearance.

The creation of the printing press (using movable type) by Johannes Gutenberg in the 1450s encouraged authors to write in their local vernacular rather than in Greek or Latin classical languages, widening the reading audience and promoting the spread of Renaissance ideas.

The impact of the Renaissance varied across the continent; countries that were predominantly Catholic or predominantly Protestant experienced the Renaissance differently. Areas where the Orthodox Church was culturally dominant, as well as those areas of Europe under Islamic rule, were more or less outside its influence. The period focused on self-actualization and one's ability to accept what is going on in one's life.

A YouTube element has been excluded from this version of the text. You can view it online here: https://milnepublishing.geneseo.edu/suny-fmcc-boundless-worldhistory-print/?p=271

Renaissance Man ("Blister in the Sun" by the Violent Femmes): Quick overview of some of the prominent men of the Renaissance.

Renaissance Writers

The 13th and 14th century Italian literary revolution helped set the stage for the Renaissance.

Learning Objectives

Identify the key contributions made by Dante, Boccaccio, and Bruni

Key Takeaways

Key Points

- The ideas characterizing the Renaissance had their origin in late 13th century Florence, in particular in the writings of Dante Alighieri (1265–1321) and Petrarch (1304–1374).
- The literature and poetry of the Renaissance was largely influenced by the developing

science and philosophy.

- The Humanist Francesco Petrarch, a key figure in the renewed sense of scholarship, was also an accomplished poet, publishing several important works of poetry in Italian as well as Latin.
- Petrarch's disciple, Giovanni Boccaccio, became a major author in his own right, whose major work, *The Decameron*, was a source of inspiration and plots for many English authors in the Renaissance.
- A generation before Petrarch and Boccaccio, Dante Alighieri set the stage for Renaissance literature with his *Divine Comedy*, widely considered the greatest literary work composed in the Italian language and a masterpiece of world literature.
- Leonardo Bruni was an Italian humanist, historian, and statesman, often recognized as the first modern historian.

Key Terms

- **humanist**: One who studies classical antiquity and the intellectual adoption of its philosophies, centered on the important role of humans in the universe.
- **metaphysics**: A branch of philosophy concerned with explaining the fundamental nature of being and the world that encompasses it.

Overview

Many argue that the ideas characterizing the Renaissance had their origin in late 13th century Florence, in particular in the writings of Dante Alighieri (1265–1321) and Petrarch (1304–1374). Italian prose of the 13th century was as abundant and varied as its poetry. In the year 1282 a period of new literature began. With the school of Lapo Gianni, Guido Cavalcanti, Cino da Pistoia, and Dante Alighieri, lyric poetry became exclusively Tuscan. The whole novelty and poetic power of this school consisted in, according to Dante, *Quando Amore spira, noto, ed a quel niodo Ch'ei detta dentro, vo significando*—that is, in a power of expressing the feelings of the soul in the way in which love inspires them, in an appropriate and graceful manner, fitting form to matter, and by art fusing one with the other. Love is a divine gift that redeems man in the eyes of God, and the poet's mistress is the angel sent from heaven to show the way to salvation.

The literature and poetry of the Renaissance was largely influenced by the developing science and philosophy. The Humanist Francesco Petrarch, a key figure in the renewed sense of scholarship, was also an accomplished poet, publishing several important works of poetry. He wrote poetry in Latin, notably the Punic War epic *Africa*, but is today remembered for his works in the Italian vernacular, especially the *Canzoniere*, a collection of love sonnets dedicated to his unrequited love, Laura. He was the foremost writer of sonnets in Italian, and translations of his work into English by Thomas Wyatt established the sonnet form in England, where it was employed by William Shakespeare and countless other poets.

Giovanni Boccaccio

Petrarch's disciple, Giovanni Boccaccio, became a major author in his own right. His major work was *The Decameron*, a collection of 100 stories told by ten storytellers who have fled to the outskirts of Florence to escape the black plague over ten nights. *The Decameron* in particular and Boccaccio's work in general were a major source of inspiration and plots for many English authors in the Renaissance, including Geoffrey Chaucer and William Shakespeare. The various tales of love in *The Decameron* range from the erotic to the tragic. Tales of wit, practical jokes, and life lessons contribute to the mosaic. In addition to its literary value and widespread influence, it provides a document of life at the time. Written in the vernacular of the Florentine language, it is considered a masterpiece of classical early Italian prose.

Boccaccio wrote his imaginative literature mostly in the Italian vernacular, as well as other works in Latin, and is particularly noted for his realistic dialogue that differed from that of his contemporaries, medieval writers who usually followed formulaic models for character and plot.

Discussions between Boccaccio and Petrarch were instrumental in Boccaccio writing the *Genealogia deorum gentilium*; the first edition was completed in 1360 and it remained one of the key reference works on classical mythology for over 400 years. It served as an extended defense for the studies of ancient literature and thought. Despite the Pagan beliefs at the core of the *Genealogia deorum gentilium,* Boccaccio believed that much could be learned from antiquity. Thus, he challenged the arguments of clerical intellectuals who wanted to limit access to classical sources to prevent any moral harm to Christian readers. The revival of classical antiquity became a foundation of the Renaissance, and his defense of the importance of ancient literature was an essential requirement for its development.

The Decameron

A depiction of Giovanni Boccaccio and Florentines who have fled from the plague, the frame story for *The Decameron*.

Dante Alighieri

A generation before Petrarch and Boccaccio, Dante Alighieri set the stage for Renaissance literature. His *Divine Comedy*, originally called *Comedìa* and later christened *Divina* by Boccaccio, is widely considered the greatest literary work composed in the Italian language and a masterpiece of world literature.

In the late Middle Ages, the overwhelming majority of poetry was written in Latin, and therefore was accessible only to affluent and educated audiences. In *De vulgari eloquentia* (On Eloquence in the Vernacular), however, Dante defended use of the vernacular in literature. He himself would even write in the Tuscan dialect for works such as *The New Life* (1295) and the aforementioned *Divine Comedy*; this choice, though highly unorthodox, set a hugely important precedent that later Italian writers such as Petrarch and Boccaccio would follow. As a result, Dante played an instrumental role in establishing the national language of Italy. Dante's significance also extends past his home country; his depictions of Hell, Purgatory, and Heaven have provided inspiration for a large body of Western art, and are cited as an influence on the works of John Milton, Geoffrey Chaucer, and Lord Alfred Tennyson, among many others.

Dante, like most Florentines of his day, was embroiled in the Guelph-Ghibelline conflict. He fought in the Battle of Campaldino (June 11, 1289) with the Florentine Guelphs against the Arezzo Ghibellines. After defeating the Ghibellines, the Guelphs divided into two factions: the White Guelphs—Dante's party, led by Vieri dei Cerchi—and the Black Guelphs, led by Corso Donati. Although the split was along family lines at first, ideological differences arose based on opposing views of the papal role in Florentine affairs, with the Blacks supporting the pope and the Whites wanting more freedom from Rome. Dante was accused of corruption and financial wrongdoing by the Black Guelphs for the time that he was serving as city prior (Florence's highest position) for two months in 1300. He was condemned to perpetual exile; if he returned to Florence without paying a fine, he could be burned at the stake.

At some point during his exile he conceived of the *Divine Comedy*, but the date is uncertain. The work is much more assured and on a larger scale than anything he had produced in Florence; it is likely he would have undertaken such a work only after he realized his political ambitions, which had been central to him up to his banishment, had been halted for some time, possibly forever. Mixing religion and private concerns in his writings, he invoked the worst anger of God against his city and suggested several particular targets that were also his personal enemies.

Portrait of Dante: *Dante Alighieri was a major Italian poet of the Late Middle Ages who influenced and set the precedent for Renaissance literature.*

Leonardo Bruni

Leonardo Bruni (c. 1370–March 9, 1444) was an Italian Humanist, historian, and statesman, often recognized as the most important Humanist historian of the early Renaissance. He has been called the first modern historian. He was the earliest person to write using the three-period view of history: Antiquity, Middle Ages, and Modern. The dates Bruni used to define the periods are not exactly what modern historians use today, but he laid the conceptual groundwork for a tripartite division of history.

Bruni's most notable work is *Historiarum Florentini populi libri XII* (History of the Florentine People, 12 Books), which has been called the first modern history book. While it probably was not Bruni's intention to secularize history, the three period view of history is unquestionably secular, and for that Bruni has been called the first modern historian. The foundation of Bruni's conception can be found with Petrarch, who distinguished the classical period from later cultural decline, or *tenebrae* (literally "darkness"). Bruni argued that Italy had revived in recent centuries and could therefore be described as entering a new age.

One of Bruni's most famous works is *New Cicero*, a biography of the Roman statesman Cicero. He was also the author of biographies in Italian of Dante and Petrarch. It was Bruni who used the phrase " studia humanitatis," meaning the study of human endeavors, as distinct from those of theology and metaphysics, which is where the term "humanists" comes from.

As a Humanist Bruni was essential in translating into Latin many works of Greek philosophy and history, such as those by Aristotle and Procopius. Bruni's translations of Aristotle's *Politics* and *Nicomachean Ethics*, as well as the pseudo-Aristotelean *Economics*, were widely distributed in manuscript and in print.

Christine de Pizan

Christine de Pizan was an Italian-French late medieval author who wrote about the positive contributions of women to European history and court life.

Learning Objectives

Discuss the significance of Christine de Pizan's work

Key Takeaways

Key Points

- Christine de Pizan was an Italian-French late medieval author, primarily a court writer, who wrote commissioned works for aristocratic families and addressed literary debates of the era.
- Her work is characterized by a prominent and positive depiction of women who encouraged ethical and judicious conduct in courtly life.
- Much of the impetus for her writing came from her need to earn a living to support her mother, a niece, and her two surviving children after being widowed at the age of 25.
- Christine's participation in a literary debate about Jean de Meun's *Romance of the Rose* allowed her to move beyond the courtly circles, and ultimately to establish her status as a writer concerned with the position of women in society.

Key Terms

- **feminism**: A range of political movements, ideologies, and social movements that share a common goal: to define, establish, and achieve political, economic, personal, and social rights for women that are equal to those of men.
- **chivalry**: A code of conduct associated with the medieval institution of knighthood, which later developed into social and moral virtues more generally.
- **alchemist**: A person who practices the philosophical and proto-scientific tradition aimed

> to purify, mature, and perfect certain objects, such as the transmutation of "base metals" (e.g., lead) into "noble" ones (particularly gold) and the creation of an elixir of immortality.

Overview

Christine de Pizan (1364–1430) was an Italian-French late medieval author. She served as a court writer for several dukes (Louis of Orleans, Philip the Bold of Burgundy, and John the Fearless of Burgundy) and the French royal court during the reign of Charles VI. She wrote both poetry and prose works such as biographies and books containing practical advice for women. She completed forty-one works during her thirty-year career from 1399 to 1429. She married in 1380 at the age of fifteen, and was widowed ten years later. Much of the impetus for her writing came from her need to earn a living to support her mother, a niece, and her two surviving children. She spent most of her childhood and all of her adult life in Paris and then the abbey at Poissy, and wrote entirely in her adopted language, Middle French.

In recent decades, Christine de Pizan's work has been returned to prominence by the efforts of scholars such as Charity Cannon Willard, Earl Jeffrey Richards, and Simone de Beauvoir. Certain scholars have argued that she should be seen as an early feminist who efficiently used language to convey that women could play an important role within society.

Christine de Pizan: *A painting of Christine de Pizan, considered by some scholars to be a proto-feminist, lecturing four men.*

Life

Christine de Pizan was born in 1364 in Venice, Italy. Following her birth, her father, Thomas de Pizan, accepted an appointment to the court of Charles V of France, as the king's astrologer, alchemist, and physician. In this atmosphere, Christine was able to pursue her intellectual interests. She successfully educated herself by immersing herself in languages, in the rediscovered classics and Humanism of the early Renaissance, and in Charles V's royal archive, which housed a vast number of manuscripts. But she did not assert her intellectual abilities, or establish her authority as a writer, until she was widowed at the age of 25.

In order to support herself and her family, Christine turned to writing. By 1393, she was writing love ballads, which caught the attention of wealthy patrons within the court. These patrons were intrigued by the novelty of a female writer and had her compose texts about their romantic exploits. Her output during this period was prolific. Between 1393 and 1412 she composed over 300 ballads, and many more shorter poems.

Christine's participation in a literary debate, in 1401–1402, allowed her to move beyond the courtly circles, and ultimately to establish her status as a writer concerned with the position of women in society. During these years, she involved herself in a renowned literary controversy, the "Querelle du Roman de la Rose." She helped to instigate this debate by beginning to question the literary merits of Jean de Meun's The The Romance of the Rose. Written in the 13th century, The Romance of the Rose satirizes the conventions of courtly love while critically depicting women as nothing more than seducers. Christine specifically objected to the use of vulgar terms in Jean de Meun's allegorical poem. She argued that these terms denigrated the proper and natural function of sexuality, and that such language was inappropriate for female characters such as Madam Reason. According to her, noble women did not use such language. Her critique primarily stemmed from her belief that Jean de Meun was purposely slandering women through the debated text.

The debate itself was extensive, and at its end the principal issue was no longer Jean de Meun's literary capabilities; it had shifted to the unjust slander of women within literary texts. This dispute helped to establish Christine's reputation as a female intellectual who could assert herself effectively and defend her claims in the male-dominated literary realm. She continued to counter abusive literary treatments of women.

Writing

Christine produced a large amount of vernacular works in both prose and verse. Her works include political treatises, mirrors for princes, epistles, and poetry.

Her early courtly poetry is marked by her knowledge of aristocratic custom and fashion of the day, particularly involving women and the practice of chivalry. Her early and later allegorical and didactic treatises reflect both autobiographical information about her life and views and also her own individualized and Humanist approach to the scholastic learned tradition of mythology, legend, and history she inherited from clerical scholars, and to the genres and courtly or scholastic subjects of contemporary French and Italian poets she admired. Supported and encouraged by important royal French and English patrons, she influenced 15th century English poetry.

By 1405, Christine had completed her most famous literary works, *The Book of the City of Ladies* and *The Treasure of the City of Ladies*. The first of these shows the importance of women's past contributions to society, and the second strives to teach women of all estates how to cultivate useful qualities. In *The Treasure of the City of Ladies*, she highlights the persuasive effect of women's speech and actions in everyday life. In this particular text, Christine argues that women must recognize and promote their ability to make peace between people. This ability will allow women to mediate between husband and subjects. She also argues that slanderous speech erodes one's honor and threatens the sisterly bond among women. Christine then argues that "skill in discourse should be a part of every woman's moral repertoire." She believed that a woman's influence is realized when her speech accords value to chastity, virtue, and restraint. She argued that rhetoric is a powerful tool that women could employ to settle differences and to assert themselves.

Additionally, *The Treasure of the City of Ladies* provides glimpses into women's lives in 1400, from the great lady in the castle down to the merchant's wife, the servant, and the peasant. She offers advice to governesses, widows, and even prostitutes.

Picture from The Book of the City of Ladies: *The Treasure of the City of Ladies is a manual of education by medieval Italian-French author Christine de Pizan.*

Machiavelli

Renaissance philosopher Niccolò Machiavelli sought to describe political life as it really was rather than its philosophical ideal, as infamously portrayed in his text *The Prince*.

Learning Objectives

Analyze Machiavelli's impact during his own lifetime and in the modern day

Key Takeaways

Key Points

- Niccolò Machiavelli was an Italian Renaissance historian, politician, diplomat, philosopher, Humanist, and writer, often called the founder of modern political science.

- His writings were innovative because of his emphasis on practical and pragmatic strategies over philosophical ideals, exemplified by such phrases as "He who neglects what is done for what ought to be done, sooner effects his ruin than his preservation."
- His most famous text, *The Prince*, has been profoundly influential, from the time of his life up to the present day, both on politicians and philosophers.
- *The Prince* describes strategies to be an effective statesman and infamously includes justifications for treachery and violence to retain power.

Key Terms

- **republicanism**: An ideology of being a citizen in a state in which power resides in elected individuals representing the citizen body.
- **realpolitik**: Politics or diplomacy based primarily on considerations of given circumstances and factors, rather than explicit ideological notions or moral and ethical premises.
- **Machiavellian**: Cunning and scheming in statecraft or in general conduct.

Overview

Niccolò Machiavelli (May 3, 1469–June 21, 1527) was an Italian Renaissance historian, politician, diplomat, philosopher, Humanist, and writer. He has often been called the founder of modern political science. He was for many years a senior official in the Florentine Republic, with responsibilities in diplomatic and military affairs. He also wrote comedies, carnival songs, and poetry. His personal correspondence is renowned in the Italian language. He was secretary to the Second Chancery of the Republic of Florence from 1498 to 1512, when the Medici were out of power. He wrote his most renowned work, *The Prince* (*Il Principe*) in 1513.

"Machiavellianism" is a widely used negative term to characterize unscrupulous politicians of the sort Machiavelli described most famously in *The Prince*. Machiavelli described immoral behavior, such as dishonesty and killing innocents, as being normal and effective in politics. He even seemed to endorse it in some situations. The book itself gained notoriety when some readers claimed that the author was teaching evil, and providing "evil recommendations to tyrants to help them maintain their power." The term " Machiavellian " is often associated with political deceit, deviousness, and *realpolitik*. On the other hand, many commentators, such as Baruch Spinoza, Jean-Jacques Rousseau, and Denis Diderot, have argued that Machiavelli was actually a republican, even when writing *The Prince*, and his writings were an inspiration to Enlightenment proponents of modern democratic political philosophy.

Portrait of Niccolò Machiavelli: *Machiavelli is a political philosopher infamous for his justification of violence in his treatise The Prince.*

The Prince

Machiavelli's best-known book, *The Prince*, contains several maxims concerning politics. Instead of the more traditional target audience of a hereditary prince, it concentrates on the possibility of a "new prince." To retain power, the hereditary prince must carefully balance the interests of a variety of institutions to which the people are accustomed. By contrast, a new prince has the more difficult task in ruling: he must first stabilize his newfound power in order to build an enduring political structure. Machiavelli suggests that the social benefits of stability and security can be achieved in the face of moral corruption. Machiavelli believed that a leader had to understand public and private morality as two different things in order to rule well. As a result, a ruler must be concerned not only with reputation, but also must be positively willing to act immorally at the right times.

As a political theorist, Machiavelli emphasized the occasional need for the methodical exercise of brute force or deceit, including extermination of entire noble families to head off any chance of a challenge to the prince's authority. He asserted that violence may be necessary for the successful stabilization of power and introduction of new legal institutions. Further, he believed that force may be used to eliminate political rivals, to coerce resistant populations, and to purge the community of other men of strong enough character to rule, who will inevitably attempt to replace the ruler. Machiavelli has become infamous for such political advice, ensuring that he would be remembered in history through the adjective "Machiavellian."

The Prince is sometimes claimed to be one of the first works of modern philosophy, especially modern political philosophy, in which the effective truth is taken to be more important than any abstract ideal. It was also in direct conflict with the dominant Catholic and scholastic doctrines of the time concerning politics and ethics. In contrast to Plato and Aristotle, Machiavelli insisted that an imaginary ideal society is not a model by which a prince should orient himself.

Influence

Machiavelli's ideas had a profound impact on political leaders throughout the modern west, helped by the new technology of the printing press. During the first generations after Machiavelli, his main influence was in non-Republican governments. One historian noted that *The Prince* was spoken of highly by Thomas Cromwell in England and had influenced Henry VIII in his turn towards Protestantism and in his tactics, for example during the Pilgrimage of Grace. A copy was also possessed by the Catholic king and emperor Charles V. In France, after an initially mixed reaction, Machiavelli came to be associated with Catherine de' Medici and the St. Bartholomew's Day massacre. As one historian reports, in the 16th century, Catholic writers "associated Machiavelli with the Protestants, whereas Protestant authors saw him as Italian and Catholic." In fact, he was apparently influencing both Catholic and Protestant kings.

Modern materialist philosophy developed in the 16th, 17th, and 18th centuries, starting in the generations after Machiavelli. This philosophy tended to be republican, more in the original spirit of Machiavellianism, but as with the Catholic authors, Machiavelli's realism and encouragement of using innovation to try to control one's own fortune were more accepted than his emphasis upon war and politics. Not only were innovative economics and politics results, but also modern science, leading some commentators to say that the 18th century Enlightenment involved a "humanitarian" moderating of Machiavellianism.

Although Jean-Jacques Rousseau is associated with very different political ideas, it is important to view Machiavelli's work from different points of view rather than just the traditional notion. For example, Rousseau viewed Machiavelli's work as a satirical piece in which Machiavelli exposes the faults of one-man rule rather than exalting amorality.

Scholars have argued that Machiavelli was a major indirect and direct influence upon the political thinking of the Founding Fathers of the United States due to his overwhelming favoritism of republicanism and the republic type of government. Benjamin Franklin, James Madison, and Thomas Jefferson followed Machiavelli's republicanism when they opposed what they saw as the emerging aristocracy that they feared Alexander Hamilton was creating with the Federalist Party. Hamilton learned from Machiavelli about the importance of foreign policy for domestic policy, but may have broken from him regarding how rapacious a republic needed to be in order to survive.

The Northern Renaissance

Erasmus

Erasmus of Rotterdam was a renowned Humanist scholar and theologian who wrote several important texts criticizing the superstition and formalism of the church while upholding its core spiritual values.

Learning Objectives

Describe Erasmus and his connection to the Renaissance

Key Takeaways

Key Points

- Erasmus was a Dutch Renaissance Humanist, Catholic priest, social critic, teacher, and theologian known as the "Prince of the Humanists" for his influential scholarship and writings.
- Erasmus lived against the backdrop of the growing European religious Reformation, but while he was critical of the abuses within the Catholic church and called for reform, he kept his distance from Luther and continued to recognize the authority of the pope.
- In *The Handbook of the Christian Soldier*, Erasmus outlines the views of the normal Christian life and critiques formalism—going through the motions of tradition without understanding their basis in the teachings of Christ.
- One of Erasmus's best-known works is *In Praise of Folly*, a satirical attack on superstitions and other traditions of European society in general and the western church in particular.

> *Key Terms*
>
> - **ecclesiastic**: The theological study of the Christian church.
> - **satirical**: Characteristic of a genre of literature in which vices, follies, abuses, and shortcomings are held up to ridicule, ideally with the intent of shaming individuals, groups, or society itself into improvement.

Overview

Erasmus of Rotterdam, or simply Erasmus, was a Dutch Renaissance Humanist, Catholic priest, social critic, teacher, and theologian.

Erasmus was a classical scholar and wrote in a pure Latin style. Among Humanists he enjoyed the name "Prince of the Humanists," and has been called "the crowning glory of the Christian Humanists." Using Humanist techniques for working on texts, he prepared important new Latin and Greek editions of the New Testament, which raised questions that would be influential in the Protestant Reformation and Catholic Counter-Reformation. He also wrote *On Free Will, The Praise of Folly, Handbook of a Christian Knight, On Civility in Children, Copia: Foundations of the Abundant Style, Julius Exclusus,* and many other works.

Erasmus lived against the backdrop of the growing European religious Reformation, but while he was critical of the abuses within the Catholic church and called for reform, he kept his distance from Luther and Melanchthon and continued to recognize the authority of the pope, emphasizing a middle path with a deep respect for traditional faith, piety, and grace, rejecting Luther's emphasis on faith alone. Erasmus remained a member of the Roman Catholic church all his life, staying committed to reforming the church and its clerics' abuses from within. He also held to the Catholic doctrine of free will, which some Reformers rejected in favor of the doctrine of predestination. His middle road ("*Via Media*") approach disappointed and even angered scholars in both camps.

Approach to Scholarship

Erasmus preferred to live the life of an independent scholar and made a conscious effort to avoid any actions or formal ties that might inhibit his freedom of intellect and literary expression. Throughout his life, he was offered many positions of honor and profit throughout the academic world but declined them all, preferring the uncertain but sufficient rewards of independent literary activity.

His residence at Leuven, where he lectured at the university, exposed Erasmus to much criticism from those ascetics, academics, and clerics hostile to the principles of literary and religious reform and the loose norms of the Renaissance adherents to which he was devoting his life.

He tried to free the methods of scholarship from the rigidity and formalism of medieval traditions, but he was not satisfied with this. His revolt against certain forms of Christian monasticism and scholasticism was not based on doubts about the truth of doctrine, nor from hostility to the organization of the church itself, nor from rejection of celibacy or monastic lifestyles. He saw himself as a preacher of righteousness by an appeal to reason, applied frankly and without fear of the magisterium. He always intended to remain faithful to Catholic doctrine, and therefore was convinced he could frankly criticize virtually everyone and everything. Aloof from entangling obligations, Erasmus was the center of the literary movement of his time, corresponding with more than 500 men in the worlds of politics and thought.

Writings

Erasmus wrote both on ecclesiastic subjects and those of general human interest. By the 1530s, the writings of Erasmus accounted for ten to twenty percent of all book sales in Europe.

His serious writings begin early, with the *Enchiridion militis Christiani*—the *Handbook of the Christian Soldier* (1503). In this short work, Erasmus outlines the views of the normal Christian life, which he was to spend the rest of his days elaborating. The chief evil of the day, he says, is formalism—going through the motions of tradition without understanding their basis in the teachings of Christ. Forms can teach the soul how to worship God, or they may hide or quench the spirit. In his examination of the dangers of formalism, Erasmus discusses monasticism, saint worship, war, the spirit of class, and the foibles of "society."

One of Erasmus's best-known works is *In Praise of Folly*, a satirical attack on superstitions and other traditions of European society in general and the western church in particular, written in 1509. *In Praise of Folly* starts off with Folly praising herself, after the manner of the Greek satirist Lucian, whose work Erasmus and Sir Thomas More had recently translated into Latin, a piece of virtuoso foolery; it then takes a darker tone in a series of orations, as Folly praises self-deception and madness and moves to a satirical examination of pious but superstitious abuses of Catholic doctrine and corrupt practices in parts of the Roman Catholic church—to which Erasmus was ever faithful—and the folly of pedants. Erasmus had recently returned disappointed from Rome, where he had turned down offers of advancement in the curia, and Folly increasingly takes on Erasmus's own chastising voice. The essay ends with a straightforward statement of Christian ideals.

Erasmus: Erasmus in 1523 as depicted by Hans Holbein the Younger. The Greek and Latin words on the book translate to "The Herculean Labours of Erasmus of Rotterdam."

The Printing Revolution

The invention of the printing press by Gutenberg led to the spread of mass communication across Europe in only a few decades.

> ### Learning Objectives
>
> Synthesize the impacts of the printing press on distribution of ideas and mass communication

> ### Key Takeaways
>
> *Key Points*
>
> - In 1436 Johannes Gutenberg began work on the invention of a new printing press that allowed precise molding of new type blocks from a uniform template and allowed for the creation of high-quality printed books.
> - Gutenberg is also credited with the introduction of an oil-based ink that was more durable than the previously used water-based inks. He tested colored inks in his Gutenberg Bible.
> - The printing press was a factor in the establishment of a community of scientists who could easily communicate their discoveries through widely disseminated scholarly journals, helping to bring on the scientific revolution.
> - Because the printing process ensured that the same information fell on the same pages, page numbering, tables of contents, and indices became common.
> - The arrival of mechanical movable type printing introduced the era of mass communication, which permanently altered the structure of society. The relatively unrestricted circulation of information and revolutionary ideas transcended borders.
>
> *Key Terms*
>
> - **Johannes Gutenberg**: (c. 1395–1468) A German blacksmith, goldsmith, printer, and publisher who introduced printing to Europe. His invention of mechanical movable type printing started the Printing Revolution and is widely regarded as the most important event of the modern period.
> - **Gutenberg Bible**: The first major book printed in the West using movable type. It marked the start of the age of the printed book in the West and is widely praised for its high aesthetic and artistic qualities.

Overview

The printing press was invented in the Holy Roman Empire by the German Johannes Gutenberg around 1440, based on existing screw presses. Gutenberg, a goldsmith by profession, developed a complete printing system that perfected the printing process through all of its stages by adapting existing technologies to printing purposes, as well as making groundbreaking inventions of his own. His newly devised hand mould made possible for the first time the precise and rapid creation of metal movable type in large quantities, a key element in the profitability of the whole printing enterprise.

The printing press spread within several decades to over 200 cities in a dozen European countries. By 1500, printing presses in operation throughout Western Europe had already produced more than 20 million volumes. In the 16th century, with presses spreading further afield, their output rose tenfold to an estimated 150 to 200 million copies. The operation of a press became so synonymous with the enterprise of printing that it lent its name to an entire new branch of media, the press.

Johannes Gutenberg

Johannes Gutenberg's work on the printing press began in approximately 1436 when he partnered with Andreas Dritzehn—a man he had previously instructed in gem-cutting—and Andreas Heilmann, owner of a paper mill. However, it was not until a 1439 lawsuit against Gutenberg that an official record exists; witnesses' testimony discussed Gutenberg's types, an inventory of metals (including lead), and his type molds.

Early wooden printing press, depicted in 1568: Such presses could produce up to 240 impressions per hour. At the left in the foreground, a "puller" removes a printed sheet from the press. The "beater" to his right is inking the form. In the background, compositors are setting type.

Having previously worked as a professional goldsmith, Gutenberg made skillful use of the knowledge of metals he had learned as a craftsman. He was the first to make type from an alloy of lead, tin, and antimony, which was critical for yielding durable type that produced high-quality printed books and proved to be much better-suited for printing than all other known materials. To create these lead types, Gutenberg used what is considered one of his most ingenious inventions, a special matrix enabling the quick and precise molding of new type blocks from a uniform template. His type case is estimated to have contained around 290 separate letter boxes, most of which were required for special characters, ligatures, punctuation marks, etc.

Mass Communication

In Renaissance Europe, the arrival of mechanical movable type printing introduced the era of mass communication, which permanently altered the structure of society. The relatively unrestricted circulation of information and (revolutionary) ideas transcended borders, captured the masses in the Reformation, and threatened the power of political and religious authorities; the sharp increase in literacy broke the monopoly of the literate elite on education and learning and bolstered the emerging middle class. Across Europe, the increasing cultural self-awareness of its peoples led to the rise of proto-nationalism, accelerated by the flowering of the European vernacular languages to the detriment of Latin's status as *lingua franca*.

As early as 1480 there were printers active in 110 different places in Germany, Italy, France, Spain, the Netherlands, Belgium, Switzerland, England, Bohemia, and Poland. From that time on, it is assumed that "the printed book was in universal use in Europe." By 1500, the printing presses in operation throughout Western Europe had already produced more than 20 million copies. In the following century, their output rose tenfold to an estimated 150 to 200 million copies.

The vast printing capacities meant that individual authors could now become true bestsellers; at least 750,000 copies of Erasmus's works were sold during his lifetime alone (1469–1536). In the period from 1518 to 1524, the publication of books in Germany alone skyrocketed sevenfold; between 1518 and 1520, Luther's tracts were distributed in 300,000 printed copies.

Spread of printing in the 15th century from Mainz, Germany: *Printing places showing the spread of incunabula printing in the 15th century. Two hundred seventy-one locations are known; the largest of them are designated by name. The term "incunabula" referred to printed materials and came to denote the printed books themselves in the late 17th century.*

Effect on Scholarship and Literacy

The printing press was also a factor in the establishment of a community of scientists who could easily communicate their discoveries through widely disseminated scholarly journals, helping to bring on the scientific revolution. Because of the printing press, authorship became more meaningful and profitable. It was suddenly important who had said or written what, and what the precise formulation and time of composition was. This allowed the exact citing of references, producing the rule, "one author, one work (title), one piece of information." Before, the author was less important, since a copy of Aristotle made in Paris would not be exactly identical to one made in Bologna. For many works prior to the printing press, the name of the author has been entirely lost.

Because the printing process ensured that the same information fell on the same pages, page numbering, tables of contents, and indices became common, though they previously had not been unknown. The process of reading also changed, gradually moving over several centuries from oral readings to silent, private reading. The wider availability of printed materials also led to a drastic rise in the adult literacy rate throughout Europe.

A YouTube element has been excluded from this version of the text. You can view it online here: https://milnepublishing.geneseo.edu/suny-fmcc-boundless-worldhistory-print/?p=277

Printing on a Gutenberg press: A demonstration of how to print on a Gutenberg printing press.

Flemish Painting in the Northern Renaissance

The Flemish School refers to artists who were active in Flanders during the 15th and 16th centuries.

Learning Objectives

Compare the artistic advances seen in the works of Robern Campin, Jan van Eyck, and Rogier van der Weyden

Key Takeaways

Key Points

- The three most prominent painters during this period, Jan van Eyck, Robert Campin, and Rogier van der Weyden, were known for making significant advances in illusionism, or the realistic and precise representation of people, space, and objects.
- The preferred subject matter of the Flemish School was typically religious in nature, and the majority of the work was presented as panels, usually in the form of diptychs or polyptychs.
- While the Italian Renaissance was based on rediscoveries of classical Greece and Rome, the Flemish school drew influence from the region's Gothic past.
- Van Eyck is known for signing and dating his work "ALS IK KAN" ("AS I CAN").
- Robert Campin has been identified with the signature "Master of Flemalle."
- Because the Flemish masters used a workshop system, they were able to mass produce high-end panels for sale and export throughout Europe.

> *Key Terms*
>
> - **illusionism**: The realistic and precise representation of people, space, and objects.
> - **tempera**: A type of painting where color pigments are mixed with a binder, usually egg. Tempera can also refers to the finished work of art itself.
> - **triptych**: A picture or series of pictures painted on three tablets connected by hinges.
> - **polyptych**: A work consisting of multiple painted or carved panels joined together, often with hinges.

The Flemish School

The Flemish School, which has also been called the Northern Renaissance, the Flemish Primitive School, and Early Netherlandish, refers to artists who were active in Flanders during the 15th and 16th centuries, especially in the cities of Bruges and Ghent. The three most prominent painters during this period—Jan van Eyck, Robert Campin, and Rogier van der Weyden—were known for making significant advances in illusionism, or the realistic and precise representation of people, space, and objects. The preferred subject matter of the Flemish School was typically religious in nature, but small portraits were common as well. The majority of this work was presented as either panels, single altarpieces, or more complex altarpieces, which were usually in the form of diptychs or polyptychs.

During the 15th and 16th centuries, the Low Countries became a political and artistic center focused around the cities of Bruges and Ghent. Because Flemish masters employed a workshop system, wherein craftsmen helped to complete their art, they were able to mass produce high-end panels for sale throughout Europe. The Flemish School emerged almost concurrently with the Italian Renaissance. However, while the Italian Renaissance was based on the rediscoveries of classical Greek and Roman culture, the Flemish school drew influence from the area's Gothic past. These artists also experimented with oil paint earlier than their Italian Renaissance peers.

Robert Campin

Robert Campin, considered the first master of the Flemish School, has been identified with the signature *"Master of Flemalle,"* which appears on numerous works of art. Campin is known for producing highly realistic works, for making great use of perspective and shading, and for being one of the first artists to work with oil paint instead of tempera. One of his best known works, the *Merode Altarpiece,* is a triptych that depicts an Annunciation Scene. The Archangel Gabriel approaches Mary as she is reading in a room that is recognized as a typical middle class Flanders home. The work is highly realistic, and the objects throughout the painting conveyed recognizable, religious meaning to viewers at the time.

The Merode Altarpiece attributed to Robert Campin: *The Merode Altarpiece is a triptych that features the Archangel Gabriel approaching Mary, who is reading in a well-decorated, typical middle class Flanders home.*

Jan Van Eyck

Jan van Eyck, a contemporary of Campin, is widely considered to be one of the most significant Northern European painters of the 15th century. He is known for signing and dating his work "ALS IK KAN" ("AS I CAN"). Signatures were not particularly customary during this time, but helped to secure his lasting reputation. Active in Bruges, and very popular within his own lifetime, van Eyck's work was highly innovative and technical. It exhibited a masterful manipulation of oil paint and a high degree of realism. While van Eyck completed many famous paintings, perhaps his most famous is the *Ghent Altarpiece*, a commissioned polyptych from around 1432.

The Ghent Altarpiece by Jan van Eyck: *The Ghent Altarpiece, a commissioned polyptych from around 1432, is perhaps van Eyck's most famous work.*

Rogier van der Weyden

Rogier van der Weyden is the last of the three most renowned Early Flemish painters. An apprentice under Robert Campin, van der Weyden exhibited many stylistic similarities, including the use of realism. Highly successful in his lifetime, his surviving works are mainly religious triptychs, altarpieces, and commissioned portraits. By the end of the 15th century, van der Weyden surpassed even van Eyck in popularity. Van der Weyden's most well-known painting is *The Descent From the Cross*, circa 1435.

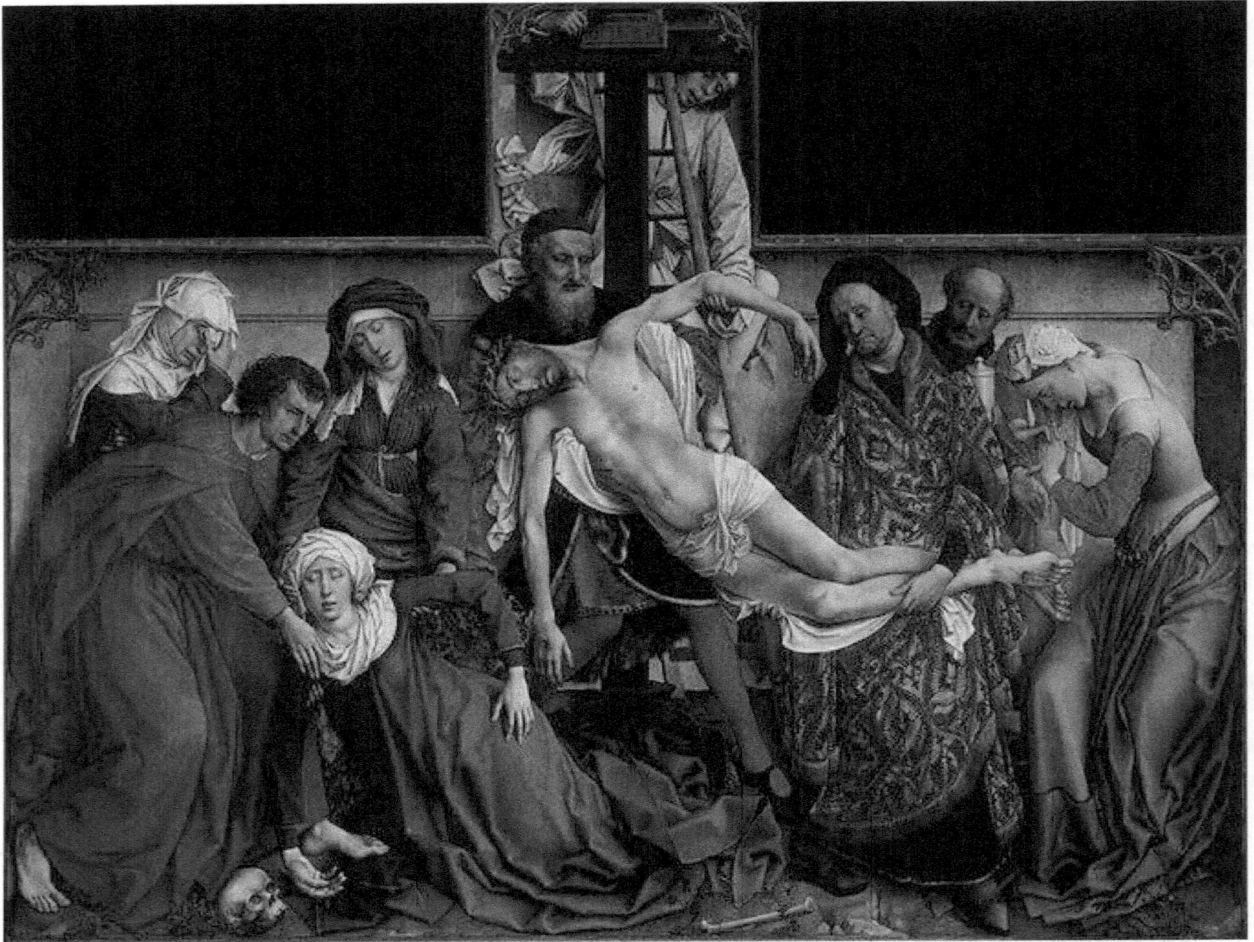

The Descent from the Cross by Rogier van der Weyden: *Van der Weyden's most well-known painting is The Descent From the Cross, circa 1435.*

Attributions

CC licensed content, Specific attribution

- Desiderius Erasmus. **Provided by**: Wikipedia. **Located at**: https://en.wikipedia.org/wiki/Desiderius_Erasmus. **License**: *CC BY-SA: Attribution-ShareAlike*
- Holbein-erasmus.jpg. **Provided by**: Wikipedia. **Located at**: https://en.wikipedia.org/wiki/Desiderius_Erasmus#/media/File:Holbein-erasmus.jpg. **License**: *CC BY-SA: Attribution-ShareAlike*
- Printing Press. **Provided by**: Wikipedia. **Located at**: http://en.wikipedia.org/wiki/Printing_press. **License**: *CC BY-SA: Attribution-ShareAlike*
- Johannes Gutenberg. **Provided by**: Wikipedia. **Located at**: http://en.wikipedia.org/wiki/Johannes_Gutenberg. **License**: *CC BY-SA: Attribution-ShareAlike*
- Gutenberg Bible. **Provided by**: Wikipedia. **Located at**: http://en.wikipedia.org/wiki/Gutenberg_Bible. **License**: *CC BY-SA: Attribution-ShareAlike*
- Incunable. **Provided by**: Wikipedia. **Located at**: http://en.wikipedia.org/wiki/Incunable. **License**: *CC BY-SA: Attribution-ShareAlike*
- Holbein-erasmus.jpg. **Provided by**: Wikipedia. **Located at**: https://en.wikipedia.org/wiki/Desiderius_Erasmus#/media/File:Holbein-erasmus.jpg. **License**: *CC BY-SA: Attribution-ShareAlike*
- Printer in 1568. **Provided by**: Wikipedia. **Located at**: http://en.wikipedia.org/wiki/File:Printer_in_1568-ce.png. **License**: *Public Domain: No Known Copyright*
- Printing towns incunabula. **Provided by**: Wikipedia. **Located at**: http://en.wikipedia.org/wiki/Global_spread_of_the_print-

THE NORTHERN RENAISSANCE • 791

- ing_press%23mediaviewer/File:Printing_towns_incunabula.svg. **License**: *CC BY-SA: Attribution-ShareAlike*
- Printing on a Gutenberg press. **Located at**: http://www.youtube.com/watch?v=ksLaBnZVRnM. **License**: *Public Domain: No Known Copyright*. **License Terms**: Standard YouTube license
- The Descent from the Cross (van der Weyden). **Provided by**: Wikipedia. **Located at**: https://en.wikipedia.org/wiki/The_Descent_from_the_Cross_(van_der_Weyden). **License**: *CC BY-SA: Attribution-ShareAlike*
- Dutch and Flemish Renaissance painting. **Provided by**: Wikipedia. **Located at**: http://en.wikipedia.org/wiki/Dutch_and_Flemish_Renaissance_painting. **License**: *CC BY-SA: Attribution-ShareAlike*
- Rogier van der Weyden. **Provided by**: Wikipedia. **Located at**: http://en.wikipedia.org/wiki/Rogier_van_der_Weyden. **License**: *CC BY-SA: Attribution-ShareAlike*
- Jan van Eyck. **Provided by**: Wikipedia. **Located at**: http://en.wikipedia.org/wiki/Jan_van_Eyck. **License**: *CC BY-SA: Attribution-ShareAlike*
- Early Netherlandish painting. **Provided by**: Wikipedia. **Located at**: http://en.wikipedia.org/wiki/Early_Netherlandish_painting. **License**: *CC BY-SA: Attribution-ShareAlike*
- Robert Campin. **Provided by**: Wikipedia. **Located at**: http://en.wikipedia.org/wiki/Robert_Campin. **License**: *CC BY-SA: Attribution-ShareAlike*
- Northern Renaissance. **Provided by**: Wikipedia. **Located at**: http://en.wikipedia.org/wiki/Northern_Renaissance. **License**: *CC BY-SA: Attribution-ShareAlike*
- The Northern Renaissance. **Provided by**: Saylor. **Located at**: http://www.saylor.org/site/wp-content/uploads/2012/08/HIST302-8.3.1-Northern-Renaissance-FINAL.pdf. **License**: *CC BY: Attribution*
- ARTH111: Introduction to Western Art History - Proto-Renaissance to Contemporary Art. **Provided by**: Saylor. **Located at**: https://legacy.saylor.org/arth111/Intro/. **License**: *CC BY: Attribution*
- tempera. **Provided by**: Wiktionary. **Located at**: http://en.wiktionary.org/wiki/tempera. **License**: *CC BY-SA: Attribution-ShareAlike*
- triptych. **Provided by**: Wiktionary. **Located at**: http://en.wiktionary.org/wiki/triptych. **License**: *CC BY-SA: Attribution-ShareAlike*
- polyptych. **Provided by**: Wiktionary. **Located at**: http://en.wiktionary.org/wiki/polyptych. **License**: *CC BY-SA: Attribution-ShareAlike*
- Holbein-erasmus.jpg. **Provided by**: Wikipedia. **Located at**: https://en.wikipedia.org/wiki/Desiderius_Erasmus#/media/File:Holbein-erasmus.jpg. **License**: *CC BY-SA: Attribution-ShareAlike*
- Printer in 1568. **Provided by**: Wikipedia. **Located at**: http://en.wikipedia.org/wiki/File:Printer_in_1568-ce.png. **License**: *Public Domain: No Known Copyright*
- Printing towns incunabula. **Provided by**: Wikipedia. **Located at**: http://en.wikipedia.org/wiki/Global_spread_of_the_printing_press%23mediaviewer/File:Printing_towns_incunabula.svg. **License**: *CC BY-SA: Attribution-ShareAlike*
- Printing on a Gutenberg press. **Located at**: http://www.youtube.com/watch?v=ksLaBnZVRnM. **License**: *Public Domain: No Known Copyright*. **License Terms**: Standard YouTube license
- El Descendimiento, by Rogier van der Weyden, from Prado in Google Earth. **Provided by**: Wikipedia. **Located at**: http://en.wikipedia.org/wiki/File:El_Descendimiento,_by_Rogier_van_der_Weyden,_from_Prado_in_Google_Earth.jpg. **License**: *Public Domain: No Known Copyright*
- Merodealtarpiece. **Provided by**: Wikipedia. **Located at**: http://en.wikipedia.org/wiki/File:Merodealtarpiece.jpg. **License**: *Public Domain: No Known Copyright*
- Lamgods open. **Provided by**: Wikipedia. **Located at**: http://en.wikipedia.org/wiki/File:Lamgods_open.jpg. **License**: *CC BY-SA: Attribution-ShareAlike*

Civilizations in the Americas

The Inca

The Inca People

The Inca Empire was the largest of the pre-Columbian mesoamerican empires.

Learning Objectives

Explain Inca agriculture, clothing, commodities, and architecture, and how these elements shaped their complex society.

Key Takeaways

Key Points

- Centered in Cusco, the Inca Empire extended from modern-day Chile to modern-day Colombia.
- Inca society was sophisticated, and boasted around seventy different crops across the empire's various climates.
- The Inca considered finely woven textiles to be an essential commodity, and spun various grades of cloth from llama and vicuña wool.

Key Terms

- **quinoa**: This grain crop produces edible seeds that are high in protein and played an essential role in the Inca diet.
- **awaska**: A lower-grade textile woven from llama wool and used for everyday household chores and cleaning.
- **Machu Picchu**: This Inca citadel was probably built for the emperor Pachacutec around 1450 CE in the Andes at a height of around 8,000 feet above sea level using dry stone

> masonry.

The Inca Empire, or Inka Empire, was the largest empire in pre-Columbian America. The civilization emerged in the 13th century and lasted until it was conquered by the Spanish in 1572. The administrative, political, and military center of the empire was located in Cusco (also spelled Cuzco) in modern-day Peru. From 1438 to 1533, the Incas used a variety of methods, from conquest to peaceful assimilation, to incorporate a large portion of western South America. Beginning with the rule of Pachacuti-Cusi Yupanqui, the Inca expanded their borders to include large parts of modern Ecuador, Peru, western and south-central Bolivia, northwest Argentina, north and north-central Chile, and southern Colombia. This vast territory was known in Quechua (the language of the Inca Empire) as Tawantin Suyu, or the Four Regions, which met in the capital of Cusco.

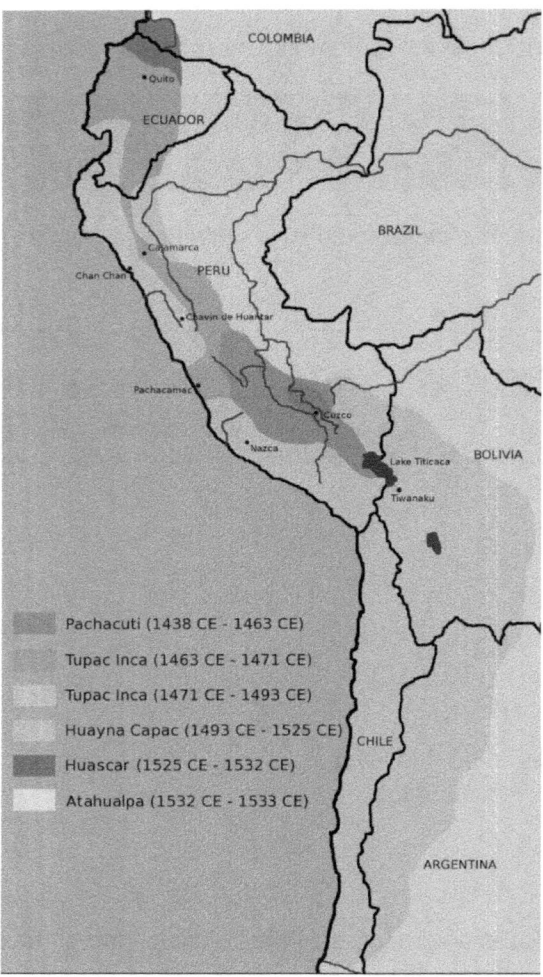

Inca Empire: *From 1438 to 1533, the Inca Empire expanded significantly.*

Architecture and Masonry

Architecture illustrates the sophistication and technical skill typical of the Inca Empire. The main example of this resilient art form was the capital city of Cusco, which drew together the Four Regions. The Inca used a mortarless construction technique, called dry stone wall, that fit stones together so well that a knife could not be fitted through the stonework. This was a process first used on a large scale by the Pucara (c. 300 BCE–300 CE) peoples to the south in Lake Titicaca, and later in the great city of Tiwanaku (c. 400–1100 CE) in present-day Bolivia. The rocks used in construction were sculpted to fit together exactly by repeatedly lowering one rock onto another and carving away any sections on the lower rock where there was compression or the pieces did not fit exactly. The tight fit and the concavity on the lower rocks made them extraordinarily stable.

Machu Picchu was built around 1450, at the height of the Inca Empire. It is a rare example of this architectural building technique and remains in remarkable condition after many centuries. The construction of Machu Picchu appears to date from the period of the two great Inca emperors, Pachacutec Inca Yupanqui (1438–1471) and Tupac Inca Yupanqui (1472–1493), and was probably built as a temple for the emperor Pachacutec. Machu Picchu was abandoned just over 100 years later, in 1572, as a belated result of the Spanish Conquest, possibly related to smallpox.

Machu Picchu: *This impressive mountain-top temple was built around 1450 CE using dry stone wall.*

Textiles, Ceramics, and Metalwork

Textiles were one of the most precious commodities of the Inca culture and denoted a person's social status, and often their profession. The brightly colored patterns on a wool tunic represented various positions and achievements. For example, a black-and-white checkerboard pattern topped with a pink triangle denoted a soldier. Because textiles were so specific to a person's class and employment, citizens could not change their wardrobe without the express permission of the government. Textiles were also manufactured that could only be used for certain tasks or social arenas. A rougher textile, spun from llama wool and called *awaska*, was used for everyday household chores. On the other hand, a fine-spun, very soft cloth made from vicuña wool could only be used in religious ceremonies.

Inca tunic: *The complex patterns woven into most Inca textiles and made into tunics, like this one, denoted a person's position in society.*

Although textiles were considered the most precious commodity in Inca culture, Incas also considered ceramics and metalwork essential commodities of the economy and class system. Incan pottery was distinctive and normally had a spherical body with a cone-shaped base. The pottery would also include curved handles and often featured animal heads, such as jaguars or birds. These ceramics were painted in bright colors, such as orange, red, black, and yellow.

The Inca also required every province to mine for precious metals like tin, silver, gold, and copper. The intricate metalwork of the Inca was heavily influenced by the Chimú culture, which was conquered and absorbed into the Inca culture around 1470. This metalwork included detailed friezes and patterns inlaid into the metal. Fine silver and gold were made into intricate decorative pieces for the emperors and elites based on these Chimú metallurgy traditions, and often included animal motifs with butterflies, jaguars, and llamas etched into the metal. Skilled metallurgists also transformed bronze and copper into farming implements, blades, axes, and pins for everyday activities.

Agriculture and Diet

The Inca culture boasted a wide variety of crops, numbering around seventy different strains in total, making it one of the most diverse crop cultures in the world. Some of these flavorful vegetables and grains included:

- Potatoes
- Sweet potatoes
- Maize
- Chili peppers
- Cotton
- Tomatoes
- Peanuts
- Oca
- Quinoa
- Amaranth

Terraced farmland in Peru: *Terraces allowed Inca farmers to utilize the mountainous terrain and grow around seventy different crops.*

These crops were grown in the high-altitude Andes by building terraced farms that allowed farmers to utilize the mineral-rich mountain soil. The quick change in altitude on these mountain farms also utilized the micro-climates of each terrace to grow a wider range of crops. The Inca also produced bounties in the Amazon rainforest and along the more arid coastline of modern-day Peru.

Alongside vegetables, the Inca supplemented their diet with fish, guinea pigs, camelid meat, and wild fowl. They also fermented maize, or corn, to create the alcoholic beverage *chicha*.

Administration of the Inca Empire

The Inca Empire utilized complex road systems, recording tools, and a hierarchical rule of law to oversee the administration of its vast population.

Learning Objectives

Understand the importance of the governing bodies, road system, recording tools, and social hierarchy of the Inca Empire

> ## Key Takeaways
>
> *Key Points*
>
> - The Inca Empire utilized a complex road system with about 25,000 miles of roads that relayed messages and goods throughout the society.
> - Inca administrators used brightly colored knotted strings called quipus to keep precise records of labor, taxes, and goods.
> - The Inca had no written legal code, but relied on magistrates and inspectors to keep people in line with established social customs.
>
> *Key Terms*
>
> - **quipus**: Brightly colored knotted strings that recorded numerical information, such as taxes, goods, and labor, using the base number of 10 to record data in knots.
> - **ayllu**: A clan-like family unit based upon a common ancestor.
> - **suyus**: Distinct districts of the Inca Empire that all reported back to the capital of Cusco. There were four major districts during the height of the empire.

Hierarchy

The Inca Empire was a hierarchical system with the emperor, or Inca Sapa, ruling over the rest of society. A number of religious officials and magistrates oversaw the administration of the empire directly below the emperor. Kurakas were magistrates that served as the head of an ayllu, or clan-like family unit based on a common ancestor. These leaders mitigated between the spiritual and physical worlds. They also collected taxes, oversaw the day-to-day administration of the empire in their regions, and even chose brides for men in their communities. Some of the privileges kurakas enjoyed included exemption from taxation, the right to ride in a litter, and the freedom to practice polygamy.

Society was broken into two distinct parts. One segment was comprised of the common people, including those cultures that had been subsumed by the Inca Empire. The second group was made up of the elite of the empire, including the emperor and the kurakas, along with various other dignitaries and blood relations. Education was vocationally based for commoners, while the elite received a formal spiritual education.

There was no codified legal system for people that broke with the cultural and social norms. Local inspectors called *okoyrikoq*, or "he who sees all," reported back to the capital and the emperor and made immediate decisions regarding punishment in cases where customs were not honored. Many times these local inspectors were blood relatives of the emperor.

Road System

The Inca civilization was able to keep populations in line, collect taxes efficiently, and move goods, messages, and military resources across such a varied landscape because of the complex road system. Measuring about 24,800 miles long, this road system connected the the regions of the empire and was the most complex and lengthy road system in South America at the time. Two main routes connected the north and the south of the empire, with many smaller branches extending to outposts to the east and west. The roads varied in width and style because often the Inca leaders utilized roads that already existed to create this powerful network. Common people could not use these official roads unless they were given permission by the government.

These roads were used for relaying messages by way of *chasqui*, or human runners, who could run up to 150 miles a day with messages for officials. Llamas and alpacas were also used to distribute goods throughout the empire and ease trade relations. The roads also had a ritual purpose because they allowed the highest leaders of the Inca Empire to ascend into the Andes to perform religious rituals in sacred spaces, such as Machu Picchu.

Chasqui carrying a quipu on official state business: *Chasquis were highly agile long-distance runners who used the complex road systems to relay messages and goods between cities.*

Record Keeping

TheInca utilized a complex recording system to keep track of the administration of the empire. Quipus (also spelled khipus) were colorful bunches of knotted strings that recorded census data, taxes, calendrical information, military organization, and accounting information. These "talking knots" could contain anything from a few threads to around 2,000, and used the base number of 10 to record information in complex variations of knots and spaces.

Inca quipu: These complex recording devices allowed officials to keep track of taxes, labor, and goods in a precise fashion.

The Spanish burned the vast majority of existing quipus when they arrived in South America. However, there is some evidence to suggest that these tools were also used to record stories and language for posterity, and were not only numerical recording devices.

Trade and Economics

Trade and the movement of goods fed into what is called the vertical archipelago. This system meant that all goods produced within the empire were immediately property of the ruling elites. These elites, such as the emperor and governors, then redistributed resources across the empire as they saw fit.

Taxes and goods were collected from four distinct *suyus*, or districts, and sent directly to the ruling emperor in Cusco. This highly organized system was most likely perfected under the emperor Pachacuti around 1460.

The Four suyus of the Inca Empire: *The economic system linked together four large suyus, or districts, that all reported back to the capital of Cusco.*

This system also required a minimum quota of manual labor from the general population. This form of labor taxation was called *mita*. The
populations of each district were expected to contribute to the wealth of the empire by mining, farming, or doing other manual labor that would benefit the entire empire. Precious metals, textiles, and crops were collected and redistributed using the the road system that snaked across the land, from the ocean to the Andes.

Religion in the Inca Empire

The Inca Empire worshipped the Sun god Inti, and expanded its hold on outlying areas by incorporating other deities into the religious system.

Learning Objectives

Learn about the forms of worship of the Sun god Inti, the religious hierarchy, and the cultural assimilation of outlying clans in the Inca Empire

Key Takeaways

Key Points

- The Inca rulers worshipped the Sun god Inti and built the central temple, Qurikancha, in Cusco.
- The Inca elite incorporated the varied populations into the empire by allowing the worship of other deities.
- Various festivals celebrated the different aspects of the Sun. The most important of these festivals was Inti Raymi, which focused on abundance.

Key Terms

- **Pachamama**: The Earth goddess worshipped by many clans in outlying areas of the Inca Empire. Inca rulers enforced a religious system that favored Inti, but they incorporated the Earth goddess as a lesser deity.
- **Inti**: The central Sun god the Inca worshipped. He represented abundance, harvests, and fertility, and was considered more important than any other deity worshipped in the region.
- **Inti Raymi**: The most important religious festival of the Inca year. It means "Sun Festival" and occurred close to the winter solstice, which happens in June in South America.

The Inca religious system utilized oral traditions to pass down the mythology of their Sun god, Inti. This benevolent male deity was often represented as a gold disk with large rays and a human face. Golden disks were commonly displayed at temples across the Inca Empire and were also associated with the ruling emperor, who was supposed to be a direct descendent of Inti, and divinely powerful. Inti was also associated with the growth of crops and material abundance, especially in the high Andes, where the Inca centered their power.

Some myths state that this benevolent entity, along with Mama Killa, the Moon goddess, had children. Inti ordered these children, named Manco Cápac and Mama Ocllo, to descend from the sky and onto Earth with a divine golden wedge. This wedge penetrated the earth, and they built the capital of Cusco and civilization on that very spot.

Inti Worship

Royalty were considered to be direct descendants of Inti and, therefore, able to act as intermediaries between the physical and spiritual realms. The
high priest of Inti was called the *Willaq Umu*. He was often the brother or a direct blood relation of the Sapa Inca, or emperor, and was the second most powerful person in the empire. The royal family oversaw the collection of goods, spiritual festivals, and the worship of Inti. Power consolidated around the cult of the Sun, and scholars suggest that the emperor Pachacuti expanded this Sun cult to garner greater power in the 15th century.

An illustrated representation of the Sun god Inti: *This image of Inti appears at the center of Argentina's modern-day flag.*

Conquered provinces were expected to dedicate a third of their resources, such as herds and crops, directly to the worship of Inti. Each province also had a temple with male and female priests worshipping the Inti cult. Becoming a priest was considered one of the most honorable positions in society. Female priests were called *mamakuna*, or "the chosen women," and they wove special cloth and brewed chicha for religious festivals.

The main temple in the Inca Empire, called Qurikancha, was built in Cusco. The temple housed the bodies of deceased emperors and also contained a vast array of physical representations of Inti, many of which were removed or destroyed when the Spanish arrived. Qurikancha was also the main site of the religious festival Inti Raymi, which means "Sun Festival." It was considered the most important festival of the year, and is still celebrated on the winter solstice in Cusco. It represents the mythical origin of the Inca and the hope for good crops in the coming year as the winter sun returns from darkness.

The festival of Inti Raymi: *This festival is celebrated in late June in the capital of Cusco every year. Thousands of visitors arrive to see the procession and rituals.*

Religious Expansion

Religious life was centered in the Andes near Cusco, but as the Inca Empire expanded its sphere of influence, they had to incorporate a wide array of
religious customs and traditions to avoid outright revolt. Ayllus, or family clans, often worshipped very localized entities and gods. The ruling Inca often incorporated these deities into the Inti cosmos. For example, Pachamama, the Earth goddess, was a long-worshipped deity before the Inca Empire. She was incorporated into Inca culture as a lower divine entity. Similarly, the Chimú along the northern coast of Peru worshipped the Moon, rather than the Sun, probably due to the hot, arid climate and their proximity to the ocean. The Inca also incorporated the Moon into their religious myths and practices in the form of Mama Killa.

Sacrifice and the Afterlife

The Inca believed in reincarnation. Death was a passage to the next world that was full of difficulties. The spirit of the dead, camaquen, would need to follow a long dark road. The trip required the assistance of a black dog that was able to see in the dark. Most Incas imagined the after world to be very similar to the Euro-American notion of heaven, with flower-covered fields and snow-capped mountains. It was important for the Inca to ensure they did not die as a result of burning or that the body of the deceased did not become incinerated. This is because of the underlying belief that a vital force would disappear and this would threaten their passage to the after world. Those who obeyed the Inca moral code (do not steal, do not lie, do not be lazy) went to live in the "Sun's warmth" while others spent their eternal days "in the cold earth."

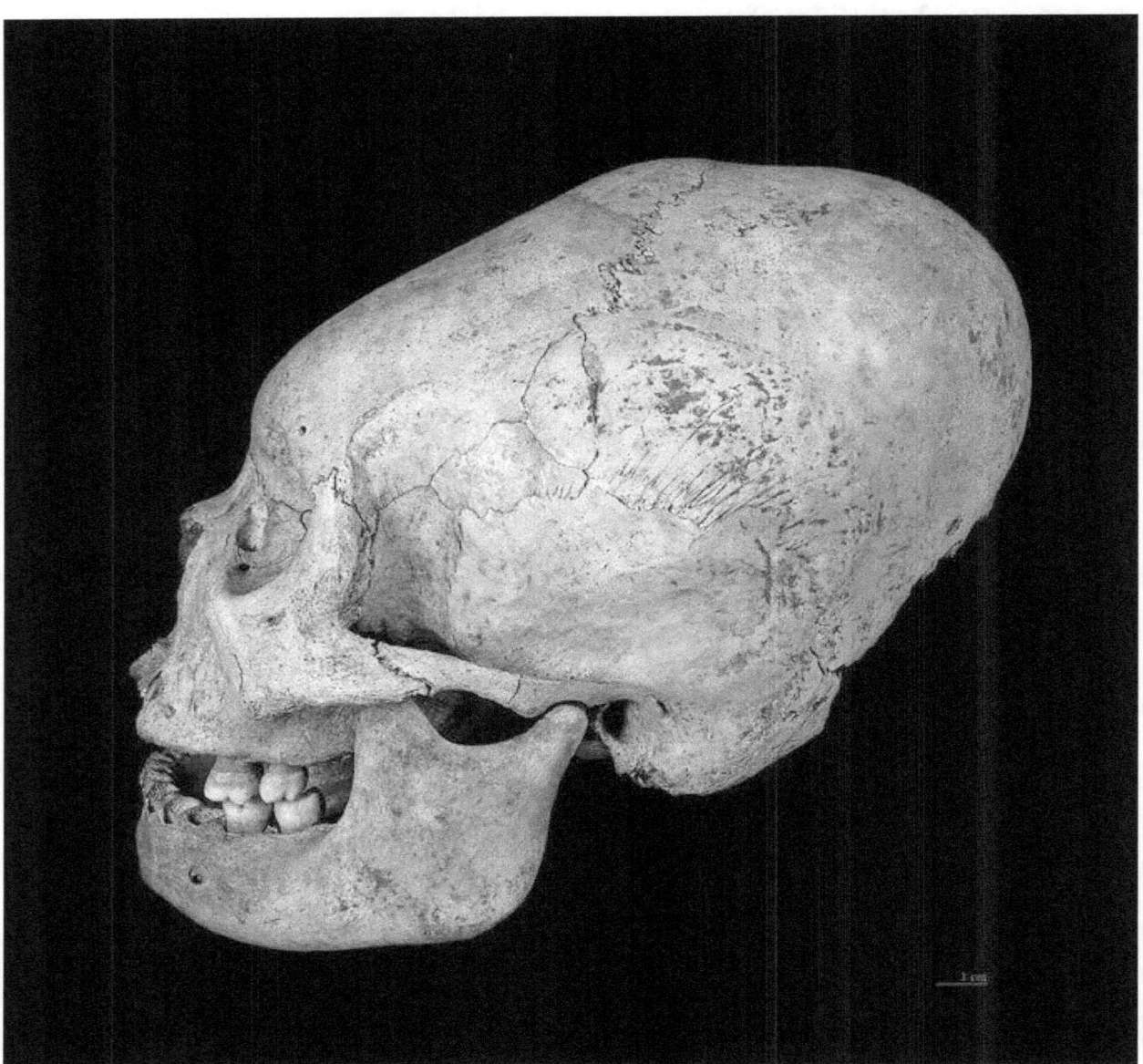

Skull showing signs of artificial cranial deformation: *Although this skull predates the Inca Empire, and is from the Nazca culture, Inca elites would reshape infants' skulls in a similar manner to illustrate a higher class status.*

Human sacrifice has been exaggerated by myth, but it did play a role in Inca religious practices. As many as 4,000 servants, court officials, favorites, and concubines were killed upon the death of the Inca uayna Capac in 1527, for example. The Incas also performed child
sacrifices during or after important events, such as the death of the Sapa Inca or during a famine. These sacrifices were known as *capacocha*.

The Inca also practiced cranial deformation. They achieved this by wrapping tight cloth straps around the heads of newborns in order to alter the shape of their soft skulls into a more conical form; this cranial deformation distinguished social classes of the communities, with only the nobility having it.

The Spanish Conquest

The Inca Empire already faced instability due to the Inca Civil War, European diseases, and internal revolt when explorer Francisco Pizarro began the conquest of Inca territory.

Learning Objectives

Learn about the contributing factors that allowed the Spanish explorers to overpower the Inca Empire and establish control of the region

Key Takeaways

Key Points

- The Inca War of Succession began after the emperor Huayna Capac died around 1528 and his two sons both wanted to seize power.
- Internal instability allowed Francisco Pizarro and his men to find allies within the Inca Empire.
- Spanish forces ousted the last Inca holdout of Vilcabamba in 1572 and enforced a harsh rule of law on the local population.

Key Terms

- **mita**: A form of labor tax that required one person from each family to work in the mines. The Spanish enforced this heavy labor tax once they gained control of the region.
- **Viceroyalty of Peru**: The Spanish forces gave the newly seized Inca region this title and started to collect taxes and labor from the local people.
- **Inca Civil War**: This internal dispute started around 1528 between two sons of the deceased emperor who both wanted control, causing instability in the Inca Empire.

Spanish Arrival

The Spanish explorer Francisco Pizarro, along with a small military retinue, landed on South American soil around 1526. The Spanish recognized the wealth and abundance that could be had in this territory; at this point the Inca Empire was at its largest, measuring around 690,000 square miles. In 1528 Pizarro went back to Spain to ask for the official blessing of the Spanish crown to the conquer the area and become governor. He returned with his blessings around 1529 and began the official takeover of the region.

Inca Civil War

Although Pizarro had a small force behind him, many problems within the Inca Empire worked to his advantage between 1528 and 1533. Foremost among these was the Inca Civil War, which is also known as the War of Succession or the War of Two Brothers. It began to brew just one year after Pizarro first landed in the region. Around 1528, the ruling Inca emperor, Huayna Capac, and his designated heir, Ninan Cuyochic, died of disease. It was most likely smallpox, which had quickly traveled down to South America after the arrival of Spanish explorers in Central America. Brothers Huascar and Atahualpa, two sons of the emperor Huayna Capac, both wanted to rule after their father's death.

Inca Emperor Atahualpa: *Although Atahualpa successfully won the Inca Civil War and ruled as emperor, he was soon captured by the Spanish and killed in 1533.*

Initially, Huascar captured the throne in Cusco, claiming legitimacy. However, Atahualpa had a keen military mind and close relations with the military generals at the time, and proved to be the deadlier force. Between 1529 and 1532 the two brothers' armies waged warfare, with one or the other gaining a stronger foothold for a time. Atahualpa initially garnered favor with northern allies and built a new capital for his forces in Quito. By 1532, Atahualpa had overpowered his brother's forces via intrigue and merciless violence, scaring many local populations away from standing up to his power. This civil war left the population in a precarious position by the time it ended.

Spanish Colonization

Around the same time that Atahualpa seized the throne in 1532, Pizarro returned to Peru with blessings from the Spanish crown. The Spanish forces went to meet with Atahualpa and demanded he take up the "true faith" (Catholicism) and the yoke of Charles I of Spain. Because of the language barrier, the Inca rulers probably did not understand much of these demands, and the meeting quickly escalated to the Battle of Cajamarca. This clash left thousands of native people dead. The Spanish also captured Atahualpa and kept him hostage, demanding ransoms of silver and gold. They also insisted that Atahualpa agree to be baptized. Although the Inca ruler was mostly cooperative in captivity, and was finally baptized, the Spanish killed him on August 29, 1533, essentially ending the potential for larger Inca attacks on Spanish forces.

An engraved representation of the Battle of Cajamarca: *This battle began in 1532, leaving thousands of native people dead and ending with the capture of Atahualpa.*

Even though the Inca Civil War made it easier for the Spanish armies to gain control initially, many other contributing factors brought about the demise of Inca rule and the crumbling of local populations. As scholar Jared Diamond points out, the Inca Empire was already facing threats:

- Local unrest in the provinces after years of paying tribute to the Inca elite created immediate allies for the Spanish against the Inca rulers.

- Demanding terrain throughout the empire made it even more difficult to keep a handle on populations and goods as the empire expanded.

- Diseases that the population had never been exposed to, such as smallpox, diphtheria, typhus, measles, and influenza, devastated large swaths of the population within fifty years.

- Superior Spanish military gear, including armor, horses, and weapons, overpowered the siege warfare more common in the Inca Empire.

The Last Incas

After Atahualpa died and the Spanish seized control, they placed Atahualpa's brother Manco Inca Yupanqui in charge of Cusco as a puppet ruler while they tried to reign in the north. After a failed attempt to recapture the city from greater Spanish rule during this time, Manco retreated to Vilcabamba and built the last stronghold of the Inca. The Inca continued to revolt against totalitarian Spanish rule until the year 1572. In that year the Spanish conquered Vilcabamba and killed the last Inca emperor, Tupac Amaru, after a summary trial.

An image of the Spanish executing Tupac Amaru: *The last Inca ruler, Tupac Amaru, was killed by Spanish forces in 1572, effectively ending any potential for an Inca uprising.*

Spanish Rule

The Spanish named this vast region the Viceroyalty of Peru and set up a Spanish system of rule, which effectively suppressed any type of uprising from local communities.

The Spanish system destroyed many of the Inca traditions and ways of life in a matter of years. Their finely honed agricultural system, which utilized tiered fields in the mountains, was completely disbanded. The Spanish also enforced heavy manual labor taxes, called mita, on the local populations. In general, this meant that every family had to offer up one person to work in the highly dangerous gold and silver mines. If that family member died, which was common, the family had to replace the fallen laborer. The Spanish also enforced heavy taxes on agriculture, metals, and other fine goods. The population continued to suffer heavy losses due to disease as Spanish rule settled into place.

Attributions

CC licensed content, Specific attribution

- Quinoa. **Provided by**: Wikipedia. **Located at**: https://en.wikipedia.org/wiki/Quinoa. **License**: *CC BY-SA: Attribution-ShareAlike*
- Dry stone. **Provided by**: Wikipedia. **Located at**: https://en.wikipedia.org/wiki/Dry_stone#Dry_stone_walls. **License**: *CC BY-SA: Attribution-ShareAlike*
- Inca Empire. **Provided by**: Wikipedia. **Located at**: http://en.wikipedia.org/wiki/Inca_Empire. **License**: *CC BY-SA: Attribution-ShareAlike*
- History of the Incas. **Provided by**: Wikipedia. **Located at**: http://en.wikipedia.org/wiki/History_of_the_Incas. **License**: *CC BY-SA: Attribution-ShareAlike*
- Andean Civilizations. **Provided by**: Wikipedia. **Located at**: http://en.wikipedia.org/wiki/Inca_civilization. **License**: *CC BY-SA: Attribution-ShareAlike*
- Spanish Conquest of the Inca Empire. **Provided by**: Wikipedia. **Located at**: http://en.wikipedia.org/wiki/Spanish_conquest_of_the_Inca_Empire. **License**: *CC BY-SA: Attribution-ShareAlike*
- Inca Society. **Provided by**: Wikipedia. **Located at**: http://en.wikipedia.org/wiki/Inca_society. **License**: *CC BY-SA: Attribution-ShareAlike*
- Machu Picchu. **Provided by**: Wikipedia. **Located at**: http://en.wikipedia.org/wiki/Machu_Picchu. **License**: *Public Domain: No Known Copyright*
- Terraced farmland in Peru. **Provided by**: Wikipedia. **Located at**: https://en.wikipedia.org/wiki/Terrace_(agriculture)#/media/File:Pisac006.jpg. **License**: *CC BY-SA: Attribution-ShareAlike*
- Machu Picchu. **Provided by**: Wikipedia. **Located at**: http://en.wikipedia.org/wiki/Machu_Picchu%23mediaviewer/File:80_-_Machu_Picchu_-_Juin_2009_-_edit.2.jpg. **License**: *CC BY-SA: Attribution-ShareAlike*
- Inca Expansion. **Provided by**: Wikipedia. **Located at**: http://en.wikipedia.org/wiki/Inca_Empire%23mediaviewer/File:Inca-expansion.png. **License**: *Public Domain: No Known Copyright*
- Tupa-inca-tunic.png. **Provided by**: Wikipedia. **Located at**: https://en.wikipedia.org/wiki/Inca_society#/media/File:Tupa-inca-tunic.png. **License**: *CC BY-SA: Attribution-ShareAlike*
- Inca society. **Provided by**: Wikipedia. **Located at**: https://en.wikipedia.org/wiki/Inca_society. **License**: *CC BY-SA: Attribution-ShareAlike*
- History of the Incas. **Provided by**: Wikipedia. **Located at**: https://en.wikipedia.org/wiki/History_of_the_Incas. **License**: *CC BY-SA: Attribution-ShareAlike*
- Inca road system. **Provided by**: Wikipedia. **Located at**: https://en.wikipedia.org/wiki/Inca_road_system. **License**: *CC BY-SA: Attribution-ShareAlike*
- Inca Empire. **Provided by**: Wikipedia. **Located at**: https://en.wikipedia.org/wiki/Inca_Empire. **License**: *CC BY-SA: Attribution-ShareAlike*
- Quipu. **Provided by**: Wikipedia. **Located at**: https://en.wikipedia.org/wiki/Quipu. **License**: *CC BY-SA: Attribution-ShareAlike*
- Kuraka. **Provided by**: Wikipedia. **Located at**: https://en.wikipedia.org/wiki/Kuraka. **License**: *CC BY-SA: Attribution-ShareAlike*
- Chasqui. **Provided by**: Wikipedia. **Located at**: https://en.wikipedia.org/wiki/Chasqui. **License**: *CC BY-SA: Attribution-ShareAlike*
- Terraced farmland in Peru. **Provided by**: Wikipedia. **Located at**: https://en.wikipedia.org/wiki/Terrace_(agriculture)#/media/

File:Pisac006.jpg. **License**: *CC BY-SA: Attribution-ShareAlike*

- Machu Picchu. **Provided by**: Wikipedia. **Located at**: http://en.wikipedia.org/wiki/Machu_Picchu%23mediaviewer/File:80_-_Machu_Picchu_-_Juin_2009_-_edit.2.jpg. **License**: *CC BY-SA: Attribution-ShareAlike*
- Inca Expansion. **Provided by**: Wikipedia. **Located at**: http://en.wikipedia.org/wiki/Inca_Empire%23mediaviewer/File:Inca-expansion.png. **License**: *Public Domain: No Known Copyright*
- Tupa-inca-tunic.png. **Provided by**: Wikipedia. **Located at**: https://en.wikipedia.org/wiki/Inca_society#/media/File:Tupa-inca-tunic.png. **License**: *CC BY-SA: Attribution-ShareAlike*
- Inca Quipu. **Provided by**: Wikipedia. **Located at**: https://en.wikipedia.org/wiki/Quipu#/media/File:Inca_Quipu.jpg. **License**: *CC BY-SA: Attribution-ShareAlike*
- Chasqui3.jpeg. **Provided by**: Wikipedia. **Located at**: https://en.wikipedia.org/wiki/Chasqui#/media/File:Chasqui3.JPG. **License**: *CC BY-SA: Attribution-ShareAlike*
- Inca_Empire_South_America.png. **Provided by**: Wikipedia. **Located at**: https://en.wikipedia.org/wiki/Government_of_the_Inca_Empire#/media/File:Inca_Empire_South_America.png. **License**: *CC BY-SA: Attribution-ShareAlike*
- Chimu. **Provided by**: Wikipedia. **Located at**: https://en.wikipedia.org/wiki/Chim%C3%BA_culture. **License**: *CC BY-SA: Attribution-ShareAlike*
- Inti Raymi. **Provided by**: Wikipedia. **Located at**: https://en.wikipedia.org/wiki/Inti_Raymi. **License**: *CC BY-SA: Attribution-ShareAlike*
- Religion in the Inca Empire. **Provided by**: Wikipedia. **Located at**: https://en.wikipedia.org/wiki/Religion_in_the_Inca_Empire. **License**: *CC BY-SA: Attribution-ShareAlike*
- Inca Empire. **Provided by**: Wikipedia. **Located at**: https://en.wikipedia.org/wiki/Inca_Empire. **License**: *CC BY-SA: Attribution-ShareAlike*
- Inti. **Provided by**: Wikipedi. **Located at**: https://en.wikipedia.org/wiki/Inti. **License**: *CC BY: Attribution*
- Terraced farmland in Peru. **Provided by**: Wikipedia. **Located at**: https://en.wikipedia.org/wiki/Terrace_(agriculture)#/media/File:Pisac006.jpg. **License**: *CC BY-SA: Attribution-ShareAlike*
- Machu Picchu. **Provided by**: Wikipedia. **Located at**: http://en.wikipedia.org/wiki/Machu_Picchu%23mediaviewer/File:80_-_Machu_Picchu_-_Juin_2009_-_edit.2.jpg. **License**: *CC BY-SA: Attribution-ShareAlike*
- Inca Expansion. **Provided by**: Wikipedia. **Located at**: http://en.wikipedia.org/wiki/Inca_Empire%23mediaviewer/File:Inca-expansion.png. **License**: *Public Domain: No Known Copyright*
- Tupa-inca-tunic.png. **Provided by**: Wikipedia. **Located at**: https://en.wikipedia.org/wiki/Inca_society#/media/File:Tupa-inca-tunic.png. **License**: *CC BY-SA: Attribution-ShareAlike*
- Inca Quipu. **Provided by**: Wikipedia. **Located at**: https://en.wikipedia.org/wiki/Quipu#/media/File:Inca_Quipu.jpg. **License**: *CC BY-SA: Attribution-ShareAlike*
- Chasqui3.jpeg. **Provided by**: Wikipedia. **Located at**: https://en.wikipedia.org/wiki/Chasqui#/media/File:Chasqui3.JPG. **License**: *CC BY-SA: Attribution-ShareAlike*
- Inca_Empire_South_America.png. **Provided by**: Wikipedia. **Located at**: https://en.wikipedia.org/wiki/Government_of_the_Inca_Empire#/media/File:Inca_Empire_South_America.png. **License**: *CC BY-SA: Attribution-ShareAlike*
- Artificial cranial deformation. **Provided by**: Wikipedia. **Located at**: https://en.wikipedia.org/wiki/Artificial_cranial_deformation#/media/File:D%C3%A9formation_P%C3%A9ruvienne_MHNT_Noir.jpg. **License**: *CC BY-SA: Attribution-ShareAlike*
- Inti_Raymi.jpg. **Provided by**: Wikimedia. **Located at**: https://commons.wikimedia.org/wiki/File:Inti_Raymi.jpg. **License**: *CC BY-SA: Attribution-ShareAlike*
- 2000px-Sol_de_Mayo-Bandera_de_Argentina.png. **Provided by**: Wikipedia. **Located at**: https://en.wikipedia.org/wiki/Inti#/media/File:Sol_de_Mayo-Bandera_de_Argentina.svg. **License**: *CC BY-SA: Attribution-ShareAlike*
- Tupac Amaru. **Provided by**: Wikipedia. **Located at**: https://en.wikipedia.org/wiki/T%C3%BApac_Amaru. **License**: *CC BY-SA: Attribution-ShareAlike*
- Spanish conquest of the Inca Empire. **Provided by**: Wikipedia. **Located at**: https://en.wikipedia.org/wiki/Spanish_conquest_of_the_Inca_Empire. **License**: *CC BY-SA: Attribution-ShareAlike*
- Inca Empire. **Provided by**: Wikipedia. **Located at**: https://en.wikipedia.org/wiki/Inca_Empire. **License**: *CC BY-SA: Attribution-ShareAlike*
- Inca Civil War. **Provided by**: Wikipedia. **Located at**: https://en.wikipedia.org/wiki/Inca_Civil_War. **License**: *CC BY-SA: Attribution-ShareAlike*
- Terraced farmland in Peru. **Provided by**: Wikipedia. **Located at**: https://en.wikipedia.org/wiki/Terrace_(agriculture)#/media/File:Pisac006.jpg. **License**: *CC BY-SA: Attribution-ShareAlike*

- Machu Picchu. **Provided by**: Wikipedia. **Located at**: http://en.wikipedia.org/wiki/Machu_Picchu%23mediaviewer/File:80_-_Machu_Picchu_-_Juin_2009_-_edit.2.jpg. **License**: *CC BY-SA: Attribution-ShareAlike*
- Inca Expansion. **Provided by**: Wikipedia. **Located at**: http://en.wikipedia.org/wiki/Inca_Empire%23mediaviewer/File:Inca-expansion.png. **License**: *Public Domain: No Known Copyright*
- Tupa-inca-tunic.png. **Provided by**: Wikipedia. **Located at**: https://en.wikipedia.org/wiki/Inca_society#/media/File:Tupa-inca-tunic.png. **License**: *CC BY-SA: Attribution-ShareAlike*
- Inca Quipu. **Provided by**: Wikipedia. **Located at**: https://en.wikipedia.org/wiki/Quipu#/media/File:Inca_Quipu.jpg. **License**: *CC BY-SA: Attribution-ShareAlike*
- Chasqui3.jpeg. **Provided by**: Wikipedia. **Located at**: https://en.wikipedia.org/wiki/Chasqui#/media/File:Chasqui3.JPG. **License**: *CC BY-SA: Attribution-ShareAlike*
- Inca_Empire_South_America.png. **Provided by**: Wikipedia. **Located at**: https://en.wikipedia.org/wiki/Government_of_the_Inca_Empire#/media/File:Inca_Empire_South_America.png. **License**: *CC BY-SA: Attribution-ShareAlike*
- Artificial cranial deformation. **Provided by**: Wikipedia. **Located at**: https://en.wikipedia.org/wiki/Artificial_cranial_deformation#/media/File:D%C3%A9formation_P%C3%A9ruvienne_MHNT_Noir.jpg. **License**: *CC BY-SA: Attribution-ShareAlike*
- Inti_Raymi.jpg. **Provided by**: Wikimedia. **Located at**: https://commons.wikimedia.org/wiki/File:Inti_Raymi.jpg. **License**: *CC BY-SA: Attribution-ShareAlike*
- 2000px-Sol_de_Mayo-Bandera_de_Argentina.png. **Provided by**: Wikipedia. **Located at**: https://en.wikipedia.org/wiki/Inti#/media/File:Sol_de_Mayo-Bandera_de_Argentina.svg. **License**: *CC BY-SA: Attribution-ShareAlike*
- Inca Civil War. **Provided by**: Wikipedia. **Located at**: https://en.wikipedia.org/wiki/Inca_Civil_War#/media/File:Ataw_Wallpa_portrait.jpg. **License**: *CC BY: Attribution*
- Spanish Conquest of the Inca. **Provided by**: Wikipedia. **Located at**: https://en.wikipedia.org/wiki/Spanish_conquest_of_the_Inca_Empire#/media/File:Tupaq_amarup_umanta_kuchunku.gif. **License**: *CC BY-SA: Attribution-ShareAlike*
- Spanish conquest of the Inca Empire. **Provided by**: Wikipedia. **Located at**: https://en.wikipedia.org/wiki/Spanish_conquest_of_the_Inca_Empire#/media/File:Inca-Spanish_confrontation.JPG. **License**: *CC BY-SA: Attribution-ShareAlike*

Early Civilizations of Mexico and Mesoamerica

The Olmec

The Olmec were the first major civilization in Mexico, lasting from approximately 1500—400 BCE.

Learning Objectives

Give an account of the society, trade, art, and religion of the Olmec

Key Takeaways

Key Points

- The Olmec lived in south-central Mexico, with their center in La Venta in Tabasco.
- Little is known about Olmec religion, though scholars believe there were eight main deities.
- People lived in small agricultural villages outside of urban centers, which were mainly for ceremonial use.
- The decline of the Olmec population from 400—350 BCE may have been due to environmental changes.

Key Terms

- **La Venta**: The main city of the Olmec civilization.
- **Mesoamerican ballgame**: An ancient ritual sport that involved keeping a rubber ball in

> play in designated courts. It most likely originated in the Olmec culture.
>
> - **Olmec colossal heads**: Basalt sculptures of human faces wearing large helmeted headdresses that stand up to 3.4 meters high. These sculptures most likely represent important rulers.

The Olmec were the first major civilization in Mexico. They lived in the tropical lowlands of south-central Mexico, in the present-day states of Veracruz and Tabasco, and had their center in the city of La Venta.

The Olmec flourished during Mesoamerica's formative period, dating roughly from as early as 1500 BCE to about 400 BCE. Pre-Olmec cultures had flourished in the area since about 2500 BCE, but by 1600–1500 BCE, Early Olmec culture had emerged. They were the first Mesoamerican civilization and laid many of the foundations for the civilizations that followed, such as the Maya. Judging from the available archeological evidence it is likely that they originated the Mesoamerican ballgame and possible that they practiced ritual bloodletting.

The Gulf of Mexico's lowlands are generally considered the birthplace of the Olmec culture, and remained the heartland of this civilization during its existence. This area is characterized by swampy lowlands punctuated by low hills, ridges, and volcanoes. The Tuxtlas Mountains rise sharply in the north, along the Gulf of Mexico's Bay of Campeche. Here the Olmec constructed permanent city-temple complexes at San Lorenzo Tenochtitlán, La Venta, Tres Zapotes, and Laguna de los Cerros. San Lorenzo remained the Olmec capital up until about 900 BCE, when the central city became La Venta, which remained functional until the demise of the Olmec around 400 BCE. Possible river or weather changes caused this movement to occur.

Trade and Village Life

There are no written records of Olmec commerce, beliefs, or customs, but from the archeological evidence it appears they were not economically confined. In fact, Olmec artifacts have been found across Mesoamerica, indicating that there were extensive interregional trade routes. The Olmec period saw a significant increase in the length of trade routes, the variety of goods, and the sources of traded items.

Trading helped the Olmec build their urban centers of San Lorenzo and La Venta. However, these cities were used predominantly for ceremonial purposes and elite activity; most people lived in small villages. Individual homes had a lean-to and a storage pit nearby. They also likely had gardens, in which the Olmec would grow medicinal herbs and small crops, like sunflowers.

The Great Pyramid in La Venta, Tabasco: *Remains of the last capital of the Olmec society, La Venta, include this religious site where elites most likely performed rituals.*

Most agriculture took place outside of the villages in fields cleared using slash-and-burn techniques. The Olmec likely grew crops such as:

- Maize
- Beans
- Squash
- Manioc
- Sweet potatoes
- Cotton

Religion

Unfortunately, there is no surviving direct account of Olmec beliefs, but their notable artwork provide clues about their life and religion.

Olmec king: *Surviving art, like this relief of a king or chief found in La Venta, help provide clues about how Olmec society functioned.*

There were eight different androgynous Olmec deities, each with its own distinct characteristics. For example, the Bird Monster was depicted as a harpy eagle associated with rulership. The Olmec Dragon was shown with flame eyebrows, a bulbous nose, and bifurcated tongue. These gods were believed to provide the rulers a mandate to lead. Deities often represented a natural element and included:

- The Maize deity
- The Rain Spirit or Were-Jaguar
- The Fish or Shark Monster

Religious activities regarding these deities probably included the elite rulers, shamans, and possibly a priest class making offerings at religious sites in La Venta and San Lorenzo.

Art

The Olmec culture was defined and unified by a specific art style, and this continues to be the hallmark of the culture. Wrought in a large number of media—jade, clay, basalt, and greenstone, among others—much Olmec art, such as The Wrestler, is surprisingly naturalistic. Other art expresses fantastic anthropomorphic creatures, often highly stylized, using an iconography reflective of a religious meaning. Common motifs include downturned mouths and a cleft head, both of which are seen in representations of were-jaguars and the rain deity.

Olmec hollow baby figurine: *Realistic ceramic objects, such as this portrayal of an infant, illustrate the highly skilled artistic style of the Olmec culture.*

Olmec Colossal Heads

The most striking art left behind by this culture are the Olmec colossal heads. Seventeen monumental stone representations of human heads sculpted from large basalt boulders have been unearthed in the region to date. The heads date from at least before 900 BCE and are a distinctive feature of the Olmec civilization. All portray mature men with fleshy cheeks, flat noses, and slightly crossed eyes. However, none of the heads are alike, and each boasts a unique headdress, which suggests they represent specific individuals.

The boulders were brought from the Sierra de los Tuxtlas mountains of Veracruz. Given that the extremely large slabs of stone used in their production were transported over large distances, requiring a great deal of human effort and resources, it is thought that the monuments represent portraits of powerful individual Olmec rulers. The heads were variously arranged in lines or groups at major Olmec centers, but the method and logistics used to transport the stone to these sites remain uncertain.

The discovery of a colossal head at Tres Zapotes in the 19th century spurred the first archaeological investigations of Olmec culture by Matthew Stirling in 1938. Most colossal heads were sculpted from spherical boulders, but two from San Lorenzo Tenochtitlán were re-carved from massive stone thrones. An additional monument, at Takalik Abaj in Guatemala, is a throne that may have been carved from a colossal head. This is the only known example from outside the Olmec heartland.

Olmec head: This sculpture is typical of the colossal heads of the Olmec.

The End of the Olmecs

The Olmec population declined sharply between 400 and 350 BCE, though it is unclear why. Archaeologists speculate that the depopulation was caused by environmental changes, specifically riverine environment changes. These changes may have been triggered by the silting up of rivers due to agricultural practices.

Another theory for the considerable population drop relates to tectonic upheavals or subsidence, as suggested by Santley and colleagues who propose relocation of settlements due to volcanism, instead of extinction. Volcanic eruptions during the Early, Late, and Terminal Formative periods would have blanketed the lands and forced the Olmec to move their settlements.

The Mixtec

The Mixtec are a group who lived in modern-day Mexico before the Spanish conquest. People still identify as Mixtec today.

> ### Learning Objectives
>
> Distinguish between the Mixtec people and the Mixtec language and identify when they were most prominent

> ### Key Takeaways
>
> *Key Points*
>
> - The Mixtec survive today, but reached peak prominence in the 11th century CE.
> - The Mixtec language is a set of up to fifty languages, and is not to be confused with the Mixtec people.
> - The Mixtec are well known in the anthropological world for their codices, or phonetic pictures in which they wrote their history and genealogies.
>
> *Key Terms*
>
> - **Mixtec**: Indigenous Mesoamerican peoples inhabiting the region known as La Mixteca, which covers parts of the Mexican states of Oaxaca, Guerrero, and Puebla.
> - **Codices**: Phonetic pictures painted on deerskin and folded into books, which recorded Mixtec history and genealogy.
> - **Tututepec**: A prominent city center during the height of the Mixtec state, situated along the coast of modern-day Oaxaca.

The Mixtec are indigenous Mesoamerican peoples inhabiting the region known as La Mixteca, which covers parts of the Mexican states of Oaxaca, Guerrero, and Puebla. Though the Mixtec remain today, they were most prominent in the 11th century and the following years, until they were conquered by the Spanish and their allies in the 16th century.

Before the arrival of Spanish hostility, a number of Mixtecan city-states competed with each other and with the Zapotec kingdoms. The major Mixtec polity was Tututepec, which rose to prominence in the 11th century under the leadership of Eight Deer Jaguar Claw. This prominent leader was the only Mixtec king to ever unite the highland and lowland polities into a single Mixtec state. During this era there were approximately 1.5 million Mixtecs populating this varied region.

Modern Mixtec People

Today there are approximately 800,000 Mixtec people in Mexico, and there are also large populations in the United States. In recent years a large exodus of indigenous peoples from Oaxaca, such as the Zapotec and Triqui, have emerged as one of the most numerous groups of Amerindians in the United States. As of 2011, an estimated 150,000 Mixtec people were living in California, and 25,000 to 30,000 were living in New York City. Large Mixtec communities exist in the border cities of Tijuana; Baja California; San Diego, California; and Tucson, Arizona. Mixtec communities are generally described as trans-national or trans-border because of their ability to maintain and reaffirm social ties between their native homelands and diasporic communities.

Mixtec Language

The word "Mixtec" is often used to refer not to the group of people of Mixtec ancestry, but to the family of languages that have developed alongside the group. There is no longer one single Mixtec language; some estimate that there are fifty distinct languages in the Mixtec family, including Cuicatec and Triqui.

Mixtec's area: The historical geographic area inhabited by the Mixtec, including the important polities, such as Tututepec.

Mixtec History

Important ancient centers of the Mixtec include the ancient capital of Tilantongo, as well as the sites of Achiutla, Cuilapan, and Yucuñudahui. The Mixtec also erected major constructions at the ancient city of Monte Albán, which had originated as a Zapotec city before the Mixtec gained control of it.

The west side platform at Monte Albán: *This ancient city remained a religious site for centuries, and was more sparsely populated during the rise of smaller Mixtec polities. However, religious sites were often reused by Mixtec elites.*

At the height of the Aztec Empire (between 1428 and 1521 CE) many Mixtec polities were forced to pay tribute. However, many Mixtec polities remained completely independent of the threatening empire, even as it expanded outward. The smaller Mixtec polities also put up resistance to Spanish forces led by Pedro de Alvarado until the invaders gained control of the region and destroyed any attempt at a revolt in 1521. Disease, weaponry, and local political fractures likely aided the Spanish takeover of the area.

Mixtex Art

The work of Mixtec artisans who produced work in stone, wood, and metal were well regarded throughout ancient Mesoamerica. Mixtec artists were known for their exceptional mastery of jewelry, in which gold and turquoise figured prominently. The intricate metalwork of Mixtec goldsmiths formed an important part of the tribute the Mixtecs had to pay to the Aztecs during parts of their history.

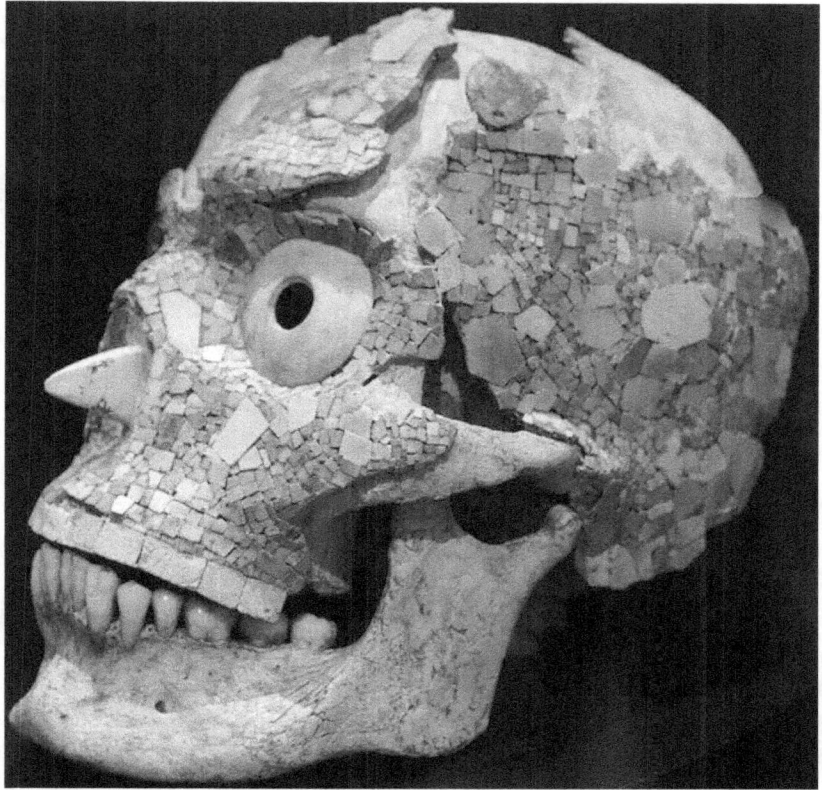

Mixtec funerary mask: *Mixtec art included the use of turquoise, gold, and carved stones, and exemplified artistry before the arrival of the Spanish.*

Codices

The Mixtec are well known in the anthropological world for their codices, or phonetic pictures, in which they wrote their history and genealogies in deerskin in the "fold-book" form. The best-known story of the Mixtec codices is that of Lord Eight Deer, named after the day on which he was born, whose personal name was Jaguar Claw, and whose epic history is related in several codices. He successfully conquered and united most of the Mixteca region.

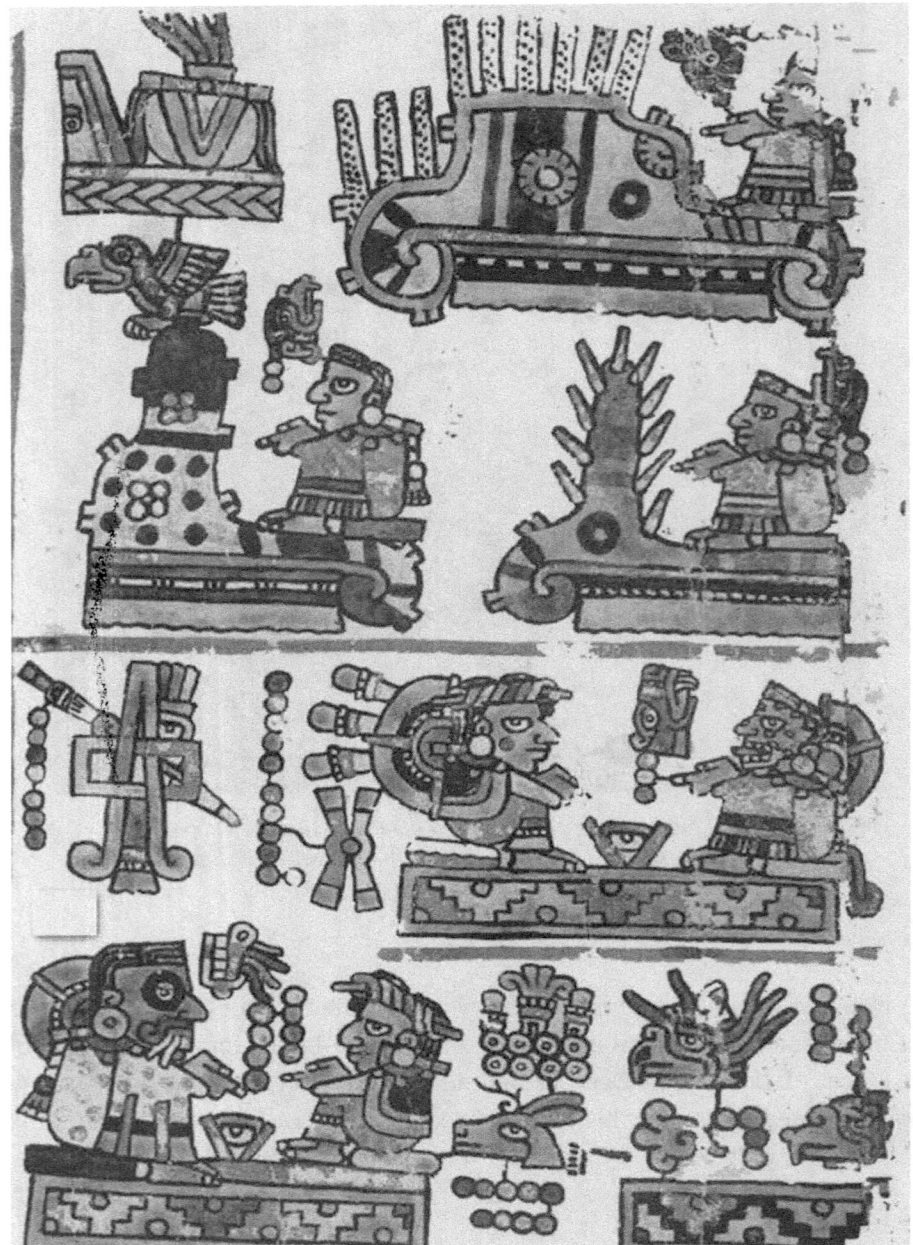

A page from the Codex Bodley: *This codex tells the story of the Tilantongo and Tiaxiaco dynasties.*

Codices can be read from right to left and often measure many feet long. The Codex Bodley measures twenty-two feet long and contains complex explanations of important family lineages and creation stories, such as the War of Heaven, that directly refer back to elite dynasties. The preservation of these extremely rare Codices paints a distinct picture of Mesoamerica right before the arrival of Spanish forces.

Teotihuacan

Teotihuacan was a city founded outside of modern Mexico City in 100 BCE and was known for its pyramids.

Learning Objectives

Discuss the diversity and notable archeological features of Teotihuacan

Key Takeaways

Key Points

- Teotihuacan was founded around 100 BCE and reached its peak population around 450 CE.
- Teotihuacan was a multi-ethnic city, with distinct quarters occupied by Otomi, Zapotec, Mixtec, Maya and Nahua peoples.
- The geographical layout of Teotihuacan is a good example of the Mesoamerican tradition of planning cities, settlements, and buildings as a reflections of their view of the Universe.

Key Terms

- **The Great Goddess**: This deity was one of the central icons of Teotihuacano religious culture. She appears in painted murals with images associated with the underworld, birth, death, and creation.
- **Teotihuacan**: A large precolumbian Mesoamerican city known for its archeological significance.
- **Pyramid of the Sun**: The largest building in Teotihuacan, which measures 246 feet high and 736 feet wide.

Just 30 miles from modern day Mexico City lies the precolumbian Mesoamerican city of Teotihuacan. It is famous for its pyramids and series of accompanying residential compounds, but was once much more than an archaeological and tourist site.

Archaeological evidence suggests that Teotihuacan was a multi-ethnic city, with distinct quarters occupied by Otomi, Totonac, Zapotec, Mixtec, Maya, and Nahua peoples. In 2001, Terrence Kaufman presented linguistic evidence suggesting that an important ethnic group in Teotihuacan was of Totonacan or Mixe–Zoquean linguistic affiliation. Other scholars maintain that the largest population group must have been of Otomi ethnicity, because the Otomi language is known to have been spoken in the area around Teotihuacan both before and after the classic period and not during the middle period.

Although it is a subject of debate whether Teotihuacan was the center of a state empire, its influence throughout Mesoamerica is well documented; evidence of Teotihuacano presence can be seen at numerous sites in Veracruz and the Maya region. Many Maya murals represent Teotihucuan and the leaders of the city during its zenith. The Aztecs were also heavily influenced by the architecture, culture, and lore of this ancient city, claiming common ancestry with the Teotihuacanos and adopting some of their artistic and architectural styles.

Founding of the City

The city and culture, which can be referred to as Teotihuacan or Teotihuacano, is thought to have been established around 100 BCE, with major monuments continuously under construction until about 250 CE. It began as a new religious center in the Mexican Highland and a large population was drawn to the city over a few centuries. It may have lasted until sometime between the 7th and 8th centuries CE, but its major monuments were sacked and systematically burned around 550 CE. At its zenith, around the first half of the first millennium CE, Teotihuacan was the largest city in the pre-Columbian Americas, with a population estimated at 125,000 or more. It's varied population made it, at minimum, the sixth largest city in the world during its epoch. The city eventually included multi-floor apartment compounds built to accommodate this large population.

Mysterious Founders and Religion

The founders of this religious and populous city remain a mystery to scholars of the area. Some have speculated that the Xitle volcano, which is located southwest of modern-day Mexico City, may have prompted a mass emigration out of the central valley and into the Teotihuacan valley. These displaced settlers may have founded, or at least helped grow, the city.

An alternate explanation is that the Totonac people, who still remain today, founded Teotihuacan. There is also evidence that at least some of the people living in Teotihuacan immigrated from those areas influenced by the Teotihuacano civilization, including the Zapotec, Mixtec, and Maya peoples.

Mural of the Great Goddess of Teotihuacan: *This powerful goddess was associated with darkness, mystery, death, and creation. She was often depicted with owls, jaguars, and spiders, all creatures of the earth, darkness and the underworld. This mural is from the Tetitla compound at Teotihuacan.*

As a religious center, Teotihuacan displayed its most prominent gods and goddesses in murals and architecture. The Great Goddess of Teotihuacan appears to be the most prominent of these deities, and she likely represented the underworld, war, creation, water, and the earth. Evidence of human sacrifices to honor the completion of buildings or special times of year has also been uncovered by archeologists. Captives from wars were decapitated, had their hearts removed, were bludgeoned, or were buried alive to commemorate these momentous occasions.

Pyramid of the Sun: *This giant pyramid dwarfs the smaller platforms surrounding it and was the largest building at Teotihuacan.*

Layout

The city's broad central avenue, called "Avenue of the Dead" (a translation from its Nahuatl name Miccoatli), is flanked by impressive ceremonial architecture, including the immense Pyramid of the Sun (third largest in the World after the Great Pyramid of Cholula and the Great Pyramid of Giza) and the Pyramid of the Moon. Along the Avenue of the Dead are many smaller talud-tablero platforms. The Aztecs believed they were tombs, inspiring the Nahuatl name of the avenue.

Pyramid of the Moon: *This pyramid is the second largest in Teotihuacan.*

Further down the Avenue of the Dead is the area known as the Citadel, containing the ruined Temple of the Feathered Serpent. This area was a large plaza surrounded by temples that formed the religious and political center of the city. Most of the common people lived in large apartment buildings spread across the city. Many of the buildings contained workshops where artisans produced pottery and other goods.

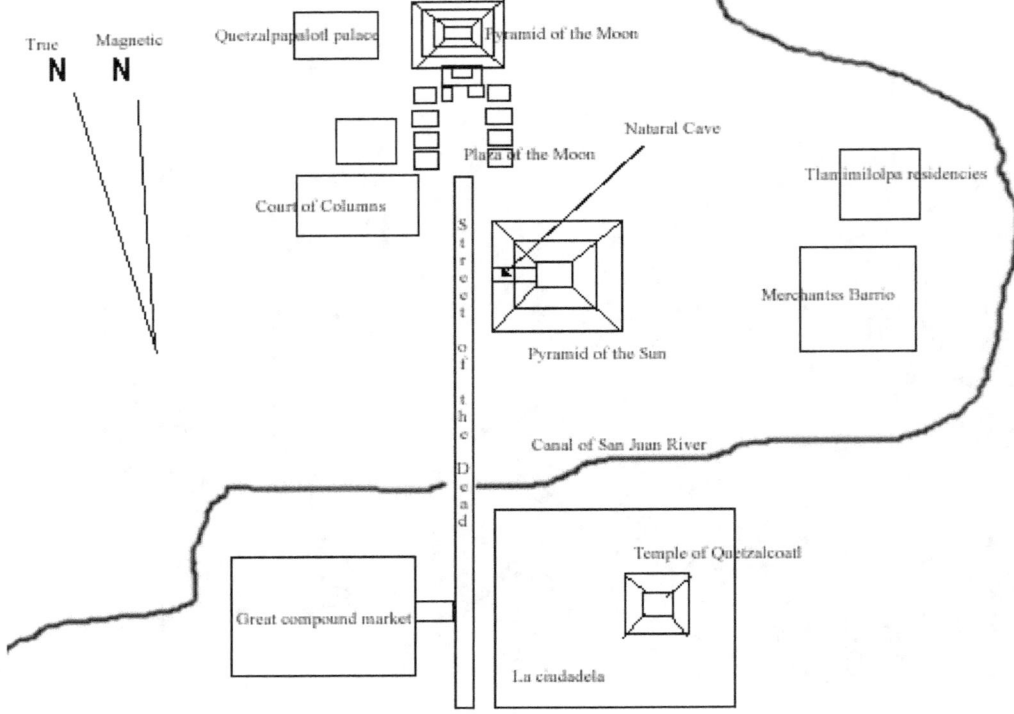

Teotihuacan City Plan: *The layout of Teotihuacan exemplifies Mesoamerican urban planning*

The geographical layout of Teotihuacan is a good example of the Mesoamerican tradition of planning cities, settlements, and buildings as a reflection of the Universe. Its urban grid is aligned to precisely 15.5° east of North. One theory says this is due to the fact that the sun rose at that same angle during the same summer day each year. Settlers used the alignment to calibrate their sense of time or as a marker for planting crops or performing certain rituals. Another theory is that there are numerous ancient sites in Mesoamerica that seem to be oriented with the tallest mountain in their given area. This appears to be the case at Teotihuacan, although the mountain to which it is oriented is not visible from within the Teotihuacan complex due to a closer mountain ridge. Pecked-cross circles throughout the city and in the surrounding regions indicate how the people managed to maintain the urban grid over long distances. It also enabled them to orient the Pyramids to the distant mountain that was out of sight.

Fall of Teotihuacan

There is an ongoing debate about why Teotihuacan collapsed and the population abandoned this city center. Evidence of climate changes, which caused severe droughts around 535 CE, suggest there was a general population decline in the region. In fact, archeological digs have revealed juvenile skeletons with signs of malnutrition, which probably forced populations to move and caused internal social strife. Further archeological evidence reveals that only the buildings associated with the elites along the Avenue of the Dead were sacked and burned. This type of activity suggests there might have been internal unrest and possibly a revolt against the elite power structure, which caused the collapse of the city.

The Zapotec

The Zapotec civilization developed in modern-day Mexico and lasted from approximately the 6th century BCE to the 16th century CE.

Learning Objectives

Explain the culture, religion, expansion, and demise of the Zapotec civilization

Key Takeaways

Key Points

- The Zapotec civilization originated in the three Central Valleys of Oaxaca in the late 6th Century BCE.
- There are five distinct Zapotec periods, denoted Monte Albán 1–5 (after the place of origin).
- The Zapotec were polytheists who developed a calendar and logosyllabic writing system.

Key Terms

- **Mitla**: The main religious city of the Zapotec culture. Elaborate buildings and artwork display the richness of religious life for the Zapotec elite.
- **Monte Alban**: The place of origin for the Zapotec civilization.
- **Cocijo**: The lightning and rain god of the Zapotec civilization. He was the most important of the religious figures and was believed to have created the universe with his breath.

The Zapotec civilization originated in the three Central Valleys of Oaxaca in the late 6th Century BCE. The valleys were divided between three different-sized societies, separated by no-man's-land in the middle, today occupied by the city of Oaxaca. Archaeological evidence from the period, such as burned temples and sacrificed captives, suggests that although the three societies shared linguistic, cultural, and religious traditions, they also competed against one another.

Panorama from Monte Albán: *The view from the site of origin of the Zapotec rulers that expanded power beyond the Central Valleys of Oaxaca.*

Five Phases

The Zapotec state formed at Monte Albán. This consolidation of power began outward political expansion during the late Monte Albán 1 phase (400–100 BCE) and throughout the Monte Albán 2 phase (100 BCE–200 CE). Zapotec rulers from Monte Albán seized control of provinces outside the valley of Oaxaca with their superior military and political clout, which quickly overtook less-developed local entities. By 200 CE, the end of the Monte Albán 2 phase, the Zapotecs had extended their influence, from Quiotepec in the North to Ocelotepec and Chiltepec in the South. The religious and cultural city of Monte Albán had become the largest city in what are today the southern Mexican highlands. This powerful city retained this status until approximately 700 CE.

Phase	Period
Monte Alban 1	ca 400–100 BC
Monte Alban 2	ca 100 BC – AD 100
Monte Alban 3	ca AD 200-900
Monte Alban 4	ca 900–1350
Monte Alban 5	ca 1350–1521

Monte Albán phases: *Historical Monte Albán phases and the duration of each phase.*

Expansion and Decline

Between Monte Albán phases 1 and 2 there was a considerable expansion of the population of the Valley of Oaxaca. As the population grew, so did the degree of social differentiation, the centralization of political power, and ceremonial activity. Another effect of this population boom and the political expansion of the military during Monte Albán 1–2 was the development of fragmented, independent states. These areas developed regional centers of power with distinct leaders and linguistic dialects. However, the Zapotec rulers retained control over vast swaths of the region. Some archeologists argue that the building centered on the main plaza of Monte Albán contains depictions of elaborate heads, which represent the rulers of conquered provinces.

Jade warrior mask from Monte Albán: *This jade replica illustrates the fierce military presence that initially expanded the Zapotec holdings during Monte Albán phase 2.*

The Zapotecs were ultimately destroyed by Spanish invaders. Having lost militarily to the Aztecs in battles from 1497–1502, the Zapotecs tried to avoid confrontation with the Spaniards, and hopefully the tragic fate of the Aztecs. The Spaniards took advantage of this pacifist stance and ultimately defeated the Zapotecs after five years of campaigns ending in 1527. The arrival of new diseases and steel weapons also weakened any attempts at a revolt from the Zapotec population. There were some subsequent uprisings against the new rulers, but for all intents and purposes, the Zapotecs were conquered. However, the seven Zapotec languages, and hundreds of Zapotec dialects, still survive with populations that have spread throughout Mexico and also Los Angeles, California.

Zapotec Writing and Religion

The Zapotecs developed a calendar and a logosyllabic system of writing that used a separate glyph to represent each of the syllables of the language. This writing system is thought to be one of the first writing systems of Mesoamerica and a predecessor of those developed by the Maya, Mixtec, and Aztec civilizations.

Like most Mesoamerican religious systems, the Zapotec religion was polytheistic. Two principal deities included Cocijo, the rain god (similar to the Aztec god Tlaloc), and Coquihani, the god of light. These deities, along with many others, centered around concepts of fertility and agriculture. It is likely that the Zapotec practiced human sacrifices to these gods of fertility, and also played elaborate and ritualistic ball games in the court at Monte Albán. They also practiced dedication rituals, which cleansed a new space. Fine pieces of rare jade, pearl, and obsidian were found in a cache in Oaxaca, and were probably used to cleanse religious sites or temples upon the completion of construction.

The ball court at Monte Albán: *A religious ball game utilizing a rubber ball was practiced throughout Mesoamerica by young men playing for sacred, and often sacrificial, purposes.*

According to historic, as well as contemporary, Zapotec legends, their ancestors emerged from the earth or from caves, or turned into people from trees or jaguars. Their governing elite apparently believed that they descended from supernatural beings that lived among the clouds, and that upon death they would return to the same status. In fact, the name by which Zapotecs are known today results from this belief. The Zapotecs of the Central Valleys call themselves "Be'ena' Za'a"—the Cloud People.

A funerary urn in the shape of a "bat god" or a jaguar: c. 300–650 CE. Height: 9.5 in (23 cm).

Mitla

Evidence of the central role of religion in the Zapotec cultural hierarchy is pronounced at the religious city of Mitla. It is the second most important archeological site in the state of Oaxaca, and the most important of the Zapotec culture. The site is located 44 kilometers from the city of Oaxaca. While Monte Albán was most important as the political center, Mitla was the main religious center, as evidenced by the elaborate buildings and artwork throughout the city. The name "Mitla" is derived from the Nahuatl name "Mictlán," which was the place of the dead or underworld. Its Zapotec name is Lyobaa, which means "place of rest." The name "Mictlán" was Hispanicized to "Mitla" by the Spanish.

Fretwork on a building in the religious capital of Mitla: *This complex fretwork illustrates the religious importance of this ancient city in the Zapotec culture.*

What makes Mitla unique among Mesoamerican sites is the elaborate and intricate mosaic fretwork and geometric designs that cover tombs, panels, friezes, and even entire walls. These mosaics are made with small, finely cut and polished stone pieces, which have been fitted together without the use of mortar. No other site in Mexico has this.

Attributions

CC licensed content, Specific attribution

- Mesoamerican ballgame. **Provided by**: Wikipedia. **Located at**: https://en.wikipedia.org/wiki/Mesoamerican_ballgame. **License**: *CC BY-SA: Attribution-ShareAlike*
- Bloodletting in Mesoamerica. **Provided by**: Wikipedia. **Located at**: https://en.wikipedia.org/wiki/Bloodletting_in_Mesoamerica. **License**: *CC BY-SA: Attribution-ShareAlike*
- Olmec Religion. **Provided by**: Wikipedia. **Located at**: http://en.wikipedia.org/wiki/Olmec_religion. **License**: *CC BY-SA: Attribution-ShareAlike*
- Olmec. **Provided by**: Wikipedia. **Located at**: http://en.wikipedia.org/wiki/Olmec. **License**: *CC BY-SA: Attribution-ShareAlike*
- Olmec. **Provided by**: Wikipedia. **Located at**: https://en.wikipedia.org/wiki/Olmec#/media/File:Olmec_baby-face_figurine,_Snite.jpg. **License**: *CC BY-SA: Attribution-ShareAlike*
- Olmec. **Provided by**: Wikipedia. **Located at**: https://en.wikipedia.org/wiki/Olmec#/media/File:La_Venta_Pir%C3%A1mide_cara_sur.jpg. **License**: *CC BY-SA: Attribution-ShareAlike*
- Olmec King. **Provided by**: Wikipedia. **Located at**: http://en.wikipedia.org/wiki/File:Olmec_King.jpg. **License**: *Public Domain: No Known Copyright*

- Olmec colossal Heads. **Provided by**: Wikipedia. **Located at**: http://en.wikipedia.org/wiki/Olmec_colossal_heads%23mediaviewer/File:Mexico.Tab.OlmecHead.01.jpg. **License**: *CC BY-SA: Attribution-ShareAlike*
- Monte Alban. **Provided by**: Wikipedia. **Located at**: https://en.wikipedia.org/wiki/Monte_Alb%C3%A1n. **License**: *CC BY-SA: Attribution-ShareAlike*
- Codex Bodley. **Provided by**: Wikipedia. **Located at**: https://en.wikipedia.org/wiki/Codex_Bodley. **License**: *CC BY-SA: Attribution-ShareAlike*
- Pedro de Alvarado. **Provided by**: Wikipedia. **Located at**: https://en.wikipedia.org/wiki/Pedro_de_Alvarado. **License**: *CC BY-SA: Attribution-ShareAlike*
- Mixtec Language. **Provided by**: Wikipedia. **Located at**: http://en.wikipedia.org/wiki/Mixtec_language. **License**: *CC BY-SA: Attribution-ShareAlike*
- Mixtec People. **Provided by**: Wikipedia. **Located at**: http://en.wikipedia.org/wiki/Mixtec_people. **License**: *CC BY-SA: Attribution-ShareAlike*
- Mixtec. **Provided by**: Wiktionary. **Located at**: http://en.wiktionary.org/wiki/Mixtec. **License**: *CC BY-SA: Attribution-ShareAlike*
- Olmec. **Provided by**: Wikipedia. **Located at**: https://en.wikipedia.org/wiki/Olmec#/media/File:Olmec_baby-face_figurine,_Snite.jpg. **License**: *CC BY-SA: Attribution-ShareAlike*
- Olmec. **Provided by**: Wikipedia. **Located at**: https://en.wikipedia.org/wiki/Olmec#/media/File:La_Venta_Pir%C3%A1mide_cara_sur.jpg. **License**: *CC BY-SA: Attribution-ShareAlike*
- Olmec King. **Provided by**: Wikipedia. **Located at**: http://en.wikipedia.org/wiki/File:Olmec_King.jpg. **License**: *Public Domain: No Known Copyright*
- Olmec colossal Heads. **Provided by**: Wikipedia. **Located at**: http://en.wikipedia.org/wiki/Olmec_colossal_heads%23mediaviewer/File:Mexico.Tab.OlmecHead.01.jpg. **License**: *CC BY-SA: Attribution-ShareAlike*
- Mixtecs. **Provided by**: Wikimedia. **Located at**: https://commons.wikimedia.org/wiki/File:Mixtecs.png. **License**: *Public Domain: No Known Copyright*
- Monte Alban. **Provided by**: Wikipedia. **Located at**: https://en.wikipedia.org/wiki/Monte_Alb%C3%A1n#/media/File:Monte_Alban_West_Side_Platform.jpg. **License**: *CC BY-SA: Attribution-ShareAlike*
- Mixtec funerary mask Grave No.n7 Monte Alban Museo de las Culturas de Oaxaca anagoria. **Provided by**: Wikimedia Commons. **Located at**: http://commons.wikimedia.org/wiki/File:2013-13-27_Mixtec_funerary_mask_Grave_No._7_Monte_Alban_Museo_de_las_Culturas_de_Oaxaca_anagoria.JPG. **License**: *CC BY: Attribution*
- Codex Bodley. **Provided by**: Wikipedia. **Located at**: https://en.wikipedia.org/wiki/Codex_Bodley#/media/File Codex_Bodley,_page_21.jpg. **License**: *CC BY-SA: Attribution-ShareAlike*
- Pyramid of the Moon. **Provided by**: Wikipedia. **Located at**: https://en.wikipedia.org/wiki/Pyramid_of_the_Moon. **License**: *CC BY-SA: Attribution-ShareAlike*
- Pyramid of the Sun. **Provided by**: Wikipedia. **Located at**: https://en.wikipedia.org/wiki/Pyramid_of_the_Sun. **License**: *CC BY-SA: Attribution-ShareAlike*
- The Great Goddess of Teotihuacan. **Provided by**: Wikipedia. **Located at**: https://en.wikipedia.org/wiki/Great_Goddess_of_Teotihuacan. **License**: *CC BY-SA: Attribution-ShareAlike*
- Otomi. **Provided by**: Wikipedia. **Located at**: https://en.wikipedia.org/wiki/Otomi_people. **License**: *CC BY-SA: Attribution-ShareAlike*
- Teotihuacan. **Provided by**: Wikipedia. **Located at**: http://en.wikipedia.org/wiki/Teotihuacan. **License**: *CC BY-SA: Attribution-ShareAlike*
- Totonac People. **Provided by**: Wikipedia. **Located at**: http://en.wikipedia.org/wiki/Totonac. **License**: *CC BY-SA: Attribution-ShareAlike*
- Teotihuacan. **Provided by**: Wikipedia. **Located at**: http://en.wikipedia.org/wiki/Teotihuacan. **License**: *CC BY-SA: Attribution-ShareAlike*
- Teotihuacan. **Provided by**: Wiktionary. **Located at**: http://en.wiktionary.org/wiki/Teotihuacan. **License**: *CC BY-SA: Attribution-ShareAlike*
- Olmec. **Provided by**: Wikipedia. **Located at**: https://en.wikipedia.org/wiki/Olmec#/media/File:Olmec_baby-face_figurine,_Snite.jpg. **License**: *CC BY-SA: Attribution-ShareAlike*
- Olmec. **Provided by**: Wikipedia. **Located at**: https://en.wikipedia.org/wiki/Olmec#/media/File:La_Venta_Pir%C3%A1mide_cara_sur.jpg. **License**: *CC BY-SA: Attribution-ShareAlike*
- Olmec King. **Provided by**: Wikipedia. **Located at**: http://en.wikipedia.org/wiki/File:Olmec_King.jpg. **License**: *Public Domain: No Known Copyright*

- Olmec colossal Heads. **Provided by**: Wikipedia. **Located at**: http://en.wikipedia.org/wiki/Olmec_colossal_heads%23mediaviewer/File:Mexico.Tab.OlmecHead.01.jpg. **License**: *CC BY-SA: Attribution-ShareAlike*

- Mixtecs. **Provided by**: Wikimedia. **Located at**: https://commons.wikimedia.org/wiki/File:Mixtecs.png. **License**: *Public Domain: No Known Copyright*

- Monte Alban. **Provided by**: Wikipedia. **Located at**: https://en.wikipedia.org/wiki/Monte_Alb%C3%A1n#/media/File:Monte_Alban_West_Side_Platform.jpg. **License**: *CC BY-SA: Attribution-ShareAlike*

- Mixtec funerary mask Grave No.n7 Monte Alban Museo de las Culturas de Oaxaca anagoria. **Provided by**: Wikimedia Commons. **Located at**: http://commons.wikimedia.org/wiki/File:2013-13-27_Mixtec_funerary_mask_Grave_No._7_Monte_Alban_Museo_de_las_Culturas_de_Oaxaca_anagoria.JPG. **License**: *CC BY: Attribution*

- Codex Bodley. **Provided by**: Wikipedia. **Located at**: https://en.wikipedia.org/wiki/Codex_Bodley#/media/File:Codex_Bodley,_page_21.jpg. **License**: *CC BY-SA: Attribution-ShareAlike*

- Pyramid of the Moon. **Provided by**: Wikipedia. **Located at**: https://en.wikipedia.org/wiki/Pyramid_of_the_Moon#/media/File:Piramide_de_la_Luna_072006.jpg. **License**: *CC BY-SA: Attribution-ShareAlike*

- Great Goddess of Teotihuacan. **Provided by**: Wikipedia. **Located at**: https://en.wikipedia.org/wiki/Great_Goddess_of_Teotihuacan#/media/File:Tetitla_Teotihuacan_Great_Goddess_mural_(Abracapocus).jpg. **License**: *CC BY-SA: Attribution-ShareAlike*

- Piru00e1mide del Sol, Teotihuacu00e1n. **Provided by**: Wikimedia Commons. **Located at**: http://commons.wikimedia.org/wiki/File:Pir%C3%A1mide_del_Sol,_Teotihuac%C3%A1n,_M%C3%A9xico.JPG. **License**: *CC BY-SA: Attribution-ShareAlike*

- Teotihuacan City Plan. **Provided by**: Wikipedia. **Located at**: http://en.wikipedia.org/wiki/File:Teotihuacancityplan.png. **License**: *CC BY-SA: Attribution-ShareAlike*

- Zapotec Civilization. **Provided by**: Wikipedia. **Located at**: http://en.wikipedia.org/wiki/Zapotec_civilization. **License**: *CC BY-SA: Attribution-ShareAlike*

- Cocijo. **Provided by**: Wikipedia. **Located at**: https://en.wikipedia.org/wiki/Cocijo. **License**: *CC BY-SA: Attribution-ShareAlike*

- Monte Alban. **Provided by**: Wikipedia. **Located at**: https://en.wikipedia.org/wiki/Monte_Alb%C3%A1n. **License**: *CC BY-SA: Attribution-ShareAlike*

- Spanish Conquest of the Aztec Empire. **Provided by**: Wikipedia. **Located at**: https://en.wikipedia.org/wiki/Spanish_conquest_of_the_Aztec_Empire. **License**: *CC BY-SA: Attribution-ShareAlike*

- Mitla. **Provided by**: Wikipedia. **Located at**: https://en.wikipedia.org/wiki/Mitla. **License**: *CC BY-SA: Attribution-ShareAlike*

- Olmec. **Provided by**: Wikipedia. **Located at**: https://en.wikipedia.org/wiki/Olmec#/media/File:Olmec_baby-face-figurine,_Snite.jpg. **License**: *CC BY-SA: Attribution-ShareAlike*

- Olmec. **Provided by**: Wikipedia. **Located at**: https://en.wikipedia.org/wiki/Olmec#/media/File:La_Venta_Pir%C3%A1mide_cara_sur.jpg. **License**: *CC BY-SA: Attribution-ShareAlike*

- Olmec King. **Provided by**: Wikipedia. **Located at**: http://en.wikipedia.org/wiki/File:Olmec_King.jpg. **License**: *Public Domain: No Known Copyright*

- Olmec colossal Heads. **Provided by**: Wikipedia. **Located at**: http://en.wikipedia.org/wiki/Olmec_colossal_heads%23mediaviewer/File:Mexico.Tab.OlmecHead.01.jpg. **License**: *CC BY-SA: Attribution-ShareAlike*

- Mixtecs. **Provided by**: Wikimedia. **Located at**: https://commons.wikimedia.org/wiki/File:Mixtecs.png. **License**: *Public Domain: No Known Copyright*

- Monte Alban. **Provided by**: Wikipedia. **Located at**: https://en.wikipedia.org/wiki/Monte_Alb%C3%A1n#/media/File:Monte_Alban_West_Side_Platform.jpg. **License**: *CC BY-SA: Attribution-ShareAlike*

- Mixtec funerary mask Grave No.n7 Monte Alban Museo de las Culturas de Oaxaca anagoria. **Provided by**: Wikimedia Commons. **Located at**: http://commons.wikimedia.org/wiki/File:2013-13-27_Mixtec_funerary_mask_Grave_No._7_Monte_Alban_Museo_de_las_Culturas_de_Oaxaca_anagoria.JPG. **License**: *CC BY: Attribution*

- Codex Bodley. **Provided by**: Wikipedia. **Located at**: https://en.wikipedia.org/wiki/Codex_Bodley#/media/File:Codex_Bodley,_page_21.jpg. **License**: *CC BY-SA: Attribution-ShareAlike*

- Pyramid of the Moon. **Provided by**: Wikipedia. **Located at**: https://en.wikipedia.org/wiki/Pyramid_of_the_Moon#/media/File:Piramide_de_la_Luna_072006.jpg. **License**: *CC BY-SA: Attribution-ShareAlike*

- Great Goddess of Teotihuacan. **Provided by**: Wikipedia. **Located at**: https://en.wikipedia.org/wiki/Great_Goddess_of_Teotihuacan#/media/File:Tetitla_Teotihuacan_Great_Goddess_mural_(Abracapocus).jpg. **License**: *CC BY-SA: Attribution-ShareAlike*

- Piru00e1mide del Sol, Teotihuacu00e1n. **Provided by**: Wikimedia Commons. **Located at**: http://commons.wikimedia.org/wiki/File:Pir%C3%A1mide_del_Sol,_Teotihuac%C3%A1n,_M%C3%A9xico.JPG. **License**: *CC BY-SA: Attribution-ShareAlike*

- Teotihuacan City Plan. **Provided by**: Wikipedia. **Located at**: http://en.wikipedia.org/wiki/File:Teotihuacancityplan.png. **License**: *CC BY-SA: Attribution-ShareAlike*

- Archaeological phases of Monte Albu00e1n history. **Provided by**: Wikipedia. **Located at:** http://en.wikipedia.org/wiki/Zapotec_civilization. **License:** *CC BY-SA: Attribution-ShareAlike*
- Monte alban panorama from northern platform. **Provided by**: Wikimedia. **Located at:** https://commons.wikimedia.org/wiki/File:Monte_alban_panorama_from_northern_platform.jpg. **License:** *Public Domain: No Known Copyright*
- Monte Alban. **Provided by**: Wikimedia. **Located at:** https://commons.wikimedia.org/wiki/File:Monte_Alb%C3%A1n-12-05oaxaca024.jpg. **License:** *CC BY: Attribution*
- Zapotec Civilization. **Provided by**: Wikimedia. **Located at:** https://commons.wikimedia.org/wiki/File:Funerary_Urn_from_Oaxaca.jpg. **License:** *CC BY-SA: Attribution-ShareAlike*
- Mitla. **Provided by**: Wikimedia. **Located at:** https://commons.wikimedia.org/wiki/File:12-05oaxaca077.jpg. **License:** *CC BY-SA: Attribution-ShareAlike*
- Zapotec civilization. **Provided by**: Wikimedia. **Located at:** https://commons.wikimedia.org/wiki/File:MonteAlbanMaskMusJadeSanCri.JPG. **License:** *Public Domain: No Known Copyright*

The Maya

The Preclassic Period of the Maya

The Preclassic period lasted from 2000 BCE to 250 CE and saw the emergence of many distinctive elements of Mayan civilization.

Learning Objectives

Describe life in the Preclassic period

Key Takeaways

Key Points

- The Preclassic period itself is further divided into four periods: Early Preclassic, Middle Preclassic, Late Preclassic, and Terminal Preclassic.
- The Early Preclassic period (2000–1000 BCE) was when the Maya transitioned into an agrarian society.
- In the Middle Preclassic period (1000–400 BCE), the Mayans built more established cities and expanded through war.
- Two powerful states emerged in the Late Preclassic period (400 BCE–100 CE).
- The Mayan civilization collapsed and left the major Preclassic capitals behind at the end of the Terminal Preclassic period (100–250 CE) for unknown reasons.

Key Terms

- **kakaw**: An Olmec word for the cacao plant. This word was borrowed and incorporated into the Mayan language, illustrating the relationship between these two cultures.

- **Southern Maya Area**: The geographic region in which Mayan civilization first emerged.
- **Kaminaljuyu**: The ruling city-state of the Middle Preclassic era. Evidence of stone monuments and complex canals illustrate the power this early capital retained for centuries.

The Preclassic period is the first of three periods in Mayan history, coming before the Classic and Postclassic periods. It extended from the emergence of the first settlements sometime between 2000 and 1500 BCE until 250 CE. The Preclassic period saw the rise of large-scale ceremonial architecture, writing, cities, and states. Many of the distinctive elements of Mesoamerican civilization can be traced back to this period, including the dominance of corn, the building of pyramids, human sacrifice, jaguar worship, the complex calendar, and many of the gods.

Mayan language speakers most likely originated in the Chiapas-Guatamalan Highlands and dispersed from there. By around 2500–2000 BCE researchers can begin to trace the arc of Mayan-language settlements and culture in what is now southeastern Mexico, Guatemala, and Belize. The Preclassic period itself is divided into four periods: Early Preclassic, Middle Preclassic, Late Preclassic, and Terminal Preclassic

Agricultural Shift – Early Preclassic (2000 BCE–1000 BCE)

Though the exact starting date of Mayan civilization is unclear, there were Mayan language speakers in the Southern Maya Area by 2000 BCE. It appears that around this time the Maya people began to transition from a hunter-gatherer lifestyle to a culture based around agricultural villages. The process appears to have been a gradual one. Analysis of bones from early Maya grave sites indicates that, although maize had already become a major component of the diet by this time, fish, meat from game animals, and other hunted or gathered foods still made up a major component of the diet. Along with the gradual development of agriculture, basic forms of pottery began to appear, with simple designs and some slipped vessels.

Around this time, the Olmec culture began to emerge in nearby Tabasco, granting the early Maya an important trading partner and beginning a period of prolonged contact that would have profound effects on Maya society and artistic production.

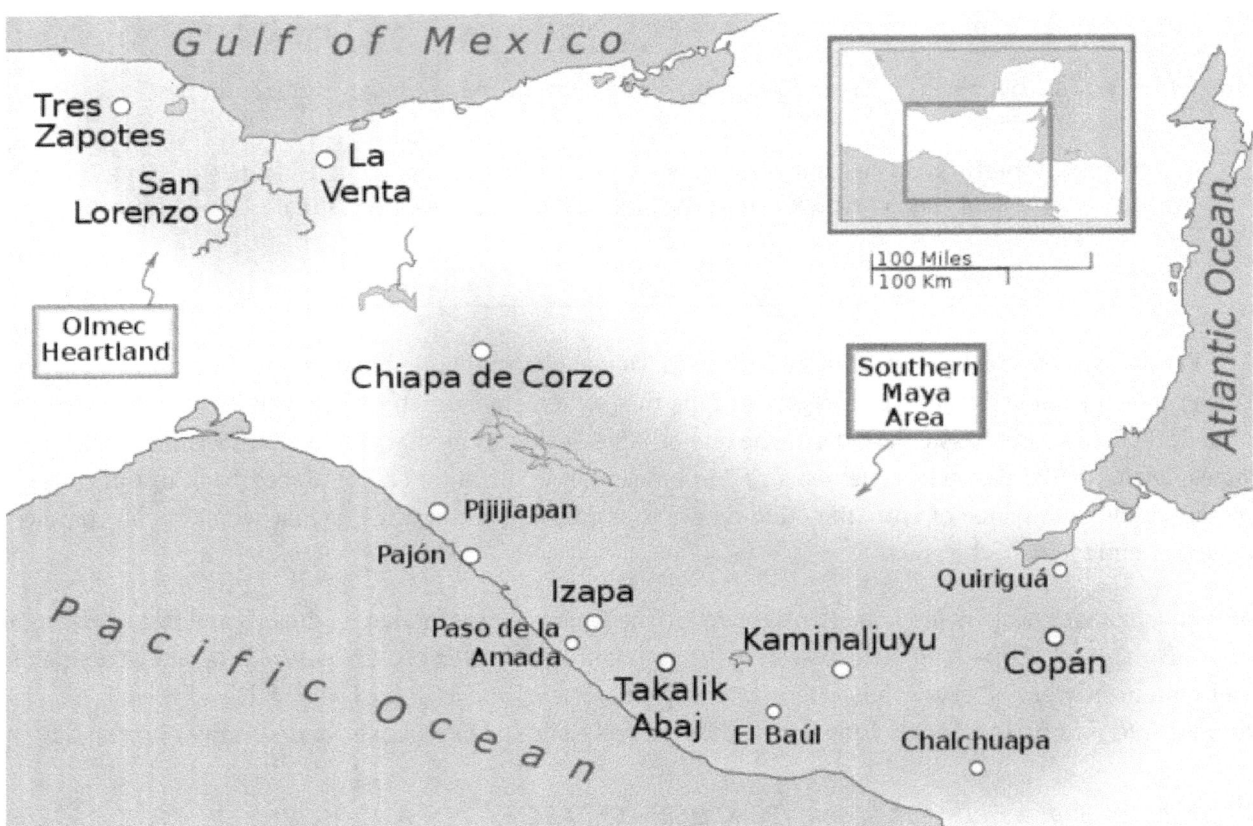

Southern Maya Area: *By 2000 BCE, there were speakers of Mayan languages in the Southern Maya Area.*

Complex Cities – Middle Preclassic (1000 BCE–400 BCE)

By around the year 1000 BCE, centuries of agricultural village life had begun to form the beginnings of a complex society, with an elite class, entrenched religious practices, and a military presence. Other developments of this era include the following:

- Prestige goods, such as obsidian mirrors and jade mosaics, began to appear, increasing the demand for more extensive trade with other language groups, including the Olmecs.

- Canals and irrigation schemes demanding coordinated human effort began to appear with increasing complexity and scale.

- Villages began to include central plazas and earthen mounds, occasionally enhanced by masonry. For instance, the site of La Blanca featured a central mound more than seventy-five feet tall. It contained a masonry fragment strongly resembling a head in the distinctive Olmec style. These plazas also suggest a developing religious and hierarchical social structure.

- Carved stone stele also began to appear during this period, adorned with portraits of rulers but still devoid of writing.

- Warfare appears to have intensified during this period, as evidenced by advanced weaponry, rulers beginning to be portrayed as warriors, and the appearance of mass graves and decapitated skeletons.

Beginning around 900 BCE, the Pacific coastal region fell under the dominance of the La Blanca statelet, which collapsed around 600 BCE, to be replaced by a polity centered around the El Ujuxte site. Another early statelet was probably based at the site of Chalchuapa, a town with extensive earthen mounds arranged around several plazas. However, it was likely ruled by the first true Mayan city-state, Kaminaljuyu.

Excavation site at Kaminaljuyu: *Complex temples, stairways, and friezes illustrate the acme of this Preclassic city's power and influence.*

Lying within modern-day Guatemala City on the shores of Lake Miraflores, Kaminaljuyu developed a powerful government structure that organized massive irrigation campaigns and built numerous intricately carved stone monuments to its rulers. These monuments clearly depict war captives and often show the rulers holding weapons. These images indicate the Kaminaljuyu polity engaged in active warfare and dominated the Guatemalan highlands for centuries.

Nakbe Palace: *The ruins of a Middle Preclassic palace at Nakbe.*

During this period, the Olmec culture reached its zenith, centered around the capital of La Venta in modern-day Tabasco near the early Maya centers. Speakers of a Mixe–Zoquean language, the Olmec are generally recognized as the first true civilization in the Americas. Their capital city of La Venta contains extensive earthworks and stone monuments, including several of the distinctive Olmec stone heads. The Olmec share several features with later Maya culture, including extensive jaguar worship, a diet dominated by maize, and the use of the cacao plant. Several words entered Mayan from a Mixe–Zoquean language, presumably due to Olmec influence. These words include the words "ajaw," meaning "lord," and "kakaw," which has become the English words "cacao" and "chocolate." Most of these borrowings relate to prestige concepts and high culture, indicating that the Middle Preclassic Maya were deeply impressed and influenced by their northwestern neighbors.

Art and Language – Late Preclassic (400 BCE–100 CE)

Some of the earliest remaining examples of the complex writing system of the Maya appear from the 3rd century BCE. The glyph-based system represents complex concepts and often reflects the religious beliefs of the Maya, including jaguar worship, elites practicing blood letting rituals, and offerings to deities. The Maya also developed the concept of the number zero during this era. The appearance of an explicit number zero in their written records might be the first example of it worldwide. The appearance of this number also helped Mayan architects and priests make exact calculations of the stars and buildings for religious and social purposes.

The Late Preclassic also saw the rise of two powerful states that rival later Classic Mayan city-states for scale and monumental architecture—Kaminaljuyu in the highlands and El Mirador in the lowlands. Both cities display the continued refinement in stonework, artistic friezes, and architecture during this era.

City Collapse – Terminal Preclassic (100 CE–250 CE)

The Late or Terminal Preclassic murals found in San Bartolo reflect the profound relationship between the Olmec and Maya civilizations over hundreds of years, due to the striking artistic similarities. These murals also provide a window into the Terminal Preclassic sacrificial and inauguration rituals, such as bloodletting, that were practiced around 100 BCE. Elites were expected to perform these painful rituals in reverence to powerful deities.

Painted mural at San Bartolo from around 100 BCE:
This colorful mural depicts a king practicing bloodletting, probably for an inauguration or other sacrificial purpose.

The collapse of the Preclassic Maya civilization remains a mystery, and little is known as to why the major cities were abandoned around 250 CE. However, there were actually two collapses, one at the end of the Preclassic and a more famous one at the end of the Classic. The Preclassic collapse refers to the systematic decline and abandoning of the major Preclassic cities, such as Kaminaljuyu and El Mirador around 100 CE. In fact, the Maya remained an essential part of the region. A number of theories have been proposed, but there is as little consensus as there is for the causes of the more famous collapse between the Classic and Postclassic periods.

The Classic Period of the Maya

The Classic period lasted from 250 to 900 CE and was the peak of the Maya civilization.

Learning Objectives

Describe life, religion, and architecture in the Classic period

Key Takeaways

Key Points

- The Maya developed an agriculturally intensive, city-centered civilization consisting of numerous independent city-states of varying power and influence.
- The Maya civilization participated in long-distance trade with many other Mesoamerican cultures and established trade routes between city-states.
- The Maya used complex calendars to calculate religious, solar, and lunar cycles.
- The cause of the collapse of the Maya civilization is unknown.

Key Terms

- **stelae**: Carved stones depicting rulers with heirogliphic texts describing their accomplishments.
- **Copán**: An important city that boasted some of the most complex architecture from the Classic period of Maya history.
- **Tzolkin**: This 365-day solar calendar utilized the movement of Earth around the Sun to calculate the year.

The Classic period lasted from 250 to 900 CE. It saw a peak in large-scale construction and urbanism, the recording of monumental inscriptions, and significant intellectual and artistic development, particularly in the southern lowland regions. During this period the Maya population numbered in the millions, with many cities containing 50,000 to 120,00o people. The Maya developed an agriculturally intensive, city-centered civilization consisting of numerous independent city-states of varying power and influence. They created a multitude of kingdoms and small empires, built monumental palaces and temples, engaged in highly developed ceremonies, and developed an elaborate hieroglyphic writing system.

The political, economic, and culturally dominant "core" Maya units of the Classic Maya world system were located in the central lowlands, while the corresponding peripheral Maya units were found along the margins of the southern highland and northern lowland areas. The semi-peripheral (mediational) units generally took the form of trade and commercial centers. But as in all world systems, the Maya core centers shifted through time, starting out during Preclassic times in the southern highlands, moving to the central lowlands during the Classic period, and finally shifting to the northern peninsula during the Postclassic period.

Monuments

The most notable monuments are the stepped pyramids the Maya built in their religious centers and the accompanying palaces of their rulers. The palace at Cancuén is the largest in the Maya area, but the site has no pyramids. On the other hand, cities like Tikal and Copán illustrate the wealth of architectural accomplishments during these prolific centuries. Copán came to its full power between the 6th and 8th centuries, and included massive temples and carvings that illustrate the full power of its ruling, and often merciless, emperors.

Tikal Temple: *Classic period temple from Tikal, Guatemala.*

The cities of Palenque and Yaxchilan were also cultural and religious centers in the southeastern Maya region, and included large temples, ball courts, and even a uniquely vaulted ceiling in the hallway of the Palenque Palace.

The Palenque Palace and aqueduct: *Cities like Palenque boasted some of the most refined architectural works in the Classic period of Maya culture.*

Other important archaeological remains include the carved stone slabs usually called stelae (the Maya called them tetun, or "tree-stones"), which depict rulers along with hieroglyphic texts describing their genealogy, military victories, and other accomplishments.

Maya mask: *Stucco frieze from Placeres, Campeche. Early Classic period (c. 250–600 CE).*

Trade

The political relationship between Classic Maya city-states has been likened to the relationships between city-states in Classical Greece and Renaissance Italy. Some cities were linked to each other by straight limestone causeways, known as sacbeob. Whether the exact function of these roads was commercial, political, or religious has not been determined.

The Maya civilization participated in long distance trade with many other Mesoamerican cultures, including Teotihuacan, the Zapotec, and other groups in central and gulf-coast Mexico. In addition, they traded with more distant, non-Mesoamerican groups, such as the Taínos of the Caribbean islands. Archeologists have also found gold from Panama in the Sacred Cenote of Chichen Itza. Important trade goods included:

- Cacao
- Salt
- Seashells
- Jade
- Obsidian

Calendars and Religion

The Maya utilized complex mathematical and astronomical calculations to build their monuments and conceptualize the cosmography of their religion. Each of the four directions represented specific deities, colors, and elements. The underworld, the cosmos, and the great tree of life at the center of the world all played their part in how buildings were built and when feasts or sacrifices were practiced. Ancestors and deities helped weave the various levels of existence together through ritual, sacrifice, and measured solar years.

The Maya developed a mathematical system that is strikingly similar to the Olmec traditions. The Maya also linked this complex system to the deity Itzamna. This deity was believed to have brought much of Maya culture to Earth. A 260-day calendar (Tzolkin) was combined with the 365-day solar calendar (Haab') to create a calendar round. This calendar round would take fifty-two solar years to return to the original first date. The Tzolkin calendar was used to calculate exact religious festival days. It utilized twenty named days that repeated thirteen times in that calendar year. The solar calendar (Haab') is very similar to the modern solar calendar year that uses Earth's orbit around the Sun to measure time. The Maya believed there were five chaotic days at the end of the solar year that allowed the portals between worlds to open up, known as Wayeb'.

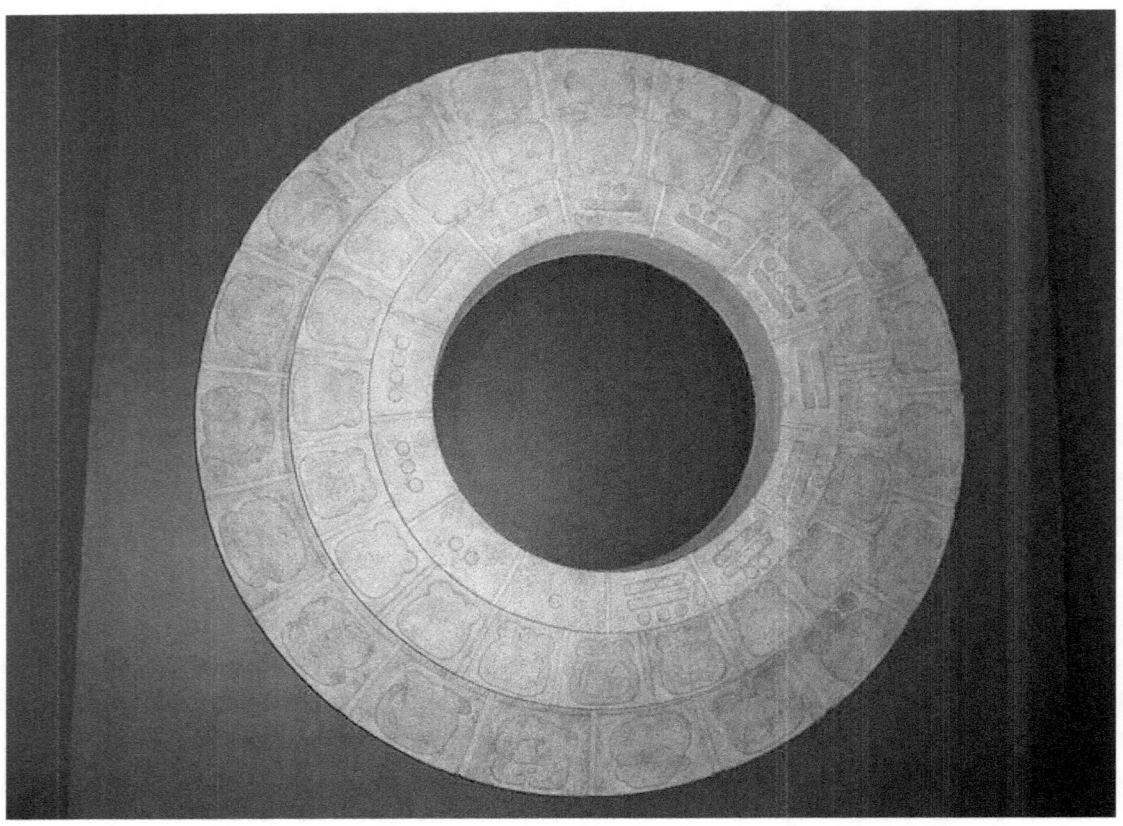

*A **Classic period Maya calendar:** Each symbol represents a specific day within the calendar. When the Tzolkin and Haab' calendar's are combined they create a fifty-two-year solar calendar.*

These calendars were recorded utilizing specific symbols for each day in the two central cycles. Calendrical stones were employed to carefully follow the movement of the solar and religious years. Although less commonly used, the Maya also employed a long count calendar that calculated dates hundreds of years in the future. They also inscribed a lengthier 819-day calendar on many religious temples throughout the region that most likely coincided with important religious days.

Decline

The Classic Maya Collapse refers to the decline of the Maya Classic Period and abandonment of the Classic Period Maya cities of the southern Maya lowlands of Mesoamerica between the 8th and 9th centuries. This should not be confused with the collapse of the Preclassic Maya in the 2nd century CE. The Classic Period of Mesoamerican chronology is generally defined as the period from 300 to 900 CE, the last 100 years of which, from 800 to 900 CE, are frequently referred to as the Terminal Classic.

It has been hypothesized that the decline of the Maya is related to the collapse of their intricate trade systems, especially those connected to the central Mexican city of Teotihuacán. Before there was a greater knowledge of the chronology of Mesoamerica, Teotihuacan was believed to have fallen during 700–750 CE, forcing the "restructuring of economic relations throughout highland Mesoamerica and the Gulf Coast." This remaking of relationships between civilizations would have then given the collapse of the Classic Maya a slightly later date. However, it is now believed that the strongest Teotihuacan influence was during the 4th and 5th centuries. In addition, the civilization of Teotihuacan started to lose its power, and maybe even abandoned the city, during 600–650 CE. The Maya civilizations are now thought to have lived on, and also prospered, perhaps for another century after the fall of Teotihuacano influence.

The Classic Maya Collapse is one of the biggest mysteries in archaeology. The classic Maya urban centers of the southern lowlands, among them Palenque, Copán, Tikal, Calakmul, and many others, went into decline during the 8th and 9th centuries and were abandoned shortly thereafter. Some 88 different theories, or variations of theories, attempting to explain the Classic Maya Collapse have been identified. From climate change, to deforestation, to lack of action by Maya kings, there is no universally accepted collapse theory, although drought is gaining momentum as the leading explanation.

The Decline of the Maya

The period after the second collapse of the Maya Empire (900 CE–1600 CE) is called the Postclassic period.

Learning Objectives

Explain what happened to the structure of the Maya Empire in the Postclassic period

Key Takeaways

Key Points

- The Maya cities of the northern lowlands in Yucatán continued to flourish.
- The center of power shifted to the northern peninsula.
- The Postclassic period was a time of technological advancement in areas of architecture, engineering, and weaponry.
- The Spanish conquest of the Maya began in the 16th century, but lasted close to 150 years.

- Mayan languages, agricultural practices, and familial cultures still exist in parts of Chiapas and Guatemala.

Key Terms

- **Mayapan**: The cultural capital of the Maya culture during the Postclassic period. It was at its height between 1220 and 1440 CE.
- **Yucatán**: A geographic area in the south of modern day Mexico near Belize.
- **Codex**: A book containing religious and cultural information written in the Mayan script. Only three of these books remain in the world.

The period after the second collapse of the Maya Empire (900 CE–1600 CE) is called the Postclassic period. The center of power shifted from the central lowlands to the northern peninsula as populations most likely searched for reliable water resources, along with greater social stability.

The Maya cities of the northern lowlands in Yucatán continued to flourish; some of the important sites in this era were Chichén Itzá, Uxmal, Edzná, and Coba. A typical Classic Maya polity was a small hierarchical state (called an *ajawil, ajawlel,* or *ajawlil*) headed by a hereditary ruler known as an *ajaw* (later *k'uhul ajaw*). However, the Postclassic period generally saw the widespread abandonment of once-thriving sites as populations gathered closer to water sources. Warfare most likely caused populations in long-inhabited religious cities, like Kuminaljuyu, to be abandoned in favor of smaller, hilltop settlements that had a better advantage against warring factions.

El Castillo (pyramid of Kukulcán) in Chichén Itzá: *Built by the pre-Columbian Maya civilization sometime between the 9th and 12th centuries CE, El Castillo served as a temple to the god Kukulkan, the Yucatec Maya Feathered Serpent deity closely related to the god Quetzalcoatl known to the Aztecs and other central Mexican cultures of the Postclassic period.*

Postclassic Cities

Maya cities during this era were dispersed settlements, often centered around the temples or palaces of a ruling dynasty or elite in that particular area. Cities remained the locales of administrative duties and royal religious practices, and the sites where luxury items were created and consumed. City centers also provided the sacred space for privileged nobles to approach the holy ruler and the places where aesthetic values of the high culture were formulated and disseminated and where aesthetic items were consumed. These more established cities were the self-proclaimed centers of social, moral, and cosmic order.

If a royal court fell out of favor with the people, as in the well-documented cases of Piedras Negras or Copan, this fall from power would cause the inevitable "death" and abandonment of the associated settlement. After the decline of the ruling dynasties of Chichén Itzá and Uxmal, Mayapan became the most important cultural site until about 1450 CE. This city's name may be the source of the word "Maya," which had a more geographically restricted meaning in Yucatec and colonial Spanish. The name only grew to its current meaning in the 19th and 20th centuries. The area degenerated into competing city-states until the Spanish arrived in the Yucatán and shifted the power dynamics.

Certain smaller Maya groups, such as the Itza Maya, Ko'woj, and Yalain of Central Peten, survived the collapse in the Postclassic period in small numbers. By around 1250 CE these groups had reconstituted themselves to form competing city-states. The Itza maintained their capital at Tayasal (also known as Noh Petén), an archaeological site thought to underlay the modern city of Flores, Guatemala, on Lake Petén Itzá. The Ko'woj had their capital at Zacpeten. Though less visible during this era, Postclassic Maya states also continued to survive in the southern highlands.

Artistry, Architecture, and Religion

The Postclassic period is often viewed as a period of cultural decline. However, it was a time of technological advancement in areas of architecture, engineering, and weaponry. Metallurgy came into use for jewelry and the development of some tools utilizing new metal alloys and metalworking techniques that developed within a few centuries. And although some of the classic cities had been abandoned after 900 CE, architecture continued to develop and thrive in newly flourishing city-states, such as Mayapan. Religious and royal architecture retained themes of death, rebirth, natural resources, and the afterlife in their motifs and designs. Ballcourts, walkways, waterways, pyramids, and temples from the Classic period continued to play essential roles in the hierarchical world of Maya city-states.

A religious building at Mayapan along the northern Yucatán Peninsula: Curved walls, complex carvings, and layered platforms illustrate the continued prevalence of architecture in Maya culture and religion during the Postclassic period.

Maya religion continued to be centered around the worship of male ancestors. These patrilineal intermediaries could vouch for mortals in the physical world from their position in the afterlife. Archeological evidence shows that deceased relatives were buried under the floor of family homes. Royal dynasties built pyramids in order to bury their ancestors. This patrilineal form of worship was used by some royal dynasties in order to justify their right to rule. The afterlife was complex, and included thirteen levels in heaven and nine levels in the underworld, which had to be navigated by an initiated priesthood, ancestors, and powerful deities.

Precise food preparation, offerings, and astronomical predictions were all required for religious practices. Powerful deities that often represented natural elements, such as jaguars, rain, and hummingbirds, needed to be placated with offerings and prayers regularly. Many of the motifs on large pyramids and temples of the royal dynasties reflect the worship of both deities and patrilineal ancestors and provide a window into the daily practices of this culture before the arrival of Spanish forces.

The Colonial Period

Shortly after their first expeditions to the region in the 16th century, the Spanish attempted to subjugate the Maya polities several times. The Maya leaders and people were understandably hostile towards the Spanish crown, and utilized bows and arrows, spears, and padded armor in defense of their city-states. The Spanish campaign, sometimes termed "The Spanish Conquest of Yucatán," would prove to be a lengthy and dangerous exercise for the invaders from the outset, and it would take some 170 years and tens of thousands of Indian auxiliaries before the Spanish established substantive control over all Maya lands.

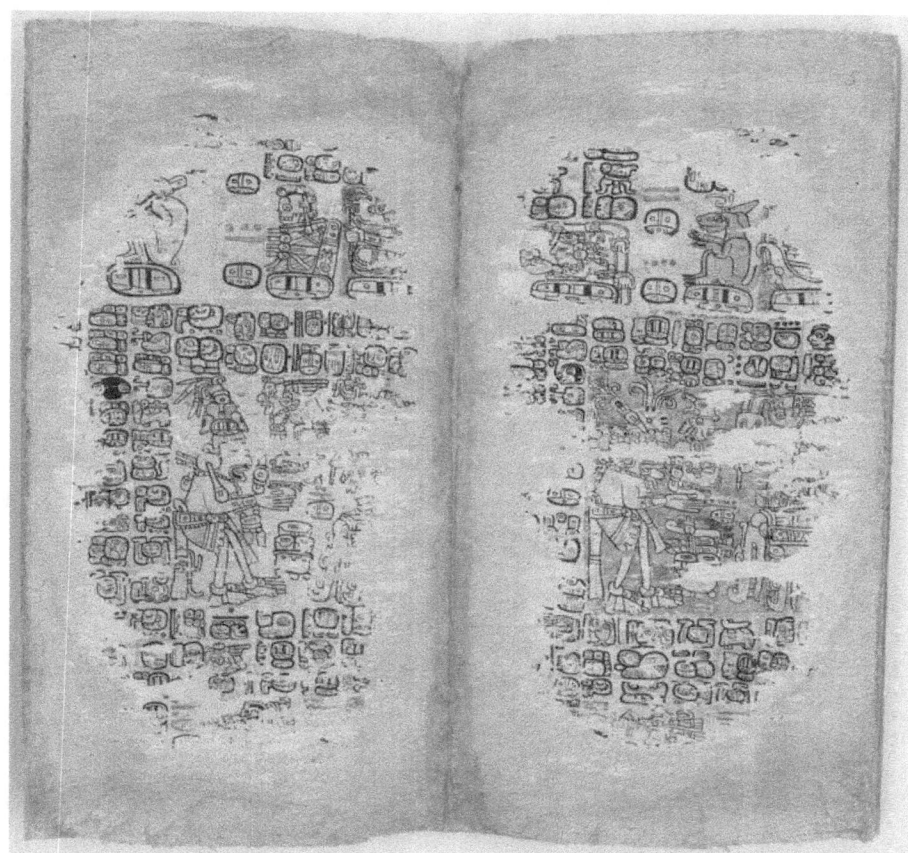

Pages from the Paris Codex: *One of three surviving examples of Mayan writing, the Paris Codex offers keen insights into religious and patrilineal traditions before the Spanish invasion.*

Unlike the Aztec and Inca Empires, there was no single Maya political center during the Postclassic period that, once overthrown, would hasten the end of collective resistance from the indigenous peoples. Instead, Spanish forces needed to subdue the numerous independent Maya polities almost one by one, many of which kept up a fierce resistance. Myths of gold and precious metals motivated many Spanish forces to capture and dominate the Maya lands. However, the Yucatán does not offer rich mining opportunities, and some areas were difficult to navigate because of the dense jungle environment.

As the battle over control of the region waged on, the Spanish church and government officials destroyed the vast majority of Maya texts and, with them, a large swath of knowledge about Maya writing and language. Fortunately, three of the pre-Columbian books dated to the Postclassic period survived the Spanish invasion and destruction of Maya culture. These are known as the Madrid Codex, the Dresden Codex, and the Paris Codex. The last Maya states (and the last indigenous holdouts from Spanish control in the Americas)—the Itza polity of Tayasal and the Ko'woj city of Zacpeten—remained independent of the Spanish until late in the 17th century. They were finally subdued by the Spanish in 1697 after many casualties.

Maya Today

Although Spanish weaponry, administration, and practices became much more dominant throughout Mesoamerica by the 17th century and onward, the Maya people persisted, along with many of their essential traditions. Today, in remote parts of Guatemala and Chiapas, similar familial configurations, uses of the 260-day Maya calendar, and agricultural practices continue to shape families of descendants. Millions of Mayan-language speakers inhabit their ancestral lands and keep these languages and traditions alive.

Attributions

CC licensed content, Specific attribution

- Mayan Civilization. **Provided by**: Ridgeaphistory. **Located at**: https://ridgeaphistory.wikispaces.com/Mayan+Civilization. **License**: *CC BY-SA: Attribution-ShareAlike*
- Southern Maya Area. **Provided by**: Wikipedia. **Located at**: https://en.wikipedia.org/wiki/Southern_Maya_area. **License**: *CC BY-SA: Attribution-ShareAlike*
- Olmec heartlad. **Provided by**: Wikipedia. **Located at**: https://en.wikipedia.org/wiki/Olmec_heartland. **License**: *CC BY-SA: Attribution-ShareAlike*
- Kaminaljuyu. **Provided by**: Wikipedia. **Located at**: https://en.wikipedia.org/wiki/Kaminaljuyu. **License**: *CC BY-SA: Attribution-ShareAlike*
- San Bartolo (Maya Site). **Provided by**: Wikipedia. **Located at**: https://en.wikipedia.org/wiki/San_Bartolo_(Maya_site). **License**: *CC BY-SA: Attribution-ShareAlike*
- Mesoamerica Chronology. **Provided by**: Wikipedia. **Located at**: http://en.wikipedia.org/wiki/Mesoamerican_chronology. **License**: *CC BY-SA: Attribution-ShareAlike*
- Preclassic Maya. **Provided by**: Wikipedia. **Located at**: http://en.wikipedia.org/wiki/Preclassic_Maya. **License**: *CC BY-SA: Attribution-ShareAlike*
- Kaminaljuyu. **Provided by**: Wikimedia. **Located at**: https://commons.wikimedia.org/wiki/File:Kaminaljuyu_2.jpg. **License**: *CC BY-SA: Attribution-ShareAlike*
- San Bartolo. **Provided by**: Wikimedia. **Located at**: https://commons.wikimedia.org/wiki/File:SBmural.jpg. **License**: *Public Domain: No Known Copyright*
- Nakbe. **Provided by**: Wikimedia. **Located at**: https://en.wikipedia.org/wiki/File:Nakbe_str.JPG. **License**: *CC BY-SA: Attribution-ShareAlike*
- Larger Southern Maya Area. **Provided by**: Wikimedia. **Located at**: https://commons.wikimedia.org/wiki/File:Larger_Southern_Maya_area_v3.svg. **License**: *Public Domain: No Known Copyright*
- Palenque. **Provided by**: Wikipedia. **Located at**: https://en.wikipedia.org/wiki/Palenque. **License**: *CC BY-SA: Attribution-ShareAlike*
- Itzamna. **Provided by**: Wikipedia. **Located at**: https://en.wikipedia.org/wiki/Itzamna. **License**: *CC BY-SA: Attribution-ShareAlike*
- Maya Calendar. **Provided by**: Wikipedia. **Located at**: https://en.wikipedia.org/wiki/Maya_calendar. **License**: *CC BY-SA: Attribution-ShareAlike*
- Copan. **Provided by**: Wikipedia. **Located at**: https://en.wikipedia.org/wiki/Cop%C3%A1n. **License**: *CC BY-SA: Attribution-ShareAlike*
- Maya Religion. **Provided by**: Wikipedia. **Located at**: https://en.wikipedia.org/wiki/Maya_religion. **License**: *CC BY-SA: Attribution-ShareAlike*
- Maya Civilization. **Provided by**: Wikipedia. **Located at**: http://en.wikipedia.org/wiki/Maya_civilization%23Classic_period. **License**: *CC BY-SA: Attribution-ShareAlike*
- Maya city. **Provided by**: Wikipedia. **Located at**: http://en.wikipedia.org/wiki/Maya_city. **License**: *CC BY-SA: Attribution-ShareAlike*
- Classic Maya Collapse. **Provided by**: Wikipedia. **Located at**: http://en.wikipedia.org/wiki/Classic_Maya_collapse. **License**: *CC BY-SA: Attribution-ShareAlike*
- Mayan Civilization. **Provided by**: Ridgeaphistory. **Located at**: https://ridgeaphistory.wikispaces.com/Mayan+Civilization. **License**: *CC BY-SA: Attribution-ShareAlike*
- Classic Maya language. **Provided by**: Wikipedia. **Located at**: http://en.wikipedia.org/wiki/Classic_Maya. **License**: *CC BY-SA: Attribution-ShareAlike*

- Maya Civilization. **Provided by**: Wikipedia. **Located at**: http://en.wikipedia.org/wiki/Maya_civilization. **License**: *CC BY-SA: Attribution-ShareAlike*
- stelae. **Provided by**: Wikipedia. **Located at**: http://en.wikipedia.org/wiki/stelae. **License**: *CC BY-SA: Attribution-ShareAlike*
- Kaminaljuyu. **Provided by**: Wikimedia. **Located at**: https://commons.wikimedia.org/wiki/File:Kaminaljuyu_2.jpg. **License**: *CC BY-SA: Attribution-ShareAlike*
- San Bartolo. **Provided by**: Wikimedia. **Located at**: https://commons.wikimedia.org/wiki/File:SBmural.jpg. **License**: *Public Domain: No Known Copyright*
- Nakbe. **Provided by**: Wikimedia. **Located at**: https://en.wikipedia.org/wiki/File:Nakbe_str.JPG. **License**: *CC BY-SA: Attribution-ShareAlike*
- Larger Southern Maya Area. **Provided by**: Wikimedia. **Located at**: https://commons.wikimedia.org/wiki/File:Larger_Southern_Maya_area_v3.svg. **License**: *Public Domain: No Known Copyright*
- Tikal Temple. **Provided by**: Wikimedia. **Located at**: https://commons.wikimedia.org/wiki/File:Tikal_temple_jaguar.jpg. **License**: *CC BY-SA: Attribution-ShareAlike*
- Classic Mayan Collapse. **Provided by**: Wikimedia. **Located at**: https://commons.wikimedia.org/wiki/File:Maya-Maske.jpg. **License**: *Public Domain: No Known Copyright*
- Maya Calendar by Matthew Bisanz. **Provided by**: Wikimedia. **Located at**: https://commons.wikimedia.org/wiki/File:Maya_Calendar_by_Matthew_Bisanz.JPG. **License**: *CC BY-SA: Attribution-ShareAlike*
- Palenque. **Provided by**: Wikimedia. **Located at**: https://commons.wikimedia.org/wiki/File:The_Palenque_Palace_Aqueduct.jpg. **License**: *CC BY-SA: Attribution-ShareAlike*
- Mayapan. **Provided by**: Wikipedia. **Located at**: https://en.wikipedia.org/wiki/Mayapan. **License**: *CC BY-SA: Attribution-ShareAlike*
- Maya Civilization. **Provided by**: Wikipedia. **Located at**: http://en.wikipedia.org/wiki/Maya_civilization%23Postclassic_period. **License**: *CC BY-SA: Attribution-ShareAlike*
- Mesoamerican Chronology. **Provided by**: Wikipedia. **Located at**: http://en.wikipedia.org/wiki/Mesoamerican_chronology. **License**: *CC BY-SA: Attribution-ShareAlike*
- Spanish Conquest of Yucatan. **Provided by**: Wikipedia. **Located at**: http://en.wikipedia.org/wiki/Spanish_conquest_of_Yucat%C3%A1n. **License**: *CC BY-SA: Attribution-ShareAlike*
- Maya Civilization. **Provided by**: Wikipedia. **Located at**: http://en.wikipedia.org/wiki/Maya_civilization. **License**: *CC BY-SA: Attribution-ShareAlike*
- Kaminaljuyu. **Provided by**: Wikimedia. **Located at**: https://commons.wikimedia.org/wiki/File:Kaminaljuyu_2.jpg. **License**: *CC BY-SA: Attribution-ShareAlike*
- San Bartolo. **Provided by**: Wikimedia. **Located at**: https://commons.wikimedia.org/wiki/File:SBmural.jpg. **License**: *Public Domain: No Known Copyright*
- Nakbe. **Provided by**: Wikimedia. **Located at**: https://en.wikipedia.org/wiki/File:Nakbe_str.JPG. **License**: *CC BY-SA: Attribution-ShareAlike*
- Larger Southern Maya Area. **Provided by**: Wikimedia. **Located at**: https://commons.wikimedia.org/wiki/File:Larger_Southern_Maya_area_v3.svg. **License**: *Public Domain: No Known Copyright*
- Tikal Temple. **Provided by**: Wikimedia. **Located at**: https://commons.wikimedia.org/wiki/File:Tikal_temple_jaguar.jpg. **License**: *CC BY-SA: Attribution-ShareAlike*
- Classic Mayan Collapse. **Provided by**: Wikimedia. **Located at**: https://commons.wikimedia.org/wiki/File:Maya-Maske.jpg. **License**: *Public Domain: No Known Copyright*
- Maya Calendar by Matthew Bisanz. **Provided by**: Wikimedia. **Located at**: https://commons.wikimedia.org/wiki/File:Maya_Calendar_by_Matthew_Bisanz.JPG. **License**: *CC BY-SA: Attribution-ShareAlike*
- Palenque. **Provided by**: Wikimedia. **Located at**: https://commons.wikimedia.org/wiki/File:The_Palenque_Palace_Aqueduct.jpg. **License**: *CC BY-SA: Attribution-ShareAlike*
- El Castillo. **Provided by**: Wikipedia. **Located at**: http://en.wikipedia.org/wiki/El_Castillo,_Chichen_Itza%23mediaviewer/File:Chichen_Itza_3.jpg. **License**: *CC BY-SA: Attribution-ShareAlike*
- Paris Codex, pages 4-5. **Provided by**: Wikipedia. **Located at**: https://en.wikipedia.org/wiki/Maya_civilization#/media/File:Paris_Codex,_pages_4-5.jpg. **License**: *CC BY-SA: Attribution-ShareAlike*
- Maya civilization. **Provided by**: Wikipedia. **Located at**: https://en.wikipedia.org/wiki/Maya_civilization#/media/File:Mayapan_chac.JPG. **License**: *CC BY-SA: Attribution-ShareAlike*

The Toltecs and the Aztecs

The Toltecs

The Toltecs were a Mesoamerican people who preceded the Aztecs and existed between 800 and 1000 CE.

Learning Objectives

Identify the Toltecs

Key Takeaways

Key Points

- Much of what is known about the Toltecs is based on what has been learned about the Aztecs.
- Historicists believe that Aztec accounts of the Toltecs can be trusted as historical sources.
- Others believe that Aztec accounts are too shrouded in myth to be trusted as sources of truth.
- Certain Mayan sites, such as Chichén Itzá, share distinctive archeological traits with religious monuments and buildings in Tula.

Key Terms

- **Quetzalcoatl**: The feathered serpent deity that appears in carvings at Tula and also in much later buildings and mythology in the Aztec Empire.
- **Historicist**: A scholar that utilizes Aztec accounts of Toltec culture to piece together the history of the Toltec people.

> - **Atlantean figures**: Gigantic stone statues of Toltec warriors that only appear at the sites of Tula, Chichén Itzá, and Potrero Nuevo.

The Toltec culture is an archaeological Mesoamerican culture that dominated a state centered in Tula in the early Postclassic period of Mesoamerican chronology (c. 800–1000 CE). Much of what is known about the Toltecs is based on what has been learned about the Aztecs, another Mesoamerican culture that postdated the Toltecs and admired the Toltecs as predecessors. Since so much of what remains on record about the Toltecs may have been tainted by Aztec glorification and mythology in the 14th through 16th centuries, it is difficult to parse out the true history.

The later Aztec culture saw the Toltecs as their intellectual and cultural predecessors, and described Toltec culture emanating from Tōllān [ˈtoːlːaːn] (Nahuatl for Tula) as the epitome of civilization. Indeed, in the Nahuatl language the word "Tōltēcatl" [toːlˈteːkat͡ɬ] (singular) or "Tōltēcah" [toːlˈteːkaʔ] (plural) came to take on the meaning "artisan." The Aztec oral and pictographic tradition also described the history of the Toltec Empire, giving lists of rulers and their exploits.

Among modern scholars it is a matter of debate whether the Aztec narratives of Toltec history should be given credence as descriptions of actual historical events. While all scholars acknowledge that there is a large mythological part of the narrative, some maintain that by using a critical comparative method some level of historicity can be salvaged from the sources. Others maintain that continued analysis of the narratives as sources of actual history is futile and hinders access to actual knowledge of the culture.

Another controversy relating to the Toltecs remains how best to understand the reasons behind the perceived similarities in architecture and iconography between the archaeological site of Tula and the Mayan site of Chichén Itzá. No consensus has yet emerged about the degree or direction of influence between these two sites.

Historicists

The historicists believe that there is truth within the stories told by the Aztecs. Theories abound about the role the Toltecs actually played in Mesoamerica, from the central Mexican valleys all the way down to certain Maya city-states.

- Désiré Charnay, the first archaeologist to work at Tula, Hidalgo, defended the historicist views based on his impression of the Toltec capital. He was the first to note similarities in architectural styles between Tula and Chichén Itzá, a famous Maya archeological site. This led him to posit the theory that Chichén Itzá had been violently taken over by a Toltec military force under the leadership of Kukulcan.
- Following Charnay, the term "Toltec" has since been associated with the influx of certain Central Mexican cultural traits into the Maya sphere of dominance during the late Classic and early Postclassic periods. The Postclassic Maya civilizations of Chichén Itzá, Mayapán, and the Guatemalan highlands have been referred to as "Toltecized" or "Mexicanized" Mayas.
- Some 20th-century historicist scholars, such as David Carrasco, Miguel León Portilla, Nigel Davies and H. B. Nicholson, argued that the Toltecs were a distinct ethnic group. This school of

thought connected the "Toltecs" to the archaeological site of Tula, which was taken to be the Tollan of Aztec myth.

- Historicists supportive of the ethnic group theory also argue that much of central Mexico was possibly dominated by a "Toltec empire" between the 10th and 12th centuries CE. One possible clue they point to is that the Aztecs referred to several Mexican city-states as Tollan, "Place of Reeds," such as "Tollan Cholollan."
- Archaeologist Laurette Sejourné, followed by the historian Enrique Florescano, argued that the "original" Tollan was probably Teotihuacán.

Anti-Historicist

On the other side of the argument lie those who believe that the Aztec stories are clouded by myth and cannot be taken as accurate accounts of the Toltec civilization. Multiple theories place the Toltec and the site of Tula within a more general framework:

- Some scholars argue that the Toltec era is best considered the fourth of the five Aztec mythical "suns" or ages. This fourth sun immediately precedes the fifth sun of the Aztec people, which was prophesied to be presided over by Quetzalcoatl.
- Some researchers argue that the only historically reliable data in the Aztec chronicles are the names of some rulers and possibly some of the conquests ascribed to them.
- Skeptics argue that the ancient city of Teotihuacán and the Aztec city of Tenochtitlan were much more influential sites for Mesoamerican culture than Tula. However, this skeptical school of thought acknowledges that Tula still contributed to central Mexican cultural heritage in unique ways.
- Recent scholarship does not frame Tula, Hidalgo, as the capital of the Toltecs as described in the Aztec accounts. Rather, it takes "Toltec" to mean simply an inhabitant of Tula during its apogee. Separating the term "Toltec" from those of the Aztec accounts, it attempts to find archaeological clues to the ethnicity, history, and social organization of the inhabitants of the site of Tula.

Archeology and Clues

While the residents of the site of Tula, Hidalgo, remain a mysterious group, and their ethnic and social dynamics are obscure, they left behind substantial archeological records that modern scholars have attempted to parse through.

Stone carving of Quetzalcoatl: *This powerful feathered serpent deity has deep mythological roots in Aztec stories. He also appears regularly in carvings at Tula.*

The city of Tula boasts 15-foot-tall warrior statues carved from stone. These same Atlantean figures, as they are called, also appear at the Mayan sites of Chichén Itzá and Potrero Nuevo.

Toltec warrior statues at Tula: *These stone statues highlight the artistic style of the city of Tula. They also connect this city with other cultural sites in Mesoamerica.*

Tula also boasts intricate carvings of eagles, jaguars, hummingbirds, and butterflies, all of which the Aztec Empire used prolifically. Furthermore, the site of Tula includes two ball courts for the religious rubber ball game that appears in many Mesoamerican civilizations. Along with these distinct relics, the Toltecs also built distinctive pyramids that mirror other sites, such as Chichén Itzá.

Many questions still remain about the inhabitants of this site, including questions about their origin and their demise. This site also raises questions about the flow of influence between multiple Mesoamerican cultures before the rise of the Aztec Empire.

The Aztec People

The Aztecs were a pre-Columbian Mesoamerican people of Central Mexico during the 14th, 15th, and 16th centuries.

Learning Objectives

Describe distinguishing factors of Aztec life

Key Takeaways

Key Points

- The Aztec "empire" was more of a collection of city-states than an empire.
- Mexico City today is built on the ruins of Tenochtitlan, which was the capital of the Aztec empire.
- Agriculture played a key role in the Aztec civilization. Irrigation and floating garden beds allowed people to grow several crops a year.

Key Terms

- **altepetl**: Small, mostly independent city-states that often paid tribute to the Aztec capital of Tenochtitlan.
- **Nahuatl**: The language spoken by the Mexica people who made up the Aztec Triple Alliance, as well as many city-states throughout the region.
- **flower wars**: The form of ritual war where warriors from the Triple Alliance fought with enemy Nahua city-states.

The Aztecs were a pre-Columbian Mesoamerican people of Central Mexico in the 14th, 15th, and 16th centuries. They called themselves Mexica. The Republic of Mexico and its capital, Mexico City, derive their names from the word "Mexica." The capital of the Aztec empire was Tenochtitlan, built on a raised island in Lake Texcoco. Modern Mexico City is built on the ruins of Tenochtitlan.

From the 13th century, the Valley of Mexico was the heart of Aztec civilization; here the capital of the Aztec Triple Alliance, the city of Tenochtitlan, was built upon raised islets in Lake Texcoco. The Triple Alliance was comprised of Tenochtitlan along with their main allies of Acolhuas of Texcoco and Tepanecs of Tlacopan. They formed a tributary empire expanding its political hegemony far beyond the Valley of Mexico, conquering other city-states throughout Mesoamerica. At its pinnacle, Aztec culture had rich and complex mythological and religious traditions, and reached remarkable architectural and artistic accomplishments. In 1521 Hernán Cortés, along with a large number of Nahuatl-speaking indigenous allies, conquered Tenochtitlan and defeated the Aztec Triple Alliance under the leadership of Hueyi Tlatoani Moctezuma II. Subsequently the Spanish founded the new settlement of Mexico City on the site of the ruined Aztec capital, from where they proceeded to colonize Central America.

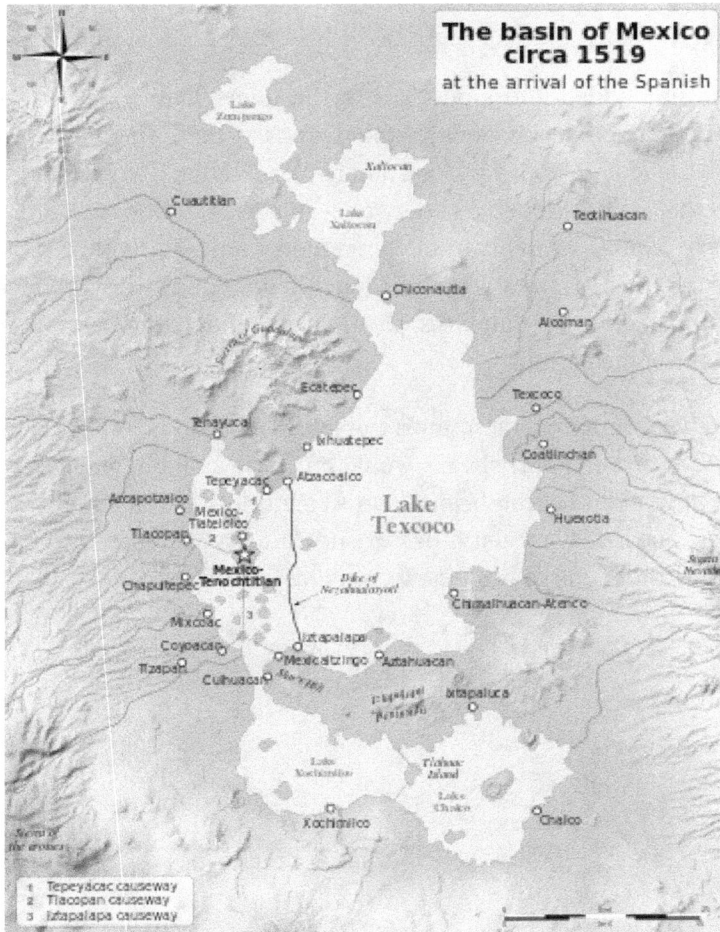

Basin in the Valley of Mexico: Circa 1519, at the time of the arrival of the Spanish.

Politics

The Aztec empire was an example of an empire that ruled by indirect means. Like most European empires, it was ethnically very diverse, but unlike most European empires, it was more of a system of tribute than a single system of government. Although the form of government is often referred to as an empire, in fact most areas within the empire were organized as city-states, known as "altepetl" in Nahuatl. These were small polities ruled by a king (tlatoani) from a legitimate dynasty.

Two of the primary architects of the Aztec empire were the half-brothers Tlacaelel and Montezuma I, nephews of Itzcoatl. Moctezuma I succeeded Itzcoatl as Hueyi Tlatoani (or king) in 1440. Although he was also offered the opportunity to be tlatoani, Tlacaelel preferred to operate as the power behind the throne. Tlacaelel focused on reforming the Aztec state and religious practices. According to some sources, he ordered the burning of most of the extant Aztec books, claiming that they contained lies. He thereupon rewrote the history of the Aztec people, thus creating a common awareness of history for the Aztecs. This rewriting led directly to the curriculum taught to scholars, and promoted the belief that the Aztecs were always a powerful and mythic nation—forgetting forever a possible true history of modest origins. One component of this reform was the institution of ritual war (the flower wars) as a way to have trained warriors, and the necessity of constant sacrifices to keep the Sun moving.

Economics

The Aztec economy can be divided into a political sector, under the control of nobles and kings, and a commercial sector that operated independently of the political sector. The political sector of the economy centered on the control of land and labor by kings and nobles. Nobles owned all land, and commoners got access to farmland and other fields through a variety of arrangements, from rental through sharecropping to serf-like labor and slavery. These payments from commoners to nobles supported both the lavish lifestyles of the high nobility and the finances of city-states. Many luxury goods were produced for consumption by nobles. The producers of featherwork, sculptures, jewelry, and other luxury items were full-time commoner specialists who worked for noble patrons.

Several forms of money were in circulation, most notably the cacao bean. These beans could be used to buy food, staples, and cloth. Around thirty beans would purchase a rabbit, while one father was recorded as selling his daughter for around 200 cacao beans. The Aztec rulers also maintained complex road systems with regular stops to rest and eat every ten miles or so. Couriers walked these roads regularly to ensure they were in good working order and to bring news back to Tenochtitlan.

Aztec headdress: *The feathers most likely came from a tropical rainforest far away, and the headdress was probably owned by an elite or noble.*

Trade also formed a central part of Aztec life. While local commoners regularly paid tribute to the nobles a few times a year, there was also extensive trade with other regions in Mesoamerica. Archeological evidence shows that jade, obsidian, feathers, and shells reached the capital through established trade routes. Rulers and nobles enjoyed wearing these more exotic goods and having them fashioned into expressive headdresses and jewelry.

Architecture and Agriculture

The capital of Tenochtitlan was divided into four even sections called *campans*. All of these sections were interlaced together with a series of canals that allowed for easy transportation throughout the islets of Lake Texcoco. Commoner housing was usually built of reeds or wood, while noble houses and religious sites were constructed from stone.

Agriculture played a large part in the economy and society of the Aztecs. They used dams to implement irrigation techniques in the valleys. They also implemented a raised bed gardening technique by layering mud and plant vegetation in the lake in order to create moist gardens. These raised beds were called *chinampas*. These extremely fertile beds could harvest seven different crops each year. Some of the most essential crops in Aztec agriculture included:

- Avocados
- Beans
- Squash

- Sweet Potatoes
- Maize
- Tomatoes
- Amarinth
- Chilies
- Cotton
- Cacao beans

Most farming occurred outside of the busy heart of Tenochtitlan. However, each family generally had a garden where they could grow maize, fruits, herbs, and medicinal plants on a smaller scale.

Aztec Religion

The Aztec religion focused on death, rebirth, and the renewal of the sun. The Aztecs practiced ritual sacrifice, ball games, and bloodletting in order to renew the sun each day.

Learning Objectives

Outline the key points of Aztec religious practices and beliefs

Key Takeaways

Key Points

- The Aztec religion incorporated deities from multiple cultures into its pantheon.
- Ritual sacrifice played an essential role in the religious practice of the Aztecs, and they believed it ensured the sun would rise again and crops would grow.
- The Aztecs utilized a 365-day calendar split into eighteen months based on agricultural traditions and different deities.

Key Terms

- **Huitzilopochtli**: The left-handed hummingbird god that mythically founded Tenochtitlan and represented war and the sun.
- **Toxcatl**: A month in the Aztec sun calendar that represented drought and ritual renewal.
- **Mesoamerican ballgame**: This ritual practice involved a rubber ball that the players hit with their elbows, knees, and hips, and tried to get through a small hoop in a special court.

The Aztecs had at least two manifestations of the supernatural: tētl and tēixiptla. Tētl, which the Spaniards and European scholars routinely mistranslated as "god" or "demon," referred rather to an impersonal, mysterious force that permeated the world. Tēixiptla, by contrast, denoted the physical representations ("idols," statues, and figurines) of the tētl as well as the human cultic activity surrounding this physical representation.

The Aztec religious cosmology included the physical earth plane, where humans lived, the underworld (or land of the dead), and the realm of the sky. Due to the flexible imperial political structure, a large pantheon of gods was incorporated into the larger cultural religious traditions. The Aztecs also worshipped deities that were central to older Mesoamerican cultures, such as the Olmecs. Some of the most central deities that the Aztecs paid homage to included:

- Huitzilopochtli – The "left-handed hummingbird" god was the god of war and the sun and also the founder of Tenochtitlan.

- Quetzalcoatl – The feathered serpent god that represented the morning star, wind, and life.

- Tlaloc – The rain and storm god.

- Mixcoatl – The "cloud serpent" god that was incorporated into Aztec belief and represented war.

- Xipe Totec – The flayed god that was associated with fertility. This deity was also incorporated from cultures under the Aztec Triple Alliance umbrella.

Huitzilopochtli as depicted in the Codex Telleriano-Remensis: *This depiction of the war and sun god shows him in all of his warrior and ritual garb.*

Founding Myth of Tenochtitlan

Veneration of Huitzilopochtli, the personification of the sun and of war, was central to the religious, social, and political practices of the Mexica people. Huitzilopochtli attained this central position after the founding of Tenochtitlan and the formation of the Mexica city-state society in the 14th century.

According to myth, Huitzilopochtli directed the wanderers to found a city on the site where they would see an eagle devouring a snake perched on a fruit-bearing nopal cactus. (It was said that Huitzilopochtli killed his nephew, Cópil, and threw his heart on the lake. Huitzilopochtli honoured Cópil by causing a cactus to grow over Cópil's heart.) This legendary vision is pictured on the coat of arms of Mexico.

Ritual and Sacrifice

Like all other Mesoamerican cultures, the Aztecs played a variant of the Mesoamerican ballgame, named "tlachtli" or "ollamaliztli" in Nahuatl. The game was played with a ball of solid rubber, called an olli. The players hit the ball with their hips, knees, and elbows, and had to pass the ball through a stone ring to automatically win. The practice of the ballgame carried religious and mythological meanings and also served

as sport. Many times players of
the game were captured during the famous Aztec flower wars with neighboring rivals. Losers of the game were often ritually sacrificed as an homage to the gods.

A depiction of human sacrifice in the Codex Magliabechiano: This Spanish rendering of human sacrifices reflects the outsider's view of these ritual traditions.

While human sacrifice was practiced throughout Mesoamerica, the Aztecs, if their own accounts are to be believed, brought this practice to an unprecedented level. For example, for the reconsecration of the Great Pyramid of Tenochtitlan in 1487, the Aztecs reported that they sacrificed 80,400 prisoners over the course of four days, reportedly by Ahuitzotl, the Great Speaker himself. This number, however, is not universally accepted. Accounts by the Tlaxcaltecas, the primary enemy of the Aztecs at the time of the Spanish Conquest, show that at least some of them considered it an honor to be sacrificed. In one legend, the warrior Tlahuicole was freed by the Aztecs but eventually returned of his own volition to die in ritual sacrifice. Tlaxcala also practiced the human sacrifice of captured Aztec citizens.

Everyone was affected by human sacrifice, and it should be considered in the context of the religious cosmology of the Aztec people. It was considered necessary in order for the world to continue and be reborn each new day. Death and ritual blood sacrifice ensured the sun would rise again and crops
would continue to grow. Not only were captives and warriors sacrificed, but nobles would often practice

ritual bloodletting during certain sacred days of the year. Every level of Aztec society was affected by the belief in the human responsibility to pay homage to the gods, and anyone could serve as a sacrificial offering.

Priests and Religious Architecture

A noble priest class played an integral role in the religious worship and sacrifices of Aztec society. They were responsible for collecting tributes and ensuring there were enough goods for sacrificial ceremonies. They also trained young men to impersonate various deities for an entire year before being sacrificed on a specific day. These priests were respected by all of society and were also responsible for practicing ritual bloodletting on themselves at regular intervals. Priests could come from the noble or common classes, but they would receive their training at different schools and perform different functions.

Aztec pyramid of St. Cecilia Acatitlan: *This pyramid is typical of Aztec religious architecture. Priests would have stood on the platform at the top to perform religious duties and sacrifices.*

Priests performed rituals from special temples and religious houses. The temples were generally huge pyramidal structures that were covered over with a new surface every fifty-two years, meaning some pyramids were gigantic in scale. These feats of architectural display were the sites of large sacrificial offerings and festivals, where Spanish reports said blood would run down the steps of the pyramids. The priests often performed smaller daily rituals in small, dark temple houses where incense and images of important gods were displayed.

Aztec Calendar

Aztec sun calendar: This calendar shows the eighteen months circling around a representation of the sun.

The Aztecs based their calendar on the sun and utilized a 365-day religious calendar. It was split into eighteen twenty-day months, and each month had its own religious, and often agricultural, theme. For example, the late winter month Altcahualo fell between February 14 and March 5 and represented a time of sowing crops and fertility. The month Toxcatl occurred in May and was a time of drought in the central valley. The Aztecs saw this month as a time of renewal, and it involved a large festival where a young man that had been impersonating the god Tezcatlipoca for a full year would be sacrificed.

The Aztec in the Colonial Period

The Aztec empire was defeated by an alliance between the Spanish and the Confederacy of Tlaxcala.

Learning Objectives

Describe the role of the Confederacy of Tlaxcala in the fall of the Aztec empire

Key Takeaways

Key Points

- The arrival of Hernándo Cortés in 1519 marked the beginning of the end for the Aztec empire.
- Cortés and the Confederacy of Tlaxcala allied to militarily defeat the Aztecs, who were further weakened by a smallpox epidemic in 1520–1521 and subsequent outbreaks.
- Aztec hegemonic structure was re-appropriated to serve the Spanish colonialists.
- Some aspects of Aztec culture, such as the language, survive.

Key Terms

- **Tlaxcalan**: The people of a pre-Columbian city and state in Central Mexico, who helped Cortés conquer the Aztec empire.
- **Bartolomé de las Casas**: (Seville, c. 1484– Madrid, July 18, 1566) Sixteenth-century Spanish historian, social reformer, and Dominican friar. Arriving as one of the first European settlers in the Americas, he participated in the atrocities committed against the Native Americans by the Spanish colonists. In 1515, he reformed his views and advocated before King Charles V, Holy Roman Emperor, on behalf of rights for the natives.

Overview

The Spanish conquest of the Aztec empire was one of the most significant events in the Spanish colonization of the Americas. The Spanish campaign began in February 1519, and was declared victorious on August 13, 1521, when a coalition army of Spanish forces and native Tlaxcalan warriors led by Hernándo Cortés and Xicotencatl the Younger captured the emperor Cuauhtemoc and Tenochtitlan, the capital of the Aztec empire. The fall of the Aztec empire was the key event in the formation of the Spanish overseas empire, with New Spain, which later became Mexico, a major component.

Hernándo Cortés

Conquest of the Aztecs

During the campaign, Cortés was given support from a number of tributaries and rivals of the Aztecs, including the Totonacs and the Tlaxcaltecas, Texcocans, and other city-states particularly bordering Lake Texcoco. In their advance, the allies were tricked and ambushed several times by the people they encountered. After eight months of battles and negotiations, which overcame the diplomatic resistance of the Aztec emperor Moctezuma II to his visit, Cortés arrived in Tenochtitlan on November 8, 1519, where he was welcomed by Moctezuma and took up residence. When news reached Cortés of the death of several of his men during the Aztec attack on the Totonacs in Veracruz, he took the opportunity to take Moctezuma captive; Moctezuma allowed himself to be captured as a diplomatic gesture. Capturing the indigenous ruler was standard operating procedure for Spaniards in their expansion in the Caribbean, so capturing Moctezuma had considerable precedent.

When Cortés left Tenochtitlan to return to the coast and deal with the expedition of Pánfilo de Narváez, Pedro de Alvarado was left in charge. Alvarado allowed a significant Aztec feast to be celebrated in Tenochtitlan, and in the pattern of the earlier massacre in Cholula closed off the square and massacred the celebrating Aztec noblemen. The biography of Cortés by Francisco López de Gómara contains a description of the massacre. The Alvarado massacre at the Main Temple of Tenochtitlan precipitated rebellion by the population of the city. When the captured emperor Moctezuma II, now seen as a mere puppet of the invading Spaniards, attempted to calm the outraged populace, he was killed by a projectile. Cortés, who by then had returned to Tenochtitlan, and his men fled the capital city during the Noche Triste in June 1520. The Spanish, Tlaxcalans, and reinforcements returned a year later, on August 13, 1521, to a civilization that had been wiped out by famine and smallpox. This made it easier to conquer the remaining Aztecs.

Aftermath

To reward Spaniards who participated in the conquest of what is now contemporary Mexico, the Spanish crown authorized grants of native labor in particular indigenous communities via the encomienda. The indigenous were not slaves, chattel bought and sold or removed from their home community, but the system was one of forced labor. The indigenous of Central Mexico had practices rendering labor and tribute products to their polity's elites, and those elites to the Mexica overlords in Tenochtitlan, so the Spanish system of encomienda was built on pre-existing patterns. The Spanish conquerors in Mexico during the early colonial era lived off the labor of the indigenous. Due to some horrifying instances of abuse against the indigenous peoples, Bishop Bartolomé de las Casas suggested importing black slaves to replace them (he later repented when he saw the even worse treatment given to the black slaves).

Nevertheless, Aztec culture survives today. Modern-day Mexico City is built on the site of the Aztec capital, Tenochtitlan. There are still 1.5 million people who speak the Aztec language of Nahuatl, and part of the Mexica migration story appears on the Mexican flag.

Attributions

CC licensed content, Specific attribution

- Aztec. **Provided by**: Wikipedia. **Located at**: https://en.wikipedia.org/wiki/Aztec. **License**: *CC BY-SA: Attribution-ShareAlike*
- Maya-Toltec Controversy in Chichen Itza. **Provided by**: Wikipedia. **Located at**: http://en.wikipedia.org/wiki/Maya-Toltec_Controversy_in_Chichen_Itza. **License**: *CC BY-SA: Attribution-ShareAlike*
- Toltec. **Provided by**: Wikipedia. **Located at**: http://en.wikipedia.org/wiki/Toltec. **License**: *CC BY-SA: Attribution-ShareAlike*
- Tenochtitlan. **Provided by**: Wikipedia. **Located at**: https://en.wikipedia.org/wiki/Tenochtitlan. **License**: *CC BY-SA: Attribution-ShareAlike*
- Teotihuacan. **Provided by**: Wikipedia. **Located at**: https://en.wikipedia.org/wiki/Teotihuacan. **License**: *CC BY-SA: Attribution-ShareAlike*
- Atlantean figures. **Provided by**: Wikipedia. **Located at**: https://en.wikipedia.org/wiki/Atlantean_figures. **License**: *CC BY-SA: Attribution-ShareAlike*
- Atlantean figures. **Provided by**: Wikipedia. **Located at**: https://en.wikipedia.org/wiki/Atlantean_figures#/media/File:Telamones_Tula.jpg. **License**: *CC BY-SA: Attribution-ShareAlike*
- Tula birdman. **Provided by**: Wikipedia. **Located at**: https://en.wikipedia.org/wiki/Toltec#/media/File:Tula_birdman.jpg. **License**: *CC BY-SA: Attribution-ShareAlike*
- History of the Aztecs. **Provided by**: Wikipedia. **Located at**: http://en.wikipedia.org/wiki/History_of_the_Aztecs. **License**: *CC BY-SA: Attribution-ShareAlike*
- Aztec. **Provided by**: Wikipedia. **Located at**: http://en.wikipedia.org/wiki/Aztec%23Cultural_patterns. **License**: *CC BY-SA: Attribution-ShareAlike*
- Aztec. **Provided by**: Wikipedia. **Located at**: http://en.wikipedia.org/wiki/Aztec. **License**: *CC BY-SA: Attribution-ShareAlike*
- The Valley of Mexico. **Provided by**: Wikipedia. **Located at**: http://en.wikipedia.org/wiki/Valley_of_Mexico. **License**: *CC BY-SA: Attribution-ShareAlike*
- Moctezuma I. **Provided by**: Wikipedia. **Located at**: http://en.wikipedia.org/wiki/Montezuma_I. **License**: *CC BY-SA: Attribution-ShareAlike*
- Flower wars. **Provided by**: Wikipedia. **Located at**: https://en.wikipedia.org/wiki/Flower_war. **License**: *CC BY-SA: Attribution-ShareAlike*
- Atlantean figures. **Provided by**: Wikipedia. **Located at**: https://en.wikipedia.org/wiki/Atlantean_figures#/media/File:Telamones_Tula.jpg. **License**: *CC BY-SA: Attribution-ShareAlike*
- Tula birdman. **Provided by**: Wikipedia. **Located at**: https://en.wikipedia.org/wiki/Toltec#/media/File:Tula_birdman.jpg. **License**: *CC BY-SA: Attribution-ShareAlike*
- Basin of Mexico. **Provided by**: Wikipedia. **Located at**: http://upload.wikimedia.org/wikipedia/commons/thumb/9/99/Basin_of_Mexico_1519_map-en.svg/360px-Basin_of_Mexico_1519_map-en.svg.png. **License**: *CC BY-SA: Attribution-ShareAlike*
- Aztec Headdress. **Provided by**: Wikimedia. **Located at**: https://commons.wikimedia.org/wiki/File:Aztecheaddress.jpg. **License**: *CC BY-SA: Attribution-ShareAlike*
- Toxcatl. **Provided by**: Wikipedia. **Located at**: https://en.wikipedia.org/wiki/Toxcatl. **License**: *CC BY-SA: Attribution-ShareAlike*
- History of the Aztecs. **Provided by**: Wikipedia. **Located at**: https://en.wikipedia.org/wiki/History_of_the_Aztecs. **License**: *CC BY-SA: Attribution-ShareAlike*

- Huitzilopochtli. **Provided by**: Wikipedia. **Located at**: https://en.wikipedia.org/wiki/Huitzilopochtli. **License**: *CC BY-SA: Attribution-ShareAlike*
- Aztec religion. **Provided by**: Wikipedia. **Located at**: https://en.wikipedia.org/wiki/Aztec_religion. **License**: *CC BY-SA: Attribution-ShareAlike*
- Aztec. **Provided by**: Wikipedia. **Located at**: https://en.wikipedia.org/wiki/Aztec. **License**: *CC BY-SA: Attribution-ShareAlike*
- Flower war. **Provided by**: Wikipedia. **Located at**: https://en.wikipedia.org/wiki/Flower_war. **License**: *CC BY-SA: Attribution-ShareAlike*
- Atlantean figures. **Provided by**: Wikipedia. **Located at**: https://en.wikipedia.org/wiki/Atlantean_figures#/media/File:Telamones_Tula.jpg. **License**: *CC BY-SA: Attribution-ShareAlike*
- Tula birdman. **Provided by**: Wikipedia. **Located at**: https://en.wikipedia.org/wiki/Toltec#/media/File:Tula_birdman.jpg. **License**: *CC BY-SA: Attribution-ShareAlike*
- Basin of Mexico. **Provided by**: Wikipedia. **Located at**: http://upload.wikimedia.org/wikipedia/commons/thumb/9/99/Basin_of_Mexico_1519_map-en.svg/360px-Basin_of_Mexico_1519_map-en.svg.png. **License**: *CC BY-SA: Attribution-ShareAlike*
- Aztec Headdress. **Provided by**: Wikimedia. **Located at**: https://commons.wikimedia.org/wiki/File:Aztecheaddress.jpg. **License**: *CC BY-SA: Attribution-ShareAlike*
- St. Cecilia Acatitlan. **Provided by**: Wikipedia. **Located at**: https://en.wikipedia.org/wiki/Aztec#/media/File:StaCeciliaAcatitlan.jpg. **License**: *Public Domain: No Known Copyright*
- Huitzilopochtli in the Codex Telleriano-Remensis. **Provided by**: Wikipedia. **Located at**: https://en.wikipedia.org/wiki/Huitzilopochtli#/media/File:Huitzilopochtli_telleriano.jpg. **License**: *Public Domain: No Known Copyright*
- Codex Magliabechiano. **Provided by**: Wikipedia. **Located at**: https://en.wikipedia.org/wiki/Aztec#/media/File:Codex_Magliabechiano_(141_cropped).jpg. **License**: *Public Domain: No Known Copyright*
- Aztec calendar. **Provided by**: Wikipedia. **Located at**: https://en.wikipedia.org/wiki/Aztec#/media/File:Aztec_calendar.svg. **License**: *CC BY-SA: Attribution-ShareAlike*
- Bartolome de las Casas. **Provided by**: Wikipedia. **Located at**: http://en.wikipedia.org/wiki/Bartolom%C3%A9_de_las_Casas. **License**: *CC BY-SA: Attribution-ShareAlike*
- Tlaxcala. **Provided by**: Wikipedia. **Located at**: http://en.wikipedia.org/wiki/Tlaxcala_(Nahua_state). **License**: *CC BY-SA: Attribution-ShareAlike*
- Spanish conquest of the Aztec Empire. **Provided by**: Wikipedia. **Located at**: http://en.wikipedia.org/wiki/Spanish_conquest_of_the_Aztec_Empire. **License**: *CC BY-SA: Attribution-ShareAlike*
- Atlantean figures. **Provided by**: Wikipedia. **Located at**: https://en.wikipedia.org/wiki/Atlantean_figures#/media/File:Telamones_Tula.jpg. **License**: *CC BY-SA: Attribution-ShareAlike*
- Tula birdman. **Provided by**: Wikipedia. **Located at**: https://en.wikipedia.org/wiki/Toltec#/media/File:Tula_birdman.jpg. **License**: *CC BY-SA: Attribution-ShareAlike*
- Basin of Mexico. **Provided by**: Wikipedia. **Located at**: http://upload.wikimedia.org/wikipedia/commons/thumb/9/99/Basin_of_Mexico_1519_map-en.svg/360px-Basin_of_Mexico_1519_map-en.svg.png. **License**: *CC BY-SA: Attribution-ShareAlike*
- Aztec Headdress. **Provided by**: Wikimedia. **Located at**: https://commons.wikimedia.org/wiki/File:Aztecheaddress.jpg. **License**: *CC BY-SA: Attribution-ShareAlike*
- St. Cecilia Acatitlan. **Provided by**: Wikipedia. **Located at**: https://en.wikipedia.org/wiki/Aztec#/media/File:StaCeciliaAcatitlan.jpg. **License**: *Public Domain: No Known Copyright*
- Huitzilopochtli in the Codex Telleriano-Remensis. **Provided by**: Wikipedia. **Located at**: https://en.wikipedia.org/wiki/Huitzilopochtli#/media/File:Huitzilopochtli_telleriano.jpg. **License**: *Public Domain: No Known Copyright*
- Codex Magliabechiano. **Provided by**: Wikipedia. **Located at**: https://en.wikipedia.org/wiki/Aztec#/media/File:Codex_Magliabechiano_(141_cropped).jpg. **License**: *Public Domain: No Known Copyright*
- Aztec calendar. **Provided by**: Wikipedia. **Located at**: https://en.wikipedia.org/wiki/Aztec#/media/File:Aztec_calendar.svg. **License**: *CC BY-SA: Attribution-ShareAlike*
- Hernan Cortes. **Provided by**: Wikipedia. **Located at**: http://upload.wikimedia.org/wikipedia/commons/5/5a/Cortes.jpg. **License**: *CC BY-SA: Attribution-ShareAlike*

www.ingramcontent.com/pod-product-compliance
Lightning Source LLC
Chambersburg PA
CBHW080717300426
44114CB00019B/2404